Pension Protection Act of 2006

WITHDRAWN
UTSA Libraries

Text of H.R. 4, as Passed by
the House on July 28, 2006, and
the Senate on August 3, 2006
JCT Technical Explanation of H.R. 4

CCH
a Wolters Kluwer business

This publication is designed to provide accurate and authoritative information in regard to the subject matter covered. It is sold with the understanding that the publisher is not engaged in rendering legal, accounting, or other professional service. If legal advice or other expert assistance is required, the services of a competent professional person should be sought.

ISBN 0-8080-1570-2

4025 W. Peterson Ave.
Chicago, IL 60646-6085
1 800 248 3248
www.CCHGroup.com

Printed in the United States of America

About This Report

This CCH publication reproduces Titles I through XIII of the Pension Protection Act of 2006 (H.R. 4), as passed by the House on July 28, 2006 and the Senate on August 3, 2006. This Report also includes the text of the Joint Committee on Taxation's Technical Explanation of the Act (JCX-38-06). On November 16, 2005, the Senate passed the Pension Security and Transparency Bill of 2005 (Sen. 1783). About a month later, on December 15, 2005, the House passed its version of a pension bill, the Pension Protection Bill of 2005 (H.R. 2830). A conference committee, then, began negotiating a compromise of the two bills. After the conference negotiations were unable to reach an agreement, the House passed the Pension Protection Act of 2006 (H.R. 4) by a vote of 279-131.

The Senate, then, passed the Act without amendment by a vote of 93 to 5 and it is expected to be signed by the President.

The Pension Act contains provisions that strengthen traditional pension plans, extend over 20 retirement tax-savings benefits, add new rules governing specific charitable donations, impose tighter controls on exempt organizations, and also covers over a dozen other major tax provisions.

The Act contains pension reform provisions that:

- Strengthen funding rules for defined benefit pension plans;
- Provide funding relief for airlines;
- Provide investment advice to plan participants;
- Make permanent the retirement savings incentives enacted under the Economic Growth and Tax Relief Reconciliation Act of 2001 (P.L. 107-16);
- Create a safe harbor to encourage employers to offer automatic enrollment in their cash or deferred arrangements;
- Strengthen disclosure rules for plan administrators;
- Make the "saver's credit" permanent;
- Allow direct rollovers from retirement plans to Roth IRAs; and
- Allow small employers to establish a combined defined benefit/401(k) (DB/K) plan.

The new law also contains a number of provisions that impact charities and charitable donations, technical corrections, and a handful of miscellaneous provisions. Among the provisions included are:

- New recordkeeping requirements for cash donations;
- Federal oversight of charitable organizations;
- Stricter rules for donations of used clothing and household goods;
- New treatment of donations of fractional interests;
- Special contribution rules for buildings in registered historical districts; and
- An extension of the rules allowing for Sec. 529 qualified tuition programs.

TECHNICAL EXPLANATION OF H.R. 4, THE "PENSION PROTECTION ACT OF 2006," AS PASSED BY THE HOUSE ON JULY 28, 2006, AND AS CONSIDERED BY THE SENATE ON AUGUST 3, 2006

Prepared by the Staff
of the
JOINT COMMITTEE ON TAXATION

August 3, 2006
JCX-38-06

CONTENTS

vii

INTRODUCTION

This document,[1] prepared by the staff of the Joint Committee on Taxation, provides a technical explanation of the "Pension Protection Act of 2006," as passed by the House of Representatives on July 28, 2006, and as considered by the Senate on August 3, 2006.

---

[1] This document may be cited as follows: Joint Committee on Taxation, *Technical Explanation of H.R. 4, the "Pension Protection Act of 2006," as Passed by the House on July 28, 2006, and as Considered by the Senate on August 3, 2006* (JCX-38-06), August 3, 2006.

TITLE I: REFORM OF FUNDING RULES FOR SINGLE-EMPLOYER DEFINED BENEFIT PENSION PLANS[2]

A. Minimum Funding Standards for Single-Employer Defined Benefit Pension Plans
(secs. 302-308 of ERISA, and sec. 412 and new sec. 430 of the Code)

Present Law

In general

Single-employer defined benefit pension plans are subject to minimum funding requirements under the Employee Retirement Income Security Act of 1974 ("ERISA") and the Internal Revenue Code (the "Code").[3] The amount of contributions required for a plan year under the minimum funding rules is generally the amount needed to fund benefits earned during that year plus that year's portion of other liabilities that are amortized over a period of years, such as benefits resulting from a grant of past service credit. The amount of required annual contributions is determined under one of a number of acceptable actuarial cost methods. Additional contributions are required under the deficit reduction contribution rules in the case of certain underfunded plans. No contribution is required under the minimum funding rules in excess of the full funding limit (described below).

General minimum funding rules

Funding standard account

As an administrative aid in the application of the funding requirements, a defined benefit pension plan is required to maintain a special account called a "funding standard account" to which specified charges and credits are made for each plan year, including a charge for normal cost and credits for contributions to the plan. Other charges or credits may apply as a result of decreases or increases in past service liability as a result of plan amendments, experience gains or losses, gains or losses resulting from a change in actuarial assumptions, or a waiver of minimum required contributions.

In determining plan funding under an actuarial cost method, a plan's actuary generally makes certain assumptions regarding the future experience of a plan. These assumptions

---

[2] Some provisions that are identical or similar to the pension provisions in the bill were contained in other bills reported by the House Committees on Ways and Means and Education and the Workforce and the Senate Committees on Finance and Health, Education, Labor and Pensions, or passed by the House or the Senate during the 109th Congress. These bills include H.R. 2830, S. 1953, and S. 1783.

[3] Multiemployer defined benefit pension plans are also subject to the minimum funding requirements, but the rules for multiemployer plans differ in various respects from the rules applicable to single-employer plans. Governmental plans and church plans are generally exempt from the minimum funding requirements.

typically involve rates of interest, mortality, disability, salary increases, and other factors affecting the value of assets and liabilities. If the plan's actual unfunded liabilities are less than those anticipated by the actuary on the basis of these assumptions, then the excess is an experience gain. If the actual unfunded liabilities are greater than those anticipated, then the difference is an experience loss. Experience gains and losses for a year are generally amortized as credits or charges to the funding standard account over five years.

If the actuarial assumptions used for funding a plan are revised and, under the new assumptions, the accrued liability of a plan is less than the accrued liability computed under the previous assumptions, the decrease is a gain from changes in actuarial assumptions. If the new assumptions result in an increase in the plan's accrued liability, the plan has a loss from changes in actuarial assumptions. The accrued liability of a plan is the actuarial present value of projected pension benefits under the plan that will not be funded by future contributions to meet normal cost or future employee contributions. The gain or loss for a year from changes in actuarial assumptions is amortized as credits or charges to the funding standard account over ten years.

If minimum required contributions are waived (as discussed below), the waived amount (referred to as a "waived funding deficiency") is credited to the funding standard account. The waived funding deficiency is then amortized over a period of five years, beginning with the year following the year in which the waiver is granted. Each year, the funding standard account is charged with the amortization amount for that year unless the plan becomes fully funded.

If, as of the close of a plan year, the funding standard account reflects credits at least equal to charges, the plan is generally treated as meeting the minimum funding standard for the year. If, as of the close of the plan year, charges to the funding standard account exceed credits to the account, then the excess is referred to as an "accumulated funding deficiency." Thus, as a general rule, the minimum contribution for a plan year is determined as the amount by which the charges to the funding standard account would exceed credits to the account if no contribution were made to the plan. For example, if the balance of charges to the funding standard account of a plan for a year would be $200,000 without any contributions, then a minimum contribution equal to that amount would be required to meet the minimum funding standard for the year to prevent an accumulated funding deficiency.

Credit balances

If credits to the funding standard account exceed charges, a "credit balance" results. A credit balance results, for example, if contributions in excess of minimum required contributions are made. Similarly, a credit balance may result from large net experience gains. The amount of the credit balance, increased with interest at the rate used under the plan to determine costs, is applied against charges to the funding standard account, thus reducing required contributions.

Funding methods and general concepts

A defined benefit pension plan is required to use an acceptable actuarial cost method to determine the elements included in its funding standard account for a year. Generally, an actuarial cost method breaks up the cost of benefits under the plan into annual charges consisting of two elements for each plan year. These elements are referred to as: (1) normal cost; and (2) supplemental cost.

The plan's normal cost for a plan year generally represents the cost of future benefits allocated to the year by the funding method used by the plan for current employees and, under some funding methods, for separated employees. Specifically, it is the amount actuarially determined that would be required as a contribution by the employer for the plan year in order to maintain the plan if the plan had been in effect from the beginning of service of the included employees and if the costs for prior years had been paid, and all assumptions as to interest, mortality, time of payment, etc., had been fulfilled. The normal cost will be funded by future contributions to the plan: (1) in level dollar amounts; (2) as a uniform percentage of payroll; (3) as a uniform amount per unit of service (e.g., $1 per hour); or (4) on the basis of the actuarial present values of benefits considered accruing in particular plan years.

The supplemental cost for a plan year is the cost of future benefits that would not be met by future normal costs, future employee contributions, or plan assets. The most common supplemental cost is that attributable to past service liability, which represents the cost of future benefits under the plan: (1) on the date the plan is first effective; or (2) on the date a plan amendment increasing plan benefits is first effective. Other supplemental costs may be attributable to net experience losses, changes in actuarial assumptions, and amounts necessary to make up funding deficiencies for which a waiver was obtained. Supplemental costs must be amortized (i.e., recognized for funding purposes) over a specified number of years, depending on the source. For example, the cost attributable to a past service liability is generally amortized over 30 years.

Normal costs and supplemental costs under a plan are computed on the basis of an actuarial valuation of the assets and liabilities of a plan. An actuarial valuation is generally required annually and is made as of a date within the plan year or within one month before the beginning of the plan year. However, a valuation date within the preceding plan year may be used if, as of that date, the value of the plan's assets is at least 100 percent of the plan's current liability (i.e., the present value of benefits under the plan, as described below).

For funding purposes, the actuarial value of plan assets may be used, rather than fair market value. The actuarial value of plan assets is the value determined on the basis of a reasonable actuarial valuation method that takes into account fair market value and is permitted under Treasury regulations. Any actuarial valuation method used must result in a value of plan assets that is not less than 80 percent of the fair market value of the assets and not more than 120 percent of the fair market value. In addition, if the valuation method uses average value of the plan assets, values may be used for a stated period not to exceed the five most recent plan years, including the current year.

In applying the funding rules, all costs, liabilities, interest rates, and other factors are required to be determined on the basis of actuarial assumptions and methods, each of which is reasonable (taking into account the experience of the plan and reasonable expectations), or which, in the aggregate, result in a total plan contribution equivalent to a contribution that would

4

be determined if each assumption and method were reasonable. In addition, the assumptions are required to offer the actuary's best estimate of anticipated experience under the plan.[4]

Additional contributions for underfunded plans

In general

Under special funding rules (referred to as the "deficit reduction contribution" rules),[5] an additional charge to a plan's funding standard account is generally required for a plan year if the plan's funded current liability percentage for the plan year is less than 90 percent.[6] A plan's "funded current liability percentage" is generally the actuarial value of plan assets as a percentage of the plan's current liability.[7] In general, a plan's current liability means all liabilities to employees and their beneficiaries under the plan, determined on a present-value basis.

The amount of the additional charge required under the deficit reduction contribution rules is the sum of two amounts: (1) the excess, if any, of (a) the deficit reduction contribution (as described below), over (b) the contribution required under the normal funding rules; and (2) the amount (if any) required with respect to unpredictable contingent event benefits. The amount of the additional charge cannot exceed the amount needed to increase the plan's funded current liability percentage to 100 percent (taking into account the expected increase in current liability due to benefits accruing during the plan year).

The deficit reduction contribution is generally the sum of (1) the "unfunded old liability amount," (2) the "unfunded new liability amount," and (3) the expected increase in current

---

[4] Under present law, certain changes in actuarial assumptions that decrease the liabilities of an underfunded single-employer plan must be approved by the Secretary of the Treasury.

[5] The deficit reduction contribution rules apply to single-employer plans, other than single-employer plans with no more than 100 participants on any day in the preceding plan year. Single-employer plans with more than 100 but not more than 150 participants are generally subject to lower contribution requirements under these rules.

[6] Under an alternative test, a plan is not subject to the deficit reduction contribution rules for a plan year if (1) the plan's funded current liability percentage for the plan year is at least 80 percent, and (2) the plan's funded current liability percentage was at least 90 percent for each of the two immediately preceding plan years or each of the second and third immediately preceding plan years.

[7] In determining a plan's funded current liability percentage for a plan year, the value of the plan's assets is generally reduced by the amount of any credit balance under the plan's funding standard account. However, this reduction does not apply in determining the plan's funded current liability percentage for purposes of whether an additional charge is required under the deficit reduction contribution rules.

liability due to benefits accruing during the plan year.[8] The "unfunded old liability amount" is the amount needed to amortize certain unfunded liabilities under 1987 and 1994 transition rules. The "unfunded new liability amount" is the applicable percentage of the plan's unfunded new liability. Unfunded new liability generally means the unfunded current liability of the plan (i.e., the amount by which the plan's current liability exceeds the actuarial value of plan assets), but determined without regard to certain liabilities (such as the plan's unfunded old liability and unpredictable contingent event benefits). The applicable percentage is generally 30 percent, but decreases by .40 of one percentage point for each percentage point by which the plan's funded current liability percentage exceeds 60 percent. For example, if a plan's funded current liability percentage is 85 percent (i.e., it exceeds 60 percent by 25 percentage points), the applicable percentage is 20 percent (30 percent minus 10 percentage points (25 multiplied by .4)).[9]

A plan may provide for unpredictable contingent event benefits, which are benefits that depend on contingencies that are not reliably and reasonably predictable, such as facility shutdowns or reductions in workforce. The value of any unpredictable contingent event benefit is not considered in determining additional contributions until the event has occurred. The event on which an unpredictable contingent event benefit is contingent is generally not considered to have occurred until all events on which the benefit is contingent have occurred.

Required interest rate and mortality table

Specific interest rate and mortality assumptions must be used in determining a plan's current liability for purposes of the special funding rule. For plans years beginning before January 1, 2004, and after December 31, 2005, the interest rate used to determine a plan's current liability must be within a permissible range of the weighted average of the interest rates on 30-year Treasury securities for the four-year period ending on the last day before the plan year begins.[10] The permissible range is generally from 90 percent to 105 percent (120 percent for plan years beginning in 2002 or 2003).[11] The interest rate used under the plan generally must be consistent with the assumptions which reflect the purchase rates that would be used by insurance companies to satisfy the liabilities under the plan.[12]

_____

[8] The deficit reduction contribution may also include an additional amount as a result of the use of a new mortality table prescribed by the Secretary of the Treasury in determining current liability for plan years beginning after 2006, as described below.

[9] In making these computations, the value of the plan's assets is reduced by the amount of any credit balance under the plan's funding standard account.

[10] The weighting used for this purpose is 40 percent, 30 percent, 20 percent and 10 percent, starting with the most recent year in the four-year period. Notice 88-73, 1988-2 C.B. 383.

[11] If the Secretary of the Treasury determines that the lowest permissible interest rate in this range is unreasonably high, the Secretary may prescribe a lower rate, but not less than 80 percent of the weighted average of the 30-year Treasury rate.

[12] Code sec. 412(b)(5)(B)(iii)(II); ERISA sec. 302(b)(5)(B)(iii)(II). Under Notice 90-11, 1990-1 C.B. 319, the interest rates in the permissible range are deemed to be consistent with the assumptions

6

Under the Pension Funding Equity Act of 2004 ("PFEA 2004"),[13] a special interest rate applies in determining current liability for plan years beginning in 2004 or 2005.[14] For these years, the interest rate used must be within a permissible range of the weighted average of the rates of interest on amounts invested conservatively in long-term investment-grade corporate bonds during the four-year period ending on the last day before the plan year begins. The permissible range for these years is from 90 percent to 100 percent. The interest rate is to be determined by the Secretary of the Treasury on the basis of two or more indices that are selected periodically by the Secretary and are in the top three quality levels available.

In determining current liability, the 1983 Group Annuity Mortality Table has been used since 1995.[15] Under present law, the Secretary of the Treasury may prescribe other tables to be used based on the actual experience of pension plans and projected trends in such experience. In addition, the Secretary of the Treasury is required to periodically review (at least every five years) any tables in effect and, to the extent the Secretary determines necessary, update such tables to reflect the actuarial experience of pension plans and projected trends in such experience.[16] Under Prop. Treas. Reg. 1.412(l)(7)-1, beginning in 2007, RP-2000 Mortality Tables are used with improvements in mortality (including future improvements) projected to the current year and with separate tables for annuitants and nonannuitants.[17]

Other rules

Full funding limitation

No contributions are required under the minimum funding rules in excess of the full funding limitation. The full funding limitation is the excess, if any, of (1) the accrued liability under the plan (including normal cost), over (2) the lesser of (a) the market value of plan assets or (b) the actuarial value of plan assets.[18] However, the full funding limitation may not be less

---

reflecting the purchase rates that would be used by insurance companies to satisfy the liabilities under the plan.

[13] Pub. L. No. 108-218 (2004).

[14] In addition, under PFEA 2004, if certain requirements are met, reduced contributions under the deficit reduction contribution rules apply for plan years beginning after December 27, 2003, and before December 28, 2005, in the case of plans maintained by commercial passenger airlines, employers primarily engaged in the production or manufacture of a steel mill product or in the processing of iron ore pellets, or a certain labor organization.

[15] Rev. Rul. 95-28, 1995-1 C.B. 74. Separate mortality tables are required to be used with respect to disabled participants.

[16] Code sec. 412(l)(7)(C)(ii)(III); ERISA sec. 302(d)(7)(C)(ii)(III).

[17] Separate tables continue to apply with respect to disabled participants.

[18] For plan years beginning before 2004, the full funding limitation was generally defined as the excess, if any, of (1) the lesser of (a) the accrued liability under the plan (including normal cost) or (b) a

than the excess, if any, of 90 percent of the plan's current liability (including the expected increase in current liability due to benefits accruing during the plan year) over the actuarial value of plan assets. In general, current liability is all liabilities to plan participants and beneficiaries accrued to date, whereas the accrued liability under the full funding limitation may be based on projected future benefits, including future salary increases.

Timing of plan contributions

In general, plan contributions required to satisfy the funding rules must be made within 8½ months after the end of the plan year. If the contribution is made by such due date, the contribution is treated as if it were made on the last day of the plan year.

In the case of a plan with a funded current liability percentage of less than 100 percent for the preceding plan year, estimated contributions for the current plan year must be made in quarterly installments during the current plan year.[19] The amount of each required installment is generally 25 percent of the lesser of (1) 90 percent of the amount required to be contributed for the current plan year or (2) 100 percent of the amount required to be contributed for the preceding plan year.[20] If a required installment is not made, interest applies for the period of underpayment at a rate of the greater of (1) 175 percent of the Federal mid-term rate, or (2) the plan rate.

Funding waivers

Within limits, the Secretary of the Treasury is permitted to waive all or a portion of the contributions required under the minimum funding standard for a plan year (a "waived funding deficiency").[21] A waiver may be granted if the employer (or employers) responsible for the contribution could not make the required contribution without temporary substantial business hardship and if requiring the contribution would be adverse to the interests of plan participants in the aggregate. Generally, no more than three waivers may be granted within any period of 15 consecutive plan years.

---

percentage (170 percent for 2003) of the plan's current liability (including the current liability normal cost), over (2) the lesser of (a) the market value of plan assets or (b) the actuarial value of plan assets, but in no case less than the excess, if any, of 90 percent of the plan's current liability over the actuarial value of plan assets. Under the Economic Growth and Tax Relief Reconciliation Act of 2001 ("EGTRRA"), the full funding limitation based on 170 percent of current liability is repealed for plan years beginning in 2004 and thereafter. The provisions of EGTRRA generally do not apply for years beginning after December 31, 2010.

[19] Code sec. 412(m); ERISA sec. 302(e).

[20] If quarterly contributions are required with respect to a plan, the amount of a quarterly installment must also be sufficient to cover any shortfall in the plan's liquid assets (a "liquidity shortfall").

[21] Code sec. 412(d); ERISA sec. 303. Under similar rules, the amortization period applicable to an unfunded past service liability or loss may also be extended.

The IRS is authorized to require security to be provided as a condition of granting a waiver of the minimum funding standard if the sum of the plan's accumulated funding deficiency and the balance of any outstanding waived funding deficiencies exceeds $1 million.

Failure to make required contributions

An employer is generally subject to an excise tax if it fails to make minimum required contributions and fails to obtain a waiver from the IRS.[22] The excise tax is 10 percent of the amount of the accumulated funding deficiency. In addition, a tax of 100 percent may be imposed if the accumulated funding deficiency is not corrected within a certain period.

If the total of the contributions the employer fails to make (plus interest) exceeds $1 million and the plan's funded current liability percentage is less than 100 percent, a lien arises in favor of the plan with respect to all property of the employer and the members of the employer's controlled group. The amount of the lien is the total amount of the missed contributions (plus interest).

Explanation of Provision

Interest rate required for plan years beginning in 2006 and 2007

For plan years beginning after December 31, 2005, and before January 1, 2008, the provision applies the present-law funding rules, with an extension of the interest rate applicable in determining current liability for plan years beginning in 2004 and 2005. Thus, in determining current liability for funding purposes for plan years beginning in 2006 and 2007, the interest rate used must be within the permissible range (90 to 100 percent) of the weighted average of the rates of interest on amounts invested conservatively in long-term investment-grade corporate bonds during the four-year period ending on the last day before the plan year begins.

Funding rules for plan years beginning after 2007 - in general

For plan years beginning after December 31, 2007, in the case of single-employer defined benefit plans, the provision repeals the present-law funding rules (including the requirement that a funding standard account be maintained) and provides a new set of rules for determining minimum required contributions.[23] Under the provision, the minimum required contribution to a single-employer defined benefit pension plan for a plan year generally depends on a comparison of the value of the plan's assets with the plan's funding target and target normal cost. As described in more detail below, under the provision, credit balances generated under present law

---

[22] Code sec. 4971. An excise tax applies also if a quarterly installment is less than the amount required to cover the plan's liquidity shortfall.

[23] A delayed effective date applies to certain plans as discussed in Items C, D and E below. Changes to the funding rules for multiemployer plans are discussed in Title II below. Governmental plans and church plans continue to be exempt from the funding rules to the extent provided under present law.

are carried over (into a "funding standard carryover balance") and generally may be used in certain circumstances to reduce otherwise required minimum contributions. In addition, as described more fully below, contributions in excess of the minimum contributions required under the provision for plan years beginning after 2007 generally are credited to a prefunding balance that may be used in certain circumstances to reduce otherwise required minimum contributions. To facilitate the use of such balances to reduce minimum required contributions, while avoiding use of such balances for more than one purpose, in some circumstances the value of plan assets is reduced by the prefunding balance and/or the funding standard carryover balance.

The minimum required contribution for a plan year, based on the value of plan assets (reduced by any prefunding balance and funding standard carryover balance) compared to the funding target, is shown in the following table:

If:	*The minimum required contribution is:*
the value of plan assets (reduced by any prefunding balance and funding standard carryover balance) is less than the funding target,	the sum of: (1) target normal cost; (2) any shortfall amortization charge; and (3) any waiver amortization charge.
the value of plan assets (reduced by any prefunding balance and funding standard carryover balance) equals or exceeds the funding target,	the target normal cost, reduced (but not below zero) by the excess of (1) the value of plan assets (reduced by any prefunding balance and funding standard carryover balance), over (2) the funding target.

Under the provision, a plan's funding target is the present value of all benefits accrued or earned as of the beginning of the plan year. A plan's target normal cost for a plan year is the present value of benefits expected to accrue or be earned during the plan year. A shortfall amortization charge is generally the sum of the amounts required to amortize any shortfall amortization bases for the plan year and the six preceding plan years. A shortfall amortization base is generally required to be established for a plan year if the plan has a funding shortfall for a plan year.[24] A shortfall amortization base may be positive or negative, i.e., an offsetting amortization base is established for gains. In general, a plan has a funding shortfall if the plan's funding target for the year exceeds the value of the plan's assets (reduced by any prefunding balance and funding standard carryover balance). A waiver amortization charge is the amount required to amortize a waived funding deficiency.

The provision specifies the interest rates and mortality table that must be used in determining a plan's target normal cost and funding target, as well as certain other actuarial

---

[24] Under a special rule, discussed below, a shortfall amortization base does not have to be established if the value of a plan's assets (reduced by any prefunding balance, but only if the employer elects to use any portion of the prefunding balance to reduce required contributions for the year) is at least equal to the plan's funding target for the plan year.

10

assumptions, including special assumptions ("at-risk" assumptions) for a plan in at-risk status. A plan is in at-risk status for a year if the value of the plan's assets (reduced by any prefunding and funding standard carryover balances) for the preceding year was less than (1) 80 percent of the plan's funding target determined without regard to the at-risk assumptions, and (2) 70 percent of the plan's funding target determined using the at-risk assumptions. Under a transition rule, instead of 80 percent, the following percentages apply: 65 percent for 2008, 70 percent for 2009, and 75 percent for 2010.

Target normal cost

Under the provision, the minimum required contribution for a plan year generally includes the plan's target normal cost for the plan year. A plan's target normal cost is the present value of all benefits expected to accrue or be earned under the plan during the plan year (the "current" year). For this purpose, an increase in any benefit attributable to services performed in a preceding year by reason of a compensation increase during the current year is treated as having accrued during the current year.

If the value of a plan's assets (reduced by any funding standard carryover balance and prefunding balance) exceeds the plan's funding target for a plan year, the minimum required contribution for the plan year is target normal cost reduced by such excess (but not below zero).

Funding target and shortfall amortization charges

In general

If the value of a plan's assets (reduced by any funding standard carryover balance and prefunding balance) is less than the plan's funding target for a plan year, so that the plan has a funding shortfall,[25] the minimum required contribution is generally increased by a shortfall amortization charge. As discussed more fully below, the shortfall amortization charge is the aggregate total (not less than zero) of the shortfall amortization installments for the plan year with respect to any shortfall amortization bases for the plan year and the six preceding plan years.

Funding target

A plan's funding target for a plan year is the present value of all benefits accrued or earned under the plan as of the beginning of the plan year. For this purpose, all benefits (including early retirement or similar benefits) are taken into account. Benefits accruing in the

---

[25] Under a special rule, in determining a plan's funding shortfall, the value of plan assets is not reduced by any funding standard carryover balance or prefunding balance if, with respect to the funding standard carryover balance or prefunding balance, there is in effect for the year a binding written with the Pension Benefit Guaranty Corporation which provides that such balance is not available to reduce the minimum required contribution for the plan year.

plan year are not taken into account in determining the plan's funding target, regardless of whether the valuation date for the plan year is later than the first day of the plan year.[26]

Shortfall amortization charge

The shortfall amortization charge for a plan year is the aggregate total (not less than zero) of the shortfall amortization installments for the plan year with respect to any shortfall amortization bases for that plan year and the six preceding plan years. The shortfall amortization installments with respect to a shortfall amortization base for a plan year are the amounts necessary to amortize the shortfall amortization base in level annual installments over the seven-plan-year period beginning with the plan year. The shortfall amortization installment with respect to a shortfall amortization base for any plan year in the seven-year period is the annual installment determined for that year for that shortfall amortization base. Shortfall amortization installments are determined using the appropriate segment interest rates (discussed below).

Shortfall amortization base and phase-in of funding target

A shortfall amortization base is determined for a plan year based on the plan's funding shortfall for the plan year. The funding shortfall is the amount (if any) by which the plan's funding target for the year exceeds the value of the plan's assets (reduced by any funding standard carryover balance and prefunding balance).

The shortfall amortization base for a plan year is (1) the plan's funding shortfall, minus (2) the present value, determined using the segment interest rates (discussed below), of the aggregate total of the shortfall amortization installments and waiver amortization installments that have been determined for the plan year and any succeeding plan year with respect to any shortfall amortization bases and waiver amortization bases for preceding plan years.

A shortfall amortization base may be positive or negative, depending on whether the present value of remaining installments with respect to prior year amortization bases is more or less than the plan's funding shortfall. In either case, the shortfall amortization base is amortized over seven years. Shortfall amortization installments for a particular plan year with respect to positive and negative shortfall amortization bases are netted in determining the shortfall amortization charge for the plan year, but the resulting shortfall amortization charge cannot be less than zero. Thus, negative amortization installments may not offset waiver amortization installments or normal cost.

Under a special rule, a shortfall amortization base does not have to be established for a plan year if the value of a plan's assets (reduced by any prefunding balance, but only if the employer elects to use any portion of the prefunding balance to reduce required contributions for the year) is at least equal to the plan's funding target for the plan year. For purposes of the special rule, a transition rule applies for plan years beginning after 2007 and before 2011. The transition rule does not apply to a plan that (1) is not in effect for 2007, or (2) is subject to the

---

[26] Benefits accruing during the plan year are taken into account in determining normal cost for the plan year.

present-law deficit reduction contribution rules for 2007 (i.e., a plan covering more than 100 participants and with a funded current liability below the applicable threshold).

Under the transition rule, a shortfall amortization base does not have to be established for a plan year during the transition period if the value of plan assets (reduced by any prefunding balance, but only if the employer elects to use the prefunding balance to reduce required contributions for the year) for the plan year is at least equal to the applicable percentage of the plan's funding target for the year. The applicable percentage is 92 percent for 2008, 94 percent for 2009, and 96 percent for 2010. However, the transition rule does not apply to a plan for any plan year after 2008 unless, for each preceding plan year after 2007, the plan's shortfall amortization base was zero (i.e., the plan was eligible for the special rule each preceding year).

Early deemed amortization of funding shortfalls for preceding years

If a plan's funding shortfall for a plan year is zero (i.e., the value of the plan's assets, reduced by any funding standard carryover balance and prefunding balance, is at least equal to the plan's funding target for the year), any shortfall amortization bases for preceding plan years are eliminated. That is, for purposes of determining any shortfall amortization charges for that year and succeeding years, the shortfall amortization bases for all preceding years (and all shortfall amortization installments determined with respect to such bases) are reduced to zero.

Waiver amortization charges

The provision retains the present-law rules under which the Secretary of the Treasury may waive all or a portion of the contributions required under the minimum funding standard for a plan year (referred to as a "waived funding deficiency").[27] If a plan has a waived funding deficiency for any of the five preceding plan years, the minimum required contribution for the plan year is increased by the waiver amortization charge for the plan year.

The waiver amortization charge for a plan year is the aggregate total of the waiver amortization installments for the plan year with respect to any waiver amortization bases for the five preceding plan years. The waiver amortization installments with respect to a waiver amortization base for a plan year are the amounts necessary to amortize the waiver amortization base in level annual installments over the five-year plan period beginning with the succeeding plan year. The waiver amortization installment with respect to that waiver amortization base for any plan year in the five-year period is the annual installment determined for the shortfall amortization base. Waiver amortization installments are determined using the appropriate segment interest rates (discussed below). The waiver amortization base for a plan year is the amount of the waived funding deficiency (if any) for the plan year.

If a plan's funding shortfall for a plan year is zero (i.e., the value of the plan's assets, reduced by any funding standard carryover balance and prefunding balance, is at least equal to the plan's funding target for the year), any waiver amortization bases for preceding plan years

---

[27] In the case of single-employer plans, the provision repeals the present-law rules under which the amortization period applicable to an unfunded past service liability or loss may be extended.

are eliminated. That is, for purposes of determining any waiver amortization charges for that year and succeeding years, the waiver amortization bases for all preceding years (and all waiver amortization installments determined with respect to such bases) are reduced to zero.

Actuarial assumptions used in determining a plan's target normal cost and funding target

Interest rates

The provision specifies the interest rates that must be used in determining a plan's target normal cost and funding target. Under the provision, present value is determined using three interest rates ("segment" rates), each of which applies to benefit payments expected to be made from the plan during a certain period. The first segment rate applies to benefits reasonably determined to be payable during the five-year period beginning on the first day of the plan year; the second segment rate applies to benefits reasonably determined to be payable during the 15-year period following the initial five-year period; and the third segment rate applies to benefits reasonably determined to be payable the end of the 15-year period. Each segment rate is a single interest rate determined monthly by the Secretary of the Treasury on the basis of a corporate bond yield curve, taking into account only the portion of the yield curve based on corporate bonds maturing during the particular segment rate period.

The corporate bond yield curve used for this purpose is to be prescribed on a monthly basis by the Secretary of the Treasury and reflect the average, for the 24-month period ending with the preceding month, of yields on investment grade corporate bonds with varying maturities and that are in the top three quality levels available. The yield curve should reflect the average of the rates on all bonds in the top three quality levels on which the yield curve is based.

The Secretary of the Treasury is directed to publish each month the corporate bond yield curve and each of the segment rates for the month. In addition, such Secretary is directed to publish a description of the methodology used to determine the yield curve and segment rates, which is sufficiently detailed to enable plans to make reasonable projections regarding the yield curve and segment rates for future months, based on a plan's projection of future interest rates.

Under the provision, the present value of liabilities under a plan is determined using the segment rates for the "applicable month" for the plan year. The applicable month is the month that includes the plan's valuation date for the plan year, or, at the election of the plan sponsor, any of the four months preceding the month that includes the valuation date. An election of a preceding month applies to the plan year for which it is made and all succeeding plan years unless revoked with the consent of the Secretary of the Treasury.

Solely for purposes of determining minimum required contributions, in lieu of the segment rates described above, an employer may elect to use interest rates on a yield curve based on the yields on investment grade corporate bonds for the month preceding the month in which the plan year begins (i.e., without regard to the 24-month averaging described above). Such an election may be revoked only with consent of the Secretary of the Treasury.

The provision provides a transition rule for plan years beginning in 2008 and 2009 (other than for plans first effective after December 31, 2007). Under this rule, for plan years beginning in 2008, the first, second, or third segment rate with respect to any month is the sum of: (1) the product of the segment rate otherwise determined for the month, multiplied by 33-⅓ percent; and (2) the product of the applicable long-term corporate bond rate,[28] multiplied by 66-⅔ percent. For plan years beginning in 2009, the first, second, or third segment rate with respect to any month is the sum of: (1) the product of the segment rate otherwise determined for the month, multiplied by 66⅔ percent; and (2) the product of applicable long-term corporate bond rate multiplied by 33⅓ percent. An employer may elect not to have the transition rule apply with respect to a plan. Such an election may be revoked only with consent of the Secretary of the Treasury.

Under the provision, certain amounts are determined using the plan's "effective interest rate" for a plan year. The effective interest rate with respect to a plan for a plan year is the single rate of interest which, if used to determine the present value of the benefits taken into account in determining the plan's funding target for the year, would result in an amount equal to the plan's funding target (as determined using the first, second, and third segment rates).

Mortality table

Under the provision, the Secretary of the Treasury is directed to prescribe by regulation the mortality tables to be used in determining present value or making any computation under the funding rules.[29] Such tables are to be based on the actual experience of pension plans and projected trends in such experience. In prescribing tables, the Secretary is to take into account results of available independent studies of mortality of individuals covered by pension plans. In addition, the Secretary is required (at least every 10 years) to revise any table in effect to reflect the actual experience of pension plans and projected trends in such experience.

The provision also provides for the use of a separate mortality table upon request of the plan sponsor and approval by the Secretary of the Treasury in accordance with procedures described below. In order for the table to be used: (1) the table must reflect the actual experience of the pension plans maintained by the plan sponsor and projected trends in general mortality experience, and (2) there must be a sufficient number of plan participants, and the pension plans must have been maintained for a sufficient period of time, to have credible information necessary for that purpose. A separate mortality table can be a mortality table constructed by the plan's enrolled actuary from the plan's own experience or a table that is an adjustment to the table prescribed by the Secretary which sufficiently reflects the plan's experience. Except as provided by the Secretary, a separate table may not be used for any plan unless (1) a separate table is established and used for each other plan maintained by the plan sponsor and, if the plan sponsor is a member of a controlled group, each member of the

---

[28] The applicable long-term corporate bond rate is a rate that is from 90 to 100 percent of the weighted average of the rates of interest on amounts invested conservatively in long-term investment-grade corporate bonds during the four-year period ending on the last day before the plan year begins as determined by the Secretary under the method in effect for 2007.

[29] As under present law, separate mortality tables are required to be used with respect to disabled participants.

controlled group,[30] and (2) the requirements for using a separate table are met with respect to the table established for each plan, taking into account only the participants of that plan, the time that plan has been in existence, and the actual experience of that plan. In general, a separate plan may be used during the period of consecutive year plan years (not to exceed 10) specified in the request. However, a separate mortality table ceases to be in effect as of the earlier of (1) the date on which there is a significant change in the participants in the plan by reason of a plan spinoff or merger or otherwise, or (2) the date on which the plan actuary determines that the table does not meet the requirements for being used.

A plan sponsor must submit a separate mortality table to the Secretary for approval at least seven months before the first day of the period for which the table is to be used. A mortality table submitted to the Secretary for approval is treated as in effect as of the first day of the period unless the Secretary, during the 180-day period beginning on the date of the submission, disapproves of the table and provides the reasons that the table fails to meet the applicable criteria. The 180-day period is to be extended upon mutual agreement of the Secretary and the plan sponsor.

Other assumptions

Under the provision, in determining any present value or making any computation, the probability that future benefits will be paid in optional forms of benefit provided under the plan must be taken into account (including the probability of lump-sum distributions determined on the basis of the plan's experience and other related assumptions). The assumptions used to determine optional forms of benefit under a plan may differ from the assumptions used to determine present value for purposes of the funding rules under the provision. Differences in the present value of future benefit payments that result from the different assumptions used to determine optional forms of benefit under a plan must be taken into account in determining any present value or making any computation for purposes of the funding rules.

The provision generally does not require other specified assumptions to be used in determining the plan's target normal cost and funding target except in the case of at-risk plans (discussed below). However, similar to present law, the determination of present value or other computation must be made on the basis of actuarial assumptions and methods, each of which is reasonable (taking into account the experience of the plan and reasonable expectations), and which, in combination, offer the actuary's best estimate of anticipated experience under the plan.[31]

---

[30] For example, the Secretary may deem it appropriate to provide an exception in the case of a small plan.

[31] The provision retains the present-law rule under which certain changes in actuarial assumptions that decrease the liabilities of an underfunded single-employer plan must be approved by the Secretary of the Treasury.

Special assumptions for at-risk plans

The provision applies special assumptions ("at-risk" assumptions) in determining the funding target and normal cost of a plan in at-risk status. Whether a plan is in at-risk status for a plan year depends on its funding target attainment percentage for the preceding year. A plan's funding target attainment percentage for a plan year is the ratio, expressed as a percentage, that the value of the plan's assets (reduced by any funding standard carryover balance and prefunding balance) bears to the plan's funding target for the year. For this purpose, the plan's funding target is determined using the actuarial assumptions for plans that are not at-risk.

Under the provision, a plan is in at-risk status for a year if, for the preceding year: (1) the plan's funding target attainment percentage, determined without regard to the at-risk assumptions, was less than 80 percent (with a transition rule discussed below), and (2) the plan's funding target attainment percentage, determined using the at-risk assumptions (without regard to whether the plan was in at-risk status for the preceding year), was less than 70 percent. Under a transition rule applicable for plan years beginning in 2008, 2009, and 2010, instead of 80 percent, the following percentages apply: 65 percent for 2008, 70 percent for 2009, and 75 percent for 2010. In the case of plan years beginning in 2008, the plan's funding target attainment percentage for the preceding plan year may be determined using such methods of estimation as the Secretary of Treasury may provide.

Under the provision, the at-risk rules do not apply if a plan had 500 or fewer participants on each day during the preceding plan year. For this purpose, all defined benefit pension plans (other than multiemployer plans) maintained by the same employer (or a predecessor employer), or by any member of such employer's controlled group, are treated as a single plan, but only participants with respect to such employer or controlled group member are taken into account.

If a plan is in at-risk status, the plan's funding target and normal cost are determined using the assumptions that: (1) all employees who are not otherwise assumed to retire as of the valuation date, but who will be eligible to elect benefits in the current and 10 succeeding years, are assumed to retire at the earliest retirement date under plan, but not before the end of the plan year; and (2) all employees are assumed to elect the retirement benefit available under the plan at the assumed retirement age that results in the highest present value. In some cases, a loading factor also applies.

The at-risk assumptions are not applied to certain employees of specified automobile manufacturers for purposes of determining whether a plan is in at-risk status, i.e., whether the plan's funding target attainment percentage, determined using the at-risk assumptions, was less than 70 percent for the preceding plan year. An employee is disregarded for this purpose if: (1) the employee is employed by a specified automobile manufacturer; (2) the employee is offered, pursuant to a bona fide retirement incentive program, a substantial amount of additional cash compensation, substantially enhanced retirement benefits under the plan, or materially reduced employment duties, on the condition that by a specified date no later than December 31, 2010, the employee retires (as defined under the terms of the plan; (3) the offer is made during 2006 pursuant to a bona fide retirement incentive program and requires that the offer can be accepted no later than a specified date (not later than December 31, 2006); and (4) the employee does not accept the offer before the specified date on which the offer expires. For this purpose, a

17

specified automobile manufacturer is (1) any automobile manufacturer and (2) any manufacturer of automobile parts that supplies parts directly to an automobile manufacturer and which, after a transaction or series of transactions ending in 1999, ceased to be a member of the automobile manufacturer's controlled group.

The funding target of a plan in at-risk status for a plan year is generally the sum of: (1) the present value of all benefits accrued or earned as of the beginning of the plan year, determined using the at-risk assumptions described above, and (2) in the case of a plan that has also been in at-risk status for at least two of the four preceding plans years, a loading factor. The loading factor is the sum of (1) $700 times the number of participants in the plan, plus (2) four percent of the funding target determined without regard to the loading factor.[32] The at-risk funding target is in no event less than the funding target determined without regard to the at-risk rules.

The target normal cost of a plan in at-risk status for a plan year is generally the sum of: (1) the present value of benefits expected to accrue or be earned under the plan during the plan year, determined using the special assumptions described above, and (2) in the case of a plan that has also been in at-risk status for at least two of the four preceding plans years, a loading factor of four percent of the target normal cost determined without regard to the loading factor.[33] The at-risk target normal is in no event less than at-risk normal cost determined without regard to the at-risk rules.

If a plan has been in at-risk status for fewer than five consecutive plan years, the amount of a plan's funding target for a plan year is the sum of: (1) the amount of the funding target determined without regard to the at-risk rules, plus (2) the transition percentage for the plan year of the excess of the amount of the funding target determined under the at-risk rules over the amount determined without regard to the at-risk rules. Similarly, if a plan has been in at-risk status for fewer than five consecutive plan years, the amount of a plan's target normal cost for a plan year is the sum of: (1) the amount of the target normal cost determined without regard to the at-risk rules, plus (2) the transition percentage for the plan year of the excess of the amount of the target normal cost determined under the at-risk rules over the amount determined without regard to the at-risk rules. The transition percentage is the product of 20 percent times the number of consecutive plan years for which the plan has been in at-risk status. In applying this rule, plan years beginning before 2008 are not taken into account.

---

[32] This loading factor is intended to reflect the cost of purchasing group annuity contracts in the case of termination of the plan.

[33] Target normal cost for a plan in at-risk status does not include a loading factor of $700 per plan participant.

Funding standard carryover balance or prefunding balance

In general

The provision preserves credit balances that have accumulated under present law (referred to as "funding standard carryover balances"). In addition, for plan years beginning after 2007, new credit balances (referred to as "prefunding balances") result if an employer makes contributions greater than those required under the new funding rules. In general, under the bill, employers may choose whether to count funding standard carryover balances and prefunding balances in determining the value of plan assets or to use the balances to reduce required contributions, but not both. In this regard, the provision provides more favorable rules with respect to the use of funding standard carryover balances.

Under the provision, if the value of a plan's assets (reduced by any prefunding balance) is at least 80 percent of the plan's funding target (determined without regard to the at-risk rules) for the preceding plan year,[34] the plan sponsor may elect to credit all or a portion of the funding standard carryover balance or prefunding balance against the minimum required contribution for the current plan year (determined after any funding waiver), thus reducing the amount that must be contributed for the current plan year.

The value of plan assets is generally reduced by any funding standard carryover balance or prefunding balance for purposes of determining minimum required contributions, including a plan's funding shortfall, and a plan's funding target attainment percentage (discussed above). However, the plan sponsor may elect to permanently reduce a funding standard carryover balance or prefunding balance, so that the value of plan assets is not required to be reduced by that amount in determining the minimum required contribution for the plan year. Any reduction of a funding standard carryover balance or prefunding balance applies before determining the balance that is available for crediting against minimum required contributions for the plan year.

Funding standard carryover balance

In the case of a single-employer plan that is in effect for a plan year beginning in 2007 and, as of the end of the 2007 plan year, has a positive balance in the funding standard account maintained under the funding rules as in effect for 2007, the plan sponsor may elect to maintain a funding standard carryover balance. The funding standard carryover balance consists of a beginning balance in the amount of the positive balance in the funding standard account as of the end of the 2007 plan year, decreased (as described below) and adjusted to reflect the rate of net gain or loss on plan assets.

For subsequent years (i.e., as of the first day of each plan year beginning after 2008), the funding standard carryover balance of a plan is decreased (but not below zero) by the sum of: (1) any amount credited to reduce the minimum required contribution for the preceding plan year, plus (2) any amount elected by the plan sponsor as a reduction in the funding standard carryover

---

[34] In the case of plan years beginning in 2008, the percentage for the preceding plan year may be determined using such methods of estimation as the Secretary of Treasury may provide.

balance (thus reducing the amount by which the value of plan assets must be reduced in determining minimum required contributions).

Prefunding balance

The plan sponsor may elect to maintain a prefunding balance, which consists of a beginning balance of zero for the 2008 plan year, increased and decreased (as described below) and adjusted to reflect the rate of net gain or loss on plan assets.

For subsequent years, i.e., as of the first day of plan year beginning after 2008 (the "current" plan year), the plan sponsor may increase the prefunding balance by an amount, not to exceed (1) the excess (if any) of the aggregate total employer contributions for the preceding plan year, over (2) the minimum required contribution for the preceding plan year. For this purpose, any excess contribution for the preceding plan year is adjusted for interest accruing for the periods between the first day of the current plan year and the dates on which the excess contributions were made, determined using the effective interest rate of the plan for the preceding plan year and treating contributions as being first used to satisfy the minimum required contribution.

The amount by which the aggregate total employer contributions for the preceding plan year exceeds the minimum required contribution for the preceding plan year is reduced (but not below zero) by the amount of contributions an employer would need to make to avoid a benefit limitation that would otherwise be imposed for the preceding plan year under the provisions of the provision relating to benefit limitations for single-employer plans.[35] Thus, contributions needed to avoid a benefit limitation do not result in an increase in the plan's prefunding balance.[36]

As of the first day of each plan year beginning after 2008, the prefunding balance of a plan is decreased (but not below zero) by the sum of: (1) any amount credited to reduce the minimum required contribution for the preceding plan year, plus (2) any amount elected by the plan sponsor as a reduction in the prefunding balance (thus reducing the amount by which the value of plan assets must be reduced in determining minimum required contributions). As discussed above, if any portion of the prefunding balance is used to reduce a minimum required contribution, the value of plan assets must be reduced by the prefunding balance in determining whether a shortfall amortization base must be established for the plan year (i.e., whether the value of plan assets for a plan year is less than the plan's funding target for the plan year). Thus, the prefunding balance may not be included in the value of plan assets in order to avoid a shortfall amortization base for a plan year and also used to reduce the minimum required contribution for the same year.

---

[35] Any contribution that may be taken into account in satisfying the requirement to make additional contributions with respect to more than one type of benefit limitation is taken into account only once for purposes of this reduction.

[36] The benefit limitations are discussed in Part B below.

Other rules

In determining the prefunding balance or funding standard carryover balance as of the first day of a plan year, the plan sponsor must adjust the balance in accordance with regulations prescribed by the Secretary of the Treasury to reflect the rate of return on plan assets for the preceding year. The rate of return is determined on the basis of the fair market value of the plan assets and must properly take into account, in accordance with regulations, all contributions, distributions, and other plan payments made during the period.

To the extent that a plan has a funding standard carryover balance of more than zero for a plan year, none of the plan's prefunding balance may be credited to reduce a minimum required contribution, nor may an election be made to reduce the prefunding balance for purposes of determining the value of plan assets. Thus, the funding standard carryover balance must be used for these purposes before the prefunding balance may be used.

Any election relating to the prefunding balance and funding standard carryover balance is to be made in such form and manner as the Secretary of the Treasury prescribes.

Other rules and definitions

Valuation date

Under the provision, all determinations made with respect to minimum required contributions for a plan year (such as the value of plan assets and liabilities) must be made as of the plan's valuation date for the plan year. In general, the valuation date for a plan year must be the first day of the plan year. However, any day in the plan year may be designated as the plan's valuation date if, on each day during the preceding plan year, the plan had 100 or fewer participants.[37] For this purpose, all defined benefit pension plans (other than multiemployer plans) maintained by the same employer (or a predecessor employer), or by any member of such employer's controlled group, are treated as a single plan, but only participants with respect to such employer or controlled group member are taken into account.

Value of plan assets

Under the provision, the value of plan assets is generally fair market value. However, the value of plan assets may be determined on the basis of the averaging of fair market values, but only if such method: (1) is permitted under regulations; (2) does not provide for averaging of fair market values over more than the period beginning on the last day of the 25th month preceding the month in which the plan's valuation date occurs and ending on the valuation date (or similar period in the case of a valuation date that's not the first day of a month); and (3) does not result in a determination of the value of plan assets that at any time is less than 90 percent or

---

[37] In the case of a plan's first plan year, the ability to use a valuation date other than the first day of the plan year is determined by taking into account the number of participants the plan is reasonably expected to have on each day during that first plan year.

more than 110 percent of the fair market value of the assets at that time. Any averaging must be adjusted for contributions and distributions as provided by the Secretary of the Treasury.

If a required contribution for a preceding plan year is made after the valuation date for the current year, the contribution is taken into account in determining the value of plan assets for the current plan year. For plan years beginning after 2008, only the present value of the contribution is taken into account, determined as of the valuation date for the current plan year, using the plan's effective interest rate for the preceding plan year. In addition, any required contribution for the current plan year is not taken into account in determining the value of plan assets. If any contributions for the current plan year are made before the valuation date, plan assets as of the valuation date does not include (1) the contributions, and (2) interest on the contributions for the period between the date of the contributions and the valuation date, determined using the plan's effective interest rate for the current plan year.

Timing rules for contributions

As under present law, the due date for the payment of a minimum required contribution for a plan year is generally 8½ months after the end of the plan year. Any payment made on a date other than the valuation date for the plan year must be adjusted for interest accruing at the plan's effective interest rate for the plan year for the period between the valuation date and the payment date. Quarterly contributions must be made during a plan year if the plan had a funding shortfall for the preceding plan year (that is, if the value of the plan's assets, reduced by the funding standard carryover balance and prefunding balance, was less than the plan's funding target for the preceding plan year).[38] If a quarterly installment is not made, interest applies for the period of underpayment at the rate of interest otherwise applicable (i.e., the plan's effective interest rate) plus 5 percentage points.

Excise tax on failure to make minimum required contributions

The provision retains the present-law rules under which an employer is generally subject to an excise tax if it fails to make minimum required contributions and fails to obtain a waiver from the IRS.[39] The excise tax is 10 percent of the aggregate unpaid minimum required contributions for all plan years remaining unpaid as of the end of any plan year. In addition, a tax of 100 percent may be imposed if any unpaid minimum required contributions remain unpaid after a certain period.

---

[38] The provision retains the present-law rules under which the amount of any quarterly installment must be sufficient to cover any liquidity shortfall.

[39] The provision retains the present-law rules under which a lien in favor of the plan with respect to property of the employer (and members of the employer's controlled group) arises in certain circumstances in which the employer fails to make required contributions.

<u>Conforming changes</u>

The provision makes various technical and conforming changes to reflect the new funding requirements.

Effective Date

The extension of the interest rate applicable in determining current liability for plan years beginning in 2004 and 2005 is effective for plan years beginning after December 31, 2005, and before January 1, 2008. The modifications to the single-employer plan funding rules are effective for plan years beginning after December 31, 2007.

B. Benefit Limitations Under Single-Employer Defined Benefit Pension Plans (new secs. 101(j) and 206(g) and (h) of ERISA, and new secs. 436-437 of the Code)

Present Law

Plant shutdown and other unpredictable contingent event benefits

A plan may provide for unpredictable contingent event benefits, which are benefits that depend on contingencies other than age, service, compensation, death or disability or that are not reliably and reasonably predictable as determined by the Secretary. Some of these benefits are commonly referred to as "plant shutdown" benefits. Under present law, unpredictable contingent event benefits generally are not taken into account for funding purposes until the event has occurred.

Defined benefit pension plans are not permitted to provide "layoff" benefits (i.e., severance benefits).[40] However, defined benefit pension plans may provide subsidized early retirement benefits, including early retirement window benefits.[41]

Limitation on certain benefit increases while funding waivers in effect

Within limits, the IRS is permitted to waive all or a portion of the contributions required under the minimum funding standard for a plan year.[42] In the case of a single-employer plan, a waiver may be granted if the employer responsible for the contribution could not make the required contribution without temporary substantial business hardship for the employer (and members of the employer's controlled group) and if requiring the contribution would be adverse to the interests of plan participants in the aggregate.

If a funding waiver is in effect for a plan, subject to certain exceptions, no plan amendment may be adopted that increases the liabilities of the plan by reason of any increase in benefits, any change in the accrual of benefits, or any change in the rate at which benefits vest under the plan.[43]

Security for certain plan amendments

In the case of a single-employer defined benefit pension plan, if a plan amendment increasing current liability is adopted and the plan's funded current liability percentage is less than 60 percent (taking into account the effect of the amendment, but disregarding any

---

[40] Treas. Reg. sec. 1.401-1(b)(1)(i).

[41] See, e.g., Treas. Reg. secs. 1.401(a)(4)-3(f)(4) and 1.411(a)-7(c).

[42] Code sec. 412(d); ERISA sec. 303.

[43] Code sec. 412(f); ERISA sec. 304(b)(1).

24

unamortized unfunded old liability), the employer and members of the employer's controlled group must provide security in favor of the plan.[44] The amount of security required is the excess of: (1) the lesser of (a) the amount by which the plan's assets are less than 60 percent of current liability, taking into account the benefit increase, or (b) the amount of the benefit increase and prior benefit increases after December 22, 1987, over (2) $10 million. The amendment is not effective until the security is provided.

The security must be in the form of a surety bond, cash, certain U.S. government obligations, or such other form as is satisfactory to the Secretary of the Treasury and the parties involved. The security is released after the funded liability of the plan reaches 60 percent.

Prohibition on benefit increases during bankruptcy

Subject to certain exceptions, if an employer maintaining a single-employer defined benefit pension plan is involved in bankruptcy proceedings, no plan amendment may be adopted that increases the liabilities of the plan by reason of any increase in benefits, any change in the accrual of benefits, or any change in the rate at which benefits vest under the plan.[45] This limitation does not apply if the plan's funded current liability percentage is at least 100 percent, taking into account the amendment.

Restrictions on benefit payments due to liquidity shortfalls

In the case of a single-employer plan with a funded current liability percentage of less than 100 percent for the preceding plan year, estimated contributions for the current plan year must be made in quarterly installments during the current plan year. If quarterly contributions are required with respect to a plan, the amount of a quarterly installment must also be sufficient to cover any shortfall in the plan's liquid assets (a "liquidity shortfall"). In general, a plan has a liquidity shortfall for a quarter if the plan's liquid assets (such as cash and marketable securities) are less than a certain amount (generally determined by reference to disbursements from the plan in the preceding 12 months).

If a quarterly installment is less than the amount required to cover the plan's liquidity shortfall, limits apply to the benefits that can be paid from a plan during the period of underpayment. During that period, the plan may not make any prohibited payment, defined as: (1) any payment in excess of the monthly amount paid under a single life annuity (plus any social security supplement provided under the plan) to a participant or beneficiary whose annuity starting date occurs during the period; (2) any payment for the purchase of an irrevocable commitment from an insurer to pay benefits (e.g., an annuity contract); or (3) any other payment specified by the Secretary of the Treasury by regulations.[46]

---

[44] Code sec. 401(a)(29); ERISA sec. 307.

[45] Code sec. 401(a)(33); ERISA sec. 204(i).

[46] Code sec. 401(a)(32); ERISA sec. 206(e).

25

Explanation of Provision

Plant shutdown and other unpredictable contingent event benefits

Under the provision, if a participant is entitled to an unpredictable contingent event benefit payable with respect to any event occurring during any plan year, the plan must provide that such benefits may not be provided if the plan's adjusted funding target attainment percentage for that plan year: (1) is less than 60 percent; or (2) would be less than 60 percent taking into account the occurrence of the event. For this purpose, the term unpredictable contingent event benefit means any benefit payable solely by reason of: (1) a plant shutdown (or similar event, as determined by the Secretary of the Treasury); or (2) any event other than attainment of any age, performance of any service, receipt or derivation of any compensation, or the occurrence of death or disability.

The determination of whether the limitation applies is made in the year the unpredictable contingent event occurs. For example, suppose a plan provides for benefits upon the occurrence of a plant shutdown, and a plant shut down occurs in 2010. Taking into account the plan shutdown, the plan's adjusted funding target attainment percentage is less than 60 percent. Thus, the limitation applies, and benefits payable solely by reason of the plant shutdown may not be paid (unless the employer makes contributions to the plan as described below), regardless of whether the benefits will be paid in the 2010 plan year or a later plan year.[47]

The limitation ceases to apply with respect to any plan year, effective as of the first day of the plan year, if the plan sponsor makes a contribution (in addition to any minimum required contribution for the plan year) equal to: (1) if the plan's adjusted funding target attainment percentage is less than 60 percent, the amount of the increase in the plan's funding target for the plan year attributable to the occurrence of the event; or (2) if the plan's adjusted funding target attainment percentage would be less than 60 percent taking into account the occurrence of the event, the amount sufficient to result in a adjusted funding target attainment percentage of 60 percent.

The limitation does not apply for the first five years a plan (or a predecessor plan) is in effect.

Plan amendments increasing benefit liabilities

Certain plan amendments may not take effect during a plan year if the plan's adjusted funding target attainment percentage for the plan year: (1) is less than 80 percent; or (2) would be less than 80 percent taking into account the amendment.[48] In such a case, no amendment may take effect if it has the effect of increasing the liabilities of the plan by reason of any increase in

---

[47] Benefits already being paid as a result of a plant shutdown or other event that occurred in a preceding year are not affected by the limitation.

[48] Under the provision, the present-law rules limiting benefit increases while an employer is in bankruptcy continue to apply.

benefits, the establishment of new benefits, any change in the rate of benefit accrual, or any change in the rate at which benefits vest under the plan. The limitation does not apply to an amendment that provides for an increase in benefits under a formula which is not based on compensation, but only if the rate of increase does not exceed the contemporaneous rate of increase in average wages of the participants covered by the amendment.

The limitation ceases to apply with respect to any plan year, effective as of the first day of the plan year (or, if later, the effective date of the amendment), if the plan sponsor makes a contribution (in addition to any minimum required contribution for the plan year) equal to: (1) if the plan's adjusted funding target attainment percentage is less than 80 percent, the amount of the increase in the plan's funding target for the plan year attributable to the amendment; or (2) if the plan's adjusted funding target attainment percentage would be less than 80 percent taking into account the amendment, the amount sufficient to result in a adjusted funding target attainment percentage of 80 percent.

The limitation does not apply for the first five years a plan (or a predecessor plan) is in effect.

Prohibited payments

A plan must provide that, if the plan's adjusted funding target attainment percentage for a plan year is less than 60 percent, the plan will not make any prohibited payments after the valuation date for the plan year.

A plan must also provide that, if the plan's adjusted funding target attainment percentage for a plan year is 60 percent or greater, but less than 80 percent, the plan may not pay any prohibited payments exceeding the lesser of: (1) 50 percent of the amount otherwise payable under the plan, and (2) the present value of the maximum PBGC guarantee with respect to the participant (determined under guidance prescribed by the PBGC, using the interest rates and mortality table applicable in determining minimum lump-sum benefits). The plan must provide that only one payment under this exception may be made with respect to any participant during any period of consecutive plan years to which the limitation applies. For this purpose, a participant and any beneficiary of the participant (including an alternate payee) is treated as one participant. If the participant's accrued benefit is allocated to an alternate payee and one or more other persons, the amount that may be distributed is allocated in the same manner unless the applicable qualified domestic relations order provides otherwise.

In addition, a plan must provide that, during any period in which the plan sponsor is in bankruptcy proceedings, the plan may not pay any prohibited payment. However, this limitation does not apply on or after the date the plan's enrolled actuary certifies that the adjusted funding target attainment percentage of the plan is not less than 100 percent.

For purposes of these limitations, "prohibited payment" is defined as under the present-law rule restricting distributions during a period of a liquidity shortfall and means (1) any payment in excess of the monthly amount paid under a single life annuity (plus any social security supplement provided under the plan) to a participant or beneficiary whose annuity starting date occurs during the period, (2) any payment for the purchase of an irrevocable commitment from an insurer to pay benefits (e.g., an annuity contract), or (3) any other payment specified by the Secretary of the Treasury by regulations.

The prohibited payment limitation does not apply to a plan for any plan year if the terms of the plan (as in effect for the period beginning on September 1, 2005, and ending with the plan year) provide for no benefit accruals with respect to any participant during the period.

Cessation of benefit accruals

A plan must provide that, if the plan's adjusted funding target attainment percentage is less than 60 percent for a plan year, all future benefit accruals under the plan must cease as of the valuation date for the plan year. The limitation applies only for purposes of the accrual of benefits; service during the freeze period is counted for other purposes. For example, if accruals are frozen under the provision, service earned during the freeze period still counts for vesting purposes. Or, as another example, suppose a plan provides that payment of benefits begins when a participant terminates employment after age 55 and with 25 years of service. Under this example, if a participant who is age 55 and has 23 years of service when the freeze on accruals becomes applicable terminates employment two years later, the participant has 25 years of service for this purpose and thus can begin receiving benefits. However (assuming the freeze on accruals is still in effect), the amount of the benefit is based on the benefit accrued before the freeze (i.e., counting only 23 years of service).

The limitation ceases to apply with respect to any plan year, effective as of the first day of the plan year, if the plan sponsor makes a contribution (in addition to any minimum required contribution for the plan year) equal to the amount sufficient to result in an adjusted funding target attainment percentage of 60 percent.

The limitation does not apply for the first five years a plan (or a predecessor plan) is in effect.

Adjusted funding target attainment percentage

In general

The term "funding target attainment percentage" is defined as under the minimum funding rules, i.e., the ratio, expressed as a percentage, that the value of the plan's assets (reduced by any funding standard carryover balance and prefunding balance) bears to the plan's funding target for the year (determined without regard to at-risk status). A plan's adjusted funding target attainment percentage is determined in the same way, except that the value of the plan's assets and the plan's funding target are both increased by the aggregate amount of purchases of annuities for employees other than highly compensated employees made by the plan during the two preceding plan years.

Special rule for fully funded plans

Under a special rule, if a plan's funding target attainment percentage is at least 100 percent, determined by not reducing the value of the plan's assets by any funding standard carryover balance or prefunding balance, the value of the plan's assets is not so reduced in determining the plan's funding target attainment percentage for purposes of whether the benefit limitations apply. Under a transition rule for a plan year beginning after 2007 and before 2011, the "applicable percentage" for the plan year is substituted for 100 percent in applying the special rule. For this purpose, the applicable percentage is 92 percent for 2007, 94 percent for 2008, 96 percent for 2009, and 98 percent for 2010. However, for any plan year beginning after 2008, the transition rule does not apply unless the plan's funding target attainment percentage (determined by not reducing the value of the plan's assets by any funding standard carryover balance or prefunding balance) for each preceding plan year in the transition period is at least equal to the applicable percentage for the preceding year.

Presumptions as to funded status

Under the provision, certain presumptions apply in determining whether limitations apply with respect to a plan, subject to certification of the plan's adjusted funding target attainment percentage by the plan's enrolled actuary.

If a plan was subject to a limitation for the preceding year, the plan's adjusted funding target attainment percentage for the current year is presumed to be the same as for the preceding year until the plan actuary certifies the plan's actual adjusted funding target attainment percentage for the current year.

If (1) a plan was not subject to a limitation for the preceding year, but its adjusted funding target attainment percentage for the preceding year was not more than 10 percentage points greater than the threshold for a limitation, and (2) as of the first day of the fourth month of the current plan year, the plan actuary has not certified the plan's actual adjusted funding target attainment percentage for the current year, the plan's funding target attainment percentage is presumed to be reduced by 10 percentage points as of that day and that day is deemed to be the plan's valuation date for purposes of applying the benefit limitation. As a result, the limitation applies as of that date until the actuary certifies the plan's actual adjusted funding target attainment percentage.

In any other case, if the plan actuary has not certified the plan's actual adjusted funding target attainment percentage by the first day of the tenth month of the current plan year, for purposes of the limitations, the plan's adjusted funding target attainment percentage is conclusively presumed to be less than 60 percent as of that day and that day is deemed to be the valuation date for purposes of applying the benefit limitations.[49]

---

[49] For purposes of applying the presumptions to plan years beginning in 2008, the funding target attainment percentage for the preceding year may be determined using such methods of estimation as the Secretary of Treasury may provide.

Reduction of funding standard carryover and prefunding balances

Election to reduce balances

As discussed above, the value of plan assets is generally reduced by any funding standard carryover or prefunding in determining a plan's funding target attainment percentage. As provided for under the funding rules applicable to single-employer plans, a plan sponsor may elect to reduce a funding standard carryover balance or prefunding balance, so that the value of plan assets is not required to be reduced by that amount in determining the plan's funding target attainment percentage.

Deemed reduction of balances in the case of collectively bargained plans

If a benefit limitation would otherwise apply to a plan maintained pursuant to one or more collective bargaining agreements between employee representatives and one or more employers, the plan sponsor is treated as having made an election to reduce any prefunding balance or funding standard carryover balance by the amount necessary to prevent the benefit limitation from applying. However, the employer is not treated as having made such an election if the election would not prevent the benefit limitation from applying to the plan.

Deemed reduction of balances in the case of other plans

If the prohibited payment limitation would otherwise apply to a plan that is not maintained pursuant to a collective bargaining agreement, the plan sponsor is treated as having made an election to reduce any prefunding balance or funding standard carryover balance by the amount necessary to prevent the benefit limitation from applying. However, the employer is not treated as having made such an election if the election would not prevent the benefit limitation from applying to the plan.

Contributions made to avoid a benefit limitation

Under the provision, an employer may make contributions (in addition to any minimum required contribution) in an amount sufficient to increase the plan's adjusted funding target attainment percentage to a level to avoid a limitation on unpredictable contingent event benefits, a plan amendment increasing benefits, or additional accruals. An employer may not use a prefunding balance or funding standard carryover balance in lieu of such a contribution, and such a contribution does not result in an increase in any prefunding balance.

Instead of making additional contributions to avoid a benefit limitation, an employer may provide security in the form of a surety bond, cash, certain U.S. government obligations, or such other form as is satisfactory to the Secretary of the Treasury and the parties involved. In such a case, the plan's adjusted funding target attainment percentage is determined by treating the security as a plan asset. Any such security may be perfected and enforced at any time after the earlier of: (1) the date on which the plan terminates; (2) if the plan sponsor fails to make a required contribution for any subsequent plan year, the due date for the contribution; or (3) if the plan's adjusted funding target attainment percentage is less than 60 percent for a consecutive period of seven years, the valuation date for the last year in the period. The security will be released (and any related amounts will be refunded with any accrued interest) at such time as the

Secretary of the Treasury may prescribe in regulations (including partial releases by reason of increases in the plan's funding target attainment percentage).

Treatment of plan as of close of prohibited or cessation period

Under the provision, if a limitation on prohibited payments or future benefit accruals ceases to apply to a plan, all such payments and benefit accruals resume, effective as of the day following the close of the period for which the limitation applies.[50] Nothing in this rule is to be construed as affecting a plan's treatment of benefits which would have been paid or accrued but for the limitation.

Notice to participants

The plan administrator must provide written notice to participants and beneficiaries within 30 days: (1) after the plan has become subject to the limitation on unpredictable uncontingent event benefits or prohibited payments; (2) in the case of a plan to which the limitation on benefit accruals applies, after the valuation date for the plan year in which the plan's adjusted target attainment percentage is less than 60 percent (or, if earlier, the date the adjusted target attainment percentage is deemed to be less than 60 percent). Notice must also be provided at such other times as may be determined by the Secretary of the Treasury. The notice may be in electronic or other form to the extent such form is reasonably accessible to the recipient.

If the plan administrator fails to provide the required notice, the Secretary of Labor may impose a civil penalty of up to $1,000 a day from the time of the failure.

Effective Date

The provision generally applies with respect to plan years beginning after December 31, 2007.

In the case of a plan maintained pursuant to one or more collective bargaining agreements between employee representatives and one or more employers ratified before January 1, 2008, the provision does not apply to plan years beginning before the earlier of: (1) the later of (a) the date on which the last collective bargaining agreement relating to the plan terminates (determined without regard to any extension thereof agreed to after the date of enactment), or (b) the first day of the first plan year to which the provision would otherwise apply; or (2) January 1, 2010. For this purpose, any plan amendment made pursuant to a collective bargaining agreement relating to the plan that amends the plan solely to conform to any requirement under the provision is not to be treated as a termination of the collective bargaining agreement.

---

[50] This rule does not apply to limitations on unpredictable contingent event benefits and plan amendments increasing liabilities.

C. Special Rules for Multiple-Employer Plans of Certain Cooperatives

Present Law

Defined benefit pension plans are required to meet certain minimum funding rules. In some cases, additional contributions are required under the deficit reduction contribution rules if a single-employer defined benefit pension plan is underfunded. Additional contributions generally are not required in the case of a plan with a funded current liability percentage of at least 90 percent. A plan's funded current liability percentage is the value of plan assets as a percentage of current liability. In general, a plan's current liability means all liabilities to employees and their beneficiaries under the plan, determined using specified interest and mortality assumptions. In the case of a plan with a funded current liability percentage of less than 100 percent for the preceding plan year, estimated contributions for the current plan year must be made in quarterly installments during the current plan year.

The PBGC insures benefits under most single-employer defined benefit pension plans in the event the plan is terminated with insufficient assets to pay for plan benefits. The PBGC is funded in part by a flat-rate premium per plan participant, and variable-rate premiums based on the amount of unfunded vested benefits under the plan. A specified interest rate and a specified mortality table apply in determining unfunded vested benefits for this purpose.

A multiple-employer plan is a plan that is maintained by more than one employer and is not maintained pursuant to a collective bargaining agreement.[51] A multiple-employer plan is subject to the minimum funding rules for single-employer plans and to PBGC variable-rate premiums.

Explanation of Provision

The provision provides a delayed effective date for the new single-employer plan funding rules in the case of a plan that was in existence on July 26, 2005, and was an eligible cooperative plan for the plan year including that date. The new funding rules do not apply with respect to such a plan for plan years beginning before the earlier of: (1) the first plan year for which the plan ceases to be an eligible cooperative plan, or (2) January 1, 2017. In addition, in applying the present-law funding rules to an eligible cooperative plan to such a plan for plan years beginning after December 31, 2007, and before the first plan year for which the new funding rules apply, the interest rate used is the interest rate applicable under the new funding rules with respect to payments expected to be made from the plan after the 20-year period beginning on the first day of the plan year (i.e., the third segment rate under the new funding rules).

A plan is treated as an eligible cooperative plan for a plan year if it is maintained by more than one employer and at least 85 percent of the employers are: (1) certain rural cooperatives;[52]

---

[51] A plan maintained by more than one employer pursuant to a collective bargaining agreement is referred to as a multiemployer plan.

[52] This is as defined in Code section 401(k)(7)(B) without regard to (iv) thereof and includes (1) organizations engaged primarily in providing electric service on a mutual or cooperative basis, or

or (2) certain cooperative organizations that are more than 50-percent owned by agricultural producers or by cooperatives owned by agricultural producers, or organizations that are more than 50-percent owned, or controlled by, one or more such cooperative organizations. A plan is also treated as an eligible cooperative plan for any plan year for which it is maintained by more than one employer and is maintained by a rural telephone cooperative association.

Effective Date

The provision is effective on the date of enactment.

---

engaged primarily in providing electric service to the public in its service area and which is exempt from tax or which is a State or local government, other than a municipality; (2) certain civic leagues and business leagues exempt from tax 80 percent of the members of which are described in (1); (3) certain cooperative telephone companies; and (4) any organization that is a national association of organizations described above.

D. Temporary Relief for Certain PBGC Settlement Plans

Present Law

Defined benefit pension plans are required to meet certain minimum funding rules. In some cases, additional contributions are required under the deficit reduction contribution rules if a single-employer defined benefit pension plan is underfunded. Additional contributions generally are not required in the case of a plan with a funded current liability percentage of at least 90 percent. A plan's funded current liability percentage is the value of plan assets as a percentage of current liability. In general, a plan's current liability means all liabilities to employees and their beneficiaries under the plan, determined using specified interest and mortality assumptions. In the case of a plan with a funded current liability percentage of less than 100 percent for the preceding plan year, estimated contributions for the current plan year must be made in quarterly installments during the current plan year.

The PBGC insures benefits under most single-employer defined benefit pension plans in the event the plan is terminated with insufficient assets to pay for plan benefits. The PBGC is funded in part by a flat-rate premium per plan participant, and variable-rate premiums based on the amount of unfunded vested benefits under the plan. A specified interest rate and a specified mortality table apply in determining unfunded vested benefits for this purpose.

Explanation of Provision

The provision agreement provides a delayed effective date for the new single-employer plan funding rules in the case of a plan that was in existence on July 26, 2005, and was a "PBGC settlement plan" as of that date. The new funding rules do not apply with respect to such a plan for plan years beginning before January 1, 2014. In addition, in applying the present-law funding rules to a such a plan for plan years beginning after December 31, 2007, and before January 1, 2014, the interest rate used is the interest rate applicable under the new funding rules with respect to payments expected to be made from the plan after the 20-year period beginning on the first day of the plan year (i.e., the third segment rate under the new funding rules).

Under the provision, the term "PBGC settlement plan" means a single-employer defined benefit plan: (1) that was sponsored by an employer in bankruptcy proceedings giving rise to a claim by the PBGC of not greater than $150 million, and the sponsorship of which was assumed by another employer (not a member of the same controlled group as the bankrupt sponsor) and the PBGC's claim was settled or withdrawn in connection with the assumption of the sponsorship; or (2) that, by agreement with the PBGC, was spun off from a plan subsequently terminated by the PBGC in an involuntary termination.

Effective Date

The provision is effective on the date of enactment.

34

E. Special Rules for Plans of Certain Government Contractors

Present Law

Defined benefit pension plans are required to meet certain minimum funding rules. In some cases, additional contributions are required under the deficit reduction contribution rules if a single-employer defined benefit pension plan is underfunded. Additional contributions generally are not required in the case of a plan with a funded current liability percentage of at least 90 percent. A plan's funded current liability percentage is the value of plan assets as a percentage of current liability. In general, a plan's current liability means all liabilities to employees and their beneficiaries under the plan, determined using specified interest and mortality assumptions. In the case of a plan with a funded current liability percentage of less than 100 percent for the preceding plan year, estimated contributions for the current plan year must be made in quarterly installments during the current plan year.

The PBGC insures benefits under most single-employer defined benefit pension plans in the event the plan is terminated with insufficient assets to pay for plan benefits. The PBGC is funded in part by a flat-rate premium per plan participant, and variable-rate premiums based on the amount of unfunded vested benefits under the plan. A specified interest rate and a specified mortality table apply in determining unfunded vested benefits for this purpose.

Explanation of Provision

The provision provides a delayed effective date for the new single-employer plan funding rules in the case of an eligible government contractor plan. The new funding rules do not apply with respect to such a plan for plan years beginning before the earliest of: (1) the first plan year for which the plan ceases to be an eligible government contractor plan, (2) the effective date of the Cost Accounting Standards Pension Harmonization Rule, and (3) the first plan year beginning after December 31, 2010. In addition, in applying the present-law funding rules to a such a plan for plan years beginning after December 31, 2007, and before the first plan year for which the new funding rules apply, the interest rate used is the interest rate applicable under the new funding rules with respect to payments expected to be made from the plan after the 20-year period beginning on the first day of the plan year (i.e., the third segment rate under the new funding rules).

Under the provision, a plan is treated as an eligible government contractor plan if it is maintained by a corporation (or member of the same affiliated group): (1) whose primary source of revenue is derived from business performed under contracts with the United States that are subject to the Federal Acquisition Regulations and also to the Defense Federal Acquisition Regulation Supplement; (2) whose revenue derived from such business in the previous fiscal year exceeded $5 billion; and (3) whose pension plan costs that are assignable under those contracts are subject to certain provisions of the Cost Accounting Standards.

The provision also requires the Cost Accounting Standards Board, not later than January 1, 2010, to review and revise the relevant provisions of the Cost Accounting Standards to harmonize minimum contributions required under ERISA of eligible government contractor plans and government reimbursable pension plan costs. Any final rule adopted by the Cost

Accounting Standards Board shall be deemed the Cost Accounting Standards Pension Harmonization Rule.

Effective Date

The provision is effective on the date of enactment.

F. Modification of Transition Rule to Pension Funding
Requirements for Interstate Bus Company
(769(c) of the Retirement Protection Act, as added by sec. 1508
of the Taxpayer Relief Act of 1997)

Present Law

Defined benefit pension plans are required to meet certain minimum funding rules. In some cases, additional contributions are required under the deficit reduction contribution rules if a single-employer defined benefit pension plan is underfunded. Additional contributions generally are not required in the case of a plan with a funded current liability percentage of at least 90 percent. A plan's funded current liability percentage is the value of plan assets as a percentage of current liability. In general, a plan's current liability means all liabilities to employees and their beneficiaries under the plan, determined using specified interest and mortality assumptions. In the case of a plan with a funded current liability percentage of less than 100 percent for the preceding plan year, estimated contributions for the current plan year must be made in quarterly installments during the current plan year.

The PBGC insures benefits under most single-employer defined benefit pension plans in the event the plan is terminated with insufficient assets to pay for plan benefits. The PBGC is funded in part by a flat-rate premium per plan participant, and variable rate premiums based on the amount of unfunded vested benefits under the plan. A specified interest rate and a specified mortality table apply in determining unfunded vested benefits for this purpose.

A special rule modifies the minimum funding requirements in the case of certain plans. The special rule applies in the case of plans that: (1) were not required to pay a variable rate PBGC premium for the plan year beginning in 1996; (2) do not, in plan years beginning after 1995 and before 2009, merge with another plan (other than a plan sponsored by an employer that was a member of the controlled group of the employer in 1996); and (3) are sponsored by a company that is engaged primarily in interurban or interstate passenger bus service.

The special rule generally treats a plan to which it applies as having a funded current liability percentage of at least 90 percent for plan years beginning after 1996 and before 2004 if for such plan year the funded current liability percentage is at least 85 percent. If the funded current liability of the plan is less than 85 percent for any plan year beginning after 1996 and before 2004, the relief from the minimum funding requirements generally applies only if certain specified contributions are made.

For plan years beginning in 2004 and 2005, the funded current liability percentage of the plan is treated as at least 90 percent for purposes of determining the amount of required contributions (100 percent for purposes of determining whether quarterly contributions are required). As a result, for these years, additional contributions under the deficit reduction contribution rules and quarterly contributions are not required with respect to the plan. In addition, for these years, the mortality table used under the plan is used in calculating PBGC variable rate premiums.

For plan years beginning after 2005 and before 2010, the funded current liability percentage generally will be deemed to be at least 90 percent if the actual funded current liability percentage is at least at certain specified levels. The relief from the minimum funding requirements generally applies for a plan year beginning in 2006, 2007, or 2008 only if contributions to the plan for the plan year equal at least the expected increase in current liability due to benefits accruing during the plan year.

Explanation of Provision

The provision revises the special rule for a plan that is sponsored by a company engaged primarily in interurban or interstate passenger bus service and that meets the other requirements for the special rule under present law. The provision extends the application of the special rule under present law for plan years beginning in 2004 and 2005 to plan years beginning in 2006 and 2007. The provision also provides several special rules relating to determining minimum required contributions and variable rate premiums for plan years beginning after 2007 when the new funding rules for single-employer plans apply.

Under the provision, for the plan year beginning in 2006 or 2007, a plan's funded current liability percentage of a plan is treated as at least 90 percent for purposes of determining the amount of required contributions (100 percent for purposes of determining whether quarterly contributions are required). As a result, for the 2006 and 2007 plan years, additional contributions under the deficit reduction contribution rules and quarterly contributions are not required with respect to the plan. In addition, the mortality table used under the plan is used in calculating PBGC variable rate premiums.

Under the provision, for plan years beginning after 2007, the mortality table used under the plan is used in: (1) determining any present value or making any computation under the minimum funding rules applicable to the plan; and (2) calculating PBGC variable rate premiums. Under a special phase-in (in lieu of the phase-in otherwise applicable under the provision relating to funding rules for single-employer plans), for purposes of determining whether a shortfall amortization base is required for plan years beginning after 2007 and before 2012, the applicable percentage of the plan's funding shortfall is the following: 90 percent for 2008, 92 percent for 2009, 94 percent for 2010, and 96 percent for 2011. In addition, for purposes of the quarterly contributions requirement, the plan is treated as not having a funding shortfall for any plan year. As a result, quarterly contributions are not required with respect to the plan.

Effective Date

The provision is effective for plan years beginning after December 31, 2005.

G. Restrictions on Funding of Nonqualified Deferred Compensation Plans by Employers Maintaining Underfunded or Terminated Single-Employer Plans
(sec. 409A of the Code)

Present Law

Amounts deferred under a nonqualified deferred compensation plan for all taxable years are currently includible in gross income to the extent not subject to a substantial risk of forfeiture and not previously included in gross income, unless certain requirements are satisfied.[53] For example, distributions from a nonqualified deferred compensation plan may be allowed only upon certain times and events. Rules also apply for the timing of elections. If the requirements are not satisfied, in addition to current income inclusion, interest at the underpayment rate plus one percentage point is imposed on the underpayments that would have occurred had the compensation been includible in income when first deferred, or if later, when not subject to a substantial risk of forfeiture. The amount required to be included in income is also subject to a 20-percent additional tax.

In the case of assets set aside in a trust (or other arrangement) for purposes of paying nonqualified deferred compensation, such assets are treated as property transferred in connection with the performance of services under Code section 83 at the time set aside if such assets (or trust or other arrangement) are located outside of the United States or at the time transferred if such assets (or trust or other arrangement) are subsequently transferred outside of the United States. A transfer of property in connection with the performance of services under Code section 83 also occurs with respect to compensation deferred under a nonqualified deferred compensation plan if the plan provides that upon a change in the employer's financial health, assets will be restricted to the payment of nonqualified deferred compensation.

Explanation of Provision

Under the provision, if during any restricted period in which a defined benefit pension plan of an employer is in at-risk status,[54] assets are set aside (directly or indirectly) in a trust (or other arrangement as determined by the Secretary of the Treasury), or transferred to such a trust or other arrangement, for purposes of paying deferred compensation of an applicable covered employee, such transferred assets are treated as property transferred in connection with the performance of services (whether or not such assets are available to satisfy the claims of general creditors) under Code section 83. The rule does not apply in the case of assets that are set aside before the defined benefit pension plan is in at-risk status.

If a nonqualified deferred compensation plan of an employer provides that assets will be restricted to the provision of benefits under the plan in connection with a restricted period (or

---

[53] Code sec. 409A.

[54] At-risk status is defined as under the provision relating to funding rules for single-employer defined benefit pension plans and applies if a plan's funding target attainment percentage for the preceding year was less than 60 percent.

other similar financial measure determined by the Secretary of Treasury) of any defined benefit pension plan of the employer, or assets are so restricted, such assets are treated as property transferred in connection with the performance of services (whether or not such assets are available to satisfy the claims of general creditors) under Code section 83.

A restricted period is (1) any period in which a single-employer defined benefit pension plan of an employer is in at risk-status, (2) any period in which the employer is in bankruptcy, and (3) the period that begins six months before and ends six months after the date any defined benefit pension plan of the employer is terminated in an involuntary or distress termination. The provision does not apply with respect to assets set aside before a restricted period.

In general, applicable covered employees include the chief executive officer (or individual acting in such capacity), the four highest compensated officers for the taxable year (other than the chief executive officer), and individuals subject to section 16(a) of the Securities Exchange Act of 1934. An applicable covered employee includes any (1) covered employee of a plan sponsor; (2) covered employee of a member of a controlled group which includes the plan sponsor; and (3) former employee who was a covered employee at the time of termination of employment with the plan sponsor or a member of a controlled group which includes the plan sponsor.

A nonqualified deferred compensation plan is any plan that provides for the deferral of compensation other than a qualified employer plan or any bona fide vacation leave, sick leave, compensatory time, disability pay, or death benefit plan. A qualified employer plan means a qualified retirement plan, tax-deferred annuity, simplified employee pension, and SIMPLE.[55] A qualified governmental excess benefit arrangement (sec. 415(m)) is a qualified employer plan. An eligible deferred compensation plan (sec. 457(b)) is also a qualified employer plan under the provision. The term plan includes any agreement or arrangement, including an agreement or arrangement that includes one person.

Any subsequent increases in the value of, or any earnings with respect to, transferred or restricted assets are treated as additional transfers of property. Interest at the underpayment rate plus one percentage point is imposed on the underpayments that would have occurred had the amounts been includible in income for the taxable year in which first deferred or, if later, the first taxable year not subject to a substantial risk of forfeiture. The amount required to be included in income is also subject to an additional 20-percent tax.

Under the provision, if an employer provides directly or indirectly for the payment of any Federal, State or local income taxes with respect to any compensation required to be included in income under the provision, interest is imposed on the amount of such payment in the same manner as if the payment were part of the deferred compensation to which it related. As under present law, such payment is included in income; in addition, under the provision, such payment is subject to a 20 percent additional tax. The payment is also nondeductible by the employer.

---

[55] A qualified employer plan also includes a section 501(c)(18) trust.

Effective Date

The provision is effective for transfers or other reservations of assets after date of enactment.

TITLE II: FUNDING RULES FOR MULTIEMPLOYER DEFINED BENEFIT PLANS

A. Funding Rules for Multiemployer Defined Benefit Plans
(new sec. 304 of ERISA and new sec. 431 of the Code)

Present Law

Multiemployer plans

A multiemployer plan is a plan to which more than one unrelated employer contributes, which is established pursuant to one or more collective bargaining agreements, and which meets such other requirements as specified by the Secretary of Labor. Multiemployer plans are governed by a board of trustees consisting of an equal number of employer and employee representatives. In general, the level of contributions to a multiemployer plan is specified in the applicable collective bargaining agreements, and the level of plan benefits is established by the plan trustees.

Defined benefit multiemployer plans are subject to the same general minimum funding rules as single-employer plans, except that different rules apply in some cases. For example, different amortization periods apply for some costs in the case of multiemployer plans. In addition, the deficit reduction contribution rules do not apply to multiemployer plans.

Funding standard account

As an administrative aid in the application of the funding requirements, a defined benefit pension plan is required to maintain a special account called a "funding standard account" to which specified charges and credits are made for each plan year, including a charge for normal cost and credits for contributions to the plan. Other credits or charges or credits may apply as a result of decreases or increases in past service liability as a result of plan amendments or experience gains or losses, gains or losses resulting from a change in actuarial assumptions, or a waiver of minimum required contributions.

If, as of the close of the plan year, charges to the funding standard account exceed credits to the account, then the excess is referred to as an "accumulated funding deficiency." For example, if the balance of charges to the funding standard account of a plan for a year would be $200,000 without any contributions, then a minimum contribution equal to that amount would be required to meet the minimum funding standard for the year to prevent an accumulated funding deficiency. If credits to the funding standard account exceed charges, a "credit balance" results. The amount of the credit balance, increased with interest, can be used to reduce future required contributions.

Funding methods and general concepts

In general

A defined benefit pension plan is required to use an acceptable actuarial cost method to determine the elements included in its funding standard account for a year. Generally, an actuarial cost method breaks up the cost of benefits under the plan into annual charges consisting

42

of two elements for each plan year. These elements are referred to as: (1) normal cost; and (2) supplemental cost.

Normal cost

The plan's normal cost for a plan year generally represents the cost of future benefits allocated to the year by the funding method used by the plan for current employees and, under some funding methods, for separated employees. Specifically, it is the amount actuarially determined that would be required as a contribution by the employer for the plan year in order to maintain the plan if the plan had been in effect from the beginning of service of the included employees and if the costs for prior years had been paid, and all assumptions as to interest, mortality, time of payment, etc., had been fulfilled.

Supplemental cost

The supplemental cost for a plan year is the cost of future benefits that would not be met by future normal costs, future employee contributions, or plan assets. The most common supplemental cost is that attributable to past service liability, which represents the cost of future benefits under the plan: (1) on the date the plan is first effective; or (2) on the date a plan amendment increasing plan benefits is first effective. Other supplemental costs may be attributable to net experience losses, changes in actuarial assumptions, and amounts necessary to make up funding deficiencies for which a waiver was obtained. Supplemental costs must be amortized (i.e., recognized for funding purposes) over a specified number of years, depending on the source.

Valuation of assets

For funding purposes, the actuarial value of plan assets may be used, rather than fair market value. The actuarial value of plan assets is the value determined under a reasonable actuarial valuation method that takes into account fair market value and is permitted under Treasury regulations. Any actuarial valuation method used must result in a value of plan assets that is not less than 80 percent of the fair market value of the assets and not more than 120 percent of the fair market value. In addition, if the valuation method uses average value of the plan assets, values may be used for a stated period not to exceed the five most recent plan years, including the current year.

Reasonableness of assumptions

In applying the funding rules, all costs, liabilities, interest rates, and other factors are required to be determined on the basis of actuarial assumptions and methods, each of which is reasonable (taking into account the experience of the plan and reasonable expectations), or which, in the aggregate, result in a total plan contribution equivalent to a contribution that would be obtained if each assumption and method were reasonable. In addition, the assumptions are required to offer the actuary's best estimate of anticipated experience under the plan.

Charges and credits to the funding standard account

In general

Under the minimum funding standard, the portion of the cost of a plan that is required to be paid for a particular year depends upon the nature of the cost. For example, the normal cost for a year is generally required to be funded currently. Other costs are spread (or amortized) over a period of years. In the case of a multiemployer plan, past service liability is amortized over 40 or 30 years depending on how the liability arose, experience gains and losses are amortized over 15 years, gains and losses from changes in actuarial assumptions are amortized over 30 years, and waived funding deficiencies are amortized over 15 years.

Normal cost

Each plan year, a plan's funding standard account is charged with the normal cost assigned to that year under the particular acceptable actuarial cost method adopted by the plan. The charge for normal cost will require an offsetting credit in the funding standard account. Usually, an employer contribution is required to create the credit. For example, if the normal cost for a plan year is $150,000, the funding standard account would be charged with that amount for the year. Assuming that there are no other credits in the account to offset the charge for normal cost, an employer contribution of $150,000 will be required for the year to avoid an accumulated funding deficiency.

Past service liability

There are three separate charges to the funding standard account one or more of which may apply to a multiemployer plan as the result of past service liabilities. In the case of a plan in existence on January 1, 1974, past service liability under the plan on the first day on which the plan was first subject to ERISA is amortized over 40 years. In the case of a plan which was not in existence on January 1, 1974, past service liability under the plan on the first day on which the plan was first subject to ERISA is amortized over 30 years. Past service liability due to plan amendments is amortized over 30 years.

Experience gains and losses

In determining plan funding under an actuarial cost method, a plan's actuary generally makes certain assumptions regarding the future experience of a plan. These assumptions typically involve rates of interest, mortality, disability, salary increases, and other factors affecting the value of assets and liabilities. The actuarial assumptions are required to be reasonable, as discussed above. If the plan's actual unfunded liabilities are less than those anticipated by the actuary on the basis of these assumptions, then the excess is an experience gain. If the actual unfunded liabilities are greater than those anticipated, then the difference is an experience loss. In the case of a multiemployer plan, experience gains and losses for a year are generally amortized over a 15-year period, resulting in credits or charges to the funding standard account.

Gains and losses from changes in assumptions

If the actuarial assumptions used for funding a plan are revised and, under the new assumptions, the accrued liability of a plan is less than the accrued liability computed under the previous assumptions, the decrease is a gain from changes in actuarial assumptions. If the new assumptions result in an increase in the accrued liability, the plan has a loss from changes in actuarial assumptions. The accrued liability of a plan is the actuarial present value of projected pension benefits under the plan that will not be funded by future contributions to meet normal cost or future employee contributions. In the case of a multiemployer plan, the gain or loss for a year from changes in actuarial assumptions is amortized over a period of 30 years, resulting in credits or charges to the funding standard account.

Shortfall funding method

Certain plans may elect to determine the required charges to the funding standard account under the shortfall method. Under such method, the charges are computed on the basis of an estimated number of units of service or production for which a certain amount per unit is to be charged. The difference between the net amount charged under this method and the net amount that otherwise would have been charged for the same period is a shortfall loss or gain that is amortized over subsequent plan years. The use of the shortfall method and changes to use of the shortfall method are generally subject to IRS approval.

Funding waivers and amortization of waived funding deficiencies

Within limits, the Secretary of the Treasury is permitted to waive all or a portion of the contributions required under the minimum funding standard for the year (a "waived funding deficiency"). In the case of a multiemployer plan, a waiver may be granted if 10 percent or more of the number of employers contributing to the plan could not make the required contribution without temporary substantial business hardship and if requiring the contribution would be adverse to the interests of plan participants in the aggregate. The minimum funding requirements may not be waived with respect to a multiemployer plan for more five out of any 15 consecutive years.

If a funding deficiency is waived, the waived amount is credited to the funding standard account. In the case of a multiemployer plan, the waived amount is then amortized over a period of 15 years, beginning with the year following the year in which the waiver is granted. Each year, the funding standard account is charged with the amortization amount for that year unless the plan becomes fully funded. In the case of a multiemployer plan, the interest rate used for purposes of determining the amortization on the waived amount is the rate determined under section 6621(b) of the Internal Revenue Code (relating to the Federal short-term rate).

Extension of amortization periods

Amortization periods may be extended for up to 10 years by the Secretary of the Treasury if the Secretary finds that the extension would carry out the purposes of ERISA and would provide adequate protection for participants under the plan and if such Secretary determines that the failure to permit such an extension would (1) result in a substantial risk to the voluntary continuation of the plan or a substantial curtailment of pension benefit levels or employee

45

compensation, and (2) be adverse to the interests of plan participants in the aggregate. The interest rate with respect to extensions of amortization periods is the same as that used with respect to waived funding deficiencies.

Alternative funding standard account

As an alternative to applying the rules described above, a plan which uses the entry age normal cost method may satisfy an alternative minimum funding standard. Under the alternative, the minimum required contribution for the year is generally based on the amount necessary to bring the plan's assets up to the present value of accrued benefits, determine using the actuarial assumptions that apply when a plan terminates. The alternative standard has been rarely used.

Controlled group liability for required contributions

Unlike the rule for single-employer plans which imposes liability for minimum required contributions to all members of the employer's controlled group, controlled-group liability does not apply to contributions an employer is required to make to a multiemployer plan.

Explanation of Provision

Amortization periods

The provision modifies the amortization periods applicable to multiemployer plans so that the amortization period for most charges is 15 years. Under the provision, past service liability under the plan is amortized over 15 years (rather than 30); past service liability due to plan amendments is amortized over 15 years (rather than 30); and experience gains and losses resulting from a change in actuarial assumptions are amortized over 15 years (rather than 30). As under present law, experience gains and losses and waived funding deficiencies are amortized over 15 years. The new amortization periods do not apply to amounts being amortized under present-law amortization periods, that is, no recalculation of amortization schedules already in effect is required under the provision. The provision eliminates the alternative funding standard account.

Actuarial assumptions

The provision provides that in applying the funding rules, all costs, liabilities, interest rates, and other factors are required to be determined on the basis of actuarial assumptions and methods, each of which is reasonable (taking into account the experience of the plan and reasonable expectations). In addition, as under present law, the assumptions are required to offer the actuary's best estimate of anticipated experience under the plan.

Extension of amortization periods

The provision provides that, upon application to the Secretary of the Treasury, the Secretary is required to grant an extension of the amortization period for up to five years with respect to any unfunded past service liability, investment loss, or experience loss. Included with the application must be a certification by the plan's actuary that (1) absent the extension, the plan would have an accumulated funding deficiency in the current plan year and any of the nine succeeding plan years, (2) the plan sponsor has adopted a plan to improve the plan's funding status, (3) taking into account the extension, the plan is projected to have sufficient assets to timely pay its expected benefit liabilities and other anticipated expenditures, and (4) that required notice is provided. The automatic extension provision does not apply with respect to any application submitted after December 31, 2014.

The Secretary of the Treasury may also grant an additional extension of such amortization periods for an additional five years. The standards for determining whether such an extension may be granted are the same as under present law. In addition, the provision requires the Secretary of the Treasury to act upon an application for an additional extension within 180 days after submission. If the Secretary rejects the application, the Secretary must provide notice to the plan detailing the specific reasons for the rejection.

As under present law, these extensions do not apply unless the applicant demonstrates to the satisfaction of the Treasury Secretary that notice of the application has been provided to each affected party (as defined in ERISA section 4001(a)(21)).

Interest rate applicable to funding waivers and extension of amortization periods

The provision eliminates the special interest rate rule for funding waivers and extensions of amortization periods so that the plan rate applies.

Additional provisions

Controlled group liability for required contributions

The provision imposes joint and several liability to all members of the employer's controlled group for minimum required contributions to single-employer or multiemployer plans.

Shortfall funding method

The provision provides that, for plan years beginning before January 1, 2015, certain multiemployer plans may adopt, use or cease using the shortfall funding method and such adoption, use, or cessation of use is deemed approved by the Secretary of the Treasury. Plans are eligible if (1) the plan has not used the shortfall funding method during the five-year period ending on the day before the date the plan is to use the shortfall funding method; and (2) the plan is not operating under an amortization period extension and did not operate under such an extension during such five-year period. Benefit restrictions apply during a period that a multiemployer plan is using the shortfall funding method. In general, plan amendments increasing benefits cannot be adopted while the shortfall funding method is in use. The provision is not intended to affect a plan's ability to adopt the shortfall funding method with IRS approval or to affect a plan's right to change funding methods as otherwise permitted.

Effective Date

The provision is effective for plan years beginning after 2007.

B. Additional Funding Rules for Multiemployer Plans in Endangered or Critical Status
(new sec. 305 of ERISA and new sec. 432 of the Code)

Present Law

In general

Multiemployer defined benefit plans are subject to minimum funding rules similar to those applicable to single-employer plans.[56] If a multiemployer plan has an accumulated funding deficiency for a year, an excise tax of five percent generally applies, increasing to 100 percent if contributions sufficient to eliminate the funding deficiency are not made within a certain period.

Additional required contributions and benefit reductions may apply if a multiemployer plan is in reorganization status or is insolvent.

Reorganization status

Certain modifications to the single-employer plan funding rules apply to multiemployer plans that experience financial difficulties, referred to as "reorganization status." A plan is in reorganization status for a year if the contribution needed to balance the charges and credits to its funding standard account exceeds its "vested benefits charge."[57] The plan's vested benefits charge is generally the amount needed to amortize, in equal annual installments, unfunded vested benefits under the plan over: (1) 10 years in the case of obligations attributable to participants in pay status; and (2) 25 years in the case of obligations attributable to other participants. A plan in reorganization status is eligible for a special funding credit. In addition, a cap on year-to-year contribution increases and other relief is available to employers that continue to contribute to the plan.

Subject to certain requirements, a multiemployer plan in reorganization status may also be amended to reduce or eliminate accrued benefits in excess of the amount of benefits guaranteed by the PBGC.[58] In order for accrued benefits to be reduced, at least six months before the beginning of the plan year in which the amendment is adopted, notice must be given that the plan is in reorganization status and that, if contributions to the plan are not increased, accrued benefits will be reduced or an excise tax will be imposed on employers obligated to contribute to the plan. The notice must be provided to plan participants and beneficiaries, any

---

[56] See the explanation of the preceding provision for a discussion of the minimum funding rules for multiemployer defined benefit plans. Under Treasury regulations, certain noncollectively bargained employees covered by a multiemployer plan may be treated as collectively bargained employees for purposes of applying the minimum coverage rules of the Code. Treas. Reg. sec. 1.410(b)-6(d)(2)(ii)(D).

[57] ERISA sec. 4241.

[58] ERISA sec. 4244A.

employer who has an obligation to contribute to the plan, and any employee organization representing employees in the plan.

Insolvency

In the case of multiemployer plans, the PBGC insures plan insolvency, rather than plan termination. A plan is insolvent when its available resources are not sufficient to pay the plan benefits for the plan year in question, or when the sponsor of a plan in reorganization reasonably determines, taking into account the plan's recent and anticipated financial experience, that the plan's available resources will not be sufficient to pay benefits that come due in the next plan year.[59] An insolvent plan is required to reduce benefits to the level that can be covered by the plan's assets. However, benefits cannot be reduced below the level guaranteed by the PBGC.[60] If a multiemployer plan is insolvent, the PBGC guarantee is provided in the form of loans to the plan trustees. If the plan recovers from insolvency status, loans from the PBGC can be repaid. Plans in reorganization status are required to compare assets and liabilities to determine if the plan will become insolvent in the future.

Explanation of Provision

In general

The provision provides additional funding rules for multiemployer defined benefit plans in effect on July 16, 2006, that are in endangered or critical status. The provision requires the adoption of and compliance with (1) a funding improvement plan in the case of a multiemployer plan in endangered status, and (2) a rehabilitation plan in the case of a multiemployer plan in critical status.

Under the provision, in the case of a plan in critical status, additional required contributions and benefit reductions apply and employers are relieved of liability for minimum required contributions under the otherwise applicable funding rules, provided that a rehabilitation plan is adopted and followed.

Annual certification of status; notice; annual reports

Not later than the 90th day of each plan year, the plan actuary must certify to the Secretary of the Treasury and to the plan sponsor whether or not the plan is in endangered or critical status for the plan year. In the case of a plan that is in a funding improvement or rehabilitation period, the actuary must certify whether or not the plan is making scheduled progress in meeting the requirements of its funding improvement or rehabilitation plan.

---

[59] ERISA sec. 4245.

[60] The limit of benefits that the PBGC guarantees under a multiemployer plan is the sum of 100 percent of the first $11 of monthly benefits and 75 percent of the next $33 of monthly benefits for each year of service. ERISA sec. 4022A(c).

In making the determinations and projections applicable under the endangered and critical status rules, the plan actuary must make projections for the current and succeeding plan years of the current value of the assets of the plan and the present value of all liabilities to participants and beneficiaries under the plan for the current plan year as of the beginning of such year. The actuary's projections must be based on reasonable actuarial estimates, assumptions, and methods that offer the actuary's best estimate of anticipated experience under the plan. An exception to this rule applies in the case of projected industry activity. Any projection of activity in the industry or industries covered by the plan, including future covered employment and contribution levels, must be based on information provided by the plan sponsor, which shall act reasonably and in good faith. The projected present value of liabilities as of the beginning of the year must be based on the most recent actuarial statement required with respect to the most recently filed annual report or the actuarial valuation for the preceding plan year.

Any actuarial projection of plan assets must assume (1) reasonably anticipated employer contributions for the current and succeeding plan years, assuming that the terms of one or more collective bargaining agreements pursuant to which the plan is maintained for the current plan year continue in effect for the succeeding plan years, or (2) that employer contributions for the most recent plan year will continue indefinitely, but only if the plan actuary determines that there have been no significant demographic changes that would make continued application of such terms unreasonable.

Failure of the plan's actuary to certify the status of the plan is treated as a failure to file the annual report (thus, an ERISA penalty of up to $1,100 per day applies).

If a plan is certified to be in endangered or critical status, notification of the endangered or critical status must be provided within 30 days after the date of certification to the participants and beneficiaries, the bargaining parties, the PBGC and the Secretary of Labor.[61] If it is certified that a plan is or will be in critical status, the plan sponsor must included in the notice an explanation of the possibility that (1) adjustable benefits may be reduced and (2) such reductions may apply to participants and beneficiaries whose benefit commencement date is on or after the date such notice is provided for the first plan year in which the plan is in critical status. The Secretary of Labor is required to prescribe a model notice to satisfy these requirements.

The plan sponsor must annually update the funding improvement or rehabilitation plan. Updates are required to be filed with the plan's annual report.

Endangered status

Definition of endangered status

A multiemployer plan is in endangered status if the plan is not in critical status and, as of the beginning of the plan year, (1) the plan's funded percentage for the plan year is less than 80

---

[61] If a plan actuary certifies that it is reasonably expected that a plan will be in critical status with respect to the first plan year after 2007, notice may be provided at any time after date of enactment, as long as it is provided on or before the date otherwise required.

percent, or (2) the plan has an accumulated funding deficiency for the plan year or is projected to have an accumulated funding deficiency in any of the six succeeding plan years (taking into account amortization extensions). A plan's funded percentage is the percentage of plan assets over accrued liability of the plan. A plan that meets the requirements of both (1) and (2) is treated as in seriously endangered status.

Information to be provided to bargaining parties

Within 30 days of the adoption of a funding improvement plan, the plan sponsor must provide to the bargaining parties schedules showing revised benefit structures, revised contribution structures, or both, which, if adopted, may reasonably be expected to enable the multiemployer plan to meet the applicable benchmarks in accordance with the funding improvement plan, including (1) one proposal for reductions in the amount of future benefit accruals necessary to achieve the applicable benchmarks, assuming no amendments increasing contributions under the plan (other than amendments increasing contributions necessary to achieve the applicable benchmarks after amendments have reduced future benefit accruals to the maximum extent permitted by law) (the "default schedule"), and (2) one proposal for increases in contributions under the plan necessary to achieve the applicable benchmarks, assuming no amendments reducing future benefit accruals under the plan. The applicable benchmarks are the requirements of the funding improvement plan (discussed below). The plan sponsor may provide the bargaining parties with additional information if deemed appropriate.

The plan sponsor must annually update any schedule of contribution rates to reflect the experience of the plan.

Funding improvement plan and funding improvement period

In the case of a multiemployer plan in endangered status, a funding improvement plan must be adopted within 240 days following the deadline for certifying a plan's status.[62] A funding improvement plan is a plan which consists of the actions, including options or a range of options, to be proposed to the bargaining parties, formulated to provide, based on reasonably anticipated experience and reasonable actuarial assumptions, for the attainment by the plan of certain requirements.

The funding improvement plan must provide that during the funding improvement period, the plan will have a certain required increase in the funded percentage and no accumulated funding deficiency for any plan year during the funding improvement period, taking into account amortization extensions (the "applicable benchmarks"). In the case of a plan that is not in seriously endangered status, under the applicable benchmarks, the plan's funded percentage must increase such that the funded percentage as of the close of the funding improvement period equals or exceeds a percentage equal to the sum of (1) the funded percentage at the beginning of the period, plus (2) 33 percent of the difference between 100 percent and the percentage in (1). Thus, the difference between 100 percent and the plan's

---

[62] This requirement applies for the initial determination year (i.e., the first plan year that the plan is in endangered status).

funded percentage at the beginning of the period must be reduced by at least one-third during the funding improvement period.

The funding improvement period is the 10-year period beginning on the first day of the first plan year beginning after the earlier of (1) the second anniversary of the date of adoption of the funding improvement plan, or (2) the expiration of collective bargaining agreements that were in effect on the due date for the actuarial certification of endangered status for the initial determination year and covering, as of such date, at least 75 percent of the plan's active participants. The period ends if the plan is no longer in endangered status or if the plan enters critical status.

In the case of a plan in seriously endangered status that is funded 70 percent or less, under the applicable benchmarks, the difference between 100 percent and the plan's funded percentage at the beginning of the period must be reduced by at least one-fifth during the funding improvement period. In the case of such plans, a 15-year funding improvement period is used.

In the case of a seriously endangered plan that is more than 70 percent funded as of the beginning of the initial determination year, the same benchmarks apply for plan years beginning on or before the date on which the last collective bargaining agreements in effect on the date for actuarial certification for the initial determination year and covering at least 75 percent of active employees in the multiemployer plan have expired if the plan actuary certifies within 30 days after certification of endangered status that the plan is not projected to attain the funding percentage increase otherwise required by the provision. Thus, for such plans, the difference between 100 percent and the plan's funded percentage at the beginning of the period must be reduced by at least one-fifth during the 15-year funding improvement period. For subsequent years for such plans, if the plan actuary certifies that the plan is not able to attain the increase generally required under the provision, the same benchmarks continue to apply.

As previously discussed, the plan sponsor must annually update the funding improvement plan and must file the update with the plan's annual report.

If, for the first plan year following the close of the funding improvement period, the plan's actuary certifies that the plan is in endangered status, such year is treated as an initial determination year. Thus, a new funding improvement plan must be adopted within 240 days of the required certification date. In such case, the plan may not be amended in a manner inconsistent with the funding improvement plan in effect for the preceding plan year until a new funding improvement plan is adopted.

Requirements pending approval of plan and during funding improvement period

Certain restrictions apply during the period beginning on the date of certification for the initial determination year and ending on the day before the first day of the funding improvement period (the "funding plan adoption period").

During the funding plan adoption period, the plan sponsor may not accept a collective bargaining agreement or participation agreement that provides for (1) a reduction in the level of contributions for any participants; (2) a suspension of contributions with respect to any period of service; or (3) any new or indirect exclusion of younger or newly hired employees from plan participation.

In addition, during the funding plan adoption period, except in the case of amendments required as a condition of qualification under the Internal Revenue Code or to apply with other applicable law, no amendment may be adopted which increases liabilities of the plan by reason of any increase in benefits, any change in accrual of benefits, or any change in the rate at which benefits become nonforfeitable under the plan.

In the case of a plan in seriously endangered status, during the funding plan adoption period, the plan sponsor must take all reasonable actions (consistent with the terms of the plan and present law) which are expected, based on reasonable assumptions, to achieve an increase in the plan's funded percentage and a postponement of an accumulated funding deficiency for at least one additional plan year. These actions include applications for extensions of amortization periods, use of the shortfall funding method in making funding standard account computations, amendments to the plan's benefit structure, reductions in future benefit accruals, and other reasonable actions.

Upon adoption of a funding improvement plan, the plan may not be amended to be inconsistent with the funding improvement plan. During the funding improvement period, a plan sponsor may not accept a collective bargaining agreement or participation agreement with respect to the multiemployer plan that provides for (1) a reduction in the level of contributions for any participants; (2) a suspension of contributions with respect to any period of service, or (3) any new direct or indirect exclusion of younger or newly hired employees from plan participation.

After the adoption of a funding improvement plan, a plan may not be amended to increase benefits, including future benefit accruals, unless the plan actuary certifies that the benefit increase is consistent with the funding improvement plan and is paid for out of contributions not required by the funding improvement plan to meet the applicable benchmark in accordance with the schedule contemplated in the funding improvement plan.

Effect of and penalty for failure to adopt a funding improvement plan

If a collective bargaining agreement providing for contributions under a multiemployer plan that was in effect at the time the plan entered endangered status expires, and after receiving one or more schedules from the plan sponsor, the bargaining parties fail to agree on changes to contribution or benefit schedules necessary to meet the applicable benchmarks, the plan sponsor must implement the default schedule. The schedule must be implemented on the earlier of the date (1) on which the Secretary of Labor certifies that the parties are at an impasse, or (2) which is 180 days after the date on which the collective bargaining agreement expires.

In the case of the failure of a plan sponsor to adopt a funding improvement plan by the end of the 240-day period after the required certification date, an ERISA penalty of up to $1,100 a day applies.

Excise tax on employers failing to meet required contributions

If the funding improvement plan requires an employer to make contributions to the plan, an excise tax applies upon the failure of the employer to make such required contributions within the time required under the plan. The amount of tax is equal to the amount of the required contribution the employer failed to make in a timely manner.

Application of excise tax to plans in endangered status/penalty for failure to achieve benchmarks

In the case of a plan in endangered status, which is not in seriously endangered status, a civil penalty of $1,100 a day applies for the failure of the plan to meet the applicable benchmarks by the end of the funding improvement period.

In the case of a plan in seriously endangered status, an excise tax applies for the failure to meet the benchmarks by the end of the funding improvement period. In such case, an excise tax applies based on the greater of (1) the amount of the contributions necessary to meet such benchmarks or (2) the plan's accumulated funding deficiency. The excise tax applies for each succeeding plan year until the benchmarks are met.

Waiver of excise tax

In the case of a failure which is due to reasonable cause and not to willful neglect, the Secretary of the Treasury may waive all or part of the excise tax on employers failing to make required contributions and the excise tax for failure to achieve the applicable benchmarks. The party against whom the tax is imposed has the burden of establishing that the failure was due to reasonable cause and not willful neglect. Reasonable cause includes unanticipated and material market fluctuations, the loss of a significant contributing employer, or other factors to the extent that the payment of tax would be excessive or otherwise inequitable relative to the failure involved. The determination of reasonable cause is based on the facts and circumstances of each case and requires the parties to act with ordinary business care and prudence. The standard requires the funding improvement plan to be based on reasonably foreseeable events. It is expected that reasonable cause would include instances in which the plan experiences a net equity loss of at least ten percent during the funding improvement period, a change in plan demographics such as the bankruptcy of a significant contributing employer, a legal change (including the outcome of litigation) that unexpectedly increases the plan's benefit obligations, or a strike or lockout for a significant period.

Critical status

Definition of critical status

A multiemployer plan is in critical status for a plan year if as of the beginning of the plan year:

1. The funded percentage of the plan is less than 65 percent and the sum of (A) the market value of plan assets, plus (B) the present value of reasonably anticipated employer and employee contributions for the current plan year and each of the six

succeeding plan years (assuming that the terms of the collective bargaining agreements continue in effect) is less than the present value of all benefits projected to be payable under the plan during the current plan year and each of the six succeeding plan years (plus administrative expenses),

2. (A) The plan has an accumulated funding deficiency for the current plan year, not taking into account any amortization extension, or (B) the plan is projected to have an accumulated funding deficiency for any of the three succeeding plan years (four succeeding plan years if the funded percentage of the plan is 65 percent or less), not taking into account any amortization extension,

3. (A) The plan's normal cost for the current plan year, plus interest for the current plan year on the amount of unfunded benefit liabilities under the plan as of the last day of the preceding year, exceeds the present value of the reasonably anticipated employer contributions for the current plan year, (B) the present value of nonforfeitable benefits of inactive participants is greater than the present value of nonforfeitable benefits of active participants, and (C) the plan has an accumulated funding deficiency for the current plan year, or is projected to have an accumulated funding deficiency for any of the four succeeding plan years (not taking into account amortization period extensions), or

4. The sum of (A) the market value of plan assets, plus (B) the present value of the reasonably anticipated employer contributions for the current plan year and each of the four succeeding plan years (assuming that the terms of the collective bargaining agreements continue in effect) is less than the present value of all benefits projected to be payable under the plan during the current plan year and each of the four succeeding plan years (plus administrative expenses).

Additional contributions during critical status

In the case of a plan in critical status, the provision imposes an additional required contribution ("surcharge") on employers otherwise obligated to make a contribution in the initial critical year, i.e., the first plan year for which the plan is in critical status. The amount of the surcharge is five percent of the contribution otherwise required to be made under the applicable collective bargaining agreement. The surcharge is 10 percent of contributions otherwise required in the case of succeeding plan years in which the plan is in critical status. The surcharge applies 30 days after the employer is notified by the plan sponsor that the plan is in critical status and the surcharge is in effect. The surcharges are due and payable on the same schedule as the contributions on which the surcharges are based. Failure to make the surcharge payment is treated as a delinquent contribution. The surcharge is not required with respect to employees covered by a collective bargaining agreement (or other agreement pursuant to which the employer contributes), beginning on the effective date of a collective bargaining agreement (or other agreement) that includes terms consistent with a schedule presented by the plan sponsor. The amount of the surcharge may not be the basis for any benefit accrual under the plan.

Surcharges are disregarded in determining an employer's withdrawal liability except for purposes of determining the unfunded vested benefits attributable to an employer under ERISA section 4211(c)(4) or a comparable method approved under ERISA section 4211(c)(5).[63]

Reductions to previously earned benefits

Notwithstanding the anti-cutback rules, the plan sponsor may make any reductions to adjustable benefits which the plan sponsor deems appropriate, based upon the outcome of collective bargaining over the schedules required to be provided by the plan sponsor as discussed below. Adjustable benefits means (1) benefits, rights, and features under the plan, including post-retirement death benefits, 60-month guarantees, disability benefits not yet in pay status, and similar benefits; (2) any early retirement benefit or retirement-type subsidy and any benefit payment option (other than the qualified joint-and-survivor annuity); and (3) benefit increase that would not be eligible for PBGC guarantee on the first day of the initial critical year because the increases were adopted (or, if later, took effect) less than 60 months before such first day. Except as provided in (3), nothing should be construed to permit a plan to reduce the level of a participant's accrued benefit payable at normal retirement age.

The plan sponsor may not reduce adjustable benefits of any participant or beneficiary whose benefit commencement date is before the date on which the plan provides notice to the participant or beneficiary that the plan is in critical status and that benefits may be reduced. An exception applies in the case of benefit increases that would not be eligible for PBGC guarantee because the increases were adopted less than 60 months before the first day of the initial critical year.

The plan sponsor must include in the schedules provided to the bargaining parties an allowance for funding the benefits of participants with respect to whom contributions are not currently required to be made, and shall reduce their benefits to the extent permitted under the Code and ERISA and considered appropriate by the plan sponsor based on the plan's then current overall funding status.

Notice of any reduction of adjustable benefits must be provided at least 30 days before the general effective date of the reduction for all participants and beneficiaries. Benefits may not be reduced until the notice requirement is satisfied. Notice must be provided to (1) plan participants and beneficiaries; (2) each employer who has an obligation to contribute under the plans; and (3) each employee organization which, for purposes of collective bargaining, represents plan participants employed by such employer. The notice must contain (1) sufficient information to enable participants and beneficiaries to understand the effect of any reduction of their benefits, including an estimate (on an annual or monthly basis) of any affected adjustable benefit that a participant or beneficiary would otherwise have been eligible for as of the general effective date for benefit reductions; and (2) information as to the rights and remedies of plan participants and beneficiaries as well as how to contact the Department of Labor for further

---

[63] The PBGC is directed to prescribe simplified methods for determining withdrawal liability in this case.

information and assistance where appropriate. The notice must be provided in a form and manner prescribed in regulations of the Secretary of Labor. In such regulations, the Secretary of Labor must establish a model notice.

Benefit reduction are disregarded in determining a plan's unfunded vested benefits for purposes of determining an employer's withdrawal liability.[64]

Information to be provided to bargaining parties

Within 30 days after adoption of the rehabilitation plan, the plan sponsor must provide to the bargaining parties schedules showing revised benefit structures, revised contribution structures, or both which, if adopted, may reasonably be expected to enable the multiemployer plan to emerge from critical status in accordance with the rehabilitation plan.[65] The schedules must reflect reductions in future benefit accruals and adjustable benefits and increases in contributions that the plan sponsor determined are reasonably necessary to emerge from critical status. One schedule must be designated as the default schedule and must assume no increases in contributions other than increases necessary to emerge from critical status after future benefit accruals and other benefits (other than benefits the reduction or elimination of which are not permitted under the anti-cutback rules) have been reduced. The plan sponsor may also provide additional information as appropriate.

The plan sponsor must periodically update any schedule of contributions rates to reflect the experience of the plan.

Rehabilitation plan

If a plan is in critical status for a plan year, the plan sponsor must adopt a rehabilitation plan within 240 days following the required date for the actuarial certification of critical status.[66]

A rehabilitation plan is a plan which consists of actions, including options or a range of options to be proposed to the bargaining parties, formulated, based on reasonable anticipated experience and reasonable actuarial assumptions, to enable the plan to cease to be in critical status by the end of the rehabilitation period and may include reductions in plan expenditures (including plan mergers and consolidations), reductions in future benefits accruals or increases in contributions, if agreed to by the bargaining parties, or any combination of such actions.

---

[64] The PBGC is directed to prescribe simplified methods for determining withdrawal liability in this case.

[65] A schedule of contribution rates provided by the plan sponsor and relied upon by bargaining parties in negotiating a collective bargaining agreement must remain in effect for the duration of the collective bargaining agreement.

[66] The requirement applies with respect to the initial critical year.

A rehabilitation plan must provide annual standards for meeting the requirements of the rehabilitation. The plan must also include the schedules required to be provided to the bargaining parties.

If the plan sponsor determines that, based on reasonable actuarial assumptions and upon exhaustion of all reasonable measures, the plan cannot reasonably be expected to emerge from critical status by the end of the rehabilitation period, the plan must include reasonable measures to emerge from critical status at a later time or to forestall possible insolvency. In such case, the plan must set forth alternatives considered, explain why the plan is not reasonable expected to emerge from critical status by the end of the rehabilitation period, and specify when, if ever, the plan is expected to emerge from critical status in accordance with the rehabilitation plan.

As previously discussed, the plan sponsor must annually update the rehabilitation plan and must file the update with the plan's annual report.

Rehabilitation period

The rehabilitation period is the 10-year period beginning on the first day of the first plan year following the earlier of (1) the second anniversary of the date of adoption of the rehabilitation plan or (2) the expiration of collective bargaining agreements that were in effect on the due date for the actuarial certification of critical status for the initial critical year and covering at least 75 percent of the active participants in the plan.

The rehabilitation period ends if the plan emerges from critical status. A plan in critical status remains in critical status until a plan year for which the plan actuary certifies that the plan is not projected to have an accumulated funding deficiency for the plan year or any of the nine succeeding plan years, without regard to the use of the shortfall method and taking into account amortization period extensions.

Rules for reductions in future benefit accrual rates

Any schedule including reductions in future benefit accruals forming part of a rehabilitation plan must not reduce the rate of benefit accruals below (1) a monthly benefit (payable as a single life annuity commencing at the participant's normal retirement age) equal to one percent of the contributions required to be made with respect to a participant or the equivalent standard accrual rate for a participant or group of participants under the collective bargaining agreements in effect as of the first day of the initial critical year, or (2) if lower, the accrual rate under the plan on such first day.

The equivalent standard accrual rate is determined by the plan sponsor based on the standard or average contribution base units which the plan sponsor determines to be representative for active participants and such other factors that the plan sponsor determines to be relevant.

Benefit reductions are disregarded in determining an employer's withdrawal liability.

Requirements pending approval and during rehabilitation period

Rehabilitation plan adoption period.–Certain restrictions apply during the period beginning on the date of certification and ending on the day before the first day of the rehabilitation period (defined as the "rehabilitation plan adoption period").

During the rehabilitation plan adoption period, the plan sponsor may not accept a collective bargaining agreement or participation agreement that provides for (1) a reduction in the level of contributions for any participants; (2) a suspension of contributions with respect to any period of service; or (3) any new direct or indirect exclusion of younger or newly hired employees from plan participation. Except in the case of amendments required as a condition of qualification under the Internal Revenue Code or to comply with other applicable law, during the rehabilitation plan adoption period, no amendments that increase the liabilities of the plan by reason of any increase in benefits, any change in the accrual of benefits, or any change in the rate at which benefits become nonforfeitable may be adopted.

During rehabilitation period.–A plan may not be amended after the date of adoption of a rehabilitation plan to be inconsistent with the rehabilitation plan.

A plan may not be amended after the date of adoption of a rehabilitation plan to increase benefits (including future benefit accruals) unless the plan actuary certifies that such increase is paid for out of additional contributions not contemplated by the rehabilitation plan and, after taking into account the benefit increases, the plan is still reasonably expected to emerge from critical status by the end of the rehabilitation period on the schedule contemplated by the rehabilitation plan.

Beginning on the date that notice of certification of the plan's critical status is sent, lump sum and other similar benefits may not be paid. The restriction does not apply if the present value of the participant's accrued benefit does not exceed $5,000. The restriction also does not apply to any makeup payment in the case of a retroactive annuity starting date or any similar payment of benefits owed with respect to a prior period.

The plan sponsor must annually update the plan and must file updates with the plan's annual report. Schedules must be annually updated to reflect experience of the plan.

Effect and penalty for failure to adopt a rehabilitation plan

If a collective bargaining agreement providing for contributions under a multiemployer plan that was in effect at the time the plan entered endangered status expires, and after receiving one of more schedules from the plan sponsor, the bargaining parties fail to adopt a contribution or benefit schedule with terms consistent with the rehabilitation plan and the scheduled from the plan sponsor, the plan sponsor must implement the default schedule. The schedule must be implemented on the earlier of the date (1) on which the Secretary of Labor certifies that the parties are at an impasse, or (2) which is 180 days after the date on which the collective bargaining agreement expires.

Upon the failure of a plan sponsor to adopt a rehabilitation plan within 240 days after the date required for certification, an ERISA penalty of $1,100 a day applies. In addition, upon the failure to timely adopt a rehabilitation plan, an excise tax is imposed on the plan sponsor equal to the greater of (1) the present law excise tax or (2) $1,100 per day. The tax must be paid by the plan sponsor.

Excise tax on employers failing to meet required contributions

If the rehabilitation plan requires an employer to make contributions to the plan, an excise tax applies upon the failure of the employer to make such required contributions within the time required under the plan. The amount of tax is equal to the amount of the required contribution the employer failed to make in a timely manner.

Application of excise tax to plans in critical status/penalty for failure to meet benchmarks or make scheduled progress

In the case of a plan in critical status, if a rehabilitation plan is adopted and complied with, employers are not liable for contributions otherwise required under the general funding rules. In addition, the present-law excise tax does not apply.

If a plan fails to leave critical status at the end of the rehabilitation period or fails to make scheduled progress in meeting its requirements under the rehabilitation plan for three consecutive years, the present law excise tax applies based on the greater of (1) the amount of the contributions necessary to leave critical status or make scheduled progress or (2) the plan's accumulated funding deficiency. The excise tax applies for each succeeding plan year until the requirements are met.

Waiver of excise tax

In the case of a failure which is due to reasonable cause and not to willful neglect, the Secretary of the Treasury may waive all or part of the excise tax on employers failing to make required contributions and the excise tax for failure to meet the rehabilitation plan requirements or make scheduled progress. The standards applicable to waivers of the excise tax for plans in endangered status apply to waivers of plans in critical status.

Additional rules

In general

The actuary's determination with respect to a plan's normal cost, actuarial accrued liability, and improvements in a plan's funded percentage must be based on the unit credit funding method (whether or not that method is used for the plan's actuarial valuation).

In the case of a plan sponsor described under section 404(c) of the Code, the term "plan sponsor" means the bargaining parties.

Expedited resolution of plan sponsor decisions

If, within 60 days of the due date for the adoption of a funding improvement plan or a rehabilitation plan, the plan sponsor has not agreed on a funding improvement plan or a rehabilitation plan, any member of the board or group that constitutes the plan sponsor may require that the plan sponsor enter into an expedited dispute resolution procedure for the development and adoption of a funding improvement plan or rehabilitation plan.

Nonbargained participation

In the case of an employer who contributes to a multiemployer plan with respect to both employees who are covered by one or more collective bargaining agreements and to employees who are not so covered, if the plan is in endangered or critical status, benefits of and contributions for the nonbargained employees, including surcharges on those contributions, must be determined as if the nonbargained employees were covered under the first to expire of the employer's collective bargaining agreements in effect when the plan entered endangered or critical status. [67] In the case of an employer who contributes to a multiemployer plan only with respect to employees who are not covered by a collective bargaining agreement, the additional funding rules apply as if the employer were the bargaining party, and its participation agreement with the plan was a collective bargaining agreement with a term ending on the first day of the plan year beginning after the employer is provided the schedule requires to be provided by the plan sponsor.

Special rule for certain restored benefits

In the case of benefits which were reduced pursuant to a plan amendment adopted on or after January 1, 2002, and before June 30, 2005, if, pursuant to the plan document, the trust agreement, or a formal written communication from the plan sponsor to participants provided before June 30, 2005, such benefits were restored, the rules under the provision do not apply to such benefit restorations to the extent that any restriction on the providing or accrual of such benefits would otherwise apply by reason of the provision.

Cause of action to compel adoption of funding improvement or rehabilitation plan

The provision creates a cause of action under ERISA in the case that the plan sponsor of a plan certified to be endangered or critical (1) has not adopted a funding improvement or rehabilitation plan within 240 days of certification of endangered or critical or (2) fails to update or comply with the terms of the funding improvement or rehabilitation plan. In such case, a civil action may be brought by an employer that has an obligation to contribute with respect to the plan, or an employee organization that represents active participants, for an order compelling the plan sponsor to adopt a funding improvement or rehabilitation plan or to update or comply with the terms of the funding improvement or rehabilitation plan.

---

[67] Treasury regulations allowing certain noncollectively bargained employees covered by a multiemployer plan to be treated as collectively bargained employees for purposes of the minimum coverage rules of the Code do not apply in making determinations under the provision.

Effective Date

The provision is effective for plan years beginning after 2007. The additional funding rules for plans in endangered or critical status do not apply to plan years beginning after December 31, 2014.

If a plan is operating under a funding improvement or rehabilitation plan for its last year beginning before January 1, 2015, the plan shall continue to operate under such funding improvement or rehabilitation plan during any period after December 31, 2014, that such funding improvement or rehabilitation plan is in effect.

C. Measures to Forestall Insolvency of Multiemployer Plans
(sec. 4245 of ERISA and sec. 418E of the Code)

Present Law

In the case of multiemployer plans, the PBGC insures plan insolvency, rather than plan termination. A plan is insolvent when its available resources are not sufficient to pay the plan benefits for the plan year in question, or when the sponsor of a plan in reorganization reasonably determines, taking into account the plan's recent and anticipated financial experience, that the plan's available resources will not be sufficient to pay benefits that come due in the next plan year.

In order to anticipate future insolvencies, at the end of the first plan year in which a plan is in reorganization and at least every three plans year thereafter, the plan sponsor must compare the value of plan assets for the plan year with the total amount of benefit payments made under the plan for the plan year.[68] Unless the plan sponsor determines that the value of plan assets exceeds three times the total amount of benefit payments, the plan sponsor must determine whether the plan will be insolvent for any of the next three plan years.

Explanation of Provision

The provision modifies the requirements for anticipating future insolvencies of plans in reorganization status. Under the provision, unless the plan sponsor determines that the value of plan assets exceeds three times the total amount of benefit payments, the plan sponsor must determine whether the plan will be insolvent for any of the next five plan years, rather than three plan years as under present law. If the plan sponsor makes a determination that the plan will be insolvent for any of the next five plan years, the plan sponsor must make the comparison of plan assets and benefit payments under the plan at least annually until the plan sponsor makes a determination that the plan will not be insolvent in any of the next five plan years.

Effective Date

The provision is effective with respect to determinations made in plan years beginning after 2007.

---

[68] Code sec. 418E(d)(1); ERISA sec. 4245(d)(1).

D. Withdrawal Liability Reforms
(secs. 4203, 4205, 4210, 4219, 4221 and 4225 of ERISA)

1. Repeal of limitation on withdrawal liability in certain cases

Present Law

Under ERISA, an employer which withdraws from a multiemployer plan in a complete or partial withdrawal is liable to the plan in the amount determined to be the employer's withdrawal liability.[69] In general, a "complete withdrawal" means the employer has permanently ceased operations under the plan or has permanently ceased to have an obligation to contribute.[70] A "partial withdrawal" generally occurs if, on the last day of a plan year, there is a 70-percent contribution decline for such plan year or there is a partial cessation of the employer's contribution obligation.[71]

When an employer withdraws from a multiemployer plan, the plan sponsor is required to determine the amount of the employer's withdrawal liability, notify the employer of the amount of the withdrawal liability, and collect the amount of the withdrawal liability from the employer.[72] The employer's withdrawal liability generally is based on the extent of the plan's unfunded vested benefits for the plan years preceding the withdrawal.[73]

ERISA section 4225 provides rules limiting or subordinating withdrawal liability in certain cases. The amount of unfunded vested benefits allocable to an employer is limited in the case of certain sales of all or substantially all of the employer's assets and in the case of an insolvent employer undergoing liquidation or dissolution.

In the case of a bona fide sale of all or substantially all of the employer's assets in an arm's length transaction to an unrelated party, the unfunded vested benefits allocable to an employer is limited to the greater of (1) a portion of the liquidation or dissolution value of the employer (determined after the sale or exchange of such assets), or (2) the unfunded vested benefits attributable to the employees of the employer. The portion to be used in (1) is determined in accordance with a table described in ERISA section 4225(a)(2). Other limitations on withdrawal liability also apply.

---

[69] ERISA sec. 4201.

[70] ERISA sec. 4203.

[71] ERISA sec. 4205.

[72] ERISA sec. 4202.

[73] ERISA secs. 4209 and 4211.

Explanation of Provision

The provision prescribes a new table under ERISA section 4225(a)(2) to be used in determining the portion of the liquidation or dissolution value of the employer for the calculation of the limitation of unfunded vested benefits allocable to an employer in the case of a bona fide sale of all or substantially all of the employer's assets in an arm's length transaction to an unrelated party. The provision also modifies the calculation of the limit so that the unfunded vested benefits allocable to an employer do not exceed the greater of (1) a portion of the liquidation or dissolution value of the employer (determined after the sale or exchange of such assets), or (2) in the case of a plan using the attributable method of allocating withdrawal liability, the unfunded vested benefits attributable to the employees of the employer. Present law ERISA section 4225(b) is not amended by the provision.

Effective Date

The provisions are effective for sales occurring on or after January 1, 2007.

2. Withdrawal liability continues if work contracted out

Present Law

Under ERISA, an employer which withdraws from a multiemployer plan in a complete or partial withdrawal is liable to the plan in the amount determined to be the employer's withdrawal liability.[74] In general, a "complete withdrawal" means the employer has permanently ceased operations under the plan or has permanently ceased to have an obligation to contribute.[75]

A "partial withdrawal" generally occurs if, on the last day of a plan year, there is a 70-percent contribution decline for such plan year or there is a partial cessation of the employer's contribution obligation.[76] A partial cessation of the employer's obligation occurs if (1) the employer permanently ceases to have an obligation to contribute under one or more, but fewer than all collective bargaining agreements under which obligated to contribute, but the employer continues to perform work in the jurisdiction of the collective bargaining agreement or transfers such work to another location or (2) an employer permanently ceases to have an obligation to contribute under the plan with respect to work performed at one or more, but fewer than all of its facilities, but continues to perform work at the facility of the type for which the obligation to contribute ceased.[77]

---

[74] ERISA sec. 4201.

[75] ERISA sec. 4203.

[76] ERISA sec. 4205.

[77] ERISA sec. 4205(b)(2).

Explanation of Provision

Under the provision, a partial withdrawal also occurs if the employer permanently ceases to have an obligation to contribute under one or more, but fewer than all collective bargaining agreements under which obligated to contribute, but the employer transfers such work to an entity or entities owned or controlled by the employer.

Effective Date

The provision is effective with respect to work transferred on or after the date of enactment.

3. Application of forgiveness rule to plans primarily covering employees in building and construction

Present Law

Under ERISA, an employer which withdraws from a multiemployer plan in a complete or partial withdrawal is liable to the plan in the amount determined to be the employer's withdrawal liability.[78] A multiemployer plan, other than a plan which primarily covers employees in the building and construction industry, may adopt a rule that an employer who withdraws from the plan is not subject to withdrawal liability if certain requirements are satisfied.[79] In general, the employer is not liable if the employer (1) first had an obligation to contribute to the plan after the date of enactment of the Multiemployer Pension Plan Amendments Act of 1980; (2) contributed to the plan for no more than the lesser of six plan years or the number of years required for vesting under the plan; (3) was required to make contributions to the plan for each year in an amount equal to less than two percent of all employer contributions for the year; and (4) never avoided withdrawal liability because of the special rule.

A multiemployer plan, other than a plan that primarily covers employees in the building and construction industry, may be amended to provide that the amount of unfunded benefits allocable to an employer that withdraws from the plan is determined under an alternative method.[80]

Explanation of Provision

The provision extends the rule allowing plans to exempt certain employers from withdrawal liability to plans primarily covering employees in the building and construction industries. In addition, the provision also provides that a plan (including a plan which primarily covers employees in the building and construction industry) may be amended to provide that the

---

[78] ERISA sec. 4201.

[79] ERISA sec. 4210.

[80] ERISA sec. 4211(c)(1).

withdrawal liability method otherwise applicable shall be applied by substituting the plan year which is specified in the amendment and for which the plan has no unfunded vested benefits for the plan year ending before September 26, 1980.

Effective Date

The provision is effective with respect to plan withdrawals occurring on or after January 1, 2007.

4. Procedures applicable to disputes involving withdrawal liability

Present Law

Under ERISA, when an employer withdraws from a multiemployer plan, the employer is generally liable for its share of unfunded vested benefits, determined as of the date of withdrawal (generally referred to as the "withdrawal liability"). Whether and when a withdrawal has occurred and the amount of the withdrawal liability is determined by the plan sponsor. The plan sponsor's assessment of withdrawal liability is presumed correct unless the employer shows by a preponderance of the evidence that the plan sponsor's determination of withdrawal liability was unreasonable or clearly erroneous. A similar standard applies in the event the amount of the plan's unfunded vested benefits is challenged.

The first payment of withdrawal liability determined by the plan sponsor is generally due no later than 60 days after demand, even if the employer contests the determination of liability. Disputes between an employer and plan sponsor concerning withdrawal liability are resolved through arbitration, which can be initiated by either party. Even if the employer contests the determination, payments of withdrawal liability must be made by the employer until the arbitrator issues a final decision with respect to the determination submitted for arbitration.

For purposes of withdrawal liability, all trades or businesses under common control are treated as a single employer. In addition, the plan sponsor may disregard a transaction in order to assess withdrawal liability if the sponsor determines that the principal purpose of the transaction was to avoid or evade withdrawal liability. For example, if a subsidiary of a parent company is sold and the subsidiary then withdraws from a multiemployer plan, the plan sponsor may assess withdrawal liability as if the subsidiary were still part of the parent company's controlled group if the sponsor determines that a principal purpose of the sale of the subsidiary was to evade or avoid withdrawal liability.

In the case of an employer that receives a notification of withdrawal liability and demand for payment after October 31, 2003, a special rule may apply if a transaction is disregarded by a plan sponsor in determining that a withdrawal has occurred or that an employer is liable for withdrawal liability. If the transaction that is disregarded by the plan sponsor occurred before January 1, 1999, and at least five years before the date of the withdrawal, then (1) the determination by the plan sponsor that a principal purpose of the transaction was to evade or avoid withdrawal liability is not be presumed to be correct, (2) the plan sponsor, rather than the employer, has the burden to establish, by a preponderance of the evidence, the elements of the claim that a principal purpose of the transaction was to evade or avoid withdrawal liability, and (3) if an employer contests the plan sponsor's determination through an arbitration proceeding,

67

or through a claim brought in a court of competent jurisdiction, the employer is not obligated to make any withdrawal liability payments until a final decision in the arbitration proceeding, or in court, upholds the plan sponsor's determination.

Explanation of Provision

Under the provision, if (1) a plan sponsor determines that a complete or partial withdrawal of an employer has occurred or an employer is liable for withdrawal liability payments with respect to the complete or partial withdrawal from the plan and (2) such determination is based in whole or in part on a finding by the plan sponsor that a principal purpose of any transaction that occurred after December 31, 1998, and at least five years (two years in the case of a small employer) before the date of complete or partial withdrawal was to evade or avoid withdrawal liability, the person against which the withdrawal liability is assessed may elect to use a special rule relating to required payments. Under the special rule, if the electing person contests the plan sponsor's determination with respect to withdrawal liability payments through an arbitration proceeding, through a claim brought in a court of competent jurisdiction, or as otherwise permitted by law, the electing person is not obligated to make the withdrawal liability payments until a final decision in the arbitration proceeding, or in court, upholds the plan sponsor's determination. The special rule applies only if the electing person (1) provides notice to the plan sponsor of its election to apply the special rule within 90 days after the plan sponsor notifies the electing person of its liability, and (2) if a final decision on the arbitration proceeding, or in court, of the withdrawal liability dispute has not been rendered within 12 months from the date of such notice, the electing person provides to the plan, effective as of the first day following the 12-month period, a bond issued by a corporate surety, or an amount held on escrow by a bank or similar financial institution satisfactory to the plan, in an amount equal to the sum of the withdrawal liability payments that would otherwise be due for the 12-month period beginning with the first anniversary of such notice. The bond or escrow must remain in effect until there is a final decision in the arbitration proceeding, or on court, of the withdrawal liability dispute. At such time, the bond or escrow must be paid to the plan if the final decision upholds the plan sponsor's determination. If the withdrawal liability dispute is not concluded by 12 months after the electing person posts the bond or escrow, the electing person must, at the start of each succeeding 12-month period, provide an additional bond or amount held in escrow equal to the sum of the withdrawal liability payments that would otherwise be payable to the plan during that period.

A small employer is an employer which, for the calendar year in which the transaction occurred, and for each of the three preceding years, on average (1) employs no more than 500 employees, and (2) is required to make contributions to the plan on behalf of not more than 250 employees.

Effective Date

The provision is effective for any person that receives a notification of withdrawal liability and demand for payment on or after the date of enactment with respect to a transaction that occurred after December 31, 1998.

E. Prohibition on Retaliation against Employers Exercising their Rights to Petition the Federal Government (sec. 510 of ERISA)

Present Law

Under ERISA section 510, it is unlawful for any person to discharge, fine, suspend, expel, discipline, or discriminate against a participant or beneficiary for exercising any right to which he is entitled under the provisions of an employee benefit plan, Title I or section 3001 of ERISA, or the Welfare and Pension Plans Disclosure Act, or for the purpose of interfering with the attainment of any right to which a participant may become entitled. It is also unlawful for any person to discharge, fine, suspend, expel or discriminate against any person because he has given information or has testified or is about to testify in any inquiry or proceeding relating to ERISA or the Welfare and Pension Plans Disclosure Act. The civil enforcement provisions under ERISA section 503 are applicable in the enforcement of such provisions.

Explanation of Provision

The provision provides that in the case of a multiemployer plan, it is unlawful for the plan sponsor or any other person to discriminate against any contributing employer for exercising rights under ERISA or for giving information or testifying in an inquiry or proceedings relating to ERISA before Congress. The provision amends the anti-retaliation section of ERISA to provide protection for employers who contribute to multiemployer plans and others. The provision is intended to close a loophole in the existing whistleblower protections. In June 2005, a witness who appeared on behalf of several other companies testified before the Retirement Security & Aging Subcommittee of the Senate Health, Education, Labor & Pensions Committee. Subsequent to that testimony there was an allegation that some of these companies may have been targeted for possible audits.

It is intended that retaliation against any employer who has an obligation to contribute to a plan due to testifying before Congress or exercising his or her rights to petition for redress of grievances would amount to unlawful retaliation under ERISA as amended by the provision. Exercising rights under ERISA, testifying before Congress, and giving information in any inquiry or proceeding relating to this Act are intended to be protected under the provision.

Effective Date

The provision is effective on the date of enactment.

F. Special Rule for Certain Benefits Funded under an Agreement Approved by the PBGC

Present Law

No provision.

Explanation of Provision

The provision provides that in the case of a multiemployer plan that is a party to an agreement that was approved by the PBGC before June 30, 2005, that increases benefits and provides for special withdrawal liability rules, certain benefit increases funded pursuant to the agreement are not subject to the multiemployer plan funding rules under the provision (including the additional funding rules for plans in endangered or critical status) if the multiemployer plan is funded in compliance with the agreement (or any amendment thereto).

Effective Date

The provision is effective on the date of enactment.

G. Exception from Excise Tax for Certain Multiemployer Pension Plans
(sec. 4971 of the Code)

Present Law

If a multiemployer plan has an accumulated funding deficiency for a year, an excise tax of five percent generally applies, increasing to 100 percent if contributions sufficient to eliminate the funding deficiency are not made within a certain period.[81]

Explanation of Provision

Under the provision, the present-law excise tax does not apply with respect to any accumulated funding deficiency of a multiemployer plan (1) with less than 100 participants; (2) with respect to which the contributing employers participated in a Federal fishery capacity reduction program; (3) with respect to which employers under the plan participated in the Northeast Fisheries Assistance Program; and (4) with respect to which the annual normal cost is less than $100,000 and the plan is experiencing a funding deficiency on the date of enactment. The tax does not apply to any taxable year beginning before the earlier of (1) the taxable year in which the plan sponsor adopts a rehabilitation plan, or (2) the taxable year that contains January 1, 2009.

Effective Date

The provision is effective for any taxable year beginning before the earlier of (1) the taxable year in which the plan sponsor adopts a rehabilitation plan, or (2) the taxable year that contains January 1, 2009.

---

[81] Code sec. 4971.

H. Sunset of Multiemployer Plan Funding Provisions

Present Law

No provision.

Explanation of Provision

The provision directs the Secretary of Labor, the Secretary of Treasury, and the Executive Director of the PBGC, not later than December 31, 2011, to conduct a study of the effect of the changes made by the provision on the operation and funding status of multiemployer plans and report the results of the study, including recommendations for legislation, to Congress. The study must include (1) the effect of funding difficulties, funding rules in effect before the date of enactment, and the changes made by the provision on small businesses participating in multiemployer plans; (2) the effect on the financial status of small employers of funding targets set in funding improvement and rehabilitation plans and associated contribution increases, funding deficiencies, excise taxes, withdrawal liability, the possibility of alternative schedules and procedures for financially-troubled employers, and other aspects of the multiemployer system; and (3) the role of the multiemployer pension plan system in helping small employers to offer pension benefits.

The provision provides that the rules applicable to plans in endangered and critical status and the rules relating to the automatic amortization extension and shortfall funding method under the general funding rules for multiemployer plans do not apply to plan years beginning after December 31, 2014. The present-law rules are reinstated for such years except that funding improvement and rehabilitation plans and amortization schedules in effect at the time of the sunset continue.

Effective Date

The provision is effective on the date of enactment.

TITLE III: INTEREST RATE ASSUMPTIONS

A. Extension of Replacement of 30-Year Treasury Rates
(secs. 302 and 4006 of ERISA, and sec. 412 of the Code)

The provisions relating to extension of the replacement of the 30-year Treasury rate for purposes of single-employer funding rules are described above, under Title I. The provision relating to extension of the replacement of the 30-year Treasury rate for PBGC premium purposes is described below, under Title IV.

B. Interest Rate Assumption for Determination of Lump-Sum Distributions
(sec. 205(g) of ERISA and sec. 417(e) of the Code)

Present law

Accrued benefits under a defined benefit pension plan generally must be paid in the form of an annuity for the life of the participant unless the participant consents to a distribution in another form. Defined benefit pension plans generally provide that a participant may choose among other forms of benefit offered under the plan, such as a lump-sum distribution. These optional forms of benefit generally must be actuarially equivalent to the life annuity benefit payable to the participant.

A defined benefit pension plan must specify the actuarial assumptions that will be used in determining optional forms of benefit under the plan in a manner that precludes employer discretion in the assumptions to be used. For example, a plan may specify that a variable interest rate will be used in determining actuarial equivalent forms of benefit, but may not give the employer discretion to choose the interest rate.

Statutory interest and mortality assumptions must be used in determining the minimum value of certain optional forms of benefit, such as a lump sum. That is, the lump sum payable under the plan may not be less than the amount of the lump sum that is actuarially equivalent to the life annuity payable to the participant, determined using the statutory assumptions. The statutory assumptions consist of an applicable interest rate and an applicable mortality table (as published by the IRS).

The applicable interest rate is the annual interest rate on 30-year Treasury securities for the month before the date of distribution or such other time as prescribed by Treasury regulations. The regulations provide various options for determining the interest rate to be used under the plan, such as the period for which the interest rate will remain constant ("stability period") and the use of averaging.

The applicable mortality table is a mortality table based on the 1994 Group Annuity Reserving Table ("94 GAR"), projected through 2002.

An amendment of a qualified retirement plan may not decrease the accrued benefit of a plan participant.[82] This restriction is sometimes referred to as the "anticutback" rule and applies to benefits that have already accrued. For purposes of the anticutback rule, an amendment is also treated as reducing an accrued benefit if, with respect to benefits accrued before the amendment is adopted, the amendment has the effect of either (1) eliminating or reducing an early retirement benefit or a retirement-type subsidy, or (2) except as provided by Treasury regulations, eliminating an optional form of benefit.

---

[82] Code sec. 411(d)(6); ERISA sec. 204(g).

Explanation of Provision

The provision changes the interest rate and mortality table used in calculating the minimum value of certain optional forms of benefit, such as lump sums.[83]

Minimum value is calculated using the first, second, and third segment rates as applied under the funding rules, with certain adjustments, for the month before the date of distribution or such other time as prescribed by Treasury regulations. The adjusted first, second, and third segment rates are derived from a corporate bond yield curve prescribed by the Secretary of the Treasury for such month which reflects the yields on investment grade corporate bonds with varying maturities (rather than a 24-month average, as under the minimum funding rules). Thus, the interest rate that applies depends upon how many years in the future a participant's annuity payment will be made. Typically, a higher interest applies for payments made further out in the future.

A transition rule applies for distributions in 2008 through 2011. For distributions in 2008 through 2011, minimum lump-sum values are determined as the weighted average of two values: (1) the value of the lump sum determined under the methodology under present law (the "old" methodology); and (2) the value of the lump sum determined using the methodology applicable for 2008 and thereafter (the "new" methodology). For distributions in 2008, the weighting factor is 80 percent for the lump-sum value determined under the old methodology and 20 percent for the lump-sum determined under the new methodology. For distributions in 2009, the weighting factor is 60 percent for the lump-sum value determined under the old methodology and 40 percent for the lump-sum determined under the new methodology. For distributions in 2010, the weighting factor is 40 percent for the lump-sum value determined under the old methodology and 60 percent for the lump-sum determined under the new methodology. For distributions in 2011, the weighting factor is 20 percent for the lump-sum value determined under the old methodology and 80 percent for the lump-sum determined under the new methodology.

The mortality table that must be used for calculating lump sums under the bill is based on the mortality table required for minimum funding purposes under the bill, modified as appropriate by the Secretary of the Treasury. The Secretary is to prescribe gender-neutral tables for use in determining minimum lump sums.

Effective Date

The provision is effective for plan years beginning after December 31, 2007.

---

[83] Under the provision of the bill relating to plan amendments, if certain requirements are met, a plan amendment to implement the changes made to the minimum value requirements may be made retroactively and without violating the anticutback rule.

C. Interest Rate Assumption for Applying Benefit Limitations to Lump-Sum Distributions (sec. 415(b) of the Code)

Present Law

Annual benefits payable under a defined benefit pension plan generally may not exceed the lesser of (1) 100 percent of average compensation, or (2) $175,000 (for 2006). The dollar limit generally applies to a benefit payable in the form of a straight life annuity. If the benefit is not in the form of a straight life annuity (e.g., a lump sum), the benefit generally is adjusted to an equivalent straight life annuity. For purposes of adjusting a benefit in a form that is subject to the minimum value rules, such as a lump-sum benefit, the interest rate used generally must be not less than the greater of: (1) the rate applicable in determining minimum lump sums, i.e., the interest rate on 30-year Treasury securities; or (2) the interest rate specified in the plan. In the case of plan years beginning in 2004 or 2005, the interest rate used generally must be not less than the greater of: (1) 5.5 percent; or (2) the interest rate specified in the plan.[84]

An amendment of a qualified retirement plan may not decrease the accrued benefit of a plan participant.[85] This restriction is sometimes referred to as the "anticutback" rule and applies to benefits that have already accrued. For purposes of the anticutback rule, an amendment is also treated as reducing an accrued benefit if, with respect to benefits accrued before the amendment is adopted, the amendment has the effect of either (1) eliminating or reducing an early retirement benefit or a retirement-type subsidy, or (2) except as provided by Treasury regulations, eliminating an optional form of benefit.

Explanation of Provision

Under the bill, for purposes of adjusting a benefit in a form that is subject to the minimum value rules, such as a lump-sum benefit, the interest rate used generally must be not less than the greater of: (1) 5.5 percent; (2) the rate that provides a benefit of not more than 105 percent of the benefit that would be provided if the rate (or rates) applicable in determining minimum lump sums were used; or (3) the interest rate specified in the plan.[86]

---

[84] In the case of a plan under which lump-sum benefits are determined solely as required under the minimum value rules (rather than using an interest rate that results in larger lump-sum benefits), the interest rate specified in the plan is the interest rate applicable under the minimum value rules. Thus, for purposes of applying the benefit limits to lump-sum benefits under the plan, the interest rate used must be not less than the greater of: (1) 5.5 percent; or (2) the interest rate applicable under the minimum value rules.

[85] Code sec. 411(d)(6); ERISA sec. 204(g).

[86] Under the provision of the bill relating to plan amendments, if certain requirements are met, a plan amendment to implement the change made to the interest rate used in adjusting a benefit in a form that is subject to the minimum value rules may be made retroactively and without violating the anticutback rule.

Effective Date

The provision is effective for years beginning after December 31, 2005.

TITLE IV: PBGC GUARANTEE AND RELATED PROVISIONS

A. PBGC Premiums
(sec. 4006 of ERISA)

Present Law

The PBGC

The minimum funding requirements permit an employer to fund defined benefit plan benefits over a period of time. Thus, it is possible that a plan may be terminated at a time when plan assets are not sufficient to provide all benefits accrued by employees under the plan. In order to protect plan participants from losing retirement benefits in such circumstances, the Pension Benefit Guaranty Corporation ("PBGC"), a corporation within the Department of Labor, was created in 1974 under ERISA to provide an insurance program for benefits under most defined benefit plans maintained by private employers.

Termination of single-employer defined benefit plans

An employer may voluntarily terminate a single-employer plan only in a standard termination or a distress termination. The PBGC may also involuntarily terminate a plan (that is, the termination is not voluntary on the part of the employer).

A standard termination is permitted only if plan assets are sufficient to cover benefit liabilities. If assets in a defined benefit plan are not sufficient to cover benefit liabilities, the employer may not terminate the plan unless the employer (and members of the employer's controlled group) meets one of four criteria of financial distress.[87]

The PBGC may institute proceedings to terminate a plan if it determines that the plan in question has not met the minimum funding standards, will be unable to pay benefits when due, has a substantial owner who has received a distribution greater than $10,000 (other than by reason of death) while the plan has unfunded nonforfeitable benefits, or may reasonably be expected to increase PBGC's long-run loss unreasonably. The PBGC must institute proceedings to terminate a plan if the plan is unable to pay benefits that are currently due.

---

[87] The four criteria for a distress termination are: (1) the contributing sponsor, and every member of the controlled group of which the sponsor is a member, is being liquidated in bankruptcy or any similar Federal law or other similar State insolvency proceedings; (2) the contributing sponsor and every member of the sponsor's controlled group is being reorganized in bankruptcy or similar State proceeding; (3) the PBGC determines that termination is necessary to allow the employer to pay its debts when due; or (4) the PBGC determines that termination is necessary to avoid unreasonably burdensome pension costs caused solely by a decline in the employer's work force.

Guaranteed benefits

When an underfunded plan terminates, the amount of benefits that the PBGC will pay depends on legal limits, asset allocation, and recovery on the PBGC's employer liability claim. The PBGC guarantee applies to "basic benefits." Basic benefits generally are benefits accrued before a plan terminates, including (1) benefits at normal retirement age; (2) most early retirement benefits; (3) disability benefits for disabilities that occurred before the plan was terminated; and (4) certain benefits for survivors of plan participants. Generally only that part of the retirement benefit that is payable in monthly installments (rather than, for example, lump-sum benefits payable to encourage early retirement) is guaranteed.[88]

Retirement benefits that begin before normal retirement age are guaranteed, provided they meet the other conditions of guarantee (such as that before the date the plan terminates, the participant had satisfied the conditions of the plan necessary to establish the right to receive the benefit other than application for the benefit). Contingent benefits (for example, subsidized early retirement benefits) are guaranteed only if the triggering event occurs before plan termination.

For plans terminating in 2006, the maximum guaranteed benefit for an individual retiring at age 65 and receiving a single life annuity is $3,971.59 per month or $47,659.08 per year.[89] The dollar limit is indexed annually for inflation. The guaranteed amount is reduced for benefits starting before age 65.

The dollar limit is indexed annually for wage inflation. The guaranteed amount is reduced for benefits starting before age 65.

In the case of a plan or a plan amendment that has been in effect for less than five years before a plan termination, the amount guaranteed is phased in by 20 percent a year.[90]

---

[88] ERISA sec. 4022(b) and (c).

[89] The PBGC generally pays the greater of the guaranteed benefit amount and the amount that was covered by plan assets when it terminated. Thus, depending on the amount of assets in the terminating plan, participants may receive more than the amount guaranteed by PBGC.

Special rules limit the guaranteed benefits of individuals who are substantial owners covered by a plans whose benefits have not been increased by reason of any plan amendment. A substantial owner generally is an individual who: (1) owns the entire interest in an unincorporated trade or business; (2) in the case of a partnership, is a partner who owns, directly or indirectly, more than 10 percent of either the capital interest or the profits interest in the partnership; (3) in the case of a corporation, owns, directly or indirectly, more than 10 percent in value of either the voting stock of the corporation or all the stock of the corporation; or (4) at any time within the preceding 60 months was a substantial owner under the plan. ERISA sec. 4022(b)(5).

[90] The phase in does not apply if the benefit is less than $20 per month.

PBGC premiums

In general

The PBGC is funded by assets in terminated plans, amounts recovered from employers who terminate underfunded plans, premiums paid with respect to covered plans, and investment earnings. All covered single-employer plans are required to pay a flat per-participant premium and underfunded plans are subject to an additional variable rate premium based on the level of underfunding. The amount of both the flat rate premium and the variable rate premium are set by statute; the premiums are not indexed for inflation.

Flat rate premium

Under the Deficit Reduction Act of 2005,[91] the flat-rate premium is $30 for plan years beginning after December, 31, 2005, with indexing after 2006 based on increases in average wages.

Variable rate premium

The variable rate premium is equal to $9 per $1,000 of unfunded vested benefits. "Unfunded vested benefits" is the amount which would be the unfunded current liability (as defined under the minimum funding rules) if only vested benefits were taken into account and if benefits were valued at the variable premium interest rate. No variable rate premium is imposed for a year if contributions to the plan for the prior year were at least equal to the full funding limit for that year.

In determining the amount of unfunded vested benefits, the interest rate used is generally 85 percent of the interest rate on 30 year Treasury securities for the month preceding the month in which the plan year begins (100 percent of the interest rate on 30 year Treasury securities for plan years beginning in 2002 and 2003). Under the Pension Funding Equity Act of 2004, in determining the amount of unfunded vested benefits for plan years beginning after December 31, 2003, and before January 1, 2006, the interest rate used is 85 percent of the annual rate of interest determined by the Secretary of the Treasury on amounts invested conservatively in long term investment-grade corporate bonds for the month preceding the month in which the plan year begins.

Termination premium

Under the Deficit Reduction Act of 2005, a new premium generally applies in the case of certain plan terminations occurring after 2005 and before 2011. A premium of $1,250 per participant is imposed generally for the year of the termination and each of the following two years. The premium applies in the case of a plan termination by the PBGC or a distress termination due to reorganization in bankruptcy, the inability of the employer to pay its debts when due, or a determination that a termination is necessary to avoid unreasonably burdensome

---

[91] Pub. L. No. 109-171, enacted February 8, 2006.

pension costs caused solely by a decline in the workforce. In the case of a termination due to reorganization, the liability for the premium does not arise until the employer is discharged from the reorganization proceeding. The premium does not apply with respect to a plan terminated during bankruptcy reorganization proceedings pursuant to a bankruptcy filing before October 18, 2005.

Explanation of Provision

Variable rate premium

For 2006 and 2007, the bill extends the present-law rule under which, in determining the amount of unfunded vested benefits for variable rate premium purposes, the interest rate used is 85 percent of the annual rate of interest determined by the Secretary of the Treasury on amounts invested conservatively in long term investment-grade corporate bonds for the month preceding the month in which the plan year begins.

Beginning in 2008, the determination of unfunded vested benefits for purposes of the variable rate premium is modified to reflect the changes to the funding rules of the provision. Thus, under the provision, unfunded vested benefits are equal to the excess (if any) of (1) the plan's funding target[92] for the year determined as under the minimum funding rules, but taking into account only vested benefits over (2) the fair market value of plan assets. In valuing unfunded vested benefits the interest rate is the first, second, and third segment rates which would be determined under the funding rules of the provision, if the segment rates were based on the yields of corporate bond rates, rather than a 24-month average of such rates. Under the bill, deductible contributions are no longer limited by the full funding limit; thus, the rule providing that no variable rate premium is required if contributions for the prior plan year were at least equal to the full funding limit no longer applies under the provision.

Termination premium

The bill makes permanent the termination premium enacted in the Deficit Reduction Act of 2005.

Effective Date

The extension of the present-law interest rate for purposes of calculating the variable rate premium is effective for plan years beginning in 2006 and 2007. The modifications to the variable rate premium are effective for plan years beginning after December 31, 2007. The provision extending the termination premium is effective on the date of enactment.

---

[92] The assumptions used in determining funded target are the same as under the minimum funding rules. Thus, for a plan in at-risk status, the at-risk assumptions are used.

B. Special Funding Rules for Plans Maintained by Commercial Airlines

Present Law

Minimum funding rules in general

Single-employer defined benefit pension plans are subject to minimum funding requirements under the Employee Retirement Income Security Act of 1974 ("ERISA") and the Internal Revenue Code (the "Code").[93] The amount of contributions required for a plan year under the minimum funding rules is generally the amount needed to fund benefits earned during that year plus that year's portion of other liabilities that are amortized over a period of years, such as benefits resulting from a grant of past service credit. The amount of required annual contributions is determined under one of a number of acceptable actuarial cost methods. Additional contributions are required under the deficit reduction contribution rules in the case of certain underfunded plans. No contribution is required under the minimum funding rules in excess of the full funding limit. A detailed description of the present-law funding rules is provided in Title I, above.

Notice of certain plan amendments

A notice requirement must be met if an amendment to a defined benefit pension plan provides for a significant reduction in the rate of future benefit accrual. In that case, the plan administrator must furnish a written notice concerning the amendment. Notice may also be required if a plan amendment eliminates or reduces an early retirement benefit or retirement-type subsidy. The plan administrator is required to provide the notice to any participant or alternate payee whose rate of future benefit accrual may reasonably be expected to be significantly reduced by the plan amendment (and to any employee organization representing affected participants). The notice must be written in a manner calculated to be understood by the average plan participant and must provide sufficient information to allow recipients to understand the effect of the amendment. In the case of a single-employer plan, the plan administrator is generally required to provide the notice at least 45 days before the effective date of the plan amendment. In the case of a multiemployer plan, the notice is generally required to be provided 15 days before the effective date of the plan amendment.

PBGC termination insurance program

The minimum funding requirements permit an employer to fund defined benefit plan benefits over a period of time. Thus, it is possible that a plan may be terminated at a time when plan assets are not sufficient to provide all benefits accrued by employees under the plan. In order to protect plan participants from losing retirement benefits in such circumstances, the PBGC guarantees basic benefits under most defined benefit plans. When an underfunded plan terminates, the amount of benefits that the PBGC will pay depends on legal limits, asset

---

[93] Code sec. 412. The minimum funding rules also apply to multiemployer plans, but the rules for multiemployer plans differ in various respects from the rules applicable to single-employer plans.

allocation, and recovery on the PBGC's employer liability claim. There is a dollar limit on the amount of otherwise guaranteed benefits based on the year in which the plan terminates. For plans terminating in 2006, the maximum guaranteed benefit for an individual retiring at age 65 and receiving a single life annuity is $3,971.59 per month or $47,659.08 per year.[94] The dollar limit is indexed annually for inflation. The guaranteed amount is reduced for benefits starting before age 65. In the case of a plan or a plan amendment that has been in effect for less than five years before a plan termination, the amount guaranteed is phased in by 20 percent a year.[95]

Termination premiums

Under the Deficit Reduction Act of 2005, a new premium generally applies in the case of certain plan terminations occurring after 2005 and before 2011. A premium of $1,250 per participant is imposed generally for the year of the termination and each of the following two years. The premium applies in the case of a plan termination by the PBGC or a distress termination due to reorganization in bankruptcy, the inability of the employer to pay its debts when due, or a determination that a termination is necessary to avoid unreasonably burdensome pension costs caused solely by a decline in the workforce. In the case of a termination due to reorganization, the liability for the premium does not arise until the employer is discharged from the reorganization proceeding. The premium does not apply with respect to a plan terminated during bankruptcy reorganization proceedings pursuant to a bankruptcy filing before October 18, 2005.

Minimum coverage requirements

The Code imposes minimum coverage requirements on qualified retirement plans in order to ensure that plans cover a broad cross section of employees.[96] In general, the minimum coverage requirements are satisfied if one of the following criteria are met: (1) the plan benefits at least 70 percent of employees who are not highly compensated employees; (2) the plan benefits a percentage of employees who are not highly compensated employees which is at least

---

[94] The PBGC generally pays the greater of the guaranteed benefit amount and the amount that was covered by plan assets when it terminated. Thus, depending on the amount of assets in the terminating plan, participants may receive more than the amount guaranteed by PBGC.

Special rules limit the guaranteed benefits of individuals who are substantial owners covered by a plans whose benefits have not been increased by reason of any plan amendment. A substantial owner generally is an individual who: (1) owns the entire interest in an unincorporated trade or business; (2) in the case of a partnership, is a partner who owns, directly or indirectly, more than 10 percent of either the capital interest or the profits interest in the partnership; (3) in the case of a corporation, owns, directly or indirectly, more than 10 percent in value of either the voting stock of the corporation or all the stock of the corporation; or (4) at any time within the preceding 60 months was a substantial owner under the plan. ERISA sec. 4022(b)(5).

[95] The phase in does not apply if the benefit is less than $20 per month.

[96] Code sec. 410(b).

70 percent of the percentage of highly compensated employees participating under the plan; or (3) the plan meets the average benefits test.

Certain employees may be disregarded in applying the minimum coverage requirements. Under one exclusion, in the case of a plan established or maintained pursuant to an agreement which the Secretary of Labor finds to be a collective bargaining agreement between air pilots represented in accordance with title II of the Railway Labor Act and one or more employers, all employees not covered by such agreement may be disregarded. This exclusion does not apply in the case of a plan which provides contributions or benefits for employees whose principal duties are not customarily performed aboard aircraft in flight.

Alternative deficit reduction contribution for certain plans

Under present law, certain employers ("applicable employers") may elect a reduced amount of additional required contribution under the deficit reduction contribution rules (an "alternative deficit reduction contribution") with respect to certain plans for applicable plan years. An applicable plan year is a plan year beginning after December 27, 2003, and before December 28, 2005, for which the employer elects a reduced contribution. If an employer so elects, the amount of the additional deficit reduction contribution for an applicable plan year is the greater of: (1) 20 percent of the amount of the additional contribution that would otherwise be required; or (2) the additional contribution that would be required if the deficit reduction contribution for the plan year were determined as the expected increase in current liability due to benefits accruing during the plan year.

An applicable employer is an employer that is: (1) a commercial passenger airline; (2) primarily engaged in the production or manufacture of a steel mill product, or the processing of iron ore pellets; or (3) an organization described in section 501(c)(5) that established the plan for which an alternative deficit reduction contribution is elected on June 30, 1955.

Explanation of Provision

In general

The provision provides special funding rules for certain eligible plans. For purposes of the provision, an eligible plan is a single-employer defined benefit pension plan sponsored by an employer that is a commercial passenger airline or the principal business of which is providing catering services to a commercial passenger airline.

The plan sponsor of an eligible plan may make one of two alternative elections. In the case of a plan that meets certain benefit accrual and benefit increase restrictions, an election allowing a 17-year amortization of the plan's unfunded liability is available. A plan that does not meet such requirements may elect to use a 10-year amortization period in amortizing the plan's shortfall amortization base for the first taxable year beginning in 2008.

84

Election for plans that meet benefit accrual and benefit increase restriction requirements

In general

Under the provision, if an election of a 17-year amortization period is made with respect to an eligible plan for a plan year (an "applicable" plan year), the minimum required contribution is determined under a special method.[97] If minimum required contributions as determined under the provision are made: (1) for an applicable plan year beginning before January 1, 2008 (for which the present-law funding rules apply), the plan does not have an accumulated funding deficiency; and (2) for an applicable plan year beginning on or after January 1, 2008 (for which the funding rules under the provision apply), the minimum required contribution is the contribution determined under the provision.

The employer may select either a plan year beginning in 2006 or 2007 as the first plan year to which the election applies. The election applies to such plan year and all subsequent plan years, unless the election is revoked with the approval of the Secretary of the Treasury. The election must be made (1) no later than December 31, 2006, in the case of an election for a plan year beginning in 2006, or (2) not later than December 31, 2007, in the case of a plan year beginning in 2007. An election under the provision must be made in such manner as prescribed by the Secretary of the Treasury. The employer may change the plan year with respect to the plan by specifying a new plan year in the election. Such a change in plan year does not require approval of the Secretary of the Treasury.

Determination of required contribution

Under the provision, the minimum required contribution for any applicable plan year during the amortization period is the amount required to amortize the plan's unfunded liability, determined as of the first day of the plan year, in equal annual installments over the remaining amortization period. For this purpose, the amortization period is the 17-plan-year period beginning with the first applicable plan year. Thus, the annual amortization amount is redetermined each year, based on the plan's unfunded liability at that time and the remainder of the amortization period. For any plan years beginning after the end of the amortization period, the plan is subject to the generally applicable minimum funding rules (as provided under the bill, including the benefit limitations applicable to underfunded plans). The plan's prefunding balance and funding standard carryover balance as of the first day of the first year beginning after the end of the amortization period is zero.[98]

---

[97] Any charge or credit in the funding standard account determined under the present-law rules or any prefunding balance or funding standard carryover balance (determined under the funding provisions of the bill) as of the end of the last year preceding the first applicable year is reduced to zero.

[98] If an election to use the special method is revoked before the end of the amortization period, the plan is subject to the generally applicable minimum funding rules beginning with the first plan year for which the election is revoked, and the plan's prefunding balance as of the beginning of that year is zero.

Any waived funding deficiency as of the day before the first day of the first applicable plan year is deemed satisfied and the amount of such waived funding deficiency must be taken into account in determining the plan's unfunded liability under the provision. Any plan amendment adopted to satisfy the benefit accrual restrictions of the provision (discussed below) or any increase in benefits provided to such plan's participants under a defined contribution or multiemployer plan will not be deemed to violate the prohibition against benefit increases during a waiver period.[99]

For purposes of the provision, a plan's unfunded liability is the unfunded accrued liability under the plan, determined under the unit credit funding method. As under present law, minimum required contributions (including the annual amortization amount) under the provision must be determined using actuarial assumptions and methods, each of which is reasonable (taking into account the experience of the plan and reasonable expectations), or which, in the aggregate, result in a total plan contribution equivalent to a contribution that would be obtained if each assumption and method were reasonable. The assumptions are required also to offer the actuary's best estimate of anticipated experience under the plan. Under the election, a rate of interest of 8.85 percent is used in determining the plan's accrued liability. The value of plan assets used must be the fair market value.

If any applicable plan year with respect to an eligible plan using the special method includes the date of enactment of the provision and a plan was spun off from such eligible plan during the plan year, but before the date of enactment, the minimum required contribution under the special method for the applicable plan year is an aggregate amount determined as if the plans were a single plan for that plan year (based on the full 12-month plan year in effect prior to the spin off). The employer is to designate the allocation of the aggregate amount between the plans for the applicable plan year.

Benefit accrual and benefit increase restrictions

Benefit accrual restrictions. - Under the provision, effective as of the first day of the first applicable plan year and at all times thereafter while an election under the provision is in effect, an eligible plan must include two accrual restrictions. First, the plan must provide that, with respect to each participant: (1) the accrued benefit, any death or disability benefit, and any social security supplement are frozen at the amount of the benefit or supplement immediately before such first day; and (2) all other benefits under the plan are eliminated. However, such freezing or elimination of benefits or supplements is required only to the extent that it would be permitted under the anticutback rule if implemented by a plan amendment adopted immediately before such first day.

Second, if an accrued benefit of a participant has been subject to the limitations on benefits under section 415 of the Code and would otherwise be increased if such limitation is increased, the plan must provide that, effective as of the first day of the first applicable plan year

---

[99] ERISA sec. 304(b); Code sec. 412(f).

86

(or, if later, the date of enactment) any such increase will not take effect. The plan does not fail to meet the anticutback rule solely because the plan is amended to meet this requirement.

Benefit increase restriction. – No applicable benefit increase under an eligible plan may take effect at any time during the period beginning on July 26, 2005, and ending on the day before the first day of the first applicable plan year. For this purpose, an applicable benefit increase is any increase in liabilities of the plan by plan amendment (or otherwise as specified by the Secretary) which would occur by reason of: (1) any increase in benefits; (2) any change in the accrual of benefits; or (3) any change in the rate at which benefits become nonforfeitable under the plan.

Exception for imputed disability service.– The benefit accrual and benefit increase restrictions do not apply to any accrual or increase with respect to imputed serviced provided to a participant during any period of the participant's disability occurring on or after the effective date of the plan amendment providing for the benefit accrual restrictions (on or after July 26, 2005, in the case of benefit increase restrictions) if the participant was: (1) was receiving disability benefits as of such date or (2) was receiving sick pay and subsequently determined to be eligible for disability benefits as of such date.

Rules relating to PBGC guarantee and plan terminations

Under the provision, if a plan to which an election applies is terminated before the end of the 10-year period beginning on the first day of the first applicable plan year, certain aspects of the PBGC guarantee provisions are applied as if the plan terminated on the first day of the first applicable plan year. Specifically, the amount of guaranteed benefits payable by the PBGC is determined based on plan assets and liabilities as of the assumed termination date. The difference between the amount of guaranteed benefits determined as of the assumed termination date and the amount of guaranteed benefits determined as of the actual termination date is to be paid from plan assets before other benefits.

The provision of the bill under which defined benefit plans that are covered by the PBGC insurance program are not taken into account in applying the overall limit on deductions for contributions to combinations of defined benefit and defined contribution plans, does not apply to an eligible plan to which the special method applies. Thus, the overall deduction limit applies.

In the case of notice required with respect to an amendment that is made to an eligible plan maintained pursuant to one or more collective bargaining agreements in order to comply with the benefit accrual and benefit increase restrictions under the provision, the provision allows the notice to be provided 15 days before the effective date of the plan amendment.

Termination premiums

If a plan terminates during the five-year period beginning on the first day of the first applicable plan year, termination premiums are imposed at a rate of $2,500 per participant (in lieu of the present-law $1,250 amount). The increased termination premium applies notwithstanding that a plan was terminated during bankruptcy reorganization proceedings pursuant to a bankruptcy filing before October 18, 2005 (i.e., the present-law grandfather rule does not apply).

The Secretary of Labor may waive the additional termination premium if the Secretary determines that the termination occurred as the result of extraordinary circumstances such as a terrorist attack or other similar event. It is intended that extraordinary circumstances means a substantial, system-wide adverse effect on the airline industry such as the terrorist attack which occurred on September 11, 2001. It is intended that the waiver of the additional premiums occur only in rare and unpredictable events. Extraordinary circumstances would not include a mere economic event such as the high price of oil or fuel, or a downturn in the market.

Alternative election in the case of plans not meeting benefit accrual and benefit increase restrictions

In lieu of the election above, a plan sponsor may elect, for the first taxable year beginning in 2008, to amortize the shortfall amortization base for such taxable year over a period of 10 plan years (rather than seven plan years) beginning with such plan year. Under such election, the benefit accrual, benefit increase and other restrictions discussed above do not apply. This 10-year amortization election must be made by December 31, 2007.

Authority of Treasury to disqualify successor plans

If either election is made under the provision and the eligible plan is maintained by an employer that establishes or maintains one or more other single-employer defined benefit plans, and such other plans in combination provide benefit accruals to any substantial number of successor employees, the Secretary of Treasury may disqualify such successor plans unless all benefit obligations of the eligible plan have been satisfied. Successor employees include any employee who is or was covered by the eligible plan and any employee who performs substantially the same type of work with respect to the same business operations as an employee covered by the eligible plan.

Alternative deficit reduction contribution for certain plans

In the case of an employer which is a commercial passenger airline, the provision extends the alternative deficit reduction contributions rules to plan years beginning before December 28, 2007.

Application of minimum coverage rules

In applying the minimum coverage rules to a plan, management pilots who are not represented in accordance with title II of the Railway Labor Act are treated as covered by a collective bargaining agreement if the management pilots manage the flight operations of air pilots who are so represented and the management pilots are, pursuant to the terms of the agreement, included in the group of employees benefiting under the plan.

The exclusion under the minimum coverage rules for air pilots represented in accordance with title II of the Railway Labor Act does not apply in the case of a plan which provides contributions or benefits for employees whose principal duties are not customarily performed aboard an aircraft in flight (other than management pilots described above).

Effective Date

The provision is effective for plan years ending after the date of enactment except that the modifications to the minimum coverage rules apply to years beginning before, on, or after the date of enactment.

C. Limitations on PBGC Guarantee of Shutdown and Other Benefits
(sec. 4022 of ERISA)

Present Law

A plan may provide for unpredictable contingent event benefits, which are benefits that depend on contingencies that are not reliably and reasonably predictable, such as facility shutdowns or reductions in workforce. Under present law, unpredictable contingent event benefits generally are not taken into account for funding purposes until the event has occurred.

Under present law, defined benefit pension plans are not permitted to provide "layoff" benefits (i.e., severance benefits).[100] However, defined benefit pension plans may provide subsidized early retirement benefits, including early retirement window benefits.[101]

Within certain limits, the PBGC guarantees any retirement benefit that was vested on the date of plan termination (other than benefits that vest solely on account of the termination), and any survivor or disability benefit that was owed or was in payment status at the date of plan termination.[102] Generally only that part of the retirement benefit that is payable in monthly installments is guaranteed.[103]

Retirement benefits that begin before normal retirement age are guaranteed, provided they meet the other conditions of guarantee (such as that, before the date the plan terminates, the participant had satisfied the conditions of the plan necessary to establish the right to receive the benefit other than application for the benefit). Contingent benefits (for example, early retirement benefits provided only if a plant shuts down) are guaranteed only if the triggering event occurs before plan termination.

In the case of a plan or a plan amendment that has been in effect for less than five years before a plan termination, the amount guaranteed is phased in by 20 percent a year.

Explanation of Provision

Under the bill, the PBGC guarantee applies to unpredictable contingent event benefits as if a plan amendment had been adopted on the date the event giving rise to the benefits occurred. An unpredictable contingent event benefit is defined as under the benefit limitations applicable to single-employer plans (described above) and means a benefit payable solely by reason of (1) a plant shutdown (or similar event as determined by the Secretary of the Treasury), or (2) an event other than the attainment of any age, performance of any service, receipt or derivation of any compensation, or occurrence of death or disability.

---

[100] Treas. Reg. sec. 1.401-1(b)(1)(i).

[101] Treas. Reg. secs. 1.401(a)(4)-3(f)(4) and 1.411(a)-7(c).

[102] ERISA sec. 4022(a).

[103] ERISA sec. 4022(b) and (c).

Effective Date

The provision applies to benefits that become payable as a result of an event which occurs after July 26, 2005.

D. Rules Relating to Bankruptcy of the Employer
(secs. 4022 and 4044 of ERISA)

Present Law

Guaranteed benefits

When an underfunded plan terminates, the amount of benefits that the PBGC will pay depends on legal limits, asset allocation, and recovery on the PBGC's employer liability claim. The PBGC guarantee applies to "basic benefits." Basic benefits generally are benefits accrued before a plan terminates, including (1) benefits at normal retirement age; (2) most early retirement benefits; (3) disability benefits for disabilities that occurred before the plan was terminated; and (4) certain benefits for survivors of plan participants. Generally only that part of the retirement benefit that is payable in monthly installments is guaranteed.[104]

Retirement benefits that begin before normal retirement age are guaranteed, provided they meet the other conditions of guarantee (such as that before the date the plan terminates, the participant had satisfied the conditions of the plan necessary to establish the right to receive the benefit other than application for the benefit). Contingent benefits (for example, subsidized early retirement benefits) are guaranteed only if the triggering event occurs before plan termination.

For plans terminating in 2006, the maximum guaranteed benefit for an individual retiring at age 65 and receiving a single life annuity is $3,971.59 per month or $47,659.08 per year.[105] The dollar limit is indexed annually for inflation. The guaranteed amount is reduced for benefits starting before age 65.

In the case of a plan or a plan amendment that has been in effect for less than five years before a plan termination, the amount guaranteed is phased in by 20 percent a year.[106]

---

[104] ERISA sec. 4022(b) and (c).

[105] The PBGC generally pays the greater of the guaranteed benefit amount and the amount that was covered by plan assets when it terminated. Thus, depending on the amount of assets in the terminating plan, participants may receive more than the amount guaranteed by PBGC.

Special rules limit the guaranteed benefits of individuals who are substantial owners covered by a plans whose benefits have not been increased by reason of any plan amendment. A substantial owner generally is an individual who: (1) owns the entire interest in an unincorporated trade or business; (2) in the case of a partnership, is a partner who owns, directly or indirectly, more than 10 percent of either the capital interest or the profits interest in the partnership; (3) in the case of a corporation, owns, directly or indirectly, more than 10 percent in value of either the voting stock of the corporation or all the stock of the corporation; or (4) at any time within the preceding 60 months was a substantial owner under the plan. ERISA sec. 4022(b)(5).

[106] The phase in does not apply if the benefit is less than $20 per month.

Asset allocation

ERISA contains rules for allocating the assets of a single-employer plan when the plan terminates. Plan assets available to pay for benefits under a terminating plan include all plan assets remaining after subtracting all liabilities (other than liabilities for future benefit payments), paid or payable from plan assets under the provisions of the plan. On termination, the plan administrator must allocate plan assets available to pay for benefits under the plan in the manner prescribed by ERISA. In general, plan assets available to pay for benefits under the plan are allocated to six priority categories. If the plan has sufficient assets to pay for all benefits in a particular priority category, the remaining assets are allocated to the next lower priority category. This process is repeated until all benefits in the priority categories are provided or until all available plan assets have been allocated.

Explanation of Provision

Under the bill, the amount of guaranteed benefits payable by the PBGC is frozen when a contributing sponsor enters bankruptcy or a similar proceeding.[107] If the plan terminates during the contributing sponsor's bankruptcy, the amount of guaranteed benefits payable by the PBGC is determined based on plan provisions, salary, service, and the guarantee in effect on the date the employer entered bankruptcy. The priority among participants for purposes of allocating plan assets and employer recoveries to non-guaranteed benefits in the event of plan termination is determined as of the date the sponsor enters bankruptcy or a similar proceeding.

A contributing sponsor of a single-employer plan is required to notify the plan administrator when the sponsor enters bankruptcy or a similar proceeding. Within a reasonable time after a plan administrator knows or has reason to know that a contributing sponsor has entered bankruptcy (or similar proceeding), the administrator is required to notify plan participants and beneficiaries of the bankruptcy and the limitations on benefit guarantees if the plan is terminated while underfunded, taking into account the bankruptcy.

The Secretary of Labor is to prescribe the form and manner of notices required under this provision. The notice is to be written in a manner calculated to be understood by the average plan participant and may be delivered in written, electronic, or other appropriate form to the extent that such form is reasonably accessible to the applicable individual.

The Secretary of Labor may assess a civil penalty of up to $100 a day for each failure to provide the notice required by the provision. Each violation with respect to any single participant or beneficiary is treated as a separate violation.

---

[107] For purposes of the provision, a contributing sponsor is considered to have entered bankruptcy if the sponsor files or has had filed against it a petition seeking liquidation or reorganization in a case under title 11 of the United States Code or under any similar Federal law or law of a State or political subdivision.

Effective Date

The provision is effective with respect to Federal bankruptcy or similar proceedings or arrangements for the benefit of creditors which are initiated on or after the date that is 30 days after enactment.

E. PBGC Premiums for Small Plans
(sec. 4006 of ERISA)

Present Law

Under present law, the Pension Benefit Guaranty Corporation ("PBGC") provides insurance protection for participants and beneficiaries under certain defined benefit pension plans by guaranteeing certain basic benefits under the plan in the event the plan is terminated with insufficient assets to pay benefits promised under the plan. The guaranteed benefits are funded in part by premium payments from employers who sponsor defined benefit pension plans. The amount of the required annual PBGC premium for a single-employer plan is generally a flat rate premium of $19 per participant and an additional variable-rate premium based on a charge of $9 per $1,000 of unfunded vested benefits. Unfunded vested benefits under a plan generally means (1) the unfunded current liability for vested benefits under the plan, over (2) the value of the plan's assets, reduced by any credit balance in the funding standard account. No variable-rate premium is imposed for a year if contributions to the plan were at least equal to the full funding limit.

The PBGC guarantee is phased in ratably in the case of plans that have been in effect for less than five years, and with respect to benefit increases from a plan amendment that was in effect for less than five years before termination of the plan.

Explanation of Provision

In the case of a plan of a small employer, the per participant variable-rate premium is no more than $5 multiplied by the number of plan participants in the plan at the end of the preceding plan year. For purposes of the provision, a small employer is a contributing sponsor that, on the first day of the plan year, has 25 or fewer employees. For this purpose, all employees of the members of the controlled group of the contributing sponsor are to be taken into account. In the case of a plan to which more than one unrelated contributing sponsor contributed, employees of all contributing sponsors (and their controlled group members) are to be taken into account in determining whether the plan was a plan of a small employer. For example, under the provision, in the case of a plan with 20 participants, the total variable rate premium is not more than $2,000, that is, (20 x $5) x 20.

Effective Date

The provision applies to plan years beginning after December 31, 2006.

F. Authorization for PBGC to Pay Interest on Premium Overpayment Refunds
(sec. 4007(b) of ERISA)

Present Law

The PBGC charges interest on underpayments of premiums, but is not authorized to pay interest on overpayments.

Explanation of Provision

The provision allows the PBGC to pay interest on overpayments made by premium payors. Interest paid on overpayments is to be calculated at the same rate and in the same manner as interest charged on premium underpayments.

Effective Date

The provision is effective with respect to interest accruing for periods beginning not earlier than the date of enactment.

G. Rules for Substantial Owner Benefits in Terminated Plans
(secs. 4021, 4022, 4043, and 4044 of ERISA)

Present Law

Under present law, the Pension Benefit Guaranty Corporation ("PBGC") provides participants and beneficiaries in a defined benefit pension plan with certain minimal guarantees as to the receipt of benefits under the plan in case of plan termination. The employer sponsoring the defined benefit pension plan is required to pay premiums to the PBGC to provide insurance for the guaranteed benefits. In general, the PBGC will guarantee all basic benefits which are payable in periodic installments for the life (or lives) of the participant and his or her beneficiaries and are non-forfeitable at the time of plan termination. The amount of the guaranteed benefit is subject to certain limitations. One limitation is that the plan (or an amendment to the plan which increases benefits) must be in effect for 60 months before termination for the PBGC to guarantee the full amount of basic benefits for a plan participant, other than a substantial owner. In the case of a substantial owner, the guaranteed basic benefit is phased in over 30 years beginning with participation in the plan. A substantial owner is one who owns, directly or indirectly, more than 10 percent of the voting stock of a corporation or all the stock of a corporation. Special rules restricting the amount of benefit guaranteed and the allocation of assets also apply to substantial owners.

Explanation of Provision

The provision provides that the 60-month phase-in of guaranteed benefits applies to a substantial owner with less than 50 percent ownership interest. For a substantial owner with a 50 percent or more ownership interest ("majority owner"), the phase-in occurs over a 10-year period and depends on the number of years the plan has been in effect. The majority owner's guaranteed benefit is limited so that it cannot be more than the amount phased in over 60 months for other participants. The rules regarding allocation of assets apply to substantial owners, other than majority owners, in the same manner as other participants.

Effective Date

The provision is effective for plan terminations with respect to which notices of intent to terminate are provided, or for which proceedings for termination are instituted by the PBGC, after December 31, 2005.

H. Acceleration of PBGC Computation of Benefits Attributable to Recoveries from Employers (secs. 4022(c) and 4062(c) of ERISA)

Present Law

In general

The Pension Benefit Guaranty Corporation ("PBGC") provides insurance protection for participants and beneficiaries under certain defined benefit pension plans by guaranteeing certain basic benefits under the plan in the event the plan is terminated with insufficient assets to pay promised benefits.[108] The guaranteed benefits are funded in part by premium payments from employers who sponsor defined benefit plans. In general, the PBGC guarantees all basic benefits which are payable in periodic installments for the life (or lives) of the participant and his or her beneficiaries and are non-forfeitable at the time of plan termination. For plans terminating in 2006, the maximum guaranteed benefit for an individual retiring at age 65 and receiving a straight life annuity is $3971.59 per month, or $47,659.08 per year.

The PBGC pays plan benefits, subject to the guarantee limits, when it becomes trustee of a terminated plan. The PBGC also pays amounts in addition to the guarantee limits ("additional benefits") if there are sufficient plan assets, including amounts recovered from the employer for unfunded benefit liabilities and contributions owed to the plan. The employer (including members of its controlled group) is statutorily liable for these amounts.

Plan underfunding recoveries

The PBGC's recoveries on its claims for unfunded benefit liabilities are shared between the PBGC and plan participants. The amounts recovered are allocated partly to the PBGC to help cover its losses for paying unfunded guaranteed benefits and partly to participants to help cover the loss of benefits that are above the PBGC's guarantees and are not funded. In determining the portion of the recovered amounts that will be allocated to participants, present law specifies the use of a recovery ratio based on plan terminations during a specified period, rather than the actual amount recovered for each specific plan. The recovery ratio that applies to a plan includes the PBGC's actual recovery experience for plan terminations in the five-Federal fiscal year period immediately preceding the Federal fiscal year in which falls the notice of intent to terminate for the particular plan.

The recovery ratio is used for all but very large plans taken over by the PBGC. For a very large plan (i.e., a plan for which participants' benefit losses exceed $20 million) actual recovery amounts with respect to the specific plan are used to determine the portion of the amounts recovered that will be allocated to participants.

---

[108] The PBGC termination insurance program does not cover plans of professional service employers that have fewer than 25 participants.

Recoveries for due and unpaid employer contributions

Amounts recovered from an employer for contributions owed to the plan are treated as plan assets and are allocated to plan benefits in the same manner as other assets in the plan's trust on the plan termination date. The amounts recovered are determined on a plan-specific basis rather than based on an historical average recovery ratio.

Explanation of Provision

The bill changes the five-year period used to determine the recovery ratio for unfunded benefit liabilities so that the period begins two years earlier. Thus, under the bill, the recovery ratio that applies to a plan includes the PBGC's actual recovery experience for plan terminations in the five-Federal fiscal year period ending with the third fiscal year preceding the fiscal year in which falls the notice of intent to terminate for the particular plan.

In addition, the provision creates a recovery ratio for determining amounts recovered for contributions owed to the plan, based on the PBGC's recovery experience over the same five-year period.

The provision does not apply to very large plans (i.e., plans for which participants' benefit losses exceed $20 million). As under present law, in the case of a very large plan, actual amounts recovered for unfunded benefit liabilities and for contributions owed to the plan are used to determine the amount available to provide additional benefits to participants.

Effective Date

The provision is effective for any plan termination for which notices of intent to terminate are provided (or, in the case of a termination by the PBGC, a notice of determination that the plan must be terminated is issued) on or after the date that is 30 days after the date of enactment.

I. Treatment of Certain Plans Where There is a Cessation or Change in Membership of a Controlled Group (sec. 4041(b) of ERISA)

Present Law

An employer may voluntarily terminate a single-employer plan only in a standard termination or a distress termination. A standard termination is permitted only if plan assets are sufficient to cover benefit liabilities. Benefit liabilities are defined generally as the present value of all benefits due under the plan (this amount is referred to as "termination liability"). This present value is determined using interest and mortality assumptions prescribed by the PBGC.

Explanation of Provision

Under the bill, if: (1) there is a transaction or series of transactions which result in a person ceasing to be a member of a controlled group; (2) such person, immediately before the transaction or series of transactions maintained a single-employer defined benefit plan which is fully funded then the interest rate used in determining whether the plan is sufficient for benefit liabilities or to otherwise assess plan liabilities for purposes of section 4041(b) or section 4042(a)(4) shall not be less than the interest rate used in determining whether the plan is fully funded.

The provision does not apply to any transaction or series of transactions unless (1) any employer maintaining the plan immediately before or after such transactions or series of transactions (a) has a outstanding senior unsecured debt instrument which is rated investment grade by each of the nationally recognized statistical rating organizations for corporate bonds that has issued a credit rating for such instrument, or (b) if no such debt instrument of such employer has been rated by such an organization but one or more of such organizations has made an issuer credit rating for such employer, all such organizations which have so rated the employer have rated such employer investment grade and (2) the employer maintaining the plan after the transaction or series of transaction employs at least 20 percent of the employees located within United States who were employed by such employer immediately before the transaction or series of transactions.

The provision does not apply in the case of determinations of liabilities by the PBGC or a court if the plan is terminated within two years of the transaction (or first transaction in a series of transactions).

For purposes of the provision, a plan is considered fully funded with respect to a transaction or series of transactions if (1) in the case of a transaction or series of transactions which occur in a plan year beginning before January 1, 2008, the funded current liability percentage for the plan year (determined under the minimum funding rules) is at least 100 percent, or (2) in the case of a transaction or series of transactions which occur on or after January 1, 2008, the funding target attainment percentage (as determined under the minimum funding rules) as of the valuation date for the plan year is at least 100 percent.

Effective Date

The provision applies to transactions or series of transactions occurring on or after the date of enactment.

J. Missing Participants
(sec. 4050 of ERISA)

Present Law

In the case of a defined benefit pension plan that is subject to the plan termination insurance program under Title IV of the Employee Retirement Income Security Act of 1974 ("ERISA"), is maintained by a single employer, and terminates under a standard termination, the plan administrator generally must purchase annuity contracts from a private insurer to provide the benefits to which participants are entitled and distribute the annuity contracts to the participants.

If the plan administrator of a terminating single employer plan cannot locate a participant after a diligent search (a "missing participant"), the plan administrator may satisfy the distribution requirement only by purchasing an annuity from an insurer or transferring the participant's designated benefit to the Pension Benefit Guaranty Corporation ("PBGC"), which holds the benefit of the missing participant as trustee until the PBGC locates the missing participant and distributes the benefit.[109]

The PBGC missing participant program is not available to multiemployer plans or defined contribution plans and other plans not covered by Title IV of ERISA.

Explanation of Provision

Under the bill, the PBGC is directed to prescribe rules for terminating multiemployer plans similar to the present-law missing participant rules applicable to terminating single-employer plans that are subject to Title IV of ERISA.

In addition, under the bill, plan administrators of certain types of plans not subject to the PBGC termination insurance program under present law are permitted, but not required, to elect to transfer missing participants' benefits to the PBGC upon plan termination. Specifically, the provision extends the missing participants program (in accordance with regulations) to defined contribution plans, defined benefit pension plans that have no more than 25 active participants and are maintained by professional service employers, and the portion of defined benefit pension plans that provide benefits based upon the separate accounts of participants and therefore are treated as defined contribution plans under ERISA.

Effective Date

The provision is effective for distributions made after final regulations implementing the provision are prescribed.

---

[109] Secs. 4041(b)(3)(A) and 4050 of ERISA.

K. Director of the PBGC
(secs. 4002 and 4003 of ERISA)

Present Law

The PBGC is a corporation within the Department of Labor. In carrying out its functions, the PBGC is administered by the chairman of the board of directors in accordance with the policies established by the board. The board of directors consists of the Secretaries of Labor, Treasury and Commerce.[110] The Secretary of Labor is the chairman of the board. The executive director of the PBGC is selected by the chairman of the board.

The PBGC is authorized to make such investigations as it deems necessary to enforce any provisions of title IV of ERISA or any rule or regulation thereunder. For the purpose of any such investigation (or any other proceeding under title IV or ERISA), any member of the board of directors or any officer designated by the chairman of the board may administer oaths, subpoena witnesses and take other actions as provided by ERISA as the corporation deems relevant or material to the inquiry.[111]

Explanation of Provision

The bill provides that, in carrying out its functions, the PBGC will be administered by a Director, who is appointed by the President by and with the advice and consent of the Senate. The Director is to act in accordance with the policies established by the PBGC board. The Senate Committees on Finance and on Health, Education, Labor, and Pensions are given joint jurisdiction over the nomination of a person nominated by the President to be Director of the PBGC. If one of such Committees votes to order reported such a nomination, the other such Committee is to report on the nomination within 30 calendar days, or it is automatically discharged.[112]

The Director, and any officer designated by the chairman, is given the authority with respect to investigations that is provided under present law to members of the PBGC board and officers designated by the chairman of the board.

---

[110] ERISA sec. 4002.

[111] ERISA sec. 4003.

[112] The provision relating to the Senate committees is treated as an exercise of rulemaking power of the Senate and is deemed a part of the rules of the Senate. It is applicable only with respect to the procedure to be followed in the case of a nomination of the Director of the PBGC and it supersedes other Senate rules only to the extent that it is inconsistent with such rules. The provision does not change the constitutional right of the Senate to change its rules (so far as relating to the procedure of the Senate) at any time, in the same manner and to the same extent as in the case of any other rule of the Senate.

The Director is to be compensated at the rate of compensation provided under Level III of the Executive Schedule.[113] Effective January 1, 2006, such annual rate of pay is $152,000.

Effective Date

The provision is effective on the date of enactment. The term of the individual serving as Executive Director of the PBGC on the date of enactment expires on the date of enactment. Such individual, or any other individual, may serve as interim Director of the PBGC until an individual is appointed as Director in accordance with the provision.

---

[113] 5 U.S.C. sec. 5314.

L. Inclusion of Information in the PBGC Annual Report
(sec. 4008 of ERISA)

Present Law

As soon as practicable after the close of each fiscal year, the PBGC is required to transmit to the President and Congress a report relative to the conduct of its business for the year. The report must include (1) financial statements setting forth its finances and the result of its operations and (2) an actuarial evaluation of the expected operations and status of the four revolving funds used by the PBGC in carrying out its operations.

Explanation of Provision

Under the bill, additional information is required to be provided in the PBGC's annual report. The report must include (1) a summary of the Pension Insurance Modeling System microsimulation model, including the specific simulation parameters, specific initial values, temporal parameters, and policy parameters used to calculate the PBGC's financial statements; (2) a comparison of (a) the average return on investments earned with respect to assets invested by the PBGC for the year to which the report relates and (b) an amount equal to 60 percent of the average return on investment for the year in the Standard & Poor's 500 Index, plus 40 percent of the average return on investment for such year in the Lehman Aggregate Bond Index (or in a similar fixed income index), and (3) a statement regarding the deficit or surplus for the year that the PBGC would have had if it had earned the return described in (2) with respect to its invested assets.

Effective Date

The provision is effective on the date of enactment.

TITLE V: DISCLOSURE

A. Defined Benefit Plan Funding Notice
(secs. 101(f) and 4011 of ERISA)

Present Law

Defined benefit pension plans are generally required to meet certain minimum funding requirements. These requirements are designed to help ensure that such plans are adequately funded. In addition, the Pension Benefit Guaranty Corporation ("PBGC") guarantees benefits under defined benefit pension plans, subject to limits.

Certain notices must be provided to participants in a single-employer defined benefit pension plan relating to the funding status of the plan. For example, ERISA requires an employer of a single-employer defined benefit plan to notify plan participants if the employer fails to make required contributions (unless a request for a funding waiver is pending).[114] In addition, in the case of an underfunded single-employer plan for which PBGC variable rate premiums are required, the plan administrator generally must notify plan participants of the plan's funding status and the limits on the PBGC benefit guarantee if the plan terminates while underfunded.[115]

Effective for plan years beginning after December 31, 2004, the plan administrator of a multiemployer defined benefit pension plan must provide an annual funding notice to: (1) each participant and beneficiary; (2) each labor organization representing such participants or beneficiaries; (3) each employer that has an obligation to contribute under the plan; and (4) the PBGC.

Such a notice must include: (1) identifying information, including the name of the plan, the address and phone number of the plan administrator and the plan's principal administrative officer, each plan sponsor's employer identification number, and the plan identification number; (2) a statement as to whether the plan's funded current liability percentage for the plan year to which the notice relates is at least 100 percent (and if not, a statement of the percentage); (3) a statement of the value of the plan's assets, the amount of benefit payments, and the ratio of the assets to the payments for the plan year to which the notice relates; (4) a summary of the rules governing insolvent multiemployer plans, including the limitations on benefit payments and any potential benefit reductions and suspensions (and the potential effects of such limitations, reductions, and suspensions on the plan); (5) a general description of the benefits under the plan that are eligible to be guaranteed by the PBGC and the limitations of the guarantee and circumstances in which such limitations apply; and (6) any additional information the plan administrator elects to include to the extent it is not inconsistent with regulations prescribed by the Secretary of Labor.

---

[114] ERISA sec. 101(d).

[115] ERISA sec. 4011.

The annual funding notice must be provided no later than two months after the deadline (including extensions) for filing the plan's annual report for the plan year to which the notice relates (i.e., nine months after the end of the plan year unless the due date for the annual report is extended). The funding notice must be provided in a form and manner prescribed in regulations by the Secretary of Labor. Additionally, it must be written so as to be understood by the average plan participant and may be provided in written, electronic, or some other appropriate form to the extent that it is reasonably accessible to persons to whom the notice is required to be provided.

A plan administrator that fails to provide the required notice to a participant or beneficiary may be liable to the participant or beneficiary in the amount of up to $100 a day from the time of the failure and for such other relief as a court may deem proper.

Explanation of Provision

The provision expands the annual funding notice requirement that applies under present law to multiemployer plans, so that it applies also to single-employer plans and, in the case of a single-employer plan, includes a summary of the PBGC rules governing plan termination. The provision also changes the information that must be provided in the notice and accelerates the time when the notice must be provided.

In addition to the information required under present law, an annual funding notice with respect to either a single-employer or multiemployer plan must include the following additional information, as of the end of the plan year to which the notice relates: (1) a statement of the number of participants who are retired or separated from service and receiving benefits, retired or separated participants who are entitled to future benefits, and active participants); (2) a statement setting forth the funding policy of the plan and the asset allocation of investments under the plan (expressed as percentages of total assets); (3) an explanation containing specific information of any plan amendment, scheduled benefit increase or reduction, or other known event taking effect in the current plan year and having a material effect on plan liabilities or assets for the year (as defined in regulations by the Secretary); and (4) a statement that a person may obtain a copy of the plan's annual report upon request, through the Department of Labor Internet website, or through an Intranet website maintained by the applicable plan sponsor.

In the case of a single-employer plan, the notice must provide: (1) a statement as to whether the plan's funding target attainment percentage (as defined under the minimum funding rules for single-employer plans) for the plan year to which the notice relates and the two preceding plan years, is at least 100 percent (and, if not, the actual percentages); (2) a statement of (a) the total assets (separately stating any funding standard carryover or prefunding balance) and the plan's liabilities for the plan year and the two preceding years, determined in the same manner as under the funding rules, and (b) the value of the plan's assets and liabilities as of the last day of the plan year to which the notice relates, determined using fair market value and the interest rate used in determining variable rate premiums; and (3) if applicable, a statement that each contributing sponsor, and each member of the sponsor's controlled group, was required to provide the information under section 4010 for the plan year to which the notice relates.

In the case of a multiemployer plan, the notice must provide: (1) a statement as to whether the plan's funded percentage (as defined under the minimum funding rules for multiemployer plans) for the plan year to which the notice relates and the two preceding plan years, is at least 100 percent (and, if not, the actual percentages); (2) a statement of the value of the plan's assets and liabilities for the plan year to which the notice relates and the two preceding plan years; (3) whether the plan was in endangered or critical status and, if so, a summary of the plan's funding improvement or rehabilitation plan and a statement describing how a person can obtain a copy of the plan's funding improvement or rehabilitation plan and the actuarial or financial data that demonstrate any action taken by the plan toward fiscal improvement; and (4) a statement that the plan administrator will provide, on written request, a copy of the plan's annual report to any labor organization representing participants and beneficiaries and any employer that has an obligation to contribute to the plan.

The annual funding notice must be provided within 120 days after the end of the plan year to which it relates. In the case of a plan covering not more than 100 employees for the preceding year, the annual funding notice must be provided upon filing of the annual report with respect to the plan (i.e., within seven months after the end of the plan year unless the due date for the annual report is extended).

The Secretary of Labor is required to publish a model notice not later than one year after the date of enactment. In addition, the Secretary of Labor is given the authority to promulgate any interim final rules as appropriate to carry out the requirement that a model notice be published.

Under the provision, the annual funding notice includes the information provided in the notice required under present law in the case of a single-employer plan that is subject to PBGC variable rate premiums. Accordingly, that present-law notice requirement is repealed under the provision.

Effective Date

The provision is effective for plan years beginning after December 31, 2007, except that the repeal of the notice required under present law in the case of a single-employer plan that is subject to PBGC variable rate premiums is effective for plan years beginning after December 31, 2006. Under a transition rule, any requirement to report a plan's funding target attainment percentage or funded percentage for a plan year beginning before January 1, 2008, is met if (1) in the case of a plan year beginning in 2006, the plan's funded current liability percentage is reported, and (2) in the case of a plan year beginning in 2007, the funding target attainment percentage or funded percentage as determined using such methods of estimation as the Secretary of the Treasury may provide is reported.

B. Access to Multiemployer Pension Plan Information
(secs. 101, 204(h), and 502(c) of ERISA and sec. 4980F of the Code)

Present Law

Annual report

The plan administrator of a pension plan generally must file an annual return with the Secretary of the Treasury, an annual report with the Secretary of Labor, and certain information with the Pension Benefit Guaranty Corporation ("PBGC"). Form 5500, which consists of a primary form and various schedules, includes the information required to be filed with all three agencies. The plan administrator satisfies the reporting requirement with respect to each agency by filing the Form 5500 with the Department of Labor.

In the case of a defined benefit pension plan, the annual report must include an actuarial statement. The actuarial statement must include, for example, information as to the value of plan assets, the plan's accrued and current liabilities, the plan's actuarial cost method and actuarial assumptions, and plan contributions. The report must be signed by an actuary enrolled to practice before the IRS, Department of Labor and the PBGC.

The Form 5500 is due by the last day of the seventh month following the close of the plan year. The due date generally may be extended up to two and one-half months. Copies of filed Form 5500s are available for public examination at the U.S. Department of Labor.

Notice of significant reduction in benefit accruals

If an amendment to a defined benefit pension plan provides for a significant reduction in the rate of future benefit accrual, the plan administrator must furnish a written notice concerning the amendment. Notice may also be required if a plan amendment eliminates or reduces an early retirement benefit or retirement-type subsidy. The plan administrator is required to provide the notice to any participant or alternate payee whose rate of future benefit accrual may reasonably be expected to be significantly reduced by the plan amendment (and to any employee organization representing affected participants). The notice must be written in a manner calculated to be understood by the average plan participant and must provide sufficient information to allow recipients to understand the effect of the amendment. The plan administrator is generally required to provide the notice at least 45 days before the effective date of the plan amendment.

Explanation of Provision

Under the provision, a plan administrator of a multiemployer plan must, within 30 days of a written request, provide a plan participant or beneficiary, employee organization or employer that has an obligation to contribute to the plan with a copy of: (1) any periodic actuarial report (including any sensitivity testing) for any plan year that has been in the plan's possession for at least 30 days; (2) a copy of any quarterly, semi-annual, or annual financial report prepared for the plan by any plan investment manager or advisor or other person who is a plan fiduciary that has been in the plan's possession for at least 30 days; and (3) a copy of any application for an amortization extension filed with the Secretary of the Treasury. Any actuarial

109

report or financial report provided to a participant, beneficiary, or employer must not include any individually identifiable information regarding any participant, beneficiary, employee, fiduciary, or contributing employer, or reveal any proprietary information regarding the plan, any contributing employer, or any entity providing services to the plan. Regulations relating to the requirement to provide actuarial or financial reports on request must be issued within one year after the date of enactment.

In addition, the plan sponsor or administrator of a multiemployer plan must provide to any employer having an obligation to contribute to the plan, within 180 days of a written request, notice of: (1) the estimated amount that would be the employer's withdrawal liability with respect to the plan if the employer withdrew from the plan on the last day of the year preceding the date of the request; and (2) an explanation of how the estimated liability amount was determined, including the actuarial assumptions and methods used to determine the value of plan liabilities and assets, the data regarding employer contributions, unfunded vested benefits, annual changes in the plan's unfunded vested benefits, and the application of any relevant limitations on the estimated withdrawal liability. Regulations may permit a longer time than 180 days as may be necessary in the case of a plan that determines withdrawal liability using certain methods.

A person is not entitled to receive more than one copy of any actuary or financial report or more than one notice of withdrawal liability during any 12-month period. The plan administrator may make a reasonable charge to cover copying, mailing, and other costs of furnishing copies or notices, subject to a maximum amount that may be prescribed by regulations. Any information required to be provided under the provision may be provided in written, electronic, or other appropriate form to the extent such form is reasonably available to the persons to whom the information is required to be provided.

In the case of a failure to comply with these requirements, the Secretary of Labor may assess a civil penalty of up to $1,000 per day for each failure to provide a notice.

Under the provision, notice of an amendment that provides for a significant reduction in the rate of future benefit accrual must be provided also to each employer that has an obligation to contribute to the plan.

Effective Date

The provision is effective for plan years beginning after December 31, 2007.

C. Additional Annual Reporting Requirements and
Electronic Display of Annual Report Information
(secs. 103 and 104 of ERISA)

Present Law

Annual report

The plan administrator of a pension plan generally must file an annual return with the Secretary of the Treasury, an annual report with the Secretary of Labor, and certain information with the Pension Benefit Guaranty Corporation ("PBGC"). Form 5500, which consists of a primary form and various schedules, includes the information required to be filed with all three agencies. The plan administrator satisfies the reporting requirement with respect to each agency by filing the Form 5500 with the Department of Labor.

In the case of a defined benefit pension plan, the annual report must include an actuarial statement. The actuarial statement must include, for example, information as to the value of plan assets, the plan's accrued and current liabilities, the plan's actuarial cost method and actuarial assumptions, and plan contributions. The report must be signed by an actuary enrolled to practice before the IRS, Department of Labor and the PBGC.

The Form 5500 is due by the last day of the seventh month following the close of the plan year. The due date generally may be extended up to two and one-half months. Copies of filed Form 5500s are available for public examination at the U.S. Department of Labor.

Summary annual report

A participant must be provided with a copy of the full annual report on written request. In addition, the plan administrator must automatically provide participants with a summary of the annual report within two months after the due date of the annual report (i.e., by the end of the ninth month after the end of the plan year unless an extension applies). The summary annual report must include a statement whether contributions were made to keep the plan funded in accordance with minimum funding requirements, or whether contributions were not made and the amount of the deficit. The current value of plan assets is also required to be disclosed. If an extension applies for the Form 5500, the summary annual report must be provided within two months after the extended due date. A plan administrator who fails to provide a summary annual report to a participant within 30 days of the participant making a request for the report may be liable to the participant for a civil penalty of up to $100 a day from the date of the failure.

Explanation of Provision

Annual report

The provision requires additional information to be provided in the annual report filed with respect to a defined benefit pension plan. In a case in which the liabilities under the plan as of the end of a plan year consist (in whole or in part) of liabilities under two or more other pension plans as of immediately before the plan year, the annual report must include the plan's funded percentage as of the last day of the plan year and the funded percentage of each of such

111

other plans. Funded percentage is defined as: (1) in the case of a single-employer plan, the plan's funded target attainment percentage (as defined under the minimum funding rules for single-employer plans); and (2) in the case of a multiemployer plan, the plan's funded percentage (as defined under the minimum funding rules for multiemployer plans).

An annual report filed with respect to a multiemployer plan must include, as of the end of the plan year, the following additional information: (1) the number of employers obligated to contribute to the plan; (2) a list of the employers that contributed more than five percent of the total contributions to the plan during the plan year; (3) the number of participants on whose behalf no contributions were made by an employer as an employer of the participant for the plan year and two preceding years; (4) the ratio of the number of participants under the plan on whose behalf no employer had an obligation to make an employer contribution during the plan year, to the number of participants under the plan on whose behalf no employer had an obligation to make an employer contribution during each of the two preceding plan years; (5) whether the plan received an amortization extension for the plan year and, if so, the amount by which it changed the minimum required contribution for the year, what minimum contribution would have been required without the extension, and the period of the extension; (6) whether the plan used the shortfall funding method and, if so, the amount by which it changed the minimum required contribution for the year, what minimum contribution would have been required without the use of this method, and the period for which the method is used; (7) whether the plan was in critical or endangered status for the plan year, and if so, a summary of any funding improvement or rehabilitation plan (or modification thereto) adopted during the plan year, and the funding percentage of the plan; (8) the number of employers that withdrew from the plan during the preceding plan year and the aggregate amount of withdrawal liability assessed, or estimated to be assessed, against the withdrawn employers; (9) if the plan that has merged with another plan or if assets and liabilities have been transferred to the plan, the actuarial valuation of the assets and liabilities of each affected plan during the year preceding the effective date of the merger or transfer, based upon the most recent data available as of the day before the first day of the plan year, or other valuation method performed under standards and procedures as prescribed by regulation.

The Secretary of Labor is required, not later than one year after the date of enactment, to publish guidance to assist multiemployer plans to identify and enumerate plan participants for whom there is no employer with an obligation to make an employer contribution under the plan and report such information in the annual report. The Secretary may provide rules as needed to apply this requirement with respect to contributions made on a basis other than hours worked, such as on the basis of units of production.

The actuarial statement filed with the annual return must include a statement explaining the actuarial assumptions and methods used in projecting future retirements and asset distributions under the plan.

Electronic display of annual report

Identification and basic plan information and actuarial information included in the annual report must be filed with the Secretary of Labor in an electronic format that accommodates display on the Internet (in accordance with regulations). The Secretary of Labor is to provide for the display of such information, within 90 days after the filing of the annual report, on a website maintained by the Secretary of Labor on the Internet and other appropriate media. Such information is also required to be displayed on any Intranet website maintained by the plan sponsor (or by the plan administrator on behalf of the plan sponsor) in accordance with regulations.

Summary annual report

Under the provision, the requirement to provide a summary annual report to participants applies does not apply to defined benefit pension plans.[116]

Multiemployer plan summary report

The provision requires the plan administrator of a multiemployer plan to provide a report containing certain summary plan information to each employee organization and each employer with an obligation to contribute to the plan within 30 days after the due date of the plan's annual report. The report must contain: (1) a description of the contribution schedules and benefit formulas under the plan, and any modification to such schedules and formulas, during such plan year; (2) the number of employers obligated to contribute to the plan; (3) a list of the employers that contributed more than 5 percent of the total contributions to the plan during such plan year; (4) the number of participants under the plan on whose behalf no employer contributions have been made to the plan for such plan year and for each of the two preceding plan years; (5) whether the plan was in critical or endangered status for the plan year and, if so, a list of the actions taken by the plan to improve its funding status and a statement describing how to obtain a copy of the plan's improvement or rehabilitation plan, as appropriate, and the actuarial and financial data that demonstrate any action taken by the plan toward fiscal improvement; (6) the number of employers that withdrew from the plan during the preceding plan year and the aggregate amount of withdrawal liability assessed, or estimated to be assessed, against such withdrawn employers, as reported on the annual report for the plan year; (7) if the plan that has merged with another plan or if assets and liabilities have been transferred to the plan, the actuarial valuation of the assets and liabilities of each affected plan during the year preceding the effective date of the merger or transfer, based upon the most recent data available as of the day before the first day of the plan year, or other valuation method performed under standards and procedures as prescribed by regulation; (8) a description as to whether the plan sought or received an amortization extension or used the shortfall funding method for the plan year; and (9) notification of the right to obtain upon written request a copy of the annual report filed with respect to the plan, the summary annual report, the summary plan description, and the summary of any material modification of the plan, subject to a limitation of one copy of any such document in any 12-month period and any reasonable charge to cover copying, mailing, and other costs of furnishing the document. Nothing in this report requirement waives any other ERISA provision requiring plan administrators to provide, upon request, information to employers that have an obligation to contribute under the plan.

---

[116] As discussed in Part A above, detailed information about a defined benefit pension plan must be provided to participants in an annual funding notice.

Effective Date

The provisions are effective for plan years beginning after December 31, 2007.

D. Section 4010 Filings with the PBGC
(sec. 4010 of ERISA)

Present Law

Present law provides that, in certain circumstances, the contributing sponsor of a single-employer plan defined benefit pension plan covered by the PBGC (and members of the contributing sponsor's controlled group) must provide certain information to the PBGC (referred to as "section 4010 reporting"). This information includes financial information with respect to the contributing sponsor (and controlled group members) and actuarial information with respect to single-employer plans maintained by the sponsor (and controlled group members).[117] Section 4010 reporting is required if: (1) the aggregate unfunded vested benefits (determined using the interest rate used in determining variable-rate premiums) as of the end of the preceding plan year under all plans maintained by members of the controlled group exceed $50 million (disregarding plans with no unfunded vested benefits); (2) the conditions for imposition of a lien (i.e., required contributions totaling more than $1 million have not been made) have occurred with respect to an underfunded plan maintained by a member of the controlled group; or (3) minimum funding waivers in excess of $1 million have been granted with respect to a plan maintained by any member of the controlled group and any portion of the waived amount is still outstanding. Information provided to the PBGC in accordance with these requirements is not available to the public.

The PBGC may assess a penalty for a failure to provide the required information in the amount of up to $1,000 a day for each day the failure continues.[118]

Explanation of Provision

Under the provision, the requirement of section 4010 reporting applicable under present law if aggregate unfunded vested benefits exceed $50 million is replaced with a requirement of section 4010 reporting if: (1) the funding target attainment percentage at the end of the preceding plan year of a plan maintained by a contributing sponsor or any member of its controlled group is less than 80 percent. It is intended that the PBGC may waive the requirement in appropriate circumstances, such as in the case of small plans.

The provision also requires the information provided to the PBGC to include the following: (1) the amount of benefit liabilities under the plan determined using the assumptions used by the PBGC in determining liabilities; (2) the funding target of the plan determined as if the plan has been in at-risk status for at least 5 plan years; and (3) the funding target attainment percentage of the plan.

The value of plan assets, a plan's funding target, a plan's funding target attainment percentage, and at-risk status are determined under the provision relating to funding rules

---

[117] ERISA sec. 4010.

[118] ERISA sec. 4071.

applicable to single-employer plans under the provision. Thus, a plan's funding target for a plan year is the present value of the benefits earned or accrued under the plan as of the beginning of the plan year. A plan's "funding target attainment percentage" means the ratio, expressed as a percentage, that the value of the plan's assets (reduced by any funding standard carryover balance and prefunding balance) bears to the plan's funding target for the year (determined without regard to the special assumptions that apply to at-risk plans). A plan is in at-risk status for a plan year if the plan's funding target attainment percentage for the preceding year was less than (1) 80 percent, determined without regard to the special at-risk assumptions, and (2) 70 percent, determined using the special at-risk assumptions.

The provision requires the PBGC to provide the Senate Committees on Health, Education, Labor, and Pensions and Finance and the House Committees on Education and the Workforce and Ways and Means with a summary report in the aggregate of the information submitted to the PBGC under section 4010.

Effective Date

The provision is effective for filings for years beginning after December 31, 2007.

E. Disclosure of Plan Termination Information to Plan Participants
(secs. 4041 and 4042 of ERISA)

Present Law

In the case of a single-employer defined benefit pension plan covered under the PBGC insurance program, the plan sponsor may voluntarily terminate the plan in a standard termination or a distress termination.[119] A standard termination is permitted only if plan assets are sufficient to cover benefit liabilities.

If assets in a defined benefit plan are not sufficient to cover benefit liabilities, the plan sponsor may not terminate the plan unless the plan sponsor (and members of the plan sponsor's controlled group) meets one of four criteria of financial distress. The four criteria for a distress termination are: (1) the plan sponsor, and every member of the controlled group of which the sponsor is a member, is being liquidated in bankruptcy or any similar Federal law or other similar State insolvency proceedings; (2) the plan sponsor and every member of the sponsor's controlled group is being reorganized in bankruptcy or similar State proceeding; (3) the PBGC determines that termination is necessary to allow the plan sponsor to pay its debts when due; or (4) the PBGC determines that termination is necessary to avoid unreasonably burdensome pension costs caused solely by a decline in the plan sponsor's work force.

In order for a plan sponsor to terminate a plan, the plan administrator must provide each affected party with advance written notice of the intent to terminate at least 60 days before the proposed termination date. Additional information must be included as required by the PBGC. For this purpose, an affected party is: (1) a plan participant; (2) a beneficiary of a deceased participant or an alternate payee under a qualified domestic relations order; (3) any employee organization representing plan participants; and (4) the PBGC (except in the case of a standard termination). In the case of a proposed distress termination, as soon as practicable after providing notice, the plan administrator must provide the PBGC with certain information, including information necessary for the PBGC to determine whether any of the criteria for a distress termination is met.

The PBGC may institute proceedings to terminate a single-employer plan if it determines that the plan in question: (1) has not met the minimum funding standards; (2) will be unable to pay benefits when due; (3) has a substantial owner who has received a distribution greater than $10,000 (other than by reason of death) while the plan has unfunded vested benefits; or (4) may reasonably be expected to increase the PBGC's long-run loss with respect to the plan unreasonably if the plan is not terminated. The PBGC must institute proceedings to terminate a plan if the plan is unable to pay benefits that are currently due.

If the PBGC determines that the requirements for an involuntary plan termination are met, it must provide notice to the plan.

---

[119] The PBGC may not proceed with a voluntary termination if the termination would violate an existing collective bargaining agreement.

Explanation of Provision

The provision revises the rules applicable in the case of a distress termination to require a plan administrator to provide an affected party with any information provided to the PBGC in connection with the proposed plan termination. The plan administrator must provide the information not later than 15 days after: (1) the receipt of a request for the information from the affected party; or (2) the provision of new information to the PBGC relating to a previous request.

The provision also requires the plan sponsor or plan administrator of a plan that has received notice from the PBGC of a determination that the plan should be involuntarily terminated to provide an affected party with any information provided to the PBGC in connection with the plan termination. In addition, the PBGC is required to provide a copy of the administrative record, including the trusteeship decision record in connection with a plan termination. The plan sponsor, plan administrator, or PBGC must provide the required information not later than 15 days after: (1) the receipt of a request for the information from the affected party; or (2) in the case of information provided to the PBGC, the provision of new information to the PBGC relating to a previous request.

The PBGC may prescribe the form and manner in which information is to be provided, which is to include delivery in written, electronic, or other appropriate form to the extent such form is reasonably accessible to individuals to whom the information is required to be provided. A plan administrator or plan sponsor may charge a reasonable fee for any information provided under this subparagraph in other than electronic form.

A plan administrator or plan sponsor may not provide the relevant information in a form that includes any information that may directly or indirectly be associated with, or otherwise identify, an individual participant or beneficiary. In addition, a court may limit disclosure of confidential information (as described under the Freedom of Information Act) to any authorized representative of the participants or beneficiaries that agrees to ensure the confidentiality of such information. For this purposes, an authorized representative means any employee organization representing participants in the pension plan.

Effective Date

The provision generally applies with respect to any plan termination, with respect to which the notice of intent to terminate, or notice that the PBGC has determined that the requirements for an involuntary plan termination are met, occurs after the date of enactment. Under a transition rule, if notice under the provision would otherwise be required before the 90th day after the date of enactment, such notice is not required to be provided until the 90th day.

F. Notice of Freedom to Divest Employer Securities
(new sec. 101(m) of ERISA)

Present Law

Under ERISA, a plan administrator is required to furnish participants with certain notices and information about the plan. This information includes, for example, a summary plan description that includes certain information, including administrative information about the plan, the plan's requirements as to eligibility for participation and benefits, the plan's vesting provisions, and the procedures for claiming benefits under the plan. Under ERISA, if a plan administrator fails or refuses to furnish to a participant information required to be provided to the participant within 30 days of the participant's written request, the participant generally may bring a civil action to recover from the plan administrator $100 a day, within the court's discretion, or other relief that the court deems proper.

Explanation of Provision

The provision requires a new notice in connection with the right of an applicable individual to divest his or her account under an applicable defined contribution plan of employer securities, as required under the provision of the provision relating to diversification rights with respect to amounts invested in employer securities. Not later than 30 days before the first date on which an applicable individual is eligible to exercise such right with respect to any type of contribution, the administrator of the plan must provide the individual with a notice setting forth such right and describing the importance of diversifying the investment of retirement account assets. Under the diversification provision, an applicable individual's right to divest his or her account of employer securities attributable to elective deferrals and employee after-tax contributions and the right to divest his or her account of employer securities attributable to other contributions (i.e., nonelective employer contributions and employer matching contributions) may become exercisable at different times. Thus, to the extent the applicable individual is first eligible to exercise such rights at different times, separate notices are required.

The notice must be written in a manner calculated to be understood by the average plan participant and may be delivered in written, electronic, or other appropriate form to the extent such form is reasonably accessible to the applicable individual. The Secretary of Treasury has regulatory authority over the required notice and is directed to prescribe a model notice to be used for this purpose within 180 days of the date of enactment of the provision. It is expected that the Secretary of Treasury will consult with the Secretary of Labor on the description of the importance of diversifying the investment of retirement account assets. In addition, it is intended that the Secretary of Treasury will prescribe rules to enable the notice to be provided at reduced administrative expense, such as allowing the notice to be provided with the summary plan description, with a reminder of these rights within a reasonable period before they become exercisable.

In the case of a failure to provide a required notice of diversification rights, the Secretary of Labor may assess a civil penalty against the plan administrator of up to $100 a day from the date of the failure. For this purpose, each violation with respect to any single applicable individual is treated as a separate violation.

119

Effective Date

The provision generally applies to plan years beginning after December 31, 2006. Under a transition rule, if notice would otherwise be required to be provided before 90 days after the date of enactment, notice is not required until 90 days after the date of enactment.

G. Periodic Pension Benefit Statements
(secs. 105(a) and 502(c)(1) of ERISA)

Present Law

ERISA provides that the administrator of a defined contribution or defined benefit pension plan must furnish a benefit statement to any participant or beneficiary who makes a written request for such a statement. The benefit statement must indicate, on the basis of the latest available information: (1) the participant's or beneficiary's total accrued benefit; and (2) the participant's or beneficiary's vested accrued benefit or the earliest date on which the accrued benefit will become vested. A participant or beneficiary is not entitled to receive more than one benefit statement during any 12-month period. If a plan administrator fails or refuses to furnish a benefit statement to a participant or beneficiary within 30 days of a written request, the participant or beneficiary may bring a civil action to recover from the plan administrator $100 a day, within the court's discretion, or other relief that the court deems proper.

Explanation of Provision

In general

The provision revises the benefit statement requirements under ERISA. The new requirements depend in part on the type of plan and the individual to whom the statement is provided. The benefit statement requirements do not apply to a one-participant retirement plan.[120]

A benefit statement is required to indicate, on the basis of the latest available information: (1) the total benefits accrued; (2) the vested accrued benefit or the earliest date on which the accrued benefit will become vested; and (3) an explanation of any permitted disparity or floor-offset arrangement that may be applied in determining accrued benefits under the plan.[121] With respect to information on vested benefits, the Secretary of Labor is required to provide that the requirements are met if, at least annually, the plan: (1) updates the information on vested benefits that is provided in the benefit statement; or (2) provides in a separate statement information as is necessary to enable participants and beneficiaries to determine their vested benefits.

If a plan administrator fails to provide a required benefit statement to a participant or beneficiary, the participant or beneficiary may bring a civil action to recover from the plan

---

[120] A one-participant retirement plan is defined as under the provision of ERISA that requires advance notice of a blackout period to be provided to participants and beneficiaries affected by the blackout period, as discussed in Part H below.

[121] Under the permitted disparity rules, contributions or benefits may be provided at a higher rate with respect to compensation above a specified level and at a lower rate with respect to compensation up to the specified level. In addition, benefits under a defined benefit plan may be offset by a portion of a participant's expected social security benefits. Under a floor-offset arrangement, benefits under a defined benefit pension plan are reduced by benefits under a defined contribution plan.

administrator $100 a day, within the court's discretion, or other relief that the court deems proper.

Requirements for defined contribution plans

The administrator of a defined contribution plan is required to provide a benefit statement (1) to a participant or beneficiary who has the right to direct the investment of the assets in his or her account, at least quarterly, (2) to any other participant or other beneficiary who has his or her own account under the plan, at least annually, and (3) to other beneficiaries, upon written request, but limited to one request during any 12-month period.

A benefit statement provided with respect to a defined contribution plan must include the value of each investment to which assets in the individual's account are allocated (determined as of the plan's most recent valuation date), including the value of any assets held in the form of employer securities (without regard to whether the securities were contributed by the employer or acquired at the direction of the individual). A quarterly benefit statement provided to a participant or beneficiary who has the right to direct investments must also provide: (1) an explanation of any limitations or restrictions on any right of the individual to direct an investment; (2) an explanation, written in a manner calculated to be understood by the average plan participant, of the importance, for the long-term retirement security of participants and beneficiaries, of a well-balanced and diversified investment portfolio, including a statement of the risk that holding more than 20 percent of a portfolio in the security of one entity (such as employer securities) may not be adequately diversified; and (3) a notice directing the participant or beneficiary to the Internet website of the Department of Labor for sources of information on individual investing and diversification.

Requirements for defined benefit plans

The administrator of a defined benefit plan is required either: (1) to furnish a benefit statement at least once every three years to each participant who has a vested accrued benefit under the plan and who is employed by the employer at the time the benefit statements are furnished to participants; or (2) to furnish at least annually to each such participant notice of the availability of a benefit statement and the manner in which the participant can obtain it. The Secretary of Labor is authorized to provide that years in which no employee or former employee benefits under the plan need not be taken into account in determining the three-year period. It is intended that the annual notice of the availability of a benefit statement may be included with other communications to the participant if done in a manner reasonably designed to attract the attention of the participant.

The administrator of a defined benefit pension plan is also required to furnish a benefit statement to a participant or beneficiary upon written request, limited to one request during any 12-month period.

In the case of a statement provided to a participant with respect to a defined benefit plan (other than at the participant's request), information may be based on reasonable estimates determined under regulations prescribed by the Secretary of Labor in consultation with the Pension Benefit Guaranty Corporation.

Form of benefit statement

A benefit statement must be written in a manner calculated to be understood by the average plan participant. It may be delivered in written, electronic, or other appropriate form to the extent such form is reasonably accessible to the recipient. For example, regulations could permit current benefit statements to be provided on a continuous basis through a secure plan website for a participant or beneficiary who has access to the website.

The Secretary of Labor is directed, within one year after the date of enactment, to develop one or more model benefit statements that may be used by plan administrators in complying with the benefit statement requirements. The use of the model statement is optional. It is intended that the model statement include items such as the amount of vested accrued benefits as of the statement date that are payable at normal retirement age under the plan, the amount of accrued benefits that are forfeitable but that may become vested under the terms of the plan, information on how to contact the Social Security Administration to obtain a participant's personal earnings and benefit estimate statement, and other information that may be important to understanding benefits earned under the plan. The Secretary of Labor is also given the authority to promulgate any interim final rules as determined appropriate to carry out the benefit statement requirements.

Effective Date

The provision is generally effective for plan years beginning after December 31, 2006. In the case of a plan maintained pursuant to one or more collective bargaining agreements, the provision is effective for plan years beginning after the earlier of (1) the later of December 31, 2007, or the date on which the last of such collective bargaining agreements terminates (determined without regard to any extension thereof after the date of enactment), or (2) December 31, 2008.

H. Notice to Participants or Beneficiaries of Blackout Periods (sec. 101(i) of ERISA)

Present Law

In general

The Sarbanes-Oxley Act of 2002[122] amended ERISA to require that the plan administrator of an individual account plan[123] provide advance notice of a blackout period (a "blackout notice") to plan participants and beneficiaries to whom the blackout period applies.[124] Generally, notice must be provided at least 30 days before the beginning of the blackout period. In the case of a blackout period that applies with respect to employer securities, the plan administrator must also provide timely notice of the blackout period to the employer (or the affiliate of the employer that issued the securities, if applicable).

The blackout notice requirement does not apply to a one-participant retirement plan, which is defined as a plan that (1) on the first day of the plan year, covered only the employer (and the employer's spouse) and the employer owns the entire business (whether or not incorporated) or covers only one or more partners (and their spouses) in a business partnership (including partners in an S or C corporation as defined in section 1361(a) of the Code), (2) meets the minimum coverage requirements without being combined with any other plan that covers employees of the business, (3) does not provide benefits to anyone except the employer (and the employer's spouse) or the partners (and their spouses), (4) does not cover a business that is a member of an affiliated service group, a controlled group of corporations, or a group of corporations under common control, and (5) does not cover a business that leases employees.[125]

Definition of blackout period

A blackout period is any period during which any ability of participants or beneficiaries under the plan, which is otherwise available under the terms of the plan, to direct or diversify assets credited to their accounts, or to obtain loans or distributions from the plan, is temporarily suspended, limited, or restricted if the suspension, limitation, or restriction is for any period of more than three consecutive business days. However, a blackout period does not include a suspension, limitation, or restriction that (1) occurs by reason of the application of securities

---

[122] Pub. L. No. 107-204 (2002).

[123] An "individual account plan" is the term generally used under ERISA for a defined contribution plan.

[124] ERISA sec. 101(i), as enacted by section 306(b) of the Sarbanes-Oxley Act of 2002. Under section 306(a), a director or executive officer of a publicly-traded corporation is prohibited from trading in employer stock during blackout periods in certain circumstances. Section 306 is effective 180 days after enactment.

[125] Governmental plans and church plans are exempt from ERISA. Accordingly, the blackout notice requirement does not apply to these plans.

laws, (2) is a change to the plan providing for a regularly scheduled suspension, limitation, or restriction that is disclosed through a summary of material modifications to the plan or materials describing specific investment options under the plan, or changes thereto, or (3) applies only to one or more individuals, each of whom is a participant, alternate payee, or other beneficiary under a qualified domestic relations order.

Timing of notice

Notice of a blackout period is generally required at least 30 days before the beginning of the period. The 30-day notice requirement does not apply if (1) deferral of the blackout period would violate the fiduciary duty requirements of ERISA and a plan fiduciary so determines in writing, or (2) the inability to provide the 30-day advance notice is due to events that were unforeseeable or circumstances beyond the reasonable control of the plan administrator and a plan fiduciary so determines in writing. In those cases, notice must be provided as soon as reasonably practicable under the circumstances unless notice in advance of the termination of the blackout period is impracticable.

Another exception to the 30-day period applies in the case of a blackout period that applies only to one or more participants or beneficiaries in connection with a merger, acquisition, divestiture, or similar transaction involving the plan or the employer and that occurs solely in connection with becoming or ceasing to be a participant or beneficiary under the plan by reason of the merger, acquisition, divestiture, or similar transaction. Under the exception, the blackout notice requirement is treated as met if notice is provided to the participants or beneficiaries to whom the blackout period applies as soon as reasonably practicable.

The Secretary of Labor may provide additional exceptions to the notice requirement that the Secretary determines are in the interests of participants and beneficiaries.

Form and content of notice

A blackout notice must be written in a manner calculated to be understood by the average plan participant and must include (1) the reasons for the blackout period, (2) an identification of the investments and other rights affected, (3) the expected beginning date and length of the blackout period, and (4) in the case of a blackout period affecting investments, a statement that the participant or beneficiary should evaluate the appropriateness of current investment decisions in light of the inability to direct or diversify assets during the blackout period, and (5) other matters as required by regulations. If the expected beginning date or length of the blackout period changes after notice has been provided, the plan administrator must provide notice of the change (and specify any material change in other matters related to the blackout) to affected participants and beneficiaries as soon as reasonably practicable.

Notices provided in connection with a blackout period (or changes thereto) must be provided in writing and may be delivered in electronic or other form to the extent that the form is reasonably accessible to the recipient. The Secretary of Labor is required to issue guidance regarding the notice requirement and a model blackout notice.

Penalty for failure to provide notice

In the case of a failure to provide notice of a blackout period, the Secretary of Labor may assess a civil penalty against a plan administrator of up to $100 per day for each failure to provide a blackout notice. For this purpose, each violation with respect to a single participant or beneficiary is treated as a separate violation.

Explanation of Provision

The provision modifies the definition of a one-participant retirement plan to be consistent with Department of Labor regulations under which certain business owners and their spouses are not treated as employees.[126] As modified, a one-participant retirement plan is a plan that: (1) on the first day of the plan year, either covered only one individual (or the individual and his or her spouse) and the individual owned 100 percent of the plan sponsor, whether or not incorporated, or covered only one or more partners (or partners and their spouses) in the plan sponsor; and (2) does not cover a business that leases employees.

Effective Date

The provision is effective as if included in section 306 of the Sarbanes-Oxley Act of 2002.

---

[126] 29 C.F.R. sec. 2510.3-3(c) (2006).

TITLE VI: INVESTMENT ADVICE, PROHIBITED TRANSACTIONS, AND FIDUCIARY RULES

A. Investment Advice
(sec. 408 of ERISA and sec. 4975 of the Code)

Present Law

ERISA and the Code prohibit certain transactions between an employer-sponsored retirement plan and a disqualified person (referred to as a "party in interest" under ERISA).[127] Under ERISA, the prohibited transaction rules apply to employer-sponsored retirement plans and welfare benefit plans. Under the Code, the prohibited transaction rules apply to qualified retirement plans and qualified retirement annuities, as well as individual retirement accounts and annuities ("IRAs"), health savings accounts ("HSAs"), Archer MSAs, and Coverdell education savings accounts.[128]

Disqualified persons include a fiduciary of the plan, a person providing services to the plan, and an employer with employees covered by the plan. For this purpose, a fiduciary includes any person who (1) exercises any authority or control respecting management or disposition of the plan's assets, (2) renders investment advice for a fee or other compensation with respect to any plan moneys or property, or has the authority or responsibility to do so, or (3) has any discretionary authority or responsibility in the administration of the plan.

Prohibited transactions include (1) the sale, exchange or leasing of property, (2) the lending of money or other extension of credit, (3) the furnishing of goods, services or facilities, (4) the transfer to, or use by or for the benefit of, the income or assets of the plan, (5) in the case of a fiduciary, any act that deals with the plan's income or assets for the fiduciary's own interest or account, and (6) the receipt by a fiduciary of any consideration for the fiduciary's own personal account from any party dealing with the plan in connection with a transaction involving the income or assets of the plan. However, certain transactions are exempt from prohibited transaction treatment, for example, certain loans to plan participants.

Under ERISA, the Secretary of Labor may assess a civil penalty against a person who engages in a prohibited transaction, other than a transaction with a plan covered by the prohibited transaction rules of the Code. The penalty may not exceed five percent of the amount involved in the transaction for each year or part of a year that the prohibited transaction continues. If the prohibited transaction is not corrected within 90 days after notice from the Secretary of Labor, the penalty may be up to 100 percent of the amount involved in the transaction. Under the Code, if a prohibited transaction occurs, the disqualified person who participates in the transaction is subject to a two-tier excise tax. The first level tax is 15 percent of the amount involved in the

---

[127] ERISA sec. 406; Code sec. 4975.

[128] The prohibited transaction rules under ERISA and the Code generally do not apply to governmental plans or church plans.

transaction. The second level tax is imposed if the prohibited transaction is not corrected within a certain period and is 100 percent of the amount involved.

Explanation of Provision

In general

The provision adds a new category of prohibited transaction exemption under ERISA and the Code in connection with the provision of investment advice through an "eligible investment advice arrangement" to participants and beneficiaries of a defined contribution plan who direct the investment of their accounts under the plan and to beneficiaries of IRAs.[129] If the requirements under the provision are met, the following are exempt from prohibited transaction treatment: (1) the provision of investment advice; (2) an investment transaction (i.e., a sale, acquisition, or holding of a security or other property) pursuant to the advice; and (3) the direct or indirect receipt of fees or other compensation in connection with the provision of the advice or an investment transaction pursuant to the advice. The prohibited transaction exemptions provided under the provision do not in any manner alter existing individual or class exemptions provided by statute or administrative action.

The provision also directs the Secretary of Labor, in consultation with the Secretary of the Treasury, to determine, based on certain information to be solicited by the Secretary of Labor, whether there is any computer model investment advice program that meets the requirements of the provision and may be used by IRAs. The determination is to be made by December 31, 2007. If the Secretary of Labor determines there is such a program, the exemptions described above apply in connection with the use of the program with respect to IRA beneficiaries. If the Secretary of Labor determines that there is not such a program, such Secretary is directed to grant a class exemption from prohibited transaction treatment (as discussed below) for the provision of investment advice, investment transactions pursuant to such advice, and related fees to beneficiaries of such arrangements.

Eligible investment advice arrangements

In general

The exemptions provided under the provision apply in connection with the provision of investment advice by a fiduciary adviser under an eligible investment advice arrangement. An eligible investment advice arrangement is an arrangement (1) meeting certain requirements (discussed below) and (2) which either (a) provides that any fees (including any commission or compensation) received by the fiduciary adviser for investment advice or with respect to an investment transaction with respect to plan assets do not vary depending on the basis of any investment option selected, or (b) uses a computer model under an investment advice program as described below in connection with the provision of investment advice to a participant or beneficiary. In the case of an eligible investment advice arrangement with respect to a defined

---

[129] The portions of the provision relating to IRAs apply to HSAs, Archer MSAs, and Coverdell education savings accounts. References here to IRAs include such other arrangements as well.

contribution plan, the arrangement must be expressly authorized by a plan fiduciary other than (1) the person offering the investment advice program, (2) any person providing investment options under the plan, or (3) any affiliate of (1) or (2).

Investment advice program using computer model

If an eligible investment advice arrangement provides investment advice pursuant to a computer model, the model must (1) apply generally accepted investment theories that take into account the historic returns of different asset classes over defined periods of time, (2) use relevant information about the participant or beneficiary, (3) use prescribed objective criteria to provide asset allocation portfolios comprised of investment options under the plan, (4) operate in a manner that is not biased in favor of any investment options offered by the fiduciary adviser or related person, and (5) take into account all the investment options under the plan in specifying how a participant's or beneficiary's account should be invested without inappropriate weighting of any investment option. An eligible investment expert must certify, before the model is used and in accordance with rules prescribed by the Secretary, that the model meets these requirements. The certification must be renewed if there are material changes to the model as determined under regulations. For this purpose, an eligible investment expert is a person who meets requirements prescribed by the Secretary and who does not bear any material affiliation or contractual relationship with any investment adviser or related person.

In addition, if a computer model is used, the only investment advice that may be provided under the arrangement is the advice generated by the computer model, and any investment transaction pursuant the advice must occur solely at the direction of the participant or beneficiary. This requirement does not preclude the participant or beneficiary from requesting other investment advice, but only if the request has not been solicited by any person connected with carrying out the investment advice arrangement.

Audit requirements

In the case of an eligible investment advice arrangement with respect to a defined contribution plan, an annual audit of the arrangement for compliance with applicable requirements must be conducted by an independent auditor (i.e., unrelated to the person offering the investment advice arrangement or any person providing investment options under the plan) who has appropriate technical training or experience and proficiency and who so represents in writing. The auditor must issue a report of the audit results to the fiduciary that authorized use of the arrangement. In the case of an eligible investment advice arrangement with respect to IRAs, an audit is required at such times and in such manner as prescribed by the Secretary of Labor.

Notice requirements

Before the initial provision of investment advice, the fiduciary adviser must provide written notice (which may be in electronic form) containing various information to the recipient of the advice, including information relating to: (1) the role of any related party in the development of the investment advice program or the selection of investment options under the plan; (2) past performance and rates of return for each investment option offered under the plan; (3) any fees or other compensation to be received by the fiduciary adviser or affiliate; (4) any material affiliation or contractual relationship of the fiduciary adviser or affiliates in the security or other property involved in the investment transaction; (5) the manner and under what circumstances any participant or beneficiary information will be used or disclosed; (6) the types of services provided by the fiduciary adviser in connection with the provision of investment advice; (7) the adviser's status as a fiduciary of the plan in connection with the provision of the advice; and (8) the ability of the recipient of the advice separately to arrange for the provision of advice by another adviser that could have no material affiliation with and receive no fees or other compensation in connection with the security or other property. This information must be maintained in accurate form and must be provided to the recipient of the investment advice, without charge, on an annual basis, on request, or in the case of any material change.

Any notification must be written in a clear and conspicuous manner, calculated to be understood by the average plan participant, and sufficiently accurate and comprehensive so as to reasonably apprise participants and beneficiaries of the required information. The Secretary is directed to issue a model form for the disclosure of fees and other compensation as required by the provision. The fiduciary adviser must maintain for at least six years any records necessary for determining whether the requirements for the prohibited transaction exemption were met. A prohibited transaction will not be considered to have occurred solely because records were lost or destroyed before the end of six years due to circumstances beyond the adviser's control.

Other requirements

In order for the exemption to apply, the following additional requirements must be satisfied: (1) the fiduciary adviser must provide disclosures applicable under securities laws; (2) an investment transaction must occur solely at the direction of the recipient of the advice; (3) compensation received by the fiduciary adviser or affiliates in connection with an investment transaction must be reasonable; and (4) the terms of the investment transaction must be at least as favorable to the plan as an arm's length transaction would be.

Fiduciary adviser

For purposes of the provision, "fiduciary adviser" is defined as a person who is a fiduciary of the plan by reason of the provision of investment advice to a participant or beneficiary and who is also: (1) registered as an investment adviser under the Investment Advisers Act of 1940 or under State laws; (2) a bank, a similar financial institution supervised by the United States or a State, or a savings association (as defined under the Federal Deposit Insurance Act), but only if the advice is provided through a trust department that is subject to periodic examination and review by Federal or State banking authorities; (3) an insurance company qualified to do business under State law; (4) registered as a broker or dealer under the Securities Exchange Act of 1934; (5) an affiliate of any of the preceding; or (6) an employee, agent or registered representative of any of the preceding who satisfies the requirements of applicable insurance, banking and securities laws relating to the provision of advice. A person who develops the computer model or markets the investment advice program or computer model is treated as a person who is a plan fiduciary by reason of the provision of investment advice and is treated as a fiduciary adviser, except that the Secretary may prescribe rules under which only one fiduciary adviser may elect treatment as a plan fiduciary. "Affiliate" means an affiliated person as defined under section 2(a)(3) of the Investment Company Act of 1940. "Registered representative" means a person described in section 3(a)(18) of the Securities Exchange Act of 1934 or a person described in section 202(a)(17) of the Investment Advisers Act of 1940.

Fiduciary rules

Subject to certain requirements, an employer or other person who is a plan fiduciary, other than a fiduciary adviser, is not treated as failing to meet the fiduciary requirements of ERISA, solely by reason of the provision of investment advice as permitted under the provision or of contracting for or otherwise arranging for the provision of the advice. This rule applies if: (1) the advice is provided under an arrangement between the employer or plan fiduciary and the fiduciary adviser for the provision of investment advice by the fiduciary adviser as permitted under the provision; (2) the terms of the arrangement require compliance by the fiduciary adviser with the requirements of the provision; and (3) the terms of the arrangement include a written acknowledgement by the fiduciary adviser that the fiduciary adviser is a plan fiduciary with respect to the provision of the advice.

The provision does not exempt the employer or a plan fiduciary from fiduciary responsibility under ERISA for the prudent selection and periodic review of a fiduciary adviser with whom the employer or plan fiduciary has arranged for the provision of investment advice. The employer or plan fiduciary does not have the duty to monitor the specific investment advice given by a fiduciary adviser. The provision also provides that nothing in the fiduciary responsibility provisions of ERISA is to be construed to preclude the use of plan assets to pay for reasonable expenses in providing investment advice.

Study and determination by the Secretary of Labor; class exemption

Under the provision, the Secretary of Labor must determine, in consultation with the Secretary of the Treasury, whether there is any computer model investment advice program that can be used by IRAs and that meets the requirements of the provision. The determination is to be made on the basis of information to be solicited by the Secretary of Labor as described below. Under the provision, a computer model investment advice program must (1) use relevant information about the beneficiary, (2) take into account the full range of investments, including equities and bonds, in determining the options for the investment portfolio of the beneficiary, and (3) allow the account beneficiary, in directing the investment of assets, sufficient flexibility in obtaining advice to evaluate and select options. The Secretary of Labor must report the results of this determination to the House Committees on Ways and Means and Education and the Workforce and the Senate Committees on Finance and Health, Education, Labor, and Pensions no later than December 31, 2007.

As soon as practicable after the date of enactment, the Secretary of Labor, in consultation with the Secretary of the Treasury, must solicit information as to the feasibility of the application of computer model investment advice programs for IRAs, including from (1) at least the top 50 trustees of IRAs, determined on the basis of assets held by such trustees, and (2) other persons offering such programs based on nonproprietary products. The information solicited by the Secretary of Labor from such trustees and other persons is to include information on their computer modeling capabilities with respect to the current year and the preceding year, including their capabilities for investment accounts they maintain. If a person from whom the Secretary of

Labor solicits information does not provide such information within 60 days after the solicitation, the person is not entitled to use any class exemption granted by the Secretary of Labor as required under the provision (as discussed below) unless such failure is due to reasonable cause and not willful neglect.

The exemptions provided under the provision with respect to an eligible investment advice arrangement involving a computer model do not apply to IRAs. If the Secretary of Labor determines that there is a computer model investment advice program that can be used by IRAs, the exemptions provided under the provision with respect to an eligible investment advice arrangement involving a computer model can apply to IRAs.

If, as a result of the study of this issue as directed by the provision, the Secretary of Labor determines that there is not such a program, the Secretary of Labor must grant a class exemption from prohibited transaction treatment for (1) the provision of investment advice by a fiduciary adviser to beneficiaries of IRAs; (2) investment transactions pursuant to the advice; and (3) the direct or indirect receipt of fees or other compensation in connection with the provision of the advice or an investment transaction pursuant to the advice. Application of the exemptions are to be subject to conditions as are set forth in the class exemption and as are (1) in the interests of the IRA and its beneficiary and protective of the rights of the beneficiary, and (2) necessary to ensure the requirements of the applicable exemptions and the investment advice provided utilizes prescribed objective criteria to provide asset allocation portfolios comprised of securities or other property available as investments under the IRA. Such conditions could require that the fiduciary adviser providing the advice (1) adopt written policies and procedures that ensure the advice provided is not biased in favor of investments offered by the fiduciary adviser or a related person, and (2) appoint an individual responsible for annually reviewing the advice provided to determine that the advice is provided in accordance with the policies and procedures in (1).

If the Secretary of Labor later determines that there is any computer model investment advice program that can be used by IRAs, the class exemption ceases to apply after the later of (1) the date two years after the Secretary's later determination, or (2) the date three years after the date the exemption first took effect.

Any person may request the Secretary of Labor to make a determination with respect to any computer model investment advice program as to whether it can be used by IRAs, and the Secretary must make such determination within 90 days of the request. If the Secretary determines that the program cannot be so used, within 10 days of the determination, the Secretary must notify the House Committees on Ways and Means and Education and the Workforce and the Senate Committees on Finance and Health, Education, Labor, and Pensions thereof and the reasons for the determination.

Effective Date

The provisions are effective with respect to investment advice provided after December 31, 2006. The provision relating to the study by the Secretary of Labor is effective on the date of enactment.

B. Prohibited Transaction Rules Relating to Financial Investments
(secs. 408, 412(a), and 502(i) and new sec. 3(42) of ERISA,
and sec. 4975 of the Code)

1. Exemption for block trading

Present Law

Present law provides statutory exemptions from the prohibited transaction rules for certain transactions.[130] Present law does not provide a statutory prohibited transaction exemption for block trades. For purposes of the prohibited transaction rules, a fiduciary means any person who (1) exercises any authority or control respecting management or disposition of the plan's assets, (2) renders investment advice for a fee or other compensation with respect to any plan moneys or property, or has the authority or responsibility to do so, or (3) has any discretionary authority or responsibility in the administration of the plan.

Explanation of Provision

The provision provides prohibited transaction exemptions under ERISA and the Code for a purchase or sale of securities or other property (as determined by the Secretary of Labor) between a plan and a disqualified person (other than a fiduciary) involving a block trade if: (1) the transaction involves a block trade; (2) at the time of the transaction, the interest of the plan (together with the interests of any other plans maintained by the same plan sponsor) does not exceed 10 percent of the aggregate size of the block trade; (3) the terms of the transaction, including the price, are at least as favorable to the plan as an arm's length transaction with an unrelated party; and (4) the compensation associated with the transaction must be no greater than the compensation associated with an arm's length transaction with an unrelated party. For purposes of the provision, block trade is defined as any trade of at least 10,000 shares or with a market value of at least $200,000 that will be allocated across two or more unrelated client accounts of a fiduciary. Examples of property other than securities that the Secretary of labor may apply the exemption to include (but are not limited to) future contracts and currency.

Effective Date

The provision is effective with respect to transactions occurring after the date of enactment.

---

[130] In addition, under ERISA section 408(a), the Secretary of Labor may grant exemptions with respect to particular transactions or classes of transactions after consultation and coordination with the Secretary of Treasury. An exemption may not be granted unless the Secretary of Labor finds that the exemption is administratively feasible, in the interests of the plan and its participants and beneficiaries, and protective of the rights of plan participants and beneficiaries.

2. Bonding relief

Present Law

Subject to certain exceptions, ERISA requires a plan fiduciary and any person handling plan assets to be bonded, generally in an amount between $1,000 and $500,000. An exception to the bonding requirement generally applies for a fiduciary (or a director, officer, or employee of the fiduciary) that is a corporation authorized to exercise trust powers or conduct an insurance business if the corporation is subject to supervision or examination by Federal or State regulators and meets certain financial requirements.

Explanation of Provision

The provision provides an exception to the ERISA bonding requirement for an entity registered as a broker or a dealer under the Securities Exchange Act of 1934 if the broker or dealer is subject to the fidelity bond requirements of a self-regulatory organization (within the meaning of the Securities Exchange Act of 1934).

Effective Date

The provision is effective for plan years beginning after the date of enactment.

3. Exemption for electronic communication network

Present Law

Present law provides statutory exemptions from the prohibited transaction rules for certain transactions.[131] Present law does not provide a statutory prohibited transaction exemption for transactions made through an electronic communication network, but such transactions may be permitted if the parties are not known to each other (a "blind" transaction).

Explanation of Provision

The provision provides a prohibited transaction exemption under ERISA and the Code for a transaction involving the purchase or sale of securities (or other property as determined under regulations) between a plan and a party in interest if: (1) the transaction is executed through an electronic communication network, alternative trading system, or similar execution system or trading venue that is subject to regulation and oversight by (a) the applicable Federal regulating entity or (b) a foreign regulatory entity as the Secretary may determine under regulations; (2) either (a) neither the execution system nor the parties to the transaction take into account the identity of the parties in the execution of trades, or (b) the transaction is effected

---

[131] In addition, under ERISA section 408(a), the Secretary of Labor may grant exemptions with respect to particular transactions or classes of transactions after consultation and coordination with the Secretary of Treasury. An exemption may not be granted unless the Secretary of Labor finds that the exemption is administratively feasible, in the interests of the plan and its participants and beneficiaries, and protective of the rights of plan participants and beneficiaries.

under rules designed to match purchases and sales at the best price available through the execution system in accordance with applicable rules of the SEC or other relevant governmental authority; (3) the price and compensation associated with the purchase and sale are not greater than an arm's length transaction with an unrelated party; (4) if the disqualified person has an ownership interest in the system or venue, the system or venue has been authorized by the plan sponsor or other independent fiduciary for this type of transaction; and (5) not less than 30 days before the first transaction of this type executed through any such system or venue, a plan fiduciary is provided written notice of the execution of the transaction through the system or venue.

Examples of other property for purposes of the exemption include (but are not limited to) futures contracts and currency.

Effective Date

The provision is effective with respect to transactions occurring after the date of enactment.

4. Exemption for service providers

Present Law

Certain transactions are exempt from prohibited transaction treatment if made for adequate consideration. For this purpose, adequate consideration means: (1) in the case of a security for which there is a generally recognized market, either the price of the security prevailing on a national securities exchange registered under the Securities Exchange Act of 1934, or, if the security is not traded on such a national securities exchange, a price not less favorable to the plan than the offering price for the security as established by the current bid and asked prices quoted by persons independent of the issuer and of any disqualified person; and (2) in the case of an asset other than a security for which there is a generally recognized market, the fair market value of the asset as determined in good faith by a trustee or named fiduciary pursuant to the terms of the plan and in accordance with regulations.[132]

Explanation of Provision

The provision provides a prohibited transaction exemption under ERISA for certain transactions (such as sales of property, loans, and transfers or use of plan assets) between a plan and a person that is a party in interest solely by reason of providing services (or solely by reason of having certain relationships with a service provider), but only if, in connection with the transaction, the plan receives no less, nor pays no more, than adequate consideration. For this purpose, adequate consideration means: (1) in the case of a security for which there is a generally recognized market, the price of the security prevailing on a national securities exchange registered under the Securities Exchange Act of 1934, taking into account factors such as the size of the transaction and marketability of the security, or, if the security is not traded on

---

[132] ERISA sec. 3(18).

such a national securities exchange, a price not less favorable to the plan than the offering price for the security as established by the current bid and asked prices quoted by persons independent of the issuer and of any disqualified person, taking into account factors such as the size of the transaction and marketability of the security; and (2) in the case of an asset other than a security for which there is a generally recognized market, the fair market value of the asset as determined in good faith by a fiduciary or named fiduciaries in accordance with regulations. The exemption does not apply to a fiduciary (or an affiliate) who has or exercises any discretionary authority or control with respect to the investment of the assets involved in the transaction or provides investment advice with respect to the assets.

Effective Date

The provision is effective with respect to transactions occurring after the date of enactment.

5. Relief for foreign exchange transactions

Present Law

Present law provides statutory exemptions from the prohibited transaction rules for certain transactions.[133] Present law does not provide a statutory prohibited transaction exemption for foreign exchange transactions.

Explanation of Provision

The provision provides a prohibited transaction exemption under ERISA and the Code for foreign exchange transactions between a bank or broker-dealer (or an affiliate of either) and a plan in connection with the sale, purchase, or holding of securities or other investment assets (other than a foreign exchange transaction unrelated to any other investment in securities or other investment assets) if: (1) at the time the foreign exchange transaction is entered into, the terms of the transaction are not less favorable to the plan than the terms generally available in comparable arm's length foreign exchange transactions between unrelated parties or the terms afforded by the bank or the broker-dealer (or any affiliate thereof) in comparable arm's-length foreign exchange transactions involving unrelated parties; (2) the exchange rate used for a particular foreign exchange transaction may not deviate by more than three percent from the interbank bid and asked rates at the time of the transaction for transactions of comparable size and maturity as displayed on an independent service that reports rates of exchange in the foreign currency market for such currency; and (3) the bank, broker-dealer (and any affiliate of either) does not have investment discretion or provide investment advice with respect to the transaction.

---

[133] In addition, under ERISA section 408(a), the Secretary of Labor may grant exemptions with respect to particular transactions or classes of transactions after consultation and coordination with the Secretary of Treasury. An exemption may not be granted unless the Secretary of Labor finds that the exemption is administratively feasible, in the interests of the plan and its participants and beneficiaries, and protective of the rights of plan participants and beneficiaries.

Effective Date

The provision is effective with respect to transactions occurring after the date of enactment.

6. Definition of plan asset vehicle

Present Law

Under ERISA regulations, applicable also for purposes of the prohibited transaction rules of the Code, when a plan holds a non-publicly-traded equity interest in an entity, the assets of the entity may be considered plan assets in certain circumstances unless equity participation in the entity by benefit plan inventors is not significant.[134] In general, such equity participation is significant if, immediately after the most recent acquisition of any equity interest in the entity, 25 percent or more of the value of any class of equity interest in the entity (disregarding certain interests) is held by benefit plan investors, defined as (1) employer-sponsored plans (including those exempt from ERISA, such as governmental plans), (2) other arrangements, such as IRAs, that are subject only to the prohibited transaction rules of the Code, and (3) any entity whose assets are plan assets by reason of a plan's investment in the entity.[135] In that case, unless an exception applies, plan assets include the plan's equity interest in the entity and an undivided interest in each of the underlying assets of the entity.

Explanation of Provision

Under the provision, the term "plan assets" means plan assets as defined under regulations prescribed by the Secretary of Labor. Under the regulations, the assets of any entity are not to be treated as plan assets if, immediately after the most recent acquisition of any equity interest in the entity, less than 25 percent of the total value of each class of equity interest in the entity (disregarding certain interests) is held by benefit plan investors. For this purpose, an entity is considered to hold plan assets only to the extent of the percentage of the equity interest held by benefit plan investors, which means an employee benefit plan subject to the fiduciary rules of ERISA, any plan to which the prohibited transaction rules of the Code applies, and any entity whose underlying assets include plan assets by reason of a plan's investment in such entity.

Effective Date

The provision is effective with respect to transactions occurring after the date of enactment.

---

[134] 29 C.F.R. sec. 2510.3-101(a) (2005). As a result, a person who exercises authority or control respecting management or disposition of the assets of the entity or renders investment advice with respect to the assets for a fee (direct or indirect) is a plan fiduciary.

[135] 29 C.F.R. sec. 2510.3-101(f) (2005).

7. Exemption for cross trading

Present Law

Present law provides statutory exemptions from the prohibited transaction rules for certain transactions.[136] Present law does not provide a statutory prohibited transaction exemption for cross trades.

Explanation of Provision

The provision provides prohibited transaction exemptions under ERISA and the Code for a transaction involving the purchase and sale of a security between a plan and any other account managed by the same investment manager if certain requirements are met. These requirements are—

- the transaction is a purchase or sale, for no consideration other than cash payment against prompt delivery of a security for which market quotations are readily available;

- the transaction is effected at the independent current market price of the security;

- no brokerage commission fee (except for customary transfer fees, the fact of which is disclosed) or other remuneration is paid in connection with the transaction;

- a fiduciary (other than the investment manager engaging in the cross trades or any affiliate) for each plan participating in the transaction authorizes in advance of any cross-trades (in a document that is separate from any other written agreement of the parties) the investment manager to engage in cross trades at the investment manager's discretion, after the fiduciary has received disclosure regarding the conditions under which cross trades may take place (but only if the disclosure is separate from any other agreement or disclosure involving the asset management relationship), including the written policies and procedures of the investment manager;

- each plan participating in the transaction has assets of at least $100,000,000, except that, if the assets of a plan are invested in a master trust containing the assets of plans maintained by employers in the same controlled group, the master trust has assets of at least $100,000,000;

- the investment manager provides to the plan fiduciary who has authorized cross trading a quarterly report detailing all cross trades executed by the investment manager in which the plan participated during such quarter, including the following information as applicable: the identity of each security bought or sold, the number of

---

[136] In addition, under ERISA section 408(a), the Secretary of Labor may grant exemptions with respect to particular transactions or classes of transactions after consultation and coordination with the Secretary of Treasury. An exemption may not be granted unless the Secretary of Labor finds that the exemption is administratively feasible, in the interests of the plan and its participants and beneficiaries, and protective of the rights of plan participants and beneficiaries.

shares or units traded, the parties involved in the cross trade, and the trade price and the method used to establish the trade price;

- the investment manager does not base its fee schedule on the plan's consent to cross trading and no other service (other than the investment opportunities and cost savings available through a cross trade) is conditioned on the plan's consent to cross trading;

- the investment manager has adopted, and cross trades are effected in accordance with, written cross-trading policies and procedures that are fair and equitable to all accounts participating in the cross-trading program and that include a description of the manager's pricing policies and procedures, and the manager's policies and procedures for allocating cross trades in an objective manner among accounts participating in the cross-trading program; and

- the investment manager has designated an individual responsible for periodically reviewing purchases and sales to ensure compliance with the written policies and procedures and, following such review, the individual must issue an annual written report no later than 90 days following the period to which it relates, signed under penalty of perjury, to the plan fiduciary who authorized the cross trading, describing the steps performed during the course of the review, the level of compliance, and any specific instances of noncompliance.

The written report must also notify the plan fiduciary of the plan's right to terminate participation in the investment manager's cross-trading program at any time.

No later than 180 days after the date of enactment, the Secretary of Labor, after consultation with the Securities and Exchange Commission, is directed to issue regulations regarding the content of policies and procedures required to be adopted by an investment manager under the requirements for the exemption.

Effective Date

The provision is effective with respect to transactions occurring after the date of enactment.

C. Correction Period for Certain Transactions Involving Securities and Commodities
(sec. 408 of ERISA, and sec. 4975 of the Code)

Present Law

ERISA and the Code prohibit certain transactions between an employer-sponsored retirement plan and a disqualified person (referred to as a "party in interest" under ERISA).[137] Disqualified persons include a fiduciary of the plan, a person providing services to the plan, and an employer with employees covered by the plan. For this purpose, a fiduciary includes any person who (1) exercises any authority or control respecting management or disposition of the plan's assets, (2) renders investment advice for a fee or other compensation with respect to any plan moneys or property, or has the authority or responsibility to do so, or (3) has any discretionary authority or responsibility in the administration of the plan.

Prohibited transactions include (1) the sale, exchange or leasing of property, (2) the lending of money or other extension of credit, (3) the furnishing of goods, services or facilities, (4) the transfer to, or use by or for the benefit of, the income or assets of the plan, (5) in the case of a fiduciary, any act that deals with the plan's income or assets for the fiduciary's own interest or account, and (6) the receipt by a fiduciary of any consideration for the fiduciary's own personal account from any party dealing with the plan in connection with a transaction involving the income or assets of the plan. However, certain transactions are exempt from prohibited transaction treatment, for example, certain loans to plan participants.

Under the Code, if a prohibited transaction occurs, the disqualified person who participates in the transaction is subject to a two-tier excise tax. The first level tax is 15 percent of the amount involved in the transaction. The second level tax is imposed if the prohibited transaction is not corrected within a certain period and is 100 percent of the amount involved. Under ERISA, the Secretary of Labor may assess a civil penalty against a person who engages in a prohibited transaction, other than a transaction with a plan covered by the prohibited transaction rules of the Code (i.e., involving a qualified retirement plan or annuity). The penalty may not exceed five percent of the amount involved in the transaction. If the prohibited transaction is not corrected within 90 days after notice from the Secretary of Labor, the penalty may be up to 100 percent of the amount involved in the transaction.[138] For purposes of these

---

[137] Under ERISA, the prohibited transaction rules apply to employer-sponsored retirement plans and welfare benefit plans. Under the Code, the prohibited transaction rules apply to qualified retirement plans and qualified retirement annuities, as well as individual retirement accounts and annuities, Archer MSAs, health savings accounts, and Coverdell education savings accounts. The prohibited transaction rules under ERISA and the Code generally do not apply to governmental plans or church plans.

[138] A prohibited transaction violates the fiduciary responsibility provisions of ERISA. Under section 502(l) of ERISA, in the case of a violation of fiduciary responsibility, a civil penalty is generally imposed of 20 percent of the amount recovered from a person with respect to the violation in a settlement agreement with the Department of Labor or a judicial proceeding, but the penalty is reduced by the amount of any excise tax or other civil penalty with respect to a prohibited transaction.

rules, the "amount involved" generally means the greater of (1) the amount of money and the fair market value of the other property given, or (2) the amount of money and the fair market value of other property received by the plan. The terms "correction" and "correct" mean, with respect to a prohibited transaction, undoing the transaction to the extent possible, but in any case placing the plan in a financial position not worse than the position in which it would be if the disqualified person were acting under the highest fiduciary standards.

For purposes of the prohibited transaction rules of the Code and ERISA, a transaction involving the sale of securities is considered to occur when the transaction is settled (that is, an actual change in ownership of the securities). Under current practice, securities transactions are commonly settled 3 days after the agreement to sell is made. Present law does not provide a statutory prohibited transaction exemption that is based solely on correction of the transaction.

Explanation of Provision

The bill provides a prohibited transaction exemption under ERISA and the Code for a transaction in connection with the acquisition, holding, or disposition of any security or commodity if the transaction is corrected within a certain period, generally within 14 days of the date the disqualified person (or other person knowingly participating in the transaction) discovers, or reasonably should have discovered, the transaction was a prohibited transaction. For this purpose, the term "correct" means, with respect to a transaction: (1) to undo the transaction to the extent possible and in any case to make good to the plan or affected account any losses resulting from the transaction; and (2) to restore to the plan or affected account any profits made through the use of assets of the plan. If the exemption applies, no excise tax is to be assessed with the transaction, any tax assessed is to be abated, and any tax collected is to be credited or refunded as a tax overpayment.

The exemption does not apply to any transaction between a plan and a plan sponsor or its affiliates that involves the acquisition or sale of an employer security or the acquisition, sale, or lease of employer real property. In addition, in the case of a disqualified person (or other person knowingly participating in the transaction), the exemption does not apply if, at the time of the transaction, the person knew (or reasonably should have known) that the transaction would constitute a prohibited transaction.

Effective Date

The provision is effective with respect to any transaction that a fiduciary or other person discovers, or reasonably should have discovered, after the date of enactment constitutes a prohibited transaction.

D. Inapplicability of Relief from Fiduciary Liability During Suspension of Ability of Participant or Beneficiary to Direct Investments (sec. 404(c) of ERISA)

Present Law

Fiduciary rules under ERISA

ERISA contains general fiduciary duty standards that apply to all fiduciary actions, including investment decisions. ERISA requires that a plan fiduciary generally must discharge its duties solely in the interests of participants and beneficiaries and with the care, skill, prudence, and diligence under the circumstances then prevailing that a prudent man acting in a like capacity and familiar with such matters would use in the conduct of an enterprise of a like character and with like aims. With respect to plan assets, ERISA requires a fiduciary to diversify the investments of the plan so as to minimize the risk of large losses, unless under the circumstances it is clearly prudent not to do so.

A plan fiduciary that breaches any of the fiduciary responsibilities, obligations, or duties imposed by ERISA is personally liable to make good to the plan any losses to the plan resulting from such breach and to restore to the plan any profits the fiduciary has made through the use of plan assets. A plan fiduciary may be liable also for a breach of responsibility by another fiduciary (a "co-fiduciary") in certain circumstances.

Special rule for participant control of assets

ERISA provides a special rule in the case of a defined contribution plan that permits participants to exercise control over the assets in their individual accounts. Under the special rule, if a participant exercises control over the assets in his or her account (as determined under regulations), the participant is not deemed to be a fiduciary by reason of such exercise and no person who is otherwise a fiduciary is liable for any loss, or by reason of any breach, that results from the participant's exercise of control.

Regulations issued by the Department of Labor describe the requirements that must be met in order for a participant to be treated as exercising control over the assets in his or her account. With respect to investment options, the regulations provide in part:

- the plan must provide at least three different investment options, each of which is diversified and has materially different risk and return characteristics;

- the plan must allow participants to give investment instructions with respect to each investment option under the plan with a frequency that is appropriate in light of the reasonably expected market volatility of the investment option (the general volatility rule);

- at a minimum, participants must be allowed to give investment instructions at least every three months with respect to least three of the investment options, and those investment options must constitute a broad range of options (the three-month minimum rule);

- participants must be provided with detailed information about the investment options, information regarding fees, investment instructions and limitations, and copies of financial data and prospectuses; and

- specific requirements must be satisfied with respect to investments in employer stock to ensure that employees' buying, selling, and voting decisions are confidential and free from employer influence.

If these and the other requirements under the regulations are met, a plan fiduciary may be liable for the investment options made available under the plan, but not for the specific investment decisions made by participants.

Blackout notice

Under ERISA, the plan administrator of a defined contribution plan generally must provide at least 30 days advance notice of a blackout period (a "blackout notice") to plan participants and beneficiaries to whom the blackout period applies.[139] Failure to provide a blackout notice may result in a civil penalty up to $100 per day for each failure with respect to a single participant or beneficiary.

A blackout period is any period during which any ability of participants or beneficiaries under the plan, which is otherwise available under the terms of the plan, to direct or diversify assets credited to their accounts, or to obtain loans or distributions from the plan, is temporarily suspended, limited, or restricted if the suspension, limitation, or restriction is for any period of more than three consecutive business days. However, a blackout period does not include a suspension, limitation, or restriction that (1) occurs by reason of the application of securities laws, (2) is a change to the plan providing for a regularly scheduled suspension, limitation, or restriction that is disclosed through a summary of material modifications to the plan or materials describing specific investment options under the plan, or changes thereto, or (3) applies only to one or more individuals, each of whom is a participant, alternate payee, or other beneficiary under a qualified domestic relations order.

A blackout notice must be written in a manner calculated to be understood by the average plan participant and must include (1) the reasons for the blackout period, (2) an identification of the investments and other rights affected, (3) the expected beginning date and length of the blackout period, and (4) in the case of a blackout period affecting investments, a statement that the participant or beneficiary should evaluate the appropriateness of current investment decisions in light of the inability to direct or diversify assets during the blackout period, and (5) other matters as required by regulations. If the expected beginning date or length of the blackout period changes after notice has been provided, the plan administrator must provide notice of the change (and specify any material change in other matters related to the blackout) to affected participants and beneficiaries as soon as reasonably practicable.

---

[139] ERISA sec. 101(i).

Explanation of Provision

The bill amends the special rule applicable if a participant exercises control over the assets in his or her account with respect to a case in which a qualified change in investment options offered under the defined contribution plan occurs. In such a case, for purposes of the special rule, a participant or beneficiary who has exercised control over the assets in his or her account before a change in investment options is not treated as not exercising control over such assets in connection with the change if certain requirements are met.

For this purpose, a qualified change in investment options means a change in the investment options offered to a participant or beneficiary under the terms of the plan, under which: (1) the participant's account is reallocated among one or more new investment options offered instead of one or more investment options that were offered immediately before the effective date of the change; and (2) the characteristics of the new investment options, including characteristics relating to risk and rate of return, are, immediately after the change, reasonably similar to the characteristics of the investment options offered immediately before the change.

The following requirements must be met in order for the rule to apply: (1) at least 30 but not more than 60 days before the effective date of the change in investment options, the plan administrator furnishes written notice of the change to participants and beneficiaries, including information comparing the existing and new investment options and an explanation that, in the absence of affirmative investment instructions from the participant or beneficiary to the contrary, the account of the participant or beneficiary will be invested in new options with characteristics reasonably similar to the characteristics of the existing investment options; (2) the participant or beneficiary has not provided to the plan administrator, in advance of the effective date of the change, affirmative investment instructions contrary to the proposed reinvestment of the participant's or beneficiary's account; and (3) the investment of the participant's or beneficiary's account as in effect immediately before the effective date of the change was the product of the exercise by such participant or beneficiary of control over the assets of the account.

In addition, the provision amends the special rule applicable if a participant or beneficiary exercises control over the assets in his or her account so that the provision under which no person who is otherwise a fiduciary is liable for any loss, or by reason of any breach, that results from the participant's or beneficiary's exercise of control does not apply in connection with a blackout period[140] in which the participant's or beneficiary's ability to direct the assets in his or her account is suspended by a plan sponsor or fiduciary. However, if a plan sponsor or fiduciary meets the requirements of ERISA in connection with authorizing and implementing a blackout period, any person who is otherwise a fiduciary is not liable under ERISA for any loss occurring during the blackout period.

Not later than one year after the date of enactment, the Secretary of Labor is to issue interim final regulations providing guidance, including safe harbors, on how plan sponsors or other affected fiduciaries can satisfy their fiduciary responsibilities during any blackout period.

---

[140] For this purpose, blackout period is defined as under the present-law provision requiring advance notice of a blackout period.

Effective Date

The provision generally applies to plan years beginning after December 31, 2007. In the case of a plan maintained pursuant to one or more collective bargaining agreements, the provision is effective for plan years beginning after the earlier of (1) the later of December 31, 2008 or the date on which the last of such collective bargaining agreements terminates (determined without regard to any extension thereof after the date of enactment), or (2) December 31, 2009.

E. Increase in Maximum Bond Amount
(sec. 412(a) of ERISA)

Present Law

ERISA generally requires every plan fiduciary and every person who handles funds or other property of a plan (a "plan official") to be bonded. The amount of the bond is fixed annually at no less than ten percent of the funds handled, but must be at least $1,000 and not more than $500,000 (unless the Secretary of Labor prescribes a larger amount after notice and an opportunity to be heard). The bond is intended to protect plans against loss from acts of fraud or dishonesty by plan officials. Qualifying bonds must have as surety a corporate surety company that is an acceptable surety on Federal bonds.

Explanation of Provision

The provision raises the maximum bond amount to $1 million in the case of a plan that holds employer securities. The provision raises the maximum bond amount to $1 million in the case of a plan that holds employer securities. A plan would not be considered to hold employer securities within the meaning of this section where the only securities held by the plan are part of a broadly diversified fund of assets, such as mutual or index funds.

Effective Date

The provision is effective for plan years beginning after December 31, 2007.

F. Increase in Penalties for Coercive Interference with Exercise of ERISA Rights (sec. 511 of ERISA)

Present Law

ERISA prohibits any person from using fraud, force or violence (or threatening force or violence) to restrain, coerce, or intimidate (or attempt to) any plan participant or beneficiary in order to interfere with or prevent the exercise of their rights under the plan, ERISA, or the Welfare and Pension Plans Disclosure Act ("WPPDA"). Willful violation of this prohibition is a criminal offense subject to a $10,000 fine or imprisonment of up to one year, or both.

Explanation of Provision

The provision increases the penalties for willful acts of coercive interference with participants' rights under a plan, ERISA, or the WPPDA. The amount of the fine is increased to $100,000, and the maximum term of imprisonment is increased to 10 years.

Effective Date

The provision is effective for violations occurring on and after the date of enactment.

G. Treatment of Investment of Assets By Plan Where Participant
Fails to Exercise Investment Election
(sec. 404(c) of ERISA)

Present Law

ERISA imposes standards on the conduct of plan fiduciaries, including persons who make investment decisions with respect to plan assets. Fiduciaries are personally liable for any losses to the plan due to a violation of fiduciary standards.

An individual account plan may permit participants to make investment decisions with respect to their accounts. ERISA fiduciary liability does not apply to investment decisions made by plan participants if participants exercise control over the investment of their individual accounts, as determined under ERISA regulations. In that case, a plan fiduciary may be responsible for the investment alternatives made available, but not for the specific investment decisions made by participants.

Explanation of Provision

Under the bill, a participant is treated as exercising control with respect to assets in an individual account plan if such amounts are invested in a default arrangement in accordance with Department of Labor regulations until the participant makes an affirmative election regarding investments. Such regulations must provide guidance on the appropriateness of certain investments for designation as default investments under the arrangement, including guidance regarding appropriate mixes of default investments and asset classes which the Secretary considers consistent with long-term capital appreciation or long-term capital preservation (or both), and the designation of other default investments. The Secretary of Labor is directed to issue regulations under the provision within six months of the date of enactment.

In order for this treatment to apply, notice of the participant's rights and obligations under the arrangement must be provided. Under the notice requirement, within a reasonable period before the plan year, the plan administrator must give each participant notice of the rights and obligations under the arrangement which is sufficiently accurate and comprehensive to apprise the participant of such rights and obligations and is written in a manner to be understood by the average participant. The notice must include an explanation of the participant's rights under the arrangement to specifically elect to exercise control over the assets in the participant's account. In addition, the participant must have a reasonable period of time after receipt of the notice and before the assets are first invested to make such an election. The notice must also explain how contributions made under the arrangement will be invested in the absence of any investment election by the employee.

Effective Date

The provision is effective for plan years beginning after December 31, 2006.

H. Clarification of Fiduciary Rules

Present Law

ERISA imposes standards on the conduct of plan fiduciaries. Fiduciaries are personally liable for any losses to the plan due to a violation of fiduciary standards.

An ERISA interpretive bulletin requires a fiduciary choosing an annuity provider for purposes of distributions from a plan (whether on separation or retirement of a participant or on termination of the plan) to take steps calculated to obtain the safest available annuity, based on the annuity provider's claims paying ability and creditworthiness, unless under the circumstances it would be in the interest of participants to do otherwise.[141]

Explanation of Provision

The bill directs the Secretary of Labor to issue final regulations within one year of the date of enactment, clarifying that the selection of an annuity contract as an optional form of distribution from a defined contribution plan is not subject to the safest available annuity requirement under the ERISA interpretive bulletin and is subject to all otherwise applicable fiduciary standards.

The regulations to be issued by the Secretary of Labor are intended to clarify that the plan sponsor or other applicable plan fiduciary is required to act in accordance with the prudence standards of ERISA section 404(a). It is not intended that there be a single safest available annuity contract since the plan fiduciary must select the most prudent option specific to its plan and its participants and beneficiaries. Furthermore, it is not intended that the regulations restate all of the factors contained in the interpretive bulletin.

Effective Date

The provision is effective on the date of enactment.

---

[141] 29 C.F.R. sec. 2509.95-1 (2005).

TITLE VII: BENEFIT ACCRUAL STANDARDS
(Secs. 203, 204, and 205 of ERISA, secs. 411 and 417 of the Code, and sec. 4(i)(2) of ADEA)

Present Law

Prohibition on age discrimination

In general

A prohibition on age discrimination applies to benefit accruals under a defined benefit pension plan.[142] Specifically, an employee's benefit accrual may not cease, and the rate of an employee's benefit accrual may not be reduced, because of the attainment of any age. However, this prohibition is not violated solely because the plan imposes (without regard to age) a limit on the amount of benefits that the plan provides or a limit on the number of years of service or years of participation that are taken into account for purposes of determining benefit accrual under the plan. Moreover, for purposes of this requirement, the subsidized portion of any early retirement benefit may be disregarded in determining benefit accruals.

In December 2002, the IRS issued proposed regulations that dealt with the application of the age discrimination rules.[143] The proposed regulations included rules for applying the age discrimination rules with respect to accrued benefits, optional forms of benefit, ancillary benefits, and other rights and features provided under a plan. Under the proposed regulations, for purposes of applying the prohibition on age discrimination to defined benefit pension plans, an employee's rate of benefit accrual for a year is generally the increase in the employee's accrued normal retirement benefit (i.e., the benefit payable at normal retirement age) for the plan year. In the preamble to the proposed regulations, the IRS requested comments on other approaches to determining the rate of benefit accrual, such as allowing accrual rates to be averaged over multiple years (for example, to accommodate plans that provide a higher rate of accrual in earlier years) or, in the case of a plan that applies an offset, determining accrual rates before application of the offset. As discussed below, in June 2004, the IRS announced the withdrawal of the proposed regulations.

Cash balance and other hybrid plans

Certain types of defined benefit pension plans, such as cash balance plans and pension equity plans, are referred to as "hybrid" plans because they combine features of a defined benefit pension plan and a defined contribution plan.

Under a cash balance plan, benefits are determined by reference to a hypothetical account balance. An employee's hypothetical account balance is determined by reference to hypothetical annual allocations to the account ("pay credits") (e.g., a certain percentage of the employee's compensation for the year) and hypothetical earnings on the account ("interest credits"). Cash

---

[142] Code sec. 411(b)(1)(H); ERISA sec. 204(b)(1)(H).

[143] 67 Fed. Reg. 76123.

balance plans are generally designed so that, when a participant receives a pay credit for a year of service, the participant also receives the right to future interest on the pay credit, regardless of whether the participant continues employment (referred to as "front-loaded" interest credits). That is, the participant's hypothetical account continues to be credited with interest after the participant stops working for the employer. As a result, if an employee terminates employment and defers distribution to a later date, interest credits will continue to be credited to that employee's hypothetical account.

Another type of hybrid plan is a pension equity plan (sometimes referred to as a "PEP"). Under a pension equity plan, benefits are generally described as a percentage of final average pay, with the percentage determined on the basis of points received for each year of service, which are often weighted for older or longer service employees. Pension equity plans commonly provide interest credits for the period between a participant's termination of employment and commencement of benefits.

Because of the front-loaded nature of accruals under cash balance plans, there is a longer time for interest credits to accrue on a pay credit to the account of a younger employee. Thus, a pay credit received at a younger age may provide a larger annuity benefit at normal retirement age than the same pay credit received at an older age. A similar effect may occur with respect to other types of hybrid plan designs, including pension equity plans.

IRS consideration of cash balance plans began in the early 1990s.[144] At that time, the focus was on the question of whether such plans satisfied the nondiscrimination requirements under section 401(a)(4), which requires that benefits or contributions not discriminate in favor of highly compensated employees. Treasury regulations issued in 1991 under section 401(a)(4) provided a safe harbor for cash balance plans that provide frontloaded interest credits and meet certain other requirements. In connection with the issuance of these regulations, Treasury spoke to the cash balance age discrimination issue. The preamble to the final regulations stated "[t]he fact that interest adjustments through normal retirement age are accrued in the year of the related hypothetical allocation will not cause a cash balance plan to fail to satisfy the requirements of section 411(b)(1)(H), relating to age-based reductions in the rate at which benefits accrue under a plan."[145] Many interpreted this language as Treasury's position that cash balance plan designs do not violate the prohibitions on age discrimination. The IRS has not to date asserted that hybrid plan formulas result in per se violations of age discrimination requirements. In 1999, Treasury and the IRS issued an announcement and a Federal Register notice stating that the question of whether cash balance conversions were age discriminatory or otherwise inconsistent with plan qualification rules was under active consideration, that further IRS determination letters on conversions to cash balance plans would therefore be suspected be referral to the IRS National Office until the IRS and Treasury had resolved the issues, and inviting public comment on the issues. Hundreds of comments were submitted. The December 2002 proposed regulations, noted above, provided that an employee's rate of benefit accrual for a year is

---

[144] Statement of Stuart L. Brown, Chief Counsel Internal Revenue Service, before the Senate Committee on Health, Education, Labor, and Pensions (Sept. 21, 1999).

[145] 56 Fed. Reg. 47528 (Sept. 19, 1991).

generally the increase in the employee's accrued normal retirement benefit (i.e., the benefit payable at normal retirement age) for the plan year. However, the proposed regulations provided a special rule under which an employee's rate of benefit accrual under a cash balance plan meeting certain requirements (an "eligible" cash balance plan) was based on the rate of pay credit provided under the plan. Thus, under the proposed regulations, an eligible cash balance plan would not violate the prohibition on age discrimination solely because pay credits for younger employees earn interest credits for a longer period.

Section 205 of the Consolidated Appropriations Act, 2004 (the "2004 Appropriations Act"), enacted January 24, 2004, provides that none of the funds made available in the 2004 Appropriations Act may be used by the Secretary of the Treasury, or his designee, to issue any rule or regulation implementing the 2002 proposed Treasury age discrimination regulations or any regulation reaching similar results.[146] The 2004 Appropriations Act also required the Secretary of the Treasury within 180 days of enactment to present to Congress a legislative proposal for providing transition relief for older and longer-service participants affected by conversions of their employers' traditional pension plans to cash balance plans. The Treasury Department complied with this requirement by including in the President's budget for fiscal year 2005 a proposal relating to cash balance and other hybrid plans that specifically addresses conversions to such plans, the application of the age discrimination rules to such plans, and the determination of minimum lump sums under such plans.[147] In June 2004, the IRS announced the withdrawal of the proposed age discrimination regulations, including the special rules for eligible cash balance plans.[148] According to the Announcement, "[t]his will provide Congress an opportunity to . . . address cash balance and other hybrid plan issues through legislation."

The application of the age discrimination rules to hybrid plans has been the subject of litigation. The decisions are divided on how ERISA requires courts to calculate the rate of benefit accrual.[149]

Calculating minimum lump-sum distributions under hybrid plans

Defined benefit pension plans, including cash balance plans and other hybrid plans, are required to provide benefits in the form of a life annuity commencing at a participant's normal retirement age. If the plan permits benefits to be paid in certain other forms, such as a lump sum,

---

[146] Pub. L. No. 108-199 (2004).

[147] A similar proposal was also contained in the President's budget proposal for fiscal year 2006.

[148] IRS Announcement 2004-57, 2004-27 I.R.B. 15.

[149] Compare *Register v. PNC Financial Services Group, Inc.* No. 04-CV-6097, 2005 WL 3120268 (E.D. Pa. Nov. 21, 2005), *Tootle v. ARINC, Inc.*, 222 F.R.D. 88 (D. Md. 2004); *Eaton v. Oanan Corp.*, 117 F. Supp. 2d 812 (S.D. Ind. 2000); with *Cooper v. IBM Personal Pension Plan*, 274 F. Supp.2d 1010 (S.D. Ill. 2003), *Richards v. Fleetboston Financial Corp.*, 427 F.Supp.2d 150 (D. Conn. 2006), *Donaldson v. Pharmacia Pension Plan*, 2006 WL 1669789, 38 E.B.C. 1006 (S.D. Ill. June 14, 2006). See also *Campbell v. BankBoston*, 327 F.3d 1 (1st Cir. 2003) and *Hirt v. Equitable Retirement Plan for Employees, Managers and Agents* No. 01 Civ. 7920 (AKH), 2006 WL 2023545 (S.D.N.Y. July 20, 2006).

minimum present value rules apply, under which the alternative form of benefit cannot be less than the present value of the life annuity payable at normal retirement age, determined using certain statutorily prescribed interest and mortality assumptions.[150]

Most cash balance plans are designed to permit a lump-sum distribution of a participant's hypothetical account balance upon termination of employment. This raises an issue as to the whether a distribution of a participant's hypothetical account balance satisfies the minimum present value rules. In 1996, the IRS issued proposed guidance (Notice 96-8) on the application of the minimum present value rules to lump-sum distributions under cash balance plans and requested public comments in anticipation of proposed regulations incorporating the proposed guidance.[151]

Under the proposed guidance, a lump-sum distribution from a cash balance plan cannot be less than the present value of the benefit payable at normal retirement age, determined using the statutory interest and mortality assumptions. For this purpose, a participant's normal retirement benefit under a cash balance plan is generally determined by projecting the participant's hypothetical account balance to normal retirement age by crediting to the account future interest credits at the plan rate, the right to which has already accrued, and converting the projected account balance to an actuarially equivalent life annuity payable at normal retirement age, using the interest and mortality assumptions specified in the plan. The proposed guidance also included rules under which cash balance plans can provide lump-sum distributions in the amount of participants' hypothetical account balances if the rate at which interest credits are provided under the plan is not greater (or is assumed not to be greater) than the statutory interest rate.

Under the approach in the proposed guidance, a difference in the rate of interest credits provided under the plan, which is used to project the account balance forward to normal retirement age, and the statutory rate used to determine the lump-sum value (i.e., present value) of the accrued benefit can cause a discrepancy between the value of the minimum lump-sum and the employee's hypothetical account balance. This effect is sometimes referred to as "whipsaw." In particular, if the plan's interest crediting rate is higher than the statutory interest rate, then the resulting lump-sum amount will generally be greater than the hypothetical account balance.

---

[150] Code sec. 417(e); ERISA sec. 205(g)(3). For years before 1995, these provisions required the use of an interest rate based on interest rates determined by the PBGC. For years after 1994, these provisions require the use of an interest rate based on interest rates on 30-year Treasury securities and a mortality table specified by the IRS.

[151] Notice 96-8, 1996-1996-1 C.B. 359. The Notice provides that regulations will be effective prospectively and, for plan years before regulations are effective, allows lump-sum distributions from cash balance plans that provide front-loaded interest credits to be based on a reasonable, good-faith interpretation of the minimum present value rules, taking into account preexisting guidance. The Notice further provides that plans that comply with the guidance in the Notice are deemed to be applying a reasonable, good-faith interpretation.

Several courts, but not all, have applied an approach similar to the approach in the proposed guidance in cases involving the determination of lump sums under cash balance plans.[152] Regulations addressing the application of the minimum present value rules to cash balance plans have not been issued.[153]

Explanation of Provision

Age discrimination rules in general

Under the provision, a plan is not treated as violating the prohibition on age discrimination under ERISA, the Code, and ADEA if a participant's accrued benefit,[154] as determined as of any date under the terms of the plan would be equal to or greater than that of any similarly situated, younger individual who is or could be a participant. For this purpose, an individual is similarly situated to a participant if the individual and the participant are (and always have been) identical in every respect (including period of service, compensation, position, date of hire, work history, and any other respect) except for age. Under the provision, the comparison of benefits for older and younger participants applies to all possible participants under all possible dates under the plan, in the same manner as the present-law application of the backloading and accrual rules.

In addition, in determining a participant's accrued benefit for this purpose, the subsidized portion of any early retirement benefit or any retirement type subsidy is disregarded. In some cases the value of an early retirement subsidy may be difficult to determine; it is therefore intended that a reasonable approximation of such value may be used for this purpose. In calculating the accrued benefit, the benefit may, under the terms of the plan, be calculated as an annuity payable at normal retirement age, the balance of a hypothetical account, or the current value of the accumulated percentage of the employee's final average compensation. That is, the

---

[152] *Berger v. Xerox Corp. Retirement Income Guarantee Plan*, 338 F.3d 755 (7th Cir. 2003); *Esden v. Bank of Boston*, 229 F.3d 154 (2d Cir. 2000), cert. dismissed, 531 U.S. 1061 (2001); *Lyons v. Georgia Pacific Salaried Employees Retirement Plan*, 221 F.3d 1235 (11th Cir. 2000) ("*Lyons II*"), cert. denied, 532 U.S. 967 (2001); and *West v. AK Steel Corp. Retirement Accumulation Plan*, 318 F. Supp.2d 579 (S.D. Ohio 2004). In *Lyons II*, the court reversed a lower court holding in *Lyons v. Georgia Pacific Salaried Employees Retirement Plan*, 66 F. Supp.2d 1328 (N.D. Ga. 1999) ("*Lyons I*"), relating to the application of the minimum present value rules in effect before 1995. The *Lyons II* court limited its analysis to the minimum present value rules in effect as of 1993 when Mr. Lyons received his lump-sum distribution; however, the court indicated that a different result could apply under the law in effect after 1994. On remand, in *Lyons v. Georgia Pacific Salaried Employees Retirement Plan*, 196 F. Supp.2d 1260 (N.D. Ga. 2002) ("*Lyons III*"), the lower court determined that payment of the hypothetical account balance did not violate the minimum present value rules in effect for years after 1994.

[153] As mentioned above, the President's budgets for fiscal years 2005 and 2006 include a proposal relating to cash balance plans that specifically addresses the determination of minimum lump sums under such plans. The President's proposal would eliminate the whipsaw effect and allow the plan to pay the hypothetical account balance, if certain requirements are satisfied.

[154] For purposes of this rule, the accrued benefit means such benefit accrued to date.

age discrimination rules may be applied on the basis of the balance of the a hypothetical account or the current value of the accumulated percentage of the employee's final average compensation, but only if the plan terms provide the accrued benefit in such form. The provision is intended to apply to hybrid plans, including pension equity plans.

The provision makes it clear that a plan is not treated as age discriminatory solely because the plan provides offsets of benefits under the plan to the extent such offsets are allowable in applying the requirements under section 401(a) of the Code. It is intended that such offsets also comply with ERISA and the ADEA.

A plan is not treated as failing to meet the age discrimination requirements solely because the plan provides a disparity in contributions and benefits with respect to which the requirements of section 401(l) of the Code are met.

A plan is not treated as failing to meet the age discrimination requirements solely because the plan provides for indexing of accrued benefits under the plan. Except in the case of any benefit provided in the form of a variable annuity, this rule does not apply with respect to any indexing which results in an accrued benefit less than the accrued benefit determined without regard to such indexing. Indexing for this purpose means, with respect to an accrued benefit, the periodic adjustment of the accrued benefit by means of the application of a recognized investment index or methodology. Under the provision, in no event may indexing be reduced or cease because of age.

Rules for applicable defined benefit plans

In general

Under the provision, an applicable defined benefit plan fails to satisfy the age discrimination rules unless the plan meets certain requirements with respect to interest credits and, in the case of a conversion, certain additional requirements. Applicable defined benefit plans must also satisfy certain vesting requirements.

Interest requirement

A plan satisfies the interest requirement if the terms of the plan provide that any interest credit (or equivalent amount) for any plan year is at a rate that is not less than zero and is not greater than a market rate of return. A plan does not fail to meet the interest requirement merely because the plan provides for a reasonable minimum guaranteed rate of return or for a rate or return that is equal to the greater of a fixed or variable rate of return. An interest credit (or an equivalent amount) of less than zero cannot result in the account balance or similar amount being less than the aggregate amount of contributions credited to the account. The Secretary of the Treasury may provide rules governing the calculation of a market rate of return and for permissible methods of crediting interest to the account (including fixed or variable interest rates) resulting in effective rates of return that meet the requirements of the provision.

If the interest credit rate (or equivalent amount) is a variable rate, the plan must provide that, upon termination of the plan, the rate of interest used to determine accrued benefits under the plan is equal to the average of the rates of interest used under the plan during the five-year period ending on the termination date.

Conversion rules

Under the provision, special rules apply if an amendment to a defined benefit plan is adopted which would have the effect of converting the plan into an applicable defined benefit plan (an "applicable plan amendment").[155] If an applicable plan amendment is adopted after June 29, 2005, the plan fails to satisfy the age discrimination rules unless the plan provides that the accrued benefit of any individual who was a participant immediately before the adoption of the amendment is not less than the sum of (1) the participant's accrued benefit for years of service before the effective date of the amendment, determined under the terms of the plan as in effect before the amendment; plus (2) the participant's accrued benefit for years of service after the effective date of the amendment, determined under the terms of the plan as in effect after the terms of the amendment.

For purposes of determining the amount in (1) above, the plan must credit the accumulation account or similar amount with the amount of any early retirement benefit or retirement-type subsidy for the plan year in which the participant retires if, as of such time, the participant has met the age, years of service, and other requirements under the plan for entitlement to such benefit or subsidy.

Vesting rules

The provision amends the ERISA and Code rules relating to vesting to provide that an applicable defined benefit plan must provide that each employee who has completed at least three years of serves has a nonforfeitable right to 100 percent of the employee's accrued benefit derived from employer contributions.

Minimum present value rules

The provision provides that an applicable defined benefit plan is not treated as failing to meet the minimum present value rules[156] solely because of the present value of the accrued benefit (or any portion thereof) of any participant is, under the terms of the plan, equal to the

---

[155] If the benefits under two or more defined benefit plans established by an employer are coordinated in such a manner as to have the effect of the adoption of an applicable plan amendment, the sponsor of the defined benefit plan or plans providing for the coordination is treated as having adopted an applicable plan amendment as of the date the coordination begins. In addition, the Secretary of Treasury is directed to issue regulations to prevent the avoidance of the requirements with respect to an applicable plan amendment through the use of two or more plan amendments rather than a single amendment.

[156] ERISA sec. 205(g), Code sec. 417(e). A plan complying with the provision also does not violate certain rules relating to vesting (ERISA sec. 203(a)(2) and Code sec. 411(a)(2)) and the determination of the accrued benefit (in the case of a plan which does not provide for employee contributions) (ERISA sec. 204(c) and Code sec. 411(c)).

amount expressed as the balance in the hypothetical account or as an accumulated percentage of the participant's final average compensation.

Rules on plan termination

The provision provides rules for making determinations of benefits upon termination of an applicable defined benefit plan. Such a plan must provide that, upon plan termination, (1) if the interest credit rate (or equivalent amount) under the plan is a variable rate, the rate of interest used to determine accrued benefits under the plan shall be equal to the average of the rates of interest used under the plan during the five-year period ending on the termination date and (2) the interest rate and mortality table used to determine the amount of any benefit under the plan payable in the form of an annuity payable at normal retirement age is the rate and table specified under the plan for such purposes as of the termination date. For purposes of (2), if the rate of interest is a variable rate, then the rate is the average of such rates during the five-year period ending on the termination date.

Definition of applicable defined benefit plan

An applicable defined benefit plan is a defined benefit plan under which the accrued benefit (or any portion thereof) is calculated as the balance of a hypothetical account maintained for the participant or as an accumulated percentage of the participant's final average compensation. The Secretary of the Treasury is to provide rules which include in the definition of an applicable defined benefit plan any defined benefit plan (or portion of such a plan) which has an effect similar to an applicable defined benefit plan.

No inference

Nothing in the provision is to be construed to infer the treatment of applicable defined benefit plans or conversions to such plans under the rules in ERISA, ADEA and the Code prohibiting age discrimination[157] as in effect before the provision is effective. In addition, no inference is to be drawn with respect to the application of the minimum benefit rules to applicable defined benefit plans before the provision is effective.

Regulations relating to mergers and acquisitions

The Secretary of the Treasury is directed to prescribe regulations for the application of the provisions relating to applicable defined benefit plans in cases where the conversion of a plan to a cash balance or similar plan is made with respect to a group of employees who become employees by reason of a merger, acquisition, or similar treatment. The regulations are to be issued not later than 12 months after the date of enactment.

Effective Date

In general, the provision is effective for periods beginning on or after June 29, 2005.

---

[157] ERISA sec. 204(b)(1)(H), ADEA sec. 4(i)(1), and Code sec. 411(b)(1)(H).

The provision relating to the minimum value rules is effective for distributions after the date of enactment.

In the case of a plan in existence on June 29, 2005, the interest credit and vesting requirements for an applicable defined benefit plan generally apply to years beginning after December 31, 2007, except that the plan sponsor may elect to have such requirements apply for any period after June 29, 2005, and before the first plan year beginning after December 31, 2007. In the case of a plan maintained pursuant to one or more collective bargaining agreements, a delayed effective date applies with respect to the interest credit and vesting requirements for an applicable defined benefit plan.

The provision relating to conversions of plans applies to plan amendments adopted after and taking effect after June 29, 2005, except that a plan sponsor may elect to have such amendments apply to plan amendments adopted before and taking affect after such date.

The direction to the Secretary of the Treasury to issue regulations relating to mergers and acquisitions is effective on the date of enactment.

TITLE VIII: PENSION RELATED REVENUE PROVISIONS

A. Deduction Limitations

1. Increase in deduction limits applicable to single-employer and multiemployer defined benefit pension plans (sec. 404 of the Code)

Present Law

In general

Employer contributions to qualified retirement plans are deductible subject to certain limits.

In the case of contributions to a defined benefit pension plan (including both single-employer and multiemployer plans), the employer generally may deduct the greater of: (1) the amount necessary to satisfy the minimum funding requirement of the plan for the year; or (2) the amount of the plan's normal cost for the year plus the amount necessary to amortize certain unfunded liabilities over 10 years, but limited to the full funding limitation for the year.[158] The maximum amount otherwise deductible generally is not less than the plan's unfunded current liability.[159] In the case of a single-employer plan covered by the PBGC insurance program that terminates during the year, the maximum deductible amount is generally not less than the amount needed to make the plan assets sufficient to fund benefit liabilities as defined for purposes of plan termination under the PBGC insurance program ("unfunded termination liability"). In applying these limits, future increases in the limits on compensation taken into account under a qualified retirement plan and on benefits payable under a defined benefit pension plan may not be taken into account.

In the case of a defined contribution plan, the employer generally may deduct contributions in an amount up to 25 percent of compensation paid or accrued during the employer's taxable year.

Overall deduction limit

If an employer sponsors one or more defined benefit pension plans and one or more defined contribution plans that cover at least one of the same employees, an overall deduction limit applies to the total contributions to all plans for a plan year. The overall deduction limit is

---

[158] The full funding limitation is the excess, if any, of (1) the accrued liability of the plan (including normal cost), over (2) the lesser of (a) the market value of plan assets or (b) the actuarial value of plan assets. However, the full funding limit is not less than the excess, if any, of 90 percent of the plan's current liability (including the current liability normal cost) over the actuarial value of plan assets.

[159] In the case of a plan with 100 or fewer participants, unfunded current liability for this purpose does not include the liability attributable to benefit increases for highly compensated employees resulting from a plan amendment that is made or becomes effective, whichever is later, within the last two years.

the greater of (1) 25 percent of compensation, or (2) the amount necessary to meet the minimum funding requirement with respect to the defined benefit plan for the year. For this purpose, the amount necessary to meet the minimum funding requirement with respect to the defined benefit plan is treated as not less than the amount of the plan's unfunded current liability.

Subject to certain exceptions, an employer that makes nondeductible contributions to a plan is subject to an excise tax equal to 10 percent of the amount of the nondeductible contributions for the year.

Explanation of Provision

Single-employer defined benefit pension plans

General deduction limit

Under the bill, for taxable years beginning in 2006 and 2007, in the case of contributions to a single-employer defined benefit plan, the maximum deductible amount is not less than the excess (if any) of (1) 150 percent of the plan's current liability, over (2) the value of plan assets.

For taxable years beginning after 2007, in the case of contributions to a single-employer defined benefit pension plan, the maximum deductible amount is equal to the greater of: (1) the excess (if any) of the sum of the plan's funding target, the plan's target normal cost, and a cushion amount for a plan year, over the value of plan assets (as determined under the minimum funding rules[160]); and (2) the minimum required contribution for the plan year.[161]

However, in the case of a plan that is not in at-risk status, the first amount above is not less than the excess (if any) of the sum of the plan's funding target and target normal cost, determined as if the plan was in at-risk status, over the value of plan assets.

The cushion amount for a plan year is the sum of (1) 50 percent of the plan's funding target for the plan year; and (2) the amount by which the plan's funding target would increase if determined by taking into account increases in participants' compensation for future years or, if the plan does not base benefits attributable to past service on compensation, increases in benefits that are expected to occur in succeeding plans year, determined on the basis of average annual benefit increases over the previous six years.[162] For this purpose, the dollar limits on benefits

---

[160] In determining the maximum deductible amount, the value of plan assets is not reduced by any pre-funding balance or funding standard account carryover balance.

[161] The bill retains the present-law rule, under which, in the case of a single-employer plan covered by the PBGC that terminates during the year, the maximum deductible amount is generally not less than the amount needed to make the plan assets sufficient to fund benefit liabilities as defined for purposes of the PBGC termination insurance program.

[162] In determining the cushion amount for a plan with 100 or fewer participants, a plan's funding target does not include the liability attributable to benefit increases for highly compensated employees resulting from a plan amendment that is made or becomes effective, whichever is later, within the last two years.

and on compensation apply, but, in the case of a plan that is covered by the PBGC insurance program, increases in the compensation limit (under sec. 401(a)(17)) that are expected to occur in succeeding plan years may be taken into account.[163] The rules relating to projecting compensation for future years are intended solely to enable employers to reduce volatility in pension contributions; the rules are not intended to create any inference that employees have any protected interest with respect to such projected increases.

Overall deduction limit

Under the bill, in applying the overall deduction limit to contributions to one or more defined benefit pension plans and one or more defined contribution plans for years beginning after December 31, 2007, single-employer defined benefit pension plans that are covered by the PBGC insurance program are not taken into account. Thus, the deduction for contributions to a defined benefit pension plan or a defined contribution plan is not affected by the overall deduction limit merely because employees are covered by both plans if the defined benefit plan is covered by the PBGC insurance program (i.e., the separate deduction limits for contributions to defined contribution plans and defined benefit pension plans apply). In addition, in applying the overall deduction limit, the amount necessary to meet the minimum funding requirement with respect to a single-employer defined benefit pension plan that is not covered by the PBGC insurance program is treated as not less than the plan's funding shortfall (as determined under the minimum funding rules).

Multiemployer defined benefit pension plans

General deduction limit

Under the bill, for taxable years beginning after 2005, in the case of contributions to a multiemployer defined benefit pension plan, the maximum deductible amount is not less than the excess (if any) of (1) 140 percent of the plan's current liability, over (2) the value of plan assets.

Overall deduction limit

Under the bill, for taxable years beginning after December 31, 2005, in applying the overall deduction limit to contributions to one or more defined benefit pension plans and one or more defined contribution plans, multiemployer plans are not taken into account. Thus, the deduction for contributions to a defined benefit pension plan or a defined contribution plan is not affected by the overall deduction limit merely because employees are covered by both plans if either plan is a multiemployer plan (i.e., the separate deduction limits for contributions to defined contribution plans and defined benefit pension plans apply).

---

[163] Expected increases in the limitations on benefits under section 415, however, may not be taken into account.

Effective Date

The effective dates of the provisions regarding deductions are described above under each provision.

2. Updating deduction rules for combination of plans (secs. 404(a)(7) and 4972 of the Code)

Present Law

Employer contributions to qualified retirement plans are deductible subject to certain limits.[164] In general, the deduction limit depends on the kind of plan.[165]

If an employer sponsors one or more defined benefit pension plans and one or more defined contribution plans that cover at least one of the same employees, an overall deduction limit applies to the total contributions to all plans for a plan year. The overall deduction limit is the greater of (1) 25 percent of compensation, or (2) the amount necessary to meet the minimum funding requirements of the defined benefit plan for the year, but not less than the amount of the plan's unfunded current liability.

Under EGTRRA, elective deferrals are not subject to the limits on deductions and are not taken into account in applying the limits to other employer contributions. The combined deduction limit of 25 percent of compensation for defined benefit and defined contribution plans does not apply if the only amounts contributed to the defined contribution plan are elective deferrals.[166]

Subject to certain exceptions, an employer that makes nondeductible contributions to a plan is subject to an excise tax equal to 10 percent of the amount of the nondeductible contributions for the year. Certain contributions to a defined contribution plan that are nondeductible solely because of the overall deduction limit are disregarded in determining the amount of nondeductible contributions for purposes of the excise tax. Contributions that are disregarded are the greater of (1) the amount of contributions not in excess of six percent of the compensation of the employees covered by the defined contribution plan, or (2) the amount of matching contributions.

Explanation of Provision

Under the bill, the overall limit on employer deductions for contributions to combinations of defined benefit and defined contribution plans applies to contributions to one or more defined contribution plans only to the extent that such contributions exceed six percent of compensation

---

[164] Code sec. 404.

[165] See the discussion under A., above, for a description of the deduction rules for defined benefit and defined contribution plans.

[166] Under the general EGTRRA sunset, this rule expires for plan years beginning after 2010.

otherwise paid or accrued during the taxable year to the beneficiaries under the plans. As under present law, for purposes of determining the excise tax on nondeductible contributions, matching contributions to a defined contribution plan that are nondeductible solely because of the overall deduction limit are disregarded.

Effective Date

The provision is effective for contributions for taxable years beginning after December 31, 2005.

B. Certain Pension Provisions Made Permanent

1. Permanency of EGTRRA pension and IRA provisions (Title X of EGTRRA)

Present Law

In general

The Economic Growth and Tax Relief Reconciliation Act of 2001 ("EGTRRA") made a number of changes to the Federal tax laws, including a variety of provisions relating to pensions and individual retirement arrangements ("IRAs"). However, in order to comply with reconciliation procedures under the Congressional Budget Act of 1974 (e.g., section 313 of the Budget Act, under which a point of order may be lodged in the Senate), EGTRRA included a "sunset" provision, pursuant to which the provisions of EGTRRA expire at the end of 2010. Specifically, EGTRRA's provisions do not apply for taxable, plan, or limitation years beginning after December 31, 2010, or to estates of decedents dying after, or gifts or generation-skipping transfers made after, December 31, 2010. EGTRRA provides that, as of the effective date of the sunset, both the Internal Revenue Code and the Employee Retirement Income Security Act of 1974 ("ERISA") will be applied as though EGTRRA had never been enacted.

Certain provisions contained in EGTRRA expire before the general sunset date of 2010.[167]

List of affected provisions

Following is a list of the provisions affected by the general EGTRRA sunset.

Individual retirement arrangements ("IRAs")

- Increases in the IRA contribution limits, including the ability to make catch-up contributions (secs. 219, 408, and 408A of the Code and sec. 601 of EGTRRA); and

- Rules relating to deemed IRAs under employer plans (sec. 408(q) of the Code and sec. 602 of EGTRRA).

Expanding coverage

- Increases in the limits on contributions, benefits, and compensation under qualified retirement plans, tax-sheltered annuities, and eligible deferred compensation plans (secs. 401(a)(17), 402(g), 408(p), 414(v), 415, and 457 of the Code and sec. 611 of EGTRRA);

- Application of prohibited transaction rules to plan loans of S corporation owners, partners, and sole proprietors (sec. 4975 of the Code and sec. 612 of EGTRRA);

---

[167] The saver's credit (sec. 25B) expires at the end of 2006. Another provision of the bill makes the saver's credit permanent.

- Modification of the top-heavy rules (sec. 416 of the Code and sec. 613 of EGTRRA);
- Elective deferrals not taken into account for purposes of deduction limits (sec. 404 of the Code and sec. 614 of EGTRRA);
- Repeal of coordination requirements for deferred compensation plans of state and local governments and tax-exempt organizations (sec. 457 of the Code and sec. 615 of EGTRRA);
- Modifications to deduction limits (sec. 404 of the Code and sec. 616 of EGTRRA);
- Option to treat elective deferrals as after-tax Roth contributions (sec. 402A of the Code and sec. 617 of EGTRRA);
- Credit for pension plan start-up costs (sec. 45E of the Code and sec. 619 of EGTRRA); and
- Certain nonresident aliens excluded in applying minimum coverage requirements (secs. 410(b)(3) and 861(a)(3) of the Code).

Enhancing fairness

- Catch-up contributions for individuals age 50 and older (sec. 414 of the Code and sec. 631 of EGTRRA);
- Equitable treatment for contributions of employees to defined contribution plans (secs. 403(b), 415, and 457 of the Code and sec. 632 of EGTRRA);
- Faster vesting of employer matching contributions (sec. 411 of the Code and sec. 633 of EGTRRA);
- Modifications to minimum distribution rules (sec. 401(a)(9) of the Code and sec. 634 of EGTRRA);
- Clarification of tax treatment of division of section 457 plan benefits upon divorce (secs. 414(p) and 457 of the Code and sec. 635 of EGTRRA);
- Provisions relating to hardship withdrawals (secs. 401(k) and 402 of the Code and sec. 636 of EGTRRA); and
- Waiver of tax on nondeductible contributions for domestic and similar workers (sec. 4972(c)(6) of the Code and sec. 637 of EGTRRA).

Increasing portability

- Rollovers of retirement plan and IRA distributions (secs. 401, 402, 403(b), 408, 457, and 3405 of the Code and secs. 641-644 of EGTRRA);
- Treatment of forms of distribution (sec. 411(d)(6) of the Code and sec. 645 of EGTRRA);
- Rationalization of restrictions on distributions (secs. 401(k), 403(b), and 457 of the Code and sec. 646 of EGTRRA);

- Purchase of service credit under governmental pension plans (secs. 403(b) and 457 of the Code and sec. 647 of EGTRRA):

- Employers may disregard rollovers for purposes of cash-out rules (sec. 411(a)(11) of the Code and sec. 648 of EGTRRA); and

- Minimum distribution and inclusion requirements for section 457 plans (sec. 457 of the Code and sec. 649 of EGTRRA).

<u>Strengthening pension security and enforcement</u>

- Phase in repeal of 160 percent of current liability funding limit; maximum deduction rules (secs. 404(a)(1), 412(c)(7), and 4972(c) of the Code and secs. 651-652 of EGTRRA);

- Excise tax relief for sound pension funding (sec. 4972 of the Code and sec. 653 of EGTRRA);

- Modifications to section 415 limits for multiemployer plans (sec. 415 of the Code and sec. 654 of EGTRRA);

- Investment of employee contributions in 401(k) plans (sec. 655 of EGTRRA);

- Prohibited allocations of stock in an S corporation ESOP (secs. 409 and 4979A of the Code and sec. 656 of EGTRRA);

- Automatic rollovers of certain mandatory distributions (secs. 401(a)(31) and 402(f)(1) of the Code and sec. 657 of EGTRRA);

- Clarification of treatment of contributions to a multiemployer plan (sec. 446 of the Code and sec. 658 of EGTRRA); and

- Treatment of plan amendments reducing future benefit accruals (sec. 4980F of the Code and sec. 659 of EGTRRA).

<u>Reducing regulatory burdens</u>

- Modification of timing of plan valuations (sec. 412 of the Code and sec. 661 of EGTRRA);

- ESOP dividends may be reinvested without loss of dividend deduction (sec. 404 of the Code and sec. 662 of EGTRRA);

- Repeal transition rule relating to certain highly compensated employees (sec. 663 of EGTRRA);

- Treatment of employees of tax-exempt entities for purposes of nondiscrimination rules (secs. 410, 401(k), and 401(m) of the Code and sec. 664 of EGTRRA);

- Treatment of employer-provided retirement advice (sec. 132 of the Code and sec. 665 of EGTRRA); and

- Repeal of the multiple use test (sec. 401(m) of the Code and sec. 666 of EGTRRA).

The provision repeals the sunset provision of EGTRRA as applied to the provisions relating to pensions and IRAs.

Effective Date

The provision is effective on the date of enactment.

2. Saver's credit made permanent (sec. 25B of the Code)

Present Law

Present law provides a temporary nonrefundable tax credit for eligible taxpayers for qualified retirement savings contributions. The maximum annual contribution eligible for the credit is $2,000. The credit rate depends on the adjusted gross income ("AGI") of the taxpayer. Joint returns with AGI of $50,000 or less, head of household returns of $37,500 or less, and single returns of $25,000 or less are eligible for the credit. The AGI limits applicable to single taxpayers apply to married taxpayers filing separate returns. The credit is in addition to any deduction or exclusion that would otherwise apply with respect to the contribution. The credit offsets minimum tax liability as well as regular tax liability. The credit is available to individuals who are 18 or older, other than individuals who are full-time students or claimed as a dependent on another taxpayer's return.

The credit is available with respect to: (1) elective deferrals to a qualified cash or deferred arrangement (a "section 401(k) plan"), a tax-sheltered annuity (a "section 403(b)" annuity), an eligible deferred compensation arrangement of a State or local government (a "section 457 plan"), a SIMPLE, or a simplified employee pension ("SEP"); (2) contributions to a traditional or Roth IRA; and (3) voluntary after-tax employee contributions to a tax-sheltered annuity or qualified retirement plan.

The amount of any contribution eligible for the credit is reduced by distributions received by the taxpayer (or by the taxpayer's spouse if the taxpayer filed a joint return with the spouse) from any plan or IRA to which eligible contributions can be made during the taxable year for which the credit is claimed, the two taxable years prior to the year the credit is claimed, and during the period after the end of the taxable year for which the credit is claimed and prior to the due date for filing the taxpayer's return for the year. Distributions that are rolled over to another retirement plan do not affect the credit.

The credit rates based on AGI are provided in Table 1, below.

Table 1.–Credit Rates for Saver's Credit

Joint Filers	Heads of Households	All Other Filers	Credit Rate
$0 – $30,000	$0 – $22,500	$0 – $15,000	50 percent
$30,001 – $32,500	$22,501 – $24,375	$15,001 – $16,250	20 percent
$32,501 – $50,000	$24,376 – $37,500	$16,251 – $25,000	10 percent
Over $50,000	Over $37,500	Over $25,000	0 percent

The credit does not apply to taxable years beginning after December 31, 2006.

Explanation of Provision

The provision makes the saver's credit permanent.

The provision also provides that an individual may direct that the amount of any refund attributable to the saver's credit be directly deposited by the Federal government into an applicable retirement plan, meaning an IRA, qualified retirement plan, section 403(b) annuity, or governmental section 457 plan designated by the individual (if the plan or other arrangement agrees to accept such direct deposits). In the case of a joint return, each spouse is entitled to designate an applicable retirement plan with respect to payments attributable to such spouse. The provision does not change the rules relating to the tax treatment of contributions to such plans or other arrangements.

Effective Date

The extension of the saver's credit is effective on enactment. The provision relating to direct deposit of refunds relating to the saver's credit is effective for taxable years beginning after December 31, 2006. (In addition, another provision of bill, described below, provides for indexing of the income limits on the saver's credit.)

C. Improvements in Portability, Distribution, and Contribution Rules

1. Purchase of permissive service credit (secs. 403(b)(13), 415(n)(3), and 457(e)(17) of the Code)

<u>Present Law</u>

In general

Present law imposes limits on contributions and benefits under qualified plans.[168] The limits on contributions and benefits under qualified plans are based on the type of plan. Under a defined benefit plan, the maximum annual benefit payable at retirement is generally the lesser of (1) a certain dollar amount ($175,000 for 2006) or (2) 100 percent of the participant's average compensation for his or her high three years.

A qualified retirement plan maintained by a State or local government employer may provide that a participant may make after-tax employee contributions in order to purchase permissive service credit, subject to certain limits.[169]

In the case of any repayment of contributions and earnings to a governmental plan with respect to an amount previously refunded upon a forfeiture of service credit under the plan (or another plan maintained by a State or local government employer within the same State), any such repayment is not taken into account for purposes of the section 415 limits on contributions and benefits. Also, service credit obtained as a result of such a repayment is not considered permissive service credit for purposes of the section 415 limits.

Permissive service credit

Definition of permissive service credit

Permissive service credit means credit for a period of service recognized by the governmental plan which the participant has not received under the plan and which the employee receives only if the employee voluntarily contributes to the plan an amount (as determined by the plan) that does not exceed the amount necessary to fund the benefit attributable to the period of service and that is in addition to the regular employee contributions, if any, under the plan.

The IRS has ruled that credit is not permissive service credit where it is purchased to provide enhanced retirement benefits for a period of service already credited under the plan, as the enhanced benefit is treated as credit for service already received.[170]

---

[168] Sec. 415.

[169] Sec. 415(n)(3).

[170] Priv. Ltr. Rul. 200229051 (April 26, 2002).

<u>Nonqualified service</u>

Service credit is not permissive service credit if more than five years of permissive service credit is purchased for nonqualified service or if nonqualified service is taken into account for an employee who has less than five years of participation under the plan. Nonqualified service is service other than service (1) as a Federal, State or local government employee, (2) as an employee of an association representing Federal, State or local government employees, (3) as an employee of an educational institution which provides elementary or secondary education, as determined under State law, or (4) for military service. Service under (1), (2) and (3) is nonqualified service if it enables a participant to receive a retirement benefit for the same service under more than one plan.

Trustee-to-trustee transfers to purchase permissive service credit

Under EGTRRA, a participant is not required to include in gross income a direct trustee-to-trustee transfer to a governmental defined benefit plan from a section 403(b) annuity or a section 457 plan if the transferred amount is used (1) to purchase permissive service credit under the plan, or (2) to repay contributions and earnings with respect to an amount previously refunded under a forfeiture of service credit under the plan (or another plan maintained by a State or local government employer within the same State).[171]

Explanation of Provision

Permissive service credit

The provision modifies the definition of permissive service credit by providing that permissive service credit means service credit which relates to benefits to which the participant is not otherwise entitled under such governmental plan, rather than service credit which such participant has not received under the plan. Credit qualifies as permissive service credit if it is purchased to provide an increased benefit for a period of service already credited under the plan (e.g., if a lower level of benefit is converted to a higher benefit level otherwise offered under the same plan) as long as it relates to benefits to which the participant is not otherwise entitled.

The provision allows participants to purchase credit for periods regardless of whether service is performed, subject to the limits on nonqualified service.

Under the provision, service as an employee of an educational organization providing elementary or secondary education can be determined under the law of the jurisdiction in which the service was performed. Thus, for example, permissive service credit can be granted for time spent teaching outside of the United States without being considered nonqualified service credit.

---

[171] Secs. 403(b)(13) and 457(e)(17).

170

Trustee-to-trustee transfers to purchase permissive service credit

The provision provides that the limits regarding nonqualified service are not applicable in determining whether a trustee-to-trustee transfer from a section 403(b) annuity or a section 457 plan to a governmental defined benefit plan is for the purchase of permissive service credit. Thus, failure of the transferee plan to satisfy the limits does not cause the transferred amounts to be included in the participant's income. As under present law, the transferee plan must satisfy the limits in providing permissive service credit as a result of the transfer.

The provision provides that trustee-to-trustee transfers under sections 457(e)(17) and 403(b)(13) may be made regardless of whether the transfer is made between plans maintained by the same employer. The provision also provides that amounts transferred from a section 403(b) annuity or a section 457 plan to a governmental defined benefit plan to purchase permissive service credit are subject to the distribution rules applicable under the Internal Revenue Code to the defined benefit plan.

Effective Date

The provision is generally effective as if included in the amendments made by section 1526 of the Taxpayer Relief Act of 1997, except that the provision regarding trustee-to-trustee transfers is effective as if included in the amendments made by section 647 of the Economic Growth and Tax Relief Reconciliation Act of 2001.

2. Rollover of after-tax amounts in annuity contracts (sec. 402(c)(2) of the Code)

Present Law

Employee after-tax contributions may be rolled over from a tax-qualified retirement plan into another tax-qualified retirement plan, if the plan to which the rollover is made is a defined contribution plan, the rollover is accomplished through a direct rollover, and the plan to which the rollover is made provides for separate accounting for such contributions (and earnings thereon). After-tax contributions can also be rolled over from a tax-sheltered annuity (a "section 403(b) annuity") to another tax-sheltered annuity if the rollover is a direct rollover, and the annuity to which the rollover is made provides for separate accounting for such contributions (and earnings thereon). After-tax contributions may also be rolled over to an IRA. If the rollover is to an IRA, the rollover need not be a direct rollover and the IRA owner has the responsibility to keep track of the amount of after-tax contributions.[172]

Explanation of Provision

The provision allows after-tax contributions to be rolled over from a qualified retirement plan to another qualified retirement plan (either a defined contribution or a defined benefit plan) or to a tax-sheltered annuity. As under present law, the rollover must be a direct rollover, and

---

[172] Sec. 402(c)(2); IRS Notice 2002-3, 2002-2 I.R.B. 289.

the plan to which the rollover is made must separately account for after-tax contributions (and earnings thereon).

Effective Date

The provision is effective for taxable years beginning after December 31, 2006.

3. Application of minimum distribution rules to governmental plans

Present Law

Minimum distribution rules apply to tax-favored retirement arrangements, including governmental plans. In general, under these rules, distribution of minimum benefits must begin no later than the required beginning date. Minimum distribution rules also apply to benefits payable with respect to a plan participant who has died. Failure to comply with the minimum distribution rules results in an excise tax imposed on the plan participant equal to 50 percent of the required minimum distribution not distributed for the year. The excise tax may be waived in certain cases.

In the case of distributions prior to the death of the plan participant, the minimum distribution rules are satisfied if either (1) the participant's entire interest in the plan is distributed by the required beginning date, or (2) the participant's interest in the plan is to be distributed (in accordance with regulations) beginning not later than the required beginning date, over a permissible period. The permissible periods are (1) the life of the participant, (2) the lives of the participant and a designated beneficiary, (3) the life expectancy of the participant, or (4) the joint life and last survivor expectancy of the participant and a designated beneficiary. In calculating minimum required distributions from account-type arrangements (e.g., a defined contribution plan or an individual retirement arrangement), life expectancies of the participant and the participant's spouse generally may be recomputed annually.

The required beginning date generally is April 1 of the calendar year following the later of (1) the calendar year in which the participant attains age 70½ or (2) the calendar year in which the participant retires.

The minimum distribution rules also apply to distributions to beneficiaries of deceased participants. In general, if the participant dies after minimum distributions have begun, the remaining interest must be distributed at least as rapidly as under the minimum distribution method being used as of the date of death. If the participant dies before minimum distributions have begun, then the entire remaining interest must generally be distributed within five years of the participant's death. The five-year rule does not apply if distributions begin within one year of the participant's death and are payable over the life of a designated beneficiary or over the life expectancy of a designated beneficiary. A surviving spouse beneficiary is not required to begin distributions until the date the deceased participant would have attained age 70½. In addition, if the surviving spouse makes a rollover from the plan into a plan or IRA of his or her own, the minimum distribution rules apply separately to the surviving spouse.

Explanation of Provision

The provision directs the Secretary of the Treasury to issue regulations under which a governmental plan is treated as complying with the minimum distribution requirements, for all years to which such requirements apply, if the plan complies with a reasonable, good faith interpretation of the statutory requirements. It is intended that the regulations apply for periods before the date of enactment.

Effective Date

The provision is effective on the date of enactment.

4. Allow direct rollovers from retirement plans to Roth IRAs (sec. 408A(e) of the Code)

Present Law

IRAs in general

There are two general types of individual retirement arrangements ("IRAs"): traditional IRAs, to which both deductible and nondeductible contributions may be made, and Roth IRAs.

Traditional IRAs

An individual may make deductible contributions to an IRA up to the lesser of a dollar limit (generally $4,000 for 2006)[173] or the individual's compensation if neither the individual nor the individual's spouse is an active participant in an employer-sponsored retirement plan.[174] If the individual (or the individual's spouse) is an active participant in an employer-sponsored retirement plan, the deduction limit is phased out for taxpayers with adjusted gross income ("AGI") over certain levels for the taxable year. A different, higher, income phaseout applies in the case of an individual who is not an active participant in an employer sponsored plan but whose spouse is.

To the extent an individual cannot or does not make deductible contributions to an IRA or contributions to a Roth IRA, the individual may make nondeductible contributions to a traditional IRA.

Amounts held in a traditional IRA are includible in income when withdrawn (except to the extent the withdrawal is a return of nondeductible contributions). Includible amounts withdrawn prior to attainment of age 59½ are subject to an additional 10-percent early

---

[173] The dollar limit is scheduled to increase until it is $5,000 in 2008-2010. Individuals age 50 and older may make additional, catch-up contributions.

[174] In the case of a married couple, deductible IRA contributions of up to the dollar limit can be made for each spouse (including, for example, a homemaker who does not work outside the home), if the combined compensation of both spouses is at least equal to the contributed amount.

withdrawal tax, unless the withdrawal is due to death or disability, is made in the form of certain periodic payments, or is used for certain specified purposes.

Roth IRAs

Individuals with AGI below certain levels may make nondeductible contributions to a Roth IRA. The maximum annual contributions that can be made to all of an individuals IRAs (both traditional and Roth) cannot exceed the maximum deductible IRA contribution limit. The maximum annual contribution that can be made to a Roth IRA is phased out for taxpayers with income above certain levels.

Amounts held in a Roth IRA that are withdrawn as a qualified distribution are not includible in income, or subject to the additional 10-percent tax on early withdrawals. A qualified distribution is a distribution that (1) is made after the five-taxable year period beginning with the first taxable year for which the individual made a contribution to a Roth IRA, and (2) which is made after attainment of age 59½, on account of death or disability, or is made for first-time homebuyer expenses of up to $10,000.

Distributions from a Roth IRA that are not qualified distributions are includible in income to the extent attributable to earnings, and subject to the 10-percent early withdrawal tax (unless an exception applies). The same exceptions to the early withdrawal tax that apply to IRAs apply to Roth IRAs.

Rollover contributions

If certain requirements are satisfied, a participant in a tax-qualified retirement plan, a tax-sheltered annuity (sec. 403(b)), or a governmental section 457 plan may roll over distributions from the plan or annuity into a traditional IRA. Distributions from such plans may not be rolled over into a Roth IRA.

Taxpayers with modified AGI of $100,000 or less generally may roll over amounts in a traditional IRA into a Roth IRA. The amount rolled over is includible in income as if a withdrawal had been made, except that the 10-percent early withdrawal tax does not apply. Married taxpayers who file separate returns cannot roll over amounts in a traditional IRA into a Roth IRA. Amounts that have been distributed from a tax-qualified retirement plan, a tax-sheltered annuity, or a governmental section 457 plan may be rolled over into a traditional IRA, and then rolled over from the traditional IRA into a Roth IRA.

Explanation of Provision

The provision allows distributions from tax-qualified retirement plans, tax-sheltered annuities, and governmental 457 plans to be rolled over directly from such plan into a Roth IRA, subject to the present law rules that apply to rollovers from a traditional IRA into a Roth IRA. For example, a rollover from a tax-qualified retirement plan into a Roth IRA is includible in gross income (except to the extent it represents a return of after-tax contributions), and the 10-percent early distribution tax does not apply. Similarly, an individual with AGI of $100,000 or more could not roll over amounts from a tax-qualified retirement plan directly into a Roth IRA.

Effective Date

The provision is effective for distributions made after December 31, 2007.

5. Eligibility for participation in eligible deferred compensation plans (sec. 457 of the Code)

Present Law

A section 457 plan is an eligible deferred compensation plan of a State or local government or tax-exempt employer that meets certain requirements. In some cases, different rules apply under section 457 to governmental plans and plans of tax-exempt employers.

Amounts deferred under an eligible deferred compensation plan of a non-governmental tax-exempt organization are includible in gross income for the year in which amounts are paid or made available. Under present law, if the amount payable to a participant does not exceed $5,000, a plan may allow a distribution up to $5,000 without such amount being treated as made available if the distribution can be made only if no amount has been deferred under the plan by the participant during the two-year period ending on the date of the distribution and there has been no prior distribution under the plan. Prior to the Small Business Job Protection Act of 1996, under former section 457(e)(9), benefits were not treated as made available because a participant could elect to receive a lump sum payable after separation from service and within 60 days of the election if (1) the total amount payable under the plan did not exceed $3,500 and (2) no additional amounts could be deferred under the plan.

Explanation of Provision

Under the provision, an individual is not precluded from participating in an eligible deferred compensation plan by reason of having received a distribution under section 457(e)(9) as in effect before the Small Business Job Protection Act of 1996.

Effective Date

The provision is effective on the date of enactment.

6. Modifications of rules governing hardships and unforeseen financial emergencies

Present Law

Distributions from a qualified cash or deferred arrangement (a "section 401(k) plan"), a tax-shelter annuity, section 457 plan, or nonqualified deferred compensation plan subject to section 409A may not be made prior to the occurrence of one or more specified events. In the case of a section 401(k) plan or tax-sheltered annuity, one event upon which distribution is permitted is the case of a hardship. Similarly, distributions from section 457 plans and nonqualified deferred compensation plans subject to section 409A may be made in the case of an unforeseeable emergency. Under regulations, a hardship or unforeseeable emergency includes a hardship or unforeseeable emergency of a participant's spouse or dependent.

175

Explanation of Provision

The provision directs the Secretary of the Treasury to revise the rules for determining whether a participant has had a hardship or unforeseeable emergency to provide that if an event would constitute a hardship or unforeseeable emergency under the plan if it occurred with respect to the participant's spouse or dependent, such event shall, to the extent permitted under the plan, constitute a hardship or unforeseeable emergency if it occurs with respect to a beneficiary under the plan. The provision requires that the revised rules be issued within 180 days after the date of enactment.

Effective Date

The provision is effective on the date of enactment.

7. Treatment of distributions to individuals called to active duty for at least 179 days (sec. 72(t) of the Code)

Present Law

Under present law, a taxpayer who receives a distribution from a qualified retirement plan prior to age 59½, death, or disability generally is subject to a 10-percent early withdrawal tax on the amount includible in income, unless an exception to the tax applies. Among other exceptions, the early distribution tax does not apply to distributions made to an employee who separates from service after age 55, or to distributions that are part of a series of substantially equal periodic payments made for the life (or life expectancy) of the employee or the joint lives (or life expectancies) of the employee and his or her beneficiary.

Certain amounts held in a qualified cash or deferred arrangement (a "401(k) plan") or in a tax-sheltered annuity (a "403(b) annuity") may not be distributed before severance from employment, age 59½, death, disability, or financial hardship of the employee.

Explanation of Provision

Under the provision, the 10-percent early withdrawal tax does not apply to a qualified reservist distribution. A qualified reservist distribution is a distribution (1) from an IRA or attributable to elective deferrals under a 401(k) plan, 403(b) annuity, or certain similar arrangements, (2) made to an individual who (by reason of being a member of a reserve component as defined in section 101 of title 37 of the U.S. Code) was ordered or called to active duty for a period in excess of 179 days or for an indefinite period, and (3) that is made during the period beginning on the date of such order or call to duty and ending at the close of the active duty period. A 401(k) plan or 403(b) annuity does not violate the distribution restrictions applicable to such plans by reason of making a qualified reservist distribution.

An individual who receives a qualified reservist distribution may, at any time during the two-year period beginning on the day after the end of the active duty period, make one or more contributions to an IRA of such individual in an aggregate amount not to exceed the amount of such distribution. The dollar limitations otherwise applicable to contributions to IRAs do not

176

apply to any contribution made pursuant to the provision. No deduction is allowed for any contribution made under the provision.

This provision applies to individuals ordered or called to active duty after September 11, 2001, and before December 31, 2007. The two-year period for making recontributions of qualified reservist distributions does not end before the date that is two years after the date of enactment.

Effective Date

The provision applies to distributions after September 11, 2001. If refund or credit of any overpayment of tax resulting from the provision would be prevented at any time before the close of the one-year period beginning on the date of the enactment by the operation of any law or rule of law (including res judicata), such refund or credit may nevertheless be made or allowed if claim therefor is filed before the close of such period.

8. Inapplicability of 10-percent additional tax on early distributions of pension plans of public safety employees (sec. 72(t) of the Code)

Present Law

Under present law, a taxpayer who receives a distribution from a qualified retirement plan prior to age 59½, death, or disability generally is subject to a 10-percent early withdrawal tax on the amount includible in income, unless an exception to the tax applies. Among other exceptions, the early distribution tax does not apply to distributions made to an employee who separates from service after age 55, or to distributions that are part of a series of substantially equal periodic payments made for the life (or life expectancy) of the employee or the joint lives (or life expectancies) of the employee and his or her beneficiary.

Explanation of Provision

Under the provision, the 10-percent early withdrawal tax does not apply to distributions from a governmental defined benefit pension plan to a qualified public safety employee who separates from service after age 50. A qualified public safety employee is an employee of a State or political subdivision of a State if the employee provides police protection, firefighting services, or emergency medical services for any area within the jurisdiction of such State or political subdivision.

Effective Date

The provision is effective for distributions made after the date of enactment.

9. Rollovers by nonspouse beneficiaries (sec. 402 of the Code)

Present Law

Tax-free rollovers

Under present law, a distribution from a qualified retirement plan, a tax-sheltered annuity ("section 403(b) annuity"), an eligible deferred compensation plan of a State or local government employer (a "governmental section 457 plan"), or an individual retirement arrangement (an "IRA") generally is included in income for the year distributed. However, eligible rollover distributions may be rolled over tax free within 60 days to another plan, annuity, or IRA.[175]

In general, an eligible rollover distribution includes any distribution to the plan participant or IRA owner other than certain periodic distributions, minimum required distributions, and distributions made on account of hardship.[176] Distributions to a participant from a qualified retirement plan, a tax-sheltered annuity, or a governmental section 457 plan generally can be rolled over to any of such plans or an IRA.[177] Similarly, distributions from an IRA to the IRA owner generally are permitted to be rolled over into a qualified retirement plan, a tax-sheltered annuity, a governmental section 457 plan, or another IRA.

Similar rollovers are permitted in the case of a distribution to the surviving spouse of the plan participant or IRA owner, but not to other persons.

If an individual inherits an IRA from the individual's deceased spouse, the IRA may be treated as the IRA of the surviving spouse. This treatment does not apply to IRAs inherited from someone other than the deceased spouse. In such cases, the IRA is not treated as the IRA of the beneficiary. Thus, for example, the beneficiary may not make contributions to the IRA and cannot roll over any amounts out of the inherited IRA. Like the original IRA owner, no amount is generally included in income until distributions are made from the IRA. Distributions from the inherited IRA must be made under the rules that apply to distributions to beneficiaries, as described below.

Minimum distribution rules

Minimum distribution rules apply to tax-favored retirement arrangements. In the case of distributions prior to the death of the participant, distributions generally must begin by the April

---

[175] The IRS has the authority to waive the 60-day requirement if failure to waive the requirement would be against equity or good conscience, including cases of casualty, disaster, or other events beyond the reasonable control of the individual. Sec. 402(c)(3)(B).

[176] Sec. 402(c)(4). Certain other distributions also are not eligible rollover distributions, e.g., corrective distributions of elective deferrals in excess of the elective deferral limits and loans that are treated as deemed distributions.

[177] Some restrictions or special rules may apply to certain distributions. For example, after-tax amounts distributed from a plan can be rolled over only to a plan of the same type or to an IRA.

1 of the calendar year following the later of the calendar year in which the participant (1) attains age 70½ or (2) retires.[178] The minimum distribution rules also apply to distributions following the death of the participant. If minimum distributions have begun prior to the participant's death, the remaining interest generally must be distributed at least as rapidly as under the minimum distribution method being used prior to the date of death. If the participant dies before minimum distributions have begun, then either (1) the entire remaining interest must be distributed within five years of the death, or (2) distributions must begin within one year of the death over the life (or life expectancy) of the designated beneficiary. A beneficiary who is the surviving spouse of the participant is not required to begin distributions until the date the deceased participant would have attained age 70½. Alternatively, if the surviving spouse makes a rollover from the plan into a plan or IRA of his or her own, minimum distributions generally would not need to begin until the surviving spouse attains age 70½.

Explanation of Provision

The provision provides that benefits of a beneficiary other than a surviving spouse may be transferred directly to an IRA. The IRA is treated as an inherited IRA of the nonspouse beneficiary. Thus, for example, distributions from the inherited IRA are subject to the distribution rules applicable to beneficiaries. The provision applies to amounts payable to a beneficiary under a qualified retirement plan, governmental section 457 plan, or a tax-sheltered annuity. To the extent provided by the Secretary, the provision applies to benefits payable to a trust maintained for a designated beneficiary to the same extent it applies to the beneficiary.

Effective Date

The provision is effective for distributions after December 31, 2006.

10. Direct deposit of tax refunds in an IRA

Present Law

Under current IRS procedures, a taxpayer may direct that his or her tax refund be deposited into a checking or savings account with a bank or other financial institution (such as a mutual fund, brokerage firm, or credit union) rather than having the refund sent to the taxpayer in the form of a check.

Explanation of Provision

The Secretary is directed to develop forms under which all or a portion of a taxpayer's refund may be deposited in an IRA of the taxpayer (or the spouse of the taxpayer in the case of a joint return). The provision does not modify the rules relating to IRAs, including the rules relating to timing and deductibility of contributions.

---

[178] In the case of five-percent owners and distributions from an IRA, distributions must begin by the April 1 of the calendar year following the year in which the individual attains age 70½.

Effective Date

The form required by the provision is to be available for taxable years beginning after December 31, 2006.

11. Additional IRA contributions for certain employees (secs. 25B and 219 of the Code)

Present Law

Under present law, favored tax treatment applies to qualified retirement plans maintained by employers and to individual retirement arrangements ("IRAs").

Qualified defined contribution plans may permit both employees and employers to make contributions to the plan. Under a qualified cash or deferred arrangement (commonly referred to as a "section 401(k) plan"), employees may elect to make pretax contributions to a plan, referred to as elective deferrals. Employees may also be permitted to make after-tax contributions to a plan. In addition, a plan may provide for employer nonelective contributions or matching contributions. Nonelective contributions are employer contributions that are made without regard to whether the employee makes elective deferrals or after-tax contributions. Matching contributions are employer contributions that are made only if the employee makes elective deferrals or after-tax contributions. Matching contributions are sometimes made in the form of employer stock.

Under present law, an individual may generally make contributions to an IRA for a taxable year up to the lesser of a certain dollar amount or the individual's compensation. The maximum annual dollar limit on IRA contributions to IRAs is $4,000 for 2005-2007 and $5,000 for 2008, with indexing thereafter. Individuals who have attained age 50 may make additional "catch-up" contributions to an IRA for a taxable year of up to $500 for 2005 and $1,000 for 2006 and thereafter.[179]

Present law provides a temporary nonrefundable tax credit for eligible taxpayers for qualified retirement savings contributions ("saver's" credit). The maximum annual contribution eligible for the credit is $2,000. The credit rate depends on the adjusted gross income ("AGI") of the taxpayer. Taxpayers filing joint returns with AGI of $50,000 or less, head of household returns of $37,500 or less, and single returns of $25,000 or less are eligible for the credit. The AGI limits applicable to single taxpayers apply to married taxpayers filing separate returns. The credit is in addition to any deduction or exclusion that would otherwise apply with respect to the contribution. The credit offsets minimum tax liability as well as regular tax liability. The credit is available to individuals who are 18 or over, other than individuals who are full-time students or claimed as a dependent on another taxpayer's return. The credit is available with respect to contributions to various types of retirement savings arrangements, including contributions to a

---

[179] These IRA limits were enacted as part of the Economic Growth and Tax Relief Reconciliation Act of 2001 ("EGTRRA"), Pub. L. No. 107-16. The provisions of EGTRRA generally do not apply for years beginning after December 31, 2010.

traditional or Roth IRA. The saver's credit does not apply to taxable years beginning after December 31, 2006.

Explanation of Provision

Under the provision, an applicable individual may elect to make additional IRA contributions of up to $3,000 per year for 2006-2009. An applicable individual must have been a participant in a section 401(k) plan under which the employer matched at least 50 percent of the employee's contributions to the plan with stock of the employer. In addition, in a taxable year preceding the taxable year of an additional contribution: (1) the employer (or any controlling corporation of the employer) must have been a debtor in a bankruptcy case, and (2) the employer or any other person must have been subject to an indictment or conviction resulting from business transactions related to the bankruptcy. The individual must also have been a participant in the section 401(k) plan on the date six months before the bankruptcy case was filed. An applicable individual who elects to make these additional IRA contributions is not permitted to make IRA catch-up contributions that apply to individuals age 50 and older.

Effective Date

The provision is effective for taxable years beginning after December 31, 2006, and before January 1, 2010.

12. Special rule for computing high-three average compensation for benefit limitation purposes (sec. 415(b)(3) of the Code)

Present Law

Annual benefits payable to a participant under a defined benefit pension plan generally may not exceed the lesser of (1) 100 percent of average compensation for the participant's high three years, or (2) $175,000 (for 2006). The dollar limit is reduced proportionately for individuals with less than 10 years of participation in the plan. The compensation limit is reduced proportionately for individuals with less than 10 years of service.

For purposes of determining average compensation for a participant's high three years, the high three years are the period of consecutive calendar years (not more than three) during which the participant was both an active participant in the plan and had the greatest aggregate compensation from the employer.

Explanation of Provision

Under the bill, for purposes of determining average compensation for a participant's high three years, the high three years are the period of consecutive calendar years (not more than three) during which the participant had the greatest aggregate compensation from the employer.

Effective Date

The provision is effective for years beginning after December 31, 2005.

13. Inflation indexing of gross income limitations on certain retirement savings incentives (secs. 25A and 219 of the Code)

Present Law

Saver's credit

Present law provides a temporary nonrefundable tax credit for eligible taxpayers for qualified retirement savings contributions. The maximum annual contribution eligible for the credit is $2,000. The credit rate depends on the adjusted gross income ("AGI") of the taxpayer. Joint returns with AGI of $50,000 or less, head of household returns of $37,500 or less, and single returns of $25,000 or less are eligible for the credit. The AGI limits applicable to single taxpayers apply to married taxpayers filing separate returns. The credit is in addition to any deduction or exclusion that would otherwise apply with respect to the contribution. The credit offsets minimum tax liability as well as regular tax liability. The credit is available to individuals who are 18 or older, other than individuals who are full-time students or claimed as a dependent on another taxpayer's return.

Under present law, the saver's credit expires after 2006.

Individual retirement arrangements

In general

There are two general types of individual retirement arrangements ("IRAs") under present law: traditional IRAs,[180] to which both deductible and nondeductible contributions may be made,[181] and Roth IRAs.[182]

The maximum annual deductible and nondeductible contributions that can be made to a traditional IRA and the maximum contribution that can be made to a Roth IRA by or on behalf of an individual varies depending on the particular circumstances, including the individual's income. However, the contribution limits for IRAs are coordinated so that the maximum annual contribution that can be made to all of an individual's IRAs is the lesser of a certain dollar amount ($4,000 for 2006) or the individual's compensation. In the case of a married couple, contributions can be made up to the dollar limit for each spouse if the combined compensation of the spouses is at least equal to the contributed amount. An individual who has attained age 50 before the end of the taxable year may also make catch-up contributions to an IRA. For this purpose, the dollar limit is increased by a certain dollar amount ($1,000 for 2006).[183]

---

[180] Sec. 408.

[181] Sec. 219.

[182] Sec. 408A.

[183] Under the Economic Growth and Tax Relief Reconciliation Act of 2001 ("EGTRRA"), the dollar limit on IRA contributions increases to $5,000 in 2008, with indexing for inflation thereafter. The

Traditional IRAs

An individual may make deductible contributions to a traditional IRA up to the IRA contribution limit if neither the individual nor the individual's spouse is an active participant in an employer-sponsored retirement plan. If an individual (or the individual's spouse) is an active participant in an employer-sponsored retirement plan, the deduction is phased out for taxpayers with adjusted gross income over certain levels for the taxable year. The adjusted gross income phase-out ranges are: (1) for single taxpayers, $50,000 to $60,000; (2) for married taxpayers filing joint returns, $75,000 to $85,000 for 2006 and $80,000 to $100,000 for years after 2006; and (3) for married taxpayers filing separate returns, $0 to $10,000. If an individual is not an active participant in an employer-sponsored retirement plan, but the individual's spouse is, the deduction is phased out for taxpayers with adjusted gross income between $150,000 and $160,000.

To the extent an individual cannot or does not make deductible contributions to an IRA or contributions to a Roth IRA, the individual may make nondeductible contributions to a traditional IRA, subject to the same limits as deductible contributions. An individual who has attained age 50 before the end of the taxable year may also make nondeductible catch-up contributions to an IRA.

Amounts held in a traditional IRA are includible in income when withdrawn, except to the extent the withdrawal is a return of nondeductible contributions. Withdrawals from an IRA before age 70½, death, or disability are subject to an additional 10-percent tax unless an exception applies.[184]

Roth IRAs

Individuals with adjusted gross income below certain levels may make nondeductible contributions to a Roth IRA, subject to the overall limit on IRA contributions described above. The maximum annual contribution that can be made to a Roth IRA is phased out for taxpayers with adjusted gross income over certain levels for the taxable year. The adjusted gross income phase-out ranges are: (1) for single taxpayers, $95,000 to $110,000; (2) for married taxpayers filing joint returns, $150,000 to $160,000; and (3) for married taxpayers filing separate returns, $0 to $10,000.

Taxpayers generally may convert a traditional IRA into a Roth IRA, except for married taxpayers filing separate returns. The amount converted is includible in income as if a withdrawal had been made, except that the 10-percent early withdrawal tax does not apply.

---

provisions of EGTRRA generally do not apply for years beginning after December 31, 2010. As a result, the dollar limit on annual IRA contributions is $2,000 for years after 2010, and catch-ups contributions are not permitted.

[184] Sec. 72(t).

Amounts held in a Roth IRA that are withdrawn as a qualified distribution are not includible in income, or subject to the additional 10-percent tax on early withdrawals. A qualified distribution is a distribution that (1) is made after the five-taxable year period beginning with the first taxable year for which the individual made a contribution to a Roth IRA, and (2) is made after attainment of age 59½, on account of death or disability, or is made for first-time homebuyer expenses of up to $10,000.

Distributions from a Roth IRA that are not qualified distributions are includible in income to the extent attributable to earnings. The amount includible in income is also subject to the 10-percent early withdrawal tax described above.

Explanation of Provision

The bill indexes the income limits applicable to the saver's credit beginning in 2007. (Another provision of the bill, described above, permanently extends the saver's credit.) Indexed amounts are rounded to the nearest multiple of $500. Under the indexed income limits, as under present law, the income limits for single taxpayers is one-half that for married taxpayers filing a joint return and the limits for heads of household are three-fourths that for married taxpayers filing a joint return.

The bill also indexes the income limits for IRA contributions beginning in 2007. The indexing applies to the income limits for deductible contributions for active participants in an employer-sponsored plan,[185] the income limits for deductible contributions if the individual is not an active participant but the individual's spouse is, and the income limits for Roth IRA contributions. Indexed amounts are rounded to the nearest multiple of $1,000. The provision does not affect the phase-out ranges under present law. Thus, for example, in the case of an active participant in an employer-sponsored plan, the phase-out range is $20,000 in the case of a married taxpayer filing a joint return and $10,000 in the case of an individual taxpayer.

Effective Date

The provision is effective for taxable years beginning after December 31, 2006.

---

[185] Under the bill, for 2007, the lower end of the income phase out for active participants filing a joint return is $80,000 as adjusted to reflect inflation.

D. Health and Medical Benefits

1. Ability to use excess pension assets for future retiree health benefits and collectively bargained retiree health benefits (sec. 420 of the Code)

Present Law

Transfer of pension assets

Defined benefit plan assets generally may not revert to an employer prior to termination of the plan and satisfaction of all plan liabilities. In addition, a reversion may occur only if the plan so provides. A reversion prior to plan termination may constitute a prohibited transaction and may result in plan disqualification. Any assets that revert to the employer upon plan termination are includible in the gross income of the employer and subject to an excise tax. The excise tax rate is 20 percent if the employer maintains a replacement plan or makes certain benefit increases in connection with the termination; if not, the excise tax rate is 50 percent. Upon plan termination, the accrued benefits of all plan participants are required to be 100-percent vested.

A pension plan may provide medical benefits to retired employees through a separate account that is part of such plan ("retiree medical accounts"). A qualified transfer of excess assets of a defined benefit plan to such a separate account within the plan may be made in order to fund retiree health benefits.[186] A qualified transfer does not result in plan disqualification, is not a prohibited transaction, and is not treated as a reversion. Thus, transferred assets are not includible in the gross income of the employer and are not subject to the excise tax on reversions. No more than one qualified transfer may be made in any taxable year. A qualified transfer may not be made from a multiemployer plan. No qualified transfer may be made after December 31, 2013.

Excess assets generally means the excess, if any, of the value of the plan's assets[187] over the greater of (1) the accrued liability under the plan (including normal cost) or (2) 125 percent of the plan's current liability.[188] In addition, excess assets transferred in a qualified transfer may not exceed the amount reasonably estimated to be the amount that the employer will pay out of such account during the taxable year of the transfer for qualified current retiree health liabilities. No deduction is allowed to the employer for (1) a qualified transfer or (2) the payment of qualified current retiree health liabilities out of transferred funds (and any income thereon). In

---

[186] Sec. 420.

[187] The value of plan assets for this purpose is the lesser of fair market value or actuarial value.

[188] In the case of plan years beginning before January 1, 2004, excess assets generally means the excess, if any, of the value of the plan's assets over the greater of (1) the lesser of (a) the accrued liability under the plan (including normal cost) or (b) 170 percent of the plan's current liability (for 2003), or (2) 125 percent of the plan's current liability. The current liability full funding limit was repealed for years beginning after 2003. Under the general sunset provision of EGTRRA, the limit is reinstated for years after 2010.

185

addition, no deduction is allowed for amounts paid other than from transferred funds for qualified current retiree health liabilities to the extent such amounts are not greater than the excess of (1) the amount transferred (and any income thereon), over (2) qualified current retiree health liabilities paid out of transferred assets (and any income thereon). An employer may not contribute any amount to a health benefits account or welfare benefit fund with respect to qualified current retiree health liabilities for which transferred assets are required to be used.

Transferred assets (and any income thereon) must be used to pay qualified current retiree health liabilities for the taxable year of the transfer. Transferred amounts generally must benefit pension plan participants, other than key employees, who are entitled upon retirement to receive retiree medical benefits through the separate account. Retiree health benefits of key employees may not be paid out of transferred assets.

Amounts not used to pay qualified current retiree health liabilities for the taxable year of the transfer are to be returned to the general assets of the plan. These amounts are not includible in the gross income of the employer, but are treated as an employer reversion and are subject to a 20-percent excise tax.

In order for the transfer to be qualified, accrued retirement benefits under the pension plan generally must be 100-percent vested as if the plan terminated immediately before the transfer (or in the case of a participant who separated in the one-year period ending on the date of the transfer, immediately before the separation).

In order to a transfer to be qualified, the employer generally must maintain retiree health benefits at the same level for the taxable year of the transfer and the following four years.

In addition, ERISA provides that, at least 60 days before the date of a qualified transfer, the employer must notify the Secretary of Labor, the Secretary of the Treasury, employee representatives, and the plan administrator of the transfer, and the plan administrator must notify each plan participant and beneficiary of the transfer.[189]

Deductions for contributions

Deductions for contributions to qualified retirement plans are subject to certain limits. Deductions for contributions to funded welfare benefit plans are generally also subject to limits, including limits on the amount that may be contributed to an account to fund the expected cost of retiree medical benefits for future years. The limit on the amount that may be contributed to an account to fund the expected cost of retiree medical benefits for future years does not apply to a separate fund established under a collective bargaining agreement.

---

[189] ERISA sec. 101(e). ERISA also provides that a qualified transfer is not a prohibited transaction under ERISA or a prohibited reversion.

Explanation of Provision

In general

If certain requirements are satisfied, the bill permits transfers of excess pension assets under a single-employer plan to retiree medical accounts to fund the expected cost of retiree medical benefits for the current and future years (a "qualified future transfer") and also allows such transfers in the case of benefits provided under a collective bargaining agreement (a "collectively bargained transfer"). Transfers must be made for at least a two-year period. An employer can elect to make a qualified future transfer or a collectively bargained transfer rather than a qualified transfer. A qualified future transfer or collectively bargained transfer must meet the requirements applicable to qualified transfers, except that the provision modifies the rules relating to (1) the determination of excess pension assets; (2) the limitation on the amount transferred; and (3) the minimum cost requirement. Additional requirements apply in the case of collectively bargained transfer.

The general sunset applicable to qualified transfer applies (i.e., transfers can be made only before January 1, 2014).

Rule applicable to qualified future transfers and collectively bargained transfers

Qualified future transfers and collectively bargained transfers can be made to the extent that plan assets exceed the greater of (1) accrued liability, or (2) 120 percent of current liability.[190] The provision requires that, during the transfer period, the plan's funded status must be maintained at the minimum level required to make transfers. If the minimum level is not maintained, the employer must make contributions to the plan to meet the minimum level or an amount required to meet the minimum level must be transferred from the health benefits account. The transfer period is the period not to exceed a total of ten consecutive taxable years beginning with the taxable year of the transfer. As previously discussed, the period must be not less than two consecutive years.

A limit applies on the amount that can be transferred. In the case of a qualified future transfer, the amount of excess pension assets that may be transferred is limited to the sum of (1) the amount that is reasonably estimated to be the amount the employer will pay out of the account during the taxable year of the transfer for current retiree health liabilities, and (2) the sum of the qualified current retiree health liabilities which the plan reasonably estimates, in accordance with guidance issued by the Secretary, will be incurred for each additional year in the transfer period. The amount that can be transferred under a collectively bargained transfer cannot exceed the amount which is reasonably estimated, in accordance with the provisions of the collective bargaining agreement and generally accepted accounting principles, to be the amount the employer maintaining the plan will pay out of such account during the collectively bargained cost maintenance period for collectively bargained retiree health liabilities.

---

[190] The single-employer plan funding concepts are updated after 2007 to reflect the changes to the single-employer plan funding rules under the bill.

The provision also modifies the minimum cost requirement which requires retiree medical benefits to be maintained at a certain level. In the case of a qualified future transfer, the minimum cost requirement will be satisfied if, during the transfer period and the four subsequent years, the annual average amount of employer costs is not less than applicable employer cost determined with respect to the transfer. An employer may elect to meet this minimum cost requirement by meeting the requirements as in effect before the amendments made by section 535 of the Tax Relief Extension Act of 1999 for each year during the transfer period and the four subsequent years. In the case of a collectively bargained transfer, the minimum cost requirements is satisfied if each collectively bargained group health plan under which collectively bargained health benefits are provided provides that the collectively bargained employer cost for each table year during the collectively bargained cost maintenance period is not less than the amount specified by the collective bargaining agreement. The collectively bargained employer cost is the average cost per covered individual of providing collectively bargained retiree health benefits as determined in accordance with the applicable collective bargaining agreement. Thus, retiree medical benefits must be provided at the level determined under the collective bargaining agreement for the shorter of (1) the remaining lifetime of each covered retiree (and any covered spouse and dependent), or (2) the period of coverage provided under the collectively bargained health plan for such covered retiree (and any covered spouse and dependent).

Additional requirements for collectively bargained transfers

As previously discussed, the bill imposes certain additional requirements in the case of a collectively bargained transfer. Collectively bargained transfers can be made only if (1) for the employer's taxable year ending in 2005, medical benefits are provided to retirees (and spouses and dependents) under all the employer's benefit plans, and (2) the aggregate cost of benefits for such year is at least five percent of the employer's gross receipts. The provision also applies to successors of such employers. Before a collectively bargained transfer, the employer must designate in writing to each employee organization that is a party to the collective bargaining agreement that the transfer is a collectively bargained transfer.

Collectively bargained retiree health liabilities means the present value, as of the beginning of a taxable year and determined in accordance with the applicable collective bargaining agreement, of all collectively bargained health benefits (including administrative expenses) for such taxable year and all subsequent taxable years during the collectively bargained cost maintenance period (with the exclusion of certain key employees) reduced by the value of assets in all health benefits accounts or welfare benefit funds set aside to pay for the collectively bargained retiree health liabilities. Collectively bargained health benefits are health benefits or coverage provided to retired employees who, immediately before the collectively bargained transfer, are entitled to receive such benefits upon retirement and who are entitled to pension benefits under the plan (and their spouses and dependents). If specified by the provisions of the collective bargaining agreement, collectively bargained health benefits also include active employees who, following their retirement, are entitled to receive such benefits and who are entitled to pension benefits under the plan (and their spouse and dependents).

Assets transferred in a collectively bargained transfer can be used to pay collectively bargained retiree health liabilities (other than liabilities of certain key employees not taken into

188

account) for the taxable year of the transfer and for any subsequent taxable year during the collectively bargained cost maintenance period. The collectively bargained cost maintenance period (with respect to a retiree) is the shorter of (1) the remaining lifetime of the covered retiree (and any covered spouse and dependents) or (2) the period of coverage provided by the collectively bargained health plan with respect to such covered retiree (and any covered spouse and dependents).

The limit on deductions in the case of certain amounts paid for qualified current retiree health liabilities other than from the health benefits account does not apply in the case of a collectively bargained transfer.

An employer may contribute additional amounts to a health benefits account or welfare benefit fund with respect to collectively bargained health liabilities for which transferred assets are required to be used. The deductibility of such contributions are subject to the limits that otherwise apply to a welfare benefit fund under a collective bargaining agreements without regard to whether such contributions are made to a health benefits account or a welfare benefit fund and without regard to the limits on deductions for contributions to qualified retirement plans (under Code section 404). The Secretary of the Treasury is directed to provide rules to prevent duplicate deductions for the same contributions or for duplicate contributions to fund the same benefits.

Effective Date

The provision is effective for transfers after the date of enactment.

2. Transfer of excess pension assets to multiemployer health plans (sec. 420 of the Code)

Present Law

Defined benefit plan assets generally may not revert to an employer prior to termination of the plan and satisfaction of all plan liabilities. In addition, a reversion may occur only if the plan so provides. A reversion prior to plan termination may constitute a prohibited transaction and may result in plan disqualification. Any assets that revert to the employer upon plan termination are includible in the gross income of the employer and subject to an excise tax. The excise tax rate is 20 percent if the employer maintains a replacement plan or makes certain benefit increases in connection with the termination; if not, the excise tax rate is 50 percent. Upon plan termination, the accrued benefits of all plan participants are required to be 100-percent vested.

A pension plan may provide medical benefits to retired employees through a separate account that is part of such plan. A qualified transfer of excess assets of a defined benefit plan to such a separate account within the plan may be made in order to fund retiree health benefits.[191] A qualified transfer does not result in plan disqualification, is not a prohibited transaction, and is not treated as a reversion. Thus, transferred assets are not includible in the gross income of the

---

[191] Sec. 420.

employer and are not subject to the excise tax on reversions. No more than one qualified transfer may be made in any taxable year. A qualified transfer may not be made from a multiemployer plan. No qualified transfer may be made after December 31, 2013.

Excess assets generally means the excess, if any, of the value of the plan's assets[192] over the greater of (1) the accrued liability under the plan (including normal cost) or (2) 125 percent of the plan's current liability.[193] In addition, excess assets transferred in a qualified transfer may not exceed the amount reasonably estimated to be the amount that the employer will pay out of such account during the taxable year of the transfer for qualified current retiree health liabilities. No deduction is allowed to the employer for (1) a qualified transfer or (2) the payment of qualified current retiree health liabilities out of transferred funds (and any income thereon).

Transferred assets (and any income thereon) must be used to pay qualified current retiree health liabilities for the taxable year of the transfer. Transferred amounts generally must benefit pension plan participants, other than key employees, who are entitled upon retirement to receive retiree medical benefits through the separate account. Retiree health benefits of key employees may not be paid out of transferred assets.

Amounts not used to pay qualified current retiree health liabilities for the taxable year of the transfer are to be returned to the general assets of the plan. These amounts are not includible in the gross income of the employer, but are treated as an employer reversion and are subject to a 20-percent excise tax.

In order for the transfer to be qualified, accrued retirement benefits under the pension plan generally must be 100-percent vested as if the plan terminated immediately before the transfer (or in the case of a participant who separated in the one-year period ending on the date of the transfer, immediately before the separation).

In order to a transfer to be qualified, the employer generally must maintain retiree health benefits at the same level for the taxable year of the transfer and the following four years.

In addition, ERISA provides that, at least 60 days before the date of a qualified transfer, the employer must notify the Secretary of Labor, the Secretary of the Treasury, employee representatives, and the plan administrator of the transfer, and the plan administrator must notify each plan participant and beneficiary of the transfer.[194]

---

[192] The value of plan assets for this purpose is the lesser of fair market value or actuarial value.

[193] In the case of plan years beginning before January 1, 2004, excess assets generally means the excess, if any, of the value of the plan's assets over the greater of (1) the lesser of (a) the accrued liability under the plan (including normal cost) or (b) 170 percent of the plan's current liability (for 2003), or (2) 125 percent of the plan's current liability. The current liability full funding limit was repealed for years beginning after 2003. Under the general sunset provision of EGTRRA, the limit is reinstated for years after 2010.

[194] ERISA sec. 101(e). ERISA also provides that a qualified transfer is not a prohibited transaction under ERISA or a prohibited reversion.

Under present law, special deduction rules apply to a multiemployer defined benefit plan established before January 1, 1954, under an agreement between the Federal government and employee representatives in a certain industry.[195]

Explanation of Provision

The bill allows qualified transfers of excess defined benefit plan assets to be made by multiemployer defined benefit plans.

Effective Date

The provision is effective for transfer made in taxable years beginning after December 31, 2006.

3. Allowance of reserve for medical benefits of plans sponsored by bona fide associations (sec. 419A of the Code)

Present Law

Under present law, deductions for contributions to funded welfare benefit plans are generally subject to limits, including limits on the amount that may be contributed to an account to fund medical benefits (other than retiree medical benefits) for future years. Deductions for contributions to a welfare benefit fund are limited to the fund's qualified cost for the taxable year. The qualified cost is the sum of (1) the qualified direct cost for the taxable year, and (2) permissible additions to a qualified asset account.

The qualified direct costs are the amount which would have been allowable as a deduction to the employer with respect to the benefits provided during the taxable year if the benefits were provided directly by the employer and the employer used the cash receipts and disbursements method of accounting. Additions to the qualified asset account are limited to the account limit. The account limit is the amount reasonably and actuarially necessary to fund claims incured but unpaid (as of the close of the taxable year) and administrative costs with respect to such claims.

These limits do not apply to a welfare benefit fund that is part of a plan (referred to a "10-or-more employer" plan), to which (1) more than one employer contributes, and (2) no employer normally contributes more than 10 percent of the total contributions, provided that the plan may not maintain experience rating arrangements with respect to individual employers.

Explanation of Provision

The bill allows deductions for contributions to fund a reserve for medical benefits (other than retiree medical benefits) for future years provided through a bona fide association as defined in section 2791(d)(3) of the Public Health Service Act. In such case, the account limit may

---

[195] Code sec. 404(c).

include a reserve not to exceed 35 percent of the sum of (1) qualified direct costs, and (2) the change in claims incurred, but unpaid for such taxable year with respect to medical benefits (other than post-retirement medical benefits).

Effective Date

The provision is effective for taxable years ending after December 31, 2006.

4. Tax treatment of combined annuity or life insurance contracts with a long-term care insurance feature (secs. 72. 1035, and 7702B and new sec. 6050U of the Code)

Present Law

Annuity contracts

In general, earnings and gains on amounts invested in a deferred annuity contract held by an individual are not subject to tax during the deferral period in the hands of the holder of the contract. When payout commences under a deferred annuity contract, the tax treatment of amounts distributed depends on whether the amount is received "as an annuity" (generally, as periodic payments under contract terms) or not.

For amounts received as an annuity by an individual, an "exclusion ratio" is provided for determining the taxable portion of each payment (sec. 72(b)). The portion of each payment that is attributable to recovery of the taxpayer's investment in the contract is not taxed. The taxable portion of each payment is ordinary income. The exclusion ratio is the ratio of the taxpayer's investment in the contract to the expected return under the contract, that is, the total of the payments expected to be received under the contract. The ratio is determined as of the taxpayer's annuity starting date. Once the taxpayer has recovered his or her investment in the contract, all further payments are included in income. If the taxpayer dies before the full investment in the contract is recovered, a deduction is allowed on the final return for the remaining investment in the contract (sec. 72(b)(3)).

Amounts not received as an annuity generally are included as ordinary income if received on or after the annuity starting date. Amounts not received as an annuity are included in income to the extent allocable to income on the contract if received before the annuity starting date, i.e., as income first (sec. 72(e)(2)). In general, loans under the annuity contract, partial withdrawals and partial surrenders are treated as amounts not received as an annuity and are subject to tax as income first (sec. 72(e)(4)). Exceptions are provided in some circumstances, such as for certain grandfathered contracts, certain life insurance and endowment contracts (other than modified endowment contracts), and contracts under qualified plans (sec. 72(e)(5)). Under these exceptions, the amount received is included in income, but only to the extent it exceeds the investment in the contract, i.e., as basis recovery first.

192

Long-term care insurance contracts

Tax treatment

Present law provides favorable tax treatment for qualified long-term care insurance contracts meeting the requirements of section 7702B.

A qualified long-term care insurance contract is treated as an accident and health insurance contract (sec. 7702B(a)(1)). Amounts received under the contract generally are excludable from income as amounts received for personal injuries or sickness (sec. 104(a)(3)). The excludable amount is subject to a dollar cap of $250 per day or $91,250 annually (for 2006), as indexed, on per diem contracts only (sec. 7702B(d)). If payments under such contracts exceed the dollar cap, then the excess is excludable only to the extent of costs in excess of the dollar cap that are incurred for long-term care services. Amounts in excess of the dollar cap, with respect to which no actual costs were incurred for long-term care services, are fully includable in income without regard to the rules relating to return of basis under section 72.

A plan of an employer providing coverage under a long-term care insurance contract generally is treated as an accident and health plan (benefits under which generally are excludable from the recipient's income under section 105).

Premiums paid for a qualified long-term care insurance contract are deductible as medical expenses, subject to a dollar cap on the deductible amount of the premium per year based on the insured person's age at the end of the taxable year (sec. 213(d)(10)). Medical expenses generally are allowed as a deduction only to the extent they exceed 7.5 percent of adjusted gross income (sec. 213(a)).

Unreimbursed expenses for qualified long-term care services provided to the taxpayer or the taxpayer's spouse or dependent are treated as medical expenses for purposes of the itemized deduction for medical expenses (subject to the floor of 7.5 percent of adjusted gross income). Amounts received under a qualified long-term care insurance contract (regardless of whether the contract reimburses expenses or pays benefits on a per diem or other periodic basis) are treated as reimbursement for expense actually incurred for medical care (sec. 7702B(a)(2)).

Definitions

A qualified long-term care insurance contract is defined as any insurance contract that provides only coverage of qualified long-term care services, and that meets additional requirements (sec. 7702B(b)). The contract is not permitted to provide for a cash surrender value or other money that can paid, assigned or pledged as collateral for a loan, or borrowed (and premium refunds are to be applied as a reduction in future premiums or to increase future benefits). Per diem-type and reimbursement-type contracts are permitted.

Qualified long-term care services are necessary diagnostic, preventive, therapeutic, curing treating, mitigating, and rehabilitative services, and maintenance or personal care services that are required by a chronically ill individual and that are provided pursuant to a plan of care prescribed by a licensed health care practitioner (sec. 7702B(c)(1)).

A chronically ill individual is generally one who has been certified within the previous 12 months by a licensed health care practitioner as being unable to perform (without substantial assistance) at least 2 activities of daily (ADLs) for at least 90 days due to a loss of functional capacity (or meeting other definitional requirements) (sec. 7702B(c)(2)).

Long-term care riders on life insurance contracts

In the case of long-term care insurance coverage provided by a rider on or as part of a life insurance contract, the requirements applicable to long-term care insurance contracts apply as if the portion of the contract providing such coverage were a separate contract (sec. 7702B(e)). The term "portion" means only the terms and benefits that are in addition to the terms and benefits under the life insurance contract without regard to long-term care coverage. As a result, if the applicable requirements are met by the long-term care portion of the contract, amounts received under the contract as provided by the rider are treated in the same manner as long-term care insurance benefits, whether or not the payment of such amounts causes a reduction in the contract's death benefit or cash surrender value.

The guideline premium limitation applicable under section 7702(c)(2) is increased by the sum of charges (but not premium payments) against the life insurance contract's cash surrender value, the imposition of which reduces premiums paid for the contract (within the meaning of sec. 7702(f)(1)). Thus, a policyholder can pre-fund to a greater degree a life insurance policy with a long-term care rider without causing the policy to lose its tax-favored treatment as life insurance.

No medical expense deduction generally is allowed under section 213 for charges against the life insurance contract's cash surrender value, unless such charges are includible in income because the life insurance contract is treated as a "modified endowment contract" under section 72(e)(10) and 7702A (sec. 7702B(e)((3)).

Tax-free exchanges of insurance contracts

Present law provides for the exchange of certain insurance contracts without recognition of gain or loss (sec. 1035). No gain or loss is recognized on the exchange of: (1) a life insurance contract for another life insurance contract or for an endowment or annuity contract; or (2) an endowment contract for another endowment contract (that provides for regular payments beginning no later than under the exchanged contract) or for an annuity contract; or (3) an annuity contract for an annuity contract. The basis of the contract received in the exchange generally is the same as the basis of the contract exchanged (sec. 1031(d)). Tax-free exchanges of long-term care insurance contracts are not permitted.

Capitalization of certain policy acquisition expenses of insurance companies

In the case of an insurance company, specified policy acquisition expenses for any taxable year are required to be capitalized, and are amortized generally over the 120-month period beginning with the first month in the second half of the taxable year (sec. 848). Specified policy acquisition expenses are determined as that portion of the insurance company's general deductions for the taxable year that does not exceed a specific percentage of the net premiums for the taxable year on each of three categories of insurance contracts. For annuity contracts, the percentage is 1.75; for group life insurance contracts, the percentage is 2.05; and for all other specified insurance contracts, the percentage is 7.7. With certain exceptions, a specified insurance contract is any life insurance, annuity, or noncancellable accident and health insurance contract or combination thereof.

Explanation of Provision

The provision provides tax rules for long-term care insurance that is provided by a rider on or as part of an annuity contract, and modifies the tax rules for long-term care insurance coverage provided by a rider on or as part of a life insurance contract.

Under the provision, any charge against the cash value of an annuity contract or the cash surrender value of a life insurance contract made as payment for coverage under a qualified long-term care insurance contract that is part of or a rider on the annuity or life insurance contract is not includable in income. The investment in the contract is reduced (but not below zero) by the charge.

The provision expands the rules for tax-free exchanges of certain insurance contracts. The provision provides that no gain or loss is recognized on the exchange of a life insurance contract, an endowment contract, an annuity contract, or a qualified long-term care insurance contract for a qualified long-term care insurance contract. The provision provides that a contract does not fail to be treated as an annuity contract, or as a life insurance contract, solely because a qualified long-term care insurance contract is a part of or a rider on such contract, for purposes of the rules for tax-free exchanges of certain insurance contracts.

The provision provides that, except as otherwise provided in regulations, for Federal tax purposes, in the case of a long-term care insurance contract (whether or not qualified) provided by a rider on or as part of a life insurance contract or an annuity contract, the portion of the contract providing long-term care insurance coverage is treated as a separate contract. The term "portion" means only the terms and benefits under a life insurance contract or annuity contract that are in addition to the terms and benefits under the contract without regard to long-term care coverage. As a result, if the applicable requirements are met by the long-term care portion of the contract, amounts received under the contract as provided by the rider are treated in the same manner as long-term care insurance benefits, whether or not the payment of such amounts causes a reduction in the life insurance contract's death benefit or cash surrender value or in the annuity contract's cash value.

No deduction as a medical expense is allowed for any payment made for coverage under a qualified long-term care insurance contract if the payment is made as a charge against the cash value of an annuity contract or the cash surrender value of a life insurance contract.

The provision provides that, for taxable years beginning after December 31, 2009, the guideline premium limitation is not directly increased by charges against a life insurance contract's cash surrender value for coverage under the qualified long-term care insurance portion of the contract. Rather, because such charges are not included in the holder's income by reason of new section 72(e)(11),[196] the charges reduce premiums paid under section 7702(f)(1), for purposes of the guideline premium limitation of section 7702. The amount by which premiums paid (under 7702(f)(1)) are reduced under this rule is intended to be the sum of any charges (but not premium payments) against the life insurance contract's cash surrender value (within the meaning of section 7702(f)(2)(a)) for long-term care coverage made to that date under the contract. For taxable years beginning before January 1, 2010, the present-law rule of section 7702B(e)(2) before amendment by the bill (the so-called "pay-as-you-go" rule) increases the guideline premium limitation by this same amount, reduced by charges the imposition of which reduces the premiums paid under the contract. Thus, the provision of the bill recreates the result of the "pay-as-you-go" rule (which is repealed by the provision) as a reduction in premiums paid rather than as an increase in the guideline premium limitation.

The provision provides that certain retirement-related arrangements are not treated as annuity contracts, for purposes of the provision.

The provision requires information reporting by any person who makes a charge against the cash value of an annuity contract, or the cash surrender value of a life insurance contract, that is excludible from gross income under the provision. The information required to be reported includes the amount of the aggregate of such charges against each such contract for the calendar year, the amount of the reduction in the investment in the contract by reason of the charges, and the name, address, and taxpayer identification number of the holder of the contract. A statement is required to be furnished to each individual identified in the information report. Penalties apply for failure to file the information report or furnish the statement required under the provision.

The provision modifies the application of the rules relating to capitalization of policy acquisition expenses of insurance companies. In the case of an annuity or life insurance contract that includes a qualified long-term care insurance contract as a part of or rider on the annuity or life insurance contract, the specified policy acquisition expenses that must be capitalized is determined using 7.7 percent of the net premiums for the taxable year on such contracts.

The provision clarifies that, effective as if included in the Health Insurance Portability and Accountability Act of 1996 (when section 7702B was enacted), except as otherwise provided in regulations, for Federal tax purposes (not just for purposes of section 7702B), in the case of a long-term care insurance contract (whether or not qualified) provided by a rider on or as part of a life insurance contract, the portion of the contract providing long-term care insurance coverage is treated as a separate contract.

---

[196] Because such charges are not included in the holder's income under new section 72(e)(11), the effect would be to increase the guideline premium limitation under present-law section 7702B(e)(2)(A) by the amount of the charges and simultaneously to reduce it by the same charges under section 7702B(e)(2)(B). Such charges that are not included in income serve to reduce premiums paid under section 7702(f)(1), and therefore would cancel each other out under 7702B(e)(2)(A) and (B).

Effective Date

The provisions are effective generally for contracts issued after December 31, 1996, but only with respect to taxable years beginning after December 31, 200**9**. The provisions relating to tax-free exchanges apply with respect to exchanges occurring after December 31, 2009. The provision relating to information reporting applies to charges made after December 31, 2009. The provision relating to policy acquisition expenses applies to specified policy acquisition expenses determined for taxable years beginning after December 31, 2009. The technical amendment relating to long-term care insurance coverage under section 7702B(e) is effective as if included with the underlying provisions of the Health Insurance Portability and Accountability Act of 1996.

5. Permit tax-free distributions from governmental retirement plans for premiums for health and long-term care insurance for public safety officers (sec. 402 of the Code)

Present Law

Under present law, a distribution from a qualified retirement plan under section 401(a), a qualified annuity plan under section 403(a), a tax-sheltered annuity under section 403(b) (a "403(b) annuity"), an eligible deferred compensation plan maintained by a State or local government under section 457 (a "governmental 457 plan"), or an individual retirement arrangement under section 408 (an "IRA") generally is included in income for the year distributed (except to the extent the amount received constitutes a return of after-tax contributions or a qualified distribution from a Roth IRA).[197] In addition, a distribution from a qualified retirement or annuity plan, a 403(b) annuity, or an IRA received before age 59½, death, or disability generally is subject to a 10-percent early withdrawal tax on the amount includible in income, unless an exception applies.[198]

Explanation of Provision

The bill provides that certain pension distributions from an eligible retirement plan used to pay for qualified health insurance premiums are excludible from income, up to a maximum exclusion of $3,000 annually. An eligible retirement plan includes a governmental qualified retirement or annuity plan, 403(b) annuity, or 457 plan. The exclusion applies with respect to eligible retired public safety officers who make an election to have qualified health insurance premiums deducted from amounts distributed from an eligible retirement plan and paid directly to the insurer. An eligible retired public safety officer is an individual who, by reason of disability or attainment of normal retirement age, is separated from service as a public safety

---

[197] Secs. 402(a), 403(a), 403(b), 408(d), and 457(a).

[198] Sec. 72(t).

officer[199] with the employer who maintains the eligible retirement plan from which pension distributions are made.

Qualified health insurance premiums include premiums for accident or health insurance or qualified long-term care insurance contracts covering the taxpayer, the taxpayer's spouse, and the taxpayer's dependents. The qualified health insurance premiums do not have to be for a plan sponsored by the employer; however, the exclusion does not apply to premiums paid by the employee and reimbursed with pension distributions. Amounts excluded from income under the provision are not taken into account in determining the itemized deduction for medical expenses under section 213 or the deduction for health insurance of self-employed individuals under section 162.

Effective Date

The provision is effective for distributions in taxable years beginning after December 31, 2006.

---

[199] The term "public safety officer" has the same meaning as under section 1204(8)(A) of the Omnibus Crime Control and Safe Streets Act of 1986.

E. United States Tax Court Modernization

1. Judges of the Tax Court (secs. 7447, 7448, and 7472 of the Code)

Present Law

The Tax Court is established by the Congress pursuant to Article I of the U.S. Constitution.[200] The salary of a Tax Court judge is the same salary as received by a U.S. District Court judge.[201] Present law also provides Tax Court judges with some benefits that correspond to benefits provided to U.S. District Court judges, including specific retirement and survivor benefit programs for Tax Court judges.[202]

Under the retirement program, a Tax Court judge may elect to receive retirement pay from the Tax Court in lieu of benefits under another Federal retirement program. A Tax Court judge may also elect to participate in a plan providing annuity benefits for the judge's surviving spouse and dependent children (the "survivors' annuity plan"). Generally, benefits under the survivors' annuity plan are payable only if the judge has performed at least five years of service. Cost-of-living increases in benefits under the survivors' annuity plan are generally based on increases in pay for active judges.

Tax Court judges participate in the Federal Employees Group Life Insurance program (the "FEGLI" program). Retired Tax Court judges are eligible to participate in the FEGLI program as the result of an administrative determination of their eligibility, rather than a specific statutory provision.

Tax Court judges are not covered by the leave system for Federal Executive Branch employees. As a result, an individual who works in the Federal Executive Branch before being appointed to the Tax Court does not continue to accrue annual leave under the same leave program and may not use leave accrued prior to his or her appointment to the Tax Court.

Tax Court judges are not eligible to participate in the Thrift Savings Plan.

Under the retirement program for Tax Court judges, retired judges generally receive retired pay equal to the rate of salary of an active judge and must be available for recall to perform judicial duties as needed by the court for up to 90 days a year (unless the judge consents to more). However, retired judges may elect to freeze the amount of their retired pay, and those who do so are not available for recall.

Retired Tax Court judges on recall are subject to the limitations on outside earned income that apply to active Federal employees under the Ethics in Government Act of 1978. However, retired District Court judges on recall may receive compensation for teaching without regard to

---

[200] Sec. 7441.

[201] Sec. 7443(c).

[202] Secs. 7447 and 7448.

the limitations on outside earned income. Retired Tax Court judges who elect to freeze the amount of their retired pay (thus making themselves unavailable for recall) are not subject to the limitations on outside earned income.

Explanation of Provision

Cost-of-living adjustments for survivor annuities

The bill provides that cost–of–living increases in benefits under the survivors' annuity plan are generally based on cost–of–living increases in benefits paid under the Civil Service Retirement System.

Life insurance coverage

In the case of a Tax Court judge age 65 or over, the Tax Court is authorized to pay on behalf of the judge any increase in employee premiums under the FEGLI program that occur after the date of enactment, including expenses generated by such payment, as authorized by the chief judge of the Tax Court in a manner consistent with payments authorized by the Judicial Conference of the United States (i.e., the body with policy-making authority over the administration of the courts of the Federal judicial branch).

Thrift Savings Plan participation

Under the provision, Tax Court judges are permitted to participate in the Thrift Savings Plan. A Tax Court judge is not eligible for agency contributions to the Thrift Savings Plan.

Effective Date

The provisions are effective on the date of enactment, except that the provision relating to cost-of-living increases in benefits under the survivors' annuity plan applies with respect to increases in Civil Service Retirement benefits taking effect after the date of enactment.

2. Special trial judges of the Tax Court (sec. 7448 and new sec. 7443C of the Code)

Present Law

The Tax Court is established by the Congress pursuant to Article I of the U.S. Constitution.[203] The chief judge of the Tax Court may appoint special trial judges to handle certain cases.[204] Special trial judges serve for an indefinite term. Special trial judges receive a salary of 90 percent of the salary of a Tax Court judge and are generally covered by the benefit programs that apply to Federal executive branch employees, including the Civil Service Retirement System or the Federal Employees' Retirement System.

---

[203] Sec. 7441.

[204] Sec. 7443A.

Explanation of Provision

Survivors' annuity plan

Under the provision, magistrate judges of the Tax Court may elect to participate in the survivors' annuity plan for Tax Court judges. An election to participate in the survivors' annuity plan must be filed not later than the latest of: (1) twelve months after the date of enactment of the provision; (2) six months after the date the judge takes office; or (3) six months after the date the judge marries.

Recall of retired special trial judges

The provision provides rules under which a retired special trial judge may be recalled to perform services for up to 90 days a year.

Effective Date

The provisions are effective on the date of enactment.

3. Consolidate review of collection due process cases in the Tax Court (sec. 6330(d) of the Code)

Present Law

In general, the IRS is required to notify taxpayers that they have a right to a fair and impartial hearing before levy may be made on any property or right to property.[205] Similar rules apply with respect to liens.[206] The hearing is held by an impartial officer from the IRS Office of Appeals, who is required to issue a determination with respect to the issues raised by the taxpayer at the hearing. The taxpayer is entitled to appeal that determination to a court. The appeal must be brought to the Tax Court, unless the Tax Court does not have jurisdiction over the underlying tax liability. If that is the case, then the appeal must be brought in the district court of the United States.[207] If a court determines that an appeal was not made to the correct court, the taxpayer has 30 days after such determination to file with the correct court.

The Tax Court is established under Article I of the United States Constitution[208] and is a court of limited jurisdiction.[209] The Tax Court only has the jurisdiction that is expressly

---

[205] Sec. 6330(a).

[206] Sec. 6320.

[207] Sec. 6330(d).

[208] Sec. 7441.

[209] Sec. 7442.

conferred on it by statute.[210] For example, the jurisdiction of the Tax Court includes the authority to hear disputes concerning notices of income tax deficiency, certain types of declaratory judgment, and worker classification status, among others, but does not include jurisdiction over most excise taxes imposed by the Internal Revenue Code. Thus, the Tax Court may not have jurisdiction over the underlying tax liability with respect to an appeal of a due process hearing relating to a collections matter. As a practical matter, many cases involving appeals of a due process hearing (whether within the jurisdiction of the Tax Court or a district court) do not involve the underlying tax liability.

Explanation of Provision

The provision modifies the jurisdiction of the Tax Court by providing that all appeals of collection due process determinations are to be made to the United States Tax Court.

Effective Date

The provision applies to determinations made after the date which is 60 days after the date of enactment.

4. Extend authority for special trial judges to hear and decide certain employment status cases (sec. 7443A of the Code)

Present Law

In connection with the audit of any person, if there is an actual controversy involving a determination by the IRS as part of an examination that (1) one or more individuals performing services for that person are employees of that person or (2) that person is not entitled to relief under section 530 of the Revenue Act of 1978, the Tax Court has jurisdiction to determine whether the IRS is correct and the proper amount of employment tax under such determination.[211] Any redetermination by the Tax Court has the force and effect of a decision of the Tax Court and is reviewable.

An election may be made by the taxpayer for small case procedures if the amount of the employment taxes in dispute is $50,000 or less for each calendar quarter involved.[212] The decision entered under the small case procedure is not reviewable in any other court and should not be cited as authority.

The chief judge of the Tax Court may assign proceedings to special trial judges. The Code enumerates certain types of proceedings that may be so assigned and may be decided by a

---

[210] Sec. 7442.

[211] Sec. 7436.

[212] Sec. 7436(c).

special trial judge. In addition, the chief judge may designate any other proceeding to be heard by a special trial judge.[213]

Explanation of Provision

The provision clarifies that the chief judge of the Tax Court may assign to special trial judges any employment tax cases that are subject to the small case procedure and may authorize special trial judges to decide such small tax cases.

Effective Date

The provision is effective for any action or proceeding in the Tax Court with respect to which a decision has not become final as of the date of enactment.

5. Confirmation of Tax Court authority to apply equitable recoupment (sec. 6214(b) of the Code)

Present Law

Equitable recoupment is a common-law equitable principle that permits the defensive use of an otherwise time-barred claim to reduce or defeat an opponent's claim if both claims arise from the same transaction. U.S. District Courts and the U.S. Court of Federal Claims, the two Federal tax refund forums, may apply equitable recoupment in deciding tax refund cases.[214] In Estate of Mueller v. Commissioner,[215] the Court of Appeals for the Sixth Circuit held that the United States Tax Court (the "Tax Court") may not apply the doctrine of equitable recoupment. More recently, the Court of Appeals for the Ninth Circuit, in Branson v. Commissioner,[216] held that the Tax Court may apply the doctrine of equitable recoupment.

Explanation of Provision

The provision confirms that the Tax Court may apply the principle of equitable recoupment to the same extent that it may be applied in Federal civil tax cases by the U.S. District Courts or the U.S. Court of Claims. No implication is intended as to whether the Tax Court has the authority to continue to apply other equitable principles in deciding matters over which it has jurisdiction.

---

[213] Sec. 7443A.

[214] *See Stone v. White*, 301 U.S. 532 (1937); *Bull v. United States*, 295 U.S. 247 (1935).

[215] 153 F.3d 302 (6th Cir.), *cert. den.*, 525 U.S. 1140 (1999).

[216] 264 F.3d 904 (9th Cir.), *cert. den.*, 2002 U.S. LEXIS 1545 (U.S. Mar. 18, 2002).

Effective Date

The provision is effective for any action or proceeding in the Tax Court with respect to which a decision has not become final as of the date of enactment.

6. Tax Court filing fee (sec. 7451 of the Code)

Present Law

The Tax Court is authorized to impose a fee of up to $60 for the filing of any petition for the redetermination of a deficiency or for declaratory judgments relating to the status and classification of 501(c)(3) organizations, the judicial review of final partnership administrative adjustments, and the judicial review of partnership items if an administrative adjustment request is not allowed in full.[217] The statute does not specifically authorize the Tax Court to impose a filing fee for the filing of a petition for review of the IRS's failure to abate interest or for failure to award administrative costs and other areas of jurisdiction for which a petition may be filed. The practice of the Tax Court is to impose a $60 filing fee in all cases commenced by petition.[218]

Explanation of Provision

The provision provides that the Tax Court is authorized to charge a filing fee of up to $60 in all cases commenced by the filing of a petition. No negative inference is to be drawn as to whether the Tax Court has the authority under present law to impose a filing fee for any case commenced by the filing of a petition.

Effective Date

The provision is effective on the date of enactment.

7. Use of practitioner fee (sec. 7475(b) of the Code)

Present Law

The Tax Court is authorized to impose a fee of up to $30 per year on practitioners admitted to practice before the Tax Court.[219] These fees are to be used to employ independent counsel to pursue disciplinary matters.

Explanation of Provision

The provision provides that Tax Court fees imposed on practitioners also are available to provide services to pro se taxpayers (i.e., a taxpayer representing himself) that will assist such

---

[217] Sec. 7451.

[218] *See* Rule 20(b) of the Tax Court Rules of Practice and Procedure.

[219] Sec. 7475.

taxpayers in controversies before the Court. For example, fees could be used for programs to educate pro se taxpayers on the procedural requirements for contesting a tax deficiency before the Tax Court.

Effective Date

The provision is effective on the date of enactment.

F. Other Provisions

1. Extension to all governmental plans of moratorium on application of certain nondiscrimination rules (sec. 1505 of the Taxpayer Relief Act of 1997, and secs. 401(a) and 401(k) of the Code)

Present Law

A qualified retirement plan maintained by a State or local government is exempt from the nondiscrimination and minimum participation requirements. A cash or deferred arrangement maintained by a State or local government is also treated as meeting the participation and nondiscrimination requirements applicable to such a qualified cash or deferred arrangement. Other governmental plans are subject to these requirements.[220]

Explanation of Provision

The provision exempts all governmental plans from the nondiscrimination and minimum participation rules. The provision also treats all governmental cash or deferred arrangements as meeting the participation and nondiscrimination requirements applicable to a qualified cash or deferred arrangement.

Effective Date

The provision is effective for any year beginning after the date of enactment.

2. Eliminate aggregate limit for usage of excess funds from black lung disability trusts to pay for retiree health (secs. 501(c)(21) and 9705 of the Code)

Present Law

Qualified black lung benefit trusts

A qualified black lung benefit trust is exempt from Federal income taxation. Contributions to a qualified black lung benefit trust generally are deductible to the extent such contributions are necessary to fund the trust.

Under present law, no assets of a qualified black lung benefit trust may be used for, or diverted to, any purpose other than (1) to satisfy liabilities, or pay insurance premiums to cover liabilities, arising under the Black Lung Acts, (2) to pay administrative costs of operating the trust, (3) to pay accident and health benefits or premiums for insurance exclusively covering such benefits (including administrative and other incidental expenses relating to such benefits) for retired coal miners and their spouses and dependents (within certain limits) or (4) investment in Federal, State, or local securities and obligations, or in time demand deposits in a bank or

---

[220] The IRS has announced that governmental plans that are subject to the nondiscrimination requirements are deemed to satisfy such requirements pending the issuance of final regulations addressing this issue. Notice 2003-6, 2003-3 I.R.B. 298; Notice 2001-46, 2001-2 C.B. 122.

insured credit union. Additionally, trust assets may be paid into the national Black Lung Disability Trust Fund, or into the general fund of the U.S. Treasury.

The amount of assets in qualified black lung benefit trusts available to pay accident and health benefits or premiums for insurance exclusively covering such benefits (including administrative and other incidental expenses relating to such benefits) for retired coal miners and their spouses and dependents may not exceed a yearly limit or an aggregate limit, whichever is less. The yearly limit is the amount of trust assets in excess of 110 percent of the present value of the liability for black lung benefits determined as of the close of the preceding taxable year of the trust. The aggregate limit is the excess of the sum of the yearly limit as of the close of the last taxable year ending before October 24, 1992, plus earnings thereon as of the close of the taxable year preceding the taxable year involved over the aggregate payments for accident of health benefits for retired coal miners and their spouses and dependents made from the trust since October 24, 1992. Each of these determinations is required to be made by an independent actuary.

In general, amounts used to pay retiree accident or health benefits are not includible in the income of the company, nor is a deduction allowed for such amounts.

United Mine Workers of America Combined Benefit Fund

The United Mine Workers of America ("UMWA") Combined Benefit Fund was established by the Coal Industry Retiree Health Benefit Act of 1992 to assume responsibility of payments for medical care expenses of retired miners and their dependents who were eligible for heath care from the private 1950 and 1974 UMWA Benefit Plans. The UMWA Combined Benefit Fund is financed by assessments on current and former signatories to labor agreements with the UMWA, past transfers from an overfunded United Mine Workers pension fund, and transfers from the Abandoned Mine Reclamation Fund.

Explanation of Provision

The provision eliminates the aggregate limit on the amount of excess black lung benefit trust assets that may be used to pay accident and health benefits or premiums for insurance exclusively covering such benefits (including administrative and other incidental expenses relating to such benefits) for retired coal miners and their spouses and dependents.

Effective Date

The provision is effective for taxable years beginning after December 31, 2006.

3. Tax treatment of company-owned life insurance ("COLI") (new secs. 101(j) and 6039I of the Code)

Present Law

Amounts received under a life insurance contract

Amounts received under a life insurance contract paid by reason of the death of the insured are not includible in gross income for Federal tax purposes.[221] No Federal income tax generally is imposed on a policyholder with respect to the earnings under a life insurance contract (inside buildup).[222]

Distributions from a life insurance contract (other than a modified endowment contract) that are made prior to the death of the insured generally are includible in income to the extent that the amounts distributed exceed the taxpayer's investment in the contract (i.e., basis). Such distributions generally are treated first as a tax-free recovery of basis, and then as income.[223]

Premium and interest deduction limitations[224]

Premiums

Under present law, no deduction is permitted for premiums paid on any life insurance, annuity or endowment contract, if the taxpayer is directly or indirectly a beneficiary under the contract.[225]

---

[221] Sec. 101(a).

[222] This favorable tax treatment is available only if a life insurance contract meets certain requirements designed to limit the investment character of the contract (sec. 7702).

[223] Sec. 72(e). In the case of a modified endowment contract, however, in general, distributions are treated as income first, loans are treated as distributions (i.e., income rather than basis recovery first), and an additional 10-percent tax is imposed on the income portion of distributions made before age 59½ and in certain other circumstances (secs. 72(e) and (v)). A modified endowment contract is a life insurance contract that does not meet a statutory "7-pay" test, i.e., generally is funded more rapidly than seven annual level premiums (sec. 7702A).

[224] In addition to the statutory limitations described below, interest deductions under company-owned life insurance arrangements have also been limited by recent cases applying general principles of tax law. See *Winn-Dixie Stores, Inc. v. Commissioner*, 113 T.C. 254 (1999), aff'd 254 F.3d 1313 (11th Cir. 2001), cert. denied, April 15, 2002; *Internal Revenue Service v. CM Holdings, Inc.*, 254 B.R. 578 (D. Del. 2000), aff'd, 301 F.3d 96 (3d Cir. 2002); *American Electric Power, Inc. v. U.S.*, 136 F. Supp. 2d 762 (S. D. Ohio 2001), aff'd, 326 F.3d 737 (6th Cir. 2003), reh. denied, 338 F.3d 534 (6th Cir. 2003), cert. denied, U.S. No. 03-529 (Jan. 12, 2004); *Dow Chemical Company v. U.S.*, 435 F.3d 594 (6th Cir. 2006), rev'g 250 F. Supp. 2d 748 (E.D. Mich. 2003) as modified, 278 F. Supp. 2d 844 (E.D. Mich. 2003).

[225] Sec. 264(a)(1).

Interest paid or accrued with respect to the contract

No deduction generally is allowed for interest paid or accrued on any debt with respect to a life insurance, annuity or endowment contract covering the life of any individual.[226] An exception is provided under this provision for insurance of key persons.

Interest that is otherwise deductible (e.g., is not disallowed under other applicable rules or general principles of tax law) may be deductible under the key person exception, to the extent that the aggregate amount of the debt does not exceed $50,000 per insured individual. The deductible interest may not exceed the amount determined by applying a rate based on a Moody's Corporate Bond Yield Average-Monthly Average Corporates. A key person is an individual who is either an officer or a 20-percent owner of the taxpayer. The number of individuals that can be treated as key persons may not exceed the greater of (1) five individuals, or (2) the lesser of five percent of the total number of officers and employees of the taxpayer, or 20 individuals.[227]

Pro rata interest limitation

A pro rata interest deduction disallowance rule also applies. Under this rule, in the case of a taxpayer other than a natural person, no deduction is allowed for the portion of the taxpayer's interest expense that is allocable to unborrowed policy cash surrender values.[228] Interest expense is allocable to unborrowed policy cash values based on the ratio of (1) the taxpayer's average unborrowed policy cash values of life insurance, annuity and endowment contracts, to (2) the sum of the average unborrowed cash values (or average adjusted bases, for other assets) of all the taxpayer's assets.

Under the pro rata interest disallowance rule, an exception is provided for any contract owned by an entity engaged in a trade or business, if the contract covers an individual who is a 20-percent owner of the entity, or an officer, director, or employee of the trade or business. The exception also applies to a joint-life contract covering a 20-percent owner and his or her spouse.

"Single premium" and "4-out-of-7" limitations

Other interest deduction limitation rules also apply with respect to life insurance, annuity and endowment contracts. Present law provides that no deduction is allowed for any amount paid or accrued on debt incurred or continued to purchase or carry a single premium life insurance, annuity or endowment contract.[229] In addition, present law provides that no deduction is allowed for any amount paid or accrued on debt incurred or continued to purchase or carry a

---

[226] Sec. 264(a)(4).

[227] Sec. 264(e)(3).

[228] Sec. 264(f). This applies to any life insurance, annuity or endowment contract issued after June 8, 1997.

[229] Sec. 264(a)(2).

life insurance, annuity or endowment contract pursuant to a plan of purchase that contemplates the systematic direct or indirect borrowing of part or all of the increases in the cash value of the contract (either from the insurer or otherwise).[230] Under this rule, several exceptions are provided, including an exception if no part of four of the annual premiums due during the initial seven-year period is paid by means of such debt (known as the "4-out-of-7 rule").

Definitions of highly compensated employee

Present law defines highly compensated employees and individuals for various purposes. For purposes of nondiscrimination rules relating to qualified retirement plans, an employee, including a self-employed individual, is treated as highly compensated with respect to a year if the employee (1) was a five-percent owner of the employer at any time during the year or the preceding year or (2) either (a) had compensation for the preceding year in excess of $95,000 (for 2005) or (b) at the election of the employer had compensation in excess of $95,000 (for 2005) and was in the highest paid 20 percent of employees for such year.[231] The $95,000 dollar amount is indexed for inflation.

For purposes of nondiscrimination rules relating to self-insured medical reimbursement plans, a highly compensated individual is an employee who is one of the five highest paid officers of the employer, a shareholder who owns more than 10 percent of the value of the stock of the employer, or is among the highest paid 25 percent of all employees.[232]

Explanation of Provision

The provision provides generally that, in the case of an employer-owned life insurance contract, the amount excluded from the applicable policyholder's income as a death benefit cannot exceed the premiums and other amounts paid by such applicable policyholder for the contract. The excess death benefit is included in income.

Exceptions to this income inclusion rule are provided. In the case of an employer-owned life insurance contract with respect to which the notice and consent requirements of the provision are met, the income inclusion rule does not apply to an amount received by reason of the death of an insured individual who, with respect to the applicable policyholder, was an employee at any time during the 12-month period before the insured's death, or who, at the time the contract was issued, was a director or highly compensated employee or highly compensated individual. For this purpose, such a person is one who is either: (1) a highly compensated employee as defined under the rules relating to qualified retirement plans, determined without regard to the election regarding the top-paid 20 percent of employees; or (2) a highly compensated individual as

---

[230] Sec. 264(a)(3).

[231] Sec. 414(q). For purposes of determining the top-paid 20 percent of employees, certain employees, such as employees subject to a collective bargaining agreement, are disregarded.

[232] Sec. 105(h)(5). For purposes of determining the top-paid 25 percent of employees, certain employees, such as employees subject to a collective bargaining agreement, are disregarded.

defined under the rules relating to self-insured medical reimbursement plans, determined by substituting the highest-paid 35 percent of employees for the highest-paid 25 percent of employees.[233]

In the case of an employer-owned life insurance contract with respect to which the notice and consent requirements of the provision are met, the income inclusion rule does not apply to an amount received by reason of the death of an insured, to the extent the amount is (1) paid to a member of the family[234] of the insured, to an individual who is the designated beneficiary of the insured under the contract (other than an applicable policyholder), to a trust established for the benefit of any such member of the family or designated beneficiary, or to the estate of the insured; or (2) used to purchase an equity (or partnership capital or profits) interest in the applicable policyholder from such a family member, beneficiary, trust or estate. It is intended that such amounts be so paid or used by the due date of the tax return for the taxable year of the applicable policyholder in which they are received as a death benefit under the insurance contract, so that the payment of the amount to such a person or persons, or the use of the amount to make such a purchase, is known in the taxable year for which the exception from the income inclusion rule is claimed.

An employer-owned life insurance contract is defined for purposes of the provision as a life insurance contract which (1) is owned by a person engaged in a trade or business and under which such person (or a related person) is directly or indirectly a beneficiary, and (2) covers the life of an individual who is an employee with respect to the trade or business of the applicable policyholder on the date the contract is issued.

An applicable policyholder means, with respect to an employer-owned life insurance contract, the person (including related persons) that owns the contract, if the person is engaged in a trade or business, and if the person (or a related person) is directly or indirectly a beneficiary under the contract.

For purposes of the provision, a related person includes any person that bears a relationship specified in section 267(b) or 707(b)(1)[235] or is engaged in trades or businesses that are under common control (within the meaning of section 52(a) or (b)).

---

[233] As under present law, certain employees are disregarded in making the determinations regarding the top-paid groups.

[234] For this purpose, a member of the family is defined in section 267(c)(4) to include only the individual's brothers and sisters (whether by the whole or half blood), spouse, ancestors, and lineal descendants.

[235] The relationships include specified relationships among family members, shareholders and corporations, corporations that are members of a controlled group, trust grantors and fiduciaries, tax-exempt organizations and persons that control such organizations, commonly controlled S corporations, partnerships and C corporations, estates and beneficiaries, commonly controlled partnerships, and partners and partnerships. Detailed rules apply to determine the specific relationships.

The notice and consent requirements of the provision are met if, before the issuance of the contract, (1) the employee is notified in writing that the applicable policyholder intends to insure the employee's life, and is notified of the maximum face amount at issue of the life insurance contract that the employer might take out on the life of the employee, (2) the employee provides written consent to being insured under the contract and that such coverage may continue after the insured terminates employment, and (3) the employee is informed in writing that an applicable policyholder will be a beneficiary of any proceeds payable on the death of the employee.

For purposes of the provision, an employee includes an officer, a director, and a highly compensated employee; an insured means, with respect to an employer-owned life insurance contract, an individual covered by the contract who is a U.S. citizen or resident. In the case of a contract covering the joint lives of two individuals, references to an insured include both of the individuals.

The provision requires annual reporting and recordkeeping by applicable policyholders that own one or more employer-owned life insurance contracts. The information to be reported is (1) the number of employees of the applicable policyholder at the end of the year, (2) the number of employees insured under employer-owned life insurance contracts at the end of the year, (3) the total amount of insurance in force at the end of the year under such contracts, (4) the name, address, and taxpayer identification number of the applicable policyholder and the type of business in which it is engaged, and (5) a statement that the applicable policyholder has a valid consent (in accordance with the consent requirements under the provision) for each insured employee and, if all such consents were not obtained, the total number of insured employees for whom such consent was not obtained. The applicable policyholder is required to keep records necessary to determine whether the requirements of the reporting rule and the income inclusion rule of new section 101(j) are met.

Effective Date

The provision generally appleis to contracts issued after the date of enactment, except for contracts issued after such date pursuant to an exchange described in section 1035 of the Code. In addition, certain material increases in the death benefit or other material changes will generally cause a contract to be treated as a new contract, with an exception for existing lives under a master contract. Increases in the death benefit that occur as a result of the operation of section 7702 of the Code or the terms of the existing contract, provided that the insurer's consent to the increase is not required, will not cause a contract to be treated as a new contract. In addition, certain changes to a contract will not be considered material changes so as to cause a contract to be treated as a new contract. These changes include administrative changes, changes from general to separate account, or changes as a result of the exercise of an option or right granted under the contract as originally issued.

Examples of situations in which death benefit increases would not cause a contract to be treated as a new contract include the following:

1. Section 7702 provides that life insurance contracts need to either meet the cash value accumulation test of section 7702(b) or the guideline premium requirements of section

7702(c) and the cash value corridor of section 7702(d). Under the corridor test, the amount of the death benefit may not be less than the applicable percentage of the cash surrender value. Contracts may be written to comply with the corridor requirement by providing for automatic increases in the death benefit based on the cash surrender value. Death benefit increases required by the corridor test or the cash value accumulation test do not require the insurer's consent at the time of increase and occur in order to keep the contact in compliance with section 7702.

2. Death benefits may also increase due to normal operation of the contract. For example, for some contracts, policyholder dividends paid under the contract may be applied to purchase paid-up additions, which increase the death benefits. The insurer's consent is not required for these death benefit increases.

3. For variable contacts and universal life contracts, the death benefit may increase as a result of market performance or the contract design. For example, some contracts provide that the death benefit will equal the cash value plus a specified amount at risk. With these contracts, the amount of the death benefit at any time will vary depending on changes in the cash value of the contract. The insurance company's consent is not required for these death benefit increases.

4. Treatment of test room supervisors and proctors who assist in the administration of college entrance and placement exams (sec. 530 of the Revenue Reconciliation Act of 1978)

Present Law

Section 530 of the Revenue Act of 1978 prohibits the Internal Revenue Service from challenging a taxpayer's treatment of an individual as an independent contractor for employment tax purposes if the taxpayer (1) has a reasonable basis for such treatment and (2) consistently treats the individual, and any other individual holding a substantially similar position, as an independent contractor.

Explanation of Provision

Under the bill, section 530 of the Revenue Act of 1978 is amended to provide that in the case of an individual providing services as a test proctor or room supervisor by assisting in the administration of college entrance or placements examinations, the consistency requirement does not apply with respect to services performed after December 31, 2006 (and remuneration paid with respect to such services). The provision applies if the individual (1) is performing the services for a tax-exempt organization, and (2) is not otherwise treated as an employee of such organization for purposes of employment taxes. Thus, under the bill, if the requirements are satisfied, the IRS is prohibited from challenging the treatment of such individuals as independent contractors for employment tax purposes, even if the organization previously treated such individuals as employees.

Effective Date

The provision is effective for remuneration paid for services performed after December 31, 2006.

5. Rule for church plans which self-annuitize (sec. 401(a)(9) of the Code)

Present Law

Minimum distribution rules apply to qualified retirement plans (sec. 401(a)(9)). Special rules apply in the case of payments under an annuity contract purchased with the employee's benefit by the plan from an insurance company.[236] If certain requirements are satisfied, these special rules apply to annuity payments from a retirement income account maintained by a church (or certain other organizations as described in sec. 403(b)(9)) even though the payments are not made under an annuity purchased from an insurance company.[237]

Explanation of Provision

The bill provides that annuity payments provided with respect to any account maintained for a participant or beneficiary under a qualified church plan does not fail to meet the minimum distribution rules merely because the payments are not made under an annuity contract purchased from an insurance company if such payments would not fail such requirements if provided with respect to a retirement income account described in section 403(b)(9).

For purposes of the provision, a qualified church plan means any money purchase plan described in section 401(a) which (1) is a church plan (as defined in section 414(e)) with respect to which the election provided by section 410(d) has not been made, and (2) was in existence on April 17, 2002.

Effective Date

The provision is effective for years beginning after the date of enactment. No inference is intended from the provision with respect to the proper application of the minimum distribution rules to church plans before the effective date.

6. Exemption for income from leveraged real estate held by church plans (sec. 514(c)(9) of the Code)

Present Law

Debt-financed income of a tax-exempt entity is subject to unrelated business income tax ("UBIT") under section 514 of the Code. Debt-financed property generally is property that is held to produce income and with respect to which there is acquisition indebtedness.

There is an exception to the UBIT rules for debt-financed property held by qualifying organizations (sec. 514(c)(9)). Qualified organizations include retirement plans qualified under section 401(a).

---

[236] Treas. Reg. sec. 1.401(a)(9)-6, A-4.

[237] Treas. Reg. sec. 1.403(b)-3, A-1(c)(3).

Explanation of Provision

The bill provides that a retirement income account of a church (or certain other organizations) as defined in section 403(b)(9) is a qualified organization for purposes of the exemption from the UBIT debt-financed property rules.

Effective Date

The provision is effective for taxable years beginning on or after the date of enactment.

7. Church plan rule for benefit limitations (sec. 415 of the Code)

Present Law

Section 415 limits the amount of benefits and contributions that may be provided under a tax-qualified plan. In the case of a defined benefit plan, the limit on annual benefits payable under the plan is the lesser of: (1) a dollar amount which is adjusted for inflation ($175,000 for 2006); and (2) 100 percent of the participant's compensation for the highest three years. Special rules apply in some cases.

Explanation of Provision

The provision provides that the 100 percent of compensation limit does not apply to a plan maintained by a church or qualified church controlled organization defined in section 3121(w)(3)(A) except with respect to "highly compensated benefits". The term "highly compensated benefits" means any benefits accrued for an employee in any year on or after the first year in which such employee is a highly compensated employee (as defined in sec. 414(q)) of the organization. For purposes of applying the 100 percent of compensation limit to highly compensated benefits, all the benefits of the employee which would otherwise be taken into account in applying the limit shall be taken into account, i.e., the limit does not apply only to those benefits accrued on or after the first year in which the employee is a highly compensated employee.

Effective Date

The provision is effective for years beginning after December 31, 2006.

8. Gratuitous transfers for the benefit of employees (sec. 664 of the Code)

Present Law

Present law permits certain limited transfers of qualified employer securities by charitable remainder trusts to an employee stock ownership plan ("ESOP") without adversely affecting the status of the charitable remainder trusts under section 664. In addition, the ESOP does not fail to be a qualified plan because it complies with the requirements with respect to a qualified gratuitous transfer.

A number of requirements must be satisfied for a transfer of securities to be a qualified gratuitous transfer, including the following: (1) the securities transferred to the ESOP must previously have passed from the decedent to a charitable remainder trust; (2) at the time of the transfer to the ESOP, family members own no more than a certain percentage of the outstanding stock of the company; (3) immediately after the transfer the ESOP owns at least 60 percent of the value of the outstanding stock of company; and (4) the ESOP meets certain requirements.

Among other requirements applicable to the ESOP, securities transferred to the ESOP are required to be allocated each year up to the applicable limit (after first allocating all other annual additions for the limitation year). The applicable limit is the lesser of (1) $30,000 (as indexed) or (2) 25 percent of the participant's compensation.

Explanation of Provision

The provision clarifies that, under section 664, the amount of transferred securities required to be allocated each year is determined on the basis of fair market value of the securities when allocated to participants.

Effective Date

The provision is effective on the date of enactment.

TITLE IX: INCREASE IN PENSION PLAN DIVERSIFICATION AND PARTICIPATION

A. Defined Contribution Plans Required to Provide Employees with Freedom to Invest Their Plan Assets (new sec. 401(a)(35) of the Code and new sec. 204(j) of ERISA)

Present Law

In general

Defined contribution plans may permit both employees and employers to make contributions to the plan. Under a qualified cash or deferred arrangement (commonly referred to as a "section 401(k) plan"), employees may elect to make pretax contributions to a plan, referred to as elective deferrals. Employees may also be permitted to make after-tax contributions to a plan. In addition, a plan may provide for employer nonelective contributions or matching contributions. Nonelective contributions are employer contributions that are made without regard to whether the employee makes elective deferrals or after-tax contributions. Matching contributions are employer contributions that are made only if the employee makes elective deferrals or after-tax contributions.

Under the Code, elective deferrals, after-tax employee contributions, and employer matching contributions are subject to special nondiscrimination tests. Certain employer nonelective contributions may be used to satisfy these special nondiscrimination tests. In addition, plans may satisfy the special nondiscrimination tests by meeting certain safe harbor contribution requirements.

The Code requires employee stock ownership plans ("ESOPs") to offer certain plan participants the right to diversify investments in employer securities. The Employee Retirement Income Security Act of 1974 ("ERISA") limits the amount of employer securities and employer real property that can be acquired or held by certain employer-sponsored retirement plans. The extent to which the ERISA limits apply depends on the type of plan and the type of contribution involved.

Diversification requirements applicable to ESOPs under the Code

An ESOP is a defined contribution plan that is designated as an ESOP and is designed to invest primarily in qualifying employer securities and that meets certain other requirements under the Code. For purposes of ESOP investments, a "qualifying employer security" is defined as: (1) publicly traded common stock of the employer or a member of the same controlled group; (2) if there is no such publicly traded common stock, common stock of the employer (or member of the same controlled group) that has both voting power and dividend rights at least as great as any other class of common stock; or (3) noncallable preferred stock that is convertible into common stock described in (1) or (2) and that meets certain requirements. In some cases, an employer may design a class of preferred stock that meets these requirements and that is held only by the ESOP.

An ESOP can be an entire plan or it can be a component of a larger defined contribution plan. An ESOP may provide for different types of contributions. For example, an ESOP may include a qualified cash or deferred arrangement that permits employees to make elective deferrals.[238]

Under the Code, ESOPs are subject to a requirement that a participant who has attained age 55 and who has at least 10 years of participation in the plan must be permitted to diversify the investment of the participant's account in assets other than employer securities.[239] The diversification requirement applies to a participant for six years, starting with the year in which the individual first meets the eligibility requirements (i.e., age 55 and 10 years of participation). The participant must be allowed to elect to diversify up to 25 percent of the participant's account (50 percent in the sixth year), reduced by the portion of the account diversified in prior years.

The participant must be given 90 days after the end of each plan year in the election period to make the election to diversify. In the case of participants who elect to diversify, the plan satisfies the diversification requirement if: (1) the plan distributes the applicable amount to the participant within 90 days after the election period; (2) the plan offers at least three investment options (not inconsistent with Treasury regulations) and, within 90 days of the election period, invests the applicable amount in accordance with the participant's election; or (3) the applicable amount is transferred within 90 days of the election period to another qualified defined contribution plan of the employer providing investment options in accordance with (2).[240]

ERISA limits on investments in employer securities and real property

ERISA imposes restrictions on the investment of retirement plan assets in employer securities or employer real property.[241] A retirement plan may hold only a "qualifying" employer security and only "qualifying" employer real property.

Under ERISA, any stock issued by the employer or an affiliate of the employer is a qualifying employer security.[242] Qualifying employer securities also include certain publicly traded partnership interests and certain marketable obligations (i.e., a bond, debenture, note, certificate or other evidence of indebtedness). Qualifying employer real property means parcels of employer real property: (1) if a substantial number of the parcels are dispersed geographically;

---

[238] Such an ESOP design is sometimes referred to as a "KSOP."

[239] Sec. 401(a)(28). The present-law diversification requirements do not apply to employer securities held by an ESOP that were acquired before January 1, 1987.

[240] IRS Notice 88-56, 1988-1 C.B. 540, Q&A-16.

[241] ERISA sec. 407.

[242] Certain additional requirements apply to employer stock held by a defined benefit pension plan or a money purchase pension plan (other than certain plans in existence before the enactment of ERISA).

(2) if each parcel of real property and the improvements thereon are suitable (or adaptable without excessive cost) for more than one use; (3) even if all of the real property is leased to one lessee (which may be an employer, or an affiliate of an employer); and (4) if the acquisition and retention of such property generally comply with the fiduciary rules of ERISA (with certain specified exceptions).

ERISA also prohibits defined benefit pension plans and money purchase pension plans (other than certain plans in existence before the enactment of ERISA) from acquiring employer securities or employer real property if, after the acquisition, more than 10 percent of the assets of the plan would be invested in employer securities and real property. Except as discussed below with respect to elective deferrals, this 10-percent limitation generally does not apply to defined contribution plans other than money purchase pension plans.[243] In addition, a fiduciary generally is deemed not to violate the requirement that plan assets be diversified with respect to the acquisition or holding of employer securities or employer real property in a defined contribution plan.[244]

The 10-percent limitation on the acquisition of employer securities and real property applies separately to the portion of a plan consisting of elective deferrals (and earnings thereon) if any portion of an individual's elective deferrals (or earnings thereon) are required to be invested in employer securities or real property pursuant to plan terms or the direction of a person other than the participant. This restriction does not apply if: (1) the amount of elective deferrals required to be invested in employer securities and real property does not exceed more than one percent of any employee's compensation; (2) the fair market value of all defined contribution plans maintained by the employer is no more than 10 percent of the fair market value of all retirement plans of the employer; or (3) the plan is an ESOP.

Explanation of Provision

In general

Under the provision, in order to satisfy the plan qualification requirements of the Code and the vesting requirements of ERISA, certain defined contribution plans are required to provide diversification rights with respect to amounts invested in employer securities. Such a plan is required to permit applicable individuals to direct that the portion of the individual's account held in employer securities be invested in alternative investments. An applicable individual includes: (1) any plan participant; and (2) any beneficiary who has an account under the plan with respect to which the beneficiary is entitled to exercise the rights of a participant.

---

[243] The 10-percent limitation also applies to a defined contribution plan that is part of an arrangement under which benefits payable to a participant under a defined benefit pension plan are reduced by benefits under the defined contribution plan (i.e., a "floor-offset" arrangement).

[244] Under ERISA, a defined contribution plan is generally referred to as an individual account plan. Plans that are not subject to the 10-percent limitation on the acquisition of employer securities and employer real property are referred to as "eligible individual account plans."

The time when the diversification requirements apply depends on the type of contributions invested in employer securities.

Plans subject to requirements

The diversification requirements generally apply to an "applicable defined contribution plan,"[245] which means a defined contribution plan holding publicly-traded employer securities (i.e., securities issued by the employer or a member of the employer's controlled group of corporations[246] that are readily tradable on an established securities market).

For this purpose, a plan holding employer securities that are not publicly traded is generally treated as holding publicly–traded employer securities if the employer (or any member of the employer's controlled group of corporations) has issued a class of stock that is a publicly–traded employer security. This treatment does not apply if neither the employer nor any parent corporation[247] of the employer has issued any publicly–traded security or any special class of stock that grants particular rights to, or bears particular risks for, the holder or the issuer with respect to any member of the employer's controlled group that has issued any publicly–traded employer security. For example, a controlled group that generally consists of corporations that have not issued publicly-traded securities may include a member that has issued publicly–traded stock (the "publicly–traded member"). In the case of a plan maintained by an employer that is another member of the controlled group, the diversification requirements do not apply to the plan, provided that neither the employer nor a parent corporation of the employer has issued any publicly–traded security or any special class of stock that grants particular rights to, or bears particular risks for, the holder or issuer with respect to the member that has issued publicly–traded stock. The Secretary of the Treasury has the authority to provide other exceptions in regulations. For example, an exception may be appropriate if no stock of the employer maintaining the plan (including stock held in the plan) is publicly traded, but a member of the employer's controlled group has issued a small amount of publicly-traded stock.

The diversification requirements do not apply to an ESOP that: (1) does not hold contributions (or earnings thereon) that are subject to the special nondiscrimination tests that apply to elective deferrals, employee after-tax contributions, and matching contributions; and (2) is a separate plan from any other qualified retirement plan of the employer. Accordingly, an ESOP that holds elective deferrals, employee contributions, employer matching contributions, or nonelective employer contributions used to satisfy the special nondiscrimination tests (including

---

[245] Under ERISA, the diversification requirements apply to an "applicable individual account plan."

[246] For this purpose, "controlled group of corporations" has the same meaning as under section 1563(a), except that, in applying that section, 50 percent is substituted for 80 percent.

[247] For this purpose, "parent corporation" has the same meaning as under section 424(e), i.e., any corporation (other than the employer) in an unbroken chain of corporations ending with the employer if each corporation other than the employer owns stock possessing at least 50 percent of the total combined voting power of all classes of stock with voting rights or at least 50 percent of the total value of shares of all classes of stock in one of the other corporations in the chain.

the safe harbor methods of satisfying the tests) is subject to the diversification requirements under the Provision. The diversification rights applicable under the provision are broader than those applicable under the Code's present-law ESOP diversification rules. Thus, an ESOP that is subject to the new requirements is excepted from the present-law rules.[248]

The new diversification requirements also do not apply to a one–participant retirement plan. For purposes of the Code, a one–participant retirement plan is a plan that: (1) on the first day of the plan year, either covered only one individual (or the individual and his or her spouse) and the individual owned 100 percent of the plan sponsor (i.e., the employer maintaining the plan), whether or not incorporated, or covered only one or more partners (or partners and their spouses) in the plan sponsor; (2) meets the minimum coverage requirements without being combined with any other plan of the business that covers employees of the business; (3) does not provide benefits to anyone except the individuals and partners (and spouses) described in (1); (4) does not cover a business that is a member of an affiliated service group, a controlled group of corporations, or a group of corporations under common control; and (5) does not cover a business that uses the services of leased employees.[249] It is intended that, for this purpose, a "partner" includes an owner of a business that is treated as a partnership for tax purposes. In addition, it includes a two-percent shareholder of an S corporation.[250]

Elective deferrals and after–tax employee contributions

In the case of amounts attributable to elective deferrals under a qualified cash or deferred arrangement and employee after-tax contributions that are invested in employer securities, any applicable individual must be permitted to direct that such amounts be invested in alternative investments.

Other contributions

In the case of amounts attributable to contributions other than elective deferrals and after-tax employees contributions (i.e., nonelective employer contributions and employer matching contributions) that are invested in employer securities, an applicable individual who is a participant with three years of service,[251] a beneficiary of such a participant, or a beneficiary of a deceased participant must be permitted to direct that such amounts be invested in alternative investments.

---

[248] An ESOP will not be treated as failing to be designed to invest primarily in qualifying employer securities merely because the plan provides diversification rights as required under the provision or greater diversification rights than required under the provision.

[249] For purposes of ERISA, a one-participant retirement plan is defined as under the provision of ERISA that requires advance notice of a blackout period to be provided to participants and beneficiaries affected by the blackout period, as discussed below.

[250] Under section 1372, a two-percent shareholder of an S corporation is treated as a partner for fringe benefit purposes.

[251] Years of service is defined as under the rules relating to vesting (sec. 411(a)).

A transition rule applies to amounts attributable to these other contributions that are invested in employer securities acquired before the first plan year for which the new diversification requirements apply. Under the transition rule, for the first three years for which the new diversification requirements apply to the plan, the applicable percentage of such amounts is subject to diversification as shown in Table 1, below. The applicable percentage applies separately to each class of employer security in an applicable individual's account. The transition rule does not apply to plan participants who have three years of service and who have attained age 55 by the beginning of the first plan year beginning after December 31, 2005.

Table 1.–Applicable Percentage for Employer Securities Held on Effective Date

Plan year for which diversification applies:	Applicable percentage:
First year	33 percent
Second year	66 percent
Third year	100 percent

The application of the transition rule is illustrated by the following example. Suppose that the account of a participant with at least three years of service held 120 shares of employer common stock contributed as matching contributions before the diversification requirements became effective. In the first year for which diversification applies, 33 percent (i.e., 40 shares) of that stock is subject to the diversification requirements. In the second year for which diversification applies, a total of 66 percent of 120 shares of stock (i.e., 79 shares, or an additional 39 shares) is subject to the diversification requirements. In the third year for which diversification applies, 100 percent of the stock, or all 120 shares, is subject to the diversification requirements. In addition, in each year, employer stock in the account attributable to elective deferrals and employee after-tax contributions is fully subject to the diversification requirements, as is any new stock contributed to the account.

Rules relating to the election of investment alternatives

A plan subject to the diversification requirements is required to give applicable individuals a choice of at least three investment options, other than employer securities, each of which is diversified and has materially different risk and return characteristics. It is intended that other investment options generally offered by the plan also must be available to applicable individuals.

A plan does not fail to meet the diversification requirements merely because the plan limits the times when divestment and reinvestment can be made to periodic, reasonable opportunities that occur at least quarterly. It is intended that applicable individuals generally be given the opportunity to make investment changes with respect to employer securities on the same basis as the opportunity to make other investment changes, except in unusual circumstances. Thus, in general, applicable individuals must be given the opportunity to request changes with respect to investments in employer securities with the same frequency as the opportunity to make other investment changes and that such changes are implemented in the same timeframe as other investment changes, unless circumstances require different treatment.

Except as provided in regulations, a plan may not impose restrictions or conditions with respect to the investment of employer securities that are not imposed on the investment of other plan assets (other than restrictions or conditions imposed by reason of the application of securities laws). For example, such a restriction or condition includes a provision under which a participant who divests his or her account of employer securities receives less favorable treatment (such as a lower rate of employer contributions) than a participant whose account remains invested in employer securities. On the other hand, such a restriction does not include the imposition of fees with respect to other investment options under the plan, merely because fees are not imposed with respect to investments in employer securities.

Effective Date

The provision is effective for plan years beginning after December 31, 2006.

In the case of a plan maintained pursuant to one or more collective bargaining agreements, the provision is effective for plan years beginning after the earlier of (1) the later of December 31, 2007, or the date on which the last of such collective bargaining agreements terminates (determined without regard to any extension thereof after the date of enactment), or (2) December 31, 2008.

A special effective date applies with respect to employer matching and nonelective contributions (and earnings thereon) that are invested in employer securities that, as of September 17, 2003: (1) consist of preferred stock; and (2) are held within an ESOP, under the terms of which the value of the preferred stock is subject to a guaranteed minimum. Under the special rule, the diversification requirements apply to such preferred stock for plan years beginning after the earlier of (1) December 31, 2007; or (2) the first date as of which the actual value of the preferred stock equals or exceeds the guaranteed minimum. When the new diversification requirements become effective for the plan under the special rule, the applicable percentage of employer securities held on the effective date that is subject to diversification is determined without regard to the special rule.

B. Increasing Participation Through Automatic Enrollment Arrangements (secs. 404(c) and 514 of ERISA and secs. 401(k), 401(m), 414 and 4979 of the Code)

Present Law

Qualified cash or deferred arrangements–in general

Under present law, most defined contribution plans may include a qualified cash or deferred arrangement (commonly referred to as a "section 401(k)" or "401(k)" plan),[252] under which employees may elect to receive cash or to have contributions made to the plan by the employer on behalf of the employee in lieu of receiving cash. Contributions made to the plan at the election of the employee are referred to as "elective deferrals" or "elective contributions".[253] A 401(k) plan may be designed so that the employee will receive cash unless an affirmative election to make contributions is made. Alternatively, a plan may provide that elective contributions are made at a specified rate unless the employee elects otherwise (i.e., elects not to make contributions or to make contributions at a different rate). Arrangements that operate in this manner are sometimes referred to as "automatic enrollment" or "negative election" plans. In either case, the employee must have an effective opportunity to elect to receive cash in lieu of contributions. [254]

Nondiscrimination rules

A special nondiscrimination test applies to elective deferrals under a section 401(k) plan, called the actual deferral percentage test or the "ADP" test. The ADP test compares the actual deferral percentages ("ADPs") of the highly compensated employee group and the nonhighly compensated employee group. The ADP for each group generally is the average of the deferral percentages separately calculated for the employees in the group who are eligible to make elective deferrals for all or a portion of the relevant plan year. Each eligible employee's deferral percentage generally is the employee's elective deferrals for the year divided by the employee's compensation for the year.

The plan generally satisfies the ADP test if the ADP of the highly compensated employee group for the current plan year is either (1) not more than 125 percent of the ADP of the

---

[252] Legally, a section 401(k) plan is not a separate type of plan, but is a profit-sharing, stock bonus, or pre-ERISA money purchase plan that contains a qualified cash or deferred arrangement. The terms "section 401(k) plan" and "401(k) plan" are used here for convenience.

[253] The maximum annual amount of elective deferrals that can be made by an individual is subject to a limit ($15,000 for 2006). An individual who has attained age 50 before the end of the taxable year may also make catch-up contributions to a section 401(k) plan, subject to a limit ($5,000 for 2006).

[254] Treasury regulations provide that whether an employee has an effective opportunity to receive cash is based on all the relevant facts and circumstances, including the adequacy of notice of the availability of the election, the period of time during which an election may be made, and any other conditions on elections. Treas. Reg. sec. 1.401(k)-1(e)(2).

nonhighly compensated employee group for the prior plan year, or (2) not more than 200 percent of the ADP of the nonhighly compensated employee group for the prior plan year and not more than two percentage points greater than the ADP of the nonhighly compensated employee group for the prior plan year.

Under a safe harbor, a section 401(k) plan is deemed to satisfy the special nondiscrimination test if the plan satisfies one of two contribution requirements and satisfies a notice requirement (a "safe harbor section 401(k) plan"). A plan satisfies the contribution requirement under the safe harbor rule if the employer either (1) satisfies a matching contribution requirement or (2) makes a nonelective contribution to a defined contribution plan of at least three percent of an employee's compensation on behalf of each nonhighly compensated employee who is eligible to participate in the arrangement. A plan generally satisfies the matching contribution requirement if, under the arrangement: (1) the employer makes a matching contribution on behalf of each nonhighly compensated employee that is equal to (a) 100 percent of the employee's elective deferrals up to three percent of compensation and (b) 50 percent of the employee's elective deferrals from three to five percent of compensation; [255] and (2) the rate of match with respect to any elective deferrals for highly compensated employees is not greater than the rate of match for nonhighly compensated employees.

Employer matching contributions are also subject to a special nondiscrimination test, the "ACP test," which compares the average actual contribution percentages ("ACPs") of matching contributions for the highly compensated employee group and the nonhighly compensated employee group. The plan generally satisfies the ACP test if the ACP of the highly compensated employee group for the current plan year is either (1) not more than 125 percent of the ACP of the nonhighly compensated employee group for the prior plan year, or (2) not more than 200 percent of the ACP of the nonhighly compensated employee group for the prior plan year and not more than two percentage points greater than the ACP of the nonhighly compensated employee group for the prior plan year.

A safe harbor section 401(k) plan that provides for matching contributions is deemed to satisfy the ACP test if, in addition to meeting the safe harbor contribution and notice requirements under section 401(k), (1) matching contributions are not provided with respect to elective deferrals in excess of six percent of compensation, (2) the rate of matching contribution does not increase as the rate of an employee's elective deferrals increases, and (3) the rate of matching contribution with respect to any rate of elective deferral of a highly compensated employee is no greater than the rate of matching contribution with respect to the same rate of deferral of a nonhighly compensated employee.

---

[255] In lieu of matching contributions at rates equal to the safe harbor rates, a plan may provide for an alternative match if (1) the rate of the matching contributions does not increase as an employee's rate of elective deferrals increases and (2) the amount of matching contributions at such rate of elective deferrals is at lest equal to the aggregate amount of contributions which would be made if rate of the matching contributions equaled the safe harbor rates.

Top-heavy rules

Special rules apply in the case of a top-heavy plan. In general, a defined contribution plan is a top-heavy plan if the accounts of key employees account for more than 60 percent of the aggregate value of accounts under the plan. If a plan is a top-heavy plan, then certain minimum vesting standards and minimum contribution requirements apply.

A plan that consists solely of contributions that satisfy the safe harbor plan rules for elective and matching contributions is not considered a top-heavy plan.

Tax-sheltered annuities

Tax-sheltered annuities ("section 403(b) annuities") may provide for contributions on a salary reduction basis, similar to section 401(k) plans. Matching contributions under a section 403(b) annuity are subject to the same nondiscrimination rules under section 401(m) as matching contributions under a section 401(k) plan (sec. 403(b)(12)). Thus, for example, the safe harbor method of satisfying the section 401(m) rules for matching contributions under a 401(k) plan applies to section 403(b) annuities.

Erroneous automatic elective contributions

Present law provides special rules for distributions of elective contributions that exceed the amount permitted under the nondiscrimination rules or the dollar limit on such contributions.

Fiduciary rules applicable to default investments of individual account plans

ERISA imposes standards on the conduct of plan fiduciaries, including persons who make investment decisions with respect to plan assets. Fiduciaries are personally liable for any losses to the plan due to a violation of fiduciary standards.

An individual account plan may permit participants to make investment decisions with respect to their accounts. ERISA fiduciary liability does not apply to investment decisions made by plan participants if participants exercise control over the investment of their individual accounts, as determined under ERISA regulations. In that case, a plan fiduciary may be responsible for the investment alternatives made available, but not for the specific investment decisions made by participants.

Preemption of State law

ERISA generally preempts all State laws relating to employee benefit plans, other than generally applicable criminal laws and laws relating to insurance, banking, or securities.

Excess contributions

An excise tax is imposed on an employer making excess contributions or excess aggregate contributions to a qualified retirement plan. Excess contributions are elective contributions, including qualified nonelective contributions and qualified matching contributions that are treated as elective contributions, made to a plan on behalf of highly compensated employees to the extent that the contributions fail to satisfy the applicable nondiscrimination tests for such plan for the year. Excess aggregate contributions are the aggregate amount of employer matching contributions and employee after-tax contributions to a plan for highly compensated employees to the extent that the contributions fail to satisfy the applicable nondiscrimination tests for such plan for the year.

The excise tax is equal to 10 percent of the excess contributions or excess aggregate contributions under a plan for the plan year ending in the taxable year. The tax does not apply to any excess contributions or excess aggregate contributions that, together with income allocable to the contributions, are distributed or forfeited (if forfeitable) within 2½ months after the close of the plan year. Any excess contributions or excess aggregate contributions that are distributed within 2½ months after the close of the plan year are treated as received and earned by the recipient in the taxable year for which such contributions are made. If the total of such distributions to a recipient under a plan for any plan year is less than $100, such distributions (and any income allocable thereto) are treated as earned and received by the recipient in the taxable year in which the distributions are made.

Additionally, if certain requirements are met, excess contributions may be recharacterized as after-tax employee contributions, no later than 2½ months after the close of the plan year to which the excess contributions relate.[256]

Explanation of Provision

In general

Under the provision, a 401(k) plan that contains an automatic enrollment feature that satisfies certain requirements (a "qualified automatic enrollment feature") is treated as meeting the ADP test with respect to elective deferrals and the ACP test with respect to matching contributions. In addition, a plan consisting solely of contributions made pursuant to a qualified automatic enrollment feature is not subject to the top-heavy rules.

A qualified automatic enrollment feature must meet certain requirements with respect to: (1) automatic deferral; (2) matching or nonelective contributions; and (3) notice to employees.

Automatic deferral/amount of elective contributions

A qualified automatic enrollment feature must provide that, unless an employee elects otherwise, the employee is treated as making an election to make elective deferrals equal to a stated percentage of compensation not in excess of 10 percent and at least equal to: three percent of compensation for the first year the deemed election applies to the participant; four percent during the second year; five percent during the third year; and six percent during the fourth year and thereafter. The stated percentage must be applied uniformly to all eligible employees.

---

[256] Treas. Reg. sec. 1.401(k)-2(b)(3).

Eligible employees mean all employees eligible to participate in the arrangement, other than employees eligible to participate in the arrangement immediately before the date on which the arrangement became a qualified automatic contribution arrangement with an election in effect (either to participate at a certain percentage or not to participate).

Matching or nonelective contribution requirement

Contributions

An automatic enrollment feature satisfies the contribution requirement if the employer either (1) satisfies a matching contribution requirement or (2) makes a nonelective contribution to a defined contribution plan of at least three percent of an employee's compensation on behalf of each nonhighly compensated employee who is eligible to participate in the automatic enrollment feature. A plan generally satisfies the matching contribution requirement if, under the arrangement: (1) the employer makes a matching contribution on behalf of each nonhighly compensated employee that is equal to 100 percent of the employee's elective deferrals as do not exceed one percent of compensation and 50 percent of the employee's elective deferrals as exceeds one percent but does not exceed six percent of compensation and (2) the rate of match with respect to any elective deferrals for highly compensated employees is not greater than the rate of match for nonhighly compensated employees. It is intended that the provision apply to section 403(b) annuities.

A plan including an automatic enrollment feature that provides for matching contributions is deemed to satisfy the ACP test if, in addition to meeting the safe harbor contribution requirements applicable to the qualified automatic enrollment feature: (1) matching contributions are not provided with respect to elective deferrals in excess of six percent of compensation, (2) the rate of matching contribution does not increase as the rate of an employee's elective deferrals increases, and (3) the rate of matching contribution with respect to any rate of elective deferral of a highly compensated employee is no greater than the rate of matching contribution with respect to the same rate of deferral of a nonhighly compensated employee.

Vesting

Any matching or other employer contributions taken into account in determining whether the requirements for a qualified automatic enrollment feature are satisfied must vest at least as rapidly as under two-year cliff vesting. That is, employees with at least two years of service must be 100 percent vested with respect to such contributions.

Withdrawal restrictions

Under the provision, any matching or other employer contributions taken into account in determining whether the requirements for a qualified automatic enrollment feature are satisfied are subject to the withdrawal rules applicable to elective contributions.

Notice requirement

Under a notice requirement, each employee eligible to participate in the arrangement must receive notice of the arrangement which is sufficiently accurate and comprehensive to apprise the employee of such rights and obligations and is written in a manner calculated to be understood by the average employee to whom the arrangement applies. The notice must explain: (1) the employee's right under the arrangement to elect not to have elective contributions made on the employee's behalf or to elect to have contributions made in a different amount; and (2) how contributions made under the automatic enrollment arrangement will be invested in the absence of any investment election by the employee. The employee must be given a reasonable period of time after receipt of the notice and before the first election contribution is to be made to make an election with respect to contributions and investments.

Application to tax-sheltered annuities

The new safe harbor rules for automatic contribution plans apply with respect to matching contributions under a section 403(b) annuity through the operation of section 403(b)(12).

Corrective distributions

The provision includes rules under which erroneous automatic contributions may be distributed from the plan no later than 90 days after the date of the first elective contribution with respect to the employee under the arrangement. The amount that is treated as an erroneous contribution is limited to the amount of automatic contributions made during the 90-day period that the employee elects to treat as an erroneous contribution. It is intended that distributions of such amounts are generally treated as a payment of compensation, rather than as a contribution to and then a distribution from the plan. The 10-percent early withdrawal tax does not apply to distributions of erroneous automatic contributions. In addition, it is intended that such contributions are not taken into account for purposes of applying the nondiscrimination rules, or the limit on elective deferrals. Similarly, it is intended that distributions of such contributions are not subject to the otherwise applicable withdrawal restrictions. The rules for corrective distributions apply to distributions from (1) qualified pension plans under Code section 401(a), (2) plans under which amounts are contributed by an individual's employer for Code section 403(b) annuity contract and (3) governmental eligible deferred compensation plans under Code section 457(b).

The corrective distribution rules are not limited to arrangements meeting the requirements of a qualified enrollment feature.

Excess contributions

In the case of an eligible automatic contribution arrangement, the excise tax on excess contributions does not apply to any excess contributions or excess aggregate contributions which, together with income allocable to the contributions, are distributed or forfeited (if forfeitable) within six months after the close of the plan year. Additionally, any excess contributions or excess aggregate contributions (and any income allocable thereto) that are distributed within the period required to avoid application of the excise tax are treated as earned and received by the recipient in the taxable year in which the distribution is made (regardless of the amount distributed), and the income allocable to excess contributions or excess aggregate contributions that must be distributed is determined through the end of the year for which the contributions were made.

Preemption of State law

The provision preempts any State law that would directly or indirectly prohibit or restrict the inclusion in a plan of an automatic contribution arrangement. The Labor Secretary may establish minimum standards for such arrangements in order for preemption to apply. An automatic contribution arrangement is an arrangement: (1) under which a participant may elect to have the plan sponsor make payments as contributions under the plan on behalf of the participant, or to the participant directly in cash, (2) under which a participant is treated as having elected to have the plan sponsor make such contributions in an amount equal to a uniform percentage of compensation provided under the plan until the participant specifically elects not to have such contributions made (or elects to have contributions made at a different percentage), and (3) under which contributions are invested in accordance with regulations issued by the Secretary of Labor relating to default investments as provided under the bill. The State preemption rules under the bill are not limited to arrangements that meet the requirements of a qualified enrollment feature.

A plan administrator must provide notice to each participant to whom the automatic contribution arrangement applies. If the notice requirement is not satisfied, an ERISA penalty of $1,100 per day applies.

Effective Date

The provision is effective for years beginning after December 31, 2007. The preemption of conflicting State regulations is effective on the date of enactment. No inference is intended as to the effect of conflicting State regulations prior to date of enactment.

C. Treatment of Eligible Combined Defined Benefit Plans and Qualified Cash or Deferred Arrangements (new sec. 414(x) of the Code and new sec. 210(e) of ERISA)

Present Law

In general

Under present law, most defined contribution plans may include a qualified cash or deferred arrangement (commonly referred to as a "section 401(k)" or "401(k)" plan),[257] under which employees may elect to receive cash or to have contributions made to the plan by the employer on behalf of the employee in lieu of receiving cash (referred to as "elective deferrals" or "elective contributions").[258] A section 401(k) plan may provide that elective deferrals are made for an employee at a specified rate unless the employee elects otherwise (i.e., elects not to make contributions or to make contributions at a different rate), provided that the employee has an effective opportunity to elect to receive cash in lieu of the default contributions. Such a design is sometimes referred to as "automatic enrollment."

Besides elective deferrals, a section 401(k) plan may provide for: (1) matching contributions, which are employer contributions that are made only if an employee makes elective deferrals; and (2) nonelective contributions, which are employer contributions that are made without regard to whether an employee makes elective deferrals. Under a section 401(k) plan, no benefit other than matching contributions can be contingent on whether an employee makes elective deferrals. Thus, for example, an employee's eligibility for benefits under a defined benefit pension plan cannot be contingent on whether the employee makes elective deferrals.

A cash balance plan is a defined benefit pension plan with benefits resembling the benefits associated with defined contribution plans. Cash balance plans are sometimes referred to as "hybrid" plans because they combine features of a defined benefit pension plan and a defined contribution plan. Under a cash balance plan, benefits are determined by reference to a hypothetical account balance. An employee's hypothetical account balance is determined by reference to hypothetical annual allocations to the account ("pay credits") (e.g., a certain percentage of the employee's compensation for the year) and hypothetical earnings on the account ("interest credits"). Other types of hybrid plans exist as well, such as so-called "pension equity" plans.

---

[257] Legally, a section 401(k) plan is not a separate type of plan, but is a profit-sharing, stock bonus, or pre-ERISA money purchase plan that contains a qualified cash or deferred arrangement. The terms "section 401(k) plan" and "401(k) plan" are used here for convenience.

[258] The maximum annual amount of elective deferrals that can be made by an individual is subject to a dollar limit ($15,000 for 2006). An individual who has attained age 50 before the end of the taxable year may also make catch-up contributions to a section 401(k) plan, subject to a limit ($5,000 for 2006).

The assets of a qualified retirement plan (either a defined contribution plan or a defined benefit pension plan) must be held in trust for the exclusive benefit of participants and beneficiaries. Defined benefit pension plans are subject to funding rules, which require employers to make contributions at specified minimum levels.[259] In addition, limits apply on the extent to which defined benefit pension plan assets may be invested in employer securities or real property. The minimum funding rules and limits on investments in employer securities or real property generally do not apply to defined contribution plans.

Nondiscrimination requirements

Under a general nondiscrimination requirement, the contributions or benefits provided under a qualified retirement plan must not discriminate in favor of highly compensated employees.[260] Treasury regulations provide detailed and exclusive rules for determining whether a plan satisfies the general nondiscrimination rules. Under the regulations, the amount of contributions or benefits provided under the plan and the benefits, rights and features offered under the plan must be tested.

A special nondiscrimination test applies to elective deferrals under a section 401(k) plan, called the actual deferral percentage test or the "ADP" test. The ADP test compares the actual deferral percentages ("ADPs") of the highly compensated employee group and the nonhighly compensated employee group. The ADP for each group generally is the average of the deferral percentages separately calculated for the employees in the group who are eligible to make elective deferrals for all or a portion of the relevant plan year. Each eligible employee's deferral percentage generally is the employee's elective deferrals for the year divided by the employee's compensation for the year.

The plan generally satisfies the ADP test if the ADP of the highly compensated employee group for the current plan year is either (1) not more than 125 percent of the ADP of the nonhighly compensated employee group for the prior plan year, or (2) not more than 200 percent of the ADP of the nonhighly compensated employee group for the prior plan year and not more than two percentage points greater than the ADP of the nonhighly compensated employee group for the prior plan year.

Under a safe harbor, a section 401(k) plan is deemed to satisfy the special nondiscrimination test if the plan satisfies one of two contribution requirements and satisfies a notice requirement (a "safe harbor section 401(k) plan"). A plan satisfies the contribution requirement under the safe harbor rule if the employer either (1) satisfies a matching contribution requirement or (2) makes a nonelective contribution to a defined contribution plan of at least three percent of an employee's compensation on behalf of each nonhighly compensated

---

[259] The Pension Benefit Guaranty Corporation generally guarantees a minimum level of benefits under a defined benefit plan.

[260] Under special rules, referred to as the permitted disparity rules, higher contributions or benefits can be provided to higher-paid employees in certain circumstances without violating the general nondiscrimination rules.

employee who is eligible to participate in the arrangement. A plan generally satisfies the matching contribution requirement if, under the arrangement: (1) the employer makes a matching contribution on behalf of each nonhighly compensated employee that is equal to (a) 100 percent of the employee's elective deferrals up to three percent of compensation and (b) 50 percent of the employee's elective deferrals from three to five percent of compensation; and (2) the rate of matching contribution with respect to any rate of elective deferrals of a highly compensated employee is not greater than the rate of matching contribution with respect to the same rate of elective deferral of a nonhighly compensated employee.[261]

Employer matching contributions are also subject to a special nondiscrimination test, the "ACP test," which compares the average actual contribution percentages ("ACPs") of matching contributions for the highly compensated employee group and the nonhighly compensated employee group. The plan generally satisfies the ACP test if the ACP of the highly compensated employee group for the current plan year is either (1) not more than 125 percent of the ACP of the nonhighly compensated employee group for the prior plan year, or (2) not more than 200 percent of the ACP of the nonhighly compensated employee group for the prior plan year and not more than two percentage points greater than the ACP of the nonhighly compensated employee group for the prior plan year.

A safe harbor section 401(k) plan that provides for matching contributions must satisfy the ACP test. Alternatively, it is deemed to satisfy the ACP test if it satisfies a matching contribution safe harbor, under which (1) matching contributions are not provided with respect to elective deferrals in excess of six percent of compensation, (2) the rate of matching contribution does not increase as the rate of an employee's elective deferrals increases, and (3) the rate of matching contribution with respect to any rate of elective deferral of a highly compensated employee is no greater than the rate of matching contribution with respect to the same rate of deferral of a nonhighly compensated employee.

Vesting rules

A qualified retirement plan generally must satisfy one of two alternative minimum vesting schedules. A plan satisfies the first schedule if a participant acquires a nonforfeitable right to 100 percent of the participant's accrued benefit derived from employer contributions upon the completion of five years of service. A plan satisfies the second schedule if a participant has a nonforfeitable right to at least 20 percent of the participant's accrued benefit derived from employer contributions after three years of service, 40 percent after four years of service, 60 percent after five years of service, 80 percent after six years of service, and 100 percent after seven years of service.

Special vesting rules apply to elective deferrals and matching contributions. Elective deferrals must be immediately vested. Matching contributions generally must vest at least as

---

[261] Alternatively, matching contributions may be provided at a different rate, provided that: (1) the rate of matching contribution doesn't increase as the rate of elective deferral increases; and (2) the aggregate amount of matching contributions with respect to each rate of elective deferral is not less than the amount that would be provided under the general rule.

rapidly as under one of two alternative minimum vesting schedules. A plan satisfies the first schedule if a participant acquires a nonforfeitable right to 100 percent of matching contributions upon the completion of three years of service. A plan satisfies the second schedule if a participant has a nonforfeitable right to 20 percent of matching contributions for each year of service beginning with the participant's second year of service and ending with 100 percent after six years of service. However, matching contributions under a safe harbor section 401(k) plan must be immediately vested.

Top-heavy rules

Under present law, a top-heavy plan is a qualified retirement plan under which cumulative benefits are provided primarily to key employees. An employee is considered a key employee if, during the prior year, the employee was (1) an officer with compensation in excess of a certain amount ($140,000 for 2006), (2) a five-percent owner, or (3) a one-percent owner with compensation in excess of $150,000. A plan that is top-heavy must provide (1) minimum employer contributions or benefits to participants who are not key employees and (2) more rapid vesting for participants who are not key employees (as discussed below).

In the case of a defined contribution plan, the minimum contribution is the lesser of (1) three percent of compensation, or (2) the highest percentage of compensation at which contributions were made for any key employee. In the case of a defined benefit pension, the minimum benefit is the lesser of (1) two percent of average compensation multiplied by the participant's years of service, or (2) 20 percent of average compensation. For this purpose, a participant's average compensation is generally average compensation for the consecutive-year period (not exceeding five years) during which the participant's aggregate compensation is the greatest.

Top-heavy plans must satisfy one of two alternative minimum vesting schedules. A plan satisfies the first schedule if a participant acquires a nonforfeitable right to 100 percent of contributions or benefits upon the completion of three years of service. A plan satisfies the second schedule if a participant has a nonforfeitable right to 20 percent of contributions or benefits for each year of service beginning with the participant's second year of service and ending with 100 percent after six years of service.[262]

A safe harbor section 401(k) plan is not subject to the top-heavy rules, provided that, if the plan provides for matching contributions, it must also satisfy the matching contribution safe harbor.

Other qualified retirement plan requirements

Qualified retirement plans are subject to various other requirements, some of which depend on whether the plan is a defined contribution plan or a defined benefit pension. Such requirements include limits on contributions and benefits and spousal protections.

---

[262] The top-heavy vesting schedules are the same as the vesting schedules that apply to matching contributions.

In the case of a defined contribution plan, annual additions with respect to each plan participant cannot exceed the lesser of: (1) 100 percent of the participant's compensation; or (2) a dollar amount, indexed for inflation ($44,000 for 2006). Annual additions are the sum of employer contributions, employee contributions, and forfeitures with respect to an individual under all defined contribution plans of the same employer. In the case of a defined benefit pension, annual benefits payable under the plan generally may not exceed the lesser of: (1) 100 percent of average compensation; or (2) a dollar amount, indexed for inflation ($175,000 for 2006).

Defined benefit pension plans are required to provide benefits in the form of annuity unless the participant (and his or her spouse, in the case of a married participant) consents to another form of benefit. In addition, in the case of a married participant, benefits generally must be paid in the form of a qualified joint and survivor annuity ("QJSA") unless the participant and his or her spouse consent to a distribution in another form. A QJSA is an annuity for the life of the participant, with a survivor annuity for the life of the spouse which is not less than 50 percent (and not more than 100 percent) of the amount of the annuity payable during the joint lives of the participant and his or her spouse. These spousal protection requirements generally do not apply to a defined contribution plan that does not offer annuity distributions.

Annual reporting by qualified retirement plans

The plan administrator of a qualified retirement plan generally must file an annual return with the Secretary of the Treasury and an annual report with the Secretary of Labor. In addition, in the case of a defined benefit pension, certain information is generally required to be filed with the Pension Benefit Guaranty Corporation ("PBGC"). Form 5500, which consists of a primary form and various schedules, includes the information required to be filed with all three agencies. The plan administrator satisfies the reporting requirement with respect to each agency by filing the Form 5500 with the Department of Labor.

The Form 5500 is due by the last day of the seventh month following the close of the plan year. The due date may be extended up to two and one-half months. Copies of filed Form 5500s are available for public examination at the U.S. Department of Labor.

A plan administrator must automatically provide participants with a summary of the annual report within two months after the due date of the annual report (i.e., by the end of the ninth month after the end of the plan year unless an extension applies). In addition, a copy of the full annual report must be provided to participants on written request.

Explanation of Provision

In general

The provision provides rules for an "eligible combined plan." An eligible combined plan is a plan: (1) that is maintained by an employer that is a small employer at the time the plan is established; (2) that consists of a defined benefit plan and an "applicable" defined contribution plan; (3) the assets of which are held in a single trust forming part of the plan and are clearly identified and allocated to the defined benefit plan and the applicable defined contribution plan to the extent necessary for the separate application of the Code and ERISA; and (4) that meets certain benefit, contribution, vesting and nondiscrimination requirements as discussed below. For this purpose, an applicable defined contribution plan is a defined contribution plan that includes a qualified cash or deferred arrangement (i.e., a section 401(k) plan). A small employer is an employer that employed an average of at least two, but not more than 500, employees on business days during the preceding calendar year and at least two employees on the first day of the plan year.

Except as specified in the provision, the provisions of the Code and ERISA are applied to any defined benefit plan and any applicable defined contribution plan that are part of an eligible combined plan in the same manner as if each were not part of the eligible combined plan. Thus, for example, the present-law limits on contributions and benefits apply separately to contributions under an applicable defined contribution plan that is part of an eligible combined plan and to benefits under the defined benefit plan that is part of the eligible combined plan. In addition, the spousal protection rules apply to the defined benefit plan, but not to the applicable defined contribution plan except to the extent provided under present law. Moreover, although the assets of an eligible combined plan are held in a single trust, the funding rules apply to a defined benefit plan that is part of an eligible combined plan on the basis of the assets identified and allocated to the defined benefit, and the limits on investing defined benefit plan assets in employer securities or real property apply to such assets. Similarly, separate participant accounts are required to be maintained under the applicable defined contribution plan that is part of the eligible combined plan, and earnings (or losses) on participants' account are based on the earnings (or losses) with respect to the assets of the applicable defined contribution plan.

Requirements with respect to defined benefit plan

A defined benefit plan that is part of an eligible combined plan is required to provide each participant with a benefit of not less than the applicable percentage of the participant's final average pay. The applicable percentage is the lesser of: (1) one percent multiplied by the participant's years of service; or (2) 20 percent. For this purpose, final average pay is determined using the consecutive-year period (not exceeding five years) during which the participant has the greatest aggregate compensation.

If the defined benefit plan is an applicable defined benefit plan,[263] the plan is treated as meeting this benefit requirement if each participant receives a pay credit for each plan year of not less than the percentage of compensation determined in accordance with the following table:

---

[263] Applicable defined benefit plan is defined as under the TITLE VII of the bill.

236

Table 2.–Percentage of Compensation

Participant's age as of the beginning of the plan year:	Percentage:
30 or less	2 percent
Over 30 but less than 40	4 percent
Over 40 but less than 50	6 percent
50 or over	8 percent

A defined benefit that is part of an eligible combined plan must provide the required benefit to each participant, regardless of whether the participant makes elective deferrals to the applicable defined contribution plan that is part of the eligible combined plan.

Any benefits provided under the defined benefit plan (including any benefits provided in addition to required benefits) must be fully vested after three years of service.

Requirements with respect to applicable defined contribution plan

Certain automatic enrollment and matching contribution requirements must be met with respect to an applicable defined contribution plan that is part of an eligible combined plan. First, the qualified cash or deferred arrangement under the plan must constitute an automatic contribution arrangement, under which each employee eligible to participate is treated as having elected to make deferrals of four percent of compensation unless the employee elects otherwise (i.e., elects not to make deferrals or to make deferrals at a different rate). Participants must be given notice of their right to elect otherwise and must be given a reasonable period of time after receiving notice in which to make an election. In addition, participants must be given notice of their rights and obligations within a reasonable period before each year.

Under the applicable defined contribution plan, the employer must be required to make matching contributions on behalf of each employee eligible to participate in the arrangement in an amount equal to 50 percent of the employee's elective deferrals up to four percent of compensation, and the rate of matching contribution with respect to any elective deferrals for highly compensated employees must not be not greater than the rate of match for nonhighly compensated employees.[264] Matching contributions in addition to the required matching contributions may also be made. The employer may also make nonelective contributions under the applicable defined contribution plan, but any nonelective contributions are not taken into account in determining whether the matching contribution requirement is met.

---

[264] As under present law, matching contributions may be provided at a different rate, provided that: (1) the rate of matching contribution doesn't increase as the rate of elective deferral increases; and (2) the aggregate amount of matching contributions with respect to each rate of elective deferral is not less than the amount that would be provided under the general rule.

Any matching contributions under the applicable defined contribution plan (including any in excess of required matching contributions) must be fully vested when made. Any nonelective contributions made under the applicable defined contribution plan must be fully vested after three years of service.

Nondiscrimination and other rules

An applicable defined contribution plan satisfies the ADP test on a safe-harbor basis. Matching contributions under an applicable defined contribution plan must satisfy the ACP test or may satisfy the matching contribution safe harbor under present law, as modified to reflect the matching contribution requirements applicable under the provision.

Nonelective contributions under an applicable defined contribution plan and benefits under a defined benefit plan that are part of an eligible combined plan are generally subject to the nondiscrimination rules as under present law. However, neither a defined benefit plan nor an applicable defined contribution plan that is part of an eligible combined plan may be combined with another plan in determining whether the nondiscrimination requirements are met.[265]

An applicable defined contribution plan and a defined benefit plan that are part of an eligible combined plan are treated as meeting the top-heavy requirements.

All contributions, benefits, and other rights and features that are provided under a defined benefit plan or an applicable defined contribution plan that is part of an eligible combined plan must be provided uniformly to all participants. This requirement applies regardless of whether nonuniform contributions, benefits, or other rights or features could be provided without violating the nondiscrimination rules. However, it is intended that a plan will not violate the uniformity requirement merely because benefits accrued for periods before a defined benefit or defined contribution plan became part of an eligible combined plan are protected (as required under the anticutback rules).

Annual reporting

An eligible combined plan is treated as a single plan for purposes of annual reporting. Thus, only a single Form 5500 is required. All of the information required under present law with respect to a defined benefit plan or a defined contribution plan must be provided in the Form 5500 for the eligible combined plan. In addition, only a single summary annual report must be provided to participants.

Other rules

The provision of the bill relating to default investment options and the preemption of State laws with respect to automatic enrollment arrangements are applicable to eligible combined

---

[265] The permitted disparity rules do not apply in determining whether an applicable defined contribution plan or a defined benefit plan that is part of an eligible combined plan satisfies (1) the contribution or benefit requirements under the provision or (2) the nondiscrimination requirements.

plans. It is intended that in the case that an eligible combined plan terminates, the PBGC guarantee applies only to benefits under the defined benefit portion of the plan.

Effective Date

The provision is effective for plan years beginning after December 31, 2009.

D. Faster Vesting of Employer Nonelective Contributions
(sec. 203 of ERISA, and sec. 411 of the Code)

Present Law

Under present law, in general, a plan is not a qualified plan unless a participant's employer-provided benefit vests at least as rapidly as under one of two alternative minimum vesting schedules. A plan satisfies the first schedule if a participant acquires a nonforfeitable right to 100 percent of the participant's accrued benefit derived from employer contributions upon the completion of five years of service. A plan satisfies the second schedule if a participant has a nonforfeitable right to at least 20 percent of the participant's accrued benefit derived from employer contributions after three years of service, 40 percent after four years of service, 60 percent after five years of service, 80 percent after six years of service, and 100 percent after seven years of service.[266]

Faster vesting schedules apply to employer matching contributions. Employer matching contributions are required to vest at least as rapidly as under one of the following two alternative minimum vesting schedules. A plan satisfies the first schedule if a participant acquires a nonforfeitable right to 100 percent of employer matching contributions upon the completion of three years of service. A plan satisfies the second schedule if a participant has a nonforfeitable right to 20 percent of employer matching contributions for each year of service beginning with the participant's second year of service and ending with 100 percent after six years of service.

Explanation of Provision

The provision applies the present-law vesting schedule for matching contributions to all employer contributions to defined contribution plans.

The provision does not apply to any employee until the employee has an hour of service after the effective date. In applying the new vesting schedule, service before the effective date is taken into account.

Effective Date

The provision is generally effective for contributions for plan years beginning after December 31, 2006.

In the case of a plan maintained pursuant to one or more collective bargaining agreements, the provision is not effective for contributions (including allocations of forfeitures) for plan years beginning before the earlier of (1) the later of the date on which the last of such collective bargaining agreements terminates (determined without regard to any extension thereof on or after the date of enactment) or January 1, 2007, or (2) January 1, 2009.

---

[266] The minimum vesting requirements are also contained in Title I of the Employee Retirement Income Security Act of 1974 ("ERISA").

In the case of an employee stock ownership plan ("ESOP") which on September 26, 2005, had outstanding a loan incurred for the purpose of acquiring qualifying employer securities, the provision does not apply to any plan year beginning before the earlier of (1) the date on which the loan is fully repaid, or (2) the date on which the loan was, as of September 26, 2005, scheduled to be fully repaid.

E. Distributions During Working Retirement
(sec. 3(2) of ERISA and new sec. 401(a)(35) of the Code)

Present Law

Under ERISA, a pension plan is a plan, fund, or program established or maintained by an employer or an employee organization, or by both, to the extent that, by its express terms or surrounding circumstances, the plan, fund, or program: (1) provides retirement income to employees, or (2) results in a deferral of income by employees for periods extending to the termination of covered employment or beyond, regardless of the method of calculating contributions made to or benefits under the plan or the method of distributing benefits from the plan.

For purposes of the qualification requirements applicable to pension plans, stock bonus plans, and profit-sharing plans under the Code, a pension plan is a plan established and maintained primarily to provide systematically for the payment of definitely determinable benefits to employees over a period of years, usually life, after retirement.[267] A pension plan (i.e., a defined benefit plan or money purchase pension plan) may not provide for distributions before the attainment of normal retirement age (commonly age 65) to participants who have not separated from employment.[268]

Under proposed regulations, in the case of a phased retirement program, a pension plan is permitted to pay a portion of a participant's benefits before attainment of normal retirement age.[269] A phased retirement program is a program under which employees who are at least age 59½ and are eligible for retirement may reduce (by at least 20 percent) the number of hours they customarily work and receive a pro rata portion of their retirement benefits, based on the reduction in their work schedule.

Explanation of Provision

Under the provision, for purposes of the definition of pension plan under ERISA, a distribution from a plan, fund, or program is not treated as made in a form other than retirement income or as a distribution prior to termination of covered employment solely because the distribution is made to an employee who has attained age 62 and who is not separated from employment at the time of such distribution.

In addition, under the Code, a pension plan does not fail to be a qualified retirement plan solely because the plan provides that a distribution may be made to an employee who has attained age 62 and who is not separated from employment at the time of the distribution.

---

[267] Treas. Reg. sec. 1.401-1(b)(1)(i).

[268] See, e.g., Rev. Rul. 74-254.

[269] Prop. Treas. Reg. secs. 1.401(a)-1(b)(1)(iv) and 1.401(a)-3.

Effective Date

The provision is effective for distributions in plan years beginning after December 31, 2006.

F. Treatment of Plans Maintained by Indian Tribes
(sec. 414(d) of the Code and sec. 3(32) of ERISA)

Present Law

Governmental plans are exempt from ERISA and from Code requirements that correspond to ERISA requirements, such as the vesting rules and the funding rules. A governmental plan is generally a plan established and maintained for its employees by (1) the Federal government, (2) the government of a State or political subdivision of a State, or (3) any agency or instrumentality of any of the foregoing.

Benefits under a defined benefit pension plan generally cannot exceed the lesser of (1) 100 percent of average compensation, or (2) a dollar amount ($175,000 for 2006), subject to certain special rules for defined benefit plans maintained by State and local government employers and other special rules for employees of a police or fire department. Employee contributions to a defined benefit pension plan are generally subject to tax; however, employee contributions may be made to a State or local government defined benefit pension plan on a pretax basis (referred to as "pickup" contributions).

Governmental defined benefit pension plans are not covered by the PBGC insurance program.

Explanation of Provision

Under the provision, the term "governmental plan" for purposes of section 414 of the Code, section 3(32) of ERISA, and the PBGC termination insurance program includes a plan: (1) which is established and maintained by an Indian tribal government (as defined in Code sec. 7701(a)(40)), a subdivision of an Indian tribal government (determined in accordance with Code sec. 7871(d)), or an agency or instrumentality of either; and (2) all of the participants of which are qualified employees of such entity. A qualified employee is an employee of an entity described in (1) all of whose services for such entity are in the performance of essential governmental services and not in the performance of commercial activities (whether or not such activities are an essential governmental function). Thus, for example, a governmental plan would include a plan of a tribal government all of the participants of which are teachers in tribal schools. On the other hand, a governmental plan would not include a plan covering tribal employees who are employed by a hotel, casino, service station, convenience store, or marina operated by a tribal government.

Under the provision, the special benefit limitations applicable to employees of police and fire departments of a State or political subdivision (Code sec. 415(b)(2)(H)) apply to such employees of an Indian tribe or any political subdivision thereof. In addition, the rules relating to pick up contribution under governmental plans (Code sec. 414(h)) and special benefit limitations for governmental plans (sec. 415(b)(10)) apply to tribal plans treated as governmental plans under the provision.

Effective Date

The provision is effective for plan years beginning on or after the date of enactment.

TITLE X: SPOUSAL PENSION PROTECTION

A. Regulations on Time and Order of Issuance of Domestic Relations Orders

Present Law

Benefits provided under a qualified retirement plan for a participant may not be assigned or alienated to creditors of the participant, except in very limited circumstances.[270] One exception to the prohibition on assignment or alienation is a qualified domestic relations order ("QDRO").[271] A QDRO is a domestic relations order that creates or recognizes a right of an alternate payee, including a former spouse, to any plan benefit payable with respect to a participant and that meets certain procedural requirements. In addition, a QDRO generally may not require the plan to provide any type or form of benefit, or any option, not otherwise provided under the plan, or to provide increased benefits.

Present law also provides that a QDRO may not require the payment of benefits to an alternate payee that are required to be paid to another alternate payee under a domestic relations order previously determined to be a QDRO. This rule implicitly recognizes that a domestic relations order issued after a QDRO may also qualify as a QDRO. However, present law does not otherwise provide specific rules for the treatment of a domestic relations order as a QDRO if the order is issued after another domestic relations order or a QDRO (including an order issued after a divorce decree) or revises another domestic relations order or a QDRO.

Present law provides specific rules that apply during any period in which the status of a domestic relations order as a QDRO is being determined (by the plan administrator, by a court, or otherwise). During such a period, the plan administrator is required to account separately for the amounts that would have been payable to the alternate payee during the period if the order had been determined to be a QDRO (referred to as "segregated amounts"). If, within the 18-month period beginning with the date on which the first payment would be required to be made under the order, the order (or modification thereof) is determined to be a QDRO, the plan administrator is required to pay the segregated amounts (including any interest thereon) to the person or persons entitled thereto. If, within the 18-month period, the order is determined not to be a QDRO, or its status as a QDRO is not resolved, the plan administrator is required to pay the segregated amounts (including any interest) to the person or persons who would be entitled to such amounts if there were no order. In such a case, any subsequent determination that the order is a QDRO is applied prospectively only.

Explanation of Provision

The Secretary of Labor is directed to issue, not later than one year after the date of enactment of the provision, regulations to clarify the status of certain domestic relations orders. In particular, the regulations are to clarify that a domestic relations order otherwise meeting the

---

[270] Code sec. 401(a)(13); ERISA sec. 206(d).

[271] Code secs. 401(a)(13)(B) and 414(p); ERISA sec. 206(d)(3).

QDRO requirements will not fail to be treated as a QDRO solely because of the time it is issued or because it is issued after or revises another domestic relations order or QDRO. The regulations are also to clarify that such a domestic relations order is in all respects subject to the same requirements and protections that apply to QDROs. For example, as under present law, such a domestic relations order may not require the payment of benefits to an alternate payee that are required to be paid to another alternate payee under an earlier QDRO. In addition, the present-law rules regarding segregated amounts that apply while the status of a domestic relations order as a QDRO is being determined continue to apply.

Effective Date

The provision is effective on the date of enactment.

B. Benefits Under the Railroad Retirement System for Former Spouses
(secs. 2 and 5 of the Railroad Retirement Act of 1974)

Present Law

In general

The Railroad Retirement System has two main components. Tier I of the system is financed by taxes on employers and employees equal to the Social Security payroll tax and provides qualified railroad retirees (and their qualified spouses, dependents, widows, or widowers) with benefits that are roughly equal to Social Security. Covered railroad workers and their employers pay the Tier I tax instead of the Social Security payroll tax, and most railroad retirees collect Tier I benefits instead of Social Security. Tier II of the system replicates a private pension plan, with employers and employees contributing a certain percentage of pay toward the system to finance defined benefits to eligible railroad retirees (and qualified spouses, dependents, widows, or widowers) upon retirement; however, the Federal Government collects the Tier II payroll contribution and pays out the benefits.

Former spouses of living railroad employees

Generally, a former spouse of a railroad employee who is otherwise eligible for any Tier I or Tier II benefit cannot receive either benefit until the railroad employee actually retires and begins receiving his or her retirement benefits. This is the case regardless of whether a State divorce court has awarded such railroad retirement benefits to the former spouse.

Former spouses of deceased railroad employees

The former spouse of a railroad employee may be eligible for survivors' benefits under Tier I of the Railroad Retirement System. However, a former spouse loses eligibility for any otherwise allowable Tier II benefits upon the death of the railroad employee.

Explanation of Provision

Former spouses of living railroad employees

The provision eliminates the requirement that a railroad employee actually receive railroad retirement benefits for the former spouse to be entitled to any Tier I benefit or Tier II benefit awarded under a State divorce court decision.

Former spouses of deceased railroad employees

The provision provides that a former spouse of a railroad employee does not lose eligibility for otherwise allowable Tier II benefits upon the death of the railroad employee.

Effective Date

The provision is effective one year after the date of enactment.

C. Requirement for Additional Survivor Annuity Option
(sec. 417 of the Code and sec. 205 of ERISA)

Present Law

Defined benefit pension plans and money purchase pension plans are required to provide benefits in the form of a qualified joint and survivor annuity ("QJSA") unless the participant and his or her spouse consent to another form of benefit. A QJSA is an annuity for the life of the participant, with a survivor annuity for the life of the spouse which is not less than 50 percent (and not more than 100 percent) of the amount of the annuity payable during the joint lives of the participant and his or her spouse.[272] In the case of a married participant who dies before the commencement of retirement benefits, the surviving spouse must be provided with a qualified preretirement survivor annuity ("QPSA"), which must provide the surviving spouse with a benefit that is not less than the benefit that would have been provided under the survivor portion of a QJSA.

The participant and his or her spouse may waive the right to a QJSA and QPSA provided certain requirements are satisfied. In general, these conditions include providing the participant with a written explanation of the terms and conditions of the survivor annuity, the right to make, and the effect of, a waiver of the annuity, the rights of the spouse to waive the survivor annuity, and the right of the participant to revoke the waiver. In addition, the spouse must provide a written consent to the waiver, witnessed by a plan representative or a notary public, which acknowledges the effect of the waiver.

Defined contribution plans other than money purchase pension plans are not required to provide a QJSA or QPSA if the participant does not elect an annuity as the form of payment, the surviving spouse is the beneficiary of the participant's entire vested account balance under the plan (unless the spouse consents to designation of another beneficiary),[273] and, with respect to the participant, the plan has not received a transfer from a plan to which the QJSA and QPSA requirements applied (or separately accounts for the transferred assets). In the case of a defined contribution plan subject to the QJSA and QPSA requirements, a QPSA means an annuity for the life of the surviving spouse that has an actuarial value of at least 50 percent of the participant's vested account balance as of the date of death.

Explanation of Provision

The provision revises the minimum survivor annuity requirements to require that, at the election of the participant, benefits will be paid in the form of a "qualified optional survivor annuity." A qualified optional survivor annuity means an annuity for the life of the participant

---

[272] Thus, for example, a QJSA could consist of an annuity for the life of the participant, with a survivor annuity for the life of the spouse equal to 75 percent of the amount of the annuity payable during the joint lives of the participant and his or her spouse.

[273] Waiver and election rules apply to the waiver of the right of the spouse to be the beneficiary under a defined contribution plan that is not required to provide a QJSA.

with a survivor annuity for the life of the spouse which is equal to the applicable percentage of the amount of the annuity that is: (1) payable during the joint lives of the participant and the spouse; and (2) the actuarial equivalent of a single annuity for the life of the participant.

If the survivor annuity provided by the QJSA under the plan is less than 75 percent of the annuity payable during the joint lives of the participant and spouse, the applicable percentage is 75 percent. If the survivor annuity provided by the QJSA under the plan is greater than or equal to 75 percent of the annuity payable during the joint lives of the participant and spouse, the applicable percentage is 50 percent. Thus, for example, if the survivor annuity provided by the QJSA under the plan is 50 percent, the survivor annuity provided under the qualified optional survivor annuity must be 75 percent.

The written explanation required to be provided to participants explaining the terms and conditions of the qualified joint and survivor annuity must also include the terms and conditions of the qualified optional survivor annuity.

Under the provision of the bill relating to plan amendments, a plan amendment made pursuant to a provision of the bill generally will not violate the anticutback rule if certain requirements are met. Thus, a plan is not treated as having decreased the accrued benefit of a participant solely by reason of the adoption of a plan amendment pursuant to the provision requiring that the plan offer a qualified optional survivor annuity. The elimination of a subsidized QJSA is not protected by the anticutback provision in the bill unless an equivalent or greater subsidy is retained in one of the forms offered under the plan as amended. For example, if a plan that offers a subsidized 50 percent QJSA is amended to provide an unsubsidized 50 percent QJSA and an unsubsidized 75 percent joint and survivor annuity as its qualified optional survivor annuity, the replacement of the subsidized 50 percent QJSA with the unsubsidized 50 percent QJSA is not protected by the anticutback protection.

Effective Date

The provision applies generally to plan years beginning after December 31, 2007. In the case of a plan maintained pursuant to one or more collective bargaining agreements, the provision applies to plan years beginning on or after the earlier of (1) the later of January 1, 2008, and the last date on which an applicable collective bargaining agreement terminates (without regard to extensions), and (2) January 1, 2009.

249

TITLE XI: ADMINISTRATIVE PROVISIONS

A. Updating of Employee Plans Compliance Resolution System

Present Law

Tax-favored treatment is provided to various retirement savings arrangements that meet certain requirements under the Code, including qualified retirement plans and annuities (secs. 401(a) and 403(a)), tax-sheltered annuities (sec. 403(b)), simplified employee pensions ("SEPs") (sec. 408(k)), and SIMPLE IRAs (sec. 408(p)). The Internal Revenue Service ("IRS") has established the Employee Plans Compliance Resolution System ("EPCRS"), which is a comprehensive system of correction programs for sponsors of retirement plans and annuities that are intended to satisfy the requirements of section 401(a), section 403(a), section 403(b), section 408(k), or section 408(p), as applicable. The IRS has updated and expanded EPCRS several times.[274]

EPCRS permits employers to correct compliance failures and continue to provide their employees with retirement benefits on a tax-favored basis. EPCRS is based on the following general principles:

- Plans sponsors and administrators should be encouraged to establish administrative practices and procedures that ensure that plans are operated properly in accordance with applicable Code requirements;

- Plans sponsors and administrators should satisfy applicable plan document requirements;

- Plans sponsors and administrators should make voluntary and timely correction of any plan failures, whether involving discrimination in favor of highly compensated employees, plan operations, the terms of the plan document, or adoption of a plan by an ineligible employer; timely and efficient correction protects participating employees by providing them with their expected retirement benefits, including favorable tax treatment;

- Voluntary compliance is promoted by providing for limited fees for voluntary corrections approved by the Service, thereby reducing employers' uncertainty regarding their potential tax liability and participants' potential tax liability;

- Fees and sanctions should be graduated in a series of steps so that there is always an incentive to correct promptly;

- Sanctions for plan failures identified on audit should be reasonable in light of the nature, extent, and severity of the violation;

- Administration of EPCRS should be consistent and uniform; and

---

[274] See Rev. Proc. 2006-27, 2006-22 IRB 945.

- Sponsors should be able to rely on the availability of EPCRS in taking corrective actions to maintain the tax-favored status of their plans.

The components of EPCRS provide for self-correction, voluntary correction with IRS approval, and correction on audit. The Self-Correction Program ("SCP") generally permits a plan sponsor that has established compliance practices and procedures to correct certain insignificant failures at any time (including during an audit), and certain significant failures generally within a 2-year period, without payment of any fee or sanction. The Voluntary Correction Program ("VCP") permits an employer, at any time before an audit, to pay a limited fee and receive IRS approval of a correction. For a failure that is discovered on audit and corrected, the Audit Closing Agreement Program ("Audit CAP") provides for a sanction that bears a reasonable relationship to the nature, extent, and severity of the failure and that takes into account the extent to which correction occurred before audit.

Explanation of Provision

The provision clarifies that the Secretary has the full authority to establish and implement EPCRS (or any successor program) and any other employee plans correction policies, including the authority to waive income, excise or other taxes to ensure that any tax, penalty or sanction is not excessive and bears a reasonable relationship to the nature, extent and severity of the failure.

Under the provision, the Secretary of the Treasury is directed to continue to update and improve EPCRS (or any successor program), giving special attention to (1) increasing the awareness and knowledge of small employers concerning the availability and use of EPCRS, (2) taking into account special concerns and circumstances that small employers face with respect to compliance and correction of compliance failures, (3) extending the duration of the self-correction period under SCP for significant compliance failures, (4) expanding the availability to correct insignificant compliance failures under SCP during audit, and (5) assuring that any tax, penalty, or sanction that is imposed by reason of a compliance failure is not excessive and bears a reasonable relationship to the nature, extent, and severity of the failure.

Effective Date

The provision is effective on the date of enactment.

B. Notice and Consent Period Regarding Distributions
(sec. 417(a) of the Code, and sec. 205(c) of ERISA)

Present Law

Notice and consent requirements apply to certain distributions from qualified retirement plans. These requirements relate to the content and timing of information that a plan must provide to a participant prior to a distribution, and to whether the plan must obtain the participant's consent to the distribution. The nature and extent of the notice and consent requirements applicable to a distribution depend upon the value of the participant's vested accrued benefit and whether the joint and survivor annuity requirements apply to the participant.

If the present value of the participant's vested accrued benefit exceeds $5,000,[275] the plan may not distribute the participant's benefit without the written consent of the participant. The participant's consent to a distribution is not valid unless the participant has received from the plan a notice that contains a written explanation of (1) the material features and the relative values of the optional forms of benefit available under the plan, (2) the participant's right to defer the receipt of a distribution, or, as applicable, to have the distribution directly transferred to another retirement plan or individual retirement arrangement ("IRA"), and (3) the rules concerning taxation of a distribution. If the joint and survivor annuity requirements are applicable, this notice also must contain a written explanation of (1) the terms and conditions of the qualified joint and survivor annuity ("QJSA"), (2) the participant's right to make, and the effect of, an election to waive the QJSA, (3) the rights of the participant's spouse with respect to a participant's waiver of the QJSA, and (4) the right to make, and the effect of, a revocation of a waiver of the QJSA. The plan generally must provide this notice to the participant no less than 30 and no more than 90 days before the date distribution commences.[276]

Explanation of Provision

Under the provision, a qualified retirement plan is required to provide the applicable distribution notice no less than 30 days and no more than 180 days before the date distribution commences. The Secretary of the Treasury is directed to modify the applicable regulations to reflect the extension of the notice period to 180 days and to provide that the description of a participant's right, if any, to defer receipt of a distribution shall also describe the consequences of failing to defer such receipt.

Effective Date

The provision and the modifications required to be made under the provision apply to years beginning after December 31, 2006. In the case of a description of the consequences of a

---

[275] The portion of a participant's benefit that is attributable to amounts rolled over from another plan may be disregarded in determining the present value of the participant's vested accrued benefit.

[276] Code sec. 417(a)(6)(A); ERISA sec. 205(c)(7)(A); Treas. Reg. secs. 1.402(f)-1, 1.411(a)-11(c), and 1.417(e)-1(b).

participant's failure to defer receipt of a distribution that is made before the date 90 days after the date on which the Secretary of the Treasury makes modifications to the applicable regulations, the plan administrator is required to make a reasonable attempt to comply with the requirements of the provision.

C. Pension Plan Reporting Simplification

Present Law

The plan administrator of a pension plan generally must file an annual return with the Secretary of the Treasury, an annual report with the Secretary of Labor, and certain information with the Pension Benefit Guaranty Corporation ("PBGC"). Form 5500, which consists of a primary form and various schedules, includes the information required to be filed with all three agencies. The plan administrator satisfies the reporting requirement with respect to each agency by filing the Form 5500 with the Department of Labor.

The Form 5500 series consists of 2 different forms: Form 5500 and Form 5500-EZ. Form 5500 is the more comprehensive of the forms and requires the most detailed financial information. The plan administrator of a "one-participant plan" generally may file Form 5500-EZ. For this purpose, a plan is a one-participant plan if: (1) the only participants in the plan are the sole owner of a business that maintains the plan (and such owner's spouse), or partners in a partnership that maintains the plan (and such partners' spouses);[277] (2) the plan is not aggregated with another plan in order to satisfy the minimum coverage requirements of section 410(b); (3) the plan does not provide benefits to anyone other than the sole owner of the business (or the sole owner and spouse) or the partners in the business (or the partners and spouses); (4) the employer is not a member of a related group of employers; and (5) the employer does not use the services of leased employees. In addition, the plan administrator of a one-participant plan is not required to file a return if the plan does not have an accumulated funding deficiency and the total value of the plan assets as of the end of the plan year and all prior plan years beginning on or after January 1, 1994, does not exceed $100,000.

With respect to a plan that does not satisfy the eligibility requirements for Form 5500-EZ, the characteristics and the size of the plan determine the amount of detailed financial information that the plan administrator must provide on Form 5500. If the plan has more than 100 participants at the beginning of the plan year, the plan administrator generally must provide more information.

Explanation of Provision

The Secretary of the Treasury is directed to modify the annual return filing requirements with respect to a one-participant plan to provide that if the total value of the plan assets of such a plan as of the end of the plan year does not exceed $250,000, the plan administrator is not required to file a return. In addition, the Secretary of the Treasury and the Secretary of Labor are directed to provide simplified reporting requirements for plan years beginning after December 31, 2006, for certain plans with fewer than 25 participants.

---

[277] Under Department of Labor regulations, certain business owners and their spouses are not treated as employees. 29 C.F.R. sec. 2510.3-3(c) (2006). Thus, plans covering only such individuals are not subject to ERISA.

Effective Date

The provision relating to one-participant retirement plans is effective for plan years beginning on or after January 1, 2007. The provision relating to simplified reporting for plans with fewer than 25 participants is effective on the date of enactment.

D. Voluntary Early Retirement Incentive and Employment Retention Plans Maintained by Local Educational Agencies and Other Entities (secs. 457(e)(11) and 457(f) of the Code, sec. 3(2)(B) of ERISA, and sec. 4(l)(1) of the ADEA)

Present Law

Eligible deferred compensation plans of State and local governments and tax-exempt employers

A "section 457 plan" is an eligible deferred compensation plan of a State or local government or tax-exempt employer that meets certain requirements. For example, the amount that can be deferred annually under section 457 cannot exceed a certain dollar limit ($14,000 for 2005). Amounts deferred under a section 457 plan are generally includible in gross income when paid or made available (or, in the case of governmental section 457 plans, when paid). Subject to certain exceptions, amounts deferred under a plan that does not comply with section 457 (an "ineligible plan") are includible in income when the amounts are not subject to a substantial risk of forfeiture. Section 457 does not apply to any bona fide vacation leave, sick leave, compensatory time, severance pay, disability pay, or death benefit plan. Additionally, section 457 does not apply to qualified retirement plans or qualified governmental excess benefit plans that provide benefits in excess of those that are provided under a qualified retirement plan maintained by the governmental employer.

ERISA

ERISA provides rules governing the operation of most employee benefit plans. The rules to which a plan is subject depend on whether the plan is an employee welfare benefit plan or an employee pension benefit plan. For example, employee pension benefit plans are subject to reporting and disclosure requirements, participation and vesting requirements, funding requirements, and fiduciary provisions. Employee welfare benefit plans are not subject to all of these requirements. Governmental plans are exempt from ERISA.

Age Discrimination in Employment Act

The Age Discrimination in Employment Act ("ADEA") generally prohibits discrimination in employment because of age. However, certain defined benefit pension plans may lawfully provide payments that constitute the subsidized portion of an early retirement benefit or social security supplements pursuant to ADEA[278], and employers may lawfully provide a voluntary early retirement incentive plan that is consistent with the purposes of ADEA.[279]

---

[278] See ADEA sec. 4(l)(1).

[279] See ADEA sec. 4(f)(2).

Explanation of Provision

Early retirement incentive plans of local educational agencies and education associations

In general

The provision addresses the treatment of certain voluntary early retirement incentive plans under section 457, ERISA, and ADEA.

Code section 457

Under the provision, special rules apply under section 457 to a voluntary early retirement incentive plan that is maintained by a local educational agency or a tax-exempt education association which principally represents employees of one or more such agencies and that makes payments or supplements as an early retirement benefit, a retirement-type subsidy, or a social security supplement in coordination with a defined benefit pension plan maintained by a State or local government or by such an association. Such a voluntary early retirement incentive plan is treated as a bona fide severance plan for purposes of section 457, and therefore is not subject to the limits under section 457, to the extent the payments or supplements could otherwise be provided under the defined benefit pension plan. For purposes of the provision, the payments or supplements that could otherwise be provided under the defined benefit pension plan are to be determined by applying the accrual and vesting rules for defined benefit pension plans.[280]

ERISA

Under the provision, voluntary early retirement incentive plans (as described above) are treated as welfare benefit plans for purposes of ERISA (other than governmental plans that are exempt from ERISA).

ADEA

The provision also addresses the treatment under ADEA of voluntary early retirement incentive plans that are maintained by local educational agencies and tax-exempt education associations which principally represent employees of one or more such agencies, and that make payments or supplements that constitute the subsidized portion of an early retirement benefit or a social security supplement and that are made in coordination with a defined benefit pension plan maintained by a State or local government or by such an association. For purposes of ADEA, such a plan is treated as part of the defined benefit pension plan and the payments or supplements under the plan are not severance pay that may be subject to certain deductions under ADEA.

---

[280] The accrual and vesting rules have the effect of limiting the social security supplements and early retirement benefits that may be provided under a defined benefit pension plan; however, government plans are exempt from these rules.

Employment retention plans of local educational agencies and education associations

The provision addresses the treatment of certain employment retention plans under section 457 and ERISA. The provision applies to employment retention plans that are maintained by local educational agencies or tax-exempt education associations which principally represent employees of one or more such agencies and that provide compensation to an employee (payable on termination of employment) for purposes of retaining the services of the employee or rewarding the employee for service with educational agencies or associations.

Under the provision, special tax treatment applies to the portion of an employment retention plan that provides benefits that do not exceed twice the applicable annual dollar limit on deferrals under section 457 ($14,000 for 2005). The provision provides an exception from the rules under section 457 for ineligible plans with respect to such portion of an employment retention plan. This exception applies for years preceding the year in which benefits under the employment retention plan are paid or otherwise made available to the employee. In addition, such portion of an employment retention plan is not treated as providing for the deferral of compensation for tax purposes.

Under the provision, an employment retention plan is also treated as a welfare benefit plan for purposes of ERISA (other than a governmental plan that is exempt from ERISA).

Effective Date

The provision is generally effective on the date of enactment. The amendments to section 457 apply to taxable years ending after the date of enactment. The amendments to ERISA apply to plan years ending after the date of enactment. Nothing in the provision alters or affects the construction of the Code, ERISA, or ADEA as applied to any plan, arrangement, or conduct to which the provision does not apply.

E. No Reduction in Unemployment Compensation as a Result of Pension Rollovers
(sec. 3304(a)(15) of the Code)

Present Law

Under present law, unemployment compensation payable by a State to an individual generally is reduced by the amount of retirement benefits received by the individual. Distributions from certain employer-sponsored retirement plans or IRAs that are transferred to a similar retirement plan or IRA ("rollover distributions") generally are not includible in income. Some States currently reduce the amount of an individual's unemployment compensation by the amount of a rollover distribution.

Explanation of Provision

The provision amends the Code so that the reduction of unemployment compensation payable to an individual by reason of the receipt of retirement benefits does not apply in the case of a rollover distribution.

Effective Date

The provision is effective for weeks beginning on or after the date of enactment.

F. Revocation of Election Relating to Treatment as Multiemployer Plan
(sec. 3(37) of ERISA and sec. 414(f) of the Code)

Present Law

A multiemployer plan mean a plan (1) to which more than one employer is required to contribute; (2) which is maintained pursuant to one or more collective bargaining agreements between one or more employee organizations and more than one employer; and (3) which satisfies such other requirements as the Secretary of Labor may prescribe.[281] Present law provides that within one year after the date of enactment of the Multiemployer Pension Plan Amendments Act of 1980, a multiemployer plan could irrevocably elect for the plan not to be treated as a multiemployer plan if certain requirements were satisfied.

Explanation of Provision

The provision allows multiemployer plans to revoke an existing election not to treat the plan as a multiemployer plan if, for each of the three plan years prior to the date of enactment, the plan would have been a multiemployer plan, but for the extension in place. The revocation must be pursuant to procedures prescribed by the PBGC.

The provision also provides that a plan to which more than one employer is required to contribute which is maintained pursuant to one or more collective bargaining agreements between one or more employee organizations and more than one employer (collectively the "criteria") may, pursuant to procedures prescribed by the PBGC, elect to be a multiemployer plan if (1) for each of the three plan years prior to the date of enactment, the plan has met the criteria; (2) substantially all of the plan's employer contributions for each of those plan years were made or required to be made by organizations that were tax-exempt; and (3) the plan was established prior to September 2, 1974. Such election is also available in the case of a plan sponsored by an organization that was established in Chicago, Illinois, on August 12, 1881, and is described in Code section 501(c)(5). There is no inference that a plan that makes an election to be a multiemployer plan was not a multiemployer plan prior to the date of enactment or would not be a multiemployer plan without regard to the election.

An election made under the provision is effective beginning with the first plan year ending after date of enactment and is irrevocable. A plan that elects to be a multiemployer plan under the provision will cease to be a multiemployer plan as of the plan year beginning immediately after the first plan year for which the majority of its employer contributions were made or required to be made by organizations that were not tax-exempt. Elections and revocations under the provision must be made within one year after the date of enactment.

Not later than 30 days before an election is made, the plan administrator must provide notice of the pending election to each plan participant and beneficiary, each labor organization representing such participants or beneficiaries, and to each employer that has an obligation to

---

[281] ERISA sec. 3(36); Code sec. 414(f).

contribute to the plan. Such notice must include the principal differences between the guarantee programs and benefit restrictions for single employer and multiemployer plans. The Secretary of Labor must prescribe a model notice within 180 days after date of enactment. The plan administrator's failure to provide the notice is treated as a failure to file an annual report. Thus, an ERISA penalty of $1,100 per day applies.

Effective Date

The provision is effective on the date of enactment.

G. Provisions Relating to Plan Amendments

Present Law

Present law provides a remedial amendment period during which, under certain circumstances, a plan may be amended retroactively in order to comply with the qualification requirements.[282] In general, plan amendments to reflect changes in the law generally must be made by the time prescribed by law for filing the income tax return of the employer for the employer's taxable year in which the change in law occurs. The Secretary of the Treasury may extend the time by which plan amendments need to be made.

The Code and ERISA provide that, in general, accrued benefits cannot be reduced by a plan amendment.[283] This prohibition on the reduction of accrued benefits is commonly referred to as the "anticutback rule."

Explanation of Provision.

A plan amendment made pursuant to the changes made by the bill or regulations issued thereunder, may be retroactively effective and will not violate the anticutback rule, if, in addition to meeting the other applicable requirements, the amendment is made on or before the last day of the first plan year beginning on or after January 1, 2009 (2011 in the case of a governmental plan).

A plan amendment will not be considered to be pursuant to the bill (or applicable regulations) if it has an effective date before the effective date of the provision under the bill (or regulations) to which it relates. Similarly, the provision does not provide relief from the anticutback rule for periods prior to the effective date of the relevant provision (or regulations) or the plan amendment.   The Secretary of the Treasury is authorized to provide exceptions to the relief from the prohibition on reductions in accrued benefits. It is intended that the Secretary will not permit inappropriate reductions in contributions or benefits that are not directly related to the provisions under the bill.

Effective Date

The provision is effective on the date of enactment.

---

[282] Sec. 401(b).

[283] Code sec. 411(d)(6); ERISA sec. 204(g).

TITLE XII: PROVISIONS RELATING TO EXEMPT ORGANIZATIONS

A. Charitable Giving Incentives

1. Tax-free distributions from individual retirement plans for charitable purposes (secs. 408, 6034, 6104, and 6652 of the Code)

Present Law

In general

If an amount withdrawn from a traditional individual retirement arrangement ("IRA") or a Roth IRA is donated to a charitable organization, the rules relating to the tax treatment of withdrawals from IRAs apply to the amount withdrawn and the charitable contribution is subject to the normally applicable limitations on deductibility of such contributions.

Charitable contributions

In computing taxable income, an individual taxpayer who itemizes deductions generally is allowed to deduct the amount of cash and up to the fair market value of property contributed to a charity described in section 501(c)(3), to certain veterans' organizations, fraternal societies, and cemetery companies,[284] or to a Federal, State, or local governmental entity for exclusively public purposes.[285] The deduction also is allowed for purposes of calculating alternative minimum taxable income.

The amount of the deduction allowable for a taxable year with respect to a charitable contribution of property may be reduced depending on the type of property contributed, the type of charitable organization to which the property is contributed, and the income of the taxpayer.[286]

A taxpayer who takes the standard deduction (i.e., who does not itemize deductions) may not take a separate deduction for charitable contributions.[287]

A payment to a charity (regardless of whether it is termed a "contribution") in exchange for which the donor receives an economic benefit is not deductible, except to the extent that the donor can demonstrate, among other things, that the payment exceeds the fair market value of the benefit received from the charity. To facilitate distinguishing charitable contributions from purchases of goods or services from charities, present law provides that no charitable contribution deduction is allowed for a separate contribution of $250 or more unless the donor obtains a contemporaneous written acknowledgement of the contribution from the charity

---

[284] Secs. 170(c)(3)-(5).

[285] Sec. 170(c)(1).

[286] Secs. 170(b) and (e).

[287] Sec. 170(a).

indicating whether the charity provided any good or service (and an estimate of the value of any such good or service) to the taxpayer in consideration for the contribution.[288] In addition, present law requires that any charity that receives a contribution exceeding $75 made partly as a gift and partly as consideration for goods or services furnished by the charity (a "quid pro quo" contribution) is required to inform the contributor in writing of an estimate of the value of the goods or services furnished by the charity and that only the portion exceeding the value of the goods or services may be deductible as a charitable contribution.[289]

Under present law, total deductible contributions of an individual taxpayer to public charities, private operating foundations, and certain types of private nonoperating foundations may not exceed 50 percent of the taxpayer's contribution base, which is the taxpayer's adjusted gross income for a taxable year (disregarding any net operating loss carryback). To the extent a taxpayer has not exceeded the 50-percent limitation, (1) contributions of capital gain property to public charities generally may be deducted up to 30 percent of the taxpayer's contribution base, (2) contributions of cash to private foundations and certain other charitable organizations generally may be deducted up to 30 percent of the taxpayer's contribution base, and (3) contributions of capital gain property to private foundations and certain other charitable organizations generally may be deducted up to 20 percent of the taxpayer's contribution base.

Contributions by individuals in excess of the 50-percent, 30-percent, and 20-percent limits may be carried over and deducted over the next five taxable years, subject to the relevant percentage limitations on the deduction in each of those years.

In addition to the percentage limitations imposed specifically on charitable contributions, present law imposes a reduction on most itemized deductions, including charitable contribution deductions, for taxpayers with adjusted gross income in excess of a threshold amount, which is indexed annually for inflation. The threshold amount for 2006 is $150,500 ($75,250 for married individuals filing separate returns). For those deductions that are subject to the limit, the total amount of itemized deductions is reduced by three percent of adjusted gross income over the threshold amount, but not by more than 80 percent of itemized deductions subject to the limit. Beginning in 2006, the overall limitation on itemized deductions phases-out for all taxpayers. The overall limitation on itemized deductions is reduced by one-third in taxable years beginning in 2006 and 2007, and by two-thirds in taxable years beginning in 2008 and 2009. The overall limitation on itemized deductions is eliminated for taxable years beginning after December 31, 2009; however, this elimination of the limitation sunsets on December 31, 2010.

In general, a charitable deduction is not allowed for income, estate, or gift tax purposes if the donor transfers an interest in property to a charity (e.g., a remainder) while also either retaining an interest in that property (e.g., an income interest) or transferring an interest in that property to a noncharity for less than full and adequate consideration.[290] Exceptions to this

---

[288] Sec. 170(f)(8).

[289] Sec. 6115.

[290] Secs. 170(f), 2055(e)(2), and 2522(c)(2).

general rule are provided for, among other interests, remainder interests in charitable remainder annuity trusts, charitable remainder unitrusts, and pooled income funds, and present interests in the form of a guaranteed annuity or a fixed percentage of the annual value of the property.[291] For such interests, a charitable deduction is allowed to the extent of the present value of the interest designated for a charitable organization.

IRA rules

Within limits, individuals may make deductible and nondeductible contributions to a traditional IRA. Amounts in a traditional IRA are includible in income when withdrawn (except to the extent the withdrawal represents a return of nondeductible contributions). Individuals also may make nondeductible contributions to a Roth IRA. Qualified withdrawals from a Roth IRA are excludable from gross income. Withdrawals from a Roth IRA that are not qualified withdrawals are includible in gross income to the extent attributable to earnings. Includible amounts withdrawn from a traditional IRA or a Roth IRA before attainment of age 59-½ are subject to an additional 10-percent early withdrawal tax, unless an exception applies. Under present law, minimum distributions are required to be made from tax-favored retirement arrangements, including IRAs. Minimum required distributions from a traditional IRA must generally begin by the April 1 of the calendar year following the year in which the IRA owner attains age 70-½.[292]

If an individual has made nondeductible contributions to a traditional IRA, a portion of each distribution from an IRA is nontaxable until the total amount of nondeductible contributions has been received. In general, the amount of a distribution that is nontaxable is determined by multiplying the amount of the distribution by the ratio of the remaining nondeductible contributions to the account balance. In making the calculation, all traditional IRAs of an individual are treated as a single IRA, all distributions during any taxable year are treated as a single distribution, and the value of the contract, income on the contract, and investment in the contract are computed as of the close of the calendar year.

In the case of a distribution from a Roth IRA that is not a qualified distribution, in determining the portion of the distribution attributable to earnings, contributions and distributions are deemed to be distributed in the following order: (1) regular Roth IRA contributions; (2) taxable conversion contributions;[293] (3) nontaxable conversion contributions; and (4) earnings. In determining the amount of taxable distributions from a Roth IRA, all Roth IRA distributions in the same taxable year are treated as a single distribution, all regular Roth IRA contributions for a year are treated as a single contribution, and all conversion contributions during the year are treated as a single contribution.

---

[291] Sec. 170(f)(2).

[292] Minimum distribution rules also apply in the case of distributions after the death of a traditional or Roth IRA owner.

[293] Conversion contributions refer to conversions of amounts in a traditional IRA to a Roth IRA.

Distributions from an IRA (other than a Roth IRA) are generally subject to withholding unless the individual elects not to have withholding apply.[294] Elections not to have withholding apply are to be made in the time and manner prescribed by the Secretary.

Split-interest trust filing requirements

Split-interest trusts, including charitable remainder annuity trusts, charitable remainder unitrusts, and pooled income funds, are required to file an annual information return (Form 1041A).[295] Trusts that are not split-interest trusts but that claim a charitable deduction for amounts permanently set aside for a charitable purpose[296] also are required to file Form 1041A. The returns are required to be made publicly available.[297] A trust that is required to distribute all trust net income currently to trust beneficiaries in a taxable year is exempt from this return requirement for such taxable year. A failure to file the required return may result in a penalty on the trust of $10 a day for as long as the failure continues, up to a maximum of $5,000 per return.

In addition, split-interest trusts are required to file annually Form 5227.[298] Form 5227 requires disclosure of information regarding a trust's noncharitable beneficiaries. The penalty for failure to file this return is calculated based on the amount of tax owed. A split-interest trust generally is not subject to tax and therefore, in general, a penalty may not be imposed for the failure to file Form 5227. Form 5227 is not required to be made publicly available.

Explanation of Provision

Qualified charitable distributions from IRAs

The provision provides an exclusion from gross income for otherwise taxable IRA distributions from a traditional or a Roth IRA in the case of qualified charitable distributions.[299] The exclusion may not exceed $100,000 per taxpayer per taxable year. Special rules apply in determining the amount of an IRA distribution that is otherwise taxable. The present-law rules regarding taxation of IRA distributions and the deduction of charitable contributions continue to apply to distributions from an IRA that are not qualified charitable distributions. Qualified charitable distributions are taken into account for purposes of the minimum distribution rules applicable to traditional IRAs to the same extent the distribution would have been taken into account under such rules had the distribution not been directly distributed under the provision.

---

[294] Sec. 3405.

[295] Sec. 6034. This requirement applies to all split-interest trusts described in section 4947(a)(2).

[296] Sec. 642(c).

[297] Sec. 6104(b).

[298] Sec. 6011; Treas. Reg. sec. 53.6011-1(d).

[299] The provision does not apply to distributions from employer-sponsored retirements plans, including SIMPLE IRAs and simplified employee pensions ("SEPs").

An IRA does not fail to qualify as an IRA merely because qualified charitable distributions have been made from the IRA. It is intended that the Secretary will prescribe rules under which IRA owners are deemed to elect out of withholding if they designate that a distribution is intended to be a qualified charitable distribution.

A qualified charitable distribution is any distribution from an IRA directly by the IRA trustee to an organization described in section 170(b)(1)(A) (other than an organization described in section 509(a)(3) or a donor advised fund (as defined in section 4966(d)(2)). Distributions are eligible for the exclusion only if made on or after the date the IRA owner attains age 70-½.

The exclusion applies only if a charitable contribution deduction for the entire distribution otherwise would be allowable (under present law), determined without regard to the generally applicable percentage limitations. Thus, for example, if the deductible amount is reduced because of a benefit received in exchange, or if a deduction is not allowable because the donor did not obtain sufficient substantiation, the exclusion is not available with respect to any part of the IRA distribution.

If the IRA owner has any IRA that includes nondeductible contributions, a special rule applies in determining the portion of a distribution that is includible in gross income (but for the provision) and thus is eligible for qualified charitable distribution treatment. Under the special rule, the distribution is treated as consisting of income first, up to the aggregate amount that would be includible in gross income (but for the provision) if the aggregate balance of all IRAs having the same owner were distributed during the same year. In determining the amount of subsequent IRA distributions includible in income, proper adjustments are to be made to reflect the amount treated as a qualified charitable distribution under the special rule.

Distributions that are excluded from gross income by reason of the provision are not taken into account in determining the deduction for charitable contributions under section 170.

Qualified charitable distribution examples

The following examples illustrate the determination of the portion of an IRA distribution that is a qualified charitable distribution. In each example, it is assumed that the requirements for qualified charitable distribution treatment are otherwise met (e.g., the applicable age requirement and the requirement that contributions are otherwise deductible) and that no other IRA distributions occur during the year.

Example 1.–Individual A has a traditional IRA with a balance of $100,000, consisting solely of deductible contributions and earnings. Individual A has no other IRA. The entire IRA balance is distributed in a distribution to an organization described in section 170(b)(1)(A) (other than an organization described in section 509(a)(3) or a donor advised fund). Under present law, the entire distribution of $100,000 would be includible in Individual A's income. Accordingly, under the provision, the entire distribution of $100,000 is a qualified charitable distribution. As a result, no amount is included in Individual A's income as a result of the distribution and the distribution is not taken into account in determining the amount of Individual A's charitable deduction for the year.

Example 2.–Individual B has a traditional IRA with a balance of $100,000, consisting of $20,000 of nondeductible contributions and $80,000 of deductible contributions and earnings. Individual B has no other IRA. In a distribution to an organization described in section 170(b)(1)(A) (other than an organization described in section 509(a)(3) or a donor advised fund), $80,000 is distributed from the IRA. Under present law, a portion of the distribution from the IRA would be treated as a nontaxable return of nondeductible contributions. The nontaxable portion of the distribution would be $16,000, determined by multiplying the amount of the distribution ($80,000) by the ratio of the nondeductible contributions to the account balance ($20,000/$100,000). Accordingly, under present law, $64,000 of the distribution ($80,000 minus $16,000) would be includible in Individual B's income.

Under the provision, notwithstanding the present-law tax treatment of IRA distributions, the distribution is treated as consisting of income first, up to the total amount that would be includible in gross income (but for the provision) if all amounts were distributed from all IRAs otherwise taken into account in determining the amount of IRA distributions. The total amount that would be includible in income if all amounts were distributed from the IRA is $80,000. Accordingly, under the provision, the entire $80,000 distributed to the charitable organization is treated as includible in income (before application of the provision) and is a qualified charitable distribution. As a result, no amount is included in Individual B's income as a result of the distribution and the distribution is not taken into account in determining the amount of Individual B's charitable deduction for the year. In addition, for purposes of determining the tax treatment of other distributions from the IRA, $20,000 of the amount remaining in the IRA is treated as Individual B's nondeductible contributions (i.e., not subject to tax upon distribution).

Split-interest trust filing requirements

The provision increases the penalty on split-interest trusts for failure to file a return and for failure to include any of the information required to be shown on such return and to show the correct information. The penalty is $20 for each day the failure continues up to $10,000 for any one return. In the case of a split-interest trust with gross income in excess of $250,000, the penalty is $100 for each day the failure continues up to a maximum of $50,000. In addition, if a person (meaning any officer, director, trustee, employee, or other individual who is under a duty to file the return or include required information)[300] knowingly failed to file the return or include required information, then that person is personally liable for such a penalty, which would be imposed in addition to the penalty that is paid by the organization. Information regarding beneficiaries that are not charitable organizations as described in section 170(c) is exempt from the requirement to make information publicly available. In addition, the provision repeals the present-law exception to the filing requirement for split-interest trusts that are required in a taxable year to distribute all net income currently to beneficiaries. Such exception remains available to trusts other than split-interest trusts that are otherwise subject to the filing requirement.

---

[300] Sec. 6652(c)(4)(C).

Effective Date

The provision relating to qualified charitable distributions is effective for distributions made in taxable years beginning after December 31, 2005, and taxable years beginning before January 1, 2008. The provision relating to information returns of split-interest trusts is effective for returns for taxable years beginning after December 31, 2006.

2. Charitable deduction for contributions of food inventory (sec. 170 of the Code)

Present Law

Under present law, a taxpayer's deduction for charitable contributions of inventory generally is limited to the taxpayer's basis (typically, cost) in the inventory, or if less the fair market value of the inventory.

For certain contributions of inventory, C corporations may claim an enhanced deduction equal to the lesser of (1) basis plus one-half of the item's appreciation (i.e., basis plus one half of fair market value in excess of basis) or (2) two times basis (sec. 170(e)(3)). In general, a C corporation's charitable contribution deductions for a year may not exceed 10 percent of the corporation's taxable income (sec. 170(b)(2)). To be eligible for the enhanced deduction, the contributed property generally must be inventory of the taxpayer, contributed to a charitable organization described in section 501(c)(3) (except for private nonoperating foundations), and the donee must (1) use the property consistent with the donee's exempt purpose solely for the care of the ill, the needy, or infants, (2) not transfer the property in exchange for money, other property, or services, and (3) provide the taxpayer a written statement that the donee's use of the property will be consistent with such requirements. In the case of contributed property subject to the Federal Food, Drug, and Cosmetic Act, the property must satisfy the applicable requirements of such Act on the date of transfer and for 180 days prior to the transfer.

A donor making a charitable contribution of inventory must make a corresponding adjustment to the cost of goods sold by decreasing the cost of goods sold by the lesser of the fair market value of the property or the donor's basis with respect to the inventory (Treas. Reg. sec. 1.170A-4A(c)(3)). Accordingly, if the allowable charitable deduction for inventory is the fair market value of the inventory, the donor reduces its cost of goods sold by such value, with the result that the difference between the fair market value and the donor's basis may still be recovered by the donor other than as a charitable contribution.

To use the enhanced deduction, the taxpayer must establish that the fair market value of the donated item exceeds basis. The valuation of food inventory has been the subject of disputes between taxpayers and the IRS.[301]

---

[301] *Lucky Stores Inc. v. Commissioner,* 105 T.C. 420 (1995) (holding that the value of surplus bread inventory donated to charity was the full retail price of the bread rather than half the retail price, as the IRS asserted).

Under the Katrina Emergency Tax Relief Act of 2005, any taxpayer, whether or not a C corporation, engaged in a trade or business is eligible to claim the enhanced deduction for certain donations made after August 28, 2005, and before January 1, 2006, of food inventory. For taxpayers other than C corporations, the total deduction for donations of food inventory in a taxable year generally may not exceed 10 percent of the taxpayer's net income for such taxable year from all sole proprietorships, S corporations, or partnerships (or other entity that is not a C corporation) from which contributions of "apparently wholesome food" are made. "Apparently wholesome food" is defined as food intended for human consumption that meets all quality and labeling standards imposed by Federal, State, and local laws and regulations even though the food may not be readily marketable due to appearance, age, freshness, grade, size, surplus, or other conditions.

Explanation of Provision

The provision extends the provision enacted as part of the Katrina Emergency Tax Relief Act of 2005. As under such Act, under the provision, any taxpayer, whether or not a C corporation, engaged in a trade or business is eligible to claim the enhanced deduction for donations of food inventory. For taxpayers other than C corporations, the total deduction for donations of food inventory in a taxable year generally may not exceed 10 percent of the taxpayer's net income for such taxable year from all sole proprietorships, S corporations, or partnerships (or other non C corporation) from which contributions of apparently wholesome food are made. For example, as under the Katrina Emergency Tax Relief Act of 2005, if a taxpayer is a sole proprietor, a shareholder in an S corporation, and a partner in a partnership, and each business makes charitable contributions of food inventory, the taxpayer's deduction for donations of food inventory is limited to 10 percent of the taxpayer's net income from the sole proprietorship and the taxpayer's interests in the S corporation and partnership. However, if only the sole proprietorship and the S corporation made charitable contributions of food inventory, the taxpayer's deduction would be limited to 10 percent of the net income from the trade or business of the sole proprietorship and the taxpayer's interest in the S corporation, but not the taxpayer's interest in the partnership.[302]

Under the provision, the enhanced deduction for food is available only for food that qualifies as "apparently wholesome food." "Apparently wholesome food" is defined as it is defined under the Katrina Emergency Tax Relief Act of 2005.

---

[302] The 10 percent limitation does not affect the application of the generally applicable percentage limitations. For example, if 10 percent of a sole proprietor's net income from the proprietor's trade or business was greater than 50 percent of the proprietor's contribution base, the available deduction for the taxable year (with respect to contributions to public charities) would be 50 percent of the proprietor's contribution base. Consistent with present law, such contributions may be carried forward because they exceed the 50 percent limitation. Contributions of food inventory by a taxpayer that is not a C corporation that exceed the 10 percent limitation but not the 50 percent limitation could not be carried forward.

The provision is effective for contributions made after December 31, 2005, and before January 1, 2008.

3. Basis adjustment to stock of S corporation contributing property (sec. 1367 of the Code)

Present Law

Under present law, if an S corporation contributes money or other property to a charity, each shareholder takes into account the shareholder's pro rata share of the contribution in determining its own income tax liability.[303] A shareholder of an S corporation reduces the basis in the stock of the S corporation by the amount of the charitable contribution that flows through to the shareholder.[304]

Explanation of Provision

The provision provides that the amount of a shareholder's basis reduction in the stock of an S corporation by reason of a charitable contribution made by the corporation will be equal to the shareholder's pro rata share of the adjusted basis of the contributed property.[305]

Thus, for example, assume an S corporation with one individual shareholder makes a charitable contribution of stock with a basis of $200 and a fair market value of $500. The shareholder will be treated as having made a $500 charitable contribution (or a lesser amount if the special rules of section 170(e) apply), and will reduce the basis of the S corporation stock by $200.[306]

Effective Date

The provision applies to contributions made in taxable years beginning after December 31, 2005, and taxable years beginning before January 1, 2008.

---

[303] Sec. 1366(a)(1)(A).

[304] Sec. 1367(a)(2)(B).

[305] *See* Rev. Rul. 96-11 (1996-1 C.B. 140) for a rule reaching a similar result in the case of charitable contributions made by a partnership.

[306] This example assumes that basis of the S corporation stock (before reduction) is at least $200.

4. Charitable deduction for contributions of book inventory (sec. 170 of the Code)

Present Law

Under present law, a taxpayer's deduction for charitable contributions of inventory generally is limited to the taxpayer's basis (typically, cost) in the inventory, or if less the fair market value of the inventory.

For certain contributions of inventory, C corporations may claim an enhanced deduction equal to the lesser of (1) basis plus one-half of the item's appreciation (i.e., basis plus one half of fair market value in excess of basis) or (2) two times basis (sec. 170(e)(3)). In general, a C corporation's charitable contribution deductions for a year may not exceed 10 percent of the corporation's taxable income (sec. 170(b)(2)). To be eligible for the enhanced deduction, the contributed property generally must be inventory of the taxpayer, contributed to a charitable organization described in section 501(c)(3) (except for private nonoperating foundations), and the donee must (1) use the property consistent with the donee's exempt purpose solely for the care of the ill, the needy, or infants, (2) not transfer the property in exchange for money, other property, or services, and (3) provide the taxpayer a written statement that the donee's use of the property will be consistent with such requirements. In the case of contributed property subject to the Federal Food, Drug, and Cosmetic Act, the property must satisfy the applicable requirements of such Act on the date of transfer and for 180 days prior to the transfer.

A donor making a charitable contribution of inventory must make a corresponding adjustment to the cost of goods sold by decreasing the cost of goods sold by the lesser of the fair market value of the property or the donor's basis with respect to the inventory (Treas. Reg. sec. 1.170A-4A(c)(3)). Accordingly, if the allowable charitable deduction for inventory is the fair market value of the inventory, the donor reduces its cost of goods sold by such value, with the result that the difference between the fair market value and the donor's basis may still be recovered by the donor other than as a charitable contribution.

To use the enhanced deduction, the taxpayer must establish that the fair market value of the donated item exceeds basis.

The Katrina Emergency Tax Relief Act of 2005 extended the present-law enhanced deduction for C corporations to certain qualified book contributions made after August 28, 2005, and before January 1, 2006. For such purposes, a qualified book contribution means a charitable contribution of books to a public school that provides elementary education or secondary education (kindergarten through grade 12) and that is an educational organization that normally maintains a regular faculty and curriculum and normally has a regularly enrolled body of pupils or students in attendance at the place where its educational activities are regularly carried on. The enhanced deduction under the Katrina Emergency Tax Relief Act of 2005 is not allowed unless the donee organization certifies in writing that the contributed books are suitable, in terms of currency, content, and quantity, for use in the donee's educational programs and that the donee will use the books in such educational programs.

Explanation of Provision

The provision extends the provision enacted as part of the Katrina Emergency Tax Relief Act of 2005. As under such Act, an enhanced deduction for C corporations for qualified book contributions is allowed.

Effective Date

The provision is effective for contributions made after December 31, 2005, and before January 1, 2008.

5. Modify tax treatment of certain payments to controlling exempt organizations (secs. 512 and 6033 of the Code)

Present Law

In general, interest, rents, royalties, and annuities are excluded from the unrelated business income of tax-exempt organizations. However, section 512(b)(13) generally treats otherwise excluded rent, royalty, annuity, and interest income as unrelated business income if such income is received from a taxable or tax-exempt subsidiary that is 50 percent controlled by the parent tax-exempt organization. In the case of a stock subsidiary, "control" means ownership by vote or value of more than 50 percent of the stock. In the case of a partnership or other entity, control means ownership of more than 50 percent of the profits, capital or beneficial interests. In addition, present law applies the constructive ownership rules of section 318 for purposes of section 512(b)(13). Thus, a parent exempt organization is deemed to control any subsidiary in which it holds more than 50 percent of the voting power or value, directly (as in the case of a first-tier subsidiary) or indirectly (as in the case of a second-tier subsidiary).

Under present law, interest, rent, annuity, or royalty payments made by a controlled entity to a tax-exempt organization are includable in the latter organization's unrelated business income and are subject to the unrelated business income tax to the extent the payment reduces the net unrelated income (or increases any net unrelated loss) of the controlled entity (determined as if the entity were tax exempt).

Explanation of Provision

The provision provides that the general rule of section 512(b)(13), which includes interest, rent, annuity, or royalty payments made by a controlled entity to the controlling tax-exempt organization in the latter organization's unrelated business income to the extent the payment reduces the net unrelated income (or increases any net unrelated loss) of the controlled entity, applies only to the portion of payments received or accrued in a taxable year that exceeds the amount of the specified payment that would have been paid or accrued if such payment had been determined under the principles of section 482. Thus, if a payment of rent by a controlled subsidiary to its tax-exempt parent organization exceeds fair market value, the excess amount of such payment over fair market value (as determined in accordance with section 482) is included in the parent organization's unrelated business income, to the extent that such excess reduced the net unrelated income (or increased any net unrelated loss) of the controlled entity (determined as if the entity were tax exempt). In addition, the provision imposes a 20-percent penalty on the

273

larger of such excess determined without regard to any amendment or supplement to a return of tax, or such excess determined with regard to all such amendments and supplements. The provision applies only to payments made pursuant to a binding written contract in effect on the date of enactment (or renewal of such a contract on substantially similar terms). It is intended that there should be further study of such arrangements in light of the provision before any determination about whether to extend or expand the provision is made.

The provision requires that a tax-exempt organization that receives interest, rent, annuity, or royalty payments from a controlled entity report such payments on its annual information return as well as any loans made to any controlled entity and any transfers between such organization and a controlled entity.

The provision provides that, not later than January 1, 2009, the Secretary shall submit a report to the Committee on Finance of the Senate and the Committee on Ways and Means of the House of Representatives a report on the effectiveness of the Internal Revenue Service in administering the provision and on the extent to which payments by controlled entities to the controlling exempt organization meet the requirements of section 482 of the Code. Such report shall include the results of any audit of any controlling organization or controlled entity and recommendations relating to the tax treatment of payments from controlled entities to controlling organizations.

Effective Date

The provision related to payments to controlling organizations applies to payments received or accrued after December 31, 2005 and before January 1, 2008. The provision relating to reporting is effective for returns the due date (determined without regard to extensions) of which is after the date of enactment. The provision relating to a report is effective on the date of enactment.

6. Encourage contributions of real property made for conservation purposes (sec. 170 of the Code)

Present Law

Charitable contributions generally

In general, a deduction is permitted for charitable contributions, subject to certain limitations that depend on the type of taxpayer, the property contributed, and the donee organization. The amount of deduction generally equals the fair market value of the contributed property on the date of the contribution. Charitable deductions are provided for income, estate, and gift tax purposes.[307]

In general, in any taxable year, charitable contributions by a corporation are not deductible to the extent the aggregate contributions exceed 10 percent of the corporation's

---

[307] Secs. 170, 2055, and 2522, respectively.

taxable income computed without regard to net operating or capital loss carrybacks. For individuals, the amount deductible is a percentage of the taxpayer's contribution base, which is the taxpayer's adjusted gross income computed without regard to any net operating loss carryback. The applicable percentage of the contribution base varies depending on the type of donee organization and property contributed. Cash contributions of an individual taxpayer to public charities, private operating foundations, and certain types of private nonoperating foundations may not exceed 50 percent of the taxpayer's contribution base. Cash contributions to private foundations and certain other organizations generally may be deducted up to 30 percent of the taxpayer's contribution base.

In general, a charitable deduction is not allowed for income, estate, or gift tax purposes if the donor transfers an interest in property to a charity while also either retaining an interest in that property or transferring an interest in that property to a noncharity for less than full and adequate consideration. Exceptions to this general rule are provided for, among other interests, remainder interests in charitable remainder annuity trusts, charitable remainder unitrusts, and pooled income funds, present interests in the form of a guaranteed annuity or a fixed percentage of the annual value of the property, and qualified conservation contributions.

Capital gain property

Capital gain property means any capital asset or property used in the taxpayer's trade or business the sale of which at its fair market value, at the time of contribution, would have resulted in gain that would have been long-term capital gain. Contributions of capital gain property to a qualified charity are deductible at fair market value within certain limitations. Contributions of capital gain property to charitable organizations described in section 170(b)(1)(A) (e.g., public charities, private foundations other than private non-operating foundations, and certain governmental units) generally are deductible up to 30 percent of the taxpayer's contribution base. An individual may elect, however, to bring all these contributions of capital gain property for a taxable year within the 50-percent limitation category by reducing the amount of the contribution deduction by the amount of the appreciation in the capital gain property. Contributions of capital gain property to charitable organizations described in section 170(b)(1)(B) (e.g., private non-operating foundations) are deductible up to 20 percent of the taxpayer's contribution base.

For purposes of determining whether a taxpayer's aggregate charitable contributions in a taxable year exceed the applicable percentage limitation, contributions of capital gain property are taken into account after other charitable contributions. Contributions of capital gain property that exceed the percentage limitation may be carried forward for five years.

Qualified conservation contributions

Qualified conservation contributions are not subject to the "partial interest" rule, which generally bars deductions for charitable contributions of partial interests in property. A qualified conservation contribution is a contribution of a qualified real property interest to a qualified organization exclusively for conservation purposes. A qualified real property interest is defined as: (1) the entire interest of the donor other than a qualified mineral interest; (2) a remainder interest; or (3) a restriction (granted in perpetuity) on the use that may be made of the real property. Qualified organizations include certain governmental units, public charities that meet certain public support tests, and certain supporting organizations. Conservation purposes include: (1) the preservation of land areas for outdoor recreation by, or for the education of, the general public; (2) the protection of a relatively natural habitat of fish, wildlife, or plants, or similar ecosystem; (3) the preservation of open space (including farmland and forest land) where such preservation will yield a significant public benefit and is either for the scenic enjoyment of the general public or pursuant to a clearly delineated Federal, State, or local governmental conservation policy; and (4) the preservation of an historically important land area or a certified historic structure.

Qualified conservation contributions of capital gain property are subject to the same limitations and carryover rules of other charitable contributions of capital gain property.

Explanation of Provision

In general

Under the provision, the 30-percent contribution base limitation on contributions of capital gain property by individuals does not apply to qualified conservation contributions (as defined under present law). Instead, individuals may deduct the fair market value of any qualified conservation contribution to an organization described in section 170(b)(1)(A) to the extent of the excess of 50 percent of the contribution base over the amount of all other allowable charitable contributions. These contributions are not taken into account in determining the amount of other allowable charitable contributions.

Individuals are allowed to carryover any qualified conservation contributions that exceed the 50-percent limitation for up to 15 years.

For example, assume an individual with a contribution base of $100 makes a qualified conservation contribution of property with a fair market value of $80 and makes other charitable contributions subject to the 50-percent limitation of $60. The individual is allowed a deduction of $50 in the current taxable year for the non-conservation contributions (50 percent of the $100 contribution base) and is allowed to carryover the excess $10 for up to 5 years. No current deduction is allowed for the qualified conservation contribution, but the entire $80 qualified conservation contribution may be carried forward for up to 15 years.

Farmers and ranchers

Individuals

In the case of an individual who is a qualified farmer or rancher for the taxable year in which the contribution is made, a qualified conservation contribution is allowable up to 100 percent of the excess of the taxpayer's contribution base over the amount of all other allowable charitable contributions.

In the above example, if the individual is a qualified farmer or rancher, in addition to the $50 deduction for non-conservation contributions, an additional $50 for the qualified conservation contribution is allowed and $30 may be carried forward for up to 15 years as a contribution subject to the 100-percent limitation.

Corporations

In the case of a corporation (other than a publicly traded corporation) that is a qualified farmer or rancher for the taxable year in which the contribution is made, any qualified conservation contribution is allowable up to 100 percent of the excess of the corporation's taxable income (as computed under section 170(b)(2)) over the amount of all other allowable charitable contributions. Any excess may be carried forward for up to 15 years as a contribution subject to the 100-percent limitation.

Requirement that land be available for agriculture or livestock production

As an additional condition of eligibility for the 100 percent limitation, with respect to any contribution of property in agriculture or livestock production, or that is available for such production, by a qualified farmer or rancher, the qualified real property interest must include a restriction that the property remain generally available for such production. (There is no requirement as to any specific use in agriculture or farming, or necessarily that the property be used for such purposes, merely that the property remain available for such purposes.) Such additional condition does not apply to contributions made after December 31, 2005, and on or before the date of enactment.

Definition

A qualified farmer or rancher means a taxpayer whose gross income from the trade of business of farming (within the meaning of section 2032A(e)(5)) is greater than 50 percent of the taxpayer's gross income for the taxable year.

Effective Date

The provision applies to contributions made in taxable years beginning after December 31, 2005, and before January 1, 2008.

7. Excise tax exemptions for blood collector organizations (secs. 4041, 4221, 4253, 4483, 6416, and 7701 of the Code)

Present Law

American National Red Cross

The American National Red Cross ("Red Cross") is a Congressionally chartered corporation. It is responsible for giving aid to members of the U.S. Armed Forces, to disaster victims in the United States and abroad to help people prevent, prepare for, and respond to emergencies.[308] The Red Cross is responsible for over half of the nation's blood supply and blood products.

Exemption from certain retail and manufacturers excise taxes

The Code permits the Secretary to exempt from excise tax certain articles and services to be purchased for the exclusive use of the United States (sec. 4293). This authority is conditioned upon the Secretary determining (1) that the imposition of such taxes will cause substantial burden or expense which can be avoided by granting tax exemption and (2) that full benefit of such exemption, if granted, will accrue to the United States.

On April 18, 1979, the Secretary exercised this authority to exempt, with limited exceptions, the Red Cross from the taxes imposed by chapters 31 and 32 of the Code with respect to articles sold to the Red Cross for its exclusive use.[309] An exemption is also authorized from the taxes imposed with respect to tires and inner tubes if such tire or inner tube is sold by any person on or in connection with the sale of any article to the American National Red Cross, for its exclusive use.[310] No exemption is provided from the gas guzzler tax (sec. 4064), and the taxes imposed on aviation fuel, on fuel used on inland waterways (sec. 4042), and on coal (sec. 4121).[311] The exemption is subject to registration requirements for tax-free sales contained in Treasury regulations. Credit and refund of tax is subject to the requirements set forth in section 6416 relating to the exemption for taxable articles sold for the exclusive use of State and local governments.

Exemption from heavy highway motor vehicle use tax

An annual use tax is imposed on highway motor vehicles, at the rates below (sec. 4481).

Under 55,000 pounds	No tax
55,000-75,000 pounds	$100 plus $22 per 1,000 pounds over 55,000
Over 75,000 pounds	$550

---

[308] *See* 36 U.S.C. sec. 300102.

[309] Department of the Treasury, *Notice-Manufacturers and Retailers Excise Taxes -Exemption from Tax of Sales of Certain Articles to the American Red Cross*, 44 F.R. 23407, 1979-1 C.B. 478 (1979). At the time the notice was issued the following taxes were covered in Chapters 31 and 32: special fuels, automotive and related items (motor vehicles, tires and tubes, petroleum products, coal, and recreational equipment (sporting goods and firearms).

[310] Under present law, there is no longer a tax on inner tubes.

[311] Department of the Treasury, *Notice-Manufacturers and Retailers Excise Taxes -Exemption from Tax of Sales of Certain Articles to the American Red Cross*, 44 F.R. 23407, 1979-1 C.B. 478, at 479 (1979). The Treasury notice also exempts the Red Cross from tax on aircraft tires and tubes, however, present law currently limits the tax to highway vehicle tires (sec. 4071(a)).

The Code provides that the Secretary may authorize exemption from the heavy highway vehicle use tax as to the use by the United States of any particular highway motor vehicle or class of highway motor vehicles if the Secretary determines that the imposition of such tax with respect to such use will cause substantial burden or expense which can be avoided by granting tax exemption and that the full benefit of such exemption, if granted will accrue to the United States (sec. 4483(b)). The IRS has ruled that the Red Cross comes within the term "United States" for purposes of the exemption from the heavy highway motor vehicle use tax (Rev. Rul. 76-510).

Exemption from communications excise tax

The Code imposes a three-percent tax on amounts paid for local telephone service; toll telephone service and teletypewriter exchange service (sec. 4251). These taxes do not apply to amounts paid for services furnished to the Red Cross (sec. 4253(c)).

Certain other tax-free sales

Exemption from certain manufacturer and retail sale excise taxes

The following sales generally are exempt from certain manufacturer and retail sale excise taxes: (1) for use by the purchaser for further manufacture, or for resale to a second purchaser in further manufacture; (2) for export or for resale to a second purchaser for export; (3) for use by the purchaser as supplies for vessels or aircraft; (4) to a State or local government for the exclusive use of a State or local government; and (5) to a nonprofit educational organization for its exclusive use (sec. 4221). The exemption generally applies to manufacturers taxes imposed by chapter 32 of the Code (the gas guzzlers tax, and the taxes imposed on tires, certain vaccines, and recreational equipment) and the tax on retail sales of heavy trucks and trailers.[312]

The manufacturers excise taxes on coal (sec. 4121), on gasoline, diesel fuel, and kerosene (sec. 4081) are not covered by the exemption. The exemption for a sale to a State or local government for their exclusive use and the exemption for sales to a nonprofit educational organization does not apply to the gas guzzlers tax, and the tax on vaccines. In addition, the exemption of sales for use as supplies for vessels and aircraft does not apply to the vaccine tax.

Exempt sales of special fuels

A retail excise tax is imposed on special motor fuels, including propane, compressed natural gas, and certain alcohol mixtures (sec. 4041). Section 4041 also serves as a back-up tax for diesel fuel or kerosene that was not subject to the manufacturers taxes under section 4081 (other than the Leaking Underground Storage Tank Trust Fund tax) if such fuel is delivered into

---

[312] The tax imposed by subchapter A of chapter 31 (relating to luxury passenger vehicles) are also exempt pursuant to this provision, however, this tax expired on December 31, 2002. (sec. 4001(g).)

the fuel supply tank of a diesel-powered highway vehicle or train.[313] No tax is imposed on these fuels for nontaxable uses, including fuel: (1) sold for use or used as supplies for vessels or aircraft, (2) sold for the exclusive use of any State, any political subdivision of a State, or the District of Columbia or used by such entity as fuel, (3) sold for export, or for shipment to a possession of the United States and is actually exported or shipped, (4) sold to a nonprofit educational organization for its exclusive use, or used by such entity as fuel (sec. 4041(g)).

Credits and refunds

In general

A credit or refund is allowed for overpayment of manufacturers or retail excise taxes (sec. 6416). Overpayments include (1) certain uses and resales, (2) price adjustments, and (3) further manufacture.

Specified uses and resales

The special fuel taxes, the retail tax on heavy trucks and trailers, and any of the manufacturers excise taxes paid on any article will be a deemed overpayment subject to credit or refund if sold for certain specified uses (sec. 6416(b)(2)). These uses are (1) export, (2) used or sold for use as supplies for vessels or aircraft, (3) sold to a State or local government for the exclusive use of a State or local government, (4) sold to a nonprofit educational organization for its exclusive use; (5) taxable tires sold to any person for use in connection with a qualified bus, or (6) the case of gasoline used or sold for use in the production of a special fuel. Certain exceptions apply in that this deemed overpayment rule does not apply to the taxes imposed by sections 4041 and 4081 on diesel fuel and kerosene, and the coal taxes (sec. 4121). Additionally, the deemed overpayment rule does not apply to the gas guzzler tax in the case of an article sold to a state or local government for its exclusive use or sold to an educational organization for its exclusive use.

Special rule for tires sold in connection with other articles

If the tax imposed on tires (sec. 4071) has been paid with respect to the sale of any tire by the manufacturer, producer, or importer, and such tire is sold by any person in connection with the sale of any other article, such tax will be deemed an overpayment by person if such other article (1) is an automobile bus chassis or an automobile bus body, or (2) is by any person exported, sold to a State or local government for exclusive use of a State or local government, sold to a nonprofit educational organization for its exclusive use, or used or sold for use as supplies for vessels or aircraft (sec. 6416(b)(4)).

Gasoline used for exempt purposes

---

[313] For example, tax is imposed on the delivery of any of the following into the fuel supply tank of a diesel powered highway vehicle or train of any dyed diesel or dyed kerosene for other than a nontaxable use; any undyed diesel fuel or undyed kerosene on which a credit or refund.

If gasoline is sold to any person for certain specified purposes, the Secretary is required to pay (without interest) to such person an amount equal to the product of the number of gallons of gasoline so sold multiplied by the rate at which tax was imposed on such gasoline under section 4081 (sec. 6421(c)). Under this provision, the specified purposes are (1) for export or for resale to a second purchaser for export; (2) for use by the purchaser as supplies for vessels or aircraft; (3) to a State or local government for exclusive use of a State or local government; and (4) to a nonprofit educational organization for its exclusive use (sec. 4221(a), 6421(c)).

Diesel fuel or kerosene used in a nontaxable use

If diesel fuel or kerosene, upon which tax has been imposed is used by any person in a nontaxable use, the Code authorizes the Secretary to pay (without interest) an amount equal to the aggregate amount of tax imposed on such fuel (sec. 6427(l)). Nontaxable uses include any exemption from the tax imposed by section 4041(a) (except prior taxation).

Explanation of Provision

The provision exempts qualified blood collector organizations from certain retail and manufacturers excise taxes to the extent such items are for the exclusive use of such an organization for the distribution or collection of blood. A qualified blood collector organization means an organization that is (1) described in section 501(c)(3) and exempt from tax under section 501(a), (2) primarily engaged in the activity of the collection of blood, (3) registered with the Secretary for purposes of excise tax exemptions, and (4) registered by the Food and Drug Administration to collect blood.

Under the provision, qualified blood collector organizations are exempt from the communications excise tax as provided by Treasury regulations. The provision also provides an exemption from the special fuels tax, and certain taxes imposed by chapter 32 and subchapter A and C of chapter 31 of the Code (i.e., the retail excise tax on heavy trucks and trailers, and the manufacturers excise taxes on tires). [314] The provision also makes conforming amendments to allow for the credit or refund of these taxes and any tax paid on gasoline for the exclusive use of the blood collector organization. The provision also permits a refund of tax for diesel fuel or kerosene used by a qualified blood collector organization. Finally, the provision provides an exemption from the heavy vehicle use tax of a "qualified blood collector vehicle" by a qualified blood collector organization. A "qualified blood collector vehicle" means a vehicle at least 80 percent of the use of which during the prior taxable period was by a qualified blood collector organization in the collection, storage, or transportation of blood. A special rule is provided for the first taxable period a vehicle is placed in service by the qualified blood collector organization. For the first taxable period a vehicle is placed in service by the organization, the vehicle will be treated as a "qualified blood collector vehicle" for that period if the organization certifies that it reasonably expects that at least 80 percent of the use of the vehicle during such

---

[314] Such organizations are also exempt from the expired retail excise tax on luxury passenger vehicles. No exemption is provided from the gas guzzler tax (sec. 4064), the taxes imposed on fuel used on inland waterways (sec. 4042), on coal (sec. 4121), and on recreational equipment (sport fishing equipment, bows, arrow components, and firearms).

taxable period will be by the organization in the collection, storage, or transportation of blood. Such certification is to be provided to the Secretary on such forms and in such manner as the Secretary may require.

It is expected that the excise tax exemptions of the Red Cross will be reexamined in conjunction with a review of its charter.

Effective Date

Generally, the provision is effective on January 1, 2007. The exemption from the heavy vehicle use tax is effective for taxable periods beginning July 1, 2007.

B. Reforming Exempt Organizations

1. Reporting on certain acquisitions of interests in insurance contracts in which certain exempt organizations hold interests (new sec. 6050V of the Code)

Present Law

Amounts received under a life insurance contract

Amounts received under a life insurance contract paid by reason of the death of the insured are not includible in gross income for Federal tax purposes.[315] No Federal income tax generally is imposed on a policyholder with respect to the earnings under a life insurance contract (inside buildup).[316]

Distributions from a life insurance contract (other than a modified endowment contract) that are made prior to the death of the insured generally are includible in income to the extent that the amounts distributed exceed the taxpayer's investment in the contract (i.e., basis). Such distributions generally are treated first as a tax-free recovery of basis, and then as income.[317]

Transfers for value

A limitation on the exclusion for amounts received under a life insurance contract is provided in the case of transfers for value. If a life insurance contract (or an interest in the contract) is transferred for valuable consideration, the amount excluded from income by reason of the death of the insured is limited to the actual value of the consideration plus the premiums and other amounts subsequently paid by the acquiror of the contract.[318]

---

[315] Sec. 101(a).

[316] This favorable tax treatment is available only if a life insurance contract meets certain requirements designed to limit the investment character of the contract. Sec. 7702.

[317] Sec. 72(e). In the case of a modified endowment contract, however, in general, distributions are treated as income first, loans are treated as distributions (i.e., income rather than basis recovery first), and an additional 10-percent tax is imposed on the income portion of distributions made before age 59-½ and in certain other circumstances. Secs. 72(e) and (v). A modified endowment contract is a life insurance contract that does not meet a statutory "7-pay" test, i.e., generally is funded more rapidly than seven annual level premiums. Sec. 7702A.

[318] Section 101(a)(2). The transfer-for-value rule does not apply, however, in the case of a transfer in which the life insurance contract (or interest in the contract) transferred has a basis in the hands of the transferee that is determined by reference to the transferor's basis. Similarly, the transfer-for-value rule generally does not apply if the transfer is between certain parties (specifically, if the transfer is to the insured, a partner of the insured, a partnership in which the insured is a partner, or a corporation in which the insured is a shareholder or officer).

Tax treatment of charitable organizations and donors

Present law generally provides tax-exempt status for charitable, educational and certain other organizations, no part of the net earnings of which inures to the benefit of any private shareholder or individual, and which meet certain other requirements.[319] Governmental entities, including some educational organizations, are exempt from tax on income under other tax rules providing that gross income does not include income derived from the exercise of any essential governmental function and accruing to a State or any political subdivision thereof.[320]

In computing taxable income, a taxpayer who itemizes deductions generally is allowed to deduct the amount of cash and the fair market value of property contributed to an organization described in section 501(c)(3) or to a Federal, State, or local governmental entity for exclusively public purposes.[321]

State-law insurable interest rules

State laws generally provide that the owner of a life insurance contract must have an insurable interest in the insured person when the life insurance contract is issued. State laws vary as to the insurable interest of a charitable organization in the life of any individual. Some State laws provide that a charitable organization meeting the requirements of section 501(c)(3) of the Code is treated as having an insurable interest in the life of any donor,[322] or, in other States, in the life of any individual who consents (whether or not the individual is a donor).[323] Other States' insurable interest rules permit the purchase of a life insurance contract even though the person paying the consideration has no insurable interest in the life of the person insured if a charitable, benevolent, educational or religious institution is designated irrevocably as the beneficiary.[324]

Transactions involving charities and non-charities acquiring life insurance

Recently, there has been an increase in transactions involving the acquisition of life insurance contracts using arrangements in which both exempt organizations, primarily charities,

---

[319] Section 501(c)(3).

[320] Section 115.

[321] Section 170.

[322] See, e.g., Mass. Gen. Laws Ann. ch. 175, sec. 123A(2) (West 2005); Iowa Code Ann. sec. 511.39 (West 2004) ("a person who, when purchasing a life insurance policy, makes a donation to the charitable organization or makes the charitable organization the beneficiary of all or a part of the proceeds of the policy . . .).

[323] See, e.g., Cal. Ins. Code sec. 10110.1(f) (West 2005); 40 Pa. Cons. Stat. Ann. sec. 40-512 (2004); Fla. Stat. Ann. sec. 27.404 (2) (2004); Mich. Comp. Laws Ann. sec. 500.2212 (West 2004).

[324] Or. Rev. Stat. sec. 743.030 (2003); Del. Code Ann. Tit. 18, sec. 2705(a) (2004).

284

and private investors have an interest in the contract.[325] The exempt organization has an insurable interest in the insured individuals, either because they are donors, because they consent, or otherwise under applicable State insurable interest rules. Private investors provide capital used to fund the purchase of the life insurance contracts, sometimes together with annuity contracts. Both the private investors and the charity have an interest in the contracts, directly or indirectly, through the use of trusts, partnerships, or other arrangements for sharing the rights to the contracts. Both the charity and the private investors receive cash amounts in connection with the investment in the contracts while the life insurance is in force or as the insured individuals die.

Explanation of Provision

The provision includes a temporary reporting requirement with respect to the acquisition of interests in certain life insurance contracts by certain exempt organizations, together with a Treasury study.

The provision provides that, for reportable acquisitions occurring after the date of enactment and on or before the date two years from the date of enactment, an applicable exempt organization that makes a reportable acquisition is required to file an information return. The information return is to contain the name, address, and taxpayer identification number of the organization and of the issuer of the applicable insurance contract, and such other information as the Secretary of the Treasury prescribes. It is intended that the Treasury Department may require the reporting of other information relevant to the study required under the provision. The report is to be in the form prescribed by the Treasury Secretary and is required to be filed at the time established by the Treasury Secretary. It is intended that the Treasury Department may require the report to be filed within a certain period after the reportable acquisition takes place in order to gather information in a timely manner that is relevant to the study required under the provision.

For this purpose, a reportable acquisition means the acquisition by an applicable exempt organization of a direct or indirect interest in a contract that the applicable exempt organization knows or has reason to know is an applicable insurance contract, if such acquisition is a part of a structured transaction involving a pool of such contracts.

An applicable insurance contract means any life insurance, annuity, or endowment contract with respect to which both an applicable exempt organization and a person other than an applicable exempt organization have directly or indirectly held an interest in the contract (whether or not at the same time). Exceptions apply under this definition. First, the term does not apply if each person (other than an applicable exempt organization) with a direct or indirect interest in the contract has an insurable interest in the insured independent of any interest of the exempt organization in the contract. Second, the term does not apply if the sole interest in the contract of the applicable exempt organization or each person other than the applicable exempt

---

[325] Davis, Wendy, "Death-Pool Donations," Trusts and Estates, May 2004, 55; Francis, Theo, "Tax May Thwart Investment Plans Enlisting Charities," Wall St. J., Feb. 8, 2005, A-10.

organization is as a named beneficiary. Third, the term does not apply if the sole interest in the contract of each person other than the applicable exempt organization is either (1) as a beneficiary of a trust holding an interest in the contract, but only if the person's designation as such a beneficiary was made without consideration and solely on a purely gratuitous basis, or (2) as a trustee who holds an interest in the contract in a fiduciary capacity solely for the benefit of applicable exempt organizations or of persons otherwise meeting one of the first two exceptions.

An applicable exempt organization is any organization described in section 170(c), 168(h)(2)(A)(iv), 2055(a), or 2522(a). Thus, for example, an applicable exempt organization generally includes an organization that is exempt from Federal income tax by reason of being described in section 501(c)(3) (including one organized outside the United States), a government or political subdivision of a government, and an Indian tribal government.

Under the provision, penalties apply for failure to file the return.

The reporting requirement terminates with respect to reportable acquisitions occurring after the date that is 2 years after the date of enactment.

The provision requires the Treasury Secretary to undertake a study on the use by tax-exempt organizations of applicable insurance contracts for the purpose of sharing the benefits of the organization's insurable interest in insured individuals under such contracts with investors, and whether such activities are consistent with the tax-exempt status of the organizations. The study may, for example, address whether certain such arrangements are or may be used to improperly shelter income from tax, and whether they should be listed transactions within the meaning of Treasury Regulation section 1.6011-4(b)(2). No later than 30 months after the date of enactment, the Treasury Secretary is required to report on the study to the Committee on Finance of the Senate and the Committee on Ways and Means of the House of Representatives.

Effective Date

The reporting provision is effective for acquisitions of contracts after the date of enactment. The study provision is effective on the date of enactment.

2. Increase the amounts of excise taxes imposed relating to public charities, social welfare organizations, and private foundations (secs. 4941, 4942, 4943, 4944, 4945, and 4958 of the Code)

Present Law

Public charities and social welfare organizations

The Code imposes excise taxes on excess benefit transactions between disqualified persons (as defined in section 4958(f)) and charitable organizations (other than private foundations) or social welfare organizations (as described in section 501(c)(4)).[326] An excess benefit transaction generally is a transaction in which an economic benefit is provided by a charitable or social welfare organization directly or indirectly to or for the use of a disqualified person, if the value of the economic benefit provided exceeds the value of the consideration (including the performance of services) received for providing such benefit.

The excess benefit tax is imposed on the disqualified person and, in certain cases, on the organization manager, but is not imposed on the exempt organization. An initial tax of 25 percent of the excess benefit amount is imposed on the disqualified person that receives the excess benefit. An additional tax on the disqualified person of 200 percent of the excess benefit applies if the violation is not corrected. A tax of 10 percent of the excess benefit (not to exceed $10,000 with respect to any excess benefit transaction) is imposed on an organization manager that knowingly participated in the excess benefit transaction, if the manager's participation was willful and not due to reasonable cause, and if the initial tax was imposed on the disqualified person.[327] If more than one person is liable for the tax on disqualified persons or on management, all such persons are jointly and severally liable for the tax.[328]

Private foundations

Self-dealing by private foundations

Excise taxes are imposed on acts of self-dealing between a disqualified person (as defined in section 4946) and a private foundation.[329] In general, self-dealing transactions are any direct or indirect: (1) sale or exchange, or leasing, of property between a private foundation and a disqualified person; (2) lending of money or other extension of credit between a private foundation and a disqualified person; (3) the furnishing of goods, services, or facilities between a private foundation and a disqualified person; (4) the payment of compensation (or payment or reimbursement of expenses) by a private foundation to a disqualified person; (5) the transfer to, or use by or for the benefit of, a disqualified person of the income or assets of the private foundation; and (6) certain payments of money or property to a government official.[330] Certain exceptions apply.[331]

---

[326] Sec. 4958. The excess benefit transaction tax commonly is referred to as "intermediate sanctions," because it imposes penalties generally considered to be less punitive than revocation of the organization's exempt status.

[327] Sec. 4958(d)(2). Taxes imposed may be abated if certain conditions are met. Secs. 4961 and 4962.

[328] Sec. 4958(d)(1).

[329] Sec. 4941.

[330] Sec. 4941(d)(1).

[331] See sec. 4941(d)(2).

An initial tax of five percent of the amount involved with respect to an act of self-dealing is imposed on any disqualified person (other than a foundation manager acting only as such) who participates in the act of self-dealing. If such a tax is imposed, a 2.5-percent tax of the amount involved is imposed on a foundation manager who participated in the act of self-dealing knowing it was such an act (and such participation was not willful and was due to reasonable cause) up to $10,000 per act. Such initial taxes may not be abated.[332] Such initial taxes are imposed for each year in the taxable period, which begins on the date the act of self-dealing occurs and ends on the earliest of the date of mailing of a notice of deficiency for the tax, the date on which the tax is assessed, or the date on which correction of the act of self-dealing is completed. A government official (as defined in section 4946(c)) is subject to such initial tax only if the official participates in the act of self-dealing knowing it is such an act. If the act of self-dealing is not corrected, a tax of 200 percent of the amount involved is imposed on the disqualified person and a tax of 50 percent of the amount involved (up to $10,000 per act) is imposed on a foundation manager who refused to agree to correcting the act of self-dealing. Such additional taxes are subject to abatement.[333]

Tax on failure to distribute income

Private nonoperating foundations are required to pay out a minimum amount each year as qualifying distributions. In general, a qualifying distribution is an amount paid to accomplish one or more of the organization's exempt purposes, including reasonable and necessary administrative expenses.[334] Failure to pay out the minimum results in an initial excise tax on the foundation of 15 percent of the undistributed amount. An additional tax of 100 percent of the undistributed amount applies if an initial tax is imposed and the required distributions have not been made by the end of the applicable taxable period.[335] A foundation may include as a qualifying distribution the salaries, occupancy expenses, travel costs, and other reasonable and necessary administrative expenses that the foundation incurs in operating a grant program. A qualifying distribution also includes any amount paid to acquire an asset used (or held for use) directly in carrying out one or more of the organization's exempt purposes and certain amounts set-aside for exempt purposes.[336] Private operating foundations are not subject to the payout requirements.

---

[332] Sec. 4962(b).

[333] Sec. 4961.

[334] Sec. 4942(g)(1)(A).

[335] Sec. 4942(a) and (b). Taxes imposed may be abated if certain conditions are met. Secs. 4961 and 4962.

[336] Sec. 4942(g)(1)(B) and 4942(g)(2). In general, an organization is permitted to adjust the distributable amount in those cases where distributions during the five preceding years have exceeded the payout requirements. Sec. 4942(i).

Tax on excess business holdings

Private foundations are subject to tax on excess business holdings.[337] In general, a private foundation is permitted to hold 20 percent of the voting stock in a corporation, reduced by the amount of voting stock held by all disqualified persons (as defined in section 4946). If it is established that no disqualified person has effective control of the corporation, a private foundation and disqualified persons together may own up to 35 percent of the voting stock of a corporation. A private foundation shall not be treated as having excess business holdings in any corporation if it owns (together with certain other related private foundations) not more than two percent of the voting stock and not more than two percent in value of all outstanding shares of all classes of stock in that corporation. Similar rules apply with respect to holdings in a partnership ("profits interest" is substituted for "voting stock" and "capital interest" for "nonvoting stock") and to other unincorporated enterprises (by substituting "beneficial interest" for "voting stock"). Private foundations are not permitted to have holdings in a proprietorship. Foundations generally have a five-year period to dispose of excess business holdings (acquired other than by purchase) without being subject to tax.[338] This five-year period may be extended an additional five years in limited circumstances.[339] The excess business holdings rules do not apply to holdings in a functionally related business or to holdings in a trade or business at least 95 percent of the gross income of which is derived from passive sources.[340]

The initial tax is equal to five percent of the value of the excess business holdings held during the foundation's applicable taxable year. An additional tax is imposed if an initial tax is imposed and at the close of the applicable taxable period, the foundation continues to hold excess business holdings. The amount of the additional tax is equal to 200 percent of such holdings.

Tax on jeopardizing investments

Private foundations and foundation managers are subject to tax on investments that jeopardize the foundation's charitable purpose.[341] In general, an initial tax of five percent of the amount of the investment applies to the foundation and to foundation managers who participated in the making of the investment knowing that it jeopardized the carrying out of the foundation's exempt purposes. The initial tax on foundation managers may not exceed $5,000 per investment. If the investment is not removed from jeopardy (e.g., sold or otherwise disposed of), an additional tax of 25 percent of the amount of the investment is imposed on the foundation and five percent of the amount of the investment on a foundation manager who refused to agree to removing the investment from jeopardy. The additional tax on foundation managers may not exceed $10,000 per investment. An investment, the primary purpose of which is to accomplish a

---

[337] Sec. 4943. Taxes imposed may be abated if certain conditions are met. Secs. 4961 and 4962.

[338] Sec. 4943(c)(6).

[339] Sec. 4943(c)(7).

[340] Sec. 4943(d)(3).

[341] Sec. 4944. Taxes imposed may be abated if certain conditions are met. Secs. 4961 and 4962.

charitable purpose and no significant purpose of which is the production of income or the appreciation of property, is not considered a jeopardizing investment.[342]

Tax on taxable expenditures

Certain expenditures of private foundations are subject to tax.[343] In general, taxable expenditures are expenses: (1) for lobbying; (2) to influence the outcome of a public election or carry on a voter registration drive (unless certain requirements are met); (3) as a grant to an individual for travel, study, or similar purposes unless made pursuant to procedures approved by the Secretary; (4) as a grant to an organization that is not a public charity or exempt operating foundation unless the foundation exercises expenditure responsibility[344] with respect to the grant; or (5) for any non-charitable purpose. For each taxable expenditure, a tax is imposed on the foundation of 10 percent of the amount of the expenditure, and an additional tax of 100 percent is imposed on the foundation if the expenditure is not corrected. A tax of 2.5 percent of the expenditure (up to $5,000) also is imposed on a foundation manager who agrees to making a taxable expenditure knowing that it is a taxable expenditure. An additional tax of 50 percent of the amount of the expenditure (up to $10,000) is imposed on a foundation manager who refuses to agree to correction of such expenditure.

Explanation of Provision

Self-dealing and excess benefit transaction initial taxes and dollar limitations

For acts of self-dealing by a private foundation to a disqualified person, the provision increases the initial tax on the self-dealer from five percent of the amount involved to 10 percent of the amount involved. The provision increases the initial tax on foundation managers from 2.5 percent of the amount involved to five percent of the amount involved and increases the dollar limitation on the amount of the initial and additional taxes on foundation managers per act of self-dealing from $10,000 per act to $20,000 per act. Similarly, the provision doubles the dollar limitation on organization managers of public charities and social welfare organizations for participation in excess benefit transactions from $10,000 per transaction to $20,000 per transaction.

Failure to distribute income, excess business holdings, jeopardizing investments, and taxable expenditures

The provision doubles the amounts of the initial taxes and the dollar limitations on foundation managers with respect to the private foundation excise taxes on the failure to distribute income, excess business holdings, jeopardizing investments, and taxable expenditures.

---

[342] Sec. 4944(c).

[343] Sec. 4945. Taxes imposed may be abated if certain conditions are met. Secs. 4961 and 4962.

[344] In general, expenditure responsibility requires that a foundation make all reasonable efforts and establish reasonable procedures to ensure that the grant is spent solely for the purpose for which it was made, to obtain reports from the grantee on the expenditure of the grant, and to make reports to the Secretary regarding such expenditures. Sec. 4945(h).

Specifically, for the failure to distribute income, the initial tax on the foundation is increased from 15 percent of the undistributed amount to 30 percent of the undistributed amount.

For excess business holdings, the initial tax on excess business holdings is increased from five percent of the value of such holdings to 10 percent of such value.

For jeopardizing investments, the initial tax of five percent of the amount of the investment that is imposed on the foundation and on foundation managers is increased to 10 percent of the amount of the investment. The dollar limitation on the initial tax on foundation managers of $5,000 per investment is increased to $10,000 and the dollar limitation on the additional tax on foundation managers of $10,000 per investment is increased to $20,000.

For taxable expenditures, the initial tax on the foundation is increased from 10 percent of the amount of the expenditure to 20 percent, the initial tax on the foundation manager is increased from 2.5 percent of the amount of the expenditure to five percent, the dollar limitation on the initial tax on foundation managers is increased from $5,000 to $10,000, and the dollar limitation on the additional tax on foundation managers is increased from $10,000 to $20,000.

Effective Date

The provision is effective for taxable years beginning after the date of enactment.

3. Reform rules for charitable contributions of easements in registered historic districts and take account of rehabilitation credit in easement donations (sec. 170 of the Code)

Present Law

In general

Present law provides special rules that apply to charitable deductions of qualified conservation contributions, which include conservation easements and façade easements.[345] Qualified conservation contributions are not subject to the "partial interest" rule, which generally bars deductions for charitable contributions of partial interests in property.[346] Accordingly, qualified conservation contributions are contributions of partial interests that are eligible for a fair market value charitable deduction.

A qualified conservation contribution is a contribution of a qualified real property interest to a qualified organization exclusively for conservation purposes. A qualified real property interest is defined as: (1) the entire interest of the donor other than a qualified mineral interest; (2) a remainder interest; or (3) a restriction (granted in perpetuity) on the use that may be made

---

[345] Sec. 170(h).

[346] Sec. 170(f)(3).

of the real property.[347] Qualified organizations include certain governmental units, public charities that meet certain public support tests, and certain supporting organizations.

Conservation purposes include: (1) the preservation of land areas for outdoor recreation by, or for the education of, the general public; (2) the protection of a relatively natural habitat of fish, wildlife, or plants, or similar ecosystem; (3) the preservation of open space (including farmland and forest land) where such preservation will yield a significant public benefit and is either for the scenic enjoyment of the general public or pursuant to a clearly delineated Federal, State, or local governmental conservation policy; and (4) the preservation of an historically important land area or a certified historic structure.[348]

In general, no deduction is available if the property may be put to a use that is inconsistent with the conservation purpose of the gift.[349] A contribution is not deductible if it accomplishes a permitted conservation purpose while also destroying other significant conservation interests.[350]

Taxpayers are required to obtain a qualified appraisal for donated property with a value of $5,000 or more, and to attach an appraisal summary to the tax return.[351] Under Treasury regulations, a qualified appraisal means an appraisal document that, among other things: (1) relates to an appraisal that is made not earlier than 60 days prior to the date of contribution of the appraised property and not later than the due date (including extensions) of the return on which a deduction is first claimed under section 170;[352] (2) is prepared, signed, and dated by a qualified appraiser; (3) includes (a) a description of the property appraised; (b) the fair market value of such property on the date of contribution and the specific basis for the valuation; (c) a statement that such appraisal was prepared for income tax purposes; (d) the qualifications of the qualified appraiser; and (e) the signature and taxpayer identification number of such appraiser; and (4) does not involve an appraisal fee that violates certain prescribed rules.[353]

---

[347] Charitable contributions of interests that constitute the taxpayer's entire interest in the property are not regarded as qualified real property interests within the meaning of section 170(h), but instead are subject to the general rules applicable to charitable contributions of entire interests of the taxpayer (i.e., generally are deductible at fair market value, without regard to satisfaction of the requirements of section 170(h)).

[348] Sec. 170(h)(4)(A).

[349] Treas. Reg. sec. 1.170A-14(e)(2).

[350] Treas. Reg. sec. 1.170A-14(e)(2).

[351] Sec. 170(f)(11)(C).

[352] In the case of a deduction first claimed or reported on an amended return, the deadline is the date on which the amended return is filed.

[353] Treas. Reg. sec. 1.170A-13(c)(3).

Valuation

The value of a conservation restriction granted in perpetuity generally is determined under the "before and after approach." Such approach provides that the fair market value of the restriction is equal to the difference (if any) between the fair market value of the property the restriction encumbers before the restriction is granted and the fair market value of the encumbered property after the restriction is granted.[354]

If the granting of a perpetual restriction has the effect of increasing the value of any other property owned by the donor or a related person, the amount of the charitable deduction for the conservation contribution is to be reduced by the amount of the increase in the value of the other property.[355] In addition, the donor is to reduce the amount of the charitable deduction by the amount of financial or economic benefits that the donor or a related person receives or can reasonably be expected to receive as a result of the contribution.[356] If such benefits are greater than those that will inure to the general public from the transfer, no deduction is allowed.[357] In those instances where the grant of a conservation restriction has no material effect on the value of the property, or serves to enhance, rather than reduce, the value of the property, no deduction is allowed.[358]

Preservation of a certified historic structure

A certified historic structure means any building, structure, or land which is (i) listed in the National Register, or (ii) located in a registered historic district (as defined in section 47(c)(3)(B)) and is certified by the Secretary of the Interior to the Secretary of the Treasury as being of historic significance to the district.[359] For this purpose, a structure means any structure, whether or not it is depreciable, and, accordingly, easements on private residences may qualify.[360] If restrictions to preserve a building or land area within a registered historic district permit future development on the site, a deduction will be allowed only if the terms of the restrictions require that such development conform with appropriate local, State, or Federal standards for construction or rehabilitation within the district.[361]

---

[354] Treas. Reg. sec. 1.170A-14(h)(3).

[355] Treas. Reg. sec. 1.170A-14(h)(3)(i).

[356] *Id.*

[357] *Id.*

[358] Treas. Reg. sec. 1.170A-14(h)(3)(ii).

[359] Sec. 170(h)(4)(B).

[360] Treas. Reg. sec. 1.170A-14(d)(5)(iii).

[361] Treas. Reg. sec. 1.170A-14(d)(5)(i).

The IRS and the courts have held that a facade easement may constitute a qualifying conservation contribution.[362] In general, a facade easement is a restriction the purpose of which is to preserve certain architectural, historic, and cultural features of the facade, or front, of a building. The terms of a facade easement might permit the property owner to make alterations to the facade of the structure if the owner obtains consent from the qualified organization that holds the easement.

Rehabilitation credit

In general, present law allows as part of the general business credit an investment tax credit.[363] The amount of the investment tax credit includes the amount of a rehabilitation credit.[364] The rehabilitation credit for any taxable year is the sum of ten percent of the qualified rehabilitation expenditures with respect to any qualified rehabilitated building other than a certified historic structure and 20 percent of the qualified rehabilitation expenditures with respect to any certified historic structure.[365] In general, a qualified rehabilitated building is a depreciable building (and its structural components) if the building has been substantially rehabilitated, was placed in service before the beginning of the rehabilitation, and (except for a certified historic structure) in the rehabilitation process a certain percentage of the existing internal and external walls and internal structural framework are retained in place as internal and external walls and internal structural framework. A qualified rehabilitation expenditure is, in general, an amount properly chargeable to a capital account (i) for depreciable property that is nonresidential real property, residential rental property, real property that has a class life of more than 12.5 years, or an addition or improvement to any such property and (ii) in connection with the rehabilitation of a qualified rehabilitation building.

Explanation of Provision

Easements in registered historic districts

The provision revises the rules for qualified conservation contributions with respect to property for which a charitable deduction is allowable under section 170(h)(4)(B)(ii) by reason of a property's location in a registered historic district. Under the provision, a charitable deduction is not allowable with respect to a structure or land area located in such a district (by reason of the structure or land area's location in such a district). A charitable deduction is

---

[362] *Hillborn v. Commissioner*, 85 T.C. 677 (1985) (holding the fair market value of a facade donation generally is determined by applying the "before and after" valuation approach); *Richmond v. U.S.*, 699 F. Supp. 578 (E.D. La. 1988); Priv. Ltr. Rul. 199933029 (May 24, 1999) (ruling that a preservation and conservation easement relating to the facade and certain interior portions of a fraternity house was a qualified conservation contribution).

[363] Sec. 38(b)(1).

[364] Sec. 46.

[365] Sec. 47(a).

294

allowable with respect to buildings (as is the case under present law) but the qualified real property interest that relates to the exterior of the building must preserve the entire exterior of the building, including the space above the building, the sides, the rear, and the front of the building. In addition, such qualified real property interest must provide that no portion of the exterior of the building may be changed in a manner inconsistent with the historical character of such exterior.

For any contribution relating to a registered historic district made after the date of enactment of the provision, taxpayers must include with the return for the taxable year of the contribution a qualified appraisal of the qualified real property interest (irrespective of the claimed value of such interest) and attach the appraisal with the taxpayer's return, photographs of the entire exterior of the building,[366] and descriptions of all current restrictions on development of the building, including, for example, zoning laws, ordinances, neighborhood association rules, restrictive covenants, and other similar restrictions. Failure to obtain and attach an appraisal or to include the required information results in disallowance of the deduction. In addition, the donor and the donee must enter into a written agreement certifying, under penalty of perjury, that the donee is a qualified organization, with a purpose of environmental protection, land conservation, open space preservation, or historic preservation, and that the donee has the resources to manage and enforce the restriction and a commitment to do so.

Taxpayers claiming a deduction for a qualified conservation contribution with respect to the exterior of a building located in a registered historic district in excess of $10,000 must pay a $500 fee to the Internal Revenue Service or the deduction is not allowed. Amounts paid are required to be dedicated to Internal Revenue Service enforcement of qualified conservation contributions.

Reduction of deduction to take account of rehabilitation credit

The provision provides that in the case of any qualified conservation contribution, the amount of the deduction is reduced by an amount that bears the same ratio to the fair market value of the contribution as the sum of the rehabilitation credits under section 47 for the preceding five taxable years with respect to a building that is part of the contribution bears to the fair market value of the building on the date of the contribution. For example, if a taxpayer makes a qualified conservation contribution with respect to a building, and such taxpayer has claimed a rehabilitation credit with respect to such building in any of the five taxable years preceding the year in which the contribution is claimed, the taxpayer must reduce the amount of the contribution. If the aggregate amount of credits claimed by the taxpayer within such five year period is $100,000, and the fair market value of the building with respect to which the contribution is made is $1,000,000, the taxpayer must reduce the amount of the deduction by 10 percent (or 100,000 over 1,000,000).

---

[366] Photographs of the entire exterior of the building are required to the extent practicable. For example, if the building is a skyscraper, aerial photographs of the roof would not be required, but photographs sufficient to establish the existing exterior still must be submitted.

The provisions relating to deductions for contributions relating to structures and land areas and to the rehabilitation credit are effective for contributions made after the date of enactment. The provision relating to a filing fee is effective for contributions made 180 days after the date of enactment. The rest of the provision is effective for contributions made after July 25, 2006.

4. Reform rules relating to charitable contributions of taxidermy (sec. 170 of the Code)

Present Law

In computing taxable income, a taxpayer who itemizes deductions generally is allowed to deduct the amount of cash and the fair market value of property contributed to an organization described in section 501(c)(3) or to a Federal, State, or local governmental entity.[367] The amount of the deduction allowable for a taxable year with respect to a charitable contribution of property may be reduced or limited depending on the type of property contributed, the type of charitable organization to which the property is contributed, and the income of the taxpayer.[368] In general, more generous charitable contribution deduction rules apply to gifts made to public charities than to gifts made to private foundations. Within certain limitations, donors also are entitled to deduct their contributions to section 501(c)(3) organizations for Federal estate and gift tax purposes. By contrast, contributions to nongovernmental, non-charitable tax-exempt organizations generally are not deductible by the donor,[369] though such organizations are eligible for the exemption from Federal income tax with respect to such donations.

The amount of the deduction for charitable contributions of capital gain property generally equals the fair market value of the contributed property on the date of the contribution. Capital gain property means any capital asset, or property used in the taxpayer's trade or business, the sale of which at its fair market value, at the time of contribution, would have resulted in gain that would have been long-term capital gain. Contributions of capital gain property are subject to different percentage limitations (i.e., limitations based on the donor's income) than other contributions of property.

For certain contributions of property, the deductible amount is reduced from the fair market value of the contributed property by the amount of any gain, generally resulting in a

---

[367] The deduction also is allowed for purposes of calculating alternative minimum taxable income.

[368] Secs. 170(b) and (e).

[369] Exceptions to the general rule of non-deductibility include certain gifts made to a veterans' organization or to a domestic fraternal society. In addition, contributions to certain nonprofit cemetery companies are deductible for Federal income tax purposes, but generally are not deductible for Federal estate and gift tax purposes. Secs. 170(c)(3), 170(c)(4), 170(c)(5), 2055(a)(3), 2055(a)(4), 2106(a)(2)(A)(iii), 2522(a)(3), and 2522(a)(4).

deduction equal to the taxpayer's basis. This rule applies to contributions of: (1) ordinary income property, e.g., property that, at the time of contribution, would not have resulted in long-term capital gain if the property was sold by the taxpayer on the contribution date;[370] (2) tangible personal property that is used by the donee in a manner unrelated to the donee's exempt (or governmental) purpose; and (3) property to or for the use of a private foundation (other than a foundation defined in section 170(b)(1)(E)).

Charitable contributions of taxidermy are subject to the tangible personal property rule (number (2) above). For example, for appreciated taxidermy, if the property is used to further the donee's exempt purpose, the deduction is fair market value. But if the property is not used to further the donee's exempt purpose, the deduction is the donor's basis. If the taxidermy is depreciated, i.e., the value is less than the taxpayer's basis in such property, taxpayers generally deduct the fair market value of such contributions, regardless of whether the property is used for exempt or unrelated purposes by the donee.

Explanation of Provision

In general, the provision provides that the amount allowed as a deduction for charitable contributions of taxidermy property that is contributed by the person who prepared, stuffed, or mounted the property (or by any person who paid or incurred the cost of such preparation, stuffing, or mounting) is the lesser of the taxpayer's basis in the property or the fair market value of the property. Specifically, a taxpayer that makes such a charitable contribution of taxidermy property for a use related to the donee's exempt purpose or function must, in determining the amount of the deduction, reduce the fair market value of the property by the amount of gain that would have been long-term capital gain if the property contributed had been sold by the taxpayer at its fair market value (determined at the time of the contribution). Taxidermy property is defined as any work of art that is the reproduction or preservation of an animal in whole or in part, is prepared, stuffed or mounted for purposes of recreating one or more characteristics of such animal, and contains a part of the body of the dead animal.

For purposes of determining a taxpayer's basis in taxidermy property that is contributed by the person who prepared, stuffed, or mounted the property (or by any person who paid or incurred the cost of such preparation, stuffing, or mounting), the provision provides a special rule that the basis of such property may include only the cost of the preparing, stuffing, or mounting. For purposes of the special rule, it is intended that only the direct costs of the preparing, stuffing, or mounting may be included in basis. Indirect costs, not included in the basis, include the costs of transportation relating to any aspect of the taxidermy or the hunting of the animal, and the direct or indirect costs relating to the hunting or killing of an animal (including the cost of equipment and the costs of preparing an animal carcass for taxidermy).

---

[370] For certain contributions of inventory, C corporations may claim an enhanced deduction equal to the lesser of (1) basis plus one-half of the item's appreciation (i.e., basis plus one half of fair market value in excess of basis) or (2) two times basis. Sec. 170(e)(3), 170(e)(4), 170(e)(6).

The provision is effective for contributions made after July 25, 2006.

5. Recapture of tax benefit on property not used for an exempt use (new sec. 6720B of the Code)

Present Law

Deductibility of charitable contributions

In general

In computing taxable income, a taxpayer who itemizes deductions generally is allowed to deduct the amount of cash and the fair market value of property contributed to an organization described in section 501(c)(3) or to a Federal, State, or local governmental entity.[371] The amount of the deduction allowable for a taxable year with respect to a charitable contribution of property may be reduced or limited depending on the type of property contributed, the type of charitable organization to which the property is contributed, and the income of the taxpayer.[372] In general, more generous charitable contribution deduction rules apply to gifts made to public charities than to gifts made to private foundations. Within certain limitations, donors also are entitled to deduct their contributions to section 501(c)(3) organizations for Federal estate and gift tax purposes. By contrast, contributions to nongovernmental, non-charitable tax-exempt organizations generally are not deductible by the donor,[373] though such organizations are eligible for the exemption from Federal income tax with respect to such donations.

Contributions of property

The amount of the deduction for charitable contributions of capital gain property generally equals the fair market value of the contributed property on the date of the contribution. Capital gain property means any capital asset, or property used in the taxpayer's trade or business, the sale of which at its fair market value, at the time of contribution, would have resulted in gain that would have been long-term capital gain. Contributions of capital gain property are subject to different percentage limitations (i.e., limitations based on the donor's income) than other contributions of property.

---

[371] The deduction also is allowed for purposes of calculating alternative minimum taxable income.

[372] Secs. 170(b) and (e).

[373] Exceptions to the general rule of non-deductibility include certain gifts made to a veterans' organization or to a domestic fraternal society. In addition, contributions to certain nonprofit cemetery companies are deductible for Federal income tax purposes, but generally are not deductible for Federal estate and gift tax purposes. Secs. 170(c)(3), 170(c)(4), 170(c)(5), 2055(a)(3), 2055(a)(4), 2106(a)(2)(A)(iii), 2522(a)(3), and 2522(a)(4).

For certain contributions of property, the deductible amount is reduced from the fair market value of the contributed property by the amount of any gain, generally resulting in a deduction equal to the taxpayer's basis. This rule applies to contributions of: (1) ordinary income property, e.g., property that, at the time of contribution, would not have resulted in long-term capital gain if the property was sold by the taxpayer on the contribution date;[374] (2) tangible personal property that is used by the donee in a manner unrelated to the donee's exempt (or governmental) purpose; and (3) property to or for the use of a private foundation (other than a foundation defined in section 170(b)(1)(E)).

Substantiation

No charitable deduction is allowed for any contribution of $250 or more unless the taxpayer substantiates the contribution by a contemporaneous written acknowledgement of the contribution by the donee organization.[375] Such acknowledgement must include the amount of cash and a description (but not value) of any property other than cash contributed, whether the donee provided any goods or services in consideration for the contribution (and a good faith estimate of the value of any such goods or services).

In general, if the total charitable deduction claimed for non-cash property is more than $500, the taxpayer must attach a completed Form 8283 (Noncash Charitable Contributions) to the taxpayer's return or the deduction is not allowed.[376] C corporations (other than personal service corporations and closely-held corporations) are required to file Form 8283 only if the deduction claimed is more than $5,000. Information required on the Form 8283 includes, among other things, a description of the property, the appraised fair market value (if an appraisal is required), the donor's basis in the property, how the donor acquired the property, a declaration by the appraiser regarding the appraiser's general qualifications, an acknowledgement by the donee that it is eligible to receive deductible contributions, and an indication by the donee whether the property is intended for an unrelated use.

Taxpayers are required to obtain a qualified appraisal for donated property with a value of more than $5,000, and to attach an appraisal summary to the tax return.[377] Under Treasury regulations, a qualified appraisal means an appraisal document that, among other things: (1) relates to an appraisal that is made not earlier than 60 days prior to the date of contribution of the appraised property and not later than the due date (including extensions) of the return on which a

---

[374] For certain contributions of inventory, C corporations may claim an enhanced deduction equal to the lesser of (1) basis plus one-half of the item's appreciation (i.e., basis plus one half of fair market value in excess of basis) or (2) two times basis. Sec. 170(e)(3), 170(e)(4), 170(e)(6).

[375] Sec. 170(f)(8).

[376] Sec. 170(f)(11).

[377] Id.

deduction is first claimed under section 170;[378] (2) is prepared, signed, and dated by a qualified appraiser; (3) includes (a) a description of the property appraised; (b) the fair market value of such property on the date of contribution and the specific basis for the valuation; (c) a statement that such appraisal was prepared for income tax purposes; (d) the qualifications of the qualified appraiser; and (e) the signature and taxpayer identification number of such appraiser; and (4) does not involve an appraisal fee that violates certain prescribed rules.[379] In the case of contributions of art valued at more than $20,000 and other contributions of more than $500,000, taxpayers are required to attach the appraisal to the tax return. Taxpayers may request a Statement of Value from the Internal Revenue Service in order to substantiate the value of art with an appraised value of $50,000 or more for income, estate, or gift tax purposes.[380] The fee for such a Statement is $2,500 for one, two, or three items or art plus $250 for each additional item.

If a donee organization sells, exchanges, or otherwise disposes of contributed property with a claimed value of more than $5,000 (other than publicly traded securities) within two years of the property's receipt, the donee is required to file a return (Form 8282) with the Secretary, and to furnish a copy of the return to the donor, showing the name, address, and taxpayer identification number of the donor, a description of the property, the date of the contribution, the amount received on the disposition, and the date of the disposition.[381]

Explanation of Provision

In general, the provision recovers the tax benefit for charitable contributions of tangible personal property with respect to which a fair market value deduction is claimed and which is not used for exempt purposes. The provision applies to appreciated tangible personal property that is identified by the donee organization, for example on the Form 8283, as for a use related to the purpose or function constituting the donee's basis for tax exemption, and for which a deduction of more than $5,000 is claimed ("applicable property").[382]

Under the provision, if a donee organization disposes of applicable property within three years of the contribution of the property, the donor is subject to an adjustment of the tax benefit. If the disposition occurs in the tax year of the donor in which the contribution is made, the donor's deduction generally is basis and not fair market value.[383] If the disposition occurs in a

---

[378] In the case of a deduction first claimed or reported on an amended return, the deadline is the date on which the amended return is filed.

[379] Treas. Reg. sec. 1.170A-13(c)(3). Sec. 170(f)(11)(E).

[380] Rev. Proc. 96-15, 1996-1 C.B. 627.

[381] Sec. 6050L(a)(1).

[382] Present law rules continue to apply to any contribution of exempt use property for which a deduction of $5,000 or less is claimed.

[383] The disposition proceeds are regarded as relevant to a determination of fair market value.

subsequent year, the donor must include as ordinary income for its taxable year in which the disposition occurs an amount equal to the excess (if any) of (i) the amount of the deduction previously claimed by the donor as a charitable contribution with respect to such property, over (ii) the donor's basis in such property at the time of the contribution.

There is no adjustment of the tax benefit if the donee organization makes a certification to the Secretary, by written statement signed under penalties of perjury by an officer of the organization. The statement must either (1) certify that the use of the property by the donee was related to the purpose or function constituting the basis for the donee's exemption, and describe how the property was used and how such use furthered such purpose or function; or (2) state the intended use of the property by the donee at the time of the contribution and certify that such use became impossible or infeasible to implement. The organization must furnish a copy of the certification to the donor (for example, as part of the Form 8282, a copy of which is supplied to the donor).

A penalty of $10,000 applies to a person that identifies applicable property as having a use that is related to a purpose or function constituting the basis for the donee's exemption knowing that it is not intended for such a use.[384]

Reporting of exempt use property contributions

The provision modifies the present-law information return requirements that apply upon the disposition of contributed property by a charitable organization (Form 8282, sec. 6050L). The return requirement is extended to dispositions made within three years after receipt (from two years). The donee organization also must provide, in addition to the information already required to be provided on the return, a description of the donee's use of the property, a statement of whether use of the property was related to the purpose or function constituting the basis for the donee's exemption, and, if applicable, a certification of any such use (described above).

Effective Date

The provision is effective for contributions made and returns filed after September 1, 2006, and with respect to the penalty, for identifications made after the date of enactment.

---

[384] Other present-law penalties also may apply, such as the penalty for aiding and abetting the understatement of tax liability under section 6701.

6. Limit charitable deduction for contributions of clothing and household items (sec. 170 of the Code)

Present Law

In general

In computing taxable income, a taxpayer who itemizes deductions generally is allowed to deduct the amount of cash and the fair market value of property contributed to an organization described in section 501(c)(3) or to a Federal, State, or local governmental entity.[385] The amount of the deduction allowable for a taxable year with respect to a charitable contribution of property may be reduced or limited depending on the type of property contributed, the type of charitable organization to which the property is contributed, and the income of the taxpayer.[386] In general, more generous charitable contribution deduction rules apply to gifts made to public charities than to gifts made to private foundations. Within certain limitations, donors also are entitled to deduct their contributions to section 501(c)(3) organizations for Federal estate and gift tax purposes. By contrast, contributions to nongovernmental, non-charitable tax-exempt organizations generally are not deductible by the donor,[387] though such organizations are eligible for the exemption from Federal income tax with respect to such donations.

Contributions of property

The amount of the deduction for charitable contributions of capital gain property generally equals the fair market value of the contributed property on the date of the contribution. Capital gain property means any capital asset or property used in the taxpayer's trade or business the sale of which at its fair market value, at the time of contribution, would have resulted in gain that would have been long-term capital gain. Contributions of capital gain property are subject to different percentage limitations than other contributions of property.

For certain contributions of property, the deductible amount is reduced from the fair market value of the contributed property by the amount of any gain, generally resulting in a deduction equal to the taxpayer's basis. This rule applies to contributions of: (1) ordinary income property, e.g., property that, at the time of contribution, would not have resulted in long-

---

[385] The deduction also is allowed for purposes of calculating alternative minimum taxable income.

[386] Secs. 170(b) and (e).

[387] Exceptions to the general rule of non-deductibility include certain gifts made to a veterans' organization or to a domestic fraternal society. In addition, contributions to certain nonprofit cemetery companies are deductible for Federal income tax purposes, but generally are not deductible for Federal estate and gift tax purposes. Secs. 170(c)(3), 170(c)(4), 170(c)(5), 2055(a)(3), 2055(a)(4), 2106(a)(2)(A)(iii), 2522(a)(3), and 2522(a)(4).

term capital gain if the property was sold by the taxpayer on the contribution date;[388] (2) tangible personal property that is used by the donee in a manner unrelated to the donee's exempt (or governmental) purpose; and (3) property to or for the use of a private foundation (other than a foundation defined in section 170(b)(1)(E)).

Charitable contributions of clothing and household items are subject to the tangible personal property rule (number (2) above). If such contributed property is appreciated property in the hands of the taxpayer, and is not used to further the donee's exempt purpose, the deduction is basis. In general, however, the value of clothing and household items is less than the taxpayer's basis in such property, with the result that taxpayers generally deduct the fair market value of such contributions, regardless of whether the property is used for exempt or unrelated purposes by the donee.

Substantiation

A donor who claims a deduction for a charitable contribution must maintain reliable written records regarding the contribution, regardless of the value or amount of such contribution. For a contribution of money, the donor generally must maintain one of the following: (1) a cancelled check; (2) a receipt (or a letter or other written communication) from the donee organization showing the name of the donee organization, the date of the contribution, and the amount of the contribution; or (3) in the absence of a cancelled check or a receipt, other reliable written records showing the name of the donee, the date of the contribution, and the amount of the contribution. For a contribution of property other than money, the donor generally must maintain a receipt from the donee organization showing the name of the donee, the date and location of the contribution, and a detailed description (but not the value) of the property.[389] A donor of property other than money need not obtain a receipt, however, if circumstances make obtaining a receipt impracticable. Under such circumstances, the donor must maintain reliable written records regarding the contribution. The required content of such a record varies depending upon factors such as the type and value of property contributed.[390]

In addition to the foregoing recordkeeping requirements, substantiation requirements apply in the case of charitable contributions with a value of $250 or more. No charitable deduction is allowed for any contribution of $250 or more unless the taxpayer substantiates the contribution by a contemporaneous written acknowledgement of the contribution by the donee organization. Such acknowledgement must include the amount of cash and a description (but not value) of any property other than cash contributed, whether the donee provided any goods or services in consideration for the contribution, and a good faith estimate of the value of any such

---

[388] For certain contributions of inventory and other property, C corporations may claim an enhanced deduction equal to the lesser of (1) basis plus one-half of the item's appreciation (i.e., basis plus one half of fair market value in excess of basis) or (2) two times basis. Sec. 170(e)(3), 170(e)(4), 170(e)(6).

[389] Treas. Reg. sec. 1.170A-13(a).

[390] Treas. Reg. sec. 1.170A-13(b).

goods or services.[391] In general, if the total charitable deduction claimed for non-cash property is more than $500, the taxpayer must attach a completed Form 8283 (Noncash Charitable Contributions) to the taxpayer's return or the deduction is not allowed.[392] In general, taxpayers are required to obtain a qualified appraisal for donated property with a value of more than $5,000, and to attach an appraisal summary to the tax return.

Explanation of Provision

The provision provides that no deduction is allowed for a charitable contribution of clothing or household items unless the clothing or household item is in good used condition or better. The Secretary is authorized to deny by regulation a deduction for any contribution of clothing or a household item that has minimal monetary value, such as used socks and used undergarments. It is noted that the President's Advisory Panel on Federal Tax Reform and the staff of the Joint Committee on Taxation both have concluded that the fair market value-based deduction for contributions of clothing and household items present difficult tax administration issues, as determining the correct value of an item is a fact intensive, and thus also a resource intensive matter.[393] As recently reported by the IRS, the amount claimed as deductions in tax year 2003 for clothing and household items was more than $9 billion.[394] It is expected that the Secretary, in consultation with affected charities, will exercise assiduously the authority to disallow a deduction for some items of low value, consistent with the goals of improving tax administration and ensure that donated clothing and households items are of meaningful use to charitable organizations.

Under the provision, a deduction may be allowed for a charitable contribution of an item of clothing or a household item not in good used condition or better if the amount claimed for the item is more than $500 and the taxpayer includes with the taxpayer's return a qualified appraisal with respect to the property. Household items include furniture, furnishings, electronics, appliances, linens, and other similar items. Food, paintings, antiques, and other objects of art, jewelry and gems, and collections are excluded from the provision.

Effective Date

The provision is effective for contributions made after the date of enactment.

---

[391] Sec. 170(f)(8).

[392] Sec. 170(f)(11).

[393] See *The President's Advisory Panel on Federal Tax Reform*, 78 (2005); Joint Committee on Taxation, *Options to Improve Tax Compliance and Reform Tax Expenditures* 288 (JCS-02-05), January 27, 2005.

[394] Internal Revenue Service, Statistics of Income Division, *Individual Noncash Charitable Contributions, 2003*, Figure A (Spring 2006).

7. Modify recordkeeping and substantiation requirements for certain charitable contributions (sec. 170 of the Code)

Present Law

A donor who claims a deduction for a charitable contribution must maintain reliable written records regarding the contribution, regardless of the value or amount of such contribution. For a contribution of money, the donor generally must maintain one of the following: (1) a cancelled check; (2) a receipt (or a letter or other written communication) from the donee showing the name of the donee organization, the date of the contribution, and the amount of the contribution; or (3) in the absence of a cancelled check or a receipt, other reliable written records showing the name of the donee, the date of the contribution, and the amount of the contribution. For a contribution of property other than money, the donor generally must maintain a receipt from the donee organization showing the name of the donee, the date and location of the contribution, and a detailed description (but not the value) of the property.[395] A donor of property other than money need not obtain a receipt, however, if circumstances make obtaining a receipt impracticable. Under such circumstances, the donor must maintain reliable written records regarding the contribution. The required content of such a record varies depending upon factors such as the type and value of property contributed.[396]

In addition to the foregoing recordkeeping requirements, substantiation requirements apply in the case of charitable contributions with a value of $250 or more. No charitable deduction is allowed for any contribution of $250 or more unless the taxpayer substantiates the contribution by a contemporaneous written acknowledgement of the contribution by the donee organization. Such acknowledgement must include the amount of cash and a description (but not value) of any property other than cash contributed, whether the donee provided any goods or services in consideration for the contribution, and a good faith estimate of the value of any such goods or services.[397] In general, if the total charitable deduction claimed for non-cash property is more than $500, the taxpayer must attach a completed Form 8283 (Noncash Charitable Contributions) to the taxpayer's return or the deduction is not allowed.[398] In general, taxpayers are required to obtain a qualified appraisal for donated property with a value of more than $5,000, and to attach an appraisal summary to the tax return.

Explanation of Provision

The provision more closely aligns the substantiation rules for money to the substantiation rules for property by providing that in the case of a charitable contribution of money, regardless of the amount, applicable recordkeeping requirements are satisfied only if the donor maintains as

---

[395] Treas. Reg. sec. 1.170A-13(a).

[396] Treas. Reg. sec. 1.170A-13(b).

[397] Sec. 170(f)(8).

[398] Sec. 170(f)(11).

a record of the contribution a bank record or a written communication from the donee showing the name of the donee organization, the date of the contribution, and the amount of the contribution. The recordkeeping requirements may not be satisfied by maintaining other written records. It is noted that currently, taxpayers are required to have a contemporaneous record of contributions of money, but that many taxpayers may not be aware of the requirement and do not keep a log of such contributions. The provision is intended to provide greater certainty, both to taxpayers and to the Secretary, in determining what may be deducted as a charitable contribution.

Effective Date

The provision is effective for contributions made in taxable years beginning after the date of enactment.

8. Contributions of fractional interests in tangible personal property (secs. 170, 2055, and 2522 of the Code)

Present Law

In general, a charitable deduction is not allowable for a contribution of a partial interest in property, such as an income interest, a remainder interest, or a right to use property.[399] A gift of an undivided portion of a donor's entire interest in property generally is not treated as a nondeductible gift of a partial interest in property.[400] For this purpose, an undivided portion of a donor's entire interest in property must consist of a fraction or percentage of each and every substantial interest or right owned by the donor in such property and must extend over the entire term of the donor's interest in such property.[401] A gift generally is treated as a gift of an undivided portion of a donor's entire interest in property if the donee is given the right, as a tenant in common with the donor, to possession, dominion, and control of the property for a portion of each year appropriate to its interest in such property.[402]

A charitable contribution deduction generally is not allowable for a contribution of a future interest in tangible personal property.[403] For this purpose, a future interest is one "in which a donor purports to give tangible personal property to a charitable organization, but has an understanding, arrangement, agreement, etc., whether written or oral, with the charitable organization which has the effect of reserving to, or retaining in, such donor a right to the use, possession, or enjoyment of the property."[404] Treasury regulations provide that section

---

[399] Secs. 170(f)(3)(A) (income tax), 2055(e)(2) (estate tax), and 2522(c)(2) (gift tax).

[400] Sec. 170(f)(3)(B)(ii).

[401] Treas. Reg. sec. 1.170A-7(b)(1).

[402] Treas. Reg. sec. 1.170A-7(b)(1).

[403] Sec. 170(a)(3).

[404] Treas. Reg. sec. 1.170A-5(a)(4).

170(a)(3), which generally denies a deduction for a contribution of a future interest in tangible personal property, "[has] no application in respect of a transfer of an undivided present interest in property. For example, a contribution of an undivided one-quarter interest in a painting with respect to which the donee is entitled to possession during three months of each year shall be treated as made upon the receipt by the donee of a formally executed and acknowledged deed of gift. However, the period of initial possession by the donee may not be deferred in time for more than one year."[405]

Explanation of Provision

In general, under present law and the provision a donor may take a deduction for a charitable contribution of a fractional interest in tangible personal property (such as an artwork), provided the donor satisfies the requirements for deductibility (including the requirements concerning contributions of partial interests and future interests in property), and in subsequent years make additional charitable contributions of interests in the same property.[406] Under the provision, the value of a donor's charitable deduction for the initial contribution of a fractional interest in an item of tangible personal property (or collection of such items) shall be determined as under current law (e.g., based upon the fair market value of the artwork at the time of the contribution of the fractional interest and considering whether the use of the artwork will be related to the donee's exempt purposes). For purposes of determining the deductible amount of each additional contribution of an interest (whether or not a fractional interest) in the same item of property, the fair market value of the item is the lesser of: (1) the value used for purposes of determining the charitable deduction for the initial fractional contribution; or (2) the fair market value of the item at the time of the subsequent contribution. This portion of the provision applies for income, gift, and estate tax purposes.

The provision provides for recapture of the income tax charitable deduction and gift tax charitable deduction under certain circumstances. First, if a donor makes an initial fractional contribution, then fails to contribute all of the donor's remaining interest in such property to the same donee before the earlier of 10 years from the initial fractional contribution or the donor's death, then the donee's charitable income and gift tax deductions for all previous contributions of interests in the item shall be recaptured (plus interest). If the donee of the initial contribution is no longer in existence as of such time, the donor's remaining interest may be contributed to another organization described in section 170(c) (which describes organizations to which contributions that are deductible for income tax purposes may be made). Second, if the donee of a fractional interest in an item of tangible personal property fails to take substantial physical possession of the item during the period described above (the possession requirement) or fails to use the property for an exempt use during the period described above (the related-use requirement), then the donee's charitable income and gift tax deductions for all previous contributions of interests in the item shall be recaptured (plus interest). If, for example, an art museum described in section 501(c)(3) that is the donee of a fractional interest in a painting

---

[405] Treas. Reg. sec. 1.170A-5(a)(2).

[406] See, e.g., *Winokur v. Commissioner*, 90 T.C. 733 (1988).

307

includes the painting in an art exhibit sponsored by the museum, such use generally will be treated as satisfying the related-use requirement of the provision.

In any case in which there is a recapture of a deduction as described in the preceding paragraph, the provision also imposes an additional tax in an amount equal to 10 percent of the amount recaptured.

Under the provision, no income or gift tax charitable deduction is allowed for a contribution of a fractional interest in an item of tangible personal property unless immediately before such contribution all interests in the item are owned (1) by the donor or (2) by the donor and the donee organization. The Secretary is authorized to make exceptions to this rule in cases where all persons who hold an interest in the item make proportional contributions of undivided interests in their respective shares of such item to the donee organization. For example, if A owns an undivided 40 percent interest in a painting and B owns an undivided 60 percent interest in the same painting, the Secretary may provide that A may take a deduction for a charitable contribution of less than the entire interest held by A, provided that both A and B make proportional contributions of undivided fractional interests in their respective shares of the painting to the same donee organization (e.g., if A contributes 50 percent of A's interest and B contributes 50 percent of B's interest).

It is intended that a contribution occurring before the date of enactment not be treated as an initial fractional contribution for purposes of the provision. Instead, the first fractional contribution by a taxpayer after the date of enactment would be considered the initial fractional contribution under the provision, regardless of whether the taxpayer had made a contribution of a fractional interest in the same item of tangible personal property prior to the date of enactment.

Effective Date

The provision is applicable for contributions, bequests, and gifts made after the date of enactment.

9. Proposals relating to appraisers and substantial and gross overstatement of valuations of property (secs. 170, 6662, 6664, 6696 and new sec. 6695A of the Code)

Present Law

Taxpayer penalties

Present law imposes accuracy-related penalties on a taxpayer in cases involving a substantial valuation misstatement or gross valuation misstatement relating to an underpayment of income tax.[407] For this purpose, a substantial valuation misstatement generally means a value claimed that is at least twice (200 percent or more) the amount determined to be the correct value, and a gross valuation misstatement generally means a value claimed that is at least four times (400 percent or more) the amount determined to be the correct value.

---

[407] Sec. 6662(b)(3) and (h).

The penalty is 20 percent of the underpayment of tax resulting from a substantial valuation misstatement and rises to 40 percent for a gross valuation misstatement. No penalty is imposed unless the portion of the underpayment attributable to the valuation misstatement exceeds $5,000 ($10,000 in the case of a corporation other than an S corporation or a personal holding company). Under present law, no penalty is imposed with respect to any portion of the understatement attributable to any item if (1) the treatment of the item on the return is or was supported by substantial authority, or (2) facts relevant to the tax treatment of the item were adequately disclosed on the return or on a statement attached to the return and there is a reasonable basis for the tax treatment. Special rules apply to tax shelters.

Present law also imposes an accuracy-related penalty on substantial or gross estate or gift tax valuation understatements.[408] In general, there is a substantial estate or gift tax understatement if the value of any property claimed on any return is 50 percent or less of the amount determined to be the correct amount, and a gross estate or gift tax understatement if such value is 25 percent or less of the amount determined to be the correct amount.

In addition, the accuracy-related penalties do not apply if a taxpayer shows there was reasonable cause for an underpayment and the taxpayer acted in good faith.[409]

Penalty for aiding and abetting understatement of tax

A penalty is imposed on a person who: (1) aids or assists in or advises with respect to a tax return or other document; (2) knows (or has reason to believe) that such document will be used in connection with a material tax matter; and (3) knows that this would result in an understatement of tax of another person. In general, the amount of the penalty is $1,000. If the document relates to the tax return of a corporation, the amount of the penalty is $10,000.

Qualified appraisals

Present law requires a taxpayer to obtain a qualified appraisal for donated property with a value of more than $5,000, and to attach an appraisal summary to the tax return.[410] Treasury Regulations state that a qualified appraisal means an appraisal document that, among other things: (1) relates to an appraisal that is made not earlier than 60 days prior to the date of contribution of the appraised property and not later than the due date (including extensions) of the return on which a deduction is first claimed under section 170; (2) is prepared, signed, and dated by a qualified appraiser; (3) includes (a) a description of the property appraised; (b) the fair market value of such property on the date of contribution and the specific basis for the valuation; (c) a statement that such appraisal was prepared for income tax purposes; (d) the qualifications of

---

[408] Sec. 6662(g) and (h).

[409] Sec. 6664(c).

[410] Sec. 170(f)(11).

the qualified appraiser; and (e) the signature and taxpayer identification number of such appraiser; and (4) does not involve an appraisal fee that violates certain prescribed rules.[411]

Qualified appraisers

Treasury Regulations define a qualified appraiser as a person who holds himself or herself out to the public as an appraiser or performs appraisals on a regular basis, is qualified to make appraisals of the type of property being valued (as determined by the appraiser's background, experience, education and membership, if any, in professional appraisal associations), is independent, and understands that an intentionally false or fraudulent overstatement of the value of the appraised property may subject the appraiser to civil penalties.[412]

Appraiser oversight

The Secretary is authorized to regulate the practice of representatives of persons before the Department of the Treasury ("Department").[413] After notice and hearing, the Secretary is authorized to suspend or disbar from practice before the Department or the Internal Revenue Service ("IRS") a representative who is incompetent, who is disreputable, who violates the rules regulating practice before the Department or the IRS, or who (with intent to defraud) willfully and knowingly misleads or threatens the person being represented (or a person who may be represented).

The Secretary also is authorized to bar from appearing before the Department or the IRS, for the purpose of offering opinion evidence on the value of property or other assets, any individual against whom a civil penalty for aiding and abetting the understatement of tax has been assessed. Thus, an appraiser who aids or assists in the preparation or presentation of an appraisal will be subject to disciplinary action if the appraiser knows that the appraisal will be used in connection with the tax laws and will result in an understatement of the tax liability of another person. The Secretary has authority to provide that the appraisals of an appraiser who has been disciplined have no probative effect in any administrative proceeding before the Department or the IRS.

Explanation of Provision

Taxpayer penalties

The provision lowers the thresholds for imposing accuracy-related penalties on a taxpayer. Under the provision, a substantial valuation misstatement exists when the claimed value of any property is 150 percent or more of the amount determined to be the correct value. A

---

[411] Treas. Reg. sec. 1.170A-13(c)(3).

[412] Treas. Reg. sec. 1.170A-13(c)(5)(i).

[413] 31 U.S.C. sec. 330.

gross valuation misstatement occurs when the claimed value of any property is 200 percent or more of the amount determined to be the correct value.

The provision tightens the thresholds for imposing accuracy-related penalties with respect to the estate or gift tax. Under the provision, a substantial estate or gift tax valuation misstatement exists when the claimed value of any property is 65 percent or less of the amount determined to be the correct value. A gross estate or gift tax valuation misstatement exists when the claimed value of any property is 40 percent or less of the amount determined to be the correct value.

Under the provision, the reasonable cause exception to the accuracy-related penalty does not apply in the case of gross valuation misstatements.

Appraiser oversight

Appraiser penalties

The provision establishes a civil penalty on any person who prepares an appraisal that is to be used to support a tax position if such appraisal results in a substantial or gross valuation misstatement. The penalty is equal to the greater of $1,000 or 10 percent of the understatement of tax resulting from a substantial or gross valuation misstatement, up to a maximum of 125 percent of the gross income derived from the appraisal. Under the provision, the penalty does not apply if the appraiser establishes that it was "more likely than not" that the appraisal was correct.

Disciplinary proceeding

The provision eliminates the requirement that the Secretary assess against an appraiser the civil penalty for aiding and abetting the understatement of tax before such appraiser may be subject to disciplinary action. Thus, the Secretary is authorized to discipline appraisers after notice and hearing. Disciplinary action may include, but is not limited to, suspending or barring an appraiser from: preparing or presenting appraisals on the value of property or other assets to the Department or the IRS; appearing before the Department or the IRS for the purpose of offering opinion evidence on the value of property or other assets; and providing that the appraisals of an appraiser who has been disciplined have no probative effect in any administrative proceeding before the Department or the IRS.

Qualified appraisers

The provision defines a qualified appraiser as an individual who (1) has earned an appraisal designation from a recognized professional appraiser organization or has otherwise met minimum education and experience requirements to be determined by the IRS in regulations; (2) regularly performs appraisals for which he or she receives compensation; (3) can demonstrate verifiable education and experience in valuing the type of property for which the appraisal is being performed; (4) has not been prohibited from practicing before the IRS by the Secretary at any time during the three years preceding the conduct of the appraisal; and (5) is not excluded from being a qualified appraiser under applicable Treasury regulations.

<u>Qualified appraisals</u>

The provision defines a qualified appraisal as an appraisal of property prepared by a qualified appraiser (as defined by the provision) in accordance with generally accepted appraisal standards and any regulations or other guidance prescribed by the Secretary.

Effective Date

The provision amending the accuracy-related penalty applies to returns filed after the date of enactment. The provision establishing a civil penalty that may be imposed on any person who prepares an appraisal that is to be used to support a tax position if such appraisal results in a substantial or gross valuation misstatement applies to appraisals prepared with respect to returns or submissions filed after the date of enactment. The provisions relating to appraiser oversight apply to appraisals prepared with respect to returns or submissions filed after the date of enactment. With respect to any contribution of a qualified real property interest which is a restriction with respect to the exterior of a building described in section 170(h)(4)(C)(ii) (currently designated section 170(h)(4)(B)(ii), relating to certain property located in a registered historic district and certified as being of historic significance to the district), and any appraisal with respect to such contribution, the provision generally applies to returns filed after July 25, 2006.

10. Establish additional exemption standards for credit counseling organizations (secs. 501 and 513 of the Code)

Present Law

Under present law, a credit counseling organization may be exempt as a charitable or educational organization described in section 501(c)(3), or as a social welfare organization described in section 501(c)(4). The IRS has issued two revenue rulings holding that certain credit counseling organizations are exempt as charitable or educational organizations or as social welfare organizations.

In Revenue Ruling 65-299,[414] an organization whose purpose was to assist families and individuals with financial problems, and help reduce the incidence of personal bankruptcy, was determined to be a social welfare organization described in section 501(c)(4). The organization counseled people in financial difficulties, advised applicants on payment of debts, and negotiated with creditors and set up debt repayment plans. The organization did not restrict its services to the poor, made no charge for counseling services, and made a nominal charge for certain services to cover postage and supplies. For financial support, the organization relied on voluntary contributions from local businesses, lending agencies, and labor unions.

---

[414] Rev. Rul. 65-299, 1965-2 C.B. 165.

In Revenue Ruling 69-441,[415] the IRS ruled an organization was a charitable or educational organization exempt under section 501(c)(3) by virtue of aiding low-income people who had financial problems and providing education to the public. The organization in that ruling had two functions: (1) educating the public on personal money management, such as budgeting, buying practices, and the sound use of consumer credit through the use of films, speakers, and publications; and (2) providing individual counseling to low-income individuals and families without charge. As part of its counseling activities, the organization established debt management plans for clients who required such services, at no charge to the clients.[416] The organization was supported by contributions primarily from creditors, and its board of directors was comprised of representatives from religious organizations, civic groups, labor unions, business groups, and educational institutions.

In 1976, the IRS denied exempt status to an organization, Consumer Credit Counseling Service of Alabama, whose activities were distinguishable from those in Revenue Ruling 69-441 in that (1) it did not restrict its services to the poor, and (2) it charged a nominal fee for its debt management plans.[417] The organization provided free information to the general public through the use of speakers, films, and publications on the subjects of budgeting, buying practices, and the use of consumer credit. It also provided counseling to debt-distressed individuals, not necessarily poor or low-income, and provided debt management plans at the cost of $10 per month, which was waived in cases of financial hardship. Its debt management activities were a relatively small part of its overall activities. The district court determined the organization qualified as charitable and educational within section 501(c)(3), finding the debt management plans to be an integral part of the agency's counseling function, and that its debt management activities were incidental to its principal functions, as only approximately 12 percent of the counselors' time was applied to such programs and the charge for the service was nominal. The court also considered the facts that the agency was publicly supported, and that it had a board dominated by members of the general public, as factors indicating a charitable operation.[418]

A recent estimate shows the number of credit counseling organizations increased from approximately 200 in 1990 to over 1,000 in 2002.[419] During the period from 1994 to late 2003,

---

[415] Rev. Rul. 69-441, 1969-2 C.B. 115.

[416] Debt management plans are debt payment arrangements, including debt consolidation arrangements, entered into by a debtor and one or more of the debtor's creditors, generally structured to reduce the amount of a debtor's regular ongoing payment by modifying the interest rate, minimum payment, maturity or other terms of the debt. Such plans frequently are promoted as a means for a debtor to restructure debt without filing for bankruptcy.

[417] *Consumer Credit Counseling Service of Alabama, Inc. v. U.S.*, 44 A.F.T.R. 2d (RIA) 5122 (D.D.C. 1978). The case involved 24 agencies throughout the United States.

[418] *See also, Credit Counseling Centers of Oklahoma, Inc., v. U.S., v. U.S.*, 45 A.F.T.R. 2d (RIA) 1401 (D.D.C. 1979) (holding the same on virtually identical facts).

[419] Opening Statement of The Honorable Max Sandlin, Hearing on Non-Profit Credit Counseling Organizations, House Ways and Means Committee, Subcommittee on Oversight (November 20, 2003).

1,215 credit counseling organizations applied to the IRS for tax exempt status under section 501(c)(3), including 810 during 2000 to 2003.[420] The IRS has recognized more than 850 credit counseling organizations as tax exempt under section 501c)((3).[421] Few credit counseling organizations have sought section 501(c)(4) status, and the IRS reports it has not seen any significant increase in the number or activity of such organizations operating as social welfare organizations.[422] As of late 2003, there were 872 active tax-exempt credit counseling agencies operating in the United States.[423]

A credit counseling organization described in section 501(c)(3) is exempt from certain Federal and State consumer protection laws that provide exemptions for organizations described therein.[424] Some believe that these exclusions from Federal and State regulation may be a primary motivation for the recent increase in the number of organizations seeking and obtaining exempt status under section 501(c)(3).[425] Such regulatory exemptions generally are not available for social welfare organizations described in section 501(c)(4).

---

[420] United States Senate Permanent Subcommittee on Investigations, Committee on Governmental Affairs, *Profiteering in a Non-Profit Industry: Abusive Practices in Credit Counseling*, Report Prepared by the Majority & Minority Staffs of the Permanent Subcommittee on Investigations and Released in Conjunction with the Permanent Subcommittee Investigations' Hearing on March 24, 2004, p. 3 (citing letter dated December 18, 2003, to the Subcommittee from IRS Commissioner Everson).

[421] Testimony of Commissioner Mark Everson before the House Ways and Means Committee, Subcommittee on Oversight (November 20, 2003).

[422] Testimony of Commissioner Mark Everson before the House Ways and Means Committee, Subcommittee on Oversight (November 20, 2003).

[423] United States Senate Permanent Subcommittee on Investigations, Committee on Governmental Affairs, *Profiteering in a Non-Profit Industry: Abusive Practices in Credit Counseling*, Report Prepared by the Majority & Minority Staffs of the Permanent Subcommittee on Investigations and Released in Conjunction with the Permanent Subcommittee Investigations' Hearing on March 24, 2004, p. 3 (citing letter dated December 18, 2003 to the Subcommittee from IRS Commissioner Everson).

[424] *E.g.*, The Credit Repair Organizations Act, 15 U.S.C. section 1679 *et seq.*, effective April 1, 1997 (imposing restrictions on credit repair organizations that are enforced by the Federal Trade Commission, including forbidding the making of untrue or misleading statements and forbidding advance payments; section 501(c)(3) organizations are explicitly exempt from such regulation). Testimony of Commissioner Mark Everson before the House Ways and Means Committee, Subcommittee on Oversight (November 20, 2003) (California's consumer protections laws that impose strict standards on credit service organizations and the credit repair industry do not apply to nonprofit organizations that have received a final determination from the IRS that they are exempt from tax under section 501(c)(3) and are not private foundations).

[425] Testimony of Commissioner Mark Everson before the House Ways and Means Committee, Subcommittee on Oversight (November 20, 2003).

Congress recently conducted hearings investigating the activities of credit counseling organizations under various consumer protection laws,[426] such as the Federal Trade Commission Act.[427] In addition, the IRS commenced a broad examination and compliance program with respect to the credit counseling industry. On May 15, 2006, the IRS announced that over the past two years, it had been auditing 63 credit counseling agencies, representing more than 40 percent of the revenue in the industry. Audits of 41 organizations, representing more than 40 percent of the revenue in the industry have been completed as of that date. All of such completed audits resulted in revocation, proposed revocation, or other termination of tax-exempt status.[428] In addition, the IRS released two legal documents that provide a legal framework for determining the exempt status and related issues with respect to credit counseling organizations.[429] In CCA 200620001, the IRS found that "[t]he critical inquiry is whether a credit counseling organization conducts its counseling program to improve an individual debtor's understanding of his financial problems and improve his ability to address those problems." The CCA concluded that whether a credit counseling organization primarily furthers educational purposes

> can be determined by assessing the methodology by which the organization conducts its counseling activities. The process an organization uses to interview clients and develop recommendations, train its counselors and market its services can distinguish between an organization whose object is to improve a person's knowledge and skills to manage his personal debt, and an organization that is offering counseling primarily as a mechanism to enroll individuals in a specific option (e.g., debt management plans) without considering the individual's best interest.

Under the Bankruptcy Abuse Prevention and Consumer Protection Act of 2005, Public Law 109-8, an individual generally may not be a debtor in bankruptcy unless such individual has, within 180 days of filing a petition for bankruptcy, received from an approved nonprofit budget and credit counseling agency an individual or group briefing that outlines the opportunities for available credit counseling and assists the individual in performing a related

---

[426] United States Senate Permanent Subcommittee on Investigations, Committee on Governmental Affairs, *Profiteering in a Non-Profit Industry: Abusive Practices in Credit Counseling*, Report Prepared by the Majority & Minority Staffs of the Permanent Subcommittee on Investigations and Released in Conjunction with the Permanent Subcommittee Investigations' Hearing on March 24, 2004.

[427] 15 U.S.C. sec. 45(a) (prohibiting unfair and deceptive acts or practices in or affecting commerce; although the Federal Trade Commission generally lacks jurisdiction to enforce consumer protection laws against bona fide nonprofit organizations, it may assert jurisdiction over a nonprofit, including a credit counseling organization, if it demonstrates the organization is organized to carry on business for profit, is a mere instrumentality of a for-profit entity, or operates through a common enterprise with one or more for-profit entities).

[428] IRS News Release, IR-2006-80, May 15, 2006.

[429] Chief Counsel Advice 200431023 (July 13, 2004); Chief Counsel Advice 200620001 (May 9, 2006).

315

budget analysis.[430] The clerk of the court must maintain a publicly available list of nonprofit budget and credit counseling agencies approved by the U.S. Trustee (or bankruptcy administrator). In general, the U.S. Trustee (or bankruptcy administrator) shall only approve an agency that demonstrates that it will provide qualified counselors, maintain adequate provision for safekeeping and payment of client funds, provide adequate counseling with respect to client credit problems, and deal responsibly and effectively with other matters relating to the quality, effectiveness, and financial security of the services it provides. The minimum qualifications for approval of such an agency include: (1) in general, having an independent board of directors; (2) charging no more than a reasonable fee, and providing services without regard to ability to pay; (3) adequate provision for safekeeping and payment of client funds; (4) provision of full disclosures to clients; (5) provision of adequate counseling with respect to a client's credit problems; (6) trained counselors who receive no commissions or bonuses based on the outcome of the counseling services; (7) experience and background in providing credit counseling; and (8) adequate financial resources to provide continuing support services for budgeting plans over the life of any repayment plan. An individual debtor must file with the court a certificate from the approved nonprofit budget and credit counseling agency that provided the required services describing the services provided, and a copy of the debt management plan, if any, developed through the agency.[431]

Explanation of Provision

Requirements for exempt status of credit counseling organizations

The provision establishes standards that a credit counseling organization must satisfy, in addition to present law requirements, in order to be organized and operated either as an organization described in section 501(c)(3) or in section 501(c)(4). The provision does not diminish the requirements set forth recently by the IRS in Chief Counsel Advice 200431023 or Chief Counsel Advice 200620001 but builds on and is consistent with such requirements, and the analysis therein. The provision is not intended to raise any question about IRS actions taken, and the IRS is expected to continue its vigorous examination of the credit counseling industry, applying the additional standards provided by the provision. The provision does not and is not intended to affect the approval process for credit counseling agencies under Public Law 109-8. Public Law 109-8 requires that an approved credit counseling agency be a nonprofit, and does not require that an approved agency be a section 501(c)(3) organization. It is expected that the

---

[430] This requirement does not apply in certain circumstances, such as: (1) in general, where a debtor resides in a district for which the U.S. Trustee has determined that the approved counseling agencies for such district are not reasonably able to provide adequate services to additional individuals; (2) where exigent circumstances merit a waiver, the individual seeking bankruptcy protection files an appropriate certification with the court, and the certification is acceptable to the court; and (3) in general, where a court determines, after notice and hearing, that the individual is unable to complete the requirement because of incapacity, disability, or active military duty in a military combat zone.

[431] The Act also requires that, prior to discharge of indebtedness under chapter 7 or chapter 13, a debtor complete an approved instructional course concerning personal financial management, which course need not be conducted by a nonprofit agency.

Department of Justice shall continue to approve agencies for purposes of providing pre-bankruptcy counseling based on criteria that are consistent with such Public Law.

Under the provision, an organization that provides credit counseling services as a substantial purpose of the organization ("credit counseling organization") is eligible for exemption from Federal income tax only as a charitable or educational organization under section 501(c)(3) or as a social welfare organization under section 501(c)(4), and only if (in addition to present-law requirements) the credit counseling organization is organized and operated in accordance with the following:

1. The organization provides credit counseling services tailored to the specific needs and circumstances of the consumer;

2. The organization makes no loans to debtors (other than loans with no fees or interest) and does not negotiate the making of loans on behalf of debtors;[432]

3. The organization provides services for the purpose of improving a consumer's credit record, credit history, or credit rating only to the extent that such services are incidental to providing credit counseling services and does not charge any separately stated fee for any such services;[433]

4. The organization does not refuse to provide credit counseling services to a consumer due to inability of the consumer to pay, the ineligibility of the consumer for debt management plan enrollment, or the unwillingness of a consumer to enroll in a debt management plan;

5. The organization establishes and implements a fee policy to require that any fees charged to a consumer for its services are reasonable,[434] allows for the waiver of fees if the consumer is unable to pay, and except to the extent allowed by State law prohibits charging any fee based in whole or in part on a percentage of the consumer's debt, the consumer's payments to be made pursuant to a debt management plan, or on the projected or actual savings to the consumer resulting from enrolling in a debt management plan;

---

[432] In general, negotiation of a loan involves negotiation of the terms of a loan, rather than the processing of a loan. Organizations that provide assistance to consumers to obtain a loan from the Department of Housing and Urban Development, for example, are not necessarily negotiating a loan for a consumer.

[433] Accordingly, a credit counseling organization may provide credit repair type services, but only to the extent that the provision of such services is a direct outgrowth of the provision of credit counseling services.

[434] Whether a credit counseling organization's fees are consistent with specific State law requirements is evidence of the reasonableness of fees but is not determinative.

6. The organization at all times has a board of directors or other governing body (a) that is controlled by persons who represent the broad interests of the public, such as public officials acting in their capacities as such, persons having special knowledge or expertise in credit or financial education, and community leaders; (b) not more than 20 percent of the voting power of which is vested in persons who are employed by the organization or who will benefit financially, directly or indirectly, from the organization's activities (other than through the receipt of reasonable directors' fees or the repayment of consumer debt to creditors other than the credit counseling organization or its affiliates) and (c) not more than 49 percent of the voting power of which is vested in persons who are employed by the organization or who will benefit financially, directly or indirectly, from the organization's activities (other than through the receipt of reasonable directors' fees);[435]

7. The organization does not own (except with respect to a section 501(c)(3) organization) more than 35 percent of the total combined voting power of a corporation (or profits or beneficial interest in the case of a partnership or trust or estate) that is in the trade or business of lending money, repairing credit, or providing debt management plan services, payment processing, and similar services; and

8. The organization receives no amount for providing referrals to others for debt management plan services, and pays no amount to others for obtaining referrals of consumers.[436]

Additional requirements for charitable and educational organizations

Under the provision, a credit counseling organization is described in section 501(c)(3) only if, in addition to satisfying the above requirements and the requirements of section 501(c)(3), the organization is organized and operated such that the organization (1) does not solicit contributions from consumers during the initial counseling process or while the consumer is receiving services from the organization and (2) the aggregate revenues of the organization that are from payments of creditors of consumers of the organization and that are attributable to debt management plan services do not exceed the applicable percentage of the total revenues of the organization. For credit counseling organizations in existence on the date of enactment, the

---

[435] The requirements described in paragraphs 4, 5, and 6 above address core issues that are related to tax-exempt status and that have proved to be problematic in the credit counseling industry--the provision of services and waiver of fees without regard to ability to pay, the establishment of a reasonable fee policy, and the presence of independent board members. No inference is intended through the provision of these specific requirements on credit counseling organizations that similar or more stringent requirements should not be adhered to by other exempt organizations providing fees for services. Rather, the provision affirms the importance of these core issues to the matter of tax exemption, both to credit counseling organizations and to other types of exempt organizations.

[436] If a credit counseling organization pays or receives a fee, for example, for using or maintaining a locator service for consumers to find a credit counseling organization, such a fee is not considered a referral.

applicable percentage is 80 percent for the first taxable year of the organization beginning after the date which is one year after the date of enactment, 70 percent for the second such taxable year beginning after such date, 60 percent for the third such taxable year beginning after such date, and 50 percent thereafter. For new credit counseling organizations, the applicable percentage is 50 percent for taxable years beginning after the date of enactment. Satisfaction of the aggregate revenues requirement is not a safe harbor; all other requirements of the provision (and of section 501(c)(3)) pertaining to section 501(c)(3) organizations also must be satisfied. Satisfaction of the aggregate revenues requirement means only that an organization has not automatically failed to be organized or operated consistent with exempt purposes. Compliance with the revenues test does not mean that the organization's debt management plan services activity is at a level that organizationally or operationally is consistent with exempt status. In other words, satisfaction of the aggregate revenues requirement (as a preliminary matter in an exemption application, or on an ongoing operational basis) provides no affirmative evidence that an organization's primary purpose is an exempt purpose, or that the revenues that are subject to the limitation (or debt management plan services revenues more generally) are related to exempt purposes. As described below, whether revenues from such activity are substantially related to exempt purposes depends on the facts and circumstances, that is, satisfaction of the aggregate revenues requirement generally is not relevant for purposes of whether any of an organization's revenues are revenues from an unrelated trade or business. Failure to satisfy the aggregate revenues requirement does not disqualify the organization from recognition of exemption under section 501(c)(4).

Additional requirement for social welfare organizations

Under the provision, a credit counseling organization is described in section 501(c)(4) only if, in addition to satisfying the above requirements applicable to such organizations, the organization notifies the Secretary, in such manner as the Secretary may by regulations prescribe, that it is applying for recognition as a credit counseling organization.

Debt management plan services treated as an unrelated trade or business

Under the provision, debt management plan services are treated as an unrelated trade or business for purposes of the tax on income from an unrelated trade or business to the extent such services are provided by an organization that is not a credit counseling organization. With respect to the provision of debt management plan services by a credit counseling organization, in order for the income from such services not to be unrelated business income, it is intended that, consistent with current law, the debt management plan service with respect to such income (1) must contribute importantly to the accomplishment of credit counseling services, and (2) must not be conducted on a larger scale than reasonably is necessary for the accomplishment of such services. For example, the provision of debt management plan services would not be substantially related to accomplishing exempt purposes if the organization recommended and enrolled an individual in a debt management plan only after determining whether the individual satisfied the financial criteria established by the creditors for such plan, without (1) considering whether it was an appropriate action in light of the individual's particular needs and objectives, (2) discussing the disadvantages of a debt management plan with the consumer, and (3) presenting other possible options to such consumer.

Definitions

Credit counseling services

Credit counseling services are (a) the provision of educational information to the general public on budgeting, personal finance, financial literacy, saving and spending practices, and the sound use of consumer credit; (b) the assisting of individuals and families with financial problems by providing them with counseling; or (c) any combination of such activities.

Debt management plan services

Debt management plan services are services related to the repayment, consolidation, or restructuring of a consumer's debt, and includes the negotiation with creditors of lower interest rates, the waiver or reduction of fees, and the marketing and processing of debt management plans.

Effective Date

In general, the provision applies to taxable years beginning after the date of enactment. For a credit counseling organization that is described in section 501(c)(3) or 501(c)(4) on the date of enactment, the provision is effective for taxable years beginning after the date that is one year after the date of enactment.

11. Expand the base of the tax on private foundation net investment income (sec. 4940 of the Code)

Present Law

In general

Under section 4940(a) of the Code, private foundations that are recognized as exempt from Federal income tax under section 501(a) of the Code are subject to a two-percent excise tax on their net investment income. Private foundations that are not exempt from tax, such as certain charitable trusts,[437] also are subject to an excise tax under section 4940(b) based on net investment income and unrelated business income. The two-percent rate of tax is reduced to one-percent if certain requirements are met in a taxable year.[438] Unlike certain other excise taxes imposed on private foundations, the tax based on investment income does not result from a violation of substantive law by the private foundation; it is solely an excise tax.

The tax on taxable private foundations under section 4940(b) is equal to the excess of the sum of the excise tax that would have been imposed under section 4940(a) if the foundation were tax exempt and the amount of the unrelated business income tax that would have been imposed if

---

[437] *See* sec. 4947(a)(1).

[438] Sec. 4940(e).

the foundation were tax exempt, over the income tax imposed on the foundation under subtitle A of the Code.

Net investment income

Internal Revenue Code

In general, net investment income is defined as the amount by which the sum of gross investment income and capital gain net income exceeds the deductions relating to the production of gross investment income.[439]

Gross investment income is the gross amount of income from interest, dividends, rents, payments with respect to securities loans, and royalties. Gross investment income does not include any income that is included in computing a foundation's unrelated business taxable income.[440]

Capital gain net income takes into account only gains and losses from the sale or other disposition of property used for the production of interest, dividends, rents, and royalties, and property used for the production of income included in computing the unrelated business income tax (except to the extent the gain or loss is taken into account for purposes of such tax). Losses from sales or other dispositions of property are allowed only to the extent of gains from such sales or other dispositions, and no capital loss carryovers are allowed.[441]

Treasury Regulations and case law

The Treasury regulations elaborate on the Code definition of net investment income. The regulations cite items of investment income listed in the Code, and in addition clarify that net investment income includes interest, dividends, rents, and royalties derived from all sources, including from assets devoted to charitable activities. For example, interest received on a student loan is includible in the gross investment income of a foundation making the loan.[442]

The regulations further provide that gross investment income includes certain items of investment income that are described in the unrelated business income tax regulations.[443] Such additional items include payments with respect to securities loans (an item added to the Code in

---

[439] Sec. 4940(c)(1). Net investment income also is determined by applying section 103 (generally providing an exclusion for interest on certain State and local bonds) and section 265 (generally disallowing the deduction for interest and certain other expenses with respect to tax-exempt income). Sec. 4940(c)(5).

[440] Sec. 4940(c)(2).

[441] Sec. 4940(c)(4).

[442] Treas. Reg. sec. 53.4940-1(d)(1).

[443] *Id.*

321

1978), annuities, income from notional principal contracts, and other substantially similar income from ordinary and routine investments to the extent determined by the Commissioner.[444] These latter three categories of income are not enumerated as net investment income in the Code.

The Treasury regulations also elaborate on the Code definition of capital gain net income. The regulations provide that the only capital gains and losses that are taken into account are (1) gains and losses from the sale or other disposition of property held by a private foundation for investment purposes (other than program related investments), and (2) property used for the production of income included in computing the unrelated business income tax (except to the extent the gain or loss is taken into account for purposes of such tax).

This definition of capital gain net income builds on the definition provided in the Code by providing an exception for gain and loss from program related investments and by stating, in addition, that "gains and losses from the sale or other disposition of property used for the exempt purposes of the private foundation are excluded."[445] As an example, the regulations provide that gain or loss on the sale of buildings used for the foundation's exempt activities are not taken into account for purposes of the section 4940 tax. If a foundation uses exempt income for exempt purposes and (other than incidentally) for investment purposes, then the portion of the gain or loss received upon sale or other disposition that is allocable to the investment use is taken into account for purposes of the tax.

The regulations further provide that "property shall be treated as held for investment purposes even though such property is disposed of by the foundation immediately upon its receipt, if it is property of a type which generally produces interest, dividends, rents, royalties, or capital gains through appreciation (for example, rental real estate, stock, bonds, mineral interest, mortgages, and securities)."[446]

This regulation has been challenged in the courts. The regulation says that property is treated as held for investment purposes if it is of a type that "generally produces" certain types of income. By contrast, the Code provides that the property be "used" to produce such income. In Zemurray Foundation v. United States, 687 F.2d 97 (5th Cir. 1982), the taxpayer foundation challenged the Treasury's attempt to tax under section 4940 capital gain on the sale of timber property. The taxpayer asserted that the property was not actually used to produce investment income, and that the Treasury Regulation was invalid because the regulation would subject to tax property that is of a type that could generally be used to produce investment income. On this issue, the court upheld the Treasury regulation, reasoning that the regulation's use of the phrase "generally used," though permitting taxation "so long as the property sold is usable to produce the applicable types of income, regardless of whether the property is actually used to produce income or not" was not unreasonable or plainly inconsistent with the statute.[447] However, on

---

[444] Treas. Reg. sec. 1.512(b)-1(a)(1).

[445] Treas. Reg. sec. 53.4940-1(f)(1).

[446] *Id.*

[447] *Zemurray Foundation v. United States*, 687 F.2d 97, 100 (5th Cir. 1982).

remand to the district court, the district court concluded that the timber property at issue, though a type of property generally used to produce investment income, was not susceptible for such use.[448] Thus, the district court concluded that the Treasury could not tax the gain under this portion of the regulation.

The question then turned to the taxpayer's second challenge to the regulation. At issue was the meaning of the regulatory phrase "capital gains through appreciation." The regulation provides that if property is of a type that generally produces capital gains through appreciation, then the gain is subject to tax. The Treasury argued that the timber property at issue, although held by the court not to be property (in this case) susceptible for use to produce interest, dividends, rents, or royalties, still was held by the taxpayer to produce capital gain through appreciation and therefore the gain should be subject to tax under the regulation.

On this issue, the court held for the taxpayer, reasoning that the language of the Code clearly is limited to certain gains and losses, e.g., the court cited the Code language providing that "there shall be taken into account only gains and losses from the sale or other disposition of property used for the production of interest, dividends, rents, and royalties . . . ."[449] The court noted that "capital gains through appreciation" is not enumerated in the statute. The court used as an example a jade figurine held by a foundation. Jade figurines do not generally produce interest, dividends, rents, or royalties, but gain on the sale of such a figurine would be taxable under the "capital gains through appreciation" standard, yet such standard does not appear in the statute. After Zemurray, the Treasury generally conceded this issue.[450]

With respect to capital losses, the Code provides that carryovers are not permitted, whereas the regulations state that neither carryovers nor carrybacks are permitted.[451]

Application of Zemurray to the Code and the regulations

Applying the Zemurray case to the Code and regulations results in a general principle for purposes of present law: private foundations are subject to tax under section 4940 only on the items of income and only on gains and losses specifically enumerated therein. Under this principle, private foundations generally are not subject to the section 4940 tax on other substantially similar types of income from ordinary and routine investments, notwithstanding Treasury regulations to the contrary. In addition, the regulations provide that gain or loss from the sale or other disposition of assets used for exempt purposes, with specific reference to program-related investments, is excluded. The Code provides for no such blanket exclusion; thus, under the language of the Code and the reasoning of Zemurray, if a foundation provided

---

[448] *Zemurray Foundation v. United States*, 53 A.F.T.R. 2d (RIA) 842 (E. D. La. 1983).

[449] *Zemurray Foundation v. United States*, 755 F.2d 404 (5th Cir. 1985), 413 (citing Code sec. 4940(c)(4)(A).

[450] G.C.M. 39538 (July 23, 1986).

[451] Treas. Reg. sec. 53.4940-1(f)(3).

office space at below market rent to a charitable organization for use in the organization's exempt purposes, gain on the sale of the building by the foundation should be subject to the section 4940 tax despite the Treasury regulations.[452]

In addition, under the logic of Zemurray, capital loss carrybacks arguably are permitted, notwithstanding Treasury regulations to the contrary, because the Code mentions only a bar on use of carryovers and says nothing about carrybacks.

Explanation of Provision

The provision amends the definition of gross investment income (including for purposes of capital gain net income) to include items of income that are similar to the items presently enumerated in the Code. Such similar items include income from notional principal contracts, annuities, and other substantially similar income from ordinary and routine investments, and, with respect to capital gain net income, capital gains from appreciation, including capital gains and losses from the sale or other disposition of assets used to further an exempt purpose.

Certain gains and losses are not taken into account in determining capital gain net income. Specifically, under the provision, no gain or loss shall be taken into account with respect to any portion of property used for a period of not less than one year for a purpose or function constituting the basis of the private foundation's exemption, if the entire property is exchanged immediately following such period solely for property of like kind which is to be used primarily for a purpose or function constituting the basis for such foundation's exemption. Rules similar to the rules of section 1031 (relating to exchange of property held for productive use or investment) apply, including, but not limited to, the exceptions of section 1031(a)(2) and the rule of section 1031(a)(3) regarding completion of the exchange within 180 days.

The provision provides that there are no carrybacks of losses from sales or other dispositions of property.

Effective Date

The provision is effective for taxable years beginning after the date of enactment.

12. Definition of convention or association of churches (sec. 7701 of the Code)

Present Law

Under present law, an organization that qualifies as a "convention or association of churches" (within the meaning of sec. 170(b)(1)(A)(i)) is not required to file an annual return,[453] is subject to the church tax inquiry and church tax examination provisions applicable to

---

[452] *See also* the example in Treas. Reg. sec. 53.4940-1(f)(1).

[453] Sec. 6033(a)(2)(A)(i).

organizations claiming to be a church,[454] and is subject to certain other provisions generally applicable to churches.[455] The Internal Revenue Code does not define the term "convention or association of churches."

Explanation of Provision

The provision provides that an organization that otherwise is a convention or association of churches does not fail to so qualify merely because the membership of the organization includes individuals as well as churches, or because individuals have voting rights in the organization.

Effective Date

The provision is effective on the date of enactment.

13. Notification requirement for exempt entities not currently required to file an annual information return (secs. 6033, 6652, and 7428 of the Code)

Present Law

Under present law, the requirement that an exempt organization file an annual information return does not apply to several categories of exempt organizations. Organizations excepted from the filing requirement include organizations (other than private foundations), the gross receipts of which in each taxable year normally are not more than $25,000.[456] Also exempt from the requirement are churches, their integrated auxiliaries, and conventions or associations of churches; the exclusively religious activities of any religious order; section 501(c)(1)

---

[454] Sec. 7611(h)(1)(B).

[455] *See, e.g.*, Sec. 402(g)(8)(B) (limitation on elective deferrals); sec. 403(b)(9)(B) (definition of retirement income account); sec. 410(d) (election to have participation, vesting, funding, and certain other provisions apply to church plans); sec. 414(e) (definition of church plan); sec. 415(c)(7) (certain contributions by church plans); sec. 501(h)(5) (disqualification of certain organizations from making the sec. 501(h) election regarding lobbying expenditure limits); sec. 501(m)(3) (definition of commercial-type insurance); sec. 508(c)(1)(A) (exception from requirement to file application seeking recognition of exempt status); sec. 512(b)(12) (allowance of up to $1,000 deduction for purposes of determining unrelated business taxable income); sec. 514(b)(3)(E) (definition of debt-financed property); sec. 3121(w)(3)(A) (election regarding exemption from social security taxes); sec. 3309(b)(1) (application of federal unemployment tax provisions to services performed in the employ of certain organizations); sec. 6043(b)(1) (requirement to file a return upon liquidation or dissolution of the organization); and sec. 7702(j)(3)(A) (treatment of certain death benefit plans as life insurance).

[456] Sec. 6033(a)(2); Treas. Reg. sec. 1.6033-2(a)(2)(i); Treas. Reg. sec. 1.6033-2(g)(1). Sec. 6033(a)(2)(A)(ii) provides a $5,000 annual gross receipts exception from the annual reporting requirements for certain exempt organizations. In Announcement 82-88, 1982-25 I.R.B. 23, the IRS exercised its discretionary authority under section 6033 to increase the gross receipts exception to $25,000, and enlarge the category of exempt organizations that are not required to file Form 990.

instrumentalities of the United States; section 501(c)(21) trusts; an interchurch organization of local units of a church; certain mission societies; certain church-affiliated elementary and high schools; certain State institutions whose income is excluded from gross income under section 115; certain governmental units and affiliates of governmental units; and other organizations that the IRS has relieved from the filing requirement pursuant to its statutory discretionary authority.

Explanation of Provision

The provision requires organizations that are excused from filing an information return by reason of normally having gross receipts below a certain specified amount (generally, under $25,000) to furnish to the Secretary annually, in electronic form, the legal name of the organization, any name under which the organization operates or does business, the organization's mailing address and Internet web site address (if any), the organization's taxpayer identification number, the name and address of a principal officer, and evidence of the organization's continuing basis for its exemption from the generally applicable information return filing requirements. Upon such organization's termination of existence, the organization is required to furnish notice of such termination.

The provision provides that if an organization fails to provide the required notice for three consecutive years, the organization's tax-exempt status is revoked. In addition, if an organization that is required to file an annual information return under section 6033(a) (Form 990) fails to file such an information return for three consecutive years, the organization's tax-exempt status is revoked. If an organization fails to meet its filing obligation to the IRS for three consecutive years in cases where the organization is subject to the information return filing requirement in one or more years during a three-year period and also is subject to the notice requirement for one or more years during the same three-year period, the organization's tax-exempt status is revoked.

A revocation under the provision is effective from the date that the Secretary determines was the last day the organization could have timely filed the third required information return or notice. To again be recognized as tax-exempt, the organization must apply to the Secretary for recognition of tax-exemption, irrespective of whether the organization was required to make an application for recognition of tax-exemption in order to gain tax-exemption originally.

If, upon application for tax-exempt status after a revocation under the provision, the organization shows to the satisfaction of the Secretary reasonable cause for failing to file the required annual notices or returns, the organization's tax-exempt status may, in the discretion of the Secretary, be reinstated retroactive to the date of revocation. An organization may not challenge under the Code's declaratory judgment procedures (section 7428) a revocation of tax-exemption made pursuant to the provision.

There is no monetary penalty for failure to file the notice under the provision. Like other information returns, the notices are subject to the public disclosure and inspection rules generally applicable to exempt organizations. The provision does not affect an organization's obligation under present law to file required information returns or existing penalties for failure to file such returns.

326

The Secretary is required to notify every organization that is subject to the notice filing requirement of the new filing obligation in a timely manner. Notification by the Secretary shall be by mail, in the case of any organization the identity and address of which is included in the list of exempt organizations maintained by the Secretary, and by Internet or other means of outreach, in the case of any other organization. In addition, the Secretary is required to publicize in a timely manner in appropriate forms and instructions and other means of outreach the new penalty imposed for consecutive failures to file the information return.

The Secretary is authorized to publish a list of organizations whose exempt status is revoked under the provision.

Effective Date

The provision is effective for notices and returns with respect to annual periods beginning after 2006.

14. Disclosure to State officials relating to section 501(c) organizations (secs. 6103, 6104, 7213, 7213A, and 7431 of the Code)

Present Law

In the case of organizations that are described in section 501(c)(3) and exempt from tax under section 501(a) or that have applied for exemption as an organization so described, present law (sec. 6104(c)) requires the Secretary to notify the appropriate State officer of (1) a refusal to recognize such organization as an organization described in section 501(c)(3), (2) a revocation of a section 501(c)(3) organization's tax-exempt status, and (3) the mailing of a notice of deficiency for any tax imposed under section 507, chapter 41, or chapter 42.[457] In addition, at the request of such appropriate State officer, the Secretary is required to make available for inspection and copying, such returns, filed statements, records, reports, and other information relating to the above-described disclosures, as are relevant to any State law determination. An appropriate State officer is the State attorney general, State tax officer, or any State official charged with overseeing organizations of the type described in section 501(c)(3).

In general, returns and return information (as such terms are defined in section 6103(b)) are confidential and may not be disclosed or inspected unless expressly provided by law.[458] Present law requires the Secretary to keep records of disclosures and requests for inspection[459]

---

[457] The applicable taxes include the termination tax on private foundations; taxes on public charities for certain excess lobbying expenses; taxes on a private foundation's net investment income, self-dealing activities, undistributed income, excess business holdings, investments that jeopardize charitable purposes, and taxable expenditures (some of these taxes also apply to certain non-exempt trusts); taxes on the political expenditures and excess benefit transactions of section 501(c)(3) organizations; and certain taxes on black lung benefit trusts and foreign organizations.

[458] Sec. 6103(a).

[459] Sec. 6103(p)(3).

and requires that persons authorized to receive returns and return information maintain various safeguards to protect such information against unauthorized disclosure.[460] Willful unauthorized disclosure or inspection of returns or return information is subject to a fine and/or imprisonment.[461] The knowing or negligent unauthorized inspection or disclosure of returns or return information gives the taxpayer a right to bring a civil suit.[462] Such present-law protections against unauthorized disclosure or inspection of returns and return information do not apply to the disclosures or inspections, described above, that are authorized by section 6104(c).

Explanation of Provision

The provision provides that upon written request by an appropriate State officer, the Secretary may disclose: (1) a notice of proposed refusal to recognize an organization as a section 501(c)(3) organization; (2) a notice of proposed revocation of tax-exemption of a section 501(c)(3) organization; (3) the issuance of a proposed deficiency of tax imposed under section 507, chapter 41, or chapter 42; (4) the names, addresses, and taxpayer identification numbers of organizations that have applied for recognition as section 501(c)(3) organizations; and (5) returns and return information of organizations with respect to which information has been disclosed under (1) through (4) above.[463] Disclosure or inspection is permitted for the purpose of, and only to the extent necessary in, the administration of State laws regulating section 501(c)(3) organizations, such as laws regulating tax-exempt status, charitable trusts, charitable solicitation, and fraud. Such disclosure or inspection may be made only to or by an appropriate State officer or to an officer or employee of the State who is designated by the appropriate State officer, and may not be made by or to a contractor or agent. The Secretary also is permitted to disclose or open to inspection the returns and return information of an organization that is recognized as tax-exempt under section 501(c)(3), or that has applied for such recognition, to an appropriate State officer if the Secretary determines that disclosure or inspection may constitute evidence of noncompliance under the laws within the jurisdiction of the appropriate State officer. For this purpose, appropriate State officer means the State attorney general, the State tax officer, or any other State official charged with overseeing organizations of the type described in section 501(c)(3).

In addition, the provision provides that upon the written request by an appropriate State officer, the Secretary may make available for inspection or disclosure returns and return information of an organization described in section 501(c) (other than section 501(c)(1) or section 501(c)(3)). Such returns and return information are available for inspection or disclosure only for the purpose of, and to the extent necessary in, the administration of State laws regulating the solicitation or administration of the charitable funds or charitable assets of such

---

[460] Sec. 6103(p)(4).

[461] Secs. 7213 and 7213A.

[462] Sec. 7431.

[463] Such returns and return information also may be open to inspection by an appropriate State officer.

organizations. Such disclosure or inspection may be made only to or by an appropriate State officer or to an officer or employee of the State who is designated by the appropriate State officer, and may not be made by or to a contractor or agent. For this purpose, appropriate State officer means the State attorney general, the State tax officer, and the head of an agency designated by the State attorney general as having primary responsibility for overseeing the solicitation of funds for charitable purposes of such organizations.

In addition, the provision provides that any returns and return information disclosed under section 6104(c) may be disclosed in civil administrative and civil judicial proceedings pertaining to the enforcement of State laws regulating the applicable tax-exempt organization in a manner prescribed by the Secretary. Returns and return information are not to be disclosed under section 6104(c), or in such an administrative or judicial proceeding, to the extent that the Secretary determines that such disclosure would seriously impair Federal tax administration. The provision makes disclosures of returns and return information under section 6104(c) subject to the disclosure, recordkeeping, and safeguard provisions of section 6103, including through requirements that the Secretary maintain a permanent system of records of requests for disclosure (sec. 6103(p)(3)) and that the appropriate State officer maintain various safeguards that protect against unauthorized disclosure (sec. 6103(p)(4)). The provision provides that the willful unauthorized disclosure of returns or return information described in section 6104(c) is a felony subject to a fine of up to $5,000 and/or imprisonment of up to five years (sec. 7213(a)(2)), the willful unauthorized inspection of returns or return information described in section 6104(c) is subject to a fine of up to $1,000 and/or imprisonment of up to one year (sec. 7213A), and provides the taxpayer the right to bring a civil action for damages in the case of knowing or negligent unauthorized disclosure or inspection of such information (sec. 7431(a)(2)).

Effective Date

The provision is effective on the date of enactment but does not apply to requests made before such date.

15. Require that unrelated business income tax returns of section 501(c)(3) organizations be made publicly available (sec. 6104 of the Code)

Present Law

In general, an organization described in section 501(c) or (d) is required to make available for public inspection a copy of its annual information return (Form 990) and exemption application materials.[464] A penalty may be imposed on any person who does not make an organization's annual returns or exemption application materials available for public inspection. The penalty amount is $20 for each day during which a failure occurs. If more than one person fails to comply, each person is jointly and severally liable for the full amount of the penalty. The maximum penalty that may be imposed on all persons for any one annual return is $10,000. There is no maximum penalty amount for failing to make exemption application materials

---

[464] Sec. 6104(d).

available for public inspection. Any person who willfully fails to comply with the public inspection requirements is subject to an additional penalty of $5,000.[465]

These requirements do not apply to an organization's annual return for unrelated business income tax (generally Form 990-T).[466]

Explanation of Provision

The provision extends the present-law public inspection and disclosure requirements and penalties applicable to the Form 990 to the unrelated business income tax return (Form 990-T) of organizations described in section 501(c)(3). The provision provides that certain information may be withheld by the organization from public disclosure and inspection if public availability would adversely affect the organization, similar to the information that may be withheld under present law with respect to applications for tax exemption and the Form 990 (e.g., information relating to a trade secret, patent, process, style of work, or apparatus of the organization, if the Secretary determines that public disclosure of such information would adversely affect the organization).

Effective Date

The provision is effective for returns filed after the date of enactment.

16. Treasury study on donor advised funds and supporting organizations

Present Law

Donor advised funds

Some charitable organizations (including community foundations) establish accounts to which donors may contribute and thereafter provide nonbinding advice or recommendations with regard to distributions from the fund or the investment of assets in the fund. Such accounts are commonly referred to as "donor advised funds." Donors who make contributions to charities for maintenance in a donor advised fund generally claim a charitable contribution deduction at the time of the contribution. Although sponsoring charities frequently permit donors (or other persons appointed by donors) to provide nonbinding recommendations concerning the distribution or investment of assets in a donor advised fund, sponsoring charities generally must have legal ownership and control of such assets following the contribution. If the sponsoring charity does not have such control (or permits a donor to exercise control over amounts contributed), the donor's contributions may not qualify for a charitable deduction, and, in the case of a community foundation, the contribution may be treated as being subject to a material restriction or condition by the donor.

---

[465] Sec. 6685.

[466] Treas. Reg. sec. 301.6104(d)-1(b)(4)(ii).

In recent years, a number of financial institutions have formed charitable corporations for the principal purpose of offering donor advised funds, sometimes referred to as "commercial" donor advised funds. In addition, some established charities have begun operating donor advised funds in addition to their primary activities. The IRS has recognized several organizations that sponsor donor advised funds, including "commercial" donor advised funds, as section 501(c)(3) public charities. The term "donor advised fund" is not defined in statute or regulations.

Supporting organizations

The Code provides that certain "supporting organizations" (in general, organizations that provide support to another section 501(c)(3) organization that is not a private foundation) are classified as public charities rather than private foundations.[467] To qualify as a supporting organization, an organization must meet all three of the following tests: (1) it must be organized and at all times operated exclusively for the benefit of, to perform the functions of, or to carry out the purposes of one or more "publicly supported organizations"[468] (the "organizational and operational tests");[469] (2) it must be operated, supervised, or controlled by or in connection with one or more publicly supported organizations (the "relationship test");[470] and (3) it must not be controlled directly or indirectly by one or more disqualified persons (as defined in section 4946) other than foundation managers and other than one or more publicly supported organizations (the "lack of outside control test").[471]

To satisfy the relationship test, a supporting organization must hold one of three statutorily described close relationships with the supported organization. The organization must be: (1) operated, supervised, or controlled by a publicly supported organization (commonly referred to as "Type I" supporting organizations); (2) supervised or controlled in connection with a publicly supported organization ("Type II" supporting organizations); or (3) operated in connection with a publicly supported organization ("Type III" supporting organizations).[472]

Type I supporting organizations

In the case of supporting organizations that are operated, supervised, or controlled by one or more publicly supported organizations (Type I supporting organizations), one or more supported organizations must exercise a substantial degree of direction over the policies,

---

[467] Sec. 509(a)(3).

[468] In general, supported organizations of a supporting organization must be publicly supported charities described in sections 509(a)(1) or (a)(2).

[469] Sec. 509(a)(3)(A).

[470] Sec. 509(a)(3)(B).

[471] Sec. 509(a)(3)(C).

[472] Treas. Reg. sec. 1.509(a)-4(f)(2).

programs, and activities of the supporting organization.[473] The relationship between the Type I supporting organization and the supported organization generally is comparable to that of a parent and subsidiary. The requisite relationship may be established by the fact that a majority of the officers, directors, or trustees of the supporting organization are appointed or elected by the governing body, members of the governing body, officers acting in their official capacity, or the membership of one or more publicly supported organizations.[474]

Type II supporting organizations

Type II supporting organizations are supervised or controlled in connection with one or more publicly supported organizations. Rather than the parent-subsidiary relationship characteristic of Type I organizations, the relationship between a Type II organization and its supported organizations is more analogous to a brother-sister relationship. In order to satisfy the Type II relationship requirement, generally there must be common supervision or control by the persons supervising or controlling both the supporting organization and the publicly supported organizations.[475] An organization generally is not considered to be "supervised or controlled in connection with" a publicly supported organization merely because the supporting organization makes payments to the publicly supported organization, even if the obligation to make payments is enforceable under state law.[476]

Type III supporting organizations

Type III supporting organizations are "operated in connection with" one or more publicly supported organizations. To satisfy the "operated in connection with" relationship, Treasury regulations require that the supporting organization be responsive to, and significantly involved in the operations of, the publicly supported organization. This relationship is deemed to exist where the supporting organization meets both a "responsiveness test" and an "integral part test."[477] In general, the responsiveness test requires that the Type III supporting organization be responsive to the needs or demands of the publicly supported organizations. In general, the integral part test requires that the Type III supporting organization maintain significant involvement in the operations of one or more publicly supported organizations, and that such publicly supported organizations are in turn dependent upon the supporting organization for the type of support which it provides.

There are two alternative methods for satisfying the integral part test. The first alternative is to establish that (1) the activities engaged in for or on behalf of the publicly

---

[473] Treas. Reg. sec. 1.509(a)-4(g)(1)(i).

[474] Id.

[475] Treas. Reg. sec. 1.509(a)- 4(h)(1).

[476] Treas. Reg. sec. 1.509(a)-4(h)(2).

[477] Treas. Reg. sec. 1.509(a)-4(i)(1).

supported organization are activities to perform the functions of, or carry out the purposes of, such organizations; and (2) these activities, but for the involvement of the supporting organization, normally would be engaged in by the publicly supported organizations themselves.[478] Organizations that satisfy this "but for" test sometimes are referred to as "functionally integrated" Type III supporting organizations. The second method for satisfying the integral part test is to establish that: (1) the supporting organization pays substantially all of its income to or for the use of one or more publicly supported organizations;[479] (2) the amount of support received by one or more of the publicly supported organizations is sufficient to insure the attentiveness of the organization or organizations to the operations of the supporting organization (this is known as the "attentiveness requirement");[480] and (3) a significant amount of the total support of the supporting organization goes to those publicly supported organizations that meet the attentiveness requirement.[481]

Explanation of Provision

Elsewhere in the bill, provision is made for new rules with respect to donor advised funds and supporting organizations. Many issues arise under current law with respect to such organizations, some of which are addressed by the bill and some of which would benefit from additional study. The provision provides that the Secretary of the Treasury shall undertake a study on the organization and operation of donor advised funds (as defined in section 4966(d)(2)) and of supporting organizations (organizations described in section 509(a)(3)). The study shall specifically consider (1) whether the amount and availability of the income, gift, or estate tax charitable deductions allowed for charitable contributions to sponsoring organizations (as defined in section 4966(d)(1)) of donor advised funds or to organizations described in section 509(a)(3) is appropriate in consideration of (i) the use of contributed assets (including the type, extent, and timing of such use) or (ii) the use of the assets of such organizations for the benefit of the person making the charitable contribution (or a person related to such person), (2) whether donor advised funds should be required to distribute for charitable purposes a specified amount (whether based on the income or assets of the fund) in order to ensure that the sponsoring organization with respect to the fund is operating consistent with the purposes or functions constituting the basis for its exemption under section 501 or its status as an organization

---

[478] Treas. Reg. sec. 1.509(a)-4(i)(3)(ii).

[479] For this purpose, the IRS has defined the term "substantially all" of an organization's income to mean 85 percent or more. Rev. Rul. 76-208, 1976-1 C.B. 161.

[480] Although the regulations do not specify the requisite level of support in numerical or percentage terms, the IRS has suggested that grants that represent less than 10 percent of the beneficiary's support likely would be viewed as insufficient to ensure attentiveness. Gen. Couns. Mem. 36379 (August 15, 1975). As an alternative to satisfying the attentiveness standard by the foregoing method, a supporting organization may demonstrate attentiveness by showing that, in order to avoid the interruption of the carrying on of a particular function or activity, the beneficiary organization will be sufficiently attentive to the operations of the supporting organization. Treas. Reg. sec. 1.509(a)-4(i)(3)(iii)(b).

[481] Treas. Reg. sec. 1.509(a)-4(i)(3)(iii).

described in section 509(a), (3) whether the retention by donors to donor advised funds or supporting organizations of rights or privileges with respect to amounts transferred to such organizations (including advisory rights or privileges with respect to the making of grants or the investment of assets) is consistent with the treatment of such transfers as completed gifts that qualify for an income, gift, or estate tax charitable deduction, and (4) whether any of the issues addressed above also raise issues with respect to other forms of charities or charitable donations.

Not later than one year after the date of enactment of this Act, the Secretary shall submit a report on the study, comment on any actions (audits, guidance, regulations, etc.) taken by the Secretary with respect to the issues discussed in the study, and make recommendations to the Committee on Finance of the Senate and the Committee on Ways and Means of the House of Representatives.

Effective Date

The provision is effective on the date of enactment.

17. Improve accountability of donor advised funds (new secs. 4966 and 4967 of the Code)

Present Law

Requirements for section 501(c)(3) tax-exempt status

Charitable organizations, i.e., organizations described in section 501(c)(3), generally are exempt from Federal income tax and are eligible to receive tax deductible contributions. A charitable organization must operate primarily in pursuance of one or more tax-exempt purposes constituting the basis of its tax exemption.[482] In order to qualify as operating primarily for a purpose described in section 501(c)(3), an organization must satisfy the following operational requirements: (1) the net earnings of the organization may not inure to the benefit of any person in a position to influence the activities of the organization; (2) the organization must operate to provide a public benefit, not a private benefit;[483] (3) the organization may not be operated primarily to conduct an unrelated trade or business;[484] (4) the organization may not engage in substantial legislative lobbying; and (5) the organization may not participate or intervene in any political campaign.

---

[482] Treas. Reg. sec. 1.501(c)(3)-1(c)(1). The Code specifies such purposes as religious, charitable, scientific, testing for public safety, literary, or educational purposes, or to foster international amateur sports competition, or for the prevention of cruelty to children or animals. In general, an organization is organized and operated for charitable purposes if it provides relief for the poor and distressed or the underprivileged. Treas. Reg. sec. 1.501(c)(3)-1(d)(2).

[483] Treas. Reg. sec. 1.501(c)(3)-1(d)(1)(ii).

[484] Treas. Reg. sec. 1.501(c)(3)-1(e)(1). Conducting a certain level of unrelated trade or business activity will not jeopardize tax-exempt status.

Classification of section 501(c)(3) organizations

Section 501(c)(3) organizations are classified either as "public charities" or "private foundations."[485] Private foundations generally are defined under section 509(a) as all organizations described in section 501(c)(3) other than an organization granted public charity status by reason of: (1) being a specified type of organization (i.e., churches, educational institutions, hospitals and certain other medical organizations, certain organizations providing assistance to colleges and universities, or a governmental unit); (2) receiving a substantial part of its support from governmental units or direct or indirect contributions from the general public; or (3) providing support to another section 501(c)(3) entity that is not a private foundation. In contrast to public charities, private foundations generally are funded from a limited number of sources (e.g., an individual, family, or corporation). Donors to private foundations and persons related to such donors together often control the operations of private foundations.

Because private foundations receive support from, and typically are controlled by, a small number of supporters, private foundations are subject to a number of anti-abuse rules and excise taxes not applicable to public charities.[486] For example, the Code imposes excise taxes on acts of "self-dealing" between disqualified persons (generally, an enumerated class of foundation insiders[487]) and a private foundation. Acts of self-dealing include, for example, sales or exchanges, or leasing, of property; lending of money; or the furnishing of goods, services, or facilities between a disqualified person and a private foundation.[488] In addition, private non-operating foundations are required to pay out a minimum amount each year as qualifying distributions. In general, a qualifying distribution is an amount paid to accomplish one or more of the organization's exempt purposes, including reasonable and necessary administrative expenses.[489] Certain expenditures of private foundations are also subject to tax.[490] In general, taxable expenditures are expenditures: (1) for lobbying; (2) to influence the outcome of a public election or carry on a voter registration drive (unless certain requirements are met); (3) as a grant to an individual for travel, study, or similar purposes unless made pursuant to procedures approved by the Secretary; (4) as a grant to an organization that is not a public charity or exempt

---

[485] Sec. 509(a). Private foundations are either private operating foundations or private non-operating foundations. In general, private operating foundations operate their own charitable programs in contrast to private non-operating foundations, which generally are grant-making organizations. Most private foundations are non-operating foundations.

[486] Secs. 4940 - 4945.

[487] See sec. 4946(a).

[488] Sec. 4941.

[489] Sec. 4942(g)(1)(A). A qualifying distribution also includes any amount paid to acquire an asset used (or held for use) directly in carrying out one or more of the organization's exempt purposes and certain amounts set-aside for exempt purposes. Sec. 4942(g)(1)(B) and 4942(g)(2).

[490] Sec. 4945. Taxes imposed may be abated if certain conditions are met. Secs. 4961 and 4962.

operating foundation unless the foundation exercises expenditure responsibility[491] with respect to the grant; or (5) for any non-charitable purpose. Additional excise taxes may also apply in the event a private foundation holds certain business interests ("excess business holdings")[492] or makes an investment that jeopardizes the foundation's exempt purposes.[493]

Supporting organizations

The Code provides that certain "supporting organizations" (in general, organizations that provide support to another section 501(c)(3) organization that is not a private foundation) are classified as public charities rather than private foundations.[494] To qualify as a supporting organization, an organization must meet all three of the following tests: (1) it must be organized and at all times operated exclusively for the benefit of, to perform the functions of, or to carry out the purposes of one or more "publicly supported organizations"[495] (the "organizational and operational tests");[496] (2) it must be operated, supervised, or controlled by or in connection with one or more publicly supported organizations (the "relationship test");[497] and (3) it must not be controlled directly or indirectly by one or more disqualified persons (as defined in section 4946) other than foundation managers and other than one or more publicly supported organizations (the "lack of outside control test").[498]

To satisfy the relationship test, a supporting organization must hold one of three statutorily described close relationships with the supported organization. The organization must be: (1) operated, supervised, or controlled by a publicly supported organization (commonly referred to as "Type I" supporting organizations); (2) supervised or controlled in connection with a publicly supported organization ("Type II" supporting organizations); or (3) operated in connection with a publicly supported organization ("Type III" supporting organizations).[499]

---

[491] In general, expenditure responsibility requires that a foundation make all reasonable efforts and establish reasonable procedures to ensure that the grant is spent solely for the purpose for which it was made, to obtain reports from the grantee on the expenditure of the grant, and to make reports to the Secretary regarding such expenditures. Sec. 4945(h).

[492] Sec. 4943.

[493] Sec. 4944.

[494] Sec. 509(a)(3).

[495] In general, supported organizations of a supporting organization must be publicly supported charities described in sections 509(a)(1) or (a)(2).

[496] Sec. 509(a)(3)(A).

[497] Sec. 509(a)(3)(B).

[498] Sec. 509(a)(3)(C).

[499] Treas. Reg. sec. 1.509(a)-4(f)(2).

Type I supporting organizations

In the case of supporting organizations that are operated, supervised, or controlled by one or more publicly supported organizations (Type I supporting organizations), one or more supported organizations must exercise a substantial degree of direction over the policies, programs, and activities of the supporting organization.[500] The relationship between the Type I supporting organization and the supported organization generally is comparable to that of a parent and subsidiary. The requisite relationship may be established by the fact that a majority of the officers, directors, or trustees of the supporting organization are appointed or elected by the governing body, members of the governing body, officers acting in their official capacity, or the membership of one or more publicly supported organizations.[501]

Type II supporting organizations

Type II supporting organizations are supervised or controlled in connection with one or more publicly supported organizations. Rather than the parent-subsidiary relationship characteristic of Type I organizations, the relationship between a Type II organization and its supported organizations is more analogous to a brother-sister relationship. In order to satisfy the Type II relationship requirement, generally there must be common supervision or control by the persons supervising or controlling both the supporting organization and the publicly supported organizations.[502] An organization generally is not considered to be "supervised or controlled in connection with" a publicly supported organization merely because the supporting organization makes payments to the publicly supported organization, even if the obligation to make payments is enforceable under state law.[503]

Type III supporting organizations

Type III supporting organizations are "operated in connection with" one or more publicly supported organizations. To satisfy the "operated in connection with" relationship, Treasury regulations require that the supporting organization be responsive to, and significantly involved in the operations of, the publicly supported organization. This relationship is deemed to exist where the supporting organization meets both a "responsiveness test" and an "integral part test."[504] In general, the responsiveness test requires that the Type III supporting organization be responsive to the needs or demands of the publicly supported organizations. In general, the integral part test requires that the Type III supporting organization maintain significant involvement in the operations of one or more publicly supported organizations, and that such

---

[500] Treas. Reg. sec. 1.509(a)-4(g)(1)(i).

[501] Id.

[502] Treas. Reg. sec. 1.509(a)- 4(h)(1).

[503] Treas. Reg. sec. 1.509(a)-4(h)(2).

[504] Treas. Reg. sec. 1.509(a)-4(i)(1).

publicly supported organizations are in turn dependent upon the supporting organization for the type of support which it provides.

There are two alternative methods for satisfying the integral part test. The first alternative is to establish that (1) the activities engaged in for or on behalf of the publicly supported organization are activities to perform the functions of, or carry out the purposes of, such organizations; and (2) these activities, but for the involvement of the supporting organization, normally would be engaged in by the publicly supported organizations themselves.[505] Organizations that satisfy this "but for" test sometimes are referred to as "functionally integrated" Type III supporting organizations. The second method for satisfying the integral part test is to establish that: (1) the supporting organization pays substantially all of its income to or for the use of one or more publicly supported organizations;[506] (2) the amount of support received by one or more of the publicly supported organizations is sufficient to insure the attentiveness of the organization or organizations to the operations of the supporting organization (this is known as the "attentiveness requirement");[507] and (3) a significant amount of the total support of the supporting organization goes to those publicly supported organizations that meet the attentiveness requirement.[508]

Charitable contributions

Contributions to organizations described in section 501(c)(3) are deductible, subject to certain limitations, as an itemized deduction from Federal income taxes.[509] Such contributions also generally are deductible for estate and gift tax purposes.[510] However, if the taxpayer retains control over the assets transferred to charity, the transfer may not qualify as a completed gift for purposes of claiming an income, estate, or gift tax deduction.

Public charities enjoy certain advantages over private foundations regarding the deductibility of contributions. For example, contributions of appreciated capital gain property to

---

[505] Treas. Reg. sec. 1.509(a)-4(i)(3)(ii).

[506] For this purpose, the IRS has defined the term "substantially all" of an organization's income to mean 85 percent or more. Rev. Rul. 76-208, 1976-1 C.B. 161.

[507] Although the regulations do not specify the requisite level of support in numerical or percentage terms, the IRS has suggested that grants that represent less than 10 percent of the beneficiary's support likely would be viewed as insufficient to ensure attentiveness. Gen. Couns. Mem. 36379 (August 15, 1975). As an alternative to satisfying the attentiveness standard by the foregoing method, a supporting organization may demonstrate attentiveness by showing that, in order to avoid the interruption of the carrying on of a particular function or activity, the beneficiary organization will be sufficiently attentive to the operations of the supporting organization. Treas. Reg. sec. 1.509(a)-4(i)(3)(iii)(b).

[508] Treas. Reg. sec. 1.509(a)-4(i)(3)(iii).

[509] Sec. 170.

[510] Secs. 2055 and 2522.

a private foundation generally are deductible only to the extent of the donor's cost basis.[511] In contrast, contributions to public charities generally are deductible in an amount equal to the property's fair market value, except for gifts of inventory and other ordinary income property, short-term capital gain property, and tangible personal property the use of which is unrelated to the donee organization's exempt purpose. In addition, under present law, a taxpayer's deductible contributions generally are limited to specified percentages of the taxpayer's contribution base, which generally is the taxpayer's adjusted gross income for a taxable year. The applicable percentage limitations vary depending upon the type of property contributed and the classification of the donee organization. In general, contributions to non-operating private foundations are limited to a smaller percentage of the donor's contribution base (up to 30 percent) than contributions to public charities (up to 50 percent).[512]

In general, taxpayers who make contributions and claim a charitable deduction must satisfy recordkeeping and substantiation requirements.[513] The requirements vary depending on the type and value of property contributed. A deduction generally may be denied if the donor fails to satisfy applicable recordkeeping or substantiation requirements.

Intermediate sanctions (excess benefit transaction tax)

The Code imposes excise taxes on excess benefit transactions between disqualified persons and public charities.[514] An excess benefit transaction generally is a transaction in which an economic benefit is provided by a public charity directly or indirectly to or for the use of a disqualified person, if the value of the economic benefit provided exceeds the value of the consideration (including the performance of services) received for providing such benefit.

For purposes of the excess benefit transaction rules, a disqualified person is any person in a position to exercise substantial influence over the affairs of the public charity at any time in the five-year period ending on the date of the transaction at issue.[515] Persons holding certain powers, responsibilities, or interests (e.g., officers, directors, or trustees) are considered to be in a position to exercise substantial influence over the affairs of the public charity.

---

[511] A special rule in section 170(e)(5) provides that taxpayer are allowed a deduction equal to the fair market value of certain contributions of appreciated, publicly traded stock contributed to a private foundation.

[512] Sec. 170(b).

[513] Sec. 170(f)(8).

[514] Sec. 4958. The excess benefit transaction tax is commonly referred to as "intermediate sanctions," because it imposes penalties generally considered to be less punitive than revocation of the organization's exempt status. The tax also applies to transactions between disqualified persons and social welfare organizations (as described in section 501(c)(4)).

[515] Sec. 4958(f)(1). A disqualified person also includes certain family members of such a person, and certain entities that satisfy a control test with respect to such persons.

An excess benefit transaction tax is imposed on the disqualified person and, in certain cases, on the organization managers, but is not imposed on the public charity. An initial tax of 25 percent of the excess benefit amount is imposed on the disqualified person that receives the excess benefit. An additional tax on the disqualified person of 200 percent of the excess benefit applies if the violation is not corrected within a specified period. A tax of 10 percent of the excess benefit (not to exceed $10,000 with respect to any excess benefit transaction) is imposed on an organization manager that knowingly participated in the excess benefit transaction, if the manager's participation was willful and not due to reasonable cause, and if the initial tax was imposed on the disqualified person.

Community foundations

Community foundations generally are broadly supported section 501(c)(3) public charities that make grants to other charitable organizations located within a community foundation's particular geographic area. Donors sometimes make contributions to a community foundation through transfers to a separate trust or fund, the assets of which are held and managed by a bank or investment company.

Certain community foundations are subject to special rules that permit them to treat the separate funds or trusts maintained by the community foundation as a single entity for tax purposes. This "single entity" status allows the community foundation to be classified as a public charity. One of the requirements that community foundations must meet is that funds maintained by the community foundation may not be subject by the donor to any material restrictions or conditions. The prohibition against material restrictions or conditions is designed to prevent a donor from encumbering a fund in a manner that prevents the community foundation from freely distributing the assets and income from it in furtherance of the community foundation's charitable purposes. Under Treasury regulations, whether a particular restriction or condition placed by the donor on the transfer of assets is material must be determined from all of the facts and circumstances of the transfer. The regulations set out some of the more significant facts and circumstances to be considered in making a determination, including: (1) whether the transferee public charity is the fee owner of the assets received; (2) whether the assets are held and administered by the public charity in a manner consistent with its own exempt purposes; (3) whether the governing body of the public charity has the ultimate authority and control over the assets and the income derived from them; and (4) whether the governing body of the public charity is independent from the donor. The regulations provide several non-adverse factors for determining whether a particular restriction or condition placed by the donor on the transfer of assets is material. In addition, the regulations list numerous factors and subfactors that indicate that the community foundation is prevented from freely and effectively employing the donated assets and the income thereon.

Donor advised funds

Some charitable organizations (including community foundations) establish accounts to which donors may contribute and thereafter provide nonbinding advice or recommendations with regard to distributions from the fund or the investment of assets in the fund. Such accounts are commonly referred to as "donor advised funds." Donors who make contributions to charities for maintenance in a donor advised fund generally claim a charitable contribution deduction at the time of the contribution. Although sponsoring charities frequently permit donors (or other persons appointed by donors) to provide nonbinding recommendations concerning the distribution or investment of assets in a donor advised fund, sponsoring charities generally must have legal ownership and control of such assets following the contribution. If the sponsoring charity does not have such control (or permits a donor to exercise control over amounts contributed), the donor's contributions may not qualify for a charitable deduction, and, in the case of a community foundation, the contribution may be treated as being subject to a material restriction or condition by the donor.

In recent years, a number of financial institutions have formed charitable corporations for the principal purpose of offering donor advised funds, sometimes referred to as "commercial" donor advised funds. In addition, some established charities have begun operating donor advised funds in addition to their primary activities. The IRS has recognized several organizations that sponsor donor advised funds, including "commercial" donor advised funds, as section 501(c)(3) public charities. The term "donor advised fund" is not defined in statute or regulations.

Under the Katrina Emergency Tax Relief Act of 2005, certain of the above-described percent limitations on contributions to public charities are temporarily suspended for purposes of certain "qualified contributions" to public charities. Under the Act, qualified contributions do not include a contribution if the contribution is for establishment of a new, or maintenance in an existing, segregated fund or account with respect to which the donor (or any person appointed or designated by such donor) has, or reasonably expects to have, advisory privileges with respect to distributions or investments by reason of the donor's status as a donor.

Excess business holdings of private foundations

Private foundations are subject to tax on excess business holdings.[516] In general, a private foundation is permitted to hold 20 percent of the voting stock in a corporation, reduced by the amount of voting stock held by all disqualified persons (as defined in section 4946). If it is established that no disqualified person has effective control of the corporation, a private foundation and disqualified persons together may own up to 35 percent of the voting stock of a corporation. A private foundation shall not be treated as having excess business holdings in any corporation if it owns (together with certain other related private foundations) not more than two percent of the voting stock and not more than two percent in value of all outstanding shares of all classes of stock in that corporation. Similar rules apply with respect to holdings in a partnership ("profits interest" is substituted for "voting stock" and "capital interest" for "nonvoting stock") and to other unincorporated enterprises (by substituting "beneficial interest" for "voting stock"). Private foundations are not permitted to have holdings in a proprietorship. Foundations generally have a five-year period to dispose of excess business holdings (acquired other than by purchase) without being subject to tax.[517] This five-year period may be extended an additional five years in limited circumstances.[518] The excess business holdings rules do not apply to

---

[516] Sec. 4943. Taxes imposed may be abated if certain conditions are met. Secs. 4961 and 4962.

[517] Sec. 4943(c)(6).

[518] Sec. 4943(c)(7).

holdings in a functionally related business or to holdings in a trade or business at least 95 percent of the gross income of which is derived from passive sources.[519]

The initial tax is equal to five percent of the value of the excess business holdings held during the foundation's applicable taxable year. An additional tax is imposed if an initial tax is imposed and at the close of the applicable taxable period, the foundation continues to hold excess business holdings. The amount of the additional tax is equal to 200 percent of such holdings.

Explanation of Provision

Definition of a donor advised fund

General rule

In general, the provision defines a "donor advised fund" as a fund or account that is: (1) separately identified by reference to contributions of a donor or donors (2) owned and controlled by a sponsoring organization and (3) with respect to which a donor (or any person appointed or designated by such donor (a "donor advisor") has, or reasonably expects to have, advisory privileges with respect to the distribution or investment of amounts held in the separately identified fund or account by reason of the donor's status as a donor. All three prongs of the definition must be met in order for a fund or account to be treated as a donor advised fund.

The provision defines a "sponsoring organization" as an organization that: (1) is described in section 170(c)[520] (other than a governmental entity described in section 170(c)(1), and without regard to any requirement that the organization be organized in the United States[521]); (2) is not a private foundation (as defined in section 509(a)); and (3) maintains one or more donor advised funds.

The first prong of the definition requires that a donor advised fund be separately identified by reference to contributions of a donor or donors. A distinct fund or account of a sponsoring organization does not meet this prong of the definition unless the fund or account refers to contributions of a donor or donors, such as by naming the fund after a donor, or by treating a fund on the books of the sponsoring organization as attributable to funds contributed by a specific donor or donors. Although a sponsoring organization's general fund is a "fund or account," such fund will not, as a general matter, be treated as a donor advised fund because the general funds of an organization typically are not separately identified by reference to contributions of a specific donor or donors; rather contributions are pooled anonymously within the general fund. Similarly, a fund or account of a sponsoring organization that is distinct from the organization's general fund and that pools contributions of multiple donors generally will not

---

[519] Sec. 4943(d)(3).

[520] Section 170(c) describes organizations to which charitable contributions that are deductible for income tax purposes can be made.

[521] See sec. 170(c)(2)(A).

meet the first prong of the definition unless the contributions of specific donors are in some manner tracked and accounted for within the fund. Accordingly, if a sponsoring organization establishes a fund dedicated to the relief of poverty within a specific community, or a scholarship fund, and the fund attracts contributions from several donors but does not separately identify or refer to contributions of a donor or donors, the fund is not a donor advised fund even if a donor has advisory privileges with respect to the fund. However, a fund or account may not avoid treatment as a donor advised fund even though there is no formal recognition of such separate contributions on the books of the sponsoring organization if the fund or account operates as if contributions of a donor or donors are separately identified. The Secretary has the authority to look to the substance of an arrangement, and not merely its form. In addition, a fund or account may be treated as identified by reference to contributions of a donor or donors if the reference is to persons related to a donor. For example, if a husband made contributions to a fund or account that in turn is named after the husband's wife, the fund is treated as being separately identified by reference to contributions of a donor.

The second prong of the definition provides that the fund be owned and controlled by a sponsoring organization. To the extent that a donor or person other than the sponsoring organization owns or controls amounts deposited to a sponsoring organization, a fund or account is not a donor advised fund. (In cases where a donor retains control of an amount provided to a sponsoring organization, there may not be a completed gift for purposes of the charitable contribution deduction.)

The third prong of the definition provides that with respect to a fund or account of a sponsoring organization, a donor or donor advisor has or reasonably expects to have advisory privileges with respect to the distribution or investment of amounts held in the fund or account by reason of a donor's status as a donor. Advisory privileges are distinct from a legal right or obligation. For example, if a donor executes a gift agreement with a sponsoring organization that specifies certain enforceable rights of the donor with respect to a gift, the donor will not be treated as having "advisory privileges" due to such enforceable rights for purposes of the donor advised fund definition.

The presence of an advisory privilege may be evident through a written document that describes an arrangement between the donor or donor adviser and the sponsoring organization whereby a donor or donor advisor may provide advice to the sponsoring organization about the investment or distribution of amounts held by a sponsoring organization, even if such privileges are not exercised. The presence of an advisory privilege also may be evident through the conduct of a donor or donor advisor and the sponsoring organization. For example, even in the absence of a writing, if a donor regularly provides advice to a sponsoring organization and the sponsoring organization regularly considers such advice, the donor has advisory privileges under the provision. Even if advisory privileges do not exist at the time of a contribution, later acts by the donor (through the provision of advice) and by the sponsoring organization (through the regular consideration of advice) may establish advisory privileges subsequent to the time of the contribution. For example, if a past donor of $100,000 telephones a sponsoring organization and states that he would like the sponsoring organization to distribute $10,000 to an organization described in section 170(b)(1)(A), although the mere act of providing advice does not establish an advisory privilege, if the sponsoring organization distributed the $10,000 to the organization specified by the donor in consideration of the donor's advice, and reinforced the donor in some manner that future advice similarly would be considered, advisory privileges (or the reasonable expectation thereof) might be established. However, the mere provision of advice by a donor or donor advisor does not mean the donor or donor advisor has advisory privileges. For example, a donor's singular belief that he or she has advisory privileges with respect to the contribution does not establish an advisory privilege − there must be some reciprocity on the part of the sponsoring organization.

A person reasonably expects to have advisory privileges if both the donor or donor advisor and the sponsoring organization have reason to believe that the donor or donor advisor will provide advice and that the sponsoring organization generally will consider it. Thus, a person reasonably may expect to have advisory privileges even in the absence of the actual provision of advice. However, a donor's expectation of advisory privileges is not reasonable unless it is reinforced in some manner by the conduct of the sponsoring organization. If, at the time of the contribution, the sponsoring organization had no knowledge that the donor had an expectation of advisory privileges, or no intention of considering any advice provided by the donor, then the donor does not have a reasonable expectation of advisory privileges. Ultimately, the presence or absence of advisory privileges (or a reasonable expectation thereof) depends upon the facts and circumstances, which in turn depend upon the conduct (including any agreement) of both the donor or donor advisor and the sponsoring organization with respect to the making and consideration of advice.

A further requirement of the third prong is that the reasonable expectation of advisory privileges is by reason of the donor's status as a donor. Under this requirement, if a donor's reasonable expectation of advisory privileges is due solely to the donor's service to the organization, for example, by reason of the donor's position as an officer, employee, or director of the sponsoring organization, then the third prong of the definition is not satisfied. For instance, in general, a donor that is a member of the board of directors of the sponsoring organization may provide advice in his or her capacity as a board member with respect to the distribution or investment of amounts in a fund to which the board member contributed. However, if by reason of such donor's contribution to such fund, the donor secured an appointment on a committee of the sponsoring organization that advises how to distribute or invest amounts in such fund, the donor may have a reasonable expectation of advisory privileges, notwithstanding that the donor is an officer, employee, or director of the sponsoring organization.

The third prong of the definition is applicable to a donor or any person appointed or designated by such donor (the donor advisor). For purposes of this prong, a person appointed or designated by a donor advisor is treated as being appointed or designated by a donor. In addition, for purposes of any exception to the definition of a donor advised fund provided under the provision, to the extent a donor recommends to a sponsoring organization the selection of members of a committee that will advise as to distributions or investments of amounts in a fund or account of such sponsoring organization, such members are not treated as appointed or designated by the donor if the recommendation of such members by such donor is based on objective criteria related to the expertise of the member. For example, if a donor recommends that a committee of a sponsoring organization that will provide advice regarding scholarship grants for the advancement of science at local secondary schools should consist of persons who are the heads of the science departments of such schools, then the donor generally would not be considered to have appointed or designated such persons, i.e., they would not be treated as donor advisors.

Exceptions

A donor advised fund does not include a fund or account that makes distributions only to a single identified organization or governmental entity. For example, an endowment fund owned and controlled by a sponsoring organization that is held exclusively to for the benefit of such sponsoring organization is not a donor advised fund even if the fund is named after its principal donor and such donor has advisory privileges with respect to the distribution of amounts held in the fund to such sponsoring organization. Accordingly, a donor that contributes to a university for purposes of establishing a fund named after the donor that exclusively supports the activities of the university is not a donor advised fund even if the donor has advisory privileges regarding the distribution or investment of amounts in the fund.

A donor advised fund also does not include a fund or account with respect to which a donor or donor advisor provides advice as to which individuals receive grants for travel, study, or other similar purposes, provided that (1) the donor's or donor advisor's advisory privileges are performed exclusively by such donor or donor advisor in such person's capacity as a member of a committee all of the members of which are appointed by the sponsoring organization, (2) no combination of a donor or donor advisor or persons related to such persons, control, directly or indirectly, such committee, and (3) all grants from such fund or account are awarded on an objective and nondiscriminatory basis pursuant to a procedure approved in advance by the board of directors of the sponsoring organization, and such procedure is designed to ensure that all such grants meet the requirements described in paragraphs (1), (2), or (3) of section 4945(g) (concerning grants to individuals by private foundations).

In addition, the Secretary may exempt a fund or account from treatment as a donor advised fund if such fund or account is advised by a committee not directly or indirectly controlled by a donor, donor advisor, or persons related to a donor or donor advisor. For such purposes, it is intended that indirect control includes the ability to exercise effective control. For example, if a donor, a donor advisor, and an attorney hired by the donor to provide advice regarding the donor's contributions constitute three of the five members of such a committee, the committee would be treated as being controlled indirectly by the donor for purposes of such an exception. Board membership alone does not establish direct or indirect control. In general, under this authority, the Secretary may establish rules regarding committee advised funds generally that, if followed, would result in the fund not being treated as a donor advised fund. The Secretary also may establish rules excepting certain types of committee-advised funds, such as a fund established exclusively for disaster relief, from the donor advised fund definition.

The provision also provides that the Secretary may exempt a fund or account from treatment as a donor advised fund if such fund or account benefits a single identified charitable purpose.

Deductibility of contributions to a sponsoring organization for maintenance in a donor advised fund

Contributions to certain sponsoring organizations for maintenance in a donor advised fund not eligible for a charitable deduction

Under the provision, contributions to a sponsoring organization for maintenance in a donor advised fund are not eligible for a charitable deduction for income tax purposes if the sponsoring organization is a veterans' organization described in section 170(c)(3), a fraternal society described in section 170(c)(4), or a cemetery company described in section 170(c)(5); for gift tax purposes if the sponsoring organization is a fraternal society described in section 2522(a)(3) or a veterans' organization described in section 2522(a)(4); or for estate tax purposes if the sponsoring organization is a fraternal society described in section 2055(a)(3) or a veterans' organization described in section 2055(a)(4). In addition, contributions to a sponsoring organization for maintenance in a donor advised fund are not eligible for a charitable deduction for income, gift, or estate tax purposes if the sponsoring organization is a Type III supporting organization (other than a functionally integrated Type III supporting organization). A functionally integrated Type III supporting organization is a Type III supporting organization that is not required under regulations established by the Secretary to make payments to supported organizations due to the activities of the organization related to performing the functions of, or carrying out the purposes of, such supported organizations.[522]

Additional substantiation requirements

In addition to satisfying present-law substantiation requirements under section 170(f), a donor must obtain, with respect to each charitable contribution to a sponsoring organization to be maintained in a donor advised fund, a contemporaneous written acknowledgment from the sponsoring organization providing that the sponsoring organization has exclusive legal control over the assets contributed.

Excess business holdings

The excess business holdings rules of section 4943 are applied to donor advised funds. In applying such rules, the term disqualified person means, with respect to a donor advised fund, a donor, donor advisor, a member of the family of a donor or donor advisor, or a 35 percent controlled entity of any such person. Transition rules apply to the present holdings of a donor advised fund similar to those of section 4943(c)(4)-(6).

---

[522] The current such regulation is Treasury regulation section 1.509(a)-4(i)(3)(ii).

Automatic excess benefit transactions, disqualified persons, taxable distributions, and more than incidental benefit

Automatic excess benefit transactions

Under the provision, any grant, loan, compensation, or other similar payment from a donor advised fund to a person that with respect to such fund is a donor, donor advisor, or a person related[523] to a donor or donor advisor automatically is treated as an excess benefit transaction under section 4958, with the entire amount[524] paid to any such person treated as the amount of the excess benefit. Other similar payments include payments in the nature of a grant, loan, or payment of compensation, such as an expense reimbursement. Other similar payments do not include, for example, a payment pursuant to bona fide sale or lease of property, which instead are subject to the general rules of section 4958 under the special disqualified person rule of the provision described below. Also as described below, payment by a sponsoring organization of, for example, compensation to a person who both is a donor with respect to a donor advised fund of the sponsoring organization and a service provider with respect to the sponsoring organization generally, will not be subject to the automatic excess benefit transaction rule of the provision unless the payment (of a grant, loan, compensation, or other similar payment) properly is viewed as a payment from the donor advised fund and not from the sponsoring organization.

Any amount repaid as a result of correcting an excess benefit transaction shall not be held in any donor advised fund.

Disqualified persons

In general, the provision provides that donors and donor advisors with respect to a donor advised fund (as well as persons related to a donor or donor advisor) are treated as disqualified persons under section 4958 with respect to transactions with such donor advised fund (though not necessarily with respect to transactions with the sponsoring organization more generally). For example, if a donor to a donor advised fund purchased securities from the fund, the purchase is subject to the rules of section 4958 because, under the provision, the donor is a disqualified person with respect to the fund. Thus, if as a result of the purchase, the donor receives an excess benefit as defined under generally applicable section 4958 rules, then the donor is subject to tax under such rules. If, as generally would be the case, the purchase was of securities that were contributed by the donor, a factor that may indicate the presence of an excess benefit is if the amount paid by the donor to acquire the securities is less than the amount the donor claimed the

---

[523] For purposes of the provision, a person is treated as related to another person if (1) such person bears a relationship to such other person similar to the relationships described in sections 4958(f)(1)(B) and 4958(f)(1)(C).

[524] The requirement of the provision that the entire amount of the payment be treated as the amount of the excess benefit differs from the generally applicable rule of section 4958, which provides that the excess benefit is the amount by which the value of the economic benefit provided exceeds the value of the consideration received.

securities were worth for purposes of any charitable contribution deduction of the donor. In addition, if a donor advised fund distributes securities to the sponsoring organization of the fund prior to purchase by the donor, consideration should be given to whether the distribution to the sponsoring organization prior to the purchase was intended to circumvent the disqualified person rule of the provision. If so, such a distribution may be disregarded with the result that the purchase is treated as being made from the donor advised fund and not from the sponsoring organization.

As a factual matter, a person who is a donor to a donor advised fund and thus a disqualified person with respect to the fund also may be a service provider with respect to the sponsoring organization. In general, under the provision, as under present law, the sponsoring organization's transactions with the service provider are not subject to the rules of section 4958 unless the service provider is a disqualified person with respect to the sponsoring organization (e.g., if the service provider serves on the board of directors of the sponsoring organization), or unless the transaction is not properly viewed as a transaction with the sponsoring organization but in substance is a transaction with the service provider's donor advised fund. If the transaction properly is viewed as a transaction with the donor advised fund of a sponsoring organization, then the transaction is subject to the rules of section 4958, and, as described above, if the transaction involves payment of a grant, loan, compensation, or other similar payment, then the transaction is subject to the special automatic excess benefit transaction rule of the provision. For example, if a sponsoring organization pays an amount as part of a service contract to a service provider (a bank, for example) who also is a donor to a donor advised fund of the sponsoring organization, and such amounts reasonably are charged uniformly in whole or in part as routine fees to all of the sponsoring organization's donor advised funds, the transaction generally is considered to be between the sponsoring organization and the service provider in such service provider's capacity as a service provider. The transaction is not considered to be a transaction between a donor advised fund and the service provider even though an amount paid under the contract was charged to a donor advised fund of the service provider.

The provision provides that an investment advisor (as well as persons related to the investment advisor) is treated as a disqualified person under section 4958 with respect to the sponsoring organization. Under the provision, the term "investment advisor" means, with respect to any sponsoring organization, any person (other than an employee of the sponsoring organization) compensated by the sponsoring organization for managing the investment of, or providing investment advice with respect to, assets maintained in donor advised funds (including pools of assets all or part of which are attributed to donor advised funds) owned by the sponsoring organization.

Taxable distributions

Under the provision, certain distributions from a donor advised fund are subject to tax. A "taxable distribution" is any distribution from a donor advised fund to (1) any natural person;[525]

---

[525] Under the provision, the term disqualified supporting organization means, with respect to any distribution from a donor advised fund: (1) a Type III supporting organization, other than a functionally integrated Type III supporting organization; and (2) any other supporting organization if either (a) the

(2) to any other person for any purpose other than one specified in section 170(c)(2)(B) (generally, a charitable purpose) or, if for a charitable purpose, the sponsoring organization does not exercise expenditure responsibility with respect to the distribution in accordance with section 4945(h). The expenditure responsibility rules generally require that an organization exert all reasonable efforts and establish adequate procedures to see that the distribution is spent solely for the purposes for which made, to obtain full and complete reports from the distributee on how the funds are spent, and to make full and detailed reports with respect to such expenditures to the Secretary. A taxable distribution does not in any case include a distribution to (1) an organization described in section 170(b)(1)(A)[526] (other than to a disqualified supporting organization); (2) the sponsoring organization of such donor advised fund; or (3) to another donor advised fund.[527]

In the event of a taxable distribution, an excise tax equal to 20 percent of the amount of the distribution is imposed against the sponsoring organization. In addition, an excise tax equal to five percent of the amount of the distribution is imposed against any manager of the sponsoring organization (defined in a manner similar to the term "foundation manager" under section 4945) who knowingly approved the distribution, not to exceed $10,000 with respect to any one taxable distribution. The taxes on taxable distributions are subject to abatement under generally applicable present law rules.

More than incidental benefit

Under the provision, if a donor, a donor advisor, or a person related to a donor or donor advisor of a donor advised fund provides advice as to a distribution that results in any such person receiving, directly or indirectly, a more than incidental benefit, an excise tax equal to 125 percent of the amount of such benefit is imposed against the person who advised as to the

---

donor or donor advisor of the distributing donor advised fund directly or indirectly controls a supported organization of the supporting organization, or (b) the Secretary determines by regulations that a distribution to such supporting organization otherwise is inappropriate.

[526] For purposes of the requirement that a distribution be "to" an organization described in section 170(b)(1)(A), in general, it is intended that rules similar to the rules of Treasury regulation section 53.4945-5(a)(5) apply. Under such regulations, for purposes of determining whether a grant by a private foundation is "to" an organization described in section 509(a)(1), (2), or (3) and so not a taxable expenditure under section 4945, a foreign organization that otherwise is not a section 509(a)(1), (2), or (3) organization is considered as such if the private foundation makes a good faith determination that the grantee is such an organization. Similarly, under the provision, if a sponsoring organization makes a good faith determination (under standards similar to those currently applicable for private foundations) that a distributee organization is an organization described in section 170(b)(1)(A) (other than a disqualified supporting organization), then a distribution to such organization is not considered a taxable distribution.

[527] Under the provision, sponsoring organizations may make grants to natural persons from amounts not held in donor advised funds and may establish scholarship funds that are not donor advised funds. A donor may choose to make a contribution directly to such a scholarship fund (or advise that a donor advised fund make a distribution to such a scholarship fund).

distribution, and against the recipient of the benefit. Persons subject to the tax are jointly and severally liable for the tax. In addition, if a manager of the sponsoring organization (defined in a manner similar to the term "foundation manager" under section 4945) agreed to the making of the distribution, knowing that the distribution would confer a more than incidental benefit on a donor, a donor advisor, or a person related to a donor or donor advisor, the manager is subject to an excise tax equal to 10 percent of the amount of such benefit, not to exceed $10,000. The taxes on more than incidental benefit are subject to abatement under generally applicable present law rules.

In general, under the provision, there is a more than incidental benefit if, as a result of a distribution from a donor advised fund, a donor, donor advisor, or related person with respect to such fund receives a benefit that would have reduced (or eliminated) a charitable contribution deduction if the benefit was received as part of the contribution to the sponsoring organization. If, for example, a donor advises a that a distribution from the donor's donor advised fund be made to the Girl Scouts of America, and the donor's daughter is a member of a local unit of the Girl Scouts of America, the indirect benefit the donor receives as a result of such contribution is considered incidental under the provision, as it generally would not have reduced or eliminated the donor's deduction if it had been received as part of a contribution by donor to the sponsoring organization.[528]

Reporting and disclosure

The provision requires each sponsoring organization to disclose on its information return: (1) the total number of donor advised funds it owns; (2) the aggregate value of assets held in those funds at the end of the organization's taxable year; and (3) the aggregate contributions to and grants made from those funds during the year.

In addition, when seeking recognition of its tax-exempt status, a sponsoring organization must disclose whether it intends to maintain donor advised funds. It is intended that the organization must provide information regarding its planned operation of such funds, including, for example, a description of procedures it intends to use to: (1) communicate to donors and donor advisors that assets held in donor advised funds are the property of the sponsoring organization; and (2) ensure that distributions from donor advised funds do not result in more than incidental benefit to any person.

Effective Date

The provision generally is effective for taxable years beginning after the date of enactment. The provision relating to excess benefit transactions is effective for transactions occurring after the date of enactment. Information return requirements are effective for taxable years ending after the date of enactment. The requirements concerning disclosures on an organization's application for tax exemption are effective for organizations applying for recognition of exempt status after the date of enactment. Requirements relating to charitable

---

[528] See, e.g., Rev. Rul. 80-77, 1980-1 C.B. 56; Rev. Proc. 90-12, 1990-1 C.B. 471.

contributions to donor advised funds are effective for contributions made after 180 days from the date of enactment.

18. Improve accountability of supporting organizations (secs. 509, 4942, 4943, 4945, 4958, and 6033 of the Code)

Present Law

Requirements for section 501(c)(3) tax-exempt status

Charitable organizations, i.e., organizations described in section 501(c)(3), generally are exempt from Federal income tax and are eligible to receive tax deductible contributions. A charitable organization must operate primarily in pursuance of one or more tax-exempt purposes constituting the basis of its tax exemption.[529] In order to qualify as operating primarily for a purpose described in section 501(c)(3), an organization must satisfy the following operational requirements: (1) the net earnings of the organization may not inure to the benefit of any person in a position to influence the activities of the organization; (2) the organization must operate to provide a public benefit, not a private benefit;[530] (3) the organization may not be operated primarily to conduct an unrelated trade or business;[531] (4) the organization may not engage in substantial legislative lobbying; and (5) the organization may not participate or intervene in any political campaign.

Section 501(c)(3) organizations (with certain exceptions) are required to seek formal recognition of tax-exempt status by filing an application with the IRS (Form 1023). In response to the application, the IRS issues a determination letter or ruling either recognizing the applicant as tax-exempt or not.

In general, organizations exempt from Federal income tax under section 501(a) are required to file an annual information return with the IRS.[532] Under present law, the information return requirement does not apply to several categories of exempt organizations. Organizations

---

[529] Treas. Reg. sec. 1.501(c)(3)-1(c)(1). The Code specifies such purposes as religious, charitable, scientific, testing for public safety, literary, or educational purposes, or to foster international amateur sports competition, or for the prevention of cruelty to children or animals. In general, an organization is organized and operated for charitable purposes if it provides relief for the poor and distressed or the underprivileged. Treas. Reg. sec. 1.501(c)(3)-1(d)(2).

[530] Treas. Reg. sec. 1.501(c)(3)-1(d)(1)(ii).

[531] Treas. Reg. sec. 1.501(c)(3)-1(e)(1). Conducting a certain level of unrelated trade or business activity will not jeopardize tax-exempt status.

[532] Sec. 6033(a)(1).

exempt from the filing requirement include organizations (other than private foundations), the gross receipts of which in each taxable year normally are not more than $25,000.[533]

Classification of section 501(c)(3) organizations

In general

Section 501(c)(3) organizations are classified either as "public charities" or "private foundations."[534] Private foundations generally are defined under section 509(a) as all organizations described in section 501(c)(3) other than an organization granted public charity status by reason of: (1) being a specified type of organization (i.e., churches, educational institutions, hospitals and certain other medical organizations, certain organizations providing assistance to colleges and universities, or a governmental unit); (2) receiving a substantial part of its support from governmental units or direct or indirect contributions from the general public; or (3) providing support to another section 501(c)(3) entity that is not a private foundation. In contrast to public charities, private foundations generally are funded from a limited number of sources (e.g., an individual, family, or corporation). Donors to private foundations and persons related to such donors together often control the operations of private foundations.

Because private foundations receive support from, and typically are controlled by, a small number of supporters, private foundations are subject to a number of anti-abuse rules and excise taxes not applicable to public charities.[535] For example, the Code imposes excise taxes on acts of "self-dealing" between disqualified persons (generally, an enumerated class of foundation insiders[536]) and a private foundation. Acts of self-dealing include, for example, sales or exchanges, or leasing, of property; lending of money; or the furnishing of goods, services, or facilities between a disqualified person and a private foundation.[537] In addition, private non-operating foundations are required to pay out a minimum amount each year as qualifying distributions. In general, a qualifying distribution is an amount paid to accomplish one or more of the organization's exempt purposes, including reasonable and necessary administrative

---

[533] Sec. 6033(a)(2); Treas. Reg. sec. 1.6033-2(a)(2)(i); Treas. Reg. sec. 1.6033-2(g)(1). Sec. 6033(a)(2)(A)(ii) provides a $5,000 annual gross receipts exception from the annual reporting requirements for certain exempt organizations. In Announcement 82-88, 1982-25 I.R.B. 23, the IRS exercised its discretionary authority under section 6033 to increase the gross receipts exception to $25,000, and enlarge the category of exempt organizations that are not required to file Form 990.

[534] Sec. 509(a). Private foundations are either private operating foundations or private non-operating foundations. In general, private operating foundations operate their own charitable programs in contrast to private non-operating foundations, which generally are grant-making organizations. Most private foundations are non-operating foundations.

[535] Secs. 4940 - 4945.

[536] See sec. 4946(a).

[537] Sec. 4941.

expenses.[538] Certain expenditures of private foundations are also subject to tax.[539] In general, taxable expenditures are expenditures: (1) for lobbying; (2) to influence the outcome of a public election or carry on a voter registration drive (unless certain requirements are met); (3) as a grant to an individual for travel, study, or similar purposes unless made pursuant to procedures approved by the Secretary; (4) as a grant to an organization that is not a public charity or exempt operating foundation unless the foundation exercises expenditure responsibility[540] with respect to the grant; or (5) for any non-charitable purpose. Additional excise taxes may apply in the event a private foundation holds certain business interests ("excess business holdings")[541] or makes an investment that jeopardizes the foundation's exempt purposes.[542]

Public charities also enjoy certain advantages over private foundations regarding the deductibility of contributions. For example, contributions of appreciated capital gain property to a private foundation generally are deductible only to the extent of the donor's cost basis.[543] In contrast, contributions to public charities generally are deductible in an amount equal to the property's fair market value, except for gifts of inventory and other ordinary income property, short-term capital gain property, and tangible personal property the use of which is unrelated to the donee organization's exempt purpose. In addition, under present law, a taxpayer's deductible contributions generally are limited to specified percentages of the taxpayer's contribution base, which generally is the taxpayer's adjusted gross income for a taxable year. The applicable percentage limitations vary depending upon the type of property contributed and the classification of the donee organization. In general, contributions to non-operating private foundations are limited to a smaller percentage of the donor's contribution base (up to 30 percent) than contributions to public charities (up to 50 percent).[544]

---

[538] Sec. 4942(g)(1)(A). A qualifying distribution also includes any amount paid to acquire an asset used (or held for use) directly in carrying out one or more of the organization's exempt purposes and certain amounts set-aside for exempt purposes. Sec. 4942(g)(1)(B) and 4942(g)(2).

[539] Sec. 4945. Taxes imposed may be abated if certain conditions are met. Secs. 4961 and 4962.

[540] In general, expenditure responsibility requires that a foundation make all reasonable efforts and establish reasonable procedures to ensure that the grant is spent solely for the purpose for which it was made, to obtain reports from the grantee on the expenditure of the grant, and to make reports to the Secretary regarding such expenditures. Sec. 4945(h).

[541] Sec. 4943.

[542] Sec. 4944.

[543] A special rule in section 170(e)(5) provides that taxpayer are allowed a deduction equal to the fair market value of certain contributions of appreciated, publicly traded stock contributed to a private foundation.

[544] Sec. 170(b).

<u>Supporting organizations (section 509(a)(3))</u>

The Code provides that certain "supporting organizations" (in general, organizations that provide support to another section 501(c)(3) organization that is not a private foundation) are classified as public charities rather than private foundations.[545] To qualify as a supporting organization, an organization must meet all three of the following tests: (1) it must be organized and at all times operated exclusively for the benefit of, to perform the functions of, or to carry out the purposes of one or more "publicly supported organizations"[546] (the "organizational and operational tests");[547] (2) it must be operated, supervised, or controlled by or in connection with one or more publicly supported organizations (the "relationship test");[548] and (3) it must not be controlled directly or indirectly by one or more disqualified persons (as defined in section 4946) other than foundation managers and other than one or more publicly supported organizations (the "lack of outside control test").[549]

To satisfy the relationship test, a supporting organization must hold one of three statutorily described close relationships with the supported organization. The organization must be: (1) operated, supervised, or controlled by a publicly supported organization (commonly referred to as "Type I" supporting organizations); (2) supervised or controlled in connection with a publicly supported organization ("Type II" supporting organizations); or (3) operated in connection with a publicly supported organization ("Type III" supporting organizations).[550]

<u>Type I supporting organizations</u>

In the case of supporting organizations that are operated, supervised, or controlled by one or more publicly supported organizations (Type I supporting organizations), one or more supported organizations must exercise a substantial degree of direction over the policies, programs, and activities of the supporting organization.[551] The relationship between the Type I supporting organization and the supported organization generally is comparable to that of a parent and subsidiary. The requisite relationship may be established by the fact that a majority of the officers, directors, or trustees of the supporting organization are appointed or elected by

---

[545] Sec. 509(a)(3).

[546] In general, supported organizations of a supporting organization must be publicly supported charities described in sections 509(a)(1) or (a)(2).

[547] Sec. 509(a)(3)(A).

[548] Sec. 509(a)(3)(B).

[549] Sec. 509(a)(3)(C).

[550] Treas. Reg. sec. 1.509(a)-4(f)(2).

[551] Treas. Reg. sec. 1.509(a)-4(g)(1)(i).

the governing body, members of the governing body, officers acting in their official capacity, or the membership of one or more publicly supported organizations.[552]

Type II supporting organizations

Type II supporting organizations are supervised or controlled in connection with one or more publicly supported organizations. Rather than the parent-subsidiary relationship characteristic of Type I organizations, the relationship between a Type II organization and its supported organizations is more analogous to a brother-sister relationship. In order to satisfy the Type II relationship requirement, generally there must be common supervision or control by the persons supervising or controlling both the supporting organization and the publicly supported organizations.[553] An organization generally is not considered to be "supervised or controlled in connection with" a publicly supported organization merely because the supporting organization makes payments to the publicly supported organization, even if the obligation to make payments is enforceable under state law.[554]

Type III supporting organizations

Type III supporting organizations are "operated in connection with" one or more publicly supported organizations. To satisfy the "operated in connection with" relationship, Treasury regulations require that the supporting organization be responsive to, and significantly involved in the operations of, the publicly supported organization. This relationship is deemed to exist where the supporting organization meets both a "responsiveness test" and an "integral part test."[555]

In general, the responsiveness test requires that the Type III supporting organization be responsive to the needs or demands of the publicly supported organizations. The responsiveness test may be satisfied in one of two ways.[556] First, the supporting organization may demonstrate that: (1)(a) one or more of its officers, directors, or trustees are elected or appointed by the officers, directors, trustees, or membership of the supported organization; (b) one or more members of the governing bodies of the publicly supported organizations are also officers, directors, or trustees of the supporting organization; or (c) the officers, directors, or trustees of the supporting organization maintain a close continuous working relationship with the officers,

---

[552] Id.

[553] Treas. Reg. sec. 1.509(a)- 4(h)(1).

[554] Treas. Reg. sec. 1.509(a)-4(h)(2).

[555] Treas. Reg. sec. 1.509(a)-4(i)(1).

[556] For an organization that was supporting or benefiting one or more publicly supported organizations before November 20, 1970, additional facts and circumstances, such as an historic and continuing relationship between organizations, also may be taken into consideration to establish compliance with either of the responsiveness tests. Treas. Reg. sec. 1.509(a)-4(i)(1)(ii).

directors, or trustees of the publicly supported organizations; and (2) by reason of such arrangement, the officers, directors, or trustees of the supported organization have a significant voice in the investment policies of the supporting organization, the timing and manner of making grants, the selection of grant recipients by the supporting organization, and otherwise directing the use of the income or assets of the supporting organization.[557] Alternatively, the responsiveness test may be satisfied if the supporting organization is a charitable trust under state law, each specified supported organization is a named beneficiary under the trust's governing instrument, and the beneficiary organization has the power to enforce the trust and compel an accounting under state law.[558]

In general, the integral part test requires that the Type III supporting organization maintain significant involvement in the operations of one or more publicly supported organizations, and that such publicly supported organizations are in turn dependent upon the supporting organization for the type of support which it provides. There are two alternative methods for satisfying the integral part test. The first alternative is to establish that (1) the activities engaged in for or on behalf of the publicly supported organization are activities to perform the functions of, or carry out the purposes of, such organizations; and (2) these activities, but for the involvement of the supporting organization, normally would be engaged in by the publicly supported organizations themselves.[559] Organizations that satisfy this "but for" test sometimes are referred to as "functionally integrated" Type III supporting organizations. The second method for satisfying the integral part test is to establish that: (1) the supporting organization pays substantially all of its income to or for the use of one or more publicly supported organizations;[560] (2) the amount of support received by one or more of the publicly supported organizations is sufficient to insure the attentiveness of the organization or organizations to the operations of the supporting organization (this is known as the "attentiveness requirement");[561] and (3) a significant amount of the total support of the supporting organization goes to those publicly supported organizations that meet the "attentiveness requirement."[562]

---

[557] Treas. Reg. sec. 1.509(a)-4(i)(2)(ii).

[558] Treas. Reg. sec. 1.509(a)-4(i)(2)(iii).

[559] Treas. Reg. sec. 1.509(a)-4(i)(3)(ii).

[560] For this purpose, the IRS has defined the term "substantially all" of an organization's income to mean 85 percent or more. Rev. Rul. 76-208, 1976-1 C.B. 161.

[561] Although the regulations do not specify the requisite level of support in numerical or percentage terms, the IRS has suggested that grants that represent less than 10 percent of the beneficiary's support likely would be viewed as insufficient to ensure attentiveness. Gen. Couns. Mem. 36379 (August 15, 1975). As an alternative to satisfying the attentiveness standard by the foregoing method, a supporting organization may demonstrate attentiveness by showing that, in order to avoid the interruption of the carrying on of a particular function or activity, the beneficiary organization will be sufficiently attentive to the operations of the supporting organization. Treas. Reg. sec. 1.509(a)-4(i)(3)(iii)(b).

[562] Treas. Reg. sec. 1.509(a)-4(i)(3)(iii).

Intermediate sanctions (excess benefit transaction tax)

The Code imposes excise taxes on excess benefit transactions between disqualified persons and public charities.[563] An excess benefit transaction generally is a transaction in which an economic benefit is provided by a public charity directly or indirectly to or for the use of a disqualified person, if the value of the economic benefit provided exceeds the value of the consideration (including the performance of services) received for providing such benefit.

For purposes of the excess benefit transaction rules, a disqualified person is any person in a position to exercise substantial influence over the affairs of the public charity at any time in the five-year period ending on the date of the transaction at issue.[564] Persons holding certain powers, responsibilities, or interests (e.g., officers, directors, or trustees) are considered to be in a position to exercise substantial influence over the affairs of the public charity.

An excess benefit transaction tax is imposed on the disqualified person and, in certain cases, on the organization managers, but is not imposed on the public charity. An initial tax of 25 percent of the excess benefit amount is imposed on the disqualified person that receives the excess benefit. An additional tax on the disqualified person of 200 percent of the excess benefit applies if the violation is not corrected within a specified period. A tax of 10 percent of the excess benefit (not to exceed $10,000 with respect to any excess benefit transaction) is imposed on an organization manager that knowingly participated in the excess benefit transaction, if the manager's participation was willful and not due to reasonable cause, and if the initial tax was imposed on the disqualified person.

Excess business holdings of private foundations

Private foundations are subject to tax on excess business holdings.[565] In general, a private foundation is permitted to hold 20 percent of the voting stock in a corporation, reduced by the amount of voting stock held by all disqualified persons (as defined in section 4946). If it is established that no disqualified person has effective control of the corporation, a private foundation and disqualified persons together may own up to 35 percent of the voting stock of a corporation. A private foundation shall not be treated as having excess business holdings in any corporation if it owns (together with certain other related private foundations) not more than two percent of the voting stock and not more than two percent in value of all outstanding shares of all classes of stock in that corporation. Similar rules apply with respect to holdings in a partnership ("profits interest" is substituted for "voting stock" and "capital interest" for "nonvoting stock") and to other unincorporated enterprises (by substituting "beneficial interest" for "voting stock").

---

[563] Sec. 4958. The excess benefit transaction tax is commonly referred to as "intermediate sanctions," because it imposes penalties generally considered to be less punitive than revocation of the organization's exempt status. The tax also applies to transactions between disqualified persons and social welfare organizations (as described in section 501(c)(4)).

[564] Sec. 4958(f)(1). A disqualified person also includes certain family members of such a person, and certain entities that satisfy a control test with respect to such persons.

[565] Sec. 4943. Taxes imposed may be abated if certain conditions are met. Secs. 4961 and 4962.

Private foundations are not permitted to have holdings in a proprietorship. Foundations generally have a five-year period to dispose of excess business holdings (acquired other than by purchase) without being subject to tax.[566] This five-year period may be extended an additional five years in limited circumstances.[567] The excess business holdings rules do not apply to holdings in a functionally related business or to holdings in a trade or business at least 95 percent of the gross income of which is derived from passive sources.[568]

The initial tax is equal to five percent of the value of the excess business holdings held during the foundation's applicable taxable year. An additional tax is imposed if an initial tax is imposed and at the close of the applicable taxable period, the foundation continues to hold excess business holdings. The amount of the additional tax is equal to 200 percent of such holdings.

Explanation of Provision

Provisions relating to all supporting organizations (Type I, Type II, and Type III)

Automatic excess benefit transactions

Under the provision, if a supporting organization (Type I, Type II, or Type III) makes a grant, loan, payment of compensation, or other similar payment to a substantial contributor (or person related to the substantial contributor) of the supporting organization, for purposes of the excess benefit transaction rules (sec. 4958), the substantial contributor is treated as a disqualified person and the payment is treated automatically as an excess benefit transaction with the entire amount of the payment treated as the excess benefit.[569] Accordingly, the substantial contributor is subject to an initial tax of 25 percent of the amount of the payment under section 4958(a)(1) and an organization manager that participated in the making of the payment, knowing that the payment was a grant, loan, payment of compensation, or other similar payment to a substantial contributor, is subject to a tax of 10 percent of the amount of the payment under section 4958(a)(2). The second tier taxes and other rules of section 4958 also apply to such payments. Other similar payments include payments in the nature of a grant, loan, or payment of compensation, such as an expense reimbursement. Other similar payments do not include, for example, a payment made pursuant to a bona fide sale or lease of property with a substantial contributor. Such payments are subject to the general rules of section 4958 if the substantial contributor meets the definition of a disqualified person under section 4958(f), but are not subject to the automatic excess benefit transaction rule of the provision. The provision applies to

---

[566] Sec. 4943(c)(6).

[567] Sec. 4943(c)(7).

[568] Sec. 4943(d)(3).

[569] The requirement of the provision that the entire amount of the payment be treated as the amount of the excess benefit differs from the generally applicable rule of section 4958, which provides that the excess benefit is the amount by which the value of the economic benefit provided exceeds the value of the consideration received.

payments by a supporting organization to a substantial contributor but not to payments by a substantial contributor to a supporting organization.

Under the provision, a substantial contributor means any person who contributed or bequeathed an aggregate amount of more than $5,000 to the organization, if such amount is more than two percent of the total contributions and bequests received by the organization before the close of the taxable year of the organization in which the contribution or bequest is received by the organization from such person. In the case of a trust, a substantial contributor also includes the creator of the trust. A substantial contributor does not include a public charity (other than a supporting organization). Under the provision, mechanical rules similar to the rules that apply in determining whether a person is a substantial contributor to a private foundation (secs. 509(d)(2)(B) and (C)) apply.

Under the provision, a person is a related person ("related person") if a person is a member of the family (determined under section 4958(f)(4)) of a substantial contributor, or a 35 percent controlled entity, defined as a corporation, partnership, trust, or estate in which a substantial contributor or family member thereof owns more than 35 percent of the total combined voting power, profits interest, or beneficial interest, as the case may be.

In addition, under the provision, loans by any supporting organization (Type I, Type II, or Type III) to a disqualified person (as defined in section 4958) of the supporting organization are treated as an excess benefit transaction under section 4958 and the entire amount of the loan is treated as an excess benefit. For this purpose, a disqualified person does not include a public charity (other than a supporting organization).

Disclosure requirements

Under the provision, all supporting organizations are required to file an annual information return (Form 990 series) with the Secretary, regardless of the organization's gross receipts. A supporting organization must indicate on such annual information return whether it is a Type I, Type II, or Type III supporting organization and must identify its supported organizations.

Under the provision, supporting organizations must demonstrate annually that the organization is not controlled directly or indirectly by one or more disqualified persons (other than foundation managers and other than one or more publicly supported organizations) through a certification on the annual information return. It is intended that supporting organizations be able to certify that the majority of the organization's governing body is comprised of individuals who were selected based on their special knowledge or expertise in the particular field or discipline in which the supporting organization is operating, or because they represent the particular community that is served by the supported public charities.

Disqualified person

Under the provision, for purposes of the excess benefit transaction rules (sec. 4958), a disqualified person of a supporting organization is treated as a disqualified person of the supported organization.

Provisions that apply to Type III supporting organizations

Payout with respect to Type III supporting organizations

Under the provision, the Secretary shall promulgate new regulations on payments required by Type III supporting organizations that are not functionally integrated Type III supporting organizations.[570] Such regulations shall require such organizations to make distributions of a percentage either of income or assets to the public charities they support in order to ensure that a significant amount is paid to such supported organizations. A functionally integrated Type III supporting organization is a Type III supporting organization that is not required under regulations established by the Secretary to make payments to supported organizations due to the activities of the organization related to performing the functions of, or carrying out the purposes of, such supported organizations.[571]

Excess business holdings

Under the provision, the excess business holdings rules of section 4943 are applied to Type III supporting organizations (other than functionally integrated Type III supporting organizations). In applying such rules, the term disqualified person has the meaning provided in section 4958, and also includes substantial contributors and related persons and any organization that is effectively controlled by the same person or persons who control the supporting organization or any organization substantially all of the contributions to which were made by the same person or persons who made substantially all of the contributions to the supporting organization. The excess business holdings rules do not apply if, as of November 18, 2005, the holdings were held (and at all times thereafter, are held) for the benefit of the community pursuant to the direction (made as of such date) of a State attorney general or a State official with jurisdiction over the Type III supporting organization.

---

[570] See Treas. Reg. sec. 1.509(a)-4(i)(3)(iii).

[571] The current such regulation is Treasury regulation section 1.509(a)-4(i)(3)(ii). Under Treasury regulation section 1.509(a)-4(i)(3), the integral part test of current law may be satisfied in one of two ways, one of which requires a payout of substantially all of an organization's income to or for the use of one or more publicly supported organizations, and one of which does not require such a payout. There is concern that the current income-based payout does not result in a significant amount being paid to charity if assets held by a supporting organization produce little to no income, especially in relation to the value of the assets held by the organization, and as compared to amounts paid out by nonoperating private foundations. There also is concern that the current regulatory standards for satisfying the integral part test not by reason of a payout are not sufficiently stringent to ensure that there is a sufficient nexus between the supporting and supported organizations. In revising the regulations, the Secretary has the discretion to determine whether it is appropriate to impose a pay out requirement on any or all organizations not currently required to pay out. It is intended that, in revisiting the current regulations, if the distinction between Type III supporting organizations that are required to pay out and those that are not required to pay out is retained, which may be appropriate, the Secretary nonetheless shall strengthen the standard for qualification as an organization that is not required to pay out. For example, as one requirement, the Secretary may consider whether substantially all of the activities of such an organization should be activities in direct furtherance of the functions or purposes of supported organizations.

The Secretary has the authority not to impose the excess business holdings rules if the organization establishes to the satisfaction of the Secretary that excess holdings of an organization are consistent with the purpose or function constituting the basis of the organization's exempt status. In exercising this authority, the Secretary should consider, in addition to any other factors the Secretary considers significant, as favorable, but not determinative, factors, a reasoned determination by the State attorney general with jurisdiction over the supporting organization, that disposition of the holdings would have a severe detrimental impact on the community, and a binding commitment by the supporting organization to pay out at least five percent of the value of the organization's assets each year to its supported organizations. A reasoned determination would require, among other things, evidence that any such determination was made pursuant to serious study by the State attorney general of the issues involved in disposing of the excess holdings, and findings by the State attorney general about the detrimental economic impact that would result from such disposition. If as a result of such State attorney general's study and findings, the State attorney general directed as a matter of State law that permission of the State would be required prior to any sale of the holdings, such a factor should be given strong consideration by the Secretary.

Transition rules apply to the present holdings of an organization similar to those of section 4943(c)(4)-(6).[572]

Under the provision, the excess business holdings rules also apply to Type II supporting organizations but only if such organization accepts any gift or contribution from a person (other than a public charity, not including a supporting organization) who (1) controls, directly or indirectly, either alone or together (with persons described below) the governing body of a supported organization of the supporting organization;[573] (2) is a member of the family of such a person; or (3) is a 35 percent controlled entity.

<u>Organizational and operational requirements</u>

---

[572] Under the transition rules, in general, where the existing holdings of a supporting organization and disqualified persons are in excess of 50 percent (of a voting stock interest, profits interest, or beneficial interest), and not 20 percent or 35 percent as under the general rule, but are not in excess of 75 percent, a 10-year period is available before the holdings must be reduced to 50 percent. If such holdings are more than 75 percent, the reduction to 50 percent need not occur for a 15-year period. The 15-year period is expanded to 20 years if the holdings are more than 95 percent. After the expiration of the 10, 15, or 20 year period, if disqualified persons have holdings in a business enterprise in excess of two percent of the enterprise, the supporting organization has 15 additional years to dispose of any of its own holdings that are above 25 percent of the holdings in the enterprise. If disqualified persons do not have such holdings, then the supporting organization has 15 additional years to dispose of any of its own holdings that are above 35 percent of the holdings in the enterprise.

[573] For purposes of the provision, it is intended that indirect control includes the ability to exercise effective control. For example, if a person made a gift to a supporting organization and a combination of such person, a person related to such person, and such person's personal attorney were members of the five-member board of a supported organization of the supporting organization, the organization would be treated as being indirectly controlled by such person. Board membership alone does not establish direct or indirect control.

The provision provides that, in general, after the date of enactment, a Type III supporting organization may not support an organization that is not organized in the United States.[574] But, for Type III supporting organizations that support a foreign organization on the date of enactment, the provision provides that the general rule does not apply until the first day of the third taxable year of the organization beginning after the date of enactment.

Relationship to supported organization(s)

Under the provision, a Type III supporting organization must apprise each organization it supports of information regarding the supporting organization in order to help ensure the supporting organization's responsiveness. It is intended that such a showing could be satisfied, for example, through provision of documentation such as a copy of the supporting organization's governing documents, any changes made to the governing documents, the organization's annual information return filed with the Secretary (Form 990 series), any tax return (Form 990-T) filed with the Secretary, and an annual report (including a description of all of the support provided by the supporting organization, how such support was calculated, and a projection of the next year's support). It is intended that failure to make a sufficient showing is a factor in determining whether the responsiveness test of present law is met.

In general, under the provision, a Type III supporting organization that is organized as a trust must, in addition to present law requirements, establish to the satisfaction of the Secretary, that it has a close and continuous relationship with the supported organization such that the trust is responsive to the needs or demands of the supported organization. A transition rule for existing trusts provides that the provision is not effective until one year after the date of enactment but is effective on the date of enactment for other trusts.

Other provisions

Under the provision, if a Type I or Type III supporting organization accepts any gift or contribution from a person (other than a public charity, not including a supporting organization) who (1) controls, directly or indirectly, either alone or together (with persons described below) the governing body of a supported organization of the supporting organization; (2) is a member of the family of such a person; or (3) is a 35 percent controlled entity, then the supporting organization is treated as a private foundation for all purposes until such time as the organization can demonstrate to the satisfaction of the Secretary that it qualifies as a public charity other than as a supporting organization.

Under the provision, a nonoperating private foundation may not count as a qualifying distribution under section 4942 any amount paid to (1) a Type III supporting organization that is not a functionally integrated Type III supporting organization or (2) any other supporting

---

[574] U.S. charities established principally to provide financial and other assistance to a foreign charity, sometimes referred to as "friends of" organizations, may not be established as supporting organizations under the provision. Such organizations may continue to obtain public charity status, however, by virtue of demonstrating broad public support (as described in sections 509(a)(1) and 509(a)(2)).

organization if a disqualified person with respect to the foundation directly or indirectly controls the supporting organization or a supported organization of such supporting organization. Any amount that does not count as a qualifying distribution under this rule is treated as a taxable expenditure under section 4945.

Effective Date

The provision generally is effective on the date of enactment. The excess benefit transaction rules are effective for transactions occurring after July 25, 2006 (except that the rule relating to the definition of a disqualified person is effective for transactions occurring after the date of enactment). The excess business holdings requirements are effective for taxable years beginning after the date of enactment. The provision relating to distributions by nonoperating private foundations is effective for distributions and expenditures made after the date of enactment. The return requirements are effective for returns filed for taxable years ending after the date of enactment.

TITLE XIII: OTHER PROVISIONS

A. Technical Corrections to Mine Safety Act[575]

The bill makes technical corrections to the Mine Improvement and New Emergency Response Act ("MINER Act") of 2006 (Pub. L. No. 109-236). Specifically, the provision corrects a drafting error by recodifying the MINER Act's provisions increasing criminal penalties under the Mine Safety and Health Act at 30 U.S.C. s. 820(d), as was intended, and makes other technical and conforming changes.

B. Going To The Sun Road

Present Law

Section 1940 of the Safe, Accountable, Flexible, Efficient Transportation Equity Act: a Legacy for Users ("SAFETEA-LU") provides authorization for the appropriation of $50 million in funding for work to resurface, repair, rehabilitate and reconstruct the Going to the Sun Road at Glacier National Park Montana ($10 million per year for fiscal years 2005 through 2009).

Section 10212 of SAFETEA-LU rescinds a specified amount of unobligated balances of funds apportioned before September 30, 2009, to States for the Interstate maintenance, national highway system, bridge, congestion mitigation and air quality improvement, surface transportation (other than the STP set-aside programs), metropolitan planning, minimum guarantee, Appalachian development highway system, recreational trails, safe routes to school, freight intermodal connectors, coordinated border infrastructure, high risk rural road, and highway safety improvement programs. The specified amount is $8,543,000,000.

Explanation of Provision

The provision eliminates the authorizations for fiscal years 2005 and 2006, and redistributes those funds as $16,666,666 per year for fiscal years 2007 through 2009. The provision further provides that funds authorized to be appropriated under the provision are contract authority to be available for obligation in the same manner as if the funds were apportioned under chapter 1 of title 23 of the United States Code. The provision increases by $50 million the specified amount subject to rescission from $8,543,000,000 to $8,593,000,000.

Effective Date

The provision is effective on the date of enactment.

---

[575] The description of these provisions, which do not amend the Internal Revenue Code of 1986, was provided to the staff of the Joint Committee on Taxation by staff of the House Committee on Education and the Workforce.

C. Exception to Local Furnishing Requirements for Certain Alaska Hydroelectric Projects

Present Law

Interest on bonds issued by State and local governments generally is excluded from gross income for Federal income tax purposes if the proceeds of such bonds are used to finance direct activities of governmental units or if such bonds are repaid with revenues of governmental units. Interest on State or local government bonds issued to finance activities of private persons is taxable unless a specific exception applies ("private activity bonds").

The interest on private activity bonds is eligible for tax-exemption if such bonds are issued for certain purposes permitted by the Code ("qualified private activity bonds"). The definition of a qualified private activity bond includes bonds issued to finance certain private facilities for the "local furnishing" of electricity or gas. Generally, a facility provides local furnishing if the area served by the facility does not exceed (1) two contiguous counties or (2) a city and a contiguous county (the "two-county rule").

The Code generally limits the local furnishing exception to bonds for facilities (1) of persons who were engaged in the local furnishing of electric energy or gas on January 1, 1997 (or a successor in interest to such persons), and (2) that serve areas served by those persons on such date (the "service area limitation") (sec. 142(f)(3)). The Small Business Job Protection Act of 1996 (the "Act") provided an exception from these limitations for bonds issued to finance the acquisition of the Snettisham hydroelectric project from the Alaska Power Administration (Pub. L. No. 104-188, sec. 1804 (1996)).

Explanation of Provision

The provision provides an exception from the service area limitation under section 142(f)(3) for bonds issued prior to May 31, 2006, to finance the Lake Dorothy hydroelectric project to provide electricity to the City of Hoonah, Alaska. In addition, the furnishing of electric service to the City of Hoonah, Alaska is disregarded for purposes of applying the two-county rule to bonds issued before May 31, 2006, to finance either the Lake Dorothy hydroelectric project (as defined in the provision) or to finance the acquisition of the Snettisham hydroelectric project.

Effective Date

The provision is effective on the date of enactment.

D. Extend Certain Tax Rules for Qualified Tuition Programs
(sec. 529 of the Code)

Present Law

Overview

Section 529 provides specified income tax and transfer tax rules for the treatment of accounts and contracts established under qualified tuition programs.[576] A qualified tuition program is a program established and maintained by a State or agency or instrumentality thereof, or by one or more eligible educational institutions, which satisfies certain requirements and under which a person may purchase tuition credits or certificates on behalf of a designated beneficiary that entitle the beneficiary to the waiver or payment of qualified higher education expenses of the beneficiary (a "prepaid tuition program").[577] In the case of a program established and maintained by a State or agency or instrumentality thereof, a qualified tuition program also includes a program under which a person may make contributions to an account that is established for the purpose of satisfying the qualified higher education expenses of the designated beneficiary of the account, provided it satisfies certain specified requirements (a "savings account program").[578] Under both types of qualified tuition programs, a contributor establishes an account for the benefit of a particular designated beneficiary to provide for that beneficiary's higher education expenses.

For this purpose, qualified higher education expenses means tuition, fees, books, supplies, and equipment required for the enrollment or attendance of a designated beneficiary at an eligible educational institution, and expenses for special needs services in the case of a special needs beneficiary that are incurred in connection with such enrollment or attendance.[579] Qualified higher education expenses generally also include room and board for students who are enrolled at least half-time.[580]

Income tax treatment

A qualified tuition program, including a savings account or a prepaid tuition contract established thereunder, generally is exempt from income tax, although it is subject to the tax on unrelated business income.[581] Contributions to a qualified tuition account (or with respect to a

---

[576] The term "account" refers to a prepaid tuition benefit contract or a tuition savings account established pursuant to a qualified tuition program.

[577] Sec. 529(b)(1)(A).

[578] Sec. 529(b)(1)(A).

[579] Sec. 529(e)(3)(A).

[580] Sec. 529(e)(3)(B).

[581] Sec. 529(a). An interest in a qualified tuition account is not treated as debt for purposes of the debt-financed property rules under section 514. Sec. 529(e)(4).

prepaid tuition contract) are not deductible to the contributor or includible in income of the designated beneficiary or account owner. Earnings accumulate tax-free until a distribution is made. If a distribution is made to pay qualified higher education expenses, no portion of the distribution is subject to income tax.[582] If a distribution is not used to pay qualified higher education expenses, the earnings portion of the distribution is subject to Federal income tax[583] and a 10-percent additional tax (subject to exceptions for death, disability, or the receipt of a scholarship).[584] A change in the designated beneficiary of an account or prepaid contract is not treated as a distribution for income tax purposes if the new designated beneficiary is a member of the family of the old beneficiary.[585]

Gift and generation-skipping transfer (GST) tax treatment

A contribution to a qualified tuition account (or with respect to a prepaid tuition contract) is treated as a completed gift of a present interest from the contributor to the designated beneficiary.[586] Such contributions qualify for the per-donee annual gift tax exclusion ($12,000 for 2006), and, to the extent of such exclusions, also are exempt from the generation-skipping transfer (GST) tax. A contributor may contribute in a single year up to five times the per-donee annual gift tax exclusion amount to a qualified tuition account and, for gift tax and GST tax purposes, treat the contribution as having been made ratably over the five-year period beginning with the calendar year in which the contribution is made.[587]

A distribution from a qualified tuition account or prepaid tuition contract generally is not subject to gift tax or GST tax.[588] Those taxes may apply, however, to a change of designated

---

[582] Sec. 529(c)(3)(B). Any benefit furnished to a designated beneficiary under a qualified tuition account is treated as a distribution to the beneficiary for these purposes. Sec. 529(c)(3)(B)(iv).

[583] Sec. 529(c)(3)(A) and (B)(ii).

[584] Sec. 529(c)(6).

[585] Sec. 529(c)(3)(C)(ii). For this purpose, "member of the family" means, with respect to a designated beneficiary: (1) the spouse of such beneficiary; (2) an individual who bears a relationship to such beneficiary which is described in paragraphs (1) through (8) of section 152(a) (i.e., with respect to the beneficiary, a son, daughter, or a descendant of either; a stepson or stepdaughter; a sibling or stepsibling; a father, mother, or ancestor of either; a stepfather or stepmother; a son or daughter of a brother or sister; a brother or sister of a father or mother; and a son-in-law, daughter-in-law, father-in-law, mother-in-law, brother-in-law, or sister-in-law), or the spouse of any such individual; and (3) the first cousin of such beneficiary. Sec. 529(e)(2).

[586] Sec. 529(c)(2)(A).

[587] Sec. 529(c)(2)(B).

[588] Sec. 529(c)(5)(A).

beneficiary if the new designated beneficiary is in a generation below that of the old beneficiary or if the new beneficiary is not a member of the family of the old beneficiary.[589]

Estate tax treatment

Qualified tuition program account balances or prepaid tuition benefits generally are excluded from the gross estate of any individual.[590] Amounts distributed on account of the death of the designated beneficiary, however, are includible in the designated beneficiary's gross estate.[591] If the contributor elected the special five-year allocation rule for gift tax annual exclusion purposes, any amounts contributed that are allocable to the years within the five-year period remaining after the year of the contributor's death are includible in the contributor's gross estate.[592]

Certain provisions expiring under the Economic Growth and Tax Relief Reconciliation Act of 2001 ("EGTRRA")

The Economic Growth and Tax Relief Reconciliation Act of 2001 ("EGTRRA") made a number of changes to the rules regarding qualified tuition programs. However, in order to comply with reconciliation procedures under the Congressional Budget Act of 1974, EGTRRA included a "sunset" provision, pursuant to which the provisions of the Act expire at the end of 2010. Specifically, EGTRRA's provisions do not apply for taxable, plan, or limitation years beginning after December 31, 2010, or to estates of decedents dying after, or gifts or generation-skipping transfers made after, December 31, 2010. EGTRRA provides that, as of the effective date of the sunset, the Code will be applied as thought EGTRRA had never been enacted.

The provisions of present-law section 529 scheduled to expire by reason of the EGTRRA sunset provision include: (1) the provision that makes qualified withdrawals from qualified tuition accounts exempt from income tax; (2) the repeal of a pre-EGTRRA requirement that there be more than a de minimis penalty imposed on amounts not used for educational purposes and the imposition of the 10-percent additional tax on distributions not used for qualified higher education purposes; (3) a provision permitting certain private educational institutions to establish prepaid tuition programs that qualify under section 529 if they receive a ruling or determination to that effect from the Internal Revenue Service, and if the assets are held in a trust created or organized for the exclusive benefit of designated beneficiaries; (4) certain provisions permitting rollovers from one account to another account; (5) certain rules regarding the treatment of room and board as qualifying expenses; (6) certain rules regarding coordination with Hope and lifetime learning credit provisions; (7) the provision that treats first cousins as members of the

---

[589] Sec. 529(c)(5)(B).

[590] Sec. 529(c)(4)(A).

[591] Sec. 529(c)(4)(B).

[592] Sec. 529(c)(4)(C).

family for purposes of the rollover and change in beneficiary rules; and (8) certain provisions regarding the education expenses of special needs beneficiaries.[593]

Explanation of Provision

Permanently extend EGTRRA modifications to qualified tuition program rules

The provision repeals the sunset provision of EGTRRA insofar as it applies to the EGTRRA modifications to the rules regarding qualified tuition programs. As a result, the provision permanently extends all provisions of EGTRRA that expire at the end of 2010 that relate to qualified tuition programs.

Grant of regulatory authority to Treasury

Present law regarding the transfer tax treatment of qualified tuition program accounts is unclear and in some situations imposes tax in a manner inconsistent with generally applicable transfer tax provisions. In addition, present law creates opportunities for abuse of qualified tuition programs. For example, taxpayers may seek to avoid gift and generation skipping transfer taxes by establishing and contributing to multiple qualified tuition program accounts with different designated beneficiaries (using the provision of section 529 that permits a contributor to contribute up to five times the annual exclusion amount per donee in a single year and treat the contribution as having been made ratably over five years), with the intention of subsequently changing the designated beneficiaries of such accounts to a single, common beneficiary and distributing the entire amount to such beneficiary without further transfer tax consequences. Taxpayers also may seek to use qualified tuition program accounts as retirement accounts with all of the tax benefits but none of the restrictions and requirements of qualified retirement accounts. The provision grants the Secretary broad regulatory authority to clarify the tax treatment of certain transfers and to ensure that qualified tuition program accounts are used for the intended purpose of saving for higher education expenses of the designated beneficiary, including the authority to impose related recordkeeping and reporting requirements. The provision also authorizes the Secretary to limit the persons who may be contributors to a qualified tuition program and to determine any special rules for the operation and Federal tax consequences of such programs if such contributors are not individuals.

Effective Date

The provision is effective on the date of enactment.

---

[593] EGTRRA sec. 402.

TITLE XIV: TARIFF PROVISIONS[594]

A. Suspension of Duties on Liquid Crystal Device (LCD) Panel Assemblies for Use in LCD Direct View Televisions

Present Law

Present law provides for a 4.5 percent ad valorem customs duty on imported liquid crystal device (LCD) panel assemblies for use in LCD direct view televisions from all sources (provided for in subheading 9013.80.90 of the Harmonized Tariff Schedule of the United States).

Explanation of Provision

The provision suspends the present customs duty applicable to LCD panel assemblies for use in LCD direct view televisions through December 31, 2009.

Effective Date

The provision applies with respect to goods entered, or withdrawn from warehouse for consumption, on or after the 15th day after the date of the enactment.

B. Suspension of Duties on Ceiling Fans

Present Law

Present law provides for a 4.7-percent ad valorem customs duty on imported ceiling fans from all sources (provided for in subheading 8414.51.00 of the Harmonized Tariff Schedule of the United States), but that duty is currently suspended for all imports until December 31, 2006.

Explanation of Provision

The provision extends the current suspension of the customs duty applicable to ceiling fans through December 31, 2009.

Effective Date

The provision applies with respect to goods entered, or withdrawn from warehouse for consumption, on or after the 15th day after the date of the enactment.

---

[594] The description of these provisions, which do not amend the Internal Revenue Code of 1986, was provided to the staff of the Joint Committee on Taxation by staff of the House Committee on Ways and Means and the Senate Committee on Finance.

C. Suspension of Duties on Nuclear Steam Generators, Reactor Vessel Heads and Pressurizers

Present Law

Nuclear steam generators, as classified under heading 9902.84.02 of the Harmonized Tariff Schedule of the United States, enter the United States duty free until December 31, 2008. After December 31, 2008, the duty on nuclear steam generators returns to the column 1 rate of 5.2 percent under subheading 8402.11.00 of the Harmonized Tariff Schedule of the United States.

Nuclear reactor vessel heads and pressurizers, as classified under heading 9902.84.03 of the Harmonized Tariff Schedule of the United States, enter the United States duty free until December 31, 2008. After December 31, 2008, the duty on nuclear reactor vessel heads and pressurizers returns to the column 1 rate of 3.3 percent under subheading 8401.40.00 of the Harmonized Tariff Schedule of the United States.

Explanation of Provision

With respect to imported nuclear steam generators, reactor vessel heads, and pressurizers, that are purchased pursuant to a contract entered into on or before July 31, 2006, the provision extends the present-law suspension of applicable customs duty through December 31, 2010.

Effective Date

The provision is effective with respect to goods entered, or withdrawn from warehouse for consumption, on or after the 15th day after the date of enactment.

D. Suspension of New Shipper Bonding Privilege

Present Law

Once an antidumping or countervailing duty order is in place, importers of subject merchandise are required to post cash deposits to cover the estimated duties. An exception is made for importers of subject merchandise from new shippers (foreign producers or exporters) who were not selling to the United States at the time of the original investigation and who have requested a review of their shipments to determine individual dumping margins or countervailing duty rates. During the pendency of such a review, an importer of subject merchandise from a new shipper may choose to post a bond or security in lieu of a cash deposit of estimated duties.

Explanation of Provision

The provision temporarily suspends the ability of importers of subject merchandise from new shippers to choose to post a bond or security in lieu of a cash deposit of estimated duties during the period beginning on April 1, 2006, through June 30, 2009.

The provision requires the Secretary of the Treasury, in consultation with the Secretary of Commerce and the Secretary of Homeland Security, to submit to the Committee on Ways and Means of the House of Representatives and the Committee on Finance of the Senate a report describing: (1) any major problem encountered in the collection of duties, including any fraudulent activity intended to avoid the payment of duties; (2) an estimate of duties that were uncollected and a description of why the duties were uncollected; and (3) recommendations on any additional action needed to address problems related to the collection of duties.

In addition, the provision requires the Secretary of the Treasury, in consultation with the Secretary of Commerce, the United States Trade Representative, and the Secretary of Homeland Security, to submit to the Committee on Ways and Means of the House of Representatives and the Committee on Finance of the Senate a report containing: (1) recommendations on whether the temporary suspension of the new shipper bonding privilege should be extended beyond June 30, 2009; (2) an assessment of the effectiveness of any administrative measure taken to address problems encountered in the collection of duties from importers of subject merchandise from new shippers; and (3) an assessment of any burden imposed on legitimate trade and commerce by the temporary suspension of the new shipper bonding privilege.

Effective Date

The provision is effective on the date of enactment, and it applies to imports from new shippers during the period beginning on April 1, 2006, through June 30, 2009.

E. Wool Trust Fund and Wool Fabric Duty Suspension

Present Law

Present law enacted in the Trade Act of 2002 and extended in the Miscellaneous Trade Bill of 2004 provides for temporary duty reductions or duty suspensions of certain fabrics made from worsted wool and for payments made under the wool trust fund. The fund consists of three special refund pools for importers of wool fabric, wool yarn, and wool fiber and top, and identifies all persons eligible for the refunds including U.S. manufacturers of these products. The program expires in 2007.

Explanation of Provision

The provision extends the current program for an additional two years until 2009.

Effective Date

The provision is effective on the date of enactment.

F. Miscellaneous Trade and Technical Corrections Provisions

Present Law

Under present law, imports of the goods described in Title I of Division B of the bill enter under the specified Harmonized Tariff Schedule subheading with the associated tariff rate.

Explanation of Provision

The bill includes certain provisions taken from the House-passed H.R. 4944, the Miscellaneous Trade and Technical Corrections Act of 2006, for which there are Senate companions introduced, which suspend or reduce the tariff rate on certain selected products. The provisions also correct government errors or authorize reliquidations of duties related to certain products.

Effective Date

The effective date is the 15th day after the date of enactment.

G. Vessel Repair Duties

Present law

Under present law, section 466(h) of the Tariff Act of 1930 (19 U.S.C. 1466(h)), the cost of equipment, repair parts, and materials that are installed on a vessel documented under the laws of the United States and engaged in the foreign or coasting trade, if the installation is done by members of the regular crew of such vessel while the vessel is on the high seas, is excluded from a 50 percent ad valorem duty.

Explanation of Provision

This provision clarifies that the 50 percent ad valorem duty on vessel repairs excludes the cost of equipment, repair parts, and materials that are installed on a vessel documented under the laws of the United States and engaged in the foreign or coasting trade, if the installation is done by members of the regular crew of such vessel while the vessel is on the high seas, in foreign waters, or in a foreign port, and does not involve foreign shipyard repairs by foreign labor.

Effective Date

The provision is effective on the date of enactment, and it applies to vessel equipment, repair parts, and materials installed on or after April 25, 2001.

H. CAFTA-DR Provisions Related to Agreement Implementation

Present Law

Present law enacted in the Dominican Republic-Central America-United States Free Trade Agreement (CAFTA-DR) Implementation Act allows the President to exercise proclamation authority to implement provisions of the Agreement including tariffs and rules of origin changes, except for rules of origin changes for certain textile and apparel items. Also, current law was drafted under the assumption at the time of enactment of this legislation that the entry into force for all CAFTA-DR countries would be identical including for the purpose of determining the rule of origin covering co-produced products.

Explanation of Provision

The provision extends narrow proclamation authority to the President to implement specific proposed changes to the rules of origin for certain apparel items and certain trade preference level administrative changes as embodied in letters of understanding between the United States and several of the CAFTA-DR countries. For those countries that have not implemented the Agreement and have not negotiated letters of understanding with the United States for rules of origin changes, the provision grants limited proclamation authority to the President to proclaim changes yet to be agreed upon related to rules of origin for articles containing pocketing material, but the President's authority is subject to consultation and layover requirements and Congressional disapproval action. These limitations are considered appropriate given the extraordinary nature of granting open-ended proclamation authority to a President in this sensitive product area.

In addition, the provision provides a technical correction with respect to application of a retroactive effective date for certain liquidations and reliquidations of co-produced products. The provision also creates a reporting requirement for the U.S. Trade Representative's Office on the status of negotiations related to other CAFTA-DR textile changes concerning socks and technical corrections.

Effective Date

The effective date is the date of enactment, and the apparel proclamation authority extends until December 31, 2007.

H. R. 4

AN ACT

To provide economic security for all Americans, and for
other purposes.

1   *Be it enacted by the Senate and House of Representa-*

2   *tives of the United States of America in Congress assembled,*

3   **SECTION 1. SHORT TITLE AND TABLE OF CONTENTS.**

4   (a) SHORT TITLE.—This Act may be cited as the

5   "Pension Protection Act of 2006".

1   (b) TABLE OF CONTENTS.—The table of contents for

2 this Act (other than so much of title XIV as follows section

3 1401) is as follows:

4

TITLE I—REFORM OF FUNDING RULES FOR SINGLE-EMPLOYER DEFINED BENEFIT PENSION PLANS

Subtitle A—Amendments to Employee Retirement Income Security Act of 1974

SEC. 101. MINIMUM FUNDING STANDARDS.

(a) REPEAL OF EXISTING FUNDING RULES.—Sections 302 through 308 of the Employee Retirement Income Security Act of 1974 (29 U.S.C. 1082 through 1086) are repealed.

(b) NEW MINIMUM FUNDING STANDARDS.—Part 3 of subtitle B of title I of such Act (as amended by subsection (a)) is amended by inserting after section 301 the following new section:

"SEC. 302. MINIMUM FUNDING STANDARDS.

"(a) REQUIREMENT TO MEET MINIMUM FUNDING STANDARD.—

"(1) IN GENERAL.—A plan to which this part applies shall satisfy the minimum funding standard applicable to the plan for any plan year.

"(2) MINIMUM FUNDING STANDARD.—For purposes of paragraph (1), a plan shall be treated as satisfying the minimum funding standard for a plan year if—

  "(A) in the case of a defined benefit plan which is a single-employer plan, the employer makes contributions to or under the plan for the plan year which, in the aggregate, are not less than the minimum required contribution determined under section 303 for the plan for the plan year,

  "(B) in the case of a money purchase plan which is a single employer plan, the employer makes contributions to or under the plan for the plan year which are required under the terms of the plan, and

  "(C) in the case of a multiemployer plan, the employers make contributions to or under the plan for any plan year which, in the aggregate, are sufficient to ensure that the plan does not have an accumulated funding deficiency under section 304 as of the end of the plan year.

"(b) LIABILITY FOR CONTRIBUTIONS.—

  "(1) IN GENERAL.—Except as provided in paragraph (2), the amount of any contribution required by this section (including any required installments

under paragraphs (3) and (4) of section 303(j))
shall be paid by the employer responsible for making
contributions to or under the plan.

"(2) JOINT AND SEVERAL LIABILITY WHERE
EMPLOYER MEMBER OF CONTROLLED GROUP.—If
the employer referred to in paragraph (1) is a member of a controlled group, each member of such
group shall be jointly and severally liable for payment of such contributions.

"(c) VARIANCE FROM MINIMUM FUNDING STAND-
ARDS.—

"(1) WAIVER IN CASE OF BUSINESS HARD-
SHIP.—

"(A) IN GENERAL.—If—

"(i) an employer is (or in the case of
a multiemployer plan, 10 percent or more
of the number of employers contributing to
or under the plan is) unable to satisfy the
minimum funding standard for a plan year
without temporary substantial business
hardship (substantial business hardship in
the case of a multiemployer plan), and

"(ii) application of the standard would
be adverse to the interests of plan participants in the aggregate,

1   the Secretary of the Treasury may, subject to

2   subparagraph (C), waive the requirements of

3   subsection (a) for such year with respect to all

4   or any portion of the minimum funding stand-

5   ard. The Secretary of the Treasury shall not

6   waive the minimum funding standard with re-

7   spect to a plan for more than 3 of any 15 (5

8   of any 15 in the case of a multiemployer plan)

9   consecutive plan years.

10   "(B) EFFECTS OF WAIVER.—If a waiver is

11   granted under subparagraph (A) for any plan

12   year—

13   "(i) in the case of a single-employer

14   plan, the minimum required contribution

15   under section 303 for the plan year shall

16   be reduced by the amount of the waived

17   funding deficiency and such amount shall

18   be amortized as required under section

19   303(e), and

20   "(ii) in the case of a multiemployer

21   plan, the funding standard account shall

22   be credited under section 304(b)(3)(C)

23   with the amount of the waived funding de-

24   ficiency and such amount shall be amor-

1   tized as required under section

2   304(b)(2)(C).

3   "(C) WAIVER OF AMORTIZED PORTION

4   NOT ALLOWED.—The Secretary of the Treasury

5   may not waive under subparagraph (A) any

6   portion of the minimum funding standard

7   under subsection (a) for a plan year which is

8   attributable to any waived funding deficiency

9   for any preceding plan year.

10   "(2) DETERMINATION OF BUSINESS HARD-

11 SHIP.—For purposes of this subsection, the factors

12 taken into account in determining temporary sub-

13 stantial business hardship (substantial business

14 hardship in the case of a multiemployer plan) shall

15 include (but shall not be limited to) whether or

16 not—

17   "(A) the employer is operating at an eco-

18   nomic loss,

19   "(B) there is substantial unemployment or

20   underemployment in the trade or business and

21   in the industry concerned,

22   "(C) the sales and profits of the industry

23   concerned are depressed or declining, and

1   "(D) it is reasonable to expect that the

2   plan will be continued only if the waiver is

3   granted.

4   "(3) WAIVED FUNDING DEFICIENCY.—For pur-

5 poses of this part, the term 'waived funding defi-

6 ciency' means the portion of the minimum funding

7 standard under subsection (a) (determined without

8 regard to the waiver) for a plan year waived by the

9 Secretary of the Treasury and not satisfied by em-

10 ployer contributions.

11   "(4) SECURITY FOR WAIVERS FOR SINGLE-EM-

12 PLOYER PLANS, CONSULTATIONS.—

13   "(A) SECURITY MAY BE REQUIRED.—

14   "(i) IN GENERAL.—Except as pro-

15   vided in subparagraph (C), the Secretary

16   of the Treasury may require an employer

17   maintaining a defined benefit plan which is

18   a single-employer plan (within the meaning

19   of section 4001(a)(15)) to provide security

20   to such plan as a condition for granting or

21   modifying a waiver under paragraph (1).

22   "(ii) SPECIAL RULES.—Any security

23   provided under clause (i) may be perfected

24   and enforced only by the Pension Benefit

25   Guaranty Corporation, or at the direction

1   of the Corporation, by a contributing spon-

2   sor (within the meaning of section

3   4001(a)(13)), or a member of such spon-

4   sor's controlled group (within the meaning

5   of section 4001(a)(14)).

6   ''(B) CONSULTATION WITH THE PENSION

7 BENEFIT GUARANTY CORPORATION.—Except as

8 provided in subparagraph (C), the Secretary of

9 the Treasury shall, before granting or modi-

10 fying a waiver under this subsection with re-

11 spect to a plan described in subparagraph

12 (A)(i)—

13   ''(i) provide the Pension Benefit

14 Guaranty Corporation with—

15   ''(I) notice of the completed ap-

16 plication for any waiver or modifica-

17 tion, and

18   ''(II) an opportunity to comment

19 on such application within 30 days

20 after receipt of such notice, and

21   ''(ii) consider—

22   ''(I) any comments of the Cor-

23 poration under clause (i)(II), and

24   ''(II) any views of any employee

25 organization (within the meaning of

section 3(4)) representing participants in the plan which are submitted in writing to the Secretary of the Treasury in connection with such application.

Information provided to the Corporation under this subparagraph shall be considered tax return information and subject to the safeguarding and reporting requirements of section 6103(p) of the Internal Revenue Code of 1986.

"(C) EXCEPTION FOR CERTAIN WAIVERS.—

"(i) IN GENERAL.—The preceding provisions of this paragraph shall not apply to any plan with respect to which the sum of—

"(I) the aggregate unpaid minimum required contributions for the plan year and all preceding plan years, and

"(II) the present value of all waiver amortization installments determined for the plan year and succeeding plan years under section 303(e)(2),

1   is less than $1,000,000.

2   "(ii) TREATMENT OF WAIVERS FOR

3   WHICH APPLICATIONS ARE PENDING.—The

4   amount described in clause (i)(I) shall in-

5   clude any increase in such amount which

6   would result if all applications for waivers

7   of the minimum funding standard under

8   this subsection which are pending with re-

9   spect to such plan were denied.

10   "(iii) UNPAID MINIMUM REQUIRED

11   CONTRIBUTION.—For purposes of this sub-

12   paragraph—

13   "(I) IN GENERAL.—The term

14   'unpaid minimum required contribu-

15   tion' means, with respect to any plan

16   year, any minimum required contribu-

17   tion under section 303 for the plan

18   year which is not paid on or before

19   the due date (as determined under

20   section 303(j)(1)) for the plan year.

21   "(II) ORDERING RULE.—For

22   purposes of subclause (I), any pay-

23   ment to or under a plan for any plan

24   year shall be allocated first to unpaid

25   minimum required contributions for

17

all preceding plan years on a first-in, first-out basis and then to the minimum required contribution under section 303 for the plan year.

"(5) SPECIAL RULES FOR SINGLE-EMPLOYER PLANS.—

"(A) APPLICATION MUST BE SUBMITTED BEFORE DATE 2½ MONTHS AFTER CLOSE OF YEAR.—In the case of a single-employer plan, no waiver may be granted under this subsection with respect to any plan for any plan year unless an application therefor is submitted to the Secretary of the Treasury not later than the 15th day of the 3rd month beginning after the close of such plan year.

"(B) SPECIAL RULE IF EMPLOYER IS MEMBER OF CONTROLLED GROUP.—In the case of a single-employer plan, if an employer is a member of a controlled group, the temporary substantial business hardship requirements of paragraph (1) shall be treated as met only if such requirements are met—

"(i) with respect to such employer, and

1   "(ii) with respect to the controlled

2   group of which such employer is a member

3   (determined by treating all members of

4   such group as a single employer).

5   The Secretary of the Treasury may provide that

6 an analysis of a trade or business or industry

7 of a member need not be conducted if such Sec-

8 retary determines such analysis is not necessary

9 because the taking into account of such member

10 would not significantly affect the determination

11 under this paragraph.

12   "(6) ADVANCE NOTICE.—

13   "(A) IN GENERAL.—The Secretary of the

14 Treasury shall, before granting a waiver under

15 this subsection, require each applicant to pro-

16 vide evidence satisfactory to such Secretary that

17 the applicant has provided notice of the filing of

18 the application for such waiver to each affected

19 party (as defined in section 4001(a)(21)). Such

20 notice shall include a description of the extent

21 to which the plan is funded for benefits which

22 are guaranteed under title IV and for benefit li-

23 abilities.

24   "(B) CONSIDERATION OF RELEVANT IN-

25 FORMATION.—The Secretary of the Treasury

1 shall consider any relevant information provided

2 by a person to whom notice was given under

3 subparagraph (A).

4 "(7) RESTRICTION ON PLAN AMENDMENTS.—

5 "(A) IN GENERAL.—No amendment of a

6 plan which increases the liabilities of the plan

7 by reason of any increase in benefits, any

8 change in the accrual of benefits, or any change

9 in the rate at which benefits become nonforfeit-

10 able under the plan shall be adopted if a waiver

11 under this subsection or an extension of time

12 under section 304(d) is in effect with respect to

13 the plan, or if a plan amendment described in

14 subsection (d)(2) has been made at any time in

15 the preceding 12 months (24 months in the

16 case of a multiemployer plan). If a plan is

17 amended in violation of the preceding sentence,

18 any such waiver, or extension of time, shall not

19 apply to any plan year ending on or after the

20 date on which such amendment is adopted.

21 "(B) EXCEPTION.—Subparagraph (A)

22 shall not apply to any plan amendment which—

23 "(i) the Secretary of the Treasury de-

24 termines to be reasonable and which pro-

1   vides for only de minimis increases in the

2   liabilities of the plan,

3   "(ii) only repeals an amendment de-

4   scribed in subsection (d)(2), or

5   "(iii) is required as a condition of

6   qualification under part I of subchapter D

7   of chapter 1 of the Internal Revenue Code

8   of 1986.

9   "(8) CROSS REFERENCE.—For corresponding

10 duties of the Secretary of the Treasury with regard

11 to implementation of the Internal Revenue Code of

12 1986, see section 412(c) of such Code.

13 "(d) MISCELLANEOUS RULES.—

14   "(1) CHANGE IN METHOD OR YEAR.—If the

15 funding method, the valuation date, or a plan year

16 for a plan is changed, the change shall take effect

17 only if approved by the Secretary of the Treasury.

18   "(2) CERTAIN RETROACTIVE PLAN AMEND-

19 MENTS.—For purposes of this section, any amend-

20 ment applying to a plan year which—

21   "(A) is adopted after the close of such plan

22   year but no later than 2½ months after the

23   close of the plan year (or, in the case of a mul-

24   tiemployer plan, no later than 2 years after the

25   close of such plan year),

1   "(B) does not reduce the accrued benefit

2   of any participant determined as of the begin-

3   ning of the first plan year to which the amend-

4   ment applies, and

5   "(C) does not reduce the accrued benefit of

6   any participant determined as of the time of

7   adoption except to the extent required by the

8   circumstances,

9 shall, at the election of the plan administrator, be

10 deemed to have been made on the first day of such

11 plan year. No amendment described in this para-

12 graph which reduces the accrued benefits of any par-

13 ticipant shall take effect unless the plan adminis-

14 trator files a notice with the Secretary of the Treas-

15 ury notifying him of such amendment and such Sec-

16 retary has approved such amendment, or within 90

17 days after the date on which such notice was filed,

18 failed to disapprove such amendment. No amend-

19 ment described in this subsection shall be approved

20 by the Secretary of the Treasury unless such Sec-

21 retary determines that such amendment is necessary

22 because of a temporary substantial business hard-

23 ship (as determined under subsection (c)(2)) or a

24 substantial business hardship (as so determined) in

25 the case of a multiemployer plan and that a waiver

1   under subsection (c) (or, in the case of a multiem-

2   ployer plan, any extension of the amortization period

3   under section 304(d)) is unavailable or inadequate.

4   "(3) CONTROLLED GROUP.—For purposes of

5   this section, the term 'controlled group' means any

6   group treated as a single employer under subsection

7   (b), (c), (m), or (o) of section 414 of the Internal

8   Revenue Code of 1986.".

9   (c) CLERICAL AMENDMENT.—The table of contents

10 in section 1 of such Act is amended by striking the items

11 relating to sections 302 through 308 and inserting the fol-

12 lowing new item:

"Sec. 302. Minimum funding standards.".

13   (d) EFFECTIVE DATE.—The amendments made by

14 this section shall apply to plan years beginning after 2007.

15 **SEC. 102. FUNDING RULES FOR SINGLE-EMPLOYER DE-**

16   **FINED BENEFIT PENSION PLANS.**

17   (a) IN GENERAL.—Part 3 of subtitle B of title I of

18 the Employee Retirement Income Security Act of 1974 (as

19 amended by section 101 of this Act) is amended by insert-

20 ing after section 302 the following new section:

21 **"SEC. 303. MINIMUM FUNDING STANDARDS FOR SINGLE-**

22   **EMPLOYER DEFINED BENEFIT PENSION**

23   **PLANS.**

24   "(a) MINIMUM REQUIRED CONTRIBUTION.—For

25 purposes of this section and section 302(a)(2)(A), except

1 as provided in subsection (f), the term 'minimum required

2 contribution' means, with respect to any plan year of a

3 single-employer plan—

4   "(1) in any case in which the value of plan as-

5   sets of the plan (as reduced under subsection

6   (f)(4)(B)) is less than the funding target of the plan

7   for the plan year, the sum of—

8   "(A) the target normal cost of the plan for

9   the plan year,

10   "(B) the shortfall amortization charge (if

11   any) for the plan for the plan year determined

12   under subsection (c), and

13   "(C) the waiver amortization charge (if

14   any) for the plan for the plan year as deter-

15   mined under subsection (e); or

16   "(2) in any case in which the value of plan as-

17   sets of the plan (as reduced under subsection

18   (f)(4)(B)) equals or exceeds the funding target of

19   the plan for the plan year, the target normal cost of

20   the plan for the plan year reduced (but not below

21   zero) by such excess.

22   "(b) TARGET NORMAL COST.—For purposes of this

23 section, except as provided in subsection (i)(2) with re-

24 spect to plans in at-risk status, the term 'target normal

25 cost' means, for any plan year, the present value of all

1 benefits which are expected to accrue or to be earned

2 under the plan during the plan year. For purposes of this

3 subsection, if any benefit attributable to services per-

4 formed in a preceding plan year is increased by reason

5 of any increase in compensation during the current plan

6 year, the increase in such benefit shall be treated as hav-

7 ing accrued during the current plan year.

8   "(c) SHORTFALL AMORTIZATION CHARGE.—

9   "(1) IN GENERAL.—For purposes of this sec-

10   tion, the shortfall amortization charge for a plan for

11   any plan year is the aggregate total (not less than

12   zero) of the shortfall amortization installments for

13   such plan year with respect to the shortfall amorti-

14   zation bases for such plan year and each of the 6

15   preceding plan years.

16   "(2) SHORTFALL AMORTIZATION INSTALL-

17   MENT.—For purposes of paragraph (1)—

18   "(A) DETERMINATION.—The shortfall am-

19   ortization installments are the amounts nec-

20   essary to amortize the shortfall amortization

21   base of the plan for any plan year in level an-

22   nual installments over the 7-plan-year period

23   beginning with such plan year.

24   "(B) SHORTFALL INSTALLMENT.—The

25   shortfall amortization installment for any plan

1   year in the 7-plan-year period under subpara-
2   graph (A) with respect to any shortfall amorti-
3   zation base is the annual installment deter-
4   mined under subparagraph (A) for that year for
5   that base.

6   "(C) SEGMENT RATES.—In determining
7   any shortfall amortization installment under
8   this paragraph, the plan sponsor shall use the
9   segment rates determined under subparagraph
10   (C) of subsection (h)(2), applied under rules
11   similar to the rules of subparagraph (B) of sub-
12   section (h)(2).

13   "(3) SHORTFALL AMORTIZATION BASE.—For
14   purposes of this section, the shortfall amortization
15   base of a plan for a plan year is—

16   "(A) the funding shortfall of such plan for
17   such plan year, minus

18   "(B) the present value (determined using
19   the segment rates determined under subpara-
20   graph (C) of subsection (h)(2), applied under
21   rules similar to the rules of subparagraph (B)
22   of subsection (h)(2)) of the aggregate total of
23   the shortfall amortization installments and
24   waiver amortization installments which have
25   been determined for such plan year and any

1 succeeding plan year with respect to the short-

2 fall amortization bases and waiver amortization

3 bases of the plan for any plan year preceding

4 such plan year.

5 "(4) FUNDING SHORTFALL.—For purposes of

6 this section, the funding shortfall of a plan for any

7 plan year is the excess (if any) of—

8 "(A) the funding target of the plan for the

9 plan year, over

10 "(B) the value of plan assets of the plan

11 (as reduced under subsection (f)(4)(B)) for the

12 plan year which are held by the plan on the

13 valuation date.

14 "(5) EXEMPTION FROM NEW SHORTFALL AM-

15 ORTIZATION BASE.—

16 "(A) IN GENERAL.—In any case in which

17 the value of plan assets of the plan (as reduced

18 under subsection (f)(4)(A)) is equal to or great-

19 er than the funding target of the plan for the

20 plan year, the shortfall amortization base of the

21 plan for such plan year shall be zero.

22 "(B) TRANSITION RULE.—

23 "(i) IN GENERAL.—Except as pro-

24 vided in clauses (iii) and (iv), in the case

25 of plan years beginning after 2007 and be-

1   fore 2011, only the applicable percentage

2   of the funding target shall be taken into

3   account under paragraph (3)(A) in deter-

4   mining the funding shortfall for the plan

5   year for purposes of subparagraph (A).

6   "(ii) APPLICABLE PERCENTAGE.—For

7   purposes of subparagraph (A), the applica-

8   ble percentage shall be determined in ac-

9   cordance with the following table:

"In the case of a plan year beginning in calendar year:	The applicable percentage is
2008	92
2009	94
2010	96.

10   "(iii) LIMITATION.—Clause (i) shall

11   not apply with respect to any plan year

12   after 2008 unless the shortfall amortiza-

13   tion base for each of the preceding years

14   beginning after 2007 was zero (determined

15   after application of this subparagraph).

16   "(iv) TRANSITION RELIEF NOT AVAIL-

17   ABLE FOR NEW OR DEFICIT REDUCTION

18   PLANS.—Clause (i) shall not apply to a

19   plan—

20   "(I) which was not in effect for a

21   plan year beginning in 2007, or

22   "(II) which was in effect for a

23   plan year beginning in 2007 and

1   which was subject to section 302(d)

2   (as in effect for plan years beginning

3   in 2007), determined after the appli-

4   cation of paragraphs (6) and (9)

5   thereof.

6   "(6) EARLY DEEMED AMORTIZATION UPON AT-

7 TAINMENT OF FUNDING TARGET.—In any case in

8 which the funding shortfall of a plan for a plan year

9 is zero, for purposes of determining the shortfall am-

10 ortization charge for such plan year and succeeding

11 plan years, the shortfall amortization bases for all

12 preceding plan years (and all shortfall amortization

13 installments determined with respect to such bases)

14 shall be reduced to zero.

15 "(d) RULES RELATING TO FUNDING TARGET.—For

16 purposes of this section—

17   "(1) FUNDING TARGET.—Except as provided in

18 subsection (i)(1) with respect to plans in at-risk sta-

19 tus, the funding target of a plan for a plan year is

20 the present value of all benefits accrued or earned

21 under the plan as of the beginning of the plan year.

22   "(2) FUNDING TARGET ATTAINMENT PERCENT-

23 AGE.—The 'funding target attainment percentage' of

24 a plan for a plan year is the ratio (expressed as a

25 percentage) which—

"(A) the value of plan assets for the plan year (as reduced under subsection (f)(4)(B)), bears to

"(B) the funding target of the plan for the plan year (determined without regard to subsection (i)(1)).

"(e) WAIVER AMORTIZATION CHARGE.—

"(1) DETERMINATION OF WAIVER AMORTIZATION CHARGE.—The waiver amortization charge (if any) for a plan for any plan year is the aggregate total of the waiver amortization installments for such plan year with respect to the waiver amortization bases for each of the 5 preceding plan years.

"(2) WAIVER AMORTIZATION INSTALLMENT.— For purposes of paragraph (1)—

"(A) DETERMINATION.—The waiver amortization installments are the amounts necessary to amortize the waiver amortization base of the plan for any plan year in level annual installments over a period of 5 plan years beginning with the succeeding plan year.

"(B) WAIVER INSTALLMENT.—The waiver amortization installment for any plan year in the 5-year period under subparagraph (A) with respect to any waiver amortization base is the

1   annual installment determined under subpara-

2   graph (A) for that year for that base.

3   "(3) INTEREST RATE.—In determining any

4   waiver amortization installment under this sub-

5   section, the plan sponsor shall use the segment rates

6   determined under subparagraph (C) of subsection

7   (h)(2), applied under rules similar to the rules of

8   subparagraph (B) of subsection (h)(2).

9   "(4) WAIVER AMORTIZATION BASE.—The waiv-

10   er amortization base of a plan for a plan year is the

11   amount of the waived funding deficiency (if any) for

12   such plan year under section 302(c).

13   "(5) EARLY DEEMED AMORTIZATION UPON AT-

14   TAINMENT OF FUNDING TARGET.—In any case in

15   which the funding shortfall of a plan for a plan year

16   is zero, for purposes of determining the waiver am-

17   ortization charge for such plan year and succeeding

18   plan years, the waiver amortization bases for all pre-

19   ceding plan years (and all waiver amortization in-

20   stallments determined with respect to such bases)

21   shall be reduced to zero.

22   "(f) REDUCTION OF MINIMUM REQUIRED CONTRIBU-

23   TION BY PREFUNDING BALANCE AND FUNDING STAND-

24   ARD CARRYOVER BALANCE.—

25   "(1) ELECTION TO MAINTAIN BALANCES.—

1   "(A) PREFUNDING BALANCE.—The plan

2   sponsor of a single-employer plan may elect to

3   maintain a prefunding balance.

4   "(B) FUNDING STANDARD CARRYOVER

5   BALANCE.—

6   "(i) IN GENERAL.—In the case of a

7   single-employer plan described in clause

8   (ii), the plan sponsor may elect to maintain

9   a funding standard carryover balance, until

10   such balance is reduced to zero.

11   "(ii) PLANS MAINTAINING FUNDING

12   STANDARD ACCOUNT IN 2007.—A plan is

13   described in this clause if the plan—

14   "(I) was in effect for a plan year

15   beginning in 2007, and

16   "(II) had a positive balance in

17   the funding standard account under

18   section 302(b) as in effect for such

19   plan year and determined as of the

20   end of such plan year.

21   "(2) APPLICATION OF BALANCES.—A

22   prefunding balance and a funding standard carry-

23   over balance maintained pursuant to this para-

24   graph—

1   "(A) shall be available for crediting against

2   the minimum required contribution, pursuant to

3   an election under paragraph (3),

4   "(B) shall be applied as a reduction in the

5   amount treated as the value of plan assets for

6   purposes of this section, to the extent provided

7   in paragraph (4), and

8   "(C) may be reduced at any time, pursu-

9   ant to an election under paragraph (5).

10   "(3) ELECTION TO APPLY BALANCES AGAINST

11 MINIMUM REQUIRED CONTRIBUTION.—

12   "(A) IN GENERAL.—Except as provided in

13   subparagraphs (B) and (C), in the case of any

14   plan year in which the plan sponsor elects to

15   credit against the minimum required contribu-

16   tion for the current plan year all or a portion

17   of the prefunding balance or the funding stand-

18   ard carryover balance for the current plan year

19   (not in excess of such minimum required con-

20   tribution), the minimum required contribution

21   for the plan year shall be reduced as of the first

22   day of the plan year by the amount so credited

23   by the plan sponsor. For purposes of the pre-

24   ceding sentence, the minimum required con-

1   tribution shall be determined after taking into

2   account any waiver under section 302(c).

3   "(B) COORDINATION WITH FUNDING

4   STANDARD CARRYOVER BALANCE.—To the ex-

5   tent that any plan has a funding standard car-

6   ryover balance greater than zero, no amount of

7   the prefunding balance of such plan may be

8   credited under this paragraph in reducing the

9   minimum required contribution.

10   "(C) LIMITATION FOR UNDERFUNDED

11   PLANS.—The preceding provisions of this para-

12   graph shall not apply for any plan year if the

13   ratio (expressed as a percentage) which—

14   "(i) the value of plan assets for the

15   preceding plan year (as reduced under

16   paragraph (4)(C)), bears to

17   "(ii) the funding target of the plan for

18   the preceding plan year (determined with-

19   out regard to subsection (i)(1)),

20   is less than 80 percent. In the case of plan

21   years beginning in 2008, the ratio under this

22   subparagraph may be determined using such

23   methods of estimation as the Secretary of the

24   Treasury may prescribe.

"(4) EFFECT OF BALANCES ON AMOUNTS
TREATED AS VALUE OF PLAN ASSETS.—In the case
of any plan maintaining a prefunding balance or a
funding standard carryover balance pursuant to this
subsection, the amount treated as the value of plan
assets shall be deemed to be such amount, reduced
as provided in the following subparagraphs:

"(A) APPLICABILITY OF SHORTFALL AM-
ORTIZATION BASE.—For purposes of subsection
(c)(5), the value of plan assets is deemed to be
such amount, reduced by the amount of the
prefunding balance, but only if an election
under paragraph (2) applying any portion of
the prefunding balance in reducing the minimum required contribution is in effect for the
plan year.

"(B) DETERMINATION OF EXCESS ASSETS,
FUNDING SHORTFALL, AND FUNDING TARGET
ATTAINMENT PERCENTAGE.—

"(i) IN GENERAL.—For purposes of
subsections (a), (c)(4)(B), and (d)(2)(A),
the value of plan assets is deemed to be
such amount, reduced by the amount of
the prefunding balance and the funding
standard carryover balance.

"(ii) SPECIAL RULE FOR CERTAIN BINDING AGREEMENTS WITH PBGC.—For purposes of subsection (c)(4)(B), the value of plan assets shall not be deemed to be reduced for a plan year by the amount of the specified balance if, with respect to such balance, there is in effect for a plan year a binding written agreement with the Pension Benefit Guaranty Corporation which provides that such balance is not available to reduce the minimum required contribution for the plan year. For purposes of the preceding sentence, the term 'specified balance' means the prefunding balance or the funding standard carryover balance, as the case may be.

"(C) AVAILABILITY OF BALANCES IN PLAN YEAR FOR CREDITING AGAINST MINIMUM REQUIRED CONTRIBUTION.—For purposes of paragraph (3)(C)(i) of this subsection, the value of plan assets is deemed to be such amount, reduced by the amount of the prefunding balance.

"(5) ELECTION TO REDUCE BALANCE PRIOR TO DETERMINATIONS OF VALUE OF PLAN ASSETS AND

CREDITING AGAINST MINIMUM REQUIRED CONTRIBU-
TION.—

"(A) IN GENERAL.—The plan sponsor may
elect to reduce by any amount the balance of
the prefunding balance and the funding standard carryover balance for any plan year (but
not below zero). Such reduction shall be effective prior to any determination of the value of
plan assets for such plan year under this section and application of the balance in reducing
the minimum required contribution for such
plan for such plan year pursuant to an election
under paragraph (2).

"(B) COORDINATION BETWEEN
PREFUNDING BALANCE AND FUNDING STAND-
ARD CARRYOVER BALANCE.—To the extent that
any plan has a funding standard carryover balance greater than zero, no election may be
made under subparagraph (A) with respect to
the prefunding balance.

"(6) PREFUNDING BALANCE.—

"(A) IN GENERAL.—A prefunding balance
maintained by a plan shall consist of a beginning balance of zero, increased and decreased to
the extent provided in subparagraphs (B) and

(C), and adjusted further as provided in paragraph (8).

"(B) INCREASES.—

"(i) IN GENERAL.—As of the first day of each plan year beginning after 2008, the prefunding balance of a plan shall be increased by the amount elected by the plan sponsor for the plan year. Such amount shall not exceed the excess (if any) of—

"(I) the aggregate total of employer contributions to the plan for the preceding plan year, over—

"(II) the minimum required contribution for such preceding plan year.

"(ii) ADJUSTMENTS FOR INTEREST.—Any excess contributions under clause (i) shall be properly adjusted for interest accruing for the periods between the first day of the current plan year and the dates on which the excess contributions were made, determined by using the effective interest rate for the preceding plan year and by treating contributions as being first used to satisfy the minimum required contribution.

1   "(iii) CERTAIN CONTRIBUTIONS NEC-

2   ESSARY TO AVOID BENEFIT LIMITATIONS

3   DISREGARDED.—The excess described in

4   clause (i) with respect to any preceding

5   plan year shall be reduced (but not below

6   zero) by the amount of contributions an

7   employer would be required to make under

8   paragraph (1), (2), or (4) of section 206(g)

9   to avoid a benefit limitation which would

10   otherwise be imposed under such para-

11   graph for the preceding plan year. Any

12   contribution which may be taken into ac-

13   count in satisfying the requirements of

14   more than 1 of such paragraphs shall be

15   taken into account only once for purposes

16   of this clause.

17   "(C) DECREASE.—The prefunding balance

18   of a plan shall be decreased (but not below

19   zero) by—

20   "(i) as of the first day of each plan

21   year after 2008, the amount of such bal-

22   ance credited under paragraph (2) (if any)

23   in reducing the minimum required con-

24   tribution of the plan for the preceding plan

25   year, and

"(ii) as of the time specified in paragraph (5))(A), any reduction in such balance elected under paragraph (5).

"(7) FUNDING STANDARD CARRYOVER BALANCE.—

"(A) IN GENERAL.—A funding standard carryover balance maintained by a plan shall consist of a beginning balance determined under subparagraph (B), decreased to the extent provided in subparagraph (C), and adjusted further as provided in paragraph (8).

"(B) BEGINNING BALANCE.—The beginning balance of the funding standard carryover balance shall be the positive balance described in paragraph (1)(B)(ii)(II).

"(C) DECREASES.—The funding standard carryover balance of a plan shall be decreased (but not below zero) by—

"(i) as of the first day of each plan year after 2008, the amount of such balance credited under paragraph (2) (if any) in reducing the minimum required contribution of the plan for the preceding plan year, and

1   "(ii) as of the time specified in para-

2   graph (5))(A), any reduction in such bal-

3   ance elected under paragraph (5).

4   "(8) ADJUSTMENTS FOR INVESTMENT EXPERI-

5 ENCE.—In determining the prefunding balance or

6 the funding standard carryover balance of a plan as

7 of the first day of the plan year, the plan sponsor

8 shall, in accordance with regulations prescribed by

9 the Secretary of the Treasury, adjust such balance

10 to reflect the rate of return on plan assets for the

11 preceding plan year. Notwithstanding subsection

12 (g)(3), such rate of return shall be determined on

13 the basis of fair market value and shall properly

14 take into account, in accordance with such regula-

15 tions, all contributions, distributions, and other plan

16 payments made during such period.

17   "(9) ELECTIONS.—Elections under this sub-

18 section shall be made at such times, and in such

19 form and manner, as shall be prescribed in regula-

20 tions of the Secretary of the Treasury.

21   "(g) VALUATION OF PLAN ASSETS AND LIABIL-

22 ITIES.—

23   "(1) TIMING OF DETERMINATIONS.—Except as

24 otherwise provided under this subsection, all deter-

25 minations under this section for a plan year shall be

made as of the valuation date of the plan for such plan year.

"(2) VALUATION DATE.—For purposes of this section—

"(A) IN GENERAL.—Except as provided in subparagraph (B), the valuation date of a plan for any plan year shall be the first day of the plan year.

"(B) EXCEPTION FOR SMALL PLANS.—If, on each day during the preceding plan year, a plan had 100 or fewer participants, the plan may designate any day during the plan year as its valuation date for such plan year and succeeding plan years. For purposes of this subparagraph, all defined benefit plans which are single-employer plans and are maintained by the same employer (or any member of such employer's controlled group) shall be treated as 1 plan, but only participants with respect to such employer or member shall be taken into account.

"(C) APPLICATION OF CERTAIN RULES IN DETERMINATION OF PLAN SIZE.—For purposes of this paragraph—

1   "(i) PLANS NOT IN EXISTENCE IN
2   PRECEDING YEAR.—In the case of the first
3   plan year of any plan, subparagraph (B)
4   shall apply to such plan by taking into ac-
5   count the number of participants that the
6   plan is reasonably expected to have on
7   days during such first plan year.

8   "(ii) PREDECESSORS.—Any reference
9   in subparagraph (B) to an employer shall
10   include a reference to any predecessor of
11   such employer.

12   "(3) DETERMINATION OF VALUE OF PLAN AS-
13   SETS.—For purposes of this section—

14   "(A) IN GENERAL.—Except as provided in
15   subparagraph (B), the value of plan assets shall
16   be the fair market value of the assets.

17   "(B) AVERAGING ALLOWED.—A plan may
18   determine the value of plan assets on the basis
19   of the averaging of fair market values, but only
20   if such method—

21   "(i) is permitted under regulations
22   prescribed by the Secretary of the Treas-
23   ury,

24   "(ii) does not provide for averaging of
25   such values over more than the period be-

43

ginning on the last day of the 25th month preceding the month in which the valuation date occurs and ending on the valuation date (or a similar period in the case of a valuation date which is not the 1st day of a month), and

"(iii) does not result in a determination of the value of plan assets which, at any time, is lower than 90 percent or greater than 110 percent of the fair market value of such assets at such time.

Any such averaging shall be adjusted for contributions and distributions (as provided by the Secretary of the Treasury).

"(4) ACCOUNTING FOR CONTRIBUTION RECEIPTS.—For purposes of determining the value of assets under paragraph (3)—

"(A) PRIOR YEAR CONTRIBUTIONS.—If—

"(i) an employer makes any contribution to the plan after the valuation date for the plan year in which the contribution is made, and

"(ii) the contribution is for a preceding plan year,

44

1   the contribution shall be taken into account as

2   an asset of the plan as of the valuation date,

3   except that in the case of any plan year begin-

4   ning after 2008, only the present value (deter-

5   mined as of the valuation date) of such con-

6   tribution may be taken into account. For pur-

7   poses of the preceding sentence, present value

8   shall be determined using the effective interest

9   rate for the preceding plan year to which the

10   contribution is properly allocable.

11   "(B) SPECIAL RULE FOR CURRENT YEAR

12   CONTRIBUTIONS MADE BEFORE VALUATION

13   DATE.—If any contributions for any plan year

14   are made to or under the plan during the plan

15   year but before the valuation date for the plan

16   year, the assets of the plan as of the valuation

17   date shall not include—

18   "(i) such contributions, and

19   "(ii) interest on such contributions for

20   the period between the date of the con-

21   tributions and the valuation date, deter-

22   mined by using the effective interest rate

23   for the plan year.

24   "(h) ACTUARIAL ASSUMPTIONS AND METHODS.—

"(1) IN GENERAL.—Subject to this subsection, the determination of any present value or other computation under this section shall be made on the basis of actuarial assumptions and methods—

"(A) each of which is reasonable (taking into account the experience of the plan and reasonable expectations), and

"(B) which, in combination, offer the actuary's best estimate of anticipated experience under the plan.

"(2) INTEREST RATES.—

"(A) EFFECTIVE INTEREST RATE.—For purposes of this section, the term 'effective interest rate' means, with respect to any plan for any plan year, the single rate of interest which, if used to determine the present value of the plan's accrued or earned benefits referred to in subsection (d)(1), would result in an amount equal to the funding target of the plan for such plan year.

"(B) INTEREST RATES FOR DETERMINING FUNDING TARGET.—For purposes of determining the funding target and normal cost of a plan for any plan year, the interest rate used in

1 determining the present value of the benefits of

2 the plan shall be—

3   "(i) in the case of benefits reasonably

4   determined to be payable during the 5-year

5   period beginning on the first day of the

6   plan year, the first segment rate with re-

7   spect to the applicable month,

8   "(ii) in the case of benefits reasonably

9   determined to be payable during the 15-

10   year period beginning at the end of the pe-

11   riod described in clause (i), the second seg-

12   ment rate with respect to the applicable

13   month, and

14   "(iii) in the case of benefits reason-

15   ably determined to be payable after the pe-

16   riod described in clause (ii), the third seg-

17   ment rate with respect to the applicable

18   month.

19   "(C) SEGMENT RATES.—For purposes of

20 this paragraph—

21   "(i) FIRST SEGMENT RATE.—The

22   term 'first segment rate' means, with re-

23   spect to any month, the single rate of in-

24   terest which shall be determined by the

25   Secretary of the Treasury for such month

1   on the basis of the corporate bond yield

2   curve for such month, taking into account

3   only that portion of such yield curve which

4   is based on bonds maturing during the 5-

5   year period commencing with such month.

6   "(ii) SECOND SEGMENT RATE.—The

7   term 'second segment rate' means, with re-

8   spect to any month, the single rate of in-

9   terest which shall be determined by the

10   Secretary of the Treasury for such month

11   on the basis of the corporate bond yield

12   curve for such month, taking into account

13   only that portion of such yield curve which

14   is based on bonds maturing during the 15-

15   year period beginning at the end of the pe-

16   riod described in clause (i).

17   "(iii) THIRD SEGMENT RATE.—The

18   term 'third segment rate' means, with re-

19   spect to any month, the single rate of in-

20   terest which shall be determined by the

21   Secretary of the Treasury for such month

22   on the basis of the corporate bond yield

23   curve for such month, taking into account

24   only that portion of such yield curve which

25   is based on bonds maturing during periods

1 beginning after the period described in
2 clause (ii).

3 "(D) CORPORATE BOND YIELD CURVE.—
4 For purposes of this paragraph—

5 "(i) IN GENERAL.—The term 'cor-
6 porate bond yield curve' means, with re-
7 spect to any month, a yield curve which is
8 prescribed by the Secretary of the Treas-
9 ury for such month and which reflects the
10 average, for the 24-month period ending
11 with the month preceding such month, of
12 monthly yields on investment grade cor-
13 porate bonds with varying maturities and
14 that are in the top 3 quality levels avail-
15 able.

16 "(ii) ELECTION TO USE YIELD
17 CURVE.—Solely for purposes of deter-
18 mining the minimum required contribution
19 under this section, the plan sponsor may,
20 in lieu of the segment rates determined
21 under subparagraph (C), elect to use inter-
22 est rates under the corporate bond yield
23 curve. For purposes of the preceding sen-
24 tence such curve shall be determined with-
25 out regard to the 24-month averaging de-

1   scribed in clause (i). Such election, once
2   made, may be revoked only with the con-
3   sent of the Secretary of the Treasury.

4   "(E) APPLICABLE MONTH.—For purposes
5   of this paragraph, the term 'applicable month'
6   means, with respect to any plan for any plan
7   year, the month which includes the valuation
8   date of such plan for such plan year or, at the
9   election of the plan sponsor, any of the 4
10   months which precede such month. Any election
11   made under this subparagraph shall apply to
12   the plan year for which the election is made and
13   all succeeding plan years, unless the election is
14   revoked with the consent of the Secretary of the
15   Treasury.

16   "(F) PUBLICATION REQUIREMENTS.—The
17   Secretary of the Treasury shall publish for each
18   month the corporate bond yield curve (and the
19   corporate bond yield curve reflecting the modi-
20   fication described in section
21   205(g)(3)(B)(iii)(I)) for such month and each
22   of the rates determined under subparagraph
23   (B) for such month. The Secretary of the
24   Treasury shall also publish a description of the
25   methodology used to determine such yield curve

1   and such rates which is sufficiently detailed to

2   enable plans to make reasonable projections re-

3   garding the yield curve and such rates for fu-

4   ture months based on the plan's projection of

5   future interest rates.

6   "(G) TRANSITION RULE.—

7   "(i) IN GENERAL.—Notwithstanding

8   the preceding provisions of this paragraph,

9   for plan years beginning in 2008 or 2009,

10   the first, second, or third segment rate for

11   a plan with respect to any month shall be

12   equal to the sum of—

13   "(I) the product of such rate for

14   such month determined without re-

15   gard to this subparagraph, multiplied

16   by the applicable percentage, and

17   "(II) the product of the rate de-

18   termined under the rules of section

19   302(b)(5)(B)(ii)(II) (as in effect for

20   plan years beginning in 2007), multi-

21   plied by a percentage equal to 100

22   percent minus the applicable percent-

23   age.

24   "(ii) APPLICABLE PERCENTAGE.—For

25   purposes of clause (i), the applicable per-

1   centage is 33⅓ percent for plan years be-

2   ginning in 2008 and 66⅔ percent for plan

3   years beginning in 2009.

4   "(iii) NEW PLANS INELIGIBLE.—

5   Clause (i) shall not apply to any plan if the

6   first plan year of the plan begins after De-

7   cember 31, 2007.

8   "(iv) ELECTION.—The plan sponsor

9   may elect not to have this subparagraph

10   apply. Such election, once made, may be

11   revoked only with the consent of the Sec

12   retary of the Treasury.

13   "(3) MORTALITY TABLES.—

14   "(A) IN GENERAL.—Except as provided in

15   subparagraph (C) or (D), the Secretary of the

16   Treasury shall by regulation prescribe mortality

17   tables to be used in determining any present

18   value or making any computation under this

19   section. Such tables shall be based on the actual

20   experience of pension plans and projected

21   trends in such experience. In prescribing such

22   tables, the Secretary of the Treasury shall take

23   into account results of available independent

24   studies of mortality of individuals covered by

25   pension plans.

1   "(B) Periodic revision.—The Secretary

2   of the Treasury shall (at least every 10 years)

3   make revisions in any table in effect under sub-

4   paragraph (A) to reflect the actual experience

5   of pension plans and projected trends in such

6   experience.

7   "(C) Substitute mortality table.—

8   "(i) In general.—Upon request by

9   the plan sponsor and approval by the Sec-

10   retary of the Treasury, a mortality table

11   which meets the requirements of clause

12   (iii) shall be used in determining any

13   present value or making any computation

14   under this section during the period of

15   consecutive plan years (not to exceed 10)

16   specified in the request.

17   "(ii) Early termination of pe-

18   riod.—Notwithstanding clause (i), a mor-

19   tality table described in clause (i) shall

20   cease to be in effect as of the earliest of—

21   "(I) the date on which there is a

22   significant change in the participants

23   in the plan by reason of a plan spinoff

24   or merger or otherwise, or

1   "(II) the date on which the plan

2   actuary determines that such table

3   does not meet the requirements of

4   clause (iii).

5   "(iii) REQUIREMENTS.—A mortality

6 table meets the requirements of this clause

7 if—

8   "(I) there is a sufficient number

9   of plan participants, and the pension

10   plans have been maintained for a suf-

11   ficient period of time, to have credible

12   information necessary for purposes of

13   subclause (II), and

14   "(II) such table reflects the ac-

15   tual experience of the pension plans

16   maintained by the sponsor and pro-

17   jected trends in general mortality ex-

18   perience.

19   "(iv) ALL PLANS IN CONTROLLED

20 GROUP MUST USE SEPARATE TABLE.—Ex-

21 cept as provided by the Secretary of the

22 Treasury, a plan sponsor may not use a

23 mortality table under this subparagraph

24 for any plan maintained by the plan spon-

25 sor unless—

..

54

1   "(I) a separate mortality table is

2   established and used under this sub-

3   paragraph for each other plan main-

4   tained by the plan sponsor and if the

5   plan sponsor is a member of a con-

6   trolled group, each member of the

7   controlled group, and

8   "(II) the requirements of clause

9   (iii) are met separately with respect to

10   the table so established for each such

11   plan, determined by only taking into

12   account the participants of such plan,

13   the time such plan has been in exist-

14   ence, and the actual experience of

15   such plan.

16   "(v) DEADLINE FOR SUBMISSION AND

17 DISPOSITION OF APPLICATION.—

18   "(I) SUBMISSION.—The plan

19   sponsor shall submit a mortality table

20   to the Secretary of the Treasury for

21   approval under this subparagraph at

22   least 7 months before the 1st day of

23   the period described in clause (i).

24   "(II) DISPOSITION.—Any mor-

25   tality table submitted to the Secretary

1   of the Treasury for approval under

2   this subparagraph shall be treated as

3   in effect as of the 1st day of the pe-

4   riod described in clause (i) unless the

5   Secretary of the Treasury, during the

6   180-day period beginning on the date

7   of such submission, disapproves of

8   such table and provides the reasons

9   that such table fails to meet the re-

10   quirements of clause (iii). The 180-

11   day period shall be extended upon mu-

12   tual agreement of the Secretary of the

13   Treasury and the plan sponsor.

14   "(D) SEPARATE MORTALITY TABLES FOR

15 THE DISABLED.—Notwithstanding subpara-

16 graph (A)—

17   "(i) IN GENERAL.—The Secretary of

18   the Treasury shall establish mortality ta-

19   bles which may be used (in lieu of the ta-

20   bles under subparagraph (A)) under this

21   subsection for individuals who are entitled

22   to benefits under the plan on account of

23   disability. The Secretary of the Treasury

24   shall establish separate tables for individ-

25   uals whose disabilities occur in plan years

1   beginning before January 1, 1995, and for
2   individuals whose disabilities occur in plan
3   years beginning on or after such date.

4   "(ii) SPECIAL RULE FOR DISABILITIES
5   OCCURRING AFTER 1994.—In the case of
6   disabilities occurring in plan years begin-
7   ning after December 31, 1994, the tables
8   under clause (i) shall apply only with re-
9   spect to individuals described in such sub-
10   clause who are disabled within the meaning
11   of title II of the Social Security Act and
12   the regulations thereunder.

13   "(iii) PERIODIC REVISION.—The Sec-
14   retary of the Treasury shall (at least every
15   10 years) make revisions in any table in ef-
16   fect under clause (i) to reflect the actual
17   experience of pension plans and projected
18   trends in such experience.

19   "(4) PROBABILITY OF BENEFIT PAYMENTS IN
20   THE FORM OF LUMP SUMS OR OTHER OPTIONAL
21   FORMS.—For purposes of determining any present
22   value or making any computation under this section,
23   there shall be taken into account—

24   "(A) the probability that future benefit
25   payments under the plan will be made in the

1   form of optional forms of benefits provided

2   under the plan (including lump sum distribu-

3   tions, determined on the basis of the plan's ex-

4   perience and other related assumptions), and

5   "(B) any difference in the present value of

6   such future benefit payments resulting from the

7   use of actuarial assumptions, in determining

8   benefit payments in any such optional form of

9   benefits, which are different from those speci-

10   fied in this subsection.

11   "(5) APPROVAL OF LARGE CHANGES IN ACTU-

12   ARIAL ASSUMPTIONS.—

13   "(A) IN GENERAL.—No actuarial assump-

14   tion used to determine the funding target for a

15   plan to which this paragraph applies may be

16   changed without the approval of the Secretary

17   of the Treasury.

18   "(B) PLANS TO WHICH PARAGRAPH AP-

19   PLIES.—This paragraph shall apply to a plan

20   only if—

21   "(i) the plan is a single-employer plan

22   to which title IV applies,

23   "(ii) the aggregate unfunded vested

24   benefits as of the close of the preceding

25   plan year (as determined under section

1   4006(a)(3)(E)(iii)) of such plan and all

2   other plans maintained by the contributing

3   sponsors (as defined in section

4   4001(a)(13)) and members of such spon-

5   sors' controlled groups (as defined in sec-

6   tion 4001(a)(14)) which are covered by

7   title IV (disregarding plans with no un-

8   funded vested benefits) exceed

9     $50,000,000, and

10   "(iii) the change in assumptions (de-

11   termined after taking into account any

12   changes in interest rate and mortality

13   table) results in a decrease in the funding

14   shortfall of the plan for the current plan

15   year that exceeds $50,000,000, or that ex-

16   ceeds $5,000,000 and that is 5 percent or

17   more of the funding target of the plan be-

18   fore such change.

19 "(i) SPECIAL RULES FOR AT-RISK PLANS.—

20   "(1) FUNDING TARGET FOR PLANS IN AT-RISK

21 STATUS.—

22   "(A) IN GENERAL.—In the case of a plan

23   which is in at-risk status for a plan year, the

24   funding target of the plan for the plan year

25   shall be equal to the sum of—

"(i) the present value of all benefits accrued or earned under the plan as of the beginning of the plan year, as determined by using the additional actuarial assumptions described in subparagraph (B), and

"(ii) in the case of a plan which also has been in at-risk status for at least 2 of the 4 preceding plan years, a loading factor determined under subparagraph (C).

"(B) ADDITIONAL ACTUARIAL ASSUMPTIONS.—The actuarial assumptions described in this subparagraph are as follows:

"(i) All employees who are not otherwise assumed to retire as of the valuation date but who will be eligible to elect benefits during the plan year and the 10 succeeding plan years shall be assumed to retire at the earliest retirement date under the plan but not before the end of the plan year for which the at-risk funding target and at-risk target normal cost are being determined.

"(ii) All employees shall be assumed to elect the retirement benefit available under the plan at the assumed retirement

1   age (determined after application of clause

2   (i)) which would result in the highest

3   present value of benefits.

4   "(C) LOADING FACTOR.—The loading fac-

5   tor applied with respect to a plan under this

6   paragraph for any plan year is the sum of—

7   "(i) $700, times the number of par-

8   ticipants in the plan, plus

9   "(ii) 4 percent of the funding target

10   (determined without regard to this para-

11   graph) of the plan for the plan year.

12   "(2) TARGET NORMAL COST OF AT-RISK

13 PLANS.—In the case of a plan which is in at-risk

14 status for a plan year, the target normal cost of the

15 plan for such plan year shall be equal to the sum

16 of—

17   "(A) the present value of all benefits which

18   are expected to accrue or be earned under the

19   plan during the plan year, determined using the

20   additional actuarial assumptions described in

21   paragraph (1)(B), plus

22   "(B) in the case of a plan which also has

23   been in at-risk status for at least 2 of the 4

24   preceding plan years, a loading factor equal to

25   4 percent of the target normal cost (determined

without regard to this paragraph) of the plan for the plan year.

"(3) MINIMUM AMOUNT.—In no event shall—

"(A) the at-risk funding target be less than the funding target, as determined without regard to this subsection, or

"(B) the at-risk target normal cost be less than the target normal cost, as determined without regard to this subsection.

"(4) DETERMINATION OF AT-RISK STATUS.— For purposes of this subsection—

"(A) IN GENERAL.—A plan is in at-risk status for a plan year if—

"(i) the funding target attainment percentage for the preceding plan year (determined under this section without regard to this subsection) is less than 80 percent, and

"(ii) the funding target attainment percentage for the preceding plan year (determined under this section by using the additional actuarial assumptions described in paragraph (1)(B) in computing the funding target) is less than 70 percent.

1   "(B) Transition rule.—In the case of

2   plan years beginning in 2008, 2009, and 2010,

3   subparagraph (A)(i) shall be applied by sub-

4   stituting the following percentages for '80 per-

5   cent':

6   "(i) 65 percent in the case of 2008.

7   "(ii) 70 percent in the case of 2009.

8   "(iii) 75 percent in the case of 2010.

9   In the case of plan years beginning in 2008, the

10   funding target attainment percentage for the

11   preceding plan year under subparagraph (A)(ii)

12   may be determined using such methods of esti-

13   mation as the Secretary of the Treasury may

14   provide.

15   "(C) Special rule for employees of-

16   fered early retirement in 2006.—

17   "(i) In general.—For purposes of

18   subparagraph (A)(ii), the additional actu-

19   arial assumptions described in paragraph

20   (1)(B) shall not be taken into account with

21   respect to any employee if—

22   "(I) such employee is employed

23   by a specified automobile manufac-

24   turer,

63

1   "(II) such employee is offered a

2   substantial amount of additional cash

3   compensation, substantially enhanced

4   retirement benefits under the plan, or

5   materially reduced employment duties

6   on the condition that by a specified

7   date (not later than December 31,

8   2010) the employee retires (as defined

9   under the terms of the plan),

10   "(III) such offer is made during

11   2006 and pursuant to a bona fide re-

12   tirement incentive program and re-

13   quires, by the terms of the offer, that

14   such offer can be accepted not later

15   than a specified date (not later than

16   December 31, 2006), and

17   "(IV) such employee does not

18   elect to accept such offer before the

19   specified date on which the offer ex-

20   pires.

21   "(ii) SPECIFIED AUTOMOBILE MANU-

22   FACTURER.—For purposes of clause (i),

23   the term 'specified automobile manufac-

24   turer' means—

"(I) any manufacturer of automobiles, and

"(II) any manufacturer of automobile parts which supplies such parts directly to a manufacturer of automobiles and which, after a transaction or series of transactions ending in 1999, ceased to be a member of a controlled group which included such manufacturer of automobiles.

"(5) TRANSITION BETWEEN APPLICABLE FUNDING TARGETS AND BETWEEN APPLICABLE TARGET NORMAL COSTS.—

"(A) IN GENERAL.—In any case in which a plan which is in at-risk status for a plan year has been in such status for a consecutive period of fewer than 5 plan years, the applicable amount of the funding target and of the target normal cost shall be, in lieu of the amount determined without regard to this paragraph, the sum of—

"(i) the amount determined under this section without regard to this subsection, plus "(ii) the transition percentage for such plan year of the excess of the amount determined under this subsection (without regard to this paragraph) over the amount determined under this section without regard to this subsection.

"(B) TRANSITION PERCENTAGE.—For purposes of subparagraph (A), the transition percentage shall be determined in accordance with the following table:

"If the consecutive number of years (including the plan year) the plan is in at-risk status is—	The transition percentage is—
1	20
2	40
3	60
4	80.

"(C) YEARS BEFORE EFFECTIVE DATE.— For purposes of this paragraph, plan years beginning before 2008 shall not be taken into account.

"(6) SMALL PLAN EXCEPTION.—If, on each day during the preceding plan year, a plan had 500 or fewer participants, the plan shall not be treated as in at-risk status for the plan year. For purposes of this paragraph, all defined benefit plans (other than multiemployer plans) maintained by the same employer (or any member of such employer's controlled group) shall be treated as 1 plan, but only partici-

1   pants with respect to such employer or member shall

2   be taken into account and the rules of subsection

3   (g)(2)(C) shall apply.

4   "(j) PAYMENT OF MINIMUM REQUIRED CONTRIBU-

5 TIONS.—

6   "(1) IN GENERAL.—For purposes of this sec-

7   tion, the due date for any payment of any minimum

8   required contribution for any plan year shall be 8½

9   months after the close of the plan year.

10   "(2) INTEREST.—Any payment required under

11   paragraph (1) for a plan year that is made on a date

12   other than the valuation date for such plan year

13   shall be adjusted for interest accruing for the period

14   between the valuation date and the payment date, at

15   the effective rate of interest for the plan for such

16   plan year.

17   "(3) ACCELERATED QUARTERLY CONTRIBUTION

18   SCHEDULE FOR UNDERFUNDED PLANS.—

19   "(A) FAILURE TO TIMELY MAKE RE-

20   QUIRED INSTALLMENT.—In any case in which

21   the plan has a funding shortfall for the pre-

22   ceding plan year, the employer maintaining the

23   plan shall make the required installments under

24   this paragraph and if the employer fails to pay

25   the full amount of a required installment for

1 the plan year, then the amount of interest

2 charged under paragraph (2) on the under-

3 payment for the period of underpayment shall

4 be determined by using a rate of interest equal

5 to the rate otherwise used under paragraph (2)

6 plus 5 percentage points.

7 "(B) AMOUNT OF UNDERPAYMENT, PE-

8 RIOD OF UNDERPAYMENT.—For purposes of

9 subparagraph (A)—

10 "(i) AMOUNT.—The amount of the

11 underpayment shall be the excess of—

12 "(I) the required installment,

13 over

14 "(II) the amount (if any) of the

15 installment contributed to or under

16 the plan on or before the due date for

17 the installment.

18 "(ii) PERIOD OF UNDERPAYMENT.—

19 The period for which any interest is

20 charged under this paragraph with respect

21 to any portion of the underpayment shall

22 run from the due date for the installment

23 to the date on which such portion is con-

24 tributed to or under the plan.

1   "(iii) ORDER OF CREDITING CON-

2   TRIBUTIONS.—For purposes of clause

3   (i)(II), contributions shall be credited

4   against unpaid required installments in the

5   order in which such installments are re-

6   quired to be paid.

7   "(C) NUMBER OF REQUIRED INSTALL-

8   MENTS; DUE DATES.—For purposes of this

9   paragraph—

10   "(i) PAYABLE IN 4 INSTALLMENTS.—

11   There shall be 4 required installments for

12   each plan year.

13   "(ii) TIME FOR PAYMENT OF IN-

14   STALLMENTS.—The due dates for required

15   installments are set forth in the following

16   table:

In the case of the following required installment:	The due date is:
1st	April 15
2nd	July 15
3rd	October 15
4th	January 15 of the following year.

17   "(D) AMOUNT OF REQUIRED INSTALL-

18   MENT.—For purposes of this paragraph—

1   "(i) IN GENERAL.—The amount of

2   any required installment shall be 25 per-

3   cent of the required annual payment.

4   "(ii) REQUIRED ANNUAL PAYMENT.—

5   For purposes of clause (i), the term 're-

6   quired annual payment' means the lesser

7   of—

8   "(I) 90 percent of the minimum

9   required contribution (determined

10   without regard to this subsection) to

11   the plan for the plan year under this

12   section, or

13   "(II) 100 percent of the min-

14   imum required contribution (deter-

15   mined without regard to this sub-

16   section or to any waiver under section

17   302(c)) to the plan for the preceding

18   plan year.

19   Subclause (II) shall not apply if the pre-

20   ceding plan year referred to in such clause

21   was not a year of 12 months.

22   "(E) FISCAL YEARS AND SHORT YEARS.—

23   "(i) FISCAL YEARS.—In applying this

24   paragraph to a plan year beginning on any

25   date other than January 1, there shall be

1   substituted for the months specified in this

2   paragraph, the months which correspond

3   thereto.

4   "(ii) SHORT PLAN YEAR.—This sub-

5   paragraph shall be applied to plan years of

6   less than 12 months in accordance with

7   regulations prescribed by the Secretary of

8   the Treasury.

9   "(4) LIQUIDITY REQUIREMENT IN CONNECTION

10 WITH QUARTERLY CONTRIBUTIONS.—

11   "(A) IN GENERAL.—A plan to which this

12   paragraph applies shall be treated as failing to

13   pay the full amount of any required installment

14   under paragraph (3) to the extent that the

15   value of the liquid assets paid in such install-

16   ment is less than the liquidity shortfall (wheth-

17   er or not such liquidity shortfall exceeds the

18   amount of such installment required to be paid

19   but for this paragraph).

20   "(B) PLANS TO WHICH PARAGRAPH AP-

21   PLIES.—This paragraph shall apply to a plan

22   (other than a plan described in subsection

23   (g)(2)(B)) which—

24   "(i) is required to pay installments

25   under paragraph (3) for a plan year, and

"(ii) has a liquidity shortfall for any quarter during such plan year.

"(C) PERIOD OF UNDERPAYMENT.—For purposes of paragraph (3)(A), any portion of an installment that is treated as not paid under subparagraph (A) shall continue to be treated as unpaid until the close of the quarter in which the due date for such installment occurs.

"(D) LIMITATION ON INCREASE.—If the amount of any required installment is increased by reason of subparagraph (A), in no event shall such increase exceed the amount which, when added to prior installments for the plan year, is necessary to increase the funding target attainment percentage of the plan for the plan year (taking into account the expected increase in funding target due to benefits accruing or earned during the plan year) to 100 percent.

"(E) DEFINITIONS.—For purposes of this paragraph—

"(i) LIQUIDITY SHORTFALL.—The term 'liquidity shortfall' means, with respect to any required installment, an amount equal to the excess (as of the last

1   day of the quarter for which such install-

2   ment is made) of—

3   "(I) the base amount with re-

4   spect to such quarter, over

5   "(II) the value (as of such last

6   day) of the plan's liquid assets.

7   "(ii) BASE AMOUNT.—

8   "(I) IN GENERAL.—The term

9   'base amount' means, with respect to

10   any quarter, an amount equal to 3

11   times the sum of the adjusted dis-

12   bursements from the plan for the 12

13   months ending on the last day of such

14   quarter.

15   "(II) SPECIAL RULE.—If the

16   amount determined under subclause

17   (I) exceeds an amount equal to 2

18   times the sum of the adjusted dis-

19   bursements from the plan for the 36

20   months ending on the last day of the

21   quarter and an enrolled actuary cer-

22   tifies to the satisfaction of the Sec-

23   retary of the Treasury that such ex-

24   cess is the result of nonrecurring cir-

25   cumstances, the base amount with re-

1   spect to such quarter shall be deter-

2   mined without regard to amounts re-

3   lated to those nonrecurring cir-

4   cumstances.

5   "(iii) DISBURSEMENTS FROM THE

6   PLAN.—The term 'disbursements from the

7   plan' means all disbursements from the

8   trust, including purchases of annuities,

9   payments of single sums and other bene-

10   fits, and administrative expenses.

11   "(iv) ADJUSTED DISBURSEMENTS.—

12   The term 'adjusted disbursements' means

13   disbursements from the plan reduced by

14   the product of—

15   "(I) the plan's funding target at-

16   tainment percentage for the plan year,

17   and

18   "(II) the sum of the purchases of

19   annuities, payments of single sums,

20   and such other disbursements as the

21   Secretary of the Treasury shall pro-

22   vide in regulations.

23   "(v) LIQUID ASSETS.—The term 'liq-

24   uid assets' means cash, marketable securi-

25   ties, and such other assets as specified by

1   the Secretary of the Treasury in regula-

2   tions.

3   "(vi) QUARTER.—The term 'quarter'

4   means, with respect to any required install-

5   ment, the 3-month period preceding the

6   month in which the due date for such in-

7   stallment occurs.

8   "(F) REGULATIONS.—The Secretary of the

9   Treasury may prescribe such regulations as are

10   necessary to carry out this paragraph.

11   "(k) IMPOSITION OF LIEN WHERE FAILURE TO

12 MAKE REQUIRED CONTRIBUTIONS.—

13   "(1) IN GENERAL.—In the case of a plan to

14   which this subsection applies (as provided under

15   paragraph (2)), if—

16   "(A) any person fails to make a contribu-

17   tion payment required by section 302 and this

18   section before the due date for such payment,

19   and

20   "(B) the unpaid balance of such payment

21   (including interest), when added to the aggre-

22   gate unpaid balance of all preceding such pay-

23   ments for which payment was not made before

24   the due date (including interest), exceeds

25           $1,000,000,

1 then there shall be a lien in favor of the plan in the

2 amount determined under paragraph (3) upon all

3 property and rights to property, whether real or per-

4 sonal, belonging to such person and any other per-

5 son who is a member of the same controlled group

6 of which such person is a member.

7 "(2) PLANS TO WHICH SUBSECTION APPLIES.—

8 This subsection shall apply to a single-employer plan

9 covered under section 4021 for any plan year for

10 which the funding target attainment percentage (as

11 defined in subsection (d)(2)) of such plan is less

12 than 100 percent.

13 "(3) AMOUNT OF LIEN.—For purposes of para-

14 graph (1), the amount of the lien shall be equal to

15 the aggregate unpaid balance of contribution pay-

16 ments required under this section and section 302

17 for which payment has not been made before the due

18 date.

19 "(4) NOTICE OF FAILURE; LIEN.—

20 "(A) NOTICE OF FAILURE.—A person

21 committing a failure described in paragraph (1)

22 shall notify the Pension Benefit Guaranty Cor-

23 poration of such failure within 10 days of the

24 due date for the required contribution payment.

1   "(B) PERIOD OF LIEN.—The lien imposed

2   by paragraph (1) shall arise on the due date for

3   the required contribution payment and shall

4   continue until the last day of the first plan year

5   in which the plan ceases to be described in

6   paragraph (1)(B). Such lien shall continue to

7   run without regard to whether such plan con-

8   tinues to be described in paragraph (2) during

9   the period referred to in the preceding sentence.

10   "(C) CERTAIN RULES TO APPLY.—Any

11   amount with respect to which a lien is imposed

12   under paragraph (1) shall be treated as taxes

13   due and owing the United States and rules

14   similar to the rules of subsections (c), (d), and

15   (e) of section 4068 shall apply with respect to

16   a lien imposed by subsection (a) and the

17   amount with respect to such lien.

18   "(5) ENFORCEMENT.—Any lien created under

19   paragraph (1) may be perfected and enforced only

20   by the Pension Benefit Guaranty Corporation, or at

21   the direction of the Pension Benefit Guaranty Cor-

22   poration, by the contributing sponsor (or any mem-

23   ber of the controlled group of the contributing spon-

24   sor).

1   "(6) DEFINITIONS.—For purposes of this sub-
2 section—

3   "(A) CONTRIBUTION PAYMENT.—The term
4   'contribution payment' means, in connection
5   with a plan, a contribution payment required to
6   be made to the plan, including any required in-
7   stallment under paragraphs (3) and (4) of sub-
8   section (j).

9   "(B) DUE DATE; REQUIRED INSTALL-
10   MENT.—The terms 'due date' and 'required in-
11   stallment' have the meanings given such terms
12   by subsection (j), except that in the case of a
13   payment other than a required installment, the
14   due date shall be the date such payment is re-
15   quired to be made under section 303.

16   "(C) CONTROLLED GROUP.—The term
17   'controlled group' means any group treated as
18   a single employer under subsections (b), (c),
19   (m), and (o) of section 414 of the Internal Rev-
20   enue Code of 1986.

21 "(l) QUALIFIED TRANSFERS TO HEALTH BENEFIT
22 ACCOUNTS.—In the case of a qualified transfer (as de-
23 fined in section 420 of the Internal Revenue Code of
24 1986), any assets so transferred shall not, for purposes
25 of this section, be treated as assets in the plan.".

1   (b) CLERICAL AMENDMENT.—The table of sections
2 in section 1 of such Act (as amended by section 101) is
3 amended by inserting after the item relating to section
4 302 the following new item:

"Sec. 303. Minimum funding standards for single-employer defined benefit pension plans.".

5   (c) EFFECTIVE DATE.—The amendments made by
6 this section shall apply with respect to plan years begin-
7 ning after 2007.

8 SEC. 103. BENEFIT LIMITATIONS UNDER SINGLE-EM-
9   PLOYER PLANS.

10   (a) FUNDING-BASED LIMITS ON BENEFITS AND
11 BENEFIT ACCRUALS UNDER SINGLE-EMPLOYER
12 PLANS.—Section 206 of the Employee Retirement Income
13 Security Act of 1974 (29 U.S.C. 1056) is amended by
14 adding at the end the following new subsection:

15   "(g) FUNDING-BASED LIMITS ON BENEFITS AND
16 BENEFIT ACCRUALS UNDER SINGLE-EMPLOYER
17 PLANS.—

18   "(1) FUNDING-BASED LIMITATION ON SHUT-
19   DOWN BENEFITS AND OTHER UNPREDICTABLE CON-
20   TINGENT EVENT BENEFITS UNDER SINGLE-EM-
21   PLOYER PLANS.—

22   "(A) IN GENERAL.—If a participant of a
23   defined benefit plan which is a single-employer
24   plan is entitled to an unpredictable contingent

1   event benefit payable with respect to any event
2   occurring during any plan year, the plan shall
3   provide that such benefit may not be provided
4   if the adjusted funding target attainment per-
5   centage for such plan year—

6   "(i) is less than 60 percent, or

7   "(ii) would be less than 60 percent
8   taking into account such occurrence.

9   "(B)   EXEMPTION.—Subparagraph   (A)
10 shall cease to apply with respect to any plan
11 year, effective as of the first day of the plan
12 year, upon payment by the plan sponsor of a
13 contribution (in addition to any minimum re-
14 quired contribution under section 303) equal
15 to—

16   "(i) in the case of subparagraph
17   (A)(i), the amount of the increase in the
18   funding target of the plan (under section
19   303) for the plan year attributable to the
20   occurrence referred to in subparagraph
21   (A), and

22   "(ii) in the case of subparagraph
23   (A)(ii), the amount sufficient to result in a
24   funding target attainment percentage of 60
25   percent.

1   "(C) UNPREDICTABLE CONTINGENT

2   EVENT.—For purposes of this paragraph, the

3   term 'unpredictable contingent event benefit'

4   means any benefit payable solely by reason of—

5   "(i) a plant shutdown (or similar

6   event, as determined by the Secretary of

7   the Treasury), or

8   "(ii) an event other than the attain-

9   ment of any age, performance of any serv-

10   ice, receipt or derivation of any compensa-

11   tion, or occurrence of death or disability.

12   "(2) LIMITATIONS ON PLAN AMENDMENTS IN-

13   CREASING LIABILITY FOR BENEFITS.—

14   "(A) IN GENERAL.—No amendment to a

15   defined benefit plan which is a single-employer

16   plan which has the effect of increasing liabilities

17   of the plan by reason of increases in benefits,

18   establishment of new benefits, changing the

19   rate of benefit accrual, or changing the rate at

20   which benefits become nonforfeitable may take

21   effect during any plan year if the adjusted

22   funding target attainment percentage for such

23   plan year is—

24   "(i) less than 80 percent, or

1   "(ii) would be less than 80 percent

2   taking into account such amendment.

3   "(B)   EXEMPTION.—Subparagraph   (A)

4 shall cease to apply with respect to any plan

5 year, effective as of the first day of the plan

6 year (or if later, the effective date of the

7 amendment), upon payment by the plan sponsor

8 of a contribution (in addition to any minimum

9 required contribution under section 303) equal

10 to—

11   "(i) in the case of subparagraph

12   (A)(i), the amount of the increase in the

13   funding target of the plan (under section

14   303) for the plan year attributable to the

15   amendment, and

16   "(ii) in the case of subparagraph

17   (A)(ii), the amount sufficient to result in

18   an adjusted funding target attainment per-

19   centage of 80 percent.

20   "(C) EXCEPTION FOR CERTAIN BENEFIT

21 INCREASES.—Subparagraph (A) shall not apply

22 to any amendment which provides for an in-

23 crease in benefits under a formula which is not

24 based on a participant's compensation, but only

25 if the rate of such increase is not in excess of

1   the contemporaneous rate of increase in average

2   wages of participants covered by the amend-

3   ment.

4   "(3) LIMITATIONS ON ACCELERATED BENEFIT

5 DISTRIBUTIONS.—

6   "(A) FUNDING PERCENTAGE LESS THAN

7   60 PERCENT.—A defined benefit plan which is

8   a single-employer plan shall provide that, in any

9   case in which the plan's adjusted funding target

10   attainment percentage for a plan year is less

11   than 60 percent, the plan may not pay any pro-

12   hibited payment after the valuation date for the

13   plan year.

14   "(B) BANKRUPTCY.—A defined benefit

15   plan which is a single-employer plan shall pro-

16   vide that, during any period in which the plan

17   sponsor is a debtor in a case under title 11,

18   United States Code, or similar Federal or State

19   law, the plan may not pay any prohibited pay-

20   ment. The preceding sentence shall not apply

21   on or after the date on which the enrolled actu-

22   ary of the plan certifies that the adjusted fund-

23   ing target attainment percentage of such plan

24   is not less than 100 percent.

1   "(C) LIMITED PAYMENT IF PERCENTAGE

2   AT LEAST 60 PERCENT BUT LESS THAN 80 PER-

3   CENT.—

4   "(i) IN GENERAL.—A defined benefit

5   plan which is a single-employer plan shall

6   provide that, in any case in which the

7   plan's adjusted funding target attainment

8   percentage for a plan year is 60 percent or

9   greater but less than 80 percent, the plan

10   may not pay any prohibited payment after

11   the valuation date for the plan year to the

12   extent the amount of the payment exceeds

13   the lesser of—

14   "(I) 50 percent of the amount of

15   the payment which could be made

16   without regard to this subsection, or

17   "(II) the present value (deter-

18   mined under guidance prescribed by

19   the Pension Benefit Guaranty Cor-

20   poration, using the interest and mor-

21   tality assumptions under section

22   205(g)) of the maximum guarantee

23   with respect to the participant under

24   section 4022.

25   "(ii) ONE-TIME APPLICATION.—

1   "(I) IN GENERAL.—The plan

2   shall also provide that only 1 prohib-

3   ited payment meeting the require-

4   ments of clause (i) may be made with

5   respect to any participant during any

6   period of consecutive plan years to

7   which the limitations under either

8   subparagraph (A) or (B) or this sub-

9   paragraph applies.

10   "(II) TREATMENT OF BENE-

11   FICIARIES.—For purposes of this

12   clause, a participant and any bene-

13   ficiary on his behalf (including an al-

14   ternate payee, as defined in section

15   206(d)(3)(K)) shall be treated as 1

16   participant. If the accrued benefit of a

17   participant is allocated to such an al-

18   ternate payee and 1 or more other

19   persons, the amount under clause (i)

20   shall be allocated among such persons

21   in the same manner as the accrued

22   benefit is allocated unless the quali-

23   fied domestic relations order (as de-

24   fined in section 206(d)(3)(B)(i)) pro-

25   vides otherwise.

1   "(D) EXCEPTION.—This paragraph shall

2 not apply to any plan for any plan year if the

3 terms of such plan (as in effect for the period

4 beginning on September 1, 2005, and ending

5 with such plan year) provide for no benefit ac-

6 cruals with respect to any participant during

7 such period.

8   "(E) PROHIBITED PAYMENT.—For pur-

9 pose of this paragraph, the term 'prohibited

10 payment' means—

11   "(i) any payment, in excess of the

12   monthly amount paid under a single life

13   annuity (plus any social security supple-

14   ments described in the last sentence of sec-

15   tion 204(b)(1)(G)), to a participant or ben-

16   eficiary whose annuity starting date (as de-

17   fined in section 205(h)(2)) occurs during

18   any period a limitation under subpara-

19   graph (A) or (B) is in effect,

20   "(ii) any payment for the purchase of

21   an irrevocable commitment from an insurer

22   to pay benefits, and

23   "(iii) any other payment specified by

24   the Secretary of the Treasury by regula-

25   tions.

"(4) LIMITATION ON BENEFIT ACCRUALS FOR PLANS WITH SEVERE FUNDING SHORTFALLS.—

"(A) IN GENERAL.—A defined benefit plan which is a single-employer plan shall provide that, in any case in which the plan's adjusted funding target attainment percentage for a plan year is less than 60 percent, benefit accruals under the plan shall cease as of the valuation date for the plan year.

"(B) EXEMPTION.—Subparagraph (A) shall cease to apply with respect to any plan year, effective as of the first day of the plan year, upon payment by the plan sponsor of a contribution (in addition to any minimum required contribution under section 303) equal to the amount sufficient to result in an adjusted funding target attainment percentage of 60 percent.

"(5) RULES RELATING TO CONTRIBUTIONS REQUIRED TO AVOID BENEFIT LIMITATIONS.—

"(A) SECURITY MAY BE PROVIDED.—

"(i) IN GENERAL.—For purposes of this subsection, the adjusted funding target attainment percentage shall be determined by treating as an asset of the plan

1   any security provided by a plan sponsor in

2   a form meeting the requirements of clause

3   (ii).

4   "(ii) FORM OF SECURITY.—The secu-

5   rity required under clause (i) shall consist

6   of—

7   "(I) a bond issued by a corporate

8   surety company that is an acceptable

9   surety for purposes of section 412 of

10   this Act,

11   "(II) cash, or United States obli-

12   gations which mature in 3 years or

13   less, held in escrow by a bank or simi-

14   lar financial institution, or

15   "(III) such other form of security

16   as is satisfactory to the Secretary of

17   the Treasury and the parties involved.

18   "(iii) ENFORCEMENT.—Any security

19   provided under clause (i) may be perfected

20   and enforced at any time after the earlier

21   of—

22   "(I) the date on which the plan

23   terminates,

24   "(II) if there is a failure to make

25   a payment of the minimum required

1   contribution for any plan year begin-

2   ning after the security is provided, the

3   due date for the payment under sec-

4   tion 303(j), or

5   "(III) if the adjusted funding

6   target attainment percentage is less

7   than 60 percent for a consecutive pe-

8   riod of 7 years, the valuation date for

9   the last year in the period.

10   "(iv) RELEASE OF SECURITY.—The

11   security shall be released (and any

12   amounts thereunder shall be refunded to-

13   gether with any interest accrued thereon)

14   at such time as the Secretary of the Treas-

15   ury may prescribe in regulations, including

16   regulations for partial releases of the secu-

17   rity by reason of increases in the funding

18   target attainment percentage.

19   "(B) PREFUNDING BALANCE OR FUNDING

20   STANDARD CARRYOVER BALANCE MAY NOT BE

21   USED.—No prefunding balance or funding

22   standard carryover balance under section 303(f)

23   may be used under paragraph (1), (2), or (4)

24   to satisfy any payment an employer may make

25   under any such paragraph to avoid or terminate

1   the application of any limitation under such

2   paragraph.

3   "(C) DEEMED REDUCTION OF FUNDING

4   BALANCES.—

5   "(i) IN GENERAL.—Subject to clause

6   (iii), in any case in which a benefit limita-

7   tion under paragraph (1), (2), (3), or (4)

8   would (but for this subparagraph and de-

9   termined without regard to paragraph

10   (1)(B), (2)(B), or (4)(B)) apply to such

11   plan for the plan year, the plan sponsor of

12   such plan shall be treated for purposes of

13   this Act as having made an election under

14   section 303(f) to reduce the prefunding

15   balance or funding standard carryover bal-

16   ance by such amount as is necessary for

17   such benefit limitation to not apply to the

18   plan for such plan year.

19   "(ii) EXCEPTION FOR INSUFFICIENT

20   FUNDING BALANCES.—Clause (i) shall not

21   apply with respect to a benefit limitation

22   for any plan year if the application of

23   clause (i) would not result in the benefit

24   limitation not applying for such plan year.

"(iii) RESTRICTIONS OF CERTAIN RULES TO COLLECTIVELY BARGAINED PLANS.—With respect to any benefit limitation under paragraph (1), (2), or (4), clause (i) shall only apply in the case of a plan maintained pursuant to 1 or more collective bargaining agreements between employee representatives and 1 or more employers.

"(6) NEW PLANS.—Paragraphs (1), (2) and (4) shall not apply to a plan for the first 5 plan years of the plan. For purposes of this paragraph, the reference in this paragraph to a plan shall include a reference to any predecessor plan.

"(7) PRESUMED UNDERFUNDING FOR PURPOSES OF BENEFIT LIMITATIONS.—

"(A) PRESUMPTION OF CONTINUED UNDERFUNDING.—In any case in which a benefit limitation under paragraph (1), (2), (3), or (4) has been applied to a plan with respect to the plan year preceding the current plan year, the adjusted funding target attainment percentage of the plan for the current plan year shall be presumed to be equal to the adjusted funding target attainment percentage of the plan for

1   the preceding plan year until the enrolled actu-

2   ary of the plan certifies the actual adjusted

3   funding target attainment percentage of the

4   plan for the current plan year.

5   "(B) PRESUMPTION OF UNDERFUNDING

6   AFTER 10TH MONTH.—In any case in which no

7   certification of the adjusted funding target at-

8   tainment percentage for the current plan year

9   is made with respect to the plan before the first

10 day of the 10th month of such year, for pur-

11 poses of paragraphs (1), (2), (3), and (4), such

12 first day shall be deemed, for purposes of such

13 paragraph, to be the valuation date of the plan

14 for the current plan year and the plan's ad-

15 justed funding target attainment percentage

16 shall be conclusively presumed to be less than

17 60 percent as of such first day.

18   "(C) PRESUMPTION OF UNDERFUNDING

19 AFTER 4TH MONTH FOR NEARLY UNDER-

20 FUNDED PLANS.—In any case in which—

21   "(i) a benefit limitation under para-

22   graph (1), (2), (3), or (4) did not apply to

23   a plan with respect to the plan year pre-

24   ceding the current plan year, but the ad-

25   justed funding target attainment percent-

age of the plan for such preceding plan year was not more than 10 percentage points greater than the percentage which would have caused such paragraph to apply to the plan with respect to such preceding plan year, and

"(ii) as of the first day of the 4th month of the current plan year, the enrolled actuary of the plan has not certified the actual adjusted funding target attainment percentage of the plan for the current plan year,

until the enrolled actuary so certifies, such first day shall be deemed, for purposes of such paragraph, to be the valuation date of the plan for the current plan year and the adjusted funding target attainment percentage of the plan as of such first day shall, for purposes of such paragraph, be presumed to be equal to 10 percentage points less than the adjusted funding target attainment percentage of the plan for such preceding plan year.

"(8) TREATMENT OF PLAN AS OF CLOSE OF PROHIBITED OR CESSATION PERIOD.—For purposes of applying this part—

"(A) OPERATION OF PLAN AFTER PE-
RIOD.—Unless the plan provides otherwise, payments and accruals will resume effective as of
the day following the close of the period for
which any limitation of payment or accrual of
benefits under paragraph (3) or (4) applies.

"(B) TREATMENT OF AFFECTED BENE-
FITS.—Nothing in this paragraph shall be construed as affecting the plan's treatment of benefits which would have been paid or accrued but
for this subsection.

"(9) TERMS RELATING TO FUNDING TARGET
ATTAINMENT PERCENTAGE.—For purposes of this
subsection—

"(A) IN GENERAL.—The term 'funding
target attainment percentage' has the same
meaning given such term by section 303(d)(2).

"(B) ADJUSTED FUNDING TARGET AT-
TAINMENT PERCENTAGE.—The term 'adjusted
funding target attainment percentage' means
the funding target attainment percentage which
is determined under subparagraph (A) by increasing each of the amounts under subparagraphs (A) and (B) of section 303(d)(2) by the
aggregate amount of purchases of annuities for

1   employees other than highly compensated em-

2   ployees (as defined in section 414(q) of the In-

3   ternal Revenue Code of 1986) which were made

4   by the plan during the preceding 2 plan years.

5   "(C) APPLICATION TO PLANS WHICH ARE

6   FULLY FUNDED WITHOUT REGARD TO REDUC-

7   TIONS FOR FUNDING BALANCES.—

8   "(i) IN GENERAL.—In the case of a

9   plan for any plan year, if the funding tar-

10   get attainment percentage is 100 percent

11   or more (determined without regard to this

12   subparagraph and without regard to the

13   reduction in the value of assets under sec-

14   tion 303(f)(4)), the funding target attain-

15   ment percentage for purposes of subpara-

16   graphs (A) and (B) shall be determined

17   without regard to such reduction.

18   "(ii) TRANSITION RULE.—Clause (i)

19   shall be applied to plan years beginning

20   after 2007 and before 2011 by substituting

21   for '100 percent' the applicable percentage

22   determined in accordance with the fol-

23   lowing table:

"In the case of a plan year beginning in calendar year:	The applicable percentage is
2008	92
2009	94
2010	96.

1   "(iii) LIMITATION.—Clause (ii) shall

2   not apply with respect to any plan year

3   after 2008 unless the funding target at-

4   tainment percentage (determined without

5   regard to this subparagraph) of the plan

6   for each preceding plan year after 2007

7   was not less than the applicable percentage

8   with respect to such preceding plan year

9   determined under clause (ii).

10   "(10) SPECIAL RULE FOR 2008.—For purposes

11 of this subsection, in the case of plan years begin-

12 ning in 2008, the funding target attainment percent-

13 age for the preceding plan year may be determined

14 using such methods of estimation as the Secretary

15 of the Treasury may provide.".

16 (b) NOTICE REQUIREMENT.—

17   (1) IN GENERAL.—Section 101 of such Act (29

18 U.S.C. 1021) is amended—

19   (A) by redesignating subsection (j) as sub-

20   section (k); and

21   (B) by inserting after subsection (i) the

22   following new subsection:

23 "(j) NOTICE OF FUNDING-BASED LIMITATION ON

24 CERTAIN FORMS OF DISTRIBUTION.—The plan adminis-

25 trator of a single-employer plan shall provide a written no-

tice to plan participants and beneficiaries within 30 days—

       "(1) after the plan has become subject to a restriction described in paragraph (1) or (3) of section 206(g)),

       "(2) in the case of a plan to which section 206(g)(4) applies, after the valuation date for the plan year described in section 206(g)(4)(B) for which the plan's adjusted funding target attainment percentage for the plan year is less than 60 percent (or, if earlier, the date such percentage is deemed to be less than 60 percent under section 206(g)(7)), and

       "(3) at such other time as may be determined by the Secretary of the Treasury.

The notice required to be provided under this subsection shall be in writing, except that such notice may be in electronic or other form to the extent that such form is reasonably accessible to the recipient.".

       (2) ENFORCEMENT.—Section 502(c)(4) of such Act (29 U.S.C. 1132(c)(4)) is amended by striking "section 302(b)(7)(F)(iv)" and inserting "section 101(j) or 302(b)(7)(F)(iv)".

       (c) EFFECTIVE DATES.—

1   (1) IN GENERAL.—The amendments made by
2 this section shall apply to plan years beginning after
3 December 31, 2007.

4   (2) COLLECTIVE BARGAINING EXCEPTION.—In
5 the case of a plan maintained pursuant to 1 or more
6 collective bargaining agreements between employee
7 representatives and 1 or more employers ratified be-
8 fore January 1, 2008, the amendments made by this
9 section shall not apply to plan years beginning be-
10 fore the earlier of—

11   (A) the later of—

12   (i) the date on which the last collec-
13   tive bargaining agreement relating to the
14   plan terminates (determined without re-
15   gard to any extension thereof agreed to
16   after the date of the enactment of this
17   Act), or

18   (ii) the first day of the first plan year
19   to which the amendments made by this
20   subsection would (but for this subpara-
21   graph) apply, or

22   (B) January 1, 2010.

23 For purposes of subparagraph (A)(i), any plan
24 amendment made pursuant to a collective bargaining
25 agreement relating to the plan which amends the

1   plan solely to conform to any requirement added by

2   this section shall not be treated as a termination of

3   such collective bargaining agreement.

4 **SEC. 104. SPECIAL RULES FOR MULTIPLE EMPLOYER**

5   **PLANS OF CERTAIN COOPERATIVES.**

6   (a) GENERAL RULE.—Except as provided in this sec-

7 tion, if a plan in existence on July 26, 2005, was an eligi-

8 ble cooperative plan for its plan year which includes such

9 date, the amendments made by this subtitle and subtitle

10 B shall not apply to plan years beginning before the earlier

11 of—

12   (1) the first plan year for which the plan ceases

13   to be an eligible cooperative plan, or

14   (2) January 1, 2017.

15   (b) INTEREST RATE.—In applying section

16 302(b)(5)(B) of the Employee Retirement Income Secu-

17 rity Act of 1974 and section 412(b)(5)(B) of the Internal

18 Revenue Code of 1986 (as in effect before the amendments

19 made by this subtitle and subtitle B) to an eligible cooper-

20 ative plan for plan years beginning after December 31,

21 2007, and before the first plan year to which such amend-

22 ments apply, the third segment rate determined under sec-

23 tion 303(h)(2)(C)(iii) of such Act and section

24 430(h)(2)(C)(iii) of such Code (as added by such amend-

99

1 ments) shall be used in lieu of the interest rate otherwise

2 used.

3   (c) ELIGIBLE COOPERATIVE PLAN DEFINED.—For

4 purposes of this section, a plan shall be treated as an eligi-

5 ble cooperative plan for a plan year if the plan is main-

6 tained by more than 1 employer and at least 85 percent

7 of the employers are—

8   (1) rural cooperatives (as defined in section

9   401(k)(7)(B) of such Code without regard to clause

10   (iv) thereof), or

11   (2) organizations which are—

12   (A) cooperative organizations described in

13   section 1381(a) of such Code which are more

14   than 50-percent owned by agricultural pro-

15   ducers or by cooperatives owned by agricultural

16   producers, or

17   (B) more than 50-percent owned, or con-

18   trolled by, one or more cooperative organiza-

19   tions described in subparagraph (A).

20 A plan shall also be treated as an eligible cooperative plan

21 for any plan year for which it is described in section

22 210(a) of the Employee Retirement Income Security Act

23 of 1974 and is maintained by a rural telephone cooperative

24 association described in section 3(40)(B)(v) of such Act.

Act. Sec. 104

SEC. 105. TEMPORARY RELIEF FOR CERTAIN PBGC SETTLE-
MENT PLANS.

(a) GENERAL RULE.—Except as provided in this section, if a plan in existence on July 26, 2005, was a PBGC settlement plan as of such date, the amendments made by this subtitle and subtitle B shall not apply to plan years beginning before January 1, 2014.

(b) INTEREST RATE.—In applying section 302(b)(5)(B) of the Employee Retirement Income Security Act of 1974 and section 412(b)(5)(B) of the Internal Revenue Code of 1986 (as in effect before the amendments made by this subtitle and subtitle B), to a PBGC settlement plan for plan years beginning after December 31, 2007, and before January 1, 2014, the third segment rate determined under section 303(h)(2)(C)(iii) of such Act and section 430(h)(2)(C)(iii) of such Code (as added by such amendments) shall be used in lieu of the interest rate otherwise used.

(c) PBGC SETTLEMENT PLAN.—For purposes of this section, the term "PBGC settlement plan" means a defined benefit plan (other than a multiemployer plan) to which section 302 of such Act and section 412 of such Code apply and—

(1) which was sponsored by an employer which was in bankruptcy, giving rise to a claim by the Pension Benefit Guaranty Corporation of not great-

er than $150,000,000, and the sponsorship of which was assumed by another employer that was not a member of the same controlled group as the bankrupt sponsor and the claim of the Pension Benefit Guaranty Corporation was settled or withdrawn in connection with the assumption of the sponsorship, or

(2) which, by agreement with the Pension Benefit Guaranty Corporation, was spun off from a plan subsequently terminated by such Corporation under section 4042 of the Employee Retirement Income Security Act of 1974.

SEC. 106. SPECIAL RULES FOR PLANS OF CERTAIN GOVERNMENT CONTRACTORS.

(a) GENERAL RULE.—Except as provided in this section, if a plan is an eligible government contractor plan, this subtitle and subtitle B shall not apply to plan years beginning before the earliest of—

(1) the first plan year for which the plan ceases to be an eligible government contractor plan,

(2) the effective date of the Cost Accounting Standards Pension Harmonization Rule, or

(3) January 1, 2011.

(b) INTEREST RATE.—In applying section 302(b)(5)(B) of the Employee Retirement Income Secu-

1 rity Act of 1974 and section 412(b)(5)(B) of the Internal

2 Revenue Code of 1986 (as in effect before the amendments

3 made by this subtitle and subtitle B) to an eligible govern-

4 ment contractor plan for plan years beginning after De-

5 cember 31, 2007, and before the first plan year to which

6 such amendments apply, the third segment rate deter-

7 mined under section 303(h)(2)(C)(iii) of such Act and sec-

8 tion 430(h)(2)(C)(iii) of such Code (as added by such

9 amendments) shall be used in lieu of the interest rate oth-

10 erwise used.

11   (c) ELIGIBLE GOVERNMENT CONTRACTOR PLAN DE-

12 FINED.—For purposes of this section, a plan shall be

13 treated as an eligible government contractor plan if it is

14 maintained by a corporation or a member of the same af-

15 filiated group (as defined by section 1504(a) of the Inter-

16 nal Revenue Code of 1986), whose primary source of rev-

17 enue is derived from business performed under contracts

18 with the United States that are subject to the Federal Ac-

19 quisition Regulations (Chapter 1 of Title 48, C.F.R.) and

20 that are also subject to the Defense Federal Acquisition

21 Regulation Supplement (Chapter 2 of Title 48, C.F.R.),

22 and whose revenue derived from such business in the pre-

23 vious fiscal year exceeded $5,000,000,000, and whose pen-

24 sion plan costs that are assignable under those contracts

1 are subject to sections 412 and 413 of the Cost Account-
2 ing Standards (48 C.F.R. 9904.412 and 9904.413).

3 (d) COST ACCOUNTING STANDARDS PENSION HAR-
4 MONIZATION RULE.—The Cost Accounting Standards
5 Board shall review and revise sections 412 and 413 of the
6 Cost Accounting Standards (48 C.F.R. 9904.412 and
7 9904.413) to harmonize the minimum required contribu-
8 tion under the Employee Retirement Income Security Act
9 of 1974 of eligible government contractor plans and gov-
10 ernment reimbursable pension plan costs not later than
11 January 1, 2010. Any final rule adopted by the Cost Ac-
12 counting Standards Board shall be deemed the Cost Ac-
13 counting Standards Pension Harmonization Rule.

14 **SEC. 107. TECHNICAL AND CONFORMING AMENDMENTS.**

15 (a) MISCELLANEOUS AMENDMENTS TO TITLE I.—
16 Subtitle B of title I of such Act (29 U.S.C. 1021 et seq.)
17 is amended—

18 (1) in section 101(d)(3), by striking "section
19 302(e)" and inserting "section 303(j)";

20 (2) in section 103(d)(8)(B), by striking "the re-
21 quirements of section 302(c)(3)" and inserting "the
22 applicable requirements of sections 303(h) and
23 304(c)(3)";

24 (3) in section 103(d), by striking paragraph
25 (11) and inserting the following:

1   "(11) If the current value of the assets of the

2   plan is less than 70 percent of—

3   "(A) in the case of a single-employer plan,

4   the funding target (as defined in section

5   303(d)(1)) of the plan, or

6   "(B) in the case of a multiemployer plan,

7   the current liability (as defined in section

8   304(c)(6)(D)) under the plan,

9   the percentage which such value is of the amount

10   described in subparagraph (A) or (B).";

11   (4) in section 203(a)(3)(C), by striking "section

12   302(c)(8)" and inserting "section 302(d)(2)";

13   (5) in section 204(g)(1), by striking "section

14   302(c)(8)" and inserting "section 302(d)(2)";

15   (6) in section 204(i)(2)(B), by striking "section

16   302(c)(8)" and inserting "section 302(d)(2)";

17   (7) in section 204(i)(3), by striking "funded

18   current liability percentage (within the meaning of

19   section 302(d)(8) of this Act)" and inserting "fund-

20   ing target attainment percentage (as defined in sec-

21   tion 303(d)(2))";

22   (8) in section 204(i)(4), by striking "section

23   302(c)(11)(A), without regard to section

24   302(c)(11)(B)" and inserting "section 302(b)(1),

25   without regard to section 302(b)(2)";

1   (9) in section 206(e)(1), by striking "section

2   302(d)" and inserting "section 303(j)(4)", and by

3   striking "section 302(e)(5)" and inserting "section

4   303(j)(4)(E)(i)";

5   (10) in section 206(e)(3), by striking "section

6   302(e) by reason of paragraph (5)(A) thereof" and

7   inserting "section 303(j)(3) by reason of section

8   303(j)(4)(A)"; and

9   (11) in sections 101(e)(3), 403(c)(1), and

10   408(b)(13), by striking "American Jobs Creation

11   Act of 2004" and inserting "Pension Protection Act

12   of 2006".

13   (b) MISCELLANEOUS AMENDMENTS TO TITLE IV.—

14   Title IV of such Act is amended—

15   (1) in section 4001(a)(13) (29 U.S.C.

16   1301(a)(13)), by striking "302(c)(11)(A)" and in-

17   serting "302(b)(1)", by striking "412(c)(11)(A)"

18   and inserting "412(b)(1)", by striking

19   "302(c)(11)(B)" and inserting "302(b)(2)", and by

20   striking "412(c)(11)(B)" and inserting "412(b)(2)";

21   (2) in section 4003(e)(1) (29 U.S.C.

22   1303(e)(1)), by striking "302(f)(1)(A) and (B)" and

23   inserting "303(k)(1)(A) and (B)", and by striking

24   "412(n)(1)(A) and (B)" and inserting

25   "430(k)(1)(A) and (B)";

1   (3) in section 4010(b)(2) (29 U.S.C.

2   1310(b)(2)), by striking "302(f)(1)(A) and (B)" and

3   inserting "303(k)(1)(A) and (B)", and by striking

4   "412(n)(1)(A) and (B)" and inserting

5   "430(k)(1)(A) and (B)";

6   (4) in section 4062(c) (29 U.S.C. 1362(c)), by

7   striking paragraphs (1), (2), and (3) and inserting

8   the following:

9   "(1) the sum of the shortfall amortization

10   charge (within the meaning of section 303(c)(1) of

11   this Act and 430(d)(1) of the Internal Revenue Code

12   of 1986) with respect to the plan (if any) for the

13   plan year in which the termination date occurs, plus

14   the aggregate total of shortfall amortization install-

15   ments (if any) determined for succeeding plan years

16   under section 303(c)(2) of this Act and section

17   430(d)(2) of such Code (which, for purposes of this

18   subparagraph, shall include any increase in such

19   sum which would result if all applications for waiv-

20   ers of the minimum funding standard under section

21   302(c) of this Act and section 412(c) of such Code

22   which are pending with respect to such plan were

23   denied and if no additional contributions (other than

24   those already made by the termination date) were

1 made for the plan year in which the termination

2 date occurs or for any previous plan year), and

3   "(2) the sum of the waiver amortization charge

4 (within the meaning of section 303(e)(1) of this Act

5 and 430(e)(1) of the Internal Revenue Code of

6 1986) with respect to the plan (if any) for the plan

7 year in which the termination date occurs, plus the

8 aggregate total of waiver amortization installments

9 (if any) determined for succeeding plan years under

10 section 303(e)(2) of this Act and section 430(e)(2)

11 of such Code,";

12   (5) in section 4071 (29 U.S.C. 1371), by strik-

13 ing "302(f)(4)" and inserting "303(k)(4)";

14   (6) in section 4243(a)(1)(B) (29 U.S.C.

15 1423(a)(1)(B)), by striking "302(a)" and inserting

16 "304(a)", and, in clause (i), by striking "302(a)"

17 and inserting "304(a)";

18   (7) in section 4243(f)(1) (29 U.S.C.

19 1423(f)(1)), by striking "303(a)" and inserting

20 "302(c)";

21   (8) in section 4243(f)(2) (29 U.S.C.

22 1423(f)(2)), by striking "303(c)" and inserting

23 "302(c)(3)"; and

24   (9) in section 4243(g) (29 U.S.C. 1423(g)), by

25 striking "302(c)(3)" and inserting "304(c)(3)".

1   (c) AMENDMENTS TO REORGANIZATION PLAN No. 4

2 OF 1978.—Section 106(b)(ii) of Reorganization Plan No.

3 4 of 1978 (ratified and affirmed as law by Public Law

4 98–532 (98 Stat. 2705)) is amended by striking

5 "302(c)(8)" and inserting "302(d)(2)", by striking

6 "304(a) and (b)(2)(A)" and inserting "304(d)(1), (d)(2),

7 and (e)(2)(A)", and by striking "412(c)(8), (e), and

8 (f)(2)(A)" and inserting "412(c)(2) and 431(d)(1), (d)(2),

9 and (e)(2)(A)".

10   (d) REPEAL OF EXPIRED AUTHORITY FOR TEM-

11 PORARY VARIANCES.—Section 207 of such Act (29 U.S.C.

12 1057) is repealed.

13   (e) EFFECTIVE DATE.—The amendments made by

14 this section shall apply to plan years beginning after 2007.

Subtitle B—Amendments to
Internal Revenue Code of 1986

17 **SEC. 111. MINIMUM FUNDING STANDARDS.**

18   (a) NEW MINIMUM FUNDING STANDARDS.—Section

19 412 of the Internal Revenue Code of 1986 (relating to

20 minimum funding standards) is amended to read as fol-

21 lows:

22 **"SEC. 412. MINIMUM FUNDING STANDARDS.**

23   "(a) REQUIREMENT TO MEET MINIMUM FUNDING

24 STANDARD.—

109

"(1) IN GENERAL.—A plan to which this section applies shall satisfy the minimum funding standard applicable to the plan for any plan year.

"(2) MINIMUM FUNDING STANDARD.—For purposes of paragraph (1), a plan shall be treated as satisfying the minimum funding standard for a plan year if—

"(A) in the case of a defined benefit plan which is not a multiemployer plan, the employer makes contributions to or under the plan for the plan year which, in the aggregate, are not less than the minimum required contribution determined under section 430 for the plan for the plan year,

"(B) in the case of a money purchase plan which is not a multiemployer plan, the employer makes contributions to or under the plan for the plan year which are required under the terms of the plan, and

"(C) in the case of a multiemployer plan, the employers make contributions to or under the plan for any plan year which, in the aggregate, are sufficient to ensure that the plan does not have an accumulated funding deficiency

1   under section 431 as of the end of the plan

2   year.

3   "(b) LIABILITY FOR CONTRIBUTIONS.—

4   "(1) IN GENERAL.—Except as provided in para-

5   graph (2), the amount of any contribution required

6   by this section (including any required installments

7   under paragraphs (3) and (4) of section 430(j))

8   shall be paid by the employer responsible for making

9   contributions to or under the plan.

10   "(2) JOINT AND SEVERAL LIABILITY WHERE

11   EMPLOYER MEMBER OF CONTROLLED GROUP.—If

12   the employer referred to in paragraph (1) is a mem-

13   ber of a controlled group, each member of such

14   group shall be jointly and severally liable for pay-

15   ment of such contributions.

16   "(c) VARIANCE FROM MINIMUM FUNDING STAND-

17 ARDS.—

18   "(1) WAIVER IN CASE OF BUSINESS HARD-

19   SHIP.—

20   "(A) IN GENERAL.—If—

21   "(i) an employer is (or in the case of

22   a multiemployer plan, 10 percent or more

23   of the number of employers contributing to

24   or under the plan is) unable to satisfy the

25   minimum funding standard for a plan year

1 without temporary substantial business

2 hardship (substantial business hardship in

3 the case of a multiemployer plan), and

4 "(ii) application of the standard would

5 be adverse to the interests of plan partici-

6 pants in the aggregate,

7 the Secretary may, subject to subparagraph

8 (C), waive the requirements of subsection (a)

9 for such year with respect to all or any portion

10 of the minimum funding standard. The Sec-

11 retary shall not waive the minimum funding

12 standard with respect to a plan for more than

13 3 of any 15 (5 of any 15 in the case of a multi-

14 employer plan) consecutive plan years

15 "(B) EFFECTS OF WAIVER.—If a waiver is

16 granted under subparagraph (A) for any plan

17 year—

18 "(i) in the case of a defined benefit

19 plan which is not a multiemployer plan,

20 the minimum required contribution under

21 section 430 for the plan year shall be re-

22 duced by the amount of the waived funding

23 deficiency and such amount shall be amor-

24 tized as required under section 430(e), and

1   "(ii) in the case of a multiemployer

2   plan, the funding standard account shall

3   be credited under section 431(b)(3)(C)

4   with the amount of the waived funding de-

5   ficiency and such amount shall be amor-

6   tized as required under section

7   431(b)(2)(C).

8   "(C) WAIVER OF AMORTIZED PORTION

9   NOT ALLOWED.—The Secretary may not waive

10   under subparagraph (A) any portion of the

11   minimum funding standard under subsection

12   (a) for a plan year which is attributable to any

13   waived funding deficiency for any preceding

14   plan year.

15   "(2) DETERMINATION OF BUSINESS HARD-

16   SHIP.—For purposes of this subsection, the factors

17   taken into account in determining temporary sub-

18   stantial business hardship (substantial business

19   hardship in the case of a multiemployer plan) shall

20   include (but shall not be limited to) whether or

21   not—

22   "(A) the employer is operating at an eco-

23   nomic loss,

1   "(B) there is substantial unemployment or

2   underemployment in the trade or business and

3   in the industry concerned,

4   "(C) the sales and profits of the industry

5   concerned are depressed or declining, and

6   "(D) it is reasonable to expect that the

7   plan will be continued only if the waiver is

8   granted.

9   "(3) WAIVED FUNDING DEFICIENCY.—For pur-

10 poses of this section and part III of this subchapter,

11 the term 'waived funding deficiency' means the por-

12 tion of the minimum funding standard under sub-

13 section (a) (determined without regard to the waiv-

14 er) for a plan year waived by the Secretary and not

15 satisfied by employer contributions.

16   "(4) SECURITY FOR WAIVERS FOR SINGLE-EM-

17 PLOYER PLANS, CONSULTATIONS.—

18   "(A) SECURITY MAY BE REQUIRED.—

19   "(i) IN GENERAL.—Except as pro-

20   vided in subparagraph (C), the Secretary

21   may require an employer maintaining a de-

22   fined benefit plan which is a single-em-

23   ployer plan (within the meaning of section

24   4001(a)(15) of the Employee Retirement

25   Income Security Act of 1974) to provide

1   security to such plan as a condition for

2   granting or modifying a waiver under

3   paragraph (1).

4   "(ii) SPECIAL RULES.—Any security

5   provided under clause (i) may be perfected

6   and enforced only by the Pension Benefit

7   Guaranty Corporation, or at the direction

8   of the Corporation, by a contributing spon-

9   sor (within the meaning of section

10   4001(a)(13) of the Employee Retirement

11   Income Security Act of 1974), or a mem-

12   ber of such sponsor's controlled group

13   (within the meaning of section 4001(a)(14)

14   of such Act).

15   "(B) CONSULTATION WITH THE PENSION

16 BENEFIT GUARANTY CORPORATION.—Except as

17 provided in subparagraph (C), the Secretary

18 shall, before granting or modifying a waiver

19 under this subsection with respect to a plan de-

20 scribed in subparagraph (A)(i)—

21   "(i) provide the Pension Benefit

22   Guaranty Corporation with—

23   "(I) notice of the completed ap-

24   plication for any waiver or modifica-

25   tion, and

"(II) an opportunity to comment on such application within 30 days after receipt of such notice, and

"(ii) consider—

"(I) any comments of the Corporation under clause (i)(II), and

"(II) any views of any employee organization (within the meaning of section 3(4) of the Employee Retirement Income Security Act of 1974) representing participants in the plan which are submitted in writing to the Secretary in connection with such application.

Information provided to the Corporation under this subparagraph shall be considered tax return information and subject to the safeguarding and reporting requirements of section 6103(p).

"(C) EXCEPTION FOR CERTAIN WAIVERS.—

"(i) IN GENERAL.—The preceding provisions of this paragraph shall not apply to any plan with respect to which the sum of—

"(I) the aggregate unpaid minimum required contributions (within the meaning of section 4971(c)(4)) for the plan year and all preceding plan years, and

"(II) the present value of all waiver amortization installments determined for the plan year and succeeding plan years under section 430(e)(2),

is less than $1,000,000.

"(ii) TREATMENT OF WAIVERS FOR WHICH APPLICATIONS ARE PENDING.—The amount described in clause (i)(I) shall include any increase in such amount which would result if all applications for waivers of the minimum funding standard under this subsection which are pending with respect to such plan were denied.

"(5) SPECIAL RULES FOR SINGLE-EMPLOYER PLANS.—

"(A) APPLICATION MUST BE SUBMITTED BEFORE DATE 2½ MONTHS AFTER CLOSE OF YEAR.—In the case of a defined benefit plan which is not a multiemployer plan, no waiver

1   may be granted under this subsection with re-

2   spect to any plan for any plan year unless an

3   application therefor is submitted to the Sec-

4   retary not later than the 15th day of the 3rd

5   month beginning after the close of such plan

6   year.

7   "(B) SPECIAL RULE IF EMPLOYER IS MEM-

8   BER OF CONTROLLED GROUP.—In the case of a

9   defined benefit plan which is not a multiem-

10   ployer plan, if an employer is a member of a

11   controlled group, the temporary substantial

12   business hardship requirements of paragraph

13   (1) shall be treated as met only if such require-

14   ments are met—

15   "(i) with respect to such employer,

16   and

17   "(ii) with respect to the controlled

18   group of which such employer is a member

19   (determined by treating all members of

20   such group as a single employer).

21   The Secretary may provide that an analysis of

22   a trade or business or industry of a member

23   need not be conducted if the Secretary deter-

24   mines such analysis is not necessary because

25   the taking into account of such member would

1   not significantly affect the determination under

2   this paragraph.

3   ''(6) ADVANCE NOTICE.—

4   ''(A) IN GENERAL.—The Secretary shall,

5   before granting a waiver under this subsection,

6   require each applicant to provide evidence satis-

7   factory to the Secretary that the applicant has

8   provided notice of the filing of the application

9   for such waiver to each affected party (as de-

10   fined in section 4001(a)(21) of the Employee

11   Retirement Income Security Act of 1974). Such

12   notice shall include a description of the extent

13   to which the plan is funded for benefits which

14   are guaranteed under title IV of the Employee

15   Retirement Income Security Act of 1974 and

16   for benefit liabilities.

17   ''(B) CONSIDERATION OF RELEVANT IN-

18   FORMATION.—The Secretary shall consider any

19   relevant information provided by a person to

20   whom notice was given under subparagraph

21   (A).

22   ''(7) RESTRICTION ON PLAN AMENDMENTS.—

23   ''(A) IN GENERAL.—No amendment of a

24   plan which increases the liabilities of the plan

25   by reason of any increase in benefits, any

119

1 change in the accrual of benefits, or any change

2 in the rate at which benefits become nonforfeit-

3 able under the plan shall be adopted if a waiver

4 under this subsection or an extension of time

5 under section 431(d) is in effect with respect to

6 the plan, or if a plan amendment described in

7 subsection (d)(2) has been made at any time in

8 the preceding 12 months '(24 months in the

9 case of a multiemployer plan). If a plan is

10 amended in violation of the preceding sentence,

11 any such waiver, or extension of time, shall not

12 apply to any plan year ending on or after the

13 date on which such amendment is adopted.

14 "(B) EXCEPTION.—Subparagraph (A)

15 shall not apply to any plan amendment which—

16 "(i) the Secretary determines to be

17 reasonable and which provides for only de

18 minimis increases in the liabilities of the

19 plan,

20 "(ii) only repeals an amendment de-

21 scribed in subsection (d)(2), or

22 "(iii) is required as a condition of

23 qualification under part I of subchapter D,

24 of chapter 1.

25 "(d) MISCELLANEOUS RULES.—

1   "(1) CHANGE IN METHOD OR YEAR.—If the

2   funding method, the valuation date, or a plan year

3   for a plan is changed, the change shall take effect

4   only if approved by the Secretary.

5   "(2) CERTAIN RETROACTIVE PLAN AMEND-

6   MENTS.—For purposes of this section, any amend-

7   ment applying to a plan year which—

8   "(A) is adopted after the close of such plan

9   year but no later than 2½ months after the

10   close of the plan year (or, in the case of a mul-

11   tiemployer plan, no later than 2 years after the

12   close of such plan year),

13   "(B) does not reduce the accrued benefit

14   of any participant determined as of the begin-

15   ning of the first plan year to which the amend-

16   ment applies, and

17   "(C) does not reduce the accrued benefit of

18   any participant determined as of the time of

19   adoption except to the extent required by the

20   circumstances,

21   shall, at the election of the plan administrator, be

22   deemed to have been made on the first day of such

23   plan year. No amendment described in this para-

24   graph which reduces the accrued benefits of any par-

25   ticipant shall take effect unless the plan adminis-

1   trator files a notice with the Secretary notifying him

2   of such amendment and the Secretary has approved

3   such amendment, or within 90 days after the date

4   on which such notice was filed, failed to disapprove

5   such amendment. No amendment described in this

6   subsection shall be approved by the Secretary unless

7   the Secretary determines that such amendment is

8   necessary because of a temporary substantial busi-

9   ness hardship (as determined under subsection

10   (c)(2)) or a substantial business hardship (as so de-

11   termined) in the case of a multiemployer plan and

12   that a waiver under subsection (c) (or, in the case

13   of a multiemployer plan, any extension of the amor-

14   tization period under section 431(d)) is unavailable

15   or inadequate.

16   "(3) CONTROLLED GROUP.—For purposes of

17   this section, the term 'controlled group' means any

18   group treated as a single employer under subsection

19   (b), (c), (m), or (o) of section 414.

20   "(e) PLANS TO WHICH SECTION APPLIES.—

21   "(1) IN GENERAL.—Except as provided in para-

22   graphs (2) and (4), this section applies to a plan if,

23   for any plan year beginning on or after the effective

24   date of this section for such plan under the Em-

25   ployee Retirement Income Security Act of 1974—

1   "(A) such plan included a trust which

2   qualified (or was determined by the Secretary

3   to have qualified) under section 401(a), or

4   "(B) such plan satisfied (or was deter-

5   mined by the Secretary to have satisfied) the

6   requirements of section 403(a).

7   "(2) EXCEPTIONS.—This section shall not

8 apply to—

9   "(A) any profit-sharing or stock bonus

10   plan,

11   "(B) any insurance contract plan described

12   in paragraph (3),

13   "(C) any governmental plan (within the

14   meaning of section 414(d)),

15   "(D) any church plan (within the meaning

16   of section 414(e)) with respect to which the

17   election provided by section 410(d) has not been

18   made,

19   "(E) any plan which has not, at any time

20   after September 2, 1974, provided for employer

21   contributions, or

22   "(F) any plan established and maintained

23   by a society, order, or association described in

24   section 501(c)(8) or (9), if no part of the con-

1   tributions to or under such plan are made by

2   employers of participants in such plan.

3   No plan described in subparagraph (C), (D), or (F)

4 shall be treated as a qualified plan for purposes of

5 section 401(a) unless such plan meets the require-

6 ments of section 401(a)(7) as in effect on September

7 1, 1974.

8   "(3) CERTAIN INSURANCE CONTRACT PLANS.—

9 A plan is described in this paragraph if—

10   "(A) the plan is funded exclusively by the

11   purchase of individual insurance contracts,

12   "(B) such contracts provide for level an-

13   nual premium payments to be paid extending

14   not later than the retirement age for each indi-

15   vidual participating in the plan, and com-

16   mencing with the date the individual became a

17   participant in the plan (or, in the case of an in-

18   crease in benefits, commencing at the time such

19   increase becomes effective),

20   "(C) benefits provided by the plan are

21   equal to the benefits provided under each con-

22   tract at normal retirement age under the plan

23   and are guaranteed by an insurance carrier (li-

24   censed under the laws of a State to do business

1   with the plan) to the extent premiums have

2   been paid,

3   "(D) premiums payable for the plan year,

4   and all prior plan years, under such contracts

5   have been paid before lapse or there is rein-

6   statement of the policy,

7   "(E) no rights under such contracts have

8   been subject to a security interest at any time

9   during the plan year, and

10   "(F) no policy loans are outstanding at

11   any time during the plan year.

12 A plan funded exclusively by the purchase of group

13 insurance contracts which is determined under regu-

14 lations prescribed by the Secretary to have the same

15 characteristics as contracts described in the pre-

16 ceding sentence shall be treated as a plan described

17 in this paragraph.

18   "(4) CERTAIN TERMINATED MULTIEMPLOYER

19 PLANS.—This section applies with respect to a ter-

20 minated multiemployer plan to which section 4021

21 of the Employee Retirement Income Security Act of

22 1974 applies until the last day of the plan year in

23 which the plan terminates (within the meaning of

24 section 4041A(a)(2) of such Act).".

1   (b) EFFECTIVE DATE.—The amendments made by
2 this section shall apply to plan years beginning after De-
3 cember 31, 2007.

4 **SEC. 112. FUNDING RULES FOR SINGLE-EMPLOYER DE-**
5   **FINED BENEFIT PENSION PLANS.**

6   (a) IN GENERAL.—Subchapter D of chapter 1 of the
7 Internal Revenue Code of 1986 (relating to deferred com-
8 pensation, etc.) is amended by adding at the end the fol-
9 lowing new part:

10 **"PART III—MINIMUM FUNDING STANDARDS FOR**
11   **SINGLE-EMPLOYER DEFINED BENEFIT PEN-**
12   **SION PLANS**

13 **"SEC. 430. MINIMUM FUNDING STANDARDS FOR SINGLE-**
14   **EMPLOYER DEFINED BENEFIT PENSION**
15   **PLANS.**

16   "(a) MINIMUM REQUIRED CONTRIBUTION.—For
17 purposes of this section and section 412(a)(2)(A), except
18 as provided in subsection (f), the term 'minimum required
19 contribution' means, with respect to any plan year of a
20 defined benefit plan which is not a multiemployer plan—

21   "(1) in any case in which the value of plan as-
22   sets of the plan (as reduced under subsection
23   (f)(4)(B)) is less than the funding target of the plan
24   for the plan year, the sum of—

1   "(A) the target normal cost of the plan for

2   the plan year,

3   "(B) the shortfall amortization charge (if

4   any) for the plan for the plan year determined

5   under subsection (c), and

6   "(C) the waiver amortization charge (if

7   any) for the plan for the plan year as deter-

8   mined under subsection (e);

9   "(2) in any case in which the value of plan as-

10   sets of the plan (as reduced under subsection

11   (f)(4)(B)) equals or exceeds the funding target of

12   the plan for the plan year, the target normal cost of

13   the plan for the plan year reduced (but not below

14   zero) by such excess.

15   "(b) TARGET NORMAL COST.—For purposes of this

16 section, except as provided in subsection (i)(2) with re-

17 spect to plans in at-risk status, the term 'target normal

18 cost' means, for any plan year, the present value of all

19 benefits which are expected to accrue or to be earned

20 under the plan during the plan year. For purposes of this

21 subsection, if any benefit attributable to services per-

22 formed in a preceding plan year is increased by reason

23 of any increase in compensation during the current plan

24 year, the increase in such benefit shall be treated as hav-

25 ing accrued during the current plan year.

1   "(c) SHORTFALL AMORTIZATION CHARGE.—

2   "(1) IN GENERAL.—For purposes of this sec-

3 tion, the shortfall amortization charge for a plan for

4 any plan year is the aggregate total (not less than

5 zero) of the shortfall amortization installments for

6 such plan year with respect to the shortfall amorti-

7 zation bases for such plan year and each of the 6

8 preceding plan years.

9   "(2) SHORTFALL AMORTIZATION INSTALL-

10 MENT.—For purposes of paragraph (1)—

11   "(A) DETERMINATION.—The shortfall am-

12   ortization installments are the amounts nec-

13   essary to amortize the shortfall amortization

14   base of the plan for any plan year in level an-

15   nual installments over the 7-plan-year period

16   beginning with such plan year.

17   "(B) SHORTFALL INSTALLMENT.—The

18   shortfall amortization installment for any plan

19   year in the 7-plan-year period under subpara-

20   graph (A) with respect to any shortfall amorti-

21   zation base is the annual installment deter-

22   mined under subparagraph (A) for that year for

23   that base.

24   "(C) SEGMENT RATES.—In determining

25   any shortfall amortization installment under

1   this paragraph, the plan sponsor shall use the

2   segment rates determined under subparagraph

3   (C) of subsection (h)(2), applied under rules

4   similar to the rules of subparagraph (B) of sub-

5   section (h)(2).

6   "(3) SHORTFALL AMORTIZATION BASE.—For

7   purposes of this section, the shortfall amortization

8   base of a plan for a plan year is—

9   "(A) the funding shortfall of such plan for

10   such plan year, minus

11   "(B) the present value (determined using

12   the segment rates determined under subpara-

13   graph (C) of subsection (h)(2), applied under

14   rules similar to the rules of subparagraph (B)

15   of subsection (h)(2)) of the aggregate total of

16   the shortfall amortization installments and

17   waiver amortization installments which have

18   been determined for such plan year and any

19   succeeding plan year with respect to the short-

20   fall amortization bases and waiver amortization

21   bases of the plan for any plan year preceding

22   such plan year.

23   "(4) FUNDING SHORTFALL.—For purposes of

24   this section, the funding shortfall of a plan for any

25   plan year is the excess (if any) of—

1   "(A) the funding target of the plan for the

2   plan year, over

3   "(B) the value of plan assets of the plan

4   (as reduced under subsection (f)(4)(B)) for the

5   plan year which are held by the plan on the

6   valuation date.

7   "(5) EXEMPTION FROM NEW SHORTFALL AM-

8 ORTIZATION BASE.—

9   "(A) IN GENERAL.—In any case in which

10   the value of plan assets of the plan (as reduced

11   under subsection (f)(4)(A)) is equal to or great-

12   er than the funding target of the plan for the

13   plan year, the shortfall amortization base of the

14   plan for such plan year shall be zero.

15   "(B) TRANSITION RULE.—

16   "(i) IN GENERAL.—Except as pro-

17   vided in clauses (iii) and (iv), in the case

18   of plan years beginning after 2007 and be-

19   fore 2011, only the applicable percentage

20   of the funding target shall be taken into

21   account under paragraph (3)(A) in deter-

22   mining the funding shortfall for the plan

23   year for purposes of subparagraph (A).

24   "(ii) APPLICABLE PERCENTAGE.—For

25   purposes of subparagraph (A), the applica-

130

1 ble percentage shall be determined in ac-

2 cordance with the following table:

"In the case of a plan year beginning in calendar year:	The applicable percentage is
2008	92
2009	94
2010	96.

3   "(iii) LIMITATION.—Clause (i) shall

4 not apply with respect to any plan year

5 after 2008 unless the shortfall amortiza-

6 tion base for each of the preceding years

7 beginning after 2007 was zero (determined

8 after application of this subparagraph).

9   "(iv) TRANSITION RELIEF NOT AVAIL-

10 ABLE FOR NEW OR DEFICIT REDUCTION

11 PLANS.—Clause (i) shall not apply to a

12 plan—

13   "(I) which was not in effect for a

14 plan year beginning in 2007, or

15   "(II) which was in effect for a

16 plan year beginning in 2007 and

17 which was subject to section 412(l)

18 (as in effect for plan years beginning

19 in 2007), determined after the appli-

20 cation of paragraphs (6) and (9)

21 thereof.

22   "(6) EARLY DEEMED AMORTIZATION UPON AT-

23 TAINMENT OF FUNDING TARGET.—In any case in

1   which the funding shortfall of a plan for a plan year

2   is zero, for purposes of determining the shortfall am-

3   ortization charge for such plan year and succeeding

4   plan years, the shortfall amortization bases for all

5   preceding plan years (and all shortfall amortization

6   installments determined with respect to such bases)

7   shall be reduced to zero.

8   "(d) RULES RELATING TO FUNDING TARGET.—For

9 purposes of this section—

10   "(1) FUNDING TARGET.—Except as provided in

11   subsection (i)(1) with respect to plans in at-risk sta-

12   tus, the funding target of a plan for a plan year is

13   the present value of all benefits accrued or earned

14   under the plan as of the beginning of the plan year.

15   "(2) FUNDING TARGET ATTAINMENT PERCENT-

16   AGE.—The 'funding target attainment percentage' of

17   a plan for a plan year is the ratio (expressed as a

18   percentage) which—

19   "(A) the value of plan assets for the plan

20   year (as reduced under subsection (f)(4)(B)),

21   bears to

22   "(B) the funding target of the plan for the

23   plan year (determined without regard to sub-

24   section (i)(1)).

25   "(e) WAIVER AMORTIZATION CHARGE.—

1   "(1) DETERMINATION OF WAIVER AMORTIZA-

2 TION CHARGE.—The waiver amortization charge (if

3 any) for a plan for any plan year is the aggregate

4 total of the waiver amortization installments for

5 such plan year with respect to the waiver amortiza-

6 tion bases for each of the 5 preceding plan years.

7   "(2) WAIVER AMORTIZATION INSTALLMENT.—

8 For purposes of paragraph (1)—

9   "(A) DETERMINATION.—The waiver amor-

10   tization installments are the amounts necessary

11   to amortize the waiver amortization base of the

12   plan for any plan year in level annual install-

13   ments over a period of 5 plan years beginning

14   with the succeeding plan year.

15   "(B) WAIVER INSTALLMENT.—The waiver

16   amortization installment for any plan year in

17   the 5-year period under subparagraph (A) with

18   respect to any waiver amortization base is the

19   annual installment determined under subpara-

20   graph (A) for that year for that base.

21   "(3) INTEREST RATE.—In determining any

22 waiver amortization installment under this sub-

23 section, the plan sponsor shall use the segment rates

24 determined under subparagraph (C) of subsection

(h)(2), applied under rules similar to the rules of subparagraph (B) of subsection (h)(2).

"(4) WAIVER AMORTIZATION BASE.—The waiver amortization base of a plan for a plan year is the amount of the waived funding deficiency (if any) for such plan year under section 412(c).

"(5) EARLY DEEMED AMORTIZATION UPON ATTAINMENT OF FUNDING TARGET.—In any case in which the funding shortfall of a plan for a plan year is zero, for purposes of determining the waiver amortization charge for such plan year and succeeding plan years, the waiver amortization bases for all preceding plan years (and all waiver amortization installments determined with respect to such bases) shall be reduced to zero.

"(f) REDUCTION OF MINIMUM REQUIRED CONTRIBUTION BY PREFUNDING BALANCE AND FUNDING STANDARD CARRYOVER BALANCE.—

"(1) ELECTION TO MAINTAIN BALANCES.—

"(A) PREFUNDING BALANCE.—The plan sponsor of a defined benefit plan which is not a multiemployer plan may elect to maintain a prefunding balance.

"(B) FUNDING STANDARD CARRYOVER BALANCE.—

1   "(i) IN GENERAL.—In the case of a

2   defined benefit plan (other than a multiem-

3   ployer plan) described in clause (ii), the

4   plan sponsor may elect to maintain a fund-

5   ing standard carryover balance, until such

6   balance is reduced to zero.

7   "(ii) PLANS MAINTAINING FUNDING

8   STANDARD ACCOUNT IN 2007.—A plan is

9   described in this clause if the plan—

10   "(I) was in effect for a plan year

11   beginning in 2007, and

12   "(II) had a positive balance in

13   the funding standard account under

14   section 412(b) as in effect for such

15   plan year and determined as of the

16   end of such plan year.

17   "(2) APPLICATION OF BALANCES.—A

18 prefunding balance and a funding standard carry-

19 over balance maintained pursuant to this para-

20 graph—

21   "(A) shall be available for crediting against

22   the minimum required contribution, pursuant to

23   an election under paragraph (3),

24   "(B) shall be applied as a reduction in the

25   amount treated as the value of plan assets for

1   purposes of this section, to the extent provided

2   in paragraph (4), and

3   "(C) may be reduced at any time, pursu-

4   ant to an election under paragraph (5).

5   "(3) ELECTION TO APPLY BALANCES AGAINST

6   MINIMUM REQUIRED CONTRIBUTION.—

7   "(A) IN GENERAL.—Except as provided in

8   subparagraphs (B) and (C), in the case of any

9   plan year in which the plan sponsor elects to

10   credit against the minimum required contribu-

11   tion for the current plan year all or a portion

12   of the prefunding balance or the funding stand-

13   ard carryover balance for the current plan year

14   (not in excess of such minimum required con-

15   tribution), the minimum required contribution

16   for the plan year shall be reduced as of the first

17   day of the plan year by the amount so credited

18   by the plan sponsor as of the first day of the

19   plan year. For purposes of the preceding sen-

20   tence, the minimum required contribution shall

21   be determined after taking into account any

22   waiver under section 412(c).

23   "(B) COORDINATION WITH FUNDING

24   STANDARD CARRYOVER BALANCE.—To the ex-

25   tent that any plan has a funding standard car-

ryover balance greater than zero, no amount of
the prefunding balance of such plan may be
credited under this paragraph in reducing the
minimum required contribution.

"(C) LIMITATION FOR UNDERFUNDED
PLANS.—The preceding provisions of this paragraph shall not apply for any plan year if the
ratio (expressed as a percentage) which—

"(i) the value of plan assets for the
preceding plan year (as reduced under
paragraph (4)(C)), bears to

"(ii) the funding target of the plan for
the preceding plan year (determined without regard to subsection (i)(1)),

is less than 80 percent. In the case of plan
years beginning in 2008, the ratio under this
subparagraph may be determined using such
methods of estimation as the Secretary may
prescribe.

"(4) EFFECT OF BALANCES ON AMOUNTS
TREATED AS VALUE OF PLAN ASSETS.—In the case
of any plan maintaining a prefunding balance or a
funding standard carryover balance pursuant to this
subsection, the amount treated as the value of plan

assets shall be deemed to be such amount, reduced as provided in the following subparagraphs:

"(A) APPLICABILITY OF SHORTFALL AMORTIZATION BASE.—For purposes of subsection (c)(5), the value of plan assets is deemed to be such amount, reduced by the amount of the prefunding balance, but only if an election under paragraph (2) applying any portion of the prefunding balance in reducing the minimum required contribution is in effect for the plan year.

"(B) DETERMINATION OF EXCESS ASSETS, FUNDING SHORTFALL, AND FUNDING TARGET ATTAINMENT PERCENTAGE.—

"(i) IN GENERAL.—For purposes of subsections (a), (c)(4)(B), and (d)(2)(A), the value of plan assets is deemed to be such amount, reduced by the amount of the prefunding balance and the funding standard carryover balance.

"(ii) SPECIAL RULE FOR CERTAIN BINDING AGREEMENTS WITH PBGC.—For purposes of subsection (c)(4)(B), the value of plan assets shall not be deemed to be reduced for a plan year by the amount of the

1   specified balance if, with respect to such

2   balance, there is in effect for a plan year

3   a binding written agreement with the Pen-

4   sion Benefit Guaranty Corporation which

5   provides that such balance is not available

6   to reduce the minimum required contribu-

7   tion for the plan year. For purposes of the

8   preceding sentence, the term 'specified bal-

9   ance' means the prefunding balance or the

10   funding standard carryover balance, as the

11   case may be.

12   "(C) AVAILABILITY OF BALANCES IN PLAN

13   YEAR FOR CREDITING AGAINST MINIMUM RE-

14   QUIRED   CONTRIBUTION.—For   purposes   of

15   paragraph (3)(C)(i) of this subsection, the value

16   of plan assets is deemed to be such amount, re-

17   duced by the amount of the prefunding balance.

18   "(5) ELECTION TO REDUCE BALANCE PRIOR TO

19   DETERMINATIONS OF VALUE OF PLAN ASSETS AND

20   CREDITING AGAINST MINIMUM REQUIRED CONTRIBU-

21   TION.—

22   "(A) IN GENERAL.—The plan sponsor may

23   elect to reduce by any amount the balance of

24   the prefunding balance and the funding stand-

25   ard carryover balance for any plan year (but

1   not below zero). Such reduction shall be effec-

2   tive prior to any determination of the value of

3   plan assets for such plan year under this sec-

4   tion and application of the balance in reducing

5   the minimum required contribution for such

6   plan for such plan year pursuant to an election

7   under paragraph (2).

8   "(B) COORDINATION BETWEEN

9   PREFUNDING BALANCE AND FUNDING STAND-

10   ARD CARRYOVER BALANCE.—To the extent that

11   any plan has a funding standard carryover bal-

12   ance greater than zero, no election may be

13   made under subparagraph (A) with respect to

14   the prefunding balance.

15   "(6) PREFUNDING BALANCE.—

16   "(A) IN GENERAL.—A prefunding balance

17   maintained by a plan shall consist of a begin-

18   ning balance of zero, increased and decreased to

19   the extent provided in subparagraphs (B) and

20   (C), and adjusted further as provided in para-

21   graph (8).

22   "(B) INCREASES.—

23   "(i) IN GENERAL.—As of the first day

24   of each plan year beginning after 2008, the

25   prefunding balance of a plan shall be in-

1   creased by the amount elected by the plan

2   sponsor for the plan year. Such amount

3   shall not exceed the excess (if any) of—

4   "(I) the aggregate total of em-

5   ployer contributions to the plan for

6   the preceding plan year, over—

7   "(II) the minimum required con-

8   tribution for such preceding plan year.

9   "(ii) ADJUSTMENTS FOR INTEREST.—

10   Any excess contributions under clause (i)

11   shall be properly adjusted for interest ac-

12   cruing for the periods between the first

13   day of the current plan year and the dates

14   on which the excess contributions were

15   made, determined by using the effective in-

16   terest rate for the preceding plan year and

17   by treating contributions as being first

18   used to satisfy the minimum required con-

19   tribution.

20   "(iii) CERTAIN CONTRIBUTIONS NEC-

21   ESSARY TO AVOID BENEFIT LIMITATIONS

22   DISREGARDED.—The excess described in

23   clause (i) with respect to any preceding

24   plan year shall be reduced (but not below

25   zero) by the amount of contributions an

141

employer would be required to make under
paragraph (1), (2), or (4) of section 206(g)
to avoid a benefit limitation which would
otherwise be imposed under such paragraph for the preceding plan year. Any
contribution which may be taken into account in satisfying the requirements of
more than 1 of such paragraphs shall be
taken into account only once for purposes
of this clause.

"(C) DECREASES.—The prefunding bal-
ance of a plan shall be decreased (but not below
zero) by the sum of—

"(i) as of the first day of each plan
year after 2008, the amount of such balance credited under paragraph (2) (if any)
in reducing the minimum required contribution of the plan for the preceding plan
year, and

"(ii) as of the time specified in paragraph (5))(A), any reduction in such balance elected under paragraph (5).

"(7) FUNDING STANDARD CARRYOVER BAL-
ANCE.—

1   "(A) IN GENERAL.—A funding standard

2 carryover balance maintained by a plan shall

3 consist of a beginning balance determined

4 under subparagraph (B), decreased to the ex-

5 tent provided in subparagraph (C), and ad-

6 justed further as provided in paragraph (8).

7   "(B) BEGINNING BALANCE.—The begin-

8 ning balance of the funding standard carryover

9 balance shall be the positive balance described

10 in paragraph (1)(B)(ii)(II).

11   "(C) DECREASES.—The funding standard

12 carryover balance of a plan shall be decreased

13 (but not below zero) by—

14   "(i) as of the first day of each plan

15   year after 2008, the amount of such bal-

16   ance credited under paragraph (2) (if any)

17   in reducing the minimum required con-

18   tribution of the plan for the preceding plan

19   year, and

20   "(ii) as of the time specified in para-

21   graph (5))(A), any reduction in such bal-

22   ance elected under paragraph (5).

23 "(8) ADJUSTMENTS FOR INVESTMENT EXPERI-

24 ENCE.—In determining the prefunding balance or

25 the funding standard carryover balance of a plan as

of the first day of the plan year, the plan sponsor
shall, in accordance with regulations prescribed by
the Secretary of the Treasury, adjust such balance
to reflect the rate of return on plan assets for the
preceding plan year. Notwithstanding subsection
(g)(3), such rate of return shall be determined on
the basis of fair market value and shall properly
take into account, in accordance with such regulations, all contributions, distributions, and other plan
payments made during such period.

"(9) ELECTIONS.—Elections under this subsection shall be made at such times, and in such
form and manner, as shall be prescribed in regulations of the Secretary.

"(g) VALUATION OF PLAN ASSETS AND LIABIL-
ITIES.—

"(1) TIMING OF DETERMINATIONS.—Except as
otherwise provided under this subsection, all determinations under this section for a plan year shall be
made as of the valuation date of the plan for such
plan year.

"(2) VALUATION DATE.—For purposes of this
section—

"(A) IN GENERAL.—Except as provided in
subparagraph (B), the valuation date of a plan

1   for any plan year shall be the first day of the

2   plan year.

3   "(B) EXCEPTION FOR SMALL PLANS.—If,

4   on each day during the preceding plan year, a

5   plan had 100 or fewer participants, the plan

6   may designate any day during the plan year as

7   its valuation date for such plan year and suc-

8   ceeding plan years. For purposes of this sub-

9   paragraph, all defined benefit plans (other than

10   multiemployer plans) maintained by the same

11   employer (or any member of such employer's

12   controlled group) shall be treated as 1 plan, but

13   only participants with respect to such employer

14   or member shall be taken into account.

15   "(C) APPLICATION OF CERTAIN RULES IN

16   DETERMINATION OF PLAN SIZE.—For purposes

17   of this paragraph—

18   "(i) PLANS NOT IN EXISTENCE IN

19   PRECEDING YEAR.—In the case of the first

20   plan year of any plan, subparagraph (B)

21   shall apply to such plan by taking into ac-

22   count the number of participants that the

23   plan is reasonably expected to have on

24   days during such first plan year.

145

1   "(ii) PREDECESSORS.—Any reference

2   in subparagraph (B) to an employer shall

3   include a reference to any predecessor of

4   such employer.

5   "(3) DETERMINATION OF VALUE OF PLAN AS-

6 SETS.—For purposes of this section—

7   "(A) IN GENERAL.—Except as provided in

8   subparagraph (B), the value of plan assets shall

9   be the fair market value of the assets.

10   "(B) AVERAGING ALLOWED.—A plan may

11   determine the value of plan assets on the basis

12   of the averaging of fair market values, but only

13   if such method—

14   "(i) is permitted under regulations

15   prescribed by the Secretary,

16   "(ii) does not provide for averaging of

17   such values over more than the period be-

18   ginning on the last day of the 25th month

19   preceding the month in which the valuation

20   date occurs and ending on the valuation

21   date (or a similar period in the case of a

22   valuation date which is not the 1st day of

23   a month), and

24   "(iii) does not result in a determina-

25   tion of the value of plan assets which, at

1   any time, is lower than 90 percent or

2   greater than 110 percent of the fair mar-

3   ket value of such assets at such time.

4   Any such averaging shall be adjusted for con-

5 tributions and distributions (as provided by the

6 Secretary).

7   "(4) ACCOUNTING FOR CONTRIBUTION RE-

8 CEIPTS.—For purposes of determining the value of

9 assets under paragraph (3)—

10   "(A) PRIOR YEAR CONTRIBUTIONS.—If—

11   "(i) an employer makes any contribu-

12   tion to the plan after the valuation date for

13   the plan year in which the contribution is

14   made, and

15   "(ii) the contribution is for a pre-

16   ceding plan year,

17 the contribution shall be taken into account as

18 an asset of the plan as of the valuation date,

19 except that in the case of any plan year begin-

20 ning after 2008, only the present value (deter-

21 mined as of the valuation date) of such con-

22 tribution may be taken into account. For pur-

23 poses of the preceding sentence, present value

24 shall be determined using the effective interest

1   rate for the preceding plan year to which the

2   contribution is properly allocable.

3   "(B) SPECIAL RULE FOR CURRENT YEAR

4   CONTRIBUTIONS MADE BEFORE VALUATION

5   DATE.—If any contributions for any plan year

6   are made to or under the plan during the plan

7   year but before the valuation date for the plan

8   year, the assets of the plan as of the valuation

9   date shall not include—

10   "(i) such contributions, and

11   "(ii) interest on such contributions for

12   the period between the date of the con-

13   tributions and the valuation date, deter-

14   mined by using the effective interest rate

15   for the plan year.

16   "(h) ACTUARIAL ASSUMPTIONS AND METHODS.—

17   "(1) IN GENERAL.—Subject to this subsection,

18   the determination of any present value or other com-

19   putation under this section shall be made on the

20   basis of actuarial assumptions and methods—

21   "(A) each of which is reasonable (taking

22   into account the experience of the plan and rea-

23   sonable expectations), and

1   "(B) which, in combination, offer the actu-

2 ary's best estimate of anticipated experience

3 under the plan.

4   "(2) INTEREST RATES.—

5   "(A) EFFECTIVE INTEREST RATE.—For

6 purposes of this section, the term 'effective in-

7 terest rate' means, with respect to any plan for

8 any plan year, the single rate of interest which,

9 if used to determine the present value of the

10 plan's accrued or earned benefits referred to in

11 subsection (d)(1), would result in an amount

12 equal to the funding target of the plan for such

13 plan year.

14   "(B) INTEREST RATES FOR DETERMINING

15 FUNDING TARGET.—For purposes of deter-

16 mining the funding target of a plan for any

17 plan year, the interest rate used in determining

18 the present value of the liabilities of the plan

19 shall be—

20   "(i) in the case of benefits reasonably

21 determined to be payable during the 5-year

22 period beginning on the first day of the

23 plan year, the first segment rate with re-

24 spect to the applicable month,

149

1   "(ii) in the case of benefits reasonably

2   determined to be payable during the 15-

3   year period beginning at the end of the pe-

4   riod described in clause (i), the second seg-

5   ment rate with respect to the applicable

6   month, and

7   "(iii) in the case of benefits reason-

8   ably determined to be payable after the pe-

9   riod described in clause (ii), the third seg-

10   ment rate with respect to the applicable

11   month.

12   "(C) SEGMENT RATES.—For purposes of

13 this paragraph—

14   "(i) FIRST SEGMENT RATE.—The

15   term 'first segment rate' means, with re-

16   spect to any month, the single rate of in-

17   terest which shall be determined by the

18   Secretary for such month on the basis of

19   the corporate bond yield curve for such

20   month, taking into account only that por-

21   tion of such yield curve which is based on

22   bonds maturing during the 5-year period

23   commencing with such month.

24   "(ii) SECOND SEGMENT RATE.—The

25   term 'second segment rate' means, with re-

1 spect to any month, the single rate of in-

2 terest which shall be determined by the

3 Secretary for such month on the basis of

4 the corporate bond yield curve for such

5 month, taking into account only that por-

6 tion of such yield curve which is based on

7 bonds maturing during the 15-year period

8 beginning at the end of the period de-

9 scribed in clause (i).

10 “(iii) THIRD SEGMENT RATE.—The

11 term ‘third segment rate’ means, with re-

12 spect to any month, the single rate of in-

13 terest which shall be determined by the

14 Secretary for such month on the basis of

15 the corporate bond yield curve for such

16 month, taking into account only that por-

17 tion of such yield curve which is based on

18 bonds maturing during periods beginning

19 after the period described in clause (ii).

20 “(D) CORPORATE BOND YIELD CURVE.—

21 For purposes of this paragraph—

22 “(i) IN GENERAL.—The term ‘cor-

23 porate bond yield curve’ means, with re-

24 spect to any month, a yield curve which is

25 prescribed by the Secretary for such month

1   and which reflects the average, for the 24-

2   month period ending with the month pre-

3   ceding such month, of monthly yields on

4   investment grade corporate bonds with

5   varying maturities and that are in the top

6   3 quality levels available.

7   "(ii) ELECTION TO USE YIELD

8   CURVE.—Solely for purposes of deter-

9   mining the minimum required contribution

10   under this section, the plan sponsor may,

11   in lieu of the segment rates determined

12   under subparagraph (C), elect to use inter-

13   est rates under the corporate bond yield

14   curve. For purposes of the preceding sen-

15   tence such curve shall be determined with-

16   out regard to the 24-month averaging de-

17   scribed in clause (i). Such election, once

18   made, may be revoked only with the con-

19   sent of the Secretary.

20   "(E) APPLICABLE MONTH.—For purposes

21 of this paragraph, the term 'applicable month'

22 means, with respect to any plan for any plan

23 year, the month which includes the valuation

24 date of such plan for such plan year or, at the

25 election of the plan sponsor, any of the 4

1 months which precede such month. Any election

2 made under this subparagraph shall apply to

3 the plan year for which the election is made and

4 all succeeding plan years, unless the election is

5 revoked with the consent of the Secretary.

6   "(F) PUBLICATION REQUIREMENTS.—The

7 Secretary shall publish for each month the cor-

8 porate bond yield curve (and the corporate bond

9 yield curve reflecting the modification described

10 in section 417(e)(3)(D)(i) for such month and

11 each of the rates determined under subpara-

12 graph (B) for such month. The Secretary shall

13 also publish a description of the methodology

14 used to determine such yield curve and such

15 rates which is sufficiently detailed to enable

16 plans to make reasonable projections regarding

17 the yield curve and such rates for future

18 months based on the plan's projection of future

19 interest rates.

20   "(G) TRANSITION RULE.—

21   "(i) IN GENERAL.—Notwithstanding

22   the preceding provisions of this paragraph,

23   for plan years beginning in 2008 or 2009,

24   the first, second, or third segment rate for

1   a plan with respect to any month shall be

2   equal to the sum of—

3   "(I) the product of such rate for

4   such month determined without re-

5   gard to this subparagraph, multiplied

6   by the applicable percentage, and

7   "(II) the product of the rate de-

8   termined under the rules of section

9   412(b)(5)(B)(ii)(II) (as in effect for

10   plan years beginning in 2007), multi-

11   plied by a percentage equal to 100

12   percent minus the applicable percent-

13   age.

14   "(ii) APPLICABLE PERCENTAGE.—For

15   purposes of clause (i), the applicable per-

16   centage is 33⅓ percent for plan years be-

17   ginning in 2008 and 66⅔ percent for plan

18   years beginning in 2009.

19   "(iii) NEW PLANS INELIGIBLE.—

20   Clause (i) shall not apply to any plan if the

21   first plan year of the plan begins after De-

22   cember 31, 2007.

23   "(iv) ELECTION.—The plan sponsor

24   may elect not to have this subparagraph

25   apply. Such election, once made, may be

1   revoked only with the consent of the Sec-

2   retary.

3   "(3) MORTALITY TABLES.—

4   "(A) IN GENERAL.—Except as provided in

5   subparagraph (C) or (D), the Secretary shall by

6   regulation prescribe mortality tables to be used

7   in determining any present value or making any

8   computation under this section. Such tables

9   shall be based on the actual experience of pen-

10   sion plans and projected trends in such experi-

11   ence. In prescribing such tables, the Secretary

12   shall take into account results of available inde-

13   pendent studies of mortality of individuals cov-

14   ered by pension plans.

15   "(B) PERIODIC REVISION.—The Secretary

16   shall (at least every 10 years) make revisions in

17   any table in effect under subparagraph (A) to

18   reflect the actual experience of pension plans

19   and projected trends in such experience.

20   "(C) SUBSTITUTE MORTALITY TABLE.—

21   "(i) IN GENERAL.—Upon request by

22   the plan sponsor and approval by the Sec-

23   retary, a mortality table which meets the

24   requirements of clause (iii) shall be used in

25   determining any present value or making

1   any computation under this section during
2   the period of consecutive plan years (not to
3   exceed 10) specified in the request.

4   "(ii) EARLY TERMINATION OF PE-
5   RIOD.—Notwithstanding clause (i), a mor-
6   tality table described in clause (i) shall
7   cease to be in effect as of the earliest of—

8   "(I) the date on which there is a
9   significant change in the participants
10   in the plan by reason of a plan spinoff
11   or merger or otherwise, or

12   "(II) the date on which the plan
13   actuary determines that such table
14   does not meet the requirements of
15   clause (iii).

16   "(iii) REQUIREMENTS.—A mortality
17   table meets the requirements of this clause
18   if—

19   "(I) there is a sufficient number
20   of plan participants, and the pension
21   plans have been maintained for a suf-
22   ficient period of time, to have credible
23   information necessary for purposes of
24   subclause (II), and

1   "(II) such table reflects the ac-

2   tual experience of the pension plans

3   maintained by the sponsor and pro-

4   jected trends in general mortality ex-

5   perience.

6   "(iv) ALL PLANS IN CONTROLLED

7 GROUP MUST USE SEPARATE TABLE.—Ex-

8 cept as provided by the Secretary, a plan

9 sponsor may not use a mortality table

10 under this subparagraph for any plan

11 maintained by the plan sponsor unless—

12   "(I) a separate mortality table is

13   established and used under this sub-

14   paragraph for each other plan main-

15   tained by the plan sponsor and if the

16   plan sponsor is a member of a con-

17   trolled group, each member of the

18   controlled group, and

19   "(II) the requirements of clause

20   (iii) are met separately with respect to

21   the table so established for each such

22   plan, determined by only taking into

23   account the participants of such plan,

24   the time such plan has been in exist-

ence, and the actual experience of such plan.

"(v) DEADLINE FOR SUBMISSION AND DISPOSITION OF APPLICATION.—

"(I) SUBMISSION.—The plan sponsor shall submit a mortality table to the Secretary for approval under this subparagraph at least 7 months before the 1st day of the period described in clause (i).

"(II) DISPOSITION.—Any mortality table submitted to the Secretary for approval under this subparagraph shall be treated as in effect as of the 1st day of the period described in clause (i) unless the Secretary, during the 180-day period beginning on the date of such submission, disapproves of such table and provides the reasons that such table fails to meet the requirements of clause (iii). The 180-day period shall be extended upon mutual agreement of the Secretary and the plan sponsor.

1   "(D) SEPARATE MORTALITY TABLES FOR

2   THE DISABLED.—Notwithstanding subpara-

3   graph (A)—

4   "(i) IN GENERAL.—The Secretary

5   shall establish mortality tables which may

6   be used (in lieu of the tables under sub-

7   paragraph (A)) under this subsection for

8   individuals who are entitled to benefits

9   under the plan on account of disability.

10   The Secretary shall establish separate ta-

11   bles for individuals whose disabilities occur

12   in plan years beginning before January 1,

13   1995, and for individuals whose disabilities

14   occur in plan years beginning on or after

15   such date.

16   "(ii) SPECIAL RULE FOR DISABILITIES

17   OCCURRING AFTER 1994.—In the case of

18   disabilities occurring in plan years begin-

19   ning after December 31, 1994, the tables

20   under clause (i) shall apply only with re-

21   spect to individuals described in such sub-

22   clause who are disabled within the meaning

23   of title II of the Social Security Act and

24   the regulations thereunder.

"(iii) PERIODIC REVISION.—The Secretary shall (at least every 10 years) make revisions in any table in effect under clause (i) to reflect the actual experience of pension plans and projected trends in such experience.

"(4) PROBABILITY OF BENEFIT PAYMENTS IN THE FORM OF LUMP SUMS OR OTHER OPTIONAL FORMS.—For purposes of determining any present value or making any computation under this section, there shall be taken into account—

"(A) the probability that future benefit payments under the plan will be made in the form of optional forms of benefits provided under the plan (including lump sum distributions, determined on the basis of the plan's experience and other related assumptions), and

"(B) any difference in the present value of such future benefit payments resulting from the use of actuarial assumptions, in determining benefit payments in any such optional form of benefits, which are different from those specified in this subsection.

"(5) APPROVAL OF LARGE CHANGES IN ACTUARIAL ASSUMPTIONS.—

1   "(A) IN GENERAL.—No actuarial assump-

2 tion used to determine the funding target for a

3 plan to which this paragraph applies may be

4 changed without the approval of the Secretary.

5   "(B) PLANS TO WHICH PARAGRAPH AP-

6 PLIES.—This paragraph shall apply to a plan

7 only if—

8   "(i) the plan is a defined benefit plan

9 (other than a multiemployer plan) to which

10 title IV of the Employee Retirement In-

11 come Security Act of 1974 applies,

12   "(ii) the aggregate unfunded vested

13 benefits as of the close of the preceding

14 plan year (as determined under section

15 4006(a)(3)(E)(iii) of the Employee Retire-

16 ment Income Security Act of 1974) of such

17 plan and all other plans maintained by the

18 contributing sponsors (as defined in sec-

19 tion 4001(a)(13) of such Act) and mem-

20 bers of such sponsors' controlled groups

21 (as defined in section 4001(a)(14) of such

22 Act) which are covered by title IV (dis-

23 regarding plans with no unfunded vested

24 benefits) exceed $50,000,000, and

1   "(iii) the change in assumptions (de-

2   termined after taking into account any

3   changes in interest rate and mortality

4   table) results in a decrease in the funding

5   shortfall of the plan for the current plan

6   year that exceeds $50,000,000, or that ex-

7   ceeds $5,000,000 and that is 5 percent or

8   more of the funding target of the plan be-

9   fore such change.

10 "(i) SPECIAL RULES FOR AT-RISK PLANS.—

11   "(1) FUNDING TARGET FOR PLANS IN AT-RISK

12 STATUS.—

13   "(A) IN GENERAL.—In the case of a plan

14   which is in at-risk status for a plan year, the

15   funding target of the plan for the plan year

16   shall be equal to the sum of—

17   "(i) the present value of all benefits

18   accrued or earned under the plan as of the

19   beginning of the plan year, as determined

20   by using the additional actuarial assump-

21   tions described in subparagraph (B), and

22   "(ii) in the case of a plan which also

23   has been in at-risk status for at least 2 of

24   the 4 preceding plan years, a loading fac-

25   tor determined under subparagraph (C).

162

"(B) ADDITIONAL ACTUARIAL ASSUMP-
TIONS.—The actuarial assumptions described in
this subparagraph are as follows:

"(i) All employees who are not otherwise assumed to retire as of the valuation
date but who will be eligible to elect benefits during the plan year and the 10 succeeding plan years shall be assumed to retire at the earliest retirement date under
the plan but not before the end of the plan
year for which the at-risk funding target
and at-risk target normal cost are being
determined.

"(ii) All employees shall be assumed
to elect the retirement benefit available
under the plan at the assumed retirement
age (determined after application of clause
(i)) which would result in the highest
present value of benefits.

"(C) LOADING FACTOR.—The loading factor applied with respect to a plan under this
paragraph for any plan year is the sum of—

"(i) $700, times the number of par-
ticipants in the plan, plus

1   "(ii) 4 percent of the funding target

2   (determined without regard to this para-

3   graph) of the plan for the plan year.

4   "(2) TARGET NORMAL COST OF AT-RISK

5 PLANS.—In the case of a plan which is in at-risk

6 status for a plan year, the target normal cost of the

7 plan for such plan year shall be equal to the sum

8 of—

9   "(A) the present value of all benefits which

10   are expected to accrue or be earned under the

11   plan during the plan year, determined using the

12   additional actuarial assumptions described in

13   paragraph (1)(B), plus

14   "(B) in the case of a plan which also has

15   been in at-risk status for at least 2 of the 4

16   preceding plan years, a loading factor equal to

17   4 percent of the target normal cost (determined

18   without regard to this paragraph) of the plan

19   for the plan year.

20   "(3) MINIMUM AMOUNT.—In no event shall—

21   "(A) the at-risk funding target be less

22   than the funding target, as determined without

23   regard to this subsection, or

1   "(B) the at-risk target normal cost be less

2   than the target normal cost, as determined

3   without regard to this subsection.

4   "(4) DETERMINATION OF AT-RISK STATUS.—

5 For purposes of this subsection—

6   "(A) IN GENERAL.—A plan is in at-risk

7   status for a plan year if—

8   "(i) the funding target attainment

9   percentage for the preceding plan year (de-

10   termined under this section without regard

11   to this subsection) is less than 80 percent,

12   and

13   "(ii) the funding target attainment

14   percentage for the preceding plan year (de-

15   termined under this section by using the

16   additional actuarial assumptions described

17   in paragraph (1)(B) in computing the

18   funding target) is less than 70 percent.

19   "(B) TRANSITION RULE.—In the case of

20   plan years beginning in 2008, 2009, and 2010,

21   subparagraph (A)(i) shall be applied by sub-

22   stituting the following percentages for '80 per-

23   cent':

24   "(i) 65 percent in the case of 2008.

25   "(ii) 70 percent in the case of 2009.

"(iii) 75 percent in the case of 2010.
In the case of plan years beginning in 2008, the funding target attainment percentage for the preceding plan year under subparagraph (A)(ii) may be determined using such methods of estimation as the Secretary may provide.

"(C) SPECIAL RULE FOR EMPLOYEES OFFERED EARLY RETIREMENT IN 2006.—

"(i) IN GENERAL.—For purposes of subparagraph (A)(ii), the additional actuarial assumptions described in paragraph (1)(B) shall not be taken into account with respect to any employee if—

"(I) such employee is employed by a specified automobile manufacturer,

"(II) such employee is offered a substantial amount of additional cash compensation, substantially enhanced retirement benefits under the plan, or materially reduced employment duties on the condition that by a specified date (not later than December 31, 2010) the employee retires (as defined under the terms of the plan),

1   "(III) such offer is made during

2   2006 and pursuant to a bona fide re-

3   tirement incentive program and re-

4   quires, by the terms of the offer, that

5   such offer can be accepted not later

6   than a specified date (not later than

7   December 31, 2006), and

8   "(IV) such employee does not

9   elect to accept such offer before the

10   specified date on which the offer ex-

11   pires.

12   "(ii) SPECIFIED AUTOMOBILE MANU-

13   FACTURER.—For purposes of clause (i),

14   the term 'specified automobile manufac-

15   turer' means—

16   "(I) any manufacturer of auto-

17   mobiles, and

18   "(II) any manufacturer of auto-

19   mobile parts which supplies such parts

20   directly to a manufacturer of auto-

21   mobiles and which, after a transaction

22   or series of transactions ending in

23   1999, ceased to be a member of a

24   controlled group which included such

25   manufacturer of automobiles.

"(5) TRANSITION BETWEEN APPLICABLE FUND-
ING TARGETS AND BETWEEN APPLICABLE TARGET
NORMAL COSTS.—

"(A) IN GENERAL.—In any case in which
a plan which is in at-risk status for a plan year
has been in such status for a consecutive period
of fewer than 5 plan years, the applicable
amount of the funding target and of the target
normal cost shall be, in lieu of the amount determined without regard to this paragraph, the
sum of—

"(i) the amount determined under this
section without regard to this subsection,
plus

"(ii) the transition percentage for
such plan year of the excess of the amount
determined under this subsection (without
regard to this paragraph) over the amount
determined under this section without regard to this subsection.

"(B) TRANSITION PERCENTAGE.—For
purposes of subparagraph (A), the transition
percentage shall be determined in accordance
with the following table:

"If the consecutive number of years (including the plan year) the plan is in at-risk status is—	The transition percentage is—
1	20
2	40
3	60
4	80.

"(C) YEARS BEFORE EFFECTIVE DATE.—
For purposes of this paragraph, plan years beginning before 2008 shall not be taken into account.

"(6) SMALL PLAN EXCEPTION.—If, on each day during the preceding plan year, a plan had 500 or fewer participants, the plan shall not be treated as in at-risk status for the plan year. For purposes of this paragraph, all defined benefit plans (other than multiemployer plans) maintained by the same employer (or any member of such employer's controlled group) shall be treated as 1 plan, but only participants with respect to such employer or member shall be taken into account and the rules of subsection (g)(2)(C) shall apply.

"(j) PAYMENT OF MINIMUM REQUIRED CONTRIBUTIONS.—

"(1) IN GENERAL.—For purposes of this section, the due date for any payment of any minimum required contribution for any plan year shall be 8½ months after the close of the plan year.

1   "(2) INTEREST.—Any payment required under

2   paragraph (1) for a plan year that is made on a date

3   other than the valuation date for such plan year

4   shall be adjusted for interest accruing for the period

5   between the valuation date and the payment date, at

6   the effective rate of interest for the plan for such

7   plan year.

8   "(3) ACCELERATED QUARTERLY CONTRIBUTION

9   SCHEDULE FOR UNDERFUNDED PLANS.—

10   "(A) FAILURE TO TIMELY MAKE RE-

11   QUIRED INSTALLMENT.—In any case in which

12   the plan has a funding shortfall for the pre-

13   ceding plan year, the employer maintaining the

14   plan shall make the required installments under

15   this paragraph and if the employer fails to pay

16   the full amount of a required installment for

17   the plan year, then the amount of interest

18   charged under paragraph (2) on the under-

19   payment for the period of underpayment shall

20   be determined by using a rate of interest equal

21   to the rate otherwise used under paragraph (2)

22   plus 5 percentage points.

23   "(B) AMOUNT OF UNDERPAYMENT, PE-

24   RIOD OF UNDERPAYMENT.—For purposes of

25   subparagraph (A)—

1   "(i) AMOUNT.—The amount of the

2 underpayment shall be the excess of—

3   "(I) the required installment,

4 over

5   "(II) the amount (if any) of the

6 installment contributed to or under

7 the plan on or before the due date for

8 the installment.

9   "(ii) PERIOD OF UNDERPAYMENT.—

10 The period for which any interest is

11 charged under this paragraph with respect

12 to any portion of the underpayment shall

13 run from the due date for the installment

14 to the date on which such portion is con-

15 tributed to or under the plan.

16   "(iii) ORDER OF CREDITING CON-

17 TRIBUTIONS.—For purposes of clause

18 (i)(II), contributions shall be credited

19 against unpaid required installments in the

20 order in which such installments are re-

21 quired to be paid.

22   "(C) NUMBER OF REQUIRED INSTALL-

23 MENTS; DUE DATES.—For purposes of this

24 paragraph—

1   "(i) PAYABLE IN 4 INSTALLMENTS.—

2   There shall be 4 required installments for

3   each plan year.

4   "(ii) TIME FOR PAYMENT OF IN-

5   STALLMENTS.—The due dates for required

6   installments are set forth in the following

7   table:

In the case of the following required installment:	The due date is:
1st	April 15
2nd	July 15
3rd	October 15
4th	January 15 of the following year.

8   "(D) AMOUNT OF REQUIRED INSTALL-

9   MENT.—For purposes of this paragraph—

10   "(i) IN GENERAL.—The amount of

11   any required installment shall be 25 per-

12   cent of the required annual payment.

13   "(ii) REQUIRED ANNUAL PAYMENT.—

14   For purposes of clause (i), the term 're-

15   quired annual payment' means the lesser

16   of—

17   "(I) 90 percent of the minimum

18   required contribution (determined

19   without regard to this subsection) to

1   the plan for the plan year under this

2   section, or

3   "(II) 100 percent of the min-

4   imum required contribution (deter-

5   mined without regard to this sub-

6   section or to any waiver under section

7   302(c)) to the plan for the preceding

8   plan year.

9   Subclause (II) shall not apply if the pre-

10   ceding plan year referred to in such clause

11   was not a year of 12 months.

12   "(E) FISCAL YEARS AND SHORT YEARS.—

13   "(i) FISCAL YEARS.—In applying this

14   paragraph to a plan year beginning on any

15   date other than January 1, there shall be

16   substituted for the months specified in this

17   paragraph, the months which correspond

18   thereto.

19   "(ii) SHORT PLAN YEAR.—This sub-

20   paragraph shall be applied to plan years of

21   less than 12 months in accordance with

22   regulations prescribed by the Secretary.

23   "(4) LIQUIDITY REQUIREMENT IN CONNECTION

24   WITH QUARTERLY CONTRIBUTIONS.—

1   "(A) IN GENERAL.—A plan to which this

2   paragraph applies shall be treated as failing to

3   pay the full amount of any required installment

4   under paragraph (3) to the extent that the

5   value of the liquid assets paid in such install-

6   ment is less than the liquidity shortfall (wheth-

7   er or not such liquidity shortfall exceeds the

8   amount of such installment required to be paid

9   but for this paragraph).

10   "(B) PLANS TO WHICH PARAGRAPH AP-

11   PLIES.—This paragraph shall apply to a plan

12   (other than a plan described in subsection

13   (g)(2)(B)) which—

14   "(i) is required to pay installments

15   under paragraph (3) for a plan year, and

16   "(ii) has a liquidity shortfall for any

17   quarter during such plan year.

18   "(C) PERIOD OF UNDERPAYMENT.—For

19   purposes of paragraph (3)(A), any portion of an

20   installment that is treated as not paid under

21   subparagraph (A) shall continue to be treated

22   as unpaid until the close of the quarter in

23   which the due date for such installment occurs.

24   "(D) LIMITATION ON INCREASE.—If the

25   amount of any required installment is increased

1   by reason of subparagraph (A), in no event

2   shall such increase exceed the amount which,

3   when added to prior installments for the plan

4   year, is necessary to increase the funding target

5   attainment percentage of the plan for the plan

6   year (taking into account the expected increase

7   in funding target due to benefits accruing or

8   earned during the plan year) to 100 percent.

9   "(E) DEFINITIONS.—For purposes of this

10   paragraph—

11   "(i) LIQUIDITY SHORTFALL.—The

12   term 'liquidity shortfall' means, with re-

13   spect to any required installment, an

14   amount equal to the excess (as of the last

15   day of the quarter for which such install-

16   ment is made) of—

17   "(I) the base amount with re-

18   spect to such quarter, over

19   "(II) the value (as of such last

20   day) of the plan's liquid assets.

21   "(ii) BASE AMOUNT.—

22   "(I) IN GENERAL.—The term

23   'base amount' means, with respect to

24   any quarter, an amount equal to 3

25   times the sum of the adjusted dis-

1   bursements from the plan for the 12

2   months ending on the last day of such

3   quarter.

4   "(II) SPECIAL RULE.—If the

5   amount determined under subclause

6   (I) exceeds an amount equal to 2

7   times the sum of the adjusted dis-

8   bursements from the plan for the 36

9   months ending on the last day of the

10   quarter and an enrolled actuary cer-

11   tifies to the satisfaction of the Sec-

12   retary that such excess is the result of

13   nonrecurring circumstances, the base

14   amount with respect to such quarter

15   shall be determined without regard to

16   amounts related to those nonrecurring

17   circumstances.

18   "(iii) DISBURSEMENTS FROM THE

19   PLAN.—The term 'disbursements from the

20   plan' means all disbursements from the

21   trust, including purchases of annuities,

22   payments of single sums and other bene-

23   fits, and administrative expenses.

24   "(iv) ADJUSTED DISBURSEMENTS.—

25   The term 'adjusted disbursements' means

1 disbursements from the plan reduced by

2 the product of—

3   "(I) the plan's funding target at-

4   tainment percentage for the plan year,

5   and

6   "(II) the sum of the purchases of

7   annuities, payments of single sums,

8   and such other disbursements as the

9   Secretary shall provide in regulations.

10   "(v) LIQUID ASSETS.—The term 'liq-

11   uid assets' means cash, marketable securi-

12   ties, and such other assets as specified by

13   the Secretary in regulations.

14   "(vi) QUARTER.—The term 'quarter'

15   means, with respect to any required install-

16   ment, the 3-month period preceding the

17   month in which the due date for such in-

18   stallment occurs.

19   "(F) REGULATIONS.—The Secretary may

20 prescribe such regulations as are necessary to

21 carry out this paragraph.

22 "(k) IMPOSITION OF LIEN WHERE FAILURE TO

23 MAKE REQUIRED CONTRIBUTIONS.—

24   "(1) IN GENERAL.—In the case of a plan to

25 which this subsection applies, if—

1   "(A) any person fails to make a contribu-

2   tion payment required by section 412 and this

3   section before the due date for such payment,

4   and

5   "(B) the unpaid balance of such payment

6   (including interest), when added to the aggre-

7   gate unpaid balance of all preceding such pay-

8   ments for which payment was not made before

9   the due date (including interest), exceeds

10       $1,000,000,

11 then there shall be a lien in favor of the plan in the

12 amount determined under paragraph (3) upon all

13 property and rights to property, whether real or per-

14 sonal, belonging to such person and any other per-

15 son who is a member of the same controlled group

16 of which such person is a member.

17   "(2) PLANS TO WHICH SUBSECTION APPLIES.—

18 This subsection shall apply to a defined benefit plan

19 (other than a multiemployer plan) covered under

20 section 4021 of the Employee Retirement Income

21 Security Act of 1974 for any plan year for which the

22 funding target attainment percentage (as defined in

23 subsection (d)(2)) of such plan is less than 100 per-

24 cent.

"(3) AMOUNT OF LIEN.—For purposes of paragraph (1), the amount of the lien shall be equal to the aggregate unpaid balance of contribution payments required under this section and section 412 for which payment has not been made before the due date.

"(4) NOTICE OF FAILURE; LIEN.—

"(A) NOTICE OF FAILURE.—A person committing a failure described in paragraph (1) shall notify the Pension Benefit Guaranty Corporation of such failure within 10 days of the due date for the required contribution payment.

"(B) PERIOD OF LIEN.—The lien imposed by paragraph (1) shall arise on the due date for the required contribution payment and shall continue until the last day of the first plan year in which the plan ceases to be described in paragraph (1)(B). Such lien shall continue to run without regard to whether such plan continues to be described in paragraph (2) during the period referred to in the preceding sentence.

"(C) CERTAIN RULES TO APPLY.—Any amount with respect to which a lien is imposed under paragraph (1) shall be treated as taxes due and owing the United States and rules

1 similar to the rules of subsections (c), (d), and

2 (e) of section 4068 of the Employee Retirement

3 Income Security Act of 1974 shall apply with

4 respect to a lien imposed by subsection (a) and

5 the amount with respect to such lien.

6   "(5) ENFORCEMENT.—Any lien created under

7 paragraph (1) may be perfected and enforced only

8 by the Pension Benefit Guaranty Corporation, or at

9 the direction of the Pension Benefit Guaranty Cor-

10 poration, by the contributing sponsor (or any mem-

11 ber of the controlled group of the contributing spon-

12 sor).

13   "(6) DEFINITIONS.—For purposes of this sub-

14 section—

15   "(A) CONTRIBUTION PAYMENT.—The term

16   'contribution payment' means, in connection

17   with a plan, a contribution payment required to

18   be made to the plan, including any required in-

19   stallment under paragraphs (3) and (4) of sub-

20   section (j).

21   "(B) DUE DATE; REQUIRED INSTALL-

22   MENT.—The terms 'due date' and 'required in-

23   stallment' have the meanings given such terms

24   by subsection (j), except that in the case of a

25   payment other than a required installment, the

1   due date shall be the date such payment is re-

2   quired to be made under section 430.

3   "(C) CONTROLLED GROUP.—The term

4   'controlled group' means any group treated as

5   a single employer under subsections (b), (c),

6   (m), and (o) of section 414.

7   "(l) QUALIFIED TRANSFERS TO HEALTH BENEFIT

8 ACCOUNTS.—In the case of a qualified transfer (as de-

9 fined in section 420), any assets so transferred shall not,

10 for purposes of this section, be treated as assets in the

11 plan.".

12   (b) EFFECTIVE DATE.—The amendments made by

13 this section shall apply with respect to plan years begin-

14 ning after December 31, 2007.

15 **SEC. 113. BENEFIT LIMITATIONS UNDER SINGLE-EM-**

16   **PLOYER PLANS.**

17   (a) PROHIBITION OF SHUTDOWN BENEFITS AND

18 OTHER UNPREDICTABLE CONTINGENT EVENT BENEFITS

19 UNDER SINGLE-EMPLOYER PLANS.—

20   (1) IN GENERAL.—Part III of subchapter D of

21   chapter 1 of the Internal Revenue Code of 1986 (re-

22   lating to deferred compensation, etc.) is amended—

23   (A) by striking the heading and inserting

24   the following:

"PART III—RULES RELATING TO MINIMUM FUNDING STANDARDS AND BENEFIT LIMITATIONS

"SUBPART A. MINIMUM FUNDING STANDARDS FOR PENSION PLANS.

"SUBPART B. BENEFIT LIMITATIONS UNDER SINGLE-EMPLOYER PLANS.

"Subpart A—Minimum Funding Standards for Pension Plans

"Sec. 430. Minimum funding standards for single-employer defined benefit pension plans.", and

(B) by adding at the end the following new subpart:

"Subpart B—Benefit Limitations Under Single-Employer Plans

"Sec. 436. Funding-based limitation on shutdown benefits and other unpredictable contingent event benefits under single-employer plans.

"SEC. 436. FUNDING-BASED LIMITS ON BENEFITS AND BENEFIT ACCRUALS UNDER SINGLE-EMPLOYER PLANS.

"(a) GENERAL RULE.—For purposes of section 401(a)(29), a defined benefit plan which is a single-employer plan shall be treated as meeting the requirements of this section if the plan meets the requirements of subsections (b), (c), (d), and (e).

"(b) FUNDING-BASED LIMITATION ON SHUTDOWN BENEFITS AND OTHER UNPREDICTABLE CONTINGENT EVENT BENEFITS UNDER SINGLE-EMPLOYER PLANS.—

"(1) IN GENERAL.—If a participant of a defined benefit plan which is a single-employer plan is

1   entitled to an unpredictable contingent event benefit

2   payable with respect to any event occurring during

3   any plan year, the plan shall provide that such ben-

4   efit may not be provided if the adjusted funding tar-

5   get attainment percentage for such plan year—

6   "(A) is less than 60 percent, or

7   "(B) would be less than 60 percent taking

8   into account such occurrence.

9   "(2) EXEMPTION.—Paragraph (1) shall cease

10   to apply with respect to any plan year, effective as

11   of the first day of the plan year, upon payment by

12   the plan sponsor of a contribution (in addition to

13   any minimum required contribution under section

14   303) equal to—

15   "(A) in the case of paragraph (1)(A), the

16   amount of the increase in the funding target of

17   the plan (under section 430) for the plan year

18   attributable to the occurrence referred to in

19   paragraph (1), and

20   "(B) in the case of paragraph (1)(B), the

21   amount sufficient to result in a funding target

22   attainment percentage of 60 percent.

23   "(3) UNPREDICTABLE CONTINGENT EVENT.—

24   For purposes of this subsection, the term 'unpredict-

able contingent event benefit' means any benefit
payable solely by reason of—

    "(A) a plant shutdown (or similar event, as
determined by the Secretary), or

    "(B) any event other than the attainment
of any age, performance of any service, receipt
or derivation of any compensation, or occurrence of death or disability.

"(c) LIMITATIONS ON PLAN AMENDMENTS INCREASING LIABILITY FOR BENEFITS.—

    "(1) IN GENERAL.—No amendment to a defined benefit plan which is a single-employer plan
which has the effect of increasing liabilities of the
plan by reason of increases in benefits, establishment of new benefits, changing the rate of benefit
accrual, or changing the rate at which benefits become nonforfeitable may take effect during any plan
year if the adjusted funding target attainment percentage for such plan year is—

    "(A) less than 80 percent, or

    "(B) would be less than 80 percent taking
into account such amendment.

    "(2) EXEMPTION.—Paragraph (1) shall cease
to apply with respect to any plan year, effective as
of the first day of the plan year (or if later, the ef-

1 fective date of the amendment), upon payment by

2 the plan sponsor of a contribution (in addition to

3 any minimum required contribution under section

4 430) equal to—

5   "(A) in the case of paragraph (1)(A), the

6   amount of the increase in the funding target of

7   the plan (under section 430) for the plan year

8   attributable to the amendment, and

9   "(B) in the case of paragraph (1)(B), the

10   amount sufficient to result in an adjusted fund-

11   ing target attainment percentage of 80 percent.

12   "(3) EXCEPTION FOR CERTAIN BENEFIT IN-

13 CREASES.—Paragraph (1) shall not apply to any

14 amendment which provides for an increase in bene-

15 fits under a formula which is not based on a partici-

16 pant's compensation, but only if the rate of such in-

17 crease is not in excess of the contemporaneous rate

18 of increase in average wages of participants covered

19 by the amendment.

20   "(d) LIMITATIONS ON ACCELERATED BENEFIT DIS-

21 TRIBUTIONS.—

22   "(1) FUNDING PERCENTAGE LESS THAN 60

23 PERCENT.—A defined benefit plan which is a single-

24 employer plan shall provide that, in any case in

25 which the plan's adjusted funding target attainment

1 percentage for a plan year is less than 60 percent,

2 the plan may not pay any prohibited payment after

3 the valuation date for the plan year.

4   "(2) BANKRUPTCY.—A defined benefit plan

5 which is a single-employer plan shall provide that,

6 during any period in which the plan sponsor is a

7 debtor in a case under title 11, United States Code,

8 or similar Federal or State law, the plan may not

9 pay any prohibited payment. The preceding sentence

10 shall not apply on or after the date on which the en-

11 rolled actuary of the plan certifies that the adjusted

12 funding target attainment percentage of such plan is

13 not less than 100 percent.

14   "(3) LIMITED PAYMENT IF PERCENTAGE AT

15 LEAST 60 PERCENT BUT LESS THAN 80 PERCENT.—

16   "(A) IN GENERAL.—A defined benefit plan

17   which is a single-employer plan shall provide

18   that, in any case in which the plan's adjusted

19   funding target attainment percentage for a plan

20   year is 60 percent or greater but less than 80

21   percent, the plan may not pay any prohibited

22   payment after the valuation date for the plan

23   year to the extent the amount of the payment

24   exceeds the lesser of—

"(i) 50 percent of the amount of the payment which could be made without regard to this section, or

"(ii) the present value (determined under guidance prescribed by the Pension Benefit Guaranty Corporation, using the interest and mortality assumptions under section 417(e)) of the maximum guarantee with respect to the participant under section 4022 of the Employee Retirement Income Security Act of 1974.

"(B) ONE-TIME APPLICATION.—

"(i) IN GENERAL.—The plan shall also provide that only 1 prohibited payment meeting the requirements of subparagraph (A) may be made with respect to any participant during any period of consecutive plan years to which the limitations under either paragraph (1) or (2) or this paragraph applies.

"(ii) TREATMENT OF BENEFICIARIES.—For purposes of this subparagraph, a participant and any beneficiary on his behalf (including an alternate payee, as defined in section 414(p)(8)) shall be treated as 1 participant. If the accrued benefit of a participant is allocated to such an alternate payee and 1 or more other persons, the amount under subparagraph (A) shall be allocated among such persons in the same manner as the accrued benefit is allocated unless the qualified domestic relations order (as defined in section 414(p)(1)(A)) provides otherwise.

"(4) EXCEPTION.—This subsection shall not apply to any plan for any plan year if the terms of such plan (as in effect for the period beginning on September 1, 2005, and ending with such plan year) provide for no benefit accruals with respect to any participant during such period.

"(5) PROHIBITED PAYMENT.—For purpose of this subsection, the term 'prohibited payment' means—

"(A) any payment, in excess of the monthly amount paid under a single life annuity (plus any social security supplements described in the last sentence of section 411(a)(9)), to a participant or beneficiary whose annuity starting date (as defined in section 417(f)(2)) occurs during

1   any period a limitation under paragraph (1) or

2   (2) is in effect,

3   "(B) any payment for the purchase of an

4   irrevocable commitment from an insurer to pay

5   benefits, and

6   "(C) any other payment specified by the

7   Secretary by regulations.

8 "(e) LIMITATION ON BENEFIT ACCRUALS FOR PLANS

9 WITH SEVERE FUNDING SHORTFALLS.—

10   "(1) IN GENERAL.—A defined benefit plan

11 which is a single-employer plan shall provide that, in

12 any case in which the plan's adjusted funding target

13 attainment percentage for a plan year is less than

14 60 percent, benefit accruals under the plan shall

15 cease as of the valuation date for the plan year.

16   "(2) EXEMPTION.—Paragraph (1) shall cease

17 to apply with respect to any plan year, effective as

18 of the first day of the plan year, upon payment by

19 the plan sponsor of a contribution (in addition to

20 any minimum required contribution under section

21 430) equal to the amount sufficient to result in an

22 adjusted funding target attainment percentage of 60

23 percent.

24 "(f) RULES RELATING TO CONTRIBUTIONS RE-

25 QUIRED TO AVOID BENEFIT LIMITATIONS.—

1 "(1) SECURITY MAY BE PROVIDED.—

2   "(A) IN GENERAL.—For purposes of this

3 section, the adjusted funding target attainment

4 percentage shall be determined by treating as

5 an asset of the plan any security provided by a

6 plan sponsor in a form meeting the require-

7 ments of subparagraph (B).

8   "(B) FORM OF SECURITY.—The security

9 required under subparagraph (A) shall consist

10 of—

11   "(i) a bond issued by a corporate sur-

12 ety company that is an acceptable surety

13 for purposes of section 412 of the Em-

14 ployee Retirement Income Security Act of

15 1974,

16   "(ii) cash, or United States obliga-

17 tions which mature in 3 years or less, held

18 in escrow by a bank or similar financial in-

19 stitution, or

20   "(iii) such other form of security as is

21 satisfactory to the Secretary and the par-

22 ties involved.

23   "(C) ENFORCEMENT.—Any security pro-

24 vided under subparagraph (A) may be perfected

25 and enforced at any time after the earlier of—

1   "(i) the date on which the plan termi-

2   nates,

3   "(ii) if there is a failure to make a

4   payment of the minimum required con-

5   tribution for any plan year beginning after

6   the security is provided, the due date for

7   the payment under section 430(j), or

8   "(iii) if the adjusted funding target

9   attainment percentage is less than 60 per-

10   cent for a consecutive period of 7 years,

11   the valuation date for the last year in the

12   period.

13   "(D) RELEASE OF SECURITY.—The secu-

14   rity shall be released (and any amounts there-

15   under shall be refunded together with any inter-

16   est accrued thereon) at such time as the Sec-

17   retary may prescribe in regulations, including

18   regulations for partial releases of the security

19   by reason of increases in the funding target at-

20   tainment percentage.

21   "(2) PREFUNDING BALANCE OR FUNDING

22 STANDARD CARRYOVER BALANCE MAY NOT BE

23 USED.—No prefunding balance under section 430(f)

24 or funding standard carryover balance may be used

25 under subsection (b), (c), or (e) to satisfy any pay-

1 ment an employer may make under any such sub-
2 section to avoid or terminate the application of any
3 limitation under such subsection.

4   "(3) DEEMED REDUCTION OF FUNDING BAL-
5 ANCES.—

6   "(A) IN GENERAL.—Subject to subpara-
7   graph (C), in any case in which a benefit limita-
8   tion under subsection (b), (c), (d), or (e) would
9   (but for this subparagraph and determined
10   without regard to subsection (b)(2), (c)(2), or
11   (e)(2)) apply to such plan for the plan year, the
12   plan sponsor of such plan shall be treated for
13   purposes of this title as having made an elec-
14   tion under section 430(f) to reduce the
15   prefunding balance or funding standard carry-
16   over balance by such amount as is necessary for
17   such benefit limitation to not apply to the plan
18   for such plan year.

19   "(B) EXCEPTION FOR INSUFFICIENT
20   FUNDING BALANCES.—Subparagraph (A) shall
21   not apply with respect to a benefit limitation
22   for any plan year if the application of subpara-
23   graph (A) would not result in the benefit limita-
24   tion not applying for such plan year.

1   "(C) RESTRICTIONS OF CERTAIN RULES

2   TO COLLECTIVELY BARGAINED PLANS.—With

3   respect to any benefit limitation under sub-

4   section (b), (c), or (e), subparagraph (A) shall

5   only apply in the case of a plan maintained pur-

6   suant to 1 or more collective bargaining agree-

7   ments between employee representatives and 1

8   or more employers.

9   "(g) NEW PLANS.—Subsections (b), (c), and (e) shall

10 not apply to a plan for the first 5 plan years of the plan.

11 For purposes of this subsection, the reference in this sub-

12 section to a plan shall include a reference to any prede-

13 cessor plan.

14   "(h) PRESUMED UNDERFUNDING FOR PURPOSES OF

15 BENEFIT LIMITATIONS.—

16   "(1) PRESUMPTION OF CONTINUED UNDER-

17   FUNDING.—In any case in which a benefit limitation

18   under subsection (b), (c), (d), or (e) has been ap-

19   plied to a plan with respect to the plan year pre-

20   ceding the current plan year, the adjusted funding

21   target attainment percentage of the plan for the cur-

22   rent plan year shall be presumed to be equal to the

23   adjusted funding target attainment percentage of

24   the plan for the preceding plan year until the en-

25   rolled actuary of the plan certifies the actual ad-

1   justed funding target attainment percentage of the

2   plan for the current plan year.

3   "(2) PRESUMPTION OF UNDERFUNDING AFTER

4   10TH MONTH.—In any case in which no certification

5   of the adjusted funding target attainment percent-

6   age for the current plan year is made with respect

7   to the plan before the first day of the 10th month

8   of such year, for purposes of subsections (b), (c),

9   (d), and (e), such first day shall be deemed, for pur-

10   poses of such subsection, to be the valuation date of

11   the plan for the current plan year and the plan's ad-

12   justed funding target attainment percentage shall be

13   conclusively presumed to be less than 60 percent as

14   of such first day.

15   "(3) PRESUMPTION OF UNDERFUNDING AFTER

16   4TH MONTH FOR NEARLY UNDERFUNDED PLANS.—

17   In any case in which—

18   "(A) a benefit limitation under subsection

19   (b), (c), (d), or (e) did not apply to a plan with

20   respect to the plan year preceding the current

21   plan year, but the adjusted funding target at-

22   tainment percentage of the plan for such pre-

23   ceding plan year was not more than 10 percent-

24   age points greater than the percentage which

25   would have caused such subsection to apply to

1   the plan with respect to such preceding plan

2   year, and

3   "(B) as of the first day of the 4th month

4   of the current plan year, the enrolled actuary of

5   the plan has not certified the actual adjusted

6   funding target attainment percentage of the

7   plan for the current plan year,

8 until the enrolled actuary so certifies, such first day

9 shall be deemed, for purposes of such subsection, to

10 be the valuation date of the plan for the current

11 plan year and the adjusted funding target attain-

12 ment percentage of the plan as of such first day

13 shall, for purposes of such subsection, be presumed

14 to be equal to 10 percentage points less than the ad-

15 justed funding target attainment percentage of the

16 plan for such preceding plan year.

17 "(i) TREATMENT OF PLAN AS OF CLOSE OF PROHIB-

18 ITED OR CESSATION PERIOD.—For purposes of applying

19 this title—

20   "(1) OPERATION OF PLAN AFTER PERIOD.—

21   Unless the plan provides otherwise, payments and

22   accruals will resume effective as of the day following

23   the close of the period for which any limitation of

24   payment or accrual of benefits under subsection (d)

25   or (e) applies.

1   "(2) TREATMENT OF AFFECTED BENEFITS.—

2   Nothing in this subsection shall be construed as af-

3   fecting the plan's treatment of benefits which would

4   have been paid or accrued but for this section.

5   "(j) TERMS RELATING TO FUNDING TARGET AT-

6 TAINMENT PERCENTAGE.—For purposes of this section—

7   "(1) IN GENERAL.—The term 'funding target

8   attainment percentage' has the same meaning given

9   such term by section 430(d)(2).

10   "(2) ADJUSTED FUNDING TARGET ATTAINMENT

11   PERCENTAGE.—The term 'adjusted funding target

12   attainment percentage' means the funding target at-

13   tainment percentage which is determined under

14   paragraph (1) by increasing each of the amounts

15   under subparagraphs (A) and (B) of section

16   430(d)(2) by the aggregate amount of purchases of

17   annuities for employees other than highly com-

18   pensated employees (as defined in section 414(q))

19   which were made by the plan during the preceding

20   2 plan years.

21   "(3) APPLICATION TO PLANS WHICH ARE

22   FULLY FUNDED WITHOUT REGARD TO REDUCTIONS

23   FOR FUNDING BALANCES.—

24   "(A) IN GENERAL.—In the case of a plan

25   for any plan year, if the funding target attain-

1   ment percentage is 100 percent or more (deter-

2   mined without regard to this paragraph and

3   without regard to the reduction in the value of

4   assets under section 430(f)(4)(A)), the funding

5   target attainment percentage for purposes of

6   paragraph (1) shall be determined without re-

7   gard to such reduction.

8   "(B) TRANSITION RULE.—Subparagraph

9   (A) shall be applied to plan years beginning

10   after 2007 and before 2011 by substituting for

11   '100 percent' the applicable percentage deter-

12   mined in accordance with the following table:

"In the case of a plan year beginning in calendar year:	The applicable percentage is
2008	92
2009	94
2010	96.

13   "(C) LIMITATION.—Subparagraph (B)

14   shall not apply with respect to any plan year

15   after 2008 unless the funding target attainment

16   percentage (determined without regard to this

17   paragraph) of the plan for each preceding plan

18   year after 2007 was not less than the applicable

19   percentage with respect to such preceding plan

20   year determined under subparagraph (B).

21   "(k) SPECIAL RULE FOR 2008.—For purposes of this

22 section, in the case of plan years beginning in 2008, the

23 funding target attainment percentage for the preceding

1 plan year may be determined using such methods of esti-

2 mation as the Secretary may provide.".

3   (2) CLERICAL AMENDMENT.—The table of

4   parts for subchapter D of chapter 1 of the Internal

5   Revenue Code of 1986 is amended by adding at the

6   end the following new item:

"PART III—RULES RELATING TO MINIMUM FUNDING STANDARDS AND BENEFIT LIMITATIONS".

7 (b) EFFECTIVE DATE.—

8   (1) IN GENERAL.—The amendments made by

9   this section shall apply to plan years beginning after

10   December 31, 2007.

11   (2) COLLECTIVE BARGAINING EXCEPTION.—In

12   the case of a plan maintained pursuant to 1 or more

13   collective bargaining agreements between employee

14   representatives and 1 or more employers ratified be-

15   fore January 1, 2008, the amendments made by this

16   section shall not apply to plan years beginning be-

17   fore the earlier of—

18   (A) the later of—

19   (i) the date on which the last collec-

20   tive bargaining agreement relating to the

21   plan terminates (determined without re-

22   gard to any extension thereof agreed to

23   after the date of the enactment of this

24   Act), or

1   (ii) the first day of the first plan year

2   to which the amendments made by this

3   subsection would (but for this subpara-

4   graph) apply, or

5   (B) January 1, 2010.

6   For purposes of subparagraph (A)(i), any plan

7   amendment made pursuant to a collective bargaining

8   agreement relating to the plan which amends the

9   plan solely to conform to any requirement added by

10 this section shall not be treated as a termination of

11 such collective bargaining agreement.

12 **SEC. 114. TECHNICAL AND CONFORMING AMENDMENTS.**

13 (a) AMENDMENTS RELATED TO QUALIFICATION RE-

14 QUIREMENTS.—

15   (1) Section 401(a)(29) of the Internal Revenue

16 Code of 1986 is amended to read as follows:

17   "(29) BENEFIT LIMITATIONS ON PLANS IN AT-

18 RISK STATUS.—In the case of a defined benefit plan

19 (other than a multiemployer plan) to which the re-

20 quirements of section 412 apply, the trust of which

21 the plan is a part shall not constitute a qualified

22 trust under this subsection unless the plan meets the

23 requirements of section 436.".

24   (2) Section 401(a)(32) of such Code is amend-

25 ed—

(A) in subparagraph (A), by striking "412(m)(5)" each place it appears and inserting "section 430(j)(4)", and

(B) in subparagraph (C), by striking "section 412(m)" and inserting "section 430(j)".

(3) Section 401(a)(33) of such Code is amended—

(A) in subparagraph (B)(i), by striking "funded current liability percentage (within the meaning of section 412(l)(8))" and inserting "funding target attainment percentage (as defined in section 430(d)(2))",

(B) in subparagraph (B)(iii), by striking "subsection 412(c)(8)" and inserting "section 412(c)(2)", and

(C) in subparagraph (D), by striking "section 412(c)(11) (without regard to subparagraph (B) thereof)" and inserting "section 412(b)(2) (without regard to subparagraph (B) thereof)".

(b) VESTING RULES.—Section 411 of such Code is amended—

(1) by striking "section 412(c)(8)" in subsection (a)(3)(C) and inserting "section 412(c)(2)",

(2) in subsection (b)(1)(F)—

(A) by striking "paragraphs (2) and (3) of section 412(i)" in clause (ii) and inserting "subparagraphs (B) and (C) of section 412(e)(3)", and

(B) by striking "paragraphs (4), (5), and (6) of section 412(i)" and inserting "subparagraphs (D), (E), and (F) of section 412(e)(3)", and

(3) by striking "section 412(c)(8)" in subsection (d)(6)(A) and inserting "section 412(e)(2)".

(c) MERGERS AND CONSOLIDATIONS OF PLANS.—Subclause (I) of section 414(l)(2)(B)(i) of such Code is amended to read as follows:

"(I) the amount determined under section 431(c)(6)(A)(i) in the case of a multiemployer plan (and the sum of the funding shortfall and target normal cost determined under section 430 in the case of any other plan), over".

(d) TRANSFER OF EXCESS PENSION ASSETS TO RETIREE HEALTH ACCOUNTS.—

(1) Section 420(e)(2) of such Code is amended to read as follows:

"(2) EXCESS PENSION ASSETS.—The term 'excess pension assets' means the excess (if any) of—

"(A) the lesser of—

"(i) the fair market value of the plan's assets (reduced by the prefunding balance and funding standard carryover balance determined under section 430(f)),

or

"(ii) the value of plan assets as determined under section 430(g)(3) after reduction under section 430(f), over

"(B) 125 percent of the sum of the funding shortfall and the target normal cost determined under section 430 for such plan year.".

(2) Section 420(e)(4) of such Code is amended to read as follows:

"(4) COORDINATION WITH SECTION 430.—In the case of a qualified transfer, any assets so transferred shall not, for purposes of this section and section 430, be treated as assets in the plan.".

(e) EXCISE TAXES.—

(1) IN GENERAL.—Subsections (a) and (b) of section 4971 of such Code are amended to read as follows:

1   "(a) INITIAL TAX.—If at any time during any taxable

2 year an employer maintains a plan to which section 412

3 applies, there is hereby imposed for the taxable year a tax

4 equal to—

5   "(1) in the case of a single-employer plan, 10

6   percent of the aggregate unpaid minimum required

7   contributions for all plan years remaining unpaid as

8   of the end of any plan year ending with or within

9   the taxable year, and

10   "(2) in the case of a multiemployer plan, 5 per-

11   cent of the accumulated funding deficiency deter-

12   mined under section 431 as of the end of any plan

13   year ending with or within the taxable year.

14   "(b) ADDITIONAL TAX.—If—

15   "(1) a tax is imposed under subsection (a)(1)

16   on any unpaid required minimum contribution and

17   such amount remains unpaid as of the close of the

18   taxable period, or

19   "(2) a tax is imposed under subsection (a)(2)

20   on any accumulated funding deficiency and the accu-

21   mulated funding deficiency is not corrected within

22   the taxable period,

23 there is hereby imposed a tax equal to 100 percent of the

24 unpaid minimum required contribution or accumulated

1 funding deficiency, whichever is applicable, to the extent
2 not so paid or corrected.".

3   (2) Section 4971(c) of such Code is amended—

4   (A) by striking "the last two sentences of
5   section 412(a)" in paragraph (1) and inserting
6   "section 431", and

7   (B) by adding at the end the following new
8   paragraph:

9   "(4) UNPAID MINIMUM REQUIRED CONTRIBU-
10 TION.—

11   "(A) IN GENERAL.—The term 'unpaid
12   minimum required contribution' means, with re-
13   spect to any plan year, any minimum required
14   contribution under section 430 for the plan
15   year which is not paid on or before the due date
16   (as determined under section 430(j)(1)) for the
17   plan year.

18   "(B) ORDERING RULE.—Any payment to
19   or under a plan for any plan year shall be allo-
20   cated first to unpaid minimum required con-
21   tributions for all preceding plan years on a
22   first-in, first-out basis and then to the min-
23   imum required contribution under section 430
24   for the plan year.".

1   (3) Section 4971(e)(1) of such Code is amended

2 by striking "section 412(b)(3)(A)" and inserting

3 "section 412(a)(1)(A)".

4   (4) Section 4971(f)(1) of such Code is amend-

5 ed—

6   (A) by striking "section 412(m)(5)" and

7   inserting "section 430(j)(4)", and

8   (B) by striking "section 412(m)" and in-

9   serting "section 430(j)".

10   (5) Section 4972(c)(7) of such Code is amended

11 by striking "except to the extent that such contribu-

12 tions exceed the full-funding limitation (as defined in

13 section 412(c)(7), determined without regard to sub-

14 paragraph (A)(i)(I) thereof)" and inserting "except,

15 in the case of a multiemployer plan, to the extent

16 that such contributions exceed the full-funding limi-

17 tation (as defined in section 431(c)(6))".

18 (f) REPORTING REQUIREMENTS.—Section 6059(b) of

19 such Code is amended—

20   (1) by striking "the accumulated funding defi-

21 ciency (as defined in section 412(a))" in paragraph

22 (2) and inserting "the minimum required contribu-

23 tion determined under section 430, or the accumu-

24 lated funding deficiency determined under section

25 431,", and

1   (2) by striking paragraph (3)(B) and inserting:

2   "(B) the requirements for reasonable actu-

3   arial assumptions under section 430(h)(1) or

4   431(c)(3), whichever are applicable, have been

5   complied with.".

6 **SEC. 115. MODIFICATION OF TRANSITION RULE TO PEN-**

7   **SION FUNDING REQUIREMENTS.**

8   (a) IN GENERAL.—In the case of a plan that—

9   (1) was not required to pay a variable rate pre-

10   mium for the plan year beginning in 1996,

11   (2) has not, in any plan year beginning after

12   1995, merged with another plan (other than a plan

13   sponsored by an employer that was in 1996 within

14   the controlled group of the plan sponsor); and

15   (3) is sponsored by a company that is engaged

16   primarily in the interurban or interstate passenger

17   bus service,

18 the rules described in subsection (b) shall apply for any

19 plan year beginning after December 31, 2007.

20   (b) MODIFIED RULES.—The rules described in this

21 subsection are as follows:

22   (1) For purposes of section 430(j)(3) of the In-

23   ternal Revenue Code of 1986 and section 303(j)(3)

24   of the Employee Retirement Income Security Act of

1 1974, the plan shall be treated as not having a fund-
2 ing shortfall for any plan year.

3 (2) For purposes of—

4 (A) determining unfunded vested benefits
5 under section 4006(a)(3)(E)(iii) of such Act,
6 and

7 (B) determining any present value or mak-
8 ing any computation under section 412 of such
9 Code or section 302 of such Act,

10 the mortality table shall be the mortality table used
11 by the plan.

12 (3) Section 430(c)(5)(B) of such Code and sec-
13 tion 303(c)(5)(B) of such Act (relating to phase-in
14 of funding target for exemption from new shortfall
15 amortization base) shall each be applied by sub-
16 stituting "2012" for "2011" therein and by sub-
17 stituting for the table therein the following:

In the case of a plan year beginning in calendar year:	The applicable percentage is:
2008	90 percent
2009	92 percent
2010	94 percent
2011	96 percent.

18 (c) DEFINITIONS.—Any term used in this section
19 which is also used in section 430 of such Code or section
20 303 of such Act shall have the meaning provided such
21 term in such section. If the same term has a different

1 meaning in such Code and such Act, such term shall, for
2 purposes of this section, have the meaning provided by
3 such Code when applied with respect to such Code and
4 the meaning provided by such Act when applied with re-
5 spect to such Act.

6   (d) SPECIAL RULE FOR 2006 AND 2007.—

7   (1) IN GENERAL.—Section 769(c)(3) of the Re-
8   tirement Protection Act of 1994, as added by section
9   201 of the Pension Funding Equity Act of 2004, is
10   amended by striking "and 2005" and inserting ",
11   2005, 2006, and 2007".

12   (2) EFFECTIVE DATE.—The amendment made
13   by paragraph (1) shall apply to plan years beginning
14   after December 31, 2005.

15   (e) CONFORMING AMENDMENT.—

16   (1) Section 769 of the Retirement Protection
17   Act of 1994 is amended by striking subsection (c).

18   (2) The amendment made by paragraph (1)
19   shall take effect on December 31, 2007, and shall
20   apply to plan years beginning after such date.

SEC. 116. RESTRICTIONS ON FUNDING OF NONQUALIFIED DEFERRED COMPENSATION PLANS BY EMPLOYERS MAINTAINING UNDERFUNDED OR TERMINATED SINGLE-EMPLOYER PLANS.

(a) AMENDMENTS OF INTERNAL REVENUE CODE.— Subsection (b) of section 409A of the Internal Revenue Code of 1986 (providing rules relating to funding) is amended by redesignating paragraphs (3) and (4) as paragraphs (4) and (5), respectively, and by inserting after paragraph (2) the following new paragraph:

"(3) TREATMENT OF EMPLOYER'S DEFINED BENEFIT PLAN DURING RESTRICTED PERIOD.—

"(A) IN GENERAL.—If–

"(i) during any restricted period with respect to a single-employer defined benefit plan, assets are set aside or reserved (directly or indirectly) in a trust (or other arrangement as determined by the Secretary) or transferred to such a trust or other arrangement for purposes of paying deferred compensation of an applicable covered employee under a nonqualified deferred compensation plan of the plan sponsor or member of a controlled group which includes the plan sponsor, or

1   "(ii) a nonqualified deferred com-

2   pensation plan of the plan sponsor or

3   member of a controlled group which in-

4   cludes the plan sponsor provides that as-

5   sets will become restricted to the provision

6   of benefits under the plan in connection

7   with such restricted period (or other simi-

8   lar financial measure determined by the

9   Secretary) with respect to the defined ben-

10   efit plan, or assets are so restricted,

11   such assets shall, for purposes of section 83, be

12   treated as property transferred in connection

13   with the performance of services whether or not

14   such assets are available to satisfy claims of

15   general creditors. Clause (i) shall not apply with

16   respect to any assets which are so set aside be-

17   fore the restricted period with respect to the de-

18   fined benefit plan.

19   "(B) RESTRICTED PERIOD.—For purposes

20   of this section, the term 'restricted period'

21   means, with respect to any plan described in

22   subparagraph (A)—

23   "(i) any period during which the plan

24   is in at-risk status (as defined in section

25   430(i));

1   "(ii) any period the plan sponsor is a

2   debtor in a case under title 11, United

3   States Code, or similar Federal or State

4   law, and

5   "(iii) the 12-month period beginning

6   on the date which is 6 months before the

7   termination date of the plan if, as of the

8   termination date, the plan is not sufficient

9   for benefit liabilities (within the meaning

10   of section 4041 of the Employee Retire-

11   ment Income Security Act of 1974).

12   "(C) SPECIAL RULE FOR PAYMENT OF

13   TAXES ON DEFERRED COMPENSATION IN-

14   CLUDED IN INCOME.—If an employer provides

15   directly or indirectly for the payment of any

16   Federal, State, or local income taxes with re-

17   spect to any compensation required to be in-

18   cluded in gross income by reason of this para-

19   graph—

20   "(i) interest shall be imposed under

21   subsection (a)(1)(B)(i)(I) on the amount of

22   such payment in the same manner as if

23   such payment was part of the deferred

24   compensation to which it relates,

211

"(ii) such payment shall be taken into account in determining the amount of the additional tax under subsection (a)(1)(B)(i)(II) in the same manner as if such payment was part of the deferred compensation to which it relates, and

"(iii) no deduction shall be allowed under this title with respect to such payment.

"(D) OTHER DEFINITIONS.—For purposes of this section—

"(i) APPLICABLE COVERED EMPLOYEE.—The term 'applicable covered employee' means any—

"(I) covered employee of a plan sponsor,

"(II) covered employee of a member of a controlled group which includes the plan sponsor, and

"(III) former employee who was a covered employee at the time of termination of employment with the plan sponsor or a member of a controlled group which includes the plan sponsor.

1   "(ii) Covered employee.—The term

2   'covered employee' means an individual de-

3   scribed in section 162(m)(3) or an indi-

4   vidual subject to the requirements of sec-

5   tion 16(a) of the Securities Exchange Act

6   of 1934.".

7   (b) Conforming Amendments.—Paragraphs (4)

8 and (5) of section 409A(b) of such Code, as redesignated

9 by subsection (a) of this subsection, are each amended by

10 striking "paragraph (1) or (2)" each place it appears and

11 inserting "paragraph (1), (2), or (3)".

12   (c) Effective Date.—The amendments made by

13 this section shall apply to transfers or other reservation

14 of assets after the date of the enactment of this Act.

TITLE II—FUNDING RULES FOR MULTIEMPLOYER DEFINED BENEFIT PLANS AND RELATED PROVISIONS

Subtitle A—Amendments to Employee Retirement Income Security Act of 1974

SEC. 201. FUNDING RULES FOR MULTIEMPLOYER DEFINED BENEFIT PLANS.

24   (a) In General.—Part 3 of subtitle B of title I of

25 the Employee Retirement Income Security Act of 1974 (as

1 amended by this Act) is amended by inserting after section

2 303 the following new section:

3 "MINIMUM FUNDING STANDARDS FOR MULTIEMPLOYER

4 PLANS

5 "SEC. 304. (a) IN GENERAL.—For purposes of sec-

6 tion 302, the accumulated funding deficiency of a multi-

7 employer plan for any plan year is—

8 "(1) except as provided in paragraph (2), the

9 amount, determined as of the end of the plan year,

10 equal to the excess (if any) of the total charges to

11 the funding standard account of the plan for all plan

12 years (beginning with the first plan year for which

13 this part applies to the plan) over the total credits

14 to such account for such years, and

15 "(2) if the multiemployer plan is in reorganiza-

16 tion for any plan year, the accumulated funding de-

17 ficiency of the plan determined under section 4243.

18 "(b) FUNDING STANDARD ACCOUNT.—

19 "(1) ACCOUNT REQUIRED.—Each multiem-

20 ployer plan to which this part applies shall establish

21 and maintain a funding standard account. Such ac-

22 count shall be credited and charged solely as pro-

23 vided in this section.

24 "(2) CHARGES TO ACCOUNT.—For a plan year,

25 the funding standard account shall be charged with

26 the sum of—

1   "(A) the normal cost of the plan for the

2 plan year,

3   "(B) the amounts necessary to amortize in

4 equal annual installments (until fully amor-

5 tized)—

6   "(i) in the case of a plan which comes

7 into existence on or after January 1, 2008,

8 the unfunded past service liability under

9 the plan on the first day of the first plan

10 year to which this section applies, over a

11 period of 15 plan years,

12   "(ii) separately, with respect to each

13 plan year, the net increase (if any) in un-

14 funded past service liability under the plan

15 arising from plan amendments adopted in

16 such year, over a period of 15 plan years,

17   "(iii) separately, with respect to each

18 plan year, the net experience loss (if any)

19 under the plan, over a period of 15 plan

20 years, and

21   "(iv) separately, with respect to each

22 plan year, the net loss (if any) resulting

23 from changes in actuarial assumptions

24 used under the plan, over a period of 15

25 plan years,

"(C) the amount necessary to amortize each waived funding deficiency (within the meaning of section 302(c)(3)) for each prior plan year in equal annual installments (until fully amortized) over a period of 15 plan years,

"(D) the amount necessary to amortize in equal annual installments (until fully amortized) over a period of 5 plan years any amount credited to the funding standard account under section 302(b)(3)(D) (as in effect on the day before the date of the enactment of the Pension Protection Act of 2006), and

"(E) the amount necessary to amortize in equal annual installments (until fully amortized) over a period of 20 years the contributions which would be required to be made under the plan but for the provisions of section 302(c)(7)(A)(i)(I) (as in effect on the day before the date of the enactment of the Pension Protection Act of 2006).

"(3) CREDITS TO ACCOUNT.—For a plan year, the funding standard account shall be credited with the sum of—

1   "(A) the amount considered contributed by

2   the employer to or under the plan for the plan

3   year,

4   "(B) the amount necessary to amortize in

5   equal annual installments (until fully amor-

6   tized)—

7   "(i) separately, with respect to each

8   plan year, the net decrease (if any) in un-

9   funded past service liability under the plan

10   arising from plan amendments adopted in

11   such year, over a period of 15 plan years,

12   "(ii) separately, with respect to each

13   plan year, the net experience gain (if any)

14   under the plan, over a period of 15 plan

15   years, and

16   "(iii) separately, with respect to each

17   plan year, the net gain (if any) resulting

18   from changes in actuarial assumptions

19   used under the plan, over a period of 15

20   plan years,

21   "(C) the amount of the waived funding de-

22   ficiency (within the meaning of section

23   302(c)(3)) for the plan year, and

24   "(D) in the case of a plan year for which

25   the accumulated funding deficiency is deter-

1   mined under the funding standard account if

2   such plan year follows a plan year for which

3   such deficiency was determined under the alter-

4   native minimum funding standard under section

5   305 (as in effect on the day before the date of

6   the enactment of the Pension Protection Act of

7   2006), the excess (if any) of any debit balance

8   in the funding standard account (determined

9   without regard to this subparagraph) over any

10   debit balance in the alternative minimum fund-

11   ing standard account.

12   "(4) SPECIAL RULE FOR AMOUNTS FIRST AM-

13 ORTIZED IN PLAN YEARS BEFORE 2008.—In the case

14 of any amount amortized under section 302(b) (as

15 in effect on the day before the date of the enactment

16 of the Pension Protection Act of 2006) over any pe-

17 riod beginning with a plan year beginning before

18 2008, in lieu of the amortization described in para-

19 graphs (2)(B) and (3)(B), such amount shall con-

20 tinue to be amortized under such section as so in ef-

21 fect.

22   "(5) COMBINING AND OFFSETTING AMOUNTS

23 TO BE AMORTIZED.—Under regulations prescribed

24 by the Secretary of the Treasury, amounts required

1   to be amortized under paragraph (2) or paragraph

2   (3), as the case may be—

3   "(A) may be combined into one amount

4   under such paragraph to be amortized over a

5   period determined on the basis of the remaining

6   amortization period for all items entering into

7   such combined amount, and

8   "(B) may be offset against amounts re-

9   quired to be amortized under the other such

10   paragraph, with the resulting amount to be am-

11   ortized over a period determined on the basis of

12   the remaining amortization periods for all items

13   entering into whichever of the two amounts

14   being offset is the greater.

15   "(6) INTEREST.—The funding standard ac-

16   count (and items therein) shall be charged or cred-

17   ited (as determined under regulations prescribed by

18   the Secretary of the Treasury) with interest at the

19   appropriate rate consistent with the rate or rates of

20   interest used under the plan to determine costs.

21   "(7) SPECIAL RULES RELATING TO CHARGES

22   AND CREDITS TO FUNDING STANDARD ACCOUNT.—

23   For purposes of this part—

24   "(A) WITHDRAWAL LIABILITY.—Any

25   amount received by a multiemployer plan in

payment of all or part of an employer's withdrawal liability under part 1 of subtitle E of
title IV shall be considered an amount contributed by the employer to or under the plan. The
Secretary of the Treasury may prescribe by regulation additional charges and credits to a multiemployer plan's funding standard account to
the extent necessary to prevent withdrawal liability payments from being unduly reflected as
advance funding for plan liabilities.

"(B) ADJUSTMENTS WHEN A MULTIEM-
PLOYER PLAN LEAVES REORGANIZATION.—If a
multiemployer plan is not in reorganization in
the plan year but was in reorganization in the
immediately preceding plan year, any balance in
the funding standard account at the close of
such immediately preceding plan year—

"(i) shall be eliminated by an offsetting credit or charge (as the case may be),
but

"(ii) shall be taken into account in
subsequent plan years by being amortized
in equal annual installments (until fully
amortized) over 30 plan years.

1 The preceding sentence shall not apply to the
2 extent of any accumulated funding deficiency
3 under section 4243(a) as of the end of the last
4 plan year that the plan was in reorganization.
5   "(C) PLAN PAYMENTS TO SUPPLEMENTAL
6 PROGRAM OR WITHDRAWAL LIABILITY PAYMENT
7 FUND.—Any amount paid by a plan during a
8 plan year to the Pension Benefit Guaranty Cor-
9 poration pursuant to section 4222 of this Act or
10 to a fund exempt under section 501(c)(22) of
11 the Internal Revenue Code of 1986 pursuant to
12 section 4223 of this Act shall reduce the
13 amount of contributions considered received by
14 the plan for the plan year.
15   "(D) INTERIM WITHDRAWAL LIABILITY
16 PAYMENTS.—Any amount paid by an employer
17 pending a final determination of the employer's
18 withdrawal liability under part 1 of subtitle E
19 of title IV and subsequently refunded to the
20 employer by the plan shall be charged to the
21 funding standard account in accordance with
22 regulations prescribed by the Secretary of the
23 Treasury.
24   "(E) ELECTION FOR DEFERRAL OF
25 CHARGE FOR PORTION OF NET EXPERIENCE

1   LOSS.—If an election is in effect under section

2   302(b)(7)(F) (as in effect on the day before the

3   date of the enactment of the Pension Protection

4   Act of 2006) for any plan year, the funding

5   standard account shall be charged in the plan

6   year to which the portion of the net experience

7   loss deferred by such election was deferred with

8   the amount so deferred (and paragraph

9   (2)(B)(iii) shall not apply to the amount so

10 charged).

11   "(F) FINANCIAL ASSISTANCE.—Any

12 amount of any financial assistance from the

13 Pension Benefit Guaranty Corporation to any

14 plan, and any repayment of such amount, shall

15 be taken into account under this section and

16 section 302 in such manner as is determined by

17 the Secretary of the Treasury.

18   "(G) SHORT-TERM BENEFITS.—To the ex-

19 tent that any plan amendment increases the un-

20 funded past service liability under the plan by

21 reason of an increase in benefits which are not

22 payable as a life annuity but are payable under

23 the terms of the plan for a period that does not

24 exceed 14 years from the effective date of the

25 amendment, paragraph (2)(B)(ii) shall be ap-

plied separately with respect to such increase in unfunded past service liability by substituting the number of years of the period during which such benefits are payable for '15'.

"(c) ADDITIONAL RULES.—

"(1) DETERMINATIONS TO BE MADE UNDER FUNDING METHOD.—For purposes of this part, normal costs, accrued liability, past service liabilities, and experience gains and losses shall be determined under the funding method used to determine costs under the plan.

"(2) VALUATION OF ASSETS.—

"(A) IN GENERAL.—For purposes of this part, the value of the plan's assets shall be determined on the basis of any reasonable actuarial method of valuation which takes into account fair market value and which is permitted under regulations prescribed by the Secretary of the Treasury.

"(B) ELECTION WITH RESPECT TO BONDS.—The value of a bond or other evidence of indebtedness which is not in default as to principal or interest may, at the election of the plan administrator, be determined on an amortized basis running from initial cost at purchase

1 to par value at maturity or earliest call date.

2 Any election under this subparagraph shall be

3 made at such time and in such manner as the

4 Secretary of the Treasury shall by regulations

5 provide, shall apply to all such evidences of in-

6 debtedness, and may be revoked only with the

7 consent of such Secretary.

8 "(3) ACTUARIAL ASSUMPTIONS MUST BE REA-

9 SONABLE.—For purposes of this section, all costs, li-

10 abilities, rates of interest, and other factors under

11 the plan shall be determined on the basis of actu-

12 arial assumptions and methods—

13 "(A) each of which is reasonable (taking

14 into account the experience of the plan and rea-

15 sonable expectations), and

16 "(B) which, in combination, offer the actu-

17 ary's best estimate of anticipated experience

18 under the plan.

19 "(4) TREATMENT OF CERTAIN CHANGES AS EX-

20 PERIENCE GAIN OR LOSS.—For purposes of this sec-

21 tion, if—

22 "(A) a change in benefits under the Social

23 Security Act or in other retirement benefits cre-

24 ated under Federal or State law, or

1   "(B) a change in the definition of the term

2   'wages' under section 3121 of the Internal Rev-

3   enue Code of 1986, or a change in the amount

4   of such wages taken into account under regula-

5   tions prescribed for purposes of section

6   401(a)(5) of such Code,

7 results in an increase or decrease in accrued liability

8 under a plan, such increase or decrease shall be

9 treated as an experience loss or gain.

10   "(5) FULL FUNDING.—If, as of the close of a

11 plan year, a plan would (without regard to this para-

12 graph) have an accumulated funding deficiency in

13 excess of the full funding limitation—

14   "(A) the funding standard account shall be

15   credited with the amount of such excess, and

16   "(B) all amounts described in subpara-

17   graphs (B), (C), and (D) of subsection (b) (2)

18   and subparagraph (B) of subsection (b)(3)

19   which are required to be amortized shall be con-

20   sidered fully amortized for purposes of such

21   subparagraphs.

22   "(6) FULL-FUNDING LIMITATION.—

23   "(A) IN GENERAL.—For purposes of para-

24   graph (5), the term 'full-funding limitation'

25   means the excess (if any) of—

1   "(i) the accrued liability (including

2   normal cost) under the plan (determined

3   under the entry age normal funding meth-

4   od if such accrued liability cannot be di-

5   rectly calculated under the funding method

6   used for the plan), over

7   "(ii) the lesser of—

8   "(I) the fair market value of the

9   plan's assets, or

10   "(II) the value of such assets de-

11   termined under paragraph (2).

12   "(B) MINIMUM AMOUNT.—

13   "(i) IN GENERAL.—In no event shall

14   the full-funding limitation determined

15   under subparagraph (A) be less than the

16   excess (if any) of—

17   "(I) 90 percent of the current li-

18   ability of the plan (including the ex-

19   pected increase in current liability due

20   to benefits accruing during the plan

21   year), over

22   "(II) the value of the plan's as-

23   sets determined under paragraph (2).

24   "(ii) ASSETS.—For purposes of clause

25   (i), assets shall not be reduced by any

1   credit balance in the funding standard ac-

2   count.

3   "(C) FULL FUNDING LIMITATION.—For

4   purposes of this paragraph, unless otherwise

5   provided by the plan, the accrued liability under

6   a multiemployer plan shall not include benefits

7   which are not nonforfeitable under the plan

8   after the termination of the plan (taking into

9   consideration section 411(d)(3) of the Internal

10   Revenue Code of 1986).

11   "(D) CURRENT LIABILITY.—For purposes

12   of this paragraph—

13   "(i) IN GENERAL.—The term 'current

14   liability' means all liabilities to employees

15   and their beneficiaries under the plan.

16   "(ii) TREATMENT OF UNPREDICTABLE

17   CONTINGENT EVENT BENEFITS.—For pur-

18   poses of clause (i), any benefit contingent

19   on an event other than—

20   "(I) age, service, compensation,

21   death, or disability, or

22   "(II) an event which is reason-

23   ably and reliably predictable (as deter-

24   mined by the Secretary of the Treas-

25   ury),

shall not be taken into account until the event on which the benefit is contingent occurs.

"(iii) INTEREST RATE USED.—The rate of interest used to determine current liability under this paragraph shall be the rate of interest determined under subparagraph (E).

"(iv) MORTALITY TABLES.—

"(I) COMMISSIONERS' STANDARD TABLE.—In the case of plan years beginning before the first plan year to which the first tables prescribed under subclause (II) apply, the mortality table used in determining current liability under this paragraph shall be the table prescribed by the Secretary of the Treasury which is based on the prevailing commissioners' standard table (described in section 807(d)(5)(A) of the Internal Revenue Code of 1986) used to determine reserves for group annuity contracts issued on January 1, 1993.

1   "(II) SECRETARIAL AUTHOR-

2   ITY.—The Secretary of the Treasury

3   may by regulation prescribe for plan

4   years beginning after December 31,

5   1999, mortality tables to be used in

6   determining current liability under

7   this subsection. Such tables shall be

8   based upon the actual experience of

9   pension plans and projected trends in

10   such experience. In prescribing such

11   tables, such Secretary shall take into

12   account results of available inde-

13   pendent studies of mortality of indi-

14   viduals covered by pension plans.

15   "(v) SEPARATE MORTALITY TABLES

16   FOR THE DISABLED.—Notwithstanding

17   clause (iv)—

18   "(I) IN GENERAL.—The Sec-

19   retary of the Treasury shall establish

20   mortality tables which may be used

21   (in lieu of the tables under clause (iv))

22   to determine current liability under

23   this subsection for individuals who are

24   entitled to benefits under the plan on

25   account of disability. Such Secretary

shall establish separate tables for individuals whose disabilities occur in plan years beginning before January 1, 1995, and for individuals whose disabilities occur in plan years beginning on or after such date.

"(II) SPECIAL RULE FOR DISABILITIES OCCURRING AFTER 1994.— In the case of disabilities occurring in plan years beginning after December 31, 1994, the tables under subclause (I) shall apply only with respect to individuals described in such subclause who are disabled within the meaning of title II of the Social Security Act and the regulations thereunder.

"(vi) PERIODIC REVIEW.—The Secretary of the Treasury shall periodically (at least every 5 years) review any tables in effect under this subparagraph and shall, to the extent such Secretary determines necessary, by regulation update the tables to reflect the actual experience of pension plans and projected trends in such experience.

1   "(E) REQUIRED CHANGE OF INTEREST

2   RATE.—For purposes of determining a plan's

3   current liability for purposes of this para-

4   graph—

5   "(i) IN GENERAL.—If any rate of in-

6   terest used under the plan under sub-

7   section (b)(6) to determine cost is not

8   within the permissible range, the plan shall

9   establish a new rate of interest within the

10   permissible range.

11   "(ii) PERMISSIBLE RANGE.—For pur-

12   poses of this subparagraph—

13   "(I) IN GENERAL.—Except as

14   provided in subclause (II), the term

15   'permissible range' means a rate of in-

16   terest which is not more than 5 per-

17   cent above, and not more than 10 per-

18   cent below, the weighted average of

19   the rates of interest on 30-year Treas-

20   ury securities during the 4-year period

21   ending on the last day before the be-

22   ginning of the plan year.

23   "(II) SECRETARIAL AUTHOR-

24   ITY.—If the Secretary of the Treasury

25   finds that the lowest rate of interest

permissible under subclause (I) is unreasonably high, such Secretary may
prescribe a lower rate of interest, except that such rate may not be less
than 80 percent of the average rate
determined under such subclause.

"(iii)   ASSUMPTIONS.—Notwithstanding paragraph (3)(A), the interest
rate used under the plan shall be—

"(I) determined without taking
into account the experience of the
plan and reasonable expectations, but

"(II) consistent with the assumptions which reflect the purchase rates
which would be used by insurance
companies to satisfy the liabilities
under the plan.

"(7) ANNUAL VALUATION.—

"(A) IN GENERAL.—For purposes of this
section, a determination of experience gains and
losses and a valuation of the plan's liability
shall be made not less frequently than once
every year, except that such determination shall
be made more frequently to the extent required

1   in particular cases under regulations prescribed

2   by the Secretary of the Treasury.

3   "(B) VALUATION DATE.—

4   "(i) CURRENT YEAR.—Except as pro-

5   vided in clause (ii), the valuation referred

6   to in subparagraph (A) shall be made as of

7   a date within the plan year to which the

8   valuation refers or within one month prior

9   to the beginning of such year.

10   "(ii) USE OF PRIOR YEAR VALU-

11   ATION.—The valuation referred to in sub-

12   paragraph (A) may be made as of a date

13   within the plan year prior to the year to

14   which the valuation refers if, as of such

15   date, the value of the assets of the plan are

16   not less than 100 percent of the plan's cur-

17   rent liability (as defined in paragraph

18   (6)(D) without regard to clause (iv) there-

19   of).

20   "(iii) ADJUSTMENTS.—Information

21   under clause (ii) shall, in accordance with

22   regulations, be actuarially adjusted to re-

23   flect significant differences in participants.

24   "(iv) LIMITATION.—A change in fund-

25   ing method to use a prior year valuation,

1   as provided in clause (ii), may not be made

2   unless as of the valuation date within the

3   prior plan year, the value of the assets of

4   the plan are not less than 125 percent of

5   the plan's current liability (as defined in

6   paragraph (6)(D) without regard to clause

7   (iv) thereof).

8   "(8) TIME WHEN CERTAIN CONTRIBUTIONS

9 DEEMED MADE.—For purposes of this section, any

10 contributions for a plan year made by an employer

11 after the last day of such plan year, but not later

12 than two and one-half months after such day, shall

13 be deemed to have been made on such last day. For

14 purposes of this subparagraph, such two and one-

15 half month period may be extended for not more

16 than six months under regulations prescribed by the

17 Secretary of the Treasury.

18   "(d) EXTENSION OF AMORTIZATION PERIODS FOR

19 MULTIEMPLOYER PLANS.—

20   "(1) AUTOMATIC EXTENSION UPON APPLICA-

21 TION BY CERTAIN PLANS.—

22   "(A) IN GENERAL.—If the plan sponsor of

23 a multiemployer plan—

24   "(i) submits to the Secretary of the

25 Treasury an application for an extension of

the period of years required to amortize
any unfunded liability described in any
clause of subsection (b)(2)(B) or described
in subsection (b)(4), and

"(ii) includes with the application a
certification by the plan's actuary described in subparagraph (B),

the Secretary of the Treasury shall extend the
amortization period for the period of time (not
in excess of 5 years) specified in the application. Such extension shall be in addition to any
extension under paragraph (2).

"(B) CRITERIA.—A certification with respect to a multiemployer plan is described in
this subparagraph if the plan's actuary certifies
that, based on reasonable assumptions—

"(i) absent the extension under subparagraph (A), the plan would have an accumulated funding deficiency in the current plan year or any of the 9 succeeding
plan years,

"(ii) the plan sponsor has adopted a
plan to improve the plan's funding status,

"(iii) the plan is projected to have sufficient assets to timely pay expected bene-

fits and anticipated expenditures over the amortization period as extended, and

"(iv) the notice required under paragraph (3)(A) has been provided.

"(C) TERMINATION.—The preceding provisions of this paragraph shall not apply with respect to any application submitted after December 31, 2014.

"(2) ALTERNATIVE EXTENSION.—

"(A) IN GENERAL.—If the plan sponsor of a multiemployer plan submits to the Secretary of the Treasury an application for an extension of the period of years required to amortize any unfunded liability described in any clause of subsection (b)(2)(B) or described in subsection (b)(4), the Secretary of the Treasury may extend the amortization period for a period of time (not in excess of 10 years reduced by the number of years of any extension under paragraph (1) with respect to such unfunded liability) if the Secretary of the Treasury makes the determination described in subparagraph (B). Such extension shall be in addition to any extension under paragraph (1).

1   "(B) DETERMINATION.—The Secretary of
2 the Treasury may grant an extension under
3 subparagraph (A) if such Secretary determines
4 that—

5   "(i) such extension would carry out
6   the purposes of this Act and would provide
7   adequate protection for participants under
8   the plan and their beneficiaries, and

9   "(ii) the failure to permit such exten-
10   sion would—

11   "(I) result in a substantial risk
12   to the voluntary continuation of the
13   plan, or a substantial curtailment of
14   pension benefit levels or employee
15   compensation, and

16   "(II) be adverse to the interests
17   of plan participants in the aggregate.

18   "(C) ACTION BY SECRETARY OF THE
19 TREASURY.—The Secretary of the Treasury
20 shall act upon any application for an extension
21 under this paragraph within 180 days of the
22 submission of such application. If such Sec-
23 retary rejects the application for an extension
24 under this paragraph, such Secretary shall pro-
25 vide notice to the plan detailing the specific rea-

1   sons for the rejection, including references to

2   the criteria set forth above.

3   "(3) ADVANCE NOTICE.—

4   "(A) IN GENERAL.—The Secretary of the

5   Treasury shall, before granting an extension

6   under this subsection, require each applicant to

7   provide evidence satisfactory to such Secretary

8   that the applicant has provided notice of the fil-

9   ing of the application for such extension to each

10   affected party (as defined in section

11   4001(a)(21)) with respect to the affected plan.

12   Such notice shall include a description of the

13   extent to which the plan is funded for benefits

14   which are guaranteed under title IV and for

15   benefit liabilities.

16   "(B) CONSIDERATION OF RELEVANT IN-

17   FORMATION.—The Secretary of the Treasury

18   shall consider any relevant information provided

19   by a person to whom notice was given under

20   paragraph (1).".

21   (b) SHORTFALL FUNDING METHOD.—

22   (1) IN GENERAL.—A multiemployer plan meet-

23   ing the criteria of paragraph (2) may adopt, use, or

24   cease using, the shortfall funding method and such

25   adoption, use, or cessation of use of such method,

1   shall be deemed approved by the Secretary of the

2   Treasury under section 302(d)(1) of the Employee

3   Retirement Income Security Act of 1974 and section

4   412(d)(1) of the Internal Revenue Code of 1986.

5   (2) CRITERIA.—A multiemployer pension plan

6   meets the criteria of this clause if—

7   (A) the plan has not used the shortfall

8   funding method during the 5-year period ending

9   on the day before the date the plan is to use

10   the method under paragraph (1); and

11   (B) the plan is not operating under an am-

12   ortization period extension under section 304(d)

13   of such Act and did not operate under such an

14   extension during such 5-year period.

15   (3) SHORTFALL FUNDING METHOD DEFINED.—

16   For purposes of this subsection, the term "shortfall

17   funding method" means the shortfall funding meth-

18   od described in Treasury Regulations section

19   1.412(c)(1)–2 (26 C.F.R. 1.412(c)(1)–2).

20   (4) BENEFIT RESTRICTIONS TO APPLY.—The

21   benefit restrictions under section 302(c)(7) of such

22   Act and section 412(c)(7) of such Code shall apply

23   during any period a multiemployer plan is on the

24   shortfall funding method pursuant to this sub-

25   section.

1   (5) USE OF SHORTFALL METHOD NOT TO PRE-

2   CLUDE OTHER OPTIONS.—Nothing in this subsection

3   shall be construed to affect a multiemployer plan's

4   ability to adopt the shortfall funding method with

5   the Secretary's permission under otherwise applica-

6   ble regulations or to affect a multiemployer plan's

7   right to change funding methods, with or without

8   the Secretary's consent, as provided in applicable

9   rules and regulations.

10   (c) CONFORMING AMENDMENTS.—

11   (1) Section 301 of the Employee Retirement In-

12   come Security Act of 1974 (29 U.S.C. 1081) is

13   amended by striking subsection (d).

14   (2) The table of contents in section 1 of such

15   Act (as amended by this Act) is amended by insert-

16   ing after the item relating to section 303 the fol-

17   lowing new item:

"Sec. 304. Minimum funding standards for multiemployer plans.".

18   (d) EFFECTIVE DATE.—

19   (1) IN GENERAL.—The amendments made by

20   this section shall apply to plan years beginning after

21   2007.

22   (2) SPECIAL RULE FOR CERTAIN AMORTIZATION

23   EXTENSIONS.—If the Secretary of the Treasury

24   grants an extension under section 304 of the Em-

25   ployee Retirement Income Security Act of 1974 and

1   section 412(e) of the Internal Revenue Code of 1986

2   with respect to any application filed with the Sec-

3   retary of the Treasury on or before June 30, 2005,

4   the extension (and any modification thereof) shall be

5   applied and administered under the rules of such

6   sections as in effect before the enactment of this

7   Act, including the use of the rate of interest deter-

8   mined under section 6621(b) of such Code.

9 **SEC. 202. ADDITIONAL FUNDING RULES FOR MULTIEM-**

10   **PLOYER PLANS IN ENDANGERED OR CRIT-**

11   **ICAL STATUS.**

12   (a) IN GENERAL.—Part 3 of subtitle B of title I of

13 the Employee Retirement Income Security Act of 1974 (as

14 amended by the preceding provisions of this Act) is

15 amended by inserting after section 304 the following new

16 section:

17   "ADDITIONAL FUNDING RULES FOR MULTIEMPLOYER

18   PLANS IN ENDANGERED STATUS OR CRITICAL STATUS

19   "SEC. 305. (a) GENERAL RULE.—For purposes of

20 this part, in the case of a multiemployer plan in effect

21 on July 16, 2006—

22   "(1) if the plan is in endangered status—

23   "(A) the plan sponsor shall adopt and im-

24   plement a funding improvement plan in accord-

25   ance with the requirements of subsection (c),

26   and

241

1   "(B) the requirements of subsection (d)

2   shall apply during the funding plan adoption

3   period and the funding improvement period,

4   and

5   "(2) if the plan is in critical status—

6   "(A) the plan sponsor shall adopt and im-

7   plement a rehabilitation plan in accordance with

8   the requirements of subsection (e), and

9   "(B) the requirements of subsection (f)

10   shall apply during the rehabilitation plan adop-

11   tion period and the rehabilitation period.

12   "(b) DETERMINATION OF ENDANGERED AND CRIT-

13 ICAL STATUS.—For purposes of this section—

14   "(1) ENDANGERED STATUS.—A multiemployer

15 plan is in endangered status for a plan year if, as

16 determined by the plan actuary under paragraph

17 (3), the plan is not in critical status for the plan

18 year and, as of the beginning of the plan year, ei-

19 ther—

20   "(A) the plan's funded percentage for such

21   plan year is less than 80 percent, or

22   "(B) the plan has an accumulated funding

23   deficiency for such plan year, or is projected to

24   have such an accumulated funding deficiency

25   for any of the 6 succeeding plan years, taking

1   into account any extension of amortization peri-

2   ods under section 304(d).

3 For purposes of this section, a plan shall be treated

4 as in seriously endangered status for a plan year if

5 the plan is described in both subparagraphs (A) and

6 (B).

7   "(2) CRITICAL STATUS.—A multiemployer plan

8 is in critical status for a plan year if, as determined

9 by the plan actuary under paragraph (3), the plan

10 is described in 1 or more of the following subpara-

11 graphs as of the beginning of the plan year:

12   "(A) A plan is described in this subpara-

13   graph if—

14   "(i) the funded percentage of the plan

15   is less than 65 percent, and

16   "(ii) the sum of—

17   "(I) the fair market value of plan

18   assets, plus

19   "(II) the present value of the

20   reasonably anticipated employer con-

21   tributions for the current plan year

22   and each of the 6 succeeding plan

23   years, assuming that the terms of all

24   collective bargaining agreements pur-

25   suant to which the plan is maintained

1   for the current plan year continue in

2   effect for succeeding plan years,

3   is less than the present value of all non-

4   forfeitable benefits projected to be payable

5   under the plan during the current plan

6   year and each of the 6 succeeding plan

7   years (plus administrative expenses for

8   such plan years).

9   "(B) A plan is described in this subpara-

10   graph if—

11   "(i) the plan has an accumulated

12   funding deficiency for the current plan

13   year, not taking into account any extension

14   of amortization periods under section

15   304(d), or

16   "(ii) the plan is projected to have an

17   accumulated funding deficiency for any of

18   the 3 succeeding plan years (4 succeeding

19   plan years if the funded percentage of the

20   plan is 65 percent or less), not taking into

21   account any extension of amortization peri-

22   ods under section 304(d).

23   "(C) A plan is described in this subpara-

24   graph if—

1   "(i)(I) the plan's normal cost for the

2 current plan year, plus interest (deter-

3 mined at the rate used for determining

4 costs under the plan) for the current plan

5 year on the amount of unfunded benefit li-

6 abilities under the plan as of the last date

7 of the preceding plan year, exceeds

8   "(II) the present value of the reason-

9 ably anticipated employer and employee

10 contributions for the current plan year,

11   "(ii) the present value, as of the be-

12 ginning of the current plan year, of non-

13 forfeitable benefits of inactive participants

14 is greater than the present value of non-

15 forfeitable benefits of active participants,

16 and

17   "(iii) the plan has an accumulated

18 funding deficiency for the current plan

19 year, or is projected to have such a defi-

20 ciency for any of the 4 succeeding plan

21 years, not taking into account any exten-

22 sion of amortization periods under section

23 304(d).

24 "(D) A plan is described in this subpara-

25 graph if the sum of—

1   "(i) the fair market value of plan as-

2   sets, plus

3   "(ii) the present value of the reason-

4   ably anticipated employer contributions for

5   the current plan year and each of the 4

6   succeeding plan years, assuming that the

7   terms of all collective bargaining agree-

8   ments pursuant to which the plan is main-

9   tained for the current plan year continue

10   in effect for succeeding plan years,

11   is less than the present value of all benefits pro-

12   jected to be payable under the plan during the

13   current plan year and each of the 4 succeeding

14   plan years (plus administrative expenses for

15   such plan years).

16   "(3) ANNUAL CERTIFICATION BY PLAN ACTU-

17   ARY.—

18   "(A) IN GENERAL.—Not later than the

19   90th day of each plan year of a multiemployer

20   plan, the plan actuary shall certify to the Sec-

21   retary of the Treasury and to the plan spon-

22   sor—

23   "(i) whether or not the plan is in en-

24   dangered status for such plan year and

1   whether or not the plan is or will be in

2   critical status for such plan year, and

3   "(ii) in the case of a plan which is in

4   a funding improvement or rehabilitation

5   period, whether or not the plan is making

6   the scheduled progress in meeting the re-

7   quirements of its funding improvement or

8   rehabilitation plan.

9   "(B) ACTUARIAL PROJECTIONS OF ASSETS

10   AND LIABILITIES.—

11   "(i) IN GENERAL.—In making the de-

12   terminations and projections under this

13   subsection, the plan actuary shall make

14   projections required for the current and

15   succeeding plan years of the current value

16   of the assets of the plan and the present

17   value of all liabilities to participants and

18   beneficiaries under the plan for the current

19   plan year as of the beginning of such year.

20   The actuary's projections shall be based on

21   reasonable actuarial estimates, assump-

22   tions, and methods that, except as pro-

23   vided in clause (iii), offer the actuary's

24   best estimate of anticipated experience

25   under the plan. The projected present

value of liabilities as of the beginning of
such year shall be determined based on the
most recent of either—

"(I) the actuarial statement required under section 103(d) with respect to the most recently filed annual
report, or

"(II) the actuarial valuation for
the preceding plan year.

"(ii) DETERMINATIONS OF FUTURE
CONTRIBUTIONS.—Any actuarial projection
of plan assets shall assume—

"(I) reasonably anticipated employer contributions for the current
and succeeding plan years, assuming
that the terms of the one or more collective bargaining agreements pursuant to which the plan is maintained
for the current plan year continue in
effect for succeeding plan years, or

"(II) that employer contributions
for the most recent plan year will continue indefinitely, but only if the plan
actuary determines there have been no
significant demographic changes that

1   would make such assumption unrea-

2   sonable.

3   "(iii) PROJECTED INDUSTRY ACTIV-

4   ITY.—Any projection of activity in the in-

5   dustry or industries covered by the plan,

6   including future covered employment and

7   contribution levels, shall be based on infor-

8   mation provided by the plan sponsor,

9   which shall act reasonably and in good

10   faith.

11   "(C) PENALTY FOR FAILURE TO SECURE

12   TIMELY ACTUARIAL CERTIFICATION.—Any fail-

13   ure of the plan's actuary to certify the plan's

14   status under this subsection by the date speci-

15   fied in subparagraph (A) shall be treated for

16   purposes of section 502(c)(2) as a failure or re-

17   fusal by the plan administrator to file the an-

18   nual report required to be filed with the Sec-

19   retary under section 101(b)(4).

20   "(D) NOTICE.—

21   "(i) IN GENERAL.—In any case in

22   which it is certified under subparagraph

23   (A) that a multiemployer plan is or will be

24   in endangered or critical status for a plan

25   year, the plan sponsor shall, not later than

30 days after the date of the certification, provide notification of the endangered or critical status to the participants and beneficiaries, the bargaining parties, the Pension Benefit Guaranty Corporation, and the Secretary.

"(ii) PLANS IN CRITICAL STATUS.—If it is certified under subparagraph (A) that a multiemployer plan is or will be in critical status, the plan sponsor shall include in the notice under clause (i) an explanation of the possibility that—

"(I) adjustable benefits (as defined in subsection (e)(8)) may be reduced, and

"(II) such reductions may apply to participants and beneficiaries whose benefit commencement date is on or after the date such notice is provided for the first plan year in which the plan is in critical status.

"(iii) MODEL NOTICE.—The Secretary shall prescribe a model notice that a multiemployer plan may use to satisfy the requirements under clause (ii).

250

1   "(c) FUNDING IMPROVEMENT PLAN MUST BE
2 ADOPTED FOR MULTIEMPLOYER PLANS IN ENDANGERED
3 STATUS.—

4   "(1) IN GENERAL.—In any case in which a
5   multiemployer plan is in endangered status for a
6   plan year, the plan sponsor, in accordance with this
7   subsection—

8   "(A) shall adopt a funding improvement
9   plan not later than 240 days following the re-
10   quired date for the actuarial certification of en-
11   dangered status under subsection (b)(3)(A),
12   and

13   "(B) within 30 days after the adoption of
14   the funding improvement plan—

15   "(i) shall provide to the bargaining
16   parties 1 or more schedules showing re-
17   vised benefit structures, revised contribu-
18   tion structures, or both, which, if adopted,
19   may reasonably be expected to enable the
20   multiemployer plan to meet the applicable
21   benchmarks in accordance with the fund-
22   ing improvement plan, including—

23   "(I) one proposal for reductions
24   in the amount of future benefit accru-
25   als necessary to achieve the applicable

benchmarks, assuming no amendments increasing contributions under
the plan (other than amendments increasing contributions necessary to
achieve the applicable benchmarks
after amendments have reduced future benefit accruals to the maximum
extent permitted by law), and

"(II) one proposal for increases
in contributions under the plan necessary to achieve the applicable benchmarks, assuming no amendments reducing future benefit accruals under
the plan, and

"(ii) may, if the plan sponsor deems
appropriate, prepare and provide the bargaining parties with additional information
relating to contribution rates or benefit reductions, alternative schedules, or other information relevant to achieving the applicable benchmarks in accordance with the
funding improvement plan.

For purposes of this section, the term 'applicable benchmarks' means the requirements appli-

1   cable to the multiemployer plan under para-

2   graph (3) (as modified by paragraph (5)).

3   "(2) EXCEPTION FOR YEARS AFTER PROCESS

4   BEGINS.—Paragraph (1) shall not apply to a plan

5   year if such year is in a funding plan adoption pe-

6   riod or funding improvement period by reason of the

7   plan being in endangered status for a preceding plan

8   year. For purposes of this section, such preceding

9   plan year shall be the initial determination year with

10   respect to the funding improvement plan to which it

11   relates.

12   "(3) FUNDING IMPROVEMENT PLAN.—For pur-

13   poses of this section—

14   "(A) IN GENERAL.—A funding improve-

15   ment plan is a plan which consists of the ac-

16   tions, including options or a range of options to

17   be proposed to the bargaining parties, formu-

18   lated to provide, based on reasonably antici-

19   pated experience and reasonable actuarial as-

20   sumptions, for the attainment by the plan dur-

21   ing the funding improvement period of the fol-

22   lowing requirements:

23   "(i) INCREASE IN PLAN'S FUNDING

24   PERCENTAGE.—The plan's funded percent-

25   age as of the close of the funding improve-

1   ment period equals or exceeds a percentage

2   equal to the sum of—

3   "(I) such percentage as of the

4   beginning of such period, plus

5   "(II) 33 percent of the difference

6   between 100 percent and the percent-

7   age under subclause (I).

8   "(ii) AVOIDANCE OF ACCUMULATED

9   FUNDING DEFICIENCIES.—No accumulated

10   funding deficiency for any plan year during

11   the funding improvement period (taking

12   into account any extension of amortization

13   periods under section 304(d)).

14   "(B) SERIOUSLY ENDANGERED PLANS.—

15   In the case of a plan in seriously endangered

16   status, except as provided in paragraph (5),

17   subparagraph (A)(i)(II) shall be applied by sub-

18   stituting '20 percent' for '33 percent'.

19   "(4) FUNDING IMPROVEMENT PERIOD.—For

20   purposes of this section—

21   "(A) IN GENERAL.—The funding improve-

22   ment period for any funding improvement plan

23   adopted pursuant to this subsection is the 10-

24   year period beginning on the first day of the

1 first plan year of the multiemployer plan begin-

2 ning after the earlier of—

3   "(i) the second anniversary of the

4   date of the adoption of the funding im-

5   provement plan, or

6   "(ii) the expiration of the collective

7   bargaining agreements in effect on the due

8   date for the actuarial certification of en-

9   dangered status for the initial determina-

10   tion year under subsection (b)(3)(A) and

11   covering, as of such due date, at least 75

12   percent of the active participants in such

13   multiemployer plan.

14   "(B) SERIOUSLY ENDANGERED PLANS.—

15 In the case of a plan in seriously endangered

16 status, except as provided in paragraph (5),

17 subparagraph (A) shall be applied by sub-

18 stituting '15-year period' for '10-year period'.

19   "(C) COORDINATION WITH CHANGES IN

20 STATUS.—

21   "(i) PLANS NO LONGER IN ENDAN-

22   GERED STATUS.—If the plan's actuary cer-

23   tifies under subsection (b)(3)(A) for a plan

24   year in any funding plan adoption period

25   or funding improvement period that the

1   plan is no longer in endangered status and

2   is not in critical status, the funding plan

3   adoption period or funding improvement

4   period, whichever is applicable, shall end as

5   of the close of the preceding plan year.

6   "(ii) PLANS IN CRITICAL STATUS.—If

7   the plan's actuary certifies under sub-

8   section (b)(3)(A) for a plan year in any

9   funding plan adoption period or funding

10   improvement period that the plan is in

11   critical status, the funding plan adoption

12   period or funding improvement period,

13   whichever is applicable, shall end as of the

14   close of the plan year preceding the first

15   plan year in the rehabilitation period with

16   respect to such status.

17   "(D) PLANS IN ENDANGERED STATUS AT

18   END OF PERIOD.—If the plan's actuary certifies

19   under subsection (b)(3)(A) for the first plan

20   year following the close of the period described

21   in subparagraph (A) that the plan is in endan-

22   gered status, the provisions of this subsection

23   and subsection (d) shall be applied as if such

24   first plan year were an initial determination

25   year, except that the plan may not be amended

1   in a manner inconsistent with the funding im-

2   provement plan in effect for the preceding plan

3   year until a new funding improvement plan is

4   adopted.

5   "(5) SPECIAL RULES FOR SERIOUSLY ENDAN-

6 GERED PLANS MORE THAN 70 PERCENT FUNDED.—

7   "(A) IN GENERAL.—If the funded percent-

8   age of a plan in seriously endangered status

9   was more than 70 percent as of the beginning

10   of the initial determination year—

11   "(i) paragraphs (3)(B) and (4)(B)

12   shall apply only if the plan's actuary cer-

13   tifies, within 30 days after the certification

14   under subsection (b)(3)(A) for the initial

15   determination year, that, based on the

16   terms of the plan and the collective bar-

17   gaining agreements in effect at the time of

18   such certification, the plan is not projected

19   to meet the requirements of paragraph

20   (3)(A) (without regard to paragraphs

21   (3)(B) and (4)(B)), and

22   "(ii) if there is a certification under

23   clause (i), the plan may, in formulating its

24   funding improvement plan, only take into

25   account the rules of paragraph (3)(B) and

1   (4)(B) for plan years in the funding im-
2   provement period beginning on or before
3   the date on which the last of the collective
4   bargaining agreements described in para-
5   graph (4)(A)(ii) expires.

6   "(B) SPECIAL RULE AFTER EXPIRATION
7 OF AGREEMENTS.—Notwithstanding subpara-
8 graph (A)(ii), if, for any plan year ending after
9 the date described in subparagraph (A)(ii), the
10 plan actuary certifies (at the time of the annual
11 certification under subsection (b)(3)(A) for such
12 plan year) that, based on the terms of the plan
13 and collective bargaining agreements in effect
14 at the time of that annual certification, the plan
15 is not projected to be able to meet the require-
16 ments of paragraph (3)(A) (without regard to
17 paragraphs (3)(B) and (4)(B)), paragraphs
18 (3)(B) and (4)(B) shall continue to apply for
19 such year.

20   "(6) UPDATES TO FUNDING IMPROVEMENT
21 PLAN AND SCHEDULES.—

22   "(A) FUNDING IMPROVEMENT PLAN.—The
23 plan sponsor shall annually update the funding
24 improvement plan and shall file the update with
25 the plan's annual report under section 104.

1   "(B) SCHEDULES.—The plan sponsor shall

2 annually update any schedule of contribution

3 rates provided under this subsection to reflect

4 the experience of the plan.

5   "(C) DURATION OF SCHEDULE.—A sched-

6 ule of contribution rates provided by the plan

7 sponsor and relied upon by bargaining parties

8 in negotiating a collective bargaining agreement

9 shall remain in effect for the duration of that

10 collective bargaining agreement.

11   "(7) IMPOSITION OF DEFAULT SCHEDULE

12 WHERE FAILURE TO ADOPT FUNDING IMPROVEMENT

13 PLAN.—

14   "(A) IN GENERAL.—If—

15   "(i) a collective bargaining agreement

16 providing for contributions under a multi-

17 employer plan that was in effect at the

18 time the plan entered endangered status

19 expires, and

20   "(ii) after receiving one or more

21 schedules from the plan sponsor under

22 paragraph (1)(B), the bargaining parties

23 with respect to such agreement fail to

24 agree on changes to contribution or benefit

25 schedules necessary to meet the applicable

benchmarks in accordance with the funding improvement plan,

the plan sponsor shall implement the schedule
described in paragraph (1)(B)(i)(I) beginning
on the date specified in subparagraph (B).

"(B) DATE OF IMPLEMENTATION.—The
date specified in this subparagraph is the earlier of the date—

"(i) on which the Secretary certifies
that the parties are at an impasse, or

"(ii) which is 180 days after the date
on which the collective bargaining agreement described in subparagraph (A) expires.

"(8) FUNDING PLAN ADOPTION PERIOD.—For
purposes of this section, the term 'funding plan
adoption period' means the period beginning on the
date of the certification under subsection (b)(3)(A)
for the initial determination year and ending on the
day before the first day of the funding improvement
period.

"(d) RULES FOR OPERATION OF PLAN DURING
ADOPTION AND IMPROVEMENT PERIODS.—

"(1) SPECIAL RULES FOR PLAN ADOPTION PE-
RIOD.—During the funding plan adoption period—

1   "(A) the plan sponsor may not accept a

2   collective bargaining agreement or participation

3   agreement with respect to the multiemployer

4   plan that provides for—

5   "(i) a reduction in the level of con-

6   tributions for any participants,

7   "(ii) a suspension of contributions

8   with respect to any period of service, or

9   "(iii) any new direct or indirect exclu-

10   sion of younger or newly hired employees

11   from plan participation,

12   "(B) no amendment of the plan which in-

13   creases the liabilities of the plan by reason of

14   any increase in benefits, any change in the ac-

15   crual of benefits, or any change in the rate at

16   which benefits become nonforfeitable under the

17   plan may be adopted unless the amendment is

18   required as a condition of qualification under

19   part I of subchapter D of chapter 1 of the In-

20   ternal Revenue Code of 1986 or to comply with

21   other applicable law, and

22   "(C) in the case of a plan in seriously en-

23   dangered status, the plan sponsor shall take all

24   reasonable actions which are consistent with the

25   terms of the plan and applicable law and which

1   are expected, based on reasonable assumptions,

2   to achieve—

3   "(i) an increase in the plan's funded

4   percentage, and

5   "(ii) postponement of an accumulated

6   funding deficiency for at least 1 additional

7   plan year.

8 Actions under subparagraph (C) include applications

9 for extensions of amortization periods under section

10 304(d), use of the shortfall funding method in mak-

11 ing funding standard account computations, amend-

12 ments to the plan's benefit structure, reductions in

13 future benefit accruals, and other reasonable actions

14 consistent with the terms of the plan and applicable

15 law.

16   "(2) COMPLIANCE WITH FUNDING IMPROVE-

17 MENT PLAN.—

18   "(A) IN GENERAL.—A plan may not be

19   amended after the date of the adoption of a

20   funding improvement plan so as to be incon-

21   sistent with the funding improvement plan.

22   "(B) NO REDUCTION IN CONTRIBU-

23   TIONS.—A plan sponsor may not during any

24   funding improvement period accept a collective

25   bargaining agreement or participation agree-

ment with respect to the multiemployer plan that provides for—

    "(i) a reduction in the level of contributions for any participants,

    "(ii) a suspension of contributions with respect to any period of service, or

    "(iii) any new direct or indirect exclusion of younger or newly hired employees from plan participation.

"(C) SPECIAL RULES FOR BENEFIT INCREASES.—A plan may not be amended after the date of the adoption of a funding improvement plan so as to increase benefits, including future benefit accruals, unless the plan actuary certifies that the benefit increase is consistent with the funding improvement plan and is paid for out of contributions not required by the funding improvement plan to meet the applicable benchmark in accordance with the schedule contemplated in the funding improvement plan.

"(e) REHABILITATION PLAN MUST BE ADOPTED FOR MULTIEMPLOYER PLANS IN CRITICAL STATUS.—

    "(1) IN GENERAL.—In any case in which a multiemployer plan is in critical status for a plan year, the plan sponsor, in accordance with this sub-section—

    "(A) shall adopt a rehabilitation plan not later than 240 days following the required date for the actuarial certification of critical status under subsection (b)(3)(A), and

    "(B) within 30 days after the adoption of the rehabilitation plan—

        "(i) shall provide to the bargaining parties 1 or more schedules showing revised benefit structures, revised contribution structures, or both, which, if adopted, may reasonably be expected to enable the multiemployer plan to emerge from critical status in accordance with the rehabilitation plan, and

        "(ii) may, if the plan sponsor deems appropriate, prepare and provide the bargaining parties with additional information relating to contribution rates or benefit reductions, alternative schedules, or other information relevant to emerging from critical status in accordance with the rehabilitation plan.

1   The schedule or schedules described in subparagraph

2   (B)(i) shall reflect reductions in future benefit ac-

3   cruals and adjustable benefits, and increases in con-

4   tributions, that the plan sponsor determines are rea-

5   sonably necessary to emerge from critical status.

6   One schedule shall be designated as the default

7   schedule and such schedule shall assume that there

8   are no increases in contributions under the plan

9   other than the increases necessary to emerge from

10   critical status after future benefit accruals and other

11   benefits (other than benefits the reduction or elimi-

12   nation of which are not permitted under section

13   204(g)) have been reduced to the maximum extent

14   permitted by law.

15   "(2) EXCEPTION FOR YEARS AFTER PROCESS

16   BEGINS.—Paragraph (1) shall not apply to a plan

17   year if such year is in a rehabilitation plan adoption

18   period or rehabilitation period by reason of the plan

19   being in critical status for a preceding plan year.

20   For purposes of this section, such preceding plan

21   year shall be the initial critical year with respect to

22   the rehabilitation plan to which it relates.

23   "(3) REHABILITATION PLAN.—For purposes of

24   this section—

"(A) IN GENERAL.—A rehabilitation plan is a plan which consists of—

"(i) actions, including options or a range of options to be proposed to the bargaining parties, formulated, based on reasonably anticipated experience and reasonable actuarial assumptions, to enable the plan to cease to be in critical status by the end of the rehabilitation period and may include reductions in plan expenditures (including plan mergers and consolidations), reductions in future benefit accruals or increases in contributions, if agreed to by the bargaining parties, or any combination of such actions, or

"(ii) if the plan sponsor determines that, based on reasonable actuarial assumptions and upon exhaustion of all reasonable measures, the plan can not reasonably be expected to emerge from critical status by the end of the rehabilitation period, reasonable measures to emerge from critical status at a later time or to forestall possible insolvency (within the meaning of section 4245).

1   A rehabilitation plan must provide annual

2   standards for meeting the requirements of such

3   rehabilitation plan. Such plan shall also include

4   the schedules required to be provided under

5   paragraph (1)(B)(i) and if clause (ii) applies,

6   shall set forth the alternatives considered, ex-

7   plain why the plan is not reasonably expected to

8   emerge from critical status by the end of the re-

9   habilitation period, and specify when, if ever,

10   the plan is expected to emerge from critical sta-

11   tus in accordance with the rehabilitation plan.

12   "(B) UPDATES TO REHABILITATION PLAN

13   AND SCHEDULES.—

14   "(i) REHABILITATION PLAN.—The

15   plan sponsor shall annually update the re-

16   habilitation plan and shall file the update

17   with the plan's annual report under section

18   104.

19   "(ii) SCHEDULES.—The plan sponsor

20   shall annually update any schedule of con-

21   tribution rates provided under this sub-

22   section to reflect the experience of the

23   plan.

24   "(iii) DURATION OF SCHEDULE.—A

25   schedule of contribution rates provided by

1   the plan sponsor and relied upon by bar-

2   gaining parties in negotiating a collective

3   bargaining agreement shall remain in ef-

4   fect for the duration of that collective bar-

5   gaining agreement.

6   "(C) IMPOSITION OF DEFAULT SCHEDULE

7 WHERE FAILURE TO ADOPT REHABILITATION

8 PLAN.—

9   "(i) IN GENERAL.—If—

10   "(I) a collective bargaining agree-

11   ment providing for contributions

12   under a multiemployer plan that was

13   in effect at the time the plan entered

14   critical status expires, and

15   "(II) after receiving one or more

16   schedules from the plan sponsor under

17   paragraph (1)(B), the bargaining par-

18   ties with respect to such agreement

19   fail to adopt a contribution or benefit

20   schedules with terms consistent with

21   the rehabilitation plan and the sched-

22   ule from the plan sponsor under para-

23   graph (1)(B)(i),

24   the plan sponsor shall implement the de-

25   fault schedule described in the last sen-

1   tence of paragraph (1) beginning on the

2   date specified in clause (ii).

3   "(ii) DATE OF IMPLEMENTATION.—

4   The date specified in this clause is the ear-

5   lier of the date—

6   "(I) on which the Secretary cer-

7   tifies that the parties are at an im-

8   passe, or

9   "(II) which is 180 days after the

10   date on which the collective bar-

11   gaining agreement described in clause

12   (i) expires.

13   "(4) REHABILITATION PERIOD.—For purposes

14   of this section—

15   "(A) IN GENERAL.—The rehabilitation pe-

16   riod for a plan in critical status is the 10-year

17   period beginning on the first day of the first

18   plan year of the multiemployer plan following

19   the earlier of—

20   "(i) the second anniversary of the

21   date of the adoption of the rehabilitation

22   plan, or

23   "(ii) the expiration of the collective

24   bargaining agreements in effect on the

25   date of the due date for the actuarial cer-

tification of critical status for the initial
critical year under subsection (a)(1) and
covering, as of such date at least 75 percent of the active participants in such multiemployer plan.

If a plan emerges from critical status as provided under subparagraph (B) before the end of
such 10-year period, the rehabilitation period
shall end with the plan year preceding the plan
year for which the determination under subparagraph (B) is made.

"(B) EMERGENCE.—A plan in critical status shall remain in such status until a plan
year for which the plan actuary certifies, in accordance with subsection (b)(3)(A), that the
plan is not projected to have an accumulated
funding deficiency for the plan year or any of
the 9 succeeding plan years, without regard to
the use of the shortfall method and taking into
account any extension of amortization periods
under section 304(d).

"(5) REHABILITATION PLAN ADOPTION PE-
RIOD.—For purposes of this section, the term 'rehabilitation plan adoption period' means the period beginning on the date of the certification under sub-

1   section (b)(3)(A) for the initial critical year and end-

2   ing on the day before the first day of the rehabilita-

3   tion period.

4   "(6) LIMITATION ON REDUCTION IN RATES OF

5   FUTURE ACCRUALS.—Any reduction in the rate of

6   future accruals under the default schedule described

7   in paragraph (1)(B)(i) shall not reduce the rate of

8   future accruals below—

9   "(A) a monthly benefit (payable as a single

10   life annuity commencing at the participant's

11   normal retirement age) equal to 1 percent of

12   the contributions required to be made with re-

13   spect to a participant, or the equivalent stand-

14   ard accrual rate for a participant or group of

15   participants under the collective bargaining

16   agreements in effect as of the first day of the

17   initial critical year, or

18   "(B) if lower, the accrual rate under the

19   plan on such first day.

20   The equivalent standard accrual rate shall be deter-

21   mined by the plan sponsor based on the standard or

22   average contribution base units which the plan spon-

23   sor determines to be representative for active partici-

24   pants and such other factors as the plan sponsor de-

25   termines to be relevant. Nothing in this paragraph

shall be construed as limiting the ability of the plan sponsor to prepare and provide the bargaining parties with alternative schedules to the default schedule that established lower or higher accrual and contribution rates than the rates otherwise described in this paragraph.

"(7) AUTOMATIC EMPLOYER SURCHARGE.—

"(A) IMPOSITION OF SURCHARGE.—Each employer otherwise obligated to make contributions for the initial critical year shall be obligated to pay to the plan for such year a surcharge equal to 5 percent of the contributions otherwise required under the applicable collective bargaining agreement (or other agreement pursuant to which the employer contributes). For each succeeding plan year in which the plan is in critical status for a consecutive period of years beginning with the initial critical year, the surcharge shall be 10 percent of the contributions otherwise so required.

"(B) ENFORCEMENT OF SURCHARGE.— The surcharges under subparagraph (A) shall be due and payable on the same schedule as the contributions on which the surcharges are based. Any failure to make a surcharge pay-

1   ment shall be treated as a delinquent contribu-

2   tion under section 515 and shall be enforceable

3   as such.

4   "(C) SURCHARGE TO TERMINATE UPON

5   COLLECTIVE BARGAINING AGREEMENT RENEGO-

6   TIATION.—The surcharge under this paragraph

7   shall cease to be effective with respect to em-

8   ployees covered by a collective bargaining agree-

9   ment (or other agreement pursuant to which

10   the employer contributes), beginning on the ef-

11   fective date of a collective bargaining agreement

12   (or other such agreement) that includes terms

13   consistent with a schedule presented by the

14   plan sponsor under paragraph (1)(B)(i), as

15   modified under subparagraph (B) of paragraph

16   (3).

17   "(D) SURCHARGE NOT TO APPLY UNTIL

18   EMPLOYER RECEIVES NOTICE.—The surcharge

19   under this paragraph shall not apply to an em-

20   ployer until 30 days after the employer has

21   been notified by the plan sponsor that the plan

22   is in critical status and that the surcharge is in

23   effect.

24   "(E) SURCHARGE NOT TO GENERATE IN-

25   CREASED BENEFIT ACCRUALS.—Notwith-

standing any provision of a plan to the contrary, the amount of any surcharge under this
paragraph shall not be the basis for any benefit
accrual under the plan.

"(8) BENEFIT ADJUSTMENTS.—

"(A) ADJUSTABLE BENEFITS.—

"(i) IN GENERAL.—Notwithstanding
section 204(g), the plan sponsor shall, subject to the notice requirements in subparagraph (C), make any reductions to adjustable benefits which the plan sponsor deems
appropriate, based upon the outcome of
collective bargaining over the schedule or
schedules provided under paragraph
(1)(B)(i).

"(ii) EXCEPTION FOR RETIREES.—
Except in the case of adjustable benefits
described in clause (iv)(III), the plan sponsor of a plan in critical status shall not reduce adjustable benefits of any participant
or beneficiary whose benefit commencement date is before the date on which the
plan provides notice to the participant or
beneficiary under subsection (b)(3)(D) for
the initial critical year.

1   "(iii) PLAN SPONSOR FLEXIBILITY.—

2 The plan sponsor shall include in the

3 schedules provided to the bargaining par-

4 ties an allowance for funding the benefits

5 of participants with respect to whom con-

6 tributions are not currently required to be

7 made, and shall reduce their benefits to

8 the extent permitted under this title and

9 considered appropriate by the plan sponsor

10 based on the plan's then current overall

11 funding status.

12   "(iv) ADJUSTABLE BENEFIT DE-

13 FINED.—For purposes of this paragraph,

14 the term 'adjustable benefit' means—

15   "(I) benefits, rights, and features

16 under the plan, including post-retire-

17 ment death benefits, 60-month guar-

18 antees, disability benefits not yet in

19 pay status, and similar benefits,

20   "(II) any early retirement benefit

21 or retirement-type subsidy (within the

22 meaning of section 204(g)(2)(A)) and

23 any benefit payment option (other

24 than the qualified joint-and survivor

25 annuity), and

"(III) benefit increases that would not be eligible for a guarantee under section 4022A on the first day of initial critical year because the increases were adopted (or, if later, took effect) less than 60 months before such first day.

"(B) NORMAL RETIREMENT BENEFITS PROTECTED.—Except as provided in subparagraph (A)(iv)(III), nothing in this paragraph shall be construed to permit a plan to reduce the level of a participant's accrued benefit payable at normal retirement age.

"(C) NOTICE REQUIREMENTS.—

"(i) IN GENERAL.—No reduction may be made to adjustable benefits under subparagraph (A) unless notice of such reduction has been given at least 30 days before the general effective date of such reduction for all participants and beneficiaries to—

"(I) plan participants and beneficiaries,

"(II) each employer who has an obligation to contribute (within the

1   meaning of section 4212(a)) under the

2   plan, and

3   "(III) each employee organization

4   which, for purposes of collective bar-

5   gaining, represents plan participants

6   employed by such an employer.

7   "(ii) CONTENT OF NOTICE.—The no-

8   tice under clause (i) shall contain—

9   "(I) sufficient information to en-

10   able participants and beneficiaries to

11   understand the effect of any reduction

12   on their benefits, including an esti-

13   mate (on an annual or monthly basis)

14   of any affected adjustable benefit that

15   a participant or beneficiary would oth-

16   erwise have been eligible for as of the

17   general effective date described in

18   clause (i), and

19   "(II) information as to the rights

20   and remedies of plan participants and

21   beneficiaries as well as how to contact

22   the Department of Labor for further

23   information and assistance where ap-

24   propriate.

"(iii) FORM AND MANNER.—Any notice under clause (i)—

"(I) shall be provided in a form and manner prescribed in regulations of the Secretary,

"(II) shall be written in a manner so as to be understood by the average plan participant, and

"(III) may be provided in written, electronic, or other appropriate form to the extent such form is reasonably accessible to persons to whom the notice is required to be provided.

The Secretary shall in the regulations prescribed under subclause (I) establish a model notice that a plan sponsor may use to meet the requirements of this subparagraph.

"(9) ADJUSTMENTS DISREGARDED IN WITHDRAWAL LIABILITY DETERMINATION.—

"(A) BENEFIT REDUCTIONS.—Any benefit reductions under this subsection shall be disregarded in determining a plan's unfunded vested benefits for purposes of determining an employer's withdrawal liability under section 4201.

1   "(B) SURCHARGES.—Any surcharges

2   under paragraph (7) shall be disregarded in de-

3   termining an employer's withdrawal liability

4   under section 4211, except for purposes of de-

5   termining the unfunded vested benefits attrib-

6   utable to an employer under section 4211(c)(4)

7   or a comparable method approved under section

8   4211(c)(5).

9   "(C) SIMPLIFIED CALCULATIONS.—The

10   Pension Benefit Guaranty Corporation shall

11   prescribe simplified methods for the application

12   of this paragraph in determining withdrawal li-

13   ability.

14   "(f) RULES FOR OPERATION OF PLAN DURING

15 ADOPTION AND REHABILITATION PERIOD.—

16   "(1) COMPLIANCE WITH REHABILITATION

17   PLAN.—

18   "(A) IN GENERAL.—A plan may not be

19   amended after the date of the adoption of a re-

20   habilitation plan under subsection (e) so as to

21   be inconsistent with the rehabilitation plan.

22   "(B) SPECIAL RULES FOR BENEFIT IN-

23   CREASES.—A plan may not be amended after

24   the date of the adoption of a rehabilitation plan

25   under subsection (e) so as to increase benefits,

including future benefit accruals, unless the plan actuary certifies that such increase is paid for out of additional contributions not contemplated by the rehabilitation plan, and, after taking into account the benefit increase, the multiemployer plan still is reasonably expected to emerge from critical status by the end of the rehabilitation period on the schedule contemplated in the rehabilitation plan.

"(2) RESTRICTION ON LUMP SUMS AND SIMILAR BENEFITS.—

"(A) IN GENERAL.—Effective on the date the notice of certification of the plan's critical status for the initial critical year under subsection (b)(3)(D) is sent, and notwithstanding section 204(g), the plan shall not pay—

"(i) any payment, in excess of the monthly amount paid under a single life annuity (plus any social security supplements described in the last sentence of section 204(b)(1)(G)),

"(ii) any payment for the purchase of an irrevocable commitment from an insurer to pay benefits, and

1   "(iii) any other payment specified by

2   the Secretary of the Treasury by regula-

3   tions.

4   "(B) EXCEPTION.—Subparagraph (A)

5   shall not apply to a benefit which under section

6   203(e) may be immediately distributed without

7   the consent of the participant or to any makeup

8   payment in the case of a retroactive annuity

9   starting date or any similar payment of benefits

10   owed with respect to a prior period.

11   "(3) ADJUSTMENTS DISREGARDED IN WITH-

12 DRAWAL LIABILITY DETERMINATION.—Any benefit

13 reductions under this subsection shall be disregarded

14 in determining a plan's unfunded vested benefits for

15 purposes of determining an employer's withdrawal li-

16 ability under section 4201.

17   "(4) SPECIAL RULES FOR PLAN ADOPTION PE-

18 RIOD.—During the rehabilitation plan adoption pe-

19 riod—

20   "(A) the plan sponsor may not accept a

21   collective bargaining agreement or participation

22   agreement with respect to the multiemployer

23   plan that provides for—

24   "(i) a reduction in the level of con-

25   tributions for any participants,

"(ii) a suspension of contributions with respect to any period of service, or

"(iii) any new direct or indirect exclusion of younger or newly hired employees from plan participation, and

"(B) no amendment of the plan which increases the liabilities of the plan by reason of any increase in benefits, any change in the accrual of benefits, or any change in the rate at which benefits become nonforfeitable under the plan may be adopted unless the amendment is required as a condition of qualification under part I of subchapter D of chapter 1 of the Internal Revenue Code of 1986 or to comply with other applicable law.

"(g) EXPEDITED RESOLUTION OF PLAN SPONSOR DECISIONS.—If, within 60 days of the due date for adoption of a funding improvement plan or a rehabilitation plan under subsection (e), the plan sponsor of a plan in endangered status or a plan in critical status has not agreed on a funding improvement plan or rehabilitation plan, then any member of the board or group that constitutes the plan sponsor may require that the plan sponsor enter into an expedited dispute resolution procedure

1 for the development and adoption of a funding improve-

2 ment plan or rehabilitation plan.

3   "(h) NONBARGAINED PARTICIPATION.—

4   "(1) BOTH BARGAINED AND NONBARGAINED

5   EMPLOYEE-PARTICIPANTS.—In the case of an em-

6   ployer that contributes to a multiemployer plan with

7   respect to both employees who are covered by one or

8   more collective bargaining agreements and employ-

9   ees who are not so covered, if the plan is in endan-

10   gered status or in critical status, benefits of and

11   contributions for the nonbargained employees, in-

12   cluding surcharges on those contributions, shall be

13   determined as if those nonbargained employees were

14   covered under the first to expire of the employer's

15   collective bargaining agreements in effect when the

16   plan entered endangered or critical status.

17   "(2) NONBARGAINED EMPLOYEES ONLY.—In

18   the case of an employer that contributes to a multi-

19   employer plan only with respect to employees who

20   are not covered by a collective bargaining agreement,

21   this section shall be applied as if the employer were

22   the bargaining party, and its participation agree-

23   ment with the plan were a collective bargaining

24   agreement with a term ending on the first day of the

25   plan year beginning after the employer is provided

1   the schedule or schedules described in subsections

2   (c) and (e).

3   "(i) DEFINITIONS; ACTUARIAL METHOD.—For pur-

4 poses of this section—

5   "(1) BARGAINING PARTY.—The term 'bar-

6   gaining party' means—

7   "(A)(i) except as provided in clause (ii), an

8   employer who has an obligation to contribute

9   under the plan; or

10   "(ii) in the case of a plan described under

11   section 404(c) of the Internal Revenue Code of

12   1986, or a continuation of such a plan, the as-

13   sociation of employers that is the employer set-

14   tlor of the plan; and

15   "(B) an employee organization which, for

16   purposes of collective bargaining, represents

17   plan participants employed by an employer who

18   has an obligation to contribute under the plan.

19   "(2) FUNDED PERCENTAGE.—The term 'fund-

20   ed percentage' means the percentage equal to a frac-

21   tion—

22   "(A) the numerator of which is the value

23   of the plan's assets, as determined under sec-

24   tion 304(c)(2), and

1   "(B) the denominator of which is the ac-

2   crued liability of the plan, determined using ac-

3   tuarial assumptions described in section

4   304(c)(3).

5   "(3) ACCUMULATED FUNDING DEFICIENCY.—

6 The term 'accumulated funding deficiency' has the

7 meaning given such term in section 304(a).

8   "(4) ACTIVE PARTICIPANT.—The term 'active

9 participant' means, in connection with a multiem-

10 ployer plan, a participant who is in covered service

11 under the plan.

12   "(5) INACTIVE PARTICIPANT.—The term 'inac-

13 tive participant' means, in connection with a multi-

14 employer plan, a participant, or the beneficiary or

15 alternate payee of a participant, who—

16   "(A) is not in covered service under the

17   plan, and

18   "(B) is in pay status under the plan or has

19   a nonforfeitable right to benefits under the

20   plan.

21   "(6) PAY STATUS.—A person is in pay status

22 under a multiemployer plan if—

23   "(A) at any time during the current plan

24   year, such person is a participant or beneficiary

25   under the plan and is paid an early, late, nor-

1   mal, or disability retirement benefit under the

2   plan (or a death benefit under the plan related

3   to a retirement benefit), or

4   "(B) to the extent provided in regulations

5   of the Secretary of the Treasury, such person

6   is entitled to such a benefit under the plan.

7   "(7) OBLIGATION TO CONTRIBUTE.—The term

8   'obligation to contribute' has the meaning given such

9   term under section 4212(a).

10   "(8) ACTUARIAL METHOD.—Notwithstanding

11   any other provision of this section, the actuary's de-

12   terminations with respect to a plan's normal cost,

13   actuarial accrued liability, and improvements in a

14   plan's funded percentage under this section shall be

15   based upon the unit credit funding method (whether

16   or not that method is used for the plan's actuarial

17   valuation).

18   "(9) PLAN SPONSOR.—In the case of a plan de-

19   scribed under section 404(c) of the Internal Revenue

20   Code of 1986, or a continuation of such a plan, the

21   term 'plan sponsor' means the bargaining parties de-

22   scribed under paragraph (1).

23   "(10) BENEFIT COMMENCEMENT DATE.—The

24   term 'benefit commencement date' means the annu-

25   ity starting date (or in the case of a retroactive an-

1   nuity starting date, the date on which benefit pay-

2   ments begin).".

3   (b) ENFORCEMENT.—Section 502 of the Employee

4 Retirement Income Security Act of 1974 (29 U.S.C. 1132)

5 is amended—

6   (1) in subsection (a)(6) by striking "(6), or

7   (7)" and inserting "(6), (7), or (8)";

8   (2) by redesignating subsection (c)(8) as sub-

9   section (c)(9); and

10   (3) by inserting after subsection (c)(7) the fol-

11   lowing new paragraph:

12   "(8) The Secretary may assess against any plan

13   sponsor of a multiemployer plan a civil penalty of

14   not more than $1,100 per day—

15   "(A) for each violation by such sponsor of

16   the requirement under section 305 to adopt by

17   the deadline established in that section a fund-

18   ing improvement plan or rehabilitation plan

19   with respect to a multiemployer which is in en-

20   dangered or critical status, or

21   "(B) in the case of a plan in endangered

22   status which is not in seriously endangered sta-

23   tus, for failure by the plan to meet the applica-

24   ble benchmarks under section 305 by the end of

1   the funding improvement period with respect to

2   the plan.".

3   (c) CAUSE OF ACTION TO COMPEL ADOPTION OR IM-

4 PLEMENTATION OF FUNDING IMPROVEMENT OR REHA-

5 BILITATION PLAN.—Section 502(a) of the Employee Re-

6 tirement Income Security Act of 1974 is amended by

7 striking "or" at the end of paragraph (8), by striking the

8 period at the end of paragraph (9) and inserting "; or"

9 and by adding at the end the following:

10   "(10) in the case of a multiemployer plan that

11   has been certified by the actuary to be in endan-

12   gered or critical status under section 305, if the plan

13   sponsor—

14   "(A) has not adopted a funding improve-

15   ment or rehabilitation plan under that section

16   by the deadline established in such section, or

17   "(B) fails to update or comply with the

18   terms of the funding improvement or rehabilita-

19   tion plan in accordance with the requirements

20   of such section,

21   by an employer that has an obligation to contribute

22   with respect to the multiemployer plan or an em-

23   ployee organization that represents active partici-

24   pants in the multiemployer plan, for an order com-

25   pelling the plan sponsor to adopt a funding improve-

ment or rehabilitation plan or to update or comply with the terms of the funding improvement or rehabilitation plan in accordance with the requirements of such section and the funding improvement or rehabilitation plan.''.

(d) No Additional Contributions Required.—Section 302(b) of the Employee Retirement Income Security Act of 1974, as amended by this Act, is amended by adding at the end the following new paragraph:

"(3) Multiemployer plans in critical status.—Paragraph (1) shall not apply in the case of a multiemployer plan for any plan year in which the plan is in critical status pursuant to section 305. This paragraph shall only apply if the plan adopts a rehabilitation plan in accordance with section 305(e) and complies with the terms of such rehabilitation plan (and any updates or modifications of the plan).''.

(e) Conforming Amendment.—The table of contents in section 1 of such Act (as amended by the preceding provisions of this Act) is amended by inserting after the item relating to section 304 the following new item:

"Sec. 305. Additional funding rules for multiemployer plans in endangered status or critical status.''.

(f) Effective Dates.—

(1) IN GENERAL.—The amendments made by this section shall apply with respect to plan years beginning after 2007.

(2) SPECIAL RULE FOR CERTAIN NOTICES.—In any case in which a plan's actuary certifies that it is reasonably expected that a multiemployer plan will be in critical status under section 305(b)(3) of the Employee Retirement Income Security Act of 1974, as added by this section, with respect to the first plan year beginning after 2007, the notice required under subparagraph (D) of such section may be provided at any time after the date of enactment, so long as it is provided on or before the last date for providing the notice under such subparagraph.

(3) SPECIAL RULE FOR CERTAIN RESTORED BENEFITS.—In the case of a multiemployer plan—

    (A) with respect to which benefits were reduced pursuant to a plan amendment adopted on or after January 1, 2002, and before June 30, 2005, and

    (B) which, pursuant to the plan document, the trust agreement, or a formal written communication from the plan sponsor to participants provided before June 30, 2005, provided for the restoration of such benefits,

1 the amendments made by this section shall not apply

2 to such benefit restorations to the extent that any

3 restriction on the providing or accrual of such bene-

4 fits would otherwise apply by reason of such amend-

5 ments.

6 **SEC. 203. MEASURES TO FORESTALL INSOLVENCY OF MUL-**

7 **TIEMPLOYER PLANS.**

8 (a) ADVANCE DETERMINATION OF IMPENDING IN-

9 SOLVENCY OVER 5 YEARS.—Section 4245(d)(1) of the

10 Employee Retirement Income Security Act of 1974 (29

11 U.S.C. 1426(d)(1)) is amended—

12 (1) by striking "3 plan years" the second place

13 it appears and inserting "5 plan years"; and

14 (2) by adding at the end the following new sen-

15 tence: "If the plan sponsor makes such a determina-

16 tion that the plan will be insolvent in any of the next

17 5 plan years, the plan sponsor shall make the com-

18 parison under this paragraph at least annually until

19 the plan sponsor makes a determination that the

20 plan will not be insolvent in any of the next 5 plan

21 years.".

22 (b) EFFECTIVE DATE.—The amendments made by

23 this section shall apply with respect to determinations

24 made in plan years beginning after 2007.

SEC. 204. WITHDRAWAL LIABILITY REFORMS.

(a) UPDATE OF RULES RELATING TO LIMITATIONS ON WITHDRAWAL LIABILITY.—

(1) INCREASE IN LIMITS.—Section 4225(a)(2) of such Act (29 U.S.C. 1405(a)(2)) is amended by striking the table contained therein and inserting the following new table:

"If the liquidation or distribution value of the employer after the sale or exchange is—	The portion is—
Not more than $5,000,000	30 percent of the amount.
More than $5,000,000, but not more than $10,000,000.	$1,500,000, plus 35 percent of the amount in excess of $5,000,000.
More than $10,000,000, but not more than $15,000,000.	$3,250,000, plus 40 percent of the amount in excess of $10,000,000.
More than $15,000,000, but not more than $17,500,000.	$5,250,000, plus 45 percent of the amount in excess of $15,000,000.
More than $17,500,000, but not more than $20,000,000.	$6,375,000, plus 50 percent of the amount in excess of $17,500,000.
More than $20,000,000, but not more than $22,500,000.	$7,625,000, plus 60 percent of the amount in excess of $20,000,000.
More than $22,500,000, but not more than $25,000,000.	$9,125,000, plus 70 percent of the amount in excess of $22,500,000.
More than $25,000,000	$10,875,000, plus 80 percent of the amount in excess of $25,000,000.".

(2) PLANS USING ATTRIBUTABLE METHOD.—Section 4225(a)(1)(B) of such Act (29 U.S.C. 1405(a)(1)(B)) is amended to read as follows:

"(B) in the case of a plan using the attributable method of allocating withdrawal liability,

1   the unfunded vested benefits attributable to em-

2   ployees of the employer.''.

3   (3) EFFECTIVE DATE.—The amendments made

4 by this subsection shall apply to sales occurring on

5 or after January 1, 2007.

6   (b) WITHDRAWAL LIABILITY CONTINUES IF WORK

7 CONTRACTED OUT.—

8   (1) IN GENERAL.—Clause (i) of section

9   4205(b)(2)(A) of such Act (29 U.S.C.

10   1385(b)(2)(A)) is amended by inserting ''or to an

11   entity or entities owned or controlled by the em-

12   ployer'' after ''to another location''.

13   (2) EFFECTIVE DATE.—The amendment made

14   by this subsection shall apply with respect to work

15   transferred on or after the date of the enactment of

16   this Act.

17   (c) APPLICATION OF RULES TO PLANS PRIMARILY

18 COVERING EMPLOYEES IN THE BUILDING AND CON-

19 STRUCTION INDUSTRY.—

20   (1) IN GENERAL.—Section 4210(b) of such Act

21   (29 U.S.C. 1390(b)) is amended—

22   (A) by striking paragraph (1); and

23   (B) by redesignating paragraphs (2)

24   through (4) as paragraphs (1) through (3), re-

25   spectively.

(2) FRESH START OPTION.—Section 4211(c)(5) of such Act (29 U.S.C. 1391(c)(5)) is amended by adding at the end the following new subparagraph:

"(E) FRESH START OPTION.—Notwithstanding paragraph (1), a plan may be amended to provide that the withdrawal liability method described in subsection (b) shall be applied by substituting the plan year which is specified in the amendment and for which the plan has no unfunded vested benefits for the plan year ending before September 26, 1980.".

(3) EFFECTIVE DATE.—The amendments made by this subsection shall apply with respect to plan withdrawals occurring on or after January 1, 2007.

(d) PROCEDURES APPLICABLE TO DISPUTES INVOLVING PENSION PLAN WITHDRAWAL LIABILITY.—

(1) IN GENERAL.—Section 4221 of Employee Retirement Income Security Act of 1974 (29 U.S.C. 1401) is amended by adding at the end the following:

"(g) PROCEDURES APPLICABLE TO CERTAIN DISPUTES.—

"(1) IN GENERAL.—If—

"(A) a plan sponsor of a plan determines that—

1   "(i) a complete or partial withdrawal

2   of an employer has occurred, or

3   "(ii) an employer is liable for with-

4   drawal liability payments with respect to

5   such complete or partial withdrawal, and

6   "(B) such determination is based in whole

7   or in part on a finding by the plan sponsor

8   under section 4212(c) that a principal purpose

9   of any transaction which occurred after Decem-

10   ber 31, 1998, and at least 5 years (2 years in

11   the case of a small employer) before the date of

12   the complete or partial withdrawal was to evade

13   or avoid withdrawal liability under this subtitle,

14 then the person against which the withdrawal liabil-

15 ity is assessed based solely on the application of sec-

16 tion 4212(c) may elect to use the special rule under

17 paragraph (2) in applying subsection (d) of this sec-

18 tion and section 4219(c) to such person.

19   "(2) SPECIAL RULE.—Notwithstanding sub-

20 section (d) and section 4219(c), if an electing person

21 contests the plan sponsor's determination with re-

22 spect to withdrawal liability payments under para-

23 graph (1) through an arbitration proceeding pursu-

24 ant to subsection (a), through an action brought in

25 a court of competent jurisdiction for review of such

1   an arbitration decision, or as otherwise permitted by
2   law, the electing person shall not be obligated to
3   make the withdrawal liability payments until a final
4   decision in the arbitration proceeding, or in court,
5   upholds the plan sponsor's determination, but only if
6   the electing person—

7   "(A) provides notice to the plan sponsor of
8   its election to apply the special rule in this
9   paragraph within 90 days after the plan spon-
10   sor notifies the electing person of its liability by
11   reason of the application of section 4212(c);
12   and

13   "(B) if a final decision in the arbitration
14   proceeding, or in court, of the withdrawal liabil-
15   ity dispute has not been rendered within 12
16   months from the date of such notice, the elect-
17   ing person provides to the plan, effective as of
18   the first day following the 12-month period, a
19   bond issued by a corporate surety company that
20   is an acceptable surety for purposes of section
21   412 of this Act, or an amount held in escrow
22   by a bank or similar financial institution satis-
23   factory to the plan, in an amount equal to the
24   sum of the withdrawal liability payments that
25   would otherwise be due under subsection (d)

1   and section 4219(c) for the 12-month period

2   beginning with the first anniversary of such no-

3   tice. Such bond or escrow shall remain in effect

4   until there is a final decision in the arbitration

5   proceeding, or in court, of the withdrawal liabil-

6   ity dispute, at which time such bond or escrow

7   shall be paid to the plan if such final decision

8   upholds the plan sponsor's determination.

9   "(3) DEFINITION OF SMALL EMPLOYER.—For

10   purposes of this subsection—

11   "(A) IN GENERAL.—The term 'small em-

12   ployer' means any employer which, for the cal-

13   endar year in which the transaction referred to

14   in paragraph (1)(B) occurred and for each of

15   the 3 preceding years, on average—

16   "(i) employs not more than 500 em-

17   ployees, and

18   "(ii) is required to make contributions

19   to the plan for not more than 250 employ-

20   ees.

21   "(B) CONTROLLED GROUP.—Any group

22   treated as a single employer under subsection

23   (b)(1) of section 4001, without regard to any

24   transaction that was a basis for the plan's find-

25   ing under section 4212, shall be treated as a

1   single employer for purposes of this subpara-

2   graph.

3   "(4) ADDITIONAL SECURITY PENDING RESOLU-

4   TION OF DISPUTE.—If a withdrawal liability dispute

5   to which this subsection applies is not concluded by

6   12 months after the electing person posts the bond

7   or escrow described in paragraph (2), the electing

8   person shall, at the start of each succeeding 12-

9   month period, provide an additional bond or amount

10   held in escrow equal to the sum of the withdrawal

11   liability payments that would otherwise be payable to

12   the plan during that period.

13   "(5) The liability of the party furnishing a bond

14   or escrow under this subsection shall be reduced,

15   upon the payment of the bond or escrow to the plan,

16   by the amount thereof."

17   (2) EFFECTIVE DATE.—The amendments made

18   by this subsection shall apply to any person that re-

19   ceives a notification under section 4219(b)(1) of the

20   Employee Retirement Income Security Act of 1974

21   on or after the date of enactment of this Act with

22   respect to a transaction that occurred after Decem-

23   ber 31, 1998.

1 **SEC. 205. PROHIBITION ON RETALIATION AGAINST EM-**

2 **PLOYERS EXERCISING THEIR RIGHTS TO PE-**

3 **TITION THE FEDERAL GOVERNMENT.**

4 Section 510 of the Employee Retirement Income Se-

5 curity Act of 1974 (29 U.S.C. 1140) is amended by insert-

6 ing before the last sentence thereof the following new sen-

7 tence:"In the case of a multiemployer plan, it shall be un-

8 lawful for the plan sponsor or any other person to dis-

9 criminate against any contributing employer for exercising

10 rights under this Act or for giving information or testi-

11 fying in any inquiry or proceeding relating to this Act be-

12 fore Congress."

13 **SEC. 206. SPECIAL RULE FOR CERTAIN BENEFITS FUNDED**

14 **UNDER AN AGREEMENT APPROVED BY THE**

15 **PENSION BENEFIT GUARANTY CORPORA-**

16 **TION.**

17 In the case of a multiemployer plan that is a party

18 to an agreement that was approved by the Pension Benefit

19 Guaranty Corporation prior to June 30, 2005, and that—

20 (1) increases benefits, and

21 (2) provides for special withdrawal liability

22 rules under section 4203(f) of the Employee Retire-

23 ment Income Security Act of 1974 (29 U.S.C.

24 1383),

25 the amendments made by sections 201, 202, 211, and 212

26 of this Act shall not apply to the benefit increases under

1 any plan amendment adopted prior to June 30, 2005, that

2 are funded pursuant to such agreement if the plan is fund-

3 ed in compliance with such agreement (and any amend-

4 ments thereto).

5 Subtitle B—Amendments to
6 Internal Revenue Code of 1986

7 SEC. 211. FUNDING RULES FOR MULTIEMPLOYER DEFINED
8 BENEFIT PLANS.

9 (a) IN GENERAL.—Subpart A of part III of sub-

10 chapter D of chapter 1 of the Internal Revenue Code of

11 1986 (as added by this Act) is amended by inserting after

12 section 430 the following new section:

13 "SEC. 431. MINIMUM FUNDING STANDARDS FOR MULTIEM-
14 PLOYER PLANS.

15 "(a) IN GENERAL.—For purposes of section 412, the

16 accumulated funding deficiency of a multiemployer plan

17 for any plan year is—

18 "(1) except as provided in paragraph (2), the

19 amount, determined as of the end of the plan year,

20 equal to the excess (if any) of the total charges to

21 the funding standard account of the plan for all plan

22 years (beginning with the first plan year for which

23 this part applies to the plan) over the total credits

24 to such account for such years, and

1   "(2) if the multiemployer plan is in reorganiza-

2 tion for any plan year, the accumulated funding de-

3 ficiency of the plan determined under section 4243

4 of the Employee Retirement Income Security Act of

5 1974.

6 "(b) FUNDING STANDARD ACCOUNT.—

7   "(1) ACCOUNT REQUIRED.—Each multiem-

8 ployer plan to which this part applies shall establish

9 and maintain a funding standard account. Such ac-

10 count shall be credited and charged solely as pro-

11 vided in this section.

12   "(2) CHARGES TO ACCOUNT.—For a plan year,

13 the funding standard account shall be charged with

14 the sum of—

15   "(A) the normal cost of the plan for the

16   plan year,

17   "(B) the amounts necessary to amortize in

18   equal annual installments (until fully amor-

19   tized)—

20   "(i) in the case of a plan which comes

21   into existence on or after January 1, 2008,

22   the unfunded past service liability under

23   the plan on the first day of the first plan

24   year to which this section applies, over a

25   period of 15 plan years,

1   "(ii) separately, with respect to each

2   plan year, the net increase (if any) in un-

3   funded past service liability under the plan

4   arising from plan amendments adopted in

5   such year, over a period of 15 plan years,

6   "(iii) separately, with respect to each

7   plan year, the net experience loss (if any)

8   under the plan, over a period of 15 plan

9   years, and

10   "(iv) separately, with respect to each

11   plan year, the net loss (if any) resulting

12   from changes in actuarial assumptions

13   used under the plan, over a period of 15

14   plan years,

15   "(C) the amount necessary to amortize

16   each waived funding deficiency (within the

17   meaning of section 412(c)(3)) for each prior

18   plan year in equal annual installments (until

19   fully amortized) over a period of 15 plan years,

20   "(D) the amount necessary to amortize in

21   equal annual installments (until fully amor-

22   tized) over a period of 5 plan years any amount

23   credited to the funding standard account under

24   section 412(b)(3)(D) (as in effect on the day

before the date of the enactment of the Pension Protection Act of 2006), and

"(E) the amount necessary to amortize in equal annual installments (until fully amortized) over a period of 20 years the contributions which would be required to be made under the plan but for the provisions of section 412(c)(7)(A)(i)(I) (as in effect on the day before the date of the enactment of the Pension Protection Act of 2006).

"(3) CREDITS TO ACCOUNT.—For a plan year, the funding standard account shall be credited with the sum of—

"(A) the amount considered contributed by the employer to or under the plan for the plan year,

"(B) the amount necessary to amortize in equal annual installments (until fully amortized)—

"(i) separately, with respect to each plan year, the net decrease (if any) in unfunded past service liability under the plan arising from plan amendments adopted in such year, over a period of 15 plan years, "(ii) separately, with respect to each plan year, the net experience gain (if any) under the plan, over a period of 15 plan years, and

"(iii) separately, with respect to each plan year, the net gain (if any) resulting from changes in actuarial assumptions used under the plan, over a period of 15 plan years,

"(C) the amount of the waived funding deficiency (within the meaning of section 412(c)(3)) for the plan year, and

"(D) in the case of a plan year for which the accumulated funding deficiency is determined under the funding standard account if such plan year follows a plan year for which such deficiency was determined under the alternative minimum funding standard under section 412(g) (as in effect on the day before the date of the enactment of the Pension Protection Act of 2006), the excess (if any) of any debit balance in the funding standard account (determined without regard to this subparagraph) over any debit balance in the alternative minimum funding standard account.

1   "(4) SPECIAL RULE FOR AMOUNTS FIRST AM-

2   ORTIZED IN PLAN YEARS BEFORE 2008.—In the case

3   of any amount amortized under section 412(b) (as

4   in effect on the day before the date of the enactment

5   of the Pension Protection Act of 2006) over any pe-

6   riod beginning with a plan year beginning before

7   2008 in lieu of the amortization described in para-

8   graphs (2)(B) and (3)(B), such amount shall con-

9   tinue to be amortized under such section as so in ef-

10   fect.

11   "(5) COMBINING AND OFFSETTING AMOUNTS

12   TO BE AMORTIZED.—Under regulations prescribed

13   by the Secretary, amounts required to be amortized

14   under paragraph (2) or paragraph (3), as the case

15   may be—

16   "(A) may be combined into one amount

17   under such paragraph to be amortized over a

18   period determined on the basis of the remaining

19   amortization period for all items entering into

20   such combined amount, and

21   "(B) may be offset against amounts re-

22   quired to be amortized under the other such

23   paragraph, with the resulting amount to be am-

24   ortized over a period determined on the basis of

25   the remaining amortization periods for all items

1 entering into whichever of the two amounts
2 being offset is the greater.

3 "(6) INTEREST.—The funding standard ac-
4 count (and items therein) shall be charged or cred-
5 ited (as determined under regulations prescribed by
6 the Secretary of the Treasury) with interest at the
7 appropriate rate consistent with the rate or rates of
8 interest used under the plan to determine costs.

9 "(7) SPECIAL RULES RELATING TO CHARGES
10 AND CREDITS TO FUNDING STANDARD ACCOUNT.—
11 For purposes of this part—

12 "(A) WITHDRAWAL LIABILITY.—Any
13 amount received by a multiemployer plan in
14 payment of all or part of an employer's with-
15 drawal liability under part 1 of subtitle E of
16 title IV of the Employee Retirement Income Se-
17 curity Act of 1974 shall be considered an
18 amount contributed by the employer to or
19 under the plan. The Secretary may prescribe by
20 regulation additional charges and credits to a
21 multiemployer plan's funding standard account
22 to the extent necessary to prevent withdrawal li-
23 ability payments from being unduly reflected as
24 advance funding for plan liabilities.

"(B) ADJUSTMENTS WHEN A MULTIEM-
PLOYER PLAN LEAVES REORGANIZATION.—If a
multiemployer plan is not in reorganization in
the plan year but was in reorganization in the
immediately preceding plan year, any balance in
the funding standard account at the close of
such immediately preceding plan year—

"(i) shall be eliminated by an offsetting credit or charge (as the case may be),
but

"(ii) shall be taken into account in
subsequent plan years by being amortized
in equal annual installments (until fully
amortized) over 30 plan years.

The preceding sentence shall not apply to the
extent of any accumulated funding deficiency
under section 4243(a) of such Act as of the end
of the last plan year that the plan was in reorganization.

"(C) PLAN PAYMENTS TO SUPPLEMENTAL
PROGRAM OR WITHDRAWAL LIABILITY PAYMENT
FUND.—Any amount paid by a plan during a
plan year to the Pension Benefit Guaranty Corporation pursuant to section 4222 of such Act
or to a fund exempt under section 501(c)(22)

pursuant to section 4223 of such Act shall reduce the amount of contributions considered received by the plan for the plan year.

"(D) INTERIM WITHDRAWAL LIABILITY
PAYMENTS.—Any amount paid by an employer
pending a final determination of the employer's
withdrawal liability under part 1 of subtitle E
of title IV of such Act and subsequently refunded to the employer by the plan shall be
charged to the funding standard account in accordance with regulations prescribed by the
Secretary.

"(E) ELECTION FOR DEFERRAL OF
CHARGE FOR PORTION OF NET EXPERIENCE
LOSS.—If an election is in effect under section
412(b)(7)(F) (as in effect on the day before the
date of the enactment of the Pension Protection
Act of 2006) for any plan year, the funding
standard account shall be charged in the plan
year to which the portion of the net experience
loss deferred by such election was deferred with
the amount so deferred (and paragraph
(2)(B)(iii) shall not apply to the amount so
charged).

1   "(F)   FINANCIAL   ASSISTANCE.—Any

2   amount of any financial assistance from the

3   Pension Benefit Guaranty Corporation to any

4   plan, and any repayment of such amount, shall

5   be taken into account under this section and

6   section 412 in such manner as is determined by

7   the Secretary.

8   "(G) SHORT-TERM BENEFITS.—To the ex-

9   tent that any plan amendment increases the un-

10   funded past service liability under the plan by

11   reason of an increase in benefits which are not

12   payable as a life annuity but are payable under

13   the terms of the plan for a period that does not

14   exceed 14 years from the effective date of the

15   amendment, paragraph (2)(B)(ii) shall be ap-

16   plied separately with respect to such increase in

17   unfunded past service liability by substituting

18   the number of years of the period during which

19   such benefits are payable for '15'.

20   "(c) ADDITIONAL RULES.—

21   "(1) DETERMINATIONS TO BE MADE UNDER

22   FUNDING METHOD.—For purposes of this part, nor-

23   mal costs, accrued liability, past service liabilities,

24   and experience gains and losses shall be determined

1   under the funding method used to determine costs

2   under the plan.

3   "(2) VALUATION OF ASSETS.—

4   "(A) IN GENERAL.—For purposes of this

5   part, the value of the plan's assets shall be de-

6   termined on the basis of any reasonable actu-

7   arial method of valuation which takes into ac-

8   count fair market value and which is permitted

9   under regulations prescribed by the Secretary.

10   "(B) ELECTION WITH RESPECT TO

11   BONDS.—The value of a bond or other evidence

12   of indebtedness which is not in default as to

13   principal or interest may, at the election of the

14   plan administrator, be determined on an amor-

15   tized basis running from initial cost at purchase

16   to par value at maturity or earliest call date.

17   Any election under this subparagraph shall be

18   made at such time and in such manner as the

19   Secretary shall by regulations provide, shall

20   apply to all such evidences of indebtedness, and

21   may be revoked only with the consent of the

22   Secretary.

23   "(3) ACTUARIAL ASSUMPTIONS MUST BE REA-

24   SONABLE.—For purposes of this section, all costs, li-

25   abilities, rates of interest, and other factors under

the plan shall be determined on the basis of actuarial assumptions and methods—

      "(A) each of which is reasonable (taking
into account the experience of the plan and reasonable expectations), and

      "(B) which, in combination, offer the actu-
ary's best estimate of anticipated experience
under the plan.

    "(4) TREATMENT OF CERTAIN CHANGES AS EX-
PERIENCE GAIN OR LOSS.—For purposes of this section, if—

      "(A) a change in benefits under the Social
Security Act or in other retirement benefits created under Federal or State law, or

      "(B) a change in the definition of the term
'wages' under section 3121, or a change in the
amount of such wages taken into account under
regulations prescribed for purposes of section
401(a)(5),

results in an increase or decrease in accrued liability
under a plan, such increase or decrease shall be
treated as an experience loss or gain.

    "(5) FULL FUNDING.—If, as of the close of a
plan year, a plan would (without regard to this para-

1 graph) have an accumulated funding deficiency in

2 excess of the full funding limitation—

3   "(A) the funding standard account shall be

4 credited with the amount of such excess, and

5   "(B) all amounts described in subpara-

6 graphs (B), (C), and (D) of subsection (b) (2)

7 and subparagraph (B) of subsection (b)(3)

8 which are required to be amortized shall be con-

9 sidered fully amortized for purposes of such

10 subparagraphs.

11   "(6) FULL-FUNDING LIMITATION.—

12   "(A) IN GENERAL.—For purposes of para-

13 graph (5), the term 'full-funding limitation'

14 means the excess (if any) of—

15   "(i) the accrued liability (including

16 normal cost) under the plan (determined

17 under the entry age normal funding meth-

18 od if such accrued liability cannot be di-

19 rectly calculated under the funding method

20 used for the plan), over

21   "(ii) the lesser of—

22   "(I) the fair market value of the

23 plan's assets, or

24   "(II) the value of such assets de-

25 termined under paragraph (2).

"(B) MINIMUM AMOUNT.—

"(i) IN GENERAL.—In no event shall the full-funding limitation determined under subparagraph (A) be less than the excess (if any) of—

"(I) 90 percent of the current liability of the plan (including the expected increase in current liability due to benefits accruing during the plan year), over

"(II) the value of the plan's assets determined under paragraph (2).

"(ii) ASSETS.—For purposes of clause (i), assets shall not be reduced by any credit balance in the funding standard account.

"(C) FULL FUNDING LIMITATION.—For purposes of this paragraph, unless otherwise provided by the plan, the accrued liability under a multiemployer plan shall not include benefits which are not nonforfeitable under the plan after the termination of the plan (taking into consideration section 411(d)(3)).

"(D) CURRENT LIABILITY.—For purposes of this paragraph—

1   "(i) IN GENERAL.—The term 'current

2 liability' means all liabilities to employees

3 and their beneficiaries under the plan.

4   "(ii) TREATMENT OF UNPREDICTABLE

5 CONTINGENT EVENT BENEFITS.—For pur-

6 poses of clause (i), any benefit contingent

7 on an event other than—

8   "(I) age, service, compensation,

9   death, or disability, or

10   "(II) an event which is reason-

11   ably and reliably predictable (as deter-

12   mined by the Secretary),

13 shall not be taken into account until the

14 event on which the benefit is contingent oc-

15 curs.

16   "(iii) INTEREST RATE USED.—The

17 rate of interest used to determine current

18 liability under this paragraph shall be the

19 rate of interest determined under subpara-

20 graph (E).

21   "(iv) MORTALITY TABLES.—

22   "(I) COMMISSIONERS' STANDARD

23   TABLE.—In the case of plan years be-

24   ginning before the first plan year to

25   which the first tables prescribed under

1   subclause (II) apply, the mortality
2   table used in determining current li-
3   ability under this paragraph shall be
4   the table prescribed by the Secretary
5   which is based on the prevailing com-
6   missioners' standard table (described
7   in section 807(d)(5)(A)) used to de-
8   termine reserves for group annuity
9   contracts issued on January 1, 1993.

10 "(II) SECRETARIAL AUTHOR-
11 ITY.—The Secretary may by regula-
12 tion prescribe for plan years beginning
13 after December 31, 1999, mortality
14 tables to be used in determining cur-
15 rent liability under this subsection.
16 Such tables shall be based upon the
17 actual experience of pension plans and
18 projected trends in such experience.
19 In prescribing such tables, the Sec-
20 retary shall take into account results
21 of available independent studies of
22 mortality of individuals covered by
23 pension plans.

"(v) SEPARATE MORTALITY TABLES FOR THE DISABLED.—Notwithstanding clause (iv)—

"(I) IN GENERAL.—The Secretary shall establish mortality tables which may be used (in lieu of the tables under clause (iv)) to determine current liability under this subsection for individuals who are entitled to benefits under the plan on account of disability. The Secretary shall establish separate tables for individuals whose disabilities occur in plan years beginning before January 1, 1995, and for individuals whose disabilities occur in plan years beginning on or after such date.

"(II) SPECIAL RULE FOR DISABILITIES OCCURRING AFTER 1994.— In the case of disabilities occurring in plan years beginning after December 31, 1994, the tables under subclause (I) shall apply only with respect to individuals described in such subclause who are disabled within the meaning

1   of title II of the Social Security Act

2   and the regulations thereunder.

3   "(vi) PERIODIC REVIEW.—The Sec-

4   retary shall periodically (at least every 5

5   years) review any tables in effect under

6   this subparagraph and shall, to the extent

7   such Secretary determines necessary, by

8   regulation update the tables to reflect the

9   actual experience of pension plans and pro-

10   jected trends in such experience.

11   "(E) REQUIRED CHANGE OF INTEREST

12   RATE.—For purposes of determining a plan's

13   current liability for purposes of this para-

14   graph—

15   "(i) IN GENERAL.—If any rate of in-

16   terest used under the plan under sub-

17   section (b)(6) to determine cost is not

18   within the permissible range, the plan shall

19   establish a new rate of interest within the

20   permissible range.

21   "(ii) PERMISSIBLE RANGE.—For pur-

22   poses of this subparagraph—

23   "(I) IN GENERAL.—Except as

24   provided in subclause (II), the term

25   'permissible range' means a rate of in-

terest which is not more than 5 percent above, and not more than 10 percent below, the weighted average of the rates of interest on 30-year Treasury securities during the 4-year period ending on the last day before the beginning of the plan year.

"(II) SECRETARIAL AUTHORITY.—If the Secretary finds that the lowest rate of interest permissible under subclause (I) is unreasonably high, the Secretary may prescribe a lower rate of interest, except that such rate may not be less than 80 percent of the average rate determined under such subclause.

"(iii) ASSUMPTIONS.—Notwithstanding paragraph (3)(A), the interest rate used under the plan shall be—

"(I) determined without taking into account the experience of the plan and reasonable expectations, but

"(II) consistent with the assumptions which reflect the purchase rates which would be used by insurance

1   companies to satisfy the liabilities

2   under the plan.

3   "(7) ANNUAL VALUATION.—

4   "(A) IN GENERAL.—For purposes of this

5   section, a determination of experience gains and

6   losses and a valuation of the plan's liability

7   shall be made not less frequently than once

8   every year, except that such determination shall

9   be made more frequently to the extent required

10   in particular cases under regulations prescribed

11   by the Secretary.

12   "(B) VALUATION DATE.—

13   "(i) CURRENT YEAR.—Except as pro-

14   vided in clause (ii), the valuation referred

15   to in subparagraph (A) shall be made as of

16   a date within the plan year to which the

17   valuation refers or within one month prior

18   to the beginning of such year.

19   "(ii) USE OF PRIOR YEAR VALU-

20   ATION.—The valuation referred to in sub-

21   paragraph (A) may be made as of a date

22   within the plan year prior to the year to

23   which the valuation refers if, as of such

24   date, the value of the assets of the plan are

25   not less than 100 percent of the plan's cur-

1   rent liability (as defined in paragraph
2   (6)(D) without regard to clause (iv) there-
3   of).

4   　　"(iii)　Adjustments.—Information
5   under clause (ii) shall, in accordance with
6   regulations, be actuarially adjusted to re-
7   flect significant differences in participants.

8   　　"(iv) Limitation.—A change in fund-
9   ing method to use a prior year valuation,
10   as provided in clause (ii), may not be made
11   unless as of the valuation date within the
12   prior plan year, the value of the assets of
13   the plan are not less than 125 percent of
14   the plan's current liability (as defined in
15   paragraph (6)(D) without regard to clause
16   (iv) thereof).

17   　　"(8) Time when certain contributions
18   deemed made.—For purposes of this section, any
19   contributions for a plan year made by an employer
20   after the last day of such plan year, but not later
21   than two and one-half months after such day, shall
22   be deemed to have been made on such last day. For
23   purposes of this subparagraph, such two and one-
24   half month period may be extended for not more

1 than six months under regulations prescribed by the

2 Secretary.

3 "(d) EXTENSION OF AMORTIZATION PERIODS FOR

4 MULTIEMPLOYER PLANS.—

5 "(1) AUTOMATIC EXTENSION UPON APPLICA-

6 TION BY CERTAIN PLANS.—

7 "(A) IN GENERAL.—If the plan sponsor of

8 a multiemployer plan—

9 "(i) submits to the Secretary an appli-

10 cation for an extension of the period of

11 years required to amortize any unfunded

12 liability described in any clause of sub-

13 section (b)(2)(B) or described in subsection

14 (b)(4), and

15 "(ii) includes with the application a

16 certification by the plan's actuary de-

17 scribed in subparagraph (B),

18 the Secretary shall extend the amortization pe-

19 riod for the period of time (not in excess of 5

20 years) specified in the application. Such exten-

21 sion shall be in addition to any extension under

22 paragraph (2).

23 "(B) CRITERIA.—A certification with re-

24 spect to a multiemployer plan is described in

321

this subparagraph if the plan's actuary certifies that, based on reasonable assumptions—

"(i) absent the extension under subparagraph (A), the plan would have an accumulated funding deficiency in the current plan year or any of the 9 succeeding plan years,

"(ii) the plan sponsor has adopted a plan to improve the plan's funding status,

"(iii) the plan is projected to have sufficient assets to timely pay expected benefits and anticipated expenditures over the amortization period as extended, and

"(iv) the notice required under paragraph (3)(A) has been provided.

"(C) TERMINATION.—The preceding provisions of this paragraph shall not apply with respect to any application submitted after December 31, 2014.

"(2) ALTERNATIVE EXTENSION.—

"(A) IN GENERAL.—If the plan sponsor of a multiemployer plan submits to the Secretary an application for an extension of the period of years required to amortize any unfunded liability described in any clause of subsection

1   (b)(2)(B) or described in subsection (b)(4), the

2   Secretary may extend the amortization period

3   for a period of time (not in excess of 10 years

4   reduced by the number of years of any exten-

5   sion under paragraph (1) with respect to such

6   unfunded liability) if the Secretary makes the

7   determination described in subparagraph (B).

8   Such extension shall be in addition to any ex-

9   tension under paragraph (1).

10   "(B) DETERMINATION.—The Secretary

11   may grant an extension under subparagraph

12   (A) if the Secretary determines that—

13   "(i) such extension would carry out

14   the purposes of this Act and would provide

15   adequate protection for participants under

16   the plan and their beneficiaries, and

17   "(ii) the failure to permit such exten-

18   sion would—

19   "(I) result in a substantial risk

20   to the voluntary continuation of the

21   plan, or a substantial curtailment of

22   pension benefit levels or employee

23   compensation, and

24   "(II) be adverse to the interests

25   of plan participants in the aggregate.

1   "(C) ACTION BY SECRETARY.—The Sec-

2   retary shall act upon any application for an ex-

3   tension under this paragraph within 180 days

4   of the submission of such application. If the

5   Secretary rejects the application for an exten-

6   sion under this paragraph, the Secretary shall

7   provide notice to the plan detailing the specific

8   reasons for the rejection, including references to

9   the criteria set forth above.

10   "(3) ADVANCE NOTICE.—

11   "(A) IN GENERAL.—The Secretary shall,

12   before granting an extension under this sub-

13   section, require each applicant to provide evi-

14   dence satisfactory to such Secretary that the

15   applicant has provided notice of the filing of the

16   application for such extension to each affected

17   party (as defined in section 4001(a)(21) of the

18   Employee Retirement Income Security Act of

19   1974) with respect to the affected plan. Such

20   notice shall include a description of the extent

21   to which the plan is funded for benefits which

22   are guaranteed under title IV of such Act and

23   for benefit liabilities.

24   "(B) CONSIDERATION OF RELEVANT IN-

25   FORMATION.—The Secretary shall consider any

1   relevant information provided by a person to

2   whom notice was given under paragraph (1).".

3 (b) EFFECTIVE DATE.—

4   (1) IN GENERAL.—The amendments made by

5 this section shall apply to plan years beginning after

6 2007.

7   (2) SPECIAL RULE FOR CERTAIN AMORTIZATION

8 EXTENSIONS.—If the Secretary of the Treasury

9 grants an extension under section 304 of the Em-

10 ployee Retirement Income Security Act of 1974 and

11 section 412(e) of the Internal Revenue Code of 1986

12 with respect to any application filed with the Sec-

13 retary of the Treasury on or before June 30, 2005,

14 the extension (and any modification thereof) shall be

15 applied and administered under the rules of such

16 sections as in effect before the enactment of this

17 Act, including the use of the rate of interest deter-

18 mined under section 6621(b) of such Code.

19 **SEC. 212. ADDITIONAL FUNDING RULES FOR MULTIEM-**

20   **PLOYER PLANS IN ENDANGERED OR CRIT-**

21   **ICAL STATUS.**

22 (a) IN GENERAL.—Subpart A of part III of sub-

23 chapter D of chapter 1 of the Internal Revenue Code of

24 1986 (as amended by this Act) is amended by inserting

25 after section 431 the following new section:

"SEC. 432. ADDITIONAL FUNDING RULES FOR MULTIEM-
PLOYER PLANS IN ENDANGERED STATUS OR
CRITICAL STATUS.

"(a) GENERAL RULE.—For purposes of this part, in the case of a multiemployer plan in effect on July 16, 2006 —

"(1) if the plan is in endangered status—

"(A) the plan sponsor shall adopt and implement a funding improvement plan in accordance with the requirements of subsection (c), and

"(B) the requirements of subsection (d) shall apply during the funding plan adoption period and the funding improvement period, and

"(2) if the plan is in critical status—

"(A) the plan sponsor shall adopt and implement a rehabilitation plan in accordance with the requirements of subsection (e), and

"(B) the requirements of subsection (f) shall apply during the rehabilitation plan adoption period and the rehabilitation period.

"(b) DETERMINATION OF ENDANGERED AND CRITICAL STATUS.—For purposes of this section—

"(1) ENDANGERED STATUS.—A multiemployer plan is in endangered status for a plan year if, as

1   determined by the plan actuary under paragraph

2   (3), the plan is not in critical status for the plan

3   year and, as of the beginning of the plan year, ei-

4   ther—

5   "(A) the plan's funded percentage for such

6   plan year is less than 80 percent, or

7   "(B) the plan has an accumulated funding

8   deficiency for such plan year, or is projected to

9   have such an accumulated funding deficiency

10   for any of the 6 succeeding plan years, taking

11   into account any extension of amortization peri-

12   ods under section 431(d).

13   For purposes of this section, a plan shall be treated

14   as in seriously endangered status for a plan year if

15   the plan is described in both subparagraphs (A) and

16   (B).

17   "(2) CRITICAL STATUS.—A multiemployer plan

18   is in critical status for a plan year if, as determined

19   by the plan actuary under paragraph (3), the plan

20   is described in 1 or more of the following subpara-

21   graphs as of the beginning of the plan year:

22   "(A) A plan is described in this subpara-

23   graph if—

24   "(i) the funded percentage of the plan

25   is less than 65 percent, and

1   "(ii) the sum of—

2   "(I) the fair market value of plan

3   assets, plus

4   "(II) the present value of the

5   reasonably anticipated employer con-

6   tributions for the current plan year

7   and each of the 6 succeeding plan

8   years, assuming that the terms of all

9   collective bargaining agreements pur-

10   suant to which the plan is maintained

11   for the current plan year continue in

12   effect for succeeding plan years,

13   is less than the present value of all non-

14   forfeitable benefits projected to be payable

15   under the plan during the current plan

16   year and each of the 6 succeeding plan

17   years (plus administrative expenses for

18   such plan years).

19   "(B) A plan is described in this subpara-

20   graph if—

21   "(i) the plan has an accumulated

22   funding deficiency for the current plan

23   year, not taking into account any extension

24   of amortization periods under section

25   431(d), or

328

1   "(ii) the plan is projected to have an
2   accumulated funding deficiency for any of
3   the 3 succeeding plan years (4 succeeding
4   plan years if the funded percentage of the
5   plan is 65 percent or less), not taking into
6   account any extension of amortization peri-
7   ods under section 431(d).

8   "(C) A plan is described in this subpara-
9   graph if—

10   "(i)(I) the plan's normal cost for the
11   current plan year, plus interest (deter-
12   mined at the rate used for determining
13   costs under the plan) for the current plan
14   year on the amount of unfunded benefit li-
15   abilities under the plan as of the last date
16   of the preceding plan year, exceeds

17   "(II) the present value of the reason-
18   ably anticipated employer and employee
19   contributions for the current plan year,

20   "(ii) the present value, as of the be-
21   ginning of the current plan year, of non-
22   forfeitable benefits of inactive participants
23   is greater than the present value of non-
24   forfeitable benefits of active participants,
25   and

1   "(iii) the plan has an accumulated

2   funding deficiency for the current plan

3   year, or is projected to have such a defi-

4   ciency for any of the 4 succeeding plan

5   years, not taking into account any exten-

6   sion of amortization periods under section

7   431(d).

8   "(D) A plan is described in this subpara-

9   graph if the sum of—

10   "(i) the fair market value of plan as-

11   sets, plus

12   "(ii) the present value of the reason-

13   ably anticipated employer contributions for

14   the current plan year and each of the 4

15   succeeding plan years, assuming that the

16   terms of all collective bargaining agree-

17   ments pursuant to which the plan is main-

18   tained for the current plan year continue

19   in effect for succeeding plan years,

20   is less than the present value of all benefits pro-

21   jected to be payable under the plan during the

22   current plan year and each of the 4 succeeding

23   plan years (plus administrative expenses for

24   such plan years).

1   "(3) ANNUAL CERTIFICATION BY PLAN ACTU-

2   ARY.—

3   "(A) IN GENERAL.—Not later than the

4   90th day of each plan year of a multiemployer

5   plan, the plan actuary shall certify to the Sec-

6   retary and to the plan sponsor—

7   "(i) whether or not the plan is in en-

8   dangered status for such plan year and

9   whether or not the plan is or will be in

10   critical status for such plan year, and

11   "(ii) in the case of a plan which is in

12   a funding improvement or rehabilitation

13   period, whether or not the plan is making

14   the scheduled progress in meeting the re-

15   quirements of its funding improvement or

16   rehabilitation plan.

17   "(B) ACTUARIAL PROJECTIONS OF ASSETS

18   AND LIABILITIES.—

19   "(i) IN GENERAL.—In making the de-

20   terminations and projections under this

21   subsection, the plan actuary shall make

22   projections required for the current and

23   succeeding plan years of the current value

24   of the assets of the plan and the present

25   value of all liabilities to participants and

beneficiaries under the plan for the current plan year as of the beginning of such year. The actuary's projections shall be based on reasonable actuarial estimates, assumptions, and methods that, except as provided in clause (iii), offer the actuary's best estimate of anticipated experience under the plan. The projected present value of liabilities as of the beginning of such year shall be determined based on the most recent of either—

"(I) the actuarial statement required under section 103(d) of the Employee Retirement Income Security Act of 1974 with respect to the most recently filed annual report, or

"(II) the actuarial valuation for the preceding plan year.

"(ii) DETERMINATIONS OF FUTURE CONTRIBUTIONS.—Any actuarial projection of plan assets shall assume—

"(I) reasonably anticipated employer contributions for the current and succeeding plan years, assuming that the terms of the one or more col-

1 lective bargaining agreements pursu-

2 ant to which the plan is maintained

3 for the current plan year continue in

4 effect for succeeding plan years, or

5 "(II) that employer contributions

6 for the most recent plan year will con-

7 tinue indefinitely, but only if the plan

8 actuary determines there have been no

9 significant demographic changes that

10 would make such assumption unrea-

11 sonable.

12 "(iii) PROJECTED INDUSTRY ACTIV-

13 ITY.—Any projection of activity in the in-

14 dustry or industries covered by the plan,

15 including future covered employment and

16 contribution levels, shall be based on infor-

17 mation provided by the plan sponsor,

18 which shall act reasonably and in good

19 faith.

20 "(C) PENALTY FOR FAILURE TO SECURE

21 TIMELY ACTUARIAL CERTIFICATION.—Any fail-

22 ure of the plan's actuary to certify the plan's

23 status under this subsection by the date speci-

24 fied in subparagraph (A) shall be treated for

25 purposes of section 502(c)(2) of the Employee

333

Retirement Income Security Act of 1974 as a failure or refusal by the plan administrator to file the annual report required to be filed with the Secretary under section 101(b)(4) of such Act.

"(D) NOTICE.—

"(i) IN GENERAL.—In any case in which it is certified under subparagraph (A) that a multiemployer plan is or will be in endangered or critical status for a plan year, the plan sponsor shall, not later than 30 days after the date of the certification, provide notification of the endangered or critical status to the participants and beneficiaries, the bargaining parties, the Pension Benefit Guaranty Corporation, and the Secretary of Labor.

"(ii) PLANS IN CRITICAL STATUS.—If it is certified under subparagraph (A) that a multiemployer plan is or will be in critical status, the plan sponsor shall include in the notice under clause (i) an explanation of the possibility that—

1   "(I) adjustable benefits (as de-
2   fined in subsection (e)(8)) may be re-
3   duced, and

4   "(II) such reductions may apply
5   to participants and beneficiaries
6   whose benefit commencement date is
7   on or after the date such notice is
8   provided for the first plan year in
9   which the plan is in critical status.

10   "(iii) MODEL NOTICE.—The Secretary
11   of Labor shall prescribe a model notice
12   that a multiemployer plan may use to sat-
13   isfy the requirements under clause (ii).

14   "(c) FUNDING IMPROVEMENT PLAN MUST BE
15 ADOPTED FOR MULTIEMPLOYER PLANS IN ENDANGERED
16 STATUS.—

17   "(1) IN GENERAL.—In any case in which a
18   multiemployer plan is in endangered status for a
19   plan year, the plan sponsor, in accordance with this
20   subsection—

21   "(A) shall adopt a funding improvement
22   plan not later than 240 days following the re-
23   quired date for the actuarial certification of en-
24   dangered status under subsection (b)(3)(A),
25   and

1   "(B) within 30 days after the adoption of

2   the funding improvement plan—

3   "(i) shall provide to the bargaining

4   parties 1 or more schedules showing re-

5   vised benefit structures, revised contribu-

6   tion structures, or both, which, if adopted,

7   may reasonably be expected to enable the

8   multiemployer plan to meet the applicable

9   benchmarks in accordance with the fund-

10   ing improvement plan, including—

11   "(I) one proposal for reductions

12   in the amount of future benefit accru-

13   als necessary to achieve the applicable

14   benchmarks, assuming no amend-

15   ments increasing contributions under

16   the plan (other than amendments in-

17   creasing contributions necessary to

18   achieve the applicable benchmarks

19   after amendments have reduced fu-

20   ture benefit accruals to the maximum

21   extent permitted by law), and

22   "(II) one proposal for increases

23   in contributions under the plan nec-

24   essary to achieve the applicable bench-

25   marks, assuming no amendments re-

1   ducing future benefit accruals under

2   the plan, and

3   "(ii) may, if the plan sponsor deems

4   appropriate, prepare and provide the bar-

5   gaining parties with additional information

6   relating to contribution rates or benefit re-

7   ductions, alternative schedules, or other in-

8   formation relevant to achieving the appli-

9   cable benchmarks in accordance with the

10   funding improvement plan.

11   For purposes of this section, the term 'applica-

12 ble benchmarks' means the requirements appli-

13 cable to the multiemployer plan under para-

14 graph (3) (as modified by paragraph (5)).

15   "(2) EXCEPTION FOR YEARS AFTER PROCESS

16 BEGINS.—Paragraph (1) shall not apply to a plan

17 year if such year is in a funding plan adoption pe-

18 riod or funding improvement period by reason of the

19 plan being in endangered status for a preceding plan

20 year. For purposes of this section, such preceding

21 plan year shall be the initial determination year with

22 respect to the funding improvement plan to which it

23 relates.

24   "(3) FUNDING IMPROVEMENT PLAN.—For pur-

25 poses of this section—

"(A) IN GENERAL.—A funding improvement plan is a plan which consists of the actions, including options or a range of options to be proposed to the bargaining parties, formulated to provide, based on reasonably anticipated experience and reasonable actuarial assumptions, for the attainment by the plan during the funding improvement period of the following requirements:

"(i) INCREASE IN PLAN'S FUNDING PERCENTAGE.—The plan's funded percentage as of the close of the funding improvement period equals or exceeds a percentage equal to the sum of—

"(I) such percentage as of the beginning of such period, plus

"(II) 33 percent of the difference between 100 percent and the percentage under subclause (I).

"(ii) AVOIDANCE OF ACCUMULATED FUNDING DEFICIENCIES.—No accumulated funding deficiency for any plan year during the funding improvement period (taking into account any extension of amortization periods under section 304(d)).

1   "(B) SERIOUSLY ENDANGERED PLANS.—

2   In the case of a plan in seriously endangered

3   status, except as provided in paragraph (5),

4   subparagraph (A)(i)(II) shall be applied by sub-

5   stituting '20 percent' for '33 percent'.

6   "(4) FUNDING IMPROVEMENT PERIOD.—For

7 purposes of this section—

8   "(A) IN GENERAL.—The funding improve-

9   ment period for any funding improvement plan

10   adopted pursuant to this subsection is the 10-

11   year period beginning on the first day of the

12   first plan year of the multiemployer plan begin-

13   ning after the earlier of—

14   "(i) the second anniversary of the

15   date of the adoption of the funding im-

16   provement plan, or

17   "(ii) the expiration of the collective

18   bargaining agreements in effect on the due

19   date for the actuarial certification of en-

20   dangered status for the initial determina-

21   tion year under subsection (b)(3)(A) and

22   covering, as of such due date, at least 75

23   percent of the active participants in such

24   multiemployer plan.

1   "(B) SERIOUSLY ENDANGERED PLANS.—

2 In the case of a plan in seriously endangered

3 status, except as provided in paragraph (5),

4 subparagraph (A) shall be applied by sub-

5 stituting '15-year period' for '10-year period'.

6   "(C) COORDINATION WITH CHANGES IN

7 STATUS.—

8   "(i) PLANS NO LONGER IN ENDAN-

9 GERED STATUS.—If the plan's actuary cer-

10 tifies under subsection (b)(3)(A) for a plan

11 year in any funding plan adoption period

12 or funding improvement period that the

13 plan is no longer in endangered status and

14 is not in critical status, the funding plan

15 adoption period or funding improvement

16 period, whichever is applicable, shall end as

17 of the close of the preceding plan year.

18   "(ii) PLANS IN CRITICAL STATUS.—If

19 the plan's actuary certifies under sub-

20 section (b)(3)(A) for a plan year in any

21 funding plan adoption period or funding

22 improvement period that the plan is in

23 critical status, the funding plan adoption

24 period or funding improvement period,

25 whichever is applicable, shall end as of the

close of the plan year preceding the first plan year in the rehabilitation period with respect to such status.

"(D) PLANS IN ENDANGERED STATUS AT END OF PERIOD.—If the plan's actuary certifies under subsection (b)(3)(A) for the first plan year following the close of the period described in subparagraph (A) that the plan is in endangered status, the provisions of this subsection and subsection (d) shall be applied as if such first plan year were an initial determination year, except that the plan may not be amended in a manner inconsistent with the funding improvement plan in effect for the preceding plan year until a new funding improvement plan is adopted.

"(5) SPECIAL RULES FOR SERIOUSLY ENDANGERED PLANS MORE THAN 70 PERCENT FUNDED.—

"(A) IN GENERAL.—If the funded percentage of a plan in seriously endangered status was more than 70 percent as of the beginning of the initial determination year—

"(i) paragraphs (3)(B) and (4)(B) shall apply only if the plan's actuary certifies, within 30 days after the certification under subsection (b)(3)(A) for the initial determination year, that, based on the terms of the plan and the collective bargaining agreements in effect at the time of such certification, the plan is not projected to meet the requirements of paragraph (3)(A) (without regard to paragraphs (3)(B) and (4)(B)), and

"(ii) if there is a certification under clause (i), the plan may, in formulating its funding improvement plan, only take into account the rules of paragraph (3)(B) and (4)(B) for plan years in the funding improvement period beginning on or before the date on which the last of the collective bargaining agreements described in paragraph (4)(A)(ii) expires.

"(B) SPECIAL RULE AFTER EXPIRATION OF AGREEMENTS.—Notwithstanding subparagraph (A)(ii), if, for any plan year ending after the date described in subparagraph (A)(ii), the plan actuary certifies (at the time of the annual certification under subsection (b)(3)(A) for such plan year) that, based on the terms of the plan and collective bargaining agreements in effect

1   at the time of that annual certification, the plan

2   is not projected to be able to meet the require-

3   ments of paragraph (3)(A) (without regard to

4   paragraphs (3)(B) and (4)(B)), paragraphs

5   (3)(B) and (4)(B) shall continue to apply for

6   such year.

7   "(6) UPDATES TO FUNDING IMPROVEMENT

8 PLANS AND SCHEDULES.—

9   "(A) FUNDING IMPROVEMENT PLAN.—The

10   plan sponsor shall annually update the funding

11   improvement plan and shall file the update with

12   the plan's annual report under section 104 of

13   the Employee Retirement Income Security Act

14   of 1974.

15   "(B) SCHEDULES.—The plan sponsor shall

16   annually update any schedule of contribution

17   rates provided under this subsection to reflect

18   the experience of the plan.

19   "(C) DURATION OF SCHEDULE.—A sched-

20   ule of contribution rates provided by the plan

21   sponsor and relied upon by bargaining parties

22   in negotiating a collective bargaining agreement

23   shall remain in effect for the duration of that

24   collective bargaining agreement.

1   "(7) IMPOSITION OF DEFAULT SCHEDULE

2 WHERE FAILURE TO ADOPT FUNDING IMPROVEMENT

3 PLAN.—

4   "(A) IN GENERAL.—If—

5   "(i) a collective bargaining agreement

6 providing for contributions under a multi-

7 employer plan that was in effect at the

8 time the plan entered endangered status

9 expires, and

10   "(ii) after receiving one or more

11 schedules from the plan sponsor under

12 paragraph (1)(B), the bargaining parties

13 with respect to such agreement fail to

14 agree on changes to contribution or benefit

15 schedules necessary to meet the applicable

16 benchmarks in accordance with the fund-

17 ing improvement plan,

18 the plan sponsor shall implement the schedule

19 described in paragraph (1)(B)(i)(I) beginning

20 on the date specified in subparagraph (B).

21   "(B) DATE OF IMPLEMENTATION.—The

22 date specified in this subparagraph is the ear-

23 lier of the date—

"(i) on which the Secretary of Labor certifies that the parties are at an impasse, or

"(ii) which is 180 days after the date on which the collective bargaining agreement described in subparagraph (A) expires.

"(8) FUNDING PLAN ADOPTION PERIOD.—For purposes of this section, the term 'funding plan adoption period' means the period beginning on the date of the certification under subsection (b)(3)(A) for the initial determination year and ending on the day before the first day of the funding improvement period.

"(d) RULES FOR OPERATION OF PLAN DURING ADOPTION AND IMPROVEMENT PERIODS.—

"(1) SPECIAL RULES FOR PLAN ADOPTION PERIOD.—During the funding plan adoption period—

"(A) the plan sponsor may not accept a collective bargaining agreement or participation agreement with respect to the multiemployer plan that provides for—

"(i) a reduction in the level of contributions for any participants,

1   "(ii) a suspension of contributions

2   with respect to any period of service, or

3   "(iii) any new direct or indirect exclu-

4   sion of younger or newly hired employees

5   from plan participation,

6   "(B) no amendment of the plan which in-

7   creases the liabilities of the plan by reason of

8   any increase in benefits, any change in the ac-

9   crual of benefits, or any change in the rate at

10   which benefits become nonforfeitable under the

11   plan may be adopted unless the amendment is

12   required as a condition of qualification under

13   part I of subchapter D of chapter 1 or to com-

14   ply with other applicable law, and

15   "(C) in the case of a plan in seriously en-

16   dangered status, the plan sponsor shall take all

17   reasonable actions which are consistent with the

18   terms of the plan and applicable law and which

19   are expected, based on reasonable assumptions,

20   to achieve—

21   "(i) an increase in the plan's funded

22   percentage, and

23   "(ii) postponement of an accumulated

24   funding deficiency for at least 1 additional

25   plan year.

1 Actions under subparagraph (C) include applications

2 for extensions of amortization periods under section

3 431(d), use of the shortfall funding method in mak-

4 ing funding standard account computations, amend-

5 ments to the plan's benefit structure, reductions in

6 future benefit accruals, and other reasonable actions

7 consistent with the terms of the plan and applicable

8 law.

9 "(2) COMPLIANCE WITH FUNDING IMPROVE-

10 MENT PLAN.—

11 "(A) IN GENERAL.—A plan may not be

12 amended after the date of the adoption of a

13 funding improvement plan so as to be incon-

14 sistent with the funding improvement plan.

15 "(B) NO REDUCTION IN CONTRIBU-

16 TIONS.—A plan sponsor may not during any

17 funding improvement period accept a collective

18 bargaining agreement or participation agree-

19 ment with respect to the multiemployer plan

20 that provides for—

21 "(i) a reduction in the level of con-

22 tributions for any participants,

23 "(ii) a suspension of contributions

24 with respect to any period of service, or

1   "(iii) any new direct or indirect exclu-

2   sion of younger or newly hired employees

3   from plan participation.

4   "(C) SPECIAL RULES FOR BENEFIT IN-

5   CREASES.—A plan may not be amended after

6   the date of the adoption of a funding improve-

7   ment plan so as to increase benefits, including

8   future benefit accruals, unless the plan actuary

9   certifies that the benefit increase is consistent

10   with the funding improvement plan and is paid

11   for out of contributions not required by the

12   funding improvement plan to meet the applica-

13   ble benchmark in accordance with the schedule

14   contemplated in the funding improvement plan.

15 "(e) REHABILITATION PLAN MUST BE ADOPTED

16 FOR MULTIEMPLOYER PLANS IN CRITICAL STATUS.—

17   "(1) IN GENERAL.—In any case in which a

18 multiemployer plan is in critical status for a plan

19 year, the plan sponsor, in accordance with this sub-

20 section—

21   "(A) shall adopt a rehabilitation plan not

22   later than 240 days following the required date

23   for the actuarial certification of critical status

24   under subsection (b)(3)(A), and

1   "(B) within 30 days after the adoption of

2   the rehabilitation plan—

3   "(i) shall provide to the bargaining

4   parties 1 or more schedules showing re-

5   vised benefit structures, revised contribu-

6   tion structures, or both, which, if adopted,

7   may reasonably be expected to enable the

8   multiemployer plan to emerge from critical

9   status in accordance with the rehabilitation

10   plan, and

11   "(ii) may, if the plan sponsor deems

12   appropriate, prepare and provide the bar-

13   gaining parties with additional information

14   relating to contribution rates or benefit re-

15   ductions, alternative schedules, or other in-

16   formation relevant to emerging from crit-

17   ical status in accordance with the rehabili-

18   tation plan.

19 The schedule or schedules described in subparagraph

20 (B)(i) shall reflect reductions in future benefit ac-

21 cruals and adjustable benefits, and increases in con-

22 tributions, that the plan sponsor determines are rea-

23 sonably necessary to emerge from critical status.

24 One schedule shall be designated as the default

25 schedule and such schedule shall assume that there

1 are no increases in contributions under the plan

2 other than the increases necessary to emerge from

3 critical status after future benefit accruals and other

4 benefits (other than benefits the reduction or elimi-

5 nation of which are not permitted under section

6 411(d)(6)) have been reduced to the maximum ex-

7 tent permitted by law.

8 "(2) EXCEPTION FOR YEARS AFTER PROCESS

9 BEGINS.—Paragraph (1) shall not apply to a plan

10 year if such year is in a rehabilitation plan adoption

11 period or rehabilitation period by reason of the plan

12 being in critical status for a preceding plan year.

13 For purposes of this section, such preceding plan

14 year shall be the initial critical year with respect to

15 the rehabilitation plan to which it relates.

16 "(3) REHABILITATION PLAN.—For purposes of

17 this section—

18 "(A) IN GENERAL.—A rehabilitation plan

19 is a plan which consists of—

20 "(i) actions, including options or a

21 range of options to be proposed to the bar-

22 gaining parties, formulated, based on rea-

23 sonably anticipated experience and reason-

24 able actuarial assumptions, to enable the

25 plan to cease to be in critical status by the

1   end of the rehabilitation period and may

2   include reductions in plan expenditures (in-

3   cluding plan mergers and consolidations),

4   reductions in future benefit accruals or in-

5   creases in contributions, if agreed to by the

6   bargaining parties, or any combination of

7   such actions, or

8   "(ii) if the plan sponsor determines

9   that, based on reasonable actuarial as-

10   sumptions and upon exhaustion of all rea-

11   sonable measures, the plan can not reason-

12   ably be expected to emerge from critical

13   status by the end of the rehabilitation pe-

14   riod, reasonable measures to emerge from

15   critical status at a later time or to forestall

16   possible insolvency (within the meaning of

17   section 4245 of the Employee Retirement

18   Income Security Act of 1974).

19   A rehabilitation plan must provide annual

20   standards for meeting the requirements of such

21   rehabilitation plan. Such plan shall also include

22   the schedules required to be provided under

23   paragraph (1)(B)(i) and if clause (ii) applies,

24   shall set forth the alternatives considered, ex-

25   plain why the plan is not reasonably expected to

emerge from critical status by the end of the rehabilitation period, and specify when, if ever,
the plan is expected to emerge from critical status in accordance with the rehabilitation plan.

"(B) UPDATES TO REHABILITATION PLAN
AND SCHEDULES.—

"(i) REHABILITATION PLAN.—The
plan sponsor shall annually update the rehabilitation plan and shall file the update
with the plan's annual report under section
104 of the Employee Retirement Income
Security Act of 1974.

"(ii) SCHEDULES.—The plan sponsor
shall annually update any schedule of contribution rates provided under this subsection to reflect the experience of the
plan.

"(iii) DURATION OF SCHEDULE.—A
schedule of contribution rates provided by
the plan sponsor and relied upon by bargaining parties in negotiating a collective
bargaining agreement shall remain in effect for the duration of that collective bargaining agreement.

"(C) Imposition of default schedule
where failure to adopt rehabilitation
plan.—

"(i) In general.—If—

"(I) a collective bargaining agreement providing for contributions
under a multiemployer plan that was
in effect at the time the plan entered
critical status expires, and

"(II) after receiving one or more
schedules from the plan sponsor under
paragraph (1)(B), the bargaining parties with respect to such agreement
fail to adopt a contribution or benefit
schedules with terms consistent with
the rehabilitation plan and the schedule from the plan sponsor under paragraph (1)(B)(i),

the plan sponsor shall implement the default schedule described in the last sentence of paragraph (1) beginning on the
date specified in clause (ii).

"(ii) Date of implementation.—
The date specified in this clause is the earlier of the date—

"(I) on which the Secretary of
Labor certifies that the parties are at
an impasse, or

"(II) which is 180 days after the
date on which the collective bargaining agreement described in clause
(i) expires.

"(4) REHABILITATION PERIOD.—For purposes
of this section—

"(A) IN GENERAL.—The rehabilitation period for a plan in critical status is the 10-year
period beginning on the first day of the first
plan year of the multiemployer plan following
the earlier of—

"(i) the second anniversary of the
date of the adoption of the rehabilitation
plan, or

"(ii) the expiration of the collective
bargaining agreements in effect on the
date of the due date for the actuarial certification of critical status for the initial
critical year under subsection (a)(1) and
covering, as of such date at least 75 percent of the active participants in such multiemployer plan.

1   If a plan emerges from critical status as pro-
2   vided under subparagraph (B) before the end of
3   such 10-year period, the rehabilitation period
4   shall end with the plan year preceding the plan
5   year for which the determination under sub-
6   paragraph (B) is made.

7   "(B) EMERGENCE.—A plan in critical sta-
8   tus shall remain in such status until a plan
9   year for which the plan actuary certifies, in ac-
10   cordance with subsection (b)(3)(A), that the
11   plan is not projected to have an accumulated
12   funding deficiency for the plan year or any of
13   the 9 succeeding plan years, without regard to
14   the use of the shortfall method and taking into
15   account any extension of amortization periods
16   under section 431(d).

17   "(5) REHABILITATION PLAN ADOPTION PE-
18   RIOD.—For purposes of this section, the term 'reha-
19   bilitation plan adoption period' means the period be-
20   ginning on the date of the certification under sub-
21   section (b)(3)(A) for the initial critical year and end-
22   ing on the day before the first day of the rehabilita-
23   tion period.

24   "(6) LIMITATION ON REDUCTION IN RATES OF
25   FUTURE ACCRUALS.—Any reduction in the rate of

future accruals under the default schedule described in paragraph (1)(B)(i) shall not reduce the rate of future accruals below—

      "(A) a monthly benefit (payable as a single life annuity commencing at the participant's normal retirement age) equal to 1 percent of the contributions required to be made with respect to a participant, or the equivalent standard accrual rate for a participant or group of participants under the collective bargaining agreements in effect as of the first day of the initial critical year, or

      "(B) if lower, the accrual rate under the plan on such first day.

The equivalent standard accrual rate shall be determined by the plan sponsor based on the standard or average contribution base units which the plan sponsor determines to be representative for active participants and such other factors as the plan sponsor determines to be relevant. Nothing in this paragraph shall be construed as limiting the ability of the plan sponsor to prepare and provide the bargaining parties with alternative schedules to the default schedule that established lower or higher accrual and con-

tribution rates than the rates otherwise described in
this paragraph.

"(7) AUTOMATIC EMPLOYER SURCHARGE.—

"(A) IMPOSITION OF SURCHARGE.—Each
employer otherwise obligated to make a contribution for the initial critical year shall be obligated to pay to the plan for such year a surcharge equal to 5 percent of the contribution
otherwise required under the applicable collective bargaining agreement (or other agreement
pursuant to which the employer contributes).
For each succeeding plan year in which the
plan is in critical status for a consecutive period
of years beginning with the initial critical year,
the surcharge shall be 10 percent of the contribution otherwise so required.

"(B) ENFORCEMENT OF SURCHARGE.—
The surcharges under subparagraph (A) shall
be due and payable on the same schedule as the
contributions on which the surcharges are
based. Any failure to make a surcharge payment shall be treated as a delinquent contribution under section 515 of the Employee Retirement Income Security Act of 1974 and shall be
enforceable as such.

"(C) SURCHARGE TO TERMINATE UPON COLLECTIVE BARGAINING AGREEMENT RENEGO-TIATION.—The surcharge under this paragraph shall cease to be effective with respect to employees covered by a collective bargaining agreement (or other agreement pursuant to which the employer contributes), beginning on the effective date of a collective bargaining agreement (or other such agreement) that includes terms consistent with a schedule presented by the plan sponsor under paragraph (1)(B)(i), as modified under subparagraph (B) of paragraph (3).

"(D) SURCHARGE NOT TO APPLY UNTIL EMPLOYER RECEIVES NOTICE.—The surcharge under this paragraph shall not apply to an employer until 30 days after the employer has been notified by the plan sponsor that the plan is in critical status and that the surcharge is in effect.

"(E) SURCHARGE NOT TO GENERATE IN-CREASED BENEFIT ACCRUALS.—Notwithstanding any provision of a plan to the contrary, the amount of any surcharge under this

1 paragraph shall not be the basis for any benefit

2 accrual under the plan.

3 "(8) BENEFIT ADJUSTMENTS.—

4   "(A) ADJUSTABLE BENEFITS.—

5   "(i) IN GENERAL.—Notwithstanding

6   section 204(g), the plan sponsor shall, sub-

7   ject to the notice requirement under sub-

8   paragraph (C), make any reductions to ad-

9   justable benefits which the plan sponsor

10   deems appropriate, based upon the out-

11   come of collective bargaining over the

12   schedule or schedules provided under para-

13   graph (1)(B)(i).

14   "(ii) EXCEPTION FOR RETIREES.—

15   Except in the case of adjustable benefits

16   described in clause (iv)(III), the plan spon-

17   sor of a plan in critical status shall not re-

18   duce adjustable benefits of any participant

19   or beneficiary whose benefit commence-

20   ment date is before the date on which the

21   plan provides notice to the participant or

22   beneficiary under subsection (b)(3)(D) for

23   the initial critical year.

24   "(iii) PLAN SPONSOR FLEXIBILITY.—

25   The plan sponsor shall include in the

1 schedules provided to the bargaining par-

2 ties an allowance for funding the benefits

3 of participants with respect to whom con-

4 tributions are not currently required to be

5 made, and shall reduce their benefits to

6 the extent permitted under this title and

7 considered appropriate by the plan sponsor

8 based on the plan's then current overall

9 funding status.

10 "(iv) ADJUSTABLE BENEFIT DE-

11 FINED.—For purposes of this paragraph,

12 the term 'adjustable benefit' means—

13   "(I) benefits, rights, and features

14   under the plan, including post-retire-

15   ment death benefits, 60-month guar-

16   antees, disability benefits not yet in

17   pay status, and similar benefits,

18   "(II) any early retirement benefit

19   or retirement-type subsidy (within the

20   meaning of section 411(d)(6)(B)(i))

21   and any benefit payment option (other

22   than the qualified joint-and survivor

23   annuity), and

24   "(III) benefit increases that

25   would not be eligible for a guarantee

1   under section 4022A of the Employee

2   Retirement Income Security Act of

3   1974 on the first day of initial critical

4   year because the increases were

5   adopted (or, if later, took effect) less

6   than 60 months before such first day.

7   "(B) NORMAL RETIREMENT BENEFITS

8   PROTECTED.—Except as provided in subpara-

9   graph (A)(iv)(III), nothing in this paragraph

10   shall be construed to permit a plan to reduce

11   the level of a participant's accrued benefit pay-

12   able at normal retirement age.

13   "(C) NOTICE REQUIREMENTS.—

14   "(i) IN GENERAL.—No reduction may

15   be made to adjustable benefits under sub-

16   paragraph (A) unless notice of such reduc-

17   tion has been given at least 30 days before

18   the general effective date of such reduction

19   for all participants and beneficiaries to—

20   "(I) plan participants and bene-

21   ficiaries,

22   "(II) each employer who has an

23   obligation to contribute (within the

24   meaning of section 4212(a)) under the

25   plan, and

1   "(III) each employee organization

2   which, for purposes of collective bar-

3   gaining, represents plan participants

4   employed by such an employer.

5   "(ii) CONTENT OF NOTICE.—The no-

6 tice under clause (i) shall contain—

7   "(I) sufficient information to en-

8   able participants and beneficiaries to

9   understand the effect of any reduction

10   on their benefits, including an esti-

11   mate (on an annual or monthly basis)

12   of any affected adjustable benefit that

13   a participant or beneficiary would oth-

14   erwise have been eligible for as of the

15   general effective date described in

16   clause (i), and

17   "(II) information as to the rights

18   and remedies of plan participants and

19   beneficiaries as well as how to contact

20   the Department of Labor for further

21   information and assistance where ap-

22   propriate.

23   "(iii) FORM AND MANNER.—Any no-

24 tice under clause (i)—

1   "(I) shall be provided in a form

2   and manner prescribed in regulations

3   of the Secretary of Labor,

4   "(II) shall be written in a man-

5   ner so as to be understood by the av-

6   erage plan participant, and

7   "(III) may be provided in writ-

8   ten, electronic, or other appropriate

9   form to the extent such form is rea-

10   sonably accessible to persons to whom

11   the notice is required to be provided.

12   The Secretary of Labor shall in the regula-

13   tions prescribed under subclause (I) estab-

14   lish a model notice that a plan sponsor

15   may use to meet the requirements of this

16   subparagraph.

17   "(9) ADJUSTMENTS DISREGARDED IN WITH-

18 DRAWAL LIABILITY DETERMINATION.—

19   "(A) BENEFIT REDUCTIONS.—Any benefit

20   reductions under this subsection shall be dis-

21   regarded in determining a plan's unfunded vest-

22   ed benefits for purposes of determining an em-

23   ployer's withdrawal liability under section 4201

24   of the Employee Retirement Income Security

25   Act of 1974.

1   "(B) SURCHARGES.—Any surcharges

2 under paragraph (7) shall be disregarded in de-

3 termining an employer's withdrawal liability

4 under section 4211 of such Act, except for pur-

5 poses of determining the unfunded vested bene-

6 fits attributable to an employer under section

7 4211(c)(4) of such Act or a comparable method

8 approved under section 4211(c)(5) of such Act.

9   "(C) SIMPLIFIED CALCULATIONS.—The

10 Pension Benefit Guaranty Corporation shall

11 prescribe simplified methods for the application

12 of this paragraph in determining withdrawal li-

13 ability.

14 "(f) RULES FOR OPERATION OF PLAN DURING

15 ADOPTION AND REHABILITATION PERIOD.—

16   "(1) COMPLIANCE WITH REHABILITATION

17 PLAN.—

18   "(A) IN GENERAL.—A plan may not be

19 amended after the date of the adoption of a re-

20 habilitation plan under subsection (e) so as to

21 be inconsistent with the rehabilitation plan.

22   "(B) SPECIAL RULES FOR BENEFIT IN-

23 CREASES.—A plan may not be amended after

24 the date of the adoption of a rehabilitation plan

25 under subsection (e) so as to increase benefits,

1 including future benefit accruals, unless the

2 plan actuary certifies that such increase is paid

3 for out of additional contributions not con-

4 templated by the rehabilitation plan, and, after

5 taking into account the benefit increase, the

6 multiemployer plan still is reasonably expected

7 to emerge from critical status by the end of the

8 rehabilitation period on the schedule con-

9 templated in the rehabilitation plan.

10 "(2) RESTRICTION ON LUMP SUMS AND SIMI-

11 LAR BENEFITS.—

12 "(A) IN GENERAL.—Effective on the date

13 the notice of certification of the plan's critical

14 status for the initial critical year under sub-

15 section (b)(3)(D) is sent, and notwithstanding

16 section 411(d)(6), the plan shall not pay—

17 "(i) any payment, in excess of the

18 monthly amount paid under a single life

19 annuity (plus any social security supple-

20 ments described in the last sentence of sec-

21 tion 411(b)(1)(A)),

22 "(ii) any payment for the purchase of

23 an irrevocable commitment from an insurer

24 to pay benefits, and

1   "(iii) any other payment specified by

2   the Secretary by regulations.

3   "(B) EXCEPTION.—Subparagraph (A)

4   shall not apply to a benefit which under section

5   411(a)(11) may be immediately distributed

6   without the consent of the participant or to any

7   makeup payment in the case of a retroactive

8   annuity starting date or any similar payment of

9   benefits owed with respect to a prior period.

10   "(3) ADJUSTMENTS DISREGARDED IN WITH-

11 DRAWAL LIABILITY DETERMINATION.—Any benefit

12 reductions under this subsection shall be disregarded

13 in determining a plan's unfunded vested benefits for

14 purposes of determining an employer's withdrawal li-

15 ability under section 4201 of the Employee Retire-

16 ment Income Security Act of 1974.

17   "(4) SPECIAL RULES FOR PLAN ADOPTION PE-

18 RIOD.—During the rehabilitation plan adoption pe-

19 riod—

20   "(A) the plan sponsor may not accept a

21   collective bargaining agreement or participation

22   agreement with respect to the multiemployer

23   plan that provides for—

24   "(i) a reduction in the level of con-

25   tributions for any participants,

1   "(ii) a suspension of contributions

2   with respect to any period of service, or

3   "(iii) any new direct or indirect exclu-

4   sion of younger or newly hired employees

5   from plan participation, and

6   "(B) no amendment of the plan which in-

7   creases the liabilities of the plan by reason of

8   any increase in benefits, any change in the ac-

9   crual of benefits, or any change in the rate at

10   which benefits become nonforfeitable under the

11   plan may be adopted unless the amendment is

12   required as a condition of qualification under

13   part I of subchapter D of chapter 1 or to com-

14   ply with other applicable law.

15   "(g) EXPEDITED RESOLUTION OF PLAN SPONSOR

16 DECISIONS.—If, within 60 days of the due date for adop-

17 tion of a funding improvement plan or a rehabilitation

18 plan under subsection (e), the plan sponsor of a plan in

19 endangered status or a plan in critical status has not

20 agreed on a funding improvement plan or rehabilitation

21 plan, then any member of the board or group that con-

22 stitutes the plan sponsor may require that the plan spon-

23 sor enter into an expedited dispute resolution procedure

24 for the development and adoption of a funding improve-

25 ment plan or rehabilitation plan.

1   "(h) NONBARGAINED PARTICIPATION.—

2   "(1) BOTH BARGAINED AND NONBARGAINED

3   EMPLOYEE-PARTICIPANTS.—In the case of an em-

4   ployer that contributes to a multiemployer plan with

5   respect to both employees who are covered by one or

6   more collective bargaining agreements and employ-

7   ees who are not so covered, if the plan is in endan-

8   gered status or in critical status, benefits of and

9   contributions for the nonbargained employees, in-

10   cluding surcharges on those contributions, shall be

11   determined as if those nonbargained employees were

12   covered under the first to expire of the employer's

13   collective bargaining agreements in effect when the

14   plan entered endangered or critical status.

15   "(2) NONBARGAINED EMPLOYEES ONLY.—In

16   the case of an employer that contributes to a multi-

17   employer plan only with respect to employees who

18   are not covered by a collective bargaining agreement,

19   this section shall be applied as if the employer were

20   the bargaining party, and its participation agree-

21   ment with the plan were a collective bargaining

22   agreement with a term ending on the first day of the

23   plan year beginning after the employer is provided

24   the schedule or schedules described in subsections

25   (c) and (e).

1   "(i) DEFINITIONS; ACTUARIAL METHOD.—For pur-

2 poses of this section—

3   "(1) BARGAINING PARTY.—The term 'bar-

4   gaining party' means—

5   "(A)(i) except as provided in clause (ii), an

6   employer who has an obligation to contribute

7   under the plan; or

8   "(ii) in the case of a plan described under

9   section 404(c), or a continuation of such a plan,

10   the association of employers that is the em-

11   ployer settlor of the plan; and

12   "(B) an employee organization which, for

13   purposes of collective bargaining, represents

14   plan participants employed by an employer who

15   has an obligation to contribute under the plan.

16   "(2) FUNDED PERCENTAGE.—The term 'fund-

17   ed percentage' means the percentage equal to a frac-

18   tion—

19   "(A) the numerator of which is the value

20   of the plan's assets, as determined under sec-

21   tion 431(c)(2), and

22   "(B) the denominator of which is the ac-

23   crued liability of the plan, determined using ac-

24   tuarial assumptions described in section

25   431(c)(3).

"(3) ACCUMULATED FUNDING DEFICIENCY.—
The term 'accumulated funding deficiency' has the
meaning given such term in section 412(a).

"(4) ACTIVE PARTICIPANT.—The term 'active
participant' means, in connection with a multiemployer plan, a participant who is in covered service
under the plan.

"(5) INACTIVE PARTICIPANT.—The term 'inactive participant' means, in connection with a multiemployer plan, a participant, or the beneficiary or
alternate payee of a participant, who—

"(A) is not in covered service under the
plan, and

"(B) is in pay status under the plan or has
a nonforfeitable right to benefits under the
plan.

"(6) PAY STATUS.—A person is in pay status
under a multiemployer plan if—

"(A) at any time during the current plan
year, such person is a participant or beneficiary
under the plan and is paid an early, late, normal, or disability retirement benefit under the
plan (or a death benefit under the plan related
to a retirement benefit), or

1   "(B) to the extent provided in regulations

2   of the Secretary, such person is entitled to such

3   a benefit under the plan.

4   "(7) OBLIGATION TO CONTRIBUTE.—The term

5 'obligation to contribute' has the meaning given such

6 term under section 4212(a) of the Employee Retire-

7 ment Income Security Act of 1974.

8   "(8) ACTUARIAL METHOD.—Notwithstanding

9 any other provision of this section, the actuary's de-

10 terminations with respect to a plan's normal cost,

11 actuarial accrued liability, and improvements in a

12 plan's funded percentage under this section shall be

13 based upon the unit credit funding method (whether

14 or not that method is used for the plan's actuarial

15 valuation).

16   "(9) PLAN SPONSOR.—In the case of a plan de-

17 scribed under section 404(c), or a continuation of

18 such a plan, the term 'plan sponsor' means the bar-

19 gaining parties described under paragraph (1).

20   "(10) BENEFIT COMMENCEMENT DATE.—The

21 term 'benefit commencement date' means the annu-

22 ity starting date (or in the case of a retroactive an-

23 nuity starting date, the date on which benefit pay-

24 ments begin)."

(b) Excise Taxes on Failures Relating to Multiemployer Plans in Endangered or Critical Status.—

(1) In general.—Section 4971 of the Internal Revenue Code of 1986 is amended by redesignating subsection (g) as subsection (h) and by inserting after subsection (f) the following:

"(g) Multiemployer Plans in Endangered or Critical Status.—

"(1) In general.—Except as provided in this subsection—

"(A) no tax shall be imposed under this section for a taxable year with respect to a multiemployer plan if, for the plan years ending with or within the taxable year, the plan is in critical status pursuant to section 432, and

"(B) any tax imposed under this subsection for a taxable year with respect to a multiemployer plan if, for the plan years ending with or within the taxable year, the plan is in endangered status pursuant to section 432 shall be in addition to any other tax imposed by this section.

"(2) Failure to comply with funding improvement or rehabilitation plan.—

"(A) IN GENERAL.—If any funding improvement plan or rehabilitation plan in effect under section 432 with respect to a multiemployer plan requires an employer to make a contribution to the plan, there is hereby imposed a tax on each failure of the employer to make the required contribution within the time required under such plan.

"(B) AMOUNT OF TAX.—The amount of the tax imposed by subparagraph (A) shall be equal to the amount of the required contribution the employer failed to make in a timely manner.

"(C) LIABILITY FOR TAX.—The tax imposed by subparagraph (A) shall be paid by the employer responsible for contributing to or under the rehabilitation plan which fails to make the contribution.

"(3) FAILURE TO MEET REQUIREMENTS FOR PLANS IN ENDANGERED OR CRITICAL STATUS.—If—

"(A) a plan which is in seriously endangered status fails to meet the applicable benchmarks by the end of the funding improvement period, or

1   "(B) a plan which is in critical status ei-

2   ther—

3   "(i) fails to meet the requirements of

4   section 432(e) by the end of the rehabilita-

5   tion period, or

6   "(ii) has received a certification under

7   section 432(b)(3)(A)(ii) for 3 consecutive

8   plan years that the plan is not making the

9   scheduled progress in meeting its require-

10   ments under the rehabilitation plan,

11   the plan shall be treated as having an accumu-

12   lated funding deficiency for purposes of this

13   section for the last plan year in such funding

14   improvement, rehabilitation, or 3-consecutive

15   year period (and each succeeding plan year

16   until such benchmarks or requirements are

17   met) in an amount equal to the greater of the

18   amount of the contributions necessary to meet

19   such benchmarks or requirements or the

20   amount of such accumulated funding deficiency

21   without regard to this paragraph.

22   "(4) FAILURE TO ADOPT REHABILITATION

23 PLAN.—

24   "(A) IN GENERAL.—In the case of a multi-

25   employer plan which is in critical status, there

is hereby imposed a tax on the failure of such
plan to adopt a rehabilitation plan within the
time prescribed under section 432.

"(B) AMOUNT OF TAX.—The amount of
the tax imposed under subparagraph (A) with
respect to any plan sponsor for any taxable year
shall be the greater of—

"(i) the amount of tax imposed under
subsection (a) for the taxable year (determined without regard to this subsection),
or

"(ii) the amount equal to $1,100 mul-
tiplied by the number of days during the
taxable year which are included in the period beginning on the first day of the 240-
day period described in section
432(e)(1)(A) and ending on the day on
which the rehabilitation plan is adopted.

"(C) LIABILITY FOR TAX.—

"(i) IN GENERAL.—The tax imposed
by subparagraph (A) shall be paid by each
plan sponsor.

"(ii) PLAN SPONSOR.—For purposes
of clause (i), the term 'plan sponsor' in the
case of a multiemployer plan means the as-

1   sociation, committee, joint board of trust-

2   ees, or other similar group of representa-

3   tives of the parties who establish or main-

4   tain the plan.

5   "(5) WAIVER.—In the case of a failure de-

6 scribed in paragraph (2) or (3) which is due to rea-

7 sonable cause and not to willful neglect, the Sec-

8 retary may waive part or all of the tax imposed by

9 this subsection. For purposes of this paragraph, rea-

10 sonable cause includes unanticipated and material

11 market fluctuations, the loss of a significant contrib-

12 uting employer, or other factors to the extent that

13 the payment of tax under this subsection with re-

14 spect to the failure would be excessive or otherwise

15 inequitable relative to the failure involved.

16   "(6) TERMS USED IN SECTION 432.—For pur-

17 poses of this subsection, any term used in this sub-

18 section which is also used in section 432 shall have

19 the meaning given such term by section 432.".

20   (2) CONTROLLED GROUPS.—Section 4971(c)(2)

21 of such Code is amended—

22   (A) by striking "In the case of a plan

23   other than a multiemployer plan, if the" and in-

24   serting "If an", and

1   (B) by striking "or (f)" and inserting "(f),

2   or (g)".

3   (c) No ADDITIONAL CONTRIBUTION REQUIRED.—

4 Section 412(b) of the Internal Revenue Code of 1986, as

5 amended by this Act, is amended by adding at the end

6 the following new paragraph:

7   "(3) MULTIEMPLOYER PLANS IN CRITICAL STA-

8   TUS.—Paragraph (1) shall not apply in the case of

9   a multiemployer plan for any plan year in which the

10   plan is in critical status pursuant to section 432.

11   This paragraph shall only apply if the plan adopts

12   a rehabilitation plan in accordance with section

13   432(e) and complies with such rehabilitation plan

14   (and any modifications of the plan).".

15   (d) CLERICAL AMENDMENT.—The table of sections

16 for subpart A of part III of subchapter D of chapter 1

17 of such Code is amended by adding at the end the fol-

18 lowing new item:

> "Sec. 432. Additional funding rules for multiemployer plans in endangered sta-
> tus or critical status.".

19   (e) EFFECTIVE DATES.—

20   (1) IN GENERAL.—The amendments made by

21   this section shall apply with respect to plan years be-

22   ginning after 2007.

23   (2) SPECIAL RULE FOR CERTAIN NOTICES.—In

24   any case in which a plan's actuary certifies that it

1   is reasonably expected that a multiemployer plan will

2   be in critical status under section 305(b)(3) of the

3   Employee Retirement Income Security Act of 1974,

4   as added by this section, with respect to the first

5   plan year beginning after 2007, the notice required

6   under subparagraph (D) of such section may be pro-

7   vided at any time after the date of enactment, so

8   long as it is provided on or before the last date for

9   providing the notice under such subparagraph.

10   (3) SPECIAL RULE FOR CERTAIN RESTORED

11   BENEFITS.—In the case of a multiemployer plan—

12   (A) with respect to which benefits were re-

13   duced pursuant to a plan amendment adopted

14   on or after January 1, 2002, and before June

15   30, 2005, and

16   (B) which, pursuant to the plan document,

17   the trust agreement, or a formal written com-

18   munication from the plan sponsor to partici-

19   pants provided before June 30, 2005, provided

20   for the restoration of such benefits,

21   the amendments made by this section shall not apply

22   to such benefit restorations to the extent that any

23   restriction on the providing or accrual of such bene-

24   fits would otherwise apply by reason of such amend-

25   ments.

SEC. 213. MEASURES TO FORESTALL INSOLVENCY OF MULTIEMPLOYER PLANS.

(a) ADVANCE DETERMINATION OF IMPENDING INSOLVENCY OVER 5 YEARS.—Section 418E(d)(1) of the Internal Revenue Code of 1986 is amended—

(1) by striking "3 plan years" the second place it appears and inserting "5 plan years"; and

(2) by adding at the end the following new sentence: "If the plan sponsor makes such a determination that the plan will be insolvent in any of the next 5 plan years, the plan sponsor shall make the comparison under this paragraph at least annually until the plan sponsor makes a determination that the plan will not be insolvent in any of the next 5 plan years.".

(b) EFFECTIVE DATE.—The amendments made by this section shall apply with respect to the determinations made in plan years beginning after 2007.

SEC. 214. EXEMPTION FROM EXCISE TAXES FOR CERTAIN MULTIEMPLOYER PENSION PLANS.

(a) IN GENERAL.—Notwithstanding any other provision of law, no tax shall be imposed under subsection (a) or (b) of section 4971 of the Internal Revenue Code of 1986 with respect to any accumulated funding deficiency of a plan described in subsection (b) of this section for any taxable year beginning before the earlier of—

1   (1) the taxable year in which the plan sponsor

2   adopts a rehabilitation plan under section 305(e) of

3   the Employee Retirement Income Security Act of

4   1974 and section 432(e) of such Code (as added by

5   this Act); or

6   (2) the taxable year that contains January 1,

7   2009.

8   (b) PLAN DESCRIBED.—A plan described under this

9 subsection is a multiemployer pension plan—

10   (1) with less than 100 participants;

11   (2) with respect to which the contributing em-

12   ployers participated in a Federal fishery capacity re-

13   duction program;

14   (3) with respect to which employers under the

15   plan participated in the Northeast Fisheries Assist-

16   ance Program; and

17   (4) with respect to which the annual normal

18   cost is less than $100,000 and the plan is experi-

19   encing a funding deficiency on the date of enactment

20   of this Act.

Subtitle C—Sunset of Additional Funding Rules

21 **Subtitle C—Sunset of Additional**

22   **Funding Rules**

SEC. 221. SUNSET OF ADDITIONAL FUNDING RULES.

24   (a) REPORT.—Not later than December 31, 2011,

25 the Secretary of Labor, the Secretary of the Treasury, and

1 the Executive Director of the Pension Benefit Guaranty
2 Corporation shall conduct a study of the effect of the
3 amendments made by this subtitle on the operation and
4 funding status of multiemployer plans and shall report the
5 results of such study, including any recommendations for
6 legislation, to the Congress.

7   (b) MATTERS INCLUDED IN STUDY.—The study re-
8 quired under subsection (a) shall include—

9   (1) the effect of funding difficulties, funding
10   rules in effect before the date of the enactment of
11   this Act, and the amendments made by this subtitle
12   on small businesses participating in multiemployer
13   plans,

14   (2) the effect on the financial status of small
15   employers of—

16   (A) funding targets set in funding im-
17   provement and rehabilitation plans and associ-
18   ated contribution increases,

19   (B) funding deficiencies,

20   (C) excise taxes,

21   (D) withdrawal liability,

22   (E) the possibility of alternatives schedules
23   and procedures for financially-troubled employ-
24   ers, and

(F) other aspects of the multiemployer system, and

(3) the role of the multiemployer pension plan system in helping small employers to offer pension benefits.

(c) SUNSET.—

(1) IN GENERAL.—Except as provided in this subsection, notwithstanding any other provision of this Act, the provisions of, and the amendments made by, sections 201(b), 202, and 212 shall not apply to plan years beginning after December 31, 2014.

(2) FUNDING IMPROVEMENT AND REHABILITATION PLANS.—If a plan is operating under a funding improvement or rehabilitation plan under section 305 of such Act or 432 of such Code for its last year beginning before January 1, 2015, such plan shall continue to operate under such funding improvement or rehabilitation plan during any period after December 31, 2014, such funding improvement or rehabilitation plan is in effect and all provisions of such Act or Code relating to the operation of such funding improvement or rehabilitation plan shall continue in effect during such period.

TITLE III—INTEREST RATE ASSUMPTIONS

SEC. 301. EXTENSION OF REPLACEMENT OF 30-YEAR TREASURY RATES.

(a) AMENDMENTS OF ERISA.—

    (1) DETERMINATION OF RANGE.—Subclause (II) of section 302(b)(5)(B)(ii) of the Employee Retirement Income Security Act of 1974 is amended—

        (A) by striking "2006" and inserting "2008", and

        (B) by striking "**AND 2005**" in the heading and inserting "**, 2005, 2006, AND 2007**".

    (2) DETERMINATION OF CURRENT LIABILITY.— Subclause (IV) of section 302(d)(7)(C)(i) of such Act is amended—

        (A) by striking "or 2005" and inserting ", 2005, 2006, or 2007", and

        (B) by striking "**AND 2005**" in the heading and inserting "**, 2005, 2006, AND 2007**".

    (3) PBGC PREMIUM RATE.—Subclause (V) of section 4006(a)(3)(E)(iii) of such Act is amended by striking "2006" and inserting "2008".

(b) AMENDMENTS OF INTERNAL REVENUE CODE.—

1   (1) DETERMINATION OF RANGE.—Subclause
2   (II) of section 412(b)(5)(B)(ii) of the Internal Rev-
3   enue Code of 1986 is amended—

4   (A) by striking "2006" and inserting
5   "2008", and

6   (B) by striking "**AND 2005**" in the heading
7   and inserting "**, 2005, 2006, AND 2007**".

8   (2) DETERMINATION OF CURRENT LIABILITY.—
9   Subclause (IV) of section 412(l)(7)(C)(i) of such
10   Code is amended—

11   (A) by striking "or 2005" and inserting ",
12   2005, 2006, or 2007", and

13   (B) by striking "**AND 2005**" in the heading
14   and inserting "**, 2005, 2006, AND 2007**".

15   (c) PLAN AMENDMENTS.—Clause (ii) of section
16   101(c)(2)(A) of the Pension Funding Equity Act of 2004
17   is amended by striking "2006" and inserting "2008".

18   **SEC. 302. INTEREST RATE ASSUMPTION FOR DETERMINA-**
19   **TION OF LUMP SUM DISTRIBUTIONS.**

20   (a) AMENDMENT TO EMPLOYEE RETIREMENT IN-
21   COME SECURITY ACT OF 1974.—Paragraph (3) of section
22   205(g) of the Employee Retirement Income Security Act
23   of 1974 (29 U.S.C. 1055(g)(3)) is amended to read as
24   follows:

1   "(3)(A) For purposes of paragraphs (1) and (2), the

2 present value shall not be less than the present value cal-

3 culated by using the applicable mortality table and the ap-

4 plicable interest rate.

5   "(B) For purposes of subparagraph (A)—

6   "(i) The term 'applicable mortality table' means

7   a mortality table, modified as appropriate by the

8   Secretary of the Treasury, based on the mortality

9   table specified for the plan year under subparagraph

10   (A) of section 303(h)(3) (without regard to subpara-

11   graph (C) or (D) of such section).

12   "(ii) The term 'applicable interest rate' means

13   the adjusted first, second, and third segment rates

14   applied under rules similar to the rules of section

15   303(h)(2)(C) for the month before the date of the

16   distribution or such other time as the Secretary of

17   the Treasury may by regulations prescribe.

18   "(iii) For purposes of clause (ii), the adjusted

19   first, second, and third segment rates are the first,

20   second, and third segment rates which would be de-

21   termined under section 303(h)(2)(C) if—

22   "(I) section 303(h)(2)(D) were applied by

23   substituting the average yields for the month

24   described in clause (ii) for the average yields for

25   the 24-month period described in such section,

1   "(II) section 303(h)(2)(G)(i)(II) were ap-

2 plied   by   substituting   'section

3 205(g)(3)(B)(iii)(II)'   for   'section

4 302(b)(5)(B)(ii)(II)', and

5   "(III) the applicable percentage under sec-

6 tion 303(h)(2)(G) were determined in accord-

7 ance with the following table:

In the case of plan years beginning in:	The applicable percentage is:
2008	20 percent
2009	40 percent
2010	60 percent
2011	80 percent.".

8   (b) AMENDMENT TO INTERNAL REVENUE CODE OF

9 1986.—Paragraph (3) of section 417(e) of the Internal

10 Revenue Code of 1986 is amended to read as follows:

11   "(3) DETERMINATION OF PRESENT VALUE.—

12   "(A) IN GENERAL.—For purposes of para-

13 graphs (1) and (2), the present value shall not

14 be less than the present value calculated by

15 using the applicable mortality table and the ap-

16 plicable interest rate.

17   "(B) APPLICABLE MORTALITY TABLE.—

18 For purposes of subparagraph (A), the term

19 'applicable mortality table' means a mortality

20 table, modified as appropriate by the Secretary,

21 based on the mortality table specified for the

1   plan year under subparagraph (A) of section

2   430(h)(3) (without regard to subparagraph (C)

3   or (D) of such section).

4   "(C) APPLICABLE INTEREST RATE.—For

5   purposes of subparagraph (A), the term 'appli-

6   cable interest rate' means the adjusted first,

7   second, and third segment rates applied under

8   rules   similar   to   the   rules   of   section

9   430(h)(2)(C) for the month before the date of

10   the distribution or such other time as the Sec-

11   retary may by regulations prescribe.

12   "(D) APPLICABLE SEGMENT RATES.—For

13   purposes of subparagraph (C), the adjusted

14   first, second, and third segment rates are the

15   first, second, and third segment rates which

16   would   be   determined   under   section

17   430(h)(2)(C) if—

18   "(i) section 430(h)(2)(D) were applied

19   by substituting the average yields for the

20   month described in clause (ii) for the aver-

21   age yields for the 24-month period de-

22   scribed in such section,

23   "(ii) section 430(h)(2)(G)(i)(II) were

24   applied   by   substituting   'section

1   417(e)(3)(A)(ii)(II)'   for   'section

2   412(b)(5)(B)(ii)(II)', and

3   "(iii) the applicable percentage under

4   section 430(h)(2)(G) were determined in

5   accordance with the following table:

In the case of plan years beginning in:	The applicable percentage is:
2008	20 percent
2009	40 percent
2010	60 percent
2011	80 percent.".

6   (c) EFFECTIVE DATE.—The amendments made by

7 this section shall apply with respect to plan years begin-

8 ning after December 31, 2007.

9 **SEC. 303. INTEREST RATE ASSUMPTION FOR APPLYING**

10   **BENEFIT LIMITATIONS TO LUMP SUM DIS-**

11   **TRIBUTIONS.**

12   (a) IN GENERAL.—Clause (ii) of section

13 415(b)(2)(E) of the Internal Revenue Code of 1986 is

14 amended to read as follows:

15   "(ii) For purposes of adjusting any

16   benefit under subparagraph (B) for any

17   form of benefit subject to section

18   417(e)(3), the interest rate assumption

19   shall not be less than the greatest of—

20   "(I) 5.5 percent,

1   "(II) the rate that provides a

2   benefit of not more than 105 percent

3   of the benefit that would be provided

4   if the applicable interest rate (as de-

5   fined in section 417(e)(3)) were the

6   interest rate assumption, or

7   "(III) the rate specified under

8   the plan.".

9   (b) EFFECTIVE DATE.—The amendment made by

10 subsection (a) shall apply to distributions made in years

11 beginning after December 31, 2005.

TITLE IV—PBGC GUARANTEE AND RELATED PROVISIONS

SEC. 401. PBGC PREMIUMS.

15   (a) VARIABLE-RATE PREMIUMS.—

16   (1) CONFORMING AMENDMENTS RELATED TO

17   FUNDING RULES FOR SINGLE-EMPLOYER PLANS.—

18   Section 4006(a)(3)(E) of the Employee Retirement

19   Income and Security Act of 1974 (29 U.S.C.

20   1306(a)(3)(E)) is amended by striking clauses (iii)

21   and (iv) and inserting the following:

22   "(iii) For purposes of clause (ii), the term 'unfunded

23 vested benefits' means, for a plan year, the excess (if any)

24 of—

1   "(I) the funding target of the plan as deter-

2   mined under section 303(d) for the plan year by

3   only taking into account vested benefits and by

4   using the interest rate described in clause (iv), over

5   "(II) the fair market value of plan assets for

6   the plan year which are held by the plan on the

7   valuation date.

8   "(iv) The interest rate used in valuing benefits for

9 purposes of subclause (I) of clause (iii) shall be equal to

10 the first, second, or third segment rate for the month pre-

11 ceding the month in which the plan year begins, which

12 would be determined under section 303(h)(2)(C) if section

13 303(h)(2)(D) were applied by using the monthly yields for

14 the month preceding the month in which the plan year

15 begins on investment grade corporate bonds with varying

16 maturities and in the top 3 quality levels rather than the

17 average of such yields for a 24-month period.".

18   (2) EFFECTIVE DATE.—The amendments made

19   by paragraph (1) shall apply with respect to plan

20   years beginning after 2007.

21 (b) TERMINATION PREMIUMS.—

22   (1) REPEAL OF SUNSET PROVISION.—Subpara-

23   graph (E) of section 4006(a)(7) of such Act is re-

24   pealed.

25   (2) TECHNICAL CORRECTION.—

(A) IN GENERAL.—Section 4006(a)(7)(C)(ii) of such Act is amended by striking "subparagraph (B)(i)(I)" and inserting "subparagraph (B)".

(B) EFFECTIVE DATE.—The amendment made by this paragraph shall take effect as if included in the provision of the Deficit Reduction Act of 2005 to which it relates.

SEC. 402. SPECIAL FUNDING RULES FOR CERTAIN PLANS MAINTAINED BY COMMERCIAL AIRLINES.

(a) IN GENERAL.—The plan sponsor of an eligible plan may elect to either—

(1) have the rules of subsection (b) apply, or

(2) have section 303 of the Employee Retirement Income Security Act of 1974 and section 430 of the Internal Revenue Code of 1986 applied to its first taxable year beginning in 2008 by amortizing the shortfall amortization base for such taxable year over a period of 10 plan years (rather than 7 plan years) beginning with such plan year.

(b) ALTERNATIVE FUNDING SCHEDULE.—

(1) IN GENERAL.—If an election is made under subsection (a)(1) to have this subsection apply to an eligible plan and the requirements of paragraphs (2) and (3) are met with respect to the plan—

(A) in the case of any applicable plan year beginning before January 1, 2008, the plan shall not have an accumulated funding deficiency for purposes of section 302 of the Employee Retirement Income Security Act of 1974 and sections 412 and 4971 of the Internal Revenue Code of 1986 if contributions to the plan for the plan year are not less than the minimum required contribution determined under subsection (e) for the plan for the plan year, and

(B) in the case of any applicable plan year beginning on or after January 1, 2008, the minimum required contribution determined under sections 303 of such Act and 430 of such Code shall, for purposes of sections 302 and 303 of such Act and sections 412, 430, and 4971 of such Code, be equal to the minimum required contribution determined under subsection (e) for the plan for the plan year.

(2) ACCRUAL RESTRICTIONS.—

(A) IN GENERAL.—The requirements of this paragraph are met if, effective as of the first day of the first applicable plan year and at

1   all times thereafter while an election under this

2   section is in effect, the plan provides that—

3   (i) the accrued benefit, any death or

4   disability benefit, and any social security

5   supplement described in the last sentence

6   of section 411(a)(9) of such Code and sec-

7   tion 204(b)(1)(G) of such Act, of each par-

8   ticipant are frozen at the amount of such

9   benefit or supplement immediately before

10   such first day, and

11   (ii) all other benefits under the plan

12   are eliminated,

13   but only to the extent the freezing or elimi-

14   nation of such benefits would have been per-

15   mitted under section 411(d)(6) of such Code

16   and section 204(g) of such Act if they had been

17   implemented by a plan amendment adopted im-

18   mediately before such first day.

19   (B) INCREASES IN SECTION 415 LIMITS.—

20   If a plan provides that an accrued benefit of a

21   participant which has been subject to any limi-

22   tation under section 415 of such Code will be

23   increased if such limitation is increased, the

24   plan shall not be treated as meeting the re-

25   quirements of this section unless, effective as of

the first day of the first applicable plan year (or, if later, the date of the enactment of this Act) and at all times thereafter while an election under this section is in effect, the plan provides that any such increase shall not take effect. A plan shall not fail to meet the requirements of section 411(d)(6) of such Code and section 204(g) of such Act solely because the plan is amended to meet the requirements of this subparagraph.

(3) RESTRICTION ON APPLICABLE BENEFIT INCREASES.—

(A) IN GENERAL.—The requirements of this paragraph are met if no applicable benefit increase takes effect at any time during the period beginning on July 26, 2005, and ending on the day before the first day of the first applicable plan year.

(B) APPLICABLE BENEFIT INCREASE.— For purposes of this paragraph, the term "applicable benefit increase" means, with respect to any plan year, any increase in liabilities of the plan by plan amendment (or otherwise provided in regulations provided by the Secretary) which,

1 but for this paragraph, would occur during the

2 plan year by reason of—

3 (i) any increase in benefits,

4 (ii) any change in the accrual of bene-

5 fits, or

6 (iii) any change in the rate at which

7 benefits become nonforfeitable under the

8 plan.

9 (4) EXCEPTION FOR IMPUTED DISABILITY

10 SERVICE.—Paragraphs (2) and (3) shall not apply

11 to any accrual or increase with respect to imputed

12 service provided to a participant during any period

13 of the participant's disability occurring on or after

14 the effective date of the plan amendment providing

15 the restrictions under paragraph (2) (or on or after

16 July 26, 2005, in the case of the restrictions under

17 paragraph (3)) if the participant—

18 (A) was receiving disability benefits as of

19 such date, or

20 (B) was receiving sick pay and subse-

21 quently determined to be eligible for disability

22 benefits as of such date.

23 (c) DEFINITIONS.—For purposes of this section—

24 (1) ELIGIBLE PLAN.—The term "eligible plan"

25 means a defined benefit plan (other than a multiem-

1 ployer plan) to which sections 302 of such Act and

2 412 of such Code applies which is sponsored by an

3 employer—

4   (A) which is a commercial airline pas-

5   senger airline, or

6   (B) the principal business of which is pro-

7   viding catering services to a commercial pas-

8   senger airline.

9   (2) APPLICABLE PLAN YEAR.—The term "ap-

10 plicable plan year" means each plan year to which

11 the election under subsection (a)(1) applies under

12 subsection (d)(1)(A).

13 (d) ELECTIONS AND RELATED TERMS.—

14   (1) YEARS FOR WHICH ELECTION MADE.—

15   (A) ALTERNATIVE FUNDING SCHEDULE.—

16   If an election under subsection (a)(1) was made

17   with respect to an eligible plan, the plan spon-

18   sor may select either a plan year beginning in

19   2006 or a plan year beginning in 2007 as the

20   first plan year to which such election applies.

21   The election shall apply to such plan year and

22   all subsequent years. The election shall be

23   made—

             (i) not later than December 31, 2006, in the case of an election for a plan year beginning in 2006, or

             (ii) not later than December 31, 2007, in the case of an election for a plan year beginning in 2007.

       (B) 10 YEAR AMORTIZATION.—An election under subsection (a)(2) shall be made not later than December 31, 2007.

       (C) ELECTION OF NEW PLAN YEAR FOR ALTERNATIVE FUNDING SCHEDULE.—In the case of an election under subsection (a)(1), the plan sponsor may specify a new plan year in such election and the plan year of the plan may be changed to such new plan year without the approval of the Secretary of the Treasury.

      (2) MANNER OF ELECTION.—A plan sponsor shall make any election under subsection (a) in such manner as the Secretary of the Treasury may prescribe. Such election, once made, may be revoked only with the consent of such Secretary.

   (e) MINIMUM REQUIRED CONTRIBUTION.—In the case of an eligible plan with respect to which an election is made under subsection (a)(1)—

1   (1) IN GENERAL.—In the case of any applicable

2 plan year during the amortization period, the min-

3 imum required contribution shall be the amount nec-

4 essary to amortize the unfunded liability of the plan,

5 determined as of the first day of the plan year, in

6 equal annual installments (until fully amortized)

7 over the remainder of the amortization period. Such

8 amount shall be separately determined for each ap-

9 plicable plan year.

10   (2) YEARS AFTER AMORTIZATION PERIOD.—In

11 the case of any plan year beginning after the end of

12 the amortization period, section 302(a)(2)(A) of

13 such Act and section 412(a)(2)(A) of such Code

14 shall apply to such plan, but the prefunding balance

15 and funding standard carryover balance as of the

16 first day of the first of such years under section

17 303(f) of such Act and section 430(f) of such Code

18 shall be zero.

19   (3) DEFINITIONS.—For purposes of this sec-

20 tion—

21   (A) UNFUNDED LIABILITY.—The term

22   "unfunded liability" means the unfunded ac-

23   crued liability under the plan, determined under

24   the unit credit funding method.

1   (B) AMORTIZATION PERIOD.—The term

2   "amortization period" means the 17-plan year

3   period beginning with the first applicable plan

4   year.

5   (4) OTHER RULES.—In determining the min-

6 imum required contribution and amortization

7 amount under this subsection—

8   (A) the provisions of section 302(c)(3) of

9   such Act and section 412(c)(3) of such Code, as

10   in effect before the date of enactment of this

11   section, shall apply,

12   (B) a rate of interest of 8.85 percent shall

13   be used for all calculations requiring an interest

14   rate, and

15   (C) the value of plan assets shall be equal

16   to their fair market value.

17   (5) SPECIAL RULE FOR CERTAIN PLAN SPIN-

18 OFFS.—For purposes of subsection (b), if, with re-

19 spect to any eligible plan to which this subsection

20 applies—

21   (A) any applicable plan year includes the

22   date of the enactment of this Act,

23   (B) a plan was spun off from the eligible

24   plan during the plan year but before such date

25   of enactment,

1   the minimum required contribution under paragraph

2   (1) for the eligible plan for such applicable plan year

3   shall be an aggregate amount determined as if the

4   plans were a single plan for that plan year (based

5   on the full 12-month plan year in effect prior to the

6   spin-off). The employer shall designate the allocation

7   of such aggregate amount between such plans for

8   the applicable plan year.

9   (f) SPECIAL RULES FOR CERTAIN BALANCES AND

10 WAIVERS.—In the case of an eligible plan with respect to

11 which an election is made under subsection (a)(1)—

12   (1) FUNDING STANDARD ACCOUNT AND CREDIT

13   BALANCES.—Any charge or credit in the funding

14   standard account under section 302 of such Act or

15   section 412 of such Code, and any prefunding bal-

16   ance or funding standard carryover balance under

17   section 303 of such Act or section 430 of such Code,

18   as of the day before the first day of the first applica-

19   ble plan year, shall be reduced to zero.

20   (2) WAIVED FUNDING DEFICIENCIES.—Any

21   waived funding deficiency under sections 302 and

22   303 of such Act or section 412 of such Code, as in

23   effect before the date of enactment of this section,

24   shall be deemed satisfied as of the first day of the

25   first applicable plan year and the amount of such

1   waived funding deficiency shall be taken into ac-

2   count in determining the plan's unfunded liability

3   under subsection (e)(3)(A). In the case of a plan

4   amendment adopted to satisfy the requirements of

5   subsection (b)(2), the plan shall not be deemed to

6   violate section 304(b) of such Act or section 412(f)

7   of such Code, as so in effect, by reason of such

8   amendment or any increase in benefits provided to

9   such plan's participants under a separate plan that

10   is a defined contribution plan or a multiemployer

11   plan.

12   (g) OTHER RULES FOR PLANS MAKING ELECTION

13   UNDER THIS SECTION.—

14   (1) SUCCESSOR PLANS TO CERTAIN PLANS.—

15   If—

16   (A) an election under paragraph (1) or (2)

17   of subsection (a) is in effect with respect to any

18   eligible plan, and

19   (B) the eligible plan is maintained by an

20   employer that establishes or maintains 1 or

21   more other defined benefit plans (other than

22   any multiemployer plan), and such other plans

23   in combination provide benefit accruals to any

24   substantial number of successor employees,

1   the Secretary of the Treasury may, in the Sec-

2   retary's discretion, determine that any trust of

3   which any other such plan is a part does not con-

4   stitute a qualified trust under section 401(a) of the

5   Internal Revenue Code of 1986 unless all benefit ob-

6   ligations of the eligible plan have been satisfied. For

7   purposes of this paragraph, the term "successor em-

8   ployee" means any employee who is or was covered

9   by the eligible plan and any employees who perform

10   substantially the same type of work with respect to

11   the same business operations as an employee covered

12   by such eligible plan.

13   (2) SPECIAL RULES FOR TERMINATIONS.—

14   (A) PBGC LIABILITY LIMITED.—Section

15   4022 of the Employee Retirement Income Secu-

16   rity Act of 1974, as amended by this Act, is

17   amended by adding at the end the following

18   new subsection:

19   "(h) SPECIAL RULE FOR PLANS ELECTING CERTAIN

20   FUNDING REQUIREMENTS.—If any plan makes an elec-

21   tion under section 402(a)(1) of the Pension Protection Act

22   of 2006 and is terminated effective before the end of the

23   10-year period beginning on the first day of the first appli-

24   cable plan year—

25   "(1) this section shall be applied—

1   "(A) by treating the first day of the first

2   applicable plan year as the termination date of

3   the plan, and

4   "(B) by determining the amount of guar-

5   anteed benefits on the basis of plan assets and

6   liabilities as of such assumed termination date,

7   and

8   "(2) notwithstanding section 4044(a), plan as-

9 sets shall first be allocated to pay the amount, if

10 any, by which—

11   "(A) the amount of guaranteed benefits

12   under this section (determined without regard

13   to paragraph (1) and on the basis of plan as-

14   sets and liabilities as of the actual date of plan

15   termination), exceeds

16   "(B) the amount determined under para-

17   graph (1).".

18   (B) TERMINATION PREMIUM.—In applying

19   section 4006(a)(7)(A) of the Employee Retire-

20   ment Income Security Act of 1974 to an eligible

21   plan during any period in which an election

22   under subsection (a)(1) is in effect—

23   (i) "$2,500" shall be substituted for

24   "$1,250" in such section if such plan ter-

25   minates during the 5-year period beginning

1   on the first day of the first applicable plan

2   year with respect to such plan, and

3   (ii) such section shall be applied with-

4   out regard to subparagraph (B) of section

5   8101(d)(2) of the Deficit Reduction Act of

6   2005 (relating to special rule for plans ter-

7   minated in bankruptcy).

8   The substitution described in clause (i) shall

9   not apply with respect to any plan if the Sec-

10   retary of Labor determines that such plan ter-

11   minated as a result of extraordinary cir-

12   cumstances such as a terrorist attack or other

13   similar event.

14   (3) LIMITATION ON DEDUCTIONS UNDER CER-

15   TAIN PLANS.—Section 404(a)(7)(C)(iv) of the Inter-

16   nal Revenue Code of 1986, as added by this Act,

17   shall not apply with respect to any taxable year of

18   a plan sponsor of an eligible plan if any applicable

19   plan year with respect to such plan ends with or

20   within such taxable year.

21   (4) NOTICE.—In the case of a plan amendment

22   adopted in order to comply with this section, any no-

23   tice required under section 204(h) of such Act or

24   section 4980F(e) of such Code shall be provided

25   within 15 days of the effective date of such plan

amendment. This subsection shall not apply to any plan unless such plan is maintained pursuant to one or more collective bargaining agreements between employee representatives and 1 or more employers.

(h) EXCLUSION OF CERTAIN EMPLOYEES FROM MINIMUM COVERAGE REQUIREMENTS.—

(1) IN GENERAL.—Section 410(b)(3) of such Code is amended by striking the last sentence and inserting the following: "For purposes of subparagraph (B), management pilots who are not represented in accordance with title II of the Railway Labor Act shall be treated as covered by a collective bargaining agreement described in such subparagraph if the management pilots manage the flight operations of air pilots who are so represented and the management pilots are, pursuant to the terms of the agreement, included in the group of employees benefitting under the trust described in such subparagraph. Subparagraph (B) shall not apply in the case of a plan which provides contributions or benefits for employees whose principal duties are not customarily performed aboard an aircraft in flight (other than management pilots described in the preceding sentence)."

(2) EFFECTIVE DATE.—The amendment made by this subsection shall apply to years beginning before, on, or after the date of the enactment of this Act.

(i) EXTENSION OF SPECIAL RULE FOR ADDITIONAL FUNDING REQUIREMENTS.—In the case of an employer which is a commercial passenger airline, section 302(d)(12) of the Employee Retirement Income Security Act of 1974 and section 412(l)(12) of the Internal Revenue Code of 1986, as in effect before the date of the enactment of this Act, shall each be applied—

(1) by substituting "December 28, 2007" for "December 28, 2005" in subparagraph (D)(i) thereof, and

(2) without regard to subparagraph (D)(ii).

(j) EFFECTIVE DATE.—Except as otherwise provided in this section, the provisions of and amendments made by this section shall apply to plan years ending after the date of the enactment of this Act.

SEC. 403. LIMITATION ON PBGC GUARANTEE OF SHUT- DOWN AND OTHER BENEFITS.

(a) IN GENERAL.—Section 4022(b) of the Employee Retirement Income Security Act of 1974 (29 U.S.C. 1322(b)) is amended by adding at the end the following:

1   "(8) If an unpredictable contingent event ben-

2   efit (as defined in section 206(g)(1)) is payable by

3   reason of the occurrence of any event, this section

4   shall be applied as if a plan amendment had been

5   adopted on the date such event occurred.".

6   (b) EFFECTIVE DATE.—The amendment made by

7 this section shall apply to benefits that become payable

8 as a result of an event which occurs after July 26, 2005.

9 **SEC. 404. RULES RELATING TO BANKRUPTCY OF EM-**

10   **PLOYER.**

11   (a) GUARANTEE.—Section 4022 of the Employee Re-

12 tirement Income Security Act of 1974 (29 U.S.C. 1322)

13 is amended by adding at the end the following:

14   "(g) BANKRUPTCY FILING SUBSTITUTED FOR TER-

15 MINATION DATE.—If a contributing sponsor of a plan has

16 filed or has had filed against such person a petition seek-

17 ing liquidation or reorganization in a case under title 11,

18 United States Code, or under any similar Federal law or

19 law of a State or political subdivision, and the case has

20 not been dismissed as of the termination date of the plan,

21 then this section shall be applied by treating the date such

22 petition was filed as the termination date of the plan.".

23   (b) ALLOCATION OF ASSETS AMONG PRIORITY

24 GROUPS IN BANKRUPTCY PROCEEDINGS.—Section 4044

25 of the Employee Retirement Income Security Act of 1974

1 (29 U.S.C. 1344) is amended by adding at the end the
2 following:

3   "(e) BANKRUPTCY FILING SUBSTITUTED FOR TER-
4 MINATION DATE.—If a contributing sponsor of a plan has
5 filed or has had filed against such person a petition seek-
6 ing liquidation or reorganization in a case under title 11,
7 United States Code, or under any similar Federal law or
8 law of a State or political subdivision, and the case has
9 not been dismissed as of the termination date of the plan,
10 then subsection (a)(3) shall be applied by treating the date
11 such petition was filed as the termination date of the
12 plan.".

13   (c) EFFECTIVE DATE.—The amendments made this
14 section shall apply with respect to proceedings initiated
15 under title 11, United States Code, or under any similar
16 Federal law or law of a State or political subdivision, on
17 or after the date that is 30 days after the date of enact-
18 ment of this Act.

19 **SEC. 405. PBGC PREMIUMS FOR SMALL PLANS.**

20   (a) SMALL PLANS.—Paragraph (3) of section
21 4006(a) of the Employee Retirement Income Security Act
22 of 1974 (29 U.S.C. 1306(a)) is amended—

23   (1) by striking "The additional" in subpara-
24   graph (E)(i) and inserting "Except as provided in
25   subparagraph (H), the additional", and

1   (2) by inserting after subparagraph (G) the fol-

2   lowing new subparagraph:

3   "(H)(i) In the case of an employer who has 25 or

4 fewer employees on the first day of the plan year, the addi-

5 tional premium determined under subparagraph (E) for

6 each participant shall not exceed $5 multiplied by the

7 number of participants in the plan as of the close of the

8 preceding plan year.

9   "(ii) For purposes of clause (i), whether an employer

10 has 25 or fewer employees on the first day of the plan

11 year is determined by taking into consideration all of the

12 employees of all members of the contributing sponsor's

13 controlled group. In the case of a plan maintained by two

14 or more contributing sponsors, the employees of all con-

15 tributing sponsors and their controlled groups shall be ag-

16 gregated for purposes of determining whether the 25-or-

17 fewer-employees limitation has been satisfied."

18   (b) EFFECTIVE DATES.—The amendment made by

19 this section shall apply to plan years beginning after De-

20 cember 31, 2006.

21 **SEC. 406. AUTHORIZATION FOR PBGC TO PAY INTEREST ON**

22 **PREMIUM OVERPAYMENT REFUNDS.**

23   (a) IN GENERAL.—Section 4007(b) of the Employ-

24 ment Retirement Income Security Act of 1974 (29 U.S.C.

25 1307(b)) is amended—

1   (1) by striking "(b)" and inserting "(b)(1)",

2   and

3   (2) by inserting at the end the following new

4   paragraph:

5   "(2) The corporation is authorized to pay, subject to

6 regulations prescribed by the corporation, interest on the

7 amount of any overpayment of premium refunded to a des-

8 ignated payor. Interest under this paragraph shall be cal-

9 culated at the same rate and in the same manner as inter-

10 est is calculated for underpayments under paragraph (1)."

11   (b) EFFECTIVE DATE.—The amendments made by

12 subsection (a) shall apply to interest accruing for periods

13 beginning not earlier than the date of the enactment of

14 this Act.

15 **SEC. 407. RULES FOR SUBSTANTIAL OWNER BENEFITS IN**

16   **TERMINATED PLANS.**

17   (a) MODIFICATION OF PHASE-IN OF GUARANTEE.—

18 Section 4022(b)(5) of the Employee Retirement Income

19 Security Act of 1974 (29 U.S.C. 1322(b)(5)) is amended

20 to read as follows:

21   "(5)(A) For purposes of this paragraph, the term

22 'majority owner' means an individual who, at any time

23 during the 60-month period ending on the date the deter-

24 mination is being made—

1 "(i) owns the entire interest in an unincor-
2 porated trade or business,

3 "(ii) in the case of a partnership, is a partner
4 who owns, directly or indirectly, 50 percent or more
5 of either the capital interest or the profits interest
6 in such partnership, or

7 "(iii) in the case of a corporation, owns, directly
8 or indirectly, 50 percent or more in value of either
9 the voting stock of that corporation or all the stock
10 of that corporation.

11 For purposes of clause (iii), the constructive ownership
12 rules of section 1563(e) of the Internal Revenue Code of
13 1986 (other than paragraph (3)(C) thereof) shall apply,
14 including the application of such rules under section
15 414(c) of such Code.

16 "(B) In the case of a participant who is a majority
17 owner, the amount of benefits guaranteed under this sec-
18 tion shall equal the product of—

19 "(i) a fraction (not to exceed 1) the numerator
20 of which is the number of years from the later of the
21 effective date or the adoption date of the plan to the
22 termination date, and the denominator of which is
23 10, and

"(ii) the amount of benefits that would be guaranteed under this section if the participant were not a majority owner."

(b) MODIFICATION OF ALLOCATION OF ASSETS.—

(1) Section 4044(a)(4)(B) of the Employee Retirement Income Security Act of 1974 (29 U.S.C. 1344(a)(4)(B)) is amended by striking "section 4022(b)(5)" and inserting "section 4022(b)(5)(B)".

(2) Section 4044(b) of such Act (29 U.S.C. 1344(b)) is amended—

(A) by striking "(5)" in paragraph (2) and inserting "(4), (5),", and

(B) by redesignating paragraphs (3) through (6) as paragraphs (4) through (7), respectively, and by inserting after paragraph (2) the following new paragraph:

"(3) If assets available for allocation under paragraph (4) of subsection (a) are insufficient to satisfy in full the benefits of all individuals who are described in that paragraph, the assets shall be allocated first to benefits described in subparagraph (A) of that paragraph. Any remaining assets shall then be allocated to benefits described in subparagraph (B) of that paragraph. If assets allocated to such subparagraph (B) are insufficient to satisfy in full

1 the benefits described in that subparagraph, the as-

2 sets shall be allocated pro rata among individuals on

3 the basis of the present value (as of the termination

4 date) of their respective benefits described in that

5 subparagraph.''

6 (c) CONFORMING AMENDMENTS.—

7 (1) Section 4021 of the Employee Retirement

8 Income Security Act of 1974 (29 U.S.C. 1321) is

9 amended—

10 (A) in subsection (b)(9), by striking ''as

11 defined in section 4022(b)(6)'', and

12 (B) by adding at the end the following new

13 subsection:

14 ''(d) For purposes of subsection (b)(9), the term 'sub-

15 stantial owner' means an individual who, at any time dur-

16 ing the 60-month period ending on the date the determina-

17 tion is being made—

18 ''(1) owns the entire interest in an unincor-

19 porated trade or business,

20 ''(2) in the case of a partnership, is a partner

21 who owns, directly or indirectly, more than 10 per-

22 cent of either the capital interest or the profits inter-

23 est in such partnership, or

24 ''(3) in the case of a corporation, owns, directly

25 or indirectly, more than 10 percent in value of either

1   the voting stock of that corporation or all the stock

2   of that corporation.

3 For purposes of paragraph (3), the constructive ownership

4 rules of section 1563(e) of the Internal Revenue Code of

5 1986 (other than paragraph (3)(C) thereof) shall apply,

6 including the application of such rules under section

7 414(c) of such Code.''

8   (2) Section 4043(c)(7) of such Act (29 U.S.C.

9   1343(c)(7)) is amended by striking ''section

10   4022(b)(6)'' and inserting ''section 4021(d)''.

11   (d) EFFECTIVE DATES.—

12   (1) IN GENERAL.—Except as provided in para-

13   graph (2), the amendments made by this section

14   shall apply to plan terminations—

15   (A) under section 4041(c) of the Employee

16   Retirement Income Security Act of 1974 (29

17   U.S.C. 1341(c)) with respect to which notices

18   of intent to terminate are provided under sec-

19   tion 4041(a)(2) of such Act (29 U.S.C.

20   1341(a)(2)) after December 31, 2005, and

21   (B) under section 4042 of such Act (29

22   U.S.C. 1342) with respect to which notices of

23   determination are provided under such section

24   after such date.

1   (2) CONFORMING AMENDMENTS.—The amend-

2   ments made by subsection (c) shall take effect on

3   January 1, 2006.

4 SEC. 408. ACCELERATION OF PBGC COMPUTATION OF BEN-

5   EFITS ATTRIBUTABLE TO RECOVERIES FROM

6   EMPLOYERS.

7   (a) MODIFICATION OF AVERAGE RECOVERY PER-

8 CENTAGE OF OUTSTANDING AMOUNT OF BENEFIT LI-

9 ABILITIES PAYABLE BY CORPORATION TO PARTICIPANTS

10 AND BENEFICIARIES.—Section 4022(c)(3)(B)(ii) of the

11 Employee Retirement Income Security Act of 1974 (29

12 U.S.C. 1322(c)(3)(B)(ii)) is amended to read as follows:

13   "(ii) notices of intent to terminate

14   were provided (or in the case of a termi-

15   nation by the corporation, a notice of de-

16   termination under section 4042 was

17   issued) during the 5-Federal fiscal year pe-

18   riod ending with the third fiscal year pre-

19   ceding the fiscal year in which occurs the

20   date of the notice of intent to terminate

21   (or the notice of determination under sec-

22   tion 4042) with respect to the plan termi-

23   nation for which the recovery ratio is being

24   determined."

(b) VALUATION OF SECTION 4062(c) LIABILITY FOR
DETERMINING AMOUNTS PAYABLE BY CORPORATION TO
PARTICIPANTS AND BENEFICIARIES.—

(1) SINGLE-EMPLOYER PLAN BENEFITS GUAR-
ANTEED.—Section 4022(c)(3)(A) of the Employee
Retirement Income Security Act of 1974 (29 U.S.C.
13) is amended to read as follows:

"(A) IN GENERAL.—Except as provided in
subparagraph (C), the term 'recovery ratio'
means the ratio which—

"(i) the sum of the values of all recoveries under section 4062, 4063, or 4064,
determined by the corporation in connection with plan terminations described
under subparagraph (B), bears to

"(ii) the sum of all unfunded benefit
liabilities under such plans as of the termination date in connection with any such
prior termination.".

(2) ALLOCATION OF ASSETS.—Section 4044 of
the Employee Retirement Income Security Act of
1974 (29 U.S.C. 1362) is amended by adding at the
end the following new subsection:

"(e) VALUATION OF SECTION 4062(c) LIABILITY FOR DETERMINING AMOUNTS PAYABLE BY CORPORATION TO PARTICIPANTS AND BENEFICIARIES.—

"(1) IN GENERAL.—In the case of a terminated plan, the value of the recovery of liability under section 4062(c) allocable as a plan asset under this section for purposes of determining the amount of benefits payable by the corporation shall be determined by multiplying—

"(A) the amount of liability under section 4062(c) as of the termination date of the plan, by

"(B) the applicable section 4062(c) recovery ratio.

"(2) SECTION 4062(c) RECOVERY RATIO.—For purposes of this subsection—

"(A) IN GENERAL.—Except as provided in subparagraph (C), the term 'section 4062(c) recovery ratio' means the ratio which—

"(i) the sum of the values of all recoveries under section 4062(c) determined by the corporation in connection with plan terminations described under subparagraph (B), bears to "(ii) the sum of all the amounts of liability under section 4062(c) with respect to such plans as of the termination date in connection with any such prior termination.

"(B) PRIOR TERMINATIONS.—A plan termination described in this subparagraph is a termination with respect to which—

"(i) the value of recoveries under section 4062(c) have been determined by the corporation, and

"(ii) notices of intent to terminate were provided (or in the case of a termination by the corporation, a notice of determination under section 4042 was issued) during the 5-Federal fiscal year period ending with the third fiscal year preceding the fiscal year in which occurs the date of the notice of intent to terminate (or the notice of determination under section 4042) with respect to the plan termination for which the recovery ratio is being determined.

"(C) EXCEPTION.—In the case of a terminated plan with respect to which the outstanding amount of benefit liabilities exceeds $20,000,000, the term 'section 4062(c) recovery ratio' means, with respect to the termination of such plan, the ratio of—

"(i) the value of the recoveries on behalf of the plan under section 4062(c), to

"(ii) the amount of the liability owed under section 4062(c) as of the date of plan termination to the trustee appointed under section 4042 (b) or (c).

"(3) SUBSECTION NOT TO APPLY.—This subsection shall not apply with respect to the determination of—

"(A) whether the amount of outstanding benefit liabilities exceeds $20,000,000, or

"(B) the amount of any liability under section 4062 to the corporation or the trustee appointed under section 4042 (b) or (c).

"(4) DETERMINATIONS.—Determinations under this subsection shall be made by the corporation. Such determinations shall be binding unless shown by clear and convincing evidence to be unreasonable."

(c) EFFECTIVE DATE.—The amendments made by this section shall apply for any termination for which no-

1 tices of intent to terminate are provided (or in the case

2 of a termination by the corporation, a notice of determina-

3 tion under section 4042 under the Employee Retirement

4 Income Security Act of 1974 is issued) on or after the

5 date which is 30 days after the date of enactment of this

6 section.

7 **SEC. 409. TREATMENT OF CERTAIN PLANS WHERE CES-**

8 **SATION OR CHANGE IN MEMBERSHIP OF A**

9 **CONTROLLED GROUP.**

10 (a) IN GENERAL.—Section 4041(b) of the Employee

11 Retirement Income Security Act of 1974 (29 U.S.C.

12 1341(b)) is amended by adding at the end the following

13 new paragraph:

14 "(5) SPECIAL RULE FOR CERTAIN PLANS

15 WHERE CESSATION OR CHANGE IN MEMBERSHIP OF

16 A CONTROLLED GROUP.—

17 "(A) IN GENERAL.—Except as provided in

18 subparagraph (B), if—

19 "(i) there is transaction or series of

20 transactions which result in a person ceas-

21 ing to be a member of a controlled group,

22 and

23 "(ii) such person immediately before

24 the transaction or series of transactions

25 maintained a single-employer plan which is

1   a defined benefit plan which is fully fund-

2   ed,

3   then the interest rate used in determining

4   whether the plan is sufficient for benefit liabil-

5   ities or to otherwise assess plan liabilities for

6   purposes of this subsection or section

7   4042(a)(4) shall be not less than the interest

8   rate used in determining whether the plan is

9   fully funded.

10   "(B) LIMITATIONS.—Subparagraph (A)

11   shall not apply to any transaction or series of

12   transactions unless—

13   "(i) any employer maintaining the

14   plan immediately before or after such

15   transaction or series of transactions—

16   "(I) has an outstanding senior

17   unsecured debt instrument which is

18   rated investment grade by each of the

19   nationally recognized statistical rating

20   organizations for corporate bonds that

21   has issued a credit rating for such in-

22   strument, or

23   "(II) if no such debt instrument

24   of such employer has been rated by

25   such an organization but 1 or more of

1   such organizations has made an issuer

2   credit rating for such employer, all

3   such organizations which have so

4   rated the employer have rated such

5   employer investment grade, and

6   "(ii) the employer maintaining the

7   plan after the transaction or series of

8   transactions employs at least 20 percent of

9   the employees located in the United States

10   who were employed by such employer im-

11   mediately before the transaction or series

12   of transactions.

13   "(C) FULLY FUNDED.—For purposes of

14   subparagraph (A), a plan shall be treated as

15   fully funded with respect to any transaction or

16   series of transactions if—

17   "(i) in the case of a transaction or se-

18   ries of transactions which occur in a plan

19   year beginning before January 1, 2008,

20   the funded current liability percentage de-

21   termined under section 302(d) for the plan

22   year is at least 100 percent, and

23   "(ii) in the case of a transaction or

24   series of transactions which occur in a plan

25   year beginning on or after such date, the

funding target attainment percentage determined under section 303 is, as of the valuation date for such plan year, at least 100 percent.

"(D) 2 YEAR LIMITATION.—Subparagraph (A) shall not apply to any transaction or series of transaction if the plan referred to in subparagraph (A)(ii) is terminated under section 4041(c) or 4042 after the close of the 2-year period beginning on the date on which the first such transaction occurs."

(b) EFFECTIVE DATE.—The amendments made by this section shall apply to any transaction or series of transactions occurring on and after the date of the enactment of this Act.

SEC. 410. MISSING PARTICIPANTS.

(a) IN GENERAL.—Section 4050 of the Employee Retirement Income Security Act of 1974 (29 U.S.C. 1350) is amended by redesignating subsection (c) as subsection (e) and by inserting after subsection (b) the following new subsections:

"(c) MULTIEMPLOYER PLANS.—The corporation shall prescribe rules similar to the rules in subsection (a) for multiemployer plans covered by this title that terminate under section 4041A.

"(d) PLANS NOT OTHERWISE SUBJECT TO TITLE.—

"(1) TRANSFER TO CORPORATION.—The plan administrator of a plan described in paragraph (4) may elect to transfer a missing participant's benefits to the corporation upon termination of the plan.

"(2) INFORMATION TO THE CORPORATION.—To the extent provided in regulations, the plan administrator of a plan described in paragraph (4) shall, upon termination of the plan, provide the corporation information with respect to benefits of a missing participant if the plan transfers such benefits—

"(A) to the corporation, or

"(B) to an entity other than the corporation or a plan described in paragraph (4)(B)(ii).

"(3) PAYMENT BY THE CORPORATION.—If benefits of a missing participant were transferred to the corporation under paragraph (1), the corporation shall, upon location of the participant or beneficiary, pay to the participant or beneficiary the amount transferred (or the appropriate survivor benefit) either—

"(A) in a single sum (plus interest), or

"(B) in such other form as is specified in regulations of the corporation.

1   "(4) PLANS DESCRIBED.—A plan is described

2   in this paragraph if—

3   "(A) the plan is a pension plan (within the

4   meaning of section 3(2))—

5   "(i) to which the provisions of this

6   section do not apply (without regard to

7   this subsection), and

8   "(ii) which is not a plan described in

9   paragraphs (2) through (11) of section

10   4021(b), and

11   "(B) at the time the assets are to be dis-

12   tributed upon termination, the plan—

13   "(i) has missing participants, and

14   "(ii) has not provided for the transfer

15   of assets to pay the benefits of all missing

16   participants to another pension plan (with-

17   in the meaning of section 3(2)).

18   "(5) CERTAIN PROVISIONS NOT TO APPLY.—

19   Subsections (a)(1) and (a)(3) shall not apply to a

20   plan described in paragraph (4).".

21   (b) CONFORMING AMENDMENTS.—Section 206(f) of

22   such Act (29 U.S.C. 1056(f)) is amended—

23   (1) by striking "title IV" and inserting "section

24   4050"; and

25   (2) by striking "the plan shall provide that,".

1   (c) EFFECTIVE DATE.—The amendments made by

2 this section shall apply to distributions made after final

3 regulations implementing subsections (c) and (d) of sec-

4 tion 4050 of the Employee Retirement Income Security

5 Act of 1974 (as added by subsection (a)), respectively, are

6 prescribed.

7 **SEC. 411. DIRECTOR OF THE PENSION BENEFIT GUARANTY**

8   **CORPORATION.**

9   (a) IN GENERAL.—Title IV of the Employee Retire-

10 ment Income Security Act of 1974 (29 U.S.C. 1301 et

11 seq.) is amended—

12   (1) by striking the second sentence of section

13   4002(a) and inserting the following: "In carrying

14   out its functions under this title, the corporation

15   shall be administered by a Director, who shall be ap-

16   pointed by the President, by and with the advice and

17   consent of the Senate, and who shall act in accord-

18   ance with the policies established by the board.";

19   and

20   (2) in section 4003(b), by—

21   (A) striking "under this title, any mem-

22   ber" and inserting "under this title, the Direc-

23   tor, any member"; and

1   (B) striking "designated by the chairman"

2   and inserting "designated by the Director or

3   chairman".

4 (b) COMPENSATION OF DIRECTOR.—Section 5314 of

5 title 5, United States Code, is amended by adding at the

6 end the following new item:

7 "Director, Pension Benefit Guaranty Corporation.".

8 (c) JURISDICTION OF NOMINATION.—

9   (1) IN GENERAL.—The Committee on Finance

10   of the Senate and the Committee on Health, Edu-

11   cation, Labor, and Pensions of the Senate shall have

12   joint jurisdiction over the nomination of a person

13   nominated by the President to fill the position of Di-

14   rector of the Pension Benefit Guaranty Corporation

15   under section 4002 of the Employee Retirement In-

16   come Security Act of 1974 (29 U.S.C. 1302) (as

17   amended by this Act), and if one committee votes to

18   order reported such a nomination, the other shall re-

19   port within 30 calendar days, or be automatically

20   discharged.

21   (2) RULEMAKING OF THE SENATE.—This sub-

22   section is enacted by Congress—

23   (A) as an exercise of rulemaking power of

24   the Senate, and as such it is deemed a part of

25   the rules of the Senate, but applicable only with

1 respect to the procedure to be followed in the

2 Senate in the case of a nomination described in

3 such sentence, and it supersedes other rules

4 only to the extent that it is inconsistent with

5 such rules; and

6   (B) with full recognition of the constitu-

7 tional right of the Senate to change the rules

8 (so far as relating to the procedure of the Sen-

9 ate) at any time, in the same manner and to

10 the same extent as in the case of any other rule

11 of the Senate.

12   (d) TRANSITION.—The term of the individual serving

13 as Executive Director of the Pension Benefit Guaranty

14 Corporation on the date of enactment of this Act shall ex-

15 pire on such date of enactment. Such individual, or any

16 other individual, may serve as interim Director of such

17 Corporation until an individual is appointed as Director

18 of such Corporation under section 4002 of the Employee

19 Retirement Income Security Act of 1974 (29 U.S.C. 1302)

20 (as amended by this Act).

21 **SEC. 412. INCLUSION OF INFORMATION IN THE PBGC AN-**

22   **NUAL REPORT.**

23   Section 4008 of the Employee Retirement Income Se-

24 curity Act of 1974 (29 U.S.C. 1308) is amended by—

1   (1) striking "As soon as practicable" and in-

2 serting "(a) As soon as practicable"; and

3   (2) adding at the end the following:

4 "(b) The report under subsection (a) shall include—

5   "(1) a summary of the Pension Insurance Mod-

6 eling System microsimulation model, including the

7 specific simulation parameters, specific initial values,

8 temporal parameters, and policy parameters used to

9 calculate the financial statements for the corpora-

10 tion;

11   "(2) a comparison of—

12   "(A) the average return on investments

13   earned with respect to assets invested by the

14   corporation for the year to which the report re-

15   lates; and

16   "(B) an amount equal to 60 percent of the

17   average return on investment for such year in

18   the Standard & Poor's 500 Index, plus 40 per-

19   cent of the average return on investment for

20   such year in the Lehman Aggregate Bond

21   Index (or in a similar fixed income index); and

22   "(3) a statement regarding the deficit or sur-

23 plus for such year that the corporation would have

24 had if the corporation had earned the return de-

1 scribed in paragraph (2)(B) with respect to assets

2 invested by the corporation.".

TITLE V—DISCLOSURE

SEC. 501. DEFINED BENEFIT PLAN FUNDING NOTICE.

5 (a) IN GENERAL.—Section 101(f) of the Employee

6 Retirement Income Security Act of 1974 (29 U.S.C.

7 1021(f)) is amended to read as follows:

8 "(f) DEFINED BENEFIT PLAN FUNDING NOTICES.—

9 "(1) IN GENERAL.—The administrator of a de-

10 fined benefit plan to which title IV applies shall for

11 each plan year provide a plan funding notice to the

12 Pension Benefit Guaranty Corporation, to each plan

13 participant and beneficiary, to each labor organiza-

14 tion representing such participants or beneficiaries,

15 and, in the case of a multiemployer plan, to each

16 employer that has an obligation to contribute to the

17 plan.

18 "(2) INFORMATION CONTAINED IN NOTICES.—

19 "(A) IDENTIFYING INFORMATION.—Each

20 notice required under paragraph (1) shall con-

21 tain identifying information, including the name

22 of the plan, the address and phone number of

23 the plan administrator and the plan's principal

24 administrative officer, each plan sponsor's em-

1   ployer identification number, and the plan num-
2   ber of the plan.

3   "(B) SPECIFIC INFORMATION.—A plan
4   funding notice under paragraph (1) shall in-
5   clude—

6   "(i)(I) in the case of a single-employer
7   plan, a statement as to whether the plan's
8   funding target attainment percentage (as
9   defined in section 303(d)(2)) for the plan
10   year to which the notice relates, and for
11   the 2 preceding plan years, is at least 100
12   percent (and, if not, the actual percent-
13   ages), or

14   "(II) in the case of a multiemployer
15   plan, a statement as to whether the plan's
16   funded percentage (as defined in section
17   305(i)) for the plan year to which the no-
18   tice relates, and for the 2 preceding plan
19   years, is at least 100 percent (and, if not,
20   the actual percentages),

21   "(ii)(I) in the case of a single-em-
22   ployer plan, a statement of—

23   "(aa) the total assets (separately
24   stating the prefunding balance and
25   the funding standard carryover bal-

1 ance) and liabilities of the plan, deter-

2 mined in the same manner as under

3 section 303, for the plan year for

4 which the latest annual report filed

5 under section 104(a) was filed and for

6 the 2 preceding plan years, as re-

7 ported in the annual report for each

8 such plan year, and

9 "(bb) the value of the plan's as-

10 sets and liabilities for the plan year to

11 which the notice relates as of the last

12 day of the plan year to which the no-

13 tice relates determined using the asset

14 valuation under subclause (II) of sec-

15 tion 4006(a)(3)(E)(iii) and the inter-

16 est rate under section

17 4006(a)(3)(E)(iv), and

18 "(II) in the case of a multiemployer

19 plan, a statement of the value of the plan's

20 assets and liabilities for the plan year to

21 which the notice relates as the last day of

22 such plan year and the preceding 2 plan

23 years,

24 "(iii) a statement of the number of

25 participants who are—

432

1   "(I) retired or separated from

2   service and are receiving benefits,

3   "(II) retired or separated partici-

4   pants entitled to future benefits, and

5   "(III) active participants under

6   the plan,

7   "(iv) a statement setting forth the

8   funding policy of the plan and the asset al-

9   location of investments under the plan (ex-

10   pressed as percentages of total assets) as

11   of the end of the plan year to which the

12   notice relates,

13   "(v) in the case of a multiemployer

14   plan, whether the plan was in critical or

15   endangered status under section 305 for

16   such plan year and, if so—

17   "(I) a statement describing how

18   a person may obtain a copy of the

19   plan's funding improvement or reha-

20   bilitation plan, as appropriate, adopt-

21   ed under section 305 and the actu-

22   arial and financial data that dem-

23   onstrate any action taken by the plan

24   toward fiscal improvement, and

1   "(II) a summary of any funding

2   improvement plan, rehabilitation plan,

3   or modification thereof adopted under

4   section 305 during the plan year to

5   which the notice relates,

6   "(vi) in the case of any plan amend-

7   ment, scheduled benefit increase or reduc-

8   tion, or other known event taking effect in

9   the current plan year and having a mate-

10   rial effect on plan liabilities or assets for

11   the year (as defined in regulations by the

12   Secretary), an explanation of the amend-

13   ment, schedule increase or reduction, or

14   event, and a projection to the end of such

15   plan year of the effect of the amendment,

16   scheduled increase or reduction, or event

17   on plan liabilities,

18   "(vii)(I) in the case of a single-em-

19   ployer plan, a summary of the rules gov-

20   erning termination of single-employer plans

21   under subtitle C of title IV, or

22   "(II) in the case of a multiemployer

23   plan, a summary of the rules governing re-

24   organization or insolvency, including the

25   limitations on benefit payments,

1   "(viii) a general description of the

2   benefits under the plan which are eligible

3   to be guaranteed by the Pension Benefit

4   Guaranty Corporation, along with an ex-

5   planation of the limitations on the guar-

6   antee and the circumstances under which

7   such limitations apply,

8   "(ix) a statement that a person may

9   obtain a copy of the annual report of the

10   plan filed under section 104(a) upon re-

11   quest, through the Internet website of the

12   Department of Labor, or through an

13   Intranet website maintained by the appli-

14   cable plan sponsor (or plan administrator

15   on behalf of the plan sponsor), and

16   "(x) if applicable, a statement that

17   each contributing sponsor, and each mem-

18   ber of the contributing sponsor's controlled

19   group, of the single-employer plan was re-

20   quired to provide the information under

21   section 4010 for the plan year to which the

22   notice relates.

23   "(C) OTHER INFORMATION.—Each notice

24 under paragraph (1) shall include—

1   "(i) in the case of a multiemployer

2   plan, a statement that the plan adminis-

3   trator shall provide, upon written request,

4   to any labor organization representing plan

5   participants and beneficiaries and any em-

6   ployer that has an obligation to contribute

7   to the plan, a copy of the annual report

8   filed with the Secretary under section

9   104(a), and

10   "(ii) any additional information which

11   the plan administrator elects to include to

12   the extent not inconsistent with regulations

13   prescribed by the Secretary.

14   "(3) TIME FOR PROVIDING NOTICE.—

15   "(A) IN GENERAL.—Any notice under

16   paragraph (1) shall be provided not later than

17   120 days after the end of the plan year to

18   which the notice relates.

19   "(B) EXCEPTION FOR SMALL PLANS.—In

20   the case of a small plan (as such term is used

21   under section 303(g)(2)(B)) any notice under

22   paragraph (1) shall be provided upon filing of

23   the annual report under section 104(a).

24   "(4) FORM AND MANNER.—Any notice under

25 paragraph (1)—

1   "(A) shall be provided in a form and man-

2   ner prescribed in regulations of the Secretary,

3   "(B) shall be written in a manner so as to

4   be understood by the average plan participant,

5   and

6   "(C) may be provided in written, elec-

7   tronic, or other appropriate form to the extent

8   such form is reasonably accessible to persons to

9   whom the notice is required to be provided.".

10   (b) REPEAL OF NOTICE TO PARTICIPANTS OF FUND-

11 ING STATUS.—

12   (1) IN GENERAL.—Title IV of such Act (29

13   U.S.C. 1301 et seq.) is amended by striking section

14   4011.

15   (2) CLERICAL AMENDMENT.—Section 1 of such

16   Act is amended in the table of contents by striking

17   the item relating to section 4011.

18   (c) MODEL NOTICE.—Not later than 1 year after the

19 date of the enactment of this Act, the Secretary of Labor

20 shall publish a model version of the notice required by sec-

21 tion 101(f) of the Employee Retirement Income Security

22 Act of 1974. The Secretary of Labor may promulgate any

23 interim final rules as the Secretary determines appropriate

24 to carry out the provisions of this subsection.

25   (d) EFFECTIVE DATE.—

1   (1) IN GENERAL.—The amendments made by
2   this section shall apply to plan years beginning after
3   December 31, 2007, except that the amendment
4   made by subsection (b) shall apply to plan years be-
5   ginning after December 31, 2006.

6   (2) TRANSITION RULE.—Any requirement
7   under section 101(f) of the Employee Retirement In-
8   come Security Act of 1974 (as amended by this sec-
9   tion) to report the funding target attainment per-
10   centage or funded percentage of a plan with respect
11   to any plan year beginning before January 1, 2008,
12   shall be treated as met if the plan reports—

13   (A) in the case of a plan year beginning in
14   2006, the funded current liability percentage
15   (as defined in section 302(d)(8) of such Act) of
16   the plan for such plan year, and

17   (B) in the case of a plan year beginning in
18   2007, the funding target attainment percentage
19   or funded percentage as determined using such
20   methods of estimation as the Secretary of the
21   Treasury may provide.

22 **SEC. 502. ACCESS TO MULTIEMPLOYER PENSION PLAN IN-**
23   **FORMATION.**

24   (a) FINANCIAL INFORMATION WITH RESPECT TO
25 MULTIEMPLOYER PLANS.—

1   (1) IN GENERAL.—Section 101 of the Employee

2 Retirement Income Security Act of 1974 (29 U.S.C.

3 1021), as amended by section 103, is amended—

4   (A) by redesignating subsection (k) as sub-

5   section (l); and

6   (B) by inserting after subsection (j) the

7   following new subsection:

8 "(k) MULTIEMPLOYER PLAN INFORMATION MADE

9 AVAILABLE ON REQUEST.—

10   "(1) IN GENERAL.—Each administrator of a

11   multiemployer plan shall, upon written request, fur-

12   nish to any plan participant or beneficiary, employee

13   representative, or any employer that has an obliga-

14   tion to contribute to the plan—

15   "(A) a copy of any periodic actuarial re-

16   port (including any sensitivity testing) received

17   by the plan for any plan year which has been

18   in the plan's possession for at least 30 days,

19   "(B) a copy of any quarterly, semi-annual,

20   or annual financial report prepared for the plan

21   by any plan investment manager or advisor or

22   other fiduciary which has been in the plan's

23   possession for at least 30 days, and

24   "(C) a copy of any application filed with

25   the Secretary of the Treasury requesting an ex-

tension under section 304 of this Act or section 431(d) of the Internal Revenue Code of 1986 and the determination of such Secretary pursuant to such application.

"(2) COMPLIANCE.—Information required to be provided under paragraph (1) —

"(A) shall be provided to the requesting participant, beneficiary, or employer within 30 days after the request in a form and manner prescribed in regulations of the Secretary,

"(B) may be provided in written, electronic, or other appropriate form to the extent such form is reasonably accessible to persons to whom the information is required to be provided, and

"(C) shall not—

"(i) include any individually identifiable information regarding any plan participant, beneficiary, employee, fiduciary, or contributing employer, or

"(ii) reveal any proprietary information regarding the plan, any contributing employer, or entity providing services to the plan.

1   "(3) LIMITATIONS.—In no case shall a partici-

2   pant, beneficiary, or employer be entitled under this

3   subsection to receive more than one copy of any re-

4   port or application described in paragraph (1) dur-

5   ing any one 12-month period. The administrator

6   may make a reasonable charge to cover copying,

7   mailing, and other costs of furnishing copies of in-

8   formation pursuant to paragraph (1). The Secretary

9   may by regulations prescribe the maximum amount

10   which will constitute a reasonable charge under the

11   preceding sentence.".

12   (2) ENFORCEMENT.—Section 502(c)(4) of such

13   Act (29 U.S.C. 1132(c)(4)) is amended by striking

14   "section 101(j)" and inserting "subsection (j) or (k)

15   of section 101".

16   (3) REGULATIONS.—The Secretary shall pre-

17   scribe regulations under section 101(k)(2) of the

18   Employee Retirement Income Security Act of 1974

19   (as added by paragraph (1)) not later than 1 year

20   after the date of the enactment of this Act.

21   (b) NOTICE OF POTENTIAL WITHDRAWAL LIABILITY

22 TO MULTIEMPLOYER PLANS.—

23   (1) IN GENERAL.—Section 101 of such Act (as

24   amended by subsection (a)) is amended—

1   (A) by redesignating subsection (l) as sub-

2   section (m); and

3   (B) by inserting after subsection (k) the

4   following new subsection:

5   "(l) NOTICE OF POTENTIAL WITHDRAWAL LIABIL-

6 ITY.—

7   "(1) IN GENERAL.—The plan sponsor or ad-

8   ministrator of a multiemployer plan shall, upon writ-

9   ten request, furnish to any employer who has an ob-

10   ligation to contribute to the plan a notice of—

11   "(A) the estimated amount which would be

12   the amount of such employer's withdrawal li-

13   ability under part 1 of subtitle E of title IV if

14   such employer withdrew on the last day of the

15   plan year preceding the date of the request, and

16   "(B) an explanation of how such estimated

17   liability amount was determined, including the

18   actuarial assumptions and methods used to de-

19   termine the value of the plan liabilities and as-

20   sets, the data regarding employer contributions,

21   unfunded vested benefits, annual changes in the

22   plan's unfunded vested benefits, and the appli-

23   cation of any relevant limitations on the esti-

24   mated withdrawal liability.

For purposes of subparagraph (B), the term 'employer contribution' means, in connection with a participant, a contribution made by an employer as an employer of such participant.

"(2) COMPLIANCE.—Any notice required to be provided under paragraph (1)—

"(A) shall be provided in a form and manner prescribed in regulations of the Secretary to the requesting employer within—

"(i) 180 days after the request, or

"(ii) subject to regulations of the Secretary, such longer time as may be necessary in the case of a plan that determines withdrawal liability based on any method described under paragraph (4) or (5) of section 4211(c); and

"(B) may be provided in written, electronic, or other appropriate form to the extent such form is reasonably accessible to employers to whom the information is required to be provided.

"(3) LIMITATIONS.—In no case shall an employer be entitled under this subsection to receive more than one notice described in paragraph (1) during any one 12-month period. The person re-

1 quired to provide such notice may make a reasonable

2 charge to cover copying, mailing, and other costs of

3 furnishing such notice pursuant to paragraph (1).

4 The Secretary may by regulations prescribe the max-

5 imum amount which will constitute a reasonable

6 charge under the preceding sentence.".

7   (2) ENFORCEMENT.—Section 502(c)(4) of such

8   Act (29 U.S.C. 1132(c)(4)) is amended by striking

9   "section 101(j) or (k)" and inserting "subsection (j),

10   (k), or (l) of section 101".

11 (c) NOTICE OF AMENDMENT REDUCING FUTURE AC-

12 CRUALS.—

13   (1) AMENDMENT OF ERISA.—Section 204(h)(1)

14   of such Act (29 U.S.C. 1054(h)(1)) is amended by

15   inserting at the end before the period the following:

16   "and to each employer who has an obligation to con-

17   tribute to the plan.".

18   (2) AMENDMENT OF INTERNAL REVENUE

19   CODE.—Section 4980F(e)(1) of such Code is amend-

20   ed by adding at the end before the period the fol-

21   lowing: "and to each employer who has an obligation

22   to contribute to the plan.".

23 (d) EFFECTIVE DATE.—The amendments made by

24 this section shall apply to plan years beginning after De-

25 cember 31, 2007.

SEC. 503. ADDITIONAL ANNUAL REPORTING REQUIRE-MENTS.

(a) ADDITIONAL ANNUAL REPORTING REQUIRE-MENTS WITH RESPECT TO DEFINED BENEFIT PLANS.—

(1) IN GENERAL.—Section 103 of the Employee Retirement Income Security Act of 1974 (29 U.S.C. 1023) is amended—

(A) in subsection (a)(1)(B), by striking "subsections (d) and (e)" and inserting "subsections (d), (e), and (f)"; and

(B) by adding at the end the following new subsection:

"(f) ADDITIONAL INFORMATION WITH RESPECT TO DEFINED BENEFIT PLANS.—

"(1) LIABILITIES UNDER 2 OR MORE PLANS.—

"(A) IN GENERAL.—In any case in which any liabilities to participants or their beneficiaries under a defined benefit plan as of the end of a plan year consist (in whole or in part) of liabilities to such participants and beneficiaries under 2 or more pension plans as of immediately before such plan year, an annual report under this section for such plan year shall include the funded percentage of each of such 2 or more pension plans as of the last day of such plan year and the funded percentage of

the plan with respect to which the annual report is filed as of the last day of such plan
year.

"(B) FUNDED PERCENTAGE.—For pur-
poses of this paragraph, the term 'funded percentage'—

"(i) in the case of a single-employer
plan, means the funding target attainment
percentage, as defined in section
303(d)(2), and

"(ii) in the case of a multiemployer
plan, has the meaning given such term in
section 305(i)(2).

"(2) ADDITIONAL INFORMATION FOR MULTIEM-
PLOYER PLANS.—With respect to any defined benefit plan which is a multiemployer plan, an annual
report under this section for a plan year shall include, in addition to the information required under
paragraph (1), the following, as of the end of the
plan year to which the report relates:

"(A) The number of employers obligated to
contribute to the plan.

"(B) A list of the employers that contributed more than 5 percent of the total contributions to the plan during such plan year.

1   "(C) The number of participants under the

2   plan on whose behalf no contributions were

3   made by an employer as an employer of the

4   participant for such plan year and for each of

5   the 2 preceding plan years.

6   "(D) The ratios of—

7   "(i) the number of participants under

8   the plan on whose behalf no employer had

9   an obligation to make an employer con-

10   tribution during the plan year, to

11   "(ii) the number of participants under

12   the plan on whose behalf no employer had

13   an obligation to make an employer con-

14   tribution during each of the 2 preceding

15   plan years.

16   "(E) Whether the plan received an amorti-

17   zation extension under section 304(d) of this

18   Act or section 431(d) of the Internal Revenue

19   Code of 1986 for such plan year and, if so, the

20   amount of the difference between the minimum

21   required contribution for the year and the min-

22   imum required contribution which would have

23   been required without regard to the extension,

24   and the period of such extension.

1   "(F) Whether the plan used the shortfall

2   funding method (as such term is used in section

3   305) for such plan year and, if so, the amount

4   of the difference between the minimum required

5   contribution for the year and the minimum re-

6   quired contribution which would have been re-

7   quired without regard to the use of such meth-

8   od, and the period of use of such method.

9   "(G) Whether the plan was in critical or

10   endangered status under section 305 for such

11   plan year, and if so, a summary of any funding

12   improvement or rehabilitation plan (or modi-

13   fication thereto) adopted during the plan year,

14   and the funded percentage of the plan.

15   "(H) The number of employers that with-

16   drew from the plan during the preceding plan

17   year and the aggregate amount of withdrawal

18   liability assessed, or estimated to be assessed,

19   against such withdrawn employers.

20   "(I) In the case of a multiemployer plan

21   that has merged with another plan or to which

22   assets and liabilities have been transferred, the

23   actuarial valuation of the assets and liabilities

24   of each affected plan during the year preceding

25   the effective date of the merger or transfer,

1   based upon the most recent data available as of

2   the day before the first day of the plan year, or

3   other valuation method performed under stand-

4   ards and procedures as the Secretary may pre-

5   scribe by regulation.".

6   (2) GUIDANCE BY SECRETARY OF LABOR.—Not

7 later than 1 year after the date of enactment of this

8 Act, the Secretary of Labor shall publish guidance

9 to assist multiemployer defined benefit plans to—

10   (A) identify and enumerate plan partici-

11   pants for whom there is no employer with an

12   obligation to make an employer contribution

13   under the plan; and

14   (B) report such information under section

15   103(f)(2)(D) of the Employee Retirement In-

16   come Security Act of 1974 (as added by this

17   section).

18 (b) ADDITIONAL INFORMATION IN ANNUAL ACTU-

19 ARIAL STATEMENT REGARDING PLAN RETIREMENT PRO-

20 JECTIONS.—Section 103(d) of such Act (29 U.S.C.

21 1023(d)) is amended—

22   (1) by redesignating paragraphs (12) and (13)

23 as paragraphs (13) and (14), respectively; and

24   (2) by inserting after paragraph (11) the fol-

25 lowing new paragraph:

449

1   "(12) A statement explaining the actuarial as-

2   sumptions and methods used in projecting future re-

3   tirements and forms of benefit distributions under

4   the plan.".

5   (c) REPEAL OF SUMMARY ANNUAL REPORT RE-

6 QUIREMENT FOR DEFINED BENEFIT PLANS.—

7   (1) IN GENERAL.—Section 104(b)(3) of such

8   Act (29 U.S.C. 1024(b)(3)) is amended by inserting

9   "(other than an administrator of a defined benefit

10   plan to which the requirements of section 103(f) ap-

11   plies)" after "the administrators".

12   (2) CONFORMING AMENDMENTS.—Section

13   101(a)(2) of such Act (29 U.S.C. 1021(a)(2)) is

14   amended by inserting "subsection (f) and" before

15   "sections 104(b)(3) and 105(a) and (c)".

16   (d) FURNISHING SUMMARY PLAN INFORMATION TO

17 EMPLOYERS AND EMPLOYEE REPRESENTATIVES OF

18 MULTIEMPLOYER PLANS.—Section 104 of such Act (29

19 U.S.C. 1024) is amended—

20   (1) in the header, by striking "**PARTICI-**

21   **PANTS**" and inserting "**PARTICIPANTS AND CER-**

22   **TAIN EMPLOYERS**";

23   (2) redesignating subsection (d) as subsection

24   (e); and

25   (3) inserting after subsection (c) the following:

"(d) Furnishing Summary Plan Information to Employers and Employee Representatives of Multiemployer Plans.—

"(1) In general.—With respect to a multiemployer plan subject to this section, within 30 days after the due date under subsection (a)(1) for the filing of the annual report for the fiscal year of the plan, the administrators shall furnish to each employee organization and to each employer with an obligation to contribute to the plan a report that contains—

"(A) a description of the contribution schedules and benefit formulas under the plan, and any modification to such schedules and formulas, during such plan year;

"(B) the number of employers obligated to contribute to the plan;

"(C) a list of the employers that contributed more than 5 percent of the total contributions to the plan during such plan year;

"(D) the number of participants under the plan on whose behalf no contributions were made by an employer as an employer of the participant for such plan year and for each of the 2 preceding plan years;

1   "(E) whether the plan was in critical or

2   endangered status under section 305 for such

3   plan year and, if so, include—

4   "(i) a list of the actions taken by the

5   plan to improve its funding status; and

6   "(ii) a statement describing how a

7   person may obtain a copy of the plan's im-

8   provement or rehabilitation plan, as appli-

9   cable, adopted under section 305 and the

10   actuarial and financial data that dem-

11   onstrate any action taken by the plan to-

12   ward fiscal improvement;

13   "(F) the number of employers that with-

14   drew from the plan during the preceding plan

15   year and the aggregate amount of withdrawal

16   liability assessed, or estimated to be assessed,

17   against such withdrawn employers, as reported

18   on the annual report for the plan year to which

19   the report under this subsection relates;

20   "(G) in the case of a multiemployer plan

21   that has merged with another plan or to which

22   assets and liabilities have been transferred, the

23   actuarial valuation of the assets and liabilities

24   of each affected plan during the year preceding

25   the effective date of the merger or transfer,

1 based upon the most recent data available as of

2 the day before the first day of the plan year, or

3 other valuation method performed under stand-

4 ards and procedures as the Secretary may pre-

5 scribe by regulation;

6 "(H) a description as to whether the

7 plan—

8 "(i) sought or received an amortiza-

9 tion extension under section 304(d) of this

10 Act or section 431(d) of the Internal Rev-

11 enue Code of 1986 for such plan year; or

12 "(ii) used the shortfall funding meth-

13 od (as such term is used in section 305)

14 for such plan year; and

15 "(I) notification of the right under this

16 section of the recipient to a copy of the annual

17 report filed with the Secretary under subsection

18 (a), summary plan description, summary of any

19 material modification of the plan, upon written

20 request, but that—

21 "(i) in no case shall a recipient be en-

22 titled to receive more than one copy of any

23 such document described during any one

24 12-month period; and

1   "(ii) the administrator may make a

2   reasonable charge to cover copying, mail-

3   ing, and other costs of furnishing copies of

4   information pursuant to this subpara-

5   graph.

6   "(2) EFFECT OF SUBSECTION.—Nothing in this

7 subsection waives any other provision under this title

8 requiring plan administrators to provide, upon re-

9 quest, information to employers that have an obliga-

10 tion to contribute under the plan.".

11   (e) MODEL FORM.—Not later than 1 year after the

12 date of the enactment of this Act, the Secretary of Labor

13 shall publish a model form for providing the statements,

14 schedules, and other material required to be provided

15 under section 101(f) of the Employee Retirement Income

16 Security Act of 1974, as amended by this section. The

17 Secretary of Labor may promulgate any interim final rules

18 as the Secretary determines appropriate to carry out the

19 provisions of this subsection.

20   (f) EFFECTIVE DATE.—The amendments made by

21 this section shall apply to plan years beginning after De-

22 cember 31, 2007.

1 **SEC. 504. ELECTRONIC DISPLAY OF ANNUAL REPORT IN-**
2   **FORMATION.**

3   (a) ELECTRONIC DISPLAY OF INFORMATION.—Sec-
4 tion 104(b) of such Act (29 U.S.C. 1024(b)) is amended
5 by adding at the end the following:

6   "(5) Identification and basic plan information and ac-
7 tuarial information included in the annual report for any
8 plan year shall be filed with the Secretary in an electronic
9 format which accommodates display on the Internet, in ac-
10 cordance with regulations which shall be prescribed by the
11 Secretary. The Secretary shall provide for display of such
12 information included in the annual report, within 90 days
13 after the date of the filing of the annual report, on an
14 Internet website maintained by the Secretary and other
15 appropriate media. Such information shall also be dis-
16 played on any Intranet website maintained by the plan
17 sponsor (or by the plan administrator on behalf of the plan
18 sponsor) for the purpose of communicating with employees
19 and not the public, in accordance with regulations which
20 shall be prescribed by the Secretary.".

21   (b) EFFECTIVE DATE.—The amendments made by
22 this section shall apply to plan years beginning after De-
23 cember 31, 2007.

24 **SEC. 505. SECTION 4010 FILINGS WITH THE PBGC.**

25   (a) CHANGE IN CRITERIA FOR PERSONS REQUIRED
26 TO PROVIDE INFORMATION TO PBGC.—Section 4010(b)

1 of the Employee Retirement Income Security Act of 1974

2 (29 U.S.C. 1310(b)) is amended by striking paragraph (1)

3 and inserting the following:

4   "(1) the funding target attainment percentage

5   (as defined in subsection (d)) at the end of the pre-

6   ceding plan year of a plan maintained by the con-

7   tributing sponsor or any member of its controlled

8   group is less than 80 percent;".

9   (b) ADDITIONAL INFORMATION REQUIRED.—Section

10 4010 of the Employee Retirement Income Security Act of

11 1974 (29 U.S.C. 1310) is amended by adding at the end

12 the following new subsection:

13   "(d) ADDITIONAL INFORMATION REQUIRED.—

14   "(1) IN GENERAL.—The information submitted

15   to the corporation under subsection (a) shall in-

16   clude—

17   "(A) the amount of benefit liabilities under

18   the plan determined using the assumptions used

19   by the corporation in determining liabilities;

20   "(B) the funding target of the plan deter-

21   mined as if the plan has been in at-risk status

22   for at least 5 plan years; and

23   "(C) the funding target attainment per-

24   centage of the plan.

1   "(2) DEFINITIONS.—For purposes of this sub-

2   section:

3   "(A) FUNDING TARGET.—The term 'fund-

4   ing target' has the meaning provided under sec-

5   tion 303(d)(1).

6   "(B) FUNDING TARGET ATTAINMENT PER-

7   CENTAGE.—The term 'funding target attain-

8   ment percentage' has the meaning provided

9   under section 302(d)(2).

10   "(C) AT-RISK STATUS.—The term 'at-risk

11   status' has the meaning provided in section

12   303(i)(4).

13   "(e) NOTICE TO CONGRESS.—The corporation shall,

14 on an annual basis, submit to the Committee on Health,

15 Education, Labor, and Pensions and the Committee on Fi-

16 nance of the Senate and the Committee on Education and

17 the Workforce and the Committee on Ways and Means

18 of the House of Representatives, a summary report in the

19 aggregate of the information submitted to the corporation

20 under this section.".

21   (c) EFFECTIVE DATE.—The amendments made by

22 this section shall apply with respect to years beginning

23 after 2007.

SEC. 506. DISCLOSURE OF TERMINATION INFORMATION TO PLAN PARTICIPANTS.

(a) DISTRESS TERMINATIONS.—

(1) IN GENERAL.—Section 4041(c)(2) of the Employee Retirement Income Security Act of 1974 (29 U.S.C. 1341(c)(2)) is amended by adding at the end the following:

"(D) DISCLOSURE OF TERMINATION IN-FORMATION.—

"(i) IN GENERAL.—A plan adminis-trator that has filed a notice of intent to terminate under subsection (a)(2) shall provide to an affected party any informa-tion provided to the corporation under sub-section (a)(2) not later than 15 days after—

"(I) receipt of a request from the affected party for the information; or

"(II) the provision of new infor-mation to the corporation relating to a previous request.

"(ii) CONFIDENTIALITY.—

"(I) IN GENERAL.—The plan ad-ministrator shall not provide informa-tion under clause (i) in a form that includes any information that may di-

1   rectly or indirectly be associated with,

2   or otherwise identify, an individual

3   participant or beneficiary.

4   "(II) LIMITATION.—A court may

5   limit disclosure under this subpara-

6   graph of confidential information de-

7   scribed in section 552(b) of title 5,

8   United States Code, to any authorized

9   representative of the participants or

10   beneficiaries that agrees to ensure the

11   confidentiality of such information.

12   "(iii) FORM AND MANNER OF INFOR-

13   MATION; CHARGES.—

14   "(I) FORM AND MANNER.—The

15   corporation may prescribe the form

16   and manner of the provision of infor-

17   mation under this subparagraph,

18   which shall include delivery in written,

19   electronic, or other appropriate form

20   to the extent that such form is rea-

21   sonably accessible to individuals to

22   whom the information is required to

23   be provided.

24   "(II) REASONABLE CHARGES.—A

25   plan administrator may charge a rea-

1   sonable fee for any information pro-

2   vided under this subparagraph in

3   other than electronic form.

4   "(iv) AUTHORIZED REPRESENTA-

5   TIVE.—For purposes of this subparagraph,

6   the term 'authorized representative' means

7   any employee organization representing

8   participants in the pension plan.".

9   (2) CONFORMING AMENDMENT.—Section

10 4041(c)(1) of the Employee Retirement Income Se-

11 curity Act of 1974 (29 U.S.C. 1341(c)(1)) is amend-

12 ed in subparagraph (C) by striking "subparagraph

13 (B)" and inserting "subparagraphs (B) and (D)".

14 (b) INVOLUNTARY TERMINATIONS.—

15 (1) IN GENERAL.—Section 4042(c) of the Em-

16 ployee Retirement Income Security Act of 1974 (29

17 U.S.C. 1342(c)) is amended by—

18 (A) striking "(c) If the" and inserting

19 "(c)(1) If the";

20 (B) redesignating paragraph (3) as para-

21 graph (2); and

22 (C) adding at the end the following:

23 "(3) DISCLOSURE OF TERMINATION INFORMA-

24 TION.—

25 "(A) IN GENERAL.—

1   "(i) INFORMATION FROM PLAN SPON-

2   SOR OR ADMINISTRATOR.—A plan sponsor

3   or plan administrator of a single-employer

4   plan that has received a notice from the

5   corporation of a determination that the

6   plan should be terminated under this sec-

7   tion shall provide to an affected party any

8   information provided to the corporation in

9   connection with the plan termination.

10   "(ii) INFORMATION FROM CORPORA-

11   TION.—The corporation shall provide a

12   copy of the administrative record, includ-

13   ing the trusteeship decision record of a ter-

14   mination of a plan described under clause

15   (i).

16   "(B) TIMING OF DISCLOSURE.—The plan

17   sponsor, plan administrator, or the corporation,

18   as applicable, shall provide the information de-

19   scribed in subparagraph (A) not later than 15

20   days after—

21   "(i) receipt of a request from an af-

22   fected party for such information; or

23   "(ii) in the case of information de-

24   scribed under subparagraph (A)(i), the

25   provision of any new information to the

461

1 corporation relating to a previous request

2 by an affected party.

3 "(C) CONFIDENTIALITY.—

4 "(i) IN GENERAL.—The plan adminis-

5 trator and plan sponsor shall not provide

6 information under subparagraph (A)(i) in

7 a form which includes any information that

8 may directly or indirectly be associated

9 with, or otherwise identify, an individual

10 participant or beneficiary.

11 "(ii) LIMITATION.—A court may limit

12 disclosure under this paragraph of con-

13 fidential information described in section

14 552(b) of title 5, United States Code, to

15 authorized representatives (within the

16 meaning of section 4041(c)(2)(D)(iv)) of

17 the participants or beneficiaries that agree

18 to ensure the confidentiality of such infor-

19 mation.

20 "(D) FORM AND MANNER OF INFORMA-

21 TION; CHARGES.—

22 "(i) FORM AND MANNER.—The cor-

23 poration may prescribe the form and man-

24 ner of the provision of information under

25 this paragraph, which shall include delivery

1   in written, electronic, or other appropriate

2   form to the extent that such form is rea-

3   sonably accessible to individuals to whom

4   the information is required to be provided.

5   "(ii) REASONABLE CHARGES.—A plan

6   sponsor may charge a reasonable fee for

7   any information provided under this para-

8   graph in other than electronic form.".

9 (c) EFFECTIVE DATE.—

10   (1) IN GENERAL.—The amendments made by

11 this section shall apply to any plan termination

12 under title IV of the Employee Retirement Income

13 Security Act of 1974 (29 U.S.C. 1301 et seq.) with

14 respect to which the notice of intent to terminate (or

15 in the case of a termination by the Pension Benefit

16 Guaranty Corporation, a notice of determination

17 under section 4042 of such Act (29 U.S.C. 1342))

18 occurs after the date of enactment of this Act.

19   (2) TRANSITION RULE.—If notice under section

20 4041(c)(2)(D) or 4042(c)(3) of the Employee Re-

21 tirement Income Security Act of 1974 (as added by

22 this section) would otherwise be required to be pro-

23 vided before the 90th day after the date of the en-

24 actment of this Act, such notice shall not be re-

25 quired to be provided until such 90th day.

SEC. 507. NOTICE OF FREEDOM TO DIVEST EMPLOYER SE-CURITIES.

(a) IN GENERAL.—Section 101 of the Employee Retirement Income Security Act of 1974 (29 U.S.C. 1021), as amended by this Act, is amended by redesignating subsection (m) as subsection (n) and by inserting after subsection (l) the following:

"(m) NOTICE OF RIGHT TO DIVEST.—Not later than 30 days before the first date on which an applicable individual of an applicable individual account plan is eligible to exercise the right under section 204(j) to direct the proceeds from the divestment of employer securities with respect to any type of contribution, the administrator shall provide to such individual a notice—

"(1) setting forth such right under such section, and

"(2) describing the importance of diversifying the investment of retirement account assets.

The notice required by this subsection shall be written in a manner calculated to be understood by the average plan participant and may be delivered in written, electronic, or other appropriate form to the extent that such form is reasonably accessible to the recipient."

(b) PENALTIES.—Section 502(c)(7) of the Employee Retirement Income Security Act of 1974 (29 U.S.C.

1 1132(c)(7)) is amended by striking "section 101(i)" and

2 inserting "subsection (i) or (m) of section 101".

3 (c) MODEL NOTICE.—The Secretary of the Treasury

4 shall, within 180 days after the date of the enactment of

5 this subsection, prescribe a model notice for purposes of

6 satisfying the requirements of the amendments made by

7 this section.

8 (d) EFFECTIVE DATES.—

9 (1) IN GENERAL.—The amendments made by

10 this section shall apply to plan years beginning after

11 December 31, 2006.

12 (2) TRANSITION RULE.—If notice under section

13 101(m) of the Employee Retirement Income Secu-

14 rity Act of 1974 (as added by this section) would

15 otherwise be required to be provided before the 90th

16 day after the date of the enactment of this Act, such

17 notice shall not be required to be provided until such

18 90th day.

19 **SEC. 508. PERIODIC PENSION BENEFIT STATEMENTS.**

20 (a) AMENDMENTS OF ERISA.—

21 (1) IN GENERAL.—Section 105(a) of the Em-

22 ployee Retirement Income Security Act of 1974 (29

23 U.S.C. 1025(a)) is amended to read as follows:

24 "(a) REQUIREMENTS TO PROVIDE PENSION BEN-

25 EFIT STATEMENTS.—

"(1) REQUIREMENTS.—

"(A) INDIVIDUAL ACCOUNT PLAN.—The administrator of an individual account plan (other than a one-participant retirement plan described in section 101(i)(8)(B)) shall furnish a pension benefit statement—

"(i) at least once each calendar quarter to a participant or beneficiary who has the right to direct the investment of assets in his or her account under the plan,

"(ii) at least once each calendar year to a participant or beneficiary who has his or her own account under the plan but does not have the right to direct the investment of assets in that account, and

"(iii) upon written request to a plan beneficiary not described in clause (i) or (ii).

"(B) DEFINED BENEFIT PLAN.—The administrator of a defined benefit plan (other than a one-participant retirement plan described in section 101(i)(8)(B)) shall furnish a pension benefit statement—

"(i) at least once every 3 years to each participant with a nonforfeitable ac-

crued benefit and who is employed by the
employer maintaining the plan at the time
the statement is to be furnished, and

"(ii) to a participant or beneficiary of
the plan upon written request.

Information furnished under clause (i) to a participant may be based on reasonable estimates determined under regulations prescribed by the Secretary, in consultation with the Pension Benefit Guaranty Corporation.

"(2) STATEMENTS.—

"(A) IN GENERAL.—A pension benefit statement under paragraph (1)—

"(i) shall indicate, on the basis of the latest available information—

"(I) the total benefits accrued, and

"(II) the nonforfeitable pension benefits, if any, which have accrued, or the earliest date on which benefits will become nonforfeitable,

"(ii) shall include an explanation of any permitted disparity under section 401(l) of the Internal Revenue Code of 1986 or any floor-offset arrangement that may be applied in determining any accrued

benefits described in clause (i),

"(iii) shall be written in a manner cal-

culated to be understood by the average

plan participant, and

"(iv) may be delivered in written, elec-

tronic, or other appropriate form to the ex-

tent such form is reasonably accessible to

the participant or beneficiary.

"(B) ADDITIONAL INFORMATION.—In the

case of an individual account plan, any pension

benefit statement under clause (i) or (ii) of

paragraph (1)(A) shall include—

"(i) the value of each investment to

which assets in the individual account have

been allocated, determined as of the most

recent valuation date under the plan, in-

cluding the value of any assets held in the

form of employer securities, without regard

to whether such securities were contributed

by the plan sponsor or acquired at the di-

rection of the plan or of the participant or

beneficiary, and

"(ii) in the case of a pension benefit

statement under paragraph (1)(A)(i)—

"(I) an explanation of any limitations or restrictions on any right of the participant or beneficiary under the plan to direct an investment,

"(II) an explanation, written in a manner calculated to be understood by the average plan participant, of the importance, for the long-term retirement security of participants and beneficiaries, of a well-balanced and diversified investment portfolio, including a statement of the risk that holding more than 20 percent of a portfolio in the security of one entity (such as employer securities) may not be adequately diversified, and

"(III) a notice directing the participant or beneficiary to the Internet website of the Department of Labor for sources of information on individual investing and diversification.

"(C) ALTERNATIVE NOTICE.—The requirements of subparagraph (A)(i)(II) are met if, at least annually and in accordance with requirements of the Secretary, the plan—

"(i) updates the information described in such paragraph which is provided in the pension benefit statement, or

"(ii) provides in a separate statement such information as is necessary to enable a participant or beneficiary to determine their nonforfeitable vested benefits.

"(3) DEFINED BENEFIT PLANS.—

"(A) ALTERNATIVE NOTICE.—In the case of a defined benefit plan, the requirements of paragraph (1)(B)(i) shall be treated as met with respect to a participant if at least once each year the administrator provides to the participant notice of the availability of the pension benefit statement and the ways in which the participant may obtain such statement. Such notice may be delivered in written, electronic, or other appropriate form to the extent such form is reasonably accessible to the participant.

"(B) YEARS IN WHICH NO BENEFITS ACCRUE.—The Secretary may provide that years in which no employee or former employee benefits (within the meaning of section 410(b) of the Internal Revenue Code of 1986) under the plan need not be taken into account in determining the 3-year period under paragraph (1)(B)(i)."

(2) CONFORMING AMENDMENTS.—

(A) Section 105 of the Employee Retirement Income Security Act of 1974 (29 U.S.C. 1025) is amended by striking subsection (d).

(B) Section 105(b) of such Act (29 U.S.C. 1025(b)) is amended to read as follows:

"(b) LIMITATION ON NUMBER OF STATEMENTS.—In no case shall a participant or beneficiary of a plan be entitled to more than 1 statement described in subparagraph (A)(iii) or (B)(ii) of subsection (a)(1), whichever is applicable, in any 12-month period."

(C) Section 502(c)(1) of such Act (29 U.S.C. 1132(c)(1)) is amended by striking "or section 101(f)" and inserting "section 101(f), or section 105(a)".

(b) MODEL STATEMENTS.—

(1) IN GENERAL.—The Secretary of Labor shall, within 1 year after the date of the enactment of this section, develop 1 or more model benefit statements that are written in a manner calculated to be understood by the average plan participant and that may be used by plan administrators in com-

1   plying with the requirements of section 105 of the

2   Employee Retirement Income Security Act of 1974.

3   (2) INTERIM FINAL RULES.—The Secretary of

4   Labor may promulgate any interim final rules as the

5   Secretary determines appropriate to carry out the

6   provisions of this subsection.

7   (c) EFFECTIVE DATE.—

8   (1) IN GENERAL.—The amendments made by

9   this section shall apply to plan years beginning after

10   December 31, 2006.

11   (2) SPECIAL RULE FOR COLLECTIVELY BAR-

12   GAINED AGREEMENTS.—In the case of a plan main-

13   tained pursuant to 1 or more collective bargaining

14   agreements between employee representatives and 1

15   or more employers ratified on or before the date of

16   the enactment of this Act, paragraph (1) shall be

17   applied to benefits pursuant to, and individuals cov-

18   ered by, any such agreement by substituting for

19   "December 31, 2006" the earlier of—

20   (A) the later of—

21   (i) December 31, 2007, or

22   (ii) the date on which the last of such

23   collective bargaining agreements termi-

24   nates (determined without regard to any

1   extension thereof after such date of enact-

2   ment), or

3   (B) December 31, 2008.

SEC. 509. NOTICE TO PARTICIPANTS OR BENEFICIARIES OF

BLACKOUT PERIODS.

6   (a) IN GENERAL.—Section 101(i)(8)(B) of the Em-

7   ployee Retirement Income Security Act of 1974 (29

8   U.S.C. 1021(i)(8)(B)) is amended by striking clauses (i)

9   through (iv), by redesignating clause (v) as clause (ii), and

10   by inserting before clause (ii), as so redesignated, the fol-

11   lowing new clause:

12   "(i) on the first day of the plan

13   year—

14   "(I) covered only one individual

15   (or the individual and the individual's

16   spouse) and the individual (or the in-

17   dividual and the individual's spouse)

18   owned 100 percent of the plan spon-

19   sor (whether or not incorporated), or

20   "(II) covered only one or more

21   partners (or partners and their

22   spouses) in the plan sponsor, and".

23   (b) EFFECTIVE DATE.—The amendments made by

24   this subsection shall take effect as if included in the provi-

1 sions of section 306 of Public Law 107–204 (116 Stat.

2 745 et seq.).

TITLE VI—INVESTMENT ADVICE, PROHIBITED TRANSACTIONS, AND FIDUCIARY RULES

Subtitle A—Investment Advice

SEC. 601. PROHIBITED TRANSACTION EXEMPTION FOR PROVISION OF INVESTMENT ADVICE.

9 (a) AMENDMENTS TO THE EMPLOYEE RETIREMENT

10 INCOME SECURITY ACT OF 1974.—

11   (1) EXEMPTION FROM PROHIBITED TRANS-

12   ACTIONS.—Section 408(b) of the Employee Retire-

13   ment Income Security Act of 1974 (29 U.S.C.

14   1108(b)) is amended by adding at the end the fol-

15   lowing new paragraph:

16   "(14) Any transaction in connection with the

17   provision of investment advice described in section

18   3(21)(A)(ii) to a participant or beneficiary of an in-

19   dividual account plan that permits such participant

20   or beneficiary to direct the investment of assets in

21   their individual account, if—

22   "(A) the transaction is—

23   "(i) the provision of the investment

24   advice to the participant or beneficiary of

25   the plan with respect to a security or other

1   property available as an investment under

2   the plan,

3   "(ii) the acquisition, holding, or sale

4   of a security or other property available as

5   an investment under the plan pursuant to

6   the investment advice, or

7   "(iii) the direct or indirect receipt of

8   fees or other compensation by the fiduciary

9   adviser or an affiliate thereof (or any em-

10   ployee, agent, or registered representative

11   of the fiduciary adviser or affiliate) in con-

12   nection with the provision of the advice or

13   in connection with an acquisition, holding,

14   or sale of a security or other property

15   available as an investment under the plan

16   pursuant to the investment advice; and

17   "(B) the requirements of subsection (g)

18   are met.".

19   (2) REQUIREMENTS.—Section 408 of such Act

20   is amended further by adding at the end the fol-

21   lowing new subsection:

22   "(g) PROVISION OF INVESTMENT ADVICE TO PARTIC-

23 IPANT AND BENEFICIARIES.—

24   "(1) IN GENERAL.—The prohibitions provided

25   in section 406 shall not apply to transactions de-

1   scribed in subsection (b)(14) if the investment advice

2   provided by a fiduciary adviser is provided under an

3   eligible investment advice arrangement.

4   "(2) ELIGIBLE INVESTMENT ADVICE ARRANGE-

5   MENT.—For purposes of this subsection, the term

6   'eligible investment advice arrangement' means an

7   arrangement—

8   "(A) which either—

9   "(i) provides that any fees (including

10   any commission or other compensation) re-

11   ceived by the fiduciary adviser for invest-

12   ment advice or with respect to the sale,

13   holding, or acquisition of any security or

14   other property for purposes of investment

15   of plan assets do not vary depending on

16   the basis of any investment option selected,

17   or

18   "(ii) uses a computer model under an

19   investment advice program meeting the re-

20   quirements of paragraph (3) in connection

21   with the provision of investment advice by

22   a fiduciary adviser to a participant or ben-

23   eficiary, and

1   "(B) with respect to which the require-

2   ments of paragraph (4), (5), (6), (7), (8), and

3   (9) are met.

4   "(3) INVESTMENT ADVICE PROGRAM USING

5 COMPUTER MODEL.—

6   "(A) IN GENERAL.—An investment advice

7   program meets the requirements of this para-

8   graph if the requirements of subparagraphs

9   (B), (C), and (D) are met.

10   "(B) COMPUTER MODEL.—The require-

11   ments of this subparagraph are met if the in-

12   vestment advice provided under the investment

13   advice program is provided pursuant to a com-

14   puter model that—

15   "(i) applies generally accepted invest-

16   ment theories that take into account the

17   historic returns of different asset classes

18   over defined periods of time,

19   "(ii) utilizes relevant information

20   about the participant, which may include

21   age, life expectancy, retirement age, risk

22   tolerance, other assets or sources of in-

23   come, and preferences as to certain types

24   of investments,

"(iii) utilizes prescribed objective criteria to provide asset allocation portfolios comprised of investment options available under the plan,

"(iv) operates in a manner that is not biased in favor of investments offered by the fiduciary adviser or a person with a material affiliation or contractual relationship with the fiduciary adviser, and

"(v) takes into account all investment options under the plan in specifying how a participant's account balance should be invested and is not inappropriately weighted with respect to any investment option.

"(C) CERTIFICATION.—

"(i) IN GENERAL.—The requirements of this subparagraph are met with respect to any investment advice program if an eligible investment expert certifies, prior to the utilization of the computer model and in accordance with rules prescribed by the Secretary, that the computer model meets the requirements of subparagraph (B).

"(ii) RENEWAL OF CERTIFICATIONS.—If, as determined under regula-

1   tions prescribed by the Secretary, there are

2   material modifications to a computer

3   model, the requirements of this subpara-

4   graph are met only if a certification de-

5   scribed in clause (i) is obtained with re-

6   spect to the computer model as so modi-

7   fied.

8   "(iii) ELIGIBLE INVESTMENT EX-

9   PERT.—The term 'eligible investment ex-

10   pert' means any person—

11   "(I) which meets such require-

12   ments as the Secretary may provide,

13   and

14   "(II) does not bear any material

15   affiliation or contractual relationship

16   with any investment adviser or a re-

17   lated person thereof (or any employee,

18   agent, or registered representative of

19   the investment adviser or related per-

20   son).

21   "(D) EXCLUSIVITY OF RECOMMENDA-

22   TION.—The requirements of this subparagraph

23   are met with respect to any investment advice

24   program if—

"(i) the only investment advice provided under the program is the advice generated by the computer model described in subparagraph (B), and

"(ii) any transaction described in subsection (b)(14)(B)(ii) occurs solely at the direction of the participant or beneficiary. Nothing in the preceding sentence shall preclude the participant or beneficiary from requesting investment advice other than that described in subparagraph (A), but only if such request has not been solicited by any person connected with carrying out the arrangement.

"(4) EXPRESS AUTHORIZATION BY SEPARATE FIDUCIARY.—The requirements of this paragraph are met with respect to an arrangement if the arrangement is expressly authorized by a plan fiduciary other than the person offering the investment advice program, any person providing investment options under the plan, or any affiliate of either.

"(5) ANNUAL AUDIT.—The requirements of this paragraph are met if an independent auditor, who has appropriate technical training or experience and proficiency and so represents in writing—

1   "(A) conducts an annual audit of the ar-

2   rangement for compliance with the require-

3   ments of this subsection, and

4   "(B) following completion of the annual

5   audit, issues a written report to the fiduciary

6   who authorized use of the arrangement which

7   presents its specific findings regarding compli-

8   ance of the arrangement with the requirements

9   of this subsection.

10 For purposes of this paragraph, an auditor is con-

11 sidered independent if it is not related to the person

12 offering the arrangement to the plan and is not re-

13 lated to any person providing investment options

14 under the plan.

15   "(6) DISCLOSURE.—The requirements of this

16 paragraph are met if—

17   "(A) the fiduciary adviser provides to a

18   participant or a beneficiary before the initial

19   provision of the investment advice with regard

20   to any security or other property offered as an

21   investment option, a written notification (which

22   may consist of notification by means of elec-

23   tronic communication)—

24   "(i) of the role of any party that has

25   a material affiliation or contractual rela-

1   tionship with the financial adviser in the

2   development of the investment advice pro-

3   gram and in the selection of investment

4   options available under the plan,

5   "(ii) of the past performance and his-

6   torical rates of return of the investment

7   options available under the plan,

8   "(iii) of all fees or other compensation

9   relating to the advice that the fiduciary ad-

10   viser or any affiliate thereof is to receive

11   (including compensation provided by any

12   third party) in connection with the provi-

13   sion of the advice or in connection with the

14   sale, acquisition, or holding of the security

15   or other property,

16   "(iv) of any material affiliation or

17   contractual relationship of the fiduciary

18   adviser or affiliates thereof in the security

19   or other property,

20   "(v) the manner, and under what cir-

21   cumstances, any participant or beneficiary

22   information provided under the arrange-

23   ment will be used or disclosed,

24   "(vi) of the types of services provided

25   by the fiduciary adviser in connection with

1 the provision of investment advice by the

2 fiduciary adviser,

3   "(vii) that the adviser is acting as a

4 fiduciary of the plan in connection with the

5 provision of the advice, and

6   "(viii) that a recipient of the advice

7 may separately arrange for the provision of

8 advice by another adviser, that could have

9 no material affiliation with and receive no

10 fees or other compensation in connection

11 with the security or other property, and

12   "(B) at all times during the provision of

13 advisory services to the participant or bene-

14 ficiary, the fiduciary adviser—

15   "(i) maintains the information de-

16 scribed in subparagraph (A) in accurate

17 form and in the manner described in para-

18 graph (8),

19   "(ii) provides, without charge, accu-

20 rate information to the recipient of the ad-

21 vice no less frequently than annually,

22   "(iii) provides, without charge, accu-

23 rate information to the recipient of the ad-

24 vice upon request of the recipient, and

"(iv) provides, without charge, accurate information to the recipient of the advice concerning any material change to the information required to be provided to the recipient of the advice at a time reasonably contemporaneous to the change in information.

"(7) OTHER CONDITIONS.—The requirements of this paragraph are met if—

"(A) the fiduciary adviser provides appropriate disclosure, in connection with the sale, acquisition, or holding of the security or other property, in accordance with all applicable securities laws,

"(B) the sale, acquisition, or holding occurs solely at the direction of the recipient of the advice,

"(C) the compensation received by the fiduciary adviser and affiliates thereof in connection with the sale, acquisition, or holding of the security or other property is reasonable, and

"(D) the terms of the sale, acquisition, or holding of the security or other property are at least as favorable to the plan as an arm's length transaction would be.

"(8) STANDARDS FOR PRESENTATION OF IN-
FORMATION.—

"(A) IN GENERAL.—The requirements of
this paragraph are met if the notification required to be provided to participants and beneficiaries under paragraph (6)(A) is written in a
clear and conspicuous manner and in a manner
calculated to be understood by the average plan
participant and is sufficiently accurate and
comprehensive to reasonably apprise such participants and beneficiaries of the information
required to be provided in the notification.

"(B) MODEL FORM FOR DISCLOSURE OF
FEES AND OTHER COMPENSATION.—The Secretary shall issue a model form for the disclosure of fees and other compensation required in
paragraph (6)(A)(iii) which meets the requirements of subparagraph (A).

"(9) MAINTENANCE FOR 6 YEARS OF EVIDENCE
OF COMPLIANCE.—The requirements of this paragraph are met if a fiduciary adviser who has provided advice referred to in paragraph (1) maintains,
for a period of not less than 6 years after the provision of the advice, any records necessary for determining whether the requirements of the preceding

provisions of this subsection and of subsection (b)(14) have been met. A transaction prohibited under section 406 shall not be considered to have occurred solely because the records are lost or destroyed prior to the end of the 6-year period due to circumstances beyond the control of the fiduciary adviser.

"(10) EXEMPTION FOR PLAN SPONSOR AND CERTAIN OTHER FIDUCIARIES.—

"(A) IN GENERAL.—Subject to subparagraph (B), a plan sponsor or other person who is a fiduciary (other than a fiduciary adviser) shall not be treated as failing to meet the requirements of this part solely by reason of the provision of investment advice referred to in section 3(21)(A)(ii) (or solely by reason of contracting for or otherwise arranging for the provision of the advice), if—

"(i) the advice is provided by a fiduciary adviser pursuant to an eligible investment advice arrangement between the plan sponsor or other fiduciary and the fiduciary adviser for the provision by the fiduciary adviser of investment advice referred to in such section,

1   "(ii) the terms of the eligible invest-

2   ment advice arrangement require compli-

3   ance by the fiduciary adviser with the re-

4   quirements of this subsection, and

5   "(iii) the terms of the eligible invest-

6   ment advice arrangement include a written

7   acknowledgment by the fiduciary adviser

8   that the fiduciary adviser is a fiduciary of

9   the plan with respect to the provision of

10   the advice.

11   "(B) CONTINUED DUTY OF PRUDENT SE-

12   LECTION OF ADVISER AND PERIODIC REVIEW.—

13   Nothing in subparagraph (A) shall be construed

14   to exempt a plan sponsor or other person who

15   is a fiduciary from any requirement of this part

16   for the prudent selection and periodic review of

17   a fiduciary adviser with whom the plan sponsor

18   or other person enters into an eligible invest-

19   ment advice arrangement for the provision of

20   investment advice referred to in section

21   3(21)(A)(ii). The plan sponsor or other person

22   who is a fiduciary has no duty under this part

23   to monitor the specific investment advice given

24   by the fiduciary adviser to any particular recipi-

25   ent of the advice.

1   "(C) AVAILABILITY OF PLAN ASSETS FOR

2   PAYMENT FOR ADVICE.—Nothing in this part

3   shall be construed to preclude the use of plan

4   assets to pay for reasonable expenses in pro-

5   viding investment advice referred to in section

6   3(21)(A)(ii).

7   "(11) DEFINITIONS.—For purposes of this sub-

8 section and subsection (b)(14)—

9   "(A) FIDUCIARY ADVISER.—The term 'fi-

10   duciary adviser' means, with respect to a plan,

11   a person who is a fiduciary of the plan by rea-

12   son of the provision of investment advice re-

13   ferred to in section 3(21)(A)(ii) by the person

14   to the participant or beneficiary of the plan and

15   who is—

16   "(i) registered as an investment ad-

17   viser under the Investment Advisers Act of

18   1940 (15 U.S.C. 80b–1 et seq.) or under

19   the laws of the State in which the fiduciary

20   maintains its principal office and place of

21   business,

22   "(ii) a bank or similar financial insti-

23   tution referred to in section 408(b)(4) or a

24   savings association (as defined in section

25   3(b)(1) of the Federal Deposit Insurance

1 Act (12 U.S.C. 1813(b)(1)), but only if the

2 advice is provided through a trust depart-

3 ment of the bank or similar financial insti-

4 tution or savings association which is sub-

5 ject to periodic examination and review by

6 Federal or State banking authorities,

7 "(iii) an insurance company qualified

8 to do business under the laws of a State,

9 "(iv) a person registered as a broker

10 or dealer under the Securities Exchange

11 Act of 1934 (15 U.S.C. 78a et seq.),

12 "(v) an affiliate of a person described

13 in any of clauses (i) through (iv), or

14 "(vi) an employee, agent, or registered

15 representative of a person described in

16 clauses (i) through (v) who satisfies the re-

17 quirements of applicable insurance, bank-

18 ing, and securities laws relating to the pro-

19 vision of the advice.

20 For purposes of this part, a person who devel-

21 ops the computer model described in paragraph

22 (3)(B) or markets the investment advice pro-

23 gram or computer model shall be treated as a

24 person who is a fiduciary of the plan by reason

25 of the provision of investment advice referred to

1   in section 3(21)(A)(ii) to the participant or ben-

2   eficiary and shall be treated as a fiduciary ad-

3   viser for purposes of this subsection and sub-

4   section (b)(14), except that the Secretary may

5   prescribe rules under which only 1 fiduciary ad-

6   viser may elect to be treated as a fiduciary with

7   respect to the plan.

8   "(B) AFFILIATE.—The term 'affiliate' of

9   another entity means an affiliated person of the

10   entity (as defined in section 2(a)(3) of the In-

11   vestment Company Act of 1940 (15 U.S.C.

12   80a-2(a)(3))).

13   "(C) REGISTERED REPRESENTATIVE.—

14   The term 'registered representative' of another

15   entity means a person described in section

16   3(a)(18) of the Securities Exchange Act of

17   1934 (15 U.S.C. 78c(a)(18)) (substituting the

18   entity for the broker or dealer referred to in

19   such section) or a person described in section

20   202(a)(17) of the Investment Advisers Act of

21   1940 (15 U.S.C. 80b-2(a)(17)) (substituting

22   the entity for the investment adviser referred to

23   in such section).".

24   (3) EFFECTIVE DATE.—The amendments made

25 by this subsection shall apply with respect to advice

1   referred to in section 3(21)(A)(ii) of the Employee

2   Retirement Income Security Act of 1974 provided

3   after December 31, 2006.

4   (b) AMENDMENTS TO INTERNAL REVENUE CODE OF

5 1986.—

6   (1) EXEMPTION FROM PROHIBITED TRANS-

7   ACTIONS.—Subsection (d) of section 4975 of the In-

8   ternal Revenue Code of 1986 (relating to exemption

9   from tax on prohibited transactions) is amended—

10   (A) in paragraph (15), by striking "or" at

11   the end;

12   (B) in paragraph (16), by striking the pe-

13   riod at the end and inserting ";or"; and

14   (C) by adding at the end the following new

15   paragraph:

16   "(17) Any transaction in connection with the

17   provision of investment advice described in sub-

18   section (e)(3)(B) to a participant or beneficiary in a

19   plan and that permits such participant or bene-

20   ficiary to direct the investment of plan assets in an

21   individual account, if—

22   "(A) the transaction is—

23   "(i) the provision of the investment

24   advice to the participant or beneficiary of

25   the plan with respect to a security or other

property available as an investment under
the plan,

"(ii) the acquisition, holding, or sale
of a security or other property available as
an investment under the plan pursuant to
the investment advice, or

"(iii) the direct or indirect receipt of
fees or other compensation by the fiduciary
adviser or an affiliate thereof (or any employee, agent, or registered representative
of the fiduciary adviser or affiliate) in connection with the provision of the advice or
in connection with an acquisition, holding,
or sale of a security or other property
available as an investment under the plan
pursuant to the investment advice; and

"(B) the requirements of subsection (f)(8)
are met.".

(2) REQUIREMENTS.—Subsection (f) of such
section 4975 (relating to other definitions and special rules) is amended by adding at the end the following new paragraph:

"(8) PROVISION OF INVESTMENT ADVICE TO
PARTICIPANT AND BENEFICIARIES.—

1   "(A) IN GENERAL.—The prohibitions pro-

2 vided in subsection (c) shall not apply to trans-

3 actions described in subsection (b)(14) if the in-

4 vestment advice provided by a fiduciary adviser

5 is provided under an eligible investment advice

6 arrangement.

7   "(B) ELIGIBLE INVESTMENT ADVICE AR-

8 RANGEMENT.—For purposes of this paragraph,

9 the term 'eligible investment advice arrange-

10 ment' means an arrangement—

11   "(i) which either—

12   "(I) provides that any fees (in-

13 cluding any commission or other com-

14 pensation) received by the fiduciary

15 adviser for investment advice or with

16 respect to the sale, holding, or acqui-

17 sition of any security or other prop-

18 erty for purposes of investment of

19 plan assets do not vary depending on

20 the basis of any investment option se-

21 lected, or

22   "(II) uses a computer model

23 under an investment advice program

24 meeting the requirements of subpara-

25 graph (C) in connection with the pro-

vision of investment advice by a fiduciary adviser to a participant or beneficiary, and

"(ii) with respect to which the requirements of subparagraphs (D), (E), (F), (G), (H), and (I) are met.

"(C) INVESTMENT ADVICE PROGRAM USING COMPUTER MODEL.—

"(i) IN GENERAL.—An investment advice program meets the requirements of this subparagraph if the requirements of clauses (ii), (iii), and (iv) are met.

"(ii) COMPUTER MODEL.—The requirements of this clause are met if the investment advice provided under the investment advice program is provided pursuant to a computer model that—

"(I) applies generally accepted investment theories that take into account the historic returns of different asset classes over defined periods of time,

"(II) utilizes relevant information about the participant, which may include age, life expectancy, retirement

1   age, risk tolerance, other assets or

2   sources of income, and preferences as

3   to certain types of investments,

4   "(III) utilizes prescribed objective

5   criteria to provide asset allocation

6   portfolios comprised of investment op-

7   tions available under the plan,

8   "(IV) operates in a manner that

9   is not biased in favor of investments

10   offered by the fiduciary adviser or a

11   person with a material affiliation or

12   contractual relationship with the fidu-

13   ciary adviser, and

14   "(V) takes into account all in-

15   vestment options under the plan in

16   specifying how a participant's account

17   balance should be invested and is not

18   inappropriately weighted with respect

19   to any investment option.

20   "(iii) CERTIFICATION.—

21   "(I) IN GENERAL.—The require-

22   ments of this clause are met with re-

23   spect to any investment advice pro-

24   gram if an eligible investment expert

25   certifies, prior to the utilization of the

computer model and in accordance with rules prescribed by the Secretary of Labor, that the computer model meets the requirements of clause (ii).

"(II) RENEWAL OF CERTIFI-CATIONS.—If, as determined under regulations prescribed by the Secretary of Labor, there are material modifications to a computer model, the requirements of this clause are met only if a certification described in subclause (I) is obtained with respect to the computer model as so modified.

"(III) ELIGIBLE INVESTMENT EXPERT.—The term 'eligible investment expert' means any person which meets such requirements as the Secretary of Labor may provide and which does not bear any material affiliation or contractual relationship with any investment adviser or a related person thereof (or any employee, agent, or registered representative of the investment adviser or related person).

1   "(iv) EXCLUSIVITY OF RECOMMENDA-

2   TION.—The requirements of this clause are

3   met with respect to any investment advice

4   program if—

5   "(I) the only investment advice

6   provided under the program is the ad-

7   vice generated by the computer model

8   described in clause (ii), and

9   "(II) any transaction described in

10   subsection (b)(14)(B)(ii) occurs solely

11   at the direction of the participant or

12   beneficiary.

13   Nothing in the preceding sentence shall

14   preclude the participant or beneficiary

15   from requesting investment advice other

16   than that described in clause (i), but only

17   if such request has not been solicited by

18   any person connected with carrying out the

19   arrangement.

20   "(D) EXPRESS AUTHORIZATION BY SEPA-

21   RATE FIDUCIARY.—The requirements of this

22   subparagraph are met with respect to an ar-

23   rangement if the arrangement is expressly au-

24   thorized by a plan fiduciary other than the per-

25   son offering the investment advice program, any

1 person providing investment options under the
2 plan, or any affiliate of either.

3   "(E) AUDITS.—

4   "(i) IN GENERAL.—The requirements
5 of this subparagraph are met if an inde-
6 pendent auditor, who has appropriate tech-
7 nical training or experience and proficiency
8 and so represents in writing—

9   "(I) conducts an annual audit of
10 the arrangement for compliance with
11 the requirements of this paragraph,
12 and

13   "(II) following completion of the
14 annual audit, issues a written report
15 to the fiduciary who authorized use of
16 the arrangement which presents its
17 specific findings regarding compliance
18 of the arrangement with the require-
19 ments of this paragraph.

20   "(ii) SPECIAL RULE FOR INDIVIDUAL
21 RETIREMENT AND SIMILAR PLANS.—In the
22 case of a plan described in subparagraphs
23 (B) through (F) (and so much of subpara-
24 graph (G) as relates to such subpara-
25 graphs) of subsection (e)(1), in lieu of the

1   requirements of clause (i), audits of the ar-

2   rangement shall be conducted at such

3   times and in such manner as the Secretary

4   of Labor may prescribe.

5   "(iii) INDEPENDENT AUDITOR.—For

6   purposes of this subparagraph, an auditor

7   is considered independent if it is not re-

8   lated to the person offering the arrange-

9   ment to the plan and is not related to any

10   person providing investment options under

11   the plan.

12   "(F) DISCLOSURE.—The requirements of

13   this subparagraph are met if—

14   "(i) the fiduciary adviser provides to a

15   participant or a beneficiary before the ini-

16   tial provision of the investment advice with

17   regard to any security or other property of-

18   fered as an investment option, a written

19   notification (which may consist of notifica-

20   tion by means of electronic communica-

21   tion)—

22   "(I) of the role of any party that

23   has a material affiliation or contrac-

24   tual relationship with the financial ad-

25   viser in the development of the invest-

1   ment advice program and in the selec-

2   tion of investment options available

3   under the plan,

4   "(II) of the past performance

5   and historical rates of return of the

6   investment options available under the

7   plan,

8   "(III) of all fees or other com-

9   pensation relating to the advice that

10   the fiduciary adviser or any affiliate

11   thereof is to receive (including com-

12   pensation provided by any third

13   party) in connection with the provi-

14   sion of the advice or in connection

15   with the sale, acquisition, or holding

16   of the security or other property,

17   "(IV) of any material affiliation

18   or contractual relationship of the fidu-

19   ciary adviser or affiliates thereof in

20   the security or other property,

21   "(V) the manner, and under

22   what circumstances, any participant

23   or beneficiary information provided

24   under the arrangement will be used or

25   disclosed,

1   "(VI) of the types of services

2   provided by the fiduciary adviser in

3   connection with the provision of in-

4   vestment advice by the fiduciary ad-

5   viser,

6   "(VII) that the adviser is acting

7   as a fiduciary of the plan in connec-

8   tion with the provision of the advice,

9   and

10   "(VIII) that a recipient of the

11   advice may separately arrange for the

12   provision of advice by another adviser,

13   that could have no material affiliation

14   with and receive no fees or other com-

15   pensation in connection with the secu-

16   rity or other property, and

17   "(ii) at all times during the provision

18 of advisory services to the participant or

19 beneficiary, the fiduciary adviser—

20   "(I) maintains the information

21   described in clause (i) in accurate

22   form and in the manner described in

23   subparagraph (H),

24   "(II) provides, without charge,

25   accurate information to the recipient

of the advice no less frequently than
annually,

"(III) provides, without charge,
accurate information to the recipient
of the advice upon request of the recipient, and

"(IV) provides, without charge,
accurate information to the recipient
of the advice concerning any material
change to the information required to
be provided to the recipient of the advice at a time reasonably contemporaneous to the change in information.

"(G) OTHER CONDITIONS.—The requirements of this subparagraph are met if—

"(i) the fiduciary adviser provides appropriate disclosure, in connection with the
sale, acquisition, or holding of the security
or other property, in accordance with all
applicable securities laws,

"(ii) the sale, acquisition, or holding
occurs solely at the direction of the recipient of the advice,

"(iii) the compensation received by the
fiduciary adviser and affiliates thereof in

1   connection with the sale, acquisition, or

2   holding of the security or other property is

3   reasonable, and

4   "(iv) the terms of the sale, acquisi-

5   tion, or holding of the security or other

6   property are at least as favorable to the

7   plan as an arm's length transaction would

8   be.

9   "(H) STANDARDS FOR PRESENTATION OF

10   INFORMATION.—

11   "(i) IN GENERAL.—The requirements

12   of this subparagraph are met if the notifi-

13   cation required to be provided to partici-

14   pants and beneficiaries under subpara-

15   graph (F)(i) is written in a clear and con-

16   spicuous manner and in a manner cal-

17   culated to be understood by the average

18   plan participant and is sufficiently accu-

19   rate and comprehensive to reasonably ap-

20   prise such participants and beneficiaries of

21   the information required to be provided in

22   the notification.

23   "(ii) MODEL FORM FOR DISCLOSURE

24   OF FEES AND OTHER COMPENSATION.—

25   The Secretary of Labor shall issue a model

form for the disclosure of fees and other
compensation required in subparagraph
(F)(i)(III) which meets the requirements
of clause (i).

"(I) MAINTENANCE FOR 6 YEARS OF EVI-
DENCE OF COMPLIANCE.—The requirements of
this subparagraph are met if a fiduciary adviser
who has provided advice referred to in subparagraph (A) maintains, for a period of not less
than 6 years after the provision of the advice,
any records necessary for determining whether
the requirements of the preceding provisions of
this paragraph and of subsection (d)(17) have
been met. A transaction prohibited under section 406 shall not be considered to have occurred solely because the records are lost or destroyed prior to the end of the 6-year period
due to circumstances beyond the control of the
fiduciary adviser.

"(J) DEFINITIONS.—For purposes of this
paragraph and subsection (d)(17)—

"(i) FIDUCIARY ADVISER.—The term
'fiduciary adviser' means, with respect to a
plan, a person who is a fiduciary of the
plan by reason of the provision of invest-

1   ment advice by the person to the partici-

2   pant or beneficiary of the plan and who

3   is—

4   "(I) registered as an investment

5   adviser under the Investment Advisers

6   Act of 1940 (15 U.S.C. 80b–1 et seq.)

7   or under the laws of the State in

8   which the fiduciary maintains its prin-

9   cipal office and place of business,

10   "(II) a bank or similar financial

11   institution referred to in section

12   408(b)(4) or a savings association (as

13   defined in section 3(b)(1) of the Fed-

14   eral Deposit Insurance Act (12 U.S.C.

15   1813(b)(1)), but only if the advice is

16   provided through a trust department

17   of the bank or similar financial insti-

18   tution or savings association which is

19   subject to periodic examination and

20   review by Federal or State banking

21   authorities,

22   "(III) an insurance company

23   qualified to do business under the

24   laws of a State,

1   "(IV) a person registered as a

2   broker or dealer under the Securities

3   Exchange Act of 1934 (15 U.S.C. 78a

4   et seq.),

5   "(V) an affiliate of a person de-

6   scribed in any of subclauses (I)

7   through (IV), or

8   "(VI) an employee, agent, or reg-

9   istered representative of a person de-

10   scribed in subclauses (I) through (V)

11   who satisfies the requirements of ap-

12   plicable insurance, banking, and secu-

13   rities laws relating to the provision of

14   the advice.

15   For purposes of this title, a person who de-

16   velops the computer model described in

17   subparagraph (C)(ii) or markets the in-

18   vestment advice program or computer

19   model shall be treated as a person who is

20   a fiduciary of the plan by reason of the

21   provision of investment advice referred to

22   in subsection (e)(3)(B) to the participant

23   or beneficiary and shall be treated as a fi-

24   duciary adviser for purposes of this para-

25   graph and subsection (d)(17), except that

1   the Secretary of Labor may prescribe rules

2   under which only 1 fiduciary adviser may

3   elect to be treated as a fiduciary with re-

4   spect to the plan.

5   "(ii) AFFILIATE.—The term 'affiliate'

6   of another entity means an affiliated per-

7   son of the entity (as defined in section

8   2(a)(3) of the Investment Company Act of

9   1940 (15 U.S.C. 80a-2(a)(3))).

10   "(iii) REGISTERED REPRESENTA-

11   TIVE.—The term 'registered representa-

12   tive' of another entity means a person de-

13   scribed in section 3(a)(18) of the Securi-

14   ties Exchange Act of 1934 (15 U.S.C.

15   78c(a)(18)) (substituting the entity for the

16   broker or dealer referred to in such sec-

17   tion) or a person described in section

18   202(a)(17) of the Investment Advisers Act

19   of 1940 (15 U.S.C. 80b-2(a)(17)) (sub-

20   stituting the entity for the investment ad-

21   viser referred to in such section).".

22   (3) DETERMINATION OF FEASIBILITY OF APPLI-

23 CATION OF COMPUTER MODEL INVESTMENT ADVICE

24 PROGRAMS FOR INDIVIDUAL RETIREMENT AND SIMI-

25 LAR PLANS.—

(A) SOLICITATION OF INFORMATION.—As soon as practicable after the date of the enactment of this Act, the Secretary of Labor, in consultation with the Secretary of the Treasury, shall—

(i) solicit information as to the feasibility of the application of computer model investment advice programs for plans described in subparagraphs (B) through (F) (and so much of subparagraph (G) as relates to such subparagraphs) of section 4975(e)(1) of the Internal Revenue Code of 1986, including soliciting information from—

(I) at least the top 50 trustees of such plans, determined on the basis of assets held by such trustees, and

(II) other persons offering computer model investment advice programs based on nonproprietary products, and

(ii) shall on the basis of such information make the determination under subparagraph (B).

1   The information solicited by the Secretary of

2   Labor under clause (i) from persons described

3   in subclauses (I) and (II) of clause (i) shall in-

4   clude information on computer modeling capa-

5   bilities of such persons with respect to the cur-

6   rent year and preceding year, including such ca-

7   pabilities for investment accounts maintained

8   by such persons.

9   (B) DETERMINATION OF FEASIBILITY.—

10   The Secretary of Labor, in consultation with

11   the Secretary of the Treasury, shall, on the

12   basis of information received under subpara-

13   graph (A), determine whether there is any com-

14   puter model investment advice program which

15   may be utilized by a plan described in subpara-

16   graph (A)(i) to provide investment advice to the

17   account beneficiary of the plan which—

18   (i) utilizes relevant information about

19   the account beneficiary, which may include

20   age, life expectancy, retirement age, risk

21   tolerance, other assets or sources of in-

22   come, and preferences as to certain types

23   of investments,

24   (ii) takes into account the full range

25   of investments, including equities and

1   bonds, in determining the options for the

2   investment portfolio of the account bene-

3   ficiary, and

4   (iii) allows the account beneficiary, in

5   directing the investment of assets, suffi-

6   cient flexibility in obtaining advice to

7   evaluate and select investment options.

8   The Secretary of Labor shall report the results

9   of such determination to the committees of

10   Congress referred to in subparagraph (D)(ii)

11   not later than December 31, 2007.

12   (C) APPLICATION OF COMPUTER MODEL

13   INVESTMENT ADVICE PROGRAM.—

14   (i) CERTIFICATION REQUIRED FOR

15   USE OF COMPUTER MODEL.—

16   (I) RESTRICTION ON USE.—Sub-

17   clause (II) of section 4975(f)(8)(B)(i)

18   of the Internal Revenue Code of 1986

19   shall not apply to a plan described in

20   subparagraph (A)(i).

21   (II) RESTRICTION LIFTED IF

22   MODEL CERTIFIED.—If the Secretary

23   of Labor determines under subpara-

24   graph (B) or (D) that there is a com-

25   puter model investment advice pro-

1   gram described in subparagraph (B),

2   subclause (I) shall cease to apply as of

3   the date of such determination.

4   (ii) CLASS EXEMPTION IF NO INITIAL

5   CERTIFICATION BY SECRETARY.—If the

6   Secretary of Labor determines under sub-

7   paragraph (B) that there is no computer

8   model investment advice program described

9   in subparagraph (B), the Secretary of

10   Labor shall grant a class exemption from

11   treatment as a prohibited transaction

12   under section 4975(c) of the Internal Rev-

13   enue Code of 1986 to any transaction de-

14   scribed in section 4975(d)(17)(A) of such

15   Code with respect to plans described in

16   subparagraph (A)(i), subject to such condi-

17   tions as set forth in such exemption as are

18   in the interests of the plan and its account

19   beneficiary and protective of the rights of

20   the account beneficiary and as are nec-

21   essary to—

22   (I) ensure the requirements of

23   sections 4975(d)(17) and 4975(f)(8)

24   (other than subparagraph (C) thereof)

of the Internal Revenue Code of 1986
are met, and

(II) ensure the investment advice
provided under the investment advice
program utilizes prescribed objective
criteria to provide asset allocation
portfolios comprised of securities or
other property available as investments under the plan.

If the Secretary of Labor solicits any information under subparagraph (A) from a person and such person does not provide such information within 60 days after the solicitation, then, unless such failure was due to reasonable cause and not wilful neglect, such person shall not be entitled to utilize the class exemption under this clause.

(D) SUBSEQUENT DETERMINATION.—

(i) IN GENERAL.—If the Secretary of Labor initially makes a determination described in subparagraph (C)(ii), the Secretary may subsequently determine that there is a computer model investment advice program described in subparagraph

1   (B). If the Secretary makes such subse-

2   quent determination, then the class exemp-

3   tion described in subparagraph (C)(ii) shall

4   cease to apply after the later of—

5   (I) the date which is 2 years

6   after such subsequent determination,

7   or

8   (II) the date which is 3 years

9   after the first date on which such ex-

10   emption took effect.

11   (ii) REQUESTS FOR DETERMINA-

12   TION.—Any person may request the Sec-

13   retary of Labor to make a determination

14   under this subparagraph with respect to

15   any computer model investment advice pro-

16   gram, and the Secretary of Labor shall

17   make a determination with respect to such

18   request within 90 days. If the Secretary of

19   Labor makes a determination that such

20   program is not described in subparagraph

21   (B), the Secretary shall, within 10 days of

22   such determination, notify the Committee

23   on Ways and Means and the Committee on

24   Education and the Workforce of the House

25   of Representatives and the Committee on

1   Finance and the Committee on Health,

2   Education, Labor, and Pensions of the

3   Senate of such determination and the rea-

4   sons for such determination.

5   (E) EFFECTIVE DATE.—The provisions of

6   this paragraph shall take effect on the date of

7   the enactment of this Act.

8   (4) EFFECTIVE DATE.—Except as provided in

9   this subsection, the amendments made by this sub-

10   section shall apply with respect to advice referred to

11   in section 4975(c)(3)(B) of the Internal Revenue

12   Code of 1986 provided after December 31, 2006.

13   (c) COORDINATION WITH EXISTING EXEMPTIONS.—

14 Any exemption under section 408(b) of the Employee Re-

15 tirement Income Security Act of 1974 and section 4975(d)

16 of the Internal Revenue Code of 1986 provided by the

17 amendments made by this section shall not in any manner

18 alter existing individual or class exemptions, provided by

19 statute or administrative action.

20 # Subtitle B—Prohibited

21 # Transactions

22 **SEC. 611. PROHIBITED TRANSACTION RULES RELATING TO**

23   **FINANCIAL INVESTMENTS.**

24   (a) EXEMPTION FOR BLOCK TRADING.—

1   (1) AMENDMENTS TO EMPLOYEE RETIREMENT

2 INCOME SECURITY ACT OF 1974.—Section 408(b) of

3 such Act (29 U.S.C. 1108(b)), as amended by sec-

4 tion 601, is amended by adding at the end the fol-

5 lowing new paragraph:

6   "(15)(A) Any transaction involving the pur-

7 chase or sale of securities, or other property (as de-

8 termined by the Secretary), between a plan and a

9 party in interest (other than a fiduciary described in

10 section 3(21)(A)) with respect to a plan if—

11   "(i) the transaction involves a block trade,

12   "(ii) at the time of the transaction, the in-

13   terest of the plan (together with the interests of

14   any other plans maintained by the same plan

15   sponsor), does not exceed 10 percent of the ag-

16   gregate size of the block trade,

17   "(iii) the terms of the transaction, includ-

18   ing the price, are at least as favorable to the

19   plan as an arm's length transaction, and

20   "(iv) the compensation associated with the

21   purchase and sale is not greater than the com-

22   pensation associated with an arm's length

23   transaction with an unrelated party.

24   "(B) For purposes of this paragraph, the term

25 'block trade' means any trade of at least 10,000

shares or with a market value of at least $200,000 which will be allocated across two or more unrelated client accounts of a fiduciary.''.

(2) AMENDMENTS TO INTERNAL REVENUE CODE OF 1986.—

(A) IN GENERAL.—Subsection (d) of section 4975 of the Internal Revenue Code of 1986 (relating to exemptions), as amended by section 601, is amended by striking ''or'' at the end of paragraph (16), by striking the period at the end of paragraph (17) and inserting '', or'', and by adding at the end the following new paragraph:

''(18) any transaction involving the purchase or sale of securities, or other property (as determined by the Secretary of Labor), between a plan and a party in interest (other than a fiduciary described in subsection (e)(3)(B)) with respect to a plan if—

''(A) the transaction involves a block trade,

''(B) at the time of the transaction, the interest of the plan (together with the interests of any other plans maintained by the same plan sponsor), does not exceed 10 percent of the aggregate size of the block trade,

1   "(C) the terms of the transaction, includ-

2   ing the price, are at least as favorable to the

3   plan as an arm's length transaction, and

4   "(D) the compensation associated with the

5   purchase and sale is not greater than the com-

6   pensation associated with an arm's length

7   transaction with an unrelated party.".

8   (B) SPECIAL RULE RELATING TO BLOCK

9   TRADE.—Subsection (f) of section 4975 of such

10   Code (relating to other definitions and special

11   rules), as amended by section 601, is amended

12   by adding at the end the following new para-

13   graph:

14   "(9) BLOCK TRADE.—The term 'block trade'

15 means any trade of at least 10,000 shares or with

16 a market value of at least $200,000 which will be al-

17 located across two or more unrelated client accounts

18 of a fiduciary.".

19   (b) BONDING RELIEF.—Section 412(a) of such Act

20 (29 U.S.C. 1112(a)) is amended—

21   (1) by redesignating paragraph (2) as para-

22   graph (3),

23   (2) by striking "and" at the end of paragraph

24   (1), and

1   (3) by inserting after paragraph (1) the fol-
2   lowing new paragraph:

3   "(2) no bond shall be required of any entity
4   which is registered as a broker or a dealer under
5   section 15(b) of the Securities Exchange Act of
6   1934 (15 U.S.C. 78o(b)) if the broker or dealer is
7   subject to the fidelity bond requirements of a self-
8   regulatory organization (within the meaning of sec-
9   tion 3(a)(26) of such Act (15 U.S.C. 78c(a)(26)).".

10   (c) EXEMPTION FOR ELECTRONIC COMMUNICATION
11   NETWORK.—

12   (1) AMENDMENTS TO EMPLOYEE RETIREMENT
13   INCOME SECURITY ACT OF 1974.—Section 408(b) of
14   such Act, as amended by subsection (a), is amended
15   by adding at the end the following:

16   "(16) Any transaction involving the purchase or
17   sale of securities, or other property (as determined
18   by the Secretary), between a plan and a party in in-
19   terest if—

20   "(A) the transaction is executed through
21   an electronic communication network, alter-
22   native trading system, or similar execution sys-
23   tem or trading venue subject to regulation and
24   oversight by—

1   "(i) the applicable Federal regulating

2   entity, or

3   "(ii) such foreign regulatory entity as

4   the Secretary may determine by regulation,

5   "(B) either—

6   "(i) the transaction is effected pursu-

7   ant to rules designed to match purchases

8   and sales at the best price available

9   through the execution system in accord-

10   ance with applicable rules of the Securities

11   and Exchange Commission or other rel-

12   evant governmental authority, or

13   "(ii) neither the execution system nor

14   the parties to the transaction take into ac-

15   count the identity of the parties in the exe-

16   cution of trades,

17   "(C) the price and compensation associ-

18   ated with the purchase and sale are not greater

19   than the price and compensation associated

20   with an arm's length transaction with an unre-

21   lated party,

22   "(D) if the party in interest has an owner-

23   ship interest in the system or venue described

24   in subparagraph (A), the system or venue has

25   been authorized by the plan sponsor or other

1   independent fiduciary for transactions described

2   in this paragraph, and

3   "(E) not less than 30 days prior to the ini-

4   tial transaction described in this paragraph exe-

5   cuted through any system or venue described in

6   subparagraph (A), a plan fiduciary is provided

7   written or electronic notice of the execution of

Act. Sec. 611

8   such transaction through such system or

9   venue.".

10   (2) AMENDMENTS TO INTERNAL REVENUE

11 CODE OF 1986.—Subsection (d) of section 4975 of

12 the Internal Revenue Code of 1986 (relating to ex-

13 emptions), as amended by subsection (a), is amend-

14 ed by striking "or" at the end of paragraph (17), by

15 striking the period at the end of paragraph (18) and

16 inserting ", or", and by adding at the end the fol-

17 lowing new paragraph:

18   "(19) any transaction involving the purchase or

19 sale of securities, or other property (as determined

20 by the Secretary of Labor), between a plan and a

21 party in interest if—

22   "(A) the transaction is executed through

23   an electronic communication network, alter-

24   native trading system, or similar execution sys-

1   tem or trading venue subject to regulation and

2   oversight by—

3   "(i) the applicable Federal regulating

4   entity, or

5   "(ii) such foreign regulatory entity as

6   the Secretary of Labor may determine by

7   regulation,

8   "(B) either—

9   "(i) the transaction is effected pursu-

10   ant to rules designed to match purchases

11   and sales at the best price available

12   through the execution system in accord-

13   ance with applicable rules of the Securities

14   and Exchange Commission or other rel-

15   evant governmental authority, or

16   "(ii) neither the execution system nor

17   the parties to the transaction take into ac-

18   count the identity of the parties in the exe-

19   cution of trades,

20   "(C) the price and compensation associ-

21   ated with the purchase and sale are not greater

22   than the price and compensation associated

23   with an arm's length transaction with an unre-

24   lated party,

"(D) if the party in interest has an ownership interest in the system or venue described
in subparagraph (A), the system or venue has
been authorized by the plan sponsor or other
independent fiduciary for transactions described
in this paragraph, and

"(E) not less than 30 days prior to the initial transaction described in this paragraph executed through any system or venue described in
subparagraph (A), a plan fiduciary is provided
written or electronic notice of the execution of
such transaction through such system or
venue.".

(d) EXEMPTION FOR SERVICE PROVIDERS.—

(1) AMENDMENTS TO EMPLOYEE RETIREMENT
INCOME SECURITY ACT OF 1974.—Section 408(b) of
such Act (29 U.S.C. 1106), as amended by subsection (c), is amended by adding at the end the following new paragraph:

"(17)(A) Transactions described in subparagraphs (A), (B), and (D) of section 406(a)(1) between a plan and a person that is a party in interest
other than a fiduciary (or an affiliate) who has or
exercises any discretionary authority or control with
respect to the investment of the plan assets involved

1   in the transaction or renders investment advice

2   (within the meaning of section 3(21)(A)(ii)) with re-

3   spect to those assets, solely by reason of providing

4   services to the plan or solely by reason of a relation-

5   ship to such a service provider described in subpara-

6   graph (F), (G), (H), or (I) of section 3(14), or both,

7   but only if in connection with such transaction the

8   plan receives no less, nor pays no more, than ade-

9   quate consideration.

10   "(B) For purposes of this paragraph, the term

11   'adequate consideration' means—

12   "(i) in the case of a security for which

13   there is a generally recognized market—

14   "(I) the price of the security pre-

15   vailing on a national securities ex-

16   change which is registered under sec-

17   tion 6 of the Securities Exchange Act

18   of 1934, taking into account factors

19   such as the size of the transaction and

20   marketability of the security, or

21   "(II) if the security is not traded

22   on such a national securities ex-

23   change, a price not less favorable to

24   the plan than the offering price for

25   the security as established by the cur-

rent bid and asked prices quoted by persons independent of the issuer and of the party in interest, taking into account factors such as the size of the transaction and marketability of the security, and

"(ii) in the case of an asset other than a security for which there is a generally recognized market, the fair market value of the asset as determined in good faith by a fiduciary or fiduciaries in accordance with regulations prescribed by the Secretary.".

(2) AMENDMENT TO INTERNAL REVENUE CODE OF 1986.—

(A) IN GENERAL.—Subsection (d) of section 4975 of the Internal Revenue Code of 1986 (relating to exemptions), as amended by subsection (c), is amended by striking "or" at the end of paragraph (18), by striking the period at the end of paragraph (19) and inserting ", or", and by adding at the end the following new paragraph:

"(20) transactions described in subparagraphs (A), (B), and (D) of subsection (c)(1) between a plan and a person that is a party in interest other

1   than a fiduciary (or an affiliate) who has or exer-

2   cises any discretionary authority or control with re-

3   spect to the investment of the plan assets involved

4   in the transaction or renders investment advice

5   (within the meaning of subsection (e)(3)(B)) with

6   respect to those assets, solely by reason of providing

7   services to the plan or solely by reason of a relation-

8   ship to such a service provider described in subpara-

9   graph (F), (G), (H), or (I) of subsection (e)(2), or

10 both, but only if in connection with such transaction

11 the plan receives no less, nor pays no more, than

12 adequate consideration.''.

13   (B) SPECIAL RULE RELATING TO SERVICE

14   PROVIDERS.—Subsection (f) of section 4975 of

15   such Code (relating to other definitions and

16   special rules), as amended by subsection (a), is

17   amended by adding at the end the following

18   new paragraph:

19 ''(10) ADEQUATE CONSIDERATION.—The term

20 'adequate consideration' means—

21   ''(A) in the case of a security for which

22   there is a generally recognized market—

23   ''(i) the price of the security pre-

24   vailing on a national securities exchange

25   which is registered under section 6 of the

1   Securities Exchange Act of 1934, taking

2   into account factors such as the size of the

3   transaction and marketability of the secu-

4   rity, or

5   "(ii) if the security is not traded on

6   such a national securities exchange, a price

7   not less favorable to the plan than the of-

8   fering price for the security as established

9   by the current bid and asked prices quoted

10   by persons independent of the issuer and

11   of the party in interest, taking into ac-

12   count factors such as the size of the trans-

13   action and marketability of the security,

14   and

15   "(B) in the case of an asset other than a

16   security for which there is a generally recog-

17   nized market, the fair market value of the asset

18   as determined in good faith by a fiduciary or fi-

19   duciaries in accordance with regulations pre-

20   scribed by the Secretary of Labor.".

21   (e) RELIEF FOR FOREIGN EXCHANGE TRANS-

22   ACTIONS.—

23   (1) AMENDMENTS TO EMPLOYEE RETIREMENT

24   INCOME SECURITY ACT OF 1974.—Section 408(b) of

25   such Act (29 U.S.C. 1108(b)), as amended by sub-

section (d), is amended by adding at the end the following new paragraph:

"(18) FOREIGN EXCHANGE TRANSACTIONS.—
Any foreign exchange transactions, between a bank or broker-dealer (or any affiliate of either), and a plan (as defined in section 3(3)) with respect to which such bank or broker-dealer (or affiliate) is a trustee, custodian, fiduciary, or other party in interest, if—

"(A) the transaction is in connection with the purchase, holding, or sale of securities or other investment assets (other than a foreign exchange transaction unrelated to any other investment in securities or other investment assets),

"(B) at the time the foreign exchange transaction is entered into, the terms of the transaction are not less favorable to the plan than the terms generally available in comparable arm's length foreign exchange transactions between unrelated parties, or the terms afforded by the bank or broker-dealer (or any affiliate of either) in comparable arm's-length foreign exchange transactions involving unrelated parties,

"(C) the exchange rate used by such bank or broker-dealer (or affiliate) for a particular foreign exchange transaction does not deviate by more or less than 3 percent from the interbank bid and asked rates for transactions of comparable size and maturity at the time of the transaction as displayed on an independent service that reports rates of exchange in the foreign currency market for such currency, and

"(D) the bank or broker-dealer (or any affiliate of either) does not have investment discretion, or provide investment advice, with respect to the transaction.".

(2) AMENDMENT TO INTERNAL REVENUE CODE OF 1986.—Subsection (d) of section 4975 of the Internal Revenue Code of 1986 (relating to exemptions), as amended by subsection (d), is amended by striking "or" at the end of paragraph (19), by striking the period at the end of paragraph (20) and inserting ", or", and by adding at the end the following new paragraph:

"(21) any foreign exchange transactions, between a bank or broker-dealer (or any affiliate of either) and a plan (as defined in this section) with respect to which such bank or broker-dealer (or affil-

528

1   iate) is a trustee, custodian, fiduciary, or other party

2   in interest person, if—

3   　　　"(A) the transaction is in connection with

4   　　　the purchase, holding, or sale of securities or

5   　　　other investment assets (other than a foreign

6   　　　exchange transaction unrelated to any other in-

7   　　　vestment in securities or other investment as-

8   　　　sets),

9   　　　"(B) at the time the foreign exchange

10   　　　transaction is entered into, the terms of the

11   　　　transaction are not less favorable to the plan

12   　　　than the terms generally available in com-

13   　　　parable arm's length foreign exchange trans-

14   　　　actions between unrelated parties, or the terms

15   　　　afforded by the bank or broker-dealer (or any

16   　　　affiliate of either) in comparable arm's-length

17   　　　foreign exchange transactions involving unre-

18   　　　lated parties,

19   　　　"(C) the exchange rate used by such bank

20   　　　or broker-dealer (or affiliate) for a particular

21   　　　foreign exchange transaction does not deviate

22   　　　by more or less than 3 percent from the inter-

23   　　　bank bid and asked rates for transactions of

24   　　　comparable size and maturity at the time of the

25   　　　transaction as displayed on an independent

1   service that reports rates of exchange in the

2   foreign currency market for such currency, and

3   "(D) the bank or broker-dealer (or any af-

4   filiate of either) does not have investment dis-

5   cretion, or provide investment advice, with re-

6   spect to the transaction.".

7   (f) DEFINITION OF PLAN ASSET VEHICLE.—Section

8 3 of such Act (29 U.S.C. 1002) is amended by adding

9 at the end the following new paragraph:

10   "(42) the term 'plan assets' means plan assets as de-

11 fined by such regulations as the Secretary may prescribe,

12 except that under such regulations the assets of any entity

13 shall not be treated as plan assets if, immediately after

14 the most recent acquisition of any equity interest in the

15 entity, less than 25 percent of the total value of each class

16 of equity interest in the entity is held by benefit plan in-

17 vestors. For purposes of determinations pursuant to this

18 paragraph, the value of any equity interest held by a per-

19 son (other than such a benefit plan investor) who has dis-

20 cretionary authority or control with respect to the assets

21 of the entity or any person who provides investment advice

22 for a fee (direct or indirect) with respect to such assets,

23 or any affiliate of such a person, shall be disregarded for

24 purposes of calculating the 25 percent threshold. An entity

25 shall be considered to hold plan assets only to the extent

1 of the percentage of the equity interest held by benefit

2 plan investors. For purposes of this paragraph, the term

3 'benefit plan investor' means an employee benefit plan

4 subject to part 4, any plan to which section 4975 of the

5 Internal Revenue Code of 1986 applies, and any entity

6 whose underlying assets include plan assets by reason of

7 a plan's investment in such entity.''.

8   (g) EXEMPTION FOR CROSS TRADING.—

9   (1) AMENDMENTS TO EMPLOYEE RETIREMENT

10   INCOME SECURITY ACT OF 1974.—Section 408(b) of

11   such Act (29 U.S.C. 1108(b)), as amended by sub-

12   section (e), is amended by adding at the end the fol-

13   lowing new paragraph:

14   ''(19) CROSS TRADING.—Any transaction de-

15   scribed in sections 406(a)(1)(A) and 406(b)(2) in-

16   volving the purchase and sale of a security between

17   a plan and any other account managed by the same

18   investment manager, if—

19   ''(A) the transaction is a purchase or sale,

20   for no consideration other than cash payment

21   against prompt delivery of a security for which

22   market quotations are readily available,

23   ''(B) the transaction is effected at the

24   independent current market price of the secu-

531

rity (within the meaning of section 270.17a–
7(b) of title 17, Code of Federal Regulations),

"(C) no brokerage commission, fee (except
for customary transfer fees, the fact of which is
disclosed pursuant to subparagraph (D)), or
other remuneration is paid in connection with
the transaction,

"(D) a fiduciary (other than the investment manager engaging in the cross-trades or
any affiliate) for each plan participating in the
transaction authorizes in advance of any cross-
trades (in a document that is separate from any
other written agreement of the parties) the investment manager to engage in cross trades at
the investment manager's discretion, after such
fiduciary has received disclosure regarding the
conditions under which cross trades may take
place (but only if such disclosure is separate
from any other agreement or disclosure involving the asset management relationship), including the written policies and procedures of the
investment manager described in subparagraph
(H),

"(E) each plan participating in the transaction has assets of at least $100,000,000, ex-

cept that if the assets of a plan are invested in a master trust containing the assets of plans maintained by employers in the same controlled group (as defined in section 407(d)(7)), the master trust has assets of at least $100,000,000,

"(F) the investment manager provides to the plan fiduciary who authorized cross trading under subparagraph (D) a quarterly report detailing all cross trades executed by the investment manager in which the plan participated during such quarter, including the following information, as applicable: (i) the identity of each security bought or sold; (ii) the number of shares or units traded, (iii) the parties involved in the cross-trade; and (iv) trade price and the method used to establish the trade price,

"(G) the investment manager does not base its fee schedule on the plan's consent to cross trading, and no other service (other than the investment opportunities and cost savings available through a cross trade) is conditioned on the plan's consent to cross trading,

"(H) the investment manager has adopted, and cross-trades are effected in accordance

1   with, written cross-trading policies and proce-

2   dures that are fair and equitable to all accounts

3   participating in the cross-trading program, and

4   that include a description of the manager's

5   pricing policies and procedures, and the man-

6   ager's policies and procedures for allocating

7   cross trades in an objective manner among ac-

8   counts participating in the cross-trading pro-

9   gram, and

10   "(I) the investment manager has des-

11   ignated an individual responsible for periodi-

12   cally reviewing such purchases and sales to en-

13   sure compliance with the written policies and

14   procedures described in subparagraph (H), and

15   following such review, the individual shall issue

16   an annual written report no later than 90 days

17   following the period to which it relates signed

18   under penalty of perjury to the plan fiduciary

19   who authorized cross trading under subpara-

20   graph (D) describing the steps performed dur-

21   ing the course of the review, the level of compli-

22   ance, and any specific instances of non-compli-

23   ance.

24   The written report under subparagraph (I) shall also

25   notify the plan fiduciary of the plan's right to termi-

nate participation in the investment manager's cross-trading program at any time.''.

(2) AMENDMENTS OF INTERNAL REVENUE CODE OF 1986.—Subsection (d) of section 4975 of the Internal Revenue Code of 1986 (relating to exemptions), as amended by subsection (e), is amended by striking ''or'' at the end of paragraph (20), by striking the period at the end of paragraph (21) and inserting '', or'', and by adding at the end the following new paragraph:

''(22) any transaction described in subsection (c)(1)(A) involving the purchase and sale of a security between a plan and any other account managed by the same investment manager, if—

''(A) the transaction is a purchase or sale, for no consideration other than cash payment against prompt delivery of a security for which market quotations are readily available,

''(B) the transaction is effected at the independent current market price of the security (within the meaning of section 270.17a–7(b) of title 17, Code of Federal Regulations),

''(C) no brokerage commission, fee (except for customary transfer fees, the fact of which is disclosed pursuant to subparagraph (D)), or

1   other remuneration is paid in connection with
2   the transaction,

3   "(D) a fiduciary (other than the invest-
4   ment manager engaging in the cross-trades or
5   any affiliate) for each plan participating in the
6   transaction authorizes in advance of any cross-
7   trades (in a document that is separate from any
8   other written agreement of the parties) the in-
9   vestment manager to engage in cross trades at
10   the investment manager's discretion, after such
11   fiduciary has received disclosure regarding the
12   conditions under which cross trades may take
13   place (but only if such disclosure is separate
14   from any other agreement or disclosure involv-
15   ing the asset management relationship), includ-
16   ing the written policies and procedures of the
17   investment manager described in subparagraph
18   (H),

19   "(E) each plan participating in the trans-
20   action has assets of at least $100,000,000, ex-
21   cept that if the assets of a plan are invested in
22   a master trust containing the assets of plans
23   maintained by employers in the same controlled
24   group (as defined in section 407(d)(7) of the
25   Employee Retirement Income Security Act of

1974), the master trust has assets of at least $100,000,000,

"(F) the investment manager provides to the plan fiduciary who authorized cross trading under subparagraph (D) a quarterly report detailing all cross trades executed by the investment manager in which the plan participated during such quarter, including the following information, as applicable: (i) the identity of each security bought or sold; (ii) the number of shares or units traded, (iii) the parties involved in the cross-trade; and (iv) trade price and the method used to establish the trade price,

"(G) the investment manager does not base its fee schedule on the plan's consent to cross trading, and no other service (other than the investment opportunities and cost savings available through a cross trade) is conditioned on the plan's consent to cross trading,

"(H) the investment manager has adopted, and cross-trades are effected in accordance with, written cross-trading policies and procedures that are fair and equitable to all accounts participating in the cross-trading program, and that include a description of the manager's pricing policies and procedures, and the manager's policies and procedures for allocating cross trades in an objective manner among accounts participating in the cross-trading program, and

"(I) the investment manager has designated an individual responsible for periodically reviewing such purchases and sales to ensure compliance with the written policies and procedures described in subparagraph (H), and following such review, the individual shall issue an annual written report no later than 90 days following the period to which it relates signed under penalty of perjury to the plan fiduciary who authorized cross trading under subparagraph (D) describing the steps performed during the course of the review, the level of compliance, and any specific instances of non-compliance.

The written report shall also notify the plan fiduciary of the plan's right to terminate participation in the investment manager's cross-trading program at any time.".

(3) REGULATIONS.—No later than 180 days after the date of the enactment of this Act, the Sec-

1   retary of Labor, after consultation with the Securi-

2   ties and Exchange Commission, shall issue regula-

3   tions regarding the content of policies and proce-

4   dures required to be adopted by an investment man-

5   ager under section 408(b)(19) of the Employee Re-

6   tirement Income Security Act of 1974.

7   (h) EFFECTIVE DATES.—

8   (1) IN GENERAL.—Except as provided in para-

9   graph (2), the amendments made by this section

10 shall apply to transactions occurring after the date

11 of the enactment of this Act.

12   (2) BONDING RULE.—The amendments made

13 by subsection (b) shall apply to plan years beginning

14 after such date.

15 **SEC. 612. CORRECTION PERIOD FOR CERTAIN TRANS-**

16 **ACTIONS INVOLVING SECURITIES AND COM-**

17 **MODITIES.**

18 (a) AMENDMENT OF EMPLOYEE RETIREMENT IN-

19 COME SECURITY ACT OF 1974.—Section 408(b) of the

20 Employee Retirement Income Security Act of 1974 (29

21 U.S.C. 1108(b)), as amended by sections 601 and 611,

22 is further amended by adding at the end the following new

23 paragraph:

24   "(20)(A) Except as provided in subparagraphs

25 (B) and (C), a transaction described in section

1   406(a) in connection with the acquisition, holding,

2   or disposition of any security or commodity, if the

3   transaction is corrected before the end of the correc-

4   tion period.

5   "(B) Subparagraph (A) does not apply to any

6   transaction between a plan and a plan sponsor or its

7   affiliates that involves the acquisition or sale of an

8   employer security (as defined in section 407(d)(1))

9   or the acquisition, sale, or lease of employer real

10   property (as defined in section 407(d)(2)).

11   "(C) In the case of any fiduciary or other party

12   in interest (or any other person knowingly partici-

13   pating in such transaction), subparagraph (A) does

14   not apply to any transaction if, at the time the

15   transaction occurs, such fiduciary or party in inter-

16   est (or other person) knew (or reasonably should

17   have known) that the transaction would (without re-

18   gard to this paragraph) constitute a violation of sec-

19   tion 406(a).

20   "(D) For purposes of this paragraph, the term

21   'correction period' means, in connection with a fidu-

22   ciary or party in interest (or other person knowingly

23   participating in the transaction), the 14-day period

24   beginning on the date on which such fiduciary or

25   party in interest (or other person) discovers, or rea-

1 sonably should have discovered, that the transaction
2 would (without regard to this paragraph) constitute
3 a violation of section 406(a).

4   "(E) For purposes of this paragraph—

5   "(i) The term 'security' has the meaning
6 given such term by section 475(c)(2) of the In-
7 ternal Revenue Code of 1986 (without regard to
8 subparagraph (F)(iii) and the last sentence
9 thereof).

10   "(ii) The term 'commodity' has the mean-
11 ing given such term by section 475(e)(2) of
12 such Code (without regard to subparagraph
13 (D)(iii) thereof).

14   "(iii) The term 'correct' means, with re-
15 spect to a transaction—

16   "(I) to undo the transaction to the ex-
17 tent possible and in any case to make good
18 to the plan or affected account any losses
19 resulting from the transaction, and

20   "(II) to restore to the plan or affected
21 account any profits made through the use
22 of assets of the plan.".

23   (b) AMENDMENT OF INTERNAL REVENUE CODE OF
24 1986.—

1   (1) IN GENERAL.—Subsection (d) of section

2 4975 of the Internal Revenue Code of 1986 (relating

3 to exemptions), as amended by sections 601 and

4 611, is amended by striking "or" at the end of para-

5 graph (21), by striking the period at the end of

6 paragraph (22) and inserting ", or", and by adding

7 at the end the following new paragraph:

8   "(23) except as provided in subsection (f)(11),

9 a transaction described in subparagraph (A), (B),

10 (C), or (D) of subsection (c)(1) in connection with

11 the acquisition, holding, or disposition of any secu-

12 rity or commodity, if the transaction is corrected be-

13 fore the end of the correction period.".

14   (2) SPECIAL RULES RELATING TO CORRECTION

15 PERIOD.—Subsection (f) of section 4975 of such

16 Code (relating to other definitions and special rules),

17 as amended by sections 601 and 611, is amended by

18 adding at the end the following new paragraph:

19   "(11) CORRECTION PERIOD.—

20   "(A) IN GENERAL.—For purposes of sub-

21 section (d)(23), the term 'correction period'

22 means the 14-day period beginning on the date

23 on which the disqualified person discovers, or

24 reasonably should have discovered, that the

25 transaction would (without regard to this para-

graph and subsection (d)(23)) constitute a prohibited transaction.

"(B) EXCEPTIONS.—

"(i) EMPLOYER SECURITIES.—Subsection (d)(23) does not apply to any
transaction between a plan and a plan
sponsor or its affiliates that involves the
acquisition or sale of an employer security
(as defined in section 407(d)(1)) or the acquisition, sale, or lease of employer real
property (as defined in section 407(d)(2)).

"(ii) KNOWING PROHIBITED TRANS-
ACTION.—In the case of any disqualified
person, subsection (d)(23) does not apply
to a transaction if, at the time the transaction is entered into, the disqualified person knew (or reasonably should have
known) that the transaction would (without regard to this paragraph) constitute a
prohibited transaction.

"(C) ABATEMENT OF TAX WHERE THERE
IS A CORRECTION.—If a transaction is not
treated as a prohibited transaction by reason of
subsection (d)(23), then no tax under subsection (a) and (b) shall be assessed with re-

543

spect to such transaction, and if assessed the assessment shall be abated, and if collected shall be credited or refunded as an overpayment.

"(D) DEFINITIONS.—For purposes of this paragraph and subsection (d)(23)—

"(i) SECURITY.—The term 'security' has the meaning given such term by section 475(c)(2) (without regard to subparagraph (F)(iii) and the last sentence thereof).

"(ii) COMMODITY.—The term 'commodity' has the meaning given such term by section 475(e)(2) (without regard to subparagraph (D)(iii) thereof).

"(iii) CORRECT.—The term 'correct' means, with respect to a transaction—

"(I) to undo the transaction to the extent possible and in any case to make good to the plan or affected account any losses resulting from the transaction, and

"(II) to restore to the plan or affected account any profits made

1 through the use of assets of the

2 plan.".

3 (c) EFFECTIVE DATE.—The amendments made by

4 this section shall apply to any transaction which the fidu-

5 ciary or disqualified person discovers, or reasonably should

6 have discovered, after the date of the enactment of this

7 Act constitutes a prohibited transaction.

Subtitle C—Fiduciary and Other Rules

SEC. 621. INAPPLICABILITY OF RELIEF FROM FIDUCIARY LIABILITY DURING SUSPENSION OF ABILITY OF PARTICIPANT OR BENEFICIARY TO DIRECT INVESTMENTS.

14 (a) IN GENERAL.—Section 404(c) of the Employee

15 Retirement Income Security Act of 1974 (29 U.S.C.

16 1104(c)) is amended—

17 (1) in paragraph (1)—

18 (A) by redesignating subparagraphs (A)

19 and (B) as clauses (i) and (ii), respectively, and

20 by inserting "(A)" after "(c)(1)",

21 (B) in subparagraph (A)(ii) (as redesig-

22 nated by paragraph (1)), by inserting before the

23 period the following: ", except that this clause

24 shall not apply in connection with such partici-

25 pant or beneficiary for any blackout period dur-

1   ing which the ability of such participant or ben-

2   eficiary to direct the investment of the assets in

3   his or her account is suspended by a plan spon-

4   sor or fiduciary'', and

5   (C) by adding at the end the following new

6   subparagraphs:

7   "(B) If a person referred to in subparagraph (A)(ii)

8 meets the requirements of this title in connection with au-

9 thorizing and implementing the blackout period, any per-

10 son who is otherwise a fiduciary shall not be liable under

11 this title for any loss occurring during such period.

12   "(C) For purposes of this paragraph, the term 'black-

13 out period' has the meaning given such term by section

14 101(i)(7).''; and

15   (2) by adding at the end the following:

16   "(4)(A) In any case in which a qualified change

17   in investment options occurs in connection with an

18   individual account plan, a participant or beneficiary

19   shall not be treated for purposes of paragraph (1)

20   as not exercising control over the assets in his ac-

21   count in connection with such change if the require-

22   ments of subparagraph (C) are met in connection

23   with such change.

24   "(B) For purposes of subparagraph (A), the

25   term 'qualified change in investment options' means,

1   in connection with an individual account plan, a

2   change in the investment options offered to the par-

3   ticipant or beneficiary under the terms of the plan,

4   under which—

5   "(i) the account of the participant or bene-

6   ficiary is reallocated among one or more re-

7   maining or new investment options which are

8   offered in lieu of one or more investment op-

9   tions offered immediately prior to the effective

10   date of the change, and

11   "(ii) the stated characteristics of the re-

12   maining or new investment options provided

13   under clause (i), including characteristics relat-

14   ing to risk and rate of return, are, as of imme-

15   diately after the change, reasonably similar to

16   those of the existing investment options as of

17   immediately before the change.

18   "(C) The requirements of this subparagraph

19   are met in connection with a qualified change in in-

20   vestment options if—

21   "(i) at least 30 days and no more than 60

22   days prior to the effective date of the change,

23   the plan administrator furnishes written notice

24   of the change to the participants and bene-

25   ficiaries, including information comparing the

existing and new investment options and an explanation that, in the absence of affirmative investment instructions from the participant or beneficiary to the contrary, the account of the participant or beneficiary will be invested in the manner described in subparagraph (B),

"(ii) the participant or beneficiary has not provided to the plan administrator, in advance of the effective date of the change, affirmative investment instructions contrary to the change, and

"(iii) the investments under the plan of the participant or beneficiary as in effect immediately prior to the effective date of the change were the product of the exercise by such participant or beneficiary of control over the assets of the account within the meaning of paragraph (1).".

(b) EFFECTIVE DATE.—

(1) IN GENERAL.—The amendments made by this section shall apply to plan years beginning after December 31, 2007.

(2) SPECIAL RULE FOR COLLECTIVELY BARGAINED AGREEMENTS.—In the case of a plan maintained pursuant to 1 or more collective bargaining

1   agreements between employee representatives and 1

2   or more employers ratified on or before the date of

3   the enactment of this Act, paragraph (1) shall be

4   applied to benefits pursuant to, and individuals cov-

5   ered by, any such agreement by substituting for

6   "December 31, 2007" the earlier of—

7   (A) the later of—

8   (i) December 31, 2008, or

9   (ii) the date on which the last of such

10   collective bargaining agreements termi-

11   nates (determined without regard to any

12   extension thereof after such date of enact-

13   ment), or

14   (B) December 31, 2009.

15   **SEC. 622. INCREASE IN MAXIMUM BOND AMOUNT.**

16   (a) IN GENERAL.—Section 412(a) of the Employee

17   Retirement Income Security Act of 1974 (29 U.S.C.

18   1112), as amended by section 611(b), is amended by add-

19   ing at the end the following: "In the case of a plan that

20   holds employer securities (within the meaning of section

21   407(d)(1)), this subsection shall be applied by substituting

22   '$1,000,000' for '$500,000' each place it appears."

23   (b) EFFECTIVE DATE.—The amendment made by

24   this section shall apply to plan years beginning after De-

25   cember 31, 2007.

SEC. 623. INCREASE IN PENALTIES FOR COERCIVE INTER-FERENCE WITH EXERCISE OF ERISA RIGHTS.

(a) IN GENERAL.—Section 511 of the Employment Retirement Income Security Act of 1974 (29 U.S.C. 1141) is amended—

(1) by striking "$10,000" and inserting "$100,000", and

(2) by striking "one year" and inserting "10 years".

(b) EFFECTIVE DATE.—The amendments made by this section shall apply to violations occurring on and after the date of the enactment of this Act.

SEC. 624. TREATMENT OF INVESTMENT OF ASSETS BY PLAN WHERE PARTICIPANT FAILS TO EXERCISE IN-VESTMENT ELECTION.

(a) IN GENERAL.—Section 404(c) of the Employee Retirement Income Security Act of 1974 (29 U.S.C. 1104(c)), as amended by section 622, is amended by adding at the end the following new paragraph:

"(5) DEFAULT INVESTMENT ARRANGE-MENTS.—

"(A) IN GENERAL.—For purposes of paragraph (1), a participant in an individual account plan meeting the notice requirements of subparagraph (B) shall be treated as exercising control over the assets in the account with re-

1 spect to the amount of contributions and earn-

2 ings which, in the absence of an investment

3 election by the participant, are invested by the

4 plan in accordance with regulations prescribed

5 by the Secretary. The regulations under this

6 subparagraph shall provide guidance on the ap-

7 propriateness of designating default investments

8 that include a mix of asset classes consistent

9 with capital preservation or long-term capital

10 appreciation, or a blend of both.

11 "(B) NOTICE REQUIREMENTS.—

12 "(i) IN GENERAL.—The requirements

13 of this subparagraph are met if each par-

14 ticipant—

15 "(I) receives, within a reasonable

16 period of time before each plan year,

17 a notice explaining the employee's

18 right under the plan to designate how

19 contributions and earnings will be in-

20 vested and explaining how, in the ab-

21 sence of any investment election by

22 the participant, such contributions

23 and earnings will be invested, and

24 "(II) has a reasonable period of

25 time after receipt of such notice and

before the beginning of the plan year
to make such designation.

"(ii) FORM OF NOTICE.—The requirements of clauses (i) and (ii) of section
401(k)(12)(D) of the Internal Revenue
Code of 1986 shall apply with respect to
the notices described in this subparagraph.".

(b) EFFECTIVE DATE.—

(1) IN GENERAL.—The amendments made by
this section shall apply to plan years beginning after
December 31, 2006.

(2) REGULATIONS.—Final regulations under
section 404(c)(5)(A) of the Employee Retirement Income Security Act of 1974 (as added by this section)
shall be issued no later than 6 months after the date
of the enactment of this Act.

SEC. 625. CLARIFICATION OF FIDUCIARY RULES.

(a) IN GENERAL.—Not later than 1 year after the
date of the enactment of this Act, the Secretary of Labor
shall issue final regulations clarifying that the selection
of an annuity contract as an optional form of distribution
from an individual account plan to a participant or beneficiary—

1   (1) is not subject to the safest available annuity

2   standard under Interpretive Bulletin 95–1 (29

3   C.F.R. 2509.95–1), and

4   (2) is subject to all otherwise applicable fidu-

5   ciary standards.

6   (b) EFFECTIVE DATE.—This section shall take effect

7 on the date of enactment of this Act.

TITLE VII—BENEFIT ACCRUAL STANDARDS

10 **SEC. 701. BENEFIT ACCRUAL STANDARDS.**

11   (a) AMENDMENTS TO THE EMPLOYEE RETIREMENT

12 INCOME SECURITY ACT OF 1974.—

13   (1) RULES RELATING TO REDUCTION IN RATE

14   OF BENEFIT ACCRUAL.—Section 204(b) of the Em-

15   ployee Retirement Income Security Act of 1974 (29

16   U.S.C. 1054(b)) is amended by adding at the end

17   the following new paragraph:

18   "(5) SPECIAL RULES RELATING TO AGE.—

19   "(A) COMPARISON TO SIMILARLY SITU-

20   ATED YOUNGER INDIVIDUAL.—

21   "(i) IN GENERAL.—A plan shall not

22   be treated as failing to meet the require-

23   ments of paragraph (1)(H)(i) if a partici-

24   pant's accrued benefit, as determined as of

25   any date under the terms of the plan,

would be equal to or greater than that of any similarly situated, younger individual who is or could be a participant.

"(ii) SIMILARLY SITUATED.—For purposes of this subparagraph, a participant is similarly situated to any other individual if such participant is identical to such other individual in every respect (including period of service, compensation, position, date of hire, work history, and any other respect) except for age.

"(iii) DISREGARD OF SUBSIDIZED EARLY RETIREMENT BENEFITS.—In determining the accrued benefit as of any date for purposes of this clause, the subsidized portion of any early retirement benefit or retirement-type subsidy shall be disregarded.

"(iv) ACCRUED BENEFIT.—For purposes of this subparagraph, the accrued benefit may, under the terms of the plan, be expressed as an annuity payable at normal retirement age, the balance of a hypothetical account, or the current value of

1   the accumulated percentage of the employ-

2   ee's final average compensation.

3   "(B) APPLICABLE DEFINED BENEFIT

4   PLANS.—

5   "(i) INTEREST CREDITS.—

6   "(I) IN GENERAL.—An applicable

7   defined benefit plan shall be treated

8   as failing to meet the requirements of

9   paragraph (1)(H) unless the terms of

10   the plan provide that any interest

11   credit (or an equivalent amount) for

12   any plan year shall be at a rate which

13   is not greater than a market rate of

14   return. A plan shall not be treated as

15   failing to meet the requirements of

16   this subclause merely because the plan

17   provides for a reasonable minimum

18   guaranteed rate of return or for a

19   rate of return that is equal to the

20   greater of a fixed or variable rate of

21   return.

22   "(II) PRESERVATION OF CAP-

23   ITAL.—An interest credit (or an

24   equivalent amount) of less than zero

25   shall in no event result in the account

1   balance or similar amount being less
2   than the aggregate amount of con-
3   tributions credited to the account.

4   "(III) MARKET RATE OF RE-
5   TURN.—The Secretary of the Treas-
6   ury may provide by regulation for
7   rules governing the calculation of a
8   market rate of return for purposes of
9   subclause (I) and for permissible
10   methods of crediting interest to the
11   account (including fixed or variable
12   interest rates) resulting in effective
13   rates of return meeting the require-
14   ments of subclause (I).

15   "(ii) SPECIAL RULE FOR PLAN CON-
16   VERSIONS.—If, after June 29, 2005, an
17   applicable plan amendment is adopted, the
18   plan shall be treated as failing to meet the
19   requirements of paragraph (1)(H) unless
20   the requirements of clause (iii) are met
21   with respect to each individual who was a
22   participant in the plan immediately before
23   the adoption of the amendment.

24   "(iii) RATE OF BENEFIT ACCRUAL.—
25   Subject to clause (iv), the requirements of

1   this clause are met with respect to any

2   participant if the accrued benefit of the

3   participant under the terms of the plan as

4   in effect after the amendment is not less

5   than the sum of—

6   "(I) the participant's accrued

7   benefit for years of service before the

8   effective date of the amendment, de-

9   termined under the terms of the plan

10   as in effect before the amendment,

11   plus

12   "(II) the participant's accrued

13   benefit for years of service after the

14   effective date of the amendment, de-

15   termined under the terms of the plan

16   as in effect after the amendment.

17   "(iv) SPECIAL RULES FOR EARLY RE-

18   TIREMENT SUBSIDIES.—For purposes of

19   clause (iii)(I), the plan shall credit the ac-

20   cumulation account or similar amount with

21   the amount of any early retirement benefit

22   or retirement-type subsidy for the plan

23   year in which the participant retires if, as

24   of such time, the participant has met the

25   age, years of service, and other require-

1   ments under the plan for entitlement to

2   such benefit or subsidy.

3   "(v) APPLICABLE PLAN AMEND-

4   MENT.—For purposes of this subpara-

5   graph—

6   "(I) IN GENERAL.—The term

7   'applicable plan amendment' means

8   an amendment to a defined benefit

9   plan which has the effect of con-

10   verting the plan to an applicable de-

11   fined benefit plan.

12   "(II) SPECIAL RULE FOR CO-

13   ORDINATED BENEFITS.—If the bene-

14   fits of 2 or more defined benefit plans

15   established or maintained by an em-

16   ployer are coordinated in such a man-

17   ner as to have the effect of the adop-

18   tion of an amendment described in

19   subclause (I), the sponsor of the de-

20   fined benefit plan or plans providing

21   for such coordination shall be treated

22   as having adopted such a plan amend-

23   ment as of the date such coordination

24   begins.

1   "(III) MULTIPLE AMEND-

2   MENTS.—The Secretary of the Treas-

3   ury shall issue regulations to prevent

4   the avoidance of the purposes of this

5   subparagraph through the use of 2 or

6   more plan amendments rather than a

7   single amendment.

8   "(IV) APPLICABLE DEFINED

9   BENEFIT PLAN.—For purposes of this

10   subparagraph, the term 'applicable de-

11   fined benefit plan' has the meaning

12   given such term by section 203(f)(3).

13   "(vi) TERMINATION REQUIRE-

14   MENTS.—An applicable defined benefit

15   plan shall not be treated as meeting the re-

16   quirements of clause (i) unless the plan

17   provides that, upon the termination of the

18   plan—

19   "(I) if the interest credit rate (or

20   an equivalent amount) under the plan

21   is a variable rate, the rate of interest

22   used to determine accrued benefits

23   under the plan shall be equal to the

24   average of the rates of interest used

25   under the plan during the 5-year pe-

1   riod ending on the termination date,

2   and

3   "(II) the interest rate and mor-

4   tality table used to determine the

5   amount of any benefit under the plan

6   payable in the form of an annuity

7   payable at normal retirement age

8   shall be the rate and table specified

9   under the plan for such purpose as of

10   the termination date, except that if

11   such interest rate is a variable rate,

12   the interest rate shall be determined

13   under the rules of subclause (I).

14   "(C) CERTAIN OFFSETS PERMITTED.—A

15 plan shall not be treated as failing to meet the

16 requirements of paragraph (1)(H)(i) solely be-

17 cause the plan provides offsets against benefits

18 under the plan to the extent such offsets are al-

19 lowable in applying the requirements of section

20 401(a) of the Internal Revenue Code of 1986.

21   "(D) PERMITTED DISPARITIES IN PLAN

22 CONTRIBUTIONS OR BENEFITS.—A plan shall

23 not be treated as failing to meet the require-

24 ments of paragraph (1)(H) solely because the

25 plan provides a disparity in contributions or

1   benefits with respect to which the requirements

2   of section 401(l) of the Internal Revenue Code

3   of 1986 are met.

4   "(E) INDEXING PERMITTED.—

5   "(i) IN GENERAL.—A plan shall not

6   be treated as failing to meet the require-

7   ments of paragraph (1)(H) solely because

8   the plan provides for indexing of accrued

9   benefits under the plan.

10   "(ii) PROTECTION AGAINST LOSS.—

11   Except in the case of any benefit provided

12   in the form of a variable annuity, clause (i)

13   shall not apply with respect to any index-

14   ing which results in an accrued benefit less

15   than the accrued benefit determined with-

16   out regard to such indexing.

17   "(iii) INDEXING.—For purposes of

18   this subparagraph, the term 'indexing'

19   means, in connection with an accrued ben-

20   efit, the periodic adjustment of the accrued

21   benefit by means of the application of a

22   recognized investment index or method-

23   ology.

24   "(F) EARLY RETIREMENT BENEFIT OR RE-

25   TIREMENT-TYPE SUBSIDY.—For purposes of

1   this paragraph, the terms 'early retirement ben-

2   efit' and 'retirement-type subsidy' have the

3   meaning given such terms in subsection

4   (g)(2)(A).

5   "(G) BENEFIT ACCRUED TO DATE.—For

6   purposes of this paragraph, any reference to the

7   accrued benefit shall be a reference to such ben-

8   efit accrued to date.".

9   (2) DETERMINATIONS OF ACCRUED BENEFIT AS

10   BALANCE OF BENEFIT ACCOUNT OR EQUIVALENT

11   AMOUNTS.—Section 203 of such Act (29 U.S.C.

12   1053) is amended by adding at the end the following

13   new subsection:

14   "(f) SPECIAL RULES FOR PLANS COMPUTING AC-

15   CRUED BENEFITS BY REFERENCE TO HYPOTHETICAL AC-

16   COUNT BALANCE OR EQUIVALENT AMOUNTS.—

17   "(1) IN GENERAL.—An applicable defined ben-

18   efit plan shall not be treated as failing to meet—

19   "(A) subject to paragraph (2), the require-

20   ments of subsection (a)(2), or

21   "(B) the requirements of section 204(c) or

22   section 205(g) with respect to contributions

23   other than employee contributions,

24   solely because the present value of the accrued ben-

25   efit (or any portion thereof) of any participant is,

1   under the terms of the plan, equal to the amount ex-

2   pressed as the balance in the hypothetical account

3   described in paragraph (3) or as an accumulated

4   percentage of the participant's final average com-

5   pensation.

6   "(2) 3-YEAR VESTING.—In the case of an appli-

7   cable defined benefit plan, such plan shall be treated

8   as meeting the requirements of subsection (a)(2)

9   only if an employee who has completed at least 3

10   years of service has a nonforfeitable right to 100

11   percent of the employee's accrued benefit derived

12   from employer contributions.

13   "(3) APPLICABLE DEFINED BENEFIT PLAN AND

14   RELATED RULES.—For purposes of this sub-

15   section—

16   "(A) IN GENERAL.—The term 'applicable

17   defined benefit plan' means a defined benefit

18   plan under which the accrued benefit (or any

19   portion thereof) is calculated as the balance of

20   a hypothetical account maintained for the par-

21   ticipant or as an accumulated percentage of the

22   participant's final average compensation.

23   "(B) REGULATIONS TO INCLUDE SIMILAR

24   PLANS.—The Secretary of the Treasury shall

25   issue regulations which include in the definition

of an applicable defined benefit plan any defined benefit plan (or any portion of such a plan) which has an effect similar to an applicable defined benefit plan.''.

(b) AMENDMENTS TO THE INTERNAL REVENUE CODE OF 1986.—

(1) RULES RELATING TO REDUCTION IN RATE OF BENEFIT ACCRUAL.—Subsection (b) of section 411 of the Internal Revenue Code of 1986 is amended by adding at the end the following new paragraph:

"(5) SPECIAL RULES RELATING TO AGE.—

"(A) COMPARISON TO SIMILARLY SITUATED YOUNGER INDIVIDUAL.—

"(i) IN GENERAL.—A plan shall not be treated as failing to meet the requirements of paragraph (1)(H)(i) if a participant's accrued benefit, as determined as of any date under the terms of the plan, would be equal to or greater than that of any similarly situated, younger individual who is or could be a participant.

"(ii) SIMILARLY SITUATED.—For purposes of this subparagraph, a participant is similarly situated to any other individual if such participant is identical to such other individual in every respect (including period of service, compensation, position, date of hire, work history, and any other respect) except for age.

"(iii) DISREGARD OF SUBSIDIZED EARLY RETIREMENT BENEFITS.—In determining the accrued benefit as of any date for purposes of this clause, the subsidized portion of any early retirement benefit or retirement-type subsidy shall be disregarded.

"(iv) ACCRUED BENEFIT.—For purposes of this subparagraph, the accrued benefit may, under the terms of the plan, be expressed as an annuity payable at normal retirement age, the balance of a hypothetical account, or the current value of the accumulated percentage of the employee's final average compensation.

"(B) APPLICABLE DEFINED BENEFIT PLANS.—

"(i) INTEREST CREDITS.—

"(I) IN GENERAL.—An applicable defined benefit plan shall be treated as failing to meet the requirements of paragraph (1)(H) unless the terms of the plan provide that any interest credit (or an equivalent amount) for any plan year shall be at a rate which is not greater than a market rate of return. A plan shall not be treated as failing to meet the requirements of this subclause merely because the plan provides for a reasonable minimum guaranteed rate of return or for a rate of return that is equal to the greater of a fixed or variable rate of return.

"(II) PRESERVATION OF CAPITAL.—An interest credit (or an equivalent amount) of less than zero shall in no event result in the account balance or similar amount being less than the aggregate amount of contributions credited to the account.

"(III) MARKET RATE OF RETURN.—The Secretary may provide by regulation for rules governing the calculation of a market rate of return for purposes of subclause (I) and for permissible methods of crediting interest to the account (including fixed or variable interest rates) resulting in effective rates of return meeting the requirements of subclause (I).

"(ii) SPECIAL RULE FOR PLAN CONVERSIONS.—If, after June 29, 2005, an applicable plan amendment is adopted, the plan shall be treated as failing to meet the requirements of paragraph (1)(H) unless the requirements of clause (iii) are met with respect to each individual who was a participant in the plan immediately before the adoption of the amendment.

"(iii) RATE OF BENEFIT ACCRUAL.— Subject to clause (iv), the requirements of this clause are met with respect to any participant if the accrued benefit of the participant under the terms of the plan as in effect after the amendment is not less than the sum of—

"(I) the participant's accrued benefit for years of service before the effective date of the amendment, de-

termined under the terms of the plan
as in effect before the amendment,
plus

"(II) the participant's accrued
benefit for years of service after the
effective date of the amendment, determined under the terms of the plan
as in effect after the amendment.

"(iv) SPECIAL RULES FOR EARLY RE-
TIREMENT SUBSIDIES.—For purposes of
clause (iii)(I), the plan shall credit the accumulation account or similar amount with
the amount of any early retirement benefit
or retirement-type subsidy for the plan
year in which the participant retires if, as
of such time, the participant has met the
age, years of service, and other requirements under the plan for entitlement to
such benefit or subsidy.

"(v) APPLICABLE PLAN AMEND-
MENT.—For purposes of this subparagraph—

"(I) IN GENERAL.—The term
'applicable plan amendment' means
an amendment to a defined benefit

1   plan which has the effect of con-

2   verting the plan to an applicable de-

3   fined benefit plan.

4   "(II) SPECIAL RULE FOR CO-

5   ORDINATED BENEFITS.—If the bene-

6   fits of 2 or more defined benefit plans

7   established or maintained by an em-

8   ployer are coordinated in such a man-

9   ner as to have the effect of the adop-

10   tion of an amendment described in

11   subclause (I), the sponsor of the de-

12   fined benefit plan or plans providing

13   for such coordination shall be treated

14   as having adopted such a plan amend-

15   ment as of the date such coordination

16   begins.

17   "(III) MULTIPLE AMEND-

18   MENTS.—The Secretary shall issue

19   regulations to prevent the avoidance

20   of the purposes of this subparagraph

21   through the use of 2 or more plan

22   amendments rather than a single

23   amendment.

24   "(IV) APPLICABLE DEFINED

25   BENEFIT PLAN.—For purposes of this

subparagraph, the term 'applicable defined benefit plan' has the meaning
given such term by section
411(a)(13).

"(vi) TERMINATION REQUIRE-
MENTS.—An applicable defined benefit
plan shall not be treated as meeting the requirements of clause (i) unless the plan
provides that, upon the termination of the
plan—

"(I) if the interest credit rate (or
an equivalent amount) under the plan
is a variable rate, the rate of interest
used to determine accrued benefits
under the plan shall be equal to the
average of the rates of interest used
under the plan during the 5-year period ending on the termination date,
and

"(II) the interest rate and mortality table used to determine the
amount of any benefit under the plan
payable in the form of an annuity
payable at normal retirement age
shall be the rate and table specified

1   under the plan for such purpose as of

2   the termination date, except that if

3   such interest rate is a variable rate,

4   the interest rate shall be determined

5   under the rules of subclause (I).

6   "(C) CERTAIN OFFSETS PERMITTED.—A

7 plan shall not be treated as failing to meet the

8 requirements of paragraph (1)(H)(i) solely be-

9 cause the plan provides offsets against benefits

10 under the plan to the extent such offsets are al-

11 lowable in applying the requirements of section

12 401(a).

13   "(D) PERMITTED DISPARITIES IN PLAN

14 CONTRIBUTIONS OR BENEFITS.—A plan shall

15 not be treated as failing to meet the require-

16 ments of paragraph (1)(H) solely because the

17 plan provides a disparity in contributions or

18 benefits with respect to which the requirements

19 of section 401(l) are met.

20   "(E) INDEXING PERMITTED.—

21   "(i) IN GENERAL.—A plan shall not

22   be treated as failing to meet the require-

23   ments of paragraph (1)(H) solely because

24   the plan provides for indexing of accrued

25   benefits under the plan.

"(ii) PROTECTION AGAINST LOSS.—
Except in the case of any benefit provided
in the form of a variable annuity, clause (i)
shall not apply with respect to any indexing which results in an accrued benefit less
than the accrued benefit determined without regard to such indexing.

"(iii) INDEXING.—For purposes of
this subparagraph, the term 'indexing'
means, in connection with an accrued benefit, the periodic adjustment of the accrued
benefit by means of the application of a
recognized investment index or methodology.

"(F) EARLY RETIREMENT BENEFIT OR RE-
TIREMENT-TYPE SUBSIDY.—For purposes of
this paragraph, the terms 'early retirement benefit' and 'retirement-type subsidy' have the
meaning given such terms in subsection
(d)(6)(B)(i).

"(G) BENEFIT ACCRUED TO DATE.—For
purposes of this paragraph, any reference to the
accrued benefit shall be a reference to such benefit accrued to date.".

(2) DETERMINATIONS OF ACCRUED BENEFIT AS BALANCE OF BENEFIT ACCOUNT OR EQUIVALENT AMOUNTS.—Subsection (a) of section 411 of such Code is amended by adding at the end the following new paragraph:

"(13) SPECIAL RULES FOR PLANS COMPUTING ACCRUED BENEFITS BY REFERENCE TO HYPO-THETICAL ACCOUNT BALANCE OR EQUIVALENT AMOUNTS.—

"(A) IN GENERAL.—An applicable defined benefit plan shall not be treated as failing to meet—

"(i) subject to paragraph (2), the requirements of subsection (a)(2), or

"(ii) the requirements of subsection (c) or section 417(e) with respect to contributions other than employee contributions,

solely because the present value of the accrued benefit (or any portion thereof) of any participant is, under the terms of the plan, equal to the amount expressed as the balance in the hypothetical account described in paragraph (3) or as an accumulated percentage of the participant's final average compensation.

"(B) 3-YEAR VESTING.—In the case of an applicable defined benefit plan, such plan shall be treated as meeting the requirements of subsection (a)(2) only if an employee who has completed at least 3 years of service has a nonforfeitable right to 100 percent of the employee's accrued benefit derived from employer contributions.

"(C) APPLICABLE DEFINED BENEFIT PLAN AND RELATED RULES.—For purposes of this subsection—

"(i) IN GENERAL.—The term 'applicable defined benefit plan' means a defined benefit plan under which the accrued benefit (or any portion thereof) is calculated as the balance of a hypothetical account maintained for the participant or as an accumulated percentage of the participant's final average compensation.

"(ii) REGULATIONS TO INCLUDE SIMILAR PLANS.—The Secretary shall issue regulations which include in the definition of an applicable defined benefit plan any defined benefit plan (or any portion of

1 such a plan) which has an effect similar to

2 an applicable defined benefit plan.".

3 (c) AMENDMENTS TO AGE DISCRIMINATION IN EM-

4 PLOYMENT ACT.—Section 4(i) of the Age Discrimination

5 in Employment Act of 1967 (29 U.S.C. 623(i)) is amend-

6 ed by adding at the end the following new paragraph:

7   "(10) SPECIAL RULES RELATING TO AGE.—

8   "(A) COMPARISON TO SIMILARLY SITU-

9   ATED YOUNGER INDIVIDUAL.—

10   "(i) IN GENERAL.—A plan shall not

11   be treated as failing to meet the require-

12   ments of paragraph (1) if a participant's

13   accrued benefit, as determined as of any

14   date under the terms of the plan, would be

15   equal to or greater than that of any simi-

16   larly situated, younger individual who is or

17   could be a participant.

18   "(ii) SIMILARLY SITUATED.—For pur-

19   poses of this subparagraph, a participant

20   is similarly situated to any other individual

21   if such participant is identical to such

22   other individual in every respect (including

23   period of service, compensation, position,

24   date of hire, work history, and any other

25   respect) except for age.

"(iii) DISREGARD OF SUBSIDIZED EARLY RETIREMENT BENEFITS.—In determining the accrued benefit as of any date for purposes of this clause, the subsidized portion of any early retirement benefit or retirement-type subsidy shall be disregarded.

"(iv) ACCRUED BENEFIT.—For purposes of this subparagraph, the accrued benefit may, under the terms of the plan, be expressed as an annuity payable at normal retirement age, the balance of a hypothetical account, or the current value of the accumulated percentage of the employee's final average compensation.

"(B) APPLICABLE DEFINED BENEFIT PLANS.—

"(i) INTEREST CREDITS.—

"(I) IN GENERAL.—An applicable defined benefit plan shall be treated as failing to meet the requirements of paragraph (1) unless the terms of the plan provide that any interest credit (or an equivalent amount) for any plan year shall be at a rate which is

1   not greater than a market rate of re-

2   turn. A plan shall not be treated as

3   failing to meet the requirements of

4   this subclause merely because the plan

5   provides for a reasonable minimum

6   guaranteed rate of return or for a

7   rate of return that is equal to the

8   greater of a fixed or variable rate of

9   return.

10   "(II) PRESERVATION OF CAP-

11   ITAL.—An interest credit (or an

12   equivalent amount) of less than zero

13   shall in no event result in the account

14   balance or similar amount being less

15   than the aggregate amount of con-

16   tributions credited to the account.

17   "(III) MARKET RATE OF RE-

18   TURN.—The Secretary of the Treas-

19   ury may provide by regulation for

20   rules governing the calculation of a

21   market rate of return for purposes of

22   subclause (I) and for permissible

23   methods of crediting interest to the

24   account (including fixed or variable

25   interest rates) resulting in effective

rates of return meeting the requirements of subclause (I).

"(ii) SPECIAL RULE FOR PLAN CONVERSIONS.—If, after June 29, 2005, an applicable plan amendment is adopted, the plan shall be treated as failing to meet the requirements of paragraph (1)(H) unless the requirements of clause (iii) are met with respect to each individual who was a participant in the plan immediately before the adoption of the amendment.

"(iii) RATE OF BENEFIT ACCRUAL.— Subject to clause (iv), the requirements of this clause are met with respect to any participant if the accrued benefit of the participant under the terms of the plan as in effect after the amendment is not less than the sum of—

"(I) the participant's accrued benefit for years of service before the effective date of the amendment, determined under the terms of the plan as in effect before the amendment, plus

1   "(II) the participant's accrued

2   benefit for years of service after the

3   effective date of the amendment, de-

4   termined under the terms of the plan

5   as in effect after the amendment.

6   "(iv) SPECIAL RULES FOR EARLY RE-

7   TIREMENT SUBSIDIES.—For purposes of

8   clause (iii)(I), the plan shall credit the ac-

9   cumulation account or similar amount with

10   the amount of any early retirement benefit

11   or retirement-type subsidy for the plan

12   year in which the participant retires if, as

13   of such time, the participant has met the

14   age, years of service, and other require-

15   ments under the plan for entitlement to

16   such benefit or subsidy.

17   "(v) APPLICABLE PLAN AMEND-

18   MENT.—For purposes of this subpara-

19   graph—

20   "(I) IN GENERAL.—The term

21   'applicable plan amendment' means

22   an amendment to a defined benefit

23   plan which has the effect of con-

24   verting the plan to an applicable de-

25   fined benefit plan.

1   "(II) SPECIAL RULE FOR CO-

2   ORDINATED BENEFITS.—If the bene-

3   fits of 2 or more defined benefit plans

4   established or maintained by an em-

5   ployer are coordinated in such a man-

6   ner as to have the effect of the adop-

7   tion of an amendment described in

8   subclause (I), the sponsor of the de-

9   fined benefit plan or plans providing

10   for such coordination shall be treated

11   as having adopted such a plan amend-

12   ment as of the date such coordination

13   begins.

14   "(III) MULTIPLE AMEND-

15   MENTS.—The Secretary of the Treas-

16   ury shall issue regulations to prevent

17   the avoidance of the purposes of this

18   subparagraph through the use of 2 or

19   more plan amendments rather than a

20   single amendment.

21   "(IV) APPLICABLE DEFINED

22   BENEFIT PLAN.—For purposes of this

23   subparagraph, the term 'applicable de-

24   fined benefit plan' has the meaning

25   given such term by section 203(f)(3)

1   of the Employee Retirement Income

2   Security Act of 1974.

3   "(vi) TERMINATION REQUIRE-

4 MENTS.—An applicable defined benefit

5 plan shall not be treated as meeting the re-

6 quirements of clause (i) unless the plan

7 provides that, upon the termination of the

8 plan—

9   "(I) if the interest credit rate (or

10   an equivalent amount) under the plan

11   is a variable rate, the rate of interest

12   used to determine accrued benefits

13   under the plan shall be equal to the

14   average of the rates of interest used

15   under the plan during the 5-year pe-

16   riod ending on the termination date,

17   and

18   "(II) the interest rate and mor-

19   tality table used to determine the

20   amount of any benefit under the plan

21   payable in the form of an annuity

22   payable at normal retirement age

23   shall be the rate and table specified

24   under the plan for such purpose as of

25   the termination date, except that if

1   such interest rate is a variable rate,

2   the interest rate shall be determined

3   under the rules of subclause (I).

4   "(C) CERTAIN OFFSETS PERMITTED.—A

5 plan shall not be treated as failing to meet the

6 requirements of paragraph (1) solely because

7 the plan provides offsets against benefits under

8 the plan to the extent such offsets are allowable

9 in applying the requirements of section 401(a)

10 of the Internal Revenue Code of 1986.

11   "(D) PERMITTED DISPARITIES IN PLAN

12 CONTRIBUTIONS OR BENEFITS.—A plan shall

13 not be treated as failing to meet the require-

14 ments of paragraph (1) solely because the plan

15 provides a disparity in contributions or benefits

16 with respect to which the requirements of sec-

17 tion 401(l) of the Internal Revenue Code of

18 1986 are met.

19   "(E) INDEXING PERMITTED.—

20   "(i) IN GENERAL.—A plan shall not

21   be treated as failing to meet the require-

22   ments of paragraph (1) solely because the

23   plan provides for indexing of accrued bene-

24   fits under the plan.

1   "(ii) PROTECTION AGAINST LOSS.—

2   Except in the case of any benefit provided

3   in the form of a variable annuity, clause (i)

4   shall not apply with respect to any index-

5   ing which results in an accrued benefit less

6   than the accrued benefit determined with-

7   out regard to such indexing.

8   "(iii) INDEXING.—For purposes of

9   this subparagraph, the term 'indexing'

10   means, in connection with an accrued ben-

11   efit, the periodic adjustment of the accrued

12   benefit by means of the application of a

13   recognized investment index or method-

14   ology.

15   "(F) EARLY RETIREMENT BENEFIT OR RE-

16 TIREMENT-TYPE SUBSIDY.—For purposes of

17 this paragraph, the terms 'early retirement ben-

18 efit' and 'retirement-type subsidy' have the

19 meaning given such terms in section

20 203(g)(2)(A) of the Employee Retirement In-

21 come Security Act of 1974.

22   "(G) BENEFIT ACCRUED TO DATE.—For

23 purposes of this paragraph, any reference to the

24 accrued benefit shall be a reference to such ben-

25 efit accrued to date.".

1   (d) NO INFERENCE.—Nothing in the amendments

2 made by this section shall be construed to create an infer-

3 ence with respect to—

4   (1) the treatment of applicable defined benefit

5   plans or conversions to applicable defined benefit

6   plans under sections 204(b)(1)(H) of the Employee

7   Retirement Income Security Act of 1974, 4(i)(1) of

8   the Age Discrimination in Employment Act of 1967,

9   and 411(b)(1)(H) of the Internal Revenue Code of

10   1986, as in effect before such amendments, or

11   (2) the determination of whether an applicable

12   defined benefit plan fails to meet the requirements

13   of sections 203(a)(2), 204(c), or 204(g) of the Em-

14   ployee Retirement Income Security Act of 1974 or

15   sections 411(a)(2), 411(c), or 417(e) of such Code,

16   as in effect before such amendments, solely because

17   the present value of the accrued benefit (or any por-

18   tion thereof) of any participant is, under the terms

19   of the plan, equal to the amount expressed as the

20   balance in a hypothetical account or as an accumu-

21   lated percentage of the participant's final average

22   compensation.

23 For purposes of this subsection, the term "applicable de-

24 fined benefit plan" has the meaning given such term by

25 section 203(f)(3) of the Employee Retirement Income Se-

1 curity Act of 1974 and section 411(a)(13)(C) of such

2 Code, as in effect after such amendments.

3   (e) EFFECTIVE DATE.—

4   (1) IN GENERAL.—The amendments made by

5   this section shall apply to periods beginning on or

6   after June 29, 2005.

7   (2) PRESENT VALUE OF ACCRUED BENEFIT.—

8   The amendments made by subsections (a)(2) and

9   (b)(2) shall apply to distributions made after the

10   date of the enactment of this Act.

11   (3) VESTING AND INTEREST CREDIT REQUIRE-

12   MENTS.—In the case of a plan in existence on June

13   29, 2005, the requirements of clause (i) of section

14   411(b)(5)(B) of the Internal Revenue Code of 1986,

15   clause (i) of section 204(b)(5)(B) of the Employee

16   Retirement Income Security Act of 1974, and clause

17   (i) of section 4(i)(10)(B) of the Age Discrimination

18   in Employment Act of 1967 (as added by this Act)

19   and the requirements of 203(f)(2) of the Employee

20   Retirement Income Security Act of 1974 and section

21   411(a)(13)(B) of the Internal Revenue Code of 1986

22   (as so added) shall, for purposes of applying the

23   amendments made by subsections (a) and (b), apply

24   to years beginning after December 31, 2007, unless

25   the plan sponsor elects the application of such re-

585

1   quirements for any period after June 29, 2005, and

2   before the first year beginning after December 31,

3   2007.

4   (4) SPECIAL RULE FOR COLLECTIVELY BAR-

5   GAINED PLANS.—In the case of a plan maintained

6   pursuant to 1 or more collective bargaining agree-

7   ments between employee representatives and 1 or

8   more employers ratified on or before the date of the

9   enactment of this Act, the requirements described in

10   paragraph (3) shall, for purposes of applying the

11   amendments made by subsections (a) and (b), not

12   apply to plan years beginning before—

13   (A) the earlier of—

14   (i) the date on which the last of such

15   collective bargaining agreements termi-

16   nates (determined without regard to any

17   extension thereof on or after such date of

18   enactment), or

19   (ii) January 1, 2008, or

20   (B) January 1, 2010.

21   (5) CONVERSIONS.—The requirements of clause

22   (ii) of section 411(b)(5)(B) of the Internal Revenue

23   Code of 1986, clause (ii) of section 204(b)(5)(B) of

24   the Employee Retirement Income Security Act of

25   1974, and clause (ii) of section 4(i)(10)(B) of the

1   Age Discrimination in Employment Act of 1967 (as

2   added by this Act), shall apply to plan amendments

3   adopted after, and taking effect after, June 29,

4   2005, except that the plan sponsor may elect to have

5   such amendments apply to plan amendments adopt-

6   ed before, and taking effect after, such date.

7 SEC. 702. REGULATIONS RELATING TO MERGERS AND AC-

8   QUISITIONS.

9   The Secretary of the Treasury or his delegate shall,

10 not later than 12 months after the date of the enactment

11 of this Act, prescribe regulations for the application of the

12 amendments made by, and the provisions of, this title in

13 cases where the conversion of a plan to an applicable de-

14 fined benefit plan is made with respect to a group of em-

15 ployees who become employees by reason of a merger, ac-

16 quisition, or similar transaction.

17 TITLE VIII—PENSION RELATED
18   REVENUE PROVISIONS
19 Subtitle A—Deduction Limitations

20 SEC. 801. INCREASE IN DEDUCTION LIMIT FOR SINGLE-EM-

21   PLOYER PLANS.

22   (a) IN GENERAL.—Section 404 of the Internal Rev-

23 enue Code of 1986 (relating to deduction for contributions

24 of an employer to an employees' trust or annuity plan and

1 compensation under a deferred payment plan) is amend-

2 ed—

3   (1) in subsection (a)(1)(A), by inserting "in the

4   case of a defined benefit plan other than a multiem-

5   ployer plan, in an amount determined under sub-

6   section (o), and in the case of any other plan" after

7   "section 501(a),", and

8   (2) by inserting at the end the following new

9   subsection:

10 "(o) DEDUCTION LIMIT FOR SINGLE-EMPLOYER

11 PLANS.—For purposes of subsection (a)(1)(A)—

12   "(1) IN GENERAL.—In the case of a defined

13   benefit plan to which subsection (a)(1)(A) applies

14   (other than a multiemployer plan), the amount de-

15   termined under this subsection for any taxable year

16   shall be equal to the greater of—

17   "(A) the sum of the amounts determined

18   under paragraph (2) with respect to each plan

19   year ending with or within the taxable year, or

20   "(B) the sum of the minimum required

21   contributions under section 430 for such plan

22   years.

23   "(2) DETERMINATION OF AMOUNT.—

1   "(A) IN GENERAL.—The amount deter-

2   mined under this paragraph for any plan year

3   shall be equal to the excess (if any) of—

4   "(i) the sum of—

5   "(I) the funding target for the

6   plan year,

7   "(II) the target normal cost for

8   the plan year, and

9   "(III) the cushion amount for the

10   plan year, over

11   "(ii) the value (determined under sec-

12   tion 430(g)(2)) of the assets of the plan

13   which are held by the plan as of the valu-

14   ation date for the plan year.

15   "(B) SPECIAL RULE FOR CERTAIN EM-

16   PLOYERS.—If section 430(i) does not apply to

17   a plan for a plan year, the amount determined

18   under subparagraph (A)(i) for the plan year

19   shall in no event be less than the sum of—

20   "(i) the funding target for the plan

21   year (determined as if section 430(i) ap-

22   plied to the plan), plus

23   "(ii) the target normal cost for the

24   plan year (as so determined).

1   "(3) CUSHION AMOUNT.—For purposes of para-

2 graph (2)(A)(i)(III)—

3   "(A) IN GENERAL.—The cushion amount

4 for any plan year is the sum of—

5   "(i) 50 percent of the funding target

6 for the plan year, and

7   "(ii) the amount by which the funding

8 target for the plan year would increase if

9 the plan were to take into account—

10   "(I) increases in compensation

11 which are expected to occur in suc-

12 ceeding plan years, or

13   "(II) if the plan does not base

14 benefits for service to date on com-

15 pensation, increases in benefits which

16 are expected to occur in succeeding

17 plan years (determined on the basis of

18 the average annual increase in bene-

19 fits over the 6 immediately preceding

20 plan years).

21   "(B) LIMITATIONS.—

22   "(i) IN GENERAL.—In making the

23 computation under subparagraph (A)(ii),

24 the plan's actuary shall assume that the

1 limitations under subsection (l) and section
2 415(b) shall apply.

3   "(ii) EXPECTED INCREASES.—In the
4 case of a plan year during which a plan is
5 covered under section 4021 of the Em-
6 ployee Retirement Income Security Act of
7 1974, the plan's actuary may, notwith-
8 standing subsection (l), take into account
9 increases in the limitations which are ex-
10 pected to occur in succeeding plan years.

11   "(4) SPECIAL RULES FOR PLANS WITH 100 OR
12 FEWER PARTICIPANTS.—

13   "(A) IN GENERAL.—For purposes of deter-
14 mining the amount under paragraph (3) for any
15 plan year, in the case of a plan which has 100
16 or fewer participants for the plan year, the li-
17 ability of the plan attributable to benefit in-
18 creases for highly compensated employees (as
19 defined in section 414(q)) resulting from a plan
20 amendment which is made or becomes effective,
21 whichever is later, within the last 2 years shall
22 not be taken into account in determining the
23 target liability.

24   "(B) RULE FOR DETERMINING NUMBER
25 OF PARTICIPANTS.—For purposes of deter-

1   mining the number of plan participants, all de-

2   fined benefit plans maintained by the same em-

3   ployer (or any member of such employer's con-

4   trolled group (within the meaning of section

5   412(f)(4))) shall be treated as one plan, but

6   only participants of such member or employer

7   shall be taken into account.

8   "(5) SPECIAL RULE FOR TERMINATING

9   PLANS.—In the case of a plan which, subject to sec-

10   tion 4041 of the Employee Retirement Income Secu-

11   rity Act of 1974, terminates during the plan year,

12   the amount determined under paragraph (2) shall in

13   no event be less than the amount required to make

14   the plan sufficient for benefit liabilities (within the

15   meaning of section 4041(d) of such Act).

16   "(6) ACTUARIAL ASSUMPTIONS.—Any computa-

17   tion under this subsection for any plan year shall

18   use the same actuarial assumptions which are used

19   for the plan year under section 430.

20   "(7) DEFINITIONS.—Any term used in this sub-

21   section which is also used in section 430 shall have

22   the same meaning given such term by section 430.".

23   (b) EXCEPTION FROM LIMITATION ON DEDUCTION

24 WHERE COMBINATION OF DEFINED CONTRIBUTION AND

25 DEFINED BENEFIT PLANS.—Section 404(a)(7)(C) of

1 such Code, as amended by this Act, is amended by adding

2 at the end the following new clause:

3   "(iv) GUARANTEED PLANS.—In apply-

4   ing this paragraph, any single-employer

5   plan covered under section 4021 of the

6   Employee Retirement Income Security Act

7   of 1974 shall not be taken into account.".

8 (c) TECHNICAL AND CONFORMING AMENDMENTS.—

9   (1) The last sentence of section 404(a)(1)(A) of

10 such Code is amended by striking "section 412"

11 each place it appears and inserting "section 431".

12   (2) Section 404(a)(1)(B) of such Code is

13 amended—

14   (A) by striking "In the case of a plan" and

15 inserting "In the case of a multiemployer plan",

16   (B) by striking "section 412(c)(7)" each

17 place it appears and inserting "section

18 431(c)(6)",

19   (C) by striking "section 412(c)(7)(B)" and

20 inserting "section 431(c)(6)(A)(ii)",

21   (D) by striking "section 412(c)(7)(A)" and

22 inserting "section 431(c)(6)(A)(i)", and

23   (E) by striking "section 412" and insert-

24 ing "section 431".

1   (3) Section 404(a)(7) of such Code, as amended

2 by this Act, is amended—

3   (A) by adding at the end of subparagraph

4   (A) the following new sentence: "In the case of

5   a defined benefit plan which is a single em-

6   ployer plan, the amount necessary to satisfy the

7   minimum funding standard provided by section

8   412 shall not be less than the plan's funding

9   shortfall determined under section 430.", and

10   (B) by striking subparagraph (D) and in-

11   serting:

12   "(D) INSURANCE CONTRACT PLANS. For

13   purposes of this paragraph, a plan described in

14   section 412(e)(3) shall be treated as a defined

15   benefit plan.".

16   (4) Section 404A(g)(3)(A) of such Code is

17 amended by striking "paragraphs (3) and (7) of sec-

18 tion 412(c)" and inserting "paragraphs (3) and (6)

19 of section 431(c)".

20 (d) SPECIAL RULE FOR 2006 AND 2007.—

21   (1) IN GENERAL.—Clause (i) of section

22 404(a)(1)(D) of the Internal Revenue Code of 1986

23 (relating to special rule in case of certain plans) is

24 amended by striking "section 412(l)" and inserting

25 "section 412(l)(8)(A), except that section

1 412(l)(8)(A) shall be applied for purposes of this

2 clause by substituting '150 percent (140 percent in

3 the case of a multiemployer plan) of current liability'

4 for 'the current liability' in clause (i).''

5   (2) CONFORMING AMENDMENT.—Section

6 404(a)(1) of the Internal Revenue Code of 1986 is

7 amended by striking subparagraph (F).

8 (e) EFFECTIVE DATES.—

9   (1) IN GENERAL.—Except as provided in para-

10 graph (2), the amendments made by this section

11 shall apply to years beginning after December 31,

12 2007.

13   (2) SPECIAL RULES.—The amendments made

14 by subsection (d) shall apply to years beginning

15 after December 31, 2005.

16 **SEC. 802. DEDUCTION LIMITS FOR MULTIEMPLOYER**

17   **PLANS.**

18 (a) INCREASE IN DEDUCTION.—Section

19 404(a)(1)(D) of the Internal Revenue Code of 1986, as

20 amended by this Act, is amended to read as follows:

21   ''(D) AMOUNT DETERMINED ON BASIS OF

22   UNFUNDED CURRENT LIABILITY.—In the case

23   of a defined benefit plan which is a multiem-

24   ployer plan, except as provided in regulations,

25   the maximum amount deductible under the lim-

1   itations of this paragraph shall not be less than

2   the excess (if any) of—

3   "(i) 140 percent of the current liabil-

4   ity of the plan determined under section

5   431(c)(6)(C), over

6   "(ii) the value of the plan's assets de-

7   termined under section 431(c)(2).".

8   (b) EFFECTIVE DATE.—The amendment made by

9 subsection (a) shall apply to years beginning after Decem-

10 ber 31, 2007.

11 **SEC. 803. UPDATING DEDUCTION RULES FOR COMBINA-**

12   **TION OF PLANS.**

13   (a) IN GENERAL.—Subparagraph (C) of section

14 404(a)(7) of the Internal Revenue Code of 1986 (relating

15 to limitation on deductions where combination of defined

16 contribution plan and defined benefit plan) is amended by

17 adding after clause (ii) the following new clause:

18   "(iii) LIMITATION.—In the case of

19   employer contributions to 1 or more de-

20   fined contribution plans, this paragraph

21   shall only apply to the extent that such

22   contributions exceed 6 percent of the com-

23   pensation otherwise paid or accrued during

24   the taxable year to the beneficiaries under

25   such plans. For purposes of this clause,

1 amounts carried over from preceding tax-
2 able years under subparagraph (B) shall
3 be treated as employer contributions to 1
4 or more defined contributions to the extent
5 attributable to employer contributions to
6 such plans in such preceding taxable
7 years.".

8 (b) EXCEPTION FROM LIMITATION ON DEDUCTION
9 WHERE COMBINATION OF DEFINED CONTRIBUTION AND
10 DEFINED BENEFIT PLANS.—Section 404(a)(7)(C) of
11 such Code, as amended by this Act, is amended by adding
12 at the end the following new clause:

13 "(v) MULTIEMPLOYER PLANS.—In ap-
14 plying this paragraph, any multiemployer
15 plan shall not be taken into account.".

16 (c) CONFORMING AMENDMENT.—Subparagraph (A)
17 of section 4972(c)(6) of such Code (relating to nondeduct-
18 ible contributions) is amended to read as follows:

19 "(A) so much of the contributions to 1 or
20 more defined contribution plans which are not
21 deductible when contributed solely because of
22 section 404(a)(7) as does not exceed the
23 amount of contributions described in section
24 401(m)(4)(A), or".

1   (d) EFFECTIVE DATE.—The amendments made by

2 this section shall apply to contributions for taxable years

3 beginning after December 31, 2005.

Subtitle B—Certain Pension Provisions Made Permanent

SEC. 811. PENSIONS AND INDIVIDUAL RETIREMENT ARRANGEMENT PROVISIONS OF ECONOMIC GROWTH AND TAX RELIEF RECONCILIATION ACT OF 2001 MADE PERMANENT.

10   Title IX of the Economic Growth and Tax Relief Rec-

11 onciliation Act of 2001 shall not apply to the provisions

12 of, and amendments made by, subtitles A through F of

13 title VI of such Act (relating to pension and individual

14 retirement arrangement provisions).

SEC. 812. SAVER'S CREDIT.

16   Section 25B of the Internal Revenue Code of 1986

17 (relating to elective deferrals and IRA contributions by

18 certain individuals) is amended by striking subsection (h).

Subtitle C—Improvements in Portability, Distribution, and Contribution Rules

SEC. 821. CLARIFICATIONS REGARDING PURCHASE OF PERMISSIVE SERVICE CREDIT.

(a) IN GENERAL.—Section 415(n) of the Internal Revenue Code of 1986 (relating to special rules for the purchase of permissive service credit) is amended—

(1) by striking "an employee" in paragraph (1) and inserting "a participant", and

(2) by adding at the end of paragraph (3)(A) the following new flush sentence:

"Such term may include service credit for periods for which there is no performance of service, and, notwithstanding clause (ii), may include service credited in order to provide an increased benefit for service credit which a participant is receiving under the plan.".

(b) SPECIAL RULES FOR TRUSTEE-TO-TRUSTEE TRANSFERS.—Section 415(n)(3) of such Code is amended by adding at the end the following new subparagraph:

"(D) SPECIAL RULES FOR TRUSTEE-TO-TRUSTEE TRANSFERS.—In the case of a trustee-to-trustee transfer to which section 403(b)(13)(A) or 457(e)(17)(A) applies (with-

1   out regard to whether the transfer is made be-

2   tween plans maintained by the same em-

3   ployer)—

4   "(i) the limitations of subparagraph

5   (B) shall not apply in determining whether

6   the transfer is for the purchase of permis-

7   sive service credit, and

8   "(ii) the distribution rules applicable

9   under this title to the defined benefit gov-

10   ernmental plan to which any amounts are

11   so transferred shall apply to such amounts

12   and any benefits attributable to such

13   amounts.".

14   (c) NONQUALIFIED SERVICE.—Section 415(n)(3) of

15 such Code is amended—

16   (1) by striking "permissive service credit attrib-

17 utable to nonqualified service" each place it appears

18 in subparagraph (B) and inserting "nonqualified

19 service credit",

20   (2) by striking so much of subparagraph (C) as

21 precedes clause (i) and inserting:

22   "(C) NONQUALIFIED SERVICE CREDIT.—

23   For purposes of subparagraph (B), the term

24   'nonqualified service credit' means permissive

1   service credit other than that allowed with re-

2   spect to—'', and

3   (3) by striking "elementary or secondary edu-

4   cation (through grade 12), as determined under

5   State law" in subparagraph (C)(ii) and inserting

6   "elementary or secondary education (through grade

7   12), or a comparable level of education, as deter-

8   mined under the applicable law of the jurisdiction in

9   which the service was performed".

10   (d) EFFECTIVE DATES.—

11   (1) IN GENERAL.—The amendments made by

12   subsections (a) and (c) shall take effect as if in-

13   cluded in the amendments made by section 1526 of

14   the Taxpayer Relief Act of 1997.

15   (2) SUBSECTION (b).—The amendments made

16   by subsection (b) shall take effect as if included in

17   the amendments made by section 647 of the Eco-

18   nomic Growth and Tax Relief Reconciliation Act of

19   2001.

20 **SEC. 822. ALLOW ROLLOVER OF AFTER-TAX AMOUNTS IN**

21   **ANNUITY CONTRACTS.**

22   (a) IN GENERAL.—Subparagraph (A) of section

23 402(c)(2) (relating to the maximum amount which may

24 be rolled over) is amended—

1 (1) by striking "which is part of a plan which

2 is a defined contribution plan and which agrees to

3 separately account" and inserting "or to an annuity

4 contract described in section 403(b) and such trust

5 or contract provides for separate accounting"; and

6 (2) by inserting "(and earnings thereon)" after

7 "so transferred".

8 (b) EFFECTIVE DATE.—The amendment made by

9 subsection (a) shall apply to taxable years beginning after

10 December 31, 2006.

11 **SEC. 823. CLARIFICATION OF MINIMUM DISTRIBUTION**

12   **RULES FOR GOVERNMENTAL PLANS.**

13 The Secretary of the Treasury shall issue regulations

14 under which a governmental plan (as defined in section

15 414(d) of the Internal Revenue Code of 1986) shall, for

16 all years to which section 401(a)(9) of such Code applies

17 to such plan, be treated as having complied with such sec-

18 tion 401(a)(9) if such plan complies with a reasonable

19 good faith interpretation of such section 401(a)(9).

20 **SEC. 824. ALLOW DIRECT ROLLOVERS FROM RETIREMENT**

21   **PLANS TO ROTH IRAS.**

22 (a) IN GENERAL.—Subsection (e) of section 408A of

23 the Internal Revenue Code of 1986 (defining qualified roll-

24 over contribution) is amended to read as follows:

1   "(e) QUALIFIED ROLLOVER CONTRIBUTION.—For

2 purposes of this section, the term 'qualified rollover con-

3 tribution' means a rollover contribution—

4   "(1) to a Roth IRA from another such account,

5   "(2) from an eligible retirement plan, but only

6 if—

7   "(A) in the case of an individual retire-

8   ment plan, such rollover contribution meets the

9   requirements of section 408(d)(3), and

10   "(B) in the case of any eligible retirement

11   plan (as defined in section 402(c)(8)(B) other

12   than clauses (i) and (ii) thereof), such rollover

13   contribution meets the requirements of section

14   402(c), 403(b)(8), or 457(e)(16), as applicable.

15 For purposes of section 408(d)(3)(B), there shall be dis-

16 regarded any qualified rollover contribution from an indi-

17 vidual retirement plan (other than a Roth IRA) to a Roth

18 IRA.".

19   (b) CONFORMING AMENDMENTS.—

20   (1) Section 408A(c)(3)(B) of such Code, as in

21   effect before the Tax Increase Prevention and Rec-

22   onciliation Act of 2005, is amended—

23   (A) in the text by striking "individual re-

24   tirement plan" and inserting "an eligible retire-

1   ment   plan   (as   defined   by   section

2   402(c)(8)(B))'', and

3   (B) in the heading by striking "IRA" the

4   first place it appears and inserting "ELIGIBLE

5   RETIREMENT PLAN".

6   (2) Section 408A(d)(3) of such Code is amend-

7   ed—

8   (A) in subparagraph (A), by striking "sec-

9   tion 408(d)(3)" inserting "sections 402(c),

10   403(b)(8), 408(d)(3), and 457(e)(16)",

11   (B) in subparagraph (B), by striking "in-

12   dividual retirement plan" and inserting "eligible

13   retirement   plan   (as   defined   by   section

14   402(c)(8)(B))",

15   (C) in subparagraph (D), by inserting "or

16   6047" after "408(i)",

17   (D) in subparagraph (D), by striking "or

18   both" and inserting "persons subject to section

19   6047(d)(1), or all of the foregoing persons",

20   and

21   (E) in the heading, by striking "IRA" the

22   first place it appears and inserting "ELIGIBLE

23   RETIREMENT PLAN".

1   (c) EFFECTIVE DATE.—The amendments made by
2 this section shall apply to distributions after December 31,
3 2007.

4 **SEC. 825. ELIGIBILITY FOR PARTICIPATION IN RETIRE-**
5   **MENT PLANS.**

6   An individual shall not be precluded from partici-
7 pating in an eligible deferred compensation plan by reason
8 of having received a distribution under section 457(e)(9)
9 of the Internal Revenue Code of 1986, as in effect prior
10 to the enactment of the Small Business Job Protection
11 Act of 1996.

12 **SEC. 826. MODIFICATIONS OF RULES GOVERNING HARD-**
13   **SHIPS AND UNFORSEEN FINANCIAL EMER-**
14   **GENCIES.**

15   Within 180 days after the date of the enactment of
16 this Act, the Secretary of the Treasury shall modify the
17 rules for determining whether a participant has had a
18 hardship for purposes of section 401(k)(2)(B)(i)(IV) of
19 the Internal Revenue Code of 1986 to provide that if an
20 event (including the occurrence of a medical expense)
21 would constitute a hardship under the plan if it occurred
22 with respect to the participant's spouse or dependent (as
23 defined in section 152 of such Code), such event shall, to
24 the extent permitted under a plan, constitute a hardship
25 if it occurs with respect to a person who is a beneficiary

1 under the plan with respect to the participant. The Sec-

2 retary of the Treasury shall issue similar rules for pur-

3 poses of determining whether a participant has had—

4   (1) a hardship for purposes of section

5   403(b)(11)(B) of such Code; or

6   (2) an unforeseen financial emergency for pur-

7   poses of sections 409A(a)(2)(A)(vi),

8   409A(a)(2)(B)(ii), and 457(d)(1)(A)(iii) of such

9   Code.

10 **SEC. 827. PENALTY-FREE WITHDRAWALS FROM RETIRE-**

11   **MENT PLANS FOR INDIVIDUALS CALLED TO**

12   **ACTIVE DUTY FOR AT LEAST 179 DAYS.**

13   (a) IN GENERAL.—Paragraph (2) of section 72(t) of

14 the Internal Revenue Code of 1986 (relating to 10-percent

15 additional tax on early distributions from qualified retire-

16 ment plans) is amended by adding at the end the following

17 new subparagraph:

18   "(G) DISTRIBUTIONS FROM RETIREMENT

19   PLANS TO INDIVIDUALS CALLED TO ACTIVE

20   DUTY.—

21   "(i) IN GENERAL.—Any qualified re-

22   servist distribution.

23   "(ii) AMOUNT DISTRIBUTED MAY BE

24   REPAID.—Any individual who receives a

25   qualified reservist distribution may, at any

1 time during the 2-year period beginning on
2 the day after the end of the active duty pe-
3 riod, make one or more contributions to an
4 individual retirement plan of such indi-
5 vidual in an aggregate amount not to ex-
6 ceed the amount of such distribution. The
7 dollar limitations otherwise applicable to
8 contributions to individual retirement plans
9 shall not apply to any contribution made
10 pursuant to the preceding sentence. No de-
11 duction shall be allowed for any contribu-
12 tion pursuant to this clause.

13 "(iii) QUALIFIED RESERVIST DIS-
14 TRIBUTION.—For purposes of this sub-
15 paragraph, the term 'qualified reservist
16 distribution' means any distribution to an
17 individual if—

18 "(I) such distribution is from an
19 individual retirement plan, or from
20 amounts attributable to employer con-
21 tributions made pursuant to elective
22 deferrals described in subparagraph
23 (A) or (C) of section 402(g)(3) or sec-
24 tion 501(c)(18)(D)(iii),

"(II) such individual was (by reason of being a member of a reserve
component (as defined in section 101
of title 37, United States Code)) ordered or called to active duty for a period in excess of 179 days or for an
indefinite period, and

"(III) such distribution is made
during the period beginning on the
date of such order or call and ending
at the close of the active duty period.

"(iv) APPLICATION OF SUBPARA-
GRAPH.—This subparagraph applies to individuals ordered or called to active duty
after September 11, 2001, and before December 31, 2007. In no event shall the 2-
year period referred to in clause (ii) end
before the date which is 2 years after the
date of the enactment of this subparagraph.".

(b) CONFORMING AMENDMENTS.—

(1) Section 401(k)(2)(B)(i) of such Code is
amended by striking "or" at the end of subclause
(III), by striking "and" at the end of subclause (IV)

1 and inserting "or", and by inserting after subclause

2 (IV) the following new subclause:

3   "(V) in the case of a qualified re-

4   servist distribution (as defined in sec-

5   tion 72(t)(2)(G)(iii)), the date on

6   which a period referred to in sub-

7   clause (III) of such section begins,

8   and".

9   (2) Section 403(b)(7)(A)(ii) of such Code is

10 amended by inserting "(unless such amount is a dis-

11 tribution to which section 72(t)(2)(G) applies)" after

12 "distributee".

13   (3) Section 403(b)(11) of such Code is amend-

14 ed by striking "or" at the end of subparagraph (A),

15 by striking the period at the end of subparagraph

16 (B) and inserting ", or", and by inserting after sub-

17 paragraph (B) the following new subparagraph:

18   "(C) for distributions to which section

19   72(t)(2)(G) applies.".

20 (c) EFFECTIVE DATE; WAIVER OF LIMITATIONS.—

21   (1) EFFECTIVE DATE.—The amendment made

22 by this section shall apply to distributions after Sep-

23 tember 11, 2001.

24   (2) WAIVER OF LIMITATIONS.—If refund or

25 credit of any overpayment of tax resulting from the

1 amendments made by this section is prevented at

2 any time before the close of the 1-year period begin-

3 ning on the date of the enactment of this Act by the

4 operation of any law or rule of law (including res ju-

5 dicata), such refund or credit may nevertheless be

6 made or allowed if claim therefor is filed before the

7 close of such period.

8 SEC. 828. WAIVER OF 10 PERCENT EARLY WITHDRAWAL

9 PENALTY TAX ON CERTAIN DISTRIBUTIONS

10 OF PENSION PLANS FOR PUBLIC SAFETY EM-

11 PLOYEES.

12 (a) IN GENERAL.—Section 72(t) of the Internal Rev-

13 enue Code of 1986 (relating to subsection not to apply

14 to certain distributions) is amended by adding at the end

15 the following new paragraph:

16 "(10) DISTRIBUTIONS TO QUALIFIED PUBLIC

17 SAFETY EMPLOYEES IN GOVERNMENTAL PLANS.—

18 "(A) IN GENERAL.—In the case of a dis-

19 tribution to a qualified public safety employee

20 from a governmental plan (within the meaning

21 of section 414(d)) which is a defined benefit

22 plan, paragraph (2)(A)(v) shall be applied by

23 substituting 'age 50' for 'age 55'.

24 "(B) QUALIFIED PUBLIC SAFETY EM-

25 PLOYEE.—For purposes of this paragraph, the

1   term 'qualified public safety employee' means

2   any employee of a State or political subdivision

3   of a State who provides police protection, fire-

4   fighting services, or emergency medical services

5   for any area within the jurisdiction of such

6   State or political subdivision."

7   (b) EFFECTIVE DATE.—The amendment made by

8 this section shall apply to distributions after the date of

9 the enactment of this Act.

10 SEC. 829. ALLOW ROLLOVERS BY NONSPOUSE BENE-

11   FICIARIES OF CERTAIN RETIREMENT PLAN

12   DISTRIBUTIONS.

13   (a) IN GENERAL.—

14   (1) QUALIFIED PLANS.—Section 402(c) of the

15   Internal Revenue Code of 1986 (relating to rollovers

16   from exempt trusts) is amended by adding at the

17   end the following new paragraph:

18   "(11) DISTRIBUTIONS TO INHERITED INDI-

19   VIDUAL RETIREMENT PLAN OF NONSPOUSE BENE-

20   FICIARY.—

21   "(A) IN GENERAL.—If, with respect to any

22   portion of a distribution from an eligible retire-

23   ment plan of a deceased employee, a direct

24   trustee-to-trustee transfer is made to an indi-

25   vidual retirement plan described in clause (i) or

(ii) of paragraph (8)(B) established for the purposes of receiving the distribution on behalf of an individual who is a designated beneficiary (as defined by section 401(a)(9)(E)) of the employee and who is not the surviving spouse of the employee—

"(i) the transfer shall be treated as an eligible rollover distribution for purposes of this subsection,

"(ii) the individual retirement plan shall be treated as an inherited individual retirement account or individual retirement annuity (within the meaning of section 408(d)(3)(C)) for purposes of this title, and

"(iii) section 401(a)(9)(B) (other than clause (iv) thereof) shall apply to such plan.

"(B) CERTAIN TRUSTS TREATED AS BENE-FICIARIES.—For purposes of this paragraph, to the extent provided in rules prescribed by the Secretary, a trust maintained for the benefit of one or more designated beneficiaries shall be treated in the same manner as a trust designated beneficiary.".

1   (2) SECTION 403(a) PLANS.—Subparagraph

2   (B) of section 403(a)(4) of such Code (relating to

3   rollover amounts) is amended by inserting "and

4   (11)" after "(7)".

5   (3) SECTION 403(b) PLANS.—Subparagraph

6   (B) of section 403(b)(8) of such Code (relating to

7   rollover amounts) is amended by striking "and (9)"

8   and inserting ", (9), and (11)".

9   (4) SECTION 457 PLANS.—Subparagraph (B)

10   of section 457(e)(16) of such Code (relating to roll-

11   over amounts) is amended by striking "and (9)" and

12   inserting ", (9), and (11)".

13   (b) EFFECTIVE DATE.—The amendments made by

14 this section shall apply to distributions after December 31,

15 2006.

16 **SEC. 830. DIRECT PAYMENT OF TAX REFUNDS TO INDI-**

17   **VIDUAL RETIREMENT PLANS.**

18   (a) IN GENERAL.—The Secretary of the Treasury (or

19 the Secretary's delegate) shall make available a form (or

20 modify existing forms) for use by individuals to direct that

21 a portion of any refund of overpayment of tax imposed

22 by chapter 1 of the Internal Revenue Code of 1986 be

23 paid directly to an individual retirement plan (as defined

24 in section 7701(a)(37) of such Code) of such individual.

1   (b) EFFECTIVE DATE.—The form required by sub-
2 section (a) shall be made available for taxable years begin-
3 ning after December 31, 2006.

4 **SEC. 831. ALLOWANCE OF ADDITIONAL IRA PAYMENTS IN**
5   **CERTAIN BANKRUPTCY CASES.**

6   (a) ALLOWANCE OF CONTRIBUTIONS.—Section
7 219(b)(5) of the Internal Revenue Code of 1986 (relating
8 to deductible amount) is amended by redesignating sub-
9 paragraph (C) as subparagraph (D) and by inserting after
10 subparagraph (B) the following new subparagraph:

11   "(C) CATCHUP CONTRIBUTIONS FOR CER-
12   TAIN INDIVIDUALS.—

13   "(i) IN GENERAL.—In the case of an
14   applicable individual who elects to make a
15   qualified retirement contribution in addi-
16   tion to the deductible amount determined
17   under subparagraph (A)—

18   "(I) the deductible amount for
19   any taxable year shall be increased by
20   an amount equal to 3 times the appli-
21   cable amount determined under sub-
22   paragraph (B) for such taxable year,
23   and

24   "(II) subparagraph (B) shall not
25   apply.

1   "(ii) APPLICABLE INDIVIDUAL.—For

2   purposes of this subparagraph, the term

3   'applicable individual' means, with respect

4   to any taxable year, any individual who

5   was a qualified participant in a qualified

6   cash or deferred arrangement (as defined

7   in section 401(k)) of an employer described

8   in clause (iii) under which the employer

9   matched at least 50 percent of the employ-

10   ee's contributions to such arrangement

11   with stock of such employer.

12   "(iii) EMPLOYER DESCRIBED.—An

13   employer is described in this clause if, in

14   any taxable year preceding the taxable year

15   described in clause (ii)—

16   "(I) such employer (or any con-

17   trolling corporation of such employer)

18   was a debtor in a case under title 11

19   of the United States Code, or similar

20   Federal or State law, and

21   "(II) such employer (or any other

22   person) was subject to an indictment

23   or conviction resulting from business

24   transactions related to such case.

     "(iv) QUALIFIED PARTICIPANT.—For purposes of clause (ii), the term 'qualified participant' means any applicable individual who was a participant in the cash or deferred arrangement described in such clause on the date that is 6 months before the filing of the case described in clause (iii).

     "(v) TERMINATION.—This subparagraph shall not apply to taxable years beginning after December 31, 2009."

 (b) EFFECTIVE DATE.—The amendments made by this section shall apply to taxable years beginning after December 31, 2006.

SEC. 832. DETERMINATION OF AVERAGE COMPENSATION FOR SECTION 415 LIMITS.

 (a) IN GENERAL.—Section 415(b)(3) of the Internal Revenue Code of 1986 is amended by striking "both was an active participant in the plan and".

 (b) EFFECTIVE DATE.—The amendment made by this section shall apply to years beginning after December 31, 2005.

**SEC. 833. INFLATION INDEXING OF GROSS INCOME LIMITA-
TIONS ON CERTAIN RETIREMENT SAVINGS
INCENTIVES.**

(a) SAVER'S CREDIT.—Subsection (b) of section 25B
of the Internal Revenue Code of 1986 is amended to read
as follows:

"(b) APPLICABLE PERCENTAGE.—For purposes of
this section—

"(1) JOINT RETURNS.—In the case of a joint
return, the applicable percentage is—

"(A) if the adjusted gross income of the
taxpayer is not over $30,000, 50 percent,

"(B) if the adjusted gross income of the
taxpayer is over $30,000 but not over $32,500,
20 percent,

"(C) if the adjusted gross income of the
taxpayer is over $32,500 but not over $50,000,
10 percent, and

"(D) if the adjusted gross income of the
taxpayer is over $50,000, zero percent.

"(2) OTHER RETURNS.—In the case of—

"(A) a head of household, the applicable
percentage shall be determined under paragraph (1) except that such paragraph shall be
applied by substituting for each dollar amount
therein (as adjusted under paragraph (3)) a

1 dollar amount equal to 75 percent of such dol-
2 lar amount, and

3   "(B) any taxpayer not described in para-
4   graph (1) or subparagraph (A), the applicable
5   percentage shall be determined under para-
6   graph (1) except that such paragraph shall be
7   applied by substituting for each dollar amount
8   therein (as adjusted under paragraph (3)) a
9   dollar amount equal to 50 percent of such dol-
10   lar amount.

11   "(3) INFLATION ADJUSTMENT.—In the case of
12 any taxable year beginning in a calendar year after
13 2006, each of the dollar amount in paragraph (1)
14 shall be increased by an amount equal to—

15   "(A) such dollar amount, multiplied by
16   "(B) the cost-of-living adjustment deter-
17   mined under section 1(f)(3) for the calendar
18   year in which the taxable year begins, deter-
19   mined by substituting 'calendar year 2005' for
20   'calendar year 1992' in subparagraph (B)
21   thereof.

22   Any increase determined under the preceding sen-
23 tence shall be rounded to the nearest multiple of
24 $500.".

(b) DEDUCTION OF RETIREMENT CONTRIBUTIONS FOR ACTIVE PARTICIPANTS.—Section 219(g) of such Code is amended by adding at the end the following new paragraph:

"(8) INFLATION ADJUSTMENT.—In the case of any taxable year beginning in a calendar year after 2006, the dollar amount in the last row of the table contained in paragraph (3)(B)(i), the dollar amount in the last row of the table contained in paragraph (3)(B)(ii), and the dollar amount contained in paragraph (7)(A), shall each be increased by an amount equal to—

"(A) such dollar amount, multiplied by

"(B) the cost-of-living adjustment determined under section 1(f)(3) for the calendar year in which the taxable year begins, determined by substituting 'calendar year 2005' for 'calendar year 1992' in subparagraph (B) thereof.

Any increase determined under the preceding sentence shall be rounded to the nearest multiple of $1,000.".

(c) CONTRIBUTION LIMITATION FOR ROTH IRAS.—Section 408A(c)(3) of such Code is amended by adding at the end the following new subparagraph:

1   "(C) INFLATION ADJUSTMENT.—In the

2   case of any taxable year beginning in a calendar

3   year after 2006, the dollar amounts in sub-

4   clauses (I) and (II) of subparagraph (C)(ii)

5   shall each be increased by an amount equal

6   to—

7   "(i) such dollar amount, multiplied by

8   "(ii) the cost-of-living adjustment de-

9   termined under section 1(f)(3) for the cal-

10   endar year in which the taxable year be-

11   gins, determined by substituting 'calendar

12   year 2005' for 'calendar year 1992' in sub-

13   paragraph (B) thereof.

14   Any increase determined under the preceding

15   sentence shall be rounded to the nearest mul-

16   tiple of $1,000.".

17   (d) EFFECTIVE DATE.—The amendments made by

18 this section shall apply to taxable years beginning after

19 2006.

Subtitle D—Health and Medical Benefits

SEC. 841. USE OF EXCESS PENSION ASSETS FOR FUTURE RETIREE HEALTH BENEFITS AND COLLECTIVELY BARGAINED RETIREE HEALTH BENEFITS.

(a) IN GENERAL.—Section 420 of the Internal Revenue Code of 1986 (relating to transfers of excess pension assets to retiree health accounts) is amended by adding at the end the following new subsection:

"(f) QUALIFIED TRANSFERS TO COVER FUTURE RETIREE HEALTH COSTS AND COLLECTIVELY BARGAINED RETIREE HEALTH BENEFITS.—

"(1) IN GENERAL.—An employer maintaining a defined benefit plan (other than a multiemployer plan) may, in lieu of a qualified transfer, elect for any taxable year to have the plan make—

"(A) a qualified future transfer, or

"(B) a collectively bargained transfer.

Except as provided in this subsection, a qualified future transfer and a collectively bargained transfer shall be treated for purposes of this title and the Employee Retirement Income Security Act of 1974 as if it were a qualified transfer.

"(2) QUALIFIED FUTURE AND COLLECTIVELY BARGAINED TRANSFERS.—For purposes of this subsection—

"(A) IN GENERAL.—The terms 'qualified future transfer' and 'collectively bargained transfer' mean a transfer which meets all of the requirements for a qualified transfer, except that—

"(i) the determination of excess pension assets shall be made under subparagraph (B),

"(ii) the limitation on the amount transferred shall be determined under subparagraph (C),

"(iii) the minimum cost requirements of subsection (c)(3) shall be modified as provided under subparagraph (D), and

"(iv) in the case of a collectively bargained transfer, the requirements of subparagraph (E) shall be met with respect to the transfer.

"(B) EXCESS PENSION ASSETS.—

"(i) IN GENERAL.—In determining excess pension assets for purposes of this subsection, subsection (e)(2) shall be applied by substituting '120 percent' for '125 percent'.

"(ii) REQUIREMENT TO MAINTAIN FUNDED STATUS.—If, as of any valuation date of any plan year in the transfer period, the amount determined under subsection (e)(2)(B) (after application of clause (i)) exceeds the amount determined under subsection (e)(2)(A), either—

"(I) the employer maintaining the plan shall make contributions to the plan in an amount not less than the amount required to reduce such excess to zero as of such date, or

"(II) there is transferred from the health benefits account to the plan an amount not less than the amount required to reduce such excess to zero as of such date.

"(C) LIMITATION ON AMOUNT TRANSFERRED.—Notwithstanding subsection (b)(3), the amount of the excess pension assets which may be transferred—

"(i) in the case of a qualified future transfer shall be equal to the sum of—

1   "(I) if the transfer period in-

2   cludes the taxable year of the trans-

3   fer, the amount determined under

4   subsection (b)(3) for such taxable

5   year, plus

6   "(II) in the case of all other tax-

7   able years in the transfer period, the

8   sum of the qualified current retiree

9   health liabilities which the plan rea-

10   sonably estimates, in accordance with

11   guidance issued by the Secretary, will

12   be incurred for each of such years,

13   and

14   "(ii) in the case of a collectively bar-

15 gained transfer, shall not exceed the

16 amount which is reasonably estimated, in

17 accordance with the provisions of the col-

18 lective bargaining agreement and generally

19 accepted accounting principles, to be the

20 amount the employer maintaining the plan

21 will pay (whether directly or through reim-

22 bursement) out of such account during the

23 collectively bargained cost maintenance pe-

24 riod for collectively bargained retiree

25 health liabilities.

624

"(D) MINIMUM COST REQUIREMENTS.—

"(i) IN GENERAL.—The requirements of subsection (c)(3) shall be treated as met if—

"(I) in the case of a qualified future transfer, each group health plan or arrangement under which applicable health benefits are provided provides applicable health benefits during the period beginning with the first year of the transfer period and ending with the last day of the 4th year following the transfer period such that the annual average amount of such the applicable employer cost during such period is not less than the applicable employer cost determined under subsection (c)(3)(A) with respect to the transfer, and

"(II) in the case of a collectively bargained transfer, each collectively bargained group health plan under which collectively bargained health benefits are provided provides that the collectively bargained employer cost

1   for each taxable year during the col-

2   lectively bargained cost maintenance

3   period shall not be less than the

4   amount specified by the collective bar-

5   gaining agreement.

6   "(ii) ELECTION TO MAINTAIN BENE-

7   FITS FOR FUTURE TRANSFERS.—An em-

8   ployer may elect, in lieu of the require-

9   ments of clause (i)(I), to meet the require-

10   ments of subsection (c)(3) by meeting the

11   requirements of such subsection (as in ef-

12   fect before the amendments made by sec-

13   tion 535 of the Tax Relief Extension Act

14   of 1999) for each of the years described in

15   the period under clause (i)(I).

16   "(iii) COLLECTIVELY BARGAINED EM-

17   PLOYER COST.—For purposes of this sub-

18   paragraph, the term 'collectively bargained

19   employer cost' means the average cost per

20   covered individual of providing collectively

21   bargained retiree health benefits as deter-

22   mined in accordance with the applicable

23   collective bargaining agreement. Such

24   agreement may provide for an appropriate

25   reduction in the collectively bargained em-

1 ployer cost to take into account any por-
2 tion of the collectively bargained retiree
3 health benefits that is provided or financed
4 by a government program or other source.

5 "(E) SPECIAL RULES FOR COLLECTIVELY
6 BARGAINED TRANSFERS.—

7 "(i) IN GENERAL.—A collectively bar-
8 gained transfer shall only include a trans-
9 fer which—

10 "(I) is made in accordance with a
11 collective bargaining agreement,

12 "(II) before the transfer, the em-
13 ployer designates, in a written notice
14 delivered to each employee organiza-
15 tion that is a party to the collective
16 bargaining agreement, as a collectively
17 bargained transfer in accordance with
18 this section, and

19 "(III) involves a plan maintained
20 by an employer which, in its taxable
21 year ending in 2005, provided health
22 benefits or coverage to retirees and
23 their spouses and dependents under
24 all of the benefit plans maintained by
25 the employer, but only if the aggre-

gate cost (including administrative expenses) of such benefits or coverage which would have been allowable as a deduction to the employer (if such benefits or coverage had been provided directly by the employer and the employer used the cash receipts and disbursements method of accounting) is at least 5 percent of the gross receipts of the employer (determined in accordance with the last sentence of subsection (c)(2)(E)(ii)(II)) for such taxable year, or a plan maintained by a successor to such employer.

"(ii) USE OF ASSETS.—Any assets transferred to a health benefits account in a collectively bargained transfer (and any income allocable thereto) shall be used only to pay collectively bargained retiree health liabilities (other than liabilities of key employees not taken into account under paragraph (6)(B)(iii)) for the taxable year of the transfer or for any subsequent taxable year during the collectively bargained cost

1   maintenance period (whether directly or

2   through reimbursement).

3   "(3) COORDINATION WITH OTHER TRANS-

4 FERS.—In applying subsection (b)(3) to any subse-

5 quent transfer during a taxable year in a transfer

6 period or collectively bargained cost maintenance pe-

7 riod, qualified current retiree health liabilities shall

8 be reduced by any such liabilities taken into account

9 with respect to the qualified future transfer or col-

10 lectively bargained transfer to which such period re-

11 lates.

12   "(4) SPECIAL DEDUCTION RULES FOR COLLEC-

13 TIVELY BARGAINED TRANSFERS.—In the case of a

14 collectively bargained transfer—

15   "(A) the limitation under subsection

16   (d)(1)(C) shall not apply, and

17   "(B) notwithstanding subsection (d)(2), an

18   employer may contribute an amount to a health

19   benefits account or welfare benefit fund (as de-

20   fined in section 419(e)(1)) with respect to col-

21   lectively bargained retiree health liabilities for

22   which transferred assets are required to be used

23   under subsection (c)(1)(B), and the deduct-

24   ibility of any such contribution shall be gov-

25   erned by the limits applicable to the deduct-

1   ibility of contributions to a welfare benefit fund

2   under a collective bargaining agreement (as de-

3   termined under section 419A(f)(5)(A)) without

4   regard to whether such contributions are made

5   to a health benefits account or welfare benefit

6   fund and without regard to the provisions of

7   section 404 or the other provisions of this sec-

8   tion.

9   The Secretary shall provide rules to ensure that the

10   application of this paragraph does not result in a de-

11   duction being allowed more than once for the same

12   contribution or for 2 or more contributions or ex-

13   penditures relating to the same collectively bar-

14   gained retiree health liabilities.

15   "(5) TRANSFER PERIOD.—For purposes of this

16   subsection, the term 'transfer period' means, with

17   respect to any transfer, a period of consecutive tax-

18   able years (not less than 2) specified in the election

19   under paragraph (1) which begins and ends during

20   the 10-taxable-year period beginning with the tax-

21   able year of the transfer.

22   "(6) TERMS RELATING TO COLLECTIVELY BAR-

23   GAINED TRANSFERS.—For purposes of this sub-

24   section—

1   "(A) COLLECTIVELY BARGAINED COST

2   MAINTENANCE PERIOD.—The term 'collectively

3   bargained cost maintenance period' means, with

4   respect to each covered retiree and his covered

5   spouse and dependents, the shorter of—

6   "(i) the remaining lifetime of such

7   covered retiree and his covered spouse and

8   dependents, or

9   "(ii) the period of coverage provided

10   by the collectively bargained health plan

11   (determined as of the date of the collec-

12   tively bargained transfer) with respect to

13   such covered retiree and his covered spouse

14   and dependents.

15   "(B) COLLECTIVELY BARGAINED RETIREE

16   HEALTH LIABILITIES.—

17   "(i) IN GENERAL.—The term 'collec-

18   tively bargained retiree health liabilities'

19   means the present value, as of the begin-

20   ning of a taxable year and determined in

21   accordance with the applicable collective

22   bargaining agreement, of all collectively

23   bargained health benefits (including ad-

24   ministrative expenses) for such taxable

25   year and all subsequent taxable years dur-

ing the collectively bargained cost maintenance period.

"(ii) REDUCTION FOR AMOUNTS PRE-
VIOUSLY SET ASIDE.—The amount determined under clause (i) shall be reduced by
the value (as of the close of the plan year
preceding the year of the collectively bargained transfer) of the assets in all health
benefits accounts or welfare benefit funds
(as defined in section 419(e)(1)) set aside
to pay for the collectively bargained retiree
health liabilities.

"(iii) KEY EMPLOYEES EXCLUDED.—
If an employee is a key employee (within
the meaning of section 416(I)(1)) with respect to any plan year ending in a taxable
year, such employee shall not be taken into
account in computing collectively bargained
retiree health liabilities for such taxable
year or in calculating collectively bargained
employer cost under subsection (c)(3)(C).

"(C) COLLECTIVELY BARGAINED HEALTH
BENEFITS.—The term 'collectively bargained
health benefits' means health benefits or coverage which are provided to—

632

"(i) retired employees who, immediately before the collectively bargained transfer, are entitled to receive such benefits upon retirement and who are entitled to pension benefits under the plan, and their spouses and dependents, and

"(ii) if specified by the provisions of the collective bargaining agreement governing the collectively bargained transfer, active employees who, following their retirement, are entitled to receive such benefits and who are entitled to pension benefits under the plan, and their spouses and dependents.

"(D) COLLECTIVELY BARGAINED HEALTH PLAN.—The term 'collectively bargained health plan' means a group health plan or arrangement for retired employees and their spouses and dependents that is maintained pursuant to 1 or more collective bargaining agreements.".

(b) EFFECTIVE DATE.—The amendments made by this section shall apply to transfers after the date of the enactment of this Act.

Act. Sec. 841

**SEC. 842. TRANSFER OF EXCESS PENSION ASSETS TO MUL-
TIEMPLOYER HEALTH PLAN.**

(a) IN GENERAL.—Section 420 of the Internal Revenue Code of 1986 is amended—

(1) by striking "(other than a multiemployer plan)" in subsection (a), and

(2) by adding at the end of subsection (e) the following new paragraph:

"(5) APPLICATION TO MULTIEMPLOYER PLANS.—In the case of a multiemployer plan, this section shall be applied to any such plan—

"(A) by treating any reference in this section to an employer as a reference to all employers maintaining the plan (or, if appropriate, the plan sponsor), and

"(B) in accordance with such modifications of this section (and the provisions of this title relating to this section) as the Secretary determines appropriate to reflect the fact the plan is not maintained by a single employer."

(b) EFFECTIVE DATE.—The amendment made by this section shall apply to transfers made in taxable years beginning after December 31, 2006.

**SEC. 843. ALLOWANCE OF RESERVE FOR MEDICAL BENE-
FITS OF PLANS SPONSORED BY BONA FIDE
ASSOCIATIONS.**

(a) IN GENERAL.—Section 419A(c) of the Internal Revenue Code of 1986 (relating to account limit) is amended by adding at the end the following new paragraph:

"(6) ADDITIONAL RESERVE FOR MEDICAL BENEFITS OF BONA FIDE ASSOCIATION PLANS.—

"(A) IN GENERAL.—An applicable account limit for any taxable year may include a reserve in an amount not to exceed 35 percent of the sum of—

"(i) the qualified direct costs, and

"(ii) the change in claims incurred but unpaid,

for such taxable year with respect to medical benefits (other than post-retirement medical benefits).

"(B) APPLICABLE ACCOUNT LIMIT.—For purposes of this subsection, the term 'applicable account limit' means an account limit for a qualified asset account with respect to medical benefits provided through a plan maintained by a bona fide association (as defined in section

1   2791(d)(3) of the Public Health Service Act

2   (42 U.S.C. 300gg–91(d)(3))''.

3   (b) EFFECTIVE DATE.—The amendment made by

4 this section shall apply to taxable years beginning after

5 December 31, 2006.

6 **SEC. 844. TREATMENT OF ANNUITY AND LIFE INSURANCE**

7   **CONTRACTS WITH A LONG-TERM CARE IN-**

8   **SURANCE FEATURE.**

9   (a) EXCLUSION FROM GROSS INCOME.—Subsection

10 (e) of section 72 of the Internal Revenue Code of 1986

11 (relating to amounts not received as annuities) is amended

12 by redesignating paragraph (11) as paragraph (12) and

13 by inserting after paragraph (10) the following new para-

14 graph:

15   ''(11) SPECIAL RULES FOR CERTAIN COMBINA-

16   TION CONTRACTS PROVIDING LONG-TERM CARE IN-

17   SURANCE.—Notwithstanding paragraphs (2), (5)(C),

18   and (10), in the case of any charge against the cash

19   value of an annuity contract or the cash surrender

20   value of a life insurance contract made as payment

21   for coverage under a qualified long-term care insur-

22   ance contract which is part of or a rider on such an-

23   nuity or life insurance contract—

"(A) the investment in the contract shall be reduced (but not below zero) by such charge, and

"(B) such charge shall not be includible in gross income.".

(b) TAX-FREE EXCHANGES AMONG CERTAIN INSURANCE POLICIES.—

(1) ANNUITY CONTRACTS CAN INCLUDE QUALIFIED LONG-TERM CARE INSURANCE RIDERS.—Paragraph (2) of section 1035(b) of such Code is amended by adding at the end the following new sentence: "For purposes of the preceding sentence, a contract shall not fail to be treated as an annuity contract solely because a qualified long-term care insurance contract is a part of or a rider on such contract.".

(2) LIFE INSURANCE CONTRACTS CAN INCLUDE QUALIFIED LONG-TERM CARE INSURANCE RIDERS.—Paragraph (3) of section 1035(b) of such Code is amended by adding at the end the following new sentence: "For purposes of the preceding sentence, a contract shall not fail to be treated as a life insurance contract solely because a qualified long-term care insurance contract is a part of or a rider on such contract.".

(3) EXPANSION OF TAX-FREE EXCHANGES OF LIFE INSURANCE, ENDOWMENT, AND ANNUITY CONTRACTS FOR LONG-TERM CARE CONTRACTS.—Subsection (a) of section 1035 of such Code (relating to certain exchanges of insurance policies) is amended—

(A) in paragraph (1) by inserting "or for a qualified long-term care insurance contract" before the semicolon at the end,

(B) in paragraph (2) by inserting ", or (C) for a qualified long-term care insurance contract" before the semicolon at the end, and

(C) in paragraph (3) by inserting "or for a qualified long-term care insurance contract" before the period at the end.

(4) TAX-FREE EXCHANGES OF QUALIFIED LONG-TERM CARE INSURANCE CONTRACT.—Subsection (a) of section 1035 of such Code (relating to certain exchanges of insurance policies) is amended by striking "or" at the end of paragraph (2), by striking the period at the end of paragraph (3) and inserting "; or", and by inserting after paragraph (3) the following new paragraph:

1   "(4) a qualified long-term care insurance con-

2   tract for a qualified long-term care insurance con-

3   tract.".

4   (c) TREATMENT OF COVERAGE PROVIDED AS PART

5 OF A LIFE INSURANCE OR ANNUITY CONTRACT.—Sub-

6 section (e) of section 7702B of such Code (relating to

7 treatment of qualified long-term care insurance) is amend-

8 ed to read as follows:

9   "(e) TREATMENT OF COVERAGE PROVIDED AS PART

10 OF A LIFE INSURANCE OR ANNUITY CONTRACT.—Except

11 as otherwise provided in regulations prescribed by the Sec-

12 retary, in the case of any long-term care insurance cov-

13 erage (whether or not qualified) provided by a rider on

14 or as part of a life insurance contract or an annuity con-

15 tract—

16   "(1) IN GENERAL.—This title shall apply as if

17   the portion of the contract providing such coverage

18   is a separate contract.

19   "(2) DENIAL OF DEDUCTION UNDER SECTION

20   213.—No deduction shall be allowed under section

21   213(a) for any payment made for coverage under a

22   qualified long-term care insurance contract if such

23   payment is made as a charge against the cash sur-

24   render value of a life insurance contract or the cash

25   value of an annuity contract.

"(3) PORTION DEFINED.—For purposes of this subsection, the term 'portion' means only the terms and benefits under a life insurance contract or annuity contract that are in addition to the terms and benefits under the contract without regard to long-term care insurance coverage.

"(4) ANNUITY CONTRACTS TO WHICH PARAGRAPH (1) DOES NOT APPLY.—For purposes of this subsection, none of the following shall be treated as an annuity contract:

"(A) A trust described in section 401(a) which is exempt from tax under section 501(a).

"(B) A contract—

"(i) purchased by a trust described in subparagraph (A),

"(ii) purchased as part of a plan described in section 403(a),

"(iii) described in section 403(b),

"(iv) provided for employees of a life insurance company under a plan described in section 818(a)(3), or

"(v) from an individual retirement account or an individual retirement annuity.

1   "(C) A contract purchased by an employer

2   for the benefit of the employee (or the employ-

3   ee's spouse).

4   Any dividend described in section 404(k) which is

5 received by a participant or beneficiary shall, for

6 purposes of this paragraph, be treated as paid under

7 a separate contract to which subparagraph (B)(i)

8 applies.".

9   (d) INFORMATION REPORTING.—

10   (1) Subpart B of part III of subchapter A of

11 chapter 61 of such Code (relating to information

12 concerning transactions with other persons) is

13 amended by adding at the end the following new sec-

14 tion:

15 **"SEC. 6050U. CHARGES OR PAYMENTS FOR QUALIFIED**

16   **LONG-TERM CARE INSURANCE CONTRACTS**

17   **UNDER COMBINED ARRANGEMENTS.**

18   "(a) REQUIREMENT OF REPORTING.—Any person

19 who makes a charge against the cash value of an annuity

20 contract, or the cash surrender value of a life insurance

21 contract, which is excludible from gross income under sec-

22 tion 72(e)(11) shall make a return, according to the forms

23 or regulations prescribed by the Secretary, setting forth—

1   "(1) the amount of the aggregate of such

2   charges against each such contract for the calendar

3   year,

4   "(2) the amount of the reduction in the invest-

5   ment in each such contract by reason of such

6   charges, and

7   "(3) the name, address, and TIN of the indi-

8   vidual who is the holder of each such contract.

9 "(b) STATEMENTS TO BE FURNISHED TO PERSONS

10 WITH RESPECT TO WHOM INFORMATION IS REQUIRED.—

11 Every person required to make a return under subsection

12 (a) shall furnish to each individual whose name is required

13 to be set forth in such return a written statement show-

14 ing—

15   "(1) the name, address, and phone number of

16   the information contact of the person making the

17   payments, and

18   "(2) the information required to be shown on

19   the return with respect to such individual.

20 The written statement required under the preceding sen-

21 tence shall be furnished to the individual on or before Jan-

22 uary 31 of the year following the calendar year for which

23 the return under subsection (a) was required to be made.".

24   (2) PENALTY FOR FAILURE TO FILE.—

(A) RETURN.—Subparagraph (B) of section 6724(d)(1) of such Code is amended by striking "or" at the end of clause (xvii), by striking "and" at the end of clause (xviii) and inserting "or", and by adding at the end the following new clause:

"(xix) section 6050U (relating to charges or payments for qualified long-term care insurance contracts under combined arrangements), and".

(B) STATEMENT.—Paragraph (2) of section 6724(d) of such Code is amended by striking "or" at the end of subparagraph (AA), by striking the period at the end of subparagraph (BB), and by inserting after subparagraph (BB) the following new subparagraph:

"(CC) section 6050U (relating to charges or payments for qualified long-term care insurance contracts under combined arrangements).".

(3) CLERICAL AMENDMENT.—The table of sections for subpart B of part III of subchapter A of such chapter 61 of such Code is amended by adding at the end the following new item:

"Sec. 6050U. Charges or payments for qualified long-term care insurance contracts under combined arrangements.".

(e) TREATMENT OF POLICY ACQUISITION EX-
PENSES.—Subsection (e) of section 848 of such Code (relating to classification of contracts) is amended by adding
at the end the following new paragraph:

"(6) TREATMENT OF CERTAIN QUALIFIED
LONG-TERM CARE INSURANCE CONTRACT ARRANGE-
MENTS.—An annuity or life insurance contract
which includes a qualified long-term care insurance
contract as a part of or a rider on such annuity or
life insurance contract shall be treated as a specified
insurance contract not described in subparagraph
(A) or (B) of subsection (c)(1).".

(f) TECHNICAL AMENDMENT.—Paragraph (1) of section 7702B(e) of such Code (as in effect before amendment by subsection (c)) is amended by striking "section"
and inserting "title".

(g) EFFECTIVE DATES.—

(1) IN GENERAL.—Except as otherwise provided in this subsection, the amendments made by
this section shall apply to contracts issued after December 31, 1996, but only with respect to taxable
years beginning after December 31, 2009.

(2) TAX-FREE EXCHANGES.—The amendments
made by subsection (b) shall apply with respect to
exchanges occurring after December 31, 2009.

1   (3) INFORMATION REPORTING.—The amend-
2 ments made by subsection (d) shall apply to charges
3 made after December 31, 2009.

4   (4) POLICY ACQUISITION EXPENSES.—The
5 amendment made by subsection (e) shall apply to
6 specified policy acquisition expenses determined for
7 taxable years beginning after December 31, 2009.

8   (5) TECHNICAL AMENDMENT.—The amendment
9 made by subsection (f) shall take effect as if in-
10 cluded in section 321(a) of the Health Insurance
11 Portability and Accountability Act of 1996.

12 **SEC. 845. DISTRIBUTIONS FROM GOVERNMENTAL RETIRE-**
13   **MENT PLANS FOR HEALTH AND LONG-TERM**
14   **CARE INSURANCE FOR PUBLIC SAFETY OFFI-**
15   **CERS.**

16 (a) IN GENERAL.—Section 402 of the Internal Rev-
17 enue Code of 1986 (relating to taxability of beneficiary
18 of employees' trust) is amended by adding at the end the
19 following new subsection:

20 "(l) DISTRIBUTIONS FROM GOVERNMENTAL PLANS
21 FOR HEALTH AND LONG-TERM CARE INSURANCE.—

22   "(1) IN GENERAL.—In the case of an employee
23 who is an eligible retired public safety officer who
24 makes the election described in paragraph (6) with
25 respect to any taxable year of such employee, gross

1 income of such employee for such taxable year does

2 not include any distribution from an eligible retire-

3 ment plan to the extent that the aggregate amount

4 of such distributions does not exceed the amount

5 paid by such employee for qualified health insurance

6 premiums of the employee, his spouse, or dependents

7 (as defined in section 152) for such taxable year.

8   "(2) LIMITATION.—The amount which may be

9 excluded from gross income for the taxable year by

10 reason of paragraph (1) shall not exceed $3,000.

11   "(3) DISTRIBUTIONS MUST OTHERWISE BE IN-

12 CLUDIBLE.—

13   "(A) IN GENERAL.—An amount shall be

14   treated as a distribution for purposes of para-

15   graph (1) only to the extent that such amount

16   would be includible in gross income without re-

17   gard to paragraph (1).

18   "(B) APPLICATION OF SECTION 72.—Not-

19   withstanding section 72, in determining the ex-

20   tent to which an amount is treated as a dis-

21   tribution for purposes of subparagraph (A), the

22   aggregate amounts distributed from an eligible

23   retirement plan in a taxable year (up to the

24   amount excluded under paragraph (1)) shall be

25   treated as includible in gross income (without

1   regard to subparagraph (A)) to the extent that

2   such amount does not exceed the aggregate

3   amount which would have been so includible if

4   all amounts distributed from all eligible retire-

5   ment plans were treated as 1 contract for pur-

6   poses of determining the inclusion of such dis-

7   tribution under section 72. Proper adjustments

8   shall be made in applying section 72 to other

9   distributions in such taxable year and subse-

10   quent taxable years.

11   "(4) DEFINITIONS.—For purposes of this sub-

12   section—

13   "(A) ELIGIBLE RETIREMENT PLAN.—For

14   purposes of paragraph (1), the term 'eligible re-

15   tirement plan' means a governmental plan

16   (within the meaning of section 414(d)) which is

17   described in clause (iii), (iv), (v), or (vi) of sub-

18   section (c)(8)(B).

19   "(B) ELIGIBLE RETIRED PUBLIC SAFETY

20   OFFICER.—The term 'eligible retired public

21   safety officer' means an individual who, by rea-

22   son of disability or attainment of normal retire-

23   ment age, is separated from service as a public

24   safety officer with the employer who maintains

1   the eligible retirement plan from which distribu-

2   tions subject to paragraph (1) are made.

3   "(C) PUBLIC SAFETY OFFICER.—The term

4   'public safety officer' shall have the same mean-

5   ing given such term by section 1204(9)(A) of

6   the Omnibus Crime Control and Safe Streets

7   Act of 1968 (42 U.S.C. 3796b(9)(A)).

8   "(D) QUALIFIED HEALTH INSURANCE

9   PREMIUMS.—The term 'qualified health insur-

10   ance premiums' means premiums for coverage

11   for the eligible retired public safety officer, his

12   spouse, and dependents, by an accident or

13   health insurance plan or qualified long-term

14   care insurance contract (as defined in section

15   7702B(b)).

16   "(5) SPECIAL RULES.—For purposes of this

17 subsection—

18   "(A) DIRECT PAYMENT TO INSURER RE-

19   QUIRED.—Paragraph (1) shall only apply to a

20   distribution if payment of the premiums is

21   made directly to the provider of the accident or

22   health insurance plan or qualified long-term

23   care insurance contract by deduction from a

24   distribution from the eligible retirement plan.

648

"(B) RELATED PLANS TREATED AS 1.—All eligible retirement plans of an employer shall be treated as a single plan.

"(6) ELECTION DESCRIBED.—

"(A) IN GENERAL.—For purposes of paragraph (1), an election is described in this paragraph if the election is made by an employee after separation from service with respect to amounts not distributed from an eligible retirement plan to have amounts from such plan distributed in order to pay for qualified health insurance premiums.

"(B) SPECIAL RULE.—A plan shall not be treated as violating the requirements of section 401, or as engaging in a prohibited transaction for purposes of section 503(b), merely because it provides for an election with respect to amounts that are otherwise distributable under the plan or merely because of a distribution made pursuant to an election described in subparagraph (A).

"(7) COORDINATION WITH MEDICAL EXPENSE DEDUCTION.—The amounts excluded from gross income under paragraph (1) shall not be taken into account under section 213.

1   "(8) COORDINATION WITH DEDUCTION FOR

2   HEALTH INSURANCE COSTS OF SELF-EMPLOYED IN-

3   DIVIDUALS.—The amounts excluded from gross in-

4   come under paragraph (1) shall not be taken into

5   account under section 162(l).".

6   (b) CONFORMING AMENDMENTS.—

7   (1) Section 403(a) of such Code (relating to

8   taxability of beneficiary under a qualified annuity

9   plan) is amended by inserting after paragraph (1)

10   the following new paragraph:

11   "(2) SPECIAL RULE FOR HEALTH AND LONG-

12   TERM CARE INSURANCE.—To the extent provided in

13   section 402(l), paragraph (1) shall not apply to the

14   amount distributed under the contract which is oth-

15   erwise includible in gross income under this sub-

16   section.".

17   (2) Section 403(b) of such Code (relating to

18   taxability of beneficiary under annuity purchased by

19   section 501(c)(3) organization or public school) is

20   amended by inserting after paragraph (1) the fol-

21   lowing new paragraph:

22   "(2) SPECIAL RULE FOR HEALTH AND LONG-

23   TERM CARE INSURANCE.—To the extent provided in

24   section 402(l), paragraph (1) shall not apply to the

25   amount distributed under the contract which is oth-

1 erwise includible in gross income under this sub-
2 section.".

3   (3) Section 457(a) of such Code (relating to
4 year of inclusion in gross income) is amended by
5 adding at the end the following new paragraph:

6   "(3) SPECIAL RULE FOR HEALTH AND LONG-
7 TERM CARE INSURANCE.—In the case of a plan of
8 an eligible employer described in subsection
9 (e)(1)(A), to the extent provided in section 402(l),
10 paragraph (1) shall not apply to amounts otherwise
11 includible in gross income under this subsection.".

12   (c) EFFECTIVE DATE.—The amendments made by
13 this section shall apply to distributions in taxable years
14 beginning after December 31, 2006.

Subtitle E—United States Tax Court Modernization

SEC. 851. COST-OF-LIVING ADJUSTMENTS FOR TAX COURT JUDICIAL SURVIVOR ANNUITIES.

19   (a) IN GENERAL.—Subsection (s) of section 7448 of
20 the Internal Revenue Code of 1986 (relating to annuities
21 to surviving spouses and dependent children of judges) is
22 amended to read as follows:

23   "(s) INCREASES IN SURVIVOR ANNUITIES.—Each
24 time that an increase is made under section 8340(b) of
25 title 5, United States Code, in annuities payable under

1 subchapter III of chapter 83 of that title, each annuity
2 payable from the survivors annuity fund under this section
3 shall be increased at the same time by the same percent-
4 age by which annuities are increased under such section
5 8340(b).".

6   (b) EFFECTIVE DATE.—The amendment made by
7 this section shall apply with respect to increases made
8 under section 8340(b) of title 5, United States Code, in
9 annuities payable under subchapter III of chapter 83 of
10 that title, taking effect after the date of the enactment
11 of this Act.

12 **SEC. 852. COST OF LIFE INSURANCE COVERAGE FOR TAX**
13   **COURT JUDGES AGE 65 OR OVER.**

14   Section 7472 of the Internal Revenue Code of 1986
15 (relating to expenditures) is amended by inserting after
16 the first sentence the following new sentence: "Notwith-
17 standing any other provision of law, the Tax Court is au-
18 thorized to pay on behalf of its judges, age 65 or over,
19 any increase in the cost of Federal Employees' Group Life
20 Insurance imposed after the date of the enactment of the
21 Pension Protection Act of 2006, including any expenses
22 generated by such payments, as authorized by the chief
23 judge in a manner consistent with such payments author-
24 ized by the Judicial Conference of the United States pur-

1 suant to section 604(a)(5) of title 28, United States

2 Code."

3 **SEC. 853. PARTICIPATION OF TAX COURT JUDGES IN THE**

4   **THRIFT SAVINGS PLAN.**

5   (a) IN GENERAL.—Section 7447 of the Internal Rev-

6 enue Code of 1986 (relating to retirement of judges) is

7 amended by adding at the end the following new sub-

8 section:

9   "(j) THRIFT SAVINGS PLAN.—

10   "(1) ELECTION TO CONTRIBUTE.—

11   "(A) IN GENERAL.—A judge of the Tax

12   Court may elect to contribute to the Thrift Sav-

13   ings Fund established by section 8437 of title

14   5, United States Code.

15   "(B) PERIOD OF ELECTION.—An election

16   may be made under this paragraph only during

17   a period provided under section 8432(b) of title

18   5, United States Code, for individuals subject to

19   chapter 84 of such title.

20   "(2) APPLICABILITY OF TITLE 5 PROVISIONS.—

21   Except as otherwise provided in this subsection, the

22   provisions of subchapters III and VII of chapter 84

23   of title 5, United States Code, shall apply with re-

24   spect to a judge who makes an election under para-

25   graph (1).

"(3) SPECIAL RULES.—

"(A) AMOUNT CONTRIBUTED.—The amount contributed by a judge to the Thrift Savings Fund in any pay period shall not exceed the maximum percentage of such judge's basic pay for such period as allowable under section 8440f of title 5, United States Code. Basic pay does not include any retired pay paid pursuant to this section.

"(B) CONTRIBUTIONS FOR BENEFIT OF JUDGE.—No contributions may be made for the benefit of a judge under section 8432(c) of title 5, United States Code.

"(C) APPLICABILITY OF SECTION 8433(b) OF TITLE 5 WHETHER OR NOT JUDGE RETIRES.—Section 8433(b) of title 5, United States Code, applies with respect to a judge who makes an election under paragraph (1) and who either—

"(i) retires under subsection (b), or

"(ii) ceases to serve as a judge of the Tax Court but does not retire under subsection (b).

1   Retirement under subsection (b) is a separation

2   from service for purposes of subchapters III

3   and VII of chapter 84 of that title.

4   "(D) APPLICABILITY OF SECTION

5   8351(b)(5) OF TITLE 5.—The provisions of sec-

6   tion 8351(b)(5) of title 5, United States Code,

7   shall apply with respect to a judge who makes

8   an election under paragraph (1).

9   "(E) EXCEPTION.—Notwithstanding sub-

10   paragraph (C), if any judge retires under this

11   section, or resigns without having met the age

12   and service requirements set forth under sub-

13   section (b)(2), and such judge's nonforfeitable

14   account balance is less than an amount that the

15   Executive Director of the Federal Retirement

16   Thrift Investment Board prescribes by regula-

17   tion, the Executive Director shall pay the non-

18   forfeitable account balance to the participant in

19   a single payment.".

20   (b) EFFECTIVE DATE.—The amendment made by

21 this section shall take effect on the date of the enactment

22 of this Act, except that United States Tax Court judges

23 may only begin to participate in the Thrift Savings Plan

24 at the next open season beginning after such date.

SEC. 854. ANNUITIES TO SURVIVING SPOUSES AND DEPENDENT CHILDREN OF SPECIAL TRIAL JUDGES OF THE TAX COURT.

(a) DEFINITIONS.—Section 7448(a) of the Internal Revenue Code of 1986 (relating to definitions), as amended by this Act, is amended by redesignating paragraphs (5), (6), (7), and (8) as paragraphs (7), (8), (9), and (10), respectively, and by inserting after paragraph (4) the following new paragraphs:

"(5) The term 'special trial judge' means a judicial officer appointed pursuant to section 7443A, including any individual receiving an annuity under chapters 83 or 84 of title 5, United States Code, whether or not performing judicial duties under section 7443B.

"(6) The term 'special trial judge's salary' means the salary of a special trial judge received under section 7443A(d), any amount received as an annuity under chapters 83 or 84 of title 5, United States Code, and compensation received under section 7443B.".

(b) ELECTION.—Subsection (b) of section 7448 of such Code (relating to annuities to surviving spouses and dependent children of judges) is amended—

(1) by striking the subsection heading and inserting the following:

656

1   "(b) ELECTION.—

2   "(1) JUDGES.—",

3   (2) by moving the text 2 ems to the right, and

4   (3) by adding at the end the following new

5   paragraph:

6   "(2) SPECIAL TRIAL JUDGES.—Any special trial

7   judge may by written election filed with the chief

8   judge bring himself or herself within the purview of

9   this section. Such election shall be filed not later

10   than the later of 6 months after—

11   "(A) 6 months after the date of the enact-

12   ment of this paragraph,

13   "(B) the date the judge takes office, or

14   "(C) the date the judge marries.".

15   (c) CONFORMING AMENDMENTS.—

16   (1) The heading of section 7448 of such Code

17   is amended by inserting "**AND SPECIAL TRIAL**

18   **JUDGES**" after "**JUDGES**".

19   (2) The item relating to section 7448 in the

20   table of sections for part I of subchapter C of chap-

21   ter 76 of such Code is amended by inserting "and

22   special trial judges" after "judges".

23   (3) Subsections (c)(1), (d), (f), (g), (h), (j),

24   (m), (n), and (u) of section 7448 of such Code, as

25   amended by this Act, are each amended—

(A) by inserting "or special trial judge" after "judge" each place it appears other than in the phrase "chief judge", and

(B) by inserting "or special trial judge's" after "judge's" each place it appears.

(4) Section 7448(c) of such Code is amended—

(A) in paragraph (1), by striking "Tax Court judges" and inserting "Tax Court judicial officers",

(B) in paragraph (2)—

(i) in subparagraph (A), by inserting "and section 7443A(d)" after "(a)(4)", and

(ii) in subparagraph (B), by striking "subsection (a)(4)" and inserting "subsections (a)(4) and (a)(6)".

(5) Section 7448(j)(1) of such Code is amended—

(A) in subparagraph (A), by striking "service or retired" and inserting "service, retired", and by inserting ", or receiving any annuity under chapters 83 or 84 of title 5, United States Code," after "section 7447", and

(B) in the last sentence, by striking "subsections (a) (6) and (7)" and inserting "paragraphs (8) and (9) of subsection (a)".

(6) Section 7448(m)(1) of such Code, as amended by this Act, is amended by inserting "or any annuity under chapters 83 or 84 of title 5, United States Code" after "7447(d)".

(7) Section 7448(n) of such Code is amended by inserting "his years of service pursuant to any appointment under section 7443A," after "of the Tax Court,".

(8) Section 3121(b)(5)(E) of such Code is amended by inserting "or special trial judge" before "of the United States Tax Court".

(9) Section 210(a)(5)(E) of the Social Security Act is amended by inserting "or special trial judge" before "of the United States Tax Court".

SEC. 855. JURISDICTION OF TAX COURT OVER COLLECTION DUE PROCESS CASES.

(a) IN GENERAL.—Paragraph (1) of section 6330(d) of the Internal Revenue Code of 1986 (relating to proceeding after hearing) is amended to read as follows:

"(1) JUDICIAL REVIEW OF DETERMINATION.— The person may, within 30 days of a determination under this section, appeal such determination to the

1   Tax Court (and the Tax Court shall have jurisdic-
2   tion with respect to such matter).".

3   (b) EFFECTIVE DATE.—The amendment made by
4 this section shall apply to determinations made after the
5 date which is 60 days after the date of the enactment of
6 this Act.

7 **SEC. 856. PROVISIONS FOR RECALL.**

8   (a) IN GENERAL.—Part I of subchapter C of chapter
9 76 of the Internal Revenue Code of 1986 is amended by
10 inserting after section 7443A the following new section:

11 **"SEC. 7443B. RECALL OF SPECIAL TRIAL JUDGES OF THE**
12   **TAX COURT.**

13   "(a) RECALLING OF RETIRED SPECIAL TRIAL
14 JUDGES.—Any individual who has retired pursuant to the
15 applicable provisions of title 5, United States Code, upon
16 reaching the age and service requirements established
17 therein, may at or after retirement be called upon by the
18 chief judge of the Tax Court to perform such judicial du-
19 ties with the Tax Court as may be requested of such indi-
20 vidual for any period or periods specified by the chief
21 judge; except that in the case of any such individual—

22   "(1) the aggregate of such periods in any 1 cal-
23   endar year shall not (without such individual's con-
24   sent) exceed 90 calendar days, and

1   "(2) such individual shall be relieved of per-
2   forming such duties during any period in which ill-
3   ness or disability precludes the performance of such
4   duties.

5 Any act, or failure to act, by an individual performing ju-
6 dicial duties pursuant to this subsection shall have the
7 same force and effect as if it were the act (or failure to
8 act) of a special trial judge of the Tax Court.

9   "(b) COMPENSATION.—For the year in which a pe-
10 riod of recall occurs, the special trial judge shall receive,
11 in addition to the annuity provided under the applicable
12 provisions of title 5, United States Code, an amount equal
13 to the difference between that annuity and the current sal-
14 ary of the office to which the special trial judge is recalled.

15   "(c) RULEMAKING AUTHORITY.—The provisions of
16 this section may be implemented under such rules as may
17 be promulgated by the Tax Court."

18   (b) CONFORMING AMENDMENT.—The table of sec-
19 tions for part I of subchapter C of chapter 76 of such
20 Code is amended by inserting after the item relating to
21 section 7443A the following new item:

"Sec. 7443B. Recall of special trial judges of the Tax Court.".

SEC. 857. AUTHORITY FOR SPECIAL TRIAL JUDGES TO HEAR AND DECIDE CERTAIN EMPLOYMENT STATUS CASES.

(a) IN GENERAL.—Section 7443A(b) of the Internal Revenue Code of 1986 (relating to proceedings which may be assigned to special trial judges) is amended by striking "and" at the end of paragraph (4), by redesignating paragraph (5) as paragraph (6), and by inserting after paragraph (4) the following new paragraph:

"(5) any proceeding under section 7436(c), and".

(b) CONFORMING AMENDMENT.—Section 7443A(c) of such Code is amended by striking "or (4)" and inserting "(4), or (5)".

(c) EFFECTIVE DATE.—The amendments made by this section shall apply to any proceeding under section 7436(c) of the Internal Revenue Code of 1986 with respect to which a decision has not become final (as determined under section 7481 of such Code) before the date of the enactment of this Act.

SEC. 858. CONFIRMATION OF AUTHORITY OF TAX COURT TO APPLY DOCTRINE OF EQUITABLE RECOUPMENT.

(a) CONFIRMATION OF AUTHORITY OF TAX COURT TO APPLY DOCTRINE OF EQUITABLE RECOUPMENT.— Section 6214(b) of the Internal Revenue Code of 1986 (re-

1 lating to jurisdiction over other years and quarters) is
2 amended by adding at the end the following new sentence:
3 "Notwithstanding the preceding sentence, the Tax Court
4 may apply the doctrine of equitable recoupment to the
5 same extent that it is available in civil tax cases before
6 the district courts of the United States and the United
7 States Court of Federal Claims.".

8   (b) EFFECTIVE DATE.—The amendment made by
9 this section shall apply to any action or proceeding in the
10 United States Tax Court with respect to which a decision
11 has not become final (as determined under section 7481
12 of the Internal Revenue Code of 1986) as of the date of
13 the enactment of this Act.

14 **SEC. 859. TAX COURT FILING FEE IN ALL CASES COM-**
15   **MENCED BY FILING PETITION.**

16   (a) IN GENERAL.—Section 7451 of the Internal Rev-
17 enue Code of 1986 (relating to fee for filing a Tax Court
18 petition) is amended by striking all that follows "petition"
19 and inserting a period.

20   (b) EFFECTIVE DATE.—The amendment made by
21 this section shall take effect on the date of the enactment
22 of this Act.

SEC. 860. EXPANDED USE OF TAX COURT PRACTICE FEE FOR PRO SE TAXPAYERS.

(a) IN GENERAL.—Section 7475(b) of the Internal Revenue Code of 1986 (relating to use of fees) is amended by inserting before the period at the end "and to provide services to pro se taxpayers".

(b) EFFECTIVE DATE.—The amendment made by this section shall take effect on the date of the enactment of this Act.

Subtitle F—Other Provisions

SEC. 861. EXTENSION TO ALL GOVERNMENTAL PLANS OF CURRENT MORATORIUM ON APPLICATION OF CERTAIN NONDISCRIMINATION RULES APPLICABLE TO STATE AND LOCAL PLANS.

(a) IN GENERAL.—

(1) Subparagraph (G) of section 401(a)(5) and subparagraph (G) of section 401(a)(26) of the Internal Revenue Code of 1986 are each amended by striking "section 414(d))" and all that follows and inserting "section 414(d)).".

(2) Subparagraph (G) of section 401(k)(3) of such Code and paragraph (2) of section 1505(d) of the Taxpayer Relief Act of 1997 (Public Law 105–34; 111 Stat. 1063) are each amended by striking "maintained by a State or local government or polit-

1   ical subdivision thereof (or agency or instrumentality

2   thereof)''.

3   (b) CONFORMING AMENDMENTS.—

4   (1) The heading of subparagraph (G) of section

5   401(a)(5) of the Internal Revenue Code of 1986 is

6   amended by striking "STATE AND LOCAL GOVERN-

7   MENTAL" and inserting "GOVERNMENTAL".

8   (2) The heading of subparagraph (G) of section

9   401(a)(26) of such Code is amended by striking

10   "EXCEPTION FOR STATE AND LOCAL" and inserting

11   "EXCEPTION FOR".

12   (3) Section 401(k)(3)(G) of such Code is

13   amended by inserting "GOVERNMENTAL PLAN.—"

14   after "(G)".

15   (c) EFFECTIVE DATE.—The amendments made by

16 this section shall apply to any year beginning after the

17 date of the enactment of this Act.

18 **SEC. 862. ELIMINATION OF AGGREGATE LIMIT FOR USAGE**

19   **OF EXCESS FUNDS FROM BLACK LUNG DIS-**

20   **ABILITY TRUSTS.**

21   (a) IN GENERAL.—So much of section 501(c)(21)(C)

22 of the Internal Revenue Code of 1986 (relating to black

23 lung disability trusts) as precedes the last sentence is

24 amended to read as follows:

1   "(C) Payments described in subparagraph

2   (A)(i)(IV) may be made from such trust during

3   a taxable year only to the extent that the aggre-

4   gate amount of such payments during such tax-

5   able year does not exceed the excess (if any), as

6   of the close of the preceding taxable year, of—

7   "(i) the fair market value of the as-

8   sets of the trust, over

9   "(ii) 110 percent of the present value

10   of the liability described in subparagraph

11   (A)(i)(I) of such person.".

12   (b) EFFECTIVE DATE.—The amendments made by

13 this section shall apply to taxable years beginning after

14 December 31, 2006.

15 **SEC. 863. TREATMENT OF DEATH BENEFITS FROM COR-**

16   **PORATE-OWNED LIFE INSURANCE.**

17   (a) IN GENERAL.—Section 101 of the Internal Rev-

18 enue Code of 1986 (relating to certain death benefits) is

19 amended by adding at the end the following new sub-

20 section:

21   "(j) TREATMENT OF CERTAIN EMPLOYER-OWNED

22 LIFE INSURANCE CONTRACTS.—

23   "(1) GENERAL RULE.—In the case of an em-

24   ployer-owned life insurance contract, the amount ex-

25   cluded from gross income of an applicable policy-

1 holder by reason of paragraph (1) of subsection (a)

2 shall not exceed an amount equal to the sum of the

3 premiums and other amounts paid by the policy-

4 holder for the contract.

5   "(2) EXCEPTIONS.—In the case of an employer-

6 owned life insurance contract with respect to which

7 the notice and consent requirements of paragraph

8 (4) are met, paragraph (1) shall not apply to any of

9 the following:

10   "(A) EXCEPTIONS BASED ON INSURED'S

11   STATUS.—Any amount received by reason of

12   the death of an insured who, with respect to an

13   applicable policyholder—

14   "(i) was an employee at any time dur-

15   ing the 12-month period before the in-

16   sured's death, or

17   "(ii) is, at the time the contract is

18   issued—

19   "(I) a director,

20   "(II) a highly compensated em-

21   ployee within the meaning of section

22   414(q) (without regard to paragraph

23   (1)(B)(ii) thereof), or

24   "(III) a highly compensated indi-

25   vidual within the meaning of section

1   105(h)(5), except that '35 percent'

2   shall be substituted for '25 percent' in

3   subparagraph (C) thereof.

4   "(B) EXCEPTION FOR AMOUNTS PAID TO

5   INSURED'S HEIRS.—Any amount received by

6   reason of the death of an insured to the ex-

7   tent—

8   "(i) the amount is paid to a member

9   of the family (within the meaning of sec-

10   tion 267(c)(4)) of the insured, any indi-

11   vidual who is the designated beneficiary of

12   the insured under the contract (other than

13   the applicable policyholder), a trust estab-

14   lished for the benefit of any such member

15   of the family or designated beneficiary, or

16   the estate of the insured, or

17   "(ii) the amount is used to purchase

18   an equity (or capital or profits) interest in

19   the applicable policyholder from any person

20   described in clause (i).

21   "(3) EMPLOYER-OWNED LIFE INSURANCE CON-

22   TRACT.—

23   "(A) IN GENERAL.—For purposes of this

24   subsection, the term 'employer-owned life insur-

1   ance contract' means a life insurance contract

2   which—

3   "(i) is owned by a person engaged in

4   a trade or business and under which such

5   person (or a related person described in

6   subparagraph (B)(ii)) is directly or indi-

7   rectly a beneficiary under the contract, and

8   "(ii) covers the life of an insured who

9   is an employee with respect to the trade or

10   business of the applicable policyholder on

11   the date the contract is issued.

12 For purposes of the preceding sentence, if cov-

13 erage for each insured under a master contract

14 is treated as a separate contract for purposes of

15 sections 817(h), 7702, and 7702A, coverage for

16 each such insured shall be treated as a separate

17 contract.

18   "(B) APPLICABLE POLICYHOLDER.—For

19 purposes of this subsection—

20   "(i) IN GENERAL.—The term 'applica-

21   ble policyholder' means, with respect to

22   any employer-owned life insurance con-

23   tract, the person described in subpara-

24   graph (A)(i) which owns the contract.

669

1 "(ii) RELATED PERSONS.—The term

2 'applicable policyholder' includes any per-

3 son which—

4 "(I) bears a relationship to the

5 person described in clause (i) which is

6 specified in section 267(b) or

7 707(b)(1), or

8 "(II) is engaged in trades or

9 businesses with such person which are

10 under common control (within the

11 meaning of subsection (a) or (b) of

12 section 52).

13 "(4) NOTICE AND CONSENT REQUIREMENTS.—

14 The notice and consent requirements of this para-

15 graph are met if, before the issuance of the contract,

16 the employee—

17 "(A) is notified in writing that the applica-

18 ble policyholder intends to insure the employee's

19 life and the maximum face amount for which

20 the employee could be insured at the time the

21 contract was issued,

22 "(B) provides written consent to being in-

23 sured under the contract and that such cov-

24 erage may continue after the insured terminates

25 employment, and

1   "(C) is informed in writing that an appli-

2   cable policyholder will be a beneficiary of any

3   proceeds payable upon the death of the em-

4   ployee.

5   "(5) DEFINITIONS.—For purposes of this sub-

6 section—

7   "(A) EMPLOYEE.—The term 'employee' in-

8   cludes an officer, director, and highly com-

9   pensated employee (within the meaning of sec-

10   tion 414(q)).

11   "(B) INSURED.—The term 'insured'

12   means, with respect to an employer-owned life

13   insurance contract, an individual covered by the

14   contract who is a United States citizen or resi-

15   dent. In the case of a contract covering the

16   joint lives of 2 individuals, references to an in-

17   sured include both of the individuals.".

18   (b) REPORTING REQUIREMENTS.—Subpart A of part

19 III of subchapter A of chapter 61 of the Internal Revenue

20 Code of 1986 (relating to information concerning persons

21 subject to special provisions) is amended by inserting after

22 section 6039H the following new section:

1 **"SEC. 6039I. RETURNS AND RECORDS WITH RESPECT TO**

2 **EMPLOYER-OWNED LIFE INSURANCE CON-**

3 **TRACTS.**

4 "(a) IN GENERAL.—Every applicable policyholder

5 owning 1 or more employer-owned life insurance contracts

6 issued after the date of the enactment of this section shall

7 file a return (at such time and in such manner as the

8 Secretary shall by regulations prescribe) showing for each

9 year such contracts are owned—

10 "(1) the number of employees of the applicable

11 policyholder at the end of the year,

12 "(2) the number of such employees insured

13 under such contracts at the end of the year,

14 "(3) the total amount of insurance in force at

15 the end of the year under such contracts,

16 "(4) the name, address, and taxpayer identifica-

17 tion number of the applicable policyholder and the

18 type of business in which the policyholder is en-

19 gaged, and

20 "(5) that the applicable policyholder has a valid

21 consent for each insured employee (or, if all such

22 consents are not obtained, the number of insured

23 employees for whom such consent was not obtained).

24 "(b) RECORDKEEPING REQUIREMENT.—Each appli-

25 cable policyholder owning 1 or more employer-owned life

26 insurance contracts during any year shall keep such

1 records as may be necessary for purposes of determining

2 whether the requirements of this section and section

3 101(j) are met.

4   "(c) DEFINITIONS.—Any term used in this section

5 which is used in section 101(j) shall have the same mean-

6 ing given such term by section 101(j).".

7   (c) CONFORMING AMENDMENTS.—

8   (1) Paragraph (1) of section 101(a) of the In-

9   ternal Revenue Code of 1986 is amended by striking

10   "and subsection (f)" and inserting "subsection (f),

11   and subsection (j)".

12   (2) The table of sections for subpart A of part

13   III of subchapter A of chapter 61 of such Code is

14   amended by inserting after the item relating to sec-

15   tion 6039H the following new item:

"Sec. 6039I. Returns and records with respect to employer-owned life insurance
contracts.".

16   (d) EFFECTIVE DATE.—The amendments made by

17 this section shall apply to life insurance contracts issued

18 after the date of the enactment of this Act, except for a

19 contract issued after such date pursuant to an exchange

20 described in section 1035 of the Internal Revenue Code

21 of 1986 for a contract issued on or prior to that date.

22 For purposes of the preceding sentence, any material in-

23 crease in the death benefit or other material change shall

24 cause the contract to be treated as a new contract except

1 that, in the case of a master contract (within the meaning
2 of section 264(f)(4)(E) of such Code), the addition of cov-
3 ered lives shall be treated as a new contract only with re-
4 spect to such additional covered lives.

5 **SEC. 864. TREATMENT OF TEST ROOM SUPERVISORS AND**
6 **PROCTORS WHO ASSIST IN THE ADMINISTRA-**
7 **TION OF COLLEGE ENTRANCE AND PLACE-**
8 **MENT EXAMS.**

9 (a) IN GENERAL.—Section 530 of the Revenue Rec-
10 onciliation Act of 1978 is amended by adding at the end
11 the following new subsection:

12 "(f) TREATMENT OF TEST ROOM SUPERVISORS AND
13 PROCTORS WHO ASSIST IN THE ADMINISTRATION OF
14 COLLEGE ENTRANCE AND PLACEMENT EXAMS.—

15 "(1) IN GENERAL.—In the case of an individual
16 described in paragraph (2) who is providing services
17 as a test proctor or room supervisor by assisting in
18 the administration of college entrance or placement
19 examinations, this section shall be applied to such
20 services performed after December 31, 2006 (and
21 remuneration paid for such services) without regard
22 to subsection (a)(3) thereof.

23 "(2) APPLICABILITY.—An individual is de-
24 scribed in this paragraph if the individual—

1   "(A) is providing the services described in

2   subsection (a) to an organization described in

3   section 501(c), and exempt from tax under sec-

4   tion 501(a), of the Internal Revenue Code of

5   1986, and

6   "(B) is not otherwise treated as an em-

7   ployee of such organization for purposes of sub-

8   title C of such Code (relating to employment

9   taxes).".

10 (b) EFFECTIVE DATE.—The amendment made by

11 this section shall apply to remuneration for services per-

12 formed after December 31, 2006.

SEC. 865. GRANDFATHER RULE FOR CHURCH PLANS WHICH SELF-ANNUITIZE.

15 (a) IN GENERAL.—In the case of any plan year end-

16 ing after the date of the enactment of this Act, annuity

17 payments provided with respect to any account maintained

18 for a participant or beneficiary under a qualified church

19 plan shall not fail to satisfy the requirements of section

20 401(a)(9) of the Internal Revenue Code of 1986 merely

21 because the payments are not made under an annuity con-

22 tract purchased from an insurance company if such pay-

23 ments would not fail such requirements if provided with

24 respect to a retirement income account described in sec-

25 tion 403(b)(9) of such Code.

1   (b) QUALIFIED CHURCH PLAN.—For purposes of
2 this section, the term "qualified church plan" means any
3 money purchase pension plan described in section 401(a)
4 of such Code which—

5   (1) is a church plan (as defined in section
6   414(e) of such Code) with respect to which the elec-
7   tion provided by section 410(d) of such Code has not
8   been made, and

9   (2) was in existence on April 17, 2002.

10 **SEC. 866. EXEMPTION FOR INCOME FROM LEVERAGED**
11   **REAL ESTATE HELD BY CHURCH PLANS.**

12   (a) IN GENERAL.—Section 514(c)(9)(C) of the Inter-
13 nal Revenue Code of 1986 is amended by striking "or"
14 after clause (ii), by striking the period at the end of clause
15 (iii) and inserting "; or", and by inserting after clause (iii)
16 the following:

17   "(iv) a retirement income account de-
18   scribed in section 403(b)(9).".

19   (b) EFFECTIVE DATE.—The amendment made by
20 subsection (a) shall apply to taxable years beginning on
21 or after the date of enactment of this Act.

22 **SEC. 867. CHURCH PLAN RULE.**

23   (a) IN GENERAL.—Paragraph (11) of section 415(b)
24 of the Internal Revenue Code of 1986 is amended by add-
25 ing at the end the following: "Subparagraph (B) of para-

1 graph (1) shall not apply to a plan maintained by an orga-
2 nization described in section 3121(w)(3)(A) except with
3 respect to highly compensated benefits. For purposes of
4 this paragraph, the term 'highly compensated benefits'
5 means any benefits accrued for an employee in any year
6 on or after the first year in which such employee is a high-
7 ly compensated employee (as defined in section 414(q))
8 of the organization described in section 3121(w)(3)(A).
9 For purposes of applying paragraph (1)(B) to highly com-
10 pensated benefits, all benefits of the employee otherwise
11 taken into account (without regard to this paragraph)
12 shall be taken into account.".

13   (b) EFFECTIVE DATE.—The amendment made by
14 this section shall apply to years beginning after December
15 31, 2006.

16 **SEC. 868. GRATUITOUS TRANSFER FOR BENEFITS OF EM-**
17   **PLOYEES.**

18   (a) IN GENERAL.—Subparagraph (E) of section
19 664(g)(3) of the Internal Revenue Code of 1986 is amend-
20 ed by inserting "(determined on the basis of fair market
21 value of securities when allocated to participants)" after
22 "paragraph (7)".

23   (b) EFFECTIVE DATE.—The amendment made by
24 this section shall take effect on the date of the enactment
25 of this Act.

TITLE IX—INCREASE IN PENSION PLAN DIVERSIFICATION AND PARTICIPATION AND OTHER PENSION PROVISIONS

SEC. 901. DEFINED CONTRIBUTION PLANS REQUIRED TO PROVIDE EMPLOYEES WITH FREEDOM TO INVEST THEIR PLAN ASSETS.

(a) AMENDMENTS OF INTERNAL REVENUE CODE.—

(1) QUALIFICATION REQUIREMENT.—Section 401(a) of the Internal Revenue Code of 1986 (relating to qualified pension, profit-sharing, and stock bonus plans) is amended by inserting after paragraph (34) the following new paragraph:

"(35) DIVERSIFICATION REQUIREMENTS FOR CERTAIN DEFINED CONTRIBUTION PLANS.—

"(A) IN GENERAL.—A trust which is part of an applicable defined contribution plan shall not be treated as a qualified trust unless the plan meets the diversification requirements of subparagraphs (B), (C), and (D).

"(B) EMPLOYEE CONTRIBUTIONS AND ELECTIVE DEFERRALS INVESTED IN EMPLOYER SECURITIES.—In the case of the portion of an applicable individual's account attributable to employee contributions and elective deferrals

1   which is invested in employer securities, a plan

2   meets the requirements of this subparagraph if

3   the applicable individual may elect to direct the

4   plan to divest any such securities and to rein-

5   vest an equivalent amount in other investment

6   options meeting the requirements of subpara-

7   graph (D).

8   "(C) EMPLOYER CONTRIBUTIONS IN-

9   VESTED IN EMPLOYER SECURITIES.—In the

10   case of the portion of the account attributable

11   to employer contributions other than elective

12   deferrals which is invested in employer securi-

13   ties, a plan meets the requirements of this sub-

14   paragraph if each applicable individual who—

15   "(i) is a participant who has com-

16   pleted at least 3 years of service, or

17   "(ii) is a beneficiary of a participant

18   described in clause (i) or of a deceased

19   participant,

20   may elect to direct the plan to divest any such

21   securities and to reinvest an equivalent amount

22   in other investment options meeting the re-

23   quirements of subparagraph (D).

24   "(D) INVESTMENT OPTIONS.—

"(i) IN GENERAL.—The requirements
of this subparagraph are met if the plan
offers not less than 3 investment options,
other than employer securities, to which an
applicable individual may direct the proceeds from the divestment of employer securities pursuant to this paragraph, each
of which is diversified and has materially
different risk and return characteristics.

"(ii) TREATMENT OF CERTAIN RE-
STRICTIONS AND CONDITIONS.—

"(I) TIME FOR MAKING INVEST-
MENT CHOICES.—A plan shall not be
treated as failing to meet the requirements of this subparagraph merely because the plan limits the time for divestment and reinvestment to periodic, reasonable opportunities occurring no less frequently than quarterly.

"(II) CERTAIN RESTRICTIONS
AND CONDITIONS NOT ALLOWED.—
Except as provided in regulations, a
plan shall not meet the requirements
of this subparagraph if the plan imposes restrictions or conditions with

respect to the investment of employer securities which are not imposed on the investment of other assets of the plan. This subclause shall not apply to any restrictions or conditions imposed by reason of the application of securities laws.

"(E) APPLICABLE DEFINED CONTRIBUTION PLAN.—For purposes of this paragraph—

"(i) IN GENERAL.—The term 'applicable defined contribution plan' means any defined contribution plan which holds any publicly traded employer securities.

"(ii) EXCEPTION FOR CERTAIN ESOPS.—Such term does not include an employee stock ownership plan if—

"(I) there are no contributions to such plan (or earnings thereunder) which are held within such plan and are subject to subsection (k) or (m), and

"(II) such plan is a separate plan for purposes of section 414(l) with respect to any other defined benefit plan or defined contribution plan main-

1   tained by the same employer or em-

2   ployers.

3   "(iii) EXCEPTION FOR ONE PARTICI-

4 PANT PLANS.—Such term does not include

5 a one-participant retirement plan.

6   "(iv) ONE-PARTICIPANT RETIREMENT

7 PLAN.—For purposes of clause (iii), the

8 term 'one-participant retirement plan'

9 means a retirement plan that—

10   "(I) on the first day of the plan

11 year covered only one individual (or

12 the individual and the individual's

13 spouse) and the individual owned 100

14 percent of the plan sponsor (whether

15 or not incorporated), or covered only

16 one or more partners (or partners and

17 their spouses) in the plan sponsor,

18   "(II) meets the minimum cov-

19 erage requirements of section 410(b)

20 without being combined with any

21 other plan of the business that covers

22 the employees of the business,

23   "(III) does not provide benefits

24 to anyone except the individual (and

1   the individual's spouse) or the part-

2   ners (and their spouses),

3   "(IV) does not cover a business

4   that is a member of an affiliated serv-

5   ice group, a controlled group of cor-

6   porations, or a group of businesses

7   under common control, and

8   "(V) does not cover a business

9   that uses the services of leased em-

10   ployees (within the meaning of section

11   414(n)).

12   For purposes of this clause, the term 'part-

13   ner' includes a 2-percent shareholder (as

14   defined in section 1372(b)) of an S cor-

15   poration.

16   "(F) CERTAIN PLANS TREATED AS HOLD-

17 ING PUBLICLY TRADED EMPLOYER SECURI-

18 TIES.—

19   "(i) IN GENERAL.—Except as pro-

20   vided in regulations or in clause (ii), a plan

21   holding employer securities which are not

22   publicly traded employer securities shall be

23   treated as holding publicly traded employer

24   securities if any employer corporation, or

25   any member of a controlled group of cor-

porations which includes such employer corporation, has issued a class of stock which is a publicly traded employer security.

"(ii) EXCEPTION FOR CERTAIN CON-TROLLED GROUPS WITH PUBLICLY TRAD-ED SECURITIES.—Clause (i) shall not apply to a plan if—

"(I) no employer corporation, or parent corporation of an employer corporation, has issued any publicly traded employer security, and

"(II) no employer corporation, or parent corporation of an employer corporation, has issued any special class of stock which grants particular rights to, or bears particular risks for, the holder or issuer with respect to any corporation described in clause (i) which has issued any publicly traded employer security.

"(iii) DEFINITIONS.—For purposes of this subparagraph, the term—

"(I) 'controlled group of corpora-tions' has the meaning given such

1   term by section 1563(a), except that

2   '50 percent' shall be substituted for

3   '80 percent' each place it appears,

4   "(II) 'employer corporation'

5   means a corporation which is an em-

6   ployer maintaining the plan, and

7   "(III) 'parent corporation' has

8   the meaning given such term by sec-

9   tion 424(e).

10   "(G) OTHER DEFINITIONS.—For purposes

11   of this paragraph—

12   "(i) APPLICABLE INDIVIDUAL.—The

13   term 'applicable individual' means—

14   "(I) any participant in the plan,

15   and

16   "(II) any beneficiary who has an

17   account under the plan with respect to

18   which the beneficiary is entitled to ex-

19   ercise the rights of a participant.

20   "(ii) ELECTIVE DEFERRAL.—The

21   term 'elective deferral' means an employer

22   contribution described in section

23   402(g)(3)(A).

24   "(iii) EMPLOYER SECURITY.—The

25   term 'employer security' has the meaning

given such term by section 407(d)(1) of the Employee Retirement Income Security Act of 1974.

"(iv) EMPLOYEE STOCK OWNERSHIP PLAN.—The term 'employee stock ownership plan' has the meaning given such term by section 4975(e)(7).

"(v) PUBLICLY TRADED EMPLOYER SECURITIES.—The term 'publicly traded employer securities' means employer securities which are readily tradable on an established securities market.

"(vi) YEAR OF SERVICE.—The term 'year of service' has the meaning given such term by section 411(a)(5).

"(H) TRANSITION RULE FOR SECURITIES ATTRIBUTABLE TO EMPLOYER CONTRIBUTIONS.—

"(i) RULES PHASED IN OVER 3 YEARS.—

"(I) IN GENERAL.—In the case of the portion of an account to which subparagraph (C) applies and which consists of employer securities acquired in a plan year beginning before

1   January 1, 2007, subparagraph (C)

2   shall only apply to the applicable per-

3   centage of such securities. This sub-

4   paragraph shall be applied separately

5   with respect to each class of securi-

6   ties.

7   "(II) EXCEPTION FOR CERTAIN

8   PARTICIPANTS AGED 55 OR OVER.—

9   Subclause (I) shall not apply to an

10   applicable individual who is a partici-

11   pant who has attained age 55 and

12   completed at least 3 years of service

13   before the first plan year beginning

14   after December 31, 2005.

15   "(ii) APPLICABLE PERCENTAGE.—For

16   purposes of clause (i), the applicable per-

17   centage shall be determined as follows:

"Plan year to which subparagraph (C) applies:	The applicable percentage is:
1st	33
2d	66
3d and following	100.".

18   (2) CONFORMING AMENDMENTS.—

19   (A) Section 401(a)(28)(B) of such Code

20   (relating to additional requirements relating to

21   employee stock ownership plans) is amended by

22   adding at the end the following new clause:

"(v) EXCEPTION.—This subparagraph shall not apply to an applicable defined contribution plan (as defined in paragraph (35)(E))."

(B) Section 409(h)(7) of such Code is amended by inserting "or subparagraph (B) or (C) of section 401(a)(35)" before the period at the end.

(C) Section 4980(c)(3)(A) of such Code is amended by striking "if—" and all that follows and inserting "if the requirements of subparagraphs (B), (C), and (D) are met."

(b) AMENDMENTS OF ERISA.—

(1) IN GENERAL.—Section 204 of the Employee Retirement Income Security Act of 1974 (29 U.S.C. 1054) is amended by redesignating subsection (j) as subsection (k) and by inserting after subsection (i) the following new subsection:

"(j) DIVERSIFICATION REQUIREMENTS FOR CERTAIN INDIVIDUAL ACCOUNT PLANS.—

"(1) IN GENERAL.—An applicable individual account plan shall meet the diversification requirements of paragraphs (2), (3), and (4).

"(2) EMPLOYEE CONTRIBUTIONS AND ELECTIVE DEFERRALS INVESTED IN EMPLOYER SECURI-

1 TIES.—In the case of the portion of an applicable in-
2 dividual's account attributable to employee contribu-
3 tions and elective deferrals which is invested in em-
4 ployer securities, a plan meets the requirements of
5 this paragraph if the applicable individual may elect
6 to direct the plan to divest any such securities and
7 to reinvest an equivalent amount in other investment
8 options meeting the requirements of paragraph (4).

9 "(3) EMPLOYER CONTRIBUTIONS INVESTED IN
10 EMPLOYER SECURITIES.—In the case of the portion
11 of the account attributable to employer contributions
12 other than elective deferrals which is invested in em-
13 ployer securities, a plan meets the requirements of
14 this paragraph if each applicable individual who—

15 "(A) is a participant who has completed at
16 least 3 years of service, or

17 "(B) is a beneficiary of a participant de-
18 scribed in subparagraph (A) or of a deceased
19 participant,

20 may elect to direct the plan to divest any such secu-
21 rities and to reinvest an equivalent amount in other
22 investment options meeting the requirements of
23 paragraph (4).

24 "(4) INVESTMENT OPTIONS.—

"(A) IN GENERAL.—The requirements of this paragraph are met if the plan offers not less than 3 investment options, other than employer securities, to which an applicable individual may direct the proceeds from the divestment of employer securities pursuant to this subsection, each of which is diversified and has materially different risk and return characteristics.

"(B) TREATMENT OF CERTAIN RESTRICTIONS AND CONDITIONS.—

"(i) TIME FOR MAKING INVESTMENT CHOICES.—A plan shall not be treated as failing to meet the requirements of this paragraph merely because the plan limits the time for divestment and reinvestment to periodic, reasonable opportunities occurring no less frequently than quarterly.

"(ii) CERTAIN RESTRICTIONS AND CONDITIONS NOT ALLOWED.—Except as provided in regulations, a plan shall not meet the requirements of this paragraph if the plan imposes restrictions or conditions with respect to the investment of employer securities which are not imposed on the in-

1 vestment of other assets of the plan. This

2 subparagraph shall not apply to any re-

3 strictions or conditions imposed by reason

4 of the application of securities laws.

5 "(5) APPLICABLE INDIVIDUAL ACCOUNT

6 PLAN.—For purposes of this subsection—

7 "(A) IN GENERAL.—The term 'applicable

8 individual account plan' means any individual

9 account plan (as defined in section 3(34)) which

10 holds any publicly traded employer securities.

11 "(B) EXCEPTION FOR CERTAIN ESOPS.—

12 Such term does not include an employee stock

13 ownership plan if—

14 "(i) there are no contributions to such

15 plan (or earnings thereunder) which are

16 held within such plan and are subject to

17 subsection (k) or (m) of section 401 of the

18 Internal Revenue Code of 1986, and

19 "(ii) such plan is a separate plan (for

20 purposes of section 414(l) of such Code)

21 with respect to any other defined benefit

22 plan or individual account plan maintained

23 by the same employer or employers.

24 "(C) EXCEPTION FOR ONE PARTICIPANT

25 PLANS.—Such term shall not include a one-par-

ticipant retirement plan (as defined in section 101(i)(8)(B)).

"(D) CERTAIN PLANS TREATED AS HOLD-ING PUBLICLY TRADED EMPLOYER SECURI-TIES.—

"(i) IN GENERAL.—Except as pro-vided in regulations or in clause (ii), a plan holding employer securities which are not publicly traded employer securities shall be treated as holding publicly traded employer securities if any employer corporation, or any member of a controlled group of cor-porations which includes such employer corporation, has issued a class of stock which is a publicly traded employer secu-rity.

"(ii) EXCEPTION FOR CERTAIN CON-TROLLED GROUPS WITH PUBLICLY TRAD-ED SECURITIES.—Clause (i) shall not apply to a plan if—

"(I) no employer corporation, or parent corporation of an employer corporation, has issued any publicly traded employer security, and

1   "(II) no employer corporation, or

2   parent corporation of an employer

3   corporation, has issued any special

4   class of stock which grants particular

5   rights to, or bears particular risks for,

6   the holder or issuer with respect to

7   any corporation described in clause (i)

8   which has issued any publicly traded

9   employer security.

10   "(iii) DEFINITIONS.—For purposes of

11   this subparagraph, the term—

12   "(I) 'controlled group of corpora-

13   tions' has the meaning given such

14   term by section 1563(a) of the Inter-

15   nal Revenue Code of 1986, except

16   that '50 percent' shall be substituted

17   for '80 percent' each place it appears,

18   "(II) 'employer corporation'

19   means a corporation which is an em-

20   ployer maintaining the plan, and

21   "(III) 'parent corporation' has

22   the meaning given such term by sec-

23   tion 424(e) of such Code.

24   "(6) OTHER DEFINITIONS.—For purposes of

25   this paragraph—

"(A) APPLICABLE INDIVIDUAL.—The term 'applicable individual' means—

"(i) any participant in the plan, and

"(ii) any beneficiary who has an account under the plan with respect to which the beneficiary is entitled to exercise the rights of a participant.

"(B) ELECTIVE DEFERRAL.—The term 'elective deferral' means an employer contribution described in section 402(g)(3)(A) of the Internal Revenue Code of 1986.

"(C) EMPLOYER SECURITY.—The term 'employer security' has the meaning given such term by section 407(d)(1).

"(D) EMPLOYEE STOCK OWNERSHIP PLAN.—The term 'employee stock ownership plan' has the meaning given such term by section 4975(e)(7) of such Code.

"(E) PUBLICLY TRADED EMPLOYER SECURITIES.—The term 'publicly traded employer securities' means employer securities which are readily tradable on an established securities market.

1   "(F) YEAR OF SERVICE.—The term 'year

2   of service' has the meaning given such term by

3   section 203(b)(2).

4   "(7) TRANSITION RULE FOR SECURITIES AT-

5 TRIBUTABLE TO EMPLOYER CONTRIBUTIONS.—

6   "(A) RULES PHASED IN OVER 3 YEARS.—

7   "(i) IN GENERAL.—In the case of the

8   portion of an account to which paragraph

9   (3) applies and which consists of employer

10   securities acquired in a plan year begin-

11   ning before January 1, 2007, paragraph

12   (3) shall only apply to the applicable per-

13   centage of such securities. This subpara-

14   graph shall be applied separately with re-

15   spect to each class of securities.

16   "(ii) EXCEPTION FOR CERTAIN PAR-

17   TICIPANTS AGED 55 OR OVER.—Clause (i)

18   shall not apply to an applicable individual

19   who is a participant who has attained age

20   55 and completed at least 3 years of serv-

21   ice before the first plan year beginning

22   after December 31, 2005.

23   "(B) APPLICABLE PERCENTAGE.—For

24   purposes of subparagraph (A), the applicable

25   percentage shall be determined as follows:

"Plan year to which paragraph (3) applies:	The applicable percentage is:
1st	33
2d	66
3d	100.".

1   (2) CONFORMING AMENDMENT.—Section

2   407(b)(3) of such Act (29 U.S.C. 1107(b)(3)) is

3   amended by adding at the end the following:

4   "(D) For diversification requirements for quali-

5   fying employer securities held in certain individual

6   account plans, see section 204(j).".

7   (c) EFFECTIVE DATES.—

8   (1) IN GENERAL.—Except as provided in para-

9   graphs (2) and (3), the amendments made by this

10   section shall apply to plan years beginning after De-

11   cember 31, 2006.

12   (2) SPECIAL RULE FOR COLLECTIVELY BAR-

13   GAINED AGREEMENTS.—In the case of a plan main-

14   tained pursuant to 1 or more collective bargaining

15   agreements between employee representatives and 1

16   or more employers ratified on or before the date of

17   the enactment of this Act, paragraph (1) shall be

18   applied to benefits pursuant to, and individuals cov-

19   ered by, any such agreement by substituting for

20   "December 31, 2006" the earlier of—

21   (A) the later of—

22   (i) December 31, 2007, or

1   (ii) the date on which the last of such

2   collective bargaining agreements termi-

3   nates (determined without regard to any

4   extension thereof after such date of enact-

5   ment), or

6   (B) December 31, 2008.

7   (3) SPECIAL RULE FOR CERTAIN EMPLOYER SE-

8 CURITIES HELD IN AN ESOP.—

9   (A) IN GENERAL.—In the case of employer

10   securities to which this paragraph applies, the

11   amendments made by this section shall apply to

12   plan years beginning after the earlier of—

13   (i) December 31, 2007, or

14   (ii) the first date on which the fair

15   market value of such securities exceeds the

16   guaranteed minimum value described in

17   subparagraph (B)(ii).

18   (B) APPLICABLE SECURITIES.—This para-

19   graph shall apply to employer securities which

20   are attributable to employer contributions other

21   than elective deferrals, and which, on Sep-

22   tember 17, 2003—

23   (i) consist of preferred stock, and

24   (ii) are within an employee stock own-

25   ership plan (as defined in section

1   4975(e)(7) of the Internal Revenue Code

2   of 1986), the terms of which provide that

3   the value of the securities cannot be less

4   than the guaranteed minimum value speci-

5   fied by the plan on such date.

6   (C) COORDINATION WITH TRANSITION

7   RULE.—In applying section 401(a)(35)(H) of

8   the Internal Revenue Code of 1986 and section

9   204(j)(7) of the Employee Retirement Income

10   Security Act of 1974 (as added by this section)

11   to employer securities to which this paragraph

12   applies, the applicable percentage shall be de-

13   termined without regard to this paragraph.

14 **SEC. 902. INCREASING PARTICIPATION THROUGH AUTO-**

15   **MATIC CONTRIBUTION ARRANGEMENTS.**

16   (a) IN GENERAL.—Section 401(k) of the Internal

17 Revenue Code of 1986 (relating to cash or deferred ar-

18 rangement) is amended by adding at the end the following

19 new paragraph:

20   "(13) ALTERNATIVE METHOD FOR AUTOMATIC

21   CONTRIBUTION ARRANGEMENTS TO MEET NON-

22   DISCRIMINATION REQUIREMENTS.—

23   "(A) IN GENERAL.—A qualified automatic

24   contribution arrangement shall be treated as

1   meeting the requirements of paragraph
2   (3)(A)(ii).

3   "(B) QUALIFIED AUTOMATIC CONTRIBU-
4   TION ARRANGEMENT.—For purposes of this
5   paragraph, the term 'qualified automatic con-
6   tribution arrangement' means any cash or de-
7   ferred arrangement which meets the require-
8   ments of subparagraphs (C) through (E).

9   "(C) AUTOMATIC DEFERRAL.—

10   "(i) IN GENERAL.—The requirements
11   of this subparagraph are met if, under the
12   arrangement, each employee eligible to
13   participate in the arrangement is treated
14   as having elected to have the employer
15   make elective contributions in an amount
16   equal to a qualified percentage of com-
17   pensation.

18   "(ii) ELECTION OUT.—The election
19   treated as having been made under clause
20   (i) shall cease to apply with respect to any
21   employee if such employee makes an af-
22   firmative election—

23   "(I) to not have such contribu-
24   tions made, or

1   "(II) to make elective contribu-

2   tions at a level specified in such af-

3   firmative election.

4   "(iii) QUALIFIED PERCENTAGE.—For

5 purposes of this subparagraph, the term

6 'qualified percentage' means, with respect

7 to any employee, any percentage deter-

8 mined under the arrangement if such per-

9 centage is applied uniformly, does not ex-

10 ceed 10 percent, and is at least—

11   "(I) 3 percent during the period

12   ending on the last day of the first

13   plan year which begins after the date

14   on which the first elective contribution

15   described in clause (i) is made with

16   respect to such employee,

17   "(II) 4 percent during the first

18   plan year following the plan year de-

19   scribed in subclause (I),

20   "(III) 5 percent during the sec-

21   ond plan year following the plan year

22   described in subclause (I), and

23   "(IV) 6 percent during any sub-

24   sequent plan year.

1   "(iv) AUTOMATIC DEFERRAL FOR

2   CURRENT EMPLOYEES NOT REQUIRED.—

3   Clause (i) may be applied without taking

4   into account any employee who—

5   "(I) was eligible to participate in

6   the arrangement (or a predecessor ar-

7   rangement) immediately before the

8   date on which such arrangement be-

9   comes a qualified automatic contribu-

10   tion arrangement (determined after

11   application of this clause), and

12   "(II) had an election in effect on

13   such date either to participate in the

14   arrangement or to not participate in

15   the arrangement.

16   "(D) MATCHING OR NONELECTIVE CON-

17   TRIBUTIONS.—

18   "(i) IN GENERAL.—The requirements

19   of this subparagraph are met if, under the

20   arrangement, the employer—

21   "(I) makes matching contribu-

22   tions on behalf of each employee who

23   is not a highly compensated employee

24   in an amount equal to the sum of 100

25   percent of the elective contributions of

1   the employee to the extent that such
2   contributions do not exceed 1 percent
3   of compensation plus 50 percent of so
4   much of such compensation as exceeds
5   1 percent but does not exceed 6 per-
6   cent of compensation, or

7   "(II) is required, without regard
8   to whether the employee makes an
9   elective contribution or employee con-
10   tribution, to make a contribution to a
11   defined contribution plan on behalf of
12   each employee who is not a highly
13   compensated employee and who is eli-
14   gible to participate in the arrange-
15   ment in an amount equal to at least
16   3 percent of the employee's compensa-
17   tion.

18   "(ii) APPLICATION OF RULES FOR
19   MATCHING CONTRIBUTIONS.—The rules of
20   clauses (ii) and (iii) of paragraph (12)(B)
21   shall apply for purposes of clause (i)(I).

22   "(iii) WITHDRAWAL AND VESTING RE-
23   STRICTIONS.—An arrangement shall not be
24   treated as meeting the requirements of
25   clause (i) unless, with respect to employer

1 contributions (including matching con-
2 tributions) taken into account in deter-
3 mining whether the requirements of clause
4 (i) are met—

5   "(I) any employee who has com-
6   pleted at least 2 years of service
7   (within the meaning of section
8   411(a)) has a nonforfeitable right to
9   100 percent of the employee's accrued
10   benefit derived from such employer
11   contributions, and

12   "(II) the requirements of sub-
13   paragraph (B) of paragraph (2) are
14   met with respect to all such employer
15   contributions.

16   "(iv) APPLICATION OF CERTAIN
17 OTHER RULES.—The rules of subpara-
18 graphs (E)(ii) and (F) of paragraph (12)
19 shall apply for purposes of subclauses (I)
20 and (II) of clause (i).

21 "(E) NOTICE REQUIREMENTS.—

22   "(i) IN GENERAL.—The requirements
23 of this subparagraph are met if, within a
24 reasonable period before each plan year,
25 each employee eligible to participate in the

Act. Sec. 902

1   arrangement for such year receives written

2   notice of the employee's rights and obliga-

3   tions under the arrangement which—

4   "(I) is sufficiently accurate and

5   comprehensive to apprise the employee

6   of such rights and obligations, and

7   "(II) is written in a manner cal-

8   culated to be understood by the aver-

9   age employee to whom the arrange-

10   ment applies.

11   "(ii) TIMING AND CONTENT REQUIRE-

12   MENTS.—A notice shall not be treated as

13   meeting the requirements of clause (i) with

14   respect to an employee unless—

15   "(I) the notice explains the em-

16   ployee's right under the arrangement

17   to elect not to have elective contribu-

18   tions made on the employee's behalf

19   (or to elect to have such contributions

20   made at a different percentage),

21   "(II) in the case of an arrange-

22   ment under which the employee may

23   elect among 2 or more investment op-

24   tions, the notice explains how con-

25   tributions made under the arrange-

1   ment will be invested in the absence of

2   any investment election by the em-

3   ployee, and

4   "(III) the employee has a reason-

5   able period of time after receipt of the

6   notice described in subclauses (I) and

7   (II) and before the first elective con-

8   tribution is made to make either such

9   election.".

10   (b) MATCHING CONTRIBUTIONS.—Section 401(m) of

11 such Code (relating to nondiscrimination test for matching

12 contributions and employee contributions) is amended by

13 redesignating paragraph (12) as paragraph (13) and by

14 inserting after paragraph (11) the following new para-

15 graph:

16   "(12) ALTERNATIVE METHOD FOR AUTOMATIC

17   CONTRIBUTION ARRANGEMENTS.—A defined con-

18   tribution plan shall be treated as meeting the re-

19   quirements of paragraph (2) with respect to match-

20   ing contributions if the plan—

21   "(A) is a qualified automatic contribution

22   arrangement (as defined in subsection (k)(13)),

23   and

24   "(B) meets the requirements of paragraph

25   (11)(B).".

1 (c) Exclusion From Definition of Top-Heavy

2 Plans.—

3   (1) Elective contribution rule.—Clause

4   (i) of section 416(g)(4)(H) of such Code is amended

5   by inserting "or 401(k)(13)" after "section

6   401(k)(12)".

7   (2) Matching contribution rule.—Clause

8   (ii) of section 416(g)(4)(H) of such Code is amended

9   by inserting "or 401(m)(12)" after "section

10   401(m)(11)".

11 (d) Treatment of Withdrawals of Contribu-

12 tions During First 90 Days.—

13   (1) In general.—Section 414 of the Internal

14   Revenue Code of 1986 is amended by adding at the

15   end the following new subsection:

16 "(w) Special Rules for Certain Withdrawals

17 From Eligible Automatic Contribution Arrange-

18 ments.—

19   "(1) In general.—If an eligible automatic

20   contribution arrangement allows an employee to

21   elect to make permissible withdrawals—

22   "(A) the amount of any such withdrawal

23   shall be includible in the gross income of the

24   employee for the taxable year of the employee

25   in which the distribution is made,

"(B) no tax shall be imposed under section 72(t) with respect to the distribution, and

"(C) the arrangement shall not be treated as violating any restriction on distributions under this title solely by reason of allowing the withdrawal.

In the case of any distribution to an employee by reason of an election under this paragraph, employer matching contributions shall be forfeited or subject to such other treatment as the Secretary may prescribe.

"(2) PERMISSIBLE WITHDRAWAL.—For purposes of this subsection—

"(A) IN GENERAL.—The term 'permissible withdrawal' means any withdrawal from an eligible automatic contribution arrangement meeting the requirements of this paragraph which—

"(i) is made pursuant to an election by an employee, and

"(ii) consists of elective contributions described in paragraph (3)(B) (and earnings attributable thereto).

"(B) TIME FOR MAKING ELECTION.—Subparagraph (A) shall not apply to an election by an employee unless the election is made no later

1   than the date which is 90 days after the date

2   of the first elective contribution with respect to

3   the employee under the arrangement.

4   "(C) AMOUNT OF DISTRIBUTION.—Sub-

5   paragraph (A) shall not apply to any election by

6   an employee unless the amount of any distribu-

7   tion by reason of the election is equal to the

8   amount of elective contributions made with re-

9   spect to the first payroll period to which the eli-

10   gible automatic contribution arrangement ap-

11   plies to the employee and any succeeding pay-

12   roll period beginning before the effective date of

13   the election (and earnings attributable thereto).

14   "(3) ELIGIBLE AUTOMATIC CONTRIBUTION AR-

15   RANGEMENT.—For purposes of this subsection, the

16   term 'eligible automatic contribution arrangement'

17   means an arrangement under an applicable employer

18   plan—

19   "(A) under which a participant may elect

20   to have the employer make payments as con-

21   tributions under the plan on behalf of the par-

22   ticipant, or to the participant directly in cash,

23   "(B) under which the participant is treated

24   as having elected to have the employer make

25   such contributions in an amount equal to a uni-

form percentage of compensation provided under the plan until the participant specifically elects not to have such contributions made (or specifically elects to have such contributions made at a different percentage),

"(C) under which, in the absence of an investment election by the participant, contributions described in subparagraph (B) are invested in accordance with regulations prescribed by the Secretary of Labor under section 404(c)(5) of the Employee Retirement Income Security Act of 1974, and

"(D) which meets the requirements of paragraph (4).

"(4) NOTICE REQUIREMENTS.—

"(A) IN GENERAL.—The administrator of a plan containing an arrangement described in paragraph (3) shall, within a reasonable period before each plan year, give to each employee to whom an arrangement described in paragraph (3) applies for such plan year notice of the employee's rights and obligations under the arrangement which—

              "(i) is sufficiently accurate and comprehensive to apprise the employee of such rights and obligations, and

              "(ii) is written in a manner calculated to be understood by the average employee to whom the arrangement applies.

      "(B) TIME AND FORM OF NOTICE.—A notice shall not be treated as meeting the requirements of subparagraph (A) with respect to an employee unless—

              "(i) the notice includes an explanation of the employee's right under the arrangement to elect not to have elective contributions made on the employee's behalf (or to elect to have such contributions made at a different percentage),

              "(ii) the employee has a reasonable period of time after receipt of the notice described in clause (i) and before the first elective contribution is made to make such election, and

              "(iii) the notice explains how contributions made under the arrangement will be invested in the absence of any investment election by the employee.

1   "(5) APPLICABLE EMPLOYER PLAN.—For pur-

2 poses of this subsection, the term 'applicable em-

3 ployer plan' means—

4   "(A) an employees' trust described in sec-

5   tion 401(a) which is exempt from tax under

6   section 501(a),

7   "(B) a plan under which amounts are con-

8   tributed by an individual's employer for an an-

9   nuity contract described in section 403(b), and

10   "(C) an eligible deferred compensation

11   plan described in section 457(b) which is main-

12   tained by an eligible employer described in sec-

13   tion 457(e)(1)(A).

14   "(6) SPECIAL RULE.—A withdrawal described

15 in paragraph (1) (subject to the limitation of para-

16 graph (2)(C)) shall not be taken into account for

17 purposes of section 401(k)(3).".

18   (2) VESTING CONFORMING AMENDMENTS.—

19   (A) Section 411(a)(3)(G) of such Code is

20   amended by inserting "an erroneous automatic

21   contribution under section 414(w)," after

22   "402(g)(2)(A),".

23   (B) The heading of section 411(a)(3)(G) of

24   such Code is amended by inserting "**OR ERRO-**

NEOUS AUTOMATIC CONTRIBUTION" before the period.

(C) Section 401(k)(8)(E) of such Code is amended by inserting "an erroneous automatic contribution under section 414(w)," after "402(g)(2)(A),".

(D) The heading of section 401(k)(8)(E) of such Code is amended by inserting "**OR ER-RONEOUS AUTOMATIC CONTRIBUTION**" before the period.

(E) Section 203(a)(3)(F) of the Employee Retirement Income Security Act of 1974 (29 U.S.C. 1053(a)(3)(F)) is amended by inserting "an erroneous automatic contribution under section 414(w) of such Code," after "402(g)(2)(A) of such Code,".

(e) EXCESS CONTRIBUTIONS.—

(1) EXPANSION OF CORRECTIVE DISTRIBUTION PERIOD FOR AUTOMATIC CONTRIBUTION ARRANGE-MENTS.—Subsection (f) of section 4979 of the Internal Revenue Code of 1986 is amended—

(A) by inserting "(6 months in the case of an excess contribution or excess aggregate contribution to an eligible automatic contribution arrangement (as defined in section

414(w)(3)))" after "2½ months" in paragraph (1), and

      (B) by striking "2½ MONTHS OF" in the heading and inserting "SPECIFIED PERIOD AFTER".

(2) YEAR OF INCLUSION.—Paragraph (2) of section 4979(f) of such Code is amended to read as follows:

"(2) YEAR OF INCLUSION.—Any amount distributed as provided in paragraph (1) shall be treated as earned and received by the recipient in the recipient's taxable year in which such distributions were made.".

(3) SIMPLIFICATION OF ALLOCABLE EARNINGS.—

      (A) SECTION 4979.—Paragraph (1) of section 4979(f) of such Code is amended by adding "through the end of the plan year for which the contribution was made" after "thereto".

      (B) SECTION 401(k) AND 401(M).—

            (i) Clause (i) of section 401(k)(8)(A) of such Code is amended by adding "through the end of such year" after "such contributions".

1   (ii) Subparagraph (A) of section

2   401(m)(6) of such Code is amended by

3   adding "through the end of such year"

4   after "to such contributions".

5   (f) PREEMPTION OF CONFLICTING STATE REGULA-

6 TION.—

7   (1) IN GENERAL.—Section 514 of the Employee

8 Retirement Income Security Act of 1974 (29 U.S.C.

9 1144) is amended by adding at the end the following

10 new subsection:

11   "(e)(1) Notwithstanding any other provision of this

12 section, this title shall supersede any law of a State which

13 would directly or indirectly prohibit or restrict the inclu-

14 sion in any plan of an automatic contribution arrange-

15 ment. The Secretary may prescribe regulations which

16 would establish minimum standards that such an arrange-

17 ment would be required to satisfy in order for this sub-

18 section to apply in the case of such arrangement.

19   "(2) For purposes of this subsection, the term 'auto-

20 matic contribution arrangement' means an arrange-

21 ment——

22   "(A) under which a participant may elect to

23   have the plan sponsor make payments as contribu-

24   tions under the plan on behalf of the participant, or

25   to the participant directly in cash,

1   "(B) under which a participant is treated as

2   having elected to have the plan sponsor make such

3   contributions in an amount equal to a uniform per-

4   centage of compensation provided under the plan

5   until the participant specifically elects not to have

6   such contributions made (or specifically elects to

7   have such contributions made at a different percent-

8   age), and

9   "(C) under which such contributions are in-

10   vested in accordance with regulations prescribed by

11   the Secretary under section 404(c)(5).

12   "(3)(A) The plan administrator of an automatic con-

13 tribution arrangement shall, within a reasonable period

14 before such plan year, provide to each participant to whom

15 the arrangement applies for such plan year notice of the

16 participant's rights and obligations under the arrange-

17 ment which—

18   "(i) is sufficiently accurate and comprehensive

19   to apprise the participant of such rights and obliga-

20   tions, and

21   "(ii) is written in a manner calculated to be un-

22   derstood by the average participant to whom the ar-

23   rangement applies.

1   "(B) A notice shall not be treated as meeting the re-
2 quirements of subparagraph (A) with respect to a partici-
3 pant unless—

4   "(i) the notice includes an explanation of the
5   participant's right under the arrangement not to
6   have elective contributions made on the participant's
7   behalf (or to elect to have such contributions made
8   at a different percentage),

9   "(ii) the participant has a reasonable period of
10   time, after receipt of the notice described in clause
11   (i) and before the first elective contribution is made,
12   to make such election, and

13   "(iii) the notice explains how contributions
14   made under the arrangement will be invested in the
15   absence of any investment election by the partici-
16   pant.".

17   (2) ENFORCEMENT.—Section 502(c)(4) of such
18   Act (29 U.S.C. 1132(c)(4)) is amended by striking
19   "or section 302(b)(7)(F)(vi)" inserting ", section
20   302(b)(7)(F)(vi), or section 514(e)(3)".

21   (g) EFFECTIVE DATE.—The amendments made by
22 this section shall apply to plan years beginning after De-
23 cember 31, 2007, except that the amendments made by
24 subsection (f) shall take effect on the date of the enact-
25 ment of this Act.

SEC. 903. TREATMENT OF ELIGIBLE COMBINED DEFINED BENEFIT PLANS AND QUALIFIED CASH OR DEFERRED ARRANGEMENTS.

(a) AMENDMENTS OF INTERNAL REVENUE CODE.— Section 414 of the Internal Revenue Code of 1986, as amended by this Act, is amended by adding at the end the following new subsection:

"(x) SPECIAL RULES FOR ELIGIBLE COMBINED DEFINED BENEFIT PLANS AND QUALIFIED CASH OR DEFERRED ARRANGEMENTS.—

"(1) GENERAL RULE.—Except as provided in this subsection, the requirements of this title shall be applied to any defined benefit plan or applicable defined contribution plan which are part of an eligible combined plan in the same manner as if each such plan were not a part of the eligible combined plan.

"(2) ELIGIBLE COMBINED PLAN.—For purposes of this subsection—

"(A) IN GENERAL.—The term 'eligible combined plan' means a plan—

"(i) which is maintained by an employer which, at the time the plan is established, is a small employer, "(ii) which consists of a defined benefit plan and an applicable defined contribution plan,

"(iii) the assets of which are held in a single trust forming part of the plan and are clearly identified and allocated to the defined benefit plan and the applicable defined contribution plan to the extent necessary for the separate application of this title under paragraph (1), and

"(iv) with respect to which the benefit, contribution, vesting, and nondiscrimination requirements of subparagraphs (B), (C), (D), (E), and (F) are met.

For purposes of this subparagraph, the term 'small employer' has the meaning given such term by section 4980D(d)(2), except that such section shall be applied by substituting '500' for '50' each place it appears.

"(B) BENEFIT REQUIREMENTS.—

"(i) IN GENERAL.—The benefit requirements of this subparagraph are met with respect to the defined benefit plan forming part of the eligible combined plan

1   if the accrued benefit of each participant

2   derived from employer contributions, when

3   expressed as an annual retirement benefit,

4   is not less than the applicable percentage

5   of the participant's final average pay. For

6   purposes of this clause, final average pay

7   shall be determined using the period of

8   consecutive years (not exceeding 5) during

9   which the participant had the greatest ag-

10   gregate compensation from the employer.

11   "(ii) APPLICABLE PERCENTAGE.—For

12   purposes of clause (i), the applicable per-

13   centage is the lesser of—

14   "(I) 1 percent multiplied by the

15   number of years of service with the

16   employer, or

17   "(II) 20 percent.

18   "(iii) SPECIAL RULE FOR APPLICABLE

19   DEFINED BENEFIT PLANS.—If the defined

20   benefit plan under clause (i) is an applica-

21   ble defined benefit plan as defined in sec-

22   tion 411(a)(13)(B) which meets the inter-

23   est credit requirements of section

24   411(b)(5)(B)(i), the plan shall be treated

25   as meeting the requirements of clause (i)

1   with respect to any plan year if each par-

2   ticipant receives a pay credit for the year

3   which is not less than the percentage of

4   compensation determined in accordance

5   with the following table:

"If the participant's age as of the beginning of the year is—	The percentage is—
30 or less	2
Over 30 but less than 40	4
40 or over but less than 50	6
50 or over	8.

6   "(iv) YEARS OF SERVICE.—For pur-

7   poses of this subparagraph, years of serv-

8   ice shall be determined under the rules of

9   paragraphs (4), (5), and (6) of section

10   411(a), except that the plan may not dis-

11   regard any year of service because of a

12   participant making, or failing to make, any

13   elective deferral with respect to the quali-

14   fied cash or deferred arrangement to which

15   subparagraph (C) applies.

16   "(C) CONTRIBUTION REQUIREMENTS.—

17   "(i) IN GENERAL.—The contribution

18   requirements of this subparagraph with re-

19   spect to any applicable defined contribu-

20   tion plan forming part of an eligible com-

21   bined plan are met if—

22   "(I) the qualified cash or de-

23   ferred arrangement included in such

plan constitutes an automatic contribution arrangement, and

"(II) the employer is required to
make matching contributions on behalf of each employee eligible to participate in the arrangement in an
amount equal to 50 percent of the
elective contributions of the employee
to the extent such elective contributions do not exceed 4 percent of compensation.

Rules similar to the rules of clauses (ii)
and (iii) of section 401(k)(12)(B) shall
apply for purposes of this clause.

"(ii) NONELECTIVE CONTRIBU-
TIONS.—An applicable defined contribution
plan shall not be treated as failing to meet
the requirements of clause (i) because the
employer makes nonelective contributions
under the plan but such contributions shall
not be taken into account in determining
whether the requirements of clause (i)(II)
are met.

721

"(D) VESTING REQUIREMENTS.—The vesting requirements of this subparagraph are met if—

"(i) in the case of a defined benefit plan forming part of an eligible combined plan an employee who has completed at least 3 years of service has a nonforfeitable right to 100 percent of the employee's accrued benefit under the plan derived from employer contributions, and

"(ii) in the case of an applicable defined contribution plan forming part of eligible combined plan—

"(I) an employee has a nonforfeitable right to any matching contribution made under the qualified cash or deferred arrangement included in such plan by an employer with respect to any elective contribution, including matching contributions in excess of the contributions required under subparagraph (C)(i)(II), and

"(II) an employee who has completed at least 3 years of service has a nonforfeitable right to 100 percent

1   of the employee's accrued benefit de-

2   rived under the arrangement from

3   nonelective contributions of the em-

4   ployer.

5   For purposes of this subparagraph, the

6   rules of section 411 shall apply to the ex-

7   tent not inconsistent with this subpara-

8   graph.

9   "(E) UNIFORM PROVISION OF CONTRIBU-

10 TIONS AND BENEFITS.—In the case of a defined

11 benefit plan or applicable defined contribution

12 plan forming part of an eligible combined plan,

13 the requirements of this subparagraph are met

14 if all contributions and benefits under each

15 such plan, and all rights and features under

16 each such plan, must be provided uniformly to

17 all participants.

18   "(F) REQUIREMENTS MUST BE MET WITH-

19 OUT TAKING INTO ACCOUNT SOCIAL SECURITY

20 AND SIMILAR CONTRIBUTIONS AND BENEFITS

21 OR OTHER PLANS.—

22   "(i) IN GENERAL.—The requirements

23   of this subparagraph are met if the re-

24   quirements of clauses (ii) and (iii) are met.

"(ii) SOCIAL SECURITY AND SIMILAR CONTRIBUTIONS.—The requirements of this clause are met if—

"(I) the requirements of subparagraphs (B) and (C) are met without regard to section 401(l), and

"(II) the requirements of sections 401(a)(4) and 410(b) are met with respect to both the applicable defined contribution plan and defined benefit plan forming part of an eligible combined plan without regard to section 401(l).

"(iii) OTHER PLANS AND ARRANGEMENTS.—The requirements of this clause are met if the applicable defined contribution plan and defined benefit plan forming part of an eligible combined plan meet the requirements of sections 401(a)(4) and 410(b) without being combined with any other plan.

"(3) NONDISCRIMINATION REQUIREMENTS FOR QUALIFIED CASH OR DEFERRED ARRANGEMENT.—

"(A) IN GENERAL.—A qualified cash or deferred arrangement which is included in an applicable defined contribution plan forming part of an eligible combined plan shall be treated as meeting the requirements of section 401(k)(3)(A)(ii) if the requirements of paragraph (2)(C) are met with respect to such arrangement.

"(B) MATCHING CONTRIBUTIONS.—In applying section 401(m)(11) to any matching contribution with respect to a contribution to which paragraph (2)(C) applies, the contribution requirement of paragraph (2)(C) and the notice requirements of paragraph (5)(B) shall be substituted for the requirements otherwise applicable under clauses (i) and (ii) of section 401(m)(11)(A).

"(4) SATISFACTION OF TOP-HEAVY RULES.—A defined benefit plan and applicable defined contribution plan forming part of an eligible combined plan for any plan year shall be treated as meeting the requirements of section 416 for the plan year.

"(5) AUTOMATIC CONTRIBUTION ARRANGEMENT.—For purposes of this subsection—

"(A) IN GENERAL.—A qualified cash or deferred arrangement shall be treated as an

1   automatic contribution arrangement if the ar-
2   rangement—
3   "(i) provides that each employee eligi-
4   ble to participate in the arrangement is
5   treated as having elected to have the em-
6   ployer make elective contributions in an
7   amount equal to 4 percent of the employ-
8   ee's compensation unless the employee spe-
9   cifically elects not to have such contribu-
10   tions made or to have such contributions
11   made at a different rate, and
12   "(ii) meets the notice requirements
13   under subparagraph (B).
14   "(B) NOTICE REQUIREMENTS.—
15   "(i) IN GENERAL.—The requirements
16   of this subparagraph are met if the re-
17   quirements of clauses (ii) and (iii) are met.
18   "(ii) REASONABLE PERIOD TO MAKE
19   ELECTION.—The requirements of this
20   clause are met if each employee to whom
21   subparagraph (A)(i) applies—
22   "(I) receives a notice explaining
23   the employee's right under the ar-
24   rangement to elect not to have elective
25   contributions made on the employee's

1   behalf or to have the contributions

2   made at a different rate, and

3   "(II) has a reasonable period of

4   time after receipt of such notice and

5   before the first elective contribution is

6   made to make such election.

7   "(iii) ANNUAL NOTICE OF RIGHTS

8   AND OBLIGATIONS.—The requirements of

9   this clause are met if each employee eligi-

10   ble to participate in the arrangement is,

11   within a reasonable period before any year,

12   given notice of the employee's rights and

13   obligations under the arrangement.

14   The requirements of clauses (i) and (ii) of sec-

15   tion 401(k)(12)(D) shall be met with respect to

16   the notices described in clauses (ii) and (iii) of

17   this subparagraph.

18   "(6) COORDINATION WITH OTHER REQUIRE-

19 MENTS.—

20   "(A) TREATMENT OF SEPARATE PLANS.—

21   Section 414(k) shall not apply to an eligible

22   combined plan.

23   "(B) REPORTING.—An eligible combined

24   plan shall be treated as a single plan for pur-

25   poses of sections 6058 and 6059.

1   "(7) APPLICABLE DEFINED CONTRIBUTION

2   PLAN.—For purposes of this subsection—

3   "(A) IN GENERAL.—The term 'applicable

4   defined contribution plan' means a defined con-

5   tribution plan which includes a qualified cash or

6   deferred arrangement.

7   "(B) QUALIFIED CASH OR DEFERRED AR-

8   RANGEMENT.—The term 'qualified cash or de-

9   ferred arrangement' has the meaning given

10   such term by section 401(k)(2).".

11   (b) AMENDMENTS TO THE EMPLOYEE RETIREMENT

12 INCOME SECURITY ACT OF 1974.—

13   (1) IN GENERAL.—Section 210 of the Employee

14   Retirement Income Security Act of 1974 is amended

15   by adding at the end the following new subsection:

16   "(e) SPECIAL RULES FOR ELIGIBLE COMBINED DE-

17 FINED BENEFIT PLANS AND QUALIFIED CASH OR DE-

18 FERRED ARRANGEMENTS.—

19   "(1) GENERAL RULE.—Except as provided in

20   this subsection, this Act shall be applied to any de-

21   fined benefit plan or applicable individual account

22   plan which are part of an eligible combined plan in

23   the same manner as if each such plan were not a

24   part of the eligible combined plan.

"(2) ELIGIBLE COMBINED PLAN.—For purposes of this subsection—

"(A) IN GENERAL.—The term 'eligible
combined plan' means a plan—

"(i) which is maintained by an employer which, at the time the plan is established, is a small employer,

"(ii) which consists of a defined benefit plan and an applicable individual account plan each of which qualifies under
section 401(a) of the Internal Revenue
Code of 1986,

"(iii) the assets of which are held in
a single trust forming part of the plan and
are clearly identified and allocated to the
defined benefit plan and the applicable individual account plan to the extent necessary for the separate application of this
Act under paragraph (1), and

"(iv) with respect to which the benefit, contribution, vesting, and nondiscrimination requirements of subparagraphs (B), (C), (D), (E), and (F) are
met.

For purposes of this subparagraph, the term 'small employer' has the meaning given such term by section 4980D(d)(2) of the Internal Revenue Code of 1986, except that such section shall be applied by substituting '500' for '50' each place it appears.

"(B) BENEFIT REQUIREMENTS.—

"(i) IN GENERAL.—The benefit requirements of this subparagraph are met with respect to the defined benefit plan forming part of the eligible combined plan if the accrued benefit of each participant derived from employer contributions, when expressed as an annual retirement benefit, is not less than the applicable percentage of the participant's final average pay. For purposes of this clause, final average pay shall be determined using the period of consecutive years (not exceeding 5) during which the participant had the greatest aggregate compensation from the employer.

"(ii) APPLICABLE PERCENTAGE.—For purposes of clause (i), the applicable percentage is the lesser of—

1   "(I) 1 percent multiplied by the

2   number of years of service with the

3   employer, or

4   "(II) 20 percent.

5   "(iii) SPECIAL RULE FOR APPLICABLE

6   DEFINED BENEFIT PLANS.—If the defined

7   benefit plan under clause (i) is an applica-

8   ble defined benefit plan as defined in sec-

9   tion 203(f)(3)(B) which meets the interest

10   credit requirements of section

11   204(b)(5)(B)(i), the plan shall be treated

12   as meeting the requirements of clause (i)

13   with respect to any plan year if each par-

14   ticipant receives pay credit for the year

15   which is not less than the percentage of

16   compensation determined in accordance

17   with the following table:

"If the participant's age as of the beginning of the year is—	The percentage is—
30 or less	2
Over 30 but less than 40	4
40 or over but less than 50	6
50 or over	8.

18   "(iv) YEARS OF SERVICE.—For pur-

19   poses of this subparagraph, years of serv-

20   ice shall be determined under the rules of

21   paragraphs (1), (2), and (3) of section

22   203(b), except that the plan may not dis-

1   regard any year of service because of a

2   participant making, or failing to make, any

3   elective deferral with respect to the quali-

4   fied cash or deferred arrangement to which

5   subparagraph (C) applies.

6   "(C) CONTRIBUTION REQUIREMENTS.—

7   "(i) IN GENERAL.—The contribution

8   requirements of this subparagraph with re-

9   spect to any applicable individual account

10   plan forming part of an eligible combined

11   plan are met if—

12   "(I) the qualified cash or de-

13   ferred arrangement included in such

14   plan constitutes an automatic con-

15   tribution arrangement, and

16   "(II) the employer is required to

17   make matching contributions on be-

18   half of each employee eligible to par-

19   ticipate in the arrangement in an

20   amount equal to 50 percent of the

21   elective contributions of the employee

22   to the extent such elective contribu-

23   tions do not exceed 4 percent of com-

24   pensation.

1   Rules similar to the rules of clauses (ii)

2   and (iii) of section 401(k)(12)(B) of the

3   Internal Revenue Code of 1986 shall apply

4   for purposes of this clause.

5   "(ii) NONELECTIVE CONTRIBU-

6   TIONS.—An applicable individual account

7   plan shall not be treated as failing to meet

8   the requirements of clause (i) because the

9   employer makes nonelective contributions

10   under the plan but such contributions shall

11   not be taken into account in determining

12   whether the requirements of clause (i)(II)

13   are met.

14   "(D) VESTING REQUIREMENTS.—The vest-

15   ing requirements of this subparagraph are met

16   if—

17   "(i) in the case of a defined benefit

18   plan forming part of an eligible combined

19   plan an employee who has completed at

20   least 3 years of service has a nonforfeitable

21   right to 100 percent of the employee's ac-

22   crued benefit under the plan derived from

23   employer contributions, and

"(ii) in the case of an applicable individual account plan forming part of eligible combined plan—

"(I) an employee has a nonforfeitable right to any matching contribution made under the qualified cash or deferred arrangement included in such plan by an employer with respect to any elective contribution, including matching contributions in excess of the contributions required under subparagraph (C)(i)(II), and

"(II) an employee who has completed at least 3 years of service has a nonforfeitable right to 100 percent of the employee's accrued benefit derived under the arrangement from nonelective contributions of the employer.

For purposes of this subparagraph, the rules of section 203 shall apply to the extent not inconsistent with this subparagraph.

"(E) UNIFORM PROVISION OF CONTRIBUTIONS AND BENEFITS.—In the case of a defined

1   benefit plan or applicable individual account

2   plan forming part of an eligible combined plan,

3   the requirements of this subparagraph are met

4   if all contributions and benefits under each

5   such plan, and all rights and features under

6   each such plan, must be provided uniformly to

7   all participants.

8   "(F) REQUIREMENTS MUST BE MET WITH-

9   OUT TAKING INTO ACCOUNT SOCIAL SECURITY

10   AND SIMILAR CONTRIBUTIONS AND BENEFITS

11   OR OTHER PLANS.—

12   "(i) IN GENERAL.—The requirements

13   of this subparagraph are met if the re-

14   quirements of clauses (ii) and (iii) are met.

15   "(ii) SOCIAL SECURITY AND SIMILAR

16   CONTRIBUTIONS.—The   requirements   of

17   this clause are met if—

18   "(I) the requirements of subpara-

19   graphs (B) and (C) are met without

20   regard to section 401(l) of the Inter-

21   nal Revenue Code of 1986, and

22   "(II) the requirements of sections

23   401(a)(4) and 410(b) of the Internal

24   Revenue Code of 1986 are met with

25   respect to both the applicable defined

1   contribution plan and defined benefit

2   plan forming part of an eligible com-

3   bined plan without regard to section

4   401(l) of the Internal Revenue Code

5   of 1986.

6   "(iii) OTHER PLANS AND ARRANGE-

7   MENTS.—The requirements of this clause

8   are met if the applicable defined contribu-

9   tion plan and defined benefit plan forming

10   part of an eligible combined plan meet the

11   requirements of sections 401(a)(4) and

12   410(b) of the Internal Revenue Code of

13   1986 without being combined with any

14   other plan.

15 "(3) NONDISCRIMINATION REQUIREMENTS FOR

16 QUALIFIED CASH OR DEFERRED ARRANGEMENT.—

17   "(A) IN GENERAL.—A qualified cash or

18   deferred arrangement which is included in an

19   applicable individual account plan forming part

20   of an eligible combined plan shall be treated as

21   meeting the requirements of section

22   401(k)(3)(A)(ii) of the Internal Revenue Code

23   of 1986 if the requirements of paragraph (2)

24   are met with respect to such arrangement.

1   "(B) MATCHING CONTRIBUTIONS.—In ap-

2   plying section 401(m)(11) of such Code to any

3   matching contribution with respect to a con-

4   tribution to which paragraph (2)(C) applies, the

5   contribution requirement of paragraph (2)(C)

6   and the notice requirements of paragraph

7   (5)(B) shall be substituted for the requirements

8   otherwise applicable under clauses (i) and (ii) of

9   section 401(m)(11)(A) of such Code.

10   "(4) AUTOMATIC CONTRIBUTION ARRANGE-

11 MENT.—For purposes of this subsection—

12   "(A) IN GENERAL.—A qualified cash or

13   deferred arrangement shall be treated as an

14   automatic contribution arrangement if the ar-

15   rangement—

16   "(i) provides that each employee eligi-

17   ble to participate in the arrangement is

18   treated as having elected to have the em-

19   ployer make elective contributions in an

20   amount equal to 4 percent of the employ-

21   ee's compensation unless the employee spe-

22   cifically elects not to have such contribu-

23   tions made or to have such contributions

24   made at a different rate, and

"(ii) meets the notice requirements under subparagraph (B).

"(B) NOTICE REQUIREMENTS.—

"(i) IN GENERAL.—The requirements of this subparagraph are met if the requirements of clauses (ii) and (iii) are met.

"(ii) REASONABLE PERIOD TO MAKE ELECTION.—The requirements of this clause are met if each employee to whom subparagraph (A)(i) applies—

"(I) receives a notice explaining the employee's right under the arrangement to elect not to have elective contributions made on the employee's behalf or to have the contributions made at a different rate, and

"(II) has a reasonable period of time after receipt of such notice and before the first elective contribution is made to make such election.

"(iii) ANNUAL NOTICE OF RIGHTS AND OBLIGATIONS.—The requirements of this clause are met if each employee eligible to participate in the arrangement is, within a reasonable period before any year,

738

given notice of the employee's rights and
obligations under the arrangement.

The requirements of this subparagraph shall
not be treated as met unless the requirements
of clauses (i) and (ii) of section 401(k)(12)(D)
of the Internal Revenue Code of 1986 are met
with respect to the notices described in clauses
(ii) and (iii) of this subparagraph.

"(5) COORDINATION WITH OTHER REQUIRE-
MENTS.—

"(A) TREATMENT OF SEPARATE PLANS.—
The except clause in section 3(35) shall not
apply to an eligible combined plan.

"(B) REPORTING.—An eligible combined
plan shall be treated as a single plan for purposes of section 103.

"(6) APPLICABLE INDIVIDUAL ACCOUNT
PLAN.—For purposes of this subsection—

"(A) IN GENERAL.—The term 'applicable
individual account plan' means an individual account plan which includes a qualified cash or
deferred arrangement.

"(B) QUALIFIED CASH OR DEFERRED AR-
RANGEMENT.—The term 'qualified cash or deferred arrangement' has the meaning given

1 such term by section 401(k)(2) of the Internal

2 Revenue Code of 1986.".

3   (2) CONFORMING CHANGES.—

4   (A) The heading for section 210 of such

5   Act is amended to read as follows:

6 **"SEC. 210. MULTIPLE EMPLOYER PLANS AND OTHER SPE-**

7   **CIAL RULES.".**

8   (B) The table of contents in section 1 of

9   such Act is amended by striking the item relat-

10   ing to section 210 and inserting the following

11   new item:

"Sec. 210. Multiple employer plans and other special rules.".

12   (c) EFFECTIVE DATE.—The amendments made by

13 this section shall apply to plan years beginning after De-

14 cember 31, 2009.

15 **SEC. 904. FASTER VESTING OF EMPLOYER NONELECTIVE**

16   **CONTRIBUTIONS.**

17   (a) AMENDMENTS TO THE INTERNAL REVENUE

18 CODE OF 1986.—

19   (1) IN GENERAL.—Paragraph (2) of section

20   411(a) of the Internal Revenue Code of 1986 (relat-

21   ing to employer contributions) is amended to read as

22   follows:

23   "(2) EMPLOYER CONTRIBUTIONS.—

24   "(A) DEFINED BENEFIT PLANS.—

1   "(i) IN GENERAL.—In the case of a

2   defined benefit plan, a plan satisfies the

3   requirements of this paragraph if it satis-

4   fies the requirements of clause (ii) or (iii).

5   "(ii) 5-YEAR VESTING.—A plan satis-

6   fies the requirements of this clause if an

7   employee who has completed at least 5

8   years of service has a nonforfeitable right

9   to 100 percent of the employee's accrued

10   benefit derived from employer contribu-

11   tions.

12   "(iii) 3 TO 7 YEAR VESTING.—A plan

13   satisfies the requirements of this clause if

14   an employee has a nonforfeitable right to

15   a percentage of the employee's accrued

16   benefit derived from employer contribu-

17   tions determined under the following table:

" Years of service:	The nonforfeitable percentage is:
3	20
4	40
5	60
6	80
7 or more	100.

18   "(B) DEFINED CONTRIBUTION PLANS.—

19   "(i) IN GENERAL.—In the case of a

20   defined contribution plan, a plan satisfies

21   the requirements of this paragraph if it

1   satisfies the requirements of clause (ii) or

2   (iii).

3   "(ii) 3-YEAR VESTING.—A plan satis-

4   fies the requirements of this clause if an

5   employee who has completed at least 3

6   years of service has a nonforfeitable right

7   to 100 percent of the employee's accrued

8   benefit derived from employer contribu-

9   tions.

10   "(iii) 2 TO 6 YEAR VESTING.—A plan

11   satisfies the requirements of this clause if

12   an employee has a nonforfeitable right to

13   a percentage of the employee's accrued

14   benefit derived from employer contribu-

15   tions determined under the following table:

" Years of service:	The nonforfeitable percentage is:
2	20
3	40
4	60
5	80
6 or more	100.".

16   (2) CONFORMING AMENDMENT.—Section

17   411(a) of such Code (relating to general rule for

18   minimum vesting standards) is amended by striking

19   paragraph (12).

20   (b) AMENDMENTS TO THE EMPLOYEE RETIREMENT

21 INCOME SECURITY ACT OF 1974.—

1   (1) IN GENERAL.—Paragraph (2) of section

2   203(a) of the Employee Retirement Income Security

3   Act of 1974 (29 U.S.C. 1053(a)(2)) is amended to

4   read as follows:

5   "(2)(A)(i) In the case of a defined benefit plan,

6   a plan satisfies the requirements of this paragraph

7   if it satisfies the requirements of clause (ii) or (iii).

8   "(ii) A plan satisfies the requirements of this

9   clause if an employee who has completed at least 5

10   years of service has a nonforfeitable right to 100

11   percent of the employee's accrued benefit derived

12   from employer contributions.

13   "(iii) A plan satisfies the requirements of this

14   clause if an employee has a nonforfeitable right to

15   a percentage of the employee's accrued benefit de-

16   rived from employer contributions determined under

17   the following table:

" Years of service:	The nonforfeitable percentage is:
3	20
4	40
5	60
6	80
7 or more	100.

18   "(B)(i) In the case of an individual account

19   plan, a plan satisfies the requirements of this para-

20   graph if it satisfies the requirements of clause (ii) or

21   (iii).

1   "(ii) A plan satisfies the requirements of this

2   clause if an employee who has completed at least 3

3   years of service has a nonforfeitable right to 100

4   percent of the employee's accrued benefit derived

5   from employer contributions.

6   "(iii) A plan satisfies the requirements of this

7   clause if an employee has a nonforfeitable right to

8   a percentage of the employee's accrued benefit de-

9   rived from employer contributions determined under

10   the following table:

" Years of service:	The nonforfeitable percentage is:
2	20
3	40
4	60
5	80
6 or more	100.".

11   (2) CONFORMING AMENDMENT.—Section

12   203(a) of such Act is amended by striking para-

13   graph (4).

14 (c) EFFECTIVE DATES.—

15   (1) IN GENERAL.—Except as provided in para-

16   graphs (2) and (4), the amendments made by this

17   section shall apply to contributions for plan years

18   beginning after December 31, 2006.

19   (2) COLLECTIVE BARGAINING AGREEMENTS.—

20   In the case of a plan maintained pursuant to one or

21   more collective bargaining agreements between em-

22   ployee representatives and one or more employers

1   ratified before the date of the enactment of this Act,

2   the amendments made by this section shall not apply

3   to contributions on behalf of employees covered by

4   any such agreement for plan years beginning before

5   the earlier of—

6   (A) the later of—

7   (i) the date on which the last of such

8   collective bargaining agreements termi-

9   nates (determined without regard to any

10   extension thereof on or after such date of

11   the enactment); or

12   (ii) January 1, 2007; or

13   (B) January 1, 2009.

14   (3) SERVICE REQUIRED.—With respect to any

15   plan, the amendments made by this section shall not

16   apply to any employee before the date that such em-

17   ployee has 1 hour of service under such plan in any

18   plan year to which the amendments made by this

19   section apply.

20   (4) SPECIAL RULE FOR STOCK OWNERSHIP

21   PLANS.—Notwithstanding paragraph (1) or (2), in

22   the case of an employee stock ownership plan (as de-

23   fined in section 4975(e)(7) of the Internal Revenue

24   Code of 1986) which had outstanding on September

25   26, 2005, a loan incurred for the purpose of acquir-

1   ing qualifying employer securities (as defined in sec-

2   tion 4975(e)(8) of such Code), the amendments

3   made by this section shall not apply to any plan year

4   beginning before the earlier of—

5   (A) the date on which the loan is fully re-

6   paid, or

7   (B) the date on which the loan was, as of

8   September 26, 2005, scheduled to be fully re-

9   paid.

10   **SEC. 905. DISTRIBUTIONS DURING WORKING RETIREMENT.**

11   (a) AMENDMENT TO THE EMPLOYEE RETIREMENT

12   INCOME SECURITY ACT OF 1974.—Subparagraph (A) of

13   section 3(2) of the Employee Retirement Income Security

14   Act of 1974 (29 U.S.C. 1002(2)) is amended by adding

15   at the end the following new sentence: "A distribution

16   from a plan, fund, or program shall not be treated as

17   made in a form other than retirement income or as a dis-

18   tribution prior to termination of covered employment sole-

19   ly because such distribution is made to an employee who

20   has attained age 62 and who is not separated from em-

21   ployment at the time of such distribution.".

22   (b) AMENDMENT TO THE INTERNAL REVENUE CODE

23   OF 1986.—Subsection (a) of section 401 of the Internal

24   Revenue Code of 1986 (as amended by this Act) is amend-

746

1 ed by inserting after paragraph (35) the following new
2 paragraph:

3   "(36) DISTRIBUTIONS DURING WORKING RE-
4   TIREMENT.—A trust forming part of a pension plan
5   shall not be treated as failing to constitute a quali-
6   fied trust under this section solely because the plan
7   provides that a distribution may be made from such
8   trust to an employee who has attained age 62 and
9   who is not separated from employment at the time
10   of such distribution.".

11   (c) EFFECTIVE DATE.—The amendments made by
12 this section shall apply to distributions in plan years be-
13 ginning after December 31, 2006.

14 **SEC. 906. TREATMENT OF CERTAIN PENSION PLANS OF IN-**
15   **DIAN TRIBAL GOVERNMENTS.**

16   (a) DEFINITION OF GOVERNMENT PLAN TO INCLUDE
17 CERTAIN PENSION PLANS OF INDIAN TRIBAL GOVERN-
18 MENTS.—

19   (1) AMENDMENT TO INTERNAL REVENUE CODE
20   OF 1986.—Section 414(d) of the Internal Revenue
21   Code of 1986 (defining governmental plan) is
22   amended by adding at the end the following: "The
23   term 'governmental plan' includes a plan which is
24   established and maintained by an Indian tribal gov-
25   ernment (as defined in section 7701(a)(40)), a sub-

division of an Indian tribal government (determined
in accordance with section 7871(d)), or an agency or
instrumentality of either, and all of the participants
of which are employees of such entity substantially
all of whose services as such an employee are in the
performance of essential governmental functions but
not in the performance of commercial activities
(whether or not an essential government function).".

(2) AMENDMENT TO EMPLOYEE RETIREMENT
INCOME SECURITY ACT OF 1974.—

(A) Section 3(32) of the Employee Retirement Income Security Act of 1974 (29 U.S.C.
1002(32)) is amended by adding at the end the
following: "The term 'governmental plan' includes a plan which is established and maintained by an Indian tribal government (as defined in section 7701(a)(40) of the Internal
Revenue Code of 1986), a subdivision of an Indian tribal government (determined in accordance with section 7871(d) of such Code), or an
agency or instrumentality of either, and all of
the participants of which are employees of such
entity substantially all of whose services as such
an employee are in the performance of essential
governmental functions but not in the perform-

1 ance of commercial activities (whether or not an

2 essential government function)".

3 (B) Section 4021(b)(2) of such Act is

4 amended by adding at the end the following:

5 "or which is described in the last sentence of

6 section 3(32)".

7 (b) CLARIFICATION THAT TRIBAL GOVERNMENTS

8 ARE SUBJECT TO THE SAME PENSION PLAN RULES AND

9 REGULATIONS APPLIED TO STATE AND OTHER LOCAL

10 GOVERNMENTS AND THEIR POLICE AND FIRE-

11 FIGHTERS.—

12 (1) AMENDMENTS TO INTERNAL REVENUE

13 CODE OF 1986.—

14 (A) POLICE AND FIREFIGHTERS.—Sub-

15 paragraph (H) section 415(b)(2) of the Internal

16 Revenue Code of 1986 (defining participant) is

17 amended—

18 (i) in clause (i), by striking "State or

19 political subdivision" and inserting "State,

20 Indian tribal government (as defined in

21 section 7701(a)(40)), or any political sub-

22 division"; and

23 (ii) in clause (ii)(I), by striking "State

24 or political subdivision" each place it ap-

25 pears and inserting "State, Indian tribal

government (as so defined), or any political subdivision".

(B) STATE AND LOCAL GOVERNMENT PLANS.—

(i) IN GENERAL.—Subparagraph (A) of section 415(b)(10) of such Code (relating to limitation to equal accrued benefit) is amended by inserting "or a governmental plan described in the last sentence of section 414(d) (relating to plans of Indian tribal governments)," after "foregoing,".

(ii) CONFORMING AMENDMENT.—The heading of paragraph (1) of section 415(b) of such Code is amended by striking "SPECIAL RULE FOR STATE AND" and inserting "SPECIAL RULE FOR STATE, INDIAN TRIBAL, AND".

(C) GOVERNMENT PICK UP CONTRIBUTIONS.—Paragraph (2) of section 414(h) of such Code (relating to designation by units of government) is amended by inserting "or a governmental plan described in the last sentence of section 414(d) (relating to plans of Indian tribal governments)," after "foregoing,".

1   (2) AMENDMENTS TO EMPLOYEE RETIREMENT

2 INCOME SECURITY ACT OF 1974.—Section 4021(b) of

3 the Employee Retirement Income Security Act of

4 1974 (29 U.S.C. 1321(b)) is amended—

5   (A) in paragraph (12), by striking "or" at

6   the end;

7   (B) in paragraph (13), by striking "plan."

8   and inserting "plan; or"; and

9   (C) by adding at the end the following:

10   "(14) established and maintained by an Indian

11 tribal government (as defined in section 7701(a)(40)

12 of the Internal Revenue Code of 1986), a subdivision

13 of an Indian tribal government (determined in ac-

14 cordance with section 7871(d) of such Code), or an

15 agency or instrumentality of either, and all of the

16 participants of which are employees of such entity

17 substantially all of whose services as such an em-

18 ployee are in the performance of essential govern-

19 mental functions but not in the performance of com-

20 mercial activities (whether or not an essential gov-

21 ernment function).".

22   (c) EFFECTIVE DATE.—The amendments made by

23 this section shall apply to any year beginning on or after

24 the date of the enactment of this Act.

TITLE X—PROVISIONS RELATING TO SPOUSAL PENSION PROTECTION

SEC. 1001. REGULATIONS ON TIME AND ORDER OF ISSUANCE OF DOMESTIC RELATIONS ORDERS.

Not later than 1 year after the date of the enactment of this Act, the Secretary of Labor shall issue regulations under section 206(d)(3) of the Employee Retirement Security Act of 1974 and section 414(p) of the Internal Revenue Code of 1986 which clarify that—

    (1) a domestic relations order otherwise meeting the requirements to be a qualified domestic relations order, including the requirements of section 206(d)(3)(D) of such Act and section 414(p)(3) of such Code, shall not fail to be treated as a qualified domestic relations order solely because—

        (A) the order is issued after, or revises, another domestic relations order or qualified domestic relations order; or

        (B) of the time at which it is issued; and

    (2) any order described in paragraph (1) shall be subject to the same requirements and protections which apply to qualified domestic relations orders,

1   including the provisions of section 206(d)(3)(H) of

2   such Act and section 414(p)(7) of such Code.

3 **SEC. 1002. ENTITLEMENT OF DIVORCED SPOUSES TO RAIL-**

4   **ROAD RETIREMENT ANNUITIES INDE-**

5   **PENDENT OF ACTUAL ENTITLEMENT OF EM-**

6   **PLOYEE.**

7   (a) IN GENERAL.—Section 2 of the Railroad Retire-

8 ment Act of 1974 (45 U.S.C. 231a) is amended—

9   (1) in subsection (c)(4)(i), by striking "(A) is

10   entitled to an annuity under subsection (a)(1) and

11   (B)"; and

12   (2) in subsection (e)(5), by striking "or di-

13   vorced wife" the second place it appears.

14   (b) EFFECTIVE DATE.—The amendments made by

15 this section shall take effect 1 year after the date of the

16 enactment of this Act.

17 **SEC. 1003. EXTENSION OF TIER II RAILROAD RETIREMENT**

18   **BENEFITS TO SURVIVING FORMER SPOUSES**

19   **PURSUANT TO DIVORCE AGREEMENTS.**

20   (a) IN GENERAL.—Section 5 of the Railroad Retire-

21 ment Act of 1974 (45 U.S.C. 231d) is amended by adding

22 at the end the following:

23   "(d) Notwithstanding any other provision of law, the

24 payment of any portion of an annuity computed under sec-

25 tion 3(b) to a surviving former spouse in accordance with

1 a court decree of divorce, annulment, or legal separation
2 or the terms of any court-approved property settlement
3 incident to any such court decree shall not be terminated
4 upon the death of the individual who performed the service
5 with respect to which such annuity is so computed unless
6 such termination is otherwise required by the terms of
7 such court decree.''

8   (b) EFFECTIVE DATE.—The amendment made by
9 this section shall take effect 1 year after the date of the
10 enactment of this Act.

11 **SEC. 1004. REQUIREMENT FOR ADDITIONAL SURVIVOR AN-**
12   **NUITY OPTION.**

13   (a) AMENDMENTS TO INTERNAL REVENUE CODE.—

14   (1) ELECTION OF SURVIVOR ANNUITY.—Section

15   417(a)(1)(A) of the Internal Revenue Code of 1986

16   is amended—

17   (A) in clause (i), by striking '', and'' and

18   inserting a comma;

19   (B) by redesignating clause (ii) as clause

20   (iii); and

21   (C) by inserting after clause (i) the fol-

22   lowing:

23   ''(ii) if the participant elects a waiver

24   under clause (i), may elect the qualified op-

1   tional survivor annuity at any time during the

2   applicable election period, and''.

3   (2) DEFINITION.—Section 417 of such Code is

4 amended by adding at the end the following:

5 "(g) DEFINITION OF QUALIFIED OPTIONAL SUR-

6 VIVOR ANNUITY.—

7   "(1) IN GENERAL.—For purposes of this sec-

8   tion, the term 'qualified optional survivor annuity'

9   means an annuity—

10   "(A) for the life of the participant with a

11   survivor annuity for the life of the spouse which

12   is equal to the applicable percentage of the

13   amount of the annuity which is payable during

14   the joint lives of the participant and the spouse,

15   and

16   "(B) which is the actuarial equivalent of a

17   single annuity for the life of the participant.

18   Such term also includes any annuity in a form hav-

19   ing the effect of an annuity described in the pre-

20   ceding sentence.

21   "(2) APPLICABLE PERCENTAGE.—

22   "(A) IN GENERAL.—For purposes of para-

23   graph (1), if the survivor annuity percentage—

24   "(i) is less than 75 percent, the appli-

25   cable percentage is 75 percent, and

"(ii) is greater than or equal to 75 percent, the applicable percentage is 50 percent.

"(B) SURVIVOR ANNUITY PERCENTAGE.— For purposes of subparagraph (A), the term 'survivor annuity percentage' means the percentage which the survivor annuity under the plan's qualified joint and survivor annuity bears to the annuity payable during the joint lives of the participant and the spouse.".

(3) NOTICE.—Section 417(a)(3)(A)(i) of such Code is amended by inserting "and of the qualified optional survivor annuity" after "annuity".

(b) AMENDMENTS TO ERISA.—

(1) ELECTION OF SURVIVOR ANNUITY.—Section 205(c)(1)(A) of the Employee Retirement Income Security Act of 1974 (29 U.S.C. 1055(c)(1)(A)) is amended—

(A) in clause (i), by striking ", and" and inserting a comma;

(B) by redesignating clause (ii) as clause (iii); and

(C) by inserting after clause (i) the following:

1   "(ii) if the participant elects a waiver

2   under clause (i), may elect the qualified op-

3   tional survivor annuity at any time during the

4   applicable election period, and".

5   (2) DEFINITION.—Section 205(d) of such Act

6   (29 U.S.C. 1055(d)) is amended—

7   (A) by inserting "(1)" after "(d)";

8   (B) by redesignating paragraphs (1) and

9   (2) as subparagraphs (A) and (B), respectively;

10   and

11   (C) by adding at the end the following:

12   "(2)(A) For purposes of this section, the term 'quali-

13 fied optional survivor annuity' means an annuity—

14   "(i) for the life of the participant with a sur-

15   vivor annuity for the life of the spouse which is

16   equal to the applicable percentage of the amount of

17   the annuity which is payable during the joint lives

18   of the participant and the spouse, and

19   "(ii) which is the actuarial equivalent of a sin-

20   gle annuity for the life of the participant.

21 Such term also includes any annuity in a form having the

22 effect of an annuity described in the preceding sentence.

23   "(B)(i) For purposes of subparagraph (A), if the sur-

24 vivor annuity percentage—

1   "(I) is less than 75 percent, the applicable per-

2   centage is 75 percent, and

3   "(II) is greater than or equal to 75 percent, the

4   applicable percentage is 50 percent.

5   "(ii) For purposes of clause (i), the term 'survivor

6 annuity percentage' means the percentage which the sur-

7 vivor annuity under the plan's qualified joint and survivor

8 annuity bears to the annuity payable during the joint lives

9 of the participant and the spouse.".

10   (3) NOTICE.—Section 205(c)(3)(A)(i) of such

11   Act (29 U.S.C. 1055(c)(3)(A)(i)) is amended by in-

12   serting "and of the qualified optional survivor annu-

13   ity" after "annuity".

14   (c) EFFECTIVE DATES.—

15   (1) IN GENERAL.—The amendments made by

16   this section shall apply to plan years beginning after

17   December 31, 2007.

18   (2) SPECIAL RULE FOR COLLECTIVELY BAR-

19   GAINED PLANS.—In the case of a plan maintained

20   pursuant to 1 or more collective bargaining agree-

21   ments between employee representatives and 1 or

22   more employers ratified on or before the date of the

23   enactment of this Act, the amendments made by this

24   section shall not apply to plan years beginning be-

25   fore the earlier of—

    (A) the later of—

      (i) January 1, 2008, or

      (ii) the date on which the last collective bargaining agreement related to the plan terminates (determined without regard to any extension thereof after the date of enactment of this Act), or

    (B) January 1, 2009.

TITLE XI—ADMINISTRATIVE PROVISIONS

SEC. 1101. EMPLOYEE PLANS COMPLIANCE RESOLUTION SYSTEM.

(a) IN GENERAL.—The Secretary of the Treasury shall have full authority to establish and implement the Employee Plans Compliance Resolution System (or any successor program) and any other employee plans correction policies, including the authority to waive income, excise, or other taxes to ensure that any tax, penalty, or sanction is not excessive and bears a reasonable relationship to the nature, extent, and severity of the failure.

(b) IMPROVEMENTS.—The Secretary of the Treasury shall continue to update and improve the Employee Plans Compliance Resolution System (or any successor program), giving special attention to—

1   (1) increasing the awareness and knowledge of
2   small employers concerning the availability and use
3   of the program;

4   (2) taking into account special concerns and
5   circumstances that small employers face with respect
6   to compliance and correction of compliance failures;

7   (3) extending the duration of the self-correction
8   period under the Self-Correction Program for signifi-
9   cant compliance failures;

10   (4) expanding the availability to correct insig-
11   nificant compliance failures under the Self-Correc-
12   tion Program during audit; and

13   (5) assuring that any tax, penalty, or sanction
14   that is imposed by reason of a compliance failure is
15   not excessive and bears a reasonable relationship to
16   the nature, extent, and severity of the failure.

17   **SEC. 1102. NOTICE AND CONSENT PERIOD REGARDING DIS-**
18   **TRIBUTIONS.**

19   (a) EXPANSION OF PERIOD.—

20   (1) AMENDMENT OF INTERNAL REVENUE
21   CODE.—

22   (A) IN GENERAL.—Section 417(a)(6)(A) of
23   the Internal Revenue Code of 1986 is amended
24   by striking "90-day" and inserting "180-day".

1   (B) MODIFICATION OF REGULATIONS.—

2   The Secretary of the Treasury shall modify the

3   regulations under sections 402(f), 411(a)(11),

4   and 417 of the Internal Revenue Code of 1986

5   by substituting "180 days" for "90 days" each

6   place it appears in Treasury Regulations sec-

7   tions 1.402(f)–1, 1.411(a)–11(c), and 1.417(e)–

8   1(b).

9   (2) AMENDMENT OF ERISA.—

10   (A) IN GENERAL.—Section 205(c)(7)(A) of

11   the Employee Retirement Income Security Act

12   of 1974 (29 U.S.C. 1055(c)(7)(A)) is amended

13   by striking "90-day" and inserting "180-day".

14   (B) MODIFICATION OF REGULATIONS.—

15   The Secretary of the Treasury shall modify the

16   regulations under part 2 of subtitle B of title

17   I of the Employee Retirement Income Security

18   Act of 1974 relating to sections 203(e) and 205

19   of such Act by substituting "180 days" for "90

20   days" each place it appears.

21   (3) EFFECTIVE DATE.—The amendments and

22   modifications made or required by this subsection

23   shall apply to years beginning after December 31,

24   2006.

25   (b) NOTIFICATION OF RIGHT TO DEFER.—

761

(1) IN GENERAL.—The Secretary of the Treasury shall modify the regulations under section 411(a)(11) of the Internal Revenue Code of 1986 and under section 205 of the Employee Retirement Income Security Act of 1974 to provide that the description of a participant's right, if any, to defer receipt of a distribution shall also describe the consequences of failing to defer such receipt.

(2) EFFECTIVE DATE.—

(A) IN GENERAL.—The modifications required by paragraph (1) shall apply to years beginning after December 31, 2006.

(B) REASONABLE NOTICE.—A plan shall not be treated as failing to meet the requirements of section 411(a)(11) of such Code or section 205 of such Act with respect to any description of consequences described in paragraph (1) made within 90 days after the Secretary of the Treasury issues the modifications required by paragraph (1) if the plan administrator makes a reasonable attempt to comply with such requirements.

SEC. 1103. REPORTING SIMPLIFICATION.

(a) SIMPLIFIED ANNUAL FILING REQUIREMENT FOR OWNERS AND THEIR SPOUSES.—

(1) IN GENERAL.—The Secretary of the Treasury shall modify the requirements for filing annual returns with respect to one-participant retirement plans to ensure that such plans with assets of $250,000 or less as of the close of the plan year need not file a return for that year.

(2) ONE-PARTICIPANT RETIREMENT PLAN DEFINED.—For purposes of this subsection, the term "one-participant retirement plan" means a retirement plan with respect to which the following requirements are met:

> (A) on the first day of the plan year—
>
>> (i) the plan covered only one individual (or the individual and the individual's spouse) and the individual owned 100 percent of the plan sponsor (whether or not incorporated), or
>>
>> (ii) the plan covered only one or more partners (or partners and their spouses) in the plan sponsor;
>
> (B) the plan meets the minimum coverage requirements of section 410(b) of the Internal Revenue Code of 1986 without being combined with any other plan of the business that covers the employees of the business;

(C) the plan does not provide benefits to anyone except the individual (and the individual's spouse) or the partners (and their spouses);

(D) the plan does not cover a business that is a member of an affiliated service group, a controlled group of corporations, or a group of businesses under common control; and

(E) the plan does not cover a business that uses the services of leased employees (within the meaning of section 414(n) of such Code).

For purposes of this paragraph, the term "partner" includes a 2-percent shareholder (as defined in section 1372(b) of such Code) of an S corporation.

(3) OTHER DEFINITIONS.—Terms used in paragraph (2) which are also used in section 414 of the Internal Revenue Code of 1986 shall have the respective meanings given such terms by such section.

(4) EFFECTIVE DATE.—The provisions of this subsection shall apply to plan years beginning on or after January 1, 2007.

(b) SIMPLIFIED ANNUAL FILING REQUIREMENT FOR PLANS WITH FEWER THAN 25 PARTICIPANTS.—In the case of plan years beginning after December 31, 2006, the Secretary of the Treasury and the Secretary of Labor shall

1 provide for the filing of a simplified annual return for any

2 retirement plan which covers less than 25 participants on

3 the first day of a plan year and which meets the require-

4 ments described in subparagraphs (B), (D), and (E) of

5 subsection (a)(2).

6 SEC. 1104. VOLUNTARY EARLY RETIREMENT INCENTIVE

7 AND EMPLOYMENT RETENTION PLANS MAIN-

8 TAINED BY LOCAL EDUCATIONAL AGENCIES

9 AND OTHER ENTITIES.

10 (a) VOLUNTARY EARLY RETIREMENT INCENTIVE

11 PLANS.—

12 (1) TREATMENT AS PLAN PROVIDING SEVER-

13 ANCE PAY.—Section 457(e)(11) of the Internal Rev-

14 enue Code of 1986 (relating to certain plans ex-

15 cluded) is amended by adding at the end the fol-

16 lowing new subparagraph:

17 "(D) CERTAIN VOLUNTARY EARLY RETIRE-

18 MENT INCENTIVE PLANS.—

19 "(i) IN GENERAL.—If an applicable

20 voluntary early retirement incentive plan—

21 "(I) makes payments or supple-

22 ments as an early retirement benefit,

23 a retirement-type subsidy, or a benefit

24 described in the last sentence of sec-

25 tion 411(a)(9), and

1   "(II) such payments or supple-
2   ments are made in coordination with
3   a defined benefit plan which is de-
4   scribed in section 401(a) and includes
5   a trust exempt from tax under section
6   501(a) and which is maintained by an
7   eligible employer described in para-
8   graph (1)(A) or by an education asso-
9   ciation described in clause (ii)(II),
10   such applicable plan shall be treated for
11   purposes of subparagraph (A)(i) as a bona
12   fide severance pay plan with respect to
13   such payments or supplements to the ex-
14   tent such payments or supplements could
15   otherwise have been provided under such
16   defined benefit plan (determined as if sec-
17   tion 411 applied to such defined benefit
18   plan).

19   "(ii) APPLICABLE VOLUNTARY EARLY
20   RETIREMENT INCENTIVE PLAN.—For pur-
21   poses of this subparagraph, the term 'ap-
22   plicable voluntary early retirement incen-
23   tive plan' means a voluntary early retire-
24   ment incentive plan maintained by—

1   "(I) a local educational agency

2   (as defined in section 9101 of the Ele-

3   mentary and Secondary Education

4   Act of 1965 (20 U.S.C. 7801)), or

5   "(II) an education association

6   which principally represents employees

7   of 1 or more agencies described in

8   subclause (I) and which is described

9   in section 501(c) (5) or (6) and ex-

10   empt from tax under section 501(a)."

11   (2) AGE DISCRIMINATION IN EMPLOYMENT

12 ACT.—Section 4(l)(1) of the Age Discrimination in

13 Employment Act of 1967 (29 U.S.C. 623(l)(1)) is

14 amended—

15   (A) by inserting "(A)" after "(1)",

16   (B) by redesignating subparagraphs (A)

17 and (B) as clauses (i) and (ii), respectively,

18   (C) by redesignating clauses (i) and (ii) of

19 subparagraph (B) (as in effect before the

20 amendments made by subparagraph (B)) as

21 subclauses (I) and (II), respectively, and

22   (D) by adding at the end the following:

23 "(B) A voluntary early retirement incentive

24 plan that—

25   "(i) is maintained by—

1   "(I) a local educational agency (as de-

2   fined in section 9101 of the Elementary

3   and Secondary Education Act of 1965 (20

4   U.S.C. 7801), or

5   "(II) an education association which

6   principally represents employees of 1 or

7   more agencies described in subclause (I)

8   and which is described in section 501(c)

9   (5) or (6) of the Internal Revenue Code of

10   1986 and exempt from taxation under sec-

11   tion 501(a) of such Code, and

12   "(ii) makes payments or supplements de-

13   scribed in subclauses (I) and (II) of subpara-

14   graph (A)(ii) in coordination with a defined

15   benefit plan (as so defined) maintained by an

16   eligible employer described in section

17   457(e)(1)(A) of such Code or by an education

18   association described in clause (i)(II),

19 shall be treated solely for purposes of subparagraph

20 (A)(ii) as if it were a part of the defined benefit plan

21 with respect to such payments or supplements. Pay-

22 ments or supplements under such a voluntary early

23 retirement incentive plan shall not constitute sever-

24 ance pay for purposes of paragraph (2).".

25 (b) EMPLOYMENT RETENTION PLANS.—

(1) IN GENERAL.—Section 457(f)(2) of the Internal Revenue Code of 1986 (relating to exceptions) is amended by striking "and" at the end of subparagraph (D), by striking the period at the end of subparagraph (E) and inserting ", and", and by adding at the end the following:

"(F) that portion of any applicable employment retention plan described in paragraph (4) with respect to any participant."

(2) DEFINITIONS AND RULES RELATING TO EMPLOYMENT RETENTION PLANS.—Section 457(f) of such Code is amended by adding at the end the following new paragraph:

"(4) EMPLOYMENT RETENTION PLANS.—For purposes of paragraph (2)(F)—

"(A) IN GENERAL.—The portion of an applicable employment retention plan described in this paragraph with respect to any participant is that portion of the plan which provides benefits payable to the participant not in excess of twice the applicable dollar limit determined under subsection (e)(15).

"(B) OTHER RULES.—

"(i) LIMITATION.—Paragraph (2)(F) shall only apply to the portion of the plan

1 described in subparagraph (A) for years
2 preceding the year in which such portion is
3 paid or otherwise made available to the
4 participant.

5   "(ii) TREATMENT.—A plan shall not
6 be treated for purposes of this title as pro-
7 viding for the deferral of compensation for
8 any year with respect to the portion of the
9 plan described in subparagraph (A).

10   "(C) APPLICABLE EMPLOYMENT RETEN-
11 TION PLAN.—The term 'applicable employment
12 retention plan' means an employment retention
13 plan maintained by—

14   "(i) a local educational agency (as de-
15 fined in section 9101 of the Elementary
16 and Secondary Education Act of 1965 (20
17 U.S.C. 7801), or

18   "(ii) an education association which
19 principally represents employees of 1 or
20 more agencies described in clause (i) and
21 which is described in section 501(c) (5) or
22 (6) and exempt from taxation under sec-
23 tion 501(a).

24   "(D) EMPLOYMENT RETENTION PLAN.—
25 The term 'employment retention plan' means a

1   plan to pay, upon termination of employment,

2   compensation to an employee of a local edu-

3   cational agency or education association de-

4   scribed in subparagraph (C) for purposes of—

5   "(i) retaining the services of the em-

6   ployee, or

7   "(ii) rewarding such employee for the

8   employee's service with 1 or more such

9   agencies or associations.".

10   (c) COORDINATION WITH ERISA.—Section 3(2)(B)

11 of the Employee Retirement Income Security Act of 1974

12 (29 U.S.C. 1002(2)(B)) is amended by adding at the end

13 the following: "An applicable voluntary early retirement

14 incentive plan (as defined in section 457(e)(11)(D)(ii) of

15 the Internal Revenue Code of 1986) making payments or

16 supplements described in section 457(e)(11)(D)(i) of such

17 Code, and an applicable employment retention plan (as de-

18 fined in section 457(f)(4)(C) of such Code) making pay-

19 ments of benefits described in section 457(f)(4)(A) of such

20 Code, shall, for purposes of this title, be treated as a wel-

21 fare plan (and not a pension plan) with respect to such

22 payments and supplements."

23   (d) EFFECTIVE DATES.—

1　　　　　(1) IN GENERAL.—The amendments made by
2　　　this Act shall take effect on the date of the enact-
3　　　ment of this Act.

4　　　　　(2) TAX AMENDMENTS.—The amendments
5　　　made by subsections (a)(1) and (b) shall apply to
6　　　taxable years ending after the date of the enactment
7　　　of this Act.

8　　　　　(3) ERISA AMENDMENTS.—The amendment
9　　　made by subsection (c) shall apply to plan years
10　　　ending after the date of the enactment of this Act.

11　　　　　(4) CONSTRUCTION.—Nothing in the amend-
12　　　ments made by this section shall alter or affect the
13　　　construction of the Internal Revenue Code of 1986,
14　　　the Employee Retirement Income Security Act of
15　　　1974, or the Age Discrimination in Employment Act
16　　　of 1967 as applied to any plan, arrangement, or con-
17　　　duct to which such amendments do not apply.

18　**SEC. 1105. NO REDUCTION IN UNEMPLOYMENT COMPENSA-**
19　　　　　　　　**TION AS A RESULT OF PENSION ROLLOVERS.**

20　　　(a) IN GENERAL.—Section 3304(a) of the Internal
21　Revenue Code of 1986 (relating to requirements for State
22　unemployment laws) is amended by adding at the end the
23　following new flush sentence:
24　"Compensation shall not be reduced under paragraph (15)
25　for any pension, retirement or retired pay, annuity, or

1 similar payment which is not includible in gross income

2 of the individual for the taxable year in which paid because

3 it was part of a rollover distribution.".

4   (b) EFFECTIVE DATE.—The amendment made by

5 this section shall apply to weeks beginning on or after the

6 date of the enactment of this Act.

7 **SEC. 1106. REVOCATION OF ELECTION RELATING TO**

8   **TREATMENT AS MULTIEMPLOYER PLAN.**

9   (a) AMENDMENT TO ERISA.—Section 3(37) of the

10 Employee Retirement Income Security Act of 1974 is

11 amended by adding at the end the following new subpara-

12 graph (G):

13   "(G)(i) Within 1 year after the enactment of

14   the Pension Protection Act of 2006—

15   "(I) an election under subparagraph (E)

16   may be revoked, pursuant to procedures pre-

17   scribed by the Pension Benefit Guaranty Cor-

18   poration, if, for each of the 3 plan years prior

19   to the date of the enactment of that Act, the

20   plan would have been a multiemployer plan but

21   for the election under subparagraph (E), and

22   "(II) a plan that meets the criteria in

23   clauses (i) and (ii) of subparagraph (A) of this

24   paragraph or that is described in clause (vi)

25   may, pursuant to procedures prescribed by the

Pension Benefit Guaranty Corporation, elect to
be a multiemployer plan, if—

"(aa) for each of the 3 plan years immediately before the date of the enactment of the Pension Protection Act of 2006, the plan has met those criteria or is so described,

"(bb) substantially all of the plan's employer contributions for each of those plan years were made or required to be made by organizations that were exempt from tax under section 501 of the Internal Revenue Code of 1986, and

"(cc) the plan was established prior to September 2, 1974.

"(ii) An election under this paragraph shall be effective for all purposes under this Act and under the Internal Revenue Code of 1986, starting with the first plan year ending after the date of the enactment of the Pension Protection Act of 2006.

"(iii) Once made, an election under this paragraph shall be irrevocable, except that a plan described in subclause (i)(II) shall cease to be a multiemployer plan as of the plan year beginning immediately after the first plan year for which the major-

ity of its employer contributions were made or required to be made by organizations that were not exempt from tax under section 501 of the Internal
Revenue Code of 1986.

"(iv) The fact that a plan makes an election
under clause (i)(II) does not imply that the plan was
not a multiemployer plan prior to the date of the
election or would not be a multiemployer plan without regard to the election.

"(v)(I) No later than 30 days before an election
is made under this paragraph, the plan administrator shall provide notice of the pending election to
each plan participant and beneficiary, each labor organization representing such participants or beneficiaries, and each employer that has an obligation
to contribute to the plan, describing the principal
differences between the guarantee programs under
title IV and the benefit restrictions under this title
for single employer and multiemployer plans, along
with such other information as the plan administrator chooses to include.

"(II) Within 180 days after the date of enactment of the Pension Protection Act of 2006, the
Secretary shall prescribe a model notice under this
subparagraph.

1   "(III) A plan administrator's failure to provide

2   the notice required under this subparagraph shall be

3   treated for purposes of section 502(c)(2) as a failure

4   or refusal by the plan administrator to file the an-

5   nual report required to be filed with the Secretary

6   under section 101(b)(4).

7   "(vi) A plan is described in this clause if it is

8   a plan—

9   "(I) that was established in Chicago, Illi-

10   nois, on August 12, 1881; and

11   "(II) sponsored by an organization de-

12   scribed in section 501(c)(5) of the Internal Rev-

13   enue Code of 1986 and exempt from tax under

14   section 501(a) of such Code.".

15   (b) AMENDMENT TO INTERNAL REVENUE CODE.—

16   Subsection (f) of section 414 of the Internal Revenue Code

17   of 1986 is amended by adding at the end the following

18   new paragraph (6):

19   "(6) ELECTION WITH REGARD TO MULTIEM-

20   PLOYER STATUS.—

21   "(A) Within 1 year after the enactment of

22   the Pension Protection Act of 2006—

23   "(i) An election under paragraph (5)

24   may be revoked, pursuant to procedures

25   prescribed by the Pension Benefit Guar-

anty Corporation, if, for each of the 3 plan
years prior to the date of the enactment of
that Act, the plan would have been a multiemployer plan but for the election under
paragraph (5), and

"(ii) a plan that meets the criteria in
subparagraph (A) and (B) of paragraph
(1) of this subsection or that is described
in subparagraph (E) may, pursuant to procedures prescribed by the Pension Benefit
Guaranty Corporation, elect to be a multiemployer plan, if—

"(I) for each of the 3 plan years
immediately before the date of enactment of the Pension Protection Act of
2006, the plan has met those criteria
or is so described,

"(II) substantially all of the
plan's employer contributions for each
of those plan years were made or required to be made by organizations
that were exempt from tax under section 501, and

"(III) the plan was established
prior to September 2, 1974.

"(B) An election under this paragraph shall be effective for all purposes under this Act and under the Employee Retirement Income Security Act of 1974, starting with the first plan year ending after the date of the enactment of the Pension Protection Act of 2006.

"(C) Once made, an election under this paragraph shall be irrevocable, except that a plan described in subparagraph (A)(ii) shall cease to be a multiemployer plan as of the plan year beginning immediately after the first plan year for which the majority of its employer contributions were made or required to be made by organizations that were not exempt from tax under section 501.

"(D) The fact that a plan makes an election under subparagraph (A)(ii) does not imply that the plan was not a multiemployer plan prior to the date of the election or would not be a multiemployer plan without regard to the election.

"(E) A plan is described in this subparagraph if it is a plan—

"(i) that was established in Chicago, Illinois, on August 12, 1881; and

"(ii) sponsored by an organization described in section 501(c)(5) and exempt
from tax under section 501(a).".

SEC. 1107. PROVISIONS RELATING TO PLAN AMENDMENTS.

(a) IN GENERAL.—If this section applies to any pension plan or contract amendment—

(1) such pension plan or contract shall be treated as being operated in accordance with the terms
of the plan during the period described in subsection
(b)(2)(A), and

(2) except as provided by the Secretary of the
Treasury, such pension plan shall not fail to meet
the requirements of section 411(d)(6) of the Internal
Revenue Code of 1986 and section 204(g) of the
Employee Retirement Income Security Act of 1974
by reason of such amendment.

(b) AMENDMENTS TO WHICH SECTION APPLIES.—

(1) IN GENERAL.—This section shall apply to
any amendment to any pension plan or annuity contract which is made—

(A) pursuant to any amendment made by
this Act or pursuant to any regulation issued by
the Secretary of the Treasury or the Secretary
of Labor under this Act, and

1   (B) on or before the last day of the first

2   plan year beginning on or after January 1,

3   2009.

4 In the case of a governmental plan (as defined in

5 section 414(d) of the Internal Revenue Code of

6 1986), this paragraph shall be applied by sub-

7 stituting "2011" for "2009".

8   (2) CONDITIONS.—This section shall not apply

9 to any amendment unless—

10   (A) during the period—

11   (i) beginning on the date the legisla-

12   tive or regulatory amendment described in

13   paragraph (1)(A) takes effect (or in the

14   case of a plan or contract amendment not

15   required by such legislative or regulatory

16   amendment, the effective date specified by

17   the plan), and

18   (ii) ending on the date described in

19   paragraph (1)(B) (or, if earlier, the date

20   the plan or contract amendment is adopt-

21   ed), the plan or contract is operated as if

22   such plan or contract amendment were in

23   effect; and

24   (B) such plan or contract amendment ap-

25   plies retroactively for such period.

TITLE XII—PROVISIONS RELATING TO EXEMPT ORGANIZATIONS

Subtitle A—Charitable Giving Incentives

SEC. 1201. TAX-FREE DISTRIBUTIONS FROM INDIVIDUAL RETIREMENT PLANS FOR CHARITABLE PURPOSES.

(a) IN GENERAL.—Subsection (d) of section 408 (relating to individual retirement accounts) is amended by adding at the end the following new paragraph:

"(8) DISTRIBUTIONS FOR CHARITABLE PURPOSES.—

"(A) IN GENERAL.—So much of the aggregate amount of qualified charitable distributions with respect to a taxpayer made during any taxable year which does not exceed $100,000 shall not be includible in gross income of such taxpayer for such taxable year.

"(B) QUALIFIED CHARITABLE DISTRIBUTION.—For purposes of this paragraph, the term 'qualified charitable distribution' means any distribution from an individual retirement plan (other than a plan described in subsection (k) or (p))—

"(i) which is made directly by the trustee to an organization described in section 170(b)(1)(A) (other than any organization described in section 509(a)(3) or any fund or account described in section 4966(d)(2)), and

"(ii) which is made on or after the date that the individual for whose benefit the plan is maintained has attained age 70½.

A distribution shall be treated as a qualified charitable distribution only to the extent that the distribution would be includible in gross income without regard to subparagraph (A).

"(C) CONTRIBUTIONS MUST BE OTHERWISE DEDUCTIBLE.—For purposes of this paragraph, a distribution to an organization described in subparagraph (B)(i) shall be treated as a qualified charitable distribution only if a deduction for the entire distribution would be allowable under section 170 (determined without regard to subsection (b) thereof and this paragraph).

"(D) APPLICATION OF SECTION 72.—Notwithstanding section 72, in determining the ex-

tent to which a distribution is a qualified charitable distribution, the entire amount of the distribution shall be treated as includible in gross
income without regard to subparagraph (A) to
the extent that such amount does not exceed
the aggregate amount which would have been so
includible if all amounts distributed from all individual retirement plans were treated as 1 contract under paragraph (2)(A) for purposes of
determining the inclusion of such distribution
under section 72. Proper adjustments shall be
made in applying section 72 to other distributions in such taxable year and subsequent taxable years.

"(E) DENIAL OF DEDUCTION.—Qualified
charitable distributions which are not includible
in gross income pursuant to subparagraph (A)
shall not be taken into account in determining
the deduction under section 170.

"(F) TERMINATION.—This paragraph shall
not apply to distributions made in taxable years
beginning after December 31, 2007.".

(b) MODIFICATIONS RELATING TO INFORMATION RE-
TURNS BY CERTAIN TRUSTS.—

1   (1) RETURNS.—Section 6034 (relating to re-

2 turns by trusts described in section 4947(a)(2) or

3 claiming charitable deductions under section 642(c))

4 is amended to read as follows:

5 **"SEC. 6034. RETURNS BY CERTAIN TRUSTS.**

6   "(a) SPLIT-INTEREST TRUSTS.—Every trust de-

7 scribed in section 4947(a)(2) shall furnish such informa-

8 tion with respect to the taxable year as the Secretary may

9 by forms or regulations require.

10   "(b) TRUSTS CLAIMING CERTAIN CHARITABLE DE-

11 DUCTIONS.—

12   "(1) IN GENERAL.—Every trust not required to

13   file a return under subsection (a) but claiming a de-

14   duction under section 642(c) for the taxable year

15   shall furnish such information with respect to such

16   taxable year as the Secretary may by forms or regu-

17   lations prescribe, including—

18   "(A) the amount of the deduction taken

19   under section 642(c) within such year,

20   "(B) the amount paid out within such year

21   which represents amounts for which deductions

22   under section 642(c) have been taken in prior

23   years,

1   "(C) the amount for which such deductions

2   have been taken in prior years but which has

3   not been paid out at the beginning of such year,

4   "(D) the amount paid out of principal in

5   the current and prior years for the purposes de-

6   scribed in section 642(c),

7   "(E) the total income of the trust within

8   such year and the expenses attributable thereto,

9   and

10   "(F) a balance sheet showing the assets, li-

11   abilities, and net worth of the trust as of the

12   beginning of such year.

13   "(2) EXCEPTIONS.—Paragraph (1) shall not

14   apply to a trust for any taxable year if—

15   "(A) all the net income for such year, de-

16   termined under the applicable principles of the

17   law of trusts, is required to be distributed cur-

18   rently to the beneficiaries, or

19   "(B) the trust is described in section

20   4947(a)(1).".

21   (2) INCREASE IN PENALTY RELATING TO FIL-

22   ING OF INFORMATION RETURN BY SPLIT-INTEREST

23   TRUSTS.—Paragraph (2) of section 6652(c) (relating

24   to returns by exempt organizations and by certain

trusts) is amended by adding at the end the following new subparagraph:

"(C) SPLIT-INTEREST TRUSTS.—In the
case of a trust which is required to file a return
under section 6034(a), subparagraphs (A) and
(B) of this paragraph shall not apply and paragraph (1) shall apply in the same manner as if
such return were required under section 6033,
except that—

"(i) the 5 percent limitation in the
second sentence of paragraph (1)(A) shall
not apply,

"(ii) in the case of any trust with
gross income in excess of $250,000, the
first sentence of paragraph (1)(A) shall be
applied by substituting '$100' for '$20',
and the second sentence thereof shall be
applied by substituting '$50,000' for
'$10,000', and

"(iii) the third sentence of paragraph
(1)(A) shall be disregarded.

In addition to any penalty imposed on the trust
pursuant to this subparagraph, if the person required to file such return knowingly fails to file
the return, such penalty shall also be imposed

1   on such person who shall be personally liable

2   for such penalty.''.

3   (3) CONFIDENTIALITY OF NONCHARITABLE

4   BENEFICIARIES.—Subsection (b) of section 6104

5   (relating to inspection of annual information re-

6   turns) is amended by adding at the end the fol-

7   lowing new sentence: "In the case of a trust which

8   is required to file a return under section 6034(a),

9   this subsection shall not apply to information re-

10   garding beneficiaries which are not organizations de-

11   scribed in section 170(c).''.

12   (4) CLERICAL AMENDMENT.—The item in the

13   table of sections for subpart A of part III of sub-

14   chapter A of chapter 61 relating to section 6034 is

15   amended to read as follows:

"Sec. 6034. Returns by certain trusts.''.

16   (c) EFFECTIVE DATES.—

17   (1) SUBSECTION (a).—The amendment made

18   by subsection (a) shall apply to distributions made

19   in taxable years beginning after December 31, 2005.

20   (2) SUBSECTION (b).—The amendments made

21   by subsection (b) shall apply to returns for taxable

22   years beginning after December 31, 2006.

SEC. 1202. EXTENSION OF MODIFICATION OF CHARITABLE DEDUCTION FOR CONTRIBUTIONS OF FOOD INVENTORY.

(a) IN GENERAL.—Section 170(e)(3)(C)(iv) (relating to termination) is amended by striking "2005" and inserting "2007".

(b) EFFECTIVE DATE.—The amendment made by this section shall apply to contributions made after December 31, 2005.

SEC. 1203. BASIS ADJUSTMENT TO STOCK OF S CORPORATION CONTRIBUTING PROPERTY.

(a) IN GENERAL.—Paragraph (2) of section 1367(a) (relating to adjustments to basis of stock of shareholders, etc.) is amended by adding at the end the following new flush sentence:

"The decrease under subparagraph (B) by reason of a charitable contribution (as defined in section 170(c)) of property shall be the amount equal to the shareholder's pro rata share of the adjusted basis of such property. The preceding sentence shall not apply to contributions made in taxable years beginning after December 31, 2007.".

(b) EFFECTIVE DATE.—The amendment made by this section shall apply to contributions made in taxable years beginning after December 31, 2005.

1 **SEC. 1204. EXTENSION OF MODIFICATION OF CHARITABLE**

2   **DEDUCTION FOR CONTRIBUTIONS OF BOOK**

3   **INVENTORY.**

4   (a) IN GENERAL.—Section 170(e)(3)(D)(iv) (relating

5 to termination) is amended by striking "2005" and insert-

6 ing "2007".

7   (b) EFFECTIVE DATE.—The amendment made by

8 this section shall apply to contributions made after De-

9 cember 31, 2005.

10 **SEC. 1205. MODIFICATION OF TAX TREATMENT OF CERTAIN**

11   **PAYMENTS TO CONTROLLING EXEMPT ORGA-**

12   **NIZATIONS.**

13   (a) IN GENERAL.—Paragraph (13) of section 512(b)

14 (relating to special rules for certain amounts received from

15 controlled entities) is amended by redesignating subpara-

16 graph (E) as subparagraph (F) and by inserting after sub-

17 paragraph (D) the following new subparagraph:

18   "(E) PARAGRAPH TO APPLY ONLY TO CER-

19   TAIN EXCESS PAYMENTS.—

20   "(i) IN GENERAL.—Subparagraph (A)

21   shall apply only to the portion of a quali-

22   fying specified payment received or accrued

23   by the controlling organization that ex-

24   ceeds the amount which would have been

25   paid or accrued if such payment met the

26   requirements prescribed under section 482.

"(ii) ADDITION TO TAX FOR VALUATION MISSTATEMENTS.—The tax imposed by this chapter on the controlling organization shall be increased by an amount equal to 20 percent of the larger of—

    "(I) such excess determined without regard to any amendment or supplement to a return of tax, or

    "(II) such excess determined with regard to all such amendments and supplements.

"(iii) QUALIFYING SPECIFIED PAYMENT.—The term 'qualifying specified payment' means a specified payment which is made pursuant to—

    "(I) a binding written contract in effect on the date of the enactment of this subparagraph, or

    "(II) a contract which is a renewal, under substantially similar terms, of a contract described in subclause (I).

"(iv) TERMINATION.—This subparagraph shall not apply to payments received or accrued after December 31, 2007.".

1   (b) REPORTING.—

2   (1) IN GENERAL.—Section 6033 (relating to re-
3   turns by exempt organizations) is amended by redes-
4   ignating subsection (h) as subsection (i) and by in-
5   serting after subsection (g) the following new sub-
6   section:

7   "(h) CONTROLLING ORGANIZATIONS.—Each control-
8 ling organization (within the meaning of section
9 512(b)(13)) which is subject to the requirements of sub-
10 section (a) shall include on the return required under sub-
11 section (a)—

12   "(1) any interest, annuities, royalties, or rents
13   received from each controlled entity (within the
14   meaning of section 512(b)(13)),

15   "(2) any loans made to each such controlled en-
16   tity, and

17   "(3) any transfers of funds between such con-
18   trolling organization and each such controlled enti-
19   ty.".

20   (2) REPORT TO CONGRESS.—Not later than
21   January 1, 2009, the Secretary of the Treasury
22   shall submit to the Committee on Finance of the
23   Senate and the Committee on Ways and Means of
24   the House of Representatives a report on the effec-
25   tiveness of the Internal Revenue Service in admin-

1   istering the amendments made by subsection (a) and

2   on the extent to which payments by controlled enti-

3   ties (within the meaning of section 512(b)(13) of the

4   Internal Revenue Code of 1986) to controlling orga-

5   nizations (within the meaning of section 512(b)(13)

6   of such Code) meet the requirements under section

7   482 of such Code. Such report shall include the re-

8   sults of any audit of any controlling organization or

9   controlled entity and recommendations relating to

10   the tax treatment of payments from controlled enti-

11   ties to controlling organizations.

12   (c) EFFECTIVE DATE.—

13   (1) SUBSECTION (a).—The amendments made

14   by subsection (a) shall apply to payments received or

15   accrued after December 31, 2005.

16   (2) SUBSECTION (b).—The amendments made

17   by subsection (b) shall apply to returns the due date

18   (determined without regard to extensions) of which

19   is after the date of the enactment of this Act.

20 **SEC. 1206. ENCOURAGEMENT OF CONTRIBUTIONS OF CAP-**

21   **ITAL GAIN REAL PROPERTY MADE FOR CON-**

22   **SERVATION PURPOSES.**

23   (a) IN GENERAL.—

24   (1) INDIVIDUALS.—Paragraph (1) of section

25   170(b) (relating to percentage limitations) is amend-

ed by redesignating subparagraphs (E) and (F) as subparagraphs (F) and (G), respectively, and by inserting after subparagraph (D) the following new subparagraph:

"(E) CONTRIBUTIONS OF QUALIFIED CONSERVATION CONTRIBUTIONS.—

"(i) IN GENERAL.—Any qualified conservation contribution (as defined in subsection (h)(1)) shall be allowed to the extent the aggregate of such contributions does not exceed the excess of 50 percent of the taxpayer's contribution base over the amount of all other charitable contributions allowable under this paragraph.

"(ii) CARRYOVER.—If the aggregate amount of contributions described in clause (i) exceeds the limitation of clause (i), such excess shall be treated (in a manner consistent with the rules of subsection (d)(1)) as a charitable contribution to which clause (i) applies in each of the 15 succeeding years in order of time.

"(iii) COORDINATION WITH OTHER SUBPARAGRAPHS.—For purposes of applying this subsection and subsection (d)(1), contributions described in clause (i) shall not be treated as described in subparagraph (A), (B), (C), or (D) and such subparagraphs shall apply without regard to such contributions.

"(iv) SPECIAL RULE FOR CONTRIBUTION OF PROPERTY USED IN AGRICULTURE OR LIVESTOCK PRODUCTION.—

"(I) IN GENERAL.—If the individual is a qualified farmer or rancher for the taxable year for which the contribution is made, clause (i) shall be applied by substituting '100 percent' for '50 percent'.

"(II) EXCEPTION.—Subclause (I) shall not apply to any contribution of property made after the date of the enactment of this subparagraph which is used in agriculture or livestock production (or available for such production) unless such contribution is subject to a restriction that such property remain available for such production. This subparagraph shall be applied separately with respect to property to

1   which subclause (I) does not apply by

2   reason of the preceding sentence prior

3   to its application to property to which

4   subclause (I) does apply.

5   "(v) DEFINITION.—For purposes of

6   clause (iv), the term 'qualified farmer or

7   rancher' means a taxpayer whose gross in-

8   come from the trade or business of farm-

9   ing (within the meaning of section

10   2032A(e)(5)) is greater than 50 percent of

11   the taxpayer's gross income for the taxable

12   year.

13   "(vi) TERMINATION.—This subpara-

14   graph shall not apply to any contribution

15   made in taxable years beginning after De-

16   cember 31, 2007.".

17   (2) CORPORATIONS.—Paragraph (2) of section

18 170(b) is amended to read as follows:

19   "(2) CORPORATIONS.—In the case of a corpora-

20 tion—

21   "(A) IN GENERAL.—The total deductions

22   under subsection (a) for any taxable year (other

23   than for contributions to which subparagraph

24   (B) applies) shall not exceed 10 percent of the

25   taxpayer's taxable income.

1 "(B) QUALIFIED CONSERVATION CON-

2 TRIBUTIONS BY CERTAIN CORPORATE FARMERS

3 AND RANCHERS.—

4 "(i) IN GENERAL.—Any qualified con-

5 servation contribution (as defined in sub-

6 section (h)(1))—

7 "(I) which is made by a corpora-

8 tion which, for the taxable year during

9 which the contribution is made, is a

10 qualified farmer or rancher (as de-

11 fined in paragraph (1)(E)(v)) and the

12 stock of which is not readily tradable

13 on an established securities market at

14 any time during such year, and

15 "(II) which, in the case of con-

16 tributions made after the date of the

17 enactment of this subparagraph, is a

18 contribution of property which is used

19 in agriculture or livestock production

20 (or available for such production) and

21 which is subject to a restriction that

22 such property remain available for

23 such production,

24 shall be allowed to the extent the aggregate

25 of such contributions does not exceed the

1 excess of the taxpayer's taxable income

2 over the amount of charitable contributions

3 allowable under subparagraph (A).

4 "(ii) CARRYOVER.—If the aggregate

5 amount of contributions described in clause

6 (i) exceeds the limitation of clause (i), such

7 excess shall be treated (in a manner con-

8 sistent with the rules of subsection (d)(2))

9 as a charitable contribution to which clause

10 (i) applies in each of the 15 succeeding

11 years in order of time.

12 "(iii) TERMINATION.—This subpara-

13 graph shall not apply to any contribution

14 made in taxable years beginning after De-

15 cember 31, 2007.

16 "(C) TAXABLE INCOME.—For purposes of

17 this paragraph, taxable income shall be com-

18 puted without regard to—

19 "(i) this section,

20 "(ii) part VIII (except section 248),

21 "(iii) any net operating loss carryback

22 to the taxable year under section 172,

23 "(iv) section 199, and

24 "(v) any capital loss carryback to the

25 taxable year under section 1212(a)(1).".

(b) CONFORMING AMENDMENTS.—

    (1) Paragraph (2) of section 170(d) is amended by striking "subsection (b)(2)" each place it appears and inserting "subsection (b)(2)(A)".

    (2) Section 545(b)(2) is amended by striking "and (D)" and inserting "(D), and (E)".

(c) EFFECTIVE DATE.—The amendments made by this section shall apply to contributions made in taxable years beginning after December 31, 2005.

SEC. 1207. EXCISE TAXES EXEMPTION FOR BLOOD COLLECTOR ORGANIZATIONS.

(a) EXEMPTION FROM IMPOSITION OF SPECIAL FUELS TAX.—Section 4041(g) (relating to other exemptions) is amended by striking "and" at the end of paragraph (3), by striking the period in paragraph (4) and inserting "; and", and by inserting after paragraph (4) the following new paragraph:

    "(5) with respect to the sale of any liquid to a qualified blood collector organization (as defined in section 7701(a)(49)) for such organization's exclusive use in the collection, storage, or transportation of blood.".

(b) EXEMPTION FROM MANUFACTURERS EXCISE TAX.—

1   (1) IN GENERAL.—Section 4221(a) (relating to

2 certain tax-free sales) is amended by striking "or"

3 at the end of paragraph (4), by adding "or" at the

4 end of paragraph (5), and by inserting after para-

5 graph (5) the following new paragraph:

6   "(6) to a qualified blood collector organization

7 (as defined in section 7701(a)(49)) for such organi-

8 zation's exclusive use in the collection, storage, or

9 transportation of blood,".

10   (2) NO EXEMPTION WITH RESPECT TO VAC-

11 CINES AND RECREATIONAL EQUIPMENT.—Section

12 4221(a) is amended by adding at the end the fol-

13 lowing new sentence: "In the case of taxes imposed

14 by subchapter C or D, paragraph (6) shall not

15 apply.".

16   (3) CONFORMING AMENDMENTS.—

17   (A) The second sentence of section

18   4221(a) is amended by striking "Paragraphs

19   (4) and (5)" and inserting "Paragraphs (4),

20   (5), and (6)".

21   (B) Section 6421(c) is amended by strik-

22   ing "or (5)" and inserting "(5), or (6)".

23 (c) EXEMPTION FROM COMMUNICATION EXCISE

24 TAX.—

1   (1) IN GENERAL.—Section 4253 (relating to ex-

2 emptions) is amended by redesignating subsection

3 (k) as subsection (l) and inserting after subsection

4 (j) the following new subsection:

5 "(k) EXEMPTION FOR QUALIFIED BLOOD COL-

6 LECTOR ORGANIZATIONS.—Under regulations provided by

7 the Secretary, no tax shall be imposed under section 4251

8 on any amount paid by a qualified blood collector organi-

9 zation (as defined in section 7701(a)(49)) for services or

10 facilities furnished to such organization.".

11   (2) CONFORMING AMENDMENT.—Section

12   4253(l), as redesignated by paragraph (1), is

13   amended by striking "or (j)" and inserting "(j), or

14   (k)".

15 (d) EXEMPTION FROM TAX ON HEAVY VEHICLES.—

16 Section 4483 is amended by redesignating subsection (h)

17 as subsection (i) and by inserting after subsection (g) the

18 following new subsection:

19 "(h) EXEMPTION FOR VEHICLES USED IN BLOOD

20 COLLECTION.—

21   "(1) IN GENERAL.—No tax shall be imposed by

22   section 4481 on the use of any qualified blood col-

23   lector vehicle by a qualified blood collector organiza-

24   tion.

"(2) QUALIFIED BLOOD COLLECTOR VEHI-
CLE.—For purposes of this subsection, the term
'qualified blood collector vehicle' means a vehicle at
least 80 percent of the use of which during the prior
taxable period was by a qualified blood collector organization in the collection, storage, or transportation of blood.

"(3) SPECIAL RULE FOR VEHICLES FIRST
PLACED IN SERVICE IN A TAXABLE PERIOD.—In the
case of a vehicle first placed in service in a taxable
period, a vehicle shall be treated as a qualified blood
collector vehicle for such taxable period if such qualified blood collector organization certifies to the Secretary that the organization reasonably expects at
least 80 percent of the use of such vehicle by the organization during such taxable period will be in the
collection, storage, or transportation of blood.

"(4) QUALIFIED BLOOD COLLECTOR ORGANIZA-
TION.—The term 'qualified blood collector organization' has the meaning given such term by section
7701(a)(49).".

(e) CREDIT OR REFUND FOR CERTAIN TAXES ON
SALES AND SERVICES.—

(1) DEEMED OVERPAYMENT.—

1   (A) IN GENERAL.—Section 6416(b)(2) is

2 amended by redesignating subparagraphs (E)

3 and (F) as subparagraphs (F) and (G), respec-

4 tively, and by inserting after subparagraph (D)

5 the following new subparagraph:

6   "(E) sold to a qualified blood collector or-

7 ganization (as defined in section 7701(a)(49))

8 for such organization's exclusive use in the col-

9 lection, storage, or transportation of blood;".

10   (B) NO CREDIT OR REFUND FOR VACCINES

11 OR RECREATIONAL EQUIPMENT.—Section

12 6416(b)(2) is amended by adding at the end the

13 following new sentence: "In the case of taxes

14 imposed by subchapter C or D of chapter 32,

15 subparagraph (E) shall not apply.".

16   (C) CONFORMING AMENDMENTS.—Section

17 6416(b)(2) is amended—

18   (i) by striking "Subparagraphs (C)

19 and (D)" in the second sentence and in-

20 serting "Subparagraphs (C), (D), and

21 (E)".

22   (ii) by striking "(B), (C), and (D)"

23 and inserting "(B), (C), (D), and (E)".

24 (2) SALES OF TIRES.—Section 6416(b)(4)(B) is

25 amended by striking "or" at the end of clause (i),

1   by striking the period at the end of clause (ii) and
2   inserting ", or", and by adding after clause (ii) the
3   following:

4   "(iii) sold to a qualified blood collector
5   organization for its exclusive use in con-
6   nection with a vehicle the organization cer-
7   tifies will be primarily used in the collec-
8   tion, storage, or transportation of blood.".

9   (f) DEFINITION OF QUALIFIED BLOOD COLLECTOR
10   ORGANIZATION.—Section 7701(a) is amended by inserting
11   at the end the following new paragraph:

12   "(49) QUALIFIED BLOOD COLLECTOR ORGANI-
13   ZATION.—The term 'qualified blood collector organi-
14   zation' means an organization which is—

15   "(A) described in section 501(c)(3) and ex-
16   empt from tax under section 501(a),

17   "(B) primarily engaged in the activity of
18   the collection of human blood,

19   "(C) registered with the Secretary for pur-
20   poses of excise tax exemptions, and

21   "(D) registered by the Food and Drug Ad-
22   ministration to collect blood.".

23   (g) EFFECTIVE DATE.—

24   (1) IN GENERAL.—The amendments made by
25   this section shall take effect on January 1, 2007.

1   (2) SUBSECTION (d).—The amendment made

2 by subsection (d) shall apply to taxable periods be-

3 ginning on or after July 1, 2007.

Subtitle B—Reforming Exempt Organizations

PART 1—GENERAL REFORMS

SEC. 1211. REPORTING ON CERTAIN ACQUISITIONS OF IN-TERESTS IN INSURANCE CONTRACTS IN WHICH CERTAIN EXEMPT ORGANIZATIONS HOLD AN INTEREST.

11 (a) REPORTING REQUIREMENTS.—

12   (1) IN GENERAL.—Subpart B of part III of

13 subchapter A of chapter 61 (relating to information

14 concerning transactions with other persons), as

15 amended by this Act, is amended by adding at the

16 end the following new section:

"SEC. 6050V. RETURNS RELATING TO APPLICABLE INSUR-ANCE CONTRACTS IN WHICH CERTAIN EX-EMPT ORGANIZATIONS HOLD INTERESTS.

20   "(a) IN GENERAL.—Each applicable exempt organi-

21 zation which makes a reportable acquisition shall make the

22 return described in subsection (c).

23   "(b) TIME FOR MAKING RETURN.—Any applicable

24 exempt organization required to make a return under sub-

1 section (a) shall file such return at such time as may be
2 established by the Secretary.

3   "(c) FORM AND MANNER OF RETURNS.—A return
4 is described in this subsection if such return—

5   "(1) is in such form as the Secretary pre-
6   scribes,

7   "(2) contains the name, address, and taxpayer
8   identification number of the applicable exempt orga-
9   nization and the issuer of the applicable insurance
10   contract, and

11   "(3) contains such other information as the
12   Secretary may prescribe.

13   "(d) DEFINITIONS.—For purposes of this section—

14   "(1) REPORTABLE ACQUISITION.—The term
15   'reportable acquisition' means the acquisition by an
16   applicable exempt organization of a direct or indirect
17   interest in any applicable insurance contract in any
18   case in which such acquisition is a part of a struc-
19   tured transaction involving a pool of such contracts.

20   "(2) APPLICABLE INSURANCE CONTRACT.—

21   "(A) IN GENERAL.—The term 'applicable
22   insurance contract' means any life insurance,
23   annuity, or endowment contract with respect to
24   which both an applicable exempt organization
25   and a person other than an applicable exempt

organization have directly or indirectly held an interest in the contract (whether or not at the same time).

"(B) EXCEPTIONS.—Such term shall not include a life insurance, annuity, or endowment contract if—

"(i) all persons directly or indirectly holding any interest in the contract (other than applicable exempt organizations) have an insurable interest in the insured under the contract independent of any interest of an applicable exempt organization in the contract,

"(ii) the sole interest in the contract of an applicable exempt organization or each person other than an applicable exempt organization is as a named beneficiary, or

"(iii) the sole interest in the contract of each person other than an applicable exempt organization is—

"(I) as a beneficiary of a trust holding an interest in the contract, but only if the person's designation as such beneficiary was made without

1 consideration and solely on a purely

2 gratuitous basis, or

3   "(II) as a trustee who holds an

4   interest in the contract in a fiduciary

5   capacity solely for the benefit of appli-

6   cable exempt organizations or persons

7   otherwise described in subclause (I) or

8   clause (i) or (ii).

9 "(3) APPLICABLE EXEMPT ORGANIZATION.—

10 The term 'applicable exempt organization' means—

11   "(A) an organization described in section

12   170(c),

13   "(B) an organization described in section

14   168(h)(2)(A)(iv), or

15   "(C) an organization not described in

16   paragraph (1) or (2) which is described in sec-

17   tion 2055(a) or section 2522(a).

18 "(e) TERMINATION.—This section shall not apply to

19 reportable acquisitions occurring after the date which is

20 2 years after the date of the enactment of this section.".

21   (2) CONFORMING AMENDMENT.—The table of

22 sections for subpart B of part III of subchapter A

23 of chapter 61 is amended by adding at the end the

24 following new item:

"Sec. 6050V. Returns relating to applicable insurance contracts in which certain exempt organizations hold interests.".

(b) PENALTIES.—

(1) IN GENERAL.—Subparagraph (B) of section 6724(d)(1), as amended by this Act, is amended by redesignating clauses (xiv) through (xix) as clauses (xv) through (xx) and by inserting after clause (xiii) the following new clause:

"(xiv) section 6050V (relating to returns relating to applicable insurance contracts in which certain exempt organizations hold interests),".

(2) INTENTIONAL DISREGARD.—Section 6721(e)(2) is amended by striking "or" at the end of subparagraph (B), by striking "and" at the end of subparagraph (C) and inserting "or", and by adding at the end the following new subparagraph:

"(D) in the case of a return required to be filed under section 6050V, 10 percent of the value of the benefit of any contract with respect to which information is required to be included on the return, and".

(c) STUDY.—

(1) IN GENERAL.—The Secretary of the Treasury shall undertake a study on—

(A) the use by tax exempt organizations of applicable insurance contracts (as defined under

1   section 6050V(d)(2) of the Internal Revenue

2   Code of 1986, as added by subsection (a)) for

3   the purpose of sharing the benefits of the orga-

4   nization's insurable interest in individuals in-

5   sured under such contracts with investors, and

6   (B) whether such activities are consistent

7   with the tax exempt status of such organiza-

8   tions.

9   (2) REPORT.—Not later than 30 months after

10 the date of the enactment of this Act, the Secretary

11 of the Treasury shall report on the study conducted

12 under paragraph (1) to the Committee on Finance

13 of the Senate and the Committee on Ways and

14 Means of the House of Representatives.

15 (d) EFFECTIVE DATE.—The amendments made by

16 this section shall apply to acquisitions of contracts after

17 the date of enactment of this Act.

18 **SEC. 1212. INCREASE IN PENALTY EXCISE TAXES RELATING**

19   **TO PUBLIC CHARITIES, SOCIAL WELFARE OR-**

20   **GANIZATIONS, AND PRIVATE FOUNDATIONS.**

21 (a) TAXES ON SELF-DEALING AND EXCESS BENEFIT

22 TRANSACTIONS.—

23   (1) IN GENERAL.—Section 4941(a) (relating to

24   initial taxes) is amended—

1   (A) in paragraph (1), by striking "5 per-

2   cent" and inserting "10 percent", and

3   (B) in paragraph (2), by striking "2½

4   percent" and inserting "5 percent".

5   (2) INCREASED LIMITATION FOR MANAGERS ON

6   SELF-DEALING.—Section 4941(c)(2) is amended by

7   striking "$10,000" each place it appears in the text

8   and heading thereof and inserting "$20,000".

9   (3) INCREASED LIMITATION FOR MANAGERS ON

10   EXCESS BENEFIT TRANSACTIONS.—Section

11   4958(d)(2) is amended by striking "$10,000" and

12   inserting "$20,000".

13   (b) TAXES ON FAILURE TO DISTRIBUTE INCOME.—

14 Section 4942(a) (relating to initial tax) is amended by

15 striking "15 percent" and inserting "30 percent".

16   (c) TAXES ON EXCESS BUSINESS HOLDINGS.—Sec-

17 tion 4943(a)(1) (relating to imposition) is amended by

18 striking "5 percent" and inserting "10 percent".

19   (d) TAXES ON INVESTMENTS WHICH JEOPARDIZE

20 CHARITABLE PURPOSE.—

21   (1) IN GENERAL.—Section 4944(a) (relating to

22   initial taxes) is amended by striking "5 percent"

23   both places it appears and inserting "10 percent".

24   (2) INCREASED LIMITATION FOR MANAGERS.—

25   Section 4944(d)(2) is amended—

1   (A) by striking "$5,000," and inserting

2   "$10,000,", and

3   (B) by striking "$10,000." and inserting

4   "$20,000.".

5 (e) TAXES ON TAXABLE EXPENDITURES.—

6   (1) IN GENERAL.—Section 4945(a) (relating to

7 initial taxes) is amended—

8   (A) in paragraph (1), by striking "10 per-

9   cent" and inserting "20 percent", and

10   (B) in paragraph (2), by striking "2½

11   percent" and inserting "5 percent".

12   (2) INCREASED LIMITATION FOR MANAGERS.—

13 Section 4945(c)(2) is amended—

14   (A) by striking "$5,000," and inserting

15   "$10,000,", and

16   (B) by striking "$10,000." and inserting

17   "$20,000.".

18 (f) EFFECTIVE DATE.—The amendments made by

19 this section shall apply to taxable years beginning after

20 the date of the enactment of this Act.

SEC. 1213. REFORM OF CHARITABLE CONTRIBUTIONS OF CERTAIN EASEMENTS IN REGISTERED HISTORIC DISTRICTS AND REDUCED DEDUCTION FOR PORTION OF QUALIFIED CONSERVATION CONTRIBUTION ATTRIBUTABLE TO REHABILITATION CREDIT.

(a) SPECIAL RULES WITH RESPECT TO BUILDINGS IN REGISTERED HISTORIC DISTRICTS.—

(1) IN GENERAL.—Paragraph (4) of section 170(h) (relating to definition of conservation purpose) is amended by redesignating subparagraph (B) as subparagraph (C) and by inserting after subparagraph (A) the following new subparagraph:

"(B) SPECIAL RULES WITH RESPECT TO BUILDINGS IN REGISTERED HISTORIC DISTRICTS.—In the case of any contribution of a qualified real property interest which is a restriction with respect to the exterior of a building described in subparagraph (C)(ii), such contribution shall not be considered to be exclusively for conservation purposes unless—

"(i) such interest—

"(I) includes a restriction which preserves the entire exterior of the building (including the front, sides, rear, and height of the building), and

1   "(II) prohibits any change in the

2   exterior of the building which is incon-

3   sistent with the historical character of

4   such exterior,

5   "(ii) the donor and donee enter into a

6   written agreement certifying, under pen-

7   alty of perjury, that the donee—

8   "(I) is a qualified organization

9   (as defined in paragraph (3)) with a

10   purpose of environmental protection,

11   land conservation, open space preser-

12   vation, or historic preservation, and

13   "(II) has the resources to man-

14   age and enforce the restriction and a

15   commitment to do so, and

16   "(iii) in the case of any contribution

17   made in a taxable year beginning after the

18   date of the enactment of this subpara-

19   graph, the taxpayer includes with the tax-

20   payer's return for the taxable year of the

21   contribution—

22   "(I) a qualified appraisal (within

23   the meaning of subsection (f)(11)(E))

24   of the qualified property interest,

1   "(II) photographs of the entire

2   exterior of the building, and

3   "(III) a description of all restric-

4   tions on the development of the build-

5   ing.".

6   (b) DISALLOWANCE OF DEDUCTION FOR STRUC-

7 TURES AND LAND IN REGISTERED HISTORIC DIS-

8 TRICTS.—Subparagraph (C) of section 170(h)(4), as re-

9 designated by subsection (a), is amended—

10   (1) by striking "any building, structure, or land

11   area which",

12   (2) by inserting "any building, structure, or

13   land area which" before "is listed" in clause (i), and

14   (3) by inserting "any building which" before "is

15   located" in clause (ii).

16   (c) FILING FEE FOR CERTAIN CONTRIBUTIONS.—

17 Subsection (f) of section 170 (relating to disallowance of

18 deduction in certain cases and special rules) is amended

19 by adding at the end the following new paragraph:

20   "(13) CONTRIBUTIONS OF CERTAIN INTERESTS

21   IN BUILDINGS LOCATED IN REGISTERED HISTORIC

22   DISTRICTS.—

23   "(A) IN GENERAL.—No deduction shall be

24   allowed with respect to any contribution de-

25   scribed in subparagraph (B) unless the tax-

1   payer includes with the return for the taxable

2   year of the contribution a $500 filing fee.

3   "(B) CONTRIBUTION DESCRIBED.—A con-

4   tribution is described in this subparagraph if

5   such contribution is a qualified conservation

6   contribution (as defined in subsection (h))

7   which is a restriction with respect to the exte-

8   rior of a building described in subsection

9   (h)(4)(C)(ii) and for which a deduction is

10   claimed in excess of $10,000.

11   "(C) DEDICATION OF FEE.—Any fee col-

12   lected under this paragraph shall be used for

13   the enforcement of the provisions of subsection

14   (h).".

15   (d) REDUCED DEDUCTION FOR PORTION OF QUALI-

16 FIED CONSERVATION CONTRIBUTION ATTRIBUTABLE TO

17 THE REHABILITATION CREDIT.—Subsection (f) of section

18 170, as amended by subsection (c), is amended by adding

19 at the end the following new paragraph:

20   "(14) REDUCTION FOR AMOUNTS ATTRIB-

21   UTABLE TO REHABILITATION CREDIT.—In the case

22   of any qualified conservation contribution (as de-

23   fined in subsection (h)), the amount of the deduction

24   allowed under this section shall be reduced by an

1 amount which bears the same ratio to the fair mar-

2 ket value of the contribution as—

3   "(A) the sum of the credits allowed to the

4   taxpayer under section 47 for the 5 preceding

5   taxable years with respect to any building which

6   is a part of such contribution, bears to

7   "(B) the fair market value of the building

8   on the date of the contribution.".

9 (e) EFFECTIVE DATES.—

10   (1) SPECIAL RULES FOR BUILDINGS IN REG-

11 ISTERED HISTORIC DISTRICTS.—The amendments

12 made by subsection (a) shall apply to contributions

13 made after July 25, 2006.

14   (2) DISALLOWANCE OF DEDUCTION FOR STRUC-

15 TURES AND LAND; REDUCTION FOR REHABILITA-

16 TION CREDIT.—The amendments made by sub-

17 sections (b) and (d) shall apply to contributions

18 made after the date of the enactment of this Act.

19   (3) FILING FEE.—The amendment made by

20 subsection (c) shall apply to contributions made 180

21 days after the date of the enactment of this Act.

22 **SEC. 1214. CHARITABLE CONTRIBUTIONS OF TAXIDERMY**

23   **PROPERTY.**

24 (a) DENIAL OF LONG-TERM CAPITAL GAIN.—Sub-

25 paragraph (B) of section 170(e)(1) is amended by striking

1   "or" at the end of clause (ii), by inserting "or" at the

2   end of clause (iii), and by inserting after clause (iii) the

3   following new clause:

4   "(iv) of any taxidermy property which

5   is contributed by the person who prepared,

6   stuffed, or mounted the property or by any

7   person who paid or incurred the cost of

8   such preparation, stuffing, or mounting,".

9   (b) TREATMENT OF BASIS.—Subsection (f) of section

10   170, as amended by this Act, is amended by adding at

11   the end the following new paragraph:

12   "(15) SPECIAL RULE FOR TAXIDERMY PROP-

13   ERTY.—

14   "(A) BASIS.—For purposes of this section

15   and notwithstanding section 1012, in the case

16   of a charitable contribution of taxidermy prop-

17   erty which is made by the person who prepared,

18   stuffed, or mounted the property or by any per-

19   son who paid or incurred the cost of such prep-

20   aration, stuffing, or mounting, only the cost of

21   the preparing, stuffing, or mounting shall be in-

22   cluded in the basis of such property.

23   "(B) TAXIDERMY PROPERTY.—For pur-

24   poses of this section, the term 'taxidermy prop-

25   erty' means any work of art which—

1   "(i) is the reproduction or preserva-

2   tion of an animal, in whole or in part,

3   "(ii) is prepared, stuffed, or mounted

4   for purposes of recreating one or more

5   characteristics of such animal, and

6   "(iii) contains a part of the body of

7   the dead animal.".

8   (c) EFFECTIVE DATE.—The amendment made by

9 this section shall apply to contributions made after July

10 25, 2006.

11 **SEC. 1215. RECAPTURE OF TAX BENEFIT FOR CHARITABLE**

12   **CONTRIBUTIONS OF EXEMPT USE PROPERTY**

13   **NOT USED FOR AN EXEMPT USE.**

14   (a) RECAPTURE OF DEDUCTION ON CERTAIN SALES

15 OF EXEMPT USE PROPERTY.—

16   (1) IN GENERAL.—Clause (i) of section

17   170(e)(1)(B) (related to certain contributions of or-

18   dinary income and capital gain property) is amended

19   to read as follows:

20   "(i) of tangible personal property—

21   "(I) if the use by the donee is

22   unrelated to the purpose or function

23   constituting the basis for its exemp-

24   tion under section 501 (or, in the case

25   of a governmental unit, to any pur-

1   pose or function described in sub-

2   section (c)), or

3   "(II) which is applicable property

4   (as defined in paragraph (7)(C))

5   which is sold, exchanged, or otherwise

6   disposed of by the donee before the

7   last day of the taxable year in which

8   the contribution was made and with

9   respect to which the donee has not

10   made a certification in accordance

11   with paragraph (7)(D),".

12   (2) DISPOSITIONS AFTER CLOSE OF TAXABLE

13 YEAR.—Section 170(e) is amended by adding at the

14 end the following new paragraph:

15   "(7) RECAPTURE OF DEDUCTION ON CERTAIN

16 DISPOSITIONS OF EXEMPT USE PROPERTY.—

17   "(A) IN GENERAL.—In the case of an ap-

18   plicable disposition of applicable property, there

19   shall be included in the income of the donor of

20   such property for the taxable year of such

21   donor in which the applicable disposition occurs

22   an amount equal to the excess (if any) of—

23   "(i) the amount of the deduction al-

24   lowed to the donor under this section with

25   respect to such property, over

"(ii) the donor's basis in such property at the time such property was contributed.

"(B) APPLICABLE DISPOSITION.—For purposes of this paragraph, the term 'applicable
disposition' means any sale, exchange, or other
disposition by the donee of applicable property—

"(i) after the last day of the taxable
year of the donor in which such property
was contributed, and

"(ii) before the last day of the 3-year
period beginning on the date of the contribution of such property,

unless the donee makes a certification in accordance with subparagraph (D).

"(C) APPLICABLE PROPERTY.—For purposes of this paragraph, the term 'applicable
property' means charitable deduction property
(as defined in section 6050L(a)(2)(A))—

"(i) which is tangible personal property the use of which is identified by the
donee as related to the purpose or function
constituting the basis of the donee's exemption under section 501, and

1   "(ii) for which a deduction in excess

2   of the donor's basis is allowed.

3   "(D) CERTIFICATION.—A certification

4   meets the requirements of this subparagraph if

5   it is a written statement which is signed under

6   penalty of perjury by an officer of the donee or-

7   ganization and—

8   "(i) which—

9   "(I) certifies that the use of the

10   property by the donee was related to

11   the purpose or function constituting

12   the basis for the donee's exemption

13   under section 501, and

14   "(II) describes how the property

15   was used and how such use furthered

16   such purpose or function, or

17   "(ii) which—

18   "(I) states the intended use of

19   the property by the donee at the time

20   of the contribution, and

21   "(II) certifies that such intended

22   use has become impossible or infeasi-

23   ble to implement.".

(b) REPORTING REQUIREMENTS.—Paragraph (1) of section 6050L(a) (relating to returns relating to certain dispositions of donated property) is amended—

 (1) by striking "2 years" and inserting "3 years", and

 (2) by striking "and" at the end of subparagraph (D), by striking the period at the end of subparagraph (E) and inserting a comma, and by inserting at the end the following:

  "(F) a description of the donee's use of the property, and

  "(G) a statement indicating whether the use of the property was related to the purpose or function constituting the basis for the donee's exemption under section 501.

In any case in which the donee indicates that the use of applicable property (as defined in section 170(e)(7)(C)) was related to the purpose or function constituting the basis for the exemption of the donee under section 501 under subparagraph (G), the donee shall include with the return the certification described in section 170(e)(7)(D) if such certification is made under section 170(e)(7).".

(c) PENALTY.—

1   (1) IN GENERAL.—Part I of subchapter B of

2   chapter 68 (relating to assessable penalties) is

3   amended by inserting after section 6720A the fol-

4   lowing new section:

5 **"SEC. 6720B. FRAUDULENT IDENTIFICATION OF EXEMPT**

6   **USE PROPERTY.**

7   "In addition to any criminal penalty provided by law,

8 any person who identifies applicable property (as defined

9 in section 170(e)(7)(C)) as having a use which is related

10 to a purpose or function constituting the basis for the

11 donee's exemption under section 501 and who knows that

12 such property is not intended for such a use shall pay a

13 penalty of $10,000.".

14   (2) CLERICAL AMENDMENT.—The table of sec-

15   tions for part I of subchapter B of chapter 68 is

16   amended by adding after the item relating to section

17   6720A the following new item:

"Sec. 6720B. Fraudulent identification of exempt use property.".

18   (d) EFFECTIVE DATE.—

19   (1) RECAPTURE.—The amendments made by

20   subsection (a) shall apply to contributions after Sep-

21   tember 1, 2006.

22   (2) REPORTING.—The amendments made by

23   subsection (b) shall apply to returns filed after Sep-

24   tember 1, 2006.

1   (3) PENALTY.—The amendments made by sub-

2 section (c) shall apply to identifications made after

3 the date of the enactment of this Act.

4 **SEC. 1216. LIMITATION OF DEDUCTION FOR CHARITABLE**

5   **CONTRIBUTIONS OF CLOTHING AND HOUSE-**

6   **HOLD ITEMS.**

7   (a) IN GENERAL.—Subsection (f) of section 170, as

8 amended by this Act, is amended by adding at the end

9 the following new paragraph:

10   "(16) CONTRIBUTIONS OF CLOTHING AND

11 HOUSEHOLD ITEMS.—

12   "(A) IN GENERAL.—In the case of an indi-

13   vidual, partnership, or corporation, no deduc-

14   tion shall be allowed under subsection (a) for

15   any contribution of clothing or a household item

16   unless such clothing or household item is in

17   good used condition or better.

18   "(B) ITEMS OF MINIMAL VALUE.—Not-

19   withstanding subparagraph (A), the Secretary

20   may by regulation deny a deduction under sub-

21   section (a) for any contribution of clothing or a

22   household item which has minimal monetary

23   value.

24   "(C) EXCEPTION FOR CERTAIN PROP-

25   ERTY.—Subparagraphs (A) and (B) shall not

1   apply to any contribution of a single item of

2   clothing or a household item for which a deduc-

3   tion of more than $500 is claimed if the tax-

4   payer includes with the taxpayer's return a

5   qualified appraisal with respect to the property.

6   "(D) HOUSEHOLD ITEMS.—For purposes

7   of this paragraph—

8   "(i) IN GENERAL.—The term 'house-

9   hold items' includes furniture, furnishings,

10   electronics, appliances, linens, and other

11   similar items.

12   "(ii) EXCLUDED ITEMS.—Such term

13   does not include—

14   "(I) food,

15   "(II) paintings, antiques, and

16   other objects of art,

17   "(III) jewelry and gems, and

18   "(IV) collections.

19   "(E) SPECIAL RULE FOR PASS-THRU ENTI-

20   TIES.—In the case of a partnership or S cor-

21   poration, this paragraph shall be applied at the

22   entity level, except that the deduction shall be

23   denied at the partner or shareholder level.".

1   (b) EFFECTIVE DATE.—The amendment made by

2 this section shall apply to contributions made after the

3 date of enactment of this Act.

4 **SEC. 1217. MODIFICATION OF RECORDKEEPING REQUIRE-**

5   **MENTS FOR CERTAIN CHARITABLE CON-**

6   **TRIBUTIONS.**

7   (a) RECORDKEEPING REQUIREMENT.—Subsection

8 (f) of section 170, as amended by this Act, is amended

9 by adding at the end the following new paragraph:

10   "(17) RECORDKEEPING.—No deduction shall be

11   allowed under subsection (a) for any contribution of

12   a cash, check, or other monetary gift unless the

13   donor maintains as a record of such contribution a

14   bank record or a written communication from the

15   donee showing the name of the donee organization,

16   the date of the contribution, and the amount of the

17   contribution.".

18   (b) EFFECTIVE DATE.—The amendment made by

19 this section shall apply to contributions made in taxable

20 years beginning after the date of the enactment of this

21 Act.

22 **SEC. 1218. CONTRIBUTIONS OF FRACTIONAL INTERESTS IN**

23   **TANGIBLE PERSONAL PROPERTY.**

24   (a) INCOME TAX.—Section 170 (relating to chari-

25 table, etc., contributions and gifts) is amended by redesig-

1 nating subsection (o) as subsection (p) and by inserting

2 after subsection (n) the following new subsection:

3   "(o) SPECIAL RULES FOR FRACTIONAL GIFTS.—

4   "(1) DENIAL OF DEDUCTION IN CERTAIN

5   CASES.—

6   "(A) IN GENERAL.—No deduction shall be

7   allowed for a contribution of an undivided por-

8   tion of a taxpayer's entire interest in tangible

9   personal property unless all interest in the

10   property is held immediately before such con-

11   tribution by—

12   "(i) the taxpayer, or

13   "(ii) the taxpayer and the donee.

14   "(B) EXCEPTIONS.—The Secretary may,

15   by regulation, provide for exceptions to sub-

16   paragraph (A) in cases where all persons who

17   hold an interest in the property make propor-

18   tional contributions of an undivided portion of

19   the entire interest held by such persons.

20   "(2) VALUATION OF SUBSEQUENT GIFTS.—In

21 the case of any additional contribution, the fair mar-

22 ket value of such contribution shall be determined by

23 using the lesser of—

1   "(A) the fair market value of the property

2   at the time of the initial fractional contribution,

3   or

4   "(B) the fair market value of the property

5   at the time of the additional contribution.

6   "(3) RECAPTURE OF DEDUCTION IN CERTAIN

7 CASES; ADDITION TO TAX.—

8   "(A) RECAPTURE.—The Secretary shall

9   provide for the recapture of the amount of any

10   deduction allowed under this section (plus inter-

11   est) with respect to any contribution of an undi-

12   vided portion of a taxpayer's entire interest in

13   tangible personal property—

14   "(i) in any case in which the donor

15   does not contribute all of the remaining in-

16   terest in such property to the donee (or, if

17   such donee is no longer in existence, to any

18   person described in section 170(c)) before

19   the earlier of—

20   "(I) the date that is 10 years

21   after the date of the initial fractional

22   contribution, or

23   "(II) the date of the death of the

24   donor, and

1   "(ii) in any case in which the donee

2   has not, during the period beginning on

3   the date of the initial fractional contribu-

4   tion and ending on the date described in

5   clause (i)—

6   "(I) had substantial physical pos-

7   session of the property, and

8   "(II) used the property in a use

9   which is related to a purpose or func-

10   tion constituting the basis for the or-

11   ganizations' exemption under section

12   501.

13   "(B) ADDITION TO TAX.—The tax imposed

14 under this chapter for any taxable year for

15 which there is a recapture under subparagraph

16 (A) shall be increased by 10 percent of the

17 amount so recaptured.

18   "(4) DEFINITIONS.—For purposes of this sub-

19 section—

20   "(A) ADDITIONAL CONTRIBUTION.—The

21 term 'additional contribution' means any chari-

22 table contribution by the taxpayer of any inter-

23 est in property with respect to which the tax-

24 payer has previously made an initial fractional

25 contribution.

829

"(B) Initial fractional contribu-
tion.—The term 'initial fractional contribution'
means, with respect to any taxpayer, the first
charitable contribution of an undivided portion
of the taxpayer's entire interest in any tangible
personal property.".

(b) Estate Tax.—Section 2055 (relating to transfers for public, charitable, and religious uses) is amended
by redesignating subsection (g) as subsection (h) and by
inserting after subsection (f) the following new subsection:

"(g) Valuation of Subsequent Gifts.—

"(1) In general.—In the case of any additional contribution, the fair market value of such
contribution shall be determined by using the lesser
of—

"(A) the fair market value of the property
at the time of the initial fractional contribution,
or

"(B) the fair market value of the property
at the time of the additional contribution.

"(2) Definitions.—For purposes of this paragraph—

"(A) Additional contribution.—The
term 'additional contribution' means a bequest,
legacy, devise, or transfer described in sub-

1   section (a) of any interest in a property with re-

2   spect to which the decedent had previously

3   made an initial fractional contribution.

4   "(B) INITIAL FRACTIONAL CONTRIBU-

5   TION.—The term 'initial fractional contribution'

6   means, with respect to any decedent, any chari-

7   table contribution of an undivided portion of

8   the decedent's entire interest in any tangible

9   personal property for which a deduction was al-

10   lowed under section 170.".

11   (c) GIFT TAX.—Section 2522 (relating to charitable

12 and similar gifts) is amended by redesignating subsection

13 (e) as subsection (f) and by inserting after subsection (d)

14 the following new subsection:

15   "(e) SPECIAL RULES FOR FRACTIONAL GIFTS.—

16   "(1) DENIAL OF DEDUCTION IN CERTAIN

17   CASES.—

18   "(A) IN GENERAL.—No deduction shall be

19   allowed for a contribution of an undivided por-

20   tion of a taxpayer's entire interest in tangible

21   personal property unless all interest in the

22   property is held immediately before such con-

23   tribution by—

24   "(i) the taxpayer, or

25   "(ii) the taxpayer and the donee.

1   "(B) EXCEPTIONS.—The Secretary may,

2 by regulation, provide for exceptions to sub-

3 paragraph (A) in cases where all persons who

4 hold an interest in the property make propor-

5 tional contributions of an undivided portion of

6 the entire interest held by such persons.

7   "(2) VALUATION OF SUBSEQUENT GIFTS.—In

8 the case of any additional contribution, the fair mar-

9 ket value of such contribution shall be determined by

10 using the lesser of—

11   "(A) the fair market value of the property

12 at the time of the initial fractional contribution,

13 or

14   "(B) the fair market value of the property

15 at the time of the additional contribution.

16   "(3) RECAPTURE OF DEDUCTION IN CERTAIN

17 CASES; ADDITION TO TAX.—

18   "(A) IN GENERAL.—The Secretary shall

19 provide for the recapture of an amount equal to

20 any deduction allowed under this section (plus

21 interest) with respect to any contribution of an

22 undivided portion of a taxpayer's entire interest

23 in tangible personal property—

24   "(i) in any case in which the donor

25 does not contribute all of the remaining in-

832

1   terest in such property to the donee (or, if

2   such donee is no longer in existence, to any

3   person described in section 170(c)) before

4   the earlier of—

5   "(I) the date that is 10 years

6   after the date of the initial fractional

7   contribution, or

8   "(II) the date of the death of the

9   donor, and

10   "(ii) in any case in which the donee

11   has not, during the period beginning on

12   the date of the initial fractional contribu-

13   tion and ending on the date described in

14   clause (i)—

15   "(I) had substantial physical pos-

16   session of the property, and

17   "(II) used the property in a use

18   which is related to a purpose or func-

19   tion constituting the basis for the or-

20   ganizations' exemption under section

21   501.

22   "(B) ADDITION TO TAX.—The tax imposed

23   under this chapter for any taxable year for

24   which there is a recapture under subparagraph

(A) shall be increased by 10 percent of the amount so recaptured.

"(4) DEFINITIONS.—For purposes of this subsection—

"(A) ADDITIONAL CONTRIBUTION.—The term 'additional contribution' means any gift for which a deduction is allowed under subsection (a) or (b) of any interest in a property with respect to which the donor has previously made an initial fractional contribution.

"(B) INITIAL FRACTIONAL CONTRIBU-TION.—The term 'initial fractional contribution' means, with respect to any donor, the first gift of an undivided portion of the donor's entire interest in any tangible personal property for which a deduction is allowed under subsection (a) or (b).".

(d) EFFECTIVE DATE.—The amendments made by this section shall apply to contributions, bequests, and gifts made after the date of the enactment of this Act.

SEC. 1219. PROVISIONS RELATING TO SUBSTANTIAL AND GROSS OVERSTATEMENTS OF VALUATIONS.

(a) MODIFICATION OF THRESHOLDS FOR SUBSTAN-TIAL AND GROSS VALUATION MISSTATEMENTS.—

834

1 (1) SUBSTANTIAL VALUATION
2 MISSTATEMENT.—

3 (A) INCOME TAXES.—Subparagraph (A) of
4 section 6662(e)(1) (relating to substantial valu-
5 ation misstatement under chapter 1) is amend-
6 ed by striking "200 percent" and inserting
7 "150 percent".

8 (B) ESTATE AND GIFT TAXES.—Paragraph
9 (1) of section 6662(g) is amended by striking
10 "50 percent" and inserting "65 percent".

11 (2) GROSS VALUATION MISSTATEMENT.—

12 (A) INCOME TAXES.—Clauses (i) and (ii)
13 of section 6662(h)(2)(A) (relating to increase in
14 penalty in case of gross valuation
15 misstatements) are amended to read as follows:

16 "(i) in paragraph (1)(A), '200 per-
17 cent' for '150 percent',

18 "(ii) in paragraph (1)(B)(i)—

19 "(I) '400 percent' for '200 per-
20 cent', and

21 "(II) '25 percent' for '50 per-
22 cent', and".

23 (B) ESTATE AND GIFT TAXES.—Subpara-
24 graph (C) of section 6662(h)(2) is amended by

1   striking " '25 percent' for '50 percent' " and in-

2   serting " '40 percent' for '65 percent' ".

3   (3) ELIMINATION OF REASONABLE CAUSE EX-

4   CEPTION FOR GROSS MISSTATEMENTS.—Section

5   6664(c)(2) (relating to reasonable cause exception

6   for underpayments) is amended by striking "para-

7   graph (1) shall not apply unless" and inserting

8   "paragraph (1) shall not apply. The preceding sen-

9   tence shall not apply to a substantial valuation over-

10   statement under chapter 1 if".

11   (b) PENALTY ON APPRAISERS WHOSE APPRAISALS

12 RESULT IN SUBSTANTIAL OR GROSS VALUATION

13 MISSTATEMENTS.—

14   (1) IN GENERAL.—Part I of subchapter B of

15   chapter 68 (relating to assessable penalties) is

16   amended by inserting after section 6695 the fol-

17   lowing new section:

18 **"SEC. 6695A. SUBSTANTIAL AND GROSS VALUATION**

19   **MISSTATEMENTS ATTRIBUTABLE TO INCOR-**

20   **RECT APPRAISALS.**

21   "(a) IMPOSITION OF PENALTY.—If—

22   "(1) a person prepares an appraisal of the

23   value of property and such person knows, or reason-

24   ably should have known, that the appraisal would be

1   used in connection with a return or a claim for re-

2   fund, and

3   "(2) the claimed value of the property on a re-

4   turn or claim for refund which is based on such ap-

5   praisal results in a substantial valuation

6   misstatement under chapter 1 (within the meaning

7   of section 6662(e)), or a gross valuation

8   misstatement (within the meaning of section

9   6662(h)), with respect to such property, then such

10   person shall pay a penalty in the amount determined

11   under subsection (b).

12   "(b) AMOUNT OF PENALTY.—The amount of the

13 penalty imposed under subsection (a) on any person with

14 respect to an appraisal shall be equal to the lesser of—

15   "(1) the greater of—

16   "(A) 10 percent of the amount of the un-

17   derpayment (as defined in section 6664(a)) at-

18   tributable to the misstatement described in sub-

19   section (a)(2), or

20   "(B) $1,000, or

21   "(2) 125 percent of the gross income received

22   by the person described in subsection (a)(1) from

23   the preparation of the appraisal.

24   "(c) EXCEPTION.—No penalty shall be imposed

25 under subsection (a) if the person establishes to the satis-

1 faction of the Secretary that the value established in the

2 appraisal was more likely than not the proper value.".

3   (2) RULES APPLICABLE TO PENALTY.—Section

4   6696 (relating to rules applicable with respect to

5   sections 6694 and 6695) is amended—

6   (A) by striking "6694 and 6695" each

7   place it appears in the text and heading thereof

8   and inserting "6694, 6695, and 6695A", and

9   (B) by striking "6694 or 6695" each place

10   it appears in the text and inserting "6694,

11   6695, or 6695A".

12   (3) CONFORMING AMENDMENT.—The table of

13   sections for part I of subchapter B of chapter 68 is

14   amended by striking the item relating to section

15   6696 and inserting the following new items:

"Sec. 6695A. Substantial and gross valuation misstatements attributable to in-
        correct appraisals.
"Sec. 6696. Rules applicable with respect to sections 6694, 6695, and 6695A.".

16   (c) QUALIFIED APPRAISERS AND APPRAISALS.—

17   (1) IN GENERAL.—Subparagraph (E) of section

18   170(f)(11) is amended to read as follows:

19   "(E) QUALIFIED APPRAISAL AND AP-

20   PRAISER.—For purposes of this paragraph—

21   "(i) QUALIFIED APPRAISAL.—The

22   term 'qualified appraisal' means, with re-

23   spect to any property, an appraisal of such

24   property which—

1   "(I) is treated for purposes of

2   this paragraph as a qualified ap-

3   praisal under regulations or other

4   guidance prescribed by the Secretary,

5   and

6   "(II) is conducted by a qualified

7   appraiser in accordance with generally

8   accepted appraisal standards and any

9   regulations or other guidance pre-

10   scribed under subclause (I).

11   "(ii) QUALIFIED APPRAISER.—Except

12   as provided in clause (iii), the term 'quali-

13   fied appraiser' means an individual who—

14   "(I) has earned an appraisal des-

15   ignation from a recognized profes-

16   sional appraiser organization or has

17   otherwise met minimum education

18   and experience requirements set forth

19   in regulations prescribed by the Sec-

20   retary,

21   "(II) regularly performs apprais-

22   als for which the individual receives

23   compensation, and

24   "(III) meets such other require-

25   ments as may be prescribed by the

1   Secretary in regulations or other guid-

2   ance.

3   "(iii) SPECIFIC APPRAISALS.—An in-

4   dividual shall not be treated as a qualified

5   appraiser with respect to any specific ap-

6   praisal unless—

7   "(I) the individual demonstrates

8   verifiable education and experience in

9   valuing the type of property subject to

10   the appraisal, and

11   "(II) the individual has not been

12   prohibited from practicing before the

13   Internal Revenue Service by the Sec-

14   retary under section 330(c) of title

15   31, United States Code, at any time

16   during the 3-year period ending on

17   the date of the appraisal.".

18   (2) REASONABLE CAUSE EXCEPTION.—Sub-

19   paragraphs (B) and (C) of section 6664(c)(3) are

20   amended to read as follows:

21   "(B) QUALIFIED APPRAISAL.—The term

22   'qualified appraisal' has the meaning given such

23   term by section 170(f)(11)(E)(i).

1   "(C) QUALIFIED APPRAISER.—The term

2   'qualified appraiser' has the meaning given such

3   term by section 170(f)(11)(E)(ii).".

4   (d) DISCIPLINARY ACTIONS AGAINST APPRAISERS.—

5 Section 330(c) of title 31, United States Code, is amended

6 by striking "with respect to whom a penalty has been as-

7 sessed under section 6701(a) of the Internal Revenue

8 Code of 1986".

9   (e) EFFECTIVE DATES.—

10   (1) MISSTATEMENT PENALTIES.—Except as

11   provided in paragraph (3), the amendments made by

12   subsection (a) shall apply to returns filed after the

13   date of the enactment of this Act.

14   (2) APPRAISER PROVISIONS.—Except as pro-

15   vided in paragraph (3), the amendments made by

16   subsections (b), (c), and (d) shall apply to appraisals

17   prepared with respect to returns or submissions filed

18   after the date of the enactment of this Act.

19   (3) SPECIAL RULE FOR CERTAIN EASE-

20   MENTS.—In the case of a contribution of a qualified

21   real property interest which is a restriction with re-

22   spect to the exterior of a building described in sec-

23   tion 170(h)(4)(C)(ii) of the Internal Revenue Code

24   of 1986, and an appraisal with respect to the con-

25   tribution, the amendments made by subsections (a)

1 and (b) shall apply to returns filed after July 25,

2 2006.

3 **SEC. 1220. ADDITIONAL STANDARDS FOR CREDIT COUN-**

4 **SELING ORGANIZATIONS.**

5 (a) IN GENERAL.—Section 501 (relating to exemp-

6 tion from tax on corporations, certain trusts, etc.) is

7 amended by redesignating subsection (q) as subsection (r)

8 and by inserting after subsection (p) the following new

9 subsection:

10 "(q) SPECIAL RULES FOR CREDIT COUNSELING OR-

11 GANIZATIONS.—

12 "(1) IN GENERAL.—An organization with re-

13 spect to which the provision of credit counseling

14 services is a substantial purpose shall not be exempt

15 from tax under subsection (a) unless such organiza-

16 tion is described in paragraph (3) or (4) of sub-

17 section (c) and such organization is organized and

18 operated in accordance with the following require-

19 ments:

20 "(A) The organization—

21 "(i) provides credit counseling services

22 tailored to the specific needs and cir-

23 cumstances of consumers,

24 "(ii) makes no loans to debtors (other

25 than loans with no fees or interest) and

1   does not negotiate the making of loans on

2   behalf of debtors,

3   "(iii) provides services for the purpose

4   of improving a consumer's credit record,

5   credit history, or credit rating only to the

6   extent that such services are incidental to

7   providing credit counseling services, and

8   "(iv) does not charge any separately

9   stated fee for services for the purpose of

10   improving any consumer's credit record,

11   credit history, or credit rating.

12   "(B) The organization does not refuse to

13   provide credit counseling services to a consumer

14   due to the inability of the consumer to pay, the

15   ineligibility of the consumer for debt manage-

16   ment plan enrollment, or the unwillingness of

17   the consumer to enroll in a debt management

18   plan.

19   "(C) The organization establishes and im-

20   plements a fee policy which—

21   "(i) requires that any fees charged to

22   a consumer for services are reasonable,

23   "(ii) allows for the waiver of fees if

24   the consumer is unable to pay, and

1   "(iii) except to the extent allowed by

2   State law, prohibits charging any fee based

3   in whole or in part on a percentage of the

4   consumer's debt, the consumer's payments

5   to be made pursuant to a debt manage-

6   ment plan, or the projected or actual sav-

7   ings to the consumer resulting from enroll-

8   ing in a debt management plan.

9   "(D) At all times the organization has a

10 board of directors or other governing body—

11   "(i) which is controlled by persons

12   who represent the broad interests of the

13   public, such as public officials acting in

14   their capacities as such, persons having

15   special knowledge or expertise in credit or

16   financial education, and community lead-

17   ers,

18   "(ii) not more than 20 percent of the

19   voting power of which is vested in persons

20   who are employed by the organization or

21   who will benefit financially, directly or in-

22   directly, from the organization's activities

23   (other than through the receipt of reason-

24   able directors' fees or the repayment of

25   consumer debt to creditors other than the

1 credit counseling organization or its affili-

2 ates), and

3   "(iii) not more than 49 percent of the

4 voting power of which is vested in persons

5 who are employed by the organization or

6 who will benefit financially, directly or in-

7 directly, from the organization's activities

8 (other than through the receipt of reason-

9 able directors' fees).

10   "(E) The organization does not own more

11 than 35 percent of—

12   "(i) the total combined voting power

13 of any corporation (other than a corpora-

14 tion which is an organization described in

15 subsection (c)(3) and exempt from tax

16 under subsection (a)) which is in the trade

17 or business of lending money, repairing

18 credit, or providing debt management plan

19 services, payment processing, or similar

20 services,

21   "(ii) the profits interest of any part-

22 nership (other than a partnership which is

23 an organization described in subsection

24 (c)(3) and exempt from tax under sub-

25 section (a)) which is in the trade or busi-

ness of lending money, repairing credit, or
providing debt management plan services,
payment processing, or similar services,
and

"(iii) the beneficial interest of any
trust or estate (other than a trust which is
an organization described in subsection
(c)(3) and exempt from tax under subsection (a)) which is in the trade or business of lending money, repairing credit, or
providing debt management plan services,
payment processing, or similar services.

"(F) The organization receives no amount
for providing referrals to others for debt management plan services, and pays no amount to
others for obtaining referrals of consumers.

"(2) ADDITIONAL REQUIREMENTS FOR ORGANI-
ZATIONS DESCRIBED IN SUBSECTION (c)(3).—

"(A) IN GENERAL.—In addition to the requirements under paragraph (1), an organization with respect to which the provision of credit counseling services is a substantial purpose
and which is described in paragraph (3) of subsection (c) shall not be exempt from tax under
subsection (a) unless such organization is orga-

nized and operated in accordance with the following requirements:

"(i) The organization does not solicit
contributions from consumers during the
initial counseling process or while the consumer is receiving services from the organization.

"(ii) The aggregate revenues of the
organization which are from payments of
creditors of consumers of the organization
and which are attributable to debt management plan services do not exceed the applicable percentage of the total revenues of
the organization.

"(B) APPLICABLE PERCENTAGE.—

"(i) IN GENERAL.—For purposes of
subparagraph (A)(ii), the applicable percentage is 50 percent.

"(ii) TRANSITION RULE.—Notwithstanding clause (i), in the case of an organization with respect to which the provision of credit counseling services is a substantial purpose and which is described in
paragraph (3) of subsection (c) and exempt from tax under subsection (a) on the

1   date of the enactment of this subsection,

2   the applicable percentage is—

3   "(I) 80 percent for the first tax-

4   able year of such organization begin-

5   ning after the date which is 1 year

6   after the date of the enactment of this

7   subsection, and

8   "(II) 70 percent for the second

9   such taxable year beginning after such

10   date, and

11   "(III) 60 percent for the third

12   such taxable year beginning after such

13   date.

14   "(3) ADDITIONAL REQUIREMENT FOR ORGANI-

15 ZATIONS DESCRIBED IN SUBSECTION (c)(4).—In ad-

16 dition to the requirements under paragraph (1), an

17 organization with respect to which the provision of

18 credit counseling services is a substantial purpose

19 and which is described in paragraph (4) of sub-

20 section (c) shall not be exempt from tax under sub-

21 section (a) unless such organization notifies the Sec-

22 retary, in such manner as the Secretary may by reg-

23 ulations prescribe, that it is applying for recognition

24 as a credit counseling organization.

848

"(4) CREDIT COUNSELING SERVICES; DEBT
MANAGEMENT PLAN SERVICES.—For purposes of
this subsection—

"(A) CREDIT COUNSELING SERVICES.—
The term 'credit counseling services' means—

"(i) the providing of educational information to the general public on budgeting,
personal finance, financial literacy, saving
and spending practices, and the sound use
of consumer credit,

"(ii) the assisting of individuals and
families with financial problems by providing them with counseling, or

"(iii) a combination of the activities
described in clauses (i) and (ii).

"(B) DEBT MANAGEMENT PLAN SERV-
ICES.—The term 'debt management plan services' means services related to the repayment,
consolidation, or restructuring of a consumer's
debt, and includes the negotiation with creditors
of lower interest rates, the waiver or reduction
of fees, and the marketing and processing of
debt management plans.".

(b) DEBT MANAGEMENT PLAN SERVICES TREATED
AS AN UNRELATED BUSINESS.—Section 513 (relating to

1 unrelated trade or business) is amended by adding at the

2 end the following:

3   "(j) DEBT MANAGEMENT PLAN SERVICES.—The

4 term 'unrelated trade or business' includes the provision

5 of debt management plan services (as defined in section

6 501(q)(4)(B)) by any organization other than an organiza-

7 tion which meets the requirements of section 501(q).".

8   (c) EFFECTIVE DATE.—

9   (1) IN GENERAL.—Except as provided in para-

10   graph (2), the amendments made by this section

11   shall apply to taxable years beginning after the date

12   of the enactment of this Act.

13   (2) TRANSITION RULE FOR EXISTING ORGANI-

14   ZATIONS.—In the case of any organization described

15   in paragraph (3) or (4) section 501(c) of the Inter-

16   nal Revenue Code of 1986 and with respect to which

17   the provision of credit counseling services is a sub-

18   stantial purpose on the date of the enactment of this

19   Act, the amendments made by this section shall

20   apply to taxable years beginning after the date

21   which is 1 year after the date of the enactment of

22   this Act.

23 **SEC. 1221. EXPANSION OF THE BASE OF TAX ON PRIVATE**

24   **FOUNDATION NET INVESTMENT INCOME.**

25   (a) GROSS INVESTMENT INCOME.—

1   (1) IN GENERAL.—Paragraph (2) of section

2   4940(c) (relating to gross investment income) is

3   amended by adding at the end the following new

4   sentence: "Such term shall also include income from

5   sources similar to those in the preceding sentence.".

6   (2) CONFORMING AMENDMENT.—Subsection (e)

7   of section 509 (relating to gross investment income)

8   is amended by adding at the end the following new

9   sentence: "Such term shall also include income from

10   sources similar to those in the preceding sentence.".

11   (b) CAPITAL GAIN NET INCOME.—Paragraph (4) of

12 section 4940(c) (relating to capital gains and losses) is

13 amended—

14   (1) in subparagraph (A), by striking "used for

15   the production of interest, dividends, rents, and roy-

16   alties" and inserting "used for the production of

17   gross investment income (as defined in paragraph

18   (2))",

19   (2) in subparagraph (C), by inserting "or

20   carrybacks" after "carryovers", and

21   (3) by adding at the end the following new sub-

22   paragraph:

23   "(D) Except to the extent provided by reg-

24   ulation, under rules similar to the rules of sec-

25   tion 1031 (including the exception under sub-

1   section (a)(2) thereof), no gain or loss shall be

2   taken into account with respect to any portion

3   of property used for a period of not less than

4   1 year for a purpose or function constituting

5   the basis of the private foundation's exemption

6   if the entire property is exchanged immediately

7   following such period solely for property of like

8   kind which is to be used primarily for a purpose

9   or function constituting the basis for such foun-

10   dation's exemption.''.

11   (c) EFFECTIVE DATE.—The amendments made by

12 this section shall apply to taxable years beginning after

13 the date of the enactment of this Act.

14 **SEC. 1222. DEFINITION OF CONVENTION OR ASSOCIATION**

15   **OF CHURCHES.**

16   Section 7701 (relating to definitions) is amended by

17 redesignating subsection (o) as subsection (p) and by in-

18 serting after subsection (n) the following new subsection:

19   ''(o) CONVENTION OR ASSOCIATION OF CHURCH-

20 ES.—For purposes of this title, any organization which is

21 otherwise a convention or association of churches shall not

22 fail to so qualify merely because the membership of such

23 organization includes individuals as well as churches or be-

24 cause individuals have voting rights in such organiza-

25 tion.''.

SEC. 1223. NOTIFICATION REQUIREMENT FOR ENTITIES NOT CURRENTLY REQUIRED TO FILE.

(a) IN GENERAL.—Section 6033 (relating to returns by exempt organizations), as amended by this Act, is amended by redesignating subsection (i) as subsection (j) and by inserting after subsection (h) the following new subsection:

"(i) ADDITIONAL NOTIFICATION REQUIREMENTS.— Any organization the gross receipts of which in any taxable year result in such organization being referred to in subsection (a)(3)(A)(ii) or (a)(3)(B)—

"(1) shall furnish annually, in electronic form, and at such time and in such manner as the Secretary may by regulations prescribe, information setting forth—

"(A) the legal name of the organization,

"(B) any name under which such organization operates or does business,

"(C) the organization's mailing address and Internet web site address (if any),

"(D) the organization's taxpayer identification number,

"(E) the name and address of a principal officer, and

1   "(F) evidence of the continuing basis for

2   the organization's exemption from the filing re-

3   quirements under subsection (a)(1), and

4   "(2) upon the termination of the existence of

5   the organization, shall furnish notice of such termi-

6   nation.".

7   (b) LOSS OF EXEMPT STATUS FOR FAILURE TO FILE

8 RETURN OR NOTICE.—Section 6033 (relating to returns

9 by exempt organizations), as amended by subsection (a),

10 is amended by redesignating subsection (j) as subsection

11 (k) and by inserting after subsection (i) the following new

12 subsection:

13   "(j) LOSS OF EXEMPT STATUS FOR FAILURE TO

14 FILE RETURN OR NOTICE.—

15   "(1) IN GENERAL.—If an organization de-

16   scribed in subsection (a)(1) or (i) fails to file an an-

17   nual return or notice required under either sub-

18   section for 3 consecutive years, such organization's

19   status as an organization exempt from tax under

20   section 501(a) shall be considered revoked on and

21   after the date set by the Secretary for the filing of

22   the third annual return or notice. The Secretary

23   shall publish and maintain a list of any organization

24   the status of which is so revoked.

1   "(2) APPLICATION NECESSARY FOR REINSTATE-

2   MENT.—Any organization the tax-exempt status of

3   which is revoked under paragraph (1) must apply in

4   order to obtain reinstatement of such status regard-

5   less of whether such organization was originally re-

6   quired to make such an application.

7   "(3) RETROACTIVE REINSTATEMENT IF REA-

8   SONABLE CAUSE SHOWN FOR FAILURE.—If, upon

9   application for reinstatement of status as an organi-

10   zation exempt from tax under section 501(a), an or-

11   ganization described in paragraph (1) can show to

12   the satisfaction of the Secretary evidence of reason-

13   able cause for the failure described in such para-

14   graph, the organization's exempt status may, in the

15   discretion of the Secretary, be reinstated effective

16   from the date of the revocation under such para-

17   graph.".

18   (c) NO DECLARATORY JUDGMENT RELIEF.—Section

19 7428(b) (relating to limitations) is amended by adding at

20 the end the following new paragraph:

21   "(4) NONAPPLICATION FOR CERTAIN REVOCA-

22   TIONS.—No action may be brought under this sec-

23   tion with respect to any revocation of status de-

24   scribed in section 6033(j)(1).".

1   (d) No MONETARY PENALTY FOR FAILURE TO NO-

2 TIFY.—Section 6652(c)(1) (relating to annual returns

3 under section 6033 or 6012(a)(6)) is amended by adding

4 at the end the following new subparagraph:

5   "(E) No PENALTY FOR CERTAIN ANNUAL

6   NOTICES.—This paragraph shall not apply with

7   respect to any notice required under section

8   6033(i).".

9   (e) SECRETARIAL OUTREACH REQUIREMENTS.—

10   (1) NOTICE REQUIREMENT.—The Secretary of

11   the Treasury shall notify in a timely manner every

12   organization described in section 6033(i) of the In-

13   ternal Revenue Code of 1986 (as added by this sec-

14   tion) of the requirement under such section 6033(i)

15   and of the penalty established under section 6033(j)

16   of such Code—

17   (A) by mail, in the case of any organiza-

18   tion the identity and address of which is in-

19   cluded in the list of exempt organizations main-

20   tained by the Secretary, and

21   (B) by Internet or other means of out-

22   reach, in the case of any other organization.

23   (2) LOSS OF STATUS PENALTY FOR FAILURE TO

24   FILE RETURN.—The Secretary of the Treasury shall

25   publicize, in a timely manner in appropriate forms

1 and instructions and through other appropriate

2 means, the penalty established under section 6033(j)

3 of such Code for the failure to file a return under

4 subsection (a)(1) or (i) of section 6033 of such

5 Code.

6 (f) EFFECTIVE DATE.—The amendments made by

7 this section shall apply to notices and returns with respect

8 to annual periods beginning after 2006.

9 **SEC. 1224. DISCLOSURE TO STATE OFFICIALS RELATING TO**

10 **EXEMPT ORGANIZATIONS.**

11 (a) IN GENERAL.—Subsection (c) of section 6104 is

12 amended by striking paragraph (2) and inserting the fol-

13 lowing new paragraphs:

14 "(2) DISCLOSURE OF PROPOSED ACTIONS RE-

15 LATED TO CHARITABLE ORGANIZATIONS.—

16 "(A) SPECIFIC NOTIFICATIONS.—In the

17 case of an organization to which paragraph (1)

18 applies, the Secretary may disclose to the ap-

19 propriate State officer—

20 "(i) a notice of proposed refusal to

21 recognize such organization as an organi-

22 zation described in section 501(c)(3) or a

23 notice of proposed revocation of such orga-

24 nization's recognition as an organization

25 exempt from taxation,

1   "(ii) the issuance of a letter of pro-

2   posed deficiency of tax imposed under sec-

3   tion 507 or chapter 41 or 42, and

4   "(iii) the names, addresses, and tax-

5   payer identification numbers of organiza-

6   tions which have applied for recognition as

7   organizations described in section

8   501(c)(3).

9   "(B) ADDITIONAL DISCLOSURES.—Returns

10 and return information of organizations with

11 respect to which information is disclosed under

12 subparagraph (A) may be made available for in-

13 spection by or disclosed to an appropriate State

14 officer.

15   "(C) PROCEDURES FOR DISCLOSURE.—In-

16 formation may be inspected or disclosed under

17 subparagraph (A) or (B) only—

18   "(i) upon written request by an ap-

19   propriate State officer, and

20   "(ii) for the purpose of, and only to

21   the extent necessary in, the administration

22   of State laws regulating such organiza-

23   tions.

24 Such information may only be inspected by or

25 disclosed to a person other than the appropriate

1   State officer if such person is an officer or em-

2   ployee of the State and is designated by the ap-

3   propriate State officer to receive the returns or

4   return information under this paragraph on be-

5   half of the appropriate State officer.

6   "(D) DISCLOSURES OTHER THAN BY RE-

7   QUEST.—The Secretary may make available for

8   inspection or disclose returns and return infor-

9   mation of an organization to which paragraph

10   (1) applies to an appropriate State officer of

11   any State if the Secretary determines that such

12   returns or return information may constitute

13   evidence of noncompliance under the laws with-

14   in the jurisdiction of the appropriate State offi-

15   cer.

16   "(3) DISCLOSURE WITH RESPECT TO CERTAIN

17   OTHER EXEMPT ORGANIZATIONS.—Upon written re-

18   quest by an appropriate State officer, the Secretary

19   may make available for inspection or disclosure re-

20   turns and return information of any organization de-

21   scribed in section 501(c) (other than organizations

22   described in paragraph (1) or (3) thereof) for the

23   purpose of, and only to the extent necessary in, the

24   administration of State laws regulating the solicita-

25   tion or administration of the charitable funds or

charitable assets of such organizations. Such information may only be inspected by or disclosed to a person other than the appropriate State officer if such person is an officer or employee of the State and is designated by the appropriate State officer to receive the returns or return information under this paragraph on behalf of the appropriate State officer.

"(4) USE IN CIVIL JUDICIAL AND ADMINISTRATIVE PROCEEDINGS.—Returns and return information disclosed pursuant to this subsection may be disclosed in civil administrative and civil judicial proceedings pertaining to the enforcement of State laws regulating such organizations in a manner prescribed by the Secretary similar to that for tax administration proceedings under section 6103(h)(4).

"(5) NO DISCLOSURE IF IMPAIRMENT.—Returns and return information shall not be disclosed under this subsection, or in any proceeding described in paragraph (4), to the extent that the Secretary determines that such disclosure would seriously impair Federal tax administration.

"(6) DEFINITIONS.—For purposes of this subsection—

"(A) RETURN AND RETURN INFORMATION.—The terms 'return' and 'return informa-

1   tion' have the respective meanings given to such

2   terms by section 6103(b).

3   "(B) APPROPRIATE STATE OFFICER.—The

4   term 'appropriate State officer' means—

5   "(i) the State attorney general,

6   "(ii) the State tax officer,

7   "(iii) in the case of an organization to

8   which paragraph (1) applies, any other

9   State official charged with overseeing orga-

10   nizations of the type described in section

11   501(c)(3), and

12   "(iv) in the case of an organization to

13   which paragraph (3) applies, the head of

14   an agency designated by the State attorney

15   general as having primary responsibility

16   for overseeing the solicitation of funds for

17   charitable purposes.".

18 (b) CONFORMING AMENDMENTS.—

19   (1) Paragraph (2) of section 6103(a) is amend-

20 ed by inserting "or section 6104(c)" after "this sec-

21 tion".

22   (2) Subparagraph (A) of section 6103(p)(3) is

23 amended by inserting "and section 6104(c)" after

24 "section" in the first sentence.

1   (3) Paragraph (4) of section 6103(p) is amend-
2 ed—

3   (A) in the matter preceding subparagraph
4   (A), by inserting ", any appropriate State offi-
5   cer (as defined in section 6104(c))," before "or
6   any other person",

7   (B) in subparagraph (F)(i), by inserting
8   "any appropriate State officer (as defined in
9   section 6104(c))," before "or any other per-
10   son", and

11   (C) in the matter following subparagraph
12   (F), by inserting ", an appropriate State officer
13   (as defined in section 6104(c))," after "includ-
14   ing an agency" each place it appears.

15   (4) The heading for paragraph (1) of section
16 6104(c) is amended by inserting "FOR CHARITABLE
17 ORGANIZATIONS" after "RULE".

18   (5) Paragraph (2) of section 7213(a) is amend-
19 ed by inserting "or under section 6104(c)" after
20 "6103".

21   (6) Paragraph (2) of section 7213A(a) is
22 amended by inserting "or under section 6104(c)"
23 after "7213(a)(2)".

1   (7) Paragraph (2) of section 7431(a) is amend-

2   ed by inserting " or in violation of section 6104(c)"

3   after "6103".

4   (c) EFFECTIVE DATE.—The amendments made by

5 this section shall take effect on the date of the enactment

6 of this Act but shall not apply to requests made before

7 such date.

8 SEC. 1225. PUBLIC DISCLOSURE OF INFORMATION RELAT-

9   ING TO UNRELATED BUSINESS INCOME TAX

10   RETURNS.

11   (a) IN GENERAL.—Subparagraph (A) of section

12 6104(d)(1) is amended by redesignating clauses (ii) and

13 (iii) as clauses (iii) and (iv), respectively, and by inserting

14 after clause (i) the following new clause:

15   "(ii) any annual return filed under

16   section 6011 which relates to any tax im-

17   posed by section 511 (relating to imposi-

18   tion of tax on unrelated business income of

19   charitable, etc., organizations) by such or-

20   ganization, but only if such organization is

21   described in section 501(c)(3),".

22   (b) EFFECTIVE DATE.—The amendments made by

23 this section shall apply to returns filed after the date of

24 the enactment of this Act.

1 **SEC. 1226. STUDY ON DONOR ADVISED FUNDS AND SUP-**
2   **PORTING ORGANIZATIONS.**

3   (a) STUDY.—The Secretary of the Treasury shall un-
4 dertake a study on the organization and operation of
5 donor advised funds (as defined in section 4966(d)(2) of
6 the Internal Revenue Code of 1986, as added by this Act)
7 and of organizations described in section 509(a)(3) of such
8 Code. The study shall specifically consider—

9   (1) whether the deductions allowed for the in-
10   come, gift, or estate taxes for charitable contribu-
11   tions to sponsoring organizations (as defined in sec-
12   tion 4966(d)(1) of such Code, as added by this Act)
13   of donor advised funds or to organizations described
14   in section 509(a)(3) of such Code are appropriate in
15   consideration of—

16   (A) the use of contributed assets (including
17   the type, extent, and timing of such use), or

18   (B) the use of the assets of such organiza-
19   tions for the benefit of the person making the
20   charitable contribution (or a person related to
21   such person),

22   (2) whether donor advised funds should be re-
23   quired to distribute for charitable purposes a speci-
24   fied amount (whether based on the income or assets
25   of the fund) in order to ensure that the sponsoring
26   organization with respect to such donor advised fund

1 is operating consistent with the purposes or func-

2 tions constituting the basis for its exemption under

3 section 501, or its status as an organization de-

4 scribed in section 509(a), of such Code,

5   (3) whether the retention by donors to organi-

6 zations described in paragraph (1) of rights or privi-

7 leges with respect to amounts transferred to such or-

8 ganizations (including advisory rights or privileges

9 with respect to the making of grants or the invest-

10 ment of assets) is consistent with the treatment of

11 such transfers as completed gifts that qualify for a

12 deduction for income, gift, or estate taxes, and

13   (4) whether the issues raised by paragraphs

14 (1), (2), and (3) are also issues with respect to other

15 forms of charities or charitable donations.

16   (b) REPORT.—Not later than 1 year after the date

17 of the enactment of this Act, the Secretary of the Treasury

18 shall submit to the Committee on Finance of the Senate

19 and the Committee on Ways and Means of the House of

20 Representatives a report on the study conducted under

21 subsection (a) and make such recommendations as the

22 Secretary of the Treasury considers appropriate.

1 **PART 2—IMPROVED ACCOUNTABILITY OF DONOR**

2 **ADVISED FUNDS**

3 **SEC. 1231. EXCISE TAXES RELATING TO DONOR ADVISED**

4 **FUNDS.**

5 (a) IN GENERAL.—Chapter 42 (relating to private

6 foundations and certain other tax-exempt organizations),

7 as amended by the Tax Increase Prevention and Reconcili-

8 ation Act of 2005, is amended by adding at the end the

9 following new subchapter:

10 **"Subchapter G—Donor Advised Funds**

"Sec. 4966. Taxes on taxable distributions.
"Sec. 4967. Taxes on prohibited benefits.

11 **"SEC. 4966. TAXES ON TAXABLE DISTRIBUTIONS.**

12 "(a) IMPOSITION OF TAXES.—

13 "(1) ON THE SPONSORING ORGANIZATION.

14 There is hereby imposed on each taxable distribution

15 a tax equal to 20 percent of the amount thereof. The

16 tax imposed by this paragraph shall be paid by the

17 sponsoring organization with respect to the donor

18 advised fund.

19 "(2) ON THE FUND MANAGEMENT.—There is

20 hereby imposed on the agreement of any fund man-

21 ager to the making of a distribution, knowing that

22 it is a taxable distribution, a tax equal to 5 percent

23 of the amount thereof. The tax imposed by this

1   paragraph shall be paid by any fund manager who

2   agreed to the making of the distribution.

3   "(b) SPECIAL RULES.—For purposes of subsection

4 (a)—

5   "(1) JOINT AND SEVERAL LIABILITY.—If more

6   than one person is liable under subsection (a)(2)

7   with respect to the making of a taxable distribution,

8   all such persons shall be jointly and severally liable

9   under such paragraph with respect to such distribu-

10   tion.

11   "(2) LIMIT FOR MANAGEMENT.—With respect

12   to any one taxable distribution, the maximum

13   amount of the tax imposed by subsection (a)(2) shall

14   not exceed $10,000.

15   "(c) TAXABLE DISTRIBUTION.—For purposes of this

16 section—

17   "(1) IN GENERAL.—The term 'taxable distribu-

18   tion' means any distribution from a donor advised

19   fund—

20   "(A) to any natural person, or

21   "(B) to any other person if—

22   "(i) such distribution is for any pur-

23   pose other than one specified in section

24   170(c)(2)(B), or

1   "(ii) the sponsoring organization does

2   not exercise expenditure responsibility with

3   respect to such distribution in accordance

4   with section 4945(h).

5   "(2) EXCEPTIONS.—Such term shall not in-

6 clude any distribution from a donor advised fund—

7   "(A) to any organization described in sec-

8   tion 170(b)(1)(A) (other than a disqualified

9   supporting organization),

10   "(B) to the sponsoring organization of

11   such donor advised fund, or

12   "(C) to any other donor advised fund.

13   "(d) DEFINITIONS.—For purposes of this sub-

14 chapter—

15   "(1) SPONSORING ORGANIZATION.—The term

16 'sponsoring organization' means any organization

17 which—

18   "(A) is described in section 170(c) (other

19   than in paragraph (1) thereof, and without re-

20   gard to paragraph (2)(A) thereof),

21   "(B) is not a private foundation (as de-

22   fined in section 509(a)), and

23   "(C) maintains 1 or more donor advised

24   funds.

25   "(2) DONOR ADVISED FUND.—

1   "(A) IN GENERAL.—Except as provided in

2 subparagraph (B) or (C), the term 'donor ad-

3 vised fund' means a fund or account—

4   "(i) which is separately identified by

5 reference to contributions of a donor or do-

6 nors,

7   "(ii) which is owned and controlled by

8 a sponsoring organization, and

9   "(iii) with respect to which a donor

10 (or any person appointed or designated by

11 such donor) has, or reasonably expects to

12 have, advisory privileges with respect to

13 the distribution or investment of amounts

14 held in such fund or account by reason of

15 the donor's status as a donor.

16   "(B) EXCEPTIONS.—The term 'donor ad-

17 vised fund' shall not include any fund or ac-

18 count—

19   "(i) which makes distributions only to

20 a single identified organization or govern-

21 mental entity, or

22   "(ii) with respect to which a person

23 described in subparagraph (A)(iii) advises

24 as to which individuals receive grants for

1   travel, study, or other similar purposes,

2   if—

3   "(I) such person's advisory privi-

4   leges are performed exclusively by

5   such person in the person's capacity

6   as a member of a committee all of the

7   members of which are appointed by

8   the sponsoring organization,

9   "(II) no combination of persons

10   described in subparagraph (A)(iii) (or

11   persons related to such persons) con-

12   trol, directly or indirectly, such com-

13   mittee, and

14   "(III) all grants from such fund

15   or account are awarded on an objec-

16   tive and nondiscriminatory basis pur-

17   suant to a procedure approved in ad-

18   vance by the board of directors of the

19   sponsoring organization, and such

20   procedure is designed to ensure that

21   all such grants meet the requirements

22   of paragraphs (1), (2), or (3) of sec-

23   tion 4945(g).

24   "(C) SECRETARIAL AUTHORITY.—The Sec-

25   retary may exempt a fund or account not de-

1 scribed in subparagraph (B) from treatment as

2 a donor advised fund—

3   "(i) if such fund or account is advised

4   by a committee not directly or indirectly

5   controlled by the donor or any person ap-

6   pointed or designated by the donor for the

7   purpose of advising with respect to dis-

8   tributions from such fund (and any related

9   parties), or

10   "(ii) if such fund benefits a single

11   identified charitable purpose.

12 "(3) FUND MANAGER.—The term 'fund man-

13 ager' means, with respect to any sponsoring organi-

14 zation—

15   "(A) an officer, director, or trustee of such

16   sponsoring organization (or an individual hav-

17   ing powers or responsibilities similar to those of

18   officers, directors, or trustees of the sponsoring

19   organization), and

20   "(B) with respect to any act (or failure to

21   act), the employees of the sponsoring organiza-

22   tion having authority or responsibility with re-

23   spect to such act (or failure to act).

24 "(4) DISQUALIFIED SUPPORTING ORGANIZA-

25 TION.—

1   "(A) IN GENERAL.—The term 'disqualified

2   supporting organization' means, with respect to

3   any distribution—

4   "(i) any type III supporting organiza-

5   tion (as defined in section 4943(f)(5)(A))

6   which is not a functionally integrated type

7   III supporting organization (as defined in

8   section 4943(f)(5)(B)), and

9   "(ii) any organization which is de-

10   scribed in subparagraph (B) or (C) if—

11   "(I) the donor or any person des-

12   ignated by the donor for the purpose

13   of advising with respect to distribu-

14   tions from a donor advised fund (and

15   any related parties) directly or indi-

16   rectly controls a supported organiza-

17   tion (as defined in section 509(f)(3))

18   of such organization, or

19   "(II) the Secretary determines by

20   regulations that a distribution to such

21   organization otherwise is inappro-

22   priate.

23   "(B) TYPE I AND TYPE II SUPPORTING OR-

24   GANIZATIONS.—An organization is described in

25   this subparagraph if the organization meets the

1 requirements of subparagraphs (A) and (C) of

2 section 509(a)(3) and is—

3 "(i) operated, supervised, or controlled

4 by one or more organizations described in

5 paragraph (1) or (2) of section 509(a), or

6 "(ii) supervised or controlled in con-

7 nection with one or more such organiza-

8 tions.

9 "(C) FUNCTIONALLY INTEGRATED TYPE

10 III SUPPORTING ORGANIZATIONS.—An organiza-

11 tion is described in this subparagraph if the or-

12 ganization is a functionally integrated type III

13 supporting organization (as defined under sec-

14 tion 4943(f)(5)(B)).

15 **"SEC. 4967. TAXES ON PROHIBITED BENEFITS.**

16 "(a) IMPOSITION OF TAXES.—

17 "(1) ON THE DONOR, DONOR ADVISOR, OR RE-

18 LATED PERSON.—There is hereby imposed on the

19 advice of any person described in subsection (d) to

20 have a sponsoring organization make a distribution

21 from a donor advised fund which results in such per-

22 son or any other person described in subsection (d)

23 receiving, directly or indirectly, a more than inci-

24 dental benefit as a result of such distribution, a tax

25 equal to 125 percent of such benefit. The tax im-

1   posed by this paragraph shall be paid by any person

2   described in subsection (d) who advises as to the dis-

3   tribution or who receives such a benefit as a result

4   of the distribution.

5   "(2) ON THE FUND MANAGEMENT.—There is

6   hereby imposed on the agreement of any fund man-

7   ager to the making of a distribution, knowing that

8   such distribution would confer a benefit described in

9   paragraph (1), a tax equal to 10 percent of the

10   amount of such benefit. The tax imposed by this

11   paragraph shall be paid by any fund manager who

12   agreed to the making of the distribution.

13   "(b) EXCEPTION.—No tax shall be imposed under

14 this section with respect to any distribution if a tax has

15 been imposed with respect to such distribution under sec-

16 tion 4958.

17   "(c) SPECIAL RULES.—For purposes of subsection

18 (a)—

19   "(1) JOINT AND SEVERAL LIABILITY.—If more

20   than one person is liable under paragraph (1) or (2)

21   of subsection (a) with respect to a distribution de-

22   scribed in subsection (a), all such persons shall be

23   jointly and severally liable under such paragraph

24   with respect to such distribution.

1   "(2) LIMIT FOR MANAGEMENT.—With respect

2   to any one distribution described in subsection (a),

3   the maximum amount of the tax imposed by sub-

4   section (a)(2) shall not exceed $10,000.

5   "(d) PERSON DESCRIBED.—A person is described in

6 this subsection if such person is described in section

7 4958(f)(7) with respect to a donor advised fund.".

8   (b) CONFORMING AMENDMENTS.—

9   (1) Section 4963 is amended by inserting

10   "4966, 4967," after "4958," each place it appears

11   in subsections (a) and (c).

12   (2) The table of subchapters for chapter 42 is

13   amended by adding at the end the following new

14   item:

          "SUBCHAPTER G. DONOR ADVISED FUNDS".

15   (c) EFFECTIVE DATE.—The amendments made by

16 this section shall apply to taxable years beginning after

17 the date of the enactment of this Act.

18 **SEC. 1232. EXCESS BENEFIT TRANSACTIONS INVOLVING**

19   **DONOR ADVISED FUNDS AND SPONSORING**

20   **ORGANIZATIONS.**

21   (a) DISQUALIFIED PERSONS.—

22   (1) IN GENERAL.—Paragraph (1) of section

23   4958(f) is amended by striking "and" at the end of

24   subparagraph (B), by striking the period at the end

25   of subparagraph (C) and inserting a comma, and by

1   adding after subparagraph (C) the following new

2   subparagraphs:

3   "(D) which involves a donor advised fund

4   (as defined in section 4966(d)(2)), any person

5   who is described in paragraph (7) with respect

6   to such donor advised fund (as so defined), and

7   "(E) which involves a sponsoring organiza-

8   tion (as defined in section 4966(d)(1)), any per-

9   son who is described in paragraph (8) with re-

10   spect to such sponsoring organization (as so de-

11   fined).".

12   (2) DONORS, DONOR ADVISORS, AND INVEST-

13   MENT ADVISORS TREATED AS DISQUALIFIED PER-

14   SONS.—Section 4958(f) is amended by adding at the

15   end the following new paragraphs:

16   "(7) DONORS AND DONOR ADVISORS.—For pur-

17   poses of paragraph (1)(E), a person is described in

18   this paragraph if such person—

19   "(A)   is   described   in   section

20   4966(d)(2)(A)(iii),

21   "(B) is a member of the family of an indi-

22   vidual described in subparagraph (A), or

23   "(C) is a 35-percent controlled entity (as

24   defined in paragraph (3) by substituting 'per-

25   sons described in subparagraph (A) or (B) of

1   paragraph (7)' for 'persons described in sub-

2   paragraph (A) or (B) of paragraph (1)' in sub-

3   paragraph (A)(i) thereof).

4   "(8) INVESTMENT ADVISORS.—For purposes of

5 paragraph (1)(F)—

6   "(A) IN GENERAL.—A person is described

7   in this paragraph if such person—

8   "(i) is an investment advisor,

9   "(ii) is a member of the family of an

10   individual described in clause (i), or

11   "(iii) is a 35-percent controlled entity

12   (as defined in paragraph (3) by sub-

13   stituting 'persons described in clause (i) or

14   (ii) of paragraph (8)(A)' for 'persons de-

15   scribed in subparagraph (A) or (B) of

16   paragraph (1)' in subparagraph (A)(i)

17   thereof).

18   "(B) INVESTMENT ADVISOR DEFINED.—

19 For purposes of subparagraph (A), the term

20 'investment advisor' means, with respect to any

21 sponsoring organization (as defined in section

22 4966(d)(1)), any person (other than an em-

23 ployee of such organization) compensated by

24 such organization for managing the investment

25 of, or providing investment advice with respect

1 to, assets maintained in donor advised funds

2 (as defined in section 4966(d)(2)) owned by

3 such organization.".

4 (b) CERTAIN TRANSACTIONS TREATED AS EXCESS

5 BENEFIT TRANSACTIONS.—

6 (1) IN GENERAL.—Section 4958(c) is amended

7 by redesignating paragraph (2) as paragraph (3)

8 and by inserting after paragraph (1) the following

9 new paragraph:

10 "(2) SPECIAL RULES FOR DONOR ADVISED

11 FUNDS.—In the case of any donor advised fund (as

12 defined in section 4966(d)(2))—

13 "(A) the term 'excess benefit transaction'

14 includes any grant, loan, compensation, or other

15 similar payment from such fund to a person de-

16 scribed in subsection (f)(7) with respect to such

17 fund, and

18 "(B) the term 'excess benefit' includes,

19 with respect to any transaction described in

20 subparagraph (A), the amount of any such

21 grant, loan, compensation, or other similar pay-

22 ment.".

23 (2) SPECIAL RULE FOR CORRECTION OF TRANS-

24 ACTION.—Section 4958(f)(6) is amended by insert-

25 ing ", except that in the case of any correction of

1   an excess benefit transaction described in subsection

2   (c)(2), no amount repaid in a manner prescribed by

3   the Secretary may be held in any donor advised

4   fund'' after ''standards''.

5   (c) EFFECTIVE DATE.—The amendments made by

6 this section shall apply to transactions occurring after the

7 date of the enactment of this Act.

8 **SEC. 1233. EXCESS BUSINESS HOLDINGS OF DONOR AD-**

9   **VISED FUNDS.**

10   (a) IN GENERAL.—Section 4943 is amended by add-

11 ing at the end the following new subsection:

12   ''(e) APPLICATION OF TAX TO DONOR ADVISED

13 FUNDS.—

14   ''(1) IN GENERAL.—For purposes of this sec-

15   tion, a donor advised fund (as defined in section

16   4966(d)(2)) shall be treated as a private foundation.

17   ''(2) DISQUALIFIED PERSON.—In applying this

18   section to any donor advised fund (as so defined),

19   the term 'disqualified person' means, with respect to

20   the donor advised fund, any person who is—

21   ''(A) described in section

22   4966(d)(2)(A)(iii),

23   ''(B) a member of the family of an indi-

24   vidual described in subparagraph (A), or

1   "(C) a 35-percent controlled entity (as de-

2   fined in section 4958(f)(3) by substituting 'per-

3   sons described in subparagraph (A) or (B) of

4   section 4943(e)(2)' for 'persons described in

5   subparagraph (A) or (B) of paragraph (1)' in

6   subparagraph (A)(i) thereof).

7   "(3) PRESENT HOLDINGS.—For purposes of

8 this subsection, rules similar to the rules of para-

9 graphs (4), (5), and (6) of subsection (c) shall apply

10 to donor advised funds (as so defined), except that—

11   "(A) 'the date of the enactment of this

12   subsection' shall be substituted for 'May 26,

13   1969' each place it appears in paragraphs (4),

14   (5), and (6), and

15   "(B) 'January 1, 2007' shall be sub-

16   stituted for 'January 1, 1970' in paragraph

17   (4)(E).".

18   (b) EFFECTIVE DATE.—The amendment made by

19 this section shall apply to taxable years beginning after

20 the date of the enactment of this Act.

21 **SEC. 1234. TREATMENT OF CHARITABLE CONTRIBUTION**

22   **DEDUCTIONS TO DONOR ADVISED FUNDS.**

23   (a) INCOME.—Section 170(f) (relating to disallow-

24 ance of deduction in certain cases and special rules), as

1 amended by this Act, is amended by adding at the end

2 the following new paragraph:

3   "(18) CONTRIBUTIONS TO DONOR ADVISED

4   FUNDS.—A deduction otherwise allowed under sub-

5   section (a) for any contribution to a donor advised

6   fund (as defined in section 4966(d)(2)) shall only be

7   allowed if—

8   "(A) the sponsoring organization (as de-

9   fined in section 4966(d)(1)) with respect to

10   such donor advised fund is not—

11   "(i) described in paragraph (3), (4),

12   or (5) of subsection (c), or

13   "(ii) a type III supporting organiza-

14   tion (as defined in section 4943(f)(5)(A))

15   which is not a functionally integrated type

16   III supporting organization (as defined in

17   section 4943(f)(5)(B)), and

18   "(B) the taxpayer obtains a contempora-

19   neous written acknowledgment (determined

20   under rules similar to the rules of paragraph

21   (8)(C)) from the sponsoring organization (as so

22   defined) of such donor advised fund that such

23   organization has exclusive legal control over the

24   assets contributed.".

881

1   (b) ESTATE.—Section 2055(e) is amended by adding

2 at the end the following new paragraph:

3   "(5) CONTRIBUTIONS TO DONOR ADVISED

4   FUNDS.—A deduction otherwise allowed under sub-

5   section (a) for any contribution to a donor advised

6   fund (as defined in section 4966(d)(2)) shall only be

7   allowed if—

8   "(A) the sponsoring organization (as de-

9   fined in section 4966(d)(1)) with respect to

10   such donor advised fund is not—

11   "(i) described in paragraph (3) or (4)

12   of subsection (a), or

13   "(ii) a type III supporting organiza-

14   tion (as defined in section 4943(f)(5)(A))

15   which is not a functionally integrated type

16   III supporting organization (as defined in

17   section 4943(f)(5)(B)), and

18   "(B) the taxpayer obtains a contempora-

19   neous written acknowledgment (determined

20   under rules similar to the rules of section

21   170(f)(8)(C)) from the sponsoring organization

22   (as so defined) of such donor advised fund that

23   such organization has exclusive legal control

24   over the assets contributed.".

(c) GIFT.—Section 2522(c) is amended by adding at the end the following new paragraph:

"(5) CONTRIBUTIONS TO DONOR ADVISED FUNDS.—A deduction otherwise allowed under subsection (a) for any contribution to a donor advised fund (as defined in section 4966(d)(2)) shall only be allowed if—

"(A) the sponsoring organization (as defined in section 4966(d)(1)) with respect to such donor advised fund is not—

"(i) described in paragraph (3) or (4) of subsection (a), or

"(ii) a type III supporting organization (as defined in section 4943(f)(5)(A)) which is not a functionally integrated type III supporting organization (as defined in section 4943(f)(5)(B)), and

"(B) the taxpayer obtains a contemporaneous written acknowledgment (determined under rules similar to the rules of section 170(f)(8)(C)) from the sponsoring organization (as so defined) of such donor advised fund that such organization has exclusive legal control over the assets contributed.".

1   (d) Effective Date.—The amendments made by

2 this section shall apply to contributions made after the

3 date which is 180 days after the date of the enactment

4 of this Act.

5 **SEC. 1235. RETURNS OF, AND APPLICATIONS FOR RECOGNI-**

6 **TION BY, SPONSORING ORGANIZATIONS.**

7   (a) Matters Included on Returns.—

8   (1) In general.—Section 6033, as amended

9 by this Act, is amended by redesignating subsection

10 (k) as subsection (l) and by inserting after sub-

11 section (j) the following new subsection:

12 "(k) Additional Provisions Relating to Spon-

13 soring Organizations.—Every organization described

14 in section 4966(d)(1) shall, on the return required under

15 subsection (a) for the taxable year—

16   "(1) list the total number of donor advised

17 funds (as defined in section 4966(d)(2)) it owns at

18 the end of such taxable year,

19   "(2) indicate the aggregate value of assets held

20 in such funds at the end of such taxable year, and

21   "(3) indicate the aggregate contributions to and

22 grants made from such funds during such taxable

23 year.".

24   (2) Effective date.—The amendments made

25 by this subsection shall apply to returns filed for

1   taxable years ending after the date of the enactment

2   of this Act.

3   (b) MATTERS INCLUDED ON EXEMPT STATUS APPLI-

4   CATION.—

5   (1) IN GENERAL.—Section 508 is amended by

6   adding at the end the following new subsection:

7   "(f) ADDITIONAL PROVISIONS RELATING TO SPON-

8   SORING ORGANIZATIONS.—A sponsoring organization (as

9   defined in section 4966(d)(1)) shall give notice to the Sec-

10   retary (in such manner as the Secretary may provide)

11   whether such organization maintains or intends to main-

12   tain donor advised funds (as defined in section

13   4966(d)(2)) and the manner in which such organization

14   plans to operate such funds.".

15   (2) EFFECTIVE DATE.—The amendment made

16   by this subsection shall apply to organizations apply-

17   ing for tax-exempt status after the date of the enact-

18   ment of this Act.

19   **PART 3—IMPROVED ACCOUNTABILITY OF**

20   **SUPPORTING ORGANIZATIONS**

21   **SEC. 1241. REQUIREMENTS FOR SUPPORTING ORGANIZA-**

22   **TIONS.**

23   (a) TYPES OF SUPPORTING ORGANIZATIONS.—Sub-

24   paragraph (B) of section 509(a)(3) is amended to read

25   as follows:

1   "(B) is—

2   "(i) operated, supervised, or controlled

3   by one or more organizations described in

4   paragraph (1) or (2),

5   "(ii) supervised or controlled in con-

6   nection with one or more such organiza-

7   tions, or

8   "(iii) operated in connection with one

9   or more such organizations, and".

10   (b) REQUIREMENTS FOR SUPPORTING ORGANIZA-

11 TIONS.—Section 509 (relating to private foundation de-

12 fined) is amended by adding at the end the following new

13 subsection:

14   "(f) REQUIREMENTS FOR SUPPORTING ORGANIZA-

15 TIONS.—

16   "(1) TYPE III SUPPORTING ORGANIZATIONS.—

17   For purposes of subsection (a)(3)(B)(iii), an organi-

18   zation shall not be considered to be operated in con-

19   nection with any organization described in para-

20   graph (1) or (2) of subsection (a) unless such orga-

21   nization meets the following requirements:

22   "(A) RESPONSIVENESS.—For each taxable

23   year beginning after the date of the enactment

24   of this subsection, the organization provides to

25   each supported organization such information

1   as the Secretary may require to ensure that

2   such organization is responsive to the needs or

3   demands of the supported organization.

4   "(B) FOREIGN SUPPORTED ORGANIZA-

5   TIONS.—

6   "(i) IN GENERAL.—The organization

7   is not operated in connection with any sup-

8   ported organization that is not organized

9   in the United States.

10   "(ii) TRANSITION RULE FOR EXISTING

11   ORGANIZATIONS.—If the organization is

12   operated in connection with an organiza-

13   tion that is not organized in the United

14   States on the date of the enactment of this

15   subsection, clause (i) shall not apply until

16   the first day of the third taxable year of

17   the organization beginning after the date

18   of the enactment of this subsection.

19   "(2) ORGANIZATIONS CONTROLLED BY DO-

20   NORS.—

21   "(A) IN GENERAL.—For purposes of sub-

22   section (a)(3)(B), an organization shall not be

23   considered to be—

"(i) operated, supervised, or controlled by any organization described in paragraph (1) or (2) of subsection (a), or

"(ii) operated in connection with any organization described in paragraph (1) or (2) of subsection (a),

if such organization accepts any gift or contribution from any person described in subparagraph (B).

"(B) PERSON DESCRIBED.—A person is described in this subparagraph if, with respect to a supported organization of an organization described in subparagraph (A), such person is—

"(i) a person (other than an organization described in paragraph (1), (2), or (4) of section 509(a)) who directly or indirectly controls, either alone or together with persons described in clauses (ii) and (iii), the governing body of such supported organization,

"(ii) a member of the family (determined under section 4958(f)(4)) of an individual described in clause (i), or

1   "(iii) a 35-percent controlled entity

2   (as defined in section 4958(f)(3) by sub-

3   stituting 'persons described in clause (i) or

4   (ii) of section 509(f)(2)(B)' for 'persons

5   described in subparagraph (A) or (B) of

6   paragraph (1)' in subparagraph (A)(i)

7   thereof).

8   "(3) SUPPORTED ORGANIZATION.—For pur-

9 poses of this subsection, the term 'supported organi-

10 zation' means, with respect to an organization de-

11 scribed in subsection (a)(3), an organization de-

12 scribed in paragraph (1) or (2) of subsection (a)—

13   "(A) for whose benefit the organization de-

14   scribed in subsection (a)(3) is organized and

15   operated, or

16   "(B) with respect to which the organiza-

17   tion performs the functions of, or carries out

18   the purposes of.".

19 (c) CHARITABLE TRUSTS WHICH ARE TYPE III SUP-

20 PORTING ORGANIZATIONS.—For purposes of section

21 509(a)(3)(B)(iii) of the Internal Revenue Code of 1986,

22 an organization which is a trust shall not be considered

23 to be operated in connection with any organization de-

24 scribed in paragraph (1) or (2) of section 509(a) of such

25 Code solely because—

1   (1) it is a charitable trust under State law,

2   (2) the supported organization (as defined in

3 section 509(f)(3) of such Code) is a beneficiary of

4 such trust, and

5   (3) the supported organization (as so defined)

6 has the power to enforce the trust and compel an ac-

7 counting.

8 (d) PAYOUT REQUIREMENTS FOR TYPE III SUP-

9 PORTING ORGANIZATIONS.—

10   (1) IN GENERAL.—The Secretary of the Treas-

11 ury shall promulgate new regulations under section

12 509 of the Internal Revenue Code of 1986 on pay-

13 ments required by type III supporting organizations

14 which are not functionally integrated type III sup-

15 porting organizations. Such regulations shall require

16 such organizations to make distributions of a per-

17 centage of either income or assets to supported orga-

18 nizations (as defined in section 509(f)(3) of such

19 Code) in order to ensure that a significant amount

20 is paid to such organizations.

21   (2) TYPE III SUPPORTING ORGANIZATION;

22 FUNCTIONALLY INTEGRATED TYPE III SUPPORTING

23 ORGANIZATION.—For purposes of paragraph (1), the

24 terms "type III supporting organization" and "func-

25 tionally integrated type III supporting organization"

1   have the meanings given such terms under subpara-

2   graphs (A) and (B) section 4943(f)(5) of the Inter-

3   nal Revenue Code of 1986 (as added by this Act),

4   respectively.

5   (e) EFFECTIVE DATES.—

6   (1) IN GENERAL.—The amendments made by

7   subsections (a) and (b) shall take effect on the date

8   of the enactment of this Act.

9   (2) CHARITABLE TRUSTS WHICH ARE TYPE III

10   SUPPORTING ORGANIZATIONS.—Subsection (c) shall

11   take effect—

12   (A) in the case of trusts operated in con-

13   nection with an organization described in para-

14   graph (1) or (2) of section 509(a) of the Inter-

15   nal Revenue Code of 1986 on the date of the

16   enactment of this Act, on the date that is one

17   year after the date of the enactment of this Act,

18   and

19   (B) in the case of any other trust, on the

20   date of the enactment of this Act.

21 **SEC. 1242. EXCESS BENEFIT TRANSACTIONS INVOLVING**

22   **SUPPORTING ORGANIZATIONS.**

23   (a) DISQUALIFIED PERSONS.—Paragraph (1) of sec-

24 tion 4958(f), as amended by this Act, is amended by re-

25 designating subparagraphs (D) and (E) as subparagraphs

1 (E) and (F), respectively, and by adding after subpara-
2 graph (C) the following new subparagraph:

3   "(D) any person who is described in sub-
4   paragraph (A), (B), or (C) with respect to an
5   organization described in section 509(a)(3) and
6   organized and operated exclusively for the ben-
7   efit of, to perform the functions of, or to carry
8   out the purposes of the applicable tax-exempt
9   organization.".

10   (b) CERTAIN TRANSACTIONS TREATED AS EXCESS
11 BENEFIT TRANSACTIONS.—Section 4958(c), as amended
12 by this Act, is amended by redesignating paragraph (3)
13 as paragraph (4) and by inserting after paragraph (2) the
14 following new paragraph:

15   "(3) SPECIAL RULES FOR SUPPORTING ORGANI-
16   ZATIONS.—

17   "(A) IN GENERAL.—In the case of any or-
18   ganization described in section 509(a)(3)—

19   "(i) the term 'excess benefit trans-
20   action' includes—

21   "(I) any grant, loan, compensa-
22   tion, or other similar payment pro-
23   vided by such organization to a person
24   described in subparagraph (B), and

"(II) any loan provided by such organization to a disqualified person (other than an organization described in paragraph (1), (2), or (4) of section 509(a)), and

"(ii) the term 'excess benefit' includes, with respect to any transaction described in clause (i), the amount of any such grant, loan, compensation, or other similar payment.

"(B) PERSON DESCRIBED.—A person is described in this subparagraph if such person is—

"(i) a substantial contributor to such organization,

"(ii) a member of the family (determined under section 4958(f)(4)) of an individual described in clause (i), or

"(iii) a 35-percent controlled entity (as defined in section 4958(f)(3) by substituting 'persons described in clause (i) or (ii) of section 4958(c)(3)(B)' for 'persons described in subparagraph (A) or (B) of paragraph (1)' in subparagraph (A)(i) thereof).

"(C) SUBSTANTIAL CONTRIBUTOR.—For purposes of this paragraph—

"(i) IN GENERAL.—The term 'substantial contributor' means any person who contributed or bequeathed an aggregate amount of more than $5,000 to the organization, if such amount is more than 2 percent of the total contributions and bequests received by the organization before the close of the taxable year of the organization in which the contribution or bequest is received by the organization from such person. In the case of a trust, such term also means the creator of the trust. Rules similar to the rules of subparagraphs (B) and (C) of section 507(d)(2) shall apply for purposes of this subparagraph.

"(ii) EXCEPTION.—Such term shall not include any organization described in paragraph (1), (2), or (4) of section 509(a).".

(c) EFFECTIVE DATES.—

(1) SUBSECTION (a).—The amendments made by subsection (a) shall apply to transactions occurring after the date of the enactment of this Act.

1   (2) SUBSECTION (b).—The amendments made

2 by subsection (a) shall apply to transactions occur-

3 ring after July 25, 2006.

4 **SEC. 1243. EXCESS BUSINESS HOLDINGS OF SUPPORTING**

5   **ORGANIZATIONS.**

6   (a) IN GENERAL.—Section 4943, as amended by this

7 Act, is amended by adding at the end the following new

8 subsection:

9   "(f) APPLICATION OF TAX TO SUPPORTING ORGANI-

10 ZATIONS.—

11   "(1) IN GENERAL.—For purposes of this sec-

12   tion, an organization which is described in para-

13   graph (3) shall be treated as a private foundation.

14   "(2) EXCEPTION.—The Secretary may exempt

15   the excess business holdings of any organization

16   from the application of this subsection if the Sec-

17   retary determines that such holdings are consistent

18   with the purpose or function constituting the basis

19   for its exemption under section 501.

20   "(3) ORGANIZATIONS DESCRIBED.—An organi-

21   zation is described in this paragraph if such organi-

22   zation is—

23   "(A) a type III supporting organization

24   (other than a functionally integrated type III

25   supporting organization), or

1   "(B) an organization which meets the re-

2 quirements of subparagraphs (A) and (C) of

3 section 509(a)(3) and which is supervised or

4 controlled in connection with or one or more or-

5 ganizations described in paragraph (1) or (2) of

6 section 509(a), but only if such organization ac-

7 cepts any gift or contribution from any person

8 described in section 509(f)(2)(B).

9   "(4) DISQUALIFIED PERSON.—

10   "(A) IN GENERAL.—In applying this sec-

11 tion to any organization described in paragraph

12 (3), the term 'disqualified person' means, with

13 respect to the organization—

14   "(i) any person who was, at any time

15 during the 5-year period ending on the

16 date described in subsection (a)(2)(A), in a

17 position to exercise substantial influence

18 over the affairs of the organization,

19   "(ii) any member of the family (deter-

20 mined under section 4958(f)(4)) of an in-

21 dividual described in clause (i),

22   "(iii) any 35-percent controlled entity

23 (as defined in section 4958(f)(3) by sub-

24 stituting 'persons described in clause (i) or

25 (ii) of section 4943(f)(4)(A)' for 'persons

described in subparagraph (A) or (B) of paragraph (1)' in subparagraph (A)(i) thereof),

"(iv) any person described in section 4958(c)(3)(B), and

"(v) any organization—

"(I) which is effectively controlled (directly or indirectly) by the same person or persons who control the organization in question, or

"(II) substantially all of the contributions to which were made (directly or indirectly) by the same person or persons described in subparagraph (B) or a member of the family (within the meaning of section 4946(d)) of such a person.

"(B) PERSONS DESCRIBED.—A person is described in this subparagraph if such person is—

"(i) a substantial contributor to the organization (as defined in section 4958(c)(3)(C)),

"(ii) an officer, director, or trustee of the organization (or an individual having

1   powers or responsibilities similar to those

2   of the officers, directors, or trustees of the

3   organization), or

4   "(iii) an owner of more than 20 per-

5   cent of—

6   "(I) the total combined voting

7   power of a corporation,

8   "(II) the profits interest of a

9   partnership, or

10   "(III) the beneficial interest of a

11   trust or unincorporated enterprise,

12   which is a substantial contributor (as so

13   defined) to the organization.

14   "(5) TYPE III SUPPORTING ORGANIZATION;

15 FUNCTIONALLY INTEGRATED TYPE III SUPPORTING

16 ORGANIZATION.—For purposes of this subsection—

17   "(A) TYPE III SUPPORTING ORGANIZA-

18   TION.—The term 'type III supporting organiza-

19   tion' means an organization which meets the re-

20   quirements of subparagraphs (A) and (C) of

21   section 509(a)(3) and which is operated in con-

22   nection with one or more organizations de-

23   scribed in paragraph (1) or (2) of section

24   509(a).

1   "(B) FUNCTIONALLY INTEGRATED TYPE

2   III SUPPORTING ORGANIZATION.—The term

3   'functionally integrated type III supporting or-

4   ganization' means a type III supporting organi-

5   zation which is not required under regulations

6   established by the Secretary to make payments

7   to supported organizations (as defined under

8   section 509(f)(3)) due to the activities of the

9   organization related to performing the functions

10   of, or carrying out the purposes of, such sup-

11   ported organizations.

12   "(6) SPECIAL RULE FOR CERTAIN HOLDINGS

13 OF TYPE III SUPPORTING ORGANIZATIONS.—For

14 purposes of this subsection, the term 'excess busi-

15 ness holdings' shall not include any holdings of a

16 type III supporting organization in any business en-

17 terprise if, as of November 18, 2005, the holdings

18 were held (and at all times thereafter, are held) for

19 the benefit of the community pursuant to the direc-

20 tion of a State attorney general or a State official

21 with jurisdiction over such organization.

22   "(7) PRESENT HOLDINGS.—For purposes of

23 this subsection, rules similar to the rules of para-

24 graphs (4), (5), and (6) of subsection (c) shall apply

1   to organizations described in section 509(a)(3), ex-

2   cept that—

3   "(A) 'the date of the enactment of this

4   subsection' shall be substituted for 'May 26,

5   1969' each place it appears in paragraphs (4),

6   (5), and (6), and

7   "(B) 'January 1, 2007' shall be sub-

8   stituted for 'January 1, 1970' in paragraph

9   (4)(E).".

10   (b) EFFECTIVE DATE.—The amendment made by

11 this section shall apply to taxable years beginning after

12 the date of the enactment of this Act.

13 **SEC. 1244. TREATMENT OF AMOUNTS PAID TO SUPPORTING**

14   **ORGANIZATIONS BY PRIVATE FOUNDATIONS.**

15   (a) QUALIFYING DISTRIBUTIONS.—Paragraph (4) of

16 section 4942(g) is amended to read as follows:

17   "(4) LIMITATION ON DISTRIBUTIONS BY NON-

18 OPERATING PRIVATE FOUNDATIONS TO SUPPORTING

19 ORGANIZATIONS.—

20   "(A) IN GENERAL.—For purposes of this

21   section, the term 'qualifying distribution' shall

22   not include any amount paid by a private foun-

23   dation which is not an operating foundation

24   to—

"(i) any type III supporting organization (as defined in section 4943(f)(5)(A))
which is not a functionally integrated type
III supporting organization (as defined in
section 4943(f)(5)(B)), and

"(ii) any organization which is described in subparagraph (B) or (C) if—

"(I) a disqualified person of the
private foundation directly or indirectly controls such organization or a
supported organization (as defined in
section 509(f)(3)) of such organization, or

"(II) the Secretary determines by
regulations that a distribution to such
organization otherwise is inappropriate.

"(B) TYPE I AND TYPE II SUPPORTING OR-
GANIZATIONS.—An organization is described in
this subparagraph if the organization meets the
requirements of subparagraphs (A) and (C) of
section 509(a)(3) and is—

"(i) operated, supervised, or controlled
by one or more organizations described in
paragraph (1) or (2) of section 509(a), or

1   "(ii) supervised or controlled in con-

2   nection with one or more such organiza-

3   tions.

4   "(C) FUNCTIONALLY INTEGRATED TYPE

5   III SUPPORTING ORGANIZATIONS.—An organiza-

6   tion is described in this subparagraph if the or-

7   ganization is a functionally integrated type III

8   supporting organization (as defined under sec-

9   tion 4943(f)(5)(B)).".

10   (b) TAXABLE EXPENDITURES.—Subparagraph (A)

11 of section 4945(d)(4) is amended to read as follows:

12   "(A) such organization—

13   "(i) is described in paragraph (1) or

14   (2) of section 509(a),

15   "(ii) is an organization described in

16   section 509(a)(3) (other than an organiza-

17   tion described in clause (i) or (ii) of section

18   4942(g)(4)(A)), or

19   "(iii) is an exempt operating founda-

20   tion (as defined in section 4940(d)(2)),

21   or".

22   (c) EFFECTIVE DATE.—The amendments made by

23 this section shall apply to distributions and expenditures

24 after the date of the enactment of this Act.

1 **SEC. 1245. RETURNS OF SUPPORTING ORGANIZATIONS.**

2   (a) REQUIREMENT TO FILE RETURN.—Subpara-
3 graph (B) of section 6033(a)(3) is amended by inserting
4 "(other than an organization described in section
5 509(a)(3))" after "paragraph (1)".

6   (b) MATTERS INCLUDED ON RETURNS.—Section
7 6033, as amended by this Act, is amended by redesig-
8 nating subsection (l) as subsection (m) and by inserting
9 after subsection (k) the following new subsection:

10   "(l) ADDITIONAL PROVISIONS RELATING TO SUP-
11 PORTING ORGANIZATIONS.—Every organization described
12 in section 509(a)(3) shall, on the return required under
13 subsection (a)—

14   "(1) list the supported organizations (as de-
15   fined in section 509(f)(3)) with respect to which
16   such organization provides support,

17   "(2) indicate whether the organization meets
18   the requirements of clause (i), (ii), or (iii) of section
19   509(a)(3)(B), and

20   "(3) certify that the organization meets the re-
21   quirements of section 509(a)(3)(C).".

22   (c) EFFECTIVE DATE.—The amendments made by
23 this section shall apply to returns filed for taxable years
24 ending after the date of the enactment of this Act.

TITLE XIII—OTHER PROVISIONS

SEC. 1301. TECHNICAL CORRECTIONS RELATING TO MINE SAFETY.

Section 110 of the Federal Mine Safety and Health Act of 1977 (30 U.S.C. 820), as amended by the Mine Improvement and New Emergency Response Act of 2006 (Public Law 109–236), is amended—

 (1) by striking subsection (d); and

 (2) in subsection (a)—

  (A) by striking "(1)(1) The operator" and inserting "(1) The operator";

  (B) in the paragraph (2) added by section 8(a)(1)(B) of the Mine Improvement and New Emergency Response Act of 2006 (Public Law 109–236)—

   (i) by striking "paragraph (1)" and inserting "subsection (a)(1)"; and

   (ii) by redesignating such paragraph as subsection (d) and transferring such subsection so as to appear after subsection (c); and

 (3) in subsection (b)—

  (A) by striking "Any operator" and inserting "(1) Any operator"; and

1   (B) in the second sentence, as added by
2   section 8(a)(2) of the Mine Improvement and
3   New Emergency Response Act of 2006 (Public
4   Law 109–236), by striking "Violations" and in-
5   serting the following:
6   "(2) Violations".

7 **SEC. 1302. GOING-TO-THE-SUN ROAD.**

8   (a) IN GENERAL.—Section 1940 of the Safe, Ac-
9 countable, Flexible, Efficient Transportation Equity Act:
10 A Legacy for Users (119 Stat. 1511) is amended—
11   (1) in subsection (a)—
12   (A) by striking paragraphs (1) and (2);
13   (B) by redesignating paragraphs (3)
14   through (5) as paragraphs (1) through (3), re-
15   spectively; and
16   (C) by striking "$10,000,000" each place
17   that it appears and inserting "$16,666,666";
18   and
19   (2) by adding at the end the following:
20   "(c) CONTRACT AUTHORITY.—Except as otherwise
21 provided in this section, funds authorized to be appro-
22 priated under this section shall be available for obligation
23 in the same manner as if the funds were apportioned
24 under chapter 1 of title 23, United States Code.".

1   (b) RESCISSION.—Section 10212 of the Safe, Ac-
2 countable, Flexible, Efficient Transportation Equity Act:
3 A Legacy for Users (119 Stat. 1937) is amended by strik-
4 ing "$8,543,000,000" each place it appears and inserting
5 "$8,593,000,000".

6 **SEC. 1303. EXCEPTION TO THE LOCAL FURNISHING RE-**
7 **QUIREMENT OF THE TAX-EXEMPT BOND**
8 **RULES.**

9   (a) SNETTISHAM HYDROELECTRIC FACILITY.—For
10 purposes of determining whether any private activity bond
11 issued before May 31, 2006, and used to finance the ac-
12 quisition of the Snettisham hydroelectric facility is a quali-
13 fied bond for purposes of section 142(a)(8) of the Internal
14 Revenue Code of 1986, the electricity furnished by such
15 facility to the City of Hoonah, Alaska, shall not be taken
16 into account for purposes of section 142(f)(1) of such
17 Code.

18   (b) LAKE DOROTHY HYDROELECTRIC FACILITY.—
19 For purposes of determining whether any private activity
20 bond issued before May 31, 2006, and used to finance the
21 Lake Dorothy hydroelectric facility is a qualified bond for
22 purposes of section 142(a)(8) of the Internal Revenue
23 Code of 1986, the electricity furnished by such facility to
24 the City of Hoonah, Alaska, shall not be taken into ac-

1 count for purposes of paragraphs (1) and (3) of section

2 142(f) of such Code.

3   (c) DEFINITIONS.—For purposes of this section—

4   (1) LAKE DOROTHY HYDROELECTRIC FACIL-

5   ITY.—The term "Lake Dorothy hydroelectric facil-

6   ity" means the hydroelectric facility located approxi-

7   mately 10 miles south of Juneau, Alaska, and com-

8   monly referred to as the "Lake Dorothy project".

9   (2) SNETTISHAM HYDROELECTRIC FACILITY.—

10   The term "Snettisham hydroelectric facility" means

11   the hydroelectric project described in section 1804 of

12   the Small Business Job Protection Act of 1996.

13 **SEC. 1304. QUALIFIED TUITION PROGRAMS.**

14   (a) PERMANENT EXTENSION OF MODIFICATIONS.—

15 Section 901 of the Economic Growth and Tax Relief Rec-

16 onciliation Act of 2001 (relating to sunset provisions) shall

17 not apply to section 402 of such Act (relating to modifica-

18 tions to qualified tuition programs).

19   (b) REGULATORY AUTHORITY TO PREVENT

20 ABUSE.—Section 529 (relating to qualified tuition pro-

21 grams) is amended by adding at the end the following new

22 subsection:

23   "(f) REGULATIONS.—Notwithstanding any other pro-

24 vision of this section, the Secretary shall prescribe such

25 regulations as may be necessary or appropriate to carry

1   out the purposes of this section and to prevent abuse of

2   such purposes, including regulations under chapters 11,

3   12, and 13 of this title.''.